T

1976 CATHOLIC ALMANAC

FELICIAN A. FOY, O.F.M.
Editor

Our Sunday Visitor, Inc.
Huntington, Indiana 46750

Acknowledgements: NC News Service for coverage of news and documentary texts; *The Documents of Vatican II*, Walter M. Abbott, S.J., general editor, Herder and Herder, Association Press, New York, 1966, for quotations; *Annuario Pontificio, 1975; The Official Catholic Directory, 1975*, P. J. Kenedy & Sons, New York; The United States Mission Council, 1325 Massachusetts Ave. N.W., Washington, D.C., for U.S. foreign mission compilations and statistics; *1974 Britannica Book of the Year*, copyright 1974 by Encyclopaedia Britannica, Inc., Chicago, for reprinting with permission of statistics on religious population of the world; *Catholic Press Directory 1975; 1975 Directory of Catholic Communications Personnel*, National Catholic Office of Information. Other sources are credited in various entries.

Published with Ecclesiastical Approval

ISBN 0-87973-820-0 Paperbound Edition
ISBN 0-87973-872-3 Clothbound Edition

Library of Congress Catalog Card Number: A43-2500

Published, printed and bound in U.S.A. by
Our Sunday Visitor, Inc.
Huntington, Indiana 46750

Table of Contents

INDEX

A

Abbacy, 346
Abbess, 346
Abbey, see Monastery
Abbot, 346
Abbreviations, 700-02
Abelard, Peter, 387
Abingdon v. Schempp, 89, 479
Abjuration, 346
Ablution, 346
Abortion (Moral Principles), 346
   Declaration on, Vatican, 48, 129-32
   Pastoral Letter, Bishop Maher, 74-5
Abortion Developments, Canada, 50
   England, 61
   France, 53, 65
   Italy, 65
   Norway, 50, 85
   West Germany, 65
Abortion Developments, U.S., 125-26
   Amendments, Pro-Life, 60, 73, 123-25
   Conscience Clause, 126-27
   Federal Funds, 48
   Gallup Poll Findings, 48
   March for Life, 59-60
   1974 Estimates, 64
   Parental Consent, 48, 79
   Pastoral Letter, Bishop Maher, 74-5
     See also Birthright; Fetal Experimentation; Fetus,
     Rights of; Right to Life
Abramowicz, Alfred L., Bp., 513
Absolution, 346
   General, 346
   See also Penance; Penitential Celebrations
Abstinence, Days of, 287
   Byzantine Rite, 288
Acacius, Patriarch (484), 157
Academy of American Franciscan History, 653
Academy of California Church History, 653
Acadians, see Canada, Church in
Accessory to Sin, 346
Accommodated Senses (Bible), 240
Achillini, Alessandro, 387
Ackerman, Richard, C.S.SP., Bp., 513
Acolyte, 272
Act of Supremacy (1533), 161
Acta Apostolicae Sedis, 217
Acta Sanctae Sedis, 217
Actors' Guild, Catholic, 680
Acts of the Apostles, 235
Actual Grace, see Grace
Actual Sin, see Sin
Ad Gentes (Missions Decree), 168, 583
Ad Limina Visit, 185
Ad Purpuratorum Patrum, 197
Adam, Karl, 387
Address, Forms of, 703
   Permanent Deacons, 510
Aden, see Arabian Peninsula
Adenauer, Konrad, 387
Adjutor, St., 300
Adoptionism, 165
Adoratio (Papal Election), 374
Adoration, 346
Adrian, William H., 536
Adultery, 346-47
Advent, 285
Advent Wreath, 347
Adventists, 347
Advertising, 663
Afars and Issas, 409
Afghanistan, 409
Africa, 51, 75, 82, 95, 442
   American Bishops, 492
   Cardinals, 210
   Catholic Statistics, 443-44
   Communion in Hand, 284
   Drought, 88
   Eastern Rite Jurisdictions, 320
   Episcopal Conferences, 445
   Religious Population, 327
Africa, Missionary Srs. of Our Lady, 561
African Missions, Society of, 552
Africanization, 61, 101

Africanus Sextus, 387
Agape, 347
Agatha, St., 300
Age of Reason, 347
Aged, Eucharistic Fast, 362
Aged, Facilities for, 623-30
Agency for International Development (AID), Bolivian Ag-
   gression, 71
Aggiornamento, 347
Agnes, St., 300
Agnes, Srs. of St., 561
Agnosticism, 347
Agnus Dei, 347
Agreda, Mary of, 387
Agriculture Policies, 98
Agrimissio, 582
Ahern, Patrick V., Bp., 513
Ahr, George William, Bp., 513
Alabama, 495, 498, 499, 503, 602, 623, 636, 639
   Dates in Catholic History, 463
Alan of Walsingham, 387
Alarcon, Pedro, 387
Alaska, 496, 498, 500, 511, 604, 639
   Dates in Catholic History, 463
Alb, 257
Albania, 409
Albanian Byzantines, 318
Alberione, Giacomo, 387
Albers, Joseph, 536
Albert (Albrecht), 387
Albert the Great, St., 243
Albertus Magnus Guild, 653
Albigensianism, 165
Albornoz, Gil Alvarez Carillo de, 387
Alcoholics, 637
Alcoholism, Natl. Clergy Conference, 658
Alcuin, Albinus, 387
Alemany, Joseph S., O.P., 536
Alencastre, Stephen, SS.CC., 536
Alerding, Herman J., 536
Alessandrini, Federico, 323
Alexander of Hales, 387
Alexandrian Rite, 317
Alexian Brothers, 558
   Menominee Indian Demands, 63
Alfred the Great, 387
Alfrink, Bernard Jan, Card., 197
Algeria, 409
Alhambra, Order of, 659
Aliens ("Commuters"), 49
Aliens, Illegal, 49, 74, 137-38, 510
All Saints, 296
All Souls, 296
Allegories of Christ, 237
Alleluia, 347
Allen, Edward P., 536
Allen, Frances, 387
Allen, Francis V., Bp., 451
Allers, Rudolf, 387
Allocution, 347
Allori, Alessandro, 387
Allori, Cristofano, 387
Allouez, Claude, 406
Alms, 347
Alonso Rodriguez, Bl., 408
Aloysius Gonzaga, St., 300
Alpha and Omega, 347
Alpha Delta Gamma Fraternity, 653
Alphonsus Liguori, St., 243
Altar, 257, 259
   Cloth, 258
   Stone, 257
Alter, Karl J., Abp., 513
Altham, John, 406
Althoff, Henry, 536
Amado Blanco, Luis, 105
Amand, St., 300
Amat, Thaddeus, C.M., 536
Amazon, Indians Oppressed, 66
Ambo, 259
Ambrose, St., 243
Ambrosian Rite, 254
Ambry, 260

4

Mississippi, 495, 498, 499, 602, 642
  Dates in Catholic History, 470
Missouri, 495, 498, 500, 503, 511, 603, 616, 626-27, 631, 632, 634, 642
  Dates in Catholic History, 470
  School Aid Decision, 49
  Secular Humanism Suit, 89
  State Board of Education, 73
  Textbook Decision, 58
Mistral, Gabriela, 399
Mitchell, James, 399
Mitchell, John, 399
Mitre, 258
Mitty, John J., 544
Mixed Marriages, 280-83
Modalism, 164
Modern World, Constitution, 248-50, 250-51, 275-76, 349
Modernism, 371
  Syllabus of St. Pius X, 384
Moede, Gerald F., Dr., 49
Moeller, Henry, 544
Mogrovejo, Turibius de, St., 408
Mohammed (622), 157
Mohler, Johann, 399
Mohr, Josef, 399
Molina, Luis de, 399
Molloy, Thomas E., 544
Moluccas, **see** Indonesia
Monaco, 428
Monaghan, Francis J., 544
Monaghan, John J., 544
Monarchianism, 164
Monastery, 371
Monasticism (Sixth Century), 157
Mondino dei Luicci, 399
Monge, Gaspard, 399
Mongolian Peoples' Republic, 428
Monica, St., 304
Monk, 372
Monks of the Brotherhood of St. Francis, 556
Monophysite Churches, 325
Monophysitism, 165
Monotheism, 372
Monotheletism, 165
Monsignor (Honorary Prelates), 186
Msgr. John P. Monaghan Social Action Award, 693
Monstrance, 258
Montana, 496, 498, 500, 511, 603, 617, 627, 642
  Dates in Catholic History, 470
Montanism, 165
Montcalm, Marquis Louis, 399
Monte Cassino (c. 529), 157
Montessori, Maria, 399
Monteux, Pierre, 399
Montfort Fathers, 556
Montgomery, George T., 544
Montgomery Ward, Project Equality Rating, 84
Moon, Parker Thomas, 399
Mooney, Edward, 544
Mooney, Joe, 106
Moore, John, 544
Moore, Thomas, 400
Moore, Thomas Verner, 400
Mora, Francis, 544
Moral Law, Deviations, 71
Moral Obligations, 246-47
Morality, 372
  Christian and Religion, 53
  Crisis, U.S., 54
  Permissive, 58
  Public, 97
Morality in Media, Inc., 658
Moran, William J., Bp., 527
Moravian Church, **see** Hus, John
More, Thomas St., 305
Morgagni, Giovanni, 400
Morin, Laurent, Bp., 454
Morkovsky, John L., Bp., 528
Morley, Sylvanus Griswold, 400
Mormons, 372
Morocco, 428
Morris, John, 544
Morrow, Louis, S.D.B., Bp., 528
Mortal Sin, 381
Mortification, 372
Moslems (Muslims), 343-44
  Dialogue with Catholics, 194, 344
  Proselytism, Africa, 51
  World Statistics, 327

Mother of God, 312
  See also Mary, Catholic Teaching
Mother of God, Missionary Sisters, 573
Mother of God, Srs. Poor Servants, 573
Motta, Carlos Carmelo de Vasconcellos, Card., 204
Motu Proprio, 372
Mount Calvary, Ursuline Sisters of, 577
Mount Carmel, BVM of (July 16), 292
Mount Carmel (Religious)
  Congregation of Our Lady, 562
  Institute of Our Lady, 562
  Order of Our Lady, 553
  Third Order of Our Lady (Discalced), 582
  See also Carmelites
Movement for a Better World, 85, 651
Movies, X-Rated, Supreme Court Decision, 699
Movimiento Familiar Cristiano, 649
Moylan, Stephen, 400
Mozambique, 428
  Apostolic Delegation, 53
  Missionaries, 90
  Native Bishops, 71
Mozarabic Rite, **see** Rites
Mozart, J. C. Wolfgang, 400
Mozzoni, Umberto, Card., 204
Mrak, Ignatius, 544
Mueller, Joseph M., Bp., 528
Muench, Aloysius, 400
Mugavero, Francis J., Bp., 59, 528
Mulcahy, John J., Bp., 528
Muldoon, Peter, 544
Mullen, Tobias, 544
Muller, Johann, 400
Muller, Johannes, 400
Mulloy, William T., 544
Mulrooney, Charles R., Bp., 528
Mulvihill, James P., O.M.I., Bp., 454
Mundelein, George, 544
Munoz Duque, Anibal, Card., 204
Munoz Vega, Paolo, S.J., Card., 204
Muratorian Fragment, 228
Murillo, Bartolome, 400
Murphy, Frank, 400
Murphy, John B., 400
Murphy, Joseph A., 544
Murphy, T. Austin, Bp., 528
Murphy, Thomas W., C.SS.R., Bp., 528
Murphy, William F., 545
Murray, John C., 400
Murray, John G., 545
Murray, Philip, 400
Muscat, **see** Arabian Peninsula
Music, Sacred, 253
  Pontifical Institute, 620
  See also Liturgical Developments
Muslims, **see** Moslems
Mussio, John K., Bp., 528
Mysteries of Faith, 372
Mysteries of Rosary, 378
Mysterium Fidei **see** Transubstantiation
Mystery of Church, 219
Mystery of Eucharist, **see** Mass
Mystical Body, 220

N

Nahalka, Stefan, Msgr., 106
Nahum, 234
Namibia, 428
Napoleon, 162
Nasalli Rocca de Corneliano, Mario, Card., 204
Nathan, **see** Historical Books of Bible
Nathan, George Jean, 400
National
  Alliance of Czech Catholics, 658
  Apostolate for Mentally Retarded, 638
  Assembly of Religious Brothers, 560
  Assembly of Women Religious, 79, 95, 577-78
  Association of Catholic Chaplains, 623
  Association of Church Personnel Administrators, 658
  Association of Laity, 658
  Association of Priest Pilots, 658
  Black Sisters' Conference, 578
  Catholic Bandmasters' Assn., 658
  Catholic Cemetery Conference, 658
  Catholic Community Service, 648
  Catholic Conference for Interracial Justice, 85, 658
  Catholic Conferences, U.S., 506-11
  Catholic Development Conference, 658
  Catholic Educational Assn., 73, 605-06

Shields, Frank X., 106
Shields, James, 403
Shintos, 345
  Representatives Visit Pope, 63
  World Statistics, 327
Shipman, Andrew Jackson, 403
Shrine, Crowned, 381
Shrine, Immaculate Conception, 138
Shrines, Canada, 459
Shroud of Turin, 381
Siam, see Thailand
Siberia, 434
Sick, Anointing of, see Anointing of Sick
Sick, Eucharistic Fast, 362
Sick, Catholic Union of, 655
Sick, Clerics Regular Ministers (Camillians), 552
Sick, Oil of, 373
Sick Calls, 381
Sidarouss, Stephanos I, C.M., Patriarch, Card., 207
Sienkiewicz, Henryk, 403
Sierra Leone, 434
Signatura, Apostolic, 193
Sign of Cross, 381
Signs of the Times, 381
Signum Fidei Medal, 694
Sikkim, 434
Silva Henriquez, Raul, S.D.B., Card., 207
Similtudes of Christ, 237
Simon, Richard, 240
Simon, St. (Apostle), 242
Simony, 381
Sin, 381
  Accessory to, 346
  Punishment, 377
    See also Original Sin
Sindona, Michele, and Vatican Investments, 58
Singapore, 86, 434
Sinnot, James, M.M., 76
Sino-Korean Association, 61
Sins
  against Holy Spirit, 381
  Capital, 352
  Forgiveness, 362
    See also Penance
  Occasions, 382
  That Cry to Heaven for Vengeance, 382
Sipila, Helvi, 47
Sirach, 233
Siri, Giuseppe, Card., 207
Sister, 382
Sister Formation Conference, 577
Sisterhood, 382
Sisters, United States, 552-77
  Entrances and Departures, 551
  in Missions, 584-86
Sisters
  Meetings, 120-21
  Organizations, 577-79
    See also Religious, Women
Sisters, Urban Apostolate, 49
Sisters Uniting, 578
Situation Ethics, 382
Sitwell, Edith, 403
Sixtus II, St., 305
Skepticism, 47
Skinner, Henrietta, 403
Skinner, Patrick J., C.J.M., 455
Slander, 382
Slavery, U.S., 461
Slipyi or Slipyji, Josyf, Card., 207
  See also Ukrainian Patriarchate
Sloth, 382
Slovak Byzantine Catholics, 319
Slovak Cath. Federation of America, 659
  Catholic Sokol, 659
Slovakia, Persecution, 56, 86, 415-16
Smith, Alfred E., 403
Smith, Alphonse, 547
Smith, Eustace J., O.F.M., 106, 547
Smith, Ignatius, 403
Smith, Leo R., 547
Smith, Matthew, 403
Smith, William J., Bp., 455
Smyth, Clement, O.C.S.O., 547
Snyder, John J., Bp., 532
Sobieski, John, 403
Social Communications, Commission, 194
  Pastoral Instruction, 662-64
    See also Communications

Social Doctrine of Church, 247-51
Social Service, Sisters of, 576
Social Services, Catholic, 622-38
Socially Maladjusted, Facilities for, 631-33
Societies, Catholic, in U.S., 653-61
Societies, Religious, see Religious, Men, Women in U.S.
Society for Propagation of Faith, 660
Society of Retired Catholics, 660
  of St. Peter of Native Clergy, 660
  of St. Vincent de Paul, 622
Sodality of Our Lady, see Christian Life Communities
SODEPAX, 336
Soenneker, Henry J., Bp., 532
Solanus, Francis St., 408
Solemn Liturgical Action, 257
Solemnity of Mary, 299
Sollicitudo Omnium Ecclesiarum (Representatives of Holy
  See), 211
Solomon, see Historical Books of Bible
Solomon Islands, 435
Somalia, 435
Somaliland, French, see Afars and Issas
Somascan Fathers, 557
Song of Songs, 232
Sons of Divine Providence, 557
  Holy Family, 555
  Mary Missionary Society, 558
  Sacred Heart of Jesus (Verona Fathers), 558
Sophia, Catholic University (Japan), 619
Sorcery, 382
Sorin, Edward F., 408
Sororities, 653
Sorrowful Mother, Sisters of, 569
Sorrows (Dolors) of the Blessed Virgin Mary, 298
Soteriological Award, 694
Soteriology, 382
Souls, Holy, see All Souls
South Africa, Republic, 66, 435
  IBM Sales, 74
South America
  Cardinals, 210
  Communion in Hand, 284
  Eastern Rite Jurisdictions, 320
  Episcopal Conferences, 446
  Missionary Bishops, 493
    See also Latin America
South Carolina, 494, 497, 499, 601, 629, 643
  Dates in Catholic History, 474
South Dakota, 495, 498, 500, 603, 617, 629
  Dates in Catholic History, 475
South Korea, 76, 100, 425
  Bishop Tji Freed, 66
South West Africa, see Namibia
Southwell, Robert, St., 305
Southwest Volunteer Apostolate, 651
Soviet Union, see Union of Soviet Socialist Republics
Sowada, Alphonse, O.S.C., Bp., 532
Space, Outer, 370
Spain, 55, 60, 66, 71, 76, 81, 91, 98, 435
  Civil War (1936), 164
  Inquisition, 363
  Persecution (1931), 164
Spalding, John L., 403
Spalding, Martin, 403
Spallanzani, Lazzaro, 403
Spanish North Africa, 435
Spanish Sahara, 435
Spanish-Speaking in U.S., 94, 588-89
  Las Hermanas, 579
  PADRES, 589
  Population, 94
  Secretariat for, 588
  Seminary, Bilingual, 88
Spearman, Frank Hamilton, 404
Species, Sacred, 382
Spellman, Francis J., 404
Speltz, George H., Bp., 532
Spence, Francis J., Bp., 455
Spence, John S., 547
Spiritism, 382
Spiritual Life Institute of America, 660
Spiritual Works of Mercy, 382
Sponsor see Confirmation
Spoon, 322
Sri Lanka, 436
Staffa, Dino, Card., 207
Stamps, Vatican, 216
Stang, William, 547
Stanislaus, St., 305

ADDITIONS AND CHANGES

Roman Curia (p. 192): Most Rev. Eduardo Pironio, appointed pro-prefect of the Sacred Congregation for Religious and Secular Institutes and made titular archbishop of Thiges; he had been bishop of Mar del Plata, Argentina, from 1972.

Cardinals (pp. 197-209): Antonio Caggiano, archbishop of Buenos Aires and military vicar of Argentina, resigned Apr. 22, 1975; Luis Concha, former archbishop of Bogota, died Sept. 18 (see page 105); Luigi Raimondi, prefect of the Congregation for the Causes of Saints, died June 24 (see page 106).

Representatives of the Holy See (pp. 212-14): Canada, Archbishop Angelo Palmas, pro-nuncio; West Germany, Guido Del Mestri, pro-nuncio; Uruguay, Luigi Bellotti, nuncio.

Diplomats at the Vatican (pp. 214-15): Gabon, Mr. Marcel Sandoungout, ambassador.

Diplomatic relations were established between the Vatican City and Sri Lanka in September.

Vatican Representatives (p. 218): Most Rev. Renzo Frana, permanent observer of the Holy See to UNESCO.

Episcopal Conferences (p. 445): Cardinal Antonio Ribeiro, elected president of the Portuguese Episcopal Conference in October, 1975.

U.S. Jurisdictions, Hierarchy (pp. 484-93): New diocese of Pensacola-Tallahassee, Fla., established in October, 1975; Rene H. Gracida, auxiliary of Miami from 1972, was named bishop.

Hierarchy, Appointments: Lansing, Mich., Kenneth Povish transferred from Crookston, Minn., in October, 1975; Portland, Me., Amedee Proulx, named auxiliary in September, 1975; San Antonio, Tex., Hugo Gerbermann transferred to auxiliary in July, 1975, from Huehuetenango, Guatemala; Springfield, Ill., Joseph A. McNicholas transferred from auxiliary of St. Louis to bishop in July, 1975.

Retired: William A. O'Connor, bishop of Springfield, Ill. from 1949.

Death: J. Louis Flaherty, auxiliary of Richmond, Va., from 1966 (see page 105).

Missionary Bishops (p. 492): Hugo Gerbermann transferred to San Antonio as auxiliary bishop.

American Catholic Awards (pp. 688-95): Cardinal Gibbons Medal, Judge John J. Sirica (1975); Marian Library Medal, Rev. Giuseppe Besutti (1975); Thomas More Association Medal, John J. Delaney (1975).

PUBLICATION HISTORY

The Catholic Almanac originated, remotely from *St. Anthony's Almanac,* a 64-page annual with calendar, feature and devotional contents, published by the Franciscans of Holy Name Province from 1904 to 1929.

Completely revised and enlarged, the publication was issued under the title, *The Franciscan Almanac,* by *The Franciscan Magazine* from 1931 to 1933 and by St. Anthony's Guild from 1936 to 1971. From 1940 to 1969 its title was *The National Catholic Almanac;* the present title was adopted in 1969. The 1959 to 1971 editions were produced jointly by St. Anthony's Guild and Doubleday & Co., Inc.

The Almanac was acquired in 1971 by Our Sunday Visitor, Inc., Huntington, Ind. 46750, publisher of this edition.

OCTOBER 1975 ITEMS

Issues Discussed by Lay Council: Bishops, priests, religious and lay persons met in Vatican City in an eight-day world consultation to review and project lay participation in the life of the Church.

Suggestions and recommendations from 250 delegates to the consultation were to be evaluated by the Vatican's Council for the Laity during the week of Oct. 20-26 before being sent to Pope Paul for his decisions.

Bishop Lucas Moreira Neves, vice president of the council, told a press conference Oct. 16 that the consultation had been called for a three-fold purpose: so that the Laity Council could "take its bearings" 10 years after the Second Vatican Council, to give a new stimulus to the council's renewal movement, and to intensify the Holy Year's stimulus for reconciliation.

During the eight-day meeting questions were raised on the possibility of ordaining women to the priesthood in the Catholic Church.

"A possible future ordination of women is always raised at such meetings," said Bishop Moreira Neves.

"It is a perennial and came from Africa, Europe, the Americas and elsewhere. But this question was not within the competence of the council."

A delegate confirmed that ordination of women was widely advocated by delegates of every ethnic group and geographical area. Africans, especially, were vocal in calling for women priests.

"But over and above the cry for the priestly ordination of women was a call for a 'formal lay ministry' in which lay people would be invested in certain functions within the Church," he noted.

These functions, said this informant, would be in addition to the present lay functions of acolyte and lector. He said requests were made for creation of the ministries of musician and catechist — both to be formal ordination-type ministries.

"It would also be open to the local episcopal conferences to inaugurate other lay ministries which they might consider appropriate for the area," he said.

At the press conference, Bishop Moreira Neves noted: "How to deal with Marxist tendencies is a question that arises daily from those in areas affected. The Church tries to approach this with its clear teaching on universal justice, equality and humanity, one toward the other."

A congress delegate said that Latin American delegates tried repeatedly to get the congress to urge the Church to intervene on political levels. This was rejected by the majority of members.

"There was a very strong Latin American tendency to say that the Church had missed out on the great socio-economic movements, and that the Church should intervene politically," this delegate reported.

"However, an Irish delegate insisted on the theme of 'render unto Caesar . . .' and this was generally agreed upon, meaning that the Church had no business mixing in politics," he said.

This source stated that a "Third World liberation theology was mentioned by a number of Latin Americans, some of whom were even militant, but was not supported by the Africans.

"The tenor of the African representatives was: teach us how to pray, how to educate, how to understand the issues at stake and our simple family-life — which is the greatest apostolate in Africa."

Bishops' Meeting: Advance word about the Nov. 17 to 20, 1975, meeting of the National Conference of Catholic Bishops and the U.S. Catholic Conference indicated that it might produce a statement on housing, one of the scheduled subjects for discussion. The title was said to be "The Right to a Decent Home."

The 41st International Eucharistic Congress, to be held Aug. 1 to 8, 1976, in Philadelphia was expected to be the subject of a pastoral letter.

Other topics for consideration were to be economic issues, unemployment, the evangelization of the black community, the relationship of the Catholic and Jewish people, and bilingual, bicultural education in areas with a large Spanish-speaking population.

Probably to be deferred until the time of their spring, 1976, meeting in Chicago are actions on a projected statement on moral values (entitled "Jesus, Our Way, Truth and Life") and review of a draft of a *National Catechetical Directory.*

Vatican Policy On Jerusalem

Outlines of Vatican policy with respect to Jerusalem, and other aspects of the Holy Land, were sketched by Pope Paul VI in his 1973 Christmas address to the College of Cardinals and in another address to a general audience Apr. 19, 1974.

Related proposals are for:

• An international statute or agreement guaranteeing free access to the city of Jerusalem for all and the rights of Christians and Moslems to keep their homes there. (Christian and Moslem presence has been undermined since 1971 when Israeli authorities began expropriating non-Jewish property and carrying out a kind of urban renewal program almost exclusively for Jews.)

• A statute including "an appropriate protection" for all Holy Places in the Holy Land. (Israel agrees to this, and other nations have no objection.)

• A "just and generous response" to the plight of "hundreds of thousands" of Palestinians "who have been made refugees from their land, reduced to desperate conditions of life, or in some other way frustrated in their legitimate aspiration." (The UN officially lists as refugees 1.5 million Palestinians who have lost their homes since 1948 and have been living in Lebanon, East Jordan, on the west bank of the Jordan River, the Gaza Strip, Syria, Israel and Egypt. Another two million have moved to other places.)

Earlier Vatican policy had been in line with a resolution adopted by the United Nations Nov. 29, 1947. It called for the creation of a separate body, consisting of the city of Jerusalem and its immediate environs, under the control of an international regime. The resolution was never implemented. A trend toward the present Vatican policy became evident in December, 1967.

NOVEMBER 1974

VATICAN

CELAM and Liberation — Pope Paul told a gathering in St. Peter's Square Nov. 3 that he was "greatly impressed and comforted" by proceedings of the Oct. 29 to Nov. 2 meeting of the Latin American Bishops' Council in Rome. The meeting, marking the 20th anniversary of the council, focused attention on problems of the Church in Latin America. The Pope said, in part: "There is need to understand what socio-economic changes must be carried out, especially in the countries of the so-called Third World (of developing nations), and to bring them to a higher level of equality in the needs and rights of modern civilization and human dignity. . . . There is talk of 'liberation,' a word which the Church highly appreciates and has taken for herself, finding in it above all the basic doctrine of the liberating redemption of mankind from evil, from sin, which is the major obstacle to real freedom." He also declared that "hatred and violence" in one version of liberation theory and practice are "not the way of the Gospel" and of the Church. "The Church, rather, believes in love and thinks that love is stronger."

Church Needs Love — The Pope, at a general audience Nov. 6, rebuked both secularists and some Catholics for their antagonism toward the Church. Of the latter, he said: "These are the brothers who have left vacant the positions assigned them in the house of the Lord. They are brothers and sons who have transformed the positive witness, which the people of God awaited of them, into the arrogant functions of judges and critics of the very holy Church of God. Sometimes, usurping to themselves a faculty of free scrutiny of her doctrine and life, they have calmly aligned themselves with her adversaries — whence, with bitterness and no longer with love, they have silently moved away, perhaps protesting a desire to remain within ecclesial communion. . . . There is need for all of us to increase our love of the Church so that she may be worthy of being loved by those who do not know her or who only know her human defects and are ignorant of the strength of fidelity to the Gospel."

World Food Conference — In a Nov. 9 address to delegates to the UN World Food Conference in Rome, the Pope declared that the global food crisis stems from unwillingness to correct maldistribution of the world's resources and from the lopsided emphasis nations place on industrialization. He also warned that the issue of population growth could become an "alibi" used to sidestep the real issues behind the crisis. He called

efforts to impose restrictive population policies on nations "a new form of warfare" designed to deprive them of their "just share of the earth's goods."

Identity Crisis and Holy Year — Pope Paul, noting that reluctance to enter into the spirit of Holy Year 1975 was due to an identity crisis among some Catholics, told a general audience Nov. 13: "Happy are those who enjoy normal self-mastery and can unhesitatingly undertake the ascetic effort proposed by the Holy Year program. . . . But not all, even in the heart of the Church, are in such a favorable state. It seems that a state of uncertainty, an inner bewilderment, a lack of sureness about one's own person, prevents an easy and trusting welcome of the Holy Year's spiritual program" of reconciliation and spiritual renewal. He observed that doubt "has become common and even fashionable today," and continued: "We are anxious to recall how contrary to the genius of Catholicism, to the kingdom of God, it is to indulge in doubt and uncertainty about the doctrine of the Faith. Faith indeed invites us to a continual and progressive study, but starting from sure truths to arrive at other truths." With confidence in the meaning of man given them by their faith, Catholics can enter the Holy Year "with confidence in ourselves, in who we are, in whence we came and whither we are going."

International Women's Year — Pope Paul, during a private meeting Nov. 16 with Helvi Sipila, secretary general for the United Nations International Women's Year 1975, declared that "in the contemporary effort to promote the advancement of women in society, the Church has already recognized a 'sign of the times,' and has seen in it a call of the Spirit." Equality of the sexes, he said, "is rooted in the dignity of the human person and in the filial relationship of man and woman with God. . . ." Such equality "does not exclude . . . the specific contribution of woman to the full development of society, according to her proper and personal vocation. . . . Woman will preserve and develop, principally in the family community, in full coresponsibility with man, her task of welcoming, giving and raising life, in a growing development of its potential powers."

Skepticism and Charismatic Spirituality — For the second time in a week Pope Paul lamented at a general audience Nov. 20 a "skeptical and pessimistic doubt about one's own identity" among some Catholics. No longer is it fashionable, he said, to seek "a logical and systematic defense of religion. . . . Charismatic spiritualism is preferred to dogmatic reasoning. It is not for us to underrate this marvelous means of recovering religious truth (however) so long as the means itself is authentic."

Christian Credibility — The Holy Father declared at a general audience Nov. 27 that Christian faith and Christian conduct must go hand in hand to make Christianity credible. "Religious practice itself, isolated from observance of the moral law, is not enough to be acceptable to God and credible to those around us; it must be supported by concomitant moral and social virtues. Love of God, or religious charity, the primary commandment, cannot be separated from love of those around us or from social charity, especially toward family, those who exercise legitimate authority, the needs of the poor, the humble, the suffering, and every one of our brothers — in short, toward the man in need of bread, of love or of respect."

The Pope Also:

• Joined members of the Pontifical Academy of Sciences Nov. 13 to commemorate the centenary of the birth of Guglielmo Marconi, inventor and designer of Vatican Radio.

• Met privately with U.S. astronaut James A. McDivitt, Nov. 13.

• Met for 45 minutes with Dr. Gibreel Shukri Deeb, the representative of the Palestine Liberation Organization to the UN World Food Conference, at the latter's request, Nov. 16.

• Denounced kidnapping (37 were known in Italy during the previous year) as a "vile and atrocious" crime, Nov. 17.

• Expressed his sympathy on the deaths of Erskine Childers, president of the Irish Republic, Nov. 17, and U Thant, former secretary general of the United Nations, Nov. 26.

Vatican Briefs:

• Archbishop Luigi Poggi was named to head the Vatican's delegation for "permanent work contacts" with representatives of Poland's Communist government.

• Cardinal Humberto Medeiros of Boston was named a member of the Congregation for Bishops.

• Cardinal Jan Willebrands, president of the Secretariat for Promoting Christian Unity, praised retiring Anglican Archbishop Michael Ramsey of Canterbury for his efforts and accomplishments in pursuit of Christian unity. Archbishop Ramsey, who retired Nov. 15, was succeeded in the see of Canterbury by Archbishop Donald Coggan.

Declaration on Abortion

The Congregation for the Doctrine of the Faith made public Nov. 25 the text of a "Declaration on Procured Abortion," branding abortion as intrinsically evil and calling for action "to combat its causes." The document declared that no Christian may "conform" to an intrinsically immoral law, and that no Christian can "take part in a propaganda campaign in favor of such a law, or vote for

it. Moreover, he may not collaborate in its application."

The declaration noted, among other things:

• "Right from fertilization is begun the adventure of a human life, and each of its capacities requires time — a rather lengthy time — to find its place and to be in a position to act. The least that can be said is that present science, in its most evolved state, does not give any substantial support to those who defend abortion."

• "The tradition of the Church has always held that human life must be protected and favored from the beginning, just as it is at the various stages of its development."

• "It does not belong to society . . . to recognize this right (to life) for some and not for others. . . . It is not recognition by another that constitutes this right."

• "We proclaim . . . that none of these reasons (in defense of abortion) can ever objectively confer the right to dispose of another's life, even when that life is only beginning."

• "One cannot but be astonished to see a simultaneous increase of unqualified protests against the death penalty and every form of war, and the vindication of the liberalization of abortion, either in its entirety or in ever broader indications."

The declaration was approved by Pope Paul June 28, 1974, and the official text was published Nov. 18. (See separate entry.)

DOMESTIC

Priest Murdered — Funeral services were held Nov. 2 in Paterson, N.J., for Father Francis A. English, aged administrator of St. Boniface parish who was found dead — beaten, bound and gagged — in the rectory Oct. 29. Four suspects were charged with murder.

Abortion — A federal court enjoined Massachusetts from enforcing a law, scheduled to go into effect Nov. 1, requiring unmarried women under 18 to get written parental consent before undergoing an abortion.

In other developments:

• A Pittsburgh physician was cleared by a coroner's jury Nov. 12 of allegations that he had permitted a baby girl who survived an abortion to die.

• House-Senate conferees agreed to drop from a Department of Health, Education and Welfare appropriations bill an amendment against the use of federal funds for abortions not needed to save a mother's life.

• Gallup poll findings of Oct. 18 to 21 indicated that 52 and 48 per cent, respectively, of 1,595 adults were for and against the legality of abortion on demand during the first three months of pregnancy. The for and against percentages were 47 and 44 in April, 1974; and 46 and 45 in December, 1972, a month before the U.S. Supreme Court nullified any right to life for the unborn.

Christian Unity — Christian unity is "not an option" but an "essential element of the discipleship of anyone who would be obedient to Jesus Christ," declared Dr. Gerald F. Moede at his installation as general secretary of the Consultation on Church Union Nov. 4 in Cincinnati.

Urban Apostolate of Sisters — The Chicago archdiocese announced Nov. 11 that it was ending subsidies for the Urban Apostolate of Sisters because it had "changed its goal and purpose and . . . overlaps the efforts of other organizations." The apostolate was founded in 1968 to serve as a resource center for sisters teaching in inner-city schools, a purpose which was subsequently deemphasized in favor of social action goals. Sister Jeanne Stroh, a staff member of the apostolate, denied that it was duplicating the services of other organizations in the archdiocese. The most recent annual subsidies amounted to $29,498.

Marital Statistics — According to estimates released during the month by the National Center for Health Statistics:

• 925,000 persons — a one-year increase of 200,000 — were divorced in the year prior to March, 1974.

• More people under the age of 35 were remaining single. In 1974, 54.8 per cent of men under 35 and 44.5 per cent of women in the same age bracket had never been married.

Children of God — The attorney general of New York State issued a report containing the testimony of 74 witnesses about practices of the controversial Children of God founded by David (Moses) Berg. Reported abuses included anti-parental indoctrination, brainwashing and sexual behavior.

Supreme Court Decisions — In decisions handed down during the month, the U.S. Supreme Court:

• Let stand Nov. 11 a lower court ruling that the Church of the New Song is a religion entitled to the protection of the First Amendment. The church was founded by Harry W. Theriault while he was an inmate at the federal penitentiary in Atlanta.

• In one of three Nov. 25 decisions, ruled that "commuters" — foreign-born persons who are qualified to live in the U.S. as permanent legal aliens but live in their own countries (Mexico, Canada) — may work in the United States on a seasonal or daily basis.

• Refused to block a program providing $3 million in state aid to private colleges in Maryland, including those under religious auspices.

Parish Dispute — Archbishop Jean Jadot, apostolic delegate to the United States, declined Nov. 18 to intervene in a dispute between some members of Good Shepherd parish in Arlington, Va., and their new pastor and Bishop Thomas Welsh. At issue, according to members of the parish council, were decisions of Father Hannan to: halt work on a $1 million building program; stop the practice of in-hand reception of Holy Commun-

ion; terminate the services of six women who had been extraordinary ministers of the Eucharist; limit the parish council to an advisory capacity. In the background of the affair were innovative measures introduced by the former pastor.

10th Anniversary of Ecumenism Decree — Cardinal Jan Willebrands, president of the Vatican Secretariat for Promoting Christian Unity, was a principal participant in two interfaith assemblies marking the 10th anniversary of the Second Vatican Council's *Decree on Ecumenism.* The assemblies were for a national liturgical service in Washington, D.C., Nov. 17 and a seminar at Princeton Theological Seminary Nov. 24 to 26.

Catholics in Congress — *Christianity Today,* an evangelical Protestant weekly, reported that 123 Catholics were among the 535 representatives elected Nov. 5 to serve in the 94th Congress. Two of them were priests, Fathers Robert Drinan, S.J., of Massachusetts (reelected) and Robert W. Edgar, O. Praem., of Wisconsin. Methodists numbered 85; Episcopalians, 66; Presbyterians, 65; Jews, 24. All but six of the legislators claimed some kind of religious affiliation.

Child-Care Agency Decision — A three-judge federal court upheld Nov. 20 the constitutionality of state aid to New York's private child-care agencies. The court declared that state-aid regulations constituted a "fair and reasonable accommodation" between the No Establishment and Free Exercise clauses of the U.S. Constitution. Nearly half of the state's child-care agencies were under Catholic auspices.

Illegal Aliens — The 48 members of the New York Archdiocesan Association of Hispano Priests appealed to congressional and administration leaders "to undertake a generous, flexible immigration policy" by loosening quotas and restrictions on the residence and employment of aliens. They said that hundreds of thousands of illegal aliens in this country should be regarded "with humanitarian eyes as economic refugees" from poverty-ridden countries of Latin America, and should be granted amnesty and residential rights. Estimates regarding the number of illegals in the U.S. ran as high as eight million. A million and a half were thought to be in the New York metropolitan area.

School Aid Decisions — Parents of students attending Catholic, Protestant and Jewish schools petitioned the U.S. Supreme Court to review a July 20, 1974, decision of the Missouri Supreme Court which banned the lending of public school textbooks to students of church-related schools.

In another case, the Minnesota State Supreme Court struck down a 1971 income tax credit law which provided credits of up to $140 for parents of nonpublic school students. Basing its decision on 1973 U.S. Supreme Court rulings on school aid legislation in New York, Pennsylvania and Rhode Island, the court said Nov. 26 that the Minnesota statute violated the principle of separation of Church and state.

Butz' Insult to the Pope — Msgr. Eugene V. Clark, a spokesman for the New York archdiocese, called on Secretary of Agriculture Earl L. Butz to apologize or resign because of "his crude, pointed insult" to Pope Paul at a meeting with newsmen Nov. 27. Butz, in dismissing the view expressed by the Pope that rich nations should not seek to solve the world food crisis by telling poor nations to control population, said of the Pontiff: "He no playa the game; he no makea the rules." Butz replied to the criticism with a statement in which he said he never intended "to impugn the motives or the integrity of any religious group, ethnic group or religious leader." He attributed his remark to an Italian woman during sessions of the UN World Food Conference in Rome. It was observed in some quarters that reaction to this insult was mild in comparison with that occasioned by an army general's recent remark about Jewish influence in the United States.

Domestic Briefs:

• Dale Francis, who was fired in mid-October from the positions of editor and publisher of the *National Catholic Register,* joined the staff of *Our Sunday Visitor* as executive editor in charge of the paper's news edition. The *Register* announced Nov. 5 that its new editor would be retired Archbishop Robert J. Dwyer of Portland, Ore.

• *Commonweal* magazine marked its 50th anniversary with publication of its Nov. 15 edition.

• In a letter read to the assembly of the National Conference of Catholic Bishops Nov. 19, Cardinal Jozsef Mindszenty thanked the bishops "for all that you individually and as an episcopal body did for me during the years (1956 to 1971) of my exile in my own homeland within the precincts of the American Embassy in Budapest." The bishops paid his expenses during that time.

Bishops' Meeting

More than 250 bishops attended the Nov. 18 to 22 meeting of the National Conference of Catholic Bishops and the United States Catholic Conference in Washington, D.C. Social issues as well as internal concerns of the Church figured prominently in the proceedings. Archbishop Joseph L. Bernardin of Cincinnati was elected to a three-year term as president of both conferences. (See Meetings of the Conference of Bishops and "The World Food Crisis — A Pastoral Plan of Action.")

FOREIGN

Abortion Bill in Norway — The Norwegian parliament rejected Nov. 1, by a vote of 78 to 77, a bill that would have permitted abortion on demand up until the 12th week of pregnancy. The percentage of the population favoring unrestricted abortion increased from 13 in 1969 to 47 in August, 1974, when 44 per cent were opposed.

False Accusation — Bishop Leonidas Proana of Riobamba, Ecuador, claimed that he and his priests were being falsely accused of Communism because of their actions in defense of landless Indians in his Andean diocese. In rebuttal the bishop said, "We are fulfilling the mandate of Christ to fight the sin of social injustice," in a statement concerning incidents leading to the death of an Indian and the arrest of his vicar general.

Euthanasia Drive — What appeared to be a move in a long-expected drive for the legalization of euthanasia in England was the publication and accompanying publicity early in the month of *Confessions of a Surgeon.* The book contained accounts of numerous mercy killings carried out by George Mair during his years-long medical practice.

Sterilization in Puerto Rico — Bishop Rafael Grovas of Caguas rejected claims of the Puerto Rican government that its free sterilization program was voluntary. Referring to 300,000 women sterilized since 1973, he declared: "Contrary to what the government says, they did not submit voluntarily. . . . The position taken by government authorities regarding population problems amounts to an anti-Gospel drive." The administration had a declared goal of zero population growth by the year 2000.

Arafat at UN — Palestine Liberation Organization chief Yasir Arafat, in an address before the General Assembly of the United Nations Nov. 13, called for recognition of the Palestinians' right to self-determination, assailed Israel for violations of that right, and presented an apologia for terrorist actions of the PLO. His remarks were vigorously rebutted by Israeli spokesmen and others. The days-long UN debate on the Palestine problem was inconclusive. Arafat, whose appearance was favored by 105 UN members but opposed by the U.S. and three other nations, was only the second representative of a non-member state to address the UN. The other one was Pope Paul VI, who made a strong plea for world peace before the assembly Oct. 4, 1965.

Canadian Pro-Life Petition — The Canadian Alliance for Life reported that nearly 800,000 persons had signed a "Petition of One Million" calling upon parliament "to enact legislation providing for the child conceived but not yet born the same protection provided for any other person." The alliance planned to present the petition to Prime Minister Pierre Trudeau in January, 1975.

Press Congress — A.E.P. Wall, director and editor-in-chief of NC News Service, was elected president of the International Federation of Catholic Press Agencies during meetings of the 10th World Congress of the Catholic Press Nov. 17 to 24 in Buenos Aires. Also elected, to posts in the newly organized Federation of Church Press Associations, were John F. Fink, vice president, and James A. Doyle, treasurer, officers of the U.S. Catholic Press Association. Discussions of the congress centered on the problems and influence of religious publications.

School Aid Needed — The bishops of Argentina appealed to the government for tax relief and financial subsidies for the continuing operation of Catholic schools throughout the country. Without such aid, they said, "many schools for the poor which function on a non-tuition basis are sure to close." More than 20 per cent of the nation's five million primary and secondary students were in Catholic schools.

Moslem Proselytizing — Father Jean Paul Beyami told participants in the 10th World Congress of the Catholic Press in Buenos Aires that Arab oil profits were being used to generate a powerful drive by Moslems to spread their faith in Africa. Father Beyami, editor of a Catholic weekly in Cameroun, said: "In fact, the present situation regarding Christian churches and Moslem groups could be said to approach a cold war."

No Action on Religious Discrimination — The UN General Assembly's social, humanitarian and cultural committee again postponed efforts to formulate an international convention designed to eliminate all forms of religious intolerance by governments. The efforts, underway since 1962, were frustrated by various UN participants, especially those from Communist-dominated countries.

Conservative Jews — Delegates to an international convention of the (Conservative) World Council of Synagogues in Jerusalem accused the Israeli government of discriminating against Conservative Jews and of favoring the Orthodox. At issue, according to Samuel Rothstein of New York, president of the council, was whether the Orthodox rabbinate of Israel should exercise worldwide control over Jewry. It was noted that: Conservative rabbis are not allowed to practice their ministry in Israel; only Orthodox marriage ceremonies are regarded as valid; children of non-Orthodox marriages are not recognized as legitimate; conversions to Judaism are not recognized as valid unless they comply with Orthodox norms. Conservative Judaism claimed to be the largest movement in Jewish religious life.

No Services for Bombers — Archbishop George P. Dwyer of Birmingham, England, issued a directive prohibiting funeral services in churches of the archdiocese for anyone killed while planting bombs. "Anyone guilty of such violence is guilty of grave sin," he said.

Korean Demonstration — South Korean police burst into the U.S. Embassy grounds in Seoul Nov. 21 to arrest an American Maryknoll missionary and a score of women demonstrating for the release of political prisoners. All those arrested were freed the same day. The priest was Father James Sinnott of New York, the vicar general of the Inchon diocese.

Foreign Briefs:
• A group of Catholic societies in England formed a Prisoners in Holy Year Committee to campaign for the release or fair trial of political prisoners and prisoners of conscience throughout the world (estimated by Amnesty International to number about 500,000).

• The General Synod of the Church of England, meeting Nov. 5 to 8 in London, commended to the study of the church at large two statements drafted by the Anglican-Roman Catholic International Committee of theologians — the "Windsor Statement" on the Eucharist, published in 1971, and the "Canterbury Statement" on ministry, published in 1973.

• Awarding of the John XXIII Peace Prize to the United Nations Educational, Scientific and Cultural Organization was announced by the Vatican Nov. 14. Later in the month the organization cut off specialized aid to Israel because of its "persistence in altering the historical features" of Jerusalem by "undertaking excavations which constitute a danger" to the city's monuments.

• Personal and social spiritual renewal and reconciliation were the themes of a pastoral letter of the Polish bishops read in churches throughout the country Nov. 24.

World Food Conference

More than 1,000 delegates took part in the UN-sponsored World Food Conference which ended Nov. 16 in Rome without doing much for the immediate relief of the hungry in famine-stricken countries. Some measure of accomplishment was reflected, however, in recommendations for the establishment of a world food council, an annual grain reserve of 10 million tons, a fund for long-range development of food production in underdeveloped countries, and an early-warning information system for predicting future food shortages. The U.S., despite its many contributions, was criticized for not pledging an increase in immediate aid and for failing to announce a donation to the proposed agricultural development fund.

The Vatican delegation helped draft a resolution calling on nations to cut arms spending by 10 per cent and to contribute the money saved to development programs. A spokesman of the delegation also said: "Food and energy supplies, essential to the life of peoples, must be once and for all withdrawn from the trading and political speculation of governments and individuals so that they may become available for the security and development of all."

DECEMBER 1974

VATICAN

Jesuits — Pope Paul encouraged more than 200 members of the 32nd general congregation of the Society of Jesus to work toward "a healthy, balanced and just aggiornamento in essential fidelity to the specific character of the society and in respect for the charism of your founder" (St. Ignatius Loyola). He also said in a similar vein: "All . . . must be vigilant so that the necessary adaptation (of the society to contemporary conditions) will not be accomplished to the detriment of the fundamental identity or essential character of the role of the Jesuit. . . . This image must not be altered. It must not be distorted." The Pope gave this counsel Dec. 3, the day after the congregation was convened.

Prosperity and Nausea — The Holy Father told a general audience Dec. 4 that prosperity was causing nausea among people looking for a "messianism of the spirit and not of material abundance." He also said that "unrelenting uneasiness over political and economic changes and over the mirage of continually new revolutions" was a sign of "hopeless expectation for a superior order (of society) which man himself cannot create."

Thomism — St. Thomas Aquinas' standards for the study of philosophy and theology should be used today for the discernment of what is valid in contemporary thought, observed Pope Paul in a message to Father Vincent de Cuesnongle, master general of the Dominicans. He noted "limitations in the scholarship of St. Thomas, especially where it is tied in with medieval cosmological and biological principles," but noted: "Often the (contemporary) diffidence and aversion to St. Thomas stems from a superficial and cursory encounter and, in some cases, from a complete absence of actual reading and study of his works."

Role of Women — The Pope told members of the Italian Union of Catholic Women Jurists Dec. 7 that the Church "is directly interested" in all questions concerning the role of women in contemporary society. He spoke about principles underlying efforts for the recognition of rights due to women, cited differences between men and women, and added "that the primacy through which women hold sway in all the human sphere is where they most directly encounter the problems of life, of suffering, of assistance and, above all, of motherhood."

Anti-Christ Literature — "An entire erudite and sometimes artistic literature from the last century up to today is working hard to vivisect the Gospel, in order to throw doubt on Jesus and even on his very existence," declared Pope Paul Dec. 11. Such literature "starts out with subjective presuppositions" which undermine the objectivity of the Gos-

pel, he said. He cautioned Christians to be wary of its "hypothesis, opinion, literary artifice, scientific ambiguity, cunning humanistic praise, sentimental superficiality, and tricks relating to the interpretation or explanation of scriptural passages."

Sudanese Hierarchy, Cardinals — Pope Paul announced at a Dec. 12 consistory of cardinals:
• establishment of a hierarchy in Sudan, with two archdioceses and five dioceses;
• appointment to the rank of Cardinal Bishop of Cardinals Jean Villot, Antonio Samore and Sebastiano Baggio;
• the appointment of Cardinal Franjo Seper as Chamberlain of the College of Cardinals.

Conciliation — "Sincere conversion to God's will and complete reconciliation among Christ's disciples" are the keys to "respectful cohesion" between more progressive and more traditional Catholics, Pope Paul told seven Canadian bishops Dec. 14. He praised their efforts to find a "pastoral ministry of thought, sacrament and action" capable of meeting contemporary needs of the Church in Canada.

Christmas Reflections — Christmas was the theme of the Pope's addresses to audiences Dec. 15, 18 and 22. He called the feast a time for excitement and wonder, and a special occasion to "honor, love and protect infancy," and to help the poor and needy. On Dec. 15 he said: "The spirit of Christmas must not lack two phases which will complete its joy. The first is . . . prayer, the joy of a personal encounter with Jesus, the Messiah of all and for all. . . . The second phase . . . is the outward expression of beneficent love, sensitive to the needs of others — the small, the poor, the suffering, the abandoned, prisoners, even the indifferent and the bad. . . . There can be no authentic Christmas if it is not marked by the social love which he personified in himself and which — from him, through him and through ourselves — he desired should illumine the world."

Divorce of Morals from Religion — "No one can ignore the fact that Christian morals are under fire in their very principles," declared Pope Paul Dec. 16 in an address to members of the Pontifical International Theological Commission. As a result, he said, "contemporary man is disturbed. He does not know any longer what is good and what is bad, nor in which criteria he can place his trust. And a certain number of Christians share these doubts, having lost their faith in a concept of natural morals as well as in the positive teachings of revelation and of the Church's teaching authority." Two causes of this state of affairs were the "separation of morals from religion, and especially from the teaching of the Church regarding certain great moral problems" (such as contraception, abortion, sterilization and euthanasia); and a tendency to discount the value of the teaching of the Church, resulting in "a relativism favorable toward 'amoral' tendencies."

Hope for Peace — This was one of several topics of the Pope's address at his annual pre-Christmas meeting with cardinals Dec. 23. He called for a "just peace" in the Middle East and for an end to violence in Vietnam, Northern Ireland and other embattled parts of the world. The Holy Father also spoke about the state of the Church and the significance of Holy Year 1975.

The Pope Also:
• Called time "a pilgrimage toward fulfillment and happiness . . . in the reality of the future life promised our faith in Christ."
• Made a contribution of $11,600 to the Reno diocese for some reduction of a debt incurred because of the failure of a diocesan investment in a religious trust fund.
• Met with diplomatic representatives to the Vatican Gordian Gudenus of Austria, Dec. 16, and Gerald Woods of Ireland, Dec. 19.
• Established the first apostolic delegation in the Portuguese territory of Mozambique.
• Formally inaugurated the Vatican's new Historic Art Museum, Dec. 22.
• Told a group of Italian Catholic educators that education must be rooted in strong moral and spiritual principles, Dec. 29.

Vatican Briefs:
• *L'Osservatore Romano* called legalized abortion "only one aspect of the vaster and more dramatic relativism and permissiveness" characteristic of contemporary society. The Dec. 1 comment was a reference to passage Nov. 29 by the French National Assembly (284 to 189) of a bill permitting abortion on demand during the first 10 weeks of pregnancy.
• A press officer expressed "deep pain and grief" at the conviction of Melkite-Rite Archbishop Ilarion Capucci, patriarchal vicar for Jerusalem, by an Israeli court on charges of arms-smuggling to Palestinian terrorists.
• Diplomatic activity by the Vatican to prevent war was called a "very serious moral imperative" by Archbishop Agostino Casaroli, secretary of the Council for the Public Affairs of the Church. Such activity, he said during a Vatican Radio broadcast Dec. 11, "does not exclude the most distant nations, even if talks with them, on an ideological level, can often reveal themselves to be so difficult as to appear almost impossible."
• The news agency *Fides* reported that contributions for the missions amounted to nearly $45 million in 1973. Earlier figures were almost $31 million (1970), $35.7 million (1971) and $40.1 million (1972).

Holy Year and Reconciliation
With the words, "Open to me the doors of justice," and with three taps of a silver hammer, Pope Paul opened the Holy Door in St. Peter's Basilica during Christmas midnight Mass ceremonies marking the start of the climactic Roman celebration of Holy Year 1975. During the ceremonies, which were televised worldwide, he invited people of all faiths, and none, to take the steps of faith and "interior transformation" leading to the Holy Year objectives of spiritual renewal and reconciliation with God and their fellow men.

Reconciliation within the Church was the theme of an apostolic exhortation released Dec. 16. In it the Holy Father called for efforts throughout the Church to counteract and resolve problems connected with "ferments of infidelity to the Holy Spirit," "factional spirit," "doctrinal dissension which claims the patronage of theological pluralism," and the "polarization of dissent" which begets "seeds of disintegration." He said that loyalty to the authority of the Pope, bishops and the official teaching of the Church is the only way to maintain "sure union with Christ."

DOMESTIC

Resignation — Bishop Raymond J. Gallagher of Lafayette resigned from the steering committee of Indiana's Interreligious Consultations because of its indirect association with the Religious Coalition for Abortion Rights. He said he "could not permit any ambiguity to develop" regarding his association with other members of the committee who favored abortion.

Editor Out — Archbishop Philip M. Hannan of New Orleans asked for and received the resignation of Father Andrew Taormina from the executive editorship of the archdiocesan *Clarion Herald*. In public comment the archbishop said: "I regret very deeply his position stated in his weekly column of the Nov. 28 issue opposing the teaching of the magisterium of the Church in regard to artificial birth control." Father Taormina said on resigning that it was his "intention to devote my future efforts as a priest of the archdiocese as director of the Apostolate of the Aging program under the Office of the Social Apostolate."

School Aid Support, Church Attendance — According to the findings of a Gallup Poll survey conducted in May, 1974, 52 per cent of 1,702 adults were in favor of a U.S. constitutional amendment that would permit the government to provide financial aid to parochial schools. Approving such a proposal were 52 per cent of Catholics, 44 per cent of Protestants and 27 per cent of Jews interviewed.

In a more recent survey, Gallup pollsters estimated that 40 per cent of the adult population attended weekly church services in 1974. The percentages were reported to be 55 for Catholics, 37 for Protestants and 16 for Jews.

Catholic-Orthodox Statement — Catholic and Orthodox theologians issued an "Agreed Statement on the Church" at the conclusion of the 10th dialogue conducted under the auspices of the U.S. Bishops' Committee for Ecumenical and Interreligious Affairs and the Standing Conference of Canonical Orthodox Bishops in America. The theologians agreed that their traditions differ with respect to the kinds of authority the Pope and the Patriarch of Constantinople have and exercise in their churches.

Fair Housing — The U.S. Commission on Civil Rights, in a 379-page report, said that federal agencies, and especially the Department of Housing and Urban Development, had failed to enforce fair housing laws in an adequate manner. "This commission has found that, although there have been some positive steps taken in the area of fair housing during the past two years, they have generally had a minimal impact on the serious housing discrimination problems confronting the nation," stated Arthur S. Fleming, chairman of the commission.

Vulgar Attack — *The National Lampoon* "deserves the condemnation of all fair-minded persons" for "an incredibly scurrilous and vulgar attack on Protestant, Catholic and Jewish beliefs" in its December edition, declared Stuart Hubbell, executive director of the Catholic League for Religious and Civil Rights. He said that the league found it "incomprehensible . . . that any group of editors or writers should be so devoid of human decency and respect that they would seek to deliberately insult the religious sensibilities of their fellow Americans — Protestants, Catholics and Jews, as the *Lampoon* staff has done." The magazine lampooned the virginity of Mary, the birth of Christ and other Catholic beliefs, and carried "an extremely offensive and crude parody on the National Conference of Christians and Jews," said Hubbell.

Boston Busing — Cardinal Humberto Medeiros called for a stand of "firm principle" in the continuing controversy over "forced busing" ordered by a federal court to achieve racial balance in Boston's public schools. He made the appeal in the wake of the closing of high schools in Roxbury and South Boston districts, and two days of back-to-back demonstrations on Boston Common by groups on both sides of the issue. The cardinal restated his belief that school integration is "quite desirable and necessary for our country," and his doubt that "busing as such is an evil thing."

Budget Cuts Opposed — Budget cutbacks proposed by President Gerald Ford in Medicare, Medicaid and Food Stamp programs were called "socially unjust" by Sister Virginia Schwager, director of the Division of Health Affairs, U.S. Catholic Conference. "These proposals to reduce spending would be most costly to those already hardest hit by inflation — the poor and the elderly," she said in a letter to the President.

NOW Expels Member — With a vote of 33 to 4, with one abstention, the Columbus, O., chapter of the National Organization of Women expelled Pat Goltz because of her active and public support of Feminists for Life, an organization opposed to abortion on demand. The expelled member said she continued to believe in many NOW objectives but saw no prospect of change in its pro-abortion position.

Teacher Strike Ends — The Buffalo diocese and the Secondary Lay Teachers Association signed a new two-year wage agreement Dec. 16 that ended an 18-day strike by most of the 372 lay teachers in 16 diocesan high schools. The agreement, ending the first lay teachers' strike in the history of the diocese, was to extend to August, 1976.

Younger Bishops, Moral Crisis — Archbishop Jean Jadot, apostolic delegate to the United States, said in a *Washington Post* interview that new Vatican policies accounted for the recent trend toward appointing as bishops younger men who were open to change and had "a very wide and very strong pastoral experience." He also said that the most serious problem facing the Church in the U.S. "is the very severe moral crisis." He added: "For me, one of the most important responsibilities of the Church in the next year is to help to collaborate with all other Christians and with our Jewish co-citizens . . . to work in such a way that we are able to give back to this country a sense of moral and religious values."

Protest against Imprisonment — Provincial superiors of the Divine Word Fathers in the U.S. and Canada sent a message of protest Dec. 27 to President Ferdinand Marcos of the Philippines against "the detainment and reported serious torture" of Father Edicio de la Torre, a Filipino member of the congregation. Father de la Torre, an underground opponent of Marcos and critic of the martial law in effect since September, 1972, was arrested Dec. 13.

Drug Abuse — "The Holy Father deplores the diffusion of pseudo-philosophical . . . theories which attempt to justify narcotic abuse," declared Cardinal Jean Villot, papal secretary of state, in a letter intended for participants in the first American Congress on Alcohol and Drug Problems. More than 4,000 persons took part in the congress Dec. 13 to 18 in San Francisco.

Domestic Briefs:

• In Proclaiming Dec. 18 a National Day of Prayer, President Gerald Ford said: "I call upon all Americans to pray for Deity's blessing on our land and for peace on earth, good will among all men."

• Honored: Dr. Andre Hellegers, director of the Kennedy Institute for the Study of Human Reproduction and Bioethics, with the

Linacre Award of the National Federation of Catholic Physicians' Guilds; food service expert Brother Herman E. Zaccarelli, with the 1974 International Man of Achievement Award of the International Biographical Centre, Cambridge, England; Maryknoll Sister Edna Demanche, with the 1974 Environmental Award of the Hawaii Association of Conservation Districts; sportscaster Curt Gowdy, with the first Golden Bronco Award of the Catholic Information Office of the Cheyenne diocese.

• Elected: Episcopalian Myron B. Bloy, Jr., president of the ecumenical National Institute for Campus Ministries; Bishop Edward A. McCarthy of Phoenix, president of the Arizona Ecumenical Council.

Top News Stories of 1974

The 10 leading news stories of the year, according to the opinions of 31 editors of Catholic publications, were:

1. The world food crisis and related UN conferences on population, in Bucharest in August, and food, in Rome in November.
2. Abortion and pro-life activities.
3. Actions of the U.S. bishops at their November meeting (see separate entry).
4. Diabolical possession and "The Exorcist."
5. The 1974 assembly of the Synod of Bishops and evangelization (see separate entry).
6. Clemency or amnesty for draft evaders.
7. Divorce questions.
8. Impeachment proceedings and the resignation of President Richard M. Nixon.
9. Drought in Africa.
10. Catholic charismatics.

The top-ranked religious personality was Archbishop Joseph L. Bernardin, president of the National Conference of Catholic Bishops and the U.S. Catholic Conference.

FOREIGN

Hard To Live the Faith — An East German synod of clergy, religious and lay persons called the Church in their country a "Church of the diaspora," urged Christians to live their faith courageously in their Communist-dominated society, and offered pastoral suggestions for strengthening the faith of communities and individuals. The synodal statement defined the Church of the diaspora as "the presence of Christians in a non-Christian environment," and said in conclusion: "To some Christians in our situation the faith appears to be a heavy burden. In truth, the Lord is placing the cross on our shoulders. But, if a good majority do not stand up to the test, which will mean for them tribulation and renunciation, then it will be hard for men to persevere in their faith-decision."

Nuclear Arms — Father John Lucal, S.J., a member of the Vatican's mission to the United Nations, pleaded before the political and security committee of the General Assembly for wider adherence by governments to the treaty on non-proliferation of nuclear weapons. In his address Father Lucal traced the consistent opposition of the Vatican to armament developments over the past 85 years.

Need for Change in Spain — Bishops and lay leaders in Spain warned extreme conservatives that their hard-line policies could bring about a return of the Marxist anarchy that tore the country apart about 40 years earlier. The Spanish Bishops' Conference declared at its November meeting: "It is our duty to make a profound evolution in our institutions, to give practical implementation to the rights of citizens to form associations and to gather freely and voice their views. We consider it very necessary to insure citizens' participation in political life within the demands of the common good." The bishops also said that violence "could result from either the right's trying to block the inevitable evolution of the social, economic and political structure of the nation, or from the left's trying to force such evolution through radical means."

Parliament and Church — The British Parliament relinquished its veto power Dec. 4 over decisions of the Church of England in matters of doctrine and worship. The Dec. 4 vote of the House of Commons, 145 to 45, put final approval on the Worship and Doctrine Measure which gained overwhelming support in February, 1974, from the Church of England's General Synod, and was passed by the House of Lords in November.

Church in Ireland — The situation of the Church in Ireland contains the "elements of a crisis," and only a total mobilization of religious orders, diocesan clergy and lay persons will be able to meet the Church's needs over the next decade. This assessment was published in "Focus for Action," a report compiled under the auspices of the Conference of Major Religious Superiors. Symptomatic of the crisis, according to the report, were "attitudes of paternalism and overprotectiveness . . . reactions of immaturity among the laity," alienation of the laity from the Church, diminishing Christian belief, the prospect of a secular society, the triumph of "consumerist, non-Christian values." The document urged religious orders to lead Catholics in making changes recommended by the Second Vatican Council.

Appeal to Bolivian Government — For the sake of "Christian reconciliation among Bolivians," Cardinal Clemente Maurer of Sucre and members of the board of the Bolivian Bishops' Conference appealed to Gen. Hugo Banzer to grant a Christmas amnesty to political prisoners and exiles. They also raised questions, during a visit with the president, about social and economic policies instituted by the government following an abortive revolution early in November, policies which "deal with the conscience and conduct of Catholics." Such measures, the bishops said, could lead to "violations of the freedom of conscience and of the freedom to choose one's occupation and work."

Disabilities of Indian Christians — The Catholic Union of India asked Prime Minister Indira Ghandi to remove legal "disabilities" affecting Indian Christians so that they might enjoy the rights and privileges of members of the Hindu "scheduled castes" to which they would belong if they were not Christians.

Church Restricted in Czechoslovakia — Sources in Vienna reported that the government of Czechoslovakia was tightening restrictions on priests and nuns. At least 40 priests in Slovakia had been removed from their parishes and some had been imprisoned. The superior general of the School Sisters of St. Francis was being prevented from returning to Rome to resume her work there. Indications that these developments did not represent local policy but were part of a nationwide campaign directed from the top were refusals by the government to permit prelates to perform rites at funerals (of Bishop Karel Skoupy of Brno and Cardinal Stepan Trochta of Litomerice) of national significance during the past year.

Archbishop Found Guilty — Archbishop Ilarion Capucci, Melkite-Rite patriarchal vicar of Jerusalem, was found guilty and sentenced to 12 years in prison by an Israeli court Dec. 9 on charges of arms smuggling for Palestinian guerrillas in Israel. The counts against him were for contacting a foreign agent, possessing and carrying illegal weapons and serving an illegal organization. The archbishop's principal defense was the contention that the court was not competent to try him.

Cease-Fire — The Provisional Irish Republican Army declared a Dec. 22 to Jan. 2 ceasefire in Northern Ireland and England in a statement issued Dec. 20 in Dublin 10 days after IRA members met secretly with leading Protestant clergymen. The cease-fire was the first declared by the terrorist organization since mid-1972.

The IRA was outlawed by the British Parliament Nov. 29.

Two days later, in a message read in all Catholic churches in England and Wales, the bishops again condemned terrorism, declaring that no Catholic "can offer support or excuse" for violence like the Birmingham bombings that killed 19 persons and injured 184 Nov. 21.

Right and Left Extremists — In England, a number of Catholics known for their resistance to change in the Church, joined a Christian Affirmation Campaign in order "to promote and work for the recognition of the divine Christ in Christianity and our obligation to proclaim his Gospel." In France, 46 delegates from the dwindling membership of several Catholic groups known for their avant-

garde radicalism formed a Collective of December 1 to seek what they called "new forms of Christian existence."

Archbishop and Guerrillas — Archbishop Miguel Obando Bravo of Managua, who negotiated the release of hostages seized by guerrillas Dec. 27, flew to Cuba with them and 14 political prisoners as part of a deal guaranteeing their safety. The guerrillas, belonging to the Sandinista National Liberation Front, said their raid on a party and seizure of hostages were intended to dramatize 38 years of dictatorship by the Somoza family in Nicaragua and what they called a chain of injustices against the poor.

Foreign Briefs:

• Cardinal Stefan Wyszynski, in a pastoral letter read Dec. 1 in all churches of the Warsaw archdiocese, denounced the destruction of a 75-year-old chapel by order of city officials. He said the demolition had "no precedent in the history of postwar Poland and violates the exclusive right of the bishops to found and suppress churches."

• The 10th anniversary of the death of Sister Anwarite Nengapeto, a martyr for the sake of her vow of chastity, was celebrated in the Diocese of Isiro-Niangara, Zaire. She was killed by Congolese rebels.

• At least 375,000 bibles and selected biblical texts were distributed during 1974 in the Communist-ruled countries of Eastern Europe, according to a report issued by the Stuttgart-based World Federation of Bible Societies. It was also reported that 315,000 bibles were made available in East Germany.

• The Mexican government approved blueprints for the building of a new national shrine of Our Lady of Guadalupe, to replace the existing 265-year-old, structurally unsound building.

Paganism in Brazil

"Unbelief and religious confusion are taking increasing hold among the people (of Brazil), particularly in centers of large population. . . . Agnosticism and syncretism are bringing the Church to a critical, dangerous crossroads." So stated Cardinal Vicente Scherer of Porto Alegre in a series of radio broadcasts on the topic of evangelization.

Of special significance, he said, was the prevalence of pagan rites of Umbamba practiced by an estimated 20 million persons, most of whom were baptized Catholics. Defective evangelization in colonial times failed to result in "full acceptance of Christian teachings and rites by the native Indians or the Africans brought to Brazil as slaves. They never abandoned the beliefs and superstitions of their ancestors."

Even so, the cardinal commented, the existence of religious sentiment among the people offers "a precious tradition for social living" and the challenge for a renewed effort at true evangelization.

JANUARY 1975

VATICAN

Increase in Crime — Pope Paul, in a homily delivered at Mass on New Year's Day, deplored a "fearful increase of organized crime" (in Italy) that threatens innocent people and "makes everyone tremble." He said: "We refer to a fearful increase of organized crime, with weapons ready and aimed threateningly at innocent life, and with extremely mercenary blackmail."

Community and Vocations — "A vocation, whether priestly or . . . religious, while basically a gift of the Spirit arising within the individual, has its development in the ecclesial community," declared Pope Paul Jan. 5 in an address to some 1,500 members of the Third National Italian Congress of Vocation Promoters. He said: "It is a divine call which presupposes man's response. But this is to be found most ideally within the heart of the community. In reality, it is the community which sustains the individual with respect to freedom, option, the uniqueness of the answer to the charisms (of priestly and religious life). . . . Community action . . . is a human contribution requested by the Lord himself, and involves the responsibility of the entire community."

Counsel to Missionaries — The Holy Father presided on the feast of Epiphany over ceremonies for the commissioning of 600 missionaries. In his homily he counseled the priests, religious and lay persons from many countries: "While the Catholic missionary must recognize what is true and holy also in other religions . . . and in his apostolic zeal must abstain from any unfair proselytism, the words of the recent ecumenical council (Vatican II) likewise remain forever true; namely, that "it is through Christ's Catholic Church alone, which is the all-embracing means of salvation, that the fullness of the means of salvation can be obtained."

Authentic Christian Mentality — Christians must adopt an "authentic Christian mentality" which can critically judge the factors shaping public opinion, Pope Paul told a general audience Jan. 8. He said that the "first reform, the most personal, the most important and the most difficult" a Christian had to make during Holy Year 1975 was to adopt "a new mentality. . . . We must ask ourselves and our consciences: Do I think like a Christian? Does my mentality derive from the truth Christ taught us?"

Catholic-Jewish Relations — Pope Paul told members of the Liaison Committee between the Catholic Church and World Judaism Jan. 10 that he hoped for the establishment of "true dialogue . . . in a manner appropriate to our age" between Judaism and Catholicism. His meeting with committee members took place seven days after dialogue suggestions and guidelines were issued by the Vatican Commission for Relations with the Jews. (See separate entry for text of the guidelines and suggestions.)

Balance of Terror — Pope Paul warned against reliance on an atomic "balance of terror" as a means of safeguarding peace, in a Jan. 11 address to the diplomatic corps accredited to the Vatican. He also pointed to the Middle East, Vietnam and Cambodia as places where peace was either non-existent or in jeopardy, and defended the Vatican's diplomatic activities in the interests of peace and human rights.

The Pope said he rejected the "balance of terror" approach to peacekeeping because:

• "It has always seemed . . . to be too detached from the moral basis upon which alone peace can prosper."

• "It has likewise seemed too extravagant — through continual competition in equaling and surpassing one another in terms of powers and arms — . . . of means and energies that ought . . . to be devoted to . . . the well-being and progress of all peoples."

• "It has seemed destructive of thoughts of harmony and mutual understanding."

• "It has seemed, finally, too fragile a shield against the onslaught of so many situations of tension and conflict."

Lay Persons Are Evangelizers — In a Jan. 11 address to members of the national council of the Catholic Action movement in Italy, Pope Paul said that lay persons should be evangelizers, in close communion not only with the Holy Spirit and the hierarchy of the Church but also with contemporary society. "This mission of evangelization," he declared, "is accomplished by the Church through all of its members. The recent synod (of bishops in the fall of 1974) has reaffirmed that the duty to evangelize belongs to all the faithful."

Peace of Conscience — Penance leading to peace of conscience was called the "first breath of the spirit of the Holy Year" by Pope Paul in a talk to a throng of persons in St. Peter's Square Jan. 12. He termed peace of conscience the "heaviest responsibility borne by man . . . a responsibility which cannot be resolved by forgetting about it or by suppressing it with an evasive answer."

Can't Say "No" to Church — To say "yes" to Christ but "no" to the Church is impossible, the Pope asserted in an address to a weekly audience Jan. 15. He stated that the mediation of the Church is necessary to know Christ and to live his life. He also said that an obstacle standing in the way of Christian renewal is "opposition toward the so-called institutional Church, the real Church, the human Church, the ministering Church, which is the custodian and dispenser of the divine mysteries."

Goals — "We need to establish a scale of goals to which man can and should turn. At the top of this scale is the 'the kingdom of God and his justice.' " So stated Pope Paul during a general audience Jan. 22. If priority were not given to God's kingdom and justice, he said, the scale would be useless because it would lack Christian meaning and direction.

First Woman Envoy to Vatican — Pope Paul met Jan. 23 with Miss Bernadette Olowo of Uganda, the first woman to serve as an ambassador to the Vatican. Miss Olowo was also Uganda's envoy to West Germany.

Christian Unity — In a homily delivered at a Mass Jan. 25, the last day of the Week of Prayer for Christian Unity, Pope Paul said: "The division among Christians has . . . damaged and often even humiliated the richness of the Christian message. It has made it lose its effectiveness in the work of reconciliation with God, which is a mission the Church must continue till the end of time. . . . How, in fact, can we witness with coherence that God has reconciled us to himself if we do not show that we ourselves are reconciled to those who are believers and baptized in his name?" The Pope called ecumenism an "extremely difficult undertaking" and said that his sadness at the pace of efforts toward unity was an expression of "our desire and our love."

Permissive Morality — The Holy Father attacked permissive morality and called on Christians to strengthen any weakening sense of moral obligation, in an address before a general audience Jan. 29. He lamented that awareness of moral obligations flowing from "a superior . . . divine law is either dead or repressed" in contemporary society — in which "permissiveness appears to be a liberation from severe and wise norms, today described by too many people as 'taboos' or superstitious myths." Such norms, on the contrary, "provide reasonable limits and renewed vigor for human conduct, and give man an integrity worthy of him and a character which can meet every social confrontation."

The Pope Also:
• Sent a message of sympathy to the people of Pakistan on learning of the devastation caused by an earthquake at Rawalpindi.
• Named five new bishops and transferred four others in Hungary in a move that placed residential bishops in all but two of the country's 11 dioceses. The appointments were made in the wake of talks betweeen Vatican and Hungarian officials.
• Expressed his condolences to Maronite Catholics throughout the world on the death Jan. 11 of their Patriarch, Cardinal Paul Meouchi of Antioch.

Vatican Briefs:
• An editorial in the Jan. 2 edition of *L'Osservatore Romano* labeled as "false and absurd" a claim by German moral theologian Father Bernard Haering, C.SS.R., that the bulk of Pope Paul's speeches were ghost-written by members of the Roman Curia.
• Vatican representatives took part in 196 international conferences in 1974, according to a listing published in the Jan. 9 edition of *L'Osservatore Romano.*
• Press spokesman Federico Alessandrini denied Jan. 31 the truth of press reports "concerning considerable losses (said to be $560 million or more) which the Vatican had supposedly suffered in relation to the collapse" of Michele Sindona's financial empire.
• Inflation and rises in the cost of living were the reasons behind a Jan. 16 directive to Vatican officials to do some serious belt-tightening to improve a "serious deficit" in the Vatican budget. The deficit, according to Federico Alessandrini, was not related to developments connected with the financial failure of Michele Sindona.

Reconciliation and Peace

Pope Paul appealed for active pursuit of a peace founded on "a reconciliation of hearts" and mutual understanding — a peace "neither passive nor repressive" but "inventive, preventive and operative" — in "Reconciliation — The Way to Peace," a message for World Peace Day, Jan. 1. "Making peace," he said, "means educating for peace."

The Pontiff noted the need to settle conflicts, to counteract "jealous nationalism" and "arrogant ideologies," and to find a better way of securing peace than reliance on a balance of armed terror.

"Progress," he said, "must be made toward a peace which is loved, free and brotherly, founded, that is, on a reconciliation of hearts."

DOMESTIC

Textbook Decision — The U.S. Supreme Court refused early in the month to review a Missouri Supreme Court decision against the constitutionality of a state law allowing public school districts to lend textbooks to students of church-related schools. At issue was a statute which provided for textbook loans "to all pupils residing in the district on an equitable basis and without discrimination on the grounds of race, creed, color, national origin or school attended." The Missouri court had ruled that the law served the sectarian purposes of church-related schools.

Kissinger Suggestion — Twenty-four Catholic and Orthodox Arab-American religious leaders released a statement in Boston Jan. 15 protesting against "the suggestion that the United States might consider military intervention in the Arab oil-producing countries to avoid possible 'economic strangulation.' " The suggestion had been raised by Secretary of State Henry Kissinger during an interview published by *Business Week* Jan. 3.

Amnesty Appeals — The president of the Conference of Major Superiors of Men and

Bishop Francis J. Mugavero of Brooklyn made separate appeals for an unconditional amnesty for Vietnam war resisters to replace President Ford's clemency program. Father Joseph Francis, S.V.D., called the program "a failure . . . basically because it is not and never was intended to be a true amnesty." Bishop Mugavero said in a pastoral letter that the program was ineffective because of its limitation on "the number of eligible participants" and, in the minds of most of those covered, its punitive nature.

Due Process for Suspension from School — Catholic schools should consider themselves guided by the "spirit" of the U.S. Supreme Court ruling (Goss v. Lopez) that students suspended from school must be told the reason for their suspension and given an opportunity to respond, according to Msgr. Olin Murdick, secretary of education for the U.S. Catholic Conference. The decision calls for "due process" for students, he said, and added: "If such a process does not exist in a given school, there ought to be one."

Hartford Statement — Eighteen persons of various Christian persuasions and academic disciplines concurred Jan. 26 in an "Appeal for Theological Affirmation" at the conclusion of a three-day meeting in Hartford, Conn. The statement, which could have been entitled "A Call for Theological Sanity," dealt with 13 "false and debilitating" themes of the ultra-liberal, faddist type. The appeal repudiated trends to de-transcendentalize Christian faith and practice, to reduce the Gospel to a message of social change and liberation, and to make "human fulfillment" on earth the primary goal and norm for interpreting the Gospel.

Arlington Parish Dispute Settled — Members of Good Shepherd Parish, Arlington, Va., and Bishop Thomas Welsh agreed Jan. 26 on a "proposal of reconciliation" to end a five-month dispute over differences between the pastor, Father John Hannan, and members of the parish council. Provisions of the agreement included the establishment of a team ministry in the parish, with Father Hannan as co-pastor, and re-establishment of the parish council — with a directive for clarification of its role in parish affairs.

Arms Trade — The United States accounted for 52 per cent ($29.7 billion) of world arms sales ($57.94 billion) and 36 per cent ($765 billion) of world military expenditures ($2.5 trillion) during the period from 1963 to 1973. Expenditures by the Soviet Union amounted to $674 billion and sales to $15.68 billion. U.S. exports of arms to South Vietnam were more than double ($6.95 billion) the value of arms sent to North Vietnam by the Soviet Union ($2.09 billion) and China ($915 million). Military expenditures in Latin America, South Asia and Africa were "relatively modest," while notable increases were reported for developing nations in East Asia

and the Middle East. The figures were reported in a study by the U.S. Arms Control and Disarmament Agency entitled "World Military Expenditures and Arms Trade 1963-1973."

Hunger Relief — Dr. Eugene Carson Blake, president of Bread for the World, called on President Ford to send to needy nations between 700,000 and 800,000 tons of wheat whose purchase was cancelled by China and the Soviet Union late in the month. The sale cancellations, he said, gave the government "a new opportunity to increase dramatically its emergency food assistance to countries facing famine."

Domestic Briefs:

• Catholic and other church groups were supporting a suit seeking the right to work for Haitian refugees in the Miami area while their appeals for asylum in the U.S. were under consideration by the courts.

• Prompted by court decisions against the Minnesota Income Tax Credit Law, sisters of the St. Paul-Minneapolis archdiocese withdrew a request for a pay raise, to ease the financial condition of archdiocesan schools.

• An increasing percentage of Catholic students in the Philadelphia area was attending public schools. Percentages were 26.6 in 1970, 30.7 in 1972 and 35.7 in 1974.

• Bishop Joseph H. Hodges of Wheeling gave $250,000 to 17 religious communities serving in the diocese to care for their retired sisters.

• Auxiliary Bishop John Roach of St. Paul-Minneapolis ordered the cancellation of a scheduled talk on prison reform by former Auxiliary Bishop James Shannon at a Mass in a Minneapolis parish. Dr. Shannon was automatically excommunicated in 1969 after he left the ministry and married without due authorization.

• Democratic Representative Father Robert Drinan, S.J., of Massachusetts voted against the nomination of Nelson Rockefeller as Vice President because "the moral objectives of America would not be advanced" if a man with his "background and priorities . . . became the President of the United States."

• Three canon lawyers, in an effort to interpret existing regulations regarding priests who have left the ministry and been dispensed from priestly obligations, expressed the opinion that they "may be hired for any position in the Church for which a lay person may be employed." The canonists' study was prepared for the National Federation of Priests' Councils.

March for Life

More than 20,000 persons took part in the March for Life in Washington, D.C., Jan. 22, the second anniversary of the U.S. Supreme Court decisions which wiped out all legal protection of the right of the unborn to be born. Participants in the march from all across the country demonstrated and visited their respective members of Congress to petition for enactment of a right-to-life amendment to the U.S. Constitution.

Demonstrations of various kinds but for the same purpose were held elsewhere, and many statements of pro-life support were issued by right-to-life spokesmen and religious leaders. In one of the statements Archbishop Joseph L. Bernardin, president of the National Conference of Catholic Bishops and the U.S. Catholic Conference, attacked the widely publicized but erroneous notion that opposition to abortion was just a Catholic position. He said, rather: "It is a matter of human and civil rights — the right to life, which is one of the most basic rights of the human family." Pro-life supporters were, in fact, drawn from all sectors of the U.S. population.

The magnitude, vigor and reasoned stance of the demonstrations indicated that the pro-life movement was gaining strength despite the pro-abortion climate and momentum abetted and generated by judicial decisions.

By the end of the month right-to-life amendments proposed during the 93rd Congress were reintroduced in the 94th session by Senators James Buckley of New York and Jesse Helms of North Carolina.

In other developments:

• The Washington State Supreme Court ruled unconstitutional a statute requiring a minor to have parental permission for an abortion.

• The U.S. Supreme Court upheld a temporary injunction against the enforcement of some provisions of a Pennsylvania law restricting the conditions under which an abortion could be performed, and refused to review a lower-court ruling against the constitutionality of a Minnesota law restricting the performance of abortions.

FOREIGN

Church-State Relations in Paraguay — Reconciliation between the Church and the Paraguayan government seemed to be in the making after years of tension over human rights. Cordial relations appeared to be developing between church and state officials, and the regime was said to have relaxed some of its restrictions on civil rights. Tensions developed in the late 1960's when the bishops protested against the treatment of political prisoners charged with attempts to end the rule of Gen. Alfredo Stroessner, in power since 1954. Catholic organizations of students and farmworkers were particular targets of the regime, several priests were arrested or expelled from the country, and two high officials were excommunicated in 1971 for manhandling and detaining a bishop and torturing a priest.

Anglican Defends the Pope — Dr. Bernard C. Pawley, archdeacon of Canterbury and vice-chairman of the Anglican Commission on Roman Catholic Relations, criticized *The Times* of London for overemphasizing Pope Paul's critical comments about infidelity in the Church. He said in a letter to the newspaper: "Many of us outside the Church of Rome would agree that some of her accredited teachers have overstepped the bounds of reasonable loyalty, deserve to be called to order and should reconsider their position as Roman Catholics."

No Release for Archbishop — Justice Minister Haim Zadoc declared that the Israeli government would not release Archbishop Ilarion Capucci — sentenced in December to a 12-year prison term on gun-running charges — even if the Vatican were to request it. He said: "This matter belongs to the sphere of Israel's fight against terror, not Israel's relations with the Catholic Church and Christian communities."

Involuntary Sterilization — Bishop Gerardo Flores of Izabal told the Guatemalan Journalists Association that sterilization of Indian women against their will was contributing to "the further deterioration of family life" in Guatemala. The same type of declaration had been made since October, 1974, by bishops in Mexico, Colombia, Venezuela and Puerto Rico. The prelates called the practice an attempt by foreigners to impose drastic birth control programs in exchange for economic aid. The greatest offenders in this regard were said to be U.S. governmental and private agencies, including the Peace Corps, the Agency for International Development and the Planned Parenthood Association.

Spanish-Vatican Negotiations — Foreign Minister Pedro Cortina Mauri, in a New Year's report of world affairs, predicted it would take some time to conclude Spanish-Vatican negotiations for a new concordat to replace the one in effect since 1953. He said the objective of such an accord would be "to define well the fields in which Church and State exercise their respective jurisdictions and activity, so as to avoid interference that can lead to conflicts."

Boquen Communion Splits — An avantgarde group formed in 1969 at the Cistercian abbey in Boquen, France, split up in disagreement over its relationship with the Church (in doubt) and over its future direction (fuzzy). The Communion of Boquen had been under internal and external criticism on a number of doctrinal, pastoral and disciplinary counts.

Ordinations in Poland — Vatican Radio reported Jan. 16 that 638 priests, the largest number in six years, were ordained in 1974 — 486 diocesan clergy and 152 members of religious institutes (mostly Franciscans, Resurrectionists and Pallottines). It was also reported that 4,216 students were in the nation's seminaries.

Concordat Violations in Portugal — Nineteen bishops charged the leftist government, which came to power in the wake of a coup in

April, 1974, with violating agreements on Catholic schools (422, with some 60,000 students) and other concerns of the Church. Deploring a wave of anti-Church rallies, the bishops said Jan. 21 that the regime was "successfully maneuvering for the removal of church influence in such sectors as education, in which the Church has a right and duty to be because of existing agreements" (concordat of 1940).

Sino-Korean Association — An organization called the Sino-Korean Association of Religious Believers was established Jan. 24 at a three-day meeting in Taipei sponsored by Cardinal Paul Yu Pin. He said in an address which opened the conference: "The aim of this gathering (which included Catholics, Anglicans, Buddhists and Mohammedans) is to form an association so that religious believers of all faiths can cooperate and thus increase their influence for the welfare of their peoples and countries."

Vatican Representation at Anglican Enthronement — For the first time since the Reformation, the Vatican was officially represented — by Cardinal Jan Willebrands, President of the Secretariat for Promoting Christian Unity, and Cardinals Francois Marty of Paris and Leo J. Suenens of Malines-Brussels — at the enthronement of an Archbishop of Canterbury, Dr. Frederick D. Coggan. Dr. Coggan succeeded Archbishop Michael Ramsey, who resigned in November, 1974, as Primate of the Anglican Communion.

Repression in Equatorial Guinea — According to reports reaching exiles from Equatorial Guinea living in New York, several churches in their country had been turned into public markets, a cathedral had been converted into an armory, two bishops were expelled in 1971 and 1972, and the apostolic administrator of Bata had been arrested and jailed for seven months on charges of disrespect to President-for-life Francisco Macias Nguema. Following independence in 1968, most of 7,000 Spanish residents left the country, 50,000 to 100,000 Guineans fled to neighboring nations, foreign missionaries were expelled, and a campaign for atheism was instituted by Catholic-reared Macias. One hundred and 18 of his political enemies were put to death June 26, 1974, in a series of mass executions.

Radio Schools — Forty delegates from 14 countries attending the Inter-American Conference of Radio Schools in Guatemala City reviewed the progress of their work and planned for its future development via television. The 12-year-old federation had seven networks of schools broadcasting to rural groups, mostly Indians, basic courses in literacy, the trades, social and economic development. Schools were operating in Bolivia, Colombia, Guatemala, Honduras, other Caribbean nations, Ecuador, Mexico and Peru. The first radio schools were started in the 1940's by Father Joaquin Salcedo in Sutatenza, Colombia.

Opposition to Radio Seizure — Some 5,000 tin miners in the towns of Siglo XX and Catavi rallied in support of Canadian missionaries whose Radio Pius XII was confiscated by Bolivian authorities. The station was charged with subversion, and the missionaries were said by government officials to be foreigners interfering in domestic affairs.

Abortion Law Criticized — The Society for the Protection of the Unborn sent to all members of the British Parliament a detailed critique of the government-sponsored Lane Committee Report on the working of the Abortion Act of 1967. The critique noted that the committee admitted that the law had ushered in abortion on demand, but that it was proposing "no effective way of dealing with this abuse of the law."

Foreign Briefs:
• More than 300 nuns from various religious communities engaged in full-time parish work in Great Britain formed the Association of Parish Sisters to make their work more effective.

• According to a report from Burundi, Salesian Father Cesare Bussi, who had been sentenced to eight years' imprisonment for helping Hutu refugees flee Burundi, was pardoned.

• Church authorities in Uruguay refused to comply with a government demand that Catholic schools submit the names of principals and other personnel for approval, and called the directive "unconstitutional" and "totalitarian."

• Father Felix Morey Amengual, the oldest priest in Chile and probably in all of South America, died at the age of 105.

• It was announced in Hong Kong that the first Catholic dictionary of the Bible in Chinese, produced by the Franciscan Fathers in the city, would be published in the spring.

Africanization in Zaire

According to delayed reports from Kinshasa:

• Mabolia Imengo Tra Bwato, commissioner of state for national education, announced Dec. 13 that all religious training would be stopped in the nation's schools as of Jan. 1. He said they would be replaced by educational programs of civics, political formation and Zairean ethics.

• A government spokesman told the country's official news agency Dec. 5: "The Popular Revolutionary Movement must henceforth be considered as a church and its founder (President Mobutu Sese Seko) as a messiah." He added that there was no room in Zaire for "hierarchies of imported churches" which, he said, were harmful to ancestral values.

Mobutu's Africanization program aimed at the elimination of all but native influences, religious and otherwise, from Zaire.

FEBRUARY 1975

VATICAN

Celibacy — The service and self-sacrifice made possible by celibacy — "more a charism than a virtue" — are channeled toward "ignored brothers in need of precisely that ministry of charity with imitates and, so far as possible, equals that of Christ for men." So stated the Pope Feb. 2 in an address to hundreds of priests and nuns. He said: "Virginity is not something sterile and empty. It is not an inhuman fate, but superhuman — when the flesh is sacrificed to the spirit and the spirit is filled with a love more alive, stronger and more completely filled with God."

Selfishness and Pride — Pope Paul told a gathering of pilgrims and visitors Feb. 5: "All the great social and political disorders have their seeds in selfishness and pride, from which so many human instincts and so many actions find their inspiration, but in which there is no longer love. . . . Love has lost . . . its finest and most Christian characteristic, universality."

Nun Beatified — In the first of several beatifications and canonizations scheduled for Holy Year 1975, Pope Paul beatified Feb. 9 Mother Marie-Eugenie Millert de Brou, French foundress in 1839 of the Congregation of the Assumption.

Help of Parish Priests Asked — Pope Paul, meeting with more than 250 parish priests of his Rome diocese, spoke of problems connected with pluralism and confusion in the Church. He also asked for their help — "as indeed cooperators in our mission" — in overcoming "uneasiness, pessimism and dissatisfaction" in some quarters of the clergyn religious and laity.

Self-Denial in Lent — In a message to the Church throughout the world Feb. 11, Pope Paul pleaded for self-denial that could benefit the poor. He said: "Lent is an appropriate time for this exercise of self-denial because it reminds Christians who they are. It puts them on guard against the satisfaction of a comfortable existence and against the temptations of living in abundance. In this Holy Year, which is dedicated to reconciliation, each individual is challenged by what reconciliation implies: giving and sharing within the human family."

Penance — Pope Paul, after noting in an Ash Wednesday homily that many people would like the Church to drop "her old penitential way of thinking" and to present the Christian life as easy, said it would be "the greatest of errors . . . to remove the Cross from the center of the faith and Christian life." He added that it would be a "fatal mistake" to place trust in "economic and hedonistic well-being, in riches rather than virtue, in ideological and practical materialism which

seems to resolve all personal, social and political problems. . . . On the contrary, the Christian view (of life and penance) is based on an orientation toward a better and higher end for our existence, the final possession . . . of the fullness of immortal life with God."

The sacrament of penance was the theme of two addresses to general audiences by the Pope Feb. 26. He said: "The concept, the esteem and the use of the sacrament of penance have not always received from everyone the privileged consideration they deserve. . . . Let us give to this sacrament or, if need be, restore to it the devotion, gratitude and joy that it deserves from our faith and piety."

Conscience — Pope Paul warned a general audience Feb. 12 that a conscience based exclusively on principles of psychology can never take the place of a moral conscience which recognizes the reality of sin. He said: "Psychological conscience, detached from moral conscience which operates on the basis of religious responsibility, is no longer a good counselor. . . . This conscience stops with psychological analysis, which is in fashion today, and does not take into account ethical obligations." A conscience based only on psychological principles "enjoys a misleading and dangerous optimism which, in its application, is like that of a man who no longer consults or never consulted a real, truly human conscience. Such a man lives unscrupulously and is happy to allow himself anything that is desirable or possible."

Appeal to Children — In an Ash Wednesday broadcast to U.S. Catholic school children for the 1975 American Catholic Overseas Aid Fund, Pope Paul urged them "to share and to sacrifice in order to help once again your needy brothers and sisters in the lands across the seas."

Religious Springtime — The Holy Father, about to begin a week of retreat exercises, told a throng of people in St. Peter's Square Feb. 16 that Lent is a "religious springtime" for the practice and development of deeper and more meditative prayer; austerity; remembrance of a "neighbor in need of help, assistance, friendship, reconciliation; and "great, true, humble confidence in the goodness of God, in the mystery of the Cross."

Maronite-Rite Patriarch — The Pope officially recognized Maronite-Rite Patriarch Antoine Pierre Khoraiche of Antioch, elected Feb. 3 and installed Feb. 9, as the successor of Patriarch Paul Meouchi who died Jan. 11. The recognition was technically known as the extension of ecclesial communion by a Pope following the election of an Eastern-Rite Patriarch by an episcopal synod.

Light of the World — Noting that the panorama of the world shows "many different types of events — some distressing, threatening and sad; others consoling, new and promising," Pope Paul said Feb. 23: "Christ is the key to the solution (of problems) and the fountain of consolation and life."

Migrant Workers — In a Feb. 28 address to participants in an Italian national conference on migration, Pope Paul said: "Too many problems remain open regarding the protection of the migrants' human dignity, the need for more equality in conditions of work, housing, protection and job training — not to mention their legitimate hopes for the full enjoyment of civil rights, union rights and educational rights. There is still a long way to go before civil authorities and some sectors of society become conscious of such obligations toward this category of citizens and workers."

The Pope Also:

• Met with: Jiro Inagawa, Japanese ambassador to the Vatican, Feb. 3; Hortensia Allende, widow of the late president of Chile, Feb. 5; Kurt Waldheim, secretary general of the United Nations, Feb. 11; Mohammed el Fhafei Abdel Hamid, Egyptian ambassador to the Vatican, Feb. 13; Otto Lang, Canadian minister of justice, Feb. 15.

• Opened a special exhibit of documents pertaining to the 25 Holy Years proclaimed since 1300.

• Met Feb. 26 with 30 Shinto priests from Japan, in what *L'Osservatore Romano* called "the first official contact, for practical purposes, which the Church has had with such an authoritative group of Shinto representatives."

Vatican Briefs:

• A delayed report disclosed that the Congregation for Religious had turned down Dec. 19 an appeal for reinstatement in the Jesuits from Father Joseph O'Rourke, who was dismissed from the society for disobedience in baptizing the child of an active advocate of legalized abortion Aug. 20, 1974, in Marlboro, Mass.

• Representatives of the Vatican and Portugal agreed Feb. 15 to amend a clause in the concordat of 1940 which deprived a couple in a Catholic marriage of the civil right to sue for divorce. A new protocol acknowledged this right but reminded "the couple who have contracted canonical marriage of the serious duty encumbent on them to refrain from availing themselves of the civil faculty to seek divorce."

Father Kueng's Opinions

The Congregation for the Doctrine of the Faith, acting on a mandate from Pope Paul, admonished Father Hans Kueng for opinions expressed in two of his books, *The Church* and *Infallibility? An Inquiry.* In its admonition, issued Feb. 20, the congregation said the opinions were "in contrast with the doctrine of the Catholic Church." At issue were:

• "The opinion which places at least in

doubt the very dogma . . . of the infallibility of the Church or reduces it to a certain elementary indefectibility of the Church in matters of truthm" (According to Kueng, the Church can err in official teaching but will be preserved in fidelity to the essentials of Christian faith.)

• With respect to the teaching authority of the Church, "he does not adhere to the general concept of the authentic magisterium by which bishops are in the Church 'authentic doctors, that is, invested with the authority of Christ and who preach to the people entrusted to them the faith to believe in and to follow in daily practice" (*Dogmatic Constitution on the Church,* Second Vatican Council).

• The opinion that "the Eucharist, at least in cases of necessity, could be validly consecrated by anyone baptized but without sacerdotal status, cannot be reconciled with the doctrine of Lateran Council IV and Vatican II."

Father Kueng, a theology professor at Tuebingen University, Germany, was directed "not to continue to teach such opinions." Since early in the 1970's when his views came under scrutiny and question at the Vatican, he had been conducting an on- and off-again well-publicized campaign against the competence and procedures of the Doctrinal Congregation.

The congregation called on the bishops of Germany and elsewhere "to take care that the faithful are suitably instructed concerning the doctrine of the Church . . . and also concerning the present declaration."

DOMESTIC

Catholic Schools Week — "Visit them, choose them, support them. Catholic schools — different where it counts" (in teaching religious and moral values). This was the theme of radio spot announcements and other media presentations designed to elicit support during Catholic Schools Week Feb. 2 to 8.

Food Stamps for Unborn Child — In the first legal decision of its kind, a U.S. District Court in San Francisco granted extra food-stamp rights to a Daly City, Calif., mother because of the nutritional needs of her unborn eight-month-old child. Judge George G. Harris ruled that the child was to be treated as a separate, living human person, and that its mother was entitled to food stamps for two persons instead of for herself alone.

Menominees and the Alexian Brothers — The Alexian Brothers agreed Feb. 2 to turn over a 64-room abbey in Gresham, Wisc., to the Menominee Indian tribe, on its return to legal tribal status, for "one dollar and other considerations," following a 33-day occupation of the abbey by members of the Menominee Warrior Society. The abbey, on land which originally belonged to the tribe, had been donated to the Alexians in 1950 and used as a novitiate until 1968. The Indians based their claim for the subsequently unused property on what they said was a federal law providing that land turned over to church groups should revert to the Indians when not used for religious, educational or social-service purposes.

Pastoral on Appalachia — In the first document of its kind in U.S. history, 25 bishops issued a joint statement Feb. 3 entitled "This Land Is Home to Me: A Pastoral letter on Powerlessness in Appalachia by the Catholic Bishops of the Region." The three sections of the letter, written in free-verse, described the people's own view of their lives and social-economic conditions, summarized the social doctrine of the Church, and proposed a number of approaches to the solution of problems in the area.

1974 Abortion Estimates — The Alan Guttmacher Institute of the Planned Parenthood Federation of America reported Feb. 3 that approximately 900,000 abortions were performed in the U.S. in 1974, 745,000 in 1973 — the year in which the U.S. Supreme Court struck down anti-abortion statutes — and 600,000 in 1972. Most of the abortions were performed in private hospitals and clinics; 17 per cent of 2,100 public hospitals reported abortions in the first quarter of 1974. Reporting the highest numbers of abortions were California, the District of Columbia, Hawaii, Kansas, New Mexico, New York and Washington. The report was based on a 95 per cent return of questionnaires sent to 2,991 hospitals, clinics and physicians.

Bicentennial Hearing — Socio-economic issues of many types were aired by panelists of the Committee for the Observance of the Bicentennial, U.S. Catholic Conference, in a "Liberty and Justice for All" hearing Feb. 3 to 5 in Washington, D.C. The hearing was the first of six to be held across the country in preparation for a national Catholic bicentennial conference on liberty and justice in 1976.

Chicago TV Network — The Catholic Television Network of Chicago, the largest diocesan network in the U.S., was dedicated with formal ceremonies Feb. 6. The network, with studios at 1 N. Wacker Drive, started a full broadcast schedule of educational and adult programming.

Religious Freedom in Russia? — Assertions that constitutionally guaranteed religious freedom existed in the Soviet Union met with denials and protests during the Feb. 16 to Mar. 5 tour of the U.S. by nearly 20 religious leaders from Russia. The group, in this country on the invitation of the National Council of Churches, was headed by Russian Orthodox Metropolitan Filaret of Kiev and Galich. The party line was that Christians and Jews had such freedom but also were, as all other Soviet citizens, subject to government regulations on subversion and political activity.

Network Concerns — Network, a lobbying group of some 2,000 socially concerned sisters and other persons, reported in its February newsletter that it was primarily interested in the following subjects for consideration by the 94th Congress: global hunger, health care, domestic poverty, foreign policy and criminal justice.

Experimental Community Splits — The experimental Community of Pope John XXIII, approved in the fall of 1966, announced Feb. 28 its withdrawal from the jurisdiction of Archbishop John R. Quinn of Oklahoma City. Among reasons for the withdrawal from the Church were irregularities in liturgical and sacramental practices by the community. Archbishop Quinn did not invoke any sanctions against the community, but did rescind the pastoral assignment and faculties of Father William F. Nerin. A 1972 study of the community revealed that only 62 per cent of 59 members (total membership at that time, about 75) declared themselves to be Catholics.

Treaty with Panama — The administrative board of the U.S. Catholic Conference urged Feb. 24 the United States and Panama to negotiate a treaty in which "the main benefits from the Canal should accrue to Panama, as a nation with principal control over its natural resources." "A Resolution regarding Panama" also said that a "fair compensation should accrue to the United States for its investment in Panama."

Priest Killed — Father Thomas Quinlan, 38, principal of St. James School, Penns Grove, N.J., was killed and a second-grade teacher seriously wounded Feb. 24 by a man who fired at them with a shotgun in the school building.

Split with Girl Scouts — A two-year-long conflict between the Philadelphia Archdiocesan Department of Youth Activities and the Girl Scouts was resolved Feb. 25 with the department's announcement that it would withdraw sponsorship July 1 of 334 troops (of 8,600 girls, about one-fourth of all Girl Scouts in the city) and would form a new affiliation with Camp Fire Girls, Inc. At issue was a plan to introduce a "To Be a Woman" merit badge for 12- to 14-year-old Cadettes, with instruction on sexual intercourse, rape, pregnancy, birth control, abortion, venereal disease, menstruation and menopause.

Domestic Briefs:

• President Ford declared the week of Feb. 2 to 9 International Clergy Week in the United States.

• Honored: Msgr. Thomas G. Fahy, president of Seton Hall University, with the Brotherhood Award of the New Jersey chapter of the National Conference of Christians and Jews, for his work in ending a rent strike in Newark, N.J.; Father George B. Ford, 89, with the dedication of a Columbia University residence hall named for him, for his support of social causes especially in the 1930's and 1940's; Mary Lou Beatty, assistant managing editor of *The Washington Post*, with the 1975 By-Line Award of the Marquette University College of Journalism.

• Lenten pastorals of many U.S. bishops called on Catholics to share money or food saved from fasting with hungry people of this country and the world.

• Five members of the Hartdegen family of Philadelphia, all Franciscans — two priests and three nuns — celebrated a combined total of 259 years in religious life, at Glen Riddle, Pa.

• Joseph A. Breig, newspaperman, columnist and author, announced his retirement late in the month as full-time associate editor of three Catholic newspapers in Ohio.

Dr. Edelin Guilty

A jury of nine men and three women, after seven hours of deliberations at the end of a six-week trial, found Dr. Kenneth C. Edelin, staff physician of Boston City Hospital, guilty of manslaughter Feb. 16 in the death of a "24-week-old male child" following a legal abortion he performed Oct. 3, 1973.

The finding was that the physician, after performing a hysterotomy on the child's mother and severing the placenta, delayed for three minutes or more the removal of the child from the uterus, thus causing death by suffocation.

The legality of abortion was not at issue in the trial, despite widespread reporting and editorializing that it was.

The jury responded in its verdict to evidence presented during the trial and to the charge delivered by Suffolk Superior Court Judge James P. McGuire: "Killing or causing the death of a person who is born alive and is outside the body of his or her mother may be the subject of manslaughter. . . . In order for the defendant to be found guilty in this case, you must be satisfied beyond a reasonable doubt that the defendant caused the death of a person who had been alive outside the body of his or her mother."

Dr. Edelin was given a one-year, suspended sentence and returned to his work at the Boston City Hospital.

FOREIGN

Abortion — Cardinal Francois Marty of Paris, president of the French Bishops' Conference, restated the Church's condemnation of abortion in a televised appearance Feb. 2, the day after promulgation of a new law on the subject. He said the law, permitting abortion on demand during the first 10 weeks of pregnancy, was "inspired by the state of society's morals."

In other developments:

• The Constitutional Court of Italy struck down Feb. 18 part of the country's anti-abortion law which "does not provide for the interruption of pregnancy when continuing the pregnancy would imply injury or serious danger, medically ascertained, and when such an interruption is done for the sake of the mother's physical or mental health and is not otherwise avoidable." While acknowledging "juridical protection of the conceived," the court said it "can collide with other goods which also enjoy constitutional protection."

• West Germany's Supreme Constitutional Court, declaring that the national constitution guaranteed everyone's right to life and physical inviolability, overturned Feb. 25 a law permitting abortion on demand in the first three months of pregnancy. The ruling added that, pending more specific legislation, abortion would be legal during the first three months if undertaken to save the life of the mother, if the fetus would be born deformed, or if pregnancy resulted from rape.

• The bishops of Colombia, with reference to a proposed legalization of abortion, commented: "We gain nothing by importing the moral decadence of other nations."

Year of the Family — The bishops of Venezuela declared 1975 the Year of the Family to counteract an increase in birth control programs, rising divorce rates and an alarming spread of juvenile delinquency. They said they wanted to make the country, people and leaders, aware of poverty conditions and to prod them into programs of social reform and rehabilitation.

Anti-Violence Appeal — Cardinal Juan Landazuri Ricketts issued a call for peace in riot-torn Lima and challenged government leaders not to ask the people for sacrifices they were not making themselves. Violence erupted Feb. 5 and 6 in connection with a Peruvian army assault on a police garrison during a national police strike for higher pay and a change of command. The rioting took a toll of 100 dead, more wounded, and more than $10 million in damage.

Textbooks in Mexico — The bishops of Mexico published a strong protest against "corrupting and materialistic" parts of books scheduled for compulsory introduction in public and private schools in the spring. Their statement topped several weeks of public protests, mostly from parents and conservative circles, against passages on biology, sex education and socialism. The bishops told parents it was their responsibility to press authorities for changes in the books "to bring them into line with the respect due to all, Catholics and non-Catholics alike."

Anglicans Vote Down Patronage System — The General Synod of the Church of England, meeting Feb. 4 to 7 in London, voted to abolish the patronage system of assigning its priests to parishes. Under the system priests were appointed by the so-called "patron of the living" rather than by the bishop or the parish. The patron could be a local landowner, a commercial firm, an Oxford or Cambridge college, or perhaps a bishop. Under the new system, which required authorization by Parliament, both parish and bishop would be consulted and have the right of veto in appointments.

Nuns Barred from Nursing Schools — Vatican Radio broadcast reports Feb. 7 that the Secretariat for Religious Affairs in Czechoslovakia had issued orders forbidding enrollment and reception of diplomas by nuns in state schools of nursing. Immediately affected by the directives were 21 nuns in nurse's training in Bohemia.

Passport Withdrawals and Detention — The Catholic bishops of South Africa, in a unanimous statement Feb. 10, were sharply critical of the government's "excessive use of banning, restriction and withdrawal of passports and residential permits." While acknowledging that "countries may at times need security measures outside normal procedures," the bishops insisted that the government was going too far. Similar criticism was directed against laws permitting indefinite detention incommunicado and without legal recourse.

Indians in Amazon Hinterland — Archbishop Joao de Souza Lima of Manaus, in the heart of Amazon territory and in the path of a branch of the Trans-Amazon Highway, blamed white settlers and exploiters for driving Indians from their lands into even more remote areas, and for obstructing the government's plan for "national integration." The archbishop said: "We want the Church to lead the way in the work of integration of the national community, so it is accomplished in the light of the Gospel. . . . The work of the Church is to educate the Indians within their own surroundings, with full respect for their values, and making a selective choice of what might benefit them from the white man's culture." Contact with white civilization was said to be a significant factor in the decimation of the Indian population (118 tribes), from more than one million to approximately 120,000 since 1900.

Religion under Red Regimes — *The Times* of London concluded a survey of religion in the Communist countries of Eastern Europe with the statement: "Almost the only valid generalization is that religious practice and belief have proved remarkably durable." The newspaper observed no let-up in the ideological confrontation between Marxist materialism and any theological system, and noted that Marxist regimes viewed religious organizations as rival centers of moral authority. "But the real issues now," it said, "are the practical, political and moral ones of how to co-exist when neither system can eradicate the other in the foreseeable future."

Korean Bishop Freed — Bishop Daniel Tji Hak Soun of Won Ju, whose statements and actions for human rights brought about his trial and imprisonment by the Park Chung Hee regime, was among some 150 political prisoners released, with sentences suspended, in the middle of the month. The bishop was sentenced to a prison term of 15 years in August, 1974, by a military court which found him guilty of "inciting to rebellion."

Spanish Priests Arrested — Two hundred and 66 clergy of the Pamplona diocese, protesting the arrest and fining of seven brother priests, said that "to denounce the sin of injustice and to preach the need for conversion is a duty the Gospel demands from the priestly ministry." The convicted priests, who had expressed sympathy for striking potassium miners, were charged with aiding and abetting an illegal strike.

Violence in Argentina — An increasing number of bishops, voicing concern over the violence of guerrillas and counter-guerrillas, were supporting peace moves by the government while also pressing for social and political reforms. Cardinal Caggiano of Buenos Aires, for one, called for an end to "the fratricidal race of hate of 1974" — when more than 230 persons became the victims of clandestine groups.

Foreign Briefs:

• Cardinal Vicente Enrique Tarancon of Madrid joined a drive by the National Commission on Justice and Peace to seek amnesty for about 600 political prisoners in Spain.

• The movement of dissenting French priests called Exchanges and Dialogue, which in 1968 demanded that priests be allowed to marry and to enter the world of work and politics, declared itself dissolved. The national office of the organization urged its members to join another anti-institutional movement called Critical Christians.

• The permanent council of the Portuguese Bishops' Conference asked Feb. 26 priests in Portugal to stay out of party politics and not to become candidates for any party in national elections.

Irish Cease-Fire

The ruling army council of the Provisional Irish Republican Army announced an indefinite cease-fire in Ireland, beginning Feb. 10. The council's statement said: "In the light of discussions which have taken place between representatives of the Republican Movement and British officials, on effective arrangements to ensure that there is no breakdown of a new truce, the army council of the IRA have renewed their order suspending offensive military action."

The IRA had declared two earlier cease-fires, one in mid-1972 and another from Dec. 22, 1974, to Jan. 19. Eleven persons were killed between Jan. 19 and Feb. 10. To date five and one-half years of violence, mostly in Northern Ireland, took a toll of more than 1,150 lives.

Catholic and non-Catholic clergy, with public support, were reported to have been instrumental in events leading to the Christmas, 1974, and Feb. 10 cease-fires.

MARCH 1975

VATICAN

Family — Despite adverse influences in contemporary society, "the institution of the family itself is healthier and stronger than certain people would have us believe." So stated Pope Paul Mar. 12 at two general audiences attended by 30,000 persons. He added: "And the Christian ideal of marriage remains possible. It is more necessary than ever to proclaim it and to strengthen the good will of couples. . . . ." Regarding adverse influences, the Pope said: "Today's society accepts and encourages a relaxation of morals. Here and there civil laws observe this and foster it, which obliges Christians to heightened spiritual and moral vigor. Conditions of housing, work and environment weigh heavily on family life, and everything possible must be done to improve these conditions."

Speaking on the same subject Mar. 19, the Holy Father challenged Christian couples to "rediscover your vocation and your destiny — to preserve the incomparable human character and the spontaneously religious character of the Christian family. . . ."

Word to Pilgrims — The Pope told a gathering of pilgrims Mar. 16 that their Holy Year pilgrimage was a symbol of "life's search, leading to the Christian life and its true Catholic dimension." He said: "You distinguish yourselves from our agitated and suffering human society not in order to segregate yourselves from society but to immerse yourselves in it with your goodness and spirituality."

Knights of Columbus — Pope Paul, meeting Mar. 17 with about 450 Knights of Columbus from the U.S., Puerto Rico and Canada, urged them to give "testimony to the sanctity of life in all its stages," and to defend "the rights of all to share in the gift of God's creation." He expressed the "hope that you will lend upright and dynamic leadership in the communities in which you live. We hope that, as a body, you will address yourselves to the great religious and moral questions of the day; that your voice will be heard and that your witness will be effective in those issues that are decisive for mankind."

Conflicts — In an address Mar. 22 to the Vatican's Justice and Peace Commission, the Pope called attention to: "the agonizing tragedy which the populations of Vietnam are living through these days . . . the no less tragic situation in Cambodia, the armed struggle (rebels vs. government forces of Haile Selassie) which rages in Ethiopia, and the tensions which keep the (Turkish and Greek) populations of Cyprus divided, the climate of anxiety which still hangs over the (Arab-Israeli) truce in the Middle East." In these circumstances, "we must courageously witness to the Gospel of love, justice, peace and reconciliation, as Jesus and the prophets did. . . . But

at the same time this message must reach the practical world of today."

Challenge to Youth — Pope Paul challenged thousands of youths attending Palm Sunday celebrations to overcome an adolescent spiritual identity crisis and to accept Jesus in the clear light of the Church's doctrine. Full acceptance of Christ, he said, "is a matter of overcoming the stage of spiritual crisis which is characteristic of the transition from adolescence to youth, and then from youth to maturity. . . . It is a crisis of ideas, a crisis of faith, a crisis of moral orientation, a crisis of certainty about the meaning and value of life. . . . Only Jesus can draw out from our muddled consciousness our true personality. . . . It is he and only he who knows how to translate our religious relationship into a real social relationship, to make love of God the foundation of love for our neighbor." The conclusion of youthful search for meaning is "Christ rediscovered, Christ acclaimed, humbly and firmly believed in — not in the perpetual and hazy shadow of doubt but in the clear light of the doctrine which the Church proposes to us . . . a living Christ — the 'yes' of our choice, the 'yes' of our existence."

Earlier in the month, in a Mar. 2 address to several thousand young members of Gen ("New Generation"), the Pope asked rhetorically: "How many young people think they are free because they have cast off the habits and the authority of family life, without realizing that they have become enslaved by subjection to the arbitrary choice of a group, a social current, a collective rebellion?"

Aid for Vietnamese — The Pope, alarmed at the breakdown of the 1973 Paris agreements and the intensification of fighting in Vietnam, made a strong plea Mar. 26 for "universal solidarity" in relieving the suffering of thousands of Vietnamese. He said: "Let us do everything we can to alleviate the tragedy of those people and to prove to them that the world is not indifferent to the cries of our brethren."

Eucharistic Congress — Pope Paul hailed the development of plans for the 41st International Eucharistic Congress to be held in Philadelphia Aug. 1 to 8, 1976. Of its theme, "The Hungers of the Human Family," he said that for "the hungers of the human family the Eucharistic Congress will offer . . . the only, the perfect, solution: Jesus himself, who said 'I am the bread of life.' "

Participation in the Liturgy — The Pope told a general audience Mar. 26 that the Holy Week liturgy calls Christians to participation as actors and not as mere spectators. He said: "Yes, we may assist as spectators in the liturgical rite. But, if we truly understand its significance and purposes, we must in a certain way be actors in it, or we must at least place ourselves in harmony with the action celebrated by shifting our religious psychology to the action and to the scene from which it originated. . . . In the liturgical representation, a memorial of Christ's words and deeds is not only recalled, but his salvific action is also made operative."

Industrialization — Pope Paul told experts on industrialization to watch for its adverse effects on human dignity and international relations. In a letter addressed to the second conference of the UN's Organization for Industrial Development, he praised efforts to extend the benefits of industrialization to poorer nations, but warned: "Industrialization has also been tied to unjust situations, to benefits distributed unfairly. . . . Such conditions heavily burden international relations." The Mar. 12 to 26 conference was held in Lima, Peru.

The Pope Also:

• Spoke in praise of Michelangelo on the eve of the 500th anniversary of his birth, stating: "It is enough for us to recognize the unparalleled greatness of this artist and to recall that he was profoundly religious in sentiment." Michelangelo, an outstanding figure in the Renaissance, was the architect of St. Peter's Basilica during the last 17 years of his life.

• Met with: Canadian Prime Minister Pierre Trudeau, Mar. 7; members of the central bureau of the World Federation of Deaf Persons, Mar. 15; John Volpe, U.S. ambassador to Italy, Mar. 21; the Rev. Harry Reynolds Smythe, permanent representative of the Anglican Church and the archbishop of Canterbury, Mar. 22.

• Expressed his sympathy at the death Mar. 9 of Luis Amada Blanco, Cuban ambassador to the Vatican, and the assassination Mar. 25 of King Faisal of Saudi Arabia.

Vatican Briefs:

• Vatican Radio reported Mar. 6 that the Communist newspaper *Rude Pravo* regarded the recent visit to Prague of Archbishop Agostino Casaroli as "an important step toward improvement of relations" between the Church and the Czech government. The archbishop told Czech officials Feb. 25: "For its part, the Holy See offers its most willing cooperation, secure that it is acting not only in the interests of the Catholic Church but of the entire Czechoslovak society."

• Vatican Radio said Mar. 6 that the attack carried out that same day by Palestinian guerrillas on a Tel Aviv hotel "deserves full condemnation." The attack resulted in the death of four civilians, seven Palestinian guerrillas and three Israeli soldiers.

• The council of the general secretariat of the Synod of Bishops met with Pope Paul Mar. 8. Members of the council were in Rome Mar. 3 to 8 for work on the final reports and recommendations of the 1974 assembly of the synod.

• A Vatican source told NC News Service Mar. 18 that more than 500,000 persons had made Holy Year pilgrimages since the start of the Roman observance of the jubilee celebration on Christmas Eve. The half-million figure included only those who made their presence known to the Central Committee for the Holy Year.

Easter Message

Pope Paul proclaimed in his Easter message *"Urbi et Orbi"* ("To the City and the World") that the resurrection of Jesus has infused "new, original and inexhaustible life" into a world of dashed hopes.

Speaking before 400,000 persons in St. Peter's Square, he said: "It does not matter, brethren, if the experience of the frailty of human powers daily disappoints our fragile hopes for a stable ordering of human society. Nor does it matter if, from the very progress generated by modern development and from the sovereign exploitation of the useful secrets of nature, there seems to derive for man not fullness or certainty of life, but rather the torment of unsatisfied aspiration. It does not matter. For a new. original and inexhaustible source of life has been infused into the world by the risen Christ."

The Pope called the resurrection a "victory over sterile and deadening selfishness," and said that it provides the "example and the energy for the continual moral, spiritual and social renewal of the present life."

DOMESTIC

United Farm Workers vs. Gallo Wine Co. — More than 10,000 farm workers and their supporters, led by Cesar Chavez, rallied near the Modesto, Calif., headquarters of the E. and J. Gallo Wine Co. early in the month to bolster their national boycott of Gallo products. At issue in the dispute between the workers and the Gallo Co. was the right of the workers to decide their union representation by secret ballot.

Bread for the World — Bread for the World, an ecumenical citizen's lobby, issued a provisional nine-point policy statement on "the right to eat." The statement said: "As Christians we affirm the right of every man, woman and child on earth to a nutritionally adequate diet. This right is grounded in the value God places on human life and in the belief that 'the earth is the Lord's and the fullness thereof.' . . . We cannot rest until the fruit of God's earth is shared in a way that befits the human family."

Land Use Control — The board of directors of the National Catholic Rural Life Conference called for public restraint on private land ownership in order to control land speculation and windfall profits for large corporations. The board's statement, issued after a meeting in San Antonio, said: "Uncontrolled urban growth, energy resource exploitation, recreation development and other consumptive uses of land feed the market for speculation, drive prices beyond the reach of the average citizen and threaten the productivity of the land itself. . . . The resulting land ownership pattern, which favors corporate interests and wealthy individuals, is a threat to a stable and healthy society."

Reconciliation — Reconciliation of our Catholic past with our turbulent American present was called the Holy Year task of American Catholics by Archbishop John F. Whealon in an address before the first general assembly of the Religious Education Congress in Anaheim, Calif. He put down the idea that confusion in the Church could be blamed on the Second Vatican Council. Rather, he said: "I am convinced that we were all caught up in a massive cultural and sociological change that during the 60's swept across the entire Western world." Now, he added, the time has come "to pick up the pieces and reconstruct a faith and practice and catechesis that hold the essentials and combine the best of the past with the best of the present."

Illegal Aliens — A spokesman for the U.S. Catholic Conference supported an "across-the-board" amnesty for illegal aliens in the U.S. before an agreed-upon cut-off date. Msgr. George Higgins, secretary for research, told a House of Representatives subcommittee that the USCC also supported:

• an equitable immigration preference system for both the Eastern and Western hemispheres based primarily on family reunification and the admission of refugees;

• granting adjustment of immigration status to all, regardless of their country of birth;

• increased foreign aid and economic assistance to Mexico and other Latin American countries in particular.

Equality More Important than Integration — The moral issue of primary importance for Americans today is not integration but human dignity and equality for all, according to 30 black and white Divine Word Fathers, pastors of mostly black parishes across the country. Speaking for the group, Father William Oliver said: "We find that integration, as it is practiced in many areas of our country, does not bring with it human dignity or equality. . . . We find that, unless racial issues are attacked on moral grounds, no progress can be made which will have any lasting value. . . . We are convinced that to close black parishes and schools simply as a desegregation move is wrong. In many cases, the blacks, and especially the poor among them, are lost to the service of the Catholic Church. . . . To wish this service out of existence and to push it under the rug of integration is without Christian missionary merit. . . . In the past, outside of the religious communities so dedicated, the Catholic Church's

service to black communities, particularly poor ones, has been little realized and least supported by the whole Church in this country."

Good Friday Time Off — A state court of appeals in San Francisco ruled Mar. 14 that permitting state employes to take paid time off for a three-hour period on Good Friday violated the First Amendment to the U.S. Constitution.

Peace, Hunger, Poverty — President Gerald Ford told an audience of 10,000 at the University of Notre Dame Mar. 17 that peace could not endure unless the world hunger and poverty questions were answered. The President, after receiving an honorary doctor of laws degree, said: "There is no safety for any nation in a hungry, ill-educated and desperate world." The President also said that he had increased the Food for Peace Program from $980 million to $1.6 billion, and indicated that Notre Dame's president, Father Theodore M. Hesburgh, C.S.C., had influenced his decision to do so.

Welfare Rights for Unborn; "Hair" — In separate decisions, the U.S. Supreme Court:

• Ruled 7 to 1 that states are not required to provide welfare benefits for unborn children. The decision, in an Iowa case, left untouched current policy of the Department of Health, Education and Welfare permitting the states to decide whether or not to provide such benefits. Thirty-five states prohibited such aid.

• In the first application of obscenity law to a stage performance, struck down by a vote of 6 to 3 a ban on the performance of the musical "Hair" in the Chattanooga municipal auditorium. The court did not rule on the obscenity of the play, but said that, as a stage performance, it was subject to the same First Amendment protection (freedom of speech) as films.

Death with Dignity — A death-with-dignity bill introduced in the Illinois legislature was tabled in committee by a vote of 10 to 9. The bill would have provided that a person at least 18 years of age might execute a written document, witnessed by two others, that he or she was of sound mind and did not wish life sustained by machine. The author of the measure said it "would simply allow for a patient terminally ill to withhold heroic life support measures." Father John Quinn, executive director of the Illinois Catholic Conference, said: "We don't need legislation like this. Presently in the state of Illinois any patient can refuse treatment. . . . (The bill) could lead to euthanasia. This particular measure might have proven to be the nose of the euthanasia camel in the tent. That's the way abortion got in."

New York Charities — Catholic Charities of the New York archdiocese reported that it had spent $8,237,570 in services to more than 500,000 persons in 1974. The top priority of the federation's 205 member agencies in 1974 was the delivery of neighborhood-based family, community and child welfare services in areas of greatest need.

No Action against Episcopal Bishops — An Episcopal board of inquiry decided late in the month not to call for any disciplinary action against four bishops who ordained 11 women priests in Philadelphia in 1974. The board said that "the core of the controversy is doctrinal." As such, it had to be handled by the House of Bishops. Episcopal leaders in Washington and New York said they doubted that action against the ordaining bishops would be approved.

Atheist Rights — Madalyn Murray O'Hair, who won the 1963 Supreme Court case banning obligatory prayers in public schools, threatened to sue the Texas legislature for allegedly violating the rights of atheists. She claimed that the oath to tell the truth, "so help me, God," violates the principle of separation of Church and state.

End of Clemency Program — March 31 marked the end of the clemency program for draft evaders and deserters proclaimed by President Ford Sept. 16, 1974. Applying for clemency under the several provisions of the program were: 11,000 of 120,000 draft evaders and deserters; 4,856 of 12,500 deserters; and 501 of 4,400 draft evaders under indictment.

Domestic Briefs:
• Sister Jeannine Daigle resigned as director of the Northern Maine Medical Center following a decision by the board of directors to allow voluntary sterilization at the facility. The privately owned hospital was run under contract by the Little Franciscan Sisters of Mary.
• Twenty members of the House of Representatives, including Father Robert Drinan, S.J., introduced a bill to ban the death penalty for federal crimes.
• The National Coalition of American Nuns "adopted" as a "sister" and pledged to support Joan Little, a young North Carolina black woman accused of murder and facing a possible death sentence.
• Sufferings of the "captive nations" of Europe under Communist domination were the principal concern of participants in the Cardinal Mindszenty Foundation's Leadership Conference meeting in St. Louis.
• The Gulf Oil Corporation nominated Sister Jane Scully, president of Carlow College, Pittsburgh, to its board of directors.

NFPC Convention

More than 200 priests representing 120 senates or councils in 45 states took part in the eighth annual convention of the House of Delegates of the National Federation of Priests' Councils Mar. 10 to 13 in St. Petersburg. The theme of the meeting was "Reconciliation: Risks and Possibilities."

"Most in need of reconciliation," the delegates agreed in their agenda and statement, were divorced and remarried Catholics, resigned priests, youth, the distribution of world resources, liberal and conservative Catholics. Convention deliberations resulted in recommendations for action by priests' senates throughout the country.

In two resolutions passed, the delegates pledged themselves to give 10 per cent of their individual incomes for a year to feed the hungry, and called on priests in member councils to boycott Gallo wines in support of the United Farm Workers of America.

FOREIGN

Relations with Cuba — The head of the Colombian Bishops' Conference said that proposed renewal of relations with Cuba "could adversely affect domestic peace" in their country. Bishop Jose de Jesus Pimiento declared that, although the Church preaches brotherly relations among nations, "in the present circumstances, for the sake of peace in the nation, such relations with Cuba should not be welcomed." The circumstances referred to were waves of guerrilla attacks and kidnappings by the Marxist National Liberation Army.

Zaire Layman a Parish Leader — A married layman was officially installed as the first "parish animator" or parish leader in Zaire, according to a Vatican Radio report Mar. 4. The report said that the installation signaled "a new era in the life of the local church of Kinshasa, and should lead toward an expansion of Christian life enriched by black African values and the total dedication of the laity."

Polish Missionaries — The mission news agency *Fides* reported that 246 missionaries from Poland were sent to overseas assignments during the four years from 1970 to 1973, bringing to 826 the total number of missioners from Poland. *Fides* commented: "In spite of nearly 30 years of Communist rule, Poland, with its population of 34 million, remains a strongly Catholic country, and its contribution to the Church's missionary effort has been becoming more and more notable in recent years."

More French Students for Priesthood — France's National Center for Vocations reported that in 1974, for the first time in 11 years, the number of men (194) entering diocesan seminaries and other systems of training for the priesthood was greater than the number of entrants (151) in the previous year. The total number of men preparing for the diocesan priesthood was 1,509.

Vanguard Church — The Church in Latin America "must advance the cause of man's total liberation" from poverty and sin, a committee of the Latin American Bishops' Council declared. "We need a Church in the vanguard, filled with missionary spirit in preaching the Gospel," said the 15 bishops in charge of centralizing and coordinating efforts in such pastoral areas as teaching Christian doctrine, social action, liturgy, communications and theological research.

Priests Restricted in Czechoslovakia — More than 500 of some 4,000 Czech and Slovak priests were banned from engaging in priestly functions of any kind, with the result that about one-third of the parishes in the country were without priests. It was also reported from Prague that obstacles were being placed by the government in the way of those engaged in religious instruction. The rule seemed to be that only priests and religious as well as other teachers considered "politically safe" were given necessary licenses to function.

Mother Teresa Honored — The UN Food and Agriculture Organization struck a Ceres Medal in tribute to Mother Teresa's "exemplary love and concern for the hungry and the poorest of the poor." Proceeds from the sale of the medal were to go to the support of the work of the Missionaries of Charity. The community, founded by Mother Teresa in Calcutta in 1950, had sisters in 17 countries.

Christian Population in 2000 — A study released in Berne by the Swiss Catholic Mission Council estimated a world population of 6,126 million by the year 2000 and a Christian population of 1,914 million (31.2 per cent). It was estimated that 58.5 per cent of those professing Christian faith would be in Africa, Asia, Latin America and Oceania. In 1900, these continents had only 14.5 per cent of the world's Christians; industrialized nations had 85.5 per cent.

Missionary Expelled from Bolivia — The military government of Gen. Hugo Banzer expelled Belgian Father Eric Wasseige on charges of meddling in politics. The government based its charges on a report issued by a commission headed by the priest. The report said that social injustice and neglect of the Indian majority were the basic reasons for widespread unrest in the country. It also questioned the regime's version and figures (16 dead, more wounded) with respect to the repression of an uprising at Cochabamba in January, 1974; the report said the number of dead was nearly 100.

Meeting Banned in Madrid — Cardinal Enrique y Tarancon publicly denounced the banning by civil authorities of a public Christian meeting in a Madrid suburb. In a letter read in all of the city's churches on Mar. 19, he said: "In the minds of all is the deplorable suspension of the Christian meeting in Vallecas by the public powers, an action that neither I nor many of you can understand in a nation that has as its glorious maxim submission to the laws of God as taught by the Catholic Church." The Mar. 15 to 18 meeting was called to consider the guidance and aid the

Church might provide in solving the problems of the people.

Moral Deviations — Certain "deviations" from moral law were attacked in a pastoral letter by the bishops of Senegal and Mauritania, according to a Vatican Radio broadcast Mar. 25. The bishops "wrote in particular that practices once limited and censured — such as relations before and outside of marriage, the use of contraceptives, and procured abortion — today are becoming normal practices in the name of liberty and are accepted also by those who do not expressly follow a materialistic view of life. In view of an explosion of these deviations, the Church . . . has the duty of calling to mind the character of the total and definitive gift of the sexual act which is realized in the exclusive and indissoluble love of the couple." The bishops equated abortion with infanticide and called it an "abominable crime."

Foreign Briefs:

• It was announced in London that the Church Music Trust, an interdenominational group, would guarantee until May, 1976, the salaries of the seven-member choir of Westminster Cathedral. Cathedral officials had said earlier that, because of financial straits, they would be unable to pay the choir after the celebration of Easter 1975.

• The first two native-born bishops of Mozambique were ordained Mar. 9 in a solemn ceremony presided over by Cardinal Agnelo Rossi, prefect of the Congregation for the Evangelization of Peoples. They were Fathers Jose Maria dos Santos, O.F.M., of Lourenco Marques, and Januario Nhangumbe of Porto Amelia.

• Terrorists in Bahia Blanca, Argentina, killed Salesian Father Carlos Dorniak, the latest victim in a chain of murders that left 103 dead since January. Archbishop Jorge Mayer of Bahia Blanca called the killing "a senseless murder, blackening the humanity of those involved as killers or instigators."

Aggression against Bolivians

The bishops of Bolivia said that a 1975, $8 million birth control program funded by the U.S. Agency for International Development constituted aggression against the Bolivian people. They also singled out for criticism the International Planned Parenthood Federation and Pathfinder.

AID was underwriting birth control activities in the Ministry of Health, the National Center for the Family, and clinics run by three universities. AID and the other groups were funding "distribution of contraceptives, surgery, training of birth control personnel, and publications to propagandize birth control."

The bishops said they feared "an escalation of sterilization of women, wider use of contraceptives and legalization of abortion practices."

APRIL 1975

VATICAN

Gospel of Resurrection — The Gospel of the resurrection and "trust in the principles of justice, freedom, harmony, love and peace" can overcome armed conflicts and hatred, Pope Paul told thousands of persons Apr. 7 in a talk on Christian optimism.

In addresses to three separate general audiences Apr. 23, the Pope emphasized the reality of Christ's resurrection, saying: "It is most important that our conviction on this be clear, firm and certain." He cited "the need to define within our minds (this) doctrine of the faith, the need to make it genuine and firm for us, the need to make clear the concept and function of the faith within the plan of salvation. This is especially necessary in the face of the Protestant, Modernist and current controversies, which indeed are legion."

Newman's Work Is Relevant — Pope Paul praised 19th-century English theologian Cardinal John Henry Newman and said that his work remains relevant, in an address to scholars attending the sixth Congress on the Christian Life of Newman. He said: "Many of the problems which he treated with wisdom — although he himself was frequently misunderstood and misinterpreted in his own time — were the subjects of the discussion and study of the Fathers of the Second Vatican Council, as for example, the question of ecumenism, the relationship between Christianity and the world, the emphasis on the role of the laity in the Church, and the relationship of the Church to non-Christian religions."

Inner Peace — The Holy Father stressed the need for interior peace during three general audiences for different language groups Apr. 9. He told the pilgrims: "Innermost peace is the primary authentic happiness. It helps one to be strong in the face of adversity. It preserves the nobility and liberty of the human person under the worst conditions in which men may find themselves."

Evangelization — Pope Paul told 80 bishops in charge of missionary activities Apr. 11 that evangelization "is the backbone of the Church's action, the basic condition for the existence of the Church. . . . Evangelization is the focal point toward which must always converge the work of the entire ecclesial community."

Pastoral Ministry — This was one of the topics mentioned by Pope Paul in an address on Apr. 13, the opening day of a drive to construct new churches in Rome and its suburbs. He said: "Our pastoral activity is vertical, toward God, toward Christ. . . . But it is also horizontal — toward people, toward the masses in need of a center which can cultivate their spirit, feed their feeling of brotherhood and community, care for their most neglected and most human needs; a center which can

soothe their afflictions, strengthen their highest hopes and cultivate their moral and civic consciousness."

Religion-Life Relationship — Addressing a general audience Apr. 16, Pope Paul said: "We must learn about the saving relationship between religion and life. Life stands to gain from this relationship, meaning nobility, vigor, hope and joy at being saved. . . . We must learn about the transcendence of Christian teaching. Those who reject this higher teaching wisdom through unbelief or radical secularism blow out Christ's light shining on our lives. . . . They are really deprived of faith and vital knowledge, lovingly and freely cast in our path."

Climate for Vocations — In a message for the World Day of Vocations, Apr. 20, Pope Paul called for a new climate leading to an increase in strong vocations to the priesthood and religious life. Reflecting on the existing situation, he said that in some places "there is a heartening renewal, but in many other places there has been a disturbing decline in vocations, a decline that weighs heavily on the future."

Pilgrimage Spirit — In an open-air audience in St. Peter's Square Apr. 25, Pope Paul challenged a crowd of about 100,000 to consider their motivation for coming to the Vatican during the Holy Year. He urged them to adopt the spirit of true pilgrims, noting that "the Holy Year should be above all an awakening, an inner awakening, a search to find oneself."

Anglican Eucharist in Vatican — American and Canadian Episcopalian clergymen, in Rome for an annual conference, celebrated a first-ever Episcopalian Eucharistic service within the walls of Vatican City Apr. 27 at the invitation of Pope Paul. About 30 American and 10 Canadian deans of cathedrals participated in the service at the Church of St. Stephen of the Abyssinians, just behind the apse of St. Peter's Basilica.

Critical Christian Judgment — The Christian who confronts the world must watch with critical judgment for the signs of the times, remembering that Christians "are for the world what the soul is to the body," Pope Paul told three general audiences Apr. 30. He said: "Let us remember that being distinct from what we call the world, in a negative sense, does not separate us from the world in a positive sense — that is, from humanity, even in those aspects which are wanting, lamentable, and in need of the great light of truth and of the beneficial remedy of charity."

Concern for Vietnamese and Cambodians — On the day of South Vietnam's surrender to encircling Communist forces, a statement from the Vatican press office said that Pope Paul shared the fears of the people and hoped for the grace of a "real peace . . . after 30 years of sad struggle." The Pope expressed similar concern for the people of Cambodia Apr. 21.

The Pope Also:

• In a message to Cardinal John Cody, commended the generosity of the people of the Chicago archdiocese for their $1.5 million contribution to the Freedom from Hunger collection.

• Officiated at the marriage of 13 couples in a special Holy Year ceremony accenting the value of Christian marriage, Apr. 13.

• Established an apostolic delegation to Angola, Apr. 16.

• Awarded the Pius XI Medal to British scientist Dr. Stephen W. Hawkins during an audience with members of the Pontifical Academy of Sciences, Apr. 19.

• Took part in beatification ceremonies for Father Cesar de Bus (1544-1607), founder of the Fathers of Christian Doctrine, Apr. 27.

Vatican Briefs:

• Cardinal Egidio Vagnozzi, head of the Prefecture for Economic Affairs, stated that the value of the Vatican's "productive assets" throughout the world amounted to less than $125 million. He said published reports that the Vatican's revenue-producing assets totaled $10 billion or as much as $20 billion were "completely nonsensical." The cardinal's statement was made in an interview published in *Europa*, a monthly financial supplement.

• The Congregation for the Doctrine of the Faith issued a decree Apr. 9 simplifying rules regarding the censorship of books on matters of faith and morals. (See separate entry.)

• The Secretariat for Non-Believers launched a study late in the month of why many European youths are living only on the fringe of the Church or dropping out of it completely. A statement issued by the secretariat said: "It seems that youth's conversion to non-belief, or its confirmation in non-belief, is not merely a passing crisis of growing years, as it has usually been in the past and would normally warrant the hope of eventual reconversion with mature commitment to the faith. Rather, there is a general feeling that Europe's young people, allowing for some national differences, are immersed in a radically new milieu, a cultural setting in which faith finds no expression and is ignored."

Role of Women

The Church cannot ordain women to the priesthood because Christ's call to them — to be "disciples and collaborators," but not ordained ministers — cannot be changed, Pope Paul declared in an address Apr. 18 to a committee studying the Church's response to the 1975 UN-sponsored International Women's Year. He added, however, that "we must recognize and advance the role of women in the

mission of evangelization and in the life of the Christian community."

The liberation of women that is needed, the Pope said, will come from "progressive development," "wise discernment," and programs "corresponding to the real needs of people, so that they can walk together toward opportune and realistic goals." He called for the rejection of "utopian programs conceived by an elite for an elite."

DOMESTIC

NCEA Convention — Some 12,000 persons attended sessions of the 72nd annual convention of the National Catholic Educational Association in Atlantic City during Easter week. The theme of the meeting was "Seeking a Just Society." The mood was cautious optimism regarding the status and future of Catholic education, after a decade of doom-saying. It was observed that school closings and the flight of students from Catholic schools were the lowest in three years.

Ethnics — The Second Vatican Council's directives, to take local cultures into account in the Church, have not been implemented in the United States, according to Jerome Benno Ernst, executive director of the Catholic Conference on Ethnic and Neighborhood Affairs. He said in a Washington interview: "Although the Church in the United States has basically been an immigrant Church, it is structured so that it does not represent ethnic concerns. The Church wanted to be accepted and tended to negate and put down cultural differences out of a strong desire to be part of the melting pot." The conference, a leadership network, was organized in June, 1974, to work for the preservation and advancement of the ethnic heritages of Catholics in the United States.

Anti-Abortion Amendment Opposed — The U.S. Civil Rights Commission stated its opposition to any constitutional amendment "designed to deny the right to terminate a pregnancy." It said that such an amendment would violate the First, Ninth and Fourteenth Amendments. Cardinal Terence J. Cooke, chairman of the Committee on Pro-Life Activities, National Conference of Catholic Bishops, commented: "On the strength of the commission's assertion we are told that something barely legal in 1973 (abortion) lies at the heart of the Constitution in 1975."

Fair-Minded Education Board Wanted — The bishops of Missouri, in a letter to Gov. Christopher S. Bond, asked that fair-minded persons be appointed to the state's board of education whenever a board vacancy occurs. Their letter complained of "a considerable injustice upon the school children," and noted that the state board administered many programs that included more than just public school children. "We have found that the state board, in administering these programs over the years, has actively and consciously excluded non-public school children from receiving fair benefits," the letter said. "The state board of education has disregarded federal laws and regulations, has refused to follow the advice of the state attorney general, has failed to comply with the requests of the U.S. Commissioner of Education, has ignored requests of Missouri public officials, and has pursued a path of unending litigation, all resulting in a denial of the rights of children in non-public schools. . . . We do not think this is a reasonable path for a public board to follow."

Imaginary Visions — Officials of the Brooklyn diocese again assured homeowners and civic leaders of Bayside Hills, Queens, that no ecclesiastical authority had been given to followers of a 51-year-old woman, Mrs. Veronica Lueken, to gather semiweekly on the grounds of St. Robert Bellarmine's Parish to hear about her alleged visions of the Virgin Mary. Msgr. James P. King, chancellor of the diocese, told civic leaders that authorities "have done everything we can" to stop the gatherings of "zealots." A diocesan committee had found that the reports of miracles, miraculous photos and impending landings of comets on New York, which formed part of Mrs. Lueken's claims, were "the product of a fertile imagination," Msgr. King said.

Cooperation with Indians — The bishops of Minnesota called on Catholic people and institutions to "cooperate with the Indian people in laboring for justice." They said in a pastoral letter: "We must join in the struggle to secure equitable resolution of past injustice inflicted on the Indian people by the United States government and other private and public institutions."

Inconsistent Policy on Aliens — Three Chicano bishops, backed by the Midwest Council of La Raza and the Spanish-Speaking Coalition, sent the following telegram to President Ford about Apr. 20: "Dear Mr. President: We strongly disapprove of both your intentions of bringing 180,000 South Vietnamese persons to the United States and our government's insistence on the deportation of illegal aliens in our country. These actions are inconsistent." The prelates were: Archbishop Robert F. Sanchez of Santa Fe, Auxiliary Bishop Gilbert E. Chavez of San Diego and Auxiliary Bishop Patrick F. Flores of San Antonio.

Influence of Organized Religion — Organized religion had little influence on decisions or actions affecting the United States, according to 1,000 national leaders polled by *U.S. News and World Report.* In an Apr. 21 report on the results of the poll, they placed religion 23rd on a list of 24 "most powerful institutions," just ahead of films and just below the Republican Party.

IBM Sales to South Africa — A coalition of 14 Protestant churches and Catholic religious orders with stock in IBM urged the corporation at its annual stockholders meeting Apr. 28 in Pittsburgh to stop selling computers to the South African government, but the proposal was overwhelmingly rejected in a proxy vote. The coalition charged that IBM computers helped South Africa to maintain an oppressive and dehumanizing apartheid system of strict racial segregation that denied blacks the right to vote and rigidly controlled their lives. IBM officials said their South African operations had drawn praise even from those criticizing IBM sales there. Its work force there of 1,225 included 114 blacks, who received equal pay and special benefits and training, they said.

Personal Parish — Recognition of the first personal parish in the Cleveland diocese was announced in the last week of the month by Bishop James A. Hickey and the Community of St. Malachi. The non-territorial parish, in which membership was by choice, was approved for a period of three years. It had a membership of about 240 persons from various parts of the Cleveland metropolitan area.

Unemployment — "Unemployment is one of the worst enemies of humanity," Msgr. George G. Higgins told a rally of 60,000 persons in Washington Apr. 26. Msgr. Higgins, a 30-year veteran in the union labor movement, said widespread unemployment "seriously endangers the social order."

Domestic Briefs:

• The Catholic University of America published a supplemental volume updating the *New Catholic Encyclopedia* published in 1967.

• The Lilly Foundation of Indianapolis announced late in the month that it had given a grant of $100,000 jointly to four religious organizations cooperating regularly with NBC News in religious television programming. The organizations were the U.S. Catholic Conference, the National Council of Churches, the Southern Baptist Convention and the Jewish Theological Seminary of America.

• The Pennsylvania Catholic Conference and the Pennsylvania Council of Churches opposed repeal of the state's "blue laws" requiring businesses to close on Sunday.

• A conference of some 200 religious leaders, educators and UN non-governmental personnel, meeting in New York, marked the 60th anniversary of the massacre of an estimated 1.5 million Armenians by the Ottoman Turks. The conference voted its "clear declaration of intent" to speak out against mass violence and genocide wherever they might occur.

• Archbishop Fulton J. Sheen was awarded the first President's Patronal Medal of the Catholic University of America Apr. 16 for outstanding contributions to the Church.

Pastoral Letter on Abortion

In a pastoral letter made public Apr. 7, Bishop Leo T. Maher of San Diego declared that persons who publicly espouse abortion or who belong to organizations promoting abortion may not receive the sacraments in his diocese.

The bishop said: "In face of the shameless agitation of some groups such as the National Organization for Women, and in view of the legalization by the government of abortion under certain conditions, and since there are attempts being made to discredit those who still believe in the inviolable value of every human life, as Bishop of the Diocese of San Diego I reaffirm the universal, constant and clear doctrine of the Church on the moral evaluation of abortion. Abortion 'intended as the deliberate and direct interruption of the generative process of human life' is a serious moral crime, because it violates the fundamental right of existence which God has imparted to every human being."

"No person who claims and professes views that are contrary to the teachings of the Church can claim to be a practicing Catholic. Nor are they to be admitted to the sacraments. One who admits publicly to be a member of an organization that promotes abortions, such as the NOW organization, must be refused the sacrament of the Eucharist by priests, deacons and extraordinary ministers. Nor can they proclaim the word of God by serving as a lector, for they ignore God's law and his love."

"One can never claim freedom of opinion as a pretext for attacking the rights of others, most especially the right to life. One cannot invoke freedom of thought to destroy this life."

Demonstrations of protest against the bishop's letter were staged by abortion proponents in front of three San Diego churches Apr. 13. More than 30 people who stated their view that a woman has a right to have an abortion were refused the Eucharist.

FOREIGN

Repression of Social Works in Paraguay — The Paraguayan Bishops' Conference issued a protest against government arrests, expulsions of missionaries, and confiscations designed to cripple the social works of the Church in the country. "Arbitrary repression," they said, not only violates the constitutional rights of citizens but also the rights of the Church." They added that charges of subversion against missionaries and lay persons for social action have never been proved by the government.

Black Anger in Africa — White South Africa "could drift along to 1980 and find itself confronted with colossal black anger — within and without its frontiers — and still 75 per cent unprepared for the changes that must be made if violence is to be avoided." So stated Archbishop Denis Hurley of Durban in an address in Roma, Lesotho. He predicted that by 1980 Rhodesia and "a lot, if not all, of South West Africa will be under black rule."

Anti-Church Policy in Bolivia — The military regime of Bolivia told church authorities in La Paz that it would not permit two expelled Belgian missionaries charged with subversion to return to the country, and that any clerics or "extremist priests" caught in "subversive activities" would be arrested or deported. A government spokesman also said that Radio Station Pius XII, run by Canadian Oblate missionaries, would not be permitted on the air unless it closed its facilities to miners protesting against injustice. Luis A. Stiles, former president of the country, told newsmen in La Paz that "in 150 years of Bolivian history, no regime has been so hard on the Church, its organization and principles, as Banzer's."

Appeal to Brazilian Senate — The Brazilian Bishops' Conference, in a letter to the president of the senate, called for the passage of legislation to strengthen family life rather than to legalize divorce. The conference also urged the government to restore civil rights. Measures called for included equal pay for women, improvement of maternity benefits, wage and family subsidies, low-income housing, child welfare programs and vocational training for the young. Of civil rights, the conference said: "We call for freedom of education, for self-governing trade unions, for freedom of association among rural groups. We also stand for the rights of intellectuals and the exercise of social criticism, and for minority rights. We call for a final end of torture, kidnappings and arbitrary imprisonment of citizens."

Portuguese Elections — In the midst of an election campaign dominated by extremists representing perhaps 12 per cent of the electorate, the bishops of Portugal asked Catholics to show up at the polls in great numbers and to elect non-Communist delegates to a new constitutional assembly. "Catholics are morally forbidden to vote for parties that by their ideology, objectives, prejudices and history have shown themselves to be incompatible with the Christian concept of man and his life in society," the bishops said in a statement issued in Lisbon less than two weeks before Apr. 25 elections.

Uganda Missionaries — Ambivalent and unpredictable Idi Amin, president of Uganda, granted permanent residence in the country to four lay Catholic missionaries and a nun, according to a report from the information service of the Congregation for the Evangelization of Peoples. In 1972 Amin expelled 58 missionaries from the country, claiming that as foreigners they posed a threat to Uganda.

Northern Ireland — Cardinal William Conway and nine bishops of the Armagh Church Province appealed to Northern Irish Protestants not to seek the restoration of the political system that discriminated against Catholics for over 50 years. In a statement issued less than three weeks before the May 1 elections of delegates to a constitutional convention on the future of Northern Ireland, the bishops said: "We beg these people to look at the facts, to be realistic, and to realize that a happy and reconciled community will be impossible to achieve if there is to be a return to the system of former days. The return to such a system would mean sowing the seeds of an unending period of tension and discontent."

Priests in Spain Fined — In three years, 108 priests charged with violating security laws against subversion for preaching on social justice were fined $200,000, according to a report published in Madrid by the national Catholic weekly *Vida Nueva*. The report also said that more than 40 priests had spent time in jail for not paying fines. Bishop Antonio Infantes commented: "Denouncing real social problems, as a matter of Christian concern, should not be punished; otherwise, the right to freedom of expression is being denied."

Land Speculation in Costa Rica — Church leaders in Costa Rica were spearheading efforts to thwart land speculation by a few rich men and to foster a land-reform program for poor farmers. One of the persons involved was Robert L. Vesco, the fugitive American financier.

Pessimistic Estimates — The estimates of British sociologist Anthony Spencer that 250,000 Catholics in England were dropping out of the Church each year was challenged by Bishop Hugh Lindsay of Hexham and Newcastle. The bishop said: "There is no indication of any wholesale abandonment of Catholic identity. Mr. Spencer's estimates seem far too pessimistic."

Birth Control Policy in Dominican Republic — The bishops of the Dominican Republic told government officials in a statement that they could not cooperate in birth control programs unless they were based on "natural" methods. They made the statement in order to dispel confusion created by President Joaquin Belaguer who said during a television broadcast that "there has been no problem with the Church, which has shown itself tolerant on the matter" (of government birth control programs). The bishops said their stand was that "of the universal Church," and that their support was for a program conducted by natural family planning clinics.

Terrorism in Lebanon — The Maronite-Rite bishops of Lebanon denounced acts of terrorism in the country and appealed to Palestinians and the government to restore order, Vatican Radio reported Apr. 29. The targets of their criticism were the Palestinian Liberation Organization and the Lebanese Phalangists. The bishops cited "incidents of bloodshed and acts of violence which have brought about in recent months the deaths of hundreds of persons, the abduction and ill-treatment of innocent people and attacks on private property."

Nuncio Manhandled — A physical attack by a student mob on Archbishop Angelo Palmas brought another appeal from the bishops of Colombia to halt violence in the nation. They deplored "this shameful act" and warned: "This is a call to reflection on what the consequences might be for Colombia if mounting violence is not halted immediately." The nuncio did not suffer injury in the incident.

Foreign Briefs:
• Bethlehem University, established in October, 1973, for the higher education of Arabs living in Israeli-occupied territory, had a student body of 200 undergraduates and a staff headed by Christian Brothers from the United States.

• The number of candidates (338) for the priesthood in West Germany increased six per cent over the figure for 1973-74.

• Cardinal Vicente Enrique Tarancon established a parish in Madrid for some 20,000 English-speaking Catholics.

• Approximately 3,000 catechumens were received into the Church in the Diocese of Uvira, Zaire, at Easter Vigil ceremonies Mar. 30, according to a delayed report from the Congregation for the Evangelization of Peoples.

• The Vatican nunciature in Santiago gave asylum to 31 Chileans who claimed to be under political persecution by the ruling military junta.

• Bishop Manuel Vieira Pinto of Nampula, Mozambique, who was expelled from his diocese in April, 1974, by the Portuguese government, returned to his see from exile.

• The South Korean government gave a "note of exit" instead of an extension of his visa to American Father James Sinnot, M.M., a leading campaigner for civil rights.

Vietnamese and Cambodian Refugees

Catholic Relief Services intensified its relief efforts in South Vietnam and Cambodia, which were taken over by North Vietnamese and Khmer Rouge forces, respectively, during the month. Father Robert L. Charlebois, regional director for East Asia and the Pacific, said that CRS was ready to continue its massive relief work in both countries, provided two conditions were met. "The safety of our international staff must be assured, and our international staff must be able to monitor and account for the expenditure of commodities and funds in the refugee areas."

In this country, the Division of Migration and Refugees, U.S. Catholic Conference, under the direction of John McCarthy, joined government and other private agencies to provide resettlement and other services for some 130,000 refugees and 2,000 children cleared for adoption.

MAY 1975

VATICAN

Materialism Hinders Justice — In a message to some 50,000 persons in St. Peter's Square on the feast of St. Joseph the Worker, Pope Paul said: "Until the world of work knows how to free itself from influences which are radically materialistic and suspiciously secularist, by which it is almost bewitched today . . . we will not have a well ordered society which is truly human, much less Christian, but a weighty human society organized by complicated and impersonal economic and legal mechanisms."

Ninth World Communications Day — The Pope, at a Mass marking World Communications Day, May 11, told "readers, listeners and spectators" of all forms of communications media: "Just as you have the right in a high-minded and civil country to be served by excellent and high-minded media, so also do you have the obligation to choose for yourselves things that are good and inoffensive to your moral and Christian sensibilities — the obligation to prefer, support and defend the so-called 'good press.' You have the obligation to encourage and promote those forms of spreading thoughts and customs which are in line with a high civil and religious consciousness."

Extremists Harm the Church — The Pope severely criticized ultra-liberal and ultra-conservative Catholics, declaring that they inflict "bitter wounds" on the Church. He said in an address May 14: "These people, abusing arbitrary restorative or pluralistic criteria, have not helped in a positive building up of the Church herself, in truth and in love." He decried a "personal and perhaps selfish view" of the Church held by those who "discredit esteem for the Church before her own children and before those outside the Church, and who thus discourage ecclesiastical and religious vocations, slow down the Church's missionary thrust, and weaken its inclination toward a convincing and efficacious ecumenical dialogue."

Marian Devotion — The Holy Father told participants in two Marian meetings in Rome — of the International Marian Congress and the International Mariological Congress — that Marian devotion can be reawakened in the Church through contemplation of Mary's beauty as well as through scholarly study. He said that Mary, "full of the Spirit," is the creature "all beautiful . . . the mirror without spot and the supreme ideal of perfection."

In a letter to Cardinal Josef Suenens, president of the Mariological Congress, the Pope said: "At this particularly critical time in the history of the Church and of humanity — in which the interior renewal of Christians and their reconciliation with God and between themselves are indispensable demands — devotion to the Holy Spirit, the font of sovereign charity, unity and peace, must grow in the souls of the faithful. But, in harmony with this, kindled and given new life by the fire of divine love, devotion to the great Mother of God, Mother of the Church, incomparable model of love for God and the brethren, must also radiate in the souls of the faithful."

On May 11 the Pope recalled the first apparition of Mary at Fatima on May 13, 1917, along with the "prayers, festivals and hopes" it occasioned throughout the world. He commented: "Still today we are receiving countless messages asking that religious rebirth and just peace for entire peoples be recommended to Our Lady's intercession."

Caritas Internationalis — Works of charity and direct help to the needy and suffering performed by Caritas Internationalis, the international federation of Catholic Charities organizations, and its national counterparts received warm recognition and praise from Pope Paul on May 16. He told members of the federation: "With you we give thanks to the Lord for the past, the present and the future of Caritas Internationalis. . . . The contemporary world has more need than ever of this young charity, young but nourished and purified at its deepest level by the Holy Spirit. . . . Such charity prolongs the miracles of Christ, who was always so ready to note human suffering and to answer unforeseen appeals by persons and crowds." Father Georg Huessler was elected president of the 25-year-old federation.

Catholic Schools — In a letter written on his behalf by Cardinal Jean Villot, Pope Paul said: "In a society obsessed with efficiency and inclined to bestow privileges on an elite, the Church strongly encourages Catholic schools to open their doors to children of modest families, to slow learners, to those who suffer physical or mental handicaps, and to the children of migrant workers. Thus can private schools show that they too can render public service." The letter was addressed to Yves O'Mahony, president of the French National Union of Parents for Freedom of Education in Schools.

Christian Joy — In his second apostolic exhortation since the beginning of the Holy Year, Pope Paul asked Christians May 16 to "return to the sources of joy" by rejecting sin and by becoming "more present to God." Christian joy, he said, is gained only through "a human-divine communion, and aspires to a communion even more universal. . . . Common Christian joy . . . is not possible in truth except where the preaching of the faith is accepted in its entirety."

Pentecost Preparation and Witness — The mystery of Pentecost, when well prepared for by Christians, leads to an explosion of apostolic witness to Christ's message, declared Pope Paul in a sermon on Pentecost Sunday.

He said that Christians who prepare for Pentecost with "interior silence" will abandon themselves to the Spirit's "super love. . . . They will be almost surprised by the unusual courage . . . to speak, sing and announce to others, to everybody, 'the wonderful things of God.' "

Witness Value of Suffering — Christians who rejoice in bearing the cross should witness their joy to those who do not understand the value of suffering, Pope Paul said May 21. In an open-air audience in St. Peter's Square, he told 50,000 people: "We are happy, even under the weight of the cross, even if our cross . . . is perhaps more painful than that of others who try to shake the cross from their shoulders without wishing to acknowledge its intrinsic value and providential significance. . . . Why not give our brothers in humanity a witness that we Christians, if humble and faithful, are happy?"

Canonizations — In the first act of its kind in the Holy Year, Pope Paul canonized two Spanish saints May 25. The saints were Juan Bautista de la Concepcion, a reformer of the Trinitarian Order who died in 1613, and Vicenta Maria Lopez y Vicuna, who founded the Daughters of Mary Immaculate for domestic service in the late 19th century.

Strong Christian Witness — Christians, and especially Catholics, must be spiritually and morally strong and fearless in order to witness to Jesus, Pope Paul declared at a general audience May 28. He said: "A Christian, and especially a Catholic, must be strong — spiritually and morally strong. A follower of Christ must not be afraid. . . . He is invested with the task of witnessing which liberates him from shyness and from opportunism, and suggests to him both words and conduct at the right moment, coming forth from an interior spring which he, perhaps, did not know existed before it was tested."

The Pope Also:

• Spoke May 3 to 10,000 Croatian Holy Year pilgrims, recalling the presence of their ancestors at the first Holy Year in 1300 and praising them for their firmness in the faith.

• Told a private audience of members of the Strasbourg Council of Europe May 5 that efforts to unite Europe were in line with what the Church teaches and is seeking to accomplish.

• Reminded 50,000 pilgrims in four audiences May 7 that Christian life cannot exist without prayer. "We need prayer, the help of divine energy, which brings a remedy for our littleness," he said.

• Hailed Bishop Edward E. Swanstrom, executive director of Catholic Relief Services, as a man with understanding of the "paradox" of charity in the contemporary world.

Vatican Briefs:

• Twenty-four recruits were inducted into the Swiss Guards May 6. The ceremony commemorated the death of 147 Swiss Guards killed while protecting Pope Clement VII during the sack of Rome in 1527.

• Msgr. Silvio Luoni, head of the Vatican delegation to the UN's World Health Organization, charged that the agency's research in the field of human reproduction was oriented almost exclusively toward medical technology, instead of being guided by a sense of human dignity and responsibility, and by moral values.

Charismatic Renewal

Pope Paul told 10,000 Catholic charismatics May 19 that the spiritual renewal prompted by the Holy Spirit is "good fortune for the Church and the world."

Addressing participants in the International Conference on Charismatic Renewal in the Church, he said: "Nothing is more necessary to a world more and more secularized than the witness of this 'spiritual renewal' which we see the Holy Spirit raising up today in the most diverse regions and milieux. . . . How, then, could this 'spiritual renewal' not be 'good fortune' for the Church and the world? And, this being the case, how can we not use every means to see that it so remains?"

He told the charismatics that they must be guided by the discernment of those in authority in the Church, and offered them three principles for use in judging what is truly of the Spirit: "fidelity to the authentic doctrine of the faith"; reception of the gifts of the Spirit with gratitude and use of them for the good of the community; and, most importantly, the presence of love which communicates "the very life of the Trinity," and which can and must be communicated in love to others.

DOMESTIC

Released-Time Ruling Appealed — A ruling by a U.S. District Court judge in Harrisonburg, Va. — that a released-time program of religious instruction was unconstitutional — was appealed to the U.S. Court of Appeals. Judge James Turk declared that public school officials in Virginia may no longer grant students permission to leave school during regular hours in order to attend religion classes off public school premises. He ruled that recent Supreme Court opinions justified a decision at variance with the 1952 Zorach v. Clauson case, in which the court supported the constitutionality of programs in which public school students were released from school to attend religion classes.

Senior Recognition Month — Following the proclamation of May as Senior Recognition Month by President Ford, the health affairs representative of the U.S. Catholic Conference called for greater public awareness of the contributions made by the elderly of the nation, as well as for greater concern for their well-being. "During this month especially,"

Sister Virginia Schwager said in a statement, "we must recommit ourselves to ensuring that all older Americans enjoy a dignity and quality of life sufficient to make their lives rewarding and meaningful."

Disagreement Regarding the Ordination of Women — Speakers for several organizations of Catholic women expressed disagreement with Pope Paul's recent statement that women could not be admitted to the ordained ministries. Among the groups represented in statements were St. Joan's International Alliance, the National Coalition of American Nuns and the National Assembly of Women Religious. The head of the Canon Law Society of America, Father John T. Finnegan, also took exception to the Pope's statement.

Parental Consent Not Necessary for Abortion — A ruling by a three-judge panel in the U.S. District Court in Boston declared unconstitutional a Massachusetts statute requiring unmarried minors to have parental consent for an abortion. Two of the three judges stated: "We can attach no factual magic to that (18th) birthday. It is enough for present purposes that we find a substantial number of females under the age of 18 are capable of forming valid consent."

Support for Refugees — A statement by the president of the National Conference of Catholic Bishops urging Americans to accept Southeast Asian refugees was sent to President Ford by the conference's general secretary, Bishop James S. Rausch. In a letter which accompanied the May 8 statement by Archbishop Joseph L. Bernardin of Cincinnati, Bishop Rausch wrote: "I assure you, Mr. President, that the Catholic hierarchy of the United States will continue to support prompt and generous assistance (to the refugees); we recognize in the present situation an opportunity to serve, and we are prepared to do so."

Press Convention — Some 400 Catholic, Protestant and Orthodox journalists focused attention on higher professional standards and on ways of dealing with controversial theological issues at the May 13 to 16 joint convention of the Catholic Press Association and the Associated Church Press in New York City. Father Jeremy Harrington, O.F.M., editor of the *St. Anthony Messenger*, was elected president of the CPA. Father John B. Sheerin, C.S.P., former editor of the *Catholic World* and a leader in ecumenism, was awarded the St. Francis de Sales Award by the CPA.

Catholic Population — *The Official Catholic Directory, 1975*, published by P. J. Kenedy and Sons, reported that the Catholic population of the United States increased by 236,397 from 1973 to 1974, to a total of 48,701,835. There were declines in the numbers of brothers, sisters, seminaries and seminarians, educational institutions, elementary and secondary school students, hospitals and special institutions, and marriages. Increases were reported in the numbers of bishops, students at Catholic colleges and universities, children cared for in institutions and foster homes, patients treated in hospitals, and converts. (See statistical tables.)

Liturgy of the Hours — The first of four volumes of the revised breviary or Liturgy of the Hours was published in English late in the month. Father John Rotelle, O.S.A., director of the Bishops' Committee on the Liturgy, called the publication a major event marking the "most encompassing" revision of this official prayer of the Church in recent history.

Homosexual Rights Bills — An effort to expand Minnesota laws on human rights to include protection for homosexuals failed May 8 in the State House of Representatives, 68 to 50. The bill would have prohibited discrimination in housing, employment, education, credit and the sale of real estate on the basis of "affectional preference." In New York, several religious spokesmen and child care administrators registered opposition to a proposed City Council bill that would prohibit discriminatory employment practices against homosexuals. The bill, guaranteeing "homosexual rights," was before the council for the sixth time in four years.

National Health Insurance — Two interreligious groups issued a statement May 21 in Washington listing five "make or break" issues for national health insurance: cost controls, financing, benefits and the development of a concept of "positive health," administration and consumer participation, and distribution of health personnel and resources. The groups were the Washington Interreligious Staff Council and the Interreligious Task Force on Health Care.

Extension Society Funds — The 70-year-old Catholic Church Extension Society reported that it raised $3 million during the fiscal year which ended in February, 1975, for the support of home mission activities.

Prayer in Public Schools — Bills authorizing the reinstatement of meditation or prayer periods in public schools were passed by the legislatures of Connecticut and New Hampshire. The governors of both states indicated they would the sign the bills.

Controversial Pastor Transferred — The Arlington chancery office announced that Father John P. Hannan had been transferred from Good Shepherd Parish, Arlington, to St. Leo's, Fairfax, Va. Father Hannan had been involved for several months in a dispute with the parish council of Good Shepherd.

Domestic Briefs:

• Father J. Alcide Clement, a nun and a housekeeper of St. John the Baptist Church, Edgard, La., were found murdered in the rectory May 7, the apparent victims of robbery.

• Msgr. Pierre DuMaine, superintendent of schools in the San Francisco archdiocese, was elected to a two-year term as president of the

Catholic Television Network, a consortium of 10 U.S. broadcast stations.

• Two nuns — Dominican Sister Lucy Vazquez and Ursuline Sister Judith Anne Barnhiser — became the first women to receive the doctor of canon law degree at the Catholic University of America, the only institution in the U.S. authorized to grant the degree.

• May 25 was designated a National Day of Prayer for a Good Harvest by the National Catholic Rural Life Conference and the National Conference of Catholic Bishops.

Aid Law Unconstitutional

By a 6 to 3 vote, the U.S. Supreme Court ruled May 19 that most provisions of a Pennsylvania auxiliary services law were unconstitutional. In Meek v. Pittenger the court upheld a provision of the law allowing the lending of textbooks to nonpublic school students, but rejected major provisions of the law which approved almost $12 million in auxiliary services for students in nonpublic schools.

The court ruled that, because 75 per cent of the nonpublic schools receiving services were church-related, the law had "the unconstitutional primary effect of establishing religion." It also held that "excessive entanglement would be required for Pennyslvania to be assured that the public school professional staff members who provide the services do not advance the religious mission of the church-related schools in which they serve." The majority opinion was written by Justice Potter Stewart.

(See Meek v. Pittenger.)

FOREIGN

Aid for Refugees — Catholics on Guam were reported to be taking part in a massive, around-the-clock effort to care for the spiritual and physical needs of nearly 40,000 Vietnamese refugees flown to the island since the last week of April. It was estimated that 40 per cent of the refugees were Catholic.

Baby Lift Questions — Fourteen representatives of religious groups accredited to the UN Economic and Social Council joined in raising questions about the "Baby Lift" from Southeast Asia after the fall of South Vietnam. Concerned about possible violations of the Geneva Convention of August, 1949, they said that practices followed in the evacuation tended to separate children from their "extended" families, to make it difficult for them to continue their religious and cultural traditions, and to complicate the return of the children to their families and native country.

Portuguese Election — Religious convictions were a major factor in the election Apr. 25 of moderates to a national assembly authorized to write a new constitution for Portugal, according to Bishop Antonio Ferreira Gomes of Oporto. About 92 per cent of the electorate voted, giving two-thirds of the ballots to Socialists and Democrats, and 18 per cent to Communists.

Inter-American Bishops' Meeting — Bishops from Canada, Latin America and the United States concluded a five-day meeting May 7 in Mar del Plata, Argentina, with a declaration that the defense of human rights is crucial to the mission of the Church. Delegates "strengthened the idea of the intrinsic relationship of ministry and justice," according to a statement on evangelization, reconciliation and human rights.

Irish against Secularized Education — Most Irish people were opposed to any secularization of education, Cardinal William Conway of Armagh, president of the Irish Bishops' Conference, declared in an interview published in Dublin. He said: "To eliminate the religious dimension from education in the schools or to water it down and strip it of its familiar devotional expression, would be to strike a mortal blow at the distinctive character of the Irish people and the real source of their strength."

Divorce Bill Defeated — Despite strong lobbying by lay and Protestant groups, the Brazilian legislature rejected a bill May 9 that would have legalized divorce. Cardinal Eugenio de Araujo Sales of Rio de Janeiro commented: "This is not so much a victory for Catholics but for the common sense of legislators responding to the Christian values of our people." It was also reported that three other divorce bills were pending in the legislature.

Conception Control Program — The bishops of Ontario sharply criticized the provincial government's new $2 million conception control program for including abortion counselling and referral. "We can only deplore any government support of practices inimical to the preservation of human life," they said in a letter addressed to Frank Miller, provincial minister of health.

It was also reported that Canadian pro-life groups had succeeded in obtaining one million signatures to an anti-abortion petition to be submitted to the Canadian Parliament.

Catholic Schools in France — The French Union of Parents of Children in Private Schools, meeting May 17 to 19 in Strasbourg, accused the government of trying to "asphyxiate private schools slowly" by delaying the payment of 66 per cent of funds authorized for scholarships and teachers' salaries. Father Charles Molette said that "delaying the payment of scholarship funds to students in Catholic schools is threatening the existence of freedom of education in France." Delegates to the meeting said in a statement: "Government withholding of funds will condemn Catholic schools to become havens for children of the rich, whereas they should be open to all."

Healing Apostolate — Catholic laymen and women in Canada were urged to participate actively in the healing apostolate in order to strengthen Catholic hospitals threatened with extinction. "The time has come for the laity to come forth and take an active part in bringing Christ to the bedside," said Dr. E. G. Van Tilburg, former president of the Catholic Hospital Association of Canada. "We should all realize that our institutions cannot survive unless committed laymen and women are willing to labor in our hospitals, actively practice the philososphy of that institution, set an example in devotion to duty, restore the work ethic, be willing to take responsible jobs, support management and be prepared to make sacrifices."

No Excuse for Violence — Alarmed at the terrorism of extremists and at reports of the torture of political prisoners by police, the Spanish bishops told the Franco government there was no excuse for such violation of human rights. A statement by the steering committee of the episcopal conferences also condemned terrorist killings. "Defense of the highest goals or of public order can never, in Christian teaching, justify recourse to violence that violates the human person's basic rights" the bishops said. "Killings, attacks against persons and their property . . . deserve firm condemnation."

Patronage Right Renounced — The Portuguese government formally renounced the right, under its 89-year-old concordat with the Vatican, to present candidates for ecclesiastical posts in Goa, Daman, Diu, Dadra and Nagar Haveli. The renunciation was communicated to the government of India May 19 in accordance with provisions of the treaty of December, 1974, which restored diplomatic ties between India and Portugal.

Contraceptive Mentality — The Irish bishops criticized "the contraceptive mentality" as an "invasion of Christian attitudes toward life and marriage by typical materialist values," and linked that mentality to the practice of abortion. In the final portion of a four-part pastoral letter entitled "Human Life Is Sacred," the bishops said that the "contraceptive mentality" is characterized by a lack of generosity and of willingness to assume responsibility. They asserted it is fundamentally opposed to the Christian concept of responsible parenthood.

Archbishop at Presbyterian Assembly — The presence and address of Archbishop Thomas Winning of Glasgow at the General Assembly of the Church of Scotland May 21 in Edinburgh was regarded as a step forward in ecumenical relations in Scotland. The archbishop said: "We in the Roman Catholic Church realize that we are a stumbling block to other churches because of our convictions regarding the nature of the church and her authority. Nonetheless, we are fully committed to working with you and the other Christian churches toward unity, for we are confident that the Holy Spirit will guide all of us to an ultimate solution."

Violence in Rhodesia — A commission of the bishops of Rhodesia, in a report issued in London by the Catholic Institute for International Relations, charged Rhodesia's white-supremacist security forces with deliberate assaults on local Africans. The report alleged that security forces operating against sporadic guerrilla attacks in northeast Rhodesia showed gross disregard for the lives and property of innocent people. It called such conduct deliberate on the grounds that it followed a persistent pattern.

Foreign Briefs:
• Murals of the Holy Family, the Annunciation and other traditional subjects were discovered in Delhi, India, on the walls of a church in a group of buildings built in the 16th century.
• About 2,500 Catholics attended early morning Mass in the cathedral in Hanoi, the North Vietnamese capital, on May 4, their first day of peace in a generation, reported Dan de Luca of the Associated Press.
• An official of Catholic Relief Services disclosed that all French missionaries had left Cambodia.
• Some 300,000 persons assembled at Fatima, Portugal, May 13 for the 58th anniversary of the first apparition of the Blessed Virgin there.
• The Norwegian Nobel Committee formally accepted the nomination of Mother Teresa of Calcutta for the 1975 Nobel Peace Prize.
• Father Patrick Dodson, the first priest from one of Australia's aboriginal tribes, was ordained during the month by Bishop John P. O'Laughlin of Darwin.

Northern Ireland Elections

The results of Northern Ireland's constitutional elections of May 1 were widely regarded as worse than expected for everyone concerned except Protestant diehards, according to NC correspondent John A. Greaves.

Of the 78 men and women elected to draft the outlines for a future local government acceptable to the United Kingdom Parliament in London, 46 were United Unionists publicly pledged in advance to support the hard-line policies of a return to Protestant domination with no power-sharing for Catholics. The opposition included 17 pro-Catholic Labor Party delegates and eight moderate Alliance Party members, with five middle-of-the-road Unionists in the center. With an overall majority of 16, the United Unionists showed no sign of easing their demands for an exclusive Protestant majority rule at cabinet level in any new administration.

In the context of Northern Irish politics, the terms "Catholic" and "Protestant" were more markedly sociological than religious.

JUNE 1975

VATICAN

African Church — In an address to hundreds of African pilgrims June 1 in St. Peter's Basilica, Pope Paul said: "To keep intact a Gospel outlook and a faith which does not come from us but from God, continue to nourish yourselves on the entire living tradition of the Church which has blossomed for two millennia in the midst of the most diverse cultures." He also called on Africans to build up the Church "according to your own genius and in full fidelity to the Gospel."

Pope Paul and President Ford — Pope Paul told President Ford June 3 that his visit to the Vatican emphasized the importance he "attributes to the moral aspects of the problems" he had been discussing with government leaders on his trip to Europe. President Ford was quoted as saying that his visit to Pope Paul gave him inspiration, and that the two had "a most beneficial discussion of many problems in which we can work together for the progress of peace."

Christian Peace — Real Christian interior peace is "vigilant and active — a peace that produces," Pope Paul told a general audience June 4. He said: "Peace, which is an interior and personal obligation in Christianity, is not doing nothing, is not immobility, and possesses no such selfishness as that which idealizes a comfortable and quiet life. Yes, peace is order, but order as applied to active human life. If we want peace to be true and lasting, it must remain vigilant and active — a peace that produces continually, with joyful love and hard work. It has to be not only enjoyed, but also continually searched for."

Bishops To Implement Vatican II — Heralding what he called a "new period in church life," Pope Paul said June 6 that bishops must tirelessly implement the enactments of the Second Vatican Council and also keep a sharp eye on cultural changes in society. At a Mass concelebrated with members of the Italian Bishops' Conference in St. Peter's Basilica, he said: "The times demand from us two things as responsible and aware shepherds: a faithful application of the great treasure of doctrine and precepts of the recent council which Providence has caused to be celebrated in our generation. . . . Today we workers in the Lord's vineyard are called to a duty-bound task: the council must become the continuing stimulus and the working law of our present Church life." The Pope added that the times also demand of bishops "an attentive and vigilant perception of change in the world in which we are called to work — especially change in its cultural aspects."

Pilgrims Praised — The Holy Father extolled Holy Year pilgrims June 8 for their piety and realization that the person of Christ makes God's love for man comprehensible.

He praised the spiritual exercises of the pilgrims "for their personal character, their interior quality, their simplicity and moderation, and their divine sincerity which is proven by their authentic moral sense and frank devotion."

Pope Asks for Pardon — In what was called an extraordinary act of reconciliation, Pope Paul asked pardon of dissenting Catholics for remarks of his which may have offended them. "Have we perhaps offended them?" he asked of disgruntled Catholics in a talk at a June 11 general audience. "We would like to assure them that this was certainly not our intention. In any case, we, as leader, ask their pardon." The Pope made the gesture toward reconciliation after mentioning his apostolic exhortation of Dec. 8, 1974, on reconciliation within the Church itself.

Peace in World of Work — Peace and justice will come to the world of work only through Christian charity and not through violence or ideologies that feed on materialism and hate, declared Pope Paul at a special audience June 21 for workers from southern Italy. He said: "We who have the good fortune not to restrict the horizon of life to simply the economic and temporal sphere . . . know how to draw inspiration leading to peace and justice in the world, and especially in the world of work. That inspiration does not come from the instinct toward violence or from ideologies absorbed in materialism and hate, but from the sense of urgency of Christian charity which we feel and live, and which Christ has taught us by word and example."

African Statesmen Encouraged — The Pope expressed sympathy and encouragement for statesmen working for an independent Africa "with equality among races, with respect for the will of peoples and with assurances that citizens will be able to participate in civil, social and political life." Noting the June 25 announcement of the independence of Mozambique, he also expressed hope for speedy completion of "the irreversible process of decolonization."

Faith Needs Works — "The great sin of modern Christianity . . . is the sin of being illogical, inconsistent and unfaithful. It is faith without works." So declared the Pope during a general audience June 25. Faith, he said, must lead to fidelity. "Faith demands a profession, a logic of thought and life . . . a move from the mind to the will, a witness, effort, risk, resistance, sacrifice and a martyrdom, as so many generations of Christians have taught us." The fidelity of faith means that "an extraordinary vitality must be given to the seed of faith." Negatively, the Pope warned against the "devastating inconsistency" of dead faith.

Meeting with Gromyko — The Pope and Soviet Foreign Minister Andrei Gromyko discussed the position of the Church in the Soviet Union, disarmament and peace in a one-hour meeting June 28. Their talk came at a time when stepped-up persecution of religious groups was reported in the Soviet Union, especially in Lithuania and Armenia. The meeting was the fifth between the Pope and Gromyko since 1965.

Ordination of 359 Priests — In a ceremony Pope Paul himself described as "never before equaled," he ordained 359 priests to the priesthood in St. Peter's Square June 29. In his homily during the four-hour ceremony, the Pope stressed the priestly function of service to people in need.

The largest national group among the diocesan priests ordained were 25 Americans.

The Pope Also:

• Celebrated Mass in commemoration of the 12th anniversary of the death of Pope John XXIII, June 3.

• Told members of the European Economic Community's Court of Justice of his hopes for the progress of European collaboration, June 5.

• Named Alfred Ki Zerbo, a 102-year-old catechist in Upper Volta, a Knight of the Equestrian Order of Pope St. Sylvester.

• Met with Humayun Rasheed Choudhury, the first ambassador from Bangladesh to the Vatican, June 9; Todo Zhivkov, president of the Bulgarian Peoples Republic, June 27.

• Received 600 former French inmates of concentration camps celebrating the 30th anniversary of their liberation, June 12.

• Declared that the British decision to remain in the European Common Market offered a wider scope "for mutual friendship and shared concern for the needs of the less fortunate," on receiving Dugald Malcolm, the new British minister to the Vatican, June 19.

• Named Archbishop Mario Tagliaferri apostolic nuncio to Cuba.

Canon Law Study — A decree of the Congregation for Catholic Education, dated Apr. 2 but made public only this month, ordered a renewal of emphasis on the study of canon law in seminaries. The document said that a "lessening of interest" in canon law in recent years had a "certain disorienting effect upon the Church." It said that the Code of Canon Law had not been abrogated during the revision underway since the Second Vatican Council, and that "it is impossible to interpret pronouncements subsequent to the Second Vatican Council without a certain skill in canonical language and procedure."

Satan's Existence — The devil exists but should not be made a scapegoat for the guilt of individuals or become an obsession, according to a study prepared for the Congregation for the Doctrine of the Faith and published June 25 in *L'Osservatore Romano.* The study said: "The Catholic community, basing itself on the teachings of Jesus, of the Apostles, of the Fathers of the Church, of councils and sacred liturgy, has always believed in the mysterious reality of Satan and demons. . . . At the same time, the Church "through the centuries has always reproved various forms of superstition, obsessive preoccupation with Satan and demons, various types of veneration or morbid attachment to these spirits."

Vatican Briefs:

• Acts of violence and sacrilege against Rome's churches and the Blessed Sacrament were deplored in the name of Pope Paul by Cardinal Ugo Poletti, vicar general for Rome. In a communique in the June 7 edition of *L'Osservatore Romano,* he said: "Blasphemous graffiti on the walls of churches continually prove a rude spectacle for foreign visitors. Last May 13 the Church of St. Agnes in the Piazza Navona was the scene of hooliganism. On the evening of June 1 a molotov cocktail burst inside the Church of the Holy Twelve Apostles. During the night of June 1 and 2, three vessels with consecrated hosts were stolen from the Church of St. Hippolitus."

• Press spokesman Federico Alessandrini, writing in *L'Osservatore della Domenica,* hailed the reopening June 5 of the Suez Canal as the first bit of good news from the Middle East in months.

• An article in the June 15 edition of *L'Osservatore Romano* criticized and expressed "sorrowful surprise" over reports that several traditionalist Catholic groups were planning to celebrate the Tridentine Mass during a Holy Year pilgrimage to Rome. (The form of Mass traceable to the Council of Trent in the 16th century was supplanted by the new order of the Mass approved by Pope Paul in 1969).

New Era in the Church

In an address to the College of Cardinals on June 23, the eve of his feast day, Pope Paul declared: "A new era is unfolding of fidelity to the Holy Spirit, of love of the crucified Christ, of dedication to the brethren, of the building up of a more human and just society." He also spoke highly of Holy Year pilgrims as people willing to make sacrifices of time, money and energy to respond to the spiritual message and purposes of Holy Year 1975.

The Holy Father said, however, that reports continued to confirm that "some of our sons and daughters . . . persist in positions of doctrinal uncertainty, . . . destructive criticism, hostile diffidence or connivance with ideologies that are opposed to the Gospel and the Church." He invited them to reconciliation, stating: "Our arms are open, and our heart even more so."

The Pope also denounced certain "assaults" by society against the moral law: "artificial birth control, abortion, euthanasia, as well as all those forms of manipulation of man, whether open or disguised, which now indicate and will indicate in the future a serious debit for the contemporary world."

DOMESTIC

Sacred Heart Devotion — "It would be particularly fitting that the Solemnity of the Sacred Heart on Sunday, June 8, be the occasion for a call and response to the totality of this devotion," declared Cardinal Timothy Manning in a pastoral letter to the people of the Los Angeles archdiocese. "We call our people to a revival of this beautiful devotion and to couple with it our duty of reparation and consecration."

Catholic Hospitals — Reevaluation of the mission of the Catholic hospital to the local church, labor relations, and federal and state encroachment on hospital policies and operations were among major concerns of the fourth annual Catholic Health Assembly which met in San Francisco under the auspices of the Catholic Hospital Association. Sister Mary Maurita Sengelaub, president of the association, told some 1,200 delegates that one great concern was "the encroachment on individual and institutional freedom by way of federal legislation and the multiple regulations" regarded in some quarters as threats of "government control" and "some eventual take-over."

Project Equality Rates Montgomery Ward — Project Equality, a national interreligious organization promoting equal employment opportunities, gave Montgomery Ward, the fourth largest retailer in the nation, an "unwilling" performance rating. A report said the company had refused to allow Project Equality personnel to conduct validation reviews of its implementation of equal employment opportunities at selected facilities.

Strip-Mining Vote Disappointing — Three Catholic agencies expressed "deep disappointment" at the three-vote failure of Congress to override President Ford's veto of a strip-mining bill, and urged Congress to "renew its efforts on this urgent matter." A statement from the Social Development Office, U.S. Catholic Conference, said the office joined the National Catholic Rural Life Conference and the Catholic Committee on Appalachia in expressing "deep disappointment" over the failure. "This bill," the statement said, "would have provided sorely needed regulations to protect our valuable land and water resources, as well as to preserve the social and economic well-being of communities in areas surrounding the mines."

Protest against Supreme Court Decision — More than 60,000 persons, most of them parents of children in non-public schools, jammed Philadelphia's Independence Mall June 11 in what police officials called the largest protest demonstration in the city's history. In an orderly "Give Us Our Rights" demonstration, the parents voiced their objection to the May decision of the court which denied the constitutionality of auxiliary services to children in Pennsylvania's non-public schools. In a keynote address, Msgr. Francis B. Schulte, archdiocesan superintendent of schools, said: "Today, let the word go forth from this city . . .: to limit the freedom of some persons is to limit the freedom of all." Another speaker, Dr. Edwin Palmer, a Christian Reformed minister, declared: "The Supreme Court is neutral against religion. . . . It penalizes children because of their parents' choice of a religious education for them."

In Albany, the independent Catholic School Administrators' Association called for a "massive taxpayers' revolt" to emphasize the importance of non-public schools. A statement issued by the executive board said: "Rebellion by taxpayers throughout the land is the only argument that can convince a court blinded by its own prejudice."

Right-to-Life Convention — The National Right-to-Life Committee, meeting June 20 to 22 in Denver, was told by its vice president, Carolyn S. Gerster, M.D., that the committee is a "one-issue organization, and that issue is human life." She said: "Human life must take precedence over all personal loyalties and over all political affiliations."

Chicago School Closings — Controversy continued in Chicago over the decision of Cardinal John Cody, announced May 9, to close four schools in the predominantly black and Spanish-speaking Englewood section of the city. The archdiocesan school board, along with priests and people of the concerned parishes, objected not only to the closings but also to the manner in which the cardinal made his decision. A statement from the archdiocesan information office said: "Jurisdiction as to the closing of schools remains the discretionary right of the bishop of the diocese, using appropriate consultation."

In 1974 the archdiocese allocated subsidies of $3,261,675 to 43 needy inner-city parishes and schools. (In July, the archdiocese announced an allocation of $2,721,300 for needy parishes and schools in the 1975-76 fiscal year.)

Bishops Meet with President Ford — A White House meeting June 18 of President Ford and five bishops was called "cordial and positive" by the bishops, and "good and constructive" by an administration official. Subjects of discussion during the hour-long meeting were the world food crisis, Vietnamese refugees, illegal aliens, abortion, and aid for students of non-public schools.

Priest Cleared in Killing — Father Ralph Esposito, who said murder by rectory robbers was on his mind when he fatally shot a prowler in Mother of Sorrows rectory near Pittsburgh, was cleared of blame for the death.

Plane Crash Victims — The parents and an uncle and aunt of the Rev. Mr. Millard G.

Boyer, who was to have been ordained to the priesthood by Pope Paul at the Vatican June 29, were among those killed in the crash June 24 of an Eastern airliner during its approach to J. F. Kennedy Airport, New York.

Parish Reconciled — Byzantine-Rite Bishop Michael J. Dudick of Passaic formally accepted jurisdiction June 26 over St. Andrew's Parish, Allentown, Pa. The parish, founded in 1941 in the course of a controversy, had been chartered in civil law as independent of any higher ecclesiastical authority. Its pastor, Father Andrew Musko, was reconciled with the Church in 1965.

Domestic Briefs:

• Appointments: Attorney Gerald E. Bodell, New York regional director of the Catholic League for Religious and Civil Rights; Father David L. Mahon of Paterson, N.J., vice rector of the American College of the University of Louvain, Belgium; Sister M. Joyce Rowland, president of the College of St. Teresa of Winona, Minn., to a two-year term on the Presidential Advisory Council on Women's Educational Programs; Father Thomas A. Peyton, M.M., director of the Ministry for Justice and Peace of the National Federation of Priests' Councils.

• Approximately 250 persons attended the annual legislative seminar of Network, an organization of nuns and other persons lobbying on social justice issues.

• Father Agnellus Andrew, O.F.M., director of the Catholic Radio and Television Centre at Hatch End, England, was named "an outstanding Catholic communicator" by the Communications Committee, U.S. Catholic Conference.

• "Nothing . . . is more vital for the kingdom of God to be and to become than implanting, bringing forth and making flourish the spirit of the Lord Jesus in all his fullness in our active and future priests," declared Archbishop Jean Jadot, apostolic delegate to the U.S., in an address in Denver.

• Msgr. (Rear Admiral) John J. O'Connor was installed as chief of Navy chaplains June 27.

Study of Catholic Press

The National Catholic Conference for Interracial Justice reported June 26 that a study of the Catholic press and its concern for social justice suggested that the Catholic press "collectively pays inadequate attention to the issues of social justice, generally reporting events but giving no special educational emphasis to the subject." The study was based on an examination of 53 newspapers (38 per cent of the total publishing) during the period from Nov. 15, 1972, to May 15, 1973, and their use of stories distributed by NC News Service and Religious News Service.

In comment on the report, James J. Doyle, executive secretary of the Catholic Press Association, said the study was out of date and

that its conclusions were unjustified and misleading. Of criticism, he said: "The Catholic press is ready to accept constructive criticism of its work, and even to cooperate in professional, complete studies designed to improve its efforts to serve the Church and its people. Unfortunately, this study is seriously flawed, and it certainly creates an unjustified and misleading impression."

FOREIGN

Norway Eases Abortion Restrictions — By the slimmest possible margin, the legislature of Norway passed a bill allowing abortion for social and emotional reasons during the first 12 weeks of pregnancy. Lutheran Bishop Per Loenning, who resigned his diocese because of this action, charged that the government had ignored the state church's strong objections to abortion.

Uganda Shrine Dedicated — Cardinal Sergio Pignedoli, president of the Vatican Secretariat for Non-Christians, presided at ceremonies consecrating the national shrine of the Uganda Martyrs at Namugongo. The shrine was dedicated to the honor of more than 100 Catholic and Anglican Christians who perished between 1885 and 1887 in a persecution ordered by King Mwanga I.

Seminary Denied Approval — Bishop Pierre Mamie of Lausanne, Geneva and Fribourg, Switzerland, withdrew the Church's canonical approval from the seminary of the Priestly Fraternity of St. Pius X in Econe. The seminary was charged with "conscious and explicit rejection of the decisions of Vatican Council II and of the authority of Pope Paul VI." The action was taken by the bishop in agreement with the Vatican Congregations for the Clergy, for Religious and for Catholic Education.

Birthright Convention — More than 300 delegates from centers across the continent attended the Birthright convention in Toronto. One speaker — Father Paul Marx, O.S.B., a professor of sociology at St. John's University, Collegeville, Minn. — declared: "Abortion is only the tip of the genocidal iceberg which inevitably will lead to infanticide and mass euthanasia." Birthright's purpose was to help women distressed by pregnancy to bring their babies to term.

Resignation of Father Lombardi — Father Ricardo Lombardi, S.J., according to a delayed report, resigned as international director of the Movement for a Better World which he founded in 1952 with the approval of Pope Pius XII. Elected May 5 as his successor was Father Juan Cuberto, who had been associated with the movement since 1961.

Leftists vs. Catholics in Portugal — Hundreds of leftists attacked 500 Catholics demonstrating at archdiocesan headquarters in Lisbon against the occupation by Marxist workers of Radio Renascanza, a station owned by the Portuguese bishops. The bishops called the occupation a "most serious event" which deprived the Church of its radio voice and gave Marxists facilities for broadcasting anti-Church programs. They also cited the failure of the ruling junta of the Armed Forces Movement to take steps toward restoration of the station. They blamed the junta for "a climate of personal insecurity, intimidation and anxiety about the future," a climate which "paralyzes the exercise of authority."

Attitudes in Vietnam — Father Herbert Dargan, S.J., after his sixth official visit Apr. 24 to May 26 to Jesuits in Vietnam, said in an interview that "Roman Catholics, especially in Asia, should be prepared to see what positive contribution they can make without presuming that, given a Communist take-over, they would inevitably become non-persons or a Church of silence." He also said: "The Catholic rightists in the South are very quiet and tend to view the Church as the Church of silence and martyrs following the take-over" by the North Vietnamese. "But the South Vietnamese bishops don't. They are determined to cooperate now in the reconstruction and development of the country."

A Reuters correspondent reported that Archbishop Henri Lemaitre, apostolic delegate to Vietnam and Cambodia, was flown out of Saigon June 5 to Vientiane, Laos.

Irish Priests' Council — The Irish bishops approved plans for the establishment of a national conference to represent all the clergy of the Irish Republic and Northern Ireland. Stated purposes of the organization included the discussion of priestly life and ministry, and forms of liaison between priests and bishops.

No Endorsement — Several Brazilian bishops issued warnings that the right-wing Society for the Defense of Tradition, Family and Property was not endorsed by the Church. One of the prelates was Archbishop Aloisio Lorscheider of Fortaleza, chairman of the Brazilian Bishops' Conference. He said that, even though the organization had espoused some "Catholic causes," it could not be endorsed because of its methods and because "it defended tenets contrary to official teachings of the Church."

Soldiers Excommunicated — Bishop Arnoldo Aparicio of San Vicente, El Salvador, announced that several government officials and soldiers were excommunicated for their part in the arrest and mistreatment of Father Rafael Barahona, pastor of Tecoluca. The rural town was the scene of bloody action by the National Guard against tenant farmers protesting excessive rent charges.

Lutheran Clergy's Marriage Crisis — A deep marriage crisis was gripping Sweden's Lutheran clergy, according to Dr. Hans Cavallin, associate professor of theology at Uppsala University. Writing in a church bulletin, he said: "The difference between the percentage of divorces among marriages in Sweden on the whole and that of pastors' marriages is very likely insignificant."

Seminaries Closed — The government of Equatorial Guinea ordered the closing of three Catholic seminaries in the country,

Foreign Briefs:

• The bishops of Zaire announced a decision to provide separate maintenance for the faculty of Catholic theology of Kinshasa, which was suppressed by the government as part of the National University of Zaire.

• Slovakian Bishop Joseph Korec, who was secretly ordained after being imprisoned for opposition to the Communist government and was deprived of his state license to practice the priestly ministry, was reportedly employed as a store clerk in a Bratislava chemical plant.

• Major relics of Blessed Oliver Plunkett, the martyred 17th-century archbishop of Armagh and primate of Ireland, were given by the Benedictine monks of Downside Abbey, England, to the Armagh cathedral, according to the postulator of Blessed Oliver's canonization cause.

• Italy's Star of Solidarity Medal, for work on behalf of Italian immigrants, was presented to Father Nicholas J. Russo, head of the Brooklyn diocesan Italian Apostolate.

• Father Jose Cruz, who accompanied Philippine President Ferdinand E. Marcos on a five-day state visit to Peking, was the first foreign priest to celebrate Mass in the Chinese capital since foreign missionaries were ousted some 25 years earlier.

• Acting Prime Minister Goh Keng Swee praised the Church in Singapore for the moral instruction it imparted in Catholic schools, at a dinner commemorating the 123rd anniversary of the arrival of Christian Brothers in Singapore.

Priests Not Subversive

Priests preaching social justice throughout Latin America were not promoting violent revolution, according to a survey sponsored by the Latin American Bishops' Council.

The three-year survey of 7,000 priests in Argentina, Guatemala, Honduras, Nicaragua, Panama and Paraguay rebutted widespread accusations from governments and the extreme right that priests, including and especially foreign missionaries, were often engaged in "subversive activities." Ten per cent of the priests said they viewed their mission as "limited to preaching only." Seventy-nine per cent said their mission was "preaching and fostering the lay apostolate." None of them said they favored preaching violence or participation in violence.

Atilio Sabate, author of *The Priestly Crisis in Latin America,* commented: "The politicking many attribute to priests is non-existent, and the assertion that they are inclined toward violence is groundless."

JULY 1975

VATICAN

Apathy regarding Spread of the Faith — Pope Paul, in an address to a general audience July 2, was critical of forces in secular society and in the Church which discouraged Christians from spreading the faith among non-Christians. He said: "So-called confessional activity is opposed today at its very roots, no matter how it manifests itself ... The apostolate does not have citizenship within a secular society." He added: "No form of proselytism ... is any longer acceptable by many, including believers. Many who call themselves Catholics think that belonging to our religion does not carry with it responsibilities beyond attending Sunday Mass and making the Easter duty." The Pope declared that "free, religiously inspired activity meets obstacles today, even within the framework of the Church," especially because of the "practice of internal, anti-dogmatic and anti-institutional criticism that is fashionable in many circles."

Beatification of Father Karl Steeb — The Holy Father presided July 6 over ceremonies for the beatification of Father Karl Steeb (1773-1856), a convert at the age of 18 and founder of the Sisters of Mercy of Verona.

New Congregation in Curia — With the publication July 11 of an apostolic constitution dated six days earlier, Pope Paul merged the Congregation for the Discipline of the Sacraments and the Congregation for Divine Worship into a new Congregation for the Sacraments and Divine Worship (see separate entry). The new congregation was scheduled to begin functioning Aug. 1.

False Liberty — The Pope, in an impassioned appeal to Catholics to rekindle love for the Church, called July 16 for a halt to "the disobedience called liberty." He said: "Enough of these disintegrating interpretations of pluralism! Enough of these self-inflicted ruptures of Catholics from their indispensable cohesiveness! Enough of the disobedience called liberty! There is need today more than ever to build, not demolish, the one and Catholic Church. Love resuscitated and reinvigorated within the holy Church of God must be our first post-Jubilee action (following Holy Year 1975). ... Our first love must be that which Christ had for the Church itself, giving his life for her."

Hope for Progress in Brazil — The Pope's hope for religious and social progress in Brazil was broadcast by Vatican Radio July 20 to the concluding session of the country's ninth national Eucharistic congress in Manaus. The message spoke of the Bread of Life to be shared in a Brazil "in which the Good News of the Gospel has not yet become well known despite its (the country's) deep and rooted religiousness." Church renewal and social justice were the topics discussed at meetings during the July 16 to 20 congress. The bishops chose Manaus as the site of the congress to stress the concern of the Church for the Indian tribes in the Amazon territory. Their purpose was to urge the government to formulate and carry out development programs in the region without affecting the native population adversely.

U.S. and Soviet Astronauts Hailed — Pope Paul hailed the "embrace in the sky" of the Apollo-Soyuz astronauts July 17 as a symbol of friendly cooperation and a portent of scientific triumphs to come. He told a gathering of pilgrims at Castel Gandolfo July 20: "We are almost spellbound by this unprecedented celestial meeting and we shout our cheers to the heroic men who accomplished such a fantastic feat."

Gospel Approach — To combat groaning social ills, Christians must give fresh expression to the Gospel instead of adopting anti-religious solutions, stated Pope Paul during a general audience July 23. Asking his hearers to rekindle in themselves a "sense of the Church," he said: "There is no need to borrow from anti-religious social formulas based on conflict in order to find the wisdom and energy to bring about the good which needs to be done, as well as just reforms for human development and the continuing affirmation of justice and peace. But there is a need and a duty to express in original Christian terms the human and social view" of the Second Vatican Council's teaching on the religious and evangelical mission of the Church.

People Don't Pray — Pope Paul lamented before a general audience July 30 that "many people don't pray any more." He said: "Once it was not this way. Even people engaged in secular life had the time for a thought, an act of awareness, a moment of interior prayer, at least for an instant, every day and for a period of time on feastdays. But today modern man's lips seem sealed by a prevailing unawareness of the spiritual or the religious order, and by a deceptive idea that all reality is of the order of the senses, of temporal and material experience. ... When God is in this way excluded as the transcendent principle of the universe, along with his free and wise intervention in the world of our experience, how could man address a word to the unknown God or attempt a dialogue with him or invoke his loving providence?"

The Pope Also:
• Visited the Vatican Library to mark the fifth centenary of its founding by Pope Sixtus IV. Of the library's value in the contemporary world, he said: "What pleases us ... is the dynamism which today characterizes this enterprise. The Vatican Library remains open to students coming from everywhere, above con-

siderations of the Catholic faith, and admitting men of every religious orientation."

• Met with a delegation of churchmen and laymen from the Orthodox Patriarchate of Moscow, July 3. He told them: "It is our ardent prayer that these joint meetings (a reference to discussions by Catholic and Russian Orthodox theologians) may bear lasting fruit. We pray that the divisions of centuries will be overcome in the truth and charity of Christ, and that the Holy Spirit will bring to completion a work that has been under his inspiration — a work that is indeed manifest among the signs of our times."

• Appealed for renewed aid to drought-stricken areas of Africa during a special audience of 160 Ugandans, July 11. He said: "Today we wish to draw attention to a natural disaster, one that has been talked about in recent years but which no longer seems to attract the interest that it previously had. We mean the disaster of drought, and particularly the drought that has struck (the Sahelian region of) Africa."

• Told vacationers they should use their leisure time to examine their lives, July 13. He declared: "Such moments of relaxation are necessary and wise. They may serve to provide psychological, spiritual inner-probing. A science precious above all is that of knowing oneself, of reflecting, almost dreamlike, on one's own conscience, of freely building one's own personality."

• Was officially invited by Cardinal John J. Krol to attend the 41st International Eucharistic Congress in Philadelphia in August, 1976.

• Flew by helicopter from the Vatican to the papal summer residence at Castel Gandolfo July 17, for a two-month stay there.

Vatican Briefs:
• A Vatican Radio editorial broadcast July 4 declared: "Among the most significant expressions of . . . flourishing (renewal in the Church), it is sufficient to note the charismatic movement in America which, even if it can be made better, testifies to nothing else than a rejection of materialism and a renewal of spirituality, especially among the young."

• A Vatican communique of July 7 reported that Catholic and Russian Orthodox theologians, meeting in Trent, Italy, had "reaffirmed the traditional teaching of their churches concerning the conferring of the sacrament of the priesthood only on men."

• Nearly 4,000 Ukrainian-Rite Catholics from the free world attended a Mass concelebrated July 12 in St. Peter's Basilica for their brothers and sisters in Communist-ruled countries. The principal celebrant of the Mass was Cardinal Josyf Slipyi, the exiled major archbishop of Lvov.

Ostpolitik Tensions

The writer of an article in the July 24 edition of *L'Osservatore della Domenica* declared

that the Vatican fully understood the implications and pitfalls of its Ostpolitik policy of detente-negotiating with Communist governments in East Europe for improvements in Church-state relations.

Observers had divided opinions about the policy. Those for it held that it could not result in conditions any worse than those existing since Communist regimes came to power after World War II. Those against it contended that it amounted to abandonment of the faithful to conditions of greater or less repression and control in various countries.

Either way, tensions remained deadlocked because the normalization of relations meant one thing to Communist regimes (control and repression) and something quite different to the Church (freedom for the full practice of the faith).

DOMESTIC

Bilingual Seminary — The Immaculate Heart of Mary Collegiate Seminary in Santa Fe announced that in the fall it would become the first bilingual-tricultural (Anglo, Indo-Hispanic) seminary in the United States.

In a separate development, the Mexican American Cultural Center in San Antonio announced plans to start in September a specialized nine-month theology program to prepare seminarians for ministry in Spanish-speaking communities.

Civil Rights Commission Scored — An analysis sponsored by the Committee for Pro-Life Activities, National Conference of Catholic Bishops, blasted the U.S. Commission on Civil Rights for issuing an Apr. 14 report opposing legislation and proposed constitutional amendments that would restrict abortion. The analysis, prepared by Eugene Krasicky, general counsel of the U.S. Catholic Conference, described as "patently absurd" the commission's insinuation that using the constitutional process for amending the Constitution could undermine the Constitution.

Lutheran Convention — Rigidly conservative officers and delegates tightened their control of the Lutheran Church-Missouri Synod at the synod's biennial convention July 4 to 11 in Anaheim, Calif. They did so by outvoting liberals and moderates (representative of Evangelical Lutherans in Mission) in elections, and by resolving in the end to urge them to give in on disputed points of doctrine and discipline or to leave the synod.

Priests' Organizations — The recently formed Confraternity of Catholic Clergy, with more than 250 members in 18 cities, surfaced early in the month as an expression of "dissatisfaction at the widespread, free-swinging errors that many of the clergy propagate." Father John H. Ryder, S.J., of New York said the basic principle of the group was "total loyalty to the Holy See."

Seventy-five Priests for Equality subscribed to a new organizational charter calling for equality of women with men in law, education, economic and political life, married life, religious education, worship and decision-making processes in the Church. The chief organizer and national secretary of the group was Father William R. Callahan, S.J., of Mt. Rainier, Md.

Marriages Decline, Divorces Increase — The Bureau of the Census estimated that there were 2,233,000 marriages in the U.S. for the year ending August, 1974, a decline of 68,000 from the total of the previous year. In the same period, divorces increased by an estimated 56,000 to 948,000. Msgr. James T. McHugh, secretary of the Committee for Pro-Life Activities, National Conference of Catholic Bishops, noted that the divorce rate nearly doubled, from 2.3 to 4.4 per 1,000 married couples, between 1963 and 1973.

$2.2 Million CRS Program — Fifty-eight food and agricultural projects in 21 developing countries were parts of a $2.2 million aid program of Catholic Relief Services made possible by personal donations during the period between Dec. 15, 1974, and June 10, 1975. Bishop Edward E. Swanstrom, executive director, said the "unprecedented surge of contributions" was "concrete evidence of the concern of the American people" for the hungry and needy in Third World countries.

Captive Nations — Msgr. John Balkunas, president of the Romanian Catholic Priests' League of America, urged the bishops of the U.S. July 13 to "be concerned about those (in Communist countries) who cannot help themselves in the struggle for religious freedom and human rights. . . . Let not later generations accuse us of standing by silently while our brothers and sisters were slowly stifled to death," he said in a sermon at St. Patrick's Cathedral, New York City, during the 17th annual observance of Captive Nations Week.

Decision on Fetus — A Camden, N.J., jury found Winfield Anderson guilty of first degree murder in the death of two male fetuses after he shot and wounded their mother. The verdict was rendered after Judge Leon Wingate ruled that the fetuses were murder victims under the New Jersey homicide law.

In Boston, the Massachusetts Supreme Judicial Court ruled 4 to 3 that an unborn but viable fetus is a "person" under the state's wrongful death statute. The decision reversed an earlier ruling by the court that a fetus could not be so considered.

Day of Prayer — In accordance with a June 23 proclamation of President Ford, July 24 was observed as a National Day of Prayer for unity and the blessings of freedom throughout the land, and for peace. The first such proclamation, followed by some 180 others, was issued by the Second Continental Congress in 1775.

Kentucky Conscience Clause — The Catholic League for Religious and Civil Rights reported that it was providing legal counsel to a group of Kentucky physicians who were seeking the reversal of a court ruling against the constitutionality of the State's conscience clause with respect to abortion and sterilization. The clause declared that physicians, nurses and other hospital personnel were protected against legal penalties, claims, disciplinary action or discrimination if they refused to perform an abortion or sterilization on moral, religious or professional grounds.

Secular Humanism Charge — A lawsuit charging that public schools in St. Louis County, Mo., were teaching a form of religion — secular humanism — was cleared for eventual trial. The suit was filed by a group of taxpayers who complained that a form of "secularism," which they called a religion, was being taught in public schools in violation of the First and Fourteenth Amendments to the U.S. Constitution. The plaintiffs based their argument on the U.S. Supreme Court decision in Abington v. Schempp. The court declared that the state "may not establish a 'religion of secularism' in the sense of affirmatively opposing or showing hostility to religion, thus 'preferring those who believe in no religion over those who do believe.' "

Religious Freedom in Cuba? — The Castro regime allows Christians the right to worship within the walls of a church, but not real religious freedom. So declared Dr. Jose I. Lasaga, one-time president of the National Council of Catholic Organizations in Cuba, in testimony before a joint meeting of House subcommittees on international trade and international relations. He said: "If the Soviet definition of religious freedom, which allows people the right to worship within the walls of a church, is followed, then it may be said that there is religious freedom in Cuba. However, if we take freedom as implying that members of a religious body are able to enjoy all the basic human rights, as embodied in the Bill of Rights of the United States, we will be forced to acknowledge that there is no religious freedom in Cuba."

Bishop Mahony Heads Farm Labor Board — Gov. Edmund Brown, Jr., of California announced July 26 the appointment of Auxiliary Bishop Roger M. Mahony of Fresno to a two-year term as chairman of the Farm Labor Board designated to administer the state's recently enacted Agriculture Labor Relations Act. The bishop, as a member of the U.S. Bishops' Ad Hoc Committee on Farm Labor, had been involved in relations between the United Farm Workers of America and the Teamsters. The farm labor law, with an effective date of Aug. 29, provided for state-supervised, secret-ballot elections by farm workers for their choice of union representation.

Domestic Briefs:
• Archbishop Ignatius Strecker, president of the National Catholic Rural Life Confer-

ence, criticized the Interior Committee of the House of Representatives for killing a proposed land-use-planning bill. He said the committee's action was a "blow" and a "setback" to citizens concerned about building "a morally just national land policy" and "about the fulfillment of our moral responsibility to preserve our nation's natural resources, especially our land."

• Our Sunday Visitor, Inc., announced it had established an OSV Institute to formulate and conduct religious, educational and charitable activities.

• Dr. Verne E. Chaney, Jr., reported that the Thomas A. Dooley Foundation, named for the Catholic doctor who operated medical clinics in Southeast Asia, was moving its headquarters from San Francisco to Geneva, Switzerland. Dr. Chaney, who established the foundation in 1961, also said that the organization would be renamed in order to give it "a rightful international designation."

• Auxiliary Bishop Patrick F. Flores of San Antonio took over the sponsorship of a fund drive for the solicitation of donations from U.S. American Catholics for the construction of a new Basilica of Our Lady of Guadalupe in Mexico. The old basilica, constructed in 1709, was architecturally unsound. The new one was already under construction; completion was expected in the fall of 1976.

• The Knights of Columbus reported that members of 68 per cent of its chapters spent more than five million man-hours in community service and donated almost $11 million to charitable causes in 1974.

Soulfull Worship

"The gift of blackness is for everybody in the Church, not only blacks," declared Father Clarence Rivers at a catechetical and pastoral institute in New Orleans.

Against the background of Pope Paul's admonition, "Enrich the Church with the gift of negritude," he added: "So I'm saying to the Church in general, not only to blacks, consider the possibility that God has given us the black church in the United States as a sacrament of soul, to bring the warmth of the spirit into our presently very spiritless worship."

On another subject, Father Rivers called talk of a black separatist movement in the Church "ridiculous." "When I ask for an independent black authority, I'm not saying: 'Since you have maintained us separately, now make us really separate.' What I am saying is that, if there is to be an introduction of black culture into the Church, it is black people themselves or a black authority in the Church which must determine how this gift is to be integrated into the Church."

FOREIGN

Missionaries Will Stay — The Conference of Major Superiors of both men and women religious in Portugal voted to continue their missionary work in Guinea-Bissau and Mozambique, former Portuguese territories, and Angola (scheduled to become independent Nov. 11). A statement said: "If a presence of more than five centuries is the basis of an obligation on the part of Portugal and its people to work with the native population in achieving decolonization . . . the awareness of our missionary vocation is an even stronger motive for our missionaries to remain with these people."

Missionaries Expelled — Sixteen Verona Fathers were expelled from Uganda July 2 for undisclosed reasons. The Bolivian government deported three Spanish women missionaries July 22 on charges of illegal political activity. Father Juan Ramon Vega, a regional official of the Pontifical Commission for Justice and Peace, was prohibited July 16 from returning to his headquarters in El Salvador.

Divorce Encourages Desertion — The French Bishops' Commission on Family Life, in a statement on new relaxed divorce laws, said they would encourage desertion. The commission declared: "Divorce obtained by mutual consent will develop by the force of its logic, which is based on a weak conception of marriage, into a theory of marriage as a simple contract that is always revocable."

Oppression in Lithuania — Terror, persecution and long detention in concentration camps or mental hospitals awaited those who tried to exercise their constitutional rights in Lithuania, according to participants in a Rome meeting of the World Lithuanian Catholic Conference. They said in a declaration dated July 1: "We appeal to men of good will throughout the world and ask them to support those who are persecuted for defending their faith and human rights against the misuse of state power, against a system which punishes not those who violate the constitution but those who try to defend human rights and freedom according to the constitution."

No Persecution in Vietnam — Coadjutor Archbishop Joseph Marie Trinh Van Can of Hanoi affirmed that there was no religious persecution in North Vietnam. "There have been no attacks against religion on the radio or in the newspapers," he said. "The government is pursuing a politics of tolerance. I believe in the sincerity of the government." Nearly three months after the take-over of South Vietnam by forces from the North, Archbishop Philippe Nguyen Kim Dien of Hue wrote in a letter to his people: "We are sure that we can transform our country into a prosperous and happy one under the leadership of the Provisional Revolutionary Administration . . . The noble mission of Catholics is to cooperate with all people of good will to build a new world of fraternity and prosperity so as to make ready a new heaven and earth when Christ comes . . ."

White Fathers Returning to Mozambique — The White Fathers of Africa announced that

10 of their members would return to Mozambique by the end of the year, for the first time since their general council withdrew 40 missionaries from that territory in May, 1971. The 40 had been withdrawn because the missionaries did not want to be regarded as "accessories in the official support the bishops . . . seem to give to a (Portuguese) regime which shrewdly uses the Church for the consolidation of an anachronistic (colonial) situation in Africa." The White Fathers were encouraged to return by the replacement of the Portuguese regime June 25 by the Mozambique Liberation Front and by the return to the territory of Bishop Manuel Vieira of Nampula, who had been expelled in April, 1974.

Opus Dei Priests Ordained — Fifty-four professional men from 19 countries, all members of Opus Dei, were ordained to the priesthood by Cardinal Mario Casariego July 13 in Barcelona, Spain. The ordination was one of the largest in the history of Opus Dei.

Ordinations Down in Italy — The number of priestly ordinations in Italy dropped by 35 per cent between 1967 and 1973, according to statistics quoted in *Rogate Ergo,* a missionary life magazine. Five hundred and 66 priests were ordained in 1973. It was also reported that the number of seminarians declined between 1967 and 1973, by 45 per cent in minor seminaries and by 66 per cent in theological institutions.

Priests Killed in Honduras — A day of reparation and mourning was observed July 20 in churches throughout Honduras for 14 persons killed by soldiers and landholders in June during a demonstration for the implementation of a land reform law. Two of those killed were Father Michael J. Cypher, O.F.M. Conv., an American, and Father Ivan Betancourt of Colombia.

Mission of France — Three hundred and 25 priests were reported to be members of the Mission of France working in dioceses throughout the country to reach de-Christianized segments of the population. Head of the mission, formed in 1941, was Cardinal Francois Marty of Paris; his auxiliary, ordained in May, 1975, was Bishop Jean Remond. Most members of the mission, including Bishop Remond, were worker-priests with secular jobs.

Discrimination against Doctors — In a letter to British Prime Minister Harold Wilson, made public July 22, Cardinal John Heenan of Westminster protested governmental discrimination against doctors who opposed abortion. He said that gynecologists, anesthetists and psychiatrists conscientiously opposed to abortion were being given notice "that they have no future in the National Health Service."

Cuban Embargo Ended — The United States joined 14 of the 21 members of the Organization of American States in voting July 29 to end economic and diplomatic sanctions invoked against Cuba in 1964 because of its actions fomenting revolutionary movements in several Latin American countries. Bishop Jose M. Dominguez, head of the Cuban Bishops' Conference, in comment on the vote, said that "justice has been done" and that "the right of the Cubans to conduct trade and other forms of exchange has been justly recognized." The bishops had asked for the lifting of sanctions in 1969 and got support from the U.S. Catholic Conference in 1972. Cubans in the U.S. had mixed reactions to the OAS decision.

Foreign Briefs:

• The General Synod of the Church of England voted July 3 to retain the church's legal ban on the ordination of women.

• The Catholic Union of India, at its annual meeting in Calcutta, appointed a commission to undertake a national effort to get government assistance for Untouchables converted to Christianity.

• It was reported July 18 that the bishops of Angola had called for prayers for peace in their territory. Fighting in mid-June between the leftist Popular Movement for the Liberation of Angola and the anti-Communist National Front for the Liberation of Angola left hundreds of dead in Luanda.

• Since the beginning of Holy Year 1975, more than 1,500 visitors to the Vatican who fell ill were treated by medical teams provided by the Knights of Malta in a dispensary near St. Peter's Square.

• For the 24th year in a row, a White Train of pilgrims, many of them sick and disabled, left Rome July 30 for the Marian Shrine in Lourdes, France.

Women's Year Conference

Delegates from 135 nations attended the two-week World Conference of the International Women's Year which ended July 2 in Mexico City.

A "Plan of Action," adopted by a voice vote of the majority, was stronger in support of efforts for the establishment of a basically just international economic order than for appeals for equality of opportunities for women in all spheres of society. The shape and thrust of the plan was more in line with the aspirations of developing countries than those of the more developed nations.

In a resolution proposed by Mother Teresa of Calcutta, a member of the Vatican delegation, the plenary assembly approved a call to all women to join in solidarity with the poor of the world, and urged women enjoying at least some of the world's benefits and privileges to become co-workers with the poor.

The Vatican delegation, while in favor of much that was stated in the "Plan of Action," did not vote for it, principally because its introduction was out of line with doctrine concerning marriage and the family.

AUGUST 1975

VATICAN

Helsinki Conference — In a letter made public Aug. 1, in which he appointed Archbishop Agostino Casaroli as Vatican City's representative to the Helsinki Conference on Security and Cooperation in Europe, Pope Paul said that representatives of the 35 participating nations wanted "to establish an understanding which rests on the clear and firm principles of international law. They want to shelter Europe from the menace of new experiences of destruction and death."

Service of Scholars — Pope Paul took the occasion of the centenary of the death of Father Jacques Paul Migne to "encourage wholeheartedly those who ... work to prepare critical editions of ancient texts. ... They render a signal service to the Church," he said. Father Migne supervised the publication of a monumental "Universal Library for the Clergy" in 2,000 volumes to provide source material to replace libraries and collections destroyed in the French Revolution. His greatest publications were studies of the Latin Fathers (in 221 volumes) and the Greek Fathers (in 161 volumes) of the Church.

Prayer — "To live, it is necessary to pray," declared Pope Paul Aug. 3. Mankind, he said, "needs God. It needs to pray to him, to find in him that security, that fullness, which can come only from his concomitant goodness."

Liturgical Uplift — While stressing the importance of active participation in the liturgy, Pope Paul said Aug. 6 that the emotional uplift Catholics feel in the liturgy was not a form of escapism from the world. Rather, he stated: "It is an infusion of wisdom and energy that makes the faithful zealous, generous and active citizens in the field of earthly reality while it shows them the way and leads them to heavenly citizenship."

Renewal Means Return — The Pope, addressing a general audience Aug. 13, gave a strong "no" to two rhetorical questions: "Does ... renewal justify the bitter contestations against every traditional way of practicing our faith that have become the fashion even in ecclesiastical circles? ... Can renewal breach every dam that protects us against all kinds of arbitrary innovation?" Referring also to the social dimensions of Christian living, the Holy Father said: "Without the idea of moral obligation, without the joyous self-denial of the Cross of Christ, true justice is impossible — that same justice which today is so much called for and which is still so far from being realized in our social structure. The renewal called for in the Holy Year means a return to that unique origin which is Christ himself."

Assumption of Mary — "Mary is the anticipated first fruits of our future resurrection, the hope and guarantee of our true and real destiny," declared the Pope Aug. 15 during a Mass marking the 25th anniversary of the proclamation of Mary's Assumption as a dogma of faith.

Two days later, in an address to 7,000 pilgrims at Castel Gandolfo, the Pontiff said: "A provident and consoling feeling flows for all of us out of a better understanding of the unique, unrivaled, undeniable and most happy position assigned to Our Lady in the spiritual economy of salvation. It goes without saying that from this our modern feminism can emerge justified, strengthened and enriched." He also stated that women would find "in Christian concepts the acknowledgment of their civil and human rights and the defense of their highest natural privileges, under the directing and protecting light" of Mary.

Renewal Plan — Pope Paul outlined a three-point renewal program before some 60,000 pilgrims Aug. 20. "First, let us not be deaf or indifferent to the words of the Divine Master. Let us listen to, study and ask for what the Holy Spirit can teach us about the total truth of Christ. ... Second, let us with zealous and docile heart treasure the teaching of Christ and of those whom 'the Spirit has established as bishops to shepherd the Church of God.' Third, let us watch out for certain new theories now current and sometimes not immune from spiritual and doctrinal dangers."

Christian Inheritance vs. Pessimism — Offering an "antidote against the poison of pessimism," the Pope urged a throng of people Aug. 24 to think about the "healthy, rich, fruitful inheritance of our Christian and civil tradition. ... One need only love this inheritance to live it and to feel its regenerating power. It is an inheritance of truth, honesty, freedom, order, love of society, a spirit of service, of courage, of civil solidarity, of sacrifice for the good of one's own country. ... (Faith) can restore trust and multiply our energies in order to give a new, joyful and strong look to our generation."

Youths' Greatest Possession — "Friendship with Jesus is the greatest possession of youth; never give it up," urged Pope Paul Aug. 25 before a group of more than 3,000 young Holy Year pilgrims from Europe and Africa. He added: "But we would not be honest unless we told you that Jesus is demanding, and that his love calls for self-discipline, self-giving, self-sacrifice."

Holy Year Meaning — Pope Paul told a general audience of more than 80,000 persons Aug. 27 that "the Holy Year means a meeting with Jesus Christ, a special meeting. It signifies that everyone who celebrates it must radically reflect on his own faith, on his own opinion of Jesus Christ, on defining him, on his reality. ... He is building through us a living rock which can never collapse, neither in time nor with death. This rock is his Church, holy and immortal, to which we have the good fortune to belong and from which we receive Christ himself, the bread of eternal life."

Gypsies — During a special audience Aug. 28 at Castel Gandolfo, the Pope told more than 2,000 European Gypsies: "We hold for you deep feelings of respect, affection and of human sympathy, above all, for the singular state of your nomadic pilgrim life. But our sympathy is, above all, Christian; for in you is mirrored an aspect of the life of Jesus, Our Lord, Master and Brother." (The reference was to Christ's public career as an itinerant preacher.)

Selfishness — Human selfishness defeats the efforts of individuals and organizations for justice and peace. So stated the Pope Aug. 31 in an address before 8,000 persons. He said: "We have the impression that lofty and praiseworthy purposes lack a unifying, inspiring and efficacious idealism. Each one thinks of himself. Each strives to gain personal advantage quickly. There is lacking a truly fraternal democracy and a respect for the needs and rights of others. . . . There is a lack of the love that pardons and redeems, a lack of the charity taught by Christ which remains both obligatory and possible for us."

The Pope Also:
• Noted the 30th anniversary of the atomic bombing of Hiroshima Aug. 6, stating: "We send all the Japanese people our sorrowful greeting, respectful and filled with hope. May God bless Japan."
• Emphasized the importance of Christian-Moslem collaboration in the regulation of the Holy Places in Palestine, at a meeting with an Egyptian government delegation, Aug. 19.
• Expressed his sorrow at the death Aug. 29 of Eamon de Valera, 92, one of the principal architects of Eire, the Irish Republic.

Vatican Briefs:
• An informed Vatican source stated Aug. 4 that "for the last four or five years, Vatican Radio (unlike Radio Liberty and Radio Free Europe) has experienced little trouble in broadcasting to Eastern Europe and the Soviet Union." He attributed this to the fact that Vatican Radio "is not interested in political systems but in the possibility for those living in certain political systems to hear the radio's message, which is always pastoral."
• The repeated calls of Paul VI for nuclear disarmament as the only hope for avoiding a holocaust were recalled by Vatican Radio in a broadcast marking the 30th anniversary of the bombing of Hiroshima Aug. 6, 1945.
• A paper entitled "The Church and Human Rights" issued by the Pontifical Commission on Justice and Peace defended the basic teachings of the Church on the subject while admitting past faults in performance. "This paper," said Cardinal Maurice Roy, president of the commission, "is not,

nor does it wish to be, a directive or an official guide. . . . Rather, it is a starting point, raising questions, stimulating research, suggesting activities and offering doctrinal and theological reflections." It was noted in the paper that the mission of the Church is not to offer concrete solutions in the social, economic and political spheres for justice in the world, but to defend and promote the dignity and the fundamental rights of the human person.

Catholic Universities

Pope Paul, speaking Aug. 6 to 70 heads of Jesuit universities, said that "doctrinal relativism and moral permissiveness" could be found in some Catholic universities, and called for renewed emphasis on the Catholic character of church-sponsored colleges.

The Pope defended the mandate of the Second Vatican Council that universities should dialogue with all cultures, all faiths, and with people without any supernatural faith.

He declared, however: "But all this must be done while maintaining intact the character of the Catholic university . . . by achieving always in teaching, in publications and in all forms of academic life complete orthodoxy of doctrine, respect for the teaching authority of the Church, fidelity to the hierarchy and to the Apostolic See, without indulging in a doctrinal relativism or a moral permissiveness incompatible with the characteristics of a university that wants to call itself Catholic."

DOMESTIC

Charismatic Renewal — Father Bernard Sandheinrich of St. Louis, speaking at a gathering of charismatic prayer groups, said they wanted better understanding of the movement — which had been "grossly overplayed, overstated and misunderstood" — and closer cooperation from the clergy."

The *National Catholic Reporter* carried in its Aug. 15 edition an account of irregularities — including so-called "exorcisms" and forms of coercion — in the True House Community of South Bend, Ind., which was disbanded in 1974. The abuses, which were made known by Dr. William Storey of Notre Dame University, were not typical of practices proceeding from the principles of authentic charismatic renewal.

(In September, eight former members of the community said: "We believe that the reporting about True House has presented a distorted image of the community and misrepresented it. We also believe that the importance of True House and what happened in it have been exaggerated and unjustly and uncharitably made into a public scandal.")

Mrs. Ford Criticized — Many Catholics — from bishops to people in the pews — strongly criticized remarks, along with the judgment behind them, made by Mrs. Betty Ford during a television interview on Aug. 10. The remarks included what many regarded as endorsement of marijuana use and pre-marital sex, and unqualified approval of the Supreme Court decision of 1973 which legalized abortion on demand.

Reasons for Optimism — Reasons for optimism about the future of the Church in this country were cited by historian Msgr. John Tracy Ellis in an address to a convention of state Catholic conference leaders at South Lake Tahoe, Calif. He pointed to "the openness and honesty of the American Church in admitting and addressing its problems" as an indication that the crisis of faith was being dealt with. He also claimed that the "potential of the charismatic movement," the "alertness of the American Church to the needs of the less fortunate in the world," and the "overwhelming support for Catholic schools as evidenced by recent public polls" were grounds for optimism.

No Tie with CIA — Speaking for Catholic Relief Services, James O'Neill rejected charges of massive entanglement between CRS and the Central Intelligence Agency alleged by John D. Marks, a former State Department employe. O'Neill said: "We have to maintain contact with the U.S. embassy and the host government in any country where we have people working. But this does not put us in the CIA's pocket."

Liberation Theology — The theology of liberation — emerging from the Latin American experience of oppression and have-not socio-economics — was the central theme of an Aug. 17 to 23 meeting in Detroit attended by some 200 theologians, social scientists and other interested parties. Under discussion, which was highly rhetorical and critical of the U.S. government, American business and the Church, was a kind of theology marked by: orientation to Marxist and/or Socialist ideology; theories for changing oppressive structures and institutions of society; and difficulties about how to resolve the equation and relations between personal salvation and social reform. The main lines of liberation theology were drawn by Gustavo Gutierrez in a book published in 1971.

Conventions:

• The Catholic Central Union of America and the National Catholic Women's Union, meeting in Subiaco, Ark., called for an end to U.S. funding of birth control programs abroad as a first step toward establishing a Christian foreign policy. Officers elected during the meeting were Timothy A. Mitchell of New York, president of the Central Union, and Mary Rose Geiger of Boston, president of the Women's Union.

• "Renaissance, Reconciliation, Renewal" was the theme of the Aug. 20 to 24 sixth national convention of Black Catholics in Los Angeles. Walter Hubbard, president of the National Office for Black Catholics, said in an address that advances in black awareness

was dictating an examination of black relationships with the Church with respect to vocations to the priesthood and religious life, the role of permanent deacons, education and parish life.

• Five hundred and 43 representatives and delegates — from 42 states, Canada, Mexico, Italy and the Philippines — attended the 10th biennial convention of the National Federation of Christian Life Communities in Amherst, Mass. John R. Brown of Orchard Lake, Mich., was elected president.

Conciliation in Chicago — Conciliation was the objective of two actions by Cardinal John Cody during the month. He said in a statement Aug. 4 that he "was sorry for recent actions or tone" which might have been offensive to the archdiocesan school board — because of his intention, announced in June, to close several schools — and that he hoped to meet with the board members to discuss mutual concerns. Later in the month he invited the executive committee of the priests' senate to meet with him to iron out differences between them over the function of the senate. The committee accepted the invitation.

Released-Time Program Constitutional — The 4th U.S. Circuit Court of Appeals in Richmond ruled that a Harrisonburg, Va., released-time religious education program was constitutional. In so doing, it reversed the decision of Judge James C. Turk who had ruled earlier against the constitutionality of the program because, he said, it involved participation of public schools in advancing religion.

Girl Scouts — The Girl Scouts of the U.S.A. and the youth activities agency of the U.S. Catholic Conference announced Aug. 29 development of a national plan of cooperation. One of its purposes was to set up procedures for dealing with grievances like the one which caused a rift between the Girl Scouts and the Philadelphia archdiocese in February, 1975.

Prison Chaplains — Members of the American Catholic Correctional Chaplains' Association, noting that public concerns for prison reform had ebbed since the Attica Prison revolt in 1971, stressed the need for new community-based efforts for penal reform.

Spanish-Speaking Population — A report issued by the Census Bureau late in the month estimated that there were 11.2 million people (about five per cent of the total population) of Spanish origin in the country. About 60 per cent were from Mexico, 15 per cent from Puerto Rico and seven per cent from Cuba.

Mass on Campus Constitutional — The Delaware Supreme Court ruled that two Newman Center chaplains may celebrate Mass on the campus of the University of Delaware despite university claims that such services were in violation of the No Establishment Clause of the First Amendment to the U.S. Constitution.

Domestic Briefs:

• The Sisters' Senate of the Brooklyn diocese contributed the largest amount, almost $3,000, of any group to the defense fund of Joan Little, who was cleared of charges that she had murdered a white jailer in North Carolina.

• The Marian Icon of Kazan was featured in an Aug. 9 to 17 pilgrimage of Blue Army members to places significant in early American history.

• Several speakers at the 36th annual Tekakwitha Conference in Rapid City, S.D., called for the appointment of a bishop to supervise pastoral service to American Indians.

• The Cincinnati archdiocese pledged $3 million to help pay the retirement costs of 19 communities of sisters who had worked in schools and institutions of the archdiocese.

Conventions of Religious

Approximately 800 sisters representative of 3,500 members in 103 dioceses attended the Aug. 7 to 10 annual meeting of the National Assembly of Women Religious in San Francisco. Along with commitment to social justice, the assembly stressed the campaign for equal rights for women in the Church — in decision-making bodies, in theological education and research, in ordination to the ministry (as deacons, priests and bishops). Sister of St. Joseph Kathleen Keating was elected to chair the assembly for two years.

Some 600 administrators of 365 congregations of sisters pledged to "stand in solidarity with the women of the world." The action came on the final day of the national assembly of the Leadership Conference of Women Religious, held in St. Paul Aug. 24 to 28. The conference committed itself to a study of the UN World Plan of Action for Women "with a view to appropriate implementation . . . within the context and perspective of a Gospel vision." Participants also called for support for the International Eucharistic Congress to be held August 1 to 8, 1976, in Philadelphia, and established a "critical needs contingency fund" for world hunger and natural disasters. They echoed other calls for "opening all ministries in the Church to both men and women." Sister Barbara Thomas, superior general of the Sisters of Charity of Nazareth, Ky., was installed as president of the conference.

FOREIGN

Strife in Lebanon — Strife disruptive of political, social and economic life in their country was the major concern of a six-day meeting in late July of the Assembly of Catholic Patriarchs and Bishops of Lebanon, according to a delayed report from Beirut. Involved in the complex pattern of strife were Christian-Moslem issues, the presence of Palestinian guerrillas in Lebanon, factional disputes between a "subversive left" and an "intransigent right," the weakness of government authority and the paralysis of security forces. The assembly appealed for a comprehensive government plan to guarantee social justice to all classes and groups in the country, and pledged its efforts to bring this about.

Yugoslavian Priest Imprisoned — Reports reaching Rome said that the Supreme Court of Croatia had reversed an earlier verdict of innocent and had sentenced Father Zivko Kustic, editor of the Catholic daily *Glas Koncila* to five months in prison. He was accused of "agitating the state" in 1973 for writing two articles, one deploring the lack of priests in Yugoslavia and the other describing the life of a third-century Christian martyr, Polion. In the second article he said that Christians are bound to observe just laws but "should not conform" to unjust laws.

Violence in El Salvador — Archbishop Luis Chavez Gonzalez of San Salvador called Aug. 2 for a halt to mounting violence by government forces and protesters that left 12 dead and 40 wounded during riots on July 31. The riot broke out during a demonstration by 2,000 students demanding the release of other students arrested earlier for protesting against government financing of the Miss Universe pageant in July "while most Salvadoreans suffered privation."

Price on Bishop's Head — American-born Bishop Nicolas D'Antonio of Olancho, Honduras, where two of his priests (Fathers Ivan Betancourt and Michael J. Cypher) and several campesinos were killed in June, told an interviewer that landholders who considered him subversive had put a price of $5,000 on his head and called him a "mad Communist." The bishop was a supporter of farmers pressing for implementation of a land-reform law passed earlier in the year.

Palestinians Aided — To help "hard-core Palestinian social relief cases and permit them to become self-supporting and self-respecting wage earners," were the objectives of a loan fund program sponsored jointly by Catholic Relief Services and the Israeli Ministry of Social Welfare. Michael K. Sheehan, CRS program director in Jerusalem, said that the project had made 126 loans totaling nearly $60,000 since 1972. He called the project "a very successful field of activity."

East African Seminarians — The missionary news service *Fides* reported that East Africa, which waited three and one-half centuries for its first native priests, had 1,260 students in 11 seminaries in Kenya, Malawi, Tanzania, Uganda and Zambia.

Guadalupe Shrine — Fifty-one priests of the Cuernavaca diocese in Mexico objected to the cost (an estimated $12 million), style (modern) and manner of financing (with participation by banks and other institutions) of a new shrine of Our Lady of Guadalupe. They said in a letter that the descendants of

Juan Diego would not feel at home in the elaborate new structure near the original site of the apparitions in 1531, and that the cost did not befit the "economic crisis in the nation and the world, nor the extreme poverty of millions of Mexicans." The existing shrine, in danger of collapse, was completed in 1709.

Passion Play — The councilors of Oberammergau, Germany, announced that they had decided to replace the 1860 text of the town's world-renowned but controversial passion play with an earlier script written by Father Ferdinand Rosner, O.S.B. Reason for the change was the desire to eliminate alleged anti-Semitism in the play. The next scheduled production was for 1980, in accord with the custom of staging it every 10 years. The first presentation was staged in 1634, in thanksgiving for the preservation of Oberammergau from plague.

Defiant Traditionalist Seminary — Klaus Wodsack, a deacon studying at the seminary of the Priestly Fraternity of St. Pius X in Econe, Switzerland, told 300 traditionalists in Munich that the seminary would resume classes in the fall, despite an annulment of its charter announced May 6, 1975. Archbishop Marcel Lefebvre, founder of the fraternity, was accused by Cardinal Julius Doepfner of "causing dissension among the faithful." More of the same could be expected from the operation of similar houses of the fraternity in Italy, France and England.

Church in South Vietnam — Exiled Bishop Paul Seitz of Kontum said in a Paris radio interview Aug. 18: "The Christian life continues in Vietnam. As I was expelled, a native Vietnamese bishop took charge of administering the diocese." He added that he and other French missionaries had limited freedom under the Communist government in power since April He noted, however, that "the (Catholic) schools have not yet been reopened, and they should be."

Political Prisoners in Chile — The ecumenical Committee on Cooperation for Peace in Chile reported that, since the overthrow of the Allende government in September, 1973, it had processed about 6,500 cases involving political prisoners in Santiago and 9,000 or more in the rest of the country. More than 35,000 persons were aided since the committee began work in October, 1973.

Moral Decline in Rwanda — In a pastoral letter marking the 75th anniversary of the advent of Christianity in Rwanda, the five bishops of the country said: "Everyone can observe in his own community . . . disquieting signs of a 'quiet de-Christianization' which is always spreading. All — priests, religious and laity — must seek to find why Christian life has become less fervent than in the past." The letter, published in *L'Osservatore Romano* Aug. 27 noted: "Many baptized persons are being seduced by false doctrine . . . The reception of Communion has become irregular, if

not omitted entirely. Matrimony without benefit of the sacrament is becoming more common. The baptism of children is becoming, for some, more of a social practice than a religious duty. Moral disorder . . . is often tolerated without being fought against by the Christian community."

Witchcraft Congress — Cardinal Anibal Munoz Duque was one of several religious leaders who warned Colombians that a world witchcraft gathering in Bogota posed a threat to their faith and to their pocketbooks as well. He called for stronger efforts to "teach the people the basic truths of faith and God's plan of salvation" in order to counteract widespread superstition.

Foreign Briefs:

• Scores of thousands of pilgrims from all parts of Poland and other countries thronged to the shrine of the Black Virgin of Jasna Gora in Czestochowa to celebrate the feast of the Assumption of Mary, Aug. 15.

• Bishop Jaime Brufau of San Pedro Sula appealed for food aid to fight hunger as a four-month drought spread havoc in Honduras.

• A survey of religious practice by a random sample of 2,499 Catholics disclosed that 91 per cent of adults in the Republic of Ireland attended Mass at least once a week; 24 per cent attended more than once a week.

• Chaos ruled throughout the month in Portugal where Communists persisted in attempts to control the government despite their weakness at the polls in the most recent national elections.

Helsinki Agreement

Thirty-three European nations, the United States and Canada were signatories Aug. 1 to an agreement in which they pledged themselves to respect borders as they were at the end of World War II, to renounce the use of force as a general principle, to promote the free circulation of information and persons, and to acknowledge the principle of religious freedom.

Opinion was skeptical about the significance of the document. According to one view, the agreement recognized what was tantamount to the Soviet Union's hegemony over Eastern Europe in return for Soviet "intentions" with respect to free exchanges of persons and ideas. An editorial writer in *L'Osservatore Romano* observed, however: "Even declarations of intentions are a fact; and, in this case, a fact of major importance is that they have been imposed by a desire for security and cooperation from which even the Soviet Union was not able to withdraw."

Participation by the Vatican in the Helsinki Conference on Security and Cooperation in Europe was the first of its kind since the Congress of Vienna in 1815. The Vatican City representative was Archbishop Agostino Casaroli.

SEPTEMBER 1975

VATICAN

God Is Our Father — In a Sept. 3 address to an audience of 60,000 in St. Peter's Square, Pope Paul said: "God is Father. This announcement is repeated today to an age such as ours which has dared to proclaim the very stupid denial of God's existence." God-is-dead thinkers, he added, drew their conclusions "not from the reality of things and of life, but from negative and subjective irreligiosity." Jesus, however, "infuses in us the indisputable certainty about God — the certainty that he is, that he is the absolute and the necessary one, that he is the Creator . . . the one who keeps creatures in existence . . . and that he is Father."

Totalitarian Repression and Public Morality — At a general audience Sept. 10, the Pope deplored the "scientific and systematic repression of the most elementary and legitimate freedoms by totalitarian regimes. He also decried a "sharp decline of public morality," noting that "the law, lacking in transcendental inspiration, codifies and justifies instinctive and degrading weaknesses in public morality instead of curbing them." He urged Christians to "remain faithful to the cross of Christ, to his doctrine and his virtue."

Louvain Theologians — In a letter to Msgr. Edouard Massaux, rector of Louvain University, the Pope praised theologians of the university for being "more careful to assure the accord of their thought with the ancient faith than to court popularity in public opinion." Their stance, he observed, was in contrast to that of some theologians who, "trying to make the Christian message more accessible to the modern mentality, have actually questioned the very content of this message." He said that faith and the teaching authority of the Church belong to the very essence of theology. "Theology (and theologians) can never conceive of itself (and themselves) as an independent special-interest group in the structure of the Church or as an alternative to the teaching authority of the Church." The occasion for the Pope's letter was the transfer of the French-language section of the university's faculties of theology and canon law to a new campus (Louvain-la-Neuve) at Oppignies, about 25 miles from Louvain, Belgium. Flemish-language sections of the university remained at Louvain.

Never Be Embarrassed — Pope Paul told one of the largest crowds ever assembled for a general audience Sept. 17 that Christians must never be embarrassed because of their faith, especially at a time when the world tends to discount religion. He said: "We must never, for the sake of human respect, be embarrassed that we are a people who believe in God and Christ. . . . The modern mentality makes a distinction, or rather a separation, between the citizen of the secular world and any reference of a religious nature. . . . When a citizen of the secular world appeals to (his own) doctrinal principles . . . it is an entirely normal occurrence. . . . But when a Christian dares to do the same thing while exercising his own social or professional role, such an action often seems intolerable to people today. It seems to them to be a lack of good taste and good sense."

Second Spring in Church in the U.S. — The Holy Father told a group of about 80 U.S. bishops Sept. 15, the day after Mother Seton's canonization, that he was looking forward to a "second spring" in the life of the Church in America. "We are convinced," he said, "that the action of the Holy Spirit is ever intense in the midst of your people, stirring up new fruits of holiness and justice, and leading many to discover that the message of the cross is truly the 'power of God.' "

Safeguarding the Human Person — At a private audience Sept. 18 with participants in the 11th assembly of the European Women's Union, Pope Paul said women should "become more involved than ever in safeguarding the inalienable rights of the human person, from conception to the last breath. . . . In this way you will contribute further toward humanizing our society, which is dominated by technology. It is a serious need whose urgency is felt more deeply than ever before."

Doctors at the Service of Life — Pope Paul reaffirmed the Church's opposition to euthanasia and called upon doctors to support human life to the very last, in a Sept. 18 address to 1,000 delegates attending the Third World Congress of the College of Psychosomatic Medicine. He said: "Concerning the value of each human person, we wish to remind you that it is the physician's duty to be always at the service of life and to assist the individual to the very end, without ever accepting euthanasia or renouncing the very human duty to help a person to end his days with dignity." The Pope voiced particular concern for "the most vulnerable — the infant, the aged and the sick . . . all those who are not productive and who are abandoned by a mentality not based on a true conception of man nor on the Christian spirit."

Justice and Peace Concerns — The Pope, at a Sept. 21 meeting with members and consultors of the Commission for Justice and Peace, said he was "gratified" to note its "preoccupations" with "capital issues which cause uneasiness today: the aggravation of hunger in so many deprived nations while elsewhere there is surplus, the ceaseless multiplication and commercial sale of armaments, greater awareness of the rights of man, and a harmonious and overall concept of development."

Housing — Suitable housing is a basic

human right, and providing it for the needy is "one of the most pressing and urgent demands of justice," declared the Pope at a meeting Sept. 24 with Enrique Penalosa, secretary general of a forthcoming UN Conference on Human Settlements. He said: "We are thinking about the great many people who are still homeless or who have for a home only wretched shanties, lacking even the most elementary conveniences, which proliferate on the outskirts of cities."

Hour of Grace — Pope Paul urged Catholics to take full advantage of the Holy Year. He said Sept. 24: "This is a precious hour of grace for each of you. It is the hour of God's grace. God is passing by right next to you; so do not let such a mysterious passage be in vain." Two of the largest groups in the throng of approximately 200,000 were 20,000 devotees of the late Padre Pio and 12,000 members of the Third Order of St. Francis. In addressing the latter group, the Holy Father said: "So many centuries have passed since St. Francis walked the earth, and yet his message among generations of disciples is still so very alive and active, as your presence at this meeting shows."

Execution in Spain — Pope Paul issued a "ringing condemnation of the very harsh repression" in Spain which resulted in the execution of five terrorists on Sept. 27. Only hours after the executions, the Pontiff said he was bitter over the fact that Gen. Francisco Franco had chosen "the path of murderous repression" and had not heeded his three personal clemency appeals for the condemned.

St. John de Massias — The Holy Father presided Sept. 28 over canonization ceremonies for Blessed John de Massias (1585-1645), a Dominican brother and friend of St. Martin de Porres.

The Pope Also:

• Told Egyptian Holy Year pilgrims Sept. 3 that he rejoiced with them over the interim Israeli-Egyptian Sinai accord to be signed the following day in Geneva.

• Listed the "attempted murder of President Ford" among the world's "bad news," Sept. 7.

• Told President Idi Amin of Uganda, who expelled 58 missionaries from his country in 1972, that he was pleased at the president's recent promise that Catholic religious personnel would always be welcomed in his country, Sept. 10.

Vatican Briefs:

• The Church wants women to have an appropriate role in church life and decision-making, declared Archbishop Enrico Bartoletti during a Vatican Radio broadcast. He added, however, that the "impossible expectations" of some liberationists would be disappointed.

• Cardinal Maurice Roy, president of the Council for the Laity and the Commission for Justice and Peace, called for major changes in

world agricultural policy, including better distribution of land ownership and fair tax systems for farmers. He made the appeal Sept. 15 during meetings of the International Catholic Rural Association in Rome.

• It was announced Sept. 18 that 16 Vatican delegate-observers would attend the Fifth General Assembly of the World Council of Churches Nov. 23 to Dec. 10 in Nairobi, Kenya.

• Sent a letter of congratulations to French philosopher Etienne Gilson on the occasion of his 91st birthday, and praised him personally for his long service to the academic world and to the Church.

• Returned from a working vacation at Castel Gandolfo to Vatican City by helicopter, Sept. 13.

• Praised the Salesians of St. John Bosco for their missionary endeavors (9,000 of their 18,000 members were in missionary assignments), and especially for their work among the young, as the 100th anniversary of the congregation's first foreign mission (in Buenos Aires, Argentina) drew near.

• Cardinal John Dearden of Detroit was named a member of the Congregation for the Sacraments and Divine Worship.

Canonization of Mother Seton

Elizabeth Ann Bayley Seton was declared a saint by Pope Paul Sept. 14 during solemn ceremonies attended by more than 100,000 persons in St. Peter's Square. Hundreds of more thousands witnessed the televised event and took part in related commemorative ceremonies honoring the first native-born American raised to the dignity of the altar.

In his homily during the Mass of canonization, Pope Paul said:

"She is the first daughter of the United States of America to be glorified with this incomparable attribute of canonization."

He concluded the homily with the words:

"And to all our beloved sons and daughters in the United States and throughout the entire Church of God, we offer, in the name of Christ, the glorious heritage of Elizabeth Ann Seton. It is, above all, an ecclesiastical heritage of strong faith and pure love for God and for others — faith and love that are nourished on the Eucharist and on the word of God. Yes, brethren, and sons and daughters: the Lord is indeed wonderful in his saints. Blessed be God forever."

DOMESTIC

No Bracero Revival — A proposal to revive a program which would legalize the mass importation of farm hands under an agreement between the United States and Mexico, was called "completely unacceptable" by Msgr. George G. Higgins, secretary for research, U.S. Catholic Conference. He warned in a Labor Day statement that revival of the program, which was terminated in 1964, "would inevitably have a disastrous effect on the wages and working conditions of the American labor force and might well destroy the only viable union (United Farm Workers of America) ever to be established in the history of American agriculture."

More Poor in 1974 — The U.S. Bureau of the Census reported that there were 1.3 million more Americans with incomes below the poverty level in 1974 than in 1973. The poverty level was an annual income of $5,038 for a non-farm family of four in 1974. The median income for all families in that year was $12,840.

Holy Year Rally — More than 75,000 persons took part Sept. 7 in Holy Year ceremonies in the Louisiana Super Dome in New Orleans. It was the largest liturgical service ever in the history of the archdiocese. Pope Paul, in a special message to the gathering, urged reconciliation "with God and with all one's neighbors."

Boston Busing — Relative calm accompanied the first days of the public school year in Boston under an expanded court-ordered desegregation plan affecting nearly every neighborhood in the city. Cardinal Humberto Medeiros said in a statement that the plan, involving 26,000 children, offered "real promise of a better education for all the young people in our city." He also praised the ecumenical efforts of many religious groups and of "all men and women of good will throughout the community" in curbing the violence that marked the opening of the schools in 1974.

Catholic Universities — The mandate and mission of a Catholic university "is the defense of moral values so gravely imperiled in our own society and in that of the world at large," declared historian Msgr. John Tracy Ellis during a Mass that opened the academic year at San Francisco University. He said his statement did not imply that in Catholic universities "there has been a major betrayal in that regard." However, he added, "it would be less than honest to pretend that the last decade has not on occasion seen and heard an articulate minority speak and write in a tone and manner that reminds one of St. Paul's prophecy to Timothy when he wrote: 'The time will come when men will not listen to sound teaching but, with ears itching, will pile up for themselves teachers who suit their pleasure. They will turn their hearing away from the truth to fables' (2 Tm. 4:3-5)."

Catholic Relief Services — In an annual report, Catholic Relief Services announced that the value of goods and services is provided to 82 developing countries in the year ending June 30 reached a record high of $226.5 million. CRS received an estimated $93.6 million in U.S. government-donated commodities and $26.9 million in money support from the government, mostly in the form of payment of ocean freight charges. The agency, whose total value of services since 1943 was

$2.8 billion, had 907 employes overseas.

Clemency Board Report — Fathers Theodore Hesburgh, C.S.C., and Msgr. Francis Lally, members of the President's Clemency Board which ended its term Sept. 15, praised the clemency program but voiced their support for unconditional amnesty for Vietnam war resisters. Father Hesburgh called the program "quite fair, even quite generous." Forty per cent of the 15,500 men who applied to the board were granted unconditional pardons; 50 per cent were given alternate-service terms of less than a year; three per cent were recommended for upgraded discharges; only six per cent were denied clemency. Msgr. Lally described the program as a success for those who participated in it, but a failure because less than one-fifth of those who were eligible applied between Sept. 16, 1974, and Mar. 31, 1975.

In a related development, Bishop James Malone of Youngstown endorsed a statement by the Diocesan Pastoral Council which urged complete amnesty for those "who remain outcasts from our society because of their refusal to participate in the Vietnam war." The statement said: "Amnesty is the practical, logical next step in following the failure of President Ford's limited clemency program — a commendable but inadequate attempt to reconcile the country."

TV Family Viewing Plan — The Administrative Board of the U.S. Catholic Conference sharply criticized a new network television "family viewing" plan to rule out material considered unsuitable for younger family members during two hours of entertainment programming in prime time. In a statement issued Sept. 17, the board said the plan depended on "self-regulation by the broadcast industry," and that the networks had not demonstrated a commitment to an "open, accountable and cooperative process" necessary for self-regulation. The board questioned whether such a commitment was possible for the networks because of the "impact of commercial pressures upon their program decision-making."

Ban on Handguns — The Social Development and World Peace Committee, U.S. Catholic Conference, called for "effective and courageous action to control handguns, leading to their eventual elimination from our society." The statement, entitled "Handgun Violence: A Threat to Life," said: "The unlimited freedom to possess and use handguns must give way to the rights of all people to safety and protection against those who misuse these weapons." It was reported that in the U.S. there were 40 million handguns and more than 28,000 deaths by firearms in 1973 (13,070 murders, 13,317 suicides, etc.). Guns were the fifth largest cause of accidental death in the country.

Fewer Foreign Missionaries — The U.S. Catholic Mission Council reported that the number of U.S. Catholic missionaries in overseas assignments declined for the seventh consecutive year, from 7,418 in 1974 to 7,148 in 1975. (See separate article, United States Foreign Missionaries.)

Farm Worker Elections — In secret balloting on ranches, the United Farm Workers of American won 86 elections with a total of 13,410 votes to serve as bargaining agent for farm workers in California while the rival Teamsters won 73 elections with 8,037 votes. Some 4,175 workers declined union representation in 19 elections. The results, however, were not conclusive. Cesar Chavez, head of the UFWA, claimed the elections were "tainted" and complained of a decision by the Agriculture Labor Relations Board to delay the ballot count at some 146 farms in the Salinas Valley. Before the secret ballot elections were held, in accordance with a state law which went into effect late in August, the Teamsters had 375 contracts with growers while the UFWA had only 12.

Domestic Briefs:

• American Catholics have a lot to contribute to American society by facing and accepting their cultural and ethnic diversity, according to Msgr. Geno C. Baroni, founder and president of the National Center of Urban Ethnic Affairs. Speaking in Worcester, Mass., he said: "The Church should make the case for pluralism and for a transmission of ethnic and cultural values."

• Rear Adm. Jeremiah A. Denton, Jr., the Navy's senior prisoner of war in Vietnam, was given the Celtic Cross Award of the Catholic War Veterans at Hollywood, Fla.

• The sixth annual God Day observance, sponsored by Concerned Citizens for God and Country, was held in New York Sept. 21.

• The American Freedom from Hunger Foundation, sponsor of the National Week of Concern for World Hunger, Sept. 21 to 28, launched a campaign to collect millions of signatures on petitions pledging action to relieve domestic and world hunger.

• Father Daniel Lyons, S.J., was reported to be on a leave of absence from the Jesuits.

• Ursuline Sister Judith Anne Barnhiser, a doctor of canon law, was reported to be the first woman in the U.S. to hold the position of procurator advocate on a diocesan (Toledo) tribunal.

• The Our Sunday Visitor Institute made a grant of $25,000 to the Manresa Educational Corp., which was set up in 1974 to establish an "openly Catholic college."

Teacher Strikes

The opening of the school year was marred by lay teacher strikes in several dioceses. Among them were New York, where strikes affected nine archdiocesan high schools, and Brooklyn, where walkouts were staged at five high schools. At issue were money, seniority

and tenure claims, class size and improved insurance coverage.

In New York, the teachers returned to work Sept. 29 without a contract as a "good will gesture" to produce a cooling-off period while negotiations continued with archdiocesan officials. The strike in Brooklyn was still on at the end of the month.

FOREIGN

Chaos in Argentina — Amid political and economic crisis punctuated by armed violence, several Argentine bishops called for concerted efforts toward peace and reconstruction in the country. The alternative would be "a gradual take-over by the international forces of atheistic materialism, which (would) impose upon us their totalitarian regime so destructive of freedom and personal and family life," according to Bishop Octavio Derisi, rector of the Catholic University in Buenos Aires.

Society of the Divine Word — As the missionary Society of the Divine Word commemorated the 100th anniversary of its founding Sept. 8, it was reported that 14 per cent (437) of its priests were Asians, and that, from 1970 to 1974, 41 per cent (170) of priests ordained in the society were Asians.

Discord in Portugal — Cardinal Antonio Ribeiro of Lisbon said in a speech published Sept. 8 that important sections of the press, radio and television were sowing "seeds of hatred, promoting division and practicing ideological and religious aggression." He charged that the people had been swindled and reviled by Communist radicals striving for control of the government, despite their minority status among the electorate. He added: "The Portuguese people want a peaceful society in which minorities do not try to impose totalitarian systems or ideologies that are foreign to their Christian traditions."

Repression in Vietnam — Fourteen Jesuit missionaries recently expelled from South Vietnam reported during the month that mounting pressure in a variety of forms was being placed on the Church by the new Communist government there. They spoke about restrictions on a bishop, attacks on religion in political formation meetings, surveillance of seminarians and persons attending Mass, travel restrictions on priests, and discrimination in employment against Catholics.

Prayer Group Forced Underground — A publication of the Philippine Association of Major Religious Superiors of Men and Women reported from Manila that an ecumenical prayer group in Seoul, Korea, had been forced underground by the regime of President Park Chung Hee. Many of the several hundred participants in the group were related to political prisoners of the government.

Church in Politics — The reason for the Church's "mingling in politics" was given in a report submitted at the regional meeting in Belmopan, Belize, of the Justice and Peace Commission of the Central American Bishops' Conference. The report said: "Because of the widespread injustice afflicting the great majority of the population," pastoral action "of necessity has political consequences."

Pattern of Violence — The killing of priests and farm workers in Honduras was not an isolated phenomenon but part of a chain of violence stretching across other countries as well, according to Bishop Alfonso Lopez, secretary general of the Latin American Bishops' Council. "Violence reigns and forces strikes against those who labor for the cause of the landless peasant," he said. Other countries where such incidents occurred in recent years were Colombia, Chile, Bolivia, Ecuador, Nicaragua, the Dominican Republic, Mexico and El Salvador.

Return to Olancho — Two foreign priests and six nuns were the first missionaries to return to mission posts in Olancho Province, Honduras, after the military government said it would guarantee "their safety and rights." Another 16 priests and 19 nuns were also scheduled to return to Olancho, after 12 weeks of forced absence following raids by troops and landholders against farm workers and church personnel during a hunger march at the end of June.

Reconciliation Sought in Chile — Cardinal Raul Silva of Santiago and other bishops took part in an ecumenical thanksgiving service Sept. 18, marking the nation's independence day. During the ceremony, the cardinal reiterated the bishops' appeal for reconciliation among Chileans, and said that government leaders faced "the immense task" of laying new foundations on which "the peace and prosperity of Chile will depend." Earlier in the month, the bishops absented themselves from government-sponsored commemorations of the second anniversary of the fall of the Allende regime. The abstention was deliberate, "to keep the Church from being drawn into factional politics," stated Bishop Carlos Camus, secretary general of the bishops' conference. At the same time, the prelates called on the government to end the torture of political prisoners and discrimination against persons suspected of Marxism.

Rhodesian Bill Denounced — The Rhodesian Bishops' Conference denounced proposed legislation that would empower the government to halt criminal proceedings against a government minister for actions "in connection with the suppression of terrorism." They called the bill "a denial of justice," and said it "endangers the future of this country." In a press statement Sept. 6, they stated: "The scant respect for the rule of law which is evident in many parts of this continent, our own country included, is such as to convince us that serious consideration ought to be given by the appropriate authorities to

the establishment in Africa of a Commission for Human Rights."

Priest Hanged — The hanging of an Eastern-Rite priest in the Ukraine by Soviet police Jan. 30, 1975, was reported in the Sept. 25 edition of *L'Osservatore Romano.* The report said that Father Michele Luckyj was hanged in the village of Drohovyc for "having pursued religious activity, celebration of the Holy Mass . . . and distribution of the Eucharist." He had been warned three times "that such activity is considered illegal in the Soviet Union."

Sterilization Barred — Justice Rose Heilbron, in London, barred the proposed sterilization of a retarded 11-year-old girl whose widowed mother favored the operation. The judge said in her decision that the operation was "neither medically indicated nor necessary, and it would not be in the girl's best interest. . . . This type of operation is one which involves the deprivation of a basic human right, namely, the right of a woman to reproduce, and therefore it would be, if performed on a woman for non-therapeutic reasons and without her consent, a violation of such right."

Foreign Briefs:

• The Melkite-Rite Synod ousted controversial Archbishop Gregoire Haddad of Beirut at the end of August because of alleged "ambiguities" in theology, according to a delayed report. The action was taken despite a report from the Vatican that it had found nothing unorthodox in the archbishop's writings.

• Father Alvaro del Portillo was elected Sept. 15 president-general of Opus Dei. He succeeded Msgr. Jose Maria Escriva de Balaguer, founder of the association, who died June 26, 1975.

• Four hundred and 76 Spanish diocesan priests were reported working in 132 dioceses of 19 countries in Latin America.

• Labor Minister Michel Durafour of France announced that social security benefits would be extended to priests and religious by the beginning of 1978.

Africanization

"Africanization and localization are vigorously moving orientations which are here to stay and are well on the way," declared some 50 bishops Sept. 28 at the close of a week-long meeting near Rome of the Symposium of Episcopal Conferences of Africa and Madagascar.

They said in a report: "Not only has the Church nothing to fear from these orientations when they are properly understood and opened to the world; on the contrary, the Church has everything to gain from them."

It was made clear that support of these orientations did not imply any desire for independence of the Church in Africa from Rome.

OCTOBER 1975

VATICAN

Renewal of Faith — The Holy Year summons to renewal means a renewal of faith, Pope Paul told some 50,000 persons Oct. 1. "Faith is our answer to the word of God," he said. "It is our 'yes' to his revelation, to the offer of his light and his love."

Sympathy for the Lebanese — While receiving Boutros Dib, Lebanon's new ambassador to the Vatican, Oct. 2, the Pope said: "We follow these (many incidents of violence in Lebanon) with anxiety, suffering with the unfortunate victims and praying that a solution which is just and acceptable to all concerned will be found quickly."

Talbot's Heroic Virtue — Matt Talbot, the Dublin workingman who dragged himself from drunkenness to holiness, was recognized as having risen to a life of "heroic virtue" by a decree of the Congregation for the Causes of Saints read Oct. 3 in Pope Paul's presence. The decree, a preliminary to beatification, was one of seven relating to candidates for sainthood.

Anointing of the Sick — In an unprecedented ceremony accenting the communal aspect of Christian suffering, Pope Paul administered the sacrament of the anointing of the sick to 50 Holy Year pilgrims Oct. 5 in St. Peter's Square. Explaining the twofold aim of the sacrament, the Holy Father said: "In this sacrament the Church looks principally to the soul, to the remission of sins and to the increase of divine grace. But she also desires and aims to bring about relief and, if possible, also the cure of the infirmity."

The Kingdom of Heaven — Pope Paul, addressing a throng of some 90,000 persons Oct. 8, declared: "The kingdom of heaven that Jesus Christ preached is neither politically subversive nor morally permissive, in the ordinary meaning of those terms. Jesus Christ is the great prophet of human reform, a reform sought by all and salvific for all." The kingdom which the Gospels proclaim, he added, is not for the faint-hearted: "It is for the courageous, the stout-hearted and for those who do not refuse to bear the cross for Christ and with Christ." The reality of daily life, he declared, must be directed and shaped by a spiritual vision that sees everything in the light of divine Providence, which gives meaning and value to the changing circumstances of our existence.

Suspicion toward Missionaries — To the traditional perils and hardships of a Christian missionary, contemporary developments have added the suspicion of local peoples that he comes among them as a colonialist and exploiter, the Pope observed in a message for World Mission Day, Oct. 19. He said: "Once the great difficulty, which was an obstacle to missionary work, was the 'penetration' into lands, among peoples, under extremely arduous, difficult, hostile, perilous conditions for anxious and inexpert missionary footsteps. Today, to these obstacles another is added, perhaps even more serious, and it is 'residence' in areas which, reawakened to awareness of civilization, of their own native traditions, whatever they may be, no longer appreciate the presence of the foreign missionary who comes from other countries and who often is suspected of colonialism, as an exploiter, as the bearer of a foreign and dominating civilization. ... Mission, that is, the proclamation of the Gospel to all men, is not a thing of the past, it is not optional in itself. It is based on divine will, on the theology of salvation, on the perennially affirmed authority of the Church and on the recent solemn documentation of Vatican Council II. ... Your efforts are not in vain, your sacrifice, whatever may be the outcome, has not failed."

The Pope Also:
• Met with Greek Premier Prime Minister Konstantin Karamanlis, Oct. 1, and with Cardinal Vicente Enrique Tarancon, president of the Spanish Bishops' Conference, Oct. 2.
• Declared his "energetic condemnation" of Spain's mounting political violence, which in eight days took a toll of 13 lives, Oct. 8.
• Chose "The Real Weapons of Peace" as the theme for the Jan. 1, 1976, World Day of Peace observance.

Vatican Briefs:
• With a new outbreak of violence in Northern Ireland, Vatican Radio stated Oct. 2: "Twelve dead and 43 wounded are the tragic outcome of the terrorists in Belfast and elsewhere yesterday. ... It is difficult to hope that the precarious truce maintained since last February can hold up after these new terrorist acts."
• The Knights of Columbus pledged $76,000 annually to the Vatican to cover the major costs of around-the-world telecasts of three papal ceremonies a year — the Pope's Midnight Mass at Christmas, the Good Friday Stations of the Cross, and another event to be selected.
• An increase in the number of Catholics marrying outside the Church stems from a deep crisis of faith, declared the Committee on the Family in a "reflection document" issued Oct. 9.

Day of Peace Theme — "The Real Weapons of Peace" was chosen by Pope Paul as the theme for World Day of Peace observances Jan. 1, 1976. In announcing the theme, Vatican spokesman Federico Alessandrini said the Pope would draw attention to the 10 years since the speech he gave before the United Nations in New York, Oct. 4, 1965, by urging all chiefs of state, religious authorities, Christians and all men of good will to work for peace. In so doing, the Pope would say: "Let us not use wrong weapons such as atomic terror, passive acceptance of injustice, cowardice, violence and, above all, the arms race. . . . The arms race has become a mad machine, ruinous and scandalous. Through its quantitative and qualitative excess in mortal weaponry, the arms race transforms national and international security into a disastrous insecurity. Instead of preserving people from war, the arms race prepares for war." Alessandrini said the Pope's appeal would emphasize the "moral strength of law, respect for agreements, the effective application of recent charters for the rights of man and the rights of peoples."

DOMESTIC

New Diocese — The apostolic delegation announced establishment of the new Diocese of Pensacola-Tallahassee in northwestern Florida and the appointment of Bishop Rene H. Gracida to head the see. The 13-county area had 37,000 Catholics, 54 priests, 77 women religious, 30 parishes and nine missions.

Lunch and Nurtrition Program — The House and Senate overrode Oct. 7 a presidential veto of a $2.75 billion school lunch and child nutrition bill. The bill extended and expanded the School Lunch and Breakfast Programs, the Special Supplementary Food Program for Women, Infants and Children, and the Special Milk Program for the poor and many working-class families. Both the U.S. Catholic Conference and the National Conference of Catholic Charities had called for the override.

Petition To Permit Death — A New Jersey court had under consideration a petition from Joseph T. Quinlan for permission to order the discontinuation of extraordinary means being used to keep his adopted daughter Karen Ann alive. The 21-year-old woman had been in a coma and under artificial respiration since Apr. 15. Donald G. Collester, prosecutor for Morris County, said the "case is fraught with legal questions, not the least of which is the legal definition of death." Father Thomas Trapasso, the Quinlans' pastor, noting that Mr. Quinlan's request was not for mercy killing or euthanasia, said the Catholic point of view does not require the use of "extraordinary" means to sustain life. (See Life-Death Questions.)

Reservations about Bleeding Statue — A Philadelphia archdiocesan committee set up to investigate a "bleeding" statue of Christ said in a statement that the archdiocese "is constrained to express its serious reservations about the authenticity of the alleged phenomenon." The committee urged Catholics to exercise "grave caution and reserve" in making judgments about the figure of the Sacred Heart in the home of Mrs. Russell Poore in the Linwood section of Boothwyn, Pa.

Respect Life — Special observances marked "Respect Life Sunday" Oct. 5 in parishes across the country. The family and related concerns were the theme of the observance.

Brooklyn Teacher Strike Ends — Striking lay teachers at five Catholic high schools in the Brooklyn diocese returned to school Oct. 9 after voting 104 to 26, with four abstentions, to accept a two-year contract proposed by federal mediators. The return ended a five-week-old strike by the Lay Faculty Association of Brooklyn, an affiliate of the American Federation of Teachers. During the walkout, two of the schools were shut down.

Welfare Expenditures Up — The nation's welfare expenditures in the fiscal year which ended June 30 amounted to $22.6 billion, an increase of 20 per cent over the amount in 1974. Figures were published Oct. 16 by the Department of Health, Education and Welfare.

NLRB Elections in Seminaries — The National Labor Relations Board announced it would conduct union representation elections Oct. 17 among teachers at two Chicago archdiocesan seminaries. It was reported that Cardinal John Cody was expected to refuse to bargain with the union, regardless of how the vote went. He said in a letter to priests: "The ruling (to hold the elections) raises serious questions regarding the intrusion of government into the internal affairs of seminaries, which are among the most sensitive of ecclesiastical institutions."

Bible Study — Russell Shaw, secretary for public affairs, U.S. Catholic Conference, cautioned against Bible study undertaken without the help of interpretative guidelines. He urged that the traditional Catholic approach to Scripture be followed in the light of the upsurge of adult Bible study courses since Vatican II. The mind of the Church must be regularly consulted, he noted. "The Bible in many places is not self-explanatory, and it is easy to lose the point without a reliable guide to keep one on the track." Shaw made this observation in a talk Oct. 5 at the first of five weekly lectures sponsored by the *Catholic Universe-Bulletin,* the Cleveland diocesan newspaper, and the diocesan religious education office.

Complaint in California — An interdenominational religious group issued a strong indictment of the administration of California's farm labor election law and called upon Gov. Edmund G. Brown, Jr., to "initiate steps to enforce the law and protect the rights of farmworkers." The 72 religious leaders from 17 states did so after touring ranches in Dzlano, Oxnard and Salinas to investigate complaints that the law was being subverted. At issue were the rights of farm workers to choose the United Farm Workers of America or the Teamsters to represent them in collective bargaining.

Domestic Briefs:

• The National Catholic Disaster Relief Committee sent a grant of $10,000 for emergency relief to Catholic Social Services, San Juan, Puerto Rico, to aid victims of Hurricane Eloise.

• Sister Victoria Pastrano was elected the first woman president of the Texas Catholic Conference.

• By decision of the Naval Reserve, Oct. 10 to 12 was designated as the Navy Sabbath. All churches were asked to make it "a period of prayers of thanks for past service and intercession for the future."

• Honored: John L. Downey, a Newark, N.J., program director, to receive the Youth Minister Award of the Youth Department, U.S. Catholic Conference, Nov. 1; Dr. Eugene R. Balthazar with the 1975 Stritch Medal of Loyola University, Chicago, for his medical care of migrant workers; Mother Teresa with one of the Albert Schweitzer International Prizes, Oct. 23; singer-actress Vikki Carr with the For God and Youth Award at the convention of the National CYO Federation; U.S. District Judge John J. Sirica, of Watergate trial fame, with the alumni Cardinal Gibbons Medal of Catholic University, Oct. 25.

• Cardinal John Krol of Philadelphia announced he had accepted the honorary chairmanship of a committee seeking financial aid for the National Shrine of Our Lady of Czestochowa in Doylestown, Pa.

FOREIGN

Lithuanian Journalist Sentenced — The 17th issue of the *Chronicle of the Catholic Church in Lithuania* made it clear that the Soviet regime was keeping up its pressures on Roman Catholics. Reported was the case of Nijole Sadunaite, a 37-year-old Catholic woman arrested by Soviet secret police Aug. 27, 1974, during widespread raids aimed at closing down the underground publication. On June 20, 1975, after a four-day trial, she was sentenced to three years in a concentration camp, with an additional three years' exile, for reproduction and dissemination of the *Chronicle.*

Angolan Refugees — Vatican and Portuguese relief organizations were stepping up efforts to care for up to 300,000 Portuguese refugees from strife-torn Angola, the Portuguese African territory due to gain official independence in November. Rapid decolonization became government policy following the April, 1973, revolution against Portugal's long dictatorship.

Anti-Abortion Referendum — An Austrian pro-life group, Action for Life, reported it had collected 763,504 signatures to challenge a pro-abortion law that went into effect Jan. 1, 1975. Voting on a referendum was sched-

uled to take place from Nov. 24 to Dec. 1.

Persecution in Equatorial Africa — Refugees from Equatorial Guinea reported new mass executions there ordered by President-for-life Francisco Macias Nguema. They also said there was continued persecution of Catholics, who constituted the bulk of the population.

New Saint's Church Bombed — Twelve days before his scheduled canonization, Oct. 12, a church in Northern Ireland dedicated to the honor of Oliver Plunkett was bombed.

Peace Priests Ignored — Not one of the Czechoslovakian bishops joined two pilgrimages to Rome organized by the "peace priests," the Communist-sponsored group in Prague operating under the name of *Pacem in Terris,* according to reports reaching Vienna. When 28 of the priests in the first pilgrimage participated in a general audience in St. Peter's, Pope Paul ignored their presence, contrary to his usual custom. This was taken as an indication of the Vatican's displeasure at the constant proliferation of restrictions upon Catholics in Czechoslovakia.

Chinese Fate for Church in Vietnam — The Catholic Church in Vietnam will suffer the same fate as the Church in Communist China, according to a French Vincentian priest recently forced to leave Dalat. He said the process would be slower because of the higher percentage of Catholics in Vietnam, but insisted the objectives to be achieved and the measures being taken by the regime were similar. "As in China, the first step is the removal of all foreign missioners. It is reliably said that there is a directive to the effect that all foreign priests and sisters should be out of Vietnam by the end of October." Vietnamese priests were being pressured with ever-increasing intensity, and those considered influential were being imprisoned or removed from places where they might exert influence. The priest verified a report that the Coadjutor of Saigon, Bishop Francis Xavier Nguyen van Thuan, had been sent to an outlying village under virtual arrest.

Vatican Is Unrealistic — Anatoly Levitin-Krasnov, a Russian underground activist, told the Vatican's top negotiator with Eastern Europe that Vatican policies toward Communist regimes in that part of the world had produced nothing. He said Vatican attempts to arrive at an understanding with totalitarian regimes were unrealistic.

Bishop Won't Be Expelled — Spanish-born Bishop Pedro Casaldaliga of the San Felix prelature in Brazil, who feared expulsion because of his dispute with large land-owning companies, received assurances he would not be expelled from the country. The bishop, known as an outspoken defender of poor, landless farmers, said "presidential sources" had told the Brazilian Bishops' Conference that no action would be taken against him.

DEATHS OCTOBER 1, 1974, to OCTOBER 1, 1975

Amado Blanco, Luis, 72, Mar. 9, Rome, Italy; Cuban ambassador to Vatican City from 1962; first representative of a Communist government to be dean of diplomatic corps accredited to Vatican.

Anderson, Ian, 56, June, Edinburgh, Scotland; co-founder of Catholic Union of the Sick in Scotland.

Anson, Peter F., 86, July 10, Nunrow, Scotland; Oblate Cistercian Brother; founder of the Apostleship of the Sea Conference in Scotland.

Bailey, John M., 70, Apr. 10, Hartford, Conn.; political leader; Democratic national chairman during presidencies of John F. Kennedy and Lyndon B. Johnson.

Baker, Josephine, 68, Apr. 12, Paris, France; American-born black star of Paris show business for 50 years; became French citizen in 1937; adopted 12 children from different countries.

Brennan, Rev. Robert E., O.P., 77, June 17, Lebanon, Ky.; internationally known Dominican scholar, psychologist; author of 11 books.

Burns, John A., 66, Apr. 5, Kaiwi, Oahu, Hawaii; Hawaiian political leader; governor of Hawaii, 1962-74; instrumental in gaining statehood for Hawaii in 1959.

Collins, Rev. Joseph, S.S., 77, Jan. 23, Washington, D.C.; educator; director of National Center of Religious Education/CCD, 1942-60.

Concha, Cardinal Luis, 84, Sept. 18, Bogota, Colombia; archbishop of Bogota, 1959-72, when he retired; member of College of Cardinals from 1961.

Considine, Robert B., 68, Sept. 25, New York, N.Y.; journalist; associated with Hearst publications for almost 40 years; author.

Crowley, Patrick, 63, Nov. 20, 1974, Chicago, Ill.; lawyer; a founder and leader with his wife Patricia of the Christian Family Movement in the U.S.; president of International Confederation of Christian Family Movements.

De Valera, Eamon, 92, Aug. 29, Dublin, Ireland.; New York-born Irish independence leader; prime minister (1937-48, 1951-54, 1957-59) and president (1959-73) of Ireland.

Doherty, Rev. Edward J., 84, May 4, Renfrew, Canada; star reporter for New York *Daily News* in 1920's; author of 22 books; married Baroness Catherine De Hueck, 1943, and worked with her at Madonna House, Combermere, Ontario; ordained priest 1969 at the age of 79 in the Melkite Rite — Eastern Catholic Rite which permits ordination of married men.

Donahue, Mark, 38, Aug. 19, Graz, Austria, of injuries sustained in a crash at the Austrian Grand Prix; American race car driver; winner of 1972 Indianapolis 500 and 56 other major races.

Doyle, Sister Mary Rosaline, 101, September, Trenton, N.J.; oldest member of Sisters of St. Francis of Philadelphia; first woman religious to graduate from Georgetown University, Washington, D.C.

Duffey, Felix D., C.S.C., 71, Dec. 7, 1974, South Bend, Ind.; master of novices for Congregation of Holy Cross, 1938-49; editor of *Ave Maria* magazine, 1952-54.

Escriva de Belaguer, Msgr. Jose Maria, 73, June 26, Rome, Italy; Spanish priest; founder and president of Opus Dei (see Index).

Feltin, Cardinal Maurice, 92, Sept. 27, Thiais, France; archbishop of Paris, 1949-66, when he retired; member of College of Cardinals from 1953; supported French worker-priest movement.

Flaherty, Bishop J. Louis, 65, Aug. 9 Norfolk, Va.; auxiliary bishop of Richmond from 1966.

Foley, Raymond M., 84, Mar. 2, Grosse Pointe, Mich.; federal housing administrator and head of Housing and Home Finance Agency under Pres. Harry S. Truman; advocate of low-rent public housing.

Foley, Rev. Theodore, C.P., 61, October, 1974, Rome, Italy; superior general of Passionist Fathers and Brothers from 1964.

Frederick, Gerard (Charles R.), 44, Mar. 31, Seattle, Wash.; national leader of Catholic Charismatic Movement; convert in 1950's.

Fuller, Mother Mary, 91, June 7, Yonkers, N.Y.; mother general of Sisters of Charity of St. Vincent de Paul of New York, 1954-60; advocate of canonization cause of Mother Elizabeth Ann Seton.

Gallant, Msgr. G. Edgar, 81, September, Charlottetown, P.E.I., Canada; first Catholic priest ordained in Alaska.

Gully, Rev. Edward F., 50, July 9, Worcester, Mass.; associate editor of the *Catholic Free Press,* Worcester diocesan paper.

Hayward, Susan, 55, Mar. 14, Beverly Hills, Calif.; Academy Award-winning movie actress.

Highley, Mont Frederick, 97, Feb. 23, Oklahoma City, Okla.; lawyer; successfully defended (1918) right of Catholic priests in Oklahoma to possess altar wine for use during Mass despite state statute forbidding sale or possession of liquor; decision set precedent for other states during prohibition era.

Huber, Rev. Oscar L., C.M., 81, Jan. 21, Perryville, Mo.; gave last rites to Pres. Kennedy (was pastor of Holy Trinity parish in Dallas at time of assassination).

Jaeger, Cardinal Lorenz, 83, Apr. 1, Paderborn, W. Germany; leading German ecumenist; archbishop of Paderborn, 1941-73, when he retired; member of College of Cardinals from 1965.

Johnson, Archbishop Martin M., 75, Jan. 29, Vancouver, B.C., Canada; archbishop of Vancouver, 1965-69, when he retired.

Josi, Prof. Enrico, 90, Sept. 1, Rome, Italy; Vatican archeologist; official of the Pontifical Commission on Sacred Archeology for 45 years.

Journet, Cardinal Charles, 84, Apr. 15, Fribourg, Switzerland; noted Swiss theologian, author; member of College of Cardinals from 1965.

Jungmann, Rev. Josef Andreas, S.J., 86, Jan. 26, Innsbruck, Austria; Austrian liturgist; innovator in catechetics.

Lane, Maj. Gen. Thomas A., 68, Apr. 20, Washington, D.C.; syndicated columnist; proponent of conservative views on public and religious affairs.

Larranaga Lasa, Bishop Ignacio Gregorio, O.F.M. Cap., 82, Feb. 21, Fuenterrabia, Spain; exiled bishop of Pingliang, China.

Lavanoux, Maurice, 80, Oct. 21, 1974, New York, N.Y.; architect; church art expert; one of founders of Liturgical Arts Society.

Luetmer, Sister Nora, O.S.B., 53, Nov. 4, 1974, St. Cloud, Minn.; educator; recipient of 1974 NCEA Presidential Award for outstanding service to Catholic education.

McGann, Dora, 60, Aug. 13, New York, N.Y.; radio personality.

Marrocco, Bishop Francis A., 62, July 18, Peterborough, Ont., Canada; bishop of Peterborough from 1968.

Martin, Mother Mary, 82, Jan. 27, Drogheda, Ireland; foundress of Medical Missionaries of Mary, 1937.

Meouchi, Cardinal Paul Pierre, 80, Jan. 11, Beirut, Lebanon; Maronite-Rite patriarch of Antioch from 1955; member of College of Cardinals from 1965.

Meyer, Rev. Bernard F., M.M., 84, May 8, North Tarrytown, N.Y.; member of first ordination class of Maryknollers; one of group of first Maryknoll missionaries sent to China, 1918; served there 32 years.

Mindszenty, Cardinal Jozsef, 83, May 6, Vienna, Austria. (See separate article.)

Mooney, Joe, 65, May 12, Ft. Lauderdale, Fla.; jazz pianist, organist and singer.

Nahalka, Msgr. Stefan, 52, Mar. 6, Rome, Italy; Slovak priest in exile in Rome; founder of Slovak Institute of Sts. Cyril and Methodius in Rome.

O'Dwyer, Rev. Michael, 87, Feb. 13, Navan, Ireland; superior general of Columban Fathers, 1924-47.

O'Hara, Joseph P., 80, Mar. 4, Washington, D.C.; lawyer; U.S. representative from Minnesota for 18 years before his retirement in 1959.

O'Hayer, Eileen, Mar. 7, Blue Island, Ill.; retired editor of *Extension Magazine.*

Parker, Bishop Thomas, 87, April, near London, England; bishop of Northampton, England, 1941-67, when he retired; celebrated Mass in hundreds of village inns.

Pontamian, Brother Andrew, F.S.C., 73, Feb. 8, New York, N.Y.; dean of Manhattan College, 1942-53; professor emeritus of fine arts.

Raimondi, Cardinal Luigi, 62, June 24, Vatican City; prefect of Congregation for the Causes of Saints; apostolic delegate to the U.S., 1967-73; member of College of Cardinals from 1973.

Reid, Elizabeth, 59, Dec. 23, 1974, The Hague, Netherlands; Australian-born Grail missionary; editor of *Hong Kong Sunday Examiner;* executive director of AFPRO (Action for Food Production) in India.

Ryan, Archbishop Finbar, O.P., 93, Jan. 10, Cork, Ireland; archbishop of Port-of-Spain, Trinidad, 1940-66, when he retired.

Scheuer, Rev. Joseph, 56, June 19, Baltimore, Md.; writer; co-author of *The De-Romanization of the American Catholic Church.*

Secondari, John H., 55, Feb. 8, New York, N.Y.; producer of TV documentaries; novelist; TV script writer.

Sheehan, Arthur, 66, Aug. 7, New York, N.Y.; author; editor of *Catholic Worker* during World War II.

Shields, Frank X., 66, August, New York, N.Y.; noted tennis player.

Smith, Bishop Eustace, O.F.M., 67, June 13, Boston, Mass.; first vicar apostolic of Beirut for Latin-Rite Catholics, 1956-73, when he retired.

Staunton, Msgr. John C., 59, Mar. 30, Cincinnati, Ohio; first executive secretary of Ohio Welfare Conference (now Catholic Conference of Ohio), 1945-57.

Tabera Araoz, Cardinal Arturo, C.M.F., 71, June 13, Rome, Italy; Spanish cardinal; prefect of Sacred Congregation for Religious; archbishop of Pamplona, 1968-72; member of College of Cardinals from 1969.

Thyken, Rev. Ralph, S.V.D., 75, Jan. 11, Los Angeles, Calif.; fund raiser for foreign missions.

Walsh, William C., 85, June 17, Cumberland, Md.; prominent lawyer and political figure in Maryland; brother of Bishop James E. Walsh, M.M.

Ward, Maisie, 86, Jan. 28, New York, N.Y.: English-born publisher, biographer; charter member of Catholic Evidence Guild; founder with her husband, Frank Sheed, of publishing house of Sheed and Ward in 1926.

Warren, Rev. Cornelius, C.SS.R., 102, June 18, Saratoga Springs, N.Y.; oldest priest in history of Redemptorists.

Warren, Vincent D., S.S.J., Feb. 19, Baltimore, Md.; Josephite priest for 60 years; once kidnapped by members of Ku Klux Clan because of his work among the blacks.

Waters, Bishop Vincent S., 70, Dec. 3, 1974, Raleigh, from 1945.

Zaleski, Bishop Alexander M., 69, May 15, Miami, Fla.; bishop of Lansing, Mich., from 1965.

Special Reports

BICENTENNIAL '76: CATHOLIC OBSERVANCE

For historical background, see The Catholic Church in the United States and Background Dates in U.S. Catholic Chronology.

The Administrative Board of the National Catholic Bishops' Conference put the finishing touches to the outline of the nationwide Catholic observance of Bicentennial Year 1976 in June, 1974.

The stated theme is "Liberty and Justice for All."

The Program

The program envisioned:

• Exploration of the theme, with respect to the Church itself and the nation, in six congressional-type hearings to be held in 1975. The format of the hearings placed bishops and other church leaders in the position of listeners and speakers, at times, to issues presented by experts and those attending the hearings. (Five hearings had been conducted by the time of this writing; see below).

• Extension of the same process to parishes throughout the country.

• Compilation of findings between November, 1975, and March, 1976, and return of the subject matter for reconsideration and study to parish groups, other organizations and societies.

• Subsequent gathering of relevant information for reference to a week-long national conference on the Bicentennial theme to be held in October, 1976, in Detroit.

• Release by the Detroit meeting of a statement on liberty and justice designed to guide the social policy of the Church in the United States for the next five years or so.

Included in the program are a special liturgy to be celebrated throughout the country on July 4, 1976, and the celebration of the 41st International Eucharistic Congress Aug. 1 to 8 in Philadelphia.

Also on the schedule was participation by Catholics among 200 religious leaders in a May 21 and 22, 1976, meeting for a national consultation on "Religion and the American Experience."

The program includes parish and diocesan observances in line with local opportunity and initiative. One of them, a pilot project for parishes in their study of social issues, was initiated in Detroit in 1975, as a model for adoption in other local programs.

Directing the Program

Overall direction of the Catholic commemoration of the 200 years of American independence is in the hands of a Bishops' Committee for the Bicentennial headed by Cardinal John F. Dearden. Executive director of the staff is Dr. Francis Butler. Dominican Sister Maria Riley is one of the staff members with responsibility for services and contact with some 125 Bicentennial coordinators in dioceses throughout the country.

Archbishop Joseph L. Bernardin, by appointment of President Ford, is one of 25 members of an advisory committee charged by the American Revolutionary Bicentennial Commission to draft a "Bicentennial Declaration" commemorating the Declaration of Independence.

Purposes

The "Liberty and Justice" program "is designed to raise up for examination and action (in the light of the social doctrine of the Church and experience) those issues of justice and freedom which touch the lives and dignity of people in the United States and in our relations with other people of the world." So stated Father J. Bryan Hehir, director the Division of Justice and Peace, U.S. Catholic Conference, in the introduction to a discussion guide entitled "Liberty and Justice for All."

The major headings in the booklet, which was published by the Bishops' Bicentennial Committee, are nationhood, the Church, humankind, ethnicity and race, the neighborhood, work, the family and personhood.

Regional Hearings

Subjects discussed and recommendations made at regional hearings across the country during 1975 included the following items.

Washington, D.C., Feb. 3 to 5: Participants suggested the Church should:

• Work toward just U.S. food policies at home and abroad.

• "Unequivocally" support equality for women in every area of Church life, "including equality of ministry."

• Support the Equal Rights Amendment to the U.S. Constitution.

• Educate U.S. Catholics in the moral implications of U.S. foreign policy in many areas, including a wide range of foreign food and development assistance programs.

Jesuit Father Avery Dulles, a theologian of Catholic University, outlined a theology of social justice in the Church and criteria for the Church to engage in limited, self-critical, social-economic-political involvement, "with a bias toward the human good involved . . . in the light of the Gospel."

San Antonio, Apr. 3 to 5: The main concerns were: citizenship in this country, justice in immigration policies and in dealing with illegal aliens, racial and ethnic diversity, and the promotion of cultural identity — particularly among the Spanish-speaking, the second largest minority in this country.

Dr. Jesus Chevarria, professor of history at the University of California at Santa Barbara, told the panel of bishops and their representatives: "In my judgment, if we were to ask those Chicanos and Chicanas who have labored, struggled, and fought in the last five to 10 years for the just recognition of our national material and spiritual rights about how they feel toward the Bicentennial, they would reply simply that we have little to celebrate for our revolution of independence has not yet come."

St. Paul, June 12 to 14: More than 70 speakers repeated pleas for a sense of dignity, understanding and action. Recommendations were:

• That the Church assign its best priests to rural parishes and not use such parishes as training grounds or retirement homes.

• That the Church deal with the powerlessness of rural people by helping them understand corporate and tax structures, by working for responsible local government, and by remembering that rural people suffer from the same problems as urban people.

• That Church become involved with the problems of native Americans, especially in the areas of alcoholism, drugs, unemployment and school dropouts.

• That religious education materials be designed for the community using them, and not follow only a white, suburban-dweller approach.

• That the Church productively use land it owns on Indian reservations.

• That the Church remember middle-class Americans and their concern for family structures and moral values.

• That the Church exercise responsibility for moral concerns in its investment policies and practices.

Atlanta, Aug. 7 to 9: The overwhelming cry from witnesses was for Church support for the family and its members: more personal concern and understanding from bishops, priests and religious, and educational and supportive services from the institution. Some spoke for the rural poor of Appalachia, noting the debilitating effects of poverty and illness on family life. They urged the bishops to support unionization efforts and endeavors for healthier working conditions among sugar cane workers, migrant farmworkers, coal miners and textile workers.

Others addressed themselves to pressures against middle-class families trying to maintain Christian lifestyles in the face of changing values and social conditions.

The Church was urged to:

• Educate and lobby for respect for life at all stages.

• Support alternatives to abortion.

• Help find new alternatives to promote the dignity of the aging.

• Provide pastoral care for the mentally retarded.

• Begin programs to meet the needs of divorced Catholics.

• Respect and promote the equality of women.

• Turn parishes into centers for nurturing family life and sound values.

Sacramento, Oct. 2 to 4: Justice in the world of work was the theme, with emphasis on unions, the impact of economic and social policies on employment, farmworkers, and the employment and labor policies of the Church.

A sixth regional meeting was scheduled Dec. 4 to 6 in Newark, N.J.

A Prediction

Developments emerging from the first four hearings prompted a prediction that the year 1976 might mark a "new crossroads" for the social justice policy of the Church in the United States. Bishop James S. Rausch, general secretary of the U.S. Catholic Conference, told an NC News interviewer in Atlanta that the reason was the "Liberty and Justice for All" theme of the Catholic Bicentennial observance. He said:

"A number of bishops have told me that they are beginning to see this (program) as another 1919, a new crossroads in social action."

In 1919 the bishops issued a major document, "Bishops' Program of Social Reconstruction," which called for social policies considered revolutionary at the time, such as minimum wage laws and old age, health and unemployment insurance.

"Some of the items on that agenda were not realized in federal law until 1938, '39 or '40," Bishop Rausch added.

According to many observers, a great deal of the Church's social policy in this country today can be recognized as having its origins in the bishops' 1919 statement. Some of the leading social actionists in the U.S. Church still speak fondly of Msgr. John A. Ryan, architect of the 1919 policy, as their chief mentor and inspiration.

At the San Antonio hearing, the bishop said he thought the regional process was "basically very sound and a sign of hope to people," but added: "We still have not found a way to get a true cross-section of opinion. This to me proves that the local hearings, at the parish and diocesan level, are critical to the success of the whole undertaking."

Controversy about the Program

Not long after its publication, the "Liberty and Justice for All" discussion guide and its approaches to various subjects became items of debate.

"Perhaps in part because of its very size and avowed scope," said Jesuit Father Donald R. Campion, editor-in-chief of the national Jesuit weekly, *America*, " 'Liberty and Justice for All' has drawn more public criticism from more sources than any other episcopal initiative since the publication in 1919 of the 'socialistic' U.S. Bishops' Program of Social Reconstruction."

Also under attack were six regional hearings scheduled by the NCCB Bicentennial Committee around the country in 1975.

Greeley Criticism

One of the chief antagonists in the debate was Father Andrew Greeley, Chicago priest-sociologist. In the Feb. 7 issue of the *National Catholic Reporter,* he charged that the discussion guide and the whole consultation process was an exercise in "liberal and radical chic" dominated by a "rigidly anti-American" elite of "new social actionists" who found nothing good in the American democratic experiment. His contention was that the booklet was so filled with new-left liberation theology and "consciousness-raising" confrontation techniques that it would stifle discussion because most Catholics would be turned off from the start.

Other Views

Among other contributions to the debate:

• The Apr. 19 issue of *America* was devoted to the Catholic Bicentennial program, with articles pro and con.

• Dale Francis, executive editor of the news edition of the national weekly, *Our Sunday Visitor,* asked apropos of the guide and hearings: "Is slam Uncle Sam going to be the only game played at the party?"

• Msgr. George Higgins, secretary for research, U.S. Catholic Conference, denied that the program was an unqualified success and admitted that many of Father Greeley's criticisms were "valid up to a point." He charged him, however, with "polemical over-kill" and argued that the process of consultation was "an important step in the right direction."

Msgr. Higgins' views seemed to coincide with those of most of the officials involved in the program.

Dr. Francis Butler, executive director of the Bicentennial Committee staff, conceded that the early hearings were less successful than they could have been. He admitted that at the first hearing in Washington, D.C., the committee tried to schedule too many witnesses, left too little time for question-and-answer sessions, and did not get enough input from the local community. At the second hearing, in San Antonio, the format was better and the input from the local community was far better.

Dale Francis told NC News his reaction to the process was mixed, but said he felt there was a "sense of negativism" in the program that was not in keeping with the total celebration. Such a celebration should begin, he said, with "some sense of gratitude for what has been done in the past . . . gratitude to those Americans who have come before us, those men and women who gave us a precious heritage."

Religious educator Father Alfred McBrien saw "a healthy development" in the debate.

"Heretofore," he wrote, "the Catholic social action movement has been subject only to predictable criticism from the far right. For the first time, observers of a more moderately conservative, and even moderately liberal, point of view are raising challenging questions about the presuppositions, methods and range of certain social activists."

James Finn, editor of *Worldview* magazine and a consultor to the Bishops' Bicentennial Committee, credited Father Greeley's criticisms with "spreading the word and raising the issues" about the "Liberty and Justice for All" program. He suggested that it may be precisely the debate over Catholic social action that would be a significant contribution of the program.

Father Greeley said his widely publicized criticisms were meant "to express my own opinions" and not to start the debate. "But, if Mr. Finn's evaluation is correct, I'm pleased," he said.

Other Developments

Remote preparations for the celebration of the Bicentennial on a national scale dated back some 10 years at an expense of approximately $41 million appropriated as seed money by the Congress.

As events developed, however, there was no organization of a program by the federal government. People of Philadelphia, where Centennial and Sesqui-Centennial celebrations were centered in 1876 and 1926, turned back attempts to repeat the performance in 1976. There seemed to be no will for any kind of massive, single-event commemorating the Bicentennial.

Observers said Bicentennial celebrations were consisting of do-it-yourself projects by state and local communities, and organizations.

The American Revolutionary Bicentennial Administration was headed by John W. Warner. It had counterparts in many states where, as noted, services were rendered but commemorations were by local option.

Celebrations began in the spring of 1975 with reenactments in New England of early episodes of the Revolutionary War. New York touched off a 10-day inauguration of an 18-month program on May 22. Numerous other programs were in process or progress by July in 4,800 communities throughout the country.

A general lack of appreciation for the role of religion appeared to be the reason why the Freedom Train did not have a single item of religious significance among its 500 exhibits.

THE 41st INTERNATIONAL EUCHARISTIC CONGRESS

The 41st International Eucharistic Congress to be held Aug. 1 to 8, 1976, in Philadelphia promises to be "a milestone in the history of the Church in the United States," according to Cardinal John J. Krol of the host city. It will be the second assembly of its kind in this country and may prove to be one of the greatest in the 94-year history of such congresses.

Theme

The theme of the congress is "The Hungers of the Human Family." These hungers — for God, food, freedom and justice, love, truth, understanding, peace, and Jesus, the bread of life — will be the successive subjects of liturgical, devotional, inspirational and educational attention during the eight days of the congress. The symbol of the congress is a portrayal of two hands holding the Eucharistic host.

Events in line with the theme will include large and small gatherings for liturgical celebrations and devotional practices, lectures and discussions, displays and exhibits, and special programs for particular interest groups among the clergy, religious and all segments of the laity.

The congress is being funded by the National Conference of Catholic Bishops, foundations and private contributions.

If attendance matches estimates, it will surpass the 1.5 million figure set at Melbourne in 1973.

Purpose

Father Walter J. Conway of Philadelphia, executive secretary for the congress, said of its purpose in March, 1975:

"We plan to focus on deepening faith in, love for and devotion to Jesus Christ in the Eucharist, and to center these deepened qualities in a response to the religious and social needs of the local and universal Church. . . . Because we'll be running parallel with the Bicentennial of our nation, we want to make people aware of the need for giving thanks to God for the freedom to practice our faith, as well as the need to revivify our faith at this period of our nation's history. . . .

"This is a unique opportunity for people to give of their time, talent and energy to contribute to the success of the 41st International Eucharistic Congress and to share in this time of faith and grace by communicating the Good News to our nation and to the world. It is an opportunity which will probably never come again in the lifetime of most of us; I only hope that its spiritual renewal will be felt long after it has ended."

Statement of Pope Paul

Pope Paul, speaking of the congress and its theme, told a general audience Mar. 26:

"From many parts of the world men and women will assemble to honor the mystery of Christ in his Eucharistic sacrifice and presence, and to proclaim his lordship. At the same time they will open their hearts with new sensitivity and fresh concern to the many urgent needs of their brethren — the just aspirations and legitimate anxieties of mankind. And to all these hungers of the human family, the Eucharistic Congress will offer, with confidence and living faith, the only — the perfect — solution: Jesus himself, who said: 'I am the bread of life. He who comes to me will never be hungry and he who believes in me will never thirst' (Jn. 6:35)."

Archbishop Joseph L. Bernardin, president of the National Conference of Catholic Bishops, said that the congress theme "dramatizes in an apt way the Church's continuing concern for the Christianization of human life in all its dimensions, both spiritual and material."

Preparations

The unanimous decision of the National Conference of Catholic Bishops in November, 1973, to sponsor the congress was approved several months later by Pope Paul and the Permanent Committee for International Eucharistic Congresses. Cardinal Krol was named head of an eight-member committee on remote preparations.

In subsequent developments, a 42-member panel for general planning was set up and specific planning was handed over to 10 committees staffed by some 400 priests, religious and lay persons. The committee assignments were for program, physical preparation and sites, liturgy, communications, finances, hospitality, transportation, services, participation of other Christian churches, spiritual renewal and preparation.

Spiritual Renewal Program

The ultimate success of the congress depends largely on the response by Catholics, especially in this country, to a spiritual renewal and preparation program announced June 2, 1975, by Auxiliary Bishop Eugene Marino of Washington, D.C. The features of the program, to begin during Advent, 1975, are:

• Liturgy, with a series of Masses, devotional programs and related celebrations, along with sermons on the theme of the congress during Advent, 1975, and Lent, 1976, and a special liturgy on July 4, 1976.

• Catechetics, emphasizing instruction and inspirational experience for deepening understanding and appreciation of the Eucharist, by means of workshops, seminars, radio and television shows, and Catholic youth projects.

• Apostolates, to manifest concern for easing the spiritual hungers of the human family through sharing faith in Christ by such means as visitations of the sick, the elderly and the unchurched.

• Social Concerns, with sharing projects such as Operation Rice Bowl (donating the savings from a lenten meal to feed the hungry) and Service in God's Name (a project in which young people pledge hours of service for the needy, visiting the sick and tutoring children).

Ecumenical Dimension

The ecumenical dimension which was a feature of the Melbourne congress in 1973 will also figure in the Philadelphia congress. Archbishop William W. Baum of Washington, D.C., is the chairman of a 45-member committee responsible for handling interfaith aspects of the congress.

The vice chairmen are the Rt. Rev. John M. Allin, presiding Episcopal bishop of the United States; the Rev. Dr. Robert J. Marshall, president of the Lutheran Church in America; and Archbishop Iakovos, primate of the Greek Orthodox Church in North and South America.

Character of Congresses

The character of congresses has developed in their 94 years of history. They were devotional from the beginning, and still remain so, with focus on the sacrifice of the Mass and practices connected with the doctrine of the Real Presence of Christ in the Blessed Sacrament. Later they were associated with important events in the host countries. In the most recent period these characteristics have been combined with emphasis on the Eucharist as the inspiration of social action and on the service role of the Church within itself and to society at large.

The first congress in the U.S. was held in Chicago in 1926, the year of the Sesquicentennial celebration of national independence. The Philadelphia congress will be a highlight of Catholic participation in the Bicentennial observance.

Paul VI, who attended the international congresses in Bombay in 1964 and in Bogota in 1968, was invited to the Philadelphia celebration. It was not known at the time of writing if he would attend.

(See Glossary entry, Eucharistic Congresses.)

Prayer of the Congress

The following prayer was approved by the Congregation for Divine Worship June 21, 1975, for the 41st International Eucharistic Congress.

Father in heaven
you have made us for yourself;
our hearts are restless until they rest in you.
Fulfill this longing through Jesus, the bread of life,
so that we may witness to him
who alone satisfies the hungers of the human family.
By the power of your Spirit
lead us to the heavenly table
where we may feast on the vision of your glory for ever and ever. Amen.

HOLY YEAR 1975

(See related Vatican entries in monthly News Events and the Holy Year item in Glossary.)

Holy Year 1975, nearing its conclusion at the time of writing, was the latest in a long line of Jubilee observances celebrated in the Church nearly every 25 years since 1300.

It was unique in several respects, because of the long time it had in public attention, the emphasis it placed on local observances prior to the Roman phase, and the vast throngs — officially reported to be about 2.5 million pilgrims by mid-July — it attracted to the memorials of the Apostles.

Most significant were its purposes of spiritual renewal and reconciliation,the hope of the future of the Church and society in general.

Pope Paul, with little formality, made the first announcement of the Holy Year during a general audience on May 9, 1973. A month later he set in motion an 18-month period of local observances in advance of and preparation for the Roman phase of the celebration. He issued the formal bull of proclamation, *Apostolorum Limina* ("Memorials of the Apostles") for the Roman observance on May 23, 1974. The following Dec. 24 he ushered in this phase with the opening of the Holy Door in St. Peter's Basilica. He was prepared to close the same door on the celebration of the universal Church on Dec. 24, 1975.

During all this time, the Holy Father riveted attention on the Holy Year aims in numerous addresses, at general and private audiences for pilgrims of all nations and conditions of life, and people of all faiths. During the Roman phase of the celebration, he made himself even more visible than usual, increasing general audiences to two a week, taking part in more than the usual number of liturgical ceremonies, and taking advantage of every possible occasion, like his public recitation of the Angelus, to proclaim the message of renewal and reconciliation of people with God and with each other.

As people from all over the world moved in and about the Vatican in pilgrim fashion and for pilgrim purposes, Pope Paul presented his own "Spiritual and Pastoral Inventory of the Holy Year" in an address to members of the College of Cardinals on June 23, 1975. (Excerpts follow.)

For the first time in history, thousands of Americans had the experience of being present in St. Peter's Square when one of their own, Mother Seton, was named a saint.

SPIRITUAL AND PASTORAL INVENTORY

Following are excerpts from an address by Pope Paul to members of the College of Cardinals on June 23, 1975, in which he presented his views on the state of the Church in the midst of the Holy Year.

The excerpts are from the text circulated by the NC Documentary Service, Origins, July 3, 1975 (Vol. 5, No. 6). Lead lines have been added.

Today's meeting comes at the central moment of the Holy Year. It is exactly six months tomorrow since Christmas Eve, when, with the trepidation of holy emotion and immersed in prayer, we opened the Holy Door. Millions of the faithful have already entered through this door, with this symbolic passage starting along the ways of conversion, of encounter with God and of love for the brethren.

Intense Spirituality: A current of intense spirituality pervades the world, and one would have to be blind not to recognize it. The Roman journey is only the final point in the itinerary which the individual local churches have embarked upon. It is the worthy and logical conclusion of the celebrations on the parochial, diocesan, national and community level in all the countries of the Catholic household. These have brought and are bringing here not formless masses or wandering tourists, but people who are praying and who are confronting even difficult sacrifices — financial sacrifices, sacrifices of time, adjustment, fatigue, etc. — having been drawn not by exterior appearances but by the solemn and austere call of these places and of the great themes of the Holy Year.

Simple Pilgrims: And what is most impressive is the fact that the majority are simple people. This fact characterizes this Holy Year more than those of the past.

Gratitude: We cannot but thank God from the depths of our heart for having also visibly accompanied with his grace such a vast movement of piety, prayer and penance. And we are moved by this massive response to the request we made to the people of God in the first announcement of the Holy Year on May 9, 1973, and which we repeated in the bull of indiction, *Apostolorum Limina,* of May 23, 1974, indicating that the heart of the Jubilee celebrations consisted in renewal and reconciliation.

Two Themes: "The aspirations," we wrote, "that the two themes enunciated . . . will find a more complete realization in Rome, where the pilgrims to the tombs of the Apostles Peter and Paul and to the memorials of the other martyrs will come into more ready contact with the ancient sources of the Church's faith and life, in order to be converted by repentance, strengthened in charity and united more closely with their brethren by the grace of God. This renewal and reconciliation

pertain in the first place to the interior life, above all because the root of all good and, unfortunately, of all evil, is found in the depths of the heart. It is in the depths of the heart therefore that conversion must take place. . . ."

Plea for Reconciliation: We say . . . with the deepest regret that some of our sons and daughters (we shall always consider them in this way) persist in positions which are positions of doctrinal uncertainty, when they are not positions of destructive criticism, hostile diffidence or connivance with ideologies that are opposed to the Gospel and to the Church. To them once again and always goes our invitation . . . that they may "not wish to deprive us and themselves of the joy of new fraternal peace. Our arms are open, and our heart even more so. . . .

Response to the Holy Year Call: The call which we launched for renewal and reconciliation was received by the various local churches with an intense sharing in reflection and coresponsibility, the fruits of which are being gathered in the conclusive phase of the pilgrimage — the culmination and crowning of all the vast initiatives undertaken within the entire ecclesial community. If such consoling fruits are being gathered, and daily experience gives us the confirmation of this here in Rome, . . . it is, thank God, precisely because the local churches with marvelous and silent impulse have been able to prepare themselves over more than a year for the grace of the Jubilee by means of their own celebrations.

Significance of a Pilgrim Visit: The bishops, clergy, religious and laity have immediately understood that coming to Rome should not constitute a sporadic deed, a more or less pious distraction, or much less a "magic" act which, when performed, would set in motion — permit us to make mention of a well-known mysterious mechanism of the indulgence. Rather, the pilgrimage to the tombs of the Apostles has been prepared by a vast current of interior life and of prayer, and by an invitation to conversion in our relationship with God and with our brethren. This invitation has made it possible to understand thoroughly that "vertical dimension of life," which in the bull *Apostolorum Limina* we hoped would be intimately connected with the message of the Holy Year to ensure "the reference of all aspirations and experiences to an absolute and truly universal value. . . ."

The Future: We cannot but turn our thoughts to what still awaits us in the coming months and which will be ever more filled with deep enrichment and spiritual encounters. But we are thinking also of what is to come after the Holy Year.

In fact this current of renewal and reconciliation certainly cannot stop with the closing of the Holy Door next Christmas, when the 1975 Jubilee will be concluded. Nor can the vast spiritual movement which it has brought about be lulled until the next Jubilee.

From 1950 until today the hand of God has guided the Church through memorable events, extraordinary experiences, shining joys, and arduous and purifying tests. And today the Church is alive; despite all contrary appearances, the Church is united: the Church is and remains the yeast in the dough (cf. Mt. 13:33), the signal among nations (cf. Is. 5:26).

New Horizons: The horizon which is unfolding for these next twenty-five years is making ready for the Church new fields of apostolate, new encounters with the world that she is called to save, new purifications, in the ever-operative mystery of the cross. We are certainly not stopping here. We are open, we are available, although with the consciousness of our human limitations, to the work which the blessed Trinity wishes to continue, making use of our humble means which are without demure, without indolence, without fear.

A new era is unfolding, of faithfulness to the Holy Spirit, of love of the crucified Christ, of dedication to the brethren, of the building up of a more human and more just society. We do not want to lag behind. Forward, in the name of the Lord!

Beatifications, Canonizations

Pope Paul said in his reflections on the Holy Year that "we still recall with emotion" the beatification and canonization of Servants of God during the Jubilee. They were as follows.

Beatifications: Marie Eugenie Millaret de Brou (d. 1898), foundress of the Sisters of the Assumption, Feb. 9; Cesar de Bus (1544-1607), founder of the Fathers of Christian Doctrine, Apr. 27; Charles Steeb (1773-1856), founder of the Institute of the Sisters of Mercy, July 6; and on Oct. 19 — Arnold Janssen (1837-1909), founder of the Society of the Divine Word; John Freinademetz, an early member of that society; Charles Joseph de Mazenod (1782-1861), founder of the Oblates of Mary Immaculate; Maria Teresa Ledochowska (1863-1922), foundress of the Sodality (Sisters) of St. Peter Claver for African missions.

Canonizations: Juan Bautista de la Concepcion (d. 1613), reformer of the Trinitarian Order, and Vicenza Maria Lopez y Vicuna (d. 1890), foundress of the Religious of Mary Immaculate, May 25; Elizabeth Ann Bayley Seton (1774-1821), the first native-born American saint, foundress of the Sisters of Charity of St. Joseph, Sept. 14; John de Massias (1585-1645), Dominican brother and friend of St. Martin de Porres, Sept. 28; Oliver Plunkett (1629-1681), primate of Ireland, martyr, the first Irish saint canonized since the Middle Ages, Oct. 12; Justin de Jacobis (1800-1860), Italian missionary bishop in Ethiopia, Oct. 26.

ASSIMILATION OF VATICAN II

The Second Vatican Council still has not sufficiently penetrated the Church's life, according to Archbishop Jerome Hamer, O.P., secretary of the Congregation for the Doctrine of the Faith.

"I often express the need we should all feel to assimilate much better than we have the principles of the Second Vatican Council," he said in an October, 1975, interview with *The Mirror,* the Springfield-Cape Girardeau diocesan newspaper.

More Penetration Needed

"I have the impression that the Vatican Council still has not entered — not enough — still has not penetrated the fabric, the living tissue, shall we say, of the Church's life. The assimilation of the principles put forth by Vatican II is most important."

Describing changes he observed in the Church, he said: "As a Church, we are now more sensitive to the social dimensions of the Gospel. We can perhaps perceive the Church more in terms of a living community, in some ways in which we did not before — at least not as consciously."

He added: "We search, of course, always for further means to express this reality. There is a certain 'crisis of faith,' certain difficulties, with which we must contend, continue to study, continue to try to resolve. The atmosphere in which we live challenges us in the further study of our faith and the living of that faith."

Archbishop Hamer was in the United States on a personal, unofficial visit and for informal meetings with a group of bishops to discuss the life of the Church today, with emphasis on questions relating to the pastoral ministry.

Subjects of Discussion

"We talked about Catholic identity, about priestly identity and ministry, problems of pastoral ministry to divorced Catholics, problems affecting religious communities, signs of renewal in the Church; prayer, community experiences; collegiality and co-responsibility; the opportunities, the challenges. We talked about the teaching role and the responsibility of the local bishop to teach, clearly, the faith, as well as the collegial responsibility — that of the college of bishops as a body. We also spoke of our responsibility to the unchurched.

"We know that the Church faces somewhat the same problems the world over, but it was interesting and encouraging for me to see the vigor with which these problems are met by the bishops in the United States, to see how they try to solve them."

SAINT ELIZABETH ANN BAYLEY SETON

"We are happy to present to the world, which celebrates this year as Woman's Year, the image of Saint Elizabeth Seton — most unique in her religious feeling, most refined in personal virtue. She was a silent and intrepid promoter of works of social providence. She is a stimulating example and a protector of modern woman."

So stated Pope Paul VI in his *Angelus* talk Sunday, Sept. 14, 1975. Earlier that day he had proclaimed Elizabeth Ann Bayley Seton — wife, mother, widow, convert and foundress of a religious community — America's first native-born saint.

The canonization ceremonies took place in St. Peter's Square before an estimated crowd of 120,000, including 15,000 Americans.

Present also was an official delegation of Anglican clergymen headed by Bishop J. Stewart Wetmore, suffragan bishop of the Episcopal Diocese of New York.

In his canonization homily (see separate entry) Pope Paul praised Mother Seton's Anglican background for "having awakened and fostered the religious sentiment" that showed itself early in her life.

The day was officially designated "Woman's Day" in the Holy Year by the Vatican. In the United States, it was declared "National Saint Elizabeth Seton Day" by proclamation of President Gerald R. Ford, in accordance with a joint resolution of the Congress.

Canonization Process

The canonization climaxed a process begun in 1882 by Cardinal James Gibbons, archbishop of Baltimore, who authorized an investigation of her life and writings. The cause was formally introduced in 1940. She was beatified Mar. 17, 1963, by Pope John XXIII, and was "inscribed in the Catalogue of Saints" in the infallible decree of canonization by Pope Paul VI Sept. 14, 1975.

Biography

Elizabeth Ann Bayley was born Aug. 28, 1774, in New York, the second of the three daughters of Dr. Richard and Catherine Charlton Bayley. Her parents, of mixed French and English ancestry, were members of the Episcopal Church. Her mother died when Elizabeth was three. In 1778, her father married Charlotte Amelia Barclay whose grandfather was Jacobus Roosevelt, founder of the Roosevelt family in America.

On Jan. 24, 1794, Elizabeth married William Magee Seton, son of a wealthy importer. The couple had five children: Anna Maria, 1795-1812; William III, 1796-1868 (father of Archbishop Robert Seton); Richard, 1798-1823; Catherine, 1800-1891 (the first American postulant of the Sisters of Mercy); and Rebecca, 1802-1816. The young wife also took over the care of her husband's brothers

and sisters after her father-in-law's death in 1798.

Business failure forced William Seton to declare bankruptcy in 1799. In the spring of 1801, the family moved to 8 State Street, near Battery Park. The site of this last residence of William and Elizabeth Seton in New York now houses a shrine dedicated to the saint within the Chapel of Our Lady of the Rosary.

Death of Her Husband

By 1803 the effect of financial disaster and a recurrence of tuberculosis resulted in an alarming deterioration of William Seton's health. In October, following a physician's recommendations, the couple and their eldest daughter, Anna Maria, sailed for Leghorn (Livorno), Italy, where the Filicchis, friends and business associates, had offered them hospitality. William Seton died Dec. 27, 1803, at the Filicchi home. He was buried in the English cemetery at Leghorn. At 29, Elizabeth was a widow.

Elizabeth and Anna Maria stayed with the Filicchi family until April, 1804. The devout and practical Catholicism of the Filicchis impressed Mother Seton. "My conversion," she was to say later, "is due to the fact that I visited a Catholic country."

Conversion

She began learning about Catholicism in Italy and continued on her return to New York. She was received into the Catholic Church Mar. 14, 1805, by Father Matthew O'Brien, pastor of St. Peter's Church, Barclay Street.

Her attempts to open a school in New York met with failure because of the antagonism of family and friends after her conversion.

Educator, Religious

In 1807, Father William DuBourg, superior of the Sulpicians in Baltimore, Md., invited her to found a school near St. Mary's Seminary on Paca Street. She was joined there by several other women, and the formation of a new religious community began. Father Dubourg and Archbishop John Carroll of Baltimore approved her plans. Archbishop Carroll received the profession of her first religious vows Mar. 25, 1809.

In June, 1809, with four members of her new community, her daughters and several pupils from the Paca Street school, Mother Seton moved to a site given them in Emmitsburg, Md., about fifty miles from Baltimore. The following year she established an academy for girls and a tuition-free neighborhood school, regarded as the forerunner of the Catholic parochial school system in the United States.

In 1812, the new community — known as

the Sisters of Charity of St. Joseph — received its official rule, a modification of the one given the first Sisters of Charity by St. Vincent de Paul in 1634.

Mother Seton trained teachers and prepared textbooks. Her schools were successful and the community grew. Its work expanded to meet the charitable needs of the areas where the members worked. Sisters were sent to Philadelphia in 1814 and to New York in 1817 to take charge of orphanages there.

Mother Seton's health declined after 1818. She died Jan. 4, 1821, at the age of 46.

The Sisters of Charity

At the time of her death, her community numbered fifty sisters, some of whom were working in Philadelphia, Boston, Baltimore and New York. It remained an American community until 1849 when it was formally aggregated to the Daughters of Charity of St. Vincent de Paul whose motherhouse was (and still is) in Paris. The Emmitsburg foundation now numbers more than 2,000 sisters in five provinces in the United States. Five other communities of Sisters of Charity — with a combined membership of more than 5,500 members — trace their origin to Mother Seton's foundation at Emmitsburg: the Sisters of Charity of St. Vincent de Paul, New York; Sisters of Charity of Cincinnati, Ohio; Sisters of Charity of St. Vincent de Paul of Halifax, Nova Scotia; Sisters of Charity of St. Elizabeth, Convent Station, N.J.; and the Sisters of Charity of Seton Hill, Greensburg, Pa.

The sisters are engaged in educational, hospital and social work.

Triumph of Charity

The triumph of charity is the great poem of Elizabeth Seton, Pope John XXIII said of her in 1959 when she was given the title of Venerable.

In 1971, at ceremonies marking the 150th anniversary of her birth, her biographer, Vincentian Father Joseph Dirvin, said Mother Seton had much to say to contemporary Catholics because "she was an American woman . . . who had the best of several worlds." She undertook no extraordinary ascetical practices and her charity was such as can be practiced in ordinary everyday living. Her life, he said, was characterized by a "tremendous obedience . . . to those she considered God's guides for her."

In an address Sept. 15, 1975, to U.S. cardinals, archbishops and bishops who had attended the canonization, Pope Paul said:

Her Challenge

"The example of Elizabeth Seton presents an ever urgent challenge to the entire Church of God, and in particular to her fellow citizens. We pray that the Church in the United States will indeed be faithful to her mission on behalf of those who endure suffering in various forms — spiritual and material poverty, sickness, loneliness, lack of understanding, deprivation of rights — on behalf of those on the margin of society, those without hope."

MIRACLES

In the course of the beatification process of Mother Seton, two cures attributed to her intercession were declared miraculous Dec. 14, 1961.

• Sister Gertrude Korzendorfer, American Daughter of Charity, at Hotel Dieu, New Orleans, was cured of a malignant tumor on the pancreas so advanced at the time of its diagnosis in 1935 that it was inoperable. Within two days after members of her community began a novena to Mother Seton, an improvement in her condition was noted. Two months after the diagnosis, she was able to resume her position as administrator of a 250-bed hospital. When she died in 1942 of a pulmonary embolism, an autopsy was performed; no trace of the original tumor was found. Even the scar in the pancreas, where the tumor had been, was not apparent. The pathologist reported that, "from the medical standpoint this is a clear-cut case of complete and spontaneous cure of cancer at the head of the pancreas."

• Anne Theresa O'Neill (now Mrs. Anne Hooe) was cured of acute leukemia (lymphatic type). She was admitted to St. Agnes Hospital, Baltimore, in February, 1952, when she was four years old. Her condition was diagnosed as acute leukemia. She was transferred to University Hospital in the care of Dr. Milton Sacks, a leading expert on leukemia. She did not respond to treatment and was discharged as incurable in late March, 1952. Her condition continued to worsen and she was readmitted to St. Agnes Hospital in critical condition. The sister-supervisor of the pediatric ward persuaded the child's mother to place Anne's case in the hands of Mother Seton. A campaign of prayer was begun. Anne began to show improvement and in late April, 1952, was released from the hospital with a good report. She attended the beatification in 1963. She took part in the offertory procession at the Mass accompanying the canonization.

During the final canonization process, the following cure attributed to the intercession of Mother Seton was declared miraculous Dec. 12, 1974. At the same time Pope Paul dispensed with the customary requirement of two miracles following beatification as a prerequisite for canonization.

Carl Eric Kalin, 61 at the time, Protestant husband of a Catholic wife, was cured of meningoencephalitis complicated by primary rubeolo (red measles) in October, 1963. He was admitted to St. Joseph's Hospital, Yonkers, N.Y., Oct. 9, 1963. He lapsed into a coma and the prognosis was that he could not survive the rare illness. At the request of Mrs.

Kalin and the nun in charge of the case, a novena to Mother Seton was started at the Motherhouse of the Sisters of Charity of St. Vincent de Paul. A relic of Blessed Ann Seton was applied, and by mid-day of October 11 Mr. Kalin regained consciousness and was on his way to recovery. He was received into the Catholic Church in December, 1974, in Florida where he lives in active retirement. He attended the canonization.

NEW YORK CEREMONY

New York City Episcopalians marked the canonization of St. Elizabeth Seton by opening their doors for ecumenical services at Trinity Church, Manhattan, where she was a communicant before becoming a Catholic, and in two other churches, one in Brooklyn and one in Queens. At Trinity, the event was a joint celebration of the Rome canonization ceremony and of the 200th anniversary of the birth of Episcopal Bishop John Henry Hobart, who was her spiritual counselor.

Msgr. Myles M. Bourke, who preached, said that it was Hobart's "own devotion to the Eucharist that was communicated to Elizabeth" and that eventually resulted in her becoming a Catholic.

CANONIZATION HOMILY

Following is the text of Pope Paul's English-language homily at the canonization of St. Elizabeth Seton Sept. 14, 1975, in St. Peter's Square.

Yes, venerable brothers and beloved sons and daughters, Elizabeth Ann Seton is a saint.

We rejoice and we are deeply moved that our apostolic ministry authorizes to make this solemn declaration before all of you here present, before the holy Catholic Church, before the entire American people, and before all humanity. Elizabeth Ann Bayley Seton is a saint.

She is the first daughter of the United States of America to be glorified with this incomparable attribute.

Meaning of Being a Saint

But what do we mean when we say: "She is a saint"?

We all have some idea of the meaning of this highest title, but it is still difficult for us to make an exact analysis of it.

Being a saint means being perfect, with a perfection that attains the highest level that a human being can reach. A saint is a human creature fully conformed to the will of God. A saint is a person in whom all sin — the principle of death — is canceled out and replaced by the living splendor of divine grace.

The analysis of the concept of sanctity brings us to recognize in a soul the mingling of two elements that are entirely different but which come together to produce a single effect: sanctity.

One of these elements is the human and moral element, raised to the degree of heroism; heroic virtues are always required by the Church for the recognition of a person's sanctity.

The second element is the mystical element, which expresses the measure and form of divine action in the person chosen by God to realize in herself — always in an original way — the image of Christ (cf. Rom. 8:29).

The science of sanctity is therefore the most interesting, the most varied, the most surprising and the most fascinating of all the studies of that ever mysterious being which is man.

The Church has made this study of the life, that is, the interior and exterior history, of Elizabeth Ann Seton. And the Church has exulted with admiration and joy, and has today heard her own charism of truth poured out in the exclamation that we send up to God and announce to the world: She is a saint.

To Know and Imitate

We shall not now give a panegyric, that is, the narrative which glorifies the new saint. You already know her life and you will certainly study it further. This will be one of the most valuable fruits of the canonization of the new saint: to know her in order to admire in her an outstanding human figure, in order to praise God who is wonderful in his saints, to imitate her example — which this ceremony places in a light that will give perennial edification — to invoke her protection, now that we have the certitude of her participation in the exchange of heavenly life in the Mystical Body of Christ, which we call the communion of saints and in which we also share, although still belonging to life on earth.

We shall not, therefore, speak of the life of our St. Elizabeth Ann Seton. This is neither the time nor the place for a fitting commemoration of her.

But at least let us mention the chapters in which such a commemoration should be woven.

An American Saint

St. Elizabeth Ann Seton is an American. All of us say this with spiritual joy and with the intention of honoring the land and the nation from which she marvelously sprang forth as the first flower in the calendar of the saints. This is the title which, in his original foreword to the excellent work of (Vincentian) Father (Joseph) Dirvin, the late Cardinal (Francis) Spellman, archbishop of New York, attributed to her as primary and characteristic: "Elizabeth Ann Seton was wholly American." Rejoice, we say to the great nation of the United States of America. Rejoice for your glorious daughter. Be proud of her. And know how to preserve her fruitful heritage. This most beautiful figure of a holy woman presents to the world and to history the affirmation of new and authentic riches that are yours: that religious spirituality which your temporal prosperity seemed to obscure and almost make impossible. Your land too, America, is indeed worthy of receiving into its fertile ground the seed of evangelical holiness. And here is a splendid proof — among many others — of this fact.

May you always be able to cultivate the genuine fruitfulness of evangelical holiness, and ever experience how — far from stunting the flourishing development of your economic, cultural and civic vitality — it will be in its own way the unfailing safeguard of that vitality.

Episcopalian Background

St. Elizabeth Ann Seton was born, brought up and educated in New York and the Episcopalian communion. To this church goes the merit of having awakened and fostered the religious sense and Christian sentiment which in the young Elizabeth were naturally predisposed to the most spontaneous and lively manifestations. We willingly recognize this merit; and, knowing well how much it cost Elizabeth to pass over to the Catholic Church, we admire her courage for adhering to the religious truth and divine reality which were manifested to her therein. And we are likewise pleased to see that from this same adherence to the Catholic Church she experienced great peace and security, and found it natural to preserve all the good things which her membership in the fervent Episcopalian community had taught her, in so many beautiful expressions, especially of religious piety, and that she was always faithful in her esteem and affection for those from whom her Catholic profession had sadly separated her. For us, it is a motive of hope and a presage of ever better ecumenical relations to note the presence at this ceremony of distinguished Episcopal dignitaries, to whom — interpreting, as it were, the heartfelt sentiments of the new saint — we extend our greeting of devotion and good wishes.

Mother and Foundress

And then we must note that Elizabeth Seton was the mother of a family and at the same time the foundress of the first religious congregation of women in the United States. Although this social and ecclesial condition of hers is not unique or new (we may recall, for example, St. Birgitta, St. Frances of Rome, St. Jane Frances Fremiot de Chantal, St. Louise de Marillac), in a particular way it distinguishes St. Elizabeth Ann Bayley Seton for her complete femininity; so that, as we proclaim the supreme exaltation of a woman by the Catholic Church, we are pleased to note that this event coincides with an initiative of the United Nations' International Women's Year. This program aims at promoting an awareness of the obligation incumbent on all to recognize the true role of women in the world and to contribute to their authentic advancement in society. And we rejoice at the bond that is established between this program and today's canonization, as the Church renders the greatest honor possible to Elizabeth Ann Bayley Seton and extols her personal and extraordinary contribution as a woman — a wife, a mother, a widow, and a religious.

May the dynamism and authenticity of her life be an example in our day — and for generations to come — of what women can and must accomplish, in the fulfillment of their role, for the good of humanity.

And finally we must recall that the most notable characteristic of our saint is the fact that she was, as we said, the foundress of the first religious congregation of women in the United States. It was an offspring of the religious family of St. Vincent de Paul, which later divided into various autonomous branches — five principal ones — now spread throughout the world. And yet all of them recognize their origin in the first group, that of the Sisters of Charity of St. Joseph, personally established by St. Elizabeth Seton at Emmitsburg in the Archdiocese of Baltimore. The apostolate of helping the poor and the running of parochial schools in America had this humble, poor, courageous and glorious beginning.

This account, which constitutes the central nucleus of the earthly history and worldwide fame of the work of Mother Seton, would merit a more extended treatment. But we know that her spiritual daughters will take care to portray the work itself as it deserves.

"Be Children of the Church"

And, therefore, to these chosen daughters of the saint we direct our special and cordial greeting, with the hope that they may be enabled to be faithful to their providential and holy institution, that their fervor and their numbers may increase, in the constant conviction that they have chosen and followed a sublime vocation that is worthy of being served with the total gift of their heart, the total gift of their lives. And may they always be mindful of the final exhortation of their foundress saint — those words that she pronounced on her deathbed, like a heavenly testament, on January 2, 1821: "Be children of the Church." And we would add: "Forever."

And to all our beloved sons and daughters in the United States and throughout the entire Church of God, we offer, in the name of Christ, the glorious heritage of Elizabeth Ann Seton. It is above all an ecclesial heritage of strong faith and pure love for God and for others — faith and love that are nourished on the Eucharist and on the word of God. Yes, brethren, and sons and daughters: The Lord is indeed wonderful in his saints. Blessed be God forever.

WORLD CONFERENCE OF INTERNATIONAL WOMEN'S YEAR

This article is based primarily on an NC News story by Msgr. James T. McHugh, a member of the Vatican delegation to the conference.

Approximately 1,000 official delegates of 133 nations participated in the World Conference of the International Women's Year June 19 to July 2, 1975, in Mexico City.

The two weeks of discussion resulted in approval by consensus, but not unanimity, of a "World Plan of Action" affirming the equality of women and men and urging governments to action for appropriate reforms. Another product of the conference was a declaration on the claims of women in developing nations for social and economic justice and a new international order.

Spelling out specific rights and harmonizing the rights of women with those of men, children and society were beyond the reach of the conference.

From the standpoint of Third World nations, the conference was a launching pad for a new and organized effort to assert claims for a new worldwide economic order based on international justice. They had some success.

For those, primarily from Western nations, concerned with assuring equality of opportunity for women in all spheres of human endeavor, the achievements of the United Nations-sponsored conference were more limited.

So stated Msgr. James T. McHugh, director of the U.S. Bishops' Committee for Pro-Life Activities and a member of the Vatican delegation, in recapitulating accomplishments of the conference.

Vatican Participation

The Holy See participated actively in the conference, and a resolution on women and poverty, introduced by Mother Teresa of Calcutta as a member of the Holy See's delegation, was approved by the plenary committee. The resolution called on all women to join in solidarity with the poor of the world, and urged women enjoying at least some of the world's benefits and privileges to become "co-workers" with the poor.

Plan of Action

But, ultimately, the Holy See was unable to join the consensus in accepting the "Plan of Action." This was due to the introduction of a so-called principle stating: "Individuals and couples have the right freely and responsibly to determine the number and spacing of their children and to have the information and means to do so. The exercise of this right is basic to any real equality between the sexes, and without its achievement women are disadvantaged in their attempt to benefit from other reforms."

At first glance the proposal seemed moderate, but the discussion in the work group made it clear that the amendment was meant to establish that "individuals," married or unmarried, had the same right to decide on child-bearing and child-rearing that has commonly been accorded to married couples.

The Holy See rejected this proposal because it conflicted with the view of marriage as partnership and ignored the fact that responsible parenthood involves decision-making and mutual acceptance of responsibility by both partners.

Although the final formulation was accepted by the majority, a number of nations stated their opposition to any interpretation denying that the family is the basic social unit and that decisions concerning the size of the family or frequency of births belong to the couple.

The participating nations strongly emphasized that all recommendations of the conference would be subject to national laws and policies. The Holy See, however, saw these issues as matters of principle, and thus could not adopt a compromise position. While recognizing other positive achievements in the "Plan of Action," the Holy See could not join the majority in its favor.

Declaration of Mexico

Beyond the "Plan of Action" were the hidden agendas of individual nations and groups of nations. The best example was the "Declaration of Mexico," which was approved by a vote of 89 to 3, with 18 abstentions. Most of the abstentions, including those by the United States, Israel and Denmark, were made by Western nations.

The declaration was proposed by "Group 77," the majority of developing nations and correspondingly the majority of nations participating in the conference. This declaration was a manifesto of the claims of the Third World for social and economic justice and a new international order. It was carefully formulated, well managed, and supported by the majority. But it was also a point of confrontation between the developing nations and the western powers, and efforts by Great Britain, the United States and Western European nations to discuss the document or propose changes were completely ineffective.

Ultimate acceptance of the declaration by the overwhelming majority was an important assertion of self-identity for the developing nations, but the process created hostility and division among the participants.

Comment

The conference was called "an event of worldwide importance" and a "sign of the times" by the head of the Vatican delegation, Bishop Ramon Torrella Cascante. Writing in the July 21 edition of *L'Osservatore Romano*, he said:

"It is the Church's duty to examine it in order to perceive therein the call of the Lord. The International Women's Year is also a challenge to the Church, which must be present and active in the world, under the influence of the Spirit."

In an earlier broadcast on Vatican Radio, the bishop stated:

"The Holy See's contribution (to the conference) was, above all, a witness of solidarity toward this movement, these just aspirations of the promotion of womanhood and especially a solidarity with poor women. . . .

"Mother Teresa of Calcutta gave a living witness of this, and there was a proposal by the Holy See delegation under the heading, 'Women and Development.' Poverty and misery are obstacles to the development of women."

He described the Vatican's outstanding contribution as "that of being a universal voice, a voice above blocs, above ideology, a voice which was not neutral but prophetic, a voice of the Gospels."

Miss Rosemary Goldie, associate secretary of the Council for the Laity and a member of the Vatican delegation, said of the conference:

"Considering, as pointed out by the United Nations General Secretary, Mr. Kurt Waldheim, in his opening address, that the conference was dealing with the contribution of women to modern society in the light of the world's growing awareness of the interdependence of such major problems as food, population, environment, housing, health and education, the conference must be seen within the context of humanity's search for a better understanding of the complexities of modern society and of the long-term interests of the entire human family.

"There is little wonder that differences stood out more vividly than points of agreement. Nor is it surprising that national interests seemed to take precedence over the greater good of all.

"It is unrealistic to expect that the first U.N. World Conference in which women played such an important part would be able to achieve what all the previous work of the United Nations had not succeeded in accomplishing. At the same time, one should stress the quality of the many outstanding women who took part, many of whom already play an important role in their countries' national life."

Asked whether she considered the conference a failure, she replied:

"No. The great thing was the recognition that women can play a crucial role in reconsidering basic values and tracing new paths for the whole of society, as Mr. Waldheim pointed out, even though the conference fell far short of achieving full consensus on what

needs to be done and how to achieve it. And certainly it is encouraging that a demand for a second World Conference in 1980 was being made at its conclusion."

Msgr. McHugh, in concluding his report on the conference, said:

"Shortness of time, and incohesive agenda, and the preoccupation with development needs of the Third World partially explain the unfinished business of the conference. But it may also be that the full recognition of women's rights requires more of the working experience of equality between women and men that was proclaimed by the participating nations and was readily apparent in the work of the delegates at this conference."

EQUAL RIGHTS AMENDMENT

An Equal Rights Amendment to the U.S. Constitution was proposed to the states in 1972. It stipulates: "Equality of rights under the law shall not be abridged by the United States or by any state on account of sex."

Action by States

Thirty-four states ratified the amendment by the end of September, 1975. Four more ratifications by March, 1979, are required for adoption of the amendment.

It was voted down in a number of states, including Arizona, Georgia, Indiana, Missouri, Nevada, North Carolina, Oklahoma and Utah. Two states which ratified the amendment, Nebraska and Tennessee, were reported to be exploring the possibility of rescinding their action.

Popular Opinion

Popular opinion about the ERA was reflected in a 1975 Gallup Poll of 1,542 respondents. Fifty-eight per cent favored nondiscriminatory legislation with respect to sex, 24 per cent were opposed to the amendment, and 18 stated they had no opinion on the subject. Sixty-four per cent of the men and 54 per cent of the women polled favored adoption of the ERA.

Catholic Opinion Divided

The Catholic Church has taken no official position on the ERA, and it appeared unlikely that it would, according to Bishop Michael McAuliffe, chairman of the U.S. Bishops' Ad Hoc Committee on Women in Society and the Church.

Comments received by the committee, he said, indicated that the opinions of Catholics were "split down the middle." One evidence of this was a 20-to-20 vote by members of the Bishops' Advisory Committee with respect to ratification of the ERA.

For

Catholic support for the amendment has come from nuns' organization, a number of priests individually and in associations and senates, and lay women. Prominent in support are: the National Assembly of Women Religious, the Black Sisters' Conference, the American section of St. Joan's Alliance, a Cincinnati-based group called Catholic Women for the ERA, the Hispanic PADRES and Las Hermanas, and Network, an organization of nuns and others lobbying on issues of social justice.

Against

The most vocal Catholic opposition to the ERA has come from the National Council of Catholic Women and the Catholic Daughters of America. Their fear is that passage of the amendment would threaten family life and existing safeguards for women under law.

The national board of the Catholic Daughters of America reiterated its opposition to ratification in a statement released at a July 9 to 11, 1975, meeting in Houston. The statement said:

"The vague wording of the proposed 27th Amendment, which leaves it open to wide interpretation, would have a devastating effect on family unity. Equality of men and women can be found only in its essential foundation, which is the dignity of humans in their filial relationship to God. ... Our concern and that of all citizens should be in the effective and continued enforcement of the laws already enacted to provide equal rights for all persons."

It was reported that an unpublished critique of the ERA by the office of the General Counsel, U.S. Catholic Conference, claimed that much opposition to the ERA had no basis in fact — because interpretation would take place in the general context of constitutional rights.

It appeared that proponents of the ERA, against a background of discrimination against women in various areas, had confidence in the quality of such interpretation while those opposed did not.

1975 SISTERS' MEETINGS

Consortium: Auxiliary Bishop John Sherlock of London, Canada, urged 600 sisters attending the Apr. 4 to 6 third international assembly of the *Consortium Perfectae Caritatis* in Chicago not to give in to contemporary anti-institutional prejudice but to stay in their traditional apostolates of "health care, social welfare and education."

In his address, Bishop Sherlock rejected the argument that the increasing involvement of civil governments in the fields of health, education and welfare has made those areas unnecessary as religious apostolates.

"It may indeed be legitimate," he said, "to abandon works which were undertaken solely to fill a gap left solely by the impotence of civil authority, but surely it is rare that such works can be satisfactorily replaced by secular initiative. ..."

"Surely it is clear that, when the door of the last religious hospital closes on this continent, the last effective institutional health-care voice raised to defend the right to life of the unborn will be stilled. When that voice is stilled, then the assault will begin by the protagonists of euthanasia. Already they have identified the enemy" as the Catholic Church.

"Similarly," he continued, "the loss of schools which bear the name of Christ and strive to fashion men and women in his image is to weaken the witness of the Catholic community to the sovereignty of the spiritual dimension and destiny of man."

School Sisters of Notre Dame: Father Walter Burghardt, S.J., in an address before 1,000 School Sisters of Notre Dame meeting in Baltimore in August, spoke of the need for caution with respect to liberation movements. He said that "self-fullfillment can be perilously selfish," and that only love could harmonize liberation and reconciliation.

Noting that liberation can be a trap, Father Burghardt asserted: "You need freedom and equality to serve God and man. But focus not on what you are being freed from, but on what you are being freed for. The supreme test is service."

The great "danger in liberation movements is that I become the center of the universe," the Jesuit theologian said. "This makes for polarization. The Christian context of liberation, the human context, is not I, but others. ... Only by moving outside myself can I become a real person."

National Assembly of Women Religious: The National Assembly of Women Religious, meeting Aug. 7 to 10 in San Francisco, reemphasized its commitment to social justice and equal rights for women in the Church. Approximately 800 delegates representing a total membership of 3,500 called for:

• Including women in decision-making bodies at all levels of the Church,

• Affirmative action to equalize the involvement of women in theological education and research,

• Support for the ordination of women as deacons, priests, and bishops,

• Commitment to the passage of the Equal Rights Amendment,

• Support of the statement on equality of women in the Church by the caucus of Roman Catholic women religious at the International Women's Year tribune in Mexico City June 30,

• Solidarity with the women of the Pacific nations by supporting the terms of the Nuclear Free Pacific Conference to restrict nuclear explosions and testing in the Pacific,

• An end to colonialism, nuclear explosive devices and testings, and any functions which aid the performance of nuclear weapons delivery systems,

• Support for the bishops of the United States on the bicentennial theme of "Liberty and Justice for All," and involvement at the grassroots level,

• Support for the United Farm Workers of America and continuation of the boycott of grapes and lettuce not picked by the UFWA, and Gallo wine.

One convention speaker, Sister Margaret Foley. an associate professor of ethics at Yale Divinity School, said that sisters who are used "to fulfill the unmet needs of others through an enlightened commitment ought to demand justice for themselves, particularly in the area of Church ministry."

Sister Margaret told the sisters they should commit themselves to expand the role of women in the Church, "including ordination, in the future." (Such ordination, according to tradition and Pope Paul, is out of order.)

Sister Catherine Pinkerton, out-going president, told delegates of the NAWR's concern from the beginning "to evaluate whether or not the ministries in which they were engaged were answering the Gospel needs of the times. The movements toward diversity in ministry were not steps lightly taken or cases of advocating irresponsible freedom contrary to religious and congregational commitment. These claims came from a serious reading of the Gospel in the light of the times."

Leadership Conference of Women Religious: Some 600 administrators of 365 congregations of sisters in the U.S., meeting Aug. 24 to 28, in St. Paul, discussed some of the same topics considered at the earlier convention of the National Assembly of Women Religious. Social concerns were prominent. Ministry was the subject of several speeches but not of resolutions passed by those attending the meeting.

Ordination Conference

It was reported in September that more than 10 per cent of the women registering for a Nov. 28 to 30, 1975, convention in Detroit on "Women in Future Priesthood Now: A Call for Action," had declared their personal desire to be ordained to the priesthood. So stated publicity director Sister Patricia Hughes.

Sister Marilyn Seig, a coordinator of the conference, said:

"The conference will show how serious women are about the issue of ordination, and that these women are a force to be considered. The question of ordination of woman has surfaced as an honest question. It deserves reflective consideration and an honest answer." (Sister Marilyn failed to say that the question had been answered, in the negative but honestly, by Pope Paul in line with tradition — regarded along with Scripture as divine revelation. Not long after Sister Marilyn made her statement, Archbishop Joseph L. Bernardin gave the same kind of answer to the question.)

WOMEN NOT TO BE ORDAINED

Archbishop Joseph L. Bernardin, president of the National Conference of Catholic Bishops, issued the following statement regarding the ordination of women on Oct. 7, 1975. He was authorized to do so by the Administrative Board and the Executive Board of the conference.

The text was circulated by NC News Service.

The proclamation by the United Nations of 1975 as International Women's Year was welcomed by all. It has served as a catalyst for serious discussion and action on behalf of women within both the Church and society. When the Holy Father received Mrs. Helvi Sipila, general secretary of the International Women's Year, in November of last year, he stated that the designation of International Women's Year "does not find the Church inattentive to the problem or lacking in a clear desire to solve it. On the contrary; in the contemporary effort to promote the advancement of women in society, the Church has already recognized 'a sign of the times,' and has seen in it a call of the Spirit."

The Church owes women, both religious and lay, its own great debt of gratitude for their commitment and loving service. In a special way we must also be grateful to those who today manifest their loyalty and love by pressing the question of their role in the Church.

Both candor and a sense of responsibility impel me at this time to address a question which is in the minds of many people. Discussion of the possibility of ordaining women to the priesthood in the Roman Catholic Church is now a lively issue in the United States.

No Ordination of Women

Such discussion can contribute to a better understanding of ministry, priesthood and the role of women in the Church. But honesty and concern for the Catholic community, including those of its members who advocate the ordination of women, also require that Church leaders not seem to encourage unreasonable hopes and expectations, even by their silence. Therefore I am obliged to restate the Church's teaching that women are not to be ordained to the priesthood.

Serious Theological Obstacle

It is not correct to say that no serious theological obstacle stands in the way of ordaining women to the priesthood, and that the fact that women have not been ordained up to now can be explained simply by culturally conditioned notions of male superiority. There is a serious theological issue. Throughout its history the Catholic Church has not called women to the priesthood. Although many of the arguments presented in times gone by on this subject may not be defensible today, there are compelling reasons for this practice. In 1972 the NCCB Committee on Pastoral Research and Practices issued a report entitled "Theological Reflection on the Ordination of Women."

This report admitted that the question was complex and that there were many aspects to it which needed further study. The report, however, gave a very powerful reason for not ordaining women:

Strength of Tradition

"Revelation is made known to us from tradition as well as from Sacred Scripture (cf. *Constitution on Divine Revelation,* Nos. 8 to 10; Second Vatican Council). It is then necessary for theology in this question to look to the life and practice of the Spirit-guided Church. The constant practice and tradition of the Catholic Church has excluded women from the episcopal and priestly office. Theologians and canonists have been unanimous until modern times in considering this exclusion as absolute and of divine origin. Until recent times no theologian or canonist seemingly has judged this to be only of ecclesiastical law. It would be pointless to list the many authorities and the theological note that each assigns to this teaching. However, the constant tradition and practice of the Catholic Church against the ordination of women, interpreted (whenever interpreted) as of divine law, is of such a nature as to constitute a clear teaching of the ordinary magisterium of the Church. Though not formally defined, this is Catholic doctrine."

In commenting on this assertion, the bishops' committee went on to say:

Existing Discipline Stands

"(This reason) is of ponderous theological import. Its force will not be appreciated by those who look for Revelation and theology in Scripture alone, and who do not appreciate tradition as a source of theology. Because of (this reason) a negative answer to the possible ordination of women is indicated. The well-founded present discipline will continue to have and to hold the entire field unless and until a contrary theological development takes place, leading ultimately to a clarifying statement from the magisterium."

No Injustice

It would be a mistake, I believe, to reduce the question of the ordination of women to one of injustice, as is done at times. It would be correct to do this only if ordination were a God-given right of every individual; only if somehow one's human potential could not be fulfilled without it. In fact, however, no one, male or female, can claim a "right" to ordination. And, since the episcopal and priestly office is basically a ministry of service, ordination in no way "completes" one's humanity.

Feminine Equality and Dignity

It is true that the equality of women is an ideal which has yet to be fully realized in many fields, such as education, politics and employment. And it is not enough to show interest only in these areas of concern. To be faithful to the Spirit, who is at work among us, we must also address ourselves seriously to the question of women in the Church. As Pope Paul has said: "Although women do not receive the call to the apostolate of the Twelve and therefore to the ordained ministries, they are nonetheless invited to follow Christ as disciples and co-workers" (Statement to the Committee for International Women's Year, Apr. 18, 1975; *L'Osservatore Romano,* English edition, May 1, 1975).

Through educational efforts of the Church, we must make sure that people are truly convinced of woman's dignity and equality, an equality whose essential foundation, as the Holy Father has reminded us, is found in the "dignity of the human person, man and woman, in their filial relationship with God, of whom they are the visible image."

Contributions of Women

Women are called today to a greater leadership role in the Church; their contributions are needed in the decision-making process at the parochial, diocesan, national and universal levels. The Church has grown more aware of the variety of ministries open to women; in a very special way they are called to collaborate with all other segments of the Church in the essential work of evangelization. The Church will suffer, indeed it will be betrayed, if women are given only a secondary place in its life and mission.

Fortunately, progress is being made in all these fields and many others. More, however, needs to be done. While this is a task of the whole Church, bishops have a special pastoral responsibility in this regard. It is not enough to make statements; our statements must be matched by actions which will bring more women into the mainstream of the life of the local Church.

I know that many will welcome this statement. But many others will disagree with and be disturbed by what I have said with respect to the question of ordination. The important thing now is that we not engage in recriminations; that, instead, we approach one another with charity and mutual respect, constantly examining our own motives — not the motives of others — in order to be as certain as is humanly possible that we are indeed at all times seeking to know and do the will of Jesus Christ.

A CARDINAL'S VIEWS

The following article, with incidental changes, was written by NC News correspondent Jo-ann Price under date of Sept. 24, 1975.

Two Episcopal bishops who attended the canonization of St. Elizabeth Seton in Rome Sept. 14, 1975, reported to the Episcopal House of Bishops in Portland, Me., that their delegation had been told by Cardinal Jan Willebrands, president of the Vatican Secretariat for Promoting Christian Unity, that the issue of ordination of women to the priesthood created a "serious new element" of division in the international Anglican-Roman Catholic dialogue on the ministry.

But they said the cardinal forcefully denied reports, which circulated after his meeting with Anglican deans last April in Rome, that, if Anglicans ordained women, the on-going consultations of the Anglican-Roman Catholic International Commission would be terminated.

Significant Issue

In carefully worded documents on their audience with Pope Paul and the hour-and-20-minute session with the cardinal that followed, Bishops J. Stuart Wetmore of New York and David L. Leighton of Maryland disclosed that the cardinal said he had written to Anglican Archbishop Donald Coggan of Canterbury on the significance of ordination of women to ecumenical relations in general. They said the cardinal proposed an informal exchange of views by three theologians from each side.

They reported Cardinal Willebrands said that, if any section of the worldwide Anglican Communion proceeded to the ordination of women priests — such authorized ordinations were said to be expected by Easter, 1975, in the Anglican Church of Canada — this would create a "serious new element in the dialogue on the nature of ministry."

A Theological Matter

The bishops noted the cardinal said he felt the discussion should be approached at the theological level rather than on the cultural or social plane, or as a "matter of discipline," such as celibacy. He suggested that it was a question relating to apostolic tradition.

Cardinal Willebrands suggested that women's ordination should not be a result of sociological pressures related to women's rights movements, the bishops said.

"Why decide this now under all this pressure?" the cardinal asked the Episcopalians in reference to church-wide discussion of the issue as the Episcopal general convention in Minneapolis in September, 1976, approached. The cardinal also suggested to his visitors that bishops and deputies "should keep in mind the people of the other churches" when they come to vote on the issue.

Irresponsible Action

The bishops said Cardinal Willebrands ventured his "strong opinion" that "action to ordain by retired bishops was completely irresponsible."

During the session in Portland, the House of Bishops censured three of its members and decried the action of a fourth retired bishop for conducting unsanctioned ordinations of women priests.

Asked the extent to which pressure for ordaining women in the Roman Catholic Church was recognized, Cardinal Willebrands replied, the report said: "The Holy Father knows of the pressure and has the question under study."

Although there was evidence of "internal scriptural argument" against ordaining women, the document said, the cardinal was of the view that "anthropological arguments against ordination of women are weak and ought not to be pursued."

Other Subjects

Present with the two bishops at their meeting with the cardinal were the Rev. Robert Hunsicker, vicar of St. Paul's Chapel of Trinity Parish, New York, and American Jesuit Father John Long of the Vatican secretariat. The discussion, the bishops said, ranged in detail over the controversy in the Episcopal Church over the priestly ordination of 15 women by retired bishops in the past year and a half, in defiance of church authority. They said it also went into progress on agreed statements (Windsor and Canterbury) on the Eucharist and ministry developed by the international commission, study of the Roman Catholic position of the validity of Anglican orders (see separate entry), mutual recognition of baptism, and ecumenical experiments in the United States.

Speaking of the Anglican-Roman Catholic statements, the two bishops said Cardinal Willebrands believed there should be greater clarification in them regarding the sacrificial nature of the Eucharist and the sacramental nature of the priesthood.

The cardinal said that, if questions about the validity of Anglican orders had been reduced to "historical doubt," it would be easy to progress toward "the recognition of ministry."

The main unsettled question would then be "the priority of the bishop of Rome," the cardinal observed.

Bishop Wetmore, in presenting the documentation to the House of Bishops' meeting, recommended that "all possible opportunities" for top-level visits between Anglican and Roman Catholics be pursued. He asked that efforts be made to formulate a response to Cardinal Willebrands' opinions, to speed up study of Anglican orders, and to include St. Elizabeth Seton on the calendar of prayers of the Episcopal Church.

ANTI-ABORTION SET BACK

Spokesmen for the U.S. Bishops' Conference regarded the defeat of six proposed constitutional amendments to restrict abortion as a temporary setback in the continuing campaign to protect the life of the unborn.

The anti-abortion amendments were defeated Sept. 17, 1975, in the Senate subcommittee on constitutional amendments, chaired by Sen. Birch Bayh. Bayh said the amendments were probably dead for the current session of Congress.

Cardinal Terence Cooke of New York, chairman of the Bishops' Committee for Pro-Life Activities, called the subcommittee's action "disappointing," but said that "it is not the final word."

The cardinal went on to say that those who oppose abortion "will continue their efforts to secure full legal protection for the unborn."

Strategy Change?

There were indications that the bishops might change their strategy on constitutional amendments concerning abortion by favoring a modified state's-rights amendment such as the one offered by Sen. Quentin Burdick of North Dakota. The Bayh subcommittee voted 4-4 on the Burdick amendment, which would empower the states to "protect life, including the unborn, at all stages of biological development, irrespective of age, health or condition of physical dependency."

Burdick introduced his amendment at the request of the National Committee for a Human Life Amendment. William Cox, the committee's executive director, described the amendment as a "fallback position" or the "minimum acceptable language" that the committee could accept.

Cox said the committee, funded by individual contributions from U.S. bishops and others, would continue to press for an amendment that will define the unborn as legal persons from the point of conception or fertilization as its first choice.

Msgr. James T. McHugh, executive director of the Bishops' Pro-Life Activities Committee, said there would be a "complete reevaluation" of the Bayh Senate subcommittee vote and the amendments. He said his committee would take "a close look" at the Burdick amendment.

One source within the National Conference of Catholic Bishops said there was "a good chance, or at least a reasonable chance," that the bishops would support something close to the Burdick amendment.

Some NCCB sources said they believed the bishops could successfully support a so-called state's-rights amendment if it were made clear that they were doing so because it was the best they could hope for in a pluralistic society and within the framework of the Constitution.

HUMAN LIFE AMENDMENT

When the Senate subcommittee on constitutional amendments voted down several proposed anti-abortion amendments Sept. 17, 1975, the amendment that came closest to passage, on a 4-to-4 vote, was introduced by Sen. Quentin Burdick of North Dakota. It was introduced as the minimum acceptable at the request of the National Committee for a Human Life Amendment, sponsored by U.S. Catholic bishops. It was based on an amendment suggested by John Noonan, a professor of law at the University of California at Berkeley.

Noonan was one of the first to suggest amending the Constitution as a response to the Jan. 22, 1973, Supreme Court decisions which struck most state restrictions on abortion.

Following is Noonan's description of his amendment as it appeared in the Winter 1975 edition of the "Human Life Review," published by the Human Life Foundation.

Amendment XXVIII

The Congress within federal jurisdictions and the several States within their respective jurisdictions shall have power to protect life from the beginning of new life and at every stage of biological development irrespective of age, health, or condition of physical dependency.

What the Amendment Accomplishes

1. The Amendment negates the holdings of the Supreme Court of the United States in Roe v. Wade and Doe v. Bolton that the Constitution of the United States is violated by law which penalizes the killing of unborn life. Under the Amendment, Congress in all places particularly governed by federal law, and the States within their own borders, are empowered by the Constitution to protect life, born or unborn.

2. The Amendment negates the teaching of the Supreme Court in Roe v. Wade that life in the womb, prior to viability, is no more than "a theory of life," incapable of protection of law. Under the Amendment, Congress and the States within their respective jurisdictions may protect life from the beginning of new life.

3. The Amendment negates the teaching of the Supreme Court in Doe v. Bolton that the law must always prefer a physician's prescription for the well-being of a mother to the life itself of her child. Under the Amendment, the law may protect the child, although he or she is within the womb and physically dependent on the mother.

4. The Amendment negates the teaching of the Supreme Court in Roe v. Wade that "capability of meaningful life" is a criterion by which the protectability of life is to be determined. The Amendment assures that federal or state legislation protecting the life of the aged, the mentally-afflicted, or the chronical-

ly ill cannot be declared unconstitutional by application of such a criterion. Under the Amendment, life may be protected irrespective of the health, physical or psychological, of the life being protected.

Why the Amendment Does Not Attempt More

1. The Amendment does not make abortion murder. In Anglo-American legal tradition, discrimination has always been made between the crime of murder and the crime of abortion. No good reasons exist to end the traditional distinction.

2. The Amendment does not outlaw any particular acts of abortion. In the federal structure of the United States, it has been the responsibility of the States to design the protection of life within their borders, and the responsibility of Congress to protect life in federal areas. No good reason exists to alter the traditional allocation of responsibilities.

3. The Amendment does not mandate a particular or uniform degree, level, or kind of protection. A Constitution is not a criminal statute. If an Amendment is to act at a constitutional level, it is not the appropriate place to incorporate the detail and qualifications of a specific criminal law.

4. The Amendment does not make contraception an act which Congress or the States may prohibit under the Amendment; it does not overturn Griswold v. Connecticut. Contraception is directed to the prevention of life. The Amendment authorizes the law to act from the beginning of new life.

Advantages of the Amendment

The Amendment is modeled on the Sixteenth Amendment, overturning the decision of the Supreme Court in Pollock v. Farmers' Loan and Trust Company. The Amendment, therefore, conforms to an established pattern in which a decision of the Supreme Court is negated by Constitutional correction.

The Amendment is pro-life. Empowering the law to protect new life from the beginning, it creates the expectation that life will be protected.

The Amendment is pro-States' Rights. Restoring to the States the power taken from them by the Supreme Court, it gives the state legislatures the opportunity to shape the protection of life.

The Amendment is pro-people. Returning to the people what was taken from them by the decision of the Supreme Court, it gives the people power to safeguard the lives of future generations.

The Amendment is general enough to have the breadth, dignity, and freedom of detail appropriate for the Constitution.

The Amendment is specific enough to restore the protectability of life within the womb.

The Amendment is moderate enough not to permit *ad terrorem* arguments by advocates of abortion who will try to stretch the language of any proposed Amendment to make it appear mischievous or monstrous.

The Amendment is strong enough to withstand interpretation by a judiciary likely to be initially unsympathetic to its purpose.

The Amendment is conservative enough to satisfy not only the defenders of life but the proponents of States' Rights and the critics of judicial radicalism.

The Amendment is bold enough to win the enthusiasm of everyone dedicated to the elimination of the holdings and teachings of Roe v. Wade and Doe v. Bolton.

DEVELOPMENTS IN 1975

The trend of judicial decisions with respect to abortion was toward the elimination of all restrictions except those stated in the Jan. 22, 1973, decisions of the Supreme Court; toward authorization for payment from public funds for abortions, and toward canonization of the principle of absolutely private right to abortion on the part of women even of minority status.

Representative decisions were the following.

The Supreme Court:

• Refused to review a lower court ruling that a Minnesota law restricting the performance of abortions was unconstitutional, in January.

• Let stand a circuit court ruling that struck down a series of Chicago Board of Health regulations (regarding equipment, sanitation, procedures) for abortions during the first three months of pregnancy, in March.

Lower Courts:

• Ruled unconstitutional the policy of St. Louis in refusing abortions at the city's two municipal hospitals, in April.

• Ruled against a third anti-abortion law in Rhode Island, in June.

• Declared that two Minnesota county welfare departments must pay for elective abortions performed on welfare recipients, in view of the Equal Protection Clause of the 14th Amendment, in August.

• Declared unconstitutional laws in Washington (in January), Massachusetts (in May) and Florida (in August) requiring unmarried women under the age of 18 to have parental consent for an abortion. It was also ruled in Florida that it was constitutional for a wife to have an abortion without the consent of her husband.

In a directive with legislative effect, a memorandum from the Pentagon declared that military hospitals need not follow state laws on abortion which were more restrictive than rulings of the Supreme Court.

Legislative action, largely because of contrary judicial decisions and political reluctance, was scattered and ineffective.

It was generally acknowledged that pro-life advocates of all faiths, and none, face an uphill struggle in their efforts to seek legal protection for the life of the unborn in a climate of permissive law and opinion which claimed at least 900,000 lives in 1974.

RIGHT TO LIFE GROUPS

Representative organizations with members of all religious and philosophical convictions who are concerned with the right-to-life of the unborn and related issues include the following: the National Right-to-Life Committee, the National Committee for a Human Life Amendment, the Ad Hoc Committee in Defense of Life, National Nurses for Life, the Committee of Ten Million, the American Association of Pro-Life Obstetricians and Gynecologists, Alternatives to Abortion, Americans against Abortion, Lawyers for Life, the National Youth Pro-Life Coalition, and various groups with Concerned for Life and Right-to-Life titles.

The Alliance for Life is a Canadian organization.

Despite the opinion in some quarters that right-to-life advocates might just as well have fallen over dead after the Supreme Court decisions of 1973, pro-life organizations have shown remarkable vigor in combatting pro-abortion sentiment and relaxed legal standards.

In the process, however, they have been subject to strong counter-campaigns which have labeled them fanatical, criticized them for sensationalism, scored them as hostile to "rights" of women and privacy, and charged them with attempts to subvert the U.S. Constitution.

One of the least credible of the charges is that they are all Catholic inspired and dominated. Such is not the case. Catholic visibility is high in some sectors of the movement, but it is nowhere nearly as dominant as detractors claim.

BIRTHRIGHT

Birthright is a nondenominational guidance and referral service organization offering pregnant women alternatives to abortion, in line with the motto, "It is the right of every pregnant woman to give birth and the right of every child to be born."

Started by Mrs. Louise Summerhill of Toronto, Canada, in 1968, it has chapters in Canada, in the United States and the United Kingdom. Each of these units, manned by volunteers, operates telephone contact services for women in crises of pregnancy and aids them in what one spokesman calls the "panic period so that they can solve their problems" and avoid the decision for abortion they really do not want to make. It is believed that Birthright services have been instrumental in saving the lives of several hundred thousand babies in North America.

The executive director of Birthright, U.S.A., is Mrs. D. Cocciolone, 18 Euclid St., Woodbury, N.J. 08096.

Birthright, although it has Catholics among its volunteers and draws some support from Catholic sources, insists on its original independent and nondenominational character. Its operations have been adopted by other pro-life groups. Birthright telephone numbers are listed in scores of local directories.

A number of groups have merged the guidance function of Birthright with activist programs of their own to counteract liberalized abortion legislation and practices. Among them are groups with titles like Pro Life, Right to Life, the Coalition for Life, Citizens for Life, Spanish Right to Life in Miami, and the Human Life Amendment Committee headquartered in Washington, D.C.

HUMAN LIFE FOUNDATION

The Human Life Foundation came into being in 1968 as the bishops of the United States responded to the appeal of Pope Paul VI for the initiation of scientific research to improve methods of child spacing in keeping with the tenets of his encyclical, *Humanae Vitae.* The foundation, with a grant of $800,000 in seed money provided by the bishops, became operational in 1969. A nonprofit, tax-exempt charitable foundation, it is totally independent and self-governing with a board of 15 directors, all of whom are laymen and scientists.

Natural family planning research sponsored and funded by the foundation and carried out in the strictest fashion by independent scientists and institutions has verified the validity and reliability of natural methods — as distinct from chemical and mechanical methods — of birth regulation.

Edward B. Hanify, Esq., is chairman of the board of directors. Dr. William A. Lynch is chairman of the foundation's science committee. Lawrence J. Kane is executive director. Offices are located at 1776 K St. N.W., Washington, D.C. 20006.

CONSCIENCE CLAUSES

Conscience clauses — generally granting civil and criminal immunity to health personnel and institutions (with some exceptions) refusing to cooperate in abortion procedures for moral, ethical or religious reasons — or their equivalent have been adopted in at least 39 states.

Indiana Attorney General Theodore L. Sendak has declared in a legal opinion that the conscience clause in the state's 1973 abortion law applies to public, tax-supported hospitals as well as to private hospitals. He said the law states: "No individual may be compelled to perform an abortion against his will. No hospital may be required to permit its facilities to be utilized for the performance of abortions."

EUTHANASIA

Euthanasia — which is quite different from the morally acceptable non-use of extraordinary means to preserve life — has been the subject of bills considered by the legislatures of about 18 states, none of which adopted related statutes. A measure of this type, called a "death with dignity" bill, was denied action for the seventh time in the 1975 session of the Florida legislature.

Dr. Arthur Dyck, professor of population ethics at Harvard University, told a regional conference of the Catholic Hospital Association in Boston in March, 1974, that diminished restrictions on abortions was creating a climate of acceptance for euthanasia and infanticide.

LIFE-DEATH QUESTIONS

Following are comments made by two theologians and a physician-attorney of the Catholic University of America concerning reports of persons whose lives are sustained by machines after their vital organs have ceased to function. (See item, Permission To Permit Death, in October 1975 News Events.)

Considerations

Dr. William May, ethics specialist and associate professor of theology, drew a clear distinction between euthanasia and refusal to use extraordinary means to sustain life. "What's considered extraordinary depends on the condition of the patient and his family," he said, "but if the treatment is not therapeutic and will not result in a cure or at least an improvement, then the family is certainly justified in withholding care."

The use of extraordinary means to prolong the life of a dying patient has never been part of the Catholic tradition, he added. Pope Pius XII said: "Normally one is held to use only ordinary means — according to circumstances of persons, places, times and cultures — that do not involve any grave burden for oneself or another."

In 1971 the American bishops presented a code for the governance of Catholic hospitals which stated again that physicians and patients are not obligated to use extraordinary means to preserve life. The following year, the Commission on Catholic Hospital Ethics of the Catholic Theological Society of America issued a report on hospital ethics. The Commission asked for "clearer guidelines on the right to die in dignity, the prolongation of human life, the definition of 'extraordinary means' for preserving life, the ethics of medical heroics and the understanding of death as part of life."

Rev. John F. Dedek, author of *Contemporary Medical Ethics* and a moral theologian, agreed: "If there is still hope of respiration or brain activity, then the person should not be declared dead," he said, "but in many cases of prolonged comas the person suffers irreparable brain damage and simply cannot exist without the use of sophisticated, expensive machines. . . .

"A person is required to use only ordinary means to preserve his life and there are some amounts of money and machinery that would have to be considered extraordinary," he added.

Attorney — Physician's View

Dr. Harold Hirsh, an attorney and physician teaching in the Catholic University's Schools of Law and Nursing, pointed out that a physician is never required to perform futile acts in the care of a patient.

"The decision to discontinue an artificial respirator is based primarily on the clinical judgment of the attending physician using EEG readings of the patient's brain activity as a guide," he said. Seven states had a Brain Death Statute which stipulates that a flat EEG reading and the doctor's judgment are sufficient to make a decision to discontinue the procedure without fear of malpractice suits or homicide charges, he added. "Although a physician does not need a brain death law to stop administering treatment, many doctors feel that the law offers a certain sanctuary in their time of decision," said Hirsh.

Statement of Pope Paul

Pope Paul reaffirmed the Church's opposition to euthanasia and called upon doctors to support life to the very last, in an address to 1,000 delegates to the Third World Congress of the College of Psychosomatic Medicine Sept. 18, 1975. He said:

"Concerning the value of each human person, we wish to remind you that it is the physician's duty to be always at the service of life, and to assist the individual to the very end, without ever accepting euthanasia re renouncing the very human duty to help a person to end his days with dignity."

He recalled the teaching of Pope Pius XII on the use of pain-killing drugs, that they could be used prudently by competent people, "but never so as to diminish personal responsibility or against the rights that are proper to a human person."

FETAL EXPERIMENTATION

Regulations for federally funded fetal research — based on principles of equal treatment for all fetuses and of "minimal risk" to research subjects — were issued by the Department of Health, Education and Welfare Aug. 8, 1975.

Also effective as of that date were the lifting of a year-long ban on federally funded fetal research and provision for two ethical advisory boards to monitor observance of the regulations.

The HEW guidelines were based on recommendations made by the 11-member National Commission for the Protection of Human Subjects of Biomedical and Behavioral Research.

The commission recommended that fetal research be allowed in certain situations. It also stated that no research should be supported "which fails to treat the fetus with proper care and dignity" in a manner consistent with its "human genetic heritage."

Regulations

The HEW regulations:

• allow therapeutic research, designed to help the particular fetus;

• support non-therapeutic research, designed to gather information helpful to others, which does not involve additional risk to the fetus;

• require that all possible animal and other research be done before research is done on fetuses, and that such fetal research be done only when it can produce needed information that is available in no other way;

• require consent from the mother and father (if his identity and whereabouts are known), except in the case of research on a fetus resulting from rape.

Views

Support for the commission's recommendations, along with related HEW regulations, was registered by Father Albert Johnson, S.J., a member of the commission. General support was expressed by another commission member, David Louisell, although he objected to recommendations he regarded as a loophole for permitting non-therapeutic research on abortable or aborted fetuses. His general opinion and objection were shared by Msgr. James T. McHugh, director of Pro-Life Activities of the National Conference of Catholic Bishops.

EARLIER SUGGESTIONS

Before issuance of the foregoing regulations on fetal experimentation by the Department of Health, Education and Welfare, Msgr. McHugh told the National Commission for the Protection of Human Subjects of Biomedical and Behavioral Research in February that fetal experimentation must be considered within the context of the Supreme Court decision overturning most state abortion laws.

He criticized that decision as making it easier to think of the aborted fetus as "little more than an experimental animal."

Msgr. McHugh outlined the following guidelines for fetal experimentation:

Live Fetus

• Experimentation on the unborn fetus in the womb should be prohibited unless necessary to insure the survival or health of the fetus.

• Experiments on live aborted fetuses should be prohibited unless designed to save the life of the fetus.

• Experiments on the fetus prior to abortion should be prohibited because the fetus cannot give "informed consent" to the experiment. "Moreover, the consent of the mother, who has already decided to end the life of her yet unborn offspring, cannot be accepted as a fair or just decision on behalf of the unborn."

• Experiments on the fetus begun prior to abortion and to be completed after abortion should be prohibited.

Dead Fetus

There should be a "general disposition" against experiments on dead fetuses, Msgr. McHugh said, with the following distinctions:

• Experiments on the stillborn or spontaneously aborted fetus may be allowed to determine the cause of death and to insure survival of other infants. "The norms apply here as would apply to an autopsy of an adult."

• Experiments which are purely speculative or used to show fetal organs to medical students should be prohibited.

• Specific experiments directed toward the elimination of a particular disease may be permitted, for example, through the taking of a tissue culture. "In such a case, the intended purpose of the experiment should be carefully spelled out, there should be reasonable hope that specific scientific evidence that is otherwise unavailable will be obtained, and no other experiments will be carried out. Consent of the parents should be obtained. Once the scientific hypothesis is verified satisfactorily, such experiments should no longer be permitted."

• The physician who performs the abortion should never be allowed to perform experiments on the fetus.

Msgr. McHugh said there is "a tendency to overestimate the projected results of fetal experiments." Research on animals or study of the amniotic fluid may be sufficient, he said. "There do not seem to be any genetic diseases where experimentation on live fetuses is required."

"The basic research data in the efforts to overcome sickle cell anemia and Tay-Sachs disease (two major genetic diseases) was accumulated prior to the recent use of the live fetus as a research specimen," he said.

Question for Specialists

"There is a serious question among specialists as to whether any serious gains can be achieved by widespread experimentation on aborted fetuses," Msgr. McHugh declared.

Citing a need for more "dispassionate" discussion of fetal experimentation, he said:

"We are told that fetal experimentation is necessary to save children's lives, to gain scientific knowledge, to overcome genetic diseases. These generalizations must be tested and proven before any effective dialogue can take place."

Danger of Utilitarianism

"Moreover, even when the individual assertion can be proven to some degree, it is often basically a utilitarian argument. If experimentation on the fetus is justified to gain knowledge or overcome genetic disease for others, then the same principle can be applied to experiments on other human beings, sick or well, old or young, dying or growing better, abandoned or rejected by others."

Msgr. McHugh said the government has a duty to encourage respect for human life and should act as "guardian" of the fetus from conception to insure that it is experimented on only if necessary to insure its survival.

DECLARATION ON ABORTION

Following are excerpts from a "Declaration on Abortion" issued by the Congregation for the Doctrine of the Faith Nov. 18, 1974, nearly five months after it was approved by Pope Paul.

The excerpts are from the text circulated by the NC Documentary Service, Origins, Dec. 12, 1974 (Vol. 4, No. 25). The unnumbered subheads have been added.

I. Introduction

One cannot but be astonished to see a simultaneous increase of unqualified protests against the death penalty and every form of war and the vindication of the liberalization of abortion, either in its entirety or in ever broader indications.

In many countries the public authorities which resist the liberalization of abortion laws are the object of powerful pressures aimed at leading them to this goal. This, it is said, would violate no one's conscience, for each individual would be left free to follow his own opinion, while being prevented from imposing it on others. Ethical pluralism is claimed to be a normal consequence of ideological pluralism. There is, however, a great difference between the one and the other, for action (ethical pluralism) affects the interests of others more quickly than does mere opinion (ideological pluralism). Moreover, one can never claim freedom of opinion as a pretext for attacking the rights of others, most especially the right to life.

Obligation of Conscience

Charged with the promotion and the defense of faith and morals in the universal Church, the Sacred Congregation for the Doctrine of the Faith proposes to recall this teaching (of the Church regarding abortion) in its essential aspects to all the faithful. (In doing so) it is not a question of opposing one opinion to another, but of transmitting to the faithful a constant teaching of the supreme magisterium, which teaches moral norms in the light of faith. It is therefore clear that this declaration necessarily entails a grave obligation for Christian conscience.

II. In Light of Faith

Thus, we understand that human life, even on this earth, is precious. Infused by the Creator, life is again taken back by him (cf. Gn. 2:7; Wis. 15:11). It remains under his protection: man's blood cries out to him (cf. Gn. 4:10) and he will demand an account of it, "for in the image of God man was made" (Gn. 9:5-6). The commandment of God is formal: "You shall not kill" (Ex. 20:13). Life is at the same time a gift and a responsibility. It is received as a "talent" Tcf. Mt. 25:14-20t; it must be put to proper use.

Consistent Tradition

The tradition of the Church has always held that human life must be protected and favored from the beginning, just as at the various stages of its development.

In our days the recent Roman Pontiffs have proclaimed the same doctrine with the greatest clarity. Pius XI explicitly answered the most serious objections. Pius XII clearly excluded all direct abortion, that is, abortion which is either an end or a means. John XXIII recalled the teaching of the Fathers on the sacred character of life "which from its beginning demands the action of God the Creator." Most recently, the Second Vatican Council, presided over by Paul VI, has most severely condemned abortion: "Life must be safeguarded with extreme care from conception; abortion and infanticide are abominable crimes." The same Paul VI, speaking on this subject on many occasions, has not been afraid to declare that this teaching of the Church "has not changed and is unchangeable."

III. In Light of Reason

There is precisely a certain number of rights which society is not in a position to grant since these rights precede society; but society has the function to preserve and to enforce them. These are the greater part of those which are today called "human rights" and which our age boasts of having formulated.

Right to Life Primary

The first right of the human person is his life. He has other goods and some are more precious, but this one is fundamental — the condition of all the others. Hence it must be protected above all others. It does not belong to society, nor does it belong to public authority in any form to recognize this right for some and not for others: all discrimination is evil, whether it be founded on race, sex, color or religion. It is not recognition by another that constitutes this right. This right is antecedent to its recognition; it demands recognition and it is strictly unjust to refuse it.

Any discrimination based on the various

stages of life is no more justified than any other discrimination. The right to life remains complete in an old person, even one greatly weakened, it is not lost by one who is incurably sick. The right to life is no less to be respected in the small infant just born than in the mature person. In reality, respect for human life is called for from the time that the process of generation begins. From the time that the ovum is fertilized, a life is begun which is neither that of the father nor of the mother; it is rather the life of a new human being with his own growth. It would be made human if it were not human already.

No Scientific Support

To this perpetual evidence — perfectly independent of the discussions on the moment of animation — modern genetic science brings valuable confirmation. It has demonstrated that from the first instant there is established the program of what this living being will be: a man, this individual man with his characteristic aspects already well determined. Right from fertilization is begun the adventure of a human life, and each of its capacities requires time — a rather lengthy time — to find its place and to be in a position to act. The least that can be said is that present science, in its most evolved state, does not give any substantial support to those who defend abortion. Moreover, it is not up to biological sciences to make a definitive judgment on questions which are properly philosophical and moral, such as the moment when a human person is constituted or the legitimacy of abortion. From a moral point of view this is certain: even if a doubt existed concerning whether the fruit of conception is already a human person, it is objectively a grave sin to dare to risk murder. "The one who will be a man is already one."

IV. Reply to Objections

Divine law and natural reason, therefore, exclude all right to the direct killing of an innocent man. However, if the reasons given to justify an abortion were always manifestly evil and valueless the problem would not be so dramatic. The gravity of the problem comes from the fact that in certain cases, perhaps in quite a considerable number of cases, by denying abortion one endangers important values to which it is normal to attach great value, and which may sometimes even seem to have priority. We do not deny these very great difficulties.

No Justifying Reasons

It may be a serious question of health, sometimes of life or death, for the mother; it may be the burden represented by an additional child, especially if there are good reasons to fear that the child will be abnormal or retarded; it may be the importance attributed in different classes of society to consider-

ations of honor or dishonor, of loss of social standing, and so forth. We proclaim only that none of these reasons can ever objectively confer the right to dispose of another's life, even when that life is only beginning.

With regard to the future unhappiness of the child, no one, not even the father or mother, can act as its substitute, even if it is still in the embryonic stage, to choose in the child's name, life or death. The child itself, when grown up, will never have the right to choose suicide; no more may his parents choose death for the child while it is not of an age to decide for itself. Life is too fundamental a value to be weighed against even very serious disadvantages.

Emancipation, Sexual Freedom

The movement for the emancipation of women, insofar as it seeks essentially to free them from all unjust discrimination, is on perfectly sound ground. In the different forms of cultural background there is a great deal to be done in this regard. But one cannot change nature. Nor can one exempt women, any more than men, from what nature demands of them. Furthermore, all publicly recognized freedom is always limited by the certain rights of others.

The same must be said of the claim to sexual freedom. If by this expression one is to understand the mastery progressively acquired by reason and by authentic love over instinctive impulse, without diminishing pleasure but keeping it in its proper place — and in this sphere this is the only authentic freedom — then there is nothing to object to. But this kind of freedom will always be careful not to violate justice. If, on the contrary, one is to understand that men and women are "free" to seek sexual pleasure to the point of satiety, without taking into account any law or the essential orientation of sexual life to its fruits of fertility, then this idea has nothing Christian in it. It is even unworthy of man. In any case it does not confer any right to dispose of human life — even if embryonic — or to suppress it on the pretext that it is burdensome.

Technology vs. Morality

Scientific progress is opening to technology — and will open still more — the possibility of delicate interventions, the consequences of which can be very serious, for good as well as for evil. These are achievements of the human spirit which in themselves are admirable. But technology can never be independent of the criterion of morality, since technology exists for man and must respect his finality. Just as there is no right to use nuclear energy for every possible purpose, so there is no right to manipulate human life in every possible direction. Technology must be at the service of man, so as better to ensure the functioning of his normal abilities, to prevent or to cure his illnesses, to contribute to his better human development. It is true that the evolution of technology makes early abortion more and more easy, but the moral evaluation is in no way modified because of this.

Never Abortion

We know what seriousness the problem of birth control can assume for some families and for some countries. That is why the last council and subsequently the encyclical *Humanae Vitae* of 25 July 1968, spoke of "responsible parenthood. What we wish to say again with emphasis, as we pointed out in the conciliar constitution *Gaudium et Spes,* in the encyclical *Populorum Progressio* and in other papal documents, is that never, under any pretext, may abortion be resorted to, either by a family or by the political authority, as a legitimate means of regulating births. The damage to moral values is always a greater evil for the common good than any disadvantage in the economic or demographic order.

V. Morality and Law

Although many citizens, in particular the Catholic faithful, condemn abortion, many others hold that it is licit, at least as a lesser evil. Why force them to follow an opinion which is not theirs, especially in a country where they are in the majority? In addition it is apparent that, where they still exist, the laws condemning abortion appear difficult to apply. The crime has become too common for it to be punished every time, and the public authorities often find it is wiser to close their eyes to it. But the preservation of a law which is not applied is always to the detriment of authority and of all the other laws. It must be added that clandestine abortion puts women who resign themselves to it and have recourse to it in the most serious dangers for future pregnancies and also in many cases for their lives. Even if the legislator continues to regard abortion as an evil, may he not propose to restrict its damage?

Precedence of Child's Life

These arguments and others in addition that are heard from varying quarters are not conclusive. It is true that civil law cannot expect to cover the whole field of morality or to punish all faults. No one expects it to do so. It must often tolerate what is in fact a lesser evil, in order to avoid a greater one. One must, however, be attentive to what a change in legislation can represent. Many will take as authorization what is perhaps only the abstention from punishment. Even more, in the present case, this very renunciation seems at the very least to admit that the legislator no longer considers abortion a crime against human life, since murder is still always severely punished. It is true that it is not the task of the law to choose between points of view or to impose one rather than another. But the life of the child takes precedence over all opinions. One cannot invoke freedom of thought to destroy this life.

Natural and Human Law

The role of law is not to record what is done, but to help in promoting improvement. It is at all times the task of the state to preserve each person's rights and to protect the weakest. In order to do so the state will have to right many wrongs. The law is not obliged to sanction everything, but it cannot act contrary to a law which is deeper and more majestic than any human law: the natural law engraved in men's hearts by the Creator as a norm which reason clarifies and strives to formulate properly, and which one must always struggle to understand better, but which it is always wrong to contradict. Human law can abstain from punishment, but it cannot declare to be right what would be opposed to the natural law, for this opposition suffices to give the assurance that a law is not a law at all.

No Christian Support

It must in any case be clearly understood that a Christian can never conform to a law which is in itself immoral, and such is the case of a law which would admit in principle the licitness of abortion. Nor can a Christian take part in a propaganda campaign in favor of such a law, or vote for it. Moreover, he may not collaborate in its application. It is, for instance, inadmissible that doctors or nurses should find themselves obliged to cooperate closely in abortions and have to choose between the Christian law and their professional situation.

On the contrary it is the task of law to pursue a reform of society and of conditions of life in all milieux, starting with the most deprived, so that always and everywhere it may be possible to give every child coming into this world a welcome worthy of a person. Help for families and for unmarried mothers, assured grants for children, a statute for illegitimate children and reasonable arrangements for adoption — a whole positive policy must be put into force so that there will always be a concrete honorable and possible alternative to abortion.

VI. Conclusion

Following one's conscience in obedience to the law of God is not always the easy way. One must not fail to recognize the weight of the sacrifices and the burdens which it can impose. Heroism is sometimes called for in order to remain faithful to the requirements of the divine law. Therefore we must emphasize that the path of true progress of the human person passes through this constant fidelity to a conscience maintained in uprightness and truth; and we must exhort all those who are able to do so to lighten the burdens still crushing so many men and women, families and children, who are placed in situations to which in human terms there is no solution.

Christian Outlook

A Christian's outlook cannot be limited to the horizon of life in this world. He knows that during the present life another one is being prepared, one of such importance that it is in its light that judgments must be made. From this viewpoint there is no absolute misfortune here below, not even the terrible sorrow of bringing up a handicapped child. This is the contradiction proclaimed by the Lord: "Happy those who mourn: they shall be comforted" (Mt. 5:5). To measure happiness by the absence of sorrow and misery in this world is to turn one's back on the Gospel.

Action against Causes

But this does not mean that one can remain indifferent to these sorrows and miseries. Every man and woman with feeling, and certainly every Christian, must be ready to do what he can to remedy them. This is the law of charity, of which the first preoccupation must always be the establishment of justice. One can never approve of abortion; but it is above all necessary to combat its causes. This includes political action, which will be in particular the task of the law. But it is necessary at the same time to influence morality and to do everything possible to help families, mothers and children. Considerable progress in the service of life has been accomplished by medicine. One can hope that such progress will continue, in accordance with the vocation of doctors, which is not to suppress life but to care for it and favor it as much as possible. It is equally desirable that, in suitable institutions, or, in their absence, in the outpouring of Christian generosity and charity every form of assistance should be developed.

Ideological Action

There will be no effective action on the level of morality unless at the same time an effort is made on the level of ideas. A point of view — or even more perhaps a way of thinking — which considers fertility as an evil cannot be allowed to spread without contradiction. It is true that not all forms of culture are equally in favor of large families. Such families come up against much greater difficulties in an industrial and urban civilization. Thus the Church has in recent times insisted on the idea of responsible parenthood, the exercise

of true human and Christian prudence. Such prudence would not be authentic if it did not include generosity. It must preserve awareness of the grandeur of the task of cooperating with the Creator in the transmission of life, which gives new members to society and new children to the Church.

Christ's Church has the fundamental solicitude of protecting and favoring life. She certainly thinks before all else of the life which Christ came to bring: "I have come so that they may have life and have it to the full" (Jn. 10:10). But life at all its levels comes from God, and bodily life is for man the indispensable beginning. In this life on earth sin has introduced, multiplied and made harder to bear suffering and death. But in taking their burden upon himself Jesus Christ has transformed them: for whoever believes in him, suffering and death itself become instruments of resurrection.

SUPREME COURT DECISIONS

The U.S. Supreme Court, in a 7 to 2 ruling Jan. 22, 1973, against the constitutionality of abortion laws in Texas (Roe v. Wade) and Georgia (Doe v. Bolton), nullified all criminal abortion statutes in the 50 states, refusing in the process to acknowledge that an unborn child is a human being with right to life. Coupled with this legal denial of personhood was the canonization of the mother's absolute right to privacy, without regard for the consent of husband or parent(s), in having an abortion.

The Court ruled:

• During the first three months of pregnancy a woman's right to privacy is paramount. Accordingly, she has an unrestricted right to abortion with the consent and cooperation of a physician.

• In the second trimester, the principle controlling legislation on abortion procedures is the health or welfare of the mother, understood in the widest possible sense.

• In "the stage subsequent to viability," the controlling principles are the State's "interest in the potentiality of human life" and "the preservation of the life or health of the mother." The majority opinion stated: "For the stage subsequent to viability the State, in promoting its interest in the potentiality of human life, may, if it chooses, regulate, and even proscribe, abortion except where necessary, in appropriate medical judgment, for the preservation of the life or health of the mother."

NATIONAL CATECHETICAL DIRECTORY

Preparatory work for the development of a *National Catechetical Directory* continued during 1975 with a view toward publication of a final draft in 1976.

The purpose of the project is to compile a comprehensive, U.S.-oriented guidebook for

religious education and formation. It will incorporate the basic features of: the *General Catechetical Directory* approved by Pope Paul Mar. 18, 1971, and issued by the Congregation for the Clergy; the U.S. bishops' 1972 pastoral letter, "To Teach as Jesus Did," and their 1973 statement, "Basic

Teachings for Catholic Religious Education"; and related recommendations on contents, methods and programs made by persons concerned with Christian education.

Not a Catechism

"The directory is not a new catechism or religious education manual for the Church," according to Msgr. Wilfrid H. Paradis of Manchester, N.H., the national director of the project. "It is, rather, a sourcebook of values which hopefully will provide a sense of direction for adapting the unchanging word of God to the ever-changing needs and problems of contemporary American culture."

The directory project was approved by the National Conference of Catholic Bishops in April, 1972. Responsibility for the work was entrusted to Msgr. Paradis and his associate director, Sister Mariella Frye; a seven-member Bishops' Committee of Policy and Review; and a Directory Committee of 12 members (four bishops, two priests, two sisters, one brother, one layman and two laywomen). Collaborating in the project on local levels are diocesan directors and coordinators.

The directory is intended to be a pastoral and practical document containing norms and guidelines for teaching religion to U.S. Catholics of all ages and circumstances. It will be addressed to "those Catholics who have the responsibility of Christian education in the United States . . . parents as educators, catechists, religious, deacons and priests, writers and publishers of catechetical texts."

Origin of First Draft

Preparation for the first draft of the directory, between Dec. 1, 1973, and Mar. 31, 1974, began with a wide-ranging effort to consult the relevant opinions of members of the Church and scholars in religious education and allied sacred and human sciences. Approximately 60,000 persons across the country took part in meetings designed to elicit recommendations for the contents of the directory. Some 32,000 took part in the actual preparation of 17,400 recommendations received by the national office.

The first version of the directory, whose chapter headings are listed below, was drafted with these recommendations and standard catechetical subjects in view. It was approved

by the NCCB in November, 1974, and circulated from January to April, 1975, for further consultation and recommendations. A second working draft was to be issued for the same purpose later in the year. Plans called for publication of the final draft in 1976.

Chapter Headings

The chapter headings of the first draft of the directory were as follows.

1. The Catholic Church in the United States.

2. The Mystery of Revelation.

3. The Catholic Church and the Invitation to Community.

4. Catechesis and Catechists.

5. Catechetical Criteria and the Christian Message. (For partial contents of this chapter, see Basic Teachings for Catholic Religious Education.)

6. The Christian Life of Service.

7. Growth in Faith.

8. Liturgy and Catechesis.

9. Organization To Facilitate Religious Education.

Critique of First Draft

The first draft of the directory was the subject of discussion at regional meetings of the bishops in the spring of 1975. Summarily, recommendations made by bishops, priests, religious and lay persons at these meetings called for:

• clarification regarding those for whom the directory is intended;

• restructuring the chapters, clearer statement of the central theme, and shortening of the text;

• more pastoral orientation;

• elimination of technical vocabulary;

• more emphasis on religious education for adults;

• better coverage of the Eastern rites;

• addition of footnotes and a glossary of terms.

One view, from the meeting of the bishops of New York, regarded the draft as a splendid theological document, but called its form cumbersome and not pastoral enough.

Bishops in New England were told of the need for a "readable" document that would deepen faith and service among ordinary Catholics, as parents and educators of children, and as not-married adults.

FIRST CONFESSION AND COMMUNION

The practice of frequent confession and a directive that First Confession should precede First Communion were contained in a letter sent by Cardinal Jean Villot on behalf of Pope Paul to participants in the 26th National Liturgical Week observance which opened Aug. 25, 1975, in Florence. The letter's contents were related to the theme of the observance, "Reconcile Yourself to the Father, in Christ and in the Church."

The letter said, in part:

"The great theological-spiritual principles of penance declared by the Council of Trent are still valid and binding, (and) it is not out of place to underline also some aspects which hold great importance in the celebration of this sacrament."

Priests and Hearing Confessions: "His Holiness directs a word especially to priests so that they may love this sacred ministry, prepare their faithful in its catechesis and be always ready to hear their confessions. The new rite (see Penance, under Sacraments) offers many possibilities to enhance the sacrament, especially in the context of a celebration of the Word of God. But nothing will be so important as the willingness of pastors of souls to maintain regular attendance at the confessional. This, then, even if the new rite provides for an eventual restructuring approved by the legitimate authority, keeps its entire important function."

The Confessional: "As the Soveriegn Pontiff has said, the confessional must remain 'as a protective diaphragm between the minister and the penitent to guarantee the absolute privacy of the conversation undertaken by them and reserved to them.'" (The Pope made this statement at a general audience Apr. 3, 1974. He did not, however, rule out the hearing of confessions in an alternate type of setting.)

Frequent Confession: "Furthermore, His Holiness would like to call the attention of all — priests, religious and faithful — to the frequency of this sacrament. Unfortunately, some have little regard for frequent confession. But this is not the thought of the Church. The new rite also recommends frequent confession and presents it as a renewed commitment to increase the grace of baptism and as an opportunity and stimulus to conform more intimately to Christ and to make oneself always more docile to the voice of the Spirit. Moreover, as the Sovereign Pontiff has stressed in his apostolic exhortation on Christian joy: 'Frequent confession remains a privileged source of holiness, peace and joy.'"

First Confession before First Communion: "Finally, the Holy Father places special stress on children's confession, and especially on First Confession which must always precede First Communion even if, appropriately, there is an interval between them. From the very earliest age, the first steps toward an evangelization of penance must be taken — an evangelization which will then become an ever more valid and conscious support for a living faith in the celebration of the sacrament and, above all, in the sure and coherent guidelines for Christian life."

(See also, First Communion and Confession.)

AIMS OF NATIONAL OFFICE FOR BLACK CATHOLICS

The following article was written by NC News correspondent Bob Giles.

Active participation — not separatism — was called the objective of black American Catholics by Marianist Brother Joseph M. Davis, executive director of the National Office for Black Catholics.

Brother Davis, in Houston Sept. 18, 1975, for an address to members of the Black Catholic Community Concerns Association of Galveston-Houston, said there is a grassroots effort across the country whereby many of the 950,000 black Catholics "are trying to bring about changes within the Church we can comfortably live with — our identity as black people, our culture, music and style."

Brother Davis said that there is nothing contradictory about "our full identity as black people and being Catholic. In fact, if we really understand our Catholic teaching, we should live and practice the faith fully."

Concerns of the Office

The thrust of blacks for a "voice" in the Church, he noted, evolved from the civil rights movement of the 1960s and the so-called black experience.

He cited the recruitment of young black men and women for religious vocations as a principal concern for the five-year-old organization. "We need black priests, sisters, brothers and deacons to enter a life of service and ministry to the Church in the black community." (There are about 198 black clergy, including three auxiliary bishops, and 700 black sisters in the United States.)

The drive for religious vocations "is a specific sign that we are really mature in the Church. We no longer depend on missioners totally, and it is evident that more and more priests are evolving from the black community."

He continued: "In the Church, we need to continue to grow, be alive and healthy."

He added: "We are also promoting evangelization. Basically, of course, the idea is the spreading of the Gospel, strengthening the Catholic Church in the black community, and attracting black people to the Church."

The NOBC is striving to "give black Catholics a greater role of participation in the Church. We are trying to get black Catholics to understand it is up to us to assume responsibilities, development, vitality and growth in the community as members of the Catholic Church."

Brother Davis related that the NOBC evolved from a meeting of black priests and brothers in Detroit in April, 1968. "It was the opinion of this group that an office for black Catholics in the United States was needed," he stated. Two years later the NOBC opened in the nation's capital.

"Personally, I think NOBC was an excellent idea. It has given us insight we didn't have before, and it has led to some positive action on the part of black Catholics and the good of the Church as a whole," he said.

The NOBC is staffed by 12 blacks — priests, religious and lay persons — and the board of directors includes 24 priests, brothers, sisters and laity from across the country. It is financed by the people through the annual Black Catholics Concerned collection in October. Walter Hubbard is the president.

Black Caucus

In Cincinnati, Archbishop Joseph L. Bernardin called upon the archdiocesan Black Catholic Caucus to act as a liaison body between the Church and the total black community.

Speaking at the caucus' fifth annual meeting Sept. 28, 1975, the archbishop noted that the time of "confrontation and rhetoric" is past. "In the earlier stages of the growth of the black Catholic movement, these had their place, but now the caucus needs an accurate analysis of existing problems and their causes."

The caucus should also "reflect for the archdiocese the concerns of the black Catholic community," and "make certain that the black point of view is represented in whatever decisions are made and whatever activities are undertaken."

The caucus was commended by the archbishop for its efforts to increase black participation in Catholic affairs. He called the five-year-old association of clergy, religious and lay persons "a very timely development within the Church."

The most pressing problem confronting the caucus, according to Archbishop Bernardin, is "an apathy and general malaise of the spirit" in matters of social justice. Furthermore, "There is also among some a growing belief that the future of Catholicism among black people is very uncertain, and that no one really cares about the future of the Church in the black community." Rejecting this analysis, he declared that, "here in this archdiocese, we do care; we are concerned."

The archbishop challenged the caucus to "work positively" on problems facing the Church in the black community in the areas of liturgy, the sacraments, religious education, vocations, education, housing, criminal justice, aging and jobs. In dealing with these issues, the caucus can participate "without sacrificing black leadership or black identity," he noted.

Concerns of the National Office for Black Catholics were brought forward at 1975 regional hearings in preparation for the Catholic observance of the Bicentennial in 1976.

San Diego Committee

In San Diego, Bishop Leo T. Maher approved in late September, 1975, a policy recommendation that "a diocesan committee of black Catholics should be established," to function "as a resource and advisory board to the bishop and the Christian community regarding black Catholics."

This new committee was the most recent addition to the growing list of similar bodies in operation in many dioceses throughout the United States.

CARDINAL JOZSEF MINDSZENTY

Cardinal Jozsef Mindszenty, the personification of resistance to Communist terrorism and tyranny, died May 6, 1975, in a Viennese clinic following surgery. He was buried nine days later in the Austrian pilgrimage town of Mariazell, 60 miles southwest of Vienna.

Tragedy

The cardinal died under a cloud of tragedy. His title as primate of Hungary had been taken from him in 1974. His relations with the Vatican were strained because of a serious difference of opinion. His stature as a living sign of defiance to Communist tyranny seemed to have shrunk because of the Vatican's mandate that he leave his asylum in the U.S. Embassy in Budapest for exile in the West. He called his departure from Hungary "perhaps the heaviest cross" of his life.

His Career

Cardinal Mindszenty was born Mar. 29, 1892, in Csehimindszent, Hungary. He was ordained to the priesthood June 12, 1915, and served as a curate and pastor until his ordination as bishop of Veszprem Mar. 25, 1944. He was made archbishop of Esztergom and primate of Hungary Oct. 2, 1945, and cardinal Feb. 18, 1946.

While still a young priest, he was jailed for two months during the Communist regime of Bela Kun in 1919. While bishop of Veszprem, he was arrested Nov. 27, 1944, and jailed for several months by Nazis for his opposition to their occupation of Hungary and, especially, for their persecution of Jews.

These penal experiences were preludes to those of the rest of his life.

Trial and Sentence

The cardinal, who resisted efforts of the post-World War II Communist regime to dismantle the Church in Hungary, was arrested by government authorities Dec. 26, 1948. He was charged with "suspicion of criminal activities, including an attempt to undermine the order of the People's Republic, treason, espionage and trafficking in foreign currency." He was held in custody and underwent brutal interrogation before being brought before a kangaroo court and sentenced to life imprisonment Feb. 8, 1949.

Following sentence, he was moved from one jail to another until July, 1955, when he was placed under house confinement and surveillance. He was liberated for three and one-half days during the short-lived Freedom Fighters' revolt of October-November, 1956. He was then granted asylum in the U.S. Embassy in Budapest, where he remained until Sept. 28, 1971.

Exile

The cardinal was then placed under an order from the Vatican to leave Hungary. Under obedience, he went to Rome, where he was received warmly by Pope Paul, and stayed there for two months before taking up residence in Vienna.

It was clear that leaving Hungary was not his idea. He was convinced, and remained so until his death, that negotiations between Vatican and Hungarian officials for a kind of detente would not result in any substantial improvement of Church-state relations in the country.

Vatican's Explanation

L'Osservatore Romano explained the Vatican's decision for the removal of the cardinal at the time of his arrival in Rome. The paper said:

"The Holy See has always scrupulously respected the decision of the cardinal not to abandon . . . his own refuge and the country to which he was, and still is, linked by sacred and deep bonds.

"Nor was the position of the cardinal subordinated by the Holy See to the negotiations undertaken over several years with the government of the Hungarian People's Republic.

"But the prolongation of his singular, and in some respects abnormal, condition was progressively rendering more acute certain problems which did not concern his position but his person." (This was said to be a reference to worries over his health.)

A Vatican communique announced Feb. 5, 1974, that Pope Paul had declared the See of Esztergom vacant. It was reported at that time that the cardinal's occupancy of the see — as a refugee, an exile and an implacable opponent of Communism — had been an obstacle to hoped-for better relations between the Church and the Hungarian government.

Cardinal Mindszenty's reaction to the announcement was one of "complete and absolute exile."

Actions After Removal

While maintaining his residence in Vienna until his death, the cardinal traveled widely, visiting Hungarian communities in various countries and urging them to fidelity to the faith and to the principles of a just society. He toured the United States for two months in 1974.

In July of that year, he reiterated his opposition to Communism in an address at Stuttgart, West Germany. He said: "The Catholic people of Hungary are being trained for godlessness. I see nothing that would seem to be profitable for the people of Hungary as a result of my removal from the See of Esztergom. As a matter of fact, conditions for the Church in my homeland are as critical as ever. Nearly 2,000 priests . . . are kept from functioning as such. There is no possibility even of a gentlemen's agreement with Hungary's present rulers who practice godlessness and inhumanity."

Tributes

Pope Paul, in his first public address after the cardinal's death, said he was a protagonist of "one of the most difficult and complex periods of the thousand-year history of the Church in his noble country." He called the former primate of Hungary "zealous in faith, fierce in sentiment, and immovable in what seemed to him to be his duty and his right."

Cardinal John J. Krol of Philadelphia commented: "In life, Cardinal Mindszenty was the personification of resistance to the tyranny and terrorism of atheistic Communism. In death he will be a symbol of heroic witness to faith and a courageous defender of human dignity and rights."

Cardinal John Heenan, at a memorial Mass in London, hailed the cardinal as "the greatest confessor of the faith of the 20th century," and added: "History will tell if he was right in his uncompromising rejection of Communism."

VIETNAMESE AND CAMBODIAN REFUGEE RESETTLEMENT

In the spring of 1975, as Communist and Khmer Rouge forces completed their military takeover of South Vietnam and Cambodia, the U.S. government authorized admission to this country of 130,000 persons as refugees and another 20,000 as immigrant parolees.

Resettlement Report

By Sept. 19, reported Mrs. Julia Valada Taft, director of the Interagency Task Force for Indochinese Refugees, more than 100,000 had been resettled, 94,000 in the U.S. and 6,000 in other countries, principally Canada and France.

Nearly 35,000 were awaiting resettlement in refugee camps at Fort Chaffee, Ark., Camp Pendleton, Calif., and Indiantown Gap, Pa. An estimated 5,000 more eligibles, still to be

brought into the program, were in Laos and Thailand. Eighteen hundred refugees at Camp Pendleton and on Guam were petitioning authorities in Saigon and Hanoi for repatriation. Others remaining in camps were mostly members of large families, single men, those preferring camp to the outside world, and some handicapped.

Refugees were resettled through sponsorship by voluntary agencies, civic and religious organizations, and by individuals. Sponsorship involved assurance that housing would be available and that support and guidance would be provided refugees during the first few months of resettlement.

Some 45,000 of the resettled refugees had jobs or were in the process of getting them. Eleven thousand were reported to be in need of financial assistance. Eighteen hundred reported difficulties with sponsors. General morale, however, was said to be satisfactory.

American response to the resettlement program ranged from hostile in the beginning to gradual acceptance.

Of $505 million authorized for the evacuation and resettlement of refugees, $283 million had been spent or committed by Sept. 19, $133 million was available for continuing resettlement and about $87 million for allocation by the Department of Health, Education and Welfare for medical and social-service aid.

Catholic Participation

Catholic participation in the resettlement program was triggered by a letter from Archbishop Joseph L. Bernardin, president of the U.S. Catholic Conference, to bishops throughout the country in April. Principally, he called on them to develop local efforts to obtain sponsorships for refugees. Many subsequently appointed diocesan coordinators for this purpose.

The Southeast Asia Resettlement Program was placed under the direction of John McCarthy, head of Migration and Refugee Services, U.S. Catholic Conference. This service, which resettled 60 to 70 per cent of earlier Hungarian and Cuban refugees, had more experience in this field than any other voluntary agency. It was the largest of nine such agencies participating in the overall resettlement program.

MRS, working through field offices in the camps and through liaison with about 150 diocesan coordinators, assisted in handling the adjustment and resettlement needs of at least 34,000 refugees by the fall of 1975 and was committed to resettle 12,000 more.

By the end of July it resettled more than 20,000 refugees. Among them were the following numbers in the named dioceses: 2,017 in Los Angeles, more than 1,000 in Arlington, 881 in San Diego, 749 in New Orleans, 631 in St. Augustine, 510 in San Francisco, 484 in Richmond, 415 in Washington.

One example of parochial participation was reported from St. Paul and Minneapolis where 140 Vietnamese and Cambodians were resettled under the sponsorship of five parishes, three parish organizations, 16 individuals and families.

Sister Mary Kevin, an MRS worker at the Eglin, Fla., camp, obtained resettlement sponsorship by a Texas seafood company for 101 fishermen and their families.

A special resettlement program for the placement of some 150 Vietnamese priests, 250 religious and a number of seminarians was placed under the direction of retired Bishop Robert E. Tracy, chairman of a USCC Ad Hoc Committee on Migration and Tourism.

ILLEGAL ALIENS

Bishop James S. Rausch, general secretary of the U. S. Catholic Conference, declared Aug. 7, 1975, in Atlanta that the conference would wage a "full lobbying effort to defeat" immigration legislation pending in Congress because it failed to provide full amnesty for illegal aliens.

The Bill in Question

At issue was a bill, passed by the House Judiciary Committee on a vote of 26 to 5 near the end of July, to provide regularization of immigrant status for illegals in the country before June 30, 1968, and penalties for employers who knowingly hire illegals.

The bill resembled two others passed earlier in the House of Representatives but passed over by inaction in the Senate. The USCC committed itself to counter-action even though it appeared that no conclusive action would be taken on the measure in the near future.

The conference was on record in support of a bill providing amnesty for illegals living in the United States before Jan. 1, 1975, if they had been in continuous residence since Mar. 19, 1974. The latter date was significant as the one on which all Social Security card holders, including illegals, were cleared for rights to employment.

Civil Rights Comment

The U.S. Commission on Civil Rights, in a letter to Rep. Don Edwards of California, said that passage of a bill in the form approved by the Judiciary Committee would have a direct discriminatory effect on minority persons seeking employment, whether they are citizens or aliens authorized to work in the United States."

John Buggs, staff director of the commission, said the bill would require minority job applicants to supply proof of legal status beyond what would be required of non-minority applicants. He added that, to avoid discrimination, the bill should require proof of status from all job applicants, not just "suspected illegal aliens."

Buggs noted that one objective of the employer-penalty provisions of the bill — which would place the employer in the position of an enforcer of immigration legislation — was to reduce unemployment by freeing jobs held by illegal aliens. He said: "However, attempts to solve this country's serious economic problems cannot be made at the expense of the civil and constitutional rights of minority persons."

Civil and Economic Problem

In the same vein, Bishop Rausch commented: "In attempting to solve an economic problem, this proposal will create a civil rights problem of horrendous magnitude."

Illegals and Problems

There are no reliable statistics available on the number of illegal aliens in this country. Estimates range from two to 12 million; probably, there are about six million. Perhaps 90 per cent of them are nominally Catholic — hence the pastoral concern of the U. S. Catholic Conference — from Mexico, Middle and South America, and the Caribbean.

Problems of integration and assimilation experienced by illegal aliens in the U.S. are extremely difficult and complex because their status forces them into closed ghettos out of fear of discovery, prevents advance through education, and forces them into precarious employment at minimum and below-minimum wages. Yet, many have established themselves as responsible wage-earners and heads of families.

One set of proposals for dealing with the illegal-alien situation was framed at a meeting in March, 1975, of 150 immigration personnel from dioceses in the northeastern section of the country. The principal points were: a uniform quota and preference system for both western and eastern hemispheres, the establishment of temporary work categories for aliens, and the enforcement of existing laws imposing sanctions on exploiting practices of employers.

Church Stands in Front

The U.S. Catholic Conference is the strongest, if not the only, body of national importance that has taken a firm stand in support of fair legislation affecting illegal aliens. The reason, as stated by Father S. M. Tomasi, director of the Scalabrini Fathers' Center for Migration Studies, is:

"Migrants, immigrants, refugees and all people forced to move by economic and political violence should be special wards of the Church because of their marginality, lack of participation in political processes, poverty and uprootedness. The Church should be the ombudsman of this segment of the human family specifically because of its universal mission and structure which enables it to reach them beyond any national characteristic."

HUMAN DEVELOPMENT

The Campaign for Human Development was inaugurated by the U.S. Catholic Conference in November, 1969, to combat injustice, oppression, alienation and poverty in this country in three significant ways:

• by making people in this country, especially Catholics, aware of the poverty, oppression and/or injustice afflicting some 35 million persons, through programs of education and public instruction;

• by funding self-help programs begun and carried out by the poor or by the poor and non-poor working together;

• by seeking a re-evaluation of the priorities of individuals, families, the Church and the civic community with respect to the stewardship of God-given goods.

The campaign got under way with a collection taken up in all parishes throughout the country on Nov. 22, 1970. Seventy-five per cent of the money contributed in this and subsequent annual collections was placed in a national fund principally for funding self-help projects and also for educational purposes; 25 per cent remained in the dioceses where it was collected, for similar use on the local levels.

Approximately $38 million have been contributed on national and local levels from 1970 through November, 1974. About $26 million in grants were allocated to some 900 projects from the national fund by the end of July, 1975. It was estimated that more than $6 million in local grants were allocated by diocesan agencies during the same period. The largest campaign collection, $8.5 million, was raised in 1970.

Aid requests are reviewed by a broadly representative committee of 40 members which passes its recommendations for funding on to the Bishops' Committee for the Campaign for Human Development. Requests for aid from the national office are about 10 times greater than the 140 to 170 programs funded each year. Local-level requests and funding are handled by diocesan offices for the Campaign for Human Development.

Father Lawrence J. McNamara of Kansas City, Mo., is executive director of the campaign. Bishop Raymond J. Gallagher of Lafayette, Ind., is chairman of the bishops' committee.

The national office is located at 1312 Massachusetts Ave. N.W., Washington, D.C. 20005.

NATIONAL SHRINE

The National Shrine of the Immaculate Conception is dedicated to the honor of the Blessed Virgin Mary, who was declared patroness of the United States in 1846.

The shrine project was launched in 1914; the site and foundation stone were blessed in 1920; the crypt, an underground church, was completed in 1926; the main church and superstructure were dedicated Nov. 20, 1959; more than 56 chapels and additional interior furnishings have been installed since the dedication. The shrine has a distinctive bell tower housing a 56-bell carillon.

The shrine is the seventh largest religious building in the world, with normal seating and standing accommodations for 6,000 persons. The shrine contains some of the largest mosaics in the world.

Approximately one million persons visit the shrine each year. Open daily, it is located adjacent to the Catholic University of America, Fourth St. and Michigan Ave. N. E., Washington, D. C., 20017.

The shrine director is Msgr. John J. Murphy.

CATHOLIC CHARISMATIC RENEWAL

Approximately 10,000 persons from 60 countries attended the ninth International Conference on the Charismatic Renewal in the Catholic Church May 16 to 19, 1975, at the Catacombs of St. Callistus in Rome. The number of attendants and the fact of the convocation in Rome during the Holy Year were significant indicators of the growth of the movement since the first conference, with 90 participants, met in February, 1967, on the campus of Notre Dame University, South Bend, Ind.

Pope Paul, during a special audience May 19 with those attending the Rome conference, welcomed whatever contribution the charismatic renewal could make to the spiritual renewal of the Church. He said: "It will be very fortuitous for our times, for our brothers, that there should be a generation, your generation of young people, who shout out to the world the glory and greatness of the God of Pentecost."

Background

The movement originated with a handful of Duquesne University students and faculty members in the 1966-67 academic year and spread from there to Notre Dame, Michigan State University and the University of Michigan, other campuses and cities throughout this country. The first eight of the movement's international conferences were held at Notre Dame University; the largest, in 1974, was attended by more than 25,000 persons.

Scriptural keys to the renewal are:
• Christ's promise to send the Holy Spirit upon the Apostles;
• the description, in the Acts of the Apostles, of the effects of the coming of the Holy Spirit upon the Apostles on Pentecost;
• St. Paul's explanation, in the Letter to the Romans, of the charismatic gifts (for the good of the Church and persons) the Holy Spirit would bestow on Christians;
• New Testament evidence concerning the effects of charismatic gifts in and through the early Church.

Baptism of the Spirit

The personal key to the renewal is baptism of the Holy Spirit. This is not a new sacrament but the personally experienced actualization of grace already sacramentally received. It is variously described as "a filling with grace and power first recorded in Scripture when the Holy Spirit descended on the Apostles on the day of Pentecost" (whence the name Pentecostals), and as "the release of the power of the Holy Spirit received in the sacrament of confirmation." Its result, according to Stephen Clark, a leader of the movement, is "a change in our relationships with God such that we begin to experience in

our lives all the things which God promised that the Holy Spirit would do for believers."

Charismatic Gifts

The experience of baptism of the Holy Spirit is often accompanied by the reception of one or more charismatic gifts, such as: speaking in tongues, which is regarded as a gift of prayer; prophecy, a specific message exhorting listeners to greater love of and obedience to God; healings, which sometimes occur as a group prays for an individual, a sign of God's love and power, and a call to greater faith and reliance on him.

Charismatic gifts are understood in terms of their usefulness in building up the Church and manifesting God's love.

Among the movement's strongest points of emphasis are prayer, openness to the Holy Spirit, community experience and the sharing of spiritual gifts.

Prayer Meeting and Purpose

The characteristic form of the renewal is the weekly prayer meeting, a gathering which includes periods of spontaneous prayer, singing, sharing of experience and testimony, fellowship and teaching. Leadership teams usually guide the meetings and other activities associated with the movement, such as programs to help newcomers experience the baptism of the Spirit and seminars on subjects like personal relationships, prayer, marriage and family life, Christian growth.

The purpose of the movement is to restore the charismatic dimension of Christian life to the position of prominence and influence theologians agree it had in the early Church. Father Edward D. O'Connor, C.S.C., associate professor of theology at Notre Dame, has noted that the nature of the charismatic renewal is the same as that of the biblical and liturgical movements — to restore something to the entire Church, not to remain indefinitely as a special group within the Church. Presumably, the charismatic renewal will cease to exist as a movement when the Church becomes charismatically renewed.

Cardinal Leo J. Suenens of Belgium, a speaker at several of the international conferences, has called the charismatic renewal "a current of grace, a 'move' of the Spirit, not a movement. It will disappear as a movement as quickly as possible and enter into the blood and life of the Church."

Participation

The movement's service committee estimated in 1975 that more than 600,000 Catholics were or had been participants in prayer groups in the United States and Canada. The renewal's spread was also reported in many other countries. The movement's monthly,

New Covenant, has subscribers in 90 countries.

A substantial number of predominantly Catholic prayer groups include Protestant participants, a development called a good example of grass-roots ecumenism by several observers.

Participants in conferences and various bishops have appealed for greater interest and involvement in the renewal by bishops and priests. Auxiliary Bishop Joseph McKinney of Grand Rapids, a liaison official between the renewal's service committee and the National Conference of Catholic Bishops, estimates that about 90 per cent of the bishops are favorably disposed toward the movement itself but not toward the vagaries of some ex-

tremists. Reports in that vein were issued by the conference in 1969 and 1972.

Bishop Gerald L. Frey of Lafayette, La., is chairman for the U.S. Bishops' Ad Hoc Committee for the Charismatic Renewal.

Major services of the charismatic renewal are administered by a seven-man service committee whose operations are reviewed periodically by a 47-member advisory committee.

The address of the Communications Center, Charismatic Renewal Services, is P.O. Drawer A, Notre Dame, Ind. 46556. Ann Arbor, Mich. 48107, is the location of *New Covenant* (P.O. Box 102), the Ecumenical Communications Office (P.O. Box 331) and the International Communications Office (P.O. Box 363).

ADDRESS OF POPE PAUL: CHARISMATIC RENEWAL

On May 19, 1975, the Holy Father addressed more than 10,000 participants in the Ninth International Conference of the Charismatic Renewal at an audience in St. Peter's Basilica. Following are excerpts from the official translation of his text, distributed by the Vatican Press Office. Original lengthy paragraphs have been broken up and subheads added.

Nothing is more necessary to this more and more secularized world than the witness of this "spiritual renewal" that we see the Holy Spirit evoking in the most diverse regions and milieux.

Manifestations of Renewal

The manifestations of this renewal are varied: a profound communion of souls, intimate contact with God, in fidelity to the commitments undertaken at baptism, in prayer — frequently in group prayer — in which each person, expressing himself freely, aids, sustains, and fosters the prayer of the others and, at the basis of everything, a personal conviction, which does not have its source solely in a teaching received by faith, but also in a certain lived experience.

This lived experience shows that without God man can do nothing, that with him, on the other hand, everything becomes possible: hence this need to praise God, thank him, celebrate the marvels that he works everywhere about us and within us.

The Vertical Dimension

Human existence rediscovers its "relationship with God," what is called the "vertical dimension," without which man is irremediably crippled. Not, of course, that this "search for God" appears as a desire for conquest or possession; it wishes to be a pure acceptance of him who loves us and gives himself freely to us, desiring, because he loves us, to communicate to us a life that we have to receive freely from him, but not without a humble fidelity on our part.

And this fidelity must know how to unite

action to faith according to the teaching of St. James: "For as the body apart from the spirit is dead, so faith apart from works is dead" (Jas. 2:26).

You know the great importance that the Apostle (Paul) attributed to the "spiritual gifts." "Never try to suppress the Spirit," he wrote to the Thessalonians (1 Thess. 5:19), while immediately adding: "Test everything, hold fast what is good" (v. 21). Thus he considered that a discernment was always necessary, and he entrusted the task of testing to those whom he had placed over the community (see v. 12). . . . He indicates . . . three principles in the light of which they will more easily be able to practice this indispensable discernment.

• The first principle . . . is fidelity to the authentic doctrine of the faith (1 Cor. 12:1-3). Anything that contradicted it would not come from the Spirit; he who distributes his gifts is the same one who inspired the Scriptures and who assists the living magisterium of the Church to whom, according to the Catholic faith, Christ entrusted the authentic interpretation of these Scriptures. This is why you experience the need for an ever deeper doctrinal formation: biblical, spiritual, theological. Only a formation such as this, whose authenticity must be guaranteed by the hierarchy, will preserve you from every ever-possible deviations. . . .

• The second principle: All spiritual gifts are to be received with gratitude; and you know that the list is long (1 Cor. 12:4-10; 28-30), and does not claim to be complete (see Rm. 12:6-8; Eph. 6:11). Given, nevertheless, "for the common good" (1 Cor. 12:7), they do not all procure this common good to the same degree. Thus the Corinthians are to "desire the higher gifts (v. 31), those most useful for the community (see 14:1-5).

• The third principle is the most important one in the thought of the Apostle. . . . "Above all hovers love" (E. Osty). No matter how desirable spiritual goods are . . . only the love of charity, *agape,* makes the Christian perfect.

ECUMENICAL COLLABORATION

The Secretariat for Promoting Christian Unity released July 7, 1975, a booklet entitled "Ecumenical Collaboration at the Regional, National and Local Levels." It was intended, according to Cardinal Jan Willebrands, president of the secretariat, to give "the kind of information which can help bishops in a certain place decide about the form to be given to local ecumenical collaboration."

Following are quotations from the booklet. The text was circulated by the NC Documentary Service, Origins, July 31, 1975 (Vol. 5, No. 8).

The Ecumenical Task: "All Christian communities recognize the proclamation of the Gospel to the world, in deed as well as in word, as their first duty."

"Ecumenical initiatives must be adapted to local needs and will therefore differ from region to region, while always remaining in harmony with the bonds of Catholic communion."

"Ecumenism is an integral part of the renewal of the Church, and its promotion should be the constant concern of the local church."

"A difficulty is created if ecumenical initiatives are left solely to unofficial groups. Then there is an imbalance in which the full ecumenical responsiblity will not be adequately and prudently met. Such difficulties will best be avoided if there is an obvious and sincere commitment to ecumenism by the local church."

Ecumenism on the Local Level: "Ecumenism on the local level is a primary element of the ecumenical situation as a whole. It is not secondary, nor merely derivative. It faces specific needs and situations, and has its own resources. It has an initiative of its own, and its task is a wider one then merely implementing worldwide ecumenical directives on a small scale."

Forms of Local Ecumenism (such as sharing in prayer and worship, Bible projects, pastoral care, shared premises, education, social action): "The rule is that Catholic churches are reserved for Catholic worship. . . . Therefore, sharing them with other Christians or constructing new churches jointly with other Christians can be only by way of exception."

"In catechetics, local needs have led at times to collaboration in the teaching of religion, especially where this has to be done in non-denominational schools. But so long as Christians are not fully at one in faith, catechesis, which is formation for profession of faith, must remain necessarily the proper and inalienable task of the various churches and ecclesial communities."

Councils of Churches and Christian Councils: These are "fellowships of churches and other Christian bodies which seek to work together, to engage in dialogue, and to overcome the divisions and misunderstandings existing among them."

"Membership in local councils does not imply that membership in national councils must then be sought, just as local or national membership does not involve membership in the World Council of Churches. The question of membership must be examined separately and afresh at each level."

(Four years after exploratory talks began between the Vatican and the World Council of Churches, Pope Paul said in 1969 that the moment for Catholic membership in the body was not yet ripe.

(As of July 7, 1975, the Catholic Church had full membership in the following 19 national councils of churches: Denmark, Sweden, The Netherlands, Swaziland, Belize (British Honduras), Samoa, Fiji, New Hebrides, Solomon Islands, Papua-New Guinea, Tonga, West Germany, Botswana, St. Vincent (British Antilles), Sudan, Uganda, Finland, Guyana, Trinidad and Tobago.)

Council Statements: These are not to be considered as official utterances of member churches "unless explicitly authorized."

Pastoral and Practical Reflections: "What really matters is not the creation of new structures but the collaboration of Christians in prayer, reflection and action, based on common baptism and on a faith which on many essential points is also common."

Joint programs should be "duly authorized by the respective authorities right from the earliest stages of planning."

"It is necessary that, where there are regional, national and local doctrinal, bilateral dialogues, episcopal conferences ensure that at the right time there is contact with the Holy See."

Other Forms of Ecumenism: Some Christians prefer "to engage in local action which is ecumenical by means of informal groups of a spontaneous kind."

"In connection with the hierarchy of the Church, these informal groups can offer original and inspiring ideas; whereas, without such a contact and apart from ecclesiastical direction, they run the risk of becoming unfaithful to Catholic principles of ecumenism and even of endangering the faith."

REPORT OF COLLABORATION

The ecumenical collaboration of Catholics with other Christians was the subject of a study completed in 1974 under the auspices of the National Council of the Churches of Christ in the U.S.A. Findings of the study of 130 responding ecumenical agencies were published in 1975 under the title, "U.S. Catholic Ecumenism — Ten Years Later" (following ratification by the Second Vatican Council of its *Decree on Ecumenism in 1964).* Father David J. Bowman, S.J., associate director of the NCC commission, was the editor of the study report.

Examples of Ecumenism: During the period of the study, Catholics took part in such phases of ecumenism as "Roman Catholic ecumenism in local churches, adult education courses, social action projects, prayer, pulpit exchanges, sharing of facilities, ministerial associations, living-room dialogues, committees of all kinds, covenanted parishes, ecumenical agencies of all sorts, seminary clusters."

Evaluation: Steady progress at every level of church life was reported. However, there was a waning of popular enthusiasm after a hopeful start, coupled with apathy and a tendency to leave ecumenical effort to experts. One observer, Jerry Filteau of NC News Service, noted: "Compared with the vast effort still needed, the existing structures of local ecumenism are still spotty and inadequate."

Catholic Participation: Catholic participation was reported in 93.4 per cent of the 130 responding agencies; 45.2 per cent had full Catholic membership and participation.

"Churches came together around community issues 35.7 per cent of the time, around Faith and Order issues 16 per cent of the time, and through living-room dialogues 16 per cent of the time."

Issues:
• Divisive: Abortion, at all levels; aid to parochial schools, at state, county and city levels.
• Impeding: Denominationalism, "excessive attention to the internal structure and working of a church"; apathy, symptomatic of a low priority for ecumenism; fear; poor agency organization, "with vague means" to achieve "vague goals."
• Current: At all levels, "religion and the public schools, clergy education, criminal justice matters, the Holy Year, abortion, housing, the aged, welfare, chaplaincies, prison reform and, infrequently, Faith and Order issues."

Views and Emphases of Catholics:
• "Roman Catholics, like most other Christians, feel a bit uneasy about the way we face the hard issues of ecumenical life, but optimistic about the future and, above all, see ecumenism as a covenant community. They see ecumenical life much more with the undergirding of spiritual ecumenism than other Christians seem to do who stress social action more. There is a 20 per cent difference between Roman Catholics and the others here, and it is a significant difference which must be dealt with in coming to a better understanding of how local ecumenical life can succeed. For Catholics, a better balancing of action with prayer; for others, a better balancing of prayer with action."
• "Catholics show more concern for theological study and motivation arising from it, in regard to 'pro life' issues."
• "Many Roman Catholics feel that their ecumenical participation has included a tacit agreement to ignore issues where consensus within the ecumenical agency does not exist. In our opinion, such tacit agreements should be brought to voice and probably to vote; they do not seem to help the ecumenical movement more than they hinder it, at least in the long run."
• "There is basic, strong agreement that common prayer should be the basis for ecumenical life. . . . Twenty per cent more Catholics say prayer is essential to ecumenical life; more of them know about the bilateral theological conversations and try to apply theology to social action."
• "The Week of Prayer for Christian Unity, theological dialogue including living-room dialogues, the discipline which Catholics call 'moral theology' and Protestants usually term 'Christian ethics,' and a method which would include prayer, study and social action together — all of these seem strongly indicated whenever Catholics are moving into greater participation in ecumenical life."

CATHOLIC-JEWISH RELATIONS

Following is the text of a document issued Jan. 3, 1975, by the Vatican Commission for Religious Relations with the Jews. Its purpose is to provide suggestions and guidelines for implementing the part of the Second Vatican Council's "Declaration on Relations with Non-Christian Religions" which deals with Christian-Jewish relations. The document was dated Dec. 1, 1974.

The text was circulated by the NC Documentary Service, Origins, Jan. 9, 1975 (Vol. 4, No. 29). Several subheads have been added.

The Declaration *Nostra Aetate,* issued by the Second Vatican Council on October 28, 1965, "On the Relationship of the Church to Non-Christian Religions" (No. 4), marks an important milestone in the history of Jewish-Christian relations.

Moreover, the step taken by the council finds its historical setting in circumstances deeply affected by the memory of the persecution and massacre of Jews which took place in Europe just before and during the Second World War.

Although Christianity sprang from Judaism, taking from it certain essential elements of its faith and divine cult, the gap dividing them was deepened more and more, to such an extent that Christian and Jew hardly knew each other.

After two thousand years, too often marked by mutual ignorance and frequent confrontation, the Declaration *Nostra Aetate* provides an opportunity to open or to continue a dialogue with a view to better mutual understanding. Over the past nine years, many steps in this direction have been taken in various countries. As a result, it is easier to distinguish the conditions under which a new relationship between Jews and Christians may be worked out and developed.

Suggestions from Experience

This seems the right moment to propose, following the guidelines of the council, some concrete suggestions born of experience, hoping that they will help to bring into actual existence in the life of the Church the intentions expressed in the conciliar document.

While referring the reader back to this document, we may simply restate here that the spiritual bonds and historical links binding the Church to Judaism condemn (as opposed to the very spirit of Christianity) all forms of anti-Semitism and discrimination, which in any case the dignity of the human person alone would suffice to condemn. Further still, these links and relationships render obligatory a better mutual understanding and renewed mutual esteem. On the practical level in particular, Christians must therefore strive to acquire a better knowledge of the basic components of the religious tradition of Judaism; they must strive to learn by what essential traits the Jews define themselves in the light of their own religious experience.

With due respect for such matters of principle, we simply propose some first practical applications in different essential areas of the Church's life, with a view to launching or developing sound relations between Catholics and their Jewish brothers.

I. Dialogue

To tell the truth, such relations as there have been between Jew and Christian have scarcely ever risen above the level of monologue. From now on, real dialogue must be established.

Dialogue presupposes that each side wishes to know the other, and wishes to increase and deepen its knowledge of the other. It constitutes a particularly suitable means of favoring a better mutual knowledge and, especially in the case of dialogue between Jews and Christians, of probing the riches of one's own tradition. Dialogue demands respect for the other as he is; above all, respect for his faith and his religious convictions.

In virtue of her divine mission, and her very nature the Church must preach Jesus Christ to the world (*Ad Gentes,* "On the Church's Missionary Activity," No. 2). Lest the witness of Catholics to Jesus Christ should give offense to Jews, they must take care to live and spread their Christian faith while maintaining the strictest respect for religious liberty in line with the teaching of the Second Vatican Council (Declaration *Dignitatis Humanae,* "On Religious Freedom"). They will likewise

strive to understand the difficulties which arise for the Jewish soul — rightly imbued with an extremely high, pure notion of the divine transcendence — when faced with the mystery of the Incarnate Word.

Assessment of Responsibilities

While it is true that a widespread air of suspicion, inspired by an unfortunate past, is still dominant in this particular area, Christians, for their part, will be able to see to what extent the responsibility is theirs and deduce practical conclusions for the future.

In addition to friendly talks, competent people will be encouraged to meet and to study together the many problems deriving from the fundamental convictions of Judaism and of Christianity. In order not to hurt (even involuntarily) those taking part, it will be vital to guarantee not only tact but a great openness of spirit and diffidence with respect to one's own prejudices.

In whatever circumstances as shall prove possible and mutually acceptable, one might encourage a common meeting in the presence of God, in prayer and silent meditation, a highly efficacious way of finding that humility, that openness of heart and mind, necessary prerequisites for a deep knowledge of oneself and of others. In particular, that will be done in connection with great causes such as the struggle for peace and justice.

II. Liturgy

The existing links between the Christian liturgy and the Jewish liturgy will be borne in mind. The idea of a living community in the service of God, and in the service of men for the love of God, such as it is realized in the liturgy, is just as characteristic of the Jewish liturgy as it is of the Christian one. To improve Jewish-Christian relations, it is important to take cognizance of those common elements of the liturgical life (formulas, feasts, rites, etc.) in which the Bible holds an essential place.

An effort will be made to acquire a better understanding of whatever in the Old Testament retains its own perpetual value (cf. *Dei Verbum,* "Dogmatic Constitution on Divine Revelation," Nos. 14-15), since that has not been cancelled by the later interpretation of the New Testament. Rather, the New Testament brings out the full meaning of the Old, while both Old and New illumine and explain each other (cf. *Ibid.,* No. 16). This is all the more important since liturgical reform is now bringing the text of the Old Testament ever more frequently to the attention of Christians.

Meaning of Texts

When commenting on biblical texts, emphasis will be laid on the continuity of our faith with that of the earlier Covenant, in the perspective of the promises, without minimizing those elements of Christianity which are original. We believe that those promises were fulfilled with the first coming of Christ. But it is none-the-less true that we still await their perfect fulfillment in his glorious return at the end of time.

With respect to liturgical readings, care will be taken to see that homilies based on them will not distort their meaning, especially when it is a question of passages which seem to show the Jewish people as such in an unfavorable light. Efforts will be made so to instruct the Christian people that they will understand the true interpretation of all the texts and their meaning for the contemporary believer.

Commissions entrusted with the task of liturgical translation will pay particular attention to the way in which they express those phrases and passages which Christians, if not well informed, might musunderstand because of prejudice. Obviously, one cannot alter the text of the Bible. The point is that, with a version destined for liturgical use, there should be an overriding preoccupation to bring out explicitly the meaning of a text, while taking scriptural studies into account.

[Thus the formula "the Jews," in St. John, sometimes according to the context means "the leaders of the Jews," or "the adversaries of Jesus," terms which express better the thought of the Evangelist and avoid appearing to arraign the Jewish people as such. Another example is the use of the words "pharisee" and "pharisaism," which have taken a largely pejorative meaning.]

The preceding remarks also apply to introductions to biblical readings, to the Prayer of the Faithful, and to commentaries printed in missals used by the laity.

III. Teaching and Education

Although there is still a great deal of work to be done, a better understanding of Judaism itself and its relationship to Christianity has been achieved in recent years, thanks to the teaching of the Church, the study and research of scholars, as also to the beginning of dialogue. In this respect, the following facts deserve to be recalled.

• It is the same God, "inspirer and author of the books of both Testaments" (*Dei Verbum,* No. 16), who speaks both in the Old and New Covenants.

• Judaism in the time of Christ and the Apostles was a complex reality embracing many different trends, many spiritual, religious, social and cultural values.

• The Old Testament and the Jewish tradition founded upon it must not be set against the New Testament in such a way that the former seems to constitute a religion of only justice, fear and legalism, with no appeal to the love of God and neighbor (cf. Dt. 6:5, Lv. 19:18, Mt. 22:34-40).

• Jesus was born of the Jewish people, as were his Apostles and a large number of his first disciples. When he revealed himself as

the Messiah and Son of God (cf. Mt. 16:6), the bearer of the new Gospel message, he did so as the fulfillment and perfection of the earlier Revelation. And, although his teaching had a profoundly new character, Christ, nevertheless, in many instances, took his stand on the teaching of the Old Testament. The New Testament is profoundly marked by its relation to the Old. As the Second Vatican Council declared: "God, the inspirer and author of the books of both Testaments, wisely arranged that the New Testament be hidden in the Old and the Old be made manifest in the New" (*Dei Verbum,* No. 16), Jesus also used teaching methods similar to those employed by the rabbis of his time.

• With regard to the trial and death of Jesus, the council recalled that "what happened in his passion cannot be blamed upon all the Jews then living, without distinction, nor upon the Jews of today" (*Nostra Aetate,* No. 4).

• The history of Judaism did not end with the destruction of Jerusalem, but rather went on to develop a religious tradition. And, although we believe that the importance and meaning of that tradition were deeply affected by the coming of Christ, it is still nonetheless rich in religious values.

• With the prophets and the Apostle Paul, "the Church awaits the day, known to God alone, on which all peoples will address the Lord in a single voice and 'serve him with one accord' (Soph. 3:9)" (*Nostra Aetate,* No. 4).

Information concerning these questions is important at all levels of Christian instruction and education. Among sources of information, special attention should be paid to the following:

• —Catechisms and religious textbooks;
• —history books;
• —the mass media (press, radio, cinema, television).

The effective use of these means presupposes the thorough formation of instructors and educators in training schools, seminaries and universities.

Research into the problems bearing on Judaism and Jewish-Christian relations will be encouraged among specialists, particularly in the fields of exegesis, theology, history and sociology. Higher institutions of Catholic research, in association if possible with other similar Christian institutions and experts, are invited to contribute to the solution of such problems. Wherever possible, chairs of Jewish studies will be created, and collaboration with Jewish scholars encouraged.

IV. Joint Social Action

Jewish and Christian tradition, founded on the Word of God, is aware of the value of the human person, the image of God. Love of the same God must show itself in effective action for the good of mankind. In the spirit of the prophets, Jews and Christians will work willingly together, seeking social justice and peace at every level — local, national and international.

At the same time, such collaboration can do much to foster mutual understanding and esteem.

Conclusion

The Second Vatican Council has pointed out the path to follow in promoting deep fellowship between Jews and Christians. But there is still a long road ahead.

The problem of Jewish-Christian relations concerns the Church as such, since it is when "pondering her own mystery" that she encounters the mystery of Israel, Therefore, even in areas where no Jewish communities exist, this remains an important problem. There is also an ecumenical aspect to the question: the very return of Christians to the sources and origins of their faith, grafted on to the earlier Covenant, helps the search for unity in Christ, the cornerstone.

In this field, the bishops will know what best to do on the pastoral level, within the general disciplinary framework of the Church and in line with the common teaching of her *magisterium*. For example, they will create some suitable commissions or secretariats on a national or regional level, or appoint some competent person to promote the implementation of the conciliar directives and the suggestions made above. On October 22, 1974, the Holy Father instituted for the universal Church this commission for Religious Relations with the Jews, joined to the Secretariat for Promoting Christian Unity. This special commission, created to encourage and foster religious relations between Jews and Catholics — and to do so eventually in collaboration with other Christians — will be, within the limits of its competence, at the service of all interested organizations, providing information for them, and helping them to pursue their task in conformity with the instructions of the Holy See.

The commission wishes to develop this collaboration in order to implement, correctly and effectively, the express intentions of the council.

COMMENT

The guidelines above were praised by such representative Jewish spokesmen as Nahum Goldmann, president of the World Jewish Congress; Dr. Joseph L. Lichten, member of the International Catholic-Jewish Liaison Committee; and Rabbi Marc Tanenbaum, director of interreligious affairs for the American Jewish Committee. Each man, however, stated several reservations.

Nahum Goldmann: Called the guidelines "a very positive document" but noted that they contain "some omissions" and "some doctrinal affirmations resulting from the unavoidable divergencies between Christianity and Judaism." He added, however, that "these deficiencies do not stem from any lack of understanding of Jewish commitments."

Dr. Joseph L. Lichten: Called attention to the document's use of the word "condemn" — instead of the weaker "deplore" as in the Vatican II document on the subject—with respect to "all forms of anti-Semitism and discrimination."

In criticism, he said: (1) "The existing link between Jewish religion, people and land is not discussed at all." (2) "Further clarification seems to be required regarding 'the fulfillment and perfection' of the earlier Revelation by the New Testament, and (3) particularly the affirmation of Catholics' obligation to 'witness' to their faith."

Rabbi Marc Tanenbaum: Said that from a Jewish perspective the guidelines as a whole are "a conservative and timely contribution to the advancement of Jewish-Christian understanding and cooperation."

He stated, however, that the document "contains . . . formulations regarding conversion (which) imply a religious 'second-class' status (of Jews) in the family of faith communities."

Objections of Rabbinate

The American Orthodox Rabbinate: Deplored, in a statement issued Jan. 21, 1975, the failure of the guidelines to "forthrightly acknowledge that the land of Israel is central in the theology of Judaism." This view was expressed earlier by the International Jewish Committee on Interreligious Consultations. The rabbinate also took exception to the document's suggestion regarding joint prayers, calling such a practice "unacceptable" in traditional Judaism.

Critics Answered

Father Edward Flannery, director of the U.S. Bishops' Secretariat for Catholic-Jewish Relations: Disputed Rabbi Tanenbaum's views. He said that "nothing in the document assigns an inferior status to Judaism." Also, that the statement concerning the universal mission of the Church and its members to witness to Christ "in no sense implies a particular (conversionary) mission to Jews."

Other observers noted that fidelity to its nature and mission requires the Church, and therefore its members, to give full witness to Christ. Failure to do so — just as any failure of Jews to give witness to their covenant — would be incompatible with the faith commitment of Catholics.

Dr. Lichten declared that a few days after release of the guidelines the Catholic delegation to the International Catholic-Jewish Liaison Committee "made it clear that neither the document taken as a whole nor any part of it should be understood as an attempt at proselytising Jews."

THE WORLD FOOD CRISIS — PASTORAL PLAN

Following are excerpts from a statement with this title approved and issued by the National Conference of Catholic Bishops Nov. 21, 1974.

The text was circulated by the NC Documentary Service, Origins, Dec. 5, 1974 (Vol. 4, No. 24).

A. Public Policy/Legislative Program

The fundamental premise of the program is that food is a unique commodity and a sacred resource. The guidelines for legislative initiatives meriting USCC support are the following:

• First, increase genuine agricultural development overseas. Technical assistance and development programs must be expanded to promote greater food production in the less industrialized nations.

• Second, increase funding for Food for Peace (PL 480); as an immediate step increase substantially food allocations through Title II of Food for Peace (humanitarian aid), and resist efforts to use food as a political and strategic weapon.

• Third, modify U.S. trade policies to lower trade barriers and to provide just prices for imports from poor countries. Special trade preferences for these nations' exports and substantially increased adjustment assistance for adversely affected U.S. workers and industries must be part of this revised trade policy.

• Fourth, assure American farmers of a fair return for their capital and labor. The productivity and viability of American agriculture must be maintained. Serious disruption of this sector of the economy could adversely affect the world food crisis.

• Fifth, promote more equitable distribution of resources in the United States. Areas of legislation in this regard are the following: expanding programs of food stamps and school lunches, providing special assistance to the elderly, the unemployed and the poor, revising income tax burdens, and restructuring land-use policies.

• Sixth, protect both family farmers who are often subject to severe economic pressures in the agricultural chain of food production, processing and sales, and also consumers in middle and lower income categories.

• Seventh, modify the operation of the free market system, especially the impact of the large corporation, when it stands in the way of justice.

B. Community Information and Education

Since the food crisis is a long-term problem as well as one of immediate concern, it will be necessary to keep the structural dimensions of the issue, both in its factual and moral aspects, before the public. The Church has means of doing this through already funded programs which merit implementation at the national, diocesan and parish levels. Among them are the following:

• first, its educational system for adults, youth and children;

• second, its access to the public through the secular and religious media;

• third, workshops, special days of reflection and study for priests, religious communities and laity.

C. Pastoral Care

The most direct, universal and concrete contact the Church has with its people is at the level of pastoral ministry. Unique opportunities are available to promote the Church's deep concern about human development.

1. Liturgy: The themes of life, bread, community, solidarity and responsibility flow through the symbol and substance of the liturgical life of the Church. These can be woven into teaching, worshipping and prayer experiences which address the food crisis to the whole community. Liturgical seasons of the Church's year are especially appropriate; for example, Advent, Lent, rogation days, the Holy Year. Particularly to be encouraged are parish and diocesan programs of worship, fasting and abstinence on appointed days. The funds from such fasting would be directed toward efforts ministering to the needs of others.

2. Life Style: A major pressure on food supply is the pattern of consumption. Especially evident in our consumer-oriented way of life are the waste of food and the excessive consumption of energy. Appeals to Christian conscience of responsible stewardship, highlighting the practice of days of fast and abstinence, flow from the deepest roots of our biblical and ecclesiastical traditions. We urge the whole Catholic community — priests, religious and laity — to join with us in observing at least two days a week as days of fast. We also urge resistance to advertising and other forms of social pressure which promote affluent and wasteful eating habits.

3. Locating and Feeding the Hungry: In this time of food scarcity, inflation, economic recession and rising unemployment, methods of pastoral care require renewal and adaptation. First, awareness must be heightened about the condition of many members of our society, and efforts by priests, religious and laity must be intensified to locate and minister to those suffering severe hardships in our dioceses, parishes and local communities. Commanding attention, in particular, are the aged on limited fixed incomes, the working poor and the unemployed, and families and individuals on welfare and other public assistance programs.

Second, support for increased activities must be given to such agencies as Catholic Charities, Catholic Relief Services, the Campaign for Human Development and others. This will enable them to intensify their efforts to provide immediate short-term relief and to work for long-term structural changes for human development.

Conclusion

In this pastoral response to the food crisis the American Catholic community is called to

SYNOD OF BISHOPS, 1974

This report was written by James C. O'Neill, Rome correspondent of NC News Service.

For coverage of the nature, constitution and previous three assemblies of the synod, see separate article, Synod of Bishops.

The fourth assembly of the Synod of Bishops closed Oct. 26, 1974, on a note of hope for the Church in the future, but did not give as simple and clear a statement on evangelization as many had hoped for.

At the end of four weeks of intensive work by some 209 synodal fathers — including cardinals, bishops and the heads of major religious orders of the Church — the synod issued a general declaration stressing the "intimate connection" between human liberation and evangelization (see following article for excerpts).

It also sent the results of thousands of hours of debate and dialogue to Pope Paul for future "refinement" that would express clearly the essential thought of bishops from every continent about the prospects, hopes and problems of preaching the word of God to man today.

The Pope's Reaction

In his closing address to the synod Oct. 26, the Pope himself touched the core of the problem that the synod finally found itself faced with.

"Certainly the breadth and complexity of the theme, 'Evangelization of the Modern World,' did not allow it to be dealt with exhaustively in a short time," the Pope said. He added that the vastness and complexity of the subject did not "allow the hoped-for conclusions to be arrived at in their fullness."

Only a few days before the synod closed, the participants voted to reject three-fourths of a proposed 40-page document which had been drawn up in committee. That document had attempted to touch every point that had been brought up by hundreds of speeches and written documents submitted over a four-week period. The proposed document was rejected, primarily because it was too general, too theoretical and insufficiently profound theologically.

Estimates of Synod

Much of the world press interpreted the rejection of the proposed document as indicating a "failure" of the synod. The closing speech of Pope Paul was also seen as "nega-

address a broad agenda of issues (related to human welfare everywhere).

The goals outlined here for the Church are only a beginning. No document could possibly embrace the many activities and programs which will be required to respond to the cries of the hungry and to what Pope Paul has called this "crisis of civilization and solidarity."

tive," and "too Roman" by some newsmen and even by observers at the synod.

However, many of the participants themselves took a very positive attitude toward the entire synodal process. For instance, the five U.S. delegates who took part in the meetings made a point of issuing a statement on the closing day, beginning:

"We believe this to have been the best of the synods so far. The preparation was careful and thorough, the format was simple and well conceived, the exchange of views was candid and perceptive. It was truly a bishops' synod, in which bishops participated fully in planning and implementation."

No Simple Solutions

The U.S. participants were Cardinals John Krol of Philadelphia, John Carberry of St. Louis and John Dearden of Detroit, and Archbishops Joseph Bernardin of Cincinnati and John Quinn of Oklahoma City.

In their statement the U.S. participants also made the point: "The synod has not 'solved' the problems the Church faces in evangelization, but simple solutions to complex matters were never anticipated."

The essential problem encountered by the synod was the very simplicity of the theme put before it, "Evangelization of the Modern World." When the bishops of Asia, Africa, Europe, North and South America and the Pacific came together to discuss problems of evangelization they face on the local level, they found vast differences among their problems, although some problems such as secularization, indifference, and a pleasure-loving, non-virtue-centered society seemed to be found in many places.

However, a common note was struck in the bishops' reactions at the conclusion of the entire discussion.

As Cardinal Dearden put it: "The Holy Father seems to be saying that some of the questions raised during the synod must be seen in a broader context, because they have implications beyond the issue of evangelization."

Indigenization and Unity

The cardinal's remarks were addressed specifically to an issue raised by some of the African and Asian bishops who called for more decentralization, more "indigenization" of local churches — meaning greater adaptation to local cultures.

Cardinal Dearden said: "The Pope's comments were not negative or critical of the synod but were rather a reasonable effort to broaden the scope of the discussion by pointing to the relation between what the synod had discussed and other aspects of the Church."

Cardinal Krol, touching on the same point, noted: "There is certainly a valid kind of indigenization in the Church. However, the Holy Father was quite correct in pointing to the possible danger of carrying indigenization to the extreme of local autonomy at the expense of the unity and universality of the Church willed by Christ."

Cardinal Maurice Otunga of Nairobi, Kenya, interpreted the Pope's thought this way: "He wants to see the Church vitalized in the new situations of the world, and this is a positive approach. When he tells us to be careful, I see nothing in that because there are so many conflicting and confusing ideas flying about these days."

Experience of Unity

The African cardinal said that, for himself, "The synod personally has meant an experience of the unity of the Catholic Church. . . . The bishops present shared an anxiety which recognized the Holy Father as the physical head of the unity of the Church. . . . Without this physical unity, we are lost. There is also the fact that the world at the moment is coming together very fast and we cannot solve our problems in solitude.

"This anxiety to preserve the unity of the Church explains why the synod did not come up with what some had at first expected. We are an advisory body, and we had to ask ourselves — Are we dictating to the Pope, or are we talking to him and to ourselves? We have handed everything over to the Holy Father, and he will in time give us the guidelines."

Conflicting opinions over the results of this synod seem to grow out of the fact that it is an evolving Church organism with less than 10 years of history behind it.

As Bishop Gerald Emmett Carter of London, Ontario, Canada, put it: "The synod is a young institution and the young have a right to make mistakes, but they have no right to pessimism."

Accomplishments of Synod

Aside from the important but difficult-to-evalue conversations of bishops from around the world with themselves, with the Pope and with officials of the Church's central administrative offices in the Vatican, a major product of the synod was a general declaration on the necessity of evangelization. The synod also drew up an index of major problems of evangelization to be studied by Pope Paul and the synod's secretariat and council.

A side-result of the synod was a human-rights document drawn up by a synodal committee led by Cardinal Krol.

On Sunday noon, Oct. 27, the day after the synod closed, Pope Paul alluded publicly to the synod as an "historic moment," and made special mention of Cardinal Krol and the declaration on human rights.

EVANGELIZATION — STATEMENT OF 1974 BISHOPS' SYNOD

The following excerpts are from the "Declaration of the Synodal Fathers" which was approved by the Synod of Bishops Oct. 25, 1974, by a vote of 182 to 11.

The English translation of the statement was circulated by the NC Documentary Service, Origins, Nov. 7, 1974 (Vol. 4, No. 20). Lead lines have been added.

With this declaration of ours, we would simply like to manifest some fundamental convictions and a few of the more urgent guidelines to further promote and deepen the work we began (in this synod).

Mandate To Evangelize: We wish to confirm anew that the mandate to evangelize all men constitutes the essential mission of the Church.

The necessity to proclaim the Gospel to all nations and to every individual man, is evident and urgent, especially for those to whom the announcement of the good news of Christ has not yet been brought, wherever they might be on the face of the earth, so that the evangelization and the foundation of the Church might take root in all peoples and places.

Christian Duty: Christ's love and his man-

date urge all the faithful to dispense to others the gifts received freely from him. Therefore, the duty to proclaim the Gospel belongs to the whole people of God, gathered by the Holy Spirit in the Church through the word of God and the Eucharist.

No real Christian may absent himself from this duty which he must carry out in keeping with his state and in communion with his pastors.

The Young: In a special way we address young people whom we do not consider only as a subject to be evangelized, but also as particularly suited to evangelize others, especially their own age group. Furthermore, we are convinced that young people, to the extent that they are searching for the fundamental values of the Gospel and demanding true authenticity in conceiving and witnessing the faith, challenge us adults and compel us to renew unceasingly the new commitment to evangelize.

Interior Conversion: At the same time, we are profoundly convinced that without the grace of God, which is spread by the Father in our hearts through the Holy Spirit, we would be completely incapable of carrying out this mission as it should be done (cf.

Rom. 5:5). In fact, this work demands incessant interior conversion on the part of individual Christians and continual renewal of our communities and institutions.

In our discussions we did not ignore either old or new difficulties and obstacles which seem to hinder the work of evangelization. In fact, some phenomena of our time have been given careful examination.

Secularism: Secularization is one of them. Although it presents some positive aspects, it nevertheless inclines to the ideology of secularism, which completely excludes God from the horizon of human life and therefore from the profound meaning of existence.

Atheism: Another is atheism in its manifold forms which is widespread in many countries.

Impeded Liberty: Another major difficulty has not escaped us, a difficulty which is used with astuteness and often with violence, that is, impeding religious liberty and the life of the Church and even reducing it to silence.

The Oppressed: We did not forget those who are oppressed, especially all those who suffer persecution for the Gospel. Bearing in themselves the good news of the cross, they are performing excellent work of evangelization and are of great assistance to the whole Church in the fulfillment of its mission.

Communication Is Dynamic: Communication of the gospel is a dynamic process. This communication takes place through word, work and life, each closely connected, and is determined by various almost constitutive elements of the hearers of the word of God; that is, their needs and desires, their way of speaking, hearing, thinking, judging and entering into contact with others.

All these conditions, which differ widely according to different places and times, impel the particular churches toward an appropriate "translation" of the evangelical message.

According to the principle of incarnation, they must devise new but faithful "ways to take root."

Work of the Spirit: At the same time, we firmly believe that the Holy Spirit works unceasingly in Christ's Church, through the work of those who give witness of a holy life, through the pastoral experience of those whom God has called to govern the Church and of all their collaborators in the ecclesial ministries, and through the fruitful collaboration between pastors and theologians.

Ecumenical Collaboration: In carrying out these things we intend to collaborate more diligently with those of our Christian brothers with whom we are not yet in the union of a perfect communion, basing ourselves on the foundation of baptism and on the patrimony which we hold in common.

Thus we can henceforth render to the world a much broader common witness of Christ, while at the same time working to obtain full union in the Lord. Christ's command impels us to do so; the work of preaching and rendering witness to the Gospel demands it.

Wider Dialogue: We wish to further dialogue with other religions which are not Christian, thus to achieve a deeper understanding of the Gospel's newness and of the fullness of revelation, and to be able to show them thereby the salvific truth of God's love which fulfills itself in Christ.

We intend furthermore to seek the collaboration of all men of good will who, for reasons which are undoubtedly diverse but sincere, are in search of a deeper meaning to life or are committed to gaining more human conditions of life for their brothers.

Evangelization and Liberation: Among the many subjects dealt with by the synod, special attention was drawn to the mutual relationship between evangelization and integral salvation, of the complete liberation of man and of peoples.

In a matter of such importance we experienced profound unity in reaffirming the intimate connection between evangelization and such liberation.

That good news of salvation is to be initiated and made more manifest on earth from now on, although it is only beyond the confines of this present life that it can achieve its complete fulfillment.

Complete Liberation: Let us nurture the hope that the Church, in more faithfully fulfilling the work of evangelization, will announce the total salvation of man or rather his complete liberation, and from now on will start to bring this about.

Faithful to her evangelizing mission, the Church as a truly poor, praying and fraternal community can do much to bring about the integral salvation or the full liberation of men. She can draw from the Gospel the most profound reasons and ever new incentives to promote generous dedication to the service of all men — the poor especially, the weak and the oppressed — and to eliminate the social consequences of sin which are translated into unjust social and political structures.

The Church does not remain within merely political, social and economic limits (elements which she must certainly take into account) but leads towards freedom under all its forms — liberation from sin, from individual or collective selfishness — and to full communion with God and with men who are like brothers. In this way the Church, in her evangelical way, promotes the true and complete liberation of all men, groups and peoples.

Holy Year Hope: On the eve of Holy Year which is about to be celebrated in Rome, let us nurture the hope that all the people of God, profiting from this special occasion of grace, through the conversion of hearts, complete renewal and interior reconciliation, can better fulfill their duty to evangelize, and that the Church can more clearly appear as having been sent to the peoples to be the universal sign of salvation.

Pope Paul VI

(See additional entries under News Events, Vatican, Pope Paul, titles of documents, topical headings for coverage of 1975 and other events.)

Cardinal Giovanni Montini was elected Pope June 21, 1963, on the fifth or sixth ballot cast by the 79th and largest conclave of cardinals in the history of the Church. Taking the name Paul VI as the 261st successor to St. Peter as Bishop of Rome, he was crowned June 30 in solemn ceremonies in St. Peter's Square.

Early Career

Giovanni Battista Montini was born Sept. 26, 1897, at Concesio, near Brescia, in the foothills of the Italian Alps. He was the second of the three sons of Giorgio Montini and Giuditta Alghisi.

He suffered from ill health during his boyhood and youth and lived mostly at home while pursuing studies for the priesthood at the Cesare Arici Institute and Christ the King Seminary in Brescia. He was ordained in the cathedral there May 29, 1920. After a short period spent in parish work, he continued studies at the Gregorian University, the University of Rome and the academy for Vatican diplomats. He received degrees in civil and canon law, theology and philosophy.

Named as attaché of the nunciature at Warsaw, he served there for less than a year, returning to Rome for reasons of health in 1923. He then became chaplain of the Catholic Students' Club at the University of Rome and, in 1925, national moderator of the Italian Catholic University Federation's publications program. The student organization was suppressed by Mussolini in 1931.

He became a clerk in the Vatican Secretariat of State in 1933 and was appointed undersecretary three years later. He was named substitute secretary of state in 1944 and prosecretary for ordinary affairs in 1952.

During his period of service in the secretariat, he worked closely with Pius XII, who left the office of secretary vacant following the death of Cardinal Maglione in 1944. With a 10-year background of practical experience in Catholic Action and a longer involvement in diplomatic tasks, he is thought to have been influential in supporting the Christian Democratic parties in Europe, in helping to mobilize action against Communists at the polls in Italy in 1948, and in fostering the priest-worker experiment in France after World War II.

He was ordained archbishop of Milan Dec. 12, 1954, and was installed in the See the following Jan. 6. He was the first of 52 cardinals created by John XXIII Dec. 15, 1958, and served in the Roman Curia as a member of the Consistorial Congregation (Congregation of Bishops), the Congregation for Extraordi-nary Ecclesiastical Affairs (Secretariat of State, Council for the Public Affairs of the Church), and the Congregation of Seminaries and Universities (Congregation for Catholic Education).

In eight and one-half years in Milan he conducted a two-year visitation of the 1,000 churches in the archdiocese, built or renovated 200 churches and chapels, set up a modern system for social services, established a center for study by his priests of pastoral methods suited to contemporary conditions, stimulated Catholic Action, and made direct and effective contact with the people and their conditions of life in the Communist-affected region of northern Italy.

Renewal Commitment

On the day following his election to the papacy, Paul VI announced on Vatican Radio his intention of carrying on with the Church renewal policy and program of his predecessor. Accordingly and in his own way, he has been seeking to move forward and make last what John XXIII, in his unique and charismatic way, stimulated — despite conflicting and obstructive currents of progressivism and conservatism in the Church.

Vatican II

Immediately on his election, Paul announced he would reconvene the Second Vatican Council, which had completed only one session before the death of John XXIII.

He opened the second session Sept. 29, 1963, and at its conclusion Dec. 4 approved the promulgation of the first two conciliar documents, the *Constitution on the Sacred Liturgy* and a *Decree on Media of Social Communication*. Between the second, third and fourth sessions, he ordered that measures be taken by the various conciliar commissions to simplify and streamline the work load and to modify procedures for the smoother and faster conduct of business. At the end of the third session Nov. 21, 1964, by which time the Council had in work all of the items in its wide-ranging agenda, he approved the promulgation of the *Dogmatic Constitution on the Church*, a *Decree on Ecumenism* and a *Decree on Eastern Catholic Churches*. On Sept. 14, 1965, he opened the fourth and final session by concelebrating Mass with a group of the Council Fathers.

During the last three sessions of the Council, he generally followed the hands-off policy of John XXIII with respect to deliberations and the general conduct of business. Like John, however, who intervened during the first sesssion to prevent fruitless consideration of a draft proposal on revelation which hardly any of the Fathers favored, he took a direct hand in Council affairs on several occasions.

On June 23, 1964, he announced he was reserving to himself for study and decision a number of questions regarding birth control. Assisting him in the study was a mixed commission of some 60 persons including priests, theologians, married men and women, physicians and psychiatrists. Their reports — for and against relaxation of Church teaching and practice on the subject — were submitted to him for decision.

During the third session of the Council, at the request of a large majority of the Council Fathers, he also took under personal advisement a number of questions related to mixed marriages and similar matters.

Several weeks after the fourth session began, he cut off Council discussion of clerical celibacy because of the delicacy of the matter and the emotional manner of its treatment in communications media. His action was hailed by the Fathers of the Council.

Before action was taken on several documents at the end of the third session, he made 19 changes in the *Decree on Ecumenism* and proclaimed Mary the Mother of the Church in the *Dogmatic Constitution on the Church.*

Another incident worthy of note at the close of the third session was his refusal to order a vote on the proposed *Declaration on Religious Freedom.* A final version of several draftings of the document was proposed for balloting but was withheld by the Council's presiding board. He refused to override their decision, which was in accordance with rules of Council procedure. He stated at the time that the decree would be given first place on the agenda of the fourth session. It was so placed, and was approved.

He brought the Second Vatican Council to a close Dec. 8, 1965. He noted in a final address that the decisive phase of *aggiornamento*-in-action was already underway, and declared a special jubilee of prayer, study and work in the Church for the purpose of realizing in practice the objectives laid down in the 16 documents of the Council. He later extended the period of jubilee from May 29 to Dec. 8, 1966. He also announced at the Council closing that the beatification causes of his predecessors, John XXIII and Pius XII, were being set in motion.

He has implemented enactments of the Council in various documents. The motu proprio *Ecclesiae Sanctae* of Aug. 6, 1966, laid down executive norms for the four decrees on the pastoral office of bishops, the ministry and life of priests, the adaptation and renewal of religious life and the missionary activity of the Church. The motu proprio *Catholicam Christi Ecclesiam* of Jan. 6, 1967, established the Council of the Laity and the Commission for Justice and Peace. The encyclical *The Development of Peoples* represented an effort to implement the *Pastoral Constitution on the Church in the Modern World.* His authorization of activities and publications of the secretariats for interfaith affairs was in line with provisions of the *Decree on Ecumenism.* His approval of the establishment of scores of territorial conferences of bishops, the creation of the Synod of Bishops and the statement of norms in 1967 regarding the reestablishment of the permanent diaconate in the Roman Rite were efforts in pursuit of conciliar objectives regarding the action and composition of the hierarchy in the Church.

Two documents issued in 1966 embodied the thinking and spirit of the Council: the apostolic constitution *Paenitemini* of Feb. 17, a major statement on the revision of penitential discipline; and a decree of Mar. 18, with respect to mixed marriages. In 1967, he issued an apostolic constitution entitled *The Doctrine and Practice of Indulgences* which stated new norms in this area of Church life.

To quicken the spirit of faith in the Church, the Pope ordered observance throughout the world of a Year of Faith from June 29, 1967, to June 29, 1968, and of Holy Year 1975, with preliminaries starting in 1973.

Collegiality

The Second Vatican Council completed the work of the First by spelling out, among other things, the doctrine of collegiality of the bishops. With and under the Pope — as the successors of the Apostles with and under the leadership of Peter — the bishops as a body are the pastors of the Church whose mission, while concentrated in the sphere of their own proper jurisdictions, extends also to care, concern, and collective action with each other and the pope for the good of the universal Church.

On Nov. 21, 1964, when the third session promulgated the *Dogmatic Constitution on the Church,* Pope Paul told the assembled bishops that he intended to associate them more closely with himself in the work of the whole Church, through participation in post-conciliar commissions and in other ways.

This led to the establishment of the Synod of Bishops on paper Sept. 15, 1965. The initial meeting of the Synod from Sept. 29 to Oct. 25, 1967, represented the first papal effort in modern times to seek the consultation of bishops gathered in a collegial assembly outside of an ecumenical council. Second and third meetings in 1969 and 1971 dealt with questions concerning collegiality, territorial conferences of bishops, clerical celibacy and problems of world justice and peace.

In a move toward decentralizing and delegating authority, he increased the powers of bishops, in virtue of the motu proprio *De Episcoporum Muneribus* of July 11, 1966. In 1967, he extended the same grants of authority to bishops of the Eastern Rites. Additional faculties have since been given to bishops.

Roman Curia

He started a reorganization of the Roman

Curia in 1965 by revising the Sacred Congregation of the Holy Office. He gave the body a new name, the Sacred Congregation for the Doctrine of the Faith, made the orientation of its work more positive, and abolished the Index of Forbidden Books. He issued Aug. 15, 1967, the apostolic constitution *Regimini Ecclesiae Universae,* providing for the overall reorganization of the Curia and for the inclusion of diocesan bishops in its various departments. The constitution was put into effect in 1968.

He established an International Theological Commission in 1969, and reconstituted the Biblical Commission in 1971 and the Commission for the Codification of Oriental Canon Law in 1972.

In addition to reorganizing the Curia, he has given it a greater international complexion than it ever had in previous history.

Cardinals

By elevating 27 prelates to the rank of cardinal on Feb. 22, 1965, he increased the membership of the College of Cardinals to the high total of 103 and made it more representative (43 nations) of the Church throughout the world than it had ever been. Of greater significance than the increased geographical representation, however, was the fact that the new cardinals included three major patriarchs of Eastern Rite. Without prejudice to their patriarchal prerogatives, these prelates, and a fourth patriarch already in the Sacred College, became cardinal bishops.

He further increased the membership of the College to the all-time high total of 118 in 1967. The creation of the new cardinals, which took place in ceremonies held between June 26 and June 29, seemed to answer negatively some speculation that the College might be phased out of existence or its functions diminished. He named additional cardinals in March, 1969 (35), and February, 1973 (30).

In November, 1970, he decreed that, as of Jan. 1, 1971, cardinals 80 years of age and older could not take part in a conclave for the election of a Pope or be active in the administration of Church affairs in the Roman Curia. The decree *(Ingravescentem Aetatem)* immediately affected 25 cardinals.

He also asked for the resignation of active bishops at the age of 75.

Liturgical Renewal

He authorized promulgation of the *Constitution on the Sacred Liturgy* Dec. 8, 1963, and ordered some of its provisions into effect as of Feb. 16, 1964. On Jan. 28, 1964, he announced the formation of a post-conciliar commission with responsibility for continuing work in this field.

Progressive liturgical renewal was the subject of several documents issued by the Pope during 1967. The principal ones were instructions on sacred music, dated Mar. 5; the adaptations of rites and ceremonies, May 4; and Eucharistic worship, May 25.

In 1968, through the Consilium for Implementing the Constitution on the Sacred Liturgy, approval was given for three new Canons and eight prefaces in the Mass.

A New Order of the Mass, related to revisions of the universal liturgical calendar and the Liturgy of the Hours (revised in 1970) was decreed in 1969, to take the place of the form of Mass ordered and standardized for the Roman Rite by the Council of Trent in the 16th century. Universal adoption of these and other reforms has made the contemporary liturgical reform the most extensive in history.

Interfaith Relations

He approved promulgation of the *Decree on Ecumenism* at the conclusion of the third session of the Second Vatican Council, and gave the late Cardinal Augustin Bea, head of the Secretariat for Promoting Christian Unity, and his successor, Cardinal Jan Willebrands, a free hand in relations with members and communities of other Christian churches. To supplement interfaith relations among others, he established a Secretariat for Non-Christians May 19, 1964.

While on pilgrimage to the Holy Land Jan. 4 to 6, 1964, he held two conversations with Orthodox Patriarch Athenagoras I. He was the first Pope since St. Peter to visit the Holy Places and the first Pontiff in more than 500 years to hold conversations with an Orthodox Patriarch.

The prelates met on two more occasions, in Istanbul in July and at the Vatican in October, 1967. The visit of Athenagoras to Rome was the first by a Patriarch of Constantinople since 1451.

Between the two sets of visits, the Pope and Patriarch nullified Dec. 7, 1965, mutual Catholic-Orthodox excommunications imposed in 1054.

Also on the personal contact level, the Pope has met with numerous Orthodox prelates, Anglican Archbishop Michael Ramsey in 1966, leaders of the World Council of Churches and representatives of other religious bodies.

He authorized the initiation in May, 1965, of exploratory talks and steps toward dialogue with the World Council of Churches, and has approved of high-level talks with Anglicans and the Lutheran World Federation.

While on a visit to the Geneva headquarters of the World Council of Churches in June, 1969, he told members of the staff that the Church had great interest in the council but that the time was not yet ripe for a request for Catholic membership.

For all of his interest in ecumenism, he has repeatedly cautioned Catholics engaged in interfaith endeavors to stay within the bounds of sound doctrine. Ecumenism at any price is false, he has stated.

Encyclicals

The first of Paul's encyclicals, *Ecclesiam Suam,* dated Aug. 6, 1964, developed four principal themes related to *aggiornamento* and the aims and purposes of the Second Vatican Council: (1) the awareness the Church has of itself, and the need for this to increase and develop in depth; (2) internal renewal in the Church, and external expression of it; (3) the dialogue the Church must conduct internally among its members and externally with all men; (4) an offer of his services for furthering the cause of peace in the world.

Mense Maio, dated Apr. 29, 1965, urged prayer, especially through the intercession of the Blessed Virgin Mary during the month of May, for the success of the Second Vatican Council and for peace in the world.

Mysterium Fidei, dated Sept. 3, 1965, was a strong statement of traditional doctrine concerning the Holy Eucharist.

Prayer for peace, especially the Rosary during the month of October, was the subject of his fourth encyclical, *Christi Matri Rosarii,* Sept. 15, 1966.

The Development of Peoples was the title and subject of his fifth encyclical, dated Mar. 26, 1967. Wide in concept and definite in practical guidelines, the widely hailed document extended the social doctrine of Pope John's *Peace on Earth* and blueprinted the application to the Third World of the contents of the Second Vatican Council's *Pastoral Constitution on the Church in the Modern World.*

Priestly Celibacy dated June 24, 1967, restated the traditional doctrine and practice of the Latin Church on clerical celibacy. The well-documented and backgrounded encyclical was not received favorably by those who were arguing for change in this discipline.

Of Human Life, dated July 25, 1968, restated traditional doctrine concerning the regulation of birth.

Documents published in 1971, with the significance but not the title of encyclicals, were an apostolic letter to Cardinal Maurice Roy, on social questions; a *Pastoral Instruction: The Media, Public Opinion and Human Progress;* and an apostolic exhortation addressed to religious.

Communism

In his first encyclical, *Ecclesiam Suam,* he said he had no intention of excluding Communists from dialogue with the Church even though such dialogue would probably be incomplete and extremely difficult. In February, 1965, he urged members of an Italian workers' association to maintain contact with their fellow workers, including those with Communist leanings, but not to compromise their fidelity to Christian social principles.

One of the purposes of the Secretariat for Non-Believers, authorized and established Apr. 8, 1965, is to study and initiate relations with Communists and others on the subject of atheism. Since that time, some limited dialogue has taken place but hardly any observable results have been noted. In 1967, he approved release by the secretariat of an introductory document on dialogue of this kind. Detailed guidelines were published in October, 1968.

Negotiations with the Hungarian government, in progress for about two months before Paul's election, led to agreement in September, 1964, with respect to some Vatican freedom in making bishops' appointments and to modification of a loyalty oath expected of the clergy. The negotiations, as anticipated, left many problems unsettled, including the status of Cardinal Mindszenty who remained in seclusion in the American Embassy in Budapest until September, 1971.

Four sets of diplomatic conversations over a two-year period were concluded June 25, 1966, with the signing by Vatican and Yugoslav representatives of an agreement designed to regularize Church-State relations. Full diplomatic relations were established in 1970.

Some measure of agreement was reached with the Polish government in 1972 when Polish bishops were appointed to head four jurisdictions formerly held by German prelates in the Oder-Niesse territory.

Negotiations with Czechoslovakia, underway for several years, have had few results, and the diplomatic doors of other Communist countries have remained closed.

Peace

From the very beginning of his pontificate, he made known his dedication to the cause of world peace.

In 1963, he spoke in favor of negotiations for a nuclear test ban agreement which was finally signed by nearly 100 nations.

At the very beginning of 1964, while in Jerusalem as a pilgrim visiting the Holy Places, he sent 220 peace messages to heads of state and other international leaders. Eleven months later, while attending the 38th International Eucharistic Congress in Bombay, he again appealed for peace and disarmament, and urged nations to spend for useful and humanitarian purposes — to relieve hunger, misery, illness and ignorance — funds and efforts that could be saved through disarmament. He repeated these ideas in his annual Christmas message to the world a few weeks later.

Time and again during 1965, he raised his voice in pleas for peace — in Vietnam, the Congo, the Dominican Republic, India, Pakistan and Kashmir. In February, he told the bishops of Vietnam in a letter that he had initiated confidential approaches for the sake of peace in the divided nation. On another occasion, he decried the use of terrorist guerrilla tactics under any and all circumstances.

In one of many appeals for the outlawing of nuclear weapons, he prayed on the occasion of the 20th anniversary of the atomic bombing of Japan: "May the world never again see a day of misfortune like that of Hiroshima."

To plead, "No more war; never again war," was the simple and uncomplicated — yet extremely complex — purpose of his visit to the United Nations headquarters Oct. 4, 1965.

With the quickening of the tempo of war in Vietnam from the end of 1965, he escalated his efforts for peace. In many addresses, he pleaded for a Christmas truce, for negotiations and disarmament, and for the humane treatment of prisoners. In the fall of 1966, he sent a special delegation to Vietnam for conversations with the bishops of the country and, probably, for fact-finding purposes. Peace was the subject of many private talks, especially with persons like UN Ambassador Arthur Goldberg, U.S. Ambassador to Vietnam Henry Cabot Lodge, and Soviet Foreign Minister Andrei Gromyko.

In July, 1966, it was reported that a fundraising campaign begun the previous December in response to a papal appeal had collected almost $7.5 million for the relief of famine, particularly in India and Pakistan.

Throughout 1967, he missed no opportunity to appeal and to offer his services for peace-making in Vietnam, but without results. He made similar appeals to prevent, and then to stop, the Israeli-Arab conflict which erupted during the first week of June and continued sporadically thereafter. The most he could do was to mobilize Vatican relief forces to assist refugees.

Beginning in July, he made peace overtures to leaders of opposing factions in Nigeria where bloody tribal and political warfare took a terrible toll of life.

In 1968 and 1969, strife in these areas continued to preoccupy the Pope. He offered the Vatican as a site for Vietnam peace talks, and coupled pleas for peace in Nigeria-Biafra with appeals for stepped-up relief measures there. In August, 1968, with most other world leaders, he decried the Soviet invasion and occupation of Czechoslovakia.

The war in Indochina and Arab-Israeli hostility were subjects of frequent comment in talks from 1971 to 1975. He made several appeals in 1971 for the cessation of civil war in East Pakistan and called for international action to relieve the pressing needs of the millions of refugees in India.

He added Northern Ireland to his litany of prayers and appeals for peace as conflict continued there from 1971 to 1975.

His most recent appeals have been for peace in the Middle East and an end to violence in Portugal and Lebanon.

Pilgrimages

While John XXIII was the first Pope to venture outside the Vatican since 1870, Paul VI is the first Pontiff to travel outside of Italy since Pius VII was forced to do so by Napoleon more than 150 years ago.

Paul traveled to the Holy Land as a pilgrim to the Holy Places and to meet Ecumenical Patriarch Athenagoras I from Jan. 4 to 6, 1964.

He went to Bombay, Dec. 2 to 5, 1964, to take part in the 38th International Eucharistic Congress.

He spent nearly 14 hours in New York Oct. 4, 1965, appearing as a pilgrim to plead for peace before representatives of 116 countries at the United Nations.

In December, 1966, he made a short pilgrimage of sympathy so he could be with the people of the Florentine area of Italy which was devastated by a flood of catastrophic proportions.

To pray at the Marian shrine as a pilgrim of peace was the purpose of his one-day flying pilgrimage to Fatima, Portugal May 13, 1967.

On July 25, 1967, he flew to Turkey to see Patriarch Athenagoras I of Constantinople and to visit the ancient city of Ephesus, the locale of the house where, according to an old tradition, the Blessed Virgin Mary lived toward the end of her life, and the place of meeting of the ecumenical council which ratified her title, Mother of God (Theotokos), in 431. The purposes of the pilgrimage were plainly ecumenical and Marian.

On the sixth of his journeys outside Italy, he made a three-day flying visit to take part in the 39th International Eucharistic Congress in Bogota, Colombia, in August, 1968.

He made two visits in 1969: to Geneva, where he delivered addresses at the headquarters of the International Labor Organization and the World Council of Churches, in June; and to Kampala, to honor the martyrs of Uganda, July 31 to Aug. 2.

His ninth trip, Apr. 24, 1970, was a one-day visit to Sardinia, where he joined the islanders for a celebration in honor of their patroness, Our Lady of Bonaria.

The 10th, also in 1970, was the most extensive of all his trips with stops in Teheran, Nov. 26; Manila, the Philippines, Nov. 27 to 29; Samoa, Nov. 29; Sydney, Australia, Nov. 30 to Dec. 3; Djakarta, Indonesia, Dec. 3 and 4; Hong Kong, Dec. 4; Colombo, Ceylon, Dec. 4; and cyclone-ravaged Pakistan. Rome departure and return dates were Nov. 26 and Dec. 5. An attempt was made on the Pope's life in Manila.

He visited Udine, Italy, Sept. 16, 1972, to take part in a Eucharistic congress there. En route, he stopped in Venice.

Visits outside the Vatican since that time have been generally limited to Castel Gandolfo and the environs of Rome.

Dates and Events in Church History

First Century

Early 30's: First Christian Pentecost: gathering together of the Christian community, outpouring of the Holy Spirit, preaching of St. Peter to Jews in Jerusalem, baptism and aggregation of some 3,000 persons to the Christian community.

St. Stephen, deacon, was stoned to death at Jerusalem; he is venerated as the first Christian martyr.

34-64/67: St. Paul, formerly Saul the persecutor of Christians, was converted, baptized and joined to the college of Apostles. After three major missionary journeys, he was martyred in 64 or 67 at Rome.

39: The Gentile Cornelius and his family were baptized by St. Peter.

42: Persecution of Christians in Palestine broke out during the rule of Herod Agrippa; St. James the Greater, the first Apostle to die, was beheaded in 44; St. Peter was imprisoned for a short time; many Christians fled to Antioch and elsewhere.

At Antioch, the followers of Christ were first called Christians.

49: Christians at Rome, who were considered members of a Jewish sect, were adversely affected by a decree of Claudius which forbade Jewish worship there.

51: The Council of Jerusalem, in which all the Apostles participated under the presidency of St. Peter, decreed that circumcision, dietary regulations, and various other prescriptions of Mosaic Law were not obligatory for Gentile converts to the Christian community. The decree was issued in opposition to Judaizers who contended that observance of the Mosaic Law in its entirety was necessary for salvation.

64: Persecution under Nero: The emperor, accusing Christians of starting a fire which destroyed half of Rome, inaugurated the era of major Roman persecutions.

64/65: Martyrdom of St. Peter at Rome during the Neronian persecution. He established his see and spent his last years there after preaching in and around Jerusalem, establishing a see at Antioch, and presiding at the Council of Jerusalem.

70: Destruction of Jerusalem by Titus.

88-97: Pontificate of St. Clement I, third successor of St. Peter as bishop of Rome, one of the Apostolic Fathers. The *First Epistle of Clement to the Corinthians,* with which he has been identified, was addressed by the Church of Rome to the Church at Corinth, the scene of irregularities and divisions in the Christian community.

95: Domitian persecuted Christians, principally at Rome.

c. 100: Death of St. John, Apostle and Evangelist, marking the end of the Age of the Apostles and the first generation of the Church.

Second Century

c. 107: St. Ignatius of Antioch was martyred at Rome. He was the first writer to use the expression, "the Catholic Church."

112: Rescript to Pliny. Emperor Trajan instructed Pliny, governor of Bithynia, not to search out Christians but to punish them if they were publicly denounced and refused to do homage to the Roman gods. The rescript set a pattern of discretionary leniency for Roman magistrates in dealing with Christians.

117-138: Persecution under Hadrian. Many *Acts of Martyrs* date from this period.

c. 125: Spread of Gnosticism.

c. 155: St. Polycarp, bishop of Smyrna and disciple of St. John the Evangelist, was martyred.

c. 156: Beginning of Montanism.

161-180: Reign of Marcus Aurelius. His persecution, launched in the wake of natural disasters, was more violent than those of his predecessors.

165: St. Justin, an important early Christian writer, was martyred at Rome.

c. 180: St. Irenaeus, bishop of Lyons and one of the great early theologians, wrote *Adversus Haereses.* He stated that the teaching and tradition of the Roman See was the standard for belief.

196: Easter Controversy.

The *Didache,* written in the second century, was an important record of Christian belief, practice and government in the first century.

Latin was introduced in the West as a liturgical language.

The Catechetical School of Alexandria, founded about the middle of the century, increased in importance.

Third Century

202: Persecution under Septimius Severus, who wanted to establish one common religion in the Empire.

206: Tertullian, a convert since 197 and the first great ecclesiastical writer in Latin, joined the heretical Montanists. He died in 230.

215: Death of Clement of Alexandria, teacher of Origen and a founding father of the School of Alexandria.

217-235: St. Hippolytus, the first antipope. He was reconciled to the Church while in prison during persecution in 235.

232-254: Origen established the School of Caesarea after being deposed in 231 as head of the School of Alexandria; he died in 254. A scholar and voluminous writer, he was one of the founders of systematic theology and exerted wide influence for many years.

c. 242: Manichaeism originated in Persia.

249-251: Persecution under Decius. Many of those who denied the faith *(lapsi)* sought readmission to the Church at the end of the persecution in 251. Pope St. Cornelius had correspondence with St. Cyprian on the subject and ordered that *lapsi* were to be readmitted after suitable penance.

250-300: Neo-Platonism of Plotinus and Porphyry gained followers.

251: Novatian, an antipope, was condemned at Rome.

256: Pope St. Stephen I upheld the validity of baptism administered by heretics, in the Rebaptism Controversy.

257: Persecution under Valerian, who attempted to destroy the Church as a social structure.

258: St. Cyprian, bishop of Carthage, was martyred.

c. 260: St. Lucian founded the exegetical School of Antioch.

Pope St. Dionysius condemned teachings of Sabellius and the Marcionites.

St. Paul of Thebes became a hermit.

261: Gallienus issued an edict of toleration which ended general persecution for nearly 40 years.

c. 266: Sabellianism was condemned and Paul of Samosata deposed.

292: Diocletian divided the Roman Empire into East and West. The division emphasized political, cultural and other differences between the two parts of the Empire and influenced the Church in the East and West. The prestige of Rome began to decline.

Fourth Century

303: Persecution broke out under Diocletian. It ended in the West in 306 but continued for 10 years in the East; it was particularly violent in 304.

305: St. Anthony of Heracles established a foundation for hermits near the Red Sea in Egypt.

c. 306: The first local legislation on clerical celibacy was enacted by a council held at Elvira, Spain; bishops, priests, deacons and other ministers were forbidden to have wives.

310: St. Hilarion established a foundation for hermits in Palestine.

311: An edict of toleration issued by Galerius at the urging of Constantine and Licinius officially ended persecution in the West; some persecution continued in the East.

313: The *Edict of Milan* issued by Constantine and Licinius recognized Christianity as a lawful religion and the legal freedom of all religions in the Roman Empire.

314: The Council of Arles condemned Donatism in Africa and declared that baptism by heretics was valid.

318: St. Pachomius established the first foundation of the cenobitic (common) life, as compared with the solitary life of hermits in Upper Egypt.

325: The Ecumenical Council of Nicaea (I),

first of its kind in the history of the Church, condemned Arianism; see separate entry.

326: Discovery of the True Cross on which Christ was crucified.

337: Baptism and death of Constantine.

c. 342: Beginning of a 40-year persecution in Persia.

343-344: A local Council of Sardica reaffirmed doctrine formulated by Nicaea I and declared that bishops had the right of appeal to the pope as the highest authority in the Church.

361-363: Julian the Apostate waged an unsuccessful campaign against the Church in an attempt to restore paganism as the religion of the Empire.

c. 365: Persecution under Valens in the East.

c. 376: Beginning of the barbarian invasion in the West.

379: Death of St. Basil, the Father of Monasticism in the East. His writings contributed greatly to the development of rules for the religious life.

381: The Ecumenical Council of Constantinople (I); see separate entry.

382: The *Decree of Pope St. Damasus* listed the Canon of Sacred Scripture.

382-c. 406: St. Jerome translated the Old and New Testaments into Latin. His work is called the Vulgate Version of the Bible.

396: St. Augustine became bishop of Hippo in North Africa.

397: A local Council of Carthage published the Canon of Sacred Scripture.

Fifth Century

410: Visigoths sacked Rome.

411: Donatism was condemned by a council at Carthage.

430: St. Augustine, bishop of Hippo for 35 years, died. He was a strong defender of orthodox doctrine against Manichaeism, Donatism and Pelagianism. The depth and range of his writings made him a dominant influence in Christian thought for many centuries.

431: The Ecumenical Council of Ephesus; see separate entry.

432: St. Patrick arrived in Ireland. By the time of his death in 461 most of the country had been converted, monasteries founded and the hierarchy established.

438: The *Theodosian Code,* a compilation of decrees for the Empire, was issued by Theodosius II. It had great influence on subsequent civil and ecclesiastical law.

449: The Robber Council of Ephesus, which did not have ecclesiastical sanction, declared itself in favor of the opinions of Eutyches who contended that Christ had only one nature.

451: The Ecumenical Council of Chalcedon; see separate entry.

452: Pope St. Leo the Great persuaded Attila the Hun to spare Rome.

455: Vandals sacked Rome. The decline of

imperial Rome dates approximately from this time.

484: Patriarch Acacius of Constantinople was excommunicated for signing the *Henoticon,* a unity law published by Emperor Zeno in 482 to end the turmoil associated with the Monophysite heresy. The document capitulated to the heresy. The excommunication triggered a 35-year-long schism.

494: Pope St. Gelasius I declared in a letter to Emperor Anastasius that the pope had power and authority over the emperor in spiritual matters.

496: Clovis, King of the Franks, was converted and became the defender of Christianity in the West. The Franks became a Catholic people.

Sixth Century

520 and later: Irish monasteries flourished as centers for spiritual life, missionary training and scholarly activity.

529: The Second Council of Orange condemned Semi-Pelagianism.

c. 529: St. Benedict founded the Monte Cassino Abbey. Some years before his death in 543 he wrote a monastic rule which exercised tremendous influence on the form and style of religious life. He is called the Father of Monasticism in the West.

533: John II became the first pope to change his name. The practice did not become general until the time of Sergius IV (1009).

533-534: Emperor Justinian promulgated the *Corpus Juris Civilis* for the Roman world. Like the *Theodosian Code,* it influenced subsequent civil and ecclesiastical law.

c. 545: Death of Dionysius Exiguus who was the first to date history from the birth of Christ, a practice which resulted in use of the B.C. and A.D. abbreviations. His calculations were at least four years late.

553: The Ecumenical Council of Constantinople (II); see separate entry.

585: St. Columban founded an influential monastic school at Luxeuil. He died in 615.

589: The most important of several councils of Toledo was held. The Visigoths renounced Arianism, and St. Leander began the organization of the Church in Spain.

590-604: Pontificate of Pope St. Gregory I the Great. He set the form and style of the papacy which prevailed throughout the Middle Ages; exerted great influence on doctrine and liturgy; was strong in support of monastic discipline and clerical celibacy; authored writings on many subjects. Gregorian Chant is named in his honor.

596: Pope St. Gregory I the Great sent St. Augustine of Canterbury and 40 monks to do missionary work in England.

597: St. Columba died. He founded an important monastery at Iona, established schools and did notable missionary work in Scotland.

By the end of the century, monasteries of nuns were common; Western monasticism was flourishing; monasticism in the East, under the influence of Monophysitism and other factors, was losing its vigor.

Seventh Century

613: St. Columban established the influential Monastery of Bobbio in northern Italy.

622: The Hegira (flight) of Mohammed from Mecca to Medina signalled the beginning of Islam, which, by the end of the century, claimed almost all of the southern Mediterranean area.

629: Emperor Heraclius recovered the True Cross from the Persians.

649: A Lateran Council condemned two erroneous formulas *(Ecthesis* and *Type)* issued by emperors Heraclius and Constans II as means of reconciling Monophysites with the Church.

664: Actions of the Synod of Whitby advanced the adoption of Roman usages in England, especially regarding the date for the observance of Easter. (See Easter Controversy.)

680-681: The Ecumenical Council of Constantinople (III); see separate entry.

692: Trullan Synod. Eastern-Church discipline on clerical celibacy was settled, permitting marriage before ordination to the diaconate and continuation in marriage afterwards, but prohibiting marriage following the death of the wife thereafter. Anti-Roman canons contributed to East-West alienation.

During the century, the monastic influence of Ireland and England increased in Western Europe; schools and learning declined; regulations regarding clerical celibacy became more strict in the East.

Eighth Century

711: Moslems began the conquest of Spain.

726: Emperor Leo III, the Isaurian, launched a campaign against the veneration of sacred images and relics; called Iconoclasm (image-breaking), it caused turmoil in the East until about 843.

731: Pope Gregory II and a synod at Rome condemned Iconoclasm, with a declaration that the veneration of sacred images was in accord with Catholic tradition.

Venerable Bede issued his *Ecclesiastical History of the English People.*

732: Charles Martel defeated the Moslems at Poitiers, halting farther advance by them in the West.

744: The Monastery of Fulda was established by St. Sturm, a disciple of St. Boniface.

754: A council of more than 300 Byzantine bishops endorsed Iconoclast errors. This council and its actions were condemned by the Lateran Synod of 769.

Stephen II (III) crowned Pepin ruler of the Franks. Pepin twice invaded Italy, in 754 and 756, to defend the pope against the Lombards. His land grants to the papacy, called the Donation of Pepin, were later extended by Charlemagne (773) and formed part of the States of the Church.

c. 755: St. Boniface (Winfrid) was martyred. He was called the Apostle of Germany for his missionary work and organization of the hierarchy there.

781: Alcuin was chosen by Charlemagne to organize a Palace School, which became a center of intellectual leadership.

787: The Ecumenical Council of Nicaea (II); see separate entry.

792: A council at Ratisbon condemned Adoptionism.

The famous *Book of Kells* ("The Great Gospel of Columcille") dates from the early eighth or late seventh century.

Ninth Century

800: Charlemagne was crowned Emperor by Pope Leo III on Christmas Day.

Egbert became king of West Saxons. He unified England and strengthened the See of Canterbury.

813: Emperor Leo V, the Armenian, revived Iconoclasm, which persisted until about 843.

814: Charlemagne died.

843: The Treaty of Verdun split the Frankish kingdom among Charlemagne's three grandsons.

844: A Eucharistic controversy involving the writings of Paschasius Radbertus, Ratramnus and Rabanus Maurus occasioned the development of terminology regarding the doctrine of the Real Presence.

846: The Moslems invaded Italy and attacked Rome.

847-852: Period of composition of the *False Decretals*, a collection of forged documents attributed to popes from St. Clement (88-97) to Gregory II (715-731). The *Decretals*, which strongly supported the autonomy and rights of bishops, were suspect for a long time before being repudiated entirely about 1628.

848: The Council of Mainz condemned Gottschalk for heretical teaching regarding predestination. He was also condemned by the Council of Quierzy in 853.

857: Photius displaced Ignatius as patriarch of Constantinople. This marked the beginning of the Photian Schism, a confused state of East-West relations which has not yet been cleared up by historical research. Photius, a man of exceptional ability, died in 891.

865: St. Ansgar, Apostle of Scandinavia, died.

868: Sts. Cyril (d. 869) and Methodius (d. 885) were consecrated bishops. The Apostles of the Slavs devised an alphabet and translated the Gospels and liturgy into the Slavonic language.

869: The Ecumenical Council of Constantinople (IV); see separate entry.

871-c. 900: Reign of Alfred the Great, the only English king ever anointed by a pope at Rome.

Tenth Century

910: William, Duke of Aquitaine, founded the Benedictine Abbey of Cluny, which became a center of monastic and ecclesiastical reform.

915: Pope John X played a leading role in the expulsion of Saracens from central and southern Italy.

955: St. Olga, of the Russian royal family, was baptized.

962: Otto I, the Great, crowned by Pope John XII, revived Charlemagne's kingdom, which became the Holy Roman Empire.

966: Mieszko, first of a royal line in Poland, was baptized; he brought Latin Christianity to Poland.

989: Vladimir, ruler of Russia, was baptized. Russia was subsequently Christianized by Greek missionaries.

993: John XV was the first pope to decree the official canonization of a saint (Ulrich) for the universal Church.

997: St. Stephen became ruler of Hungary. He assisted in organizing the hierarchy and establishing Latin Christianity in that country.

999-1003: Pontificate of Sylvester II (Gerbert of Aquitaine), a Benedictine monk and the first French pope.

Eleventh Century

1009: Beginning of lasting East-West schism in the Church, marked by dropping of the name of Pope Sergius IV from the Byzantine diptychs (the listing of persons prayed for during the liturgy). The deletion was made by Patriarch Sergius II of Constantinople.

1012: St. Romuald founded the Camaldolese Hermits.

1025: The Council of Arras, and other councils later, condemned the Cathari (Neo-Manichaeans, Albigenses).

1027: The Council of Elne proclaimed the Truce of God as a means of stemming violence. The truce involved armistice periods of varying length, which were later extended.

1038: St. John Gualbert founded the Vallombrosians.

1043-1059: Constantinople patriarchate of Michael Cerularius, the key figure in a controversy concerning the primacy of the papacy. His and the Byzantine synod's refusal to acknowledge this primacy in 1054 widened and hardened the East-West schism in the Church.

1047: Pope Clement II died. He was the only pope ever buried in Germany.

1049-54: Pontificate of St. Leo IX, who inaugurated a movement of papal, diocesan, monastic and clerical reform.

1055: Condemnation of the Eucharistic doctrine of Berengarius.

1059: A Lateran Council issued new legislation regarding papal elections. Voting power was entrusted to the Roman cardinals.

1066: Death of St. Edward the Confessor, King of England from 1042 and restorer of Westminster Abbey.

Defeat, at Hastings, of Harold by William I, who subsequently exerted strong influence on the life style of the Church in England.

1073-1085: Pontificate of St. Gregory VII (Hildebrand). A strong pope, he carried forward programs of clerical and general ecclesiastical reform and struggled against Henry IV and other rulers to end the evils of lay investiture. He introduced the Latin liturgy in Spain and set definite dates for the observance of ember days.

1077: Henry IV, excommunicated and suspended from the exercise of imperial powers by Gregory VII, sought absolution from the Pope at Canossa. Henry later repudiated this action and in 1084 forced Gregory to leave Rome.

1079: The Council of Rome condemned Eucharistic errors of Berengarius, who retracted.

1084: St. Bruno founded the Carthusians.

1097-1099: The first of several Crusades undertaken between this time and 1265. Recovery of the Holy Places and gaining free access to them for Christians were the original purposes, but these were diverted to less worthy objectives in various ways. Results included: a Latin Kingdom of Jerusalem, 1099-1187; a military and political misadventure in the form of a Latin Empire of Constantinople, 1204-1261; acquisition, by treaties, of visiting rights for Christians in the Holy Land. East-West economic and cultural relationships increased during the period. In the religious sphere, actions of the Crusaders had the effect of increasing the alienation of the East from the West.

1098: St. Robert founded the Cistercians.

Twelfth Century

1108: Beginnings of the influential Abbey and School of St. Victor.

1115: St. Bernard established the Abbey of Clairvaux and inaugurated the Cistercian Reform.

1118: Christian forces captured Saragossa, Spain; the beginning of the Moslem decline in that country.

1121: St. Norbert established the original monastery of the Praemonstratensians near Laon, France.

1122: The Concordat of Worms (Pactum Callixtinum) was formulated and approved by Pope Callistus II and Emperor Henry V to settle controversy concerning the investiture of prelates. The concordat provided that the emperor could invest prelates with symbols of temporal authority but had no right to invest them with spiritual authority, which came from the Church alone, and that the emperor was not to interfere in papal elections. This was the first concordat in history.

1123: The Ecumenical Council of the Lateran (I), the first of its kind in the West; see separate entry.

1139: The Ecumenical Council of the Lateran (II); see separate entry.

1140: St. Bernard met Ábelard in debate at the Council of Sens. Abelard, whose rationalism in theology was condemned for the first time in 1121, died in 1142 at Cluny.

1148: The Synod of Rheims enacted strict disciplinary decrees for communities of women religious.

1152: The Synod of Kells reorganized the Church in Ireland.

1160: Gratian, whose *Decretum* became a basic text of Canon Law, died.

Peter Lombard, compiler of the *Four Books of Sentences,* a standard theology text for nearly 200 years, died.

1170: St. Thomas Becket, archbishop of Canterbury, who clashed with Henry II over Church-state relations, was murdered in his cathedral.

1171: Pope Alexander III reserved the process of canonization of saints to the Holy See.

1179: The Ecumenical Council of the Lateran (III); see separate entry.

1184: Waldenses and other heretics were excommunicated by Pope Lucius III.

Thirteenth Century

1198-1216: Pontificate of Innocent III, during which the papacy reached its medieval peak of authority, influence and prestige in the Church and in relations with civil rulers.

1208: Innocent III called for a crusade, the first in Christendom itself, against the Albigensians.

1209: Verbal approval was given by Innocent III to a rule of life for the Order of Friars Minor, started by St. Francis of Assisi.

1212: The Second Order of Franciscans, the Poor Clares, was founded.

1215: The Ecumenical Council of the Lateran (IV); see separate entry.

1216: Formal papal approval was given to a rule of life for the Order of Preachers, started by St. Dominic.

The Portiuncula Indulgence was granted by the Holy See at the request of St. Francis of Assisi.

1221: The Third Order of St. Francis for lay persons was founded.

1226: Death of St. Francis of Assisi.

1245: The Ecumenical Council of Lyons (I); see separate entry.

1247: Preliminary approval was given by the Holy See to a Carmelite rule of life.

1270: St. Louis IX, king of France, died.

Beginning of papal decline.

1274: The Ecumenical Council of Lyons (II); see separate entry.

Death of St. Thomas Aquinas, Doctor of the Church, of lasting influence; see separate entry.

1280: Pope Nicholas III, who made the *Breviary* the official prayer book for clergy of the Roman Church, died.

1281: The excommunication of Michael Palaeologus by Pope Martin IV ruptured the union effected with the Eastern Church in 1274.

Fourteenth Century

1302: Pope Boniface VIII issued the bull *Unam Sanctam,* concerning the unity of the Church and the temporal power of princes, against the background of a struggle with Philip IV of France; it was the most famous medieval document on the subject.

1308-1378: For a period of approximately 70 years, seven popes resided at Avignon because of unsettled conditions in Rome and other reasons; see separate entry.

1311-1312: The Ecumenical Council of Vienne; see separate entry.

1321: Dante Alighieri died a year after completing the *Divine Comedy.*

1324: Marsilius of Padua completed *Defensor Pacis,* a work condemned by Pope John XXII as heretical because of its denial of papal primacy and the hierarchical structure of the Church, and for other reasons. It was a charter for conciliarism.

1337-1453: Period of the Hundred Years' War, a dynastic struggle between France and England.

1338: Four years after the death of Pope John XXII, who had opposed Louis IV of Bavaria in a years-long controversy, electoral princes declared at the Diet of Rhense that the emperor did not need papal confirmation of his title and right to rule. Charles IV later (1356) said the same thing in a *Golden Bull,* eliminating papal rights in the election of emperors.

1347-1350: The Black Death swept across Europe, killing perhaps one-fourth to one-third of the total population; an estimated 40 per cent of the clergy succumbed.

1374: Petrarch, poet and humanist, died.

1378: Return of the papacy from Avignon to Rome.
Beginning of the Western Schism; see separate entry.

Fifteenth Century

1409: The Council of Pisa, without canonical authority, tried to end the Western Schism but succeeded only in complicating it by electing a third claimant to the papacy; see Western Schism.

1414-1418: The Ecumenical Council of Constance ended the Western Schism; see separate entry.

1431: St. Joan of Arc was burned at the stake.

1431-1449: The Council of Basle, which began with convocation by Pope Martin V in 1431, turned into an anti-papal forum of conciliarists seeking to subject the primacy and

authority of the pope to the overriding authority of an assembly of bishops. It was not an ecumenical council.

1438: The Pragmatic Sanction of Bourges was enacted by Charles VIII and the French parliament to curtail papal authority over the Church in France, in the spirit of conciliarism. It found expression in Gallicanism and had effects lasting at least until the French Revolution.

1438-1443: The Ecumenical Council of Florence affirmed the primacy of the pope in opposition to conciliarism and effected a measure of union with separated Eastern Christians; see separate entry.

1453: The fall of Constantinople to the Turks.

c. 1456: Gutenberg issued the first edition of the Bible printed from movable type, at Mainz, Germany.

1476: Pope Sixtus IV ordered observance of the feast of the Immaculate Conception on Dec. 8 throughout the Church.

1492: Columbus discovered the Americas.

1493: Pope Alexander VI issued a *Bull of Demarcation* which determined spheres of influence for the Spanish and Portuguese in the Americas.

The Renaissance, a humanistic movement which originated in Italy in the 14th century, spread to France, Germany, the Low Countries and England. A transitional period between the medieval world and the modern secular world, it introduced profound changes which affected literature and the other arts, general culture, politics and religion.

Sixteenth Century

1512-1517: The Ecumenical Council of the Lateran (V); see separate entry.

1517: Martin Luther signalled the beginning of the Reformation by posting 95 theses at Wittenberg. Subsequently, he broke completely from doctrinal orthodoxy in discourses and three published works (1519 and 1520); was excommunicated on more than 40 charges of heresy (1521); remained the dominant figure in the Reformation in Germany until his death in 1546.

1519: Zwingli triggered the Reformation in Zurich and became its leading proponent there until his death in combat in 1531.

1524: Luther's encouragement of German princes in putting down the two-year Peasants' Revolt gained political support for his cause.

1528: The Order of Friars Minor Capuchin was approved as an autonomous division of the Franciscan Order; like the Jesuits, the Capuchins became leaders in the Counter-Reformation.

1530: The *Augsburg Confession* of Lutheran faith was issued; it was later supplemented by the *Smalcald Articles* approved in 1537.

1533: Henry VIII divorced Catherine of Aragon, married Anne Boleyn, was excommunicated. In 1534 he decreed the Act of Supremacy, making the sovereign the head of the Church in England, under which Sts. John Fisher and Thomas More were executed in 1535. Despite his rejection of papal primacy and actions against monastic life in England, he generally maintained doctrinal orthodoxy until his death in 1547.

1536: John Calvin, leader of the Reformation in Switzerland until his death in 1564, issued the first edition of *Institutes of the Christian Religion*, which became the classical text of Reformed (non-Lutheran) theology.

1540: The constitutions of the Society of Jesus (Jesuits), founded by St. Ignatius of Loyola, were approved.

1541: Start of the 11-year career of St. Francis Xavier as a missionary to the East Indies and Japan.

1545-1563: The Ecumenical Council of Trent formulated statements of Catholic doctrine under attack by the Reformers and mobilized the Counter-Reformation; see separate entry.

1549: The first *Book of Common Prayer* was issued by Edward VI. Revised editions were published in 1552, 1559 and 1662.

1553: Start of the five-year reign of Mary Tudor who tried to counteract actions of Henry VIII against the Roman Church.

1555: Enactment of the Peace of Augsburg, an arrangement of religious territorialism rather than toleration, which recognized the existence of Catholicism and Lutheranism in the German Empire and provided that citizens should adopt the religion of their respective rulers.

1558: Beginning of the reign of Elizabeth I, during which the Church of England took on its definitive form.

1559: Establishment of the hierarchy of the Church of England, with the consecration of Matthew Parker as archbishop of Canterbury.

1563: The first text of the *39 Articles* of the Church of England was issued. Also enacted were a new Act of Supremacy and Oath of Succession to the English throne.

1570: Elizabeth I was excommunicated. Penal measures against Catholics subsequently became more severe.

1571: Defeat of the Turkish armada at Lepanto staved off the invasion of Eastern Europe.

1577: The *Formula of Concord*, the classical statement of Lutheran faith, was issued; it was, generally, a Lutheran counterpart of the canons of the Council of Trent. In 1580, along with other formulas of doctrine, it was included in the *Book of Concord*.

1582: The Gregorian Calendar, named for Pope Gregory XIII, was put into effect and was eventually adopted in most countries: England delayed adoption until 1752.

Seventeenth Century

1605: The Gunpowder Plot, an attempt by Catholic fanatics to blow up James I of England and the houses of Parliament, resulted in an anti-Catholic Oath of Allegiance; the Oath was condemned by Pope Paul V in 1606.

1610: Death of Matteo Ricci, outstanding Jesuit missionary to China, pioneer in cultural relations between China and Europe.

Founding of the first community of Visitation Nuns by Sts. Francis de Sales and Jane de Chantal.

1611: Founding of the Oratorians.

1613: Catholics were banned from Scandinavia.

1625: Founding of the Congregation of the Mission (Vincentians) by St. Vincent de Paul. He founded the Sisters of Charity in 1633.

1642: Death of Galileo, scientist, who was censured by the Congregation of the Holy Office for supporting the Copernican theory of the sun-centered planetary system.

Founding of the Sulpicians by Jacques Olier.

1643: Start of publication of the Bollandist *Acta Sanctorum,* a critical work on lives of the saints.

1648: Provisions in the Peace of Westphalia, ending the Thirty Years' War, extended terms of the Peace of Augsburg (1555) to Calvinists and gave equality to Catholics and Protestants in the 300 states of the Holy Roman Empire.

1649: Oliver Cromwell invaded Ireland and began a severe persecution of the Church there.

1653: Pope Innocent X condemned five propositions of Jansenism, a complex theory which distorted doctrine concerning the relations between divine grace and human freedom. Jansenism was also a rigoristic movement which seriously disturbed the Church in France, the Low Countries and Italy in this and the 18th century.

1673: The Test Act in England barred from public office Catholics who would not deny the doctrine of transubstantiation and receive Communion in the Church of England.

1678: Many English Catholics suffered death as a consequence of the Popish Plot, a false allegation by Titus Oates that Catholics planned to assassinate Charles I, land a French army in the country, burn London, and turn over the government to the Jesuits.

1682: The four articles of the *Gallican Declaration,* drawn up by Bossuet, asserted political and ecclesiastical immunities of France from papal control. The articles, which rejected the primacy of the pope, were condemned in 1690.

1689: The Toleration Act granted a measure of freedom of worship to other English dissenters but not to Catholics.

This century is called the age of Enlightenment or Reason because of the predominating rational and scientific approach of its leading philosophers, scientists and writers with respect to religion, ethics and natural law. This approach downgraded the fact and significance of revealed religion. Also characteristic of the Enlightenment were subjectivism, secularism and optimism regarding human perfectibility.

Eighteenth Century

1704: Chinese Rites—involving the Christian adaptation of elements of Confucianism, veneration of ancestors and Chinese terminology in religion — were condemned by Clement XI. An earlier ban was issued in 1645; a later one, in 1742.

1720: The Passionists were founded by St. Paul of the Cross.

1724: Persecution in China.

1732: The Redemptorists were founded by St. Alphonsus Liguori.

1738: Freemasonry was condemned by Clement XII and Catholics were forbidden to join, under penalty of excommunication; the prohibition was repeated by Benedict XIV in 1751 and by later popes.

1760's: Josephinism, a theory and system of state control of the Church, was initiated in Austria; it remained in force until about 1850.

1764: Febronianism, an unorthodox theory and practice regarding the constitution of the Church and relations between Church and state, was condemned for the first of several times. Proposed by an auxiliary bishop of Trier using the pseudonym Justinus Febronius, it had the effects of minimizing the office of the pope and supporting national churches under state control.

1773: Clement XIV issued a brief of suppression against the Jesuits, following their expulsion from Portugal in 1759, from France in 1764 and from Spain in 1767. Political intrigue and unsubstantiated accusations were principal factors in these developments. The ban, which crippled the Society, contained no condemnation of the Jesuit constitutions, particular Jesuits or Jesuit teaching. The Society was restored in 1814.

1778: Catholics in England were relieved of some civil disabilities dating back to the time of Henry VIII, by an act which permitted them to acquire, own and inherit property. Additional liberties were restored by the Roman Catholic Relief Act of 1791 and subsequent enactments of Parliament.

1789: Religious freedom in the United States was guaranteed under the First Amendment to the Constitution.

Beginning of the French Revolution which resulted in: the secularization of church property and the Civil Constitution of the Clergy in 1790; the persecution of priests, religious and lay persons loyal to papal authority; invasion of the Papal States by Napoleon in 1796; renewal of persecution from 1797-1799; attempts to dechristianize France and establish a new religion; the occupation of Rome by French troops and the forced removal of Pius VI to France in 1798.

Nineteenth Century

1809: Pius VII was made a captive by Napoleon and deported to France where he remained in exile until 1814. During this time he refused to cooperate with Napoleon who sought to bring the Church in France under his own control.

The turbulence in church-state relations in France at the beginning of the century recurred in connection with the Bourbon Restoration, the July Revolution, the second and third Republics, the Second Empire and the Dreyfus case.

1814: The Society of Jesus, suppressed since 1773, was restored.

1817: Reestablishment of the Congregation for the Propagation of the Faith (Propaganda) by Pius VII was an important factor in increasing missionary activity during the century.

1820: Years-long persecution, during which thousands died for the faith, ended in China. Thereafter, communication with the West remained cut off until about 1834. Vigorous missionary work got underway in 1842.

1822: The Pontifical Society for the Propagation of the Faith, inaugurated in France by Pauline Jaricot for the support of missionary activity, was established.

1829: The Catholic Emancipation Act relieved Catholics in England and Ireland of most of the civil disabilities to which they had been subject from the time of Henry VIII.

1832: Gregory XVI, in the encyclical *Mirari Vos,* condemned indifferentism, one of the many ideologies at odds with Christian doctrine which were proposed during the century.

1833: Start of the Oxford Movement which affected the Church of England and resulted in some notable conversions, including that of John Henry Newman in 1845, to the Catholic Church.

Frederick Ozanam founded the Society of St. Vincent de Paul in France. The society, whose objective was works of charity, became worldwide.

1848: The *Communist Manifesto,* a revolutionary document symptomatic of socioeconomic crisis, was issued.

1850: The hierarchy was reestablished in England and Nicholas Wiseman made the first archbishop of Westminster. He was succeeded in 1865 by Henry Manning, an Oxford convert and proponent of the rights of labor.

1853: The Catholic hierarchy was reestablished in Holland.

1854: Pius IX proclaimed the dogma of the Immaculate Conception in the bull *Ineffabilis Deus.*

1858: The Blessed Virgin Mary appeared to

St. Bernadette at Lourdes, France; see separate entry.

1864: Pius IX issued the encyclical *Quanta Cura* and the *Syllabus of Errors* in condemnation of some 80 propositions derived from the scientific mentality and rationalism of the century. The subjects in question had deep ramifications in many areas of thought and human endeavor; in religion, they explicitly and/or implicitly rejected divine revelation and the supernatural order.

1867: The first volume of *Das Kapital* was published. Together with the Communist First International, formed in the same year, it had great influence on the subsequent development of Communism and Socialism.

1869: The Anglican Church was disestablished in Ireland.

1869-1870: The First Vatican Council; see separate entry.

1870-1871: Victor Emmanuel II of Sardinia, crowned king of Italy after defeating Austrian and papal forces, marched into Rome in 1870 and expropriated the Papal States after a plebiscite in which Catholics, at the order of Pius IX, did not vote. In 1871, Pius IX refused to accept a Law of Guarantees. Confiscation of church property and hindrance of ecclesiastical administration by the regime followed.

1871: The German Empire, a confederation of 26 states, was formed. Government policy launched a Kulturkampf whose May Laws of 1873 were designed to annul papal jurisdiction in Prussia and other states and to place the Church under imperial control. Resistance to the enactments and the persecution they legalized forced the government to modify its anti-Church policy by 1887.

1878: Beginning of the pontificate of Leo XIII, who was pope until his death in 1903. Leo is best known for the encyclical *Rerum Novarum*, which greatly influenced the course of Christian social thought and the labor movement. His other accomplishments included promotion of a revival of Scholastic philosophy and the impetus he gave to scriptural studies.

1881: The first International Eucharistic Congress was held in Lille, France.

Alexander II of Russia died. His policies of Russification — as well as those of his two predecessors and a successor during the century — caused great suffering to Catholics, Jews and Protestants in Poland, Lithuania, the Ukraine and Bessarabia.

1882: Charles Darwin died. His theory of evolution by natural selection, one of several scientific highlights of the century, had extensive repercussions in the faith-and-science controversy.

1889: The Catholic University of America was founded in Washington, D.C.

1893: The US apostolic delegation was set up in Washington, D. C.

Twentieth Century

1901: Restrictive measures in France forced the Jesuits, Benedictines, Carmelites and other religious orders to leave the country. Subsequently, 14,000 schools were suppressed; religious orders and congregations were expelled; the concordat was renounced in 1905; church property was confiscated in 1906. For some years the Holy See, refusing to comply with government demands for the control of bishops' appointments, left some ecclesiastical offices vacant.

1903: Start of the 11-year pontificate of St. Pius X. He initiated the codification of canon law, 1904; removed the ban against participation by Catholics in Italian national elections, 1905; issued decrees calling upon the faithful to receive Holy Communion frequently and daily, and stating that children should begin receiving the Eucharist at the age of seven, 1905 and 1910, respectively; ordered the establishment of the Confraternity of Christian Doctrine in all parishes throughout the world, 1905; condemned Modernism in the decree *Lamentabili* and the encyclical *Pascendi,* 1907.

1908: The United States and England, long under the jurisdiction of the Congregation for the Propagation of the Faith as mission territories, were removed from its control and placed under the common law of the Church.

1910: Laws of separation were enacted in Portugal, marking a point of departure in church-state relations.

1911: The Catholic Foreign Mission Society of America — Maryknoll, the first US-founded society of its type — was established.

1914: Start of World War I, which lasted until 1918.

Start of the eight-year pontificate of Benedict XV. Much of his pontificate was devoted to seeking ways and means of minimizing the material and spiritual havoc of World War I. In 1917 he offered his services as a mediator to the belligerent nations, but his pleas for settlement of the conflict went unheeded.

1917: The Blessed Virgin Mary appeared to three children at Fatima, Portugal; see separate entry.

A new constitution, embodying repressive laws against the Church, was enacted in Mexico. Its implementation resulted in persecution in the 1920's and 1930's.

Bolsheviks seized power in Russia and set up a Communist dictatorship. The event marked the rise of Communism in Russian and world affairs. One of its immediate, and lasting, results was persecution of the Church, Jews and other segments of the population.

1918: The *Code of Canon Law,* in preparation for more than 10 years, went into effect in the Western Church.

1919: Benedict XV stimulated missionary work through the decree *Maximum Illud,* in which he urged the recruiting and training of native clergy in places where the Church was not firmly established.

1922: Beginning of the 17-year pontificate of Pius XI. He subscribed to the Lateran Treaty, 1929, which settled the Roman Question created by the confiscation of the Papal States in 1871; issued the encyclical *Casti Connubii,* 1930, an authoritative statement on Christian marriage; resisted the efforts of Benito Mussolini to control Catholic Action and the Church, in the encyclical *Non Abbiamo Bisogno,* 1931; opposed various Fascist policies; issued the encyclicals *Quadragesimo Anno,* 1931, developing the social doctrine of Leo XIII's *Rerum Novarum,* and *Divini Redemptoris,* 1937, calling for social justice and condemning atheistic Communism; condemned anti-Semitism, 1937.

Ireland was partitioned. All but two of the predominantly Catholic counties were included in the southern part of the country, which eventually attained the status of an independent republic in 1949.

1926: The Catholic Relief Act repealed virtually all legal disabilities of Catholics in England.

1931: Leftists proclaimed Spain a republic and proceeded to disestablish the Church, confiscate church property, deny salaries to the clergy, expel the Jesuits and ban teaching of the Catholic faith. These actions were preludes to the civil war of 1936-1939.

1933: Emergence of Adolf Hitler to power in Germany. By 1935 two of his aims were clear, the elimination of the Jews and control of a single national church. Persecution decimated the Jews over a period of years. The Church was subject to repressive measures, which Pius XI protested futilely in the encyclical *Mit Brennender Sorge* in 1937.

1936: A three-year civil war broke out in Spain between the leftist Loyalists and forces led by Francisco Franco. The Loyalists were defeated and one-man, one-party rule was established. A number of priests, religious and lay persons fell victims to Loyalist persecution.

1939: Start of World War II, which lasted until 1945.

Start of the 19-year pontificate of Pius XII; see separate entry.

1940: Start of a decade of Communist conquest in more than 13 countries, resulting in conditions of persecution for a minimum of 60 million Catholics as well as members of other faiths; see various countries.

Persecution diminished in Mexico through non-enforcement of anti-religious laws still on record.

1950: Pius XII proclaimed the dogma of the Assumption of the Blessed Virgin Mary.

1954: St. Pius X was canonized.

1957: The Communist regime of China attempted to start a national schismatic church.

1958: Beginning of the five-year pontificate of John XXIII; see separate entry.

1962: The Second Vatican Council began the first of four sessions; see separate entry.

1963: Paul VI began his pontificate; see separate entry.

HERESIES

Heresy is the formal and obstinate denial or doubt by a baptized person, who remains a nominal Christian, of any truth which must be believed as a matter of divine and Catholic faith. Formal heresy involves deliberate resistance to the authority of God who communicates revelation through Scripture and tradition and the teaching authority of the Church. Obstinate refusal to accept the infallible teaching of the Church constitutes the canonical crime of heresy.

Formal heretics automatically incur the penalty of excommunication (Canon 1325 of the Code of Canon Law). Material heretics are those who, in good faith and without formal obstinacy, do not accept articles or matters of divine and Catholic faith.

Heresies have been significant not only as disruptions of unity of faith but also as occasions for the clarification and development of doctrine.

Heresies from the beginning of the Church to the 13th century are listed below.

Judaizers: Early converts who claimed that members of the Church had to observe all the requirements of Mosaic Law as well as the obligations of Christian faith. This view was condemned by the Council of Jerusalem held in 51 under the presidency of St. Peter (Acts 15:28).

Gnosticism: A combination of elements of Platonic philosophy and Eastern mystery religions which claimed that its secret knowledge-principle gave its adherents a deeper insight into Christian doctrine than divine revelation and faith. One Gnostic thesis denied the divinity of Christ; others denied the reality of his humanity, calling it mere appearance (**Docetism, Phantasiasm**).

Modalism: A general term covering propositions (**Monarchianism, Patripassianism, Sabellianism**) that the Father, Son and Holy Spirit are not really distinct divine Persons but are only three different modes of being and self-manifestation of the one God. Various forms of Modalism, which appeared in the East in the second century and spread westward, were all condemned.

Marcionism: A Gnostic creation named for its author, who claimed there was total opposition and no connection at all between the Old Testament and the New Testament, between the God of the Jews and the God of the Christians; and that the canon of Scripture consisted only of portions of Luke's Gospel and 10 Epistles of Paul. Marcion was excommunicated in 144 at Rome, and his tenets were condemned again by a Roman council about 260. The heresy was checked at Rome by 200 but persisted for several centuries in the East and had some adherents as late as the Middle Ages.

Montanism: A form of extremism preached about 170 by Montanus of Phrygia, Asia Minor. Its principal tenets were: an imminent second coming of Christ, denial of the divine nature of the Church and its power to forgive sin, excessively rigorous morality. Condemned by Pope St. Zephyrinus (199-217). Tertullian was one of its victims.

Novatianism: A heresy of excessive rigorism named for its authŏr, a priest of Rome and antipope. Its principal tenet was that persons who fell away from the Church under persecution and/or those guilty of serious sin after baptism could not be absolved and readmitted to communion with the Church. The heresy, condemned by a Roman synod in 251, slowly subsided in the West and died in the East by the end of the seventh century.

Subordinationism, Adoptionism: Christological errors and logical antecedents of Arianism. The key tenet was that Christ, while the most excellent of creatures, was subordinate to God whose Son he was by adoption rather than by nature. First proposed at Rome late in the second century, it was condemned by Pope St. Victor in 190 and again in the following century, in 785 by Pope Adrian I, in 794 by a Council of Frankfurt, and in 1177 by Pope Alexander III.

Arianism: Denial of the divinity of Christ, the most devastating of the early heresies, authored by Arius of Alexandria and condemned by the Council of Nicaea I in 325. Arians and several kinds of **Semi-Arians** propagandized their tenets widely, raised havoc in the Church for several centuries, and established their own hierarchies and churches.

Macedonianism: Denial of the divinity of the Holy Spirit, who was said to be a creature of the Son. Condemned by the Council of Constantinople I in 381. Macedonians were also called **Pneumatomachists,** enemies of the Spirit; and **Marathonians,** after the name of one of their leaders, a bishop of Nicomedia.

Nestorianism: Denial of the real unity of divine and human natures in the single divine Person of Christ, proposed by Nestorius, patriarch of Constantinople. He also held that Mary could not be called the Mother of God *(Theotokos);* that is, of the Second Person of the Trinity made Man. Condemned by the councils of Ephesus in 431 and Chalcedon in 451.

Monophysitism: Denial of Christ's human nature; also called **Eutychianism,** after the name of one of its leading advocates. Condemned by the Council of Chalcedon in 451.

Monothelitism: Denial of the human will of Christ. Severus of Antioch and Sergius, patriarch of Constantinople, were leading advocates of the heresy, which was condemned by the Council of Constantinople III in 681.

Priscillianism: A fourth century amalgamation of elements from various sources — Sabellianism, Arianism, Docetism, Pantheism, belief in the diabolical nature of marriage, corruption of Scripture. Condemned by a Council of Braga in 563 on 17 different counts.

Donatism: A development of the error at the heart of the third century **Rebaptism Controversy** (baptism conferred by heretics is invalid because persons deprived of grace are incapable of being ministers of grace to others). Followers of Donatus the Great asserted throughout the fourth century that sacraments administered by sinners were invalid. Condemnation of the heresy is traced to Pope St. Stephen I (254-257) and the principle that sacraments have their efficacy from Christ, not from their human ministers.

Pelagianism: Denial of the supernatural order of things, proposed by Pelagius (360-420), a Breton monk. Proceeding from the assumption that Adam had a natural right to supernatural life, the theory held that man could attain salvation through the efforts of his own free will and natural powers. The theory involved errors concerning the nature of original sin, the meaning of grace and other matters. St. Augustine opposed the heresy, which was condemned by the Council of Ephesus in 431. **Semi-Pelagianism** was condemned by a Council of Orange in 529.

Iconoclasm: An image-breaking campaign which resulted from an edict issued by Eastern Emperor Leo the Isaurian in 726, that the veneration of images, pictures and relics was idolatrous. The theoretical basis of the heresy was the Monophysite error which denied the humanity of Christ. It was denounced several times before its condemnation by the Council of Nicaea II in 787.

Berengarian Heresy: Denial of the Real Presence of Christ under the appearances of bread and wine, the first clear-cut Eucharistic heresy; proposed by Berengarius of Tours (c. 1000-1088). Condemned by various synods and finally by a council held at Rome in 1079.

Waldensianism: Claimed by Peter Waldo, a merchant of Lyons, to be a return to pure Christianity, the heresy rejected the hierarchical structure of the Church, the sacramental system and other doctrines. Its adherents were excommunicated in 1184 and their tenets were condemned several times thereafter.

Albigensianism, Catharism: Related errors based on the old **Manichaean** assumption that two supreme principles of good and evil were operative in creation and life, and that the supreme objective of human endeavor was liberation from evil (matter). The heresy denied the humanity of Christ, the sacramental system and the authority of the Church (and state), and endorsed a moral code which threatened seriously the fabric of social life in southern France and northern Italy in the 12th and 13th centuries. Condemned by councils of the Lateran III and Lateran IV in 1179 and 1215.

ECUMENICAL COUNCILS

An ecumenical council is an assembly of the college of bishops, with and under the presidency of the pope, which has supreme authority over the Church in matters pertaining to faith, morals, worship and discipline.

The Second Vatican Council stated: "The supreme authority with which this college (of bishops) is empowered over the whole Church is exercised in a solemn way through an ecumenical council. A council is never ecumenical unless it is confirmed or at least accepted as such by the successor of Peter. It is the prerogative of the Roman Pontiff to convoke these councils, to preside over them, and to confirm them" *(Dogmatic Constitution on the Church,* No. 22).

Pope Presides

The pope is the head of an ecumenical council; he presides over it either personally or through legates. Conciliar decrees and other actions have binding force only when confirmed and promulgated by him. If a pope dies during a council, it is suspended until reconvened by another pope. An ecumenical council is not superior to a pope; hence, there is no appeal from a pope to a council.

Collectively, the bishops with the pope represent the whole Church. They do this not as democratic representatives of their faithful in a kind of church parliament, but as the successors of the Apostles with divinely given authority, care and responsibility over the whole Church.

Council participants with a deliberative vote are: cardinals; residential patriarchs, primates, archbishops and bishops, even if they are not yet consecrated; abbots and certain other prelates, an abbot primate, abbot superiors of monastic congregations and heads of exempt clerical religious; titular bishops, on invitation. Experts in theology and canon law may be given a consultative vote. Others, including lay persons, may address a council or observe its actions, but may not vote.

Basic legislation concerning ecumenical councils is contained in Canons 222-229 of the Code of Canon Law. Basic doctrinal considerations were stated by the Second Vatican Council in the *Dogmatic Constitution on the Church.*

Background

Ecumenical councils had their prototype in the Council of Jerusalem in 51, at which the Apostles under the leadership of St. Peter decided that converts to the Christian faith were not obliged to observe all the prescriptions of Old Testament law (Acts 15). As early as the second century, bishops got together in regional meetings, synods or councils to take common action for the doctrinal and pastoral good of their communities of faithful. The ex-

pansion of such limited assemblies to ecumenical councils was a logical and historical evolution, given the nature and needs of the Church.

Emperors were active in summoning or convoking the first eight councils, especially the first five and the eighth. Among reasons for intervention of this kind were the facts that the emperors regarded themselves as guardians of the faith; that the settlement of religious controversies, which had repercussions in political and social turmoil, served the cause of peace in the state; and that the emperors had at their disposal ways and means of facilitating gatherings of bishops. Imperial actions, however, did not account for the formally ecumenical nature of the councils.

Some councils were attended by relatively few bishops, and the ecumenical character of several was open to question for a time. However, confirmation and de facto recognition of their actions by popes and subsequent councils established them as ecumenical.

Role in History

The councils have played a highly significant role in the history of the Church by witnessing to and defining truths of revelation, by shaping forms of worship and discipline, and by promoting measures for the ever-necessary reform and renewal of Catholic life. In general, they have represented attempts of the Church to mobilize itself in times of crisis for self-preservation, self-purification and growth.

The first eight ecumenical councils were held in the East; the other 13, in the West. The majority of separated Eastern Churches — e.g., the Orthodox — recognize the ecumenical character of the first seven councils, which formulated a great deal of basic doctrine. Nestorians, however, acknowledge only the first two councils; the Monophysite Armenians, Syrians, and Copts acknowledge first three.

The 21 Councils

The 21 ecumenical councils in the history of the Church are listed below, with indication of their names or titles (taken from the names of the places where they were held); the dates; the reigning and/or approving popes; the emperors who were instrumental in convoking the eight councils in the East; the number of bishops who attended, when available; the number of sessions; the most significant actions.

1. Nicaea I, 325: St. Sylvester I (Emperor Constantine I); attended by approximately 300 bishops; sessions held between May 20 or June 19 to near the end of August. Condemned Arianism, which denied the divinity of Christ; contributed to formulation of the Nicene Creed; fixed the date of Easter; passed regulations concerning clerical discipline; adopted the civil division of the Empire as the model for the organization of the Church.

2. Constantinople I, 381: St. Damasus I (Emperor Theodosius I); attended by approximately 150 bishops; sessions held from May to July. Condemned various brands of Arianism, and Macedonianism which denied the divinity of the Holy Spirit; contributed to formulation of the Nicene Creed; approved a canon which made the bishop of Constantinople the ranking prelate in the East, with primacy next to that of the pope. Doubt about the ecumenical character of this council was resolved by the ratification of its acts by popes and the Council of Chalcedon.

3. Ephesus, 431: St. Celestine I (Emperor Theodosius II); attended by 150 to 200 bishops; five sessions held between June 22 and July 17. Condemned Nestorianism, which denied the real unity of the divine and human natures in the Person of Christ; defined *Theotokos* ("Bearer of God") as the title of Mary, Mother of the Son of God made Man; condemned Pelagianism, which reduced the supernatural to the natural order of things.

4. Chalcedon, 451: St. Leo I (Emperor Marcian); attended by approximately 600 bishops; 17 sessions held between Oct. 8 and Nov. 1. Condemned: Monophysitism, also called Eutychianism, which denied the humanity of Christ by holding that he had only one, the divine, nature; and the Monophysite Robber Synod of Ephesus, of 449.

5. Constantinople II, 553: Vigilius (Emperor Justinian I); attended by 165 bishops; eight sessions held between May 5 and June 2. Condemned the *Three Chapters,* Nestorian-tainted writings of Theodore of Mopsuestia, Theodoret of Cyprus and Ibas of Edessa.

6. Constantinople III, 680-681; St. Agatho, St. Leo II (Emperor Constantine IV); attended by approximately 170 bishops; 16 sessions held between Nov. 7, 680, and Sept. 16, 681. Condemned Monothelitism, which held that there was only one will, the divine, in Christ; censured Pope Honorius I for a letter to Sergius, bishop of Constantinople, in which he made an ambiguous but not infallible statement about the unity of will and/or operation in Christ. Constantinople III is also called the Trullan Council because its sessions were held in the domed hall, Trullos, of the imperial palace.

7. Nicaea II, 787: Adrian I (Empress Irene); attended by approximately 300 bishops: eight sessions held between Sept. 24 and Oct. 23. Condemned: Iconoclasm, which held that the use of images was idolatry; and Adoptionism, which claimed that Christ was not the Son of God by nature but only by adoption. This was the last council regarded as ecumenical by Orthodox Churches.

8. Constantinople IV, 869-870: Adrian II (Emperor Basil I); attended by 102 bishops; six sessions held between Oct. 5, 869, and Feb. 28, 870. Condemned Iconoclasm; condemned and deposed Photius as patriarch of Constantinople; restored Ignatius to the patriarchate. This was the last ecumenical council held in the East. It was first called ecumenical by canonists toward the end of the 11th century.

9. Lateran I, 1123: Callistus II; attended by approximately 300 bishops; sessions held between Mar. 18 and Apr. 6. Endorsed provisions of the Concordat of Worms concerning the investiture of prelates: approved reform measures in 25 canons.

10. Lateran II, 1139: Innocent II; attended by 900 to 1,000 bishops and abbots; three sessions held in April. Adopted measures against a schism organized by antipope Anacletus; approved 30 disciplinary measures and canons, one of which stated that holy orders is an invalidating impediment to marriage.

11. Lateran III, 1179: Alexander III; attended by at least 300 bishops; three sessions held between Mar. 5 and 19. Enacted measures against the Waldenses and Albigensians; approved reform decrees in 27 canons; provided that popes be elected by two-thirds vote of the cardinals.

12. Lateran IV, 1215: Innocent III; sessions held between Nov. 11 and 30. Ordered annual confession and Communion; defined and made first official use of the term "transubstantiation"; adopted measures to counteract the Cathari and Albigensians; approved 70 canons.

13. Lyons I, 1245: Innocent IV; attended by approximately 150 bishops; three sessions held between June 28 and July 17. Confirmed the deposition of Emperor Frederick II; approved 22 canons.

14. Lyons II, 1274: Gregory X; attended by approximately 500 bishops; six sessions held between May 7 and July 17. Accomplished a temporary reunion of separated Eastern Churches with the Roman Church; issued regulations concerning conclaves for papal elections; approved 31 canons.

15. Vienne, 1311-1312: Clement V; attended by 132 bishops; three sessions held between Oct. 16, 1311, and May 6, 1312. Suppressed the Knights Templar; enacted a number of reform decrees.

16. Constance, 1414-1418: Gregory XII, Martin V; attended by nearly 200 bishops, plus other prelates and many experts; 45 sessions held between Nov. 5, 1414, and Apr. 22, 1418. Took successful action to end the Western Schism; rejected the teachings of Wycliff; condemned Hus as a heretic. One decree, passed in the earlier stages of the council, asserted the superiority of an ecumenical council over the pope; this was later rejected.

17. Florence (also called Basel-Ferrara-Florence), 1438-1445: Eugene IV; attended by many Latin-Rite and Eastern-Rite bishops; preliminary sessions were held at Basel and Ferrara before definitive work was accomplished at Florence. Reaffirmed the primacy of the pope against the claims of Conciliarists that an ecumenical council is superior to the pope; formulated and approved decrees of union — with the Greeks, July 6, 1439; with the Armenians, Nov. 22, 1439; with the Jacobites, Feb. 4, 1442. These decrees failed to gain general or lasting acceptance in the East.

18. Lateran V, 1512-1517: Julius II, Leo X; 12 sessions held between May 3, 1512, and Mar. 16, 1517. Stated the relation and position of the pope with respect to an ecumenical council; acted to counteract the Pragmatic Sanction of Bourges and exaggerated claims of liberty by the French Church; condemned erroneous teachings concerning the nature of the human soul; stated doctrine concerning indulgences. The council reflected concern for abuses in the Church and the need for reforms but failed to take decisive action in the years immediately preceding the Reformation.

19. Trent, 1545-1563: Paul III, Julius III, Pius IV; 25 sessions held between Dec. 13, 1545, and Dec. 4, 1563. Issued a great number of decrees concerning doctrinal matters opposed by the Reformers, and mobilized the Counter-Reformation. Definitions covered the rule of faith, the nature of justification, grace, faith, original sin and its effects, the seven sacraments, the sacrificial nature of the Mass, the veneration of saints, use of sacred images, belief in purgatory, the doctrine of indulgences, the jurisdiction of the pope over the whole Church. Initiated many reforms for renewal in the liturgy and general discipline in the Church, the promotion of religious instruction, the education of the clergy through the foundation of seminaries, etc. Trent ranks with Vatican II as the greatest ecumenical council held in the West.

20. Vatican I, 1869-1870: Pius IX; attended by approximately 800 bishops and other prelates; four public sessions and 89 general meetings held between Dec. 8, 1869, and July 7, 1870. Defined papal primacy and infallibility in a dogmatic constitution on the Church; covered natural religion, revelation, faith, and the relations between faith and reason in a dogmatic constitution on the Catholic faith. The council suspended sessions Sept. 1 and was adjourned Oct. 20, 1870.

Vatican II

The Second Vatican Council, which was forecast by Pope John XXIII Jan. 25, 1959, was held in four sessions in St. Peter's Basilica.

Pope John convoked it and opened the first session, which ran from Oct. 11 to Dec. 8, 1962. Following John's death June 3, 1963, Pope Paul VI reconvened the council for the other three sessions which ran from Sept. 29 to Dec. 4, 1963; Sept. 14 to Nov. 21, 1964; Sept. 14 to Dec. 8, 1965.

A total of 2,860 Fathers participated in council proceedings, and attendance at meetings varied between 2,000 and 2,500. For various reasons, including the denial of exit from Communist-dominated countries, 274 Fathers could not attend.

The council formulated and promulgated 16 documents — two dogmatic and two pastoral constitutions, nine decrees and three declarations — all of which reflect its basic pastoral orientation toward renewal and reform in the Church. Given below are the Latin and English titles of the documents and their dates of promulgation.

• *Lumen Gentium* (Dogmatic Constitution on the Church), Nov. 21, 1964.

• *Dei Verbum* (Dogmatic Constitution on Divine Revelation), Nov. 18, 1965.

• *Sacrosanctum Concilium* (Constitution on the Sacred Liturgy), Dec. 4, 1963.

• *Gaudium et Spes* (Pastoral Constitution on the Church in the Modern World), Dec. 7, 1965.

• *Christus Dominus* (Decree on the Bishops' Pastoral Office in the Church), Oct. 28, 1965.

• *Ad Gentes* (Decree on the Church's Missionary Activity), Dec. 7, 1965.

• *Unitatis Redintegratio* (Decree on Ecumenism), Nov. 21, 1964.

• *Orientalium Ecclesiarum* (Decree on Eastern Catholic Churches), Nov. 21, 1964.

• *Presbyterorum Ordinis* (Decree on the Ministry and Life of Priests), Dec. 7, 1965.

• *Optatam Totius* (Decree on Priestly Formation), Oct. 28, 1965.

• *Perfectae Caritatis* (Decree on the Appropriate Renewal of the Religious Life), Oct. 28, 1965.

• *Apostolicam Actuositatem* (Decree on the Apostolate of the Laity), Nov. 18, 1965.

• *Inter Mirifica* (Decree on the Instruments of Social Communication), Dec. 4, 1963.

• *Dignitatis Humanae* (Declaration on Religious Freedom), Dec. 7, 1965.

• *Nostra Aetate* (Declaration on the Relationship of the Church to Non-Christian Religions), Oct. 28, 1965.

• *Gravissimum Educationis* (Declaration on Christian Education), Oct. 28, 1965.

The key documents were the four constitutions, which set the ideological basis for all the others. To date, the documents with the most visible effects are those on the liturgy, the Church, the Church in the world, ecumenism, the renewal of religious life, the life and ministry of priests, the lay apostolate.

The main business of the council was to explore and make explicit dimensions of doctrine and Christian life requiring emphasis for the full development of the Church and the better accomplishment of its mission in the contemporary world.

Archbishop Jerome Hamer, O.P., has cited the continuing need of the Church and all its members to assimilate the teachings of Vatican Council II.

Popes

LIST OF POPES

(Source: *Annuario Pontificio.*)

Information includes the name of the pope, in many cases his name before becoming pope, his birthplace or country of origin, the date of accession to the papacy, and the date of the end of reign which, in all but a few cases, was the date of death. Double dates indicate times of election and coronation.

St. Peter (Simon Bar-Jona): Bethsaida in Galilee; d. c. 67.

St. Linus: Tuscany; 67-76.

St. Anacletus (Cletus): Rome; 76-88.

St. Clement: Rome; 88-97.

St. Evaristus: Greece; 97-105.

St. Alexander I: Rome; 105-115.

St. Sixtus I: Rome; 115-125.

St. Telesphorus: Greece; 125-136.

St. Hyginus: Greece; 136-140.

St. Pius I: Aquileia; 140-155.

St. Anicetus: Syria; 155-166.

St. Soter: Campania; 166-175.

St. Eleutherius: Nicopolis in Epirus; 175-189.

Up to the time of St. Eleutherius, the years indicated for the beginning and end of pontificates are not absolutely certain. Also, up to the middle of the 11th century, there are some doubts about the exact days and months given in chronological tables.

St. Victor I: Africa; 189-199.

St. Zephyrinus: Rome; 199-217.

St. Callistus I: Rome; 217-222.

St. Urban I: Rome; 222-230.

St. Pontian: Rome; July 21, 230, to Sept. 28, 235.

St. Anterus: Greece; Nov. 21, 235, to Jan. 3, 236.

St. Fabian: Rome; Jan. 10, 236, to Jan. 20, 250.

St. Cornelius: Rome; Mar., 251, to June, 253.

St. Lucius I: Rome; June 25, 253, to Mar. 5, 254.

St. Stephen I: Rome; May 12, 254, to Aug. 2, 257.

St. Sixtus II: Greece; Aug. 30, 257, to Aug. 6, 258.

St. Dionysius: July 22, 259, to Dec. 26, 268.

St. Felix I: Rome; Jan. 5, 269, to Dec. 30, 274.

St. Eutychian: Luni; Jan. 4, 275, to Dec. 7, 283.

St. Caius: Dalmatia; Dec, 17, 283, to Apr. 22, 296.

St. Marcellinus: Rome; June 30, 296, to Oct. 25, 304.

St. Marcellus I: Rome; May 27, 308, or June 26, 308, to Jan. 16, 309.

St. Eusebius: Greece; Apr. 18, 309 or 310, to Aug. 17, 309 or 310.

St. Melchiades (Miltiades): Africa; July 2, 311, to Jan. 11, 314.

St. Sylvester I: Rome; Jan. 31, 314, to Dec. 31, 335. (Most of the popes before St. Sylvester I were martyrs.)

St. Marcus: Rome; Jan. 18, 336, to Oct. 7, 336.

St. Julius I: Rome; Feb. 6, 337, to Apr. 12, 352.

Liberius: Rome; May 17, 352, to Sept. 24, 366.

St. Damasus I: Spain; Oct. 1, 366, to Dec. 11, 384.

St. Siricius: Rome; Dec. 15, or 22 or 29, 384, to Nov. 26, 399.

St. Anastasius I: Rome; Nov. 27, 399, to Dec. 19, 401.

St. Innocent I: Albano; Dec. 22, 401, to Mar. 12, 417.

St. Zozimus: Greece; Mar. 18, 417, to Dec. 26, 418.

St. Boniface I: Rome; Dec. 28 or 29, 418, to Sept. 4, 422.

St. Celestine I: Campania; Sept. 10, 422, to July 27, 432.

St. Sixtus III: Rome; July 31, 432, to Aug. 19, 440.

St. Leo I (the Great): Tuscany; Sept. 29, 440, to Nov. 10, 461.

St. Hilary: Sardinia; Nov. 19, 461, to Feb. 29, 468.

St. Simplicius: Tivoli; Mar. 3, 468, to Mar. 10, 483.

St. Felix III (II): Rome; Mar. 13, 483, to Mar. 1, 492.

He should be called Felix II, and his successors of the same name should be numbered accordingly. The discrepancy in the numerical designation of popes named Felix was caused by the erroneous insertion in some lists of the name of St. Felix of Rome, a martyr.

St. Gelasius I: Africa; Mar. 1, 492, to Nov. 21, 496.

Anastasius II: Rome; Nov. 24, 496, to Nov. 19, 498.

St. Symmachus: Sardinia; Nov. 22, 498, to July 19, 514.

St. Hormisdas: Frosinone; July 20, 514, to Aug. 6, 523.

St. John I, Martyr: Tuscany; Aug. 13, 523, to May 18, 526.

St. Felix IV (III): Samnium; July 12, 526, to Sept. 22, 530.

Boniface II: Rome; Sept. 22, 530, to Oct. 17, 532.

John II: Rome; Jan. 2, 533, to May 8, 535.

John II was the first pope to change his name. His given name was Mercury.

St. Agapitus I: Rome; May 13, 535, to Apr. 22, 536.

St. Silverius, Martyr: Campania; June 1 or 8, 536, to Nov. 11, 537 (d. Dec. 2, 537).

St. Silverius was violently deposed in March, 537, and abdicated Nov. 11, 537. His successor, Vigilius, was not recognized as pope by all the Roman clergy until his abdication.

Vigilius: Rome; Mar. 29, 537, to June 7, 555.

Pelagius I: Rome; Apr. 16, 556, to Mar. 4, 561.

John III: Rome; July 17, 561, to July 13, 574.

Benedict I: Rome; June 2, 575, to July 30, 579.

Pelagius II: Rome; Nov. 26, 579, to Feb. 7, 590.

St. Gregory I (the Great): Rome; Sept. 3, 590, to Mar. 12, 604.

Sabinian: Blera in Tuscany; Sept. 13, 604, to Feb. 22, 606.

Boniface III: Rome; Feb. 19, 607, to Nov. 12, 607.

St. Boniface IV: Abruzzi; Aug. 25, 608, to May 8, 615.

St. Deusdedit (Adeodatus I): Rome; Oct. 19, 615, to Nov. 8, 618.

Boniface V: Naples; Dec. 23, 619, to Oct. 25, 625.

Honorius I: Campania; Oct. 27, 625, to Oct. 12, 638.

Severinus: Rome; May 28, 640, to Aug. 2, 640.

John IV: Dalmatia; Dec. 24, 640, to Oct. 12, 642.

Theodore I: Greece; Nov. 24, 642, to May 14, 649.

St. Martin I, Martyr: Todi; July, 649, to Sept. 16, 655 (in exile from June 17, 653).

St. Eugene I: Rome; Aug. 10, 654, to June 2, 657.

St. Eugene I was elected during the exile of St. Martin I, who is believed to have endorsed him as pope.

St. Vitalian: Segni; July 30, 657, to Jan. 27, 672.

Adeodatus II: Rome; Apr. 11, 672, to June 17, 676.

Donus: Rome; Nov. 2, 676, to Apr. 11, 678.

St. Agatho: Sicily; June 27, 678, to Jan. 10, 681.

St. Leo II: Sicily; Aug. 17, 682, to July 3, 683.

St. Benedict II: Rome; June 26, 684, to May 8, 685.

John V: Syria; July 23, 685, to Aug. 2, 686.

Conon: birthplace unknown; Oct. 21, 686, to Sept. 21, 687.

St. Sergius I: Syria; Dec. 15, 687, to Sept. 8, 701.

John VI: Greece; Oct. 30, 701, to Jan. 11, 705.

John VII: Greece; Mar. 1, 705, to Oct. 18, 707.

Sisinnius: Syria; Jan. 15, 708, to Feb. 4, 708.

Constantine: Syria; Mar. 25, 708, to Apr. 9, 715.

St. Gregory II: Rome; May 19, 715, to Feb. 11, 731.

St. Gregory III: Syria; Mar. 18, 731, to Nov., 741.

St. Zachary: Greece; Dec. 10, 741, to Mar. 22, 752.

Stephen II (III): Rome; Mar. 26, 752, to Apr. 26, 757.

After the death of St. Zachary, a Roman priest named Stephen was elected but died (four days later) before his consecration as bishop of Rome, which would have marked the beginning of his pontificate. Another Stephen was elected to succeed Zachary as Stephen II. (The first pope with this name was St. Stephen I, 254-57.) The ordinal III appears in parentheses after the name of Stephen II because the name of the earlier elected but deceased priest was included in some lists. Other Stephens have double numbers.

St. Paul I: Rome; Apr. (May 29), 757, to June 28, 767.

Stephen III (IV): Sicily; Aug. 1 (7), 768, to Jan. 24, 772.

Adrian I: Rome; Feb. 1 (9), 772, to Dec. 25, 795.

St. Leo III: Rome; Dec. 26 (27), 795, to June 12, 816.

Stephen IV (V): Rome; June 22, 816, to Jan. 24, 817.

St. Paschal I: Rome; Jan. 25, 817, to Feb. 11, 824.

Eugene II: Rome; Feb. (May), 824, to Aug., 827.

Valentine: Rome; Aug. 827, to Sept., 827.

Gregory IV: Rome; 827, to Jan., 844.

Sergius II: Rome; Jan., 844 to Jan. 27, 847.

St. Leo IV: Rome; Jan. (Apr. 10), 847, to July 17, 855.

Benedict III: Rome; July (Sept. 29), 855, to Apr. 17, 858.

St. Nicholas I (the Great): Rome; Apr. 24, 858, to Nov. 13, 867.

Adrian II: Rome; Dec. 14, 867, to Dec. 14, 872.

John VIII: Rome; Dec. 14, 872, to Dec. 16, 882.

Marinus I: Gallese; Dec. 16, 882, to May 15, 884.

St. Adrian III: Rome; May 17, 884, to Sept., 885. Cult confirmed June 2, 1891.

Stephen V (VI): Rome; Sept., 885, to Sept. 14, 891.

Formosus: Portus; Oct. 6, 891, to Apr. 4, 896.

Boniface VI: Rome; Apr., 896, to Apr., 896.

Stephen VI (VII): Rome; May, 896, to Aug., 897.

Romanus: Gallese; Aug., 897, to Nov., 897.

Theodore II: Rome; Dec., 897, to Dec., 897.

John IX: Tivoli; Jan., 898, to Jan., 900.

Benedict IV: Rome; Jan. (Feb.), 900, to July, 903.

Leo V: Ardea; July, 903, to Sept., 903.

Sergius III: Rome; Jan. 29, 904, to Apr. 14, 911.

Anastasius III: Rome; Apr., 911, to June, 913.

Landus: Sabina; July, 913, to Feb., 914.

John X: Tossignano (Imola); Mar., 914, to May, 928.

Leo VI: Rome; May, 928, to Dec., 928.

Stephen VII (VIII): Rome; Dec., 928, to Feb., 931.

John XI: Rome; Feb. (Mar.), 931, to Dec., 935.

Leo VII: Rome; Jan. 3, 936, to July 13, 939.

Stephen VIII (IX): Rome; July 14, 939, to Oct., 942.

Marinus II: Rome; Oct. 30, 942, to May, 946.

Agapitus II: Rome; May 10, 946, to Dec., 955.

John XII (Octavius): Tusculum; Dec. 16, 955, to May 14, 964 (date of his death).

Leo VIII: Rome; Dec. 4 (6), 963, to Mar. 1, 965.

Benedict V: Rome; May 22, 964, to July 4, 966.

Confusion exists concerning the legitimacy of claims to the pontificate by Leo VIII and Benedict V. John XII was deposed Dec. 4, 963, by a Roman council. If this deposition was invalid, Leo was an antipope. If the deposition of John was valid, Leo was the legitimate pope and Benedict was an antipope.

John XIII: Rome; Oct. 1, 965, to Sept. 6, 972.

Benedict VI: Rome; Jan. 19, 973, to June, 974.

Benedict VII: Rome; Oct. 974, to July 10, 983.

John XIV (Peter Campenora): Pavia; Dec., 983, to Aug. 20, 984.

John XV: Rome; Aug., 985, to Mar., 996.

Gregory V (Bruno of Carinthia): Saxony; May 3, 996, to Feb. 18, 999.

Sylvester II (Gerbert): Auvergne; Apr. 2, 999, to May 12, 1003.

John XVII (Siccone): Rome; June, 1003, to Dec., 1003.

John XVIII (Phasianus): Rome; Jan., 1004, to July, 1009.

Sergius IV (Peter): Rome; July 31, 1009, to May 12, 1012.

The custom of changing one's name on election to the papacy is generally considered to date from the time of Sergius IV. Before his time, several popes had changed their names. After his time, this became a regular practice, with few exceptions; e.g., Adrian VI and Marcellus II.

Benedict VIII (Theophylactus): Tusculum; May 18, 1012, to Apr. 9, 1024.

John XIX (Romanus): Tusculum; Apr. (May), 1024, to 1032.

Benedict IX (Theophylactus): Tusculum; 1032, to 1044.

Sylvester III (John): Rome; Jan. 20, 1045, to Feb. 10, 1045.

Sylvester III was an antipope if the forcible removal of Benedict IX in 1044 was not legitimate.

Benedict IX (second time): Apr. 10, 1045, to May 1, 1045.

Gregory VI (John Gratian): Rome; May 5, 1045, to Dec. 20, 1046.

Clement II (Suitger, Lord of Morsleben and Hornburg): Saxony; Dec. 24 (25), 1046, to Oct. 9, 1047.

If the resignation of Benedict IX in 1045 and his removal at the December, 1046, synod were not legitimate, Gregory VI and Clement II were antipopes.

Benedict IX (third time): Nov. 8, 1047, to July 17, 1048 (d. c. 1055).

Damasus II (Poppo): Bavaria; July 17, 1048, to Aug. 9, 1048.

St. Leo IX (Bruno): Alsace; Feb. 12, 1049, to Apr. 19, 1054.

Victor II (Gebhard): Swabia; Apr. 16, 1055, to July 28, 1057.

Stephen IX (X) (Frederick): Lorraine; Aug. 3, 1057, to Mar. 29, 1058.

Nicholas II (Gerard): Burgundy; Jan. 24, 1059, to July 27, 1061.

Alexander II (Anselmo da Baggio): Milan; Oct. 1, 1061, to Apr. 21, 1073.

St. Gregory VII (Hildebrand): Tuscany; Apr. 22 (June 30), 1073, to May 25, 1085.

Bl. Victor III (Dauferius; Desiderius): Benevento; May 24, 1086, to Sept. 16, 1087. Cult confirmed July 23, 1887.

Bl. Urban II (Otto di Lagery): France; Mar. 12, 1088, to July 29, 1099. Cult confirmed July 14, 1881.

Paschal II (Raniero): Ravenna; Aug. 13 (14), 1099, to Jan. 21, 1118.

Gelasius II (Giovanni Caetani): Gaeta; Jan. 24 (Mar. 10), 1118, to Jan. 28, 1119.

Callistus II (Guido of Burgundy): Burgundy; Feb. 2 (9), 1119, to Dec. 13, 1124.

Honorius II (Lamberto): Fiagnano (Imola); Dec. 15 (21), 1124, to Feb. 13, 1130.

Innocent II (Gregorio Papareschi): Rome; Feb. 14 (23), 1130, to Sept. 24, 1143.

Celestine II (Guido): Citta di Castello; Sept. 26 (Oct. 3), 1143, to Mar. 8, 1144.

Lucius II (Gerardo Caccianemici): Bologna: Mar. 12, 1144, to Feb. 15, 1145.

Bl. Eugene III (Bernardo Paganelli di Montemagno): Pisa; Feb. 15 (18), 1145, to July 8, 1153. Cult confirmed Oct. 3, 1872.

Anastasius IV (Corrado): Rome; July 12, 1153, to Dec, 3, 1154.

Adrian IV (Nicholas Breakspear): England; Dec. 4 (5), 1154, to Sept. 1, 1159.

Alexander III (Rolando Bandinelli): Siena; Sept. 7 (20), 1159, to Aug. 30, 1181.

Lucius III (Ubaldo Allucingoli): Lucca; Sept. 1 (6), 1181, to Sept. 25, 1185.

Urban III (Uberto Crivelli): Milan; Nov. 25 (Dec. 1), 1185, to Oct. 20, 1187.

Gregory VIII (Alberto de Morra): Benevento; Oct. 21 (25), 1187, to Dec. 17, 1187.

Clement III (Paolo Scolari): Rome; Dec. 19 (20), 1187, to Mar., 1191.

Celestine III (Giacinto Bobone): Rome; Mar. 30 (Apr. 14), 1191, to Jan. 8, 1198.

Innocent III (Lotario dei Conti di Segni): Anagni; Jan. 8 (Feb. 22), 1198, to July 16, 1216.

Honorius III (Cencio Savelli): Rome; July 18 (24), 1216, to Mar. 18, 1227.

Gregory IX (Ugolino, Count of Segni): Anagni; Mar. 19 (21), 1227, to Aug. 22, 1241.

Celestine IV (Goffredo Castiglioni): Milan; Oct. 25 (28), 1241, to Nov. 10, 1241.

Innocent IV (Sinibaldo Fieschi): Genoa; June 25 (28), 1243, to Dec. 7, 1254.

Alexander IV (Rinaldo, Count of Segni): Anagni; Dec. 12 (20), 1254, to May 25, 1261.

Urban IV (Jacques Pantaléon): Troyes; Aug. 29 (Sept. 4), 1261, to Oct. 2, 1264.

Clement IV (Guy Foulques or Guido le Gros): France; Feb. 5 (15), 1265, to Nov. 29, 1268.

Bl. Gregory X (Teobaldo Visconti): Piacenza; Sept. 1, 1271 (Mar. 27, 1272), to Jan. 10, 1276. Cult confirmed Sept. 12, 1713.

Bl. Innocent V (Peter of Tarentaise): Savoy; Jan. 21 (Feb. 22), 1276, to June 22, 1276. Cult confirmed Mar. 13, 1898.

Adrian V (Ottobono Fieschi): Genoa: July 11, 1276, to Aug. 18, 1276.

John XXI (Petrus Juliani or Petrus Hispanus): Portugal; Sept. 8 (20), 1276, to May 20, 1277.

<small>Elimination was made of the name of John XX in an effort to rectify the numerical designation of popes named John. The error dates back to the time of John XV.</small>

Nicholas III (Giovanni Gaetano Orsini): Rome; Nov. 25 (Dec. 26), 1277, to Aug. 22, 1280.

Martin IV (Simon de Brie): France; Feb. 22 (Mar. 23), 1281, to Mar. 28, 1285.

<small>The names of Marinus I (882-84) and Marinus II (942-46) were construed as Martin. In view of these two pontificates and the earlier reign of St. Martin I (649-55), this pope was called Martin IV.</small>

Honorius IV (Giacomo Savelli): Rome; Apr. 2 (May 20), 1285, to Apr. 3, 1287.

Nicholas IV (Girolamo Masci): Ascoli; Feb. 22, 1288, to Apr. 4, 1292.

St. Celestine V (Pietro del Murrone): Isernia; July 5 (Aug. 29), 1294, to Dec. 13, 1294; d. 1296. Canonized May 5, 1313.

Boniface VIII (Benedetto Caetani): Anagni; Dec. 24, 1294 (Jan. 23, 1295), to Oct. 11, 1303.

Bl. Benedict XI (Niccolo Boccasini): Treviso; Oct. 22 (27), 1303, to July 7, 1304. Cult confirmed Apr. 24, 1736.

Clement V (Bertrand de Got): France; June 5 (Nov. 14), 1305, to Apr. 20, 1314. (First of Avignon popes.)

John XXII (Jacques d'Euse): Cahors; Aug. 7 (Sept. 5), 1316, to Dec. 4, 1334.

Benedict XII (Jacques Fournier): France; Dec. 20, 1334 (Jan. 8, 1335), to Apr. 25, 1342.

Clement VI (Pierre Roger): France; May 7 (19), 1342, to Dec. 6, 1352.

Innocent VI (Etienne Aubert): France; Dec. 18 (30), 1352, to Sept. 12, 1362.

Bl. Urban V (Guillaume de Grimoard): France; Sept. 28 (Nov. 6), 1362, to Dec. 19, 1370. Cult confirmed Mar. 10, 1870.

Gregory XI (Pierre Roger de Beaufort): France; Dec. 30, 1370 (Jan. 5, 1371), to Mar. 26, 1378. (Last of Avignon popes.)

Urban VI (Bartolomeo Prignano): Naples; Apr. 8 (18), 1378, to Oct. 15, 1389.

Boniface IX (Pietro Tomacelli): Naples; Nov. 2 (9), 1389, to Oct. 1, 1404.

Innocent VII (Cosma Migliorati): Sulmona; Oct. 17 (Nov. 11), 1404, to Nov. 6, 1406.

Gregory XII (Angelo Correr): Venice; Nov. 30 (Dec. 19), 1406, to July 4, 1415, when he voluntarily resigned from the papacy to permit the election of his successor. He died Oct. 18, 1417. (See The Western Schism.)

Martin V (Oddone Colonna): Rome; Nov. 11 (21), 1417, to Feb. 20, 1431.

Eugene IV (Gabriele Condulmer): Venice; Mar. 3 (11), 1431, to Feb. 23, 1447.

Nicholas V (Tommaso Parentucelli): Sarzana; Mar. 6 (19), 1447, to Mar. 24, 1455.

Callistus III (Alfonso Borgia): Jativa (Va-

lencia); Apr. 8 (20), 1455, to Aug. 6, 1458.

Pius II (Enea Silvio Piccolomini): Siena; Aug. 19 (Sept. 3), 1458, to Aug. 15, 1464.

Paul II (Pietro Barbo): Venice; Aug. 30 (Sept. 16), 1464, to July 26, 1471.

Sixtus IV (Francesco della Rovere): Savona; Aug. 9 (25), 1471, to Aug. 12, 1484.

Innocent VIII (Giovanni Battista Cibo): Genoa; Aug. 29 (Sept. 12), 1484, to July 25, 1492.

Alexander VI (Rodrigo Borgia): Jativa (Valencia); Aug. 11 (26), 1492, to Aug. 18, 1503.

Pius III (Francesco Todeschini-Piccolomini): Siena; Sept. 22 (Oct. 1, 8), 1503, to Oct. 18, 1503.

Julius II (Giuliano della Rovere): Savona; Oct. 31 (Nov. 26), 1503, to Feb. 21, 1513.

Leo X (Giovanni de' Medici): Florence; Mar. 9 (19), 1513, to Dec. 1, 1521.

Adrian VI (Adrian Florensz): Utrecht; Jan. 9 (Aug. 31), 1522, to Sept. 14, 1523.

Clement VII (Giulio de' Medici): Florence; Nov. 19 (26), 1523, to Sept. 25, 1534.

Paul III (Alessandro Farnese): Rome; Oct. 13 (Nov. 3), 1534, to Nov. 10, 1549.

Julius III (Giovanni Maria Ciocchi del Monte): Rome; Feb. 7 (22), 1550, to Mar. 23, 1555.

Marcellus II (Marcello Cervini): Montepulciano; Apr. 9 (10), 1555, to May 1, 1555.

Paul IV (Gian Pietro Carafa): Naples; May 23 (26), 1555, to Aug. 18, 1559.

Pius IV (Giovan Angelo de' Medici): Milan; Dec. 25, 1559 (Jan. 6, 1560), to Dec. 9, 1565.

St. Pius V (Antonio-Michele Ghislieri): Bosco (Alexandria); Jan. 7 (17), 1566, to May 1, 1572. Canonized May 22, 1712.

Gregory XIII (Ugo Buoncompagni): Bologna; May 13 (25), 1572, to Apr. 10, 1585.

Sixtus V (Felice Peretti): Grottammare (Ripatransone); Apr. 24 (May 1), 1585, to Aug. 27, 1590.

Urban VII (Giovanni Battista Castagna): Rome; Sept. 15, 1590, to Sept. 27, 1590.

Gregory XIV (Niccolo Sfondrati): Cremona; Dec. 5 (8), 1590, to Oct. 16, 1591.

Innocent IX (Giovanni Antonio Facchinetti): Bologna; Oct. 29 (Nov. 3), 1591, to Dec. 30, 1591.

Clement VIII (Ippolito Aldobrandini): Florence; Jan. 30 (Feb. 9), 1592, to Mar. 3, 1605.

Leo XI (Alessandro de' Medici): Florence; Apr. 1 (10), 1605, to Apr. 27, 1605.

Paul V (Camillo Borghese): Rome; May 16 (29), 1605, to Jan. 28, 1621.

Gregory XV (Alessandro Ludovisi): Bologna; Feb. 9 (14), 1621, to July 8, 1623.

Urban VIII (Maffeo Barberini): Florence; Aug. 6 (Sept. 29), 1623, to July 29, 1644.

Innocent X (Giovanni Battista Pamfili): Rome; Sept. 15 (Oct. 4), 1644, to Jan. 7, 1655.

Alexander VII (Fabio Chigi): Siena; Apr. 7 (18), 1655, to May 22, 1667.

Clement IX (Giulio Rospigliosi): Pistoia;

June 20 (26), 1667, to Dec. 9, 1669.

Clement X (Emilio Altieri): Rome; Apr. 29 (May 11), 1670, to July 22, 1676.

Bl. Innocent XI (Benedetto Odescalchi): Como; Sept. 21 (Oct. 4), 1676, to Aug. 12, 1689.

Alexander VIII (Pietro Ottoboni): Venice; Oct. 6 (16), 1689, to Feb. 1, 1691.

Innocent XII (Antonio Pignatelli): Spinazzola; July 12 (15), 1691, to Sept. 27, 1700.

Clement XI (Giovanni Francesco Albani): Urbino; Nov. 23, 30 (Dec. 8), 1700, to Mar. 19, 1721.

Innocent XIII (Michelangelo dei Conti): Rome; May 8 (18), 1721, to Mar. 7, 1724.

Benedict XIII (Pietro Francesco — Vincenzo Maria — Orsini): Gravina (Bari); May 29 (June 4), 1724, to Feb. 21, 1730.

Clement XII (Lorenzo Corsini): Florence; July 12 (16), 1730, to Feb. 6, 1740.

Benedict XIV (Prospero Lambertini): Bologna; Aug. 17 (22), 1740, to May 3, 1758.

Clement XIII (Carlo Rezzonico): Venice; July 6 (16), 1758, to Feb. 2, 1769.

Clement XIV (Giovanni Vincenzo Antonio — Lorenzo — Ganganelli): Rimini; May 19, 28 (June 4), 1769, to Sept. 22, 1774.

Pius VI (Giovanni Angelo Braschi): Cesena; Feb. 15 (22), 1775, to Aug. 29, 1799.

Pius VII (Barnaba — Gregorio — Chiaramonti): Cesena; Mar. 14 (21), 1800, to Aug. 20, 1823.

Leo XII (Annibale della Genga): Genga (Fabriano); Sept. 28 (Oct. 5), 1823, to Feb. 10, 1829.

Pius VIII (Francesco Saverio Castiglioni): Cingoli; Mar. 31 (Apr. 5), 1829, to Nov. 30, 1830.

Gregory XVI (Bartolomeo Alberto — Mauro — Cappellari): Belluno; Feb. 2 (6), 1831, to June 1, 1846.

Pius IX (Giovanni M. Mastai Ferretti): Senigallia; June 16 (21), 1846, to Feb. 7, 1878.

Leo XIII (Gioacchino Pecci): Carpineto (Anagni); Feb. 20 (Mar. 3), 1878, to July 20, 1903.

St. Pius X (Giuseppe Sarto): Riese (Treviso); Aug. 4 (9), 1903, to Aug. 20, 1914. Canonized May 29, 1954.

Benedict XV (Giacomo della Chiesa): Genoa; Sept. 3 (6), 1914, to Jan. 22, 1922.

Pius XI (Achille Ratti): Desio (Milan); Feb. 6 (12), 1922, to Feb. 10, 1939.

Pius XII (Eugenio Pacelli): Rome; Mar. 2 (12), 1939, to Oct. 9, 1958.

John XXIII (Angelo Giuseppe Roncalli): Sotto il Monte (Bergamo); Oct. 28 (Nov. 4). 1958 to June 3, 1963.

Paul VI (Giovanni Battista Montini): Concessio (Brescia); June 21 (June 30), 1963 to —.

(See additional entries under 20th Century Popes and Pope Paul VI.)

It was not clear toward the end of 1975 whether Pope Paul would attend the 41st International Eucharistic Congress to be held in Philadelphia Aug. 1 to 8, 1976.

ANTIPOPES

(Source: *Annuario Pontificio.*)

This list of men who claimed or exercised the papal office in an uncanonical manner includes names, birthplaces and dates of alleged reigns.

St. Hippolytus: Rome; 217-235; was reconciled before his death.

Novatian: Rome; 251.

Felix II: Rome; 355 to Nov. 22, 365.

Ursinus: 366-367.

Eulalius: Dec. 27 or 29, 418, to 419.

Lawrence: 498; 501-505.

Dioscorus: Alexandria; Sept. 22, 530, to Oct. 14, 530.

Theodore: ended alleged reign, 687.

Paschal: ended alleged reign, 687.

Constantine: Nepi; June 28 (July 5), 767, to 769.

Philip: July 31, 768; retired to his monastery on the same day.

John: ended alleged reign, Jan., 844.

Anastasius: Aug., 855, to Sept., 855; d. 880.

Christopher: Rome; July or Sept., 903, to Jan., 904.

Boniface VII: Rome; June, 974, to July, 974; Aug., 984, to July, 985.

John XVI: Rossano; Apr., 997, to Feb., 998.

Gregory: ended alleged reign, 1012.

Benedict X: Rome; Apr. 5, 1058, to Jan. 24, 1059.

Honorius II: Verona; Oct. 28, 1061, to 1072.

Clement III: Parma; June 25, 1080 (Mar. 24, 1084), to Sept. 8, 1100.

Theodoric: ended alleged reign, 1100; d. 1102.

Albert: ended alleged reign, 1102.

Sylvester IV: Rome; Nov. 18, 1105, to 1111.

Gregory VIII: France; Mar. 8, 1118, to 1121.

Celestine II: Rome; ended alleged reign, Dec., 1124.

Anacletus II: Rome; Feb. 14 (23), 1130, to Jan. 25, 1138.

Victor IV: Mar., 1138, to May 29, 1138; submitted to Pope Innocent II.

Victor IV: Montecelio; Sept. 7 (Oct. 4), 1159, to Apr. 20, 1164; he did not recognize his predecessor (Victor IV, above).

Paschal III: Apr. 22 (26), 1164, to Sept. 20, 1168.

Callistus III: Arezzo; Sept., 1168, to Aug. 29, 1178; submitted to Pope Alexander III.

Innocent III: Sezze; Sept. 29, 1179, to 1180.

Nicholas V: Corvaro (Rieti); May 12 (22), 1328, to Aug. 25, 1330; d. Oct. 16, 1333.

Four antipopes of the Western Schism:

Clement VII: Sept. 20 (Oct. 31), 1378, to Sept. 16, 1394.

Benedict XIII: Aragon; Sept. 28 (Oct. 11), 1394, to May 23, 1423.

Alexander V: Crete; June 26 (July 7), 1409, to May 3, 1410.

John XXIII: Naples; May 17 (25), 1410, to May 29, 1415.

Felix V: Savoy; Nov. 5, 1439 (July 24, 1440), to April 7, 1449; d. 1451.

Avignon Papacy

Avignon was the residence of a series of French popes from Clement V to Gregory XI (1309-77). Prominent in the period were power struggles over the mixed interests of Church and state with the rulers of France (Philip IV, John II), Bavaria (Lewis IV), England (Edward III); factionalism of French and Italian churchmen; political as well as ecclesiastical turmoil in Italy, a factor of significance in prolonging the stay of popes in Avignon. Despite some positive achievements, the Avignon papacy was a prologue to the Western Schism which began in 1378.

Western Schism

The Western Schism was a confused state of affairs which divided Christendom into two and then three papal obediences from 1378 to 1417.

It occurred some 50 years after Marsilius theorized that a general (not ecumenical) council of bishops and other persons was superior to a pope and nearly 30 years before the Council of Florence stated definitively that no kind of council had such authority.

It was a period of disaster preceding the even more disastrous period of the Reformation.

Urban VI, following transfer to Rome of the 70-year papal residence at Avignon, was elected pope Apr. 8, 1378, and reigned until his death in 1389. He was succeeded by Boniface IX (1389-1404), Innocent VII (1404-1406) and Gregory XII (1406-1415). These four are considered the legitimate popes of the period.

Some of the cardinals who chose Urban pope, dissatisfied with his conduct of the office, declared that his election was invalid. They proceeded to elect Clement VII, who claimed the papacy from 1378 to 1394. He was succeeded by Benedict XIII.

Prelates seeking to end the state of divided papal loyalties convoked the Council of Pisa which, without authority, found Gregory XII and Benedict XIII, in absentia, guilty on 30-odd charges of schism and heresy, deposed them, and elected a third claimant to the papacy, Alexander V (1409-1410). He was succeeded by John XXIII (1410-1415).

The schism was ended by the Council of Constance (1414-1418). This council, although originally called into session in an irregular manner, acquired authority after being convoked by Gregory XII in 1415. In its early irregular phase, it deposed John XXIII whose election to the papacy was uncanonical anyway. After being formally convoked, it accepted the abdication of Gregory in 1415 and dismissed the claims of Benedict XIII two years later, thus clearing the way for the election of Martin V on Nov. 11, 1417. The Council of Constance also rejected the theories of John Wycliff and condemned John Hus as a heretic.

20th CENTURY POPES

Leo XIII

Leo XIII (Gioacchino Vincenzo Pecci) was born May 2, 1810, in Carpineto, Italy. Although all but three years of his life and pontificate were of the 19th century, his influence extended well into the 20th century.

He was educated at the Jesuit college in Viterbo, the Roman College, the Academy of Noble Ecclesiastics, and the University of the Sapienza. He was ordained to the priesthood in 1837.

He served as an apostolic delegate to two States of the Church, Benevento from 1838 to 1841 and Perugia in 1841 and 1842. Ordained titular archbishop of Damietta, he was papal nuncio to Belgium from January, 1843, until May, 1846; in the post, he had controversial relations with the government over education issues and acquired his first significant experience of industrialized society.

He was archbishop of Perugia from 1846 to 1878. He became a cardinal in 1853 and chamberlain of the Roman Curia in 1877. He was elected to the papacy Feb. 20, 1878. He died July 20, 1903.

Canonizations: He canonized 18 saints and beatified a group of English martyrs.

Church Administration: He established 300 new dioceses and vicariates; restored the hierarchy in Scotland, set up an English, as contrasted with the Portuguese, hierarchy in India; approved the action of the Congregation for the Propagation of the Faith in reorganizing missions in China.

Encyclicals: He issued 50 encyclicals, on subjects ranging from devotional to social. In the former category were *Annum Sacrum,* on the Sacred Heart, in 1899, and nine letters on Mary and the Rosary.

Interfaith Relations: He was unsuccessful in unity overtures made to Orthodox and Slavic Churches. He declared Anglican orders invalid in the apostolic bull *Apostolicae Curae* Sept. 13, 1896.

International Relations: Leo was frustrated in seeking solutions to the Roman Question arising from the seizure of church lands by the Kingdom of Italy in 1870. He also faced anticlerical situations in Belgium and France and in the Kulturkampf policies of Bismarck in Germany.

Social Questions: Much of Leo's influence stemmed from social doctrine stated in numerous encyclicals, concerning liberalism, liberty, the divine origin of authority; socialism, in *Quod Apostolici Muneris,* 1878; the Christian concept of the family, in *Arcanum,* 1880; socialism and economic liberalism, relations between capital and labor, in *Rerum Novarum,* 1891. Two of his social encyclicals were against the African slave trade.

Studies: In the encyclical *Aeterni Patris* of Aug. 4, 1879, he ordered a renewal of philosophical and theological studies in seminaries along scholastic, and especially Thomistic, lines, to counteract influential trends of liberalism and Modernism. He issued guidelines for biblical exegesis in *Providentissimus Deus* Nov. 18, 1893, and established the Pontifical Biblical Commission in 1902.

In other actions affecting scholarship and study, he opened the Vatican Archives to scholars in 1883 and established the Vatican Observatory.

United States: He authorized establishment of the apostolic delegation in Washington, D.C. Jan. 24, 1893. He refused to issue a condemnation of the Knights of Labor. With a document entitled *Testem Benevolentiae,* he eased resolution of questions concerning what was called an American heresy in 1899.

St. Pius X

St. Pius X (Giuseppe Melchiorre Sarto) was born in 1835 in Riese, Italy.

Educated at the college of Castelfranco and the seminary at Padua, he was ordained to the priesthood Sept. 18, 1858. He served as a curate in Trombolo for nine years before beginning an eight-year pastorate at Salzano. He was chancellor of the Treviso diocese from November, 1875, and bishop of Mantua from 1884 until 1893. He was cardinal-patriarch of Venice from that year until his election to the papacy by the conclave held from July 31 to Aug. 4, 1903.

Aims: Pius' principal objectives as pope were "to restore all things in Christ, in order that Christ may be all and in all," and "to teach (and defend) Christian truth and law."

Canonizations, Encyclicals: He canonized four saints and issued 16 encyclicals. One of the encyclicals was issued in commemoration of the 50th anniversary of the proclamation of the dogma of the Immaculate Conception of Mary.

Catechetics: He introduced a whole new era of religious instruction and formation with the encyclical *Acerbo Nimis* of Apr. 15, 1905, in which he called for vigor in establishing and conducting parochial programs of the Confraternity of Christian Doctrine.

Catholic Action: He outlined the role of official Catholic Action in two encyclicals in 1905 and 1906. Favoring organized action by Catholics themselves, he had serious reservations about interconfessional collaboration.

He stoutly maintained claims to papal rights in the anticlerical climate of Italy. He authorized bishops to relax prohibitions against participation by Catholics in some Italian elections.

Church Administration: With the motu proprio *Arduum Sane* of Mar. 19, 1904, he inaugurated the work which resulted in the Code of Canon Law; the code was completed in 1917 and went into effect in the following year. He reorganized and strengthened the

Roman Curia with the apostolic constitution *Sapienti Consilio* of June 29, 1908. While promoting the expansion of missionary work, he removed from the jurisdiction of the Congregation for the Propagation of the Faith the Church in the United States, Canada, Newfoundland, England, Ireland, Holland and Luxembourg.

International Relations: He ended traditional prerogatives of Catholic governments with respect to papal elections, in 1904. He opposed anti-Church and anticlerical actions in several countries: Bolivia in 1905, because of anti-religious legislation; France in 1906, for its 1901 action in annulling its concordat with the Holy See, and for the 1905 Law of Separation by which it decreed separation of Church and state, ordered the confiscation of church property, and blocked religious education and the activities of religious orders; Portugal in 1911, for the separation of Church and state and repressive measures which resulted in persecution later.

In 1912 he called on the bishops of Brazil to work for the improvement of conditions among Indians.

Liturgy: "The Pope of the Eucharist," he strongly recommended the frequent reception of Holy Communion in a decree dated Dec. 20, 1905; in another decree, *Quam Singulari,* of Aug. 8, 1910, he called for the early reception of the sacrament by children. He initiated measures for liturgical reform with new norms for sacred music and the start of work on revision of the *Breviary* for recitation of the Divine Office.

Modernism: Pius was a vigorous opponent of "the synthesis of all heresies," which threatened the integrity of doctrine through its influence in philosophy, theology and biblical exegesis. In opposition, he condemned 65 of its propositions as erroneous in the decree *Lamentabili* July 3, 1907; issued the encyclical *Pascendi* in the same vein Sept. 8, 1907; backed both of these with censures; and published the Oath against Modernism in September, 1910, to be taken by all the clergy. Ecclesiastical studies suffered to some extent from these actions, necessary as they were at the time.

Pius followed the lead of Leo XIII in promoting the study of scholastic philosophy. He established the Pontifical Biblical Institute May 7, 1909.

His death, Aug. 20, 1914, was hastened by the outbreak of World War I. He was beatified in 1951 and canonized May 29, 1954. His feast is observed Aug. 21.

Benedict XV

Benedict XV (Giacomo della Chiesa) was born Nov. 21, 1854, in Pegli, Italy.

He was educated at the Royal University of Genoa and Gregorian University in Rome. He was ordained to the priesthood Dec. 21, 1878.

He served in the papal diplomatic corps from 1882 to 1907; as secretary to the nuncio to Spain from 1882 to 1887, as secretary to the papal secretary of state from 1887, and as undersecretary from 1901.

He was ordained archbishop of Bologna Dec. 22, 1907, and spent four years completing a pastoral visitation therem He was made a cardinal just three months before being elected to the papacy Sept. 3, 1914, He died Jan. 22, 1922. Two key efforts of his pontificate were for peace and the relief of human suffering caused by World War I.

Canonizations: Benedict canonized three saints; one of them was Joan of Arc.

Canon Law: He published the Code of Canon Law, developed by the commission set up by St. Pius X, June 28, 1917; it went into effect the following year.

Curia: He made great changes in the personnel of the Curia. He established the Congregation for the Oriental Churches May 1, 1917, and founded the Pontifical Oriental Institute in Rome later in the year.

Encyclicals: He issued 12 encyclicals. Peace was the theme of three of them. In another, published two years after the cessation of hostilities, he wrote about child victims of the war. He followed the lead of Leo XIII in *Spiritus Paraclitus,* Sept. 15, 1920, on biblical studies.

International Relations: He was largely frustrated on the international level because of the events and attitudes of the war period, but the number of diplomats accredited to the Vatican nearly doubled, from 14 to 26, between the time of his accession to the papacy and his death.

Peace Efforts: Benedict's stance in the war was one of absolute impartiality but not of disinterested neutrality. Because he would not take sides, he was suspected by both sides and the seven-point peace plan he offered to all belligerents Aug. 1, 1917, was turned down. The points of the plan were: recognition of the moral force of right; disarmament; acceptance of arbitration in cases of dispute; guarantee of freedom of the seas; renunciation of war indemnities; evacuation and restoration of occupied territories; examination of territorial claims in dispute.

Relief Efforts: Benedict assumed personal charge of Vatican relief efforts during the war. He set up an international missing persons bureau for contacts between prisoners and their families, but was forced to close it because of the suspicion of warring nations that it was a front for espionage operations. He persuaded the Swiss government to admit into the country military victims of tuberculosis.

Roman Question: Benedict arranged a meeting of Benito Mussolini and the papal secretary of state, which marked the first step toward final settlement of the question in 1929.

Pius XI

Pius XI (Ambrogio Damiano Achille Ratti) was born May 31, 1857, in Desio, Italy.

Educated at seminaries in Seviso and Milan, and at the Lombard College, Gregorian University and Academy of St. Thomas in Rome, he was ordained to the priesthood in 1879.

He taught at the major seminary of Milan from 1882 to 1888. Appointed to the staff of the Ambrosian Library in 1888, he remained there until 1911, acquiring a reputation for publishing works on palaeography and serving as director from 1907 to 1911. He then moved to the Vatican Library, of which he was prefect from 1914 to 1918. In 1919, he was named apostolic visitor to Poland in April, nuncio in June, and was made titular archbishop of Lepanto Oct. 28. He was made archbishop of Milan and cardinal June 13, 1921, before being elected to the papacy Feb. 6, 1922. He died Feb. 10, 1939.

Aim: The objective of his pontificate, as stated in the encyclical *Ubi Arcano,* Dec. 23, 1922, was to establish the reign and peace of Christ in society.

Canonizations: He canonized 34 saints, including the Jesuit Martyrs of North America, and conferred the title of Doctor of the Church on Sts. Peter Canisius, John of the Cross, Robert Bellarmine and Albertus Magnus.

Eastern Churches: He called for better understanding of the Eastern Churches in the encyclical *Rerum Orientalium* of Sept. 8, 1928, and developed facilities for the training of Eastern-Rite priests. He inaugurated steps for the codification of Eastern-Church law in 1929. In 1935 he made Syrian Patriarch Tappouni a cardinal.

Encyclicals: His first encyclical, *Ubi Arcano,* in addition to stating the aims of his pontificate, blueprinted Catholic Action and called for its development throughout the Church. In *Quas Primas,* Dec. 11, 1925, he established the feast of Christ the King for universal observance. Subjects of some of his other encyclicals were: Christian education, in *Divini Illius Magistri,* Dec. 31, 1929; Christian marriage, in *Casti Connubii,* Dec. 30, 1930; social conditions and pressure for social change in line with the teaching in *Rerum Novarum,* in *Quadragesimo Anno,* May 15, 1931; atheistic Communism, in *Divini Redemptoris,* Mar. 19, 1937; the priesthood, in *Ad Catholici Sacerdotii,* Dec. 20, 1935.

Missions: Following the lead of Benedict XV, Pius called for the training of native clergy in the pattern of their own respective cultures, and promoted missionary developments in various ways. He ordained six native bishops for China in 1926, one for Japan in 1927, and others for regions of Asia, China and India in 1933. He placed the first 40 mission dioceses under native bishops, saw the number of native priests increase from about 2,600 to more than 7,000 and the number of Catholics in missionary areas more than double from nine million.

In the apostolic constitution *Deus Scientiarum Dominus* of May 24, 1931, he ordered the introduction of missiology into theology courses.

Interfaith Relations: Pius was negative to the ecumenical movement among Protestants but approved the Malines Conversations, 1921 to 1926, between Anglicans and Catholics.

International Relations: Relations with the Mussolini government deteriorated from 1931 on, as indicated in the encyclical *Non Abbiamo Bisogno,* when the regime took steps to curb liberties and activities of the Church; they turned critical in 1938 with the emergence of racist policies. Relations deteriorated also in Germany from 1933 on, resulting finally in condemnation of the Nazis in the encyclical *Mit Brennender Sorge,* March, 1937. Pius sparked a revival of the Church in France by encouraging Catholics to work within the democratic framework of the Republic rather than foment trouble over restoration of a monarchy. Pius was powerless before the civil war which erupted in Spain in July, 1936; sporadic persecution and repression by the Calles regime in Mexico; and systematic persecution of the Church in the Soviet Union. Many of the 10 concordats and two agreements reached with European countries after World War I became casualties of World War II.

Roman Question: Pius negotiated for two and one-half years with the Italian government to settle the Roman Question by means of the Lateran Agreement of 1929. The agreement provided independent status for the State of Vatican City; made Catholicism the official religion of Italy, with pastoral and educational freedom and state recognition of Catholic marriages, religious orders and societies; and provided a financial payment to the Vatican for expropriation of the former States of the Church.

Pius XII

Pius XII (Eugenio Maria Giovanni Pacelli) was born Mar. 2, 1876, in Rome.

Educated at the Gregorian University and the Lateran University, in Rome, he was ordained to the priesthood Apr. 2, 1899.

He entered the Vatican diplomatic service in 1901, worked on the codification of canon law, and was appointed secretary of the Congregation for Ecclesiastical Affairs in 1914. Three years later he was ordained titular archbishop of Sardis and made apostolic nuncio to Bavaria. He was nuncio to Germany from 1920 to 1929, when he was made a cardinal, and took office as papal secretary of state in the following year. His diplomatic negotiations resulted in concordats between the Vatican and Bavaria (1924), Prussia (1929), Baden (1932), Austria and the German Republic (1933). He took part in negotiations which led to settlement of the Roman Question in 1929.

He was elected to the papacy Mar. 2, 1939. He died Oct. 9, 1958, at Castel Gandolfo after the 12th longest pontificate in history.

Canonizations: He canonized 33 saints, including Mother Frances X. Cabrini, the first US citizen-Saint.

Cardinals: He raised 56 prelates to the rank of cardinal in two consistories held in 1946 and 1953. There were 57 cardinals at the time of his death.

Church Organization and Missions: He increased the number of dioceses from 1,696 to 2,048. He established native hierarchies in China (1946), Burma (1955), and parts of Africa, and extended the native structure of the Church in India. He ordained the first black bishop for Africa.

Communism: In addition to opposing and condemning Communism on numerous occasions, he decreed in 1949 the penalty of excommunication for all Catholics holding formal and willing allegiance to the Communist Party and its policies. During his reign the Church was persecuted in some 15 countries which fell under Communist domination.

Doctrine and Liturgy: He proclaimed the dogma of the Assumption of the Blessed Virgin Mary Nov. 1, 1950 (apostolic constitution, *Munificentissimus Deus*).

In various encyclicals and other enactments, he provided background for the *aggiornamento* introduced by his successor, John XXIII: by his formulations of doctrine and practice regarding the Mystical Body of Christ, the liturgy, sacred music and biblical studies; by the revision of the Rites of Holy Week; by initiation of the work which led to the calendar-missal-breviary reform ordered into effect Jan. 1, 1961; by the first of several modifications of the Eucharistic fast; by extending the time of Mass to the evening. He instituted the feasts of Mary, Queen, and of St. Joseph the Worker, and clarified teaching concerning devotion to the Sacred Heart.

His 41 encyclicals and nearly 1,000 public addresses made Pius one of the greatest teaching popes. His concern in all his communications was to deal with specific points at issue and/or to bring Christian principles to bear on contemporary world problems.

Peace Efforts: Before the start of World War II, he tried unsuccessfully to get the contending nations — Germany and Poland, France and Italy — to settle their differences peaceably. During the war, he offered his services to mediate the widened conflict, spoke out against the horrors of war and the suffering it caused, mobilized relief work for its victims, proposed a five-point program for peace in Christmas messages from 1939 to 1942, and secured a generally open status for the city of Rome. After the war, he endorsed the principles and intent of the United Nations and continued efforts for peace.

United States: Pius appointed more than 200 of the 265 American bishops resident in the US and abroad in 1958, erected 27 dioceses in this country, and raised seven dioceses to archiepiscopal rank.

John XXIII

John XXIII (Angelo Roncalli) was born Nov. 25, 1881, at Sotte il Monte, Italy.

He was educated at the seminary of the Bergamo diocese and the Pontifical Seminary in Rome, where he was ordained to the priesthood Aug. 10, 1904.

He spent the first nine or 10 years of his priesthood as secretary to the bishop of Bergamo and as an instructor in the seminary there. He served as a medic and chaplain in the Italian army during World War I. Afterwards, he resumed duties in his own diocese until he was called to Rome in 1921 for work with the Society for the Propagation of the Faith.

He began diplomatic service in 1925 as titular archbishop of Areopolis and apostolic visitor to Bulgaria. A succession of offices followed: apostolic delegate to Bulgaria (1931-1935); titular archbishop of Mesembria, apostolic delegate to Turkey and Greece, administrator of the Latin vicariate apostolic of Istanbul (1935-1944); apostolic nuncio to France (1944-1953). On these missions, he was engaged in delicate negotiations involving Roman, Eastern-Rite and Orthodox relations; the needs of people suffering from the consequences of World War II; and unsettling suspicions arising from wartime conditions.

He was made a cardinal Jan. 12, 1953, and three days later was appointed patriarch of Venice, the position he held until his election to the papacy Oct. 28, 1958. He died of stomach cancer June 3, 1963.

John was a strong and vigorous pope whose influence far outmeasured both his age and the shortness of his time in the papacy.

Second Vatican Council: John announced Jan. 25, 1959, his intention of convoking the 21st ecumenical council in history to renew life in the Church, to reform its structures and institutions, and to explore ways and means of promoting unity among Christians. Through the council, which completed its work two and one-half years after his death, he ushered in a new era in the history of the Church.

Canon Law: He established a commission Mar. 28, 1963, for revision of the Code of Canon Law. The work of this commission, still underway, will greatly influence the future course of Catholic life and the conduct of ecclesiastical affairs.

Canonizations: He canonized 10 saints. He also beatified Mother Elizabeth Ann Seton, the first native of the US ever so honored. He named St. Lawrence of Brindisi a Doctor of the Church.

Cardinals: He created 52 cardinals in five consistories, raising membership of the College of Cardinals above the traditional number of 70; at one time in 1962, the membership was 87. He made the college more international in representation than it had ever been, appointing the first cardinals from the Philippines, Japan and Africa. He ordered episcopal ordination for all cardinals. He relieved the suburban bishops of Rome of ordinary jurisdiction over their dioceses so they might devote all their time to business of the Roman Curia.

Eastern Rites: He made all Eastern-Rite patriarchs members of the Congregation for the Oriental Churches.

Ecumenism: He assigned to the Second Vatican Council the task of finding ways and means of promoting unity among Christians. He established the Vatican Secretariat for Promoting Christian Unity June 5, 1960. He showed his desire for more cordial relations with the Orthodox by sending personal representatives to visit Patriarch Athenagoras I June 27, 1961; approved a mission of five delegates to the General Assembly of the World Council of Churches which met in New Delhi, India, in November, 1961; removed a number of pejorative references to Jews in the Roman-Rite liturgy for Good Friday.

Encyclicals: Of the eight encyclicals he issued, the two outstanding ones were *Mater et Magistra* ("Christianity and Social Progress"), in which he recapitulated, updated and extended the social doctrine stated earlier by Leo XIII and Pius XI; and *Pacem in Terris* ("Peace on Earth"), the first encyclical ever addressed to all men of good will as well as to Catholics, on the natural-law principles of peace.

Liturgy: In forwarding liturgical reforms already begun by Pius XII, he ordered a calendar-missal-breviary reform into effect Jan. 1, 1961. He authorized the use of vernacular languages in the administration of the sacraments and approved giving Holy Communion to the sick in afternoon hours. He selected the liturgy as the first topic of major discussion by the Second Vatican Council.

Missions: He issued an encyclical on the missionary activity of the Church; established native hierarchies in Indonesia, Vietnam and Korea; and called on North American superiors of religious institutes to have one-tenth of their members assigned to work in Latin America by 1971.

Peace: John spoke and used his moral influence for peace in 1961 when tension developed over Berlin, in 1962 during the Algerian revolt from France, and later the same year in the Cuban missile crisis. His efforts were singled out for honor by the Balzan Peace Foundation. In 1963, he was posthumously awarded the US Presidential Medal of Freedom.

CANONIZATIONS BY LEO XIII AND HIS SUCCESSORS

Canonization is an infallible declaration by the pope that a person who suffered martyrdom and/or practiced Christian virtue to a heroic degree is in glory with God in heaven and is worthy of public honor by the universal Church and of imitation by the faithful.

Leo XIII
(1878-1903)

1881: Clare of Montefalco, virgin (d. 1308); John Baptist de Rossi, priest (1698-1764); Lawrence of Brindisi, doctor (d. 1619); Benedict J. Labre (1748-1783).

1888: Seven Holy Founders of the Servite Order; Peter Claver, priest (1581-1654); John Berchmans (1599-1621); Alphonsus Rodriguez, lay brother (1531-1617).

1897: Anthony M. Zaccaria, founder of Barnabites (1502-1539); Peter Fourier, cofounder of Augustinian Canonesses of Our Lady (1565-1640).

1900: John Baptist de La Salle, founder of Christian Brothers (1651-1719); Rita of Cascia (1381-1457).

St. Pius X
(1903-1914)

1904: Alexander Sauli, bishop (1534-1593); Gerard Majella, lay brother (1725-1755).

1909: Joseph Oriol, priest (1650-1702); Clement M. Hofbauer, priest (1751-1820).

Benedict XV
(1914-1922)

1920: Gabriel of the Sorrowful Mother (1838-1862); Margaret Mary Alacoque, virgin (1647-1690); Joan of Arc, virgin (1412-1431).

Pius XI
(1922-1939)

1925: Therese of Lisieux, virgin (1873-1897); Peter Canisius, doctor (1521-1597); Mary Magdalen Postel, foundress of Sisterhood of Christian Schools (1756-1846); Mary Magdalen Sophie Barat, foundress of Society of the Sacred Heart (1779-1865); John Eudes, founder of Eudist Fathers (1601-1680); John Baptist Vianney (Curé of Ars), priest (1786-1859).

1930: Lucy Filippini, virgin (1672-1732); Catherine Thomas, virgin (1533-1574); Jesuit North American Martyrs (see Index); Robert Bellarmine, bishop-doctor (1542-1621); Theophilus of Corte, priest (1676-1740).

1931: Albert the Great, bishop-doctor (1206-1280) (equivalent canonization).

1933: Andrew Fournet, priest (1752-1834); Bernadette Soubirous, virgin (1844-1879).

1934: Joan Antida Thouret, foundress of Sisters of Charity of St. Joan Antida (1765-1826); Mary Michaeli, foundress of Institute of Handmaids of the Blessed Sacrament (1809-1865); Louise de Marillac, foundress of Sisters of Charity (1591-1660); Joseph Benedict Cottolengo, priest (1786-1842); Pompi-

lius M. Pirotti, priest (1710-1756); Teresa Margaret Redi, virgin (1747-1770); John Bosco, founder of Salesians (1815-1888); Conrad of Parzham, lay brother (1818-1894).

1935: John Fisher, bishop-martyr (1469-1535); Thomas More, martyr (1478-1535).

1938: Andrew Bobola, martyr (1592-1657); John Leonardi, founder of Clerics Regular of the Mother of God (c. 1550-1609); Salvatore of Horta, lay brother (1520-1567).

Pius XII
(1939-1958)

1940: Gemma Galgani, virgin (1878-1903); Mary Euphrasia Pelletier, foundress of Good Shepherd Sisters (1796-1868).

1943: Margaret of Hungary, virgin (d. 1270) (equivalent canonization).

1946: Frances Xavier Cabrini, foundress of Missionary Sisters of the Sacred Heart (1850-1917).

1947: Nicholas of Flue, hermit (1417-1487); John of Britto, martyr (1647-1693); Bernard Realini, priest (1530-1616); Joseph Cafasso, priest (1811-1860); Michael Garicoits, founder of Auxiliary Priests of the Sacred Heart (1797-1863); Jeanne Elizabeth des Ages, cofoundress of Daughters of the Cross (1773-1838); Louis Marie Grignon de Montfort, founder of Montfort Fathers (1673-1716); Catherine Laboure, virgin (1806-1876).

1949: Jeanne de Lestonnac, foundress of Religious of Notre Dame of Bordeaux (1556-1640); Maria Josepha Rossello, foundress of Daughters of Our Lady of Pity (1811-1880).

1950: Emily de Rodat, foundress of Congregation of the Holy Family of Villefranche (1787-1852); Anthony Mary Claret, bishop, founder of Claretians (1807-1870); Bartolomea Capitanio (1807-1833) and Vincenza Gerosa (1784-1847), foundresses of Sisters of Charity of Lovere; Jeanne de Valois, foundress of Annonciades of Bourges (1461-1504); Vincenzo M. Strambi, bishop (1745-1824); Maria Goretti, virgin-martyr (1890-1902); Mariana Paredes of Jesus, virgin (1618-1645).

1951: Maria Domenica Mazzarello, cofoundress of Daughters of Our Lady Help of Christians (1837-1881); Emilie de Vialar, foundress of Sisters of St. Joseph "of the Apparition" (1797-1856); Anthony M. Gianelli, bishop (1789-1846); Ignatius of Laconi, lay brother (1701-1781); Francis Xavier Bianchi, priest (1743-1815).

1954: Pius X, pope (1835-1914); Dominic Savio (1842-1857); Maria Crocifissa di Rosa, foundress of Handmaids of Charity of Brescia (1813-1855); Peter Chanel, priest-martyr (1803-1841); Gaspar del Bufalo, founder of Missioners of the Most Precious Blood (1786-1837); Joseph M. Pignatelli, priest (1737-1811).

1958: Herman Joseph, O. Praem., priest (1150-1241) (equivalent canonization).

John XXIII
(1958-1963)

1959: Joaquina de Vedruna de Mas, foundress of Carmelite Sisters of Charity (1783-1854); Charles of Sezze, lay brother (1613-1670).

1960: Gregory Barbarigo, bishop (1625-1697) (equivalent canonization); John de Ribera, bishop (1532-1611).

1961: Bertilla Boscardin, virgin (1888-1922).

1962: Martin de Porres, lay brother (1569-1639); Peter Julian Eymard, founder of Blessed Sacrament Fathers (1811-1868); Anthony Pucci, priest (1819-1892); Francis Mary of Camporosso, lay brother (1804-1866).

1963: Vincent Pallotti, founder of Pallottine Fathers (1795-1850).

Paul VI
(1963-   )

1964: Twenty-two Martyrs of Uganda.

1967: Benilde, lay brother (1805-1862).

1969: Julia Billiart, foundress of Sisters of Notre Dame de Namur (1751-1816).

1970: Maria Della Dolorato Torres Acosta, foundress of Servants Sisters of Mary (1826-1887); Leonard Murialdo, priest, founder of Congregation of St. Joseph (1828-1890); Therese Couderc, foundress of Congregation of Our Lady of the Cenacle (1805-1885); John of Avila, preacher and spiritual director (1499-1569); Sts. Nicholas Tavelic, Deodatus of Aquitaine, Peter of Narbonne and Stephen of Cuneo, martyrs (d. 1391); Forty English and Welsh Martyrs (d. 16th cent.).

1974: Teresa of Jesus Jornet Ibars, foundress of Little Sisters of Abandoned Aged (1843-1897).

1975: Vicenza Maria Lopez Vicuna, foundress of Institute of Daughters of Mary Immaculate (1847-1890); Elizabeth Bayley Seton, foundress of Sisters of Charity in the U.S. (1774-1821); John de Massias, Domini-

can brother-missionary (1585-1645): Oliver Plunkett, archbishop-martyr (1629-1681); Justin de Jacobis, missionary bishop (1800-1860); John Baptist of the Conception, founder of Reformed Discalced Brothers of the Order of the Most Holy Trinity (1561-1613).

English and Welsh Martyrs

Forty Martyrs of England and Wales, victims of persecution from 1535 to 1671, were canonized by Pope Paul Oct. 25, 1970.

The martyrs were prosecuted and executed as traitors for refusal to comply with laws enacted by Henry VIII and Elizabeth I regarding supremacy (the sovereign was proclaimed the highest authority of the Church in England, acknowledgment of papal primacy was forbidden), succession and the prohibition of native-born to study for the priesthood abroad and return to England for practice of the ministry.

John Houghton, prior of the London Charterhouse, was the first of his group to die (1535) for opposing Henry's Acts of Supremacy and Succession. Cuthbert Mayne (d. 1577) was the protomartyr of the English seminary at Douay. Margaret Clitherow (d. 1586) and Swithun Wells (d. 1591) were executed for sheltering priests. Richard Gwyn (d. 1584), poet, was the protomartyr of Wales.

Others in the group were:

John Almond, Edmund Arrowsmith, Ambrose Barlow, John Boste, Alexander Briant, Edmund Campion, Philip Evans, Thomas Garnet, Edmund Gennings;

Philip Howard, John Jones, John Kemble, Luke Kirby, Robert Lawrence, David Lewis, Ann Line, John Lloyd;

Henry Morse, Nicholas Owen, John Paine, Polydore Plasden, John Plessington, Richard Reynolds, John Riggby, John Roberts;

Alban Roe, Ralph Serwin, Robert Southwell, John Southworth, John Stone, John Wall, Henry Walpole, Margaret Ward, Augustine Webster and Eustace White.

ENCYCLICALS ISSUED BY LEO XIII AND HIS SUCCESSORS

An encyclical letter is a pastoral letter addressed by a pope to the whole Church. In general, it concerns matters of doctrine, morals or discipline. Its formal title consists of the first few words of the official text. A few encyclicals, notably *Pacem in Terris* by John XXIII and *Ecclesiam Suam* by Paul VI, have been addressed to "all men of good will" as well as to bishops and the faithful in communion with the Church.

An encyclical epistle, which is like an encyclical letter in many respects, is addressed to part of the Church, that is, to the bishops and faithful of a particular country or area. Its contents may concern other than doctrinal, moral or disciplinary matters of universal significance; for example, the com-

memoration of historical events, conditions in a certain country.

The authority of encyclicals was stated by Pius XII in the encyclical *Humani Generis* Aug. 12, 1950.

"Nor must it be thought that what is contained in encyclical letters does not of itself demand assent, on the pretext that the popes do not exercise in them the supreme power of their teaching authority. Rather, such teachings belong to the ordinary magisterium, of which it is true to say: 'He who hears you, hears me' (Lk. 10:16); for the most part, too, what is expounded and inculcated in encyclical letters already appertains to Catholic doctrine for other reasonsm But if the supreme pontiffs in their official documents purposely pass judgment on a matter debated until then, it is obvious to all that the matter, according to the mind and will of the same pontiffs, cannot be considered any longer a question open for discussion among theologians."

The following list contains the titles and indicates the subject matter of encyclical letters and epistles. The latter are generally distinguishable by the limited scope of their titles or contents.

Leo XIII
(1878-1903)

1878: Inscrutabili Dei Consilio (Evils of Society), Apr. 21.

Quod Apostolici Muneris (Socialism, Communism, Nihilism), Dec. 28.

1879: Aeterni Patris (Scholastic Philosophy, Especially of Thomas Aquinas), Aug. 4.

1880: Arcanum (Christian Marriage), Feb. 10.

Grande Munus (Sts. Cyril and Methodius), Sept. 30.

Sancta Dei Civitas (Three French Societies), Dec. 3.

1881: Diuturnum (Origin of Civil Power), June 29.

1882: Etsi Nos (Conditions in Italy), Feb. 15.

Auspicato Concessum (Third Order of St. Francis), Sept. 17.

Cum Multa (Conditions in Spain), Dec. 8.

1883: Supremi Apostolatus Officio (The Rosary), Sept. 1.

1884: Nobilissima Gallorum Gens (Religious Question in France), Feb. 8.

Humanum Genus (Freemasonry), Apr. 20.

Superiore Anno (Recitation of the Rosary), Aug. 30.

1885: Immortale Dei (The Christian Constitution of States), Nov. 1.

Quod Auctoritate (Proclamation of Extraordinary Jubilee Year), Dec. 22.

1886: Quod Multum (Liberty of the Church in Hungary), Aug. 22.

Pergrata Nobis (Needs of the Church in Portugal), Sept. 14.

1888: Libertas (Human Liberty), June 20.

Paterna Caritas (Recalling the Dissenting Armenians), July 25.

Quam Aerumnosa (Italian Immigrants in America), Dec. 10.

1889: Quamquam Pluries (Patronage of St. Joseph and the Blessed Virgin Mary), Aug. 15.

1890: Sapientiae Christianae (Chief Duties of Christian Citizens), Jan. 10.

Ab Apostoli (To the Clergy and People of Italy), Oct. 15.

1891: Rerum Novarum (Condition of the Working Classes), May 15.

Octobri Mense (The Rosary), Sept. 22.

1892: Au Milieu des Sollicitudes (Church and State in France), Feb. 16.

Magnae Dei Matris (The Rosary), Sept. 8.

1893: Ad Extremas (Seminaries in the East Indies), June 24.

Constanti Hungarorum (Conditions of the Church in Hungary), Sept. 2.

Laetitiae Sanctae (The Rosary), Sept. 8.

Providentissimus Deus (Study of Holy Scripture), Nov. 18.

1894: Caritatis (Conditions in Poland), Mar. 19.

Iucunda Semper Expectatione (The Rosary), Sept. 8.

Christi Nomen (Society for the Propagation of the Faith), Dec. 24.

1895: Adiutricem (The Rosary), Sept. 5.

1896: Satis Cognitum (Church Unity), June 29.

Fidentum Piumque Animum (The Rosary), Sept. 20.

1897: Divinum Illud Munus (The Holy Spirit, doctrine and devotion), May 9.

Militantis Ecclesiae (Third Centenary of the Death of St. Peter Canisius), Aug. 1.

Augustissimae Virginis (The Rosary), Sept. 12.

Affari Vos (The Manitoba School Question), Dec. 8.

1898: Caritatis Studium (The Magisterium of the Church in Scotland), July 25.

Spesse Volte (Catholic Action in Italy) Aug. 5.

1899: Annum Sacrum (Consecration of Mankind to the Sacred Heart), May 25.

Depuis le Jour (Ecclesiastical Education in France), Sept. 8.

1900: Tametsi Futura Prospicientibus (Jesus Christ, Our Redeemer), Nov. 1.

1901: Graves de Communi Re (Christian Democracy), Jan. 18.

1902: Mirae Caritatis (The Most Holy Eucharist), May 28.

Fin dal Principio (Education of the Clergy in Italy), Dec. 8.

Saint Pius X
(1903-1914)

1903: E Supremi (Restoration of All Things in Christ), Oct. 4.

1904: Ad Diem Illum Laetissimum (Jubilee of the Immaculate Conception), Feb. 2.

Iucunda Sane (Thirteenth Centenary of the Death of St. Gregory the Great), Mar. 12.

1905: Acerbo Nimis (Teaching of Christian Doctrine), Apr. 15.

Il Fermo Proposito (Catholic Action in Italy), June 11.

1906: Vehementer Nos (French Separation Law), Feb. 11.

Tribus Circiter (Condemnation of the Mariavites), Apr. 5.

Pieni l'Animo (Clergy in Italy), July 28.

Gravissimo Officio Munere (Forbidding Associations Cultuelles), Aug. 10.

1907: Une Fois Encore (Separation of Church and State in France), Jan. 6.

Pascendi Dominici Gregis (Modernism), Sept. 8.

1909: Communium Rerum (Eighth Centenary of the Death of St. Anselm), Apr. 21.

1910: Editae Saepe (Third Centenary of the Death of St. Charles Borromeo), May 26.

1911: Iamdudum (Separation Law in Portugal), May 24.

1912: Lacrimabili Statu (Indians of South America), June 7.

Singulari Quadam (Labor Organizations in Germany), Sept. 24.

Benedict XV
(1914-1922)

1914: Ad Beatissimi Apostolorum (Appeal for Peace), Nov. 1.

1917: Humani Generis Redemptionem (Preaching), June 15.

1918: Quod Iam Diu (Peace Congress, Paris), Dec. 1.

1919: In Hac Tanta (Twelfth Centenary of St. Boniface), May 14.

Paterno Iam Diu (Christian Charity of the Children of Central Europe), Nov. 24.

1920: Pacem, Dei Munus Pulcherrimum (Peace and Christian Reconciliation), May 23.

Spiritus Paraclitus (Holy Scripture), Sept. 15.

Principi Apostolorum Petro (St. Ephrem the Syrian, declared Doctor), Oct. 5.

Annus Iam Plenus (Child War Victims), Dec. 1.

1921: Sacra Propediem (Seventh Centenary of the Third Order of St. Francis), Jan. 6.

In Praeclara Summorum (Sixth Centenary of Dante's Death), Apr. 30.

Fausto Appetente Die (Seventh Centenary of the Death of St. Dominic), June 29.

Pius XI
(1922-1939)

1922: Ubi Arcano Dei Consilio (Peace of Christ in the Kingdom of Christ), Dec. 23.

1923: Rerum Omnium Perturbationem (Third Centenary of the Death of St. Francis de Sales), Jan. 26.

Studiorum Ducem (Sixth Centenary of the Canonization of St. Thomas Aquinas), June 29.

Ecclesiam Dei (Third Centenary of the Death of St. Josaphat, Archbishop of Polotsk), Nov. 12.

1924: Maximam Gravissimamque (French Diocesan Associations), Jan. 18.

1925: Quas Primas (Feast of Christ the King), Dec. 11.

1926: Rerum Ecclesiae (Catholic Missions), Feb. 28.

Rite Expiatis (Seventh Centenary of the Death of St. Francis of Assisi), Apr. 30.

Iniquis Afflictisque (Persecution of the Church in Mexico), Nov. 18.

1928: Mortalium Animos (Promotion of True Religious Unity), Jan. 6.

Miserentissimus Redemptor (Reparation Due the Sacred Heart), May 8.

Rerum Orientalium (Reunion with the Eastern Churches), Sept. 8.

1929: Mens Nostra (Promotion of Spiritual Exercises), Dec. 20.

Quinquagesimo Ante (Sacerdotal Jubilee), Dec. 23.

Divini Illius Magistri (Rappresentanti in Terra) (Christian Education of Youth), Dec. 31.

1930: Ad Salutem (Fifteenth Centenary of the Death of St. Augustine), Apr. 20.

Casti Connubii (Christian Marriage), Dec. 31.

1931: Quadragesimo Anno (Social Reconstruction), May 15.

Non Abbiamo Bisogno (Catholic Action), June 29.

Nova Impendet (Economic Crisis, Unemployment, Armaments), Oct. 2.

Lux Veritatis (Fifteenth Centenary of the Council of Ephesus), Dec. 25.

1932: Caritate Christi Compulsi (Sacred Heart and World Distress), May 3.

Acerba Animi (Persecution of the Church in Mexico), Sept. 29.

1933: Dilectissima Nobis (Conditions in Spain), June 3.

1935: Ad Catholici Sacerdotii (Catholic Priesthood), Dec. 20.

1936: Vigilanti Cura (Clean Motion Pictures), June 29.

1937: Mit Brennender Sorge (Church in Germany), Mar. 14.

Divini Redemptoris (Atheistic Communism), Mar. 19.

Firmissimam Constantiam (Nos Es Muy Conocida) (Conditions in Mexico), Mar. 28.

Ingravescentibus Malis (The Rosary) Sept. 29.

Pius XII
(1939-1958)

1939: Summi Pontificatus (Function of the State in Modern World), Oct. 20.

Sertum Laetitiae (To the Church in the United States), Nov. 1.

1940: Saeculo Exeunte Octavo (Missions), June 13.

1943: Mystici Corporis Christi (Mystical Body), June 29.

Divino Afflante Spiritu (Biblical Studies), Sept. 30.

1944: Orientalis Ecclesiae Decus (Fifteenth Centenary of the Death of St. Cyril of Alexandria), Apr. 9.

1945: Communium Interpretes Dolorum (Appeal for Prayers), Apr. 15.

Orientales Omnes Ecclesias (Anniversary of the Ruthenian Reunion), Dec. 23.

1946: Quemadmodum (Call for Intensified Aid to Youth), Jan. 6.

Deiparae Virginis Mariae (Proposing to the Bishops the Question of the Definition of the Dogma of the Assumption), May 1.

1947: Fulgens Radiatur (Fourteenth Centenary of the Death of St. Benedict), Mar. 21.

Mediator Dei (Sacred Liturgy), Nov. 20.

Optatissima Pax (Peace and Social Disorders), Dec. 18.

1948: Auspicia Quaedam (Prayer to Blessed Virgin Mary for Peace), May 1.

In Multiplicibus Curis (Crisis in Palestine), Oct. 24.

1949: Redemptoris Nostri (Internationalization of Jerusalem), Apr. 15.

1950: Anni Sacri (Holy Year Call for Public Prayer), Mar. 12.

Summi Maeroris (Renewed Holy Year Call for Public Prayer), July 19.

Humani Generis (Warnings against Attempts to Distort Catholic Truths), Aug. 12.

Mirabile Illud (Call for Renewed Crusade of Prayers for Peace), Dec. 6.

1951: Evangelii Praecones (Call for Greater Missionary Effort), June 2.

Sempiternus Rex (Fifteenth Centenary of the Council of Chalcedon), Sept. 8.

Ingruentium Malorum (Recitation of the Rosary), Sept. 15.

1952: Orientales Ecclesias (Communist Persecution of the Church; Call for Prayers for the Persecuted), Dec. 15.

1953: Doctor Mellifluus (Eighth Centenary of Death of St. Bernard), May 24.

Fulgens Corona (Call for Catholics to Observe Marian Year), Sept. 8.

1954: Sacra Virginitas (Preeminence of Evangelical Chastity), Mar. 25.

Ecclesiae Fastos (Commemoration of St. Boniface), June 5.

Ad Sinarum Gentem (The Church in China), Oct. 7.

Ad Caeli Reginam (Feast of Queenship of Mary), Oct. 11.

1955: Musicae Sacrae (Sacred Music), Dec. 25.

1956: Haurietis Aquas (The Sacred Heart), May 15.

Luctuosissimi Eventus (Prayers for Hungary), Oct. 28.

Laetamur Admodum (Middle East Crisis), Nov. 1.

Datis Nuperrime (Prayers for Peace), Nov. 5.

1957: Fidei Donum (Missionary Effort, especially in Africa), Apr. 21.

Invicti Athletae Christi (Third Centenary of Death of St. Andrew Bobola), May 16.

Le Pelerinage de Lourdes (Centenary of Lourdes Apparitions), July 2.

Miranda Prorsus (Radio, TV and Motion Pictures), Sept. 8.

1958: Ad Apostolorum Principis (Critical Situation of the Church in China), June 29.

Meminisse Juvat (Prayers for Peace and the Persecuted Church), July 14.

John XXIII
(1958-1963)

1959: Ad Petri Cathedram (Appeal to Separated Christians to Reunite with Church), June 29.

Sacerdotii Nostri Primordia (Centenary of the Cure of Ars), Aug. 1.

Grata Recordatio (Rosary), Sept. 26.

Princeps Pastorum (Missions), Nov. 28.

1961: Mater et Magistra (Christianity and Social Progress), May 15.

Aeterna Dei Sapientia (Fifteenth Centenary of the Death of St. Leo the Great), Nov. 11.

1962: Paenitentiam Agere (Appeal for Works of Penance for Success of the Second Vatican Council), July 1.

1963: Pacem in Terris (Peace on Earth), Apr. 11.

Paul VI
(1963-   )

1964: Ecclesiam Suam (Second Vatican Council Themes), Aug. 6.

1965: Mense Maio (Prayer for Success of Vatican II, Peace), Apr. 29.

Mysterium Fidei (The Eucharist), Sept. 3.

1966: Christi Matri Rosarii (The Rosary), Sept. 15.

1967: Populorum Progressio (Development of Peoples), Mar. 26.

Sacerdotalis Caelibatus (Priestly Celibacy), June 24.

1968: Humanae Vitae (Birth Control), July 25.

THE SOCIAL QUESTION

Writing in "The Development of Peoples," Pope Paul said:

"It is undoubtedly the social problem that causes division between men. The question being raised today is that of knowing which will win — selfishness or the spirit of sacrifice. Will society be considered as an individual good exploited by the strongest, or as a common way of life in which one will rival the other in order to endure the common good, and in particular that of the most dispossessed?

"There are people who have everything and who still seek to increase their wealth. There are others also who are deprived of everything and who seek by force to acquire those things that are necessary to answer to their needs and which are being denied to them.

"Already we hear the crackling of arms. The struggle will be keen, implacable and devastating between the forces of gold on the one hand and on the other the insurrection of despair."

The pope added: "It is for each one to examine his conscience, a conscience that has a new statement for our times."

ORGANIZATION AND GOVERNMENT

As a structured society, the Catholic Church is organized and governed along lines corresponding mainly to the jurisdictions of the pope and bishops.

The pope is the supreme head of the Church. He has primacy of jurisdiction as well as honor over the entire Church.

Bishops, in union with and in subordination to the pope, are the successors of the Apostles for care of the Church and for the continuation of Christ's mission in the world. They serve the people of their own dioceses, or local churches, with ordinary authority and jurisdiction. They also share, with the pope and each other, in common concern and effort for the general welfare of the whole Church.

Bishops of exceptional status are Eastern Rite patriarchs who, subject only to the pope, are heads of the faithful belonging to their rites throughout the world.

Subject to the Holy Father and directly responsible to him for the exercise of their ministry of service to people in various jurisdictions or divisions of the Church throughout the world are: resident archbishops and metropolitans (heads of archdioceses), resident bishops (heads of dioceses), vicars and prefects apostolic (heads of vicariates apostolic and prefectures apostolic), certain abbots and prelates, apostolic administrators. Each of these, within his respective territory and according to the provisions of canon law, has ordinary jurisdiction over pastors (who are responsible for the administration of parishes), priests, religious and lay persons.

Also subject to the Holy Father are titular archbishops and bishops (who have delegated jurisdiction), religious orders and congregations of pontifical right, pontifical institutes and faculties, papal nuncios and apostolic delegates.

Assisting the pope and acting in his name in the central government and administration of the Church are cardinals and other officials of the Roman Curia.

THE HIERARCHY

The ministerial hierarchy is the orderly arrangement of the ranks and orders of the clergy to provide for the spiritual care of the faithful, the government of the Church, and the accomplishment of the Church's total mission in the world. Persons belong to this hierarchy by virtue of ordination and canonical mission.

The term hierarchy is also used to designate an entire body or group of bishops; for example, the hierarchy of the Church, the hierarchy of the United States.

Hierarchy of Order: Consists of the pope, bishops, priests and deacons, by divine law. Their purpose, for which they are ordained to holy orders, is to carry out the sacramental and pastoral ministry of the Church.

Hierarchy of Jurisdiction: Consists of the pope and bishops by divine law, and other church officials by ecclesiastical institution and mandate, who have authority to govern and direct the faithful for spiritual ends.

Prelates: Clerics with the authority of public office in the Church — i. e., the authority of jurisdiction in the external forum. They are: the pope, patriarchs, residential archbishops and bishops, certain abbots and prelates, vicars and prefects apostolic, vicars general, certain superiors in clerical exempt religious communities. Titular archbishops and bishops without ordinary jurisdiction are not prelates in the strict sense of the term; neither are pastors, who have very limited jurisdiction in the external forum.

The Pope

His Holiness the Pope is the Bishop of Rome, the Vicar of Jesus Christ, the successor of St. Peter, Prince of the Apostles, the Supreme Pontiff who has the primacy of jurisdiction and not merely of honor over the universal Church, the Patriarch of the West, the Primate of Italy, the Archbishop and Metropolitan of the Roman Province, the Sovereign of the State of Vatican City.

Cardinals
(See Index)

Patriarchs

Patriarch, a term which had its origin in the Eastern Church, is the title of a bishop who, second only to the pope, has the highest rank in the hierarchy of jurisdiction. He is the incumbent of one of the sees listed below. Subject only to the pope, an Eastern-Rite patriarch is the head of the faithful belonging to his rite throughout the world. The patriarchal sees are so called because of their special status and dignity in the history of the Church.

The Council of Nicaea (325) recognized three patriarchs — the bishops of Alexandria and Antioch in the East, and of Rome in the West. The First Council of Constantinople (381) added the bishop of Constantinople to the list of patriarchs and gave him rank second only to that of the pope, the bishop of Rome and patriarch of the West; this action was seconded by the Council of Chalcedon (451) and was given full recognition by the Fourth Lateran Council (1215). The Council of Chalcedon also acknowledged patriarchal rights of the bishop of Jerusalem. Since 451, the major patriarchates have been listed in this order of precedence: Rome, Constantinople, Alexandria, Antioch and Jerusalem.

Eastern Rite patriarchs are as follows: one of Alexandria, for the Copts; three of Antioch, one each for the Syrians, Maronites and Melkites (the latter also has the personal title of Melkite patriarch of Alexandria and of Jerusalem). The patriarch of Babylonia, for the Chaldeans, and the patriarch of Sis, or Cilicia, for the Armenians, should be called, more properly, *Katholikos* — that is, a prelate delegated for a universality of causes. These patriarchs are elected by bishops of their rites: they receive approval and the pallium, symbolic of their office, from the pope.

Latin Rite patriarchates were established for Antioch, Jerusalem, Alexandria and Constantinople during the Crusades; afterwards, they became patriarchates in name only. Jerusalem, however, was reconstituted as a patriarchate by Pius IX, in virtue of the bull *Nulla Celebrior* of July 23, 1847. In 1964, the Latin titular patriarchates of Constantinople, Alexandria and Antioch, long a bone of contention in relations with Eastern Rites, were abolished.

As of July 30, 1975, the patriarchs in the Church were:

Paul VI, Bishop of Rome, Pope, Patriarch of the West; Cardinal Stephanos I Sidarouss, C.M., of Alexandria, for the Copts; Ignace Antoine Hayek, of Antioch, for the Syrians; Maximos V Hakim, of Antioch, for the Melkites (he also has the titles of Alexandria and Jerusalem for the Melkites); Antoine Khoraiche, of Antioch, for the Maronites; Giacomo Beltritti, of Jerusalem, for the Latin Rite; Paul II Cheikho, of Babylon, for the Chaldeans; Ignace Pierre XVI Batanian, of Cilicia, for the Armenians.

The titular patriarchs (in name only) of the Latin Rite were: Jose Vieira Alvernaz, of the East Indies; Cardinal Antonio Ribeiro, of Lisbon; Cardinal Albino Luciani, of Venice. The patriarchate of the West Indies has been vacant since 1963.

Archbishops, Metropolitans

Archbishop: A bishop with the title of an archdiocese.

Metropolitan Archbishop: Head of the principal see, an archdiocese, in an ecclesiastical province consisting of several dioceses. He has the full powers of bishop in his own archdiocese and limited supervisory jurisdiction and influence over the other (suffragan) dioceses in the province.

Titular Archbishop: Has the title of an archdiocese which formerly existed in fact but now exists in title only. He does not have ordinary jurisdiction over an archdiocese.

Archbishop ad personam: A title of personal honor and distinction granted to some bishops. They do not have ordinary jurisdiction over an archdiocese.

Primate: A title given to the ranking prelate of some countries or regions.

Bishops

Residential Bishop: A bishop in charge of a diocese.

Titular Bishops: Have the titles of dioceses which formerly existed in fact but now exist in title only. They have delegated authority of jurisdiction, by grant in line with their assignments, rather than the ordinary jurisdiction of office which belongs to a residential bishop. An auxiliary bishop (titular) is an assistant to a residential bishop. A coadjutor bishop (titular) is an assistant bishop of higher status; some coadjutors have the right of succession to residential sees.

Episcopal Vicar: An assistant, who may or may not be a bishop, appointed by a residential bishop as his deputy for a certain part of a diocese, a determined type of apostolic work, or the faithful of a certain rite.

Eparch, Exarch: Titles of bishops of Eastern-Rite churches.

Nomination of Bishops: Nominees for episcopal ordination are selected in several ways. Final appointment in all cases is subject to decision by the pope.

In the US, bishops periodically submit the names of candidates to the archbishop of their province. The names are then considered at a meeting of the bishops of the province, and those receiving a favorable vote are forwarded to the apostolic delegate for transmission to the Holy See. Bishops are free to seek the counsel of priests, religious and lay persons with respect to nominees.

Eastern-Rite churches have their own procedures and synodal regulations for nominating and making final selection of candidates for episcopal ordination.

In some countries where concordat or other special arrangements are in effect, civil governments have specified privileges to express approval or disapproval of candidates for the episcopacy.

Ad Limina Visit: Residential bishops and military vicars are obliged to make a periodic *ad limina* visit ("to the threshold" of the Apostles) to the tombs of Sts. Peter and Paul, have audience with the Holy Father and present a written report of conditions in their dioceses or military jurisdictions. European bishops are required to make the visit every five years. The visits may be made every 10 years by bishops of dioceses on other continents, but a report must be submitted every five years.

Other Prelates

Some prelates and abbots, formerly called *nullius,* have jurisdiction over territories (abbacies, prefectures, prelatures) not under the authority of diocesan bishops.

Vicar Apostolic: Usually a titular bishop who has ordinary jurisdiction over a mission territory. A vicar apostolic could also serve as the administrator of a vacant diocese or a diocese whose bishop is impeded from the exercise of his office.

Prefect Apostolic: A prelate with ordinary jurisdiction over a mission territory.

Apostolic Administrator: Usually a bishop appointed to administer an ecclesiastical jurisdiction temporarily. Administrators of lesser rank are also appointed for special and more restricted supervisory duties.

Vicar General: A bishop's deputy for the administration of a diocese. Such a vicar does not have to be a bishop.

Honorary Prelates

Honorary prelates belonging to the Pontifical Household are: Apostolic Prothonotaries, Honorary Prelates of His Holiness, and Chaplains of His Holiness. Their title is Reverend Monsignor.

SYNOD OF BISHOPS

The Synod of Bishops was chartered by Pope Paul Sept. 15, 1965, in a document he issued on his own initiative under the title, *Apostolica Sollicitudo.* According to the document:

• The purposes of the Synod are: "to encourage close union and valued assistance between the Sovereign Pontiff and the bishops of the entire world; to insure that direct and real information is provided on questions and situations touching upon the internal action of the Church and its necessary activity in the world of today; to facilitate agreement on essential points of doctrine and on methods of procedure in the life of the Church."

• The Synod is a central ecclesiastical institution, permanent by nature.

• The Synod is directly and immediately subject to the Pope, who has authority to assign its agenda, to call it into session, and to give its members deliberative as well as advisory authority.

• In addition to a limited number of ex officio members and a few heads of male religious institutes, the majority of the members are elective by and representative of national or regional episcopal conferences. The Pope reserved the right to appoint the general secretary, special secretaries and no more than 15 per cent of the total membership.

The secretary general is Bishop Ladislaw Rubin of Poland. Archbishop Joseph L. Bernardin, president of the U.S. bishops' conference, is one of the 15 members of the Synod's advisory council.

First Meeting, 1967

The Synod met for the first time from Sept. 29 to Oct. 29, 1967, in Vatican City. Its objectives, as stated by Pope Paul, were "the preservation and strengthening of the Catholic faith, its integrity, its force, its development, its doctrinal and historical coherence."

One result of synodal deliberations was a recommendation to the Pope to establish an international commission of theologians to assist the Congregation for the Doctrine of the Faith and to broaden approaches to theological research. The commission was subsequently set up by Pope Paul in 1969.

In other actions, the Synod called for the formulation of a Code of Canon Law more pastoral than the one in force since 1918 and more in touch with the mentality, aspirations and needs of people in contemporary circumstances; favored the view that episcopal conferences should have major control over seminaries in their respective areas; suggested some changes in pastoral procedures with respect to mixed marriages, which were authorized in 1970; gave general approval to the New Order of the Mass which was promulgated and put into effect in 1969.

The first meeting of the Synod had 197 participants: 135 representatives of more than 90 episcopal conferences, 13 representatives of Eastern-Rite churches, 13 cardinals of the Roman Curia, 10 representatives of the Union of Superiors General of Religious, 25 members and a secretary general appointed by Pope Paul.

Extraordinary Session

The second Synod of Bishops, meeting in extraordinary session Oct. 11 to 28, 1969, opened the door to wider participation by the bishops with the Pope and each other in the government of the Church.

The business assigned to the meeting by Pope Paul was to seek and examine ways and means of putting into practice the principle of collegiality which figured largely in declarations of the Second Vatican Council on the Church and the pastoral office of bishops.

Accordingly, proceedings were oriented to three main points: (1) the nature and implications of collegiality; (2) the relationships of bishops and their conferences to the Pope; (3) the relationships of bishops and their conferences to each other. The end results were three proposals approved by the bishops and the Pope, and five times that number approved and placed under advisement by the Pope. All proposals pointed in the direction of more cooperative action by all the bishops with the Pope in the conduct of Church affairs.

The three proposals which were approved and moved for action provided for regular meetings of the Synod at two-year intervals, (later extended to three years), staff organization and operations of the general secretariat in the interim between meetings, and openness of the synodal agenda to suggestions by bishops.

The second meeting had 146 participants: 93 presidents of episcopal conferences — 22 from Europe, 14 from Asia, 29 from Africa, 24 from the Americas, four from Oceania; 13

representatives of Eastern-Rite Churches — six patriarchs, one major archbishop, six metropolitans; three religious, elected by the Union of Superiors General; 19 officials from the various departments of the Roman Curia; secretary general Bishop Ladislaw Rubin, and 17 appointees of Pope Paul.

Between the second and third meetings of the Synod, an advisory council of 15 members (12 elected, three appointed by the Pope) was formed to provide the secretariat with adequate staff for carrying on liaison with episcopal conferences and for drawing up the agenda of synodal meetings. The council, at its first meeting May 12 to 15, 1970, followed the lead of the second assembly by opening the agenda of the 1971 meeting to the suggestions of bishops from all over the world.

Synod '71

The ministerial priesthood and justice in the world were the principal topics of discussion at the third and longest meeting, the Second General Assembly of the Synod, Sept. 30 to Nov. 6, 1971.

Advisory reports on these subjects, compiled from views expressed by the bishops before and during the synodal sessions, were presented to Pope Paul at the end of the meeting. He authorized publication of the reports and said, in a letter made public Dec. 9, that he accepted conclusions reached by the bishops which "conform to the current norms" of church teaching.

The Priesthood

In its report on the priesthood, the Synod described difficulties experienced by priests, stated traditional doctrinal principles on the priesthood, and drew from these principles a set of guidelines for priestly life and ministry in the mission of Christ and the Church, and in the communion of the Church.

The report emphasized the primary and permanent dedication of priests in the Church to the ministry of word, sacrament and pastoral service as a full-time occupation.

The synodal Fathers — with 168 votes in favor without reservations, 21 votes in favor with reservations, and 10 votes against — supported the existing discipline of clerical celibacy. They favored leaving to the discretion of the Pope decisions regarding the ordination of already married men in special circumstances. They did not consider the question of permitting already ordained priests to marry. The majority voted against permitting priests who had left the ministry to resume priestly duties, although they said such priests could serve the Church in other ways and should be treated in a just and fraternal manner.

Justice in the World

In connection with "the mission of the People of God to further justice in the world," a synodal report reviewed a wide range of existing injustices; cited the social-justice imperatives of the Gospel; called for the practice of justice throughout the Church and for greater efforts in education and ecumenical collaboration for justice; and outlined an eight-point program for international action.

Behind the Synod's recommendations were the convictions:

• "The Church . . . has a proper and specific responsibility which is identified with her mission of giving witness before the world of the need for love and justice contained in the Gospel message, a witness to be carried out in church institutions themselves and in the lives of Christians."

• "Action on behalf of justice and participation in the transformation of the world fully appear to us as a constitutive dimension of the preaching of the Gospel; or, in other words, of the Church's mission for the redemption of the human race and its liberation from every oppressive situation."

• "The present situation of the world, seen in the light of faith, calls us back to the very essence of the Christian message, creating in us a deep awareness of its true meaning and of its urgent demands. The mission of preaching the Gospel dictates at the present time that we should dedicate ourselves to the liberation of man even in his present existence in this world. For, unless the Christian message of love and justice shows its effectiveness through action in the cause of justice in the world, it will only with difficulty gain credibility with the men of our times."

The assembly had 210 participants: six patriarchs, one major archbishop, seven Eastern-Rite metropolitans (one of whom was listed also as a representative of an episcopal conference), 142 elected representatives of 94 episcopal conferences, 10 men religious elected by the Union of Major Superiors, 19 cardinals of the Roman Curia, and 26 papal appointees — the general secretary, 22 bishops and three priests. Ten delegates were from the United States. American Fathers John F. Cronin and Barnabas Ahern, C.P., were among 23 priests designated by Pope Paul to attend the session.

Synod '74

"Evangelization of the Modern World" was the theme of the fourth assembly of the Synod of Bishops, Sept. 27 to Oct. 26, 1974.

The 209 participants in the month-long assembly were delegates from nearly 100 episcopal conferences, representatives of major religious orders, a limited number of Vatican officials and 21 appointees of Pope Paul. The U.S. delegation consisted of Cardinals John J. Krol, John F. Dearden, John J. Carberry, and Archbishops Joseph L. Bernardin (all elected by the National Conference of Catholic Bishops) and John R. Quinn (appointed by the Pope). Archbishop Bernardin was elected to the council of the synod Oct. 19.

(For more extensive coverage, see Synod of Bishops, 1974, and Evangelization — Statement of the 1974 Bishops' Synod.)

ROMAN CURIA

The Roman Curia consists of the Secretariat of State, the Sacred Council for the Public Affairs of the Church, nine congregations, three tribunals, three secretariats, and a complex of commissions, councils and offices which administer church affairs at the highest level.

Background

The Curia evolved gradually from advisory assemblies or synods of the Roman clergy with whose assistance the popes directed church affairs during the first 11 centuries. Its original office was the Apostolic Chancery, dating from the fourth century. The antecedents of its permanently functioning agencies and offices were special commissions of cardinals and prelates. Its establishment in a form resembling what it is now dates from the second half of the 16th century.

Pope Paul VI gave the following short account of the background of the Curia in the apostolic constitution *Regimini Ecclesiae Universae* ("For the Government of the Universal Church"), dated Aug. 15, 1967.

"The Roman Pontiffs, successors to Blessed Peter, have striven to provide for the government of the Universal Church by making use of experts to advise and assist them.

"In this connection, we should remember both the Presbyterium of the City of Rome and the College of Cardinals of the Holy Roman Church which in the course of centuries evolved from it. Then, little by little, as we know, out of that office (Apostolic Chancery) which was set up in the fourth century to transmit papal documents, many offices developed; to these was added the Auditorium, which was a well-developed tribunal in the 13th century and which was more thoroughly organized by John XXII (1316-1334).

"With an increase in the volume of things to be dealt with, bodies or commissions of cardinals selected to treat of specific questions began to be more efficiently organized in the 16th century, from which eventually arose the congregations of the Roman Curia. It is to the credit of our predecessor Sixtus V that, in the constitution *Immensa Aeterni Dei* of Jan. 22, 1588, he arranged the sacred councils in an orderly manner and wisely described the structure of the Roman Curia.

"With the progress of time, however, it happened that some of them became obsolete, others had to be added, and others had to be restructured. This is the work our predecessor St. Pius X set out to do with the constitution *Sapienti Consilio* of June 29, 1908. Its provisions, a lasting testimony to that wise

and ingenious pastor of the Church, were with a few changes incorporated into the Code of Canon Law" (Canons 242-264).

Reorganization

Pope Paul initiated a four-year reorganization study in 1963 which resulted in the constitution *Regimini Ecclesiae Universae.* The document was published Aug. 18, 1967, and went into full effect in March, 1968.

While the study was underway, the Pope took preliminary steps toward curial reorganization by reorienting and changing the title of the Sacred Congregation of the Holy Office (to the Sacred Congregation for the Doctrine of the Faith) and by appointing a number of non-Italians to key curial positions.

The stated purposes of the reorganization were to increase the efficiency of the Curia and to make it more responsive to the needs and concerns of the Universal Church. The pursuit of these objectives involved various modifications.

Curial Departments

• The Office of the Pope, including the Papal Secretariat or Secretariat of State and the Council for the Public Affairs of the Church.

• Nine congregations, instead of twelve as formerly. The functions of the Sacred Congregation of Ceremonies were transferred to the Prefecture of the Pontifical Household; the duties of the Sacred Congregation for Extraordinary Ecclesiastical Affairs were taken over by the Sacred Council for the Public Affairs of the Church; the Sacred Congregation of the Basilica of St. Peter was reduced in rank. In 1969, the Sacred Congregation of Rites was phased out of existence and its functions were assigned to the Sacred Congregation for the Causes of Saints and the Sacred Congregation for Divine Worship. In 1975 the Congregation for the Sacraments and Divine Worship was established to replace the Congregation for the Discipline of the Sacraments and the Congregation for Divine Worship.

• Three secretariats, the Council of the Laity and the Pontifical Commission on Justice and Peace.

• Three tribunals.

• Six offices, including the former Apostolic Chancery (abolished in 1973) and Apostolic Chamber, and the newly constituted Prefecture of Economic Affairs, Prefecture of the Pontifical Household, Administration of the Patrimony of the Apostolic See, and Central Statistics Office. Functions of the former Apostolic Datary and the Secretariats of State, of Briefs to Princes, and of Latin Letters were transferred to the Secretariat of State.

Operational Procedures

• The papal secretary or secretary of state has authority to take initiative in coordinating and expediting business through meetings and other cooperative procedures.

• Officials of departments have five-year terms of office, which may be renewed. Resignation is automatic on the death of a pope. The five-year terms of consultors are renewable.

• Diocesan bishops as well as full-time curial personnel have membership in curial departments, in accordance with provisions of the decree *Pro Comperto Sane* of Aug. 6, 1967. Seven diocesan bishops hold five-year membership in each congregation, with full rights to participation in the more important plenary assemblies scheduled once a year. They are also entitled to take part in routine meetings whenever they are in Rome. Three general superiors of male religious institutes hold similar membership in the Sacred Congregation for Religious and Secular Institutes.

• Lay persons are eligible to serve as consultors to curial departments.

• Close liaison with episcopal conferences is required. They should be given prior notice of forthcoming curial decrees affecting them in any special way.

• In line with customary procedure, matters in which the competence of two or more departments is involved are handled on a cooperative basis, with mutual consultation and decision.

• Although Latin remains the official language of the Curia, communication in any of the widely known modern languages is acceptable.

• Informational and financial services are centralized in the Central Statistics Office and the Prefecture of Economic Affairs, respectively.

• Heads of curial departments are required to notify the pope before conducting any serious or extraordinary business.

• Authority to act and decide on many matters belongs to departmental officials in virtue of delegation from the pope. Some matters, however, have to be referred to the pope for final decision.

Internationalization

The international complexion of personnel in the Roman Curia changed considerably during the decade from 1961 to 1970. The number of non-Italians increased from 570 to more than 1,400, a rise of 145 per cent, while the number of Italians increased from 750 to 850, a rise of only 14 per cent. In 1970, 62 per cent were from other countries, as compared with 44 per cent in 1961.

As of Aug. 1, 1975, heads or principal officers of departments of the Roman Curia (all cardinals unless indicated otherwise) were from the following countries: Italy (Baggio, Felici, Paupini, Pignedoli, Vagnozzi); France (Villot, Philippe, Garrone); Australia (Knox); Austria (Koenig); Brazil (Rossi); Dahomey

(Archbishop Gantin); India (Archbishop Lourdusamy); Netherlands (Willebrands); Poland (Msgr. Boleslaw Filipiak); United States (Wright); Yugoslavia (Seper).

DEPARTMENTS OF THE CURIA
Secretariat of State

The Secretariat of State provides the pope with the closest possible assistance in the care of the Universal Church and in dealings with all departments of the Curia.

The cardinal secretary is the key coordinator of curial operations. He has authority to call meetings of the prefects of all departments for expediting the conduct of business, for consultation and intercommunication. He handles: any and all matters entrusted to him by the pope, and ordinary matters which are not within the competence of other departments; some relations with bishops; relations with representatives of the Holy See, civil governments and their representatives, without prejudice to the competence of the Council for the Public Affairs of the Church.

The cardinal secretary has been likened to a prime minister or head of government because of the significant role he plays in coordinating curial operations at the highest level.

The secretariat has two offices for preparing and writing letters for the pope (functions formerly performed by the Secretariat of Briefs to Princes and the Secretariat of Latin Letters), and a Central Statistics Office.

It also handles work formerly done by the Apostolic Datary (the dating and countersigning of papal documents, and the management of church benefices) and the Apostolic Chancery, abolished in 1973 (care of the pope's leaden seal and the Fisherman's Ring).

It has supervisory duties over the Commission for the Instruments of Social Communication, two Vatican publications, *Acta Apostolicae Sedis* and *Annuario Pontificio*, and the Vatican Personnel Office.

The Prefecture of Vatican City is answerable to the secretary of state.

OFFICIALS: Cardinal Jean Villot, secretary of state, Most Rev. Giovanni Benelli, substitute secretary and secretary of the Cifra.

Council for Public Affairs

The Council for the Public Affairs of the Church handles diplomatic and other relations with civil governments. With the Secretariat of State, it supervises matters concerning nunciatures and apostolic delegations. It also has supervision of the Pontifical Commission for Russia.

OFFICIALS: Cardinal Jean Villot, prefect, secretary of state; Most Rev. Agostino Casaroli, secretary.

BACKGROUND: Originated by Pius VI in 1793 as the Congregation for Extraordinary Affairs from the Kingdom of the Gauls; given wider scope by Pius VII, July 19, 1814; formerly called the Sacred Congregation for Extraordinary Ecclesiastical Affairs.

CONGREGATIONS

Doctrine of the Faith

The function of the Sacred Congregation for the Doctrine of the Faith is to safeguard the doctrine of faith and morals.

Accordingly, it examines doctrinal questions; promotes studies thereon; evaluates theological opinions and, when necessary and after prior consultation with concerned bishops, reproves those regarded as opposed to principles of the faith; examines books on doctrinal matters and can reprove such works, if the contents so warrant, after giving authors the opportunity to defend themselves.

It examines matters pertaining to the Privilege of Faith (Petrine Privilege) in marriage cases, and safeguards the dignity of the sacrament of penance.

It has working relations with the Pontifical Biblical Commission.

In 1969, Pope Paul set up a Theological Commission (see separate entry) as an adjunct to the congregation, to provide it with the advisory services of additional experts in theology and allied disciplines.

OFFICIALS: Cardinal Franjo Seper, prefect; Most Rev. Jerome Hamer, O.P., secretary.

BACKGROUND: At the beginning of the 13th century, legates of Innocent III were commissioned as the Holy Office of the Inquisition to combat heresy; the same task was entrusted to the Dominican Order by Gregory IX in 1231 and to the Friars Minor by Innocent IV from 1243 to 1254. On July 21, 1542 (apostolic constitution *Licet*), Paul III instituted a permanent congregation of cardinals with supreme and universal competence over matters concerning heretics and those suspected of heresy. Pius IV, St. Pius V and Sixtus V further defined the work of the Congregation. St. Pius X changed its name to the Congregation of the Holy Office.

Paul VI, in virtue of the motu proprio *Integrae Servandae* of Dec. 7, 1965, began reorganization of the Curia with this body, to which he gave the new title, Sacred Congregation for the Doctrine of the Faith. Its orientation is not merely negative, in the condemnation of error, but positive, in the promotion of orthodox doctrine. The right of appeal, judicial representation, and the consultation of their proper regional conference of bishops, are assured to persons accused of unorthodox doctrine. The office for the censorship of books and the Roman Index of Prohibited Books were abolished.

Oriental Churches

The Sacred Congregation for the Oriental Churches has competence in matters concerning the persons and discipline of Eastern Rite Churches. It has jurisdiction over territories in which the majority of Christians belong to Oriental Rites (i. e., Egypt, the Sinai Peninsula, Eritrea, Northern Ethiopia, Southern Albania, Bulgaria, Cyprus, Greece, Iran, Iraq, Lebanon, Palestine, Syria, Jordan, Turkey, Afghanistan, the part of Thrace subject to Turkey); also, over minority communities of Orientals no matter where they live.

To assure adequate and equal representation, it has as many offices as there are rites of Oriental Churches in communion with the Holy See.

It is under mandate to consult with the Secretariat for Promoting Christian Unity on questions concerning separated Oriental Churches, and with the Secretariat for Non-Christians, especially in relations with Moslems.

It has a special commission on the liturgy and an Oriental Church Information Service.

OFFICIALS: Cardinal Paul Philippe, O.P., prefect; Most Rev. Mario Brini, secretary.

Members include all Eastern Rite patriarchs and the president of the Secretariat for Promoting Christian Unity. Consultors include the secretary of the same secretariat.

BACKGROUND: Special congregations for the affairs of the Greek and other Oriental Churches were founded long before this body was created by Pius IX Jan. 6, 1862 (apostolic constitution *Romani Pontifices*), and united with the Sacred Congregation for the Propagation of the Faith. The congregation was made autonomous by Benedict XV May 1, 1917 (motu proprio *Dei Providentis*), and given wider authority by Pius XI Mar. 25, 1938 (motu proprio *Sancta Dei Ecclesia*). John XXIII appointed six patriarchs, five of Eastern Rites and one of the Roman Rite, to the congregation and gave them the same rights as cardinals belonging to the body, in March, 1963. Paul VI named representatives of all Eastern-Rite bodies to serve as consultors of the congregation, in November, 1963.

Bishops

The Sacred Congregation for Bishops, formerly called the Sacred Consistorial Congregation, has functions related in one way or another to bishops and the jurisdictions in which they serve.

Its concerns are: the establishment and changing of dioceses, provinces, military vicariates and other jurisdictions; providing for the naming of bishops and other prelates; studying things concerning the persons, work and pastoral activity of bishops; providing for the care of bishops when they leave office; receiving and studying reports on the conditions of dioceses; general supervision of the holding and recognition of particular councils and conferences of bishops; publishing and circulating pastoral norms and guidelines through conferences of bishops.

It supervises the Pontifical Commission for

Latin America and the Pontifical Commission for Migration and Tourism.

OFFICIALS: Cardinal Sebastiano Baggio, prefect; Most Rev. Ernesto Civardi, secretary.

Ex officio members are the prefects of the Council for the Public Affairs of the Church, and of the Congregations for the Doctrine of the Faith, for the Clergy, and for Catholic Education. The substitute secretaries and undersecretaries of these curial departments are ex officio consultors.

BACKGROUND: Established by Sixtus V Jan. 22, 1588 (apostolic constitution *Immensa*); given an extension of powers by St. Pius X June 20, 1908, and Pius XII Aug. 1, 1952 (apostolic constitution *Exsul Familia*).

Sacraments and Divine Worship

The Sacred Congregation for the Sacraments and Divine Worship, established in 1975, replaces the Congregation for the Discipline of the Sacraments and the Congregation for Divine Worship.

The congregation consists of two sections — for the sacraments and for divine worship. The former supervises the discipline of the sacraments without prejudice to the competencies of the Sacred Congregation for the Doctrine of the Faith and other curial departments. The latter has general competence over the ritual and pastoral aspects of divine worship in the Roman and other Latin Rites.

OFFICIALS: Cardinal James R. Knox, prefect; Most Rev. Antonio Innocenti, secretary; Msgr. Antonio Magnoni, undersecretary, section on the sacraments; Msgr. Virgilio Noe, undersecretary, section on divine worship.

BACKGROUND: The congregation was established by Paul VI Aug. 1, 1975 (apostolic constitution, *Constans novis studium*, dated July 11, 1975). Formerly its duties were carried out by the Congregation for the Discipline of the Sacraments (instituted by St. Pius X June 29, 1908) and the Congregation for Divine Worship (established by Paul VI, May 8, 1969, to replace the Congregation of Rites instituted by Sixtus V in 1588).

Causes of Saints

The Sacred Congregation for the Causes of Saints handles all matters connected with beatification and canonization procedures, and the preservation of relics. These affairs were formerly under the supervision of the Congregation of Rites.

The congregation carries on its work through three sections or offices.

One section is a juridical office with supervisory responsibility over procedures and examinations conducted to determine the holiness of prospective saints. It includes a medical commission for the study of miracles attributed to the intercession of candidates for sainthood.

A second section, headed by the promoter general of the faith, who is popularly called the "Devil's Advocate," serves the purpose of establishing beyond reasonable doubt the evidence of holiness advanced in support of beatification and canonization causes.

Research and evaluation of documentary evidence figuring in canonization causes are the functions of the historic-hagiographical section.

OFFICIALS: Most Rev. Corrado Bafila, pro-prefect, Most Rev. Giuseppe Casoria, secretary.

BACKGROUND: The functions and title of this congregation were determined by Paul VI May 8, 1969 (apostolic constitution *Sacra Rituum Congregatio*). Formerly, its duties were carried out by the Congregation of Rites, which was established by Sixtus V in 1588 and affected by legislation of Pius XI in 1930.

Clergy

The Sacred Congregation for the Clergy, formerly called the Sacred Congregation of the Council, handles matters concerning the persons, work and pastoral ministry of clerics who exercise their apostolate in a diocese. Such clerics are diocesan deacons and priests, and religious who are engaged in ordinary parochial ministry in a diocese.

It carries on its work through three offices.

One office promotes the spiritual growth and formation as well as the professional competence of priests by encouraging the establishment and operation of pastoral institutes and other study opportunities; oversees the general discipline of the clergy, the establishment and conduct of pastoral councils and senates of priests, and resolves controversies among clerics; has a mandate to draw up a set of general principles to direct a better distribution of priests for pastoral service.

A second office, in view of its primary concern for preaching of the word of God, encourages effective apostolic programs and methods, with special emphasis on catechetical and other forms of religious training and formation for the faithful.

A third office has supervisory responsibility over church property and the temporalities of priestly life; among its functions are efforts to provide for the support of the clergy through suitable salary scales, pensions, security and health insurance programs, and other measures.

OFFICIALS: Cardinal John J. Wright, prefect; Most Rev. Maximino Romero de Lema, secretary.

BACKGROUND: Established by Pius IV Aug. 2, 1564 (apostolic constitution *Alias Nos*), under the title, Sacred Congregation of the Cardinals Interpreters of the Council of Trent; affected by legislation of Gregory XIII and Sixtus V.

Religious and Secular Institutes

The extension of the title of this congregation, which was formerly known as the Sacred Congregation of Religious or for the Affairs of Religious, indicates its dual competence over institutes of religious, together with societies of the common life without vows, and secular institutes.

One section deals with the affairs of all religious institutes and societies of the common life, and their members. It has authority in matters related to the establishment, general direction and suppression of institutes; general discipline in line with their rules and constitutions; the movement toward renewal and adaptation of institutes in contemporary circumstances; the setting up and encouragement of councils and conferences of major religious superiors for intercommunication and other purposes.

A second section has the same competence over the affairs and members of secular institutes as the first has over religious.

OFFICIALS: Most. Rev. Augustine Mayer, O.S.B., secretary.

BACKGROUND: Founded by Sixtus V May 27, 1586, with the title, Sacred Congregation for Consultations of Regulars (apostolic constitution *Romanus Pontifex*); confirmed by the apostolic constitution *Immensa* Jan. 22, 1588; made part of the Congregation for Consultations of Bishops and other Prelates in 1601; made autonomous by St. Pius X in 1908.

Catholic Education

The Sacred Congregation for Catholic Education, formerly known as the Sacred Congregation of Seminaries and Universities, has supervisory competence over institutions and works of Catholic education.

It carries on its work through three offices.

One office handles matters connected with the direction, discipline and temporal administration of seminaries, and with the education of diocesan clergy, religious and members of secular institutes.

A second office oversees Catholic universities, faculties of study and other institutions of higher learning inasmuch as they depend on the authority of the Church; encourages cooperation and mutual assistance among Catholic institutions, and the establishment of Catholic hospices and centers on campuses of non-Catholic institutions.

A third office is concerned in various ways with all Catholic schools below the college-university level, with general questions concerning education and studies, and with the cooperation of conferences of bishops and civil authorities in educational matters.

The congregation supervises Pontifical Works for Priestly Vocations.

OFFICIALS: Cardinal Gabriel Garrone,

prefect; Most Rev. Joseph Schroeffer, secretary.

BACKGROUND: The title and functions of the congregation were defined by Benedict XV Nov. 4, 1915; Pius XI, in 1931 and 1932, and Pius XII, in 1941 and 1949, extended its functions. Its work had previously been carried on by two other congregations erected by Sixtus V in 1588 and Leo XII in 1824.

Evangelization of Peoples
Propagation of the Faith

This congregation, which has alternative titles, directs and coordinates missionary work throughout the world.

Accordingly, it has competence over those matters which concern all the missions established for the spread of Christ's kingdom. These include: fostering missionary vocations; providing for the training of missionaries in seminaries; assigning missionaries to fields of work; establishing ecclesiastical jurisdictions and proposing candidates to serve them as bishops and in other capacities; encouraging the recruitment and development of indigenous clergy; mobilizing spiritual and financial support for missionary activity.

In general, the varied competence of the congregation extends to most persons and affairs of the Church in areas classified as mission territories.

To promote missionary cooperation, the congregation has a Supreme Council for the Direction of Pontifical Missionary Works. Subject to this council are the general councils of the Missionary Union of the Clergy, the Society for the Propagation of the Faith, the Society of St. Peter the Apostle for Native Clergy, the Society of the Holy Childhood, and the *Fides* news agency.

OFFICIALS: Cardinal Agnelo Rossi, prefect; Most Revs. Bernardin Gantin and Duraisamy S. Lourdusamy, secretaries.

The heads of the Secretariats for Promoting Christian Unity, for Non-Christians, and for Non-Believers are ex officio members of the congregation.

BACKGROUND: Originated as a commission of cardinals by Gregory XIII and modified by Clement VIII to promote the reconciliation of separated Eastern Christians; erected as a stable congregation by Gregory XV June 22, 1622 (apostolic constitution *Inscrutabili*).

The purpose of evangelization is to proclaim the Gospel and to do whatever can be done to form the community of faith and nourish sacramental life among those who believe. This process, which the congregation services, is intended to result in the eventual indigenization of a local church capable of self-support with respect to ministerial personnel and other resources.

TRIBUNALS
Sacred Apostolic Penitentiary
This tribunal has jurisdiction for the internal forum only (sacramental and non-sacramental). It issues decisions on questions of conscience; grants absolutions, dispensations, commutations, sanations and condonations; has charge of non-doctrinal matters pertaining to indulgences.

OFFICIALS: Cardinal Giuseppe Paupini, major penitentiary; Msgr. Giovanni Sessolo, regent.

BACKGROUND: Origin dates back to the 12th century; affected by the legislation of many popes; radically reorganized by St. Pius V in 1569; jurisdiction limited to the internal forum by St. Pius X; Benedict XV annexed the Office of Indulgences to it Mar. 25, 1917.

Apostolic Signatura
The principal concerns of this supreme court of the Church are to resolve questions concerning juridical procedure and to supervise the observance of laws and rights at the highest level. It decides the jurisdictional competence of lower courts and has jurisdiction in cases involving personnel and decisions of the Rota. It is the supreme court of the State of Vatican City.

OFFICIALS: Cardinal Dino Staffa, prefect; Most Rev. Aurelio Sabattani, secretary.

BACKGROUND: A permanent office of the Signatura has existed since the time of Eugene IV in the 15th century; affected by the legislation of many popes; reorganized by St. Pius X in 1908 and made the supreme tribunal of the Church.

Sacred Roman Rota
The Rota is the ordinary court of appeal for cases appealed to the Holy See. It is best known for its competence and decisions in cases concerning the validity of marriage.

OFFICIAL: Msgr. Boleslaw Filipiak, dean.

BACKGROUND: Originated in the Apostolic Chancery; affected by the legislation of many popes; reorganized by St. Pius X in 1908 and further revised by Pius XI in 1934.

SECRETARIATS
Christian Unity
Promoting unity among Christians is the function and competence of this secretariat.

Accordingly, it handles relations with members of other ecclesial communities; deals with the correct interpretation and execution of the principles of ecumenism; initiates or promotes Catholic ecumenical groups and coordinates on national and international levels the efforts of those promoting Christian unity; undertakes dialogue regarding ecumenical questions and activities with churches and ecclesial communities separated from the Apostolic See; sends Catholic observer-representatives to Christian gatherings, and invites to Catholic gatherings observers of other churches; orders into execution conciliar decrees dealing with ecumenical affairs.

The Commission for Catholic-Jewish Relations is attached to the secretariat.

It has two offices, for the West and for the East. Each office is under the immediate direction of a delegate.

The prefects of the Congregation for the Oriental Churches and of the Congregation for the Evangelization of Peoples are ex officio members of the secretariat. Consultors include the secretaries of these two departments.

OFFICIALS: Cardinal Jan Willebrands, president; Rev. Charles Moeller, secretary.

BACKGROUND: Established by John XXIII June 5, 1960, as a preparatory secretariat of the Second Vatican Council; raised to commission status during the first session of the council in the fall of 1962; this status confirmed Jan. 3, 1966.

For Non-Christians
This secretariat is concerned with persons who are not Christians but profess some kind of religious faith. Its function is to promote studies and dialogue for the purpose of increasing mutual understanding and respect between Christians and non-Christians.

The Commission for Catholic-Moslem Relations is attached to the secretariat.

The prefect of the Congregation for the Evangelization of Peoples is an ex officio member of the secretariat.

OFFICIALS: Cardinal Sergio Pignedoli, president; Msgr. Pietro Rossano, secretary.

BACKGROUND: Established by Paul VI May 19, 1964.

For Non-Believers
This secretariat studies the background and philosophy of atheism, and initiates and carries on dialogue with non-believers.

OFFICIALS: Cardinal Franz Koenig, president; Most Rev. Antonio Mauro, vice-president; Rev. Vincenzo Miano, S.D.B., secretary.

BACKGROUND: Established by Paul VI Apr. 9, 1965.

COUNCILS, COMMISSIONS
Council of the Laity: Instituted by Paul VI Jan. 6, 1967, to promote the development of the lay apostolate as a service agency for coordinating apostolic works, establishing liaison between lay persons and the hierarchy, compiling doctrinal studies on the role of lay persons in pastoral activity, establishing and maintaining a documentation center; Cardinal Maurice Roy, president.

Commission on Justice and Peace: Institut-

ed by Paul VI Jan. 6, 1967, to develop awareness among the People of God of their mission to promote the progress of poor nations,
to encourage international social justice, to
help underdeveloped nations work for their
own improvement, to seek ways and means of
establishing peace in the world; Cardinal
Maurice Roy, president.

Revision of the Code of Canon Law: Instituted by John XXIII Mar. 28, 1963, to replace a former commission dating from 1917;
Cardinal Pericle Felici, president.

**Revision of the Code of Oriental Canon
Law:** Reconstituted by Paul VI in 1972 to
replace a former commission dating from
July 17, 1935, "to prepare . . . the reform of
the Code of Oriental Canon Law, both in the
sections already published by . . . four motu
proprios" (1,950 canons concerning marriage; processes; religious, church property
and terminology; Eastern Rites and persons),
"and in the remaining sections which have
been completed but not published" (the balance of a total of 2,666 canons); Cardinal Joseph Parecattil, president.

**Interpretation of the Decrees of the Second
Vatican Council:** Cardinal Pericle Felici, president.

Social Communication: Instituted on an experimental basis by Pius XII in 1948; reorganized three times in the 1950's; made permanent commission by John XXIII Feb. 22,
1959; name changed to present title Apr. 11,
1964; authorized to implement the *Decree on
the Instruments of Social Communication* promulgated by the Second Vatican Council;
under supervision of the Secretariat of State
and the Council for the Public Affairs of the
Church; Most Rev. Andre-Marie Deskur,
president; Most Rev. Martin J. O'Connor,
president emeritus.

Latin America: Instituted by Pius XII Apr.
19, 1958; placed under supervision of the
Congregation for Bishops July, 1969; Cardinal Sebastiano Baggio, president.

Migration and Tourism: Instituted by Paul
VI Mar. 19, 1970, for pastoral assistance to
migrants, nomads, tourists, sea and air travelers; placed under the general supervision and
direction of the Congregation for Bishops;
Cardinal Sebastiano Baggio, president.

Cor Unum: Instituted by Paul VI July 15,
1971, to provide informational and coordinating services for Catholic aid and human development organizations and projects on a
worldwide scale; Cardinal Jean Villot, president.

Theological Commission: Instituted by Paul
VI Apr. 11, 1969, as an advisory adjunct of no
more than 30 theologians to the Congregation for the Doctrine of the Faith; Cardinal
Franjo Seper, president.

Biblical Commission: Instituted by Leo
XIII Oct. 30, 1902; completely restructured
by Paul VI June 27, 1971; Cardinal Franjo
Seper, president.

**Abbey of St. Jerome for the Revision and
Emendation of the Vulgate:** Instituted by Pius
XI June 15, 1933, to replace an earlier commission established by St. Pius X; Rev. Vincent Truijen, superior.

Revision of the New Vulgate: Instituted by
Paul VI in 1965 to augment the work of the
Abbey of St. Jerome; Most Rev. Edward
Schick, president.

Sacred Archeology: Instituted by Pius IX
Jan, 6, 1852; Most Rev. Gennaro Verolino,
president.

Historical Sciences: Instituted by Pius XII
Apr. 7, 1954, as a continuation of a commission dating from 1883; Msgr. Michael Maccarrone, president.

Ecclesiastical Archives of Italy: Instituted
by Pius XII Apr. 5, 1955; Msgr. Martino
Giusti, president.

Sacred Art in Italy: Instituted by Pius XI
Sept. 1, 1924; Most Rev. Giovanni Fallani,
president.

Sanctuaries of Pompei and Loreto: Originated by Leo XIII; under supervision of the
Congregation for the Clergy; Cardinal Umberto Mozzoni, president.

Russia: Instituted by Pius XI Apr. 6, 1930,
to handle all ecclesiastical affairs of the
country; placed under supervision of the Congregation for Extraordinary Ecclesiastical Affairs (now the Council for the Public Affairs
of the Church) in 1934, with jurisdiction limited to clergy and faithful of the Roman Rite;
under supervision of the Council for the Public Affairs of the Church; Most Rev. Agostino
Casaroli, president.

State of Vatican City: Cardinal Jean Villot,
president.

**Protection of the Historical and Artistic
Monuments of the Holy See:** Instituted by
Pius XI in 1923, reorganized by Paul VI in
1963; Most Rev. Giovanni Fallani, president.

**Preservation of the Faith, Erection of New
Churches in Rome:** Instituted by Pius XI Aug.
5, 1930, to replace a commission dating from
1902; Cardinal Ugo Poletti, president.

Works of Religion: Instituted by Pius XII
June 27, 1942, to bank and administer funds
for works of religion; replaced an earlier administration established by Leo XIII in 1887;
Most Rev. Paul C. Marcinkus, president.

Family: Instituted by Paul VI Jan. 11, 1973,
for pastoral research and supportive effort
with respect to the spiritual, moral and social
needs of the family. The president of the committee representative of bishops, priests and
lay persons is the Most Rev. Edouard Gagnon.

Catholic-Jewish Relations: Instituted by
Paul VI, Oct., 1974, to promote and foster
relations of a religious nature between Jews
and Christians; attached to the Secretariat for
Christian Unity; Cardinal Jan Willebrands,
president.

Catholic-Moslem Relations: Instituted by
Paul VI, Oct., 1974, to promote, regulate and

interpret relations between Catholics and Moslems; attached to the Secretariat for Non-Christians; Cardinal Sergio Pignedoli, president.

Commission on Role of Women

Pope Paul carried out a recommendation of the 1971 assembly of the Synod of Bishops by establishing May 3, 1973, an ad hoc Study Commission on the Role of Women in Society and the Church. The commission was authorized to continue until January, 1976. Appointed to membership were 15 women (including two nuns and American Deborah Cheloman, a 20-year-old college student), seven priests and three laymen; Archbishop Enrico Bartoletti was named president.

OFFICES
Prefecture of Economic Affairs

The Prefecture of the Economic Affairs of the Holy See is a financial office which coordinates and supervises administration of the temporalities of the Holy See.

OFFICIALS: Cardinal Egidio Vagnozzi, president; Msgr. Giovanni Angelo Abbo, secretary.

BACKGROUND: Established by Paul VI Aug. 15, 1967.

Apostolic Chamber

This office administers the temporal goods and rights of the Holy See between the death of one pope and the election of another, in accordance with special laws.

OFFICIALS: Cardinal Jean Villot, chamberlain of the Holy Roman Church; Most Rev. Vittorio Bartoccetti, vice-chamberlain.

BACKGROUND: Originated in the 11th century; reorganized by Pius XI in 1934.

Administration of Patrimony

The Administration of the Patrimony of the Apostolic See handles the estate of the Apostolic See under the direction of papal delegates acting with ordinary or extraordinary authorization.

OFFICIALS: Cardinal Jean Villot, president: Most Rev. Giuseppe Caprio, secretary.

BACKGROUND: Some of its functions date back to 1878; established by Paul VI Aug. 15, 1967.

Prefecture of Pontifical Household

This office oversees the papal chapel — which is at the service of the pope in his capacity as spiritual head of the Church — and the pontifical family — which is at the service of the pope as a sovereign. It arranges papal audiences, has charge of preparing non-liturgical elements of papal ceremonies, makes all necessary arrangements for papal visits and trips outside the Vatican, and settles questions of protocol connected with papal audiences and other formalities.

OFFICIALS: Most Rev. Jacques Martin, prefect; Msgr. Dino Monduzzi, regent.

BACKGROUND: Established by Paul VI Aug. 15, 1967, under the title, Prefecture of the Apostolic Palace; it supplanted the Sacred Congregation for Ceremonies founded by Sixtus V Jan. 22, 1588. The office was updated and reorganized under the present title by Paul VI, Mar. 28, 1968.

Central Statistics Office

The functions of this service office are to compile, systematize and analyze information on the status and condition of the Church and the needs of its pastoral ministry, from the parish level on up to the top.

The office is one of the organs of the Secretariat of State.

BACKGROUND: Established by Paul VI Aug. 15, 1967.

Eleemosynary Office

This office distributes alms and aid to the aged, sick, handicapped and other persons in need.

OFFICIAL: Most Rev. Antonio M. Travia.

BACKGROUND: The office originated as a charitable office in the time of Bl. Gregory X (1271-1276).

Vatican II Archives

The function of the office is preservation of the acts and other documents of the Second Vatican Council.

OFFICIAL: Cardinal Pericle Felici.

Personnel

This office was set up by Paul VI May 9, 1971, to handle personnel relations in the offices and other agencies of the Vatican.

OFFICIAL: Msgr. Michele Buro.

THEOLOGICAL COMMISSION

Establishment of a Theological Commission as an adjunct to the Congregation for the Doctrine of the Faith was announced by Pope Paul Apr. 28, 1969. The move had been recommended by the Second Vatican Council and was proposed by the Synod of Bishops in 1967.

The purpose of the commission is to provide the Doctrinal Congregation with the consultative and advisory services of theologians and scriptural and liturgical experts representative of various schools of thought. The international membership is restricted to 30.

Membership

The commission is headed by Cardinal Franjo Seper, prefect of the Doctrinal Congregation. Msgr. Philippe Delhaye of Belgium is secretary. Its members, all of whom were appointed by the Pope, are:

Barnabas Ahern, C.P. (U.S.); Juan Alfaro, S.J. (Spain); Catalino Arevelo, S.J. (Philippines); Hans Urs von Balthasar (Switzerland); Louis Bouyer, C.O. (France); Walter Burghardt, S.J. (U.S.); Carlo Caffara (Italy); Raniero Cantalamessa (Italy); Ives Congar, O.P. (France); Edouard Dhanis (Belgium); Wilhelm Ernst (East Germany); Olegario Gonzalez de Cardedal (Spain); Edouard Hamel, S.J. (Canada); Boguslav Inlender (Poland); Bonaventure Kloppenburg, O.F.M. (Brazil); Marie-Joseph Le Guillou, O.P. (France); Karl Lehmann (Germany); J. F. Lescrauwaet, Miss. S.C. (Holland); John Mahoney, S.J. (Great Britain); Gustave Martelet, S.J. (France); Jorge Medina Esteves (Chile); Vincent Mulago (Zaire);

Joseph Ratzinger (Germany); Georges Saber, Maronite Monk (Lebanon); Heinrich Schurmann (East Germany); Otto Semmelroth, S.J. (Germany); Anton Strle (Yugoslavia); Jean-Marie Tillard, O.P. (Canada); Cipriano Vagaggini, O.S.B. (Italy); Jan Walgrave, O.P. (Belgium).

These members were appointed to a five-year term by Pope Paul VI, Aug. 1, 1974.

Meetings

The commission met for the first time Oct. 6 to 8, 1969, for organizational purposes and the assignment of subcommissions to studies on the priesthood, the theology of hope, unity of faith and pluralism in theology, the criteria of moral knowledge, and collegiality.

Twenty-six members attending the second meeting, Oct. 5 to 10, 1970, discussed reports on the priestly ministry and collegiality. Views were exchanged about the utility of ordaining married men, but marriage was ruled out for already ordained priests wanting to continue in the ministry. With respect to collegiality, no doubt was raised about the pope's authority to act independently in the Church; the consensus, however, was that he would be prudent to engage in wide consultation before acting.

By early 1971, the commission had prepared the basis of a feasible working paper on the priesthood for the Synod of Bishops, which met for the third time in the fall. At its own meeting, held at about the same time, the commission went over some of the ground covered in synodal discussions and planned the continuation of its own work.

Pluralism in theology — concerning different ways of treating, presenting and expressing in practice the unity of faith — was the main subject under consideration at the fourth general assembly Oct. 5 to 11, 1972. The topic had been under study since the first meeting of the commission in 1969.

The October, 1973, meeting, attended by 21 members, completed work on a statement concerning apostolic succession and ordination to holy orders. The necessary sacramental sign of both, the statement said, is the imposition of hands by successors of the Apostles acting in accord with the intention of the Church.

"The Sources of Christian Moral Knowledge" was the subject of study chosen by the commission at its December, 1974, meeting in Rome. Pope Paul, addressing the commission in Latin, said he was pleased with the subject chosen for study because "no one can ignore the fact that Christian morals are under fire in their very principles." As a result, he declared, "contemporary man is disturbed. He does not know any longer what is good and what is bad, nor in which criteria he can place his trust."

COLLEGE OF CARDINALS

Cardinals are chosen by the pope to serve as his principal assistants and advisers in the central administration of church affairs. Collectively, they form the Sacred College of Cardinals.

The college evolved gradually from synods of Roman clergy with whose assistance popes directed church affairs in the first 11 centuries. The first cardinals, in about the sixth century, were priests of the leading churches of Rome who were assigned liturgical, advisory and administrative duties with the Holy See, and the regional deacons of Rome.

For all cardinals except Eastern patriarchs, membership in the college involves aggregation to the clergy of Rome. This aggregation is signified by the assignment to each cardinal, except the patriarchs, of a special or titular church in Rome.

History of the College

The Sacred College of Cardinals was not constituted in its present form and categories of membership until the 12th century, although before that time the pope had a body of advisers selected from among the bishops of dioceses neighboring Rome, priests and deacons of Rome. The college was given definite form in 1150, and in 1179 the selection of cardinals was reserved exclusively to the pope. Sixtus V fixed the number at 70, in 1586. John XXIII raised the number to 79 in 1959, to 85 in 1960 and to 87 in 1962. Paul VI increased membership to 118 in 1967, to 134 (plus two *in petto*) in 1969 and to 145 in 1973.

In 1567 the title of cardinal was reserved to members of the college; previously it had been used by priests attached to parish churches of Rome and by the leading clergy of other notable churches. The Code of Canon Law promulgated in 1918 decreed that all cardinals must be priests. Previously there had been lay cardinals (e.g., Cardinal Giacomo Antonelli, d. 1876, Secretary of State to Pius IX). John XXIII provided in the motu proprio *Cum Gravissima* Apr. 15, 1962, that all cardinals would henceforth be bishops.

Pope Paul VI placed age limits on the functions of cardinals in the apostolic letter

Ingravescentem Aetatem, dated Nov. 21, 1970, and effective as of Jan. 1, 1971. At 80, they cease to be members of curial departments and offices, and become ineligible to take part in papal elections. They retain membership in the College of Cardinals, however, with relevant rights and privileges.

Three Categories

The three categories of members of the college are cardinal bishops, cardinal priests and cardinal deacons.

Cardinal bishops include the six titular bishops of the suburban sees of Rome and two Eastern patriarchs.

First in rank are the titular bishops of the suburban sees, neighboring Rome: Ostia, Palestrina, Porto and Santa Rufina, Albano, Velletri, Frascati, Sabina and Poggio Mirteto. The dean of the college holds the title of the See of Ostia as well as his other suburban see. These cardinal bishops are engaged in full-time service in the central administration of church affairs in departments of the Roman Curia.

Four Eastern patriarchs, three of whom have since died, were made cardinal bishops by Paul VI in virtue of the motu proprio *Ad Purpuratorum Patrum* Feb. 11, 1965. Full recognition was given to their position as the heads of ancient liturgies and of sees of apostolic origin. Because of their patriarchal dignity and titles, which antedated the dignity and titles of cardinals, they were not aggregated to the Roman clergy and were not, like other cardinals, given title to Roman churches. The patriarchs were assigned rank among the cardinals in order of seniority, following the suburban titleholders. Patriarchs, at their request, were not included among the 30 new cardinals inducted into the college in 1973.

Cardinal priests, who were formerly in charge of leading churches in Rome, are bishops whose dioceses are outside Rome.

Cardinal deacons, who were formerly chosen according to regional divisions of Rome, are titular bishops assigned to full-time service in the Roman Curia.

The officers of the college are the dean and sub-dean, a chamberlain and a secretary. The dean and sub-dean are elected by the cardinal bishops, in accordance with a decree issued by Paul VI Feb. 26, 1965.

The dean of the college is Cardinal Luigi Traglia.

Selection and Duties

Cardinals are selected by the pope and are inducted into the college in a three-step process. Their nomination is announced and approved at a meeting (secret consistory) attended only by the pope and cardinals who are already members of the college; word of their election and confirmation is then communicated to the cardinals designate by means of a document called a *biglietto.* In successive and more public ceremonies, they receive the cardinalatial red biretta and ring, and concelebrate Mass with the pope and their fellow cardinals.

Cardinals under the age of 80: elect the pope when the Holy See becomes vacant (the maximum number of cardinal electors was limited to 120 by Paul VI Mar. 5, 1973); are major administrators of church affairs, serving in one or more departments of the Roman Curia. All cardinals enjoy a number of special rights and privileges. Their title, while symbolic of high honor, does not signify any extension of the powers of holy orders. They are called princes of the Church.

A **cardinal in petto** is one whose selection has been made by the pope but whose name has not been disclosed; he has no title, rights or duties until such disclosure is made, at which time he takes precedence from the time of the secret selection.

BIOGRAPHIES OF CARDINALS

Biographies of the cardinals, as of May 20, 1975, are given below in alphabetical order. For historical notes, order of seniority and geographical distribution of cardinals, see separate entries.

Alfrink, Bernard Jan: b. July 5, 1900, Nijkerk, Netherlands; ord. priest Aug. 15, 1924; professor of Sacred Scripture at Utrecht major seminary, 1933; consultor to Pontifical Biblical Commission, Rome, 1944; professor at Catholic University of Nijmegen, 1945; ord. titular archbishop of Tiana and coadjutor archbishop of Utrecht, July 17, 1951; archbishop of Utrecht, Oct. 31, 1955; cardinal Mar. 28, 1960; titular church, St. Joachim. Archbishop of Utrecht, military vicar for Netherlands, member of:

Congregations: Catholic Education, Evangelization of Peoples;

Commission: Revision of Code of Canon Law.

Antonelli, Ferdinando Giuseppe, O.F.M.: b. July 14, 1896, Subbiano, Italy; solemnly professed in Order of Friars Minor, Apr. 7, 1914; ord. priest July 25, 1922; taught church history, 1928-32, and Christian archeology, 1932-65, at Antonianum; rector magnificus of Antonianum, 1937-43, 1953-59; definitor general of Friars Minor, 1939-45; held various offices in Roman Curia; secretary of Congregation of Rites, 1965-69, and Congregation for Causes of Saints, 1969-73; ord. titular archbishop of Idicra, Mar. 19, 1966; cardinal Mar. 5, 1973; deacon, San Sebastian (on the Palatine). Member of:

Congregation: Religious and Secular Institutes.

Aponte Martinez, Luis: b. Aug. 4, 1922, Lajas, Puerto Rico; ord. priest Apr. 10, 1950; parish priest at Ponce; ord. titular bishop of Lares and auxiliary of Ponce, Oct. 12, 1960; bishop of Ponce, 1963-64; archbishop of San Juan, Nov. 4, 1964; cardinal Mar. 5, 1973;

titular church, St. Mary Mother of Providence (in Monteverde). Archbishop of San Juan, president of Puerto Rican Episcopal Conference, member of:
Congregation: Causes of Saints.
Arns, Paulo Evaristo, O.F.M.: b. Sept. 14, 1921, Forquilhinha, Brazil; ord. priest Nov. 30, 1945; held various teaching posts; director of *Sponsa Christi,* monthly review for religious, and of the Franciscan publication center in Brazil; ord. titular bishop of Respetta and auxiliary of Sao Paulo, July 3, 1966; archbishop of Sao Paulo, Oct. 22, 1970; cardinal Mar. 5, 1973; titular church, St. Anthony of Padua (in Via Tuscolana). Archbishop of Sao Paulo, member of:
Congregation: Divine Worship;
Secretariat: Non-Believers.
Baggio, Sebastiano: b. May 16, 1913, Rosa, Italy; ord. priest Dec. 21, 1935; ord. titular archbishop of Ephesus, July 26, 1953; served in Vatican diplomatic corps, 1953-69; nuncio to Chile, apostolic delegate to Canada, nuncio to Brazil; cardinal Apr. 28, 1969; archbishop of Cagliari, 1969-73; entered order of cardinal bishops as titular bishop of Velletri, Dec. 12, 1974. Prefect of Sacred Congregation for Bishops, 1973, member of:
Council for Public Affairs of Church;
Congregations: Doctrine of the Faith, Religious and Secular Institutes, Catholic Education, Evangelization of Peoples;
Commissions: Revision of Code of Canon Law, Latin America (President), Migration and Tourism (President), Sanctuaries of Pompei and Loreto;
Office: Patrimony of Holy See.
Barbieri, Antonio Maria, O.F.M. Cap.: b. Oct. 12, 1892, Montevideo, Uruguay; ord. priest Dec. 17, 1921; ord. titular archbishop of Macra and coadjutor archbishop of Montevideo, Nov. 8, 1936; founder of Catholic Action movement, major seminary in Uruguay; archbishop of Montevideo, Nov. 20, 1940; cardinal Dec. 15, 1958; titular church, St. Chrysogonus. Archbishop of Montevideo.
Bengsch, Alfred: b. Sept. 10, 1921, Berlin, Germany; called for military service while in seminary at Fulda, gravely wounded at Normandy and prisoner of Americans, 1944; resumed his studies after the war; ord. priest Apr. 2, 1950; member of faculty of seminaries at Erfurt and Neuzelle; ord. titular bishop of Tubia and auxiliary bishop of Berlin, June 11, 1959; bishop of Berlin, Aug. 16, 1961; received personal title of archbishop, Jan. 14, 1962; cardinal June 26, 1967; titular church, St. Philip Neri (in Eurosia). Archbishop of Berlin, member of:
Congregations: Religious and Secular Institutes, Divine Worship;
Commission: Revision of Code of Canon Law.
Bertoli, Paolo: b. Feb. 1, 1908, Poggio Garfagnana, Italy; ord. priest Aug. 15, 1930; ord. titular archbishop of Nicomedia May 11,

1952; served in Vatican diplomatic corps, 1952-69; apostolic delegate to Turkey, nuncio to Colombia, Lebanon and France; cardinal Apr. 28, 1969; titular church, St. Jerome. Prefect of Congregation for Causes of Saints, 1969-73. Member of:
Council for Public Affairs of Church;
Congregations: Bishops, Oriental Churches, Divine Worship, Evangelization of Peoples;
Tribunal: Apostolic Signatura;
Commission: Revision of Code of Canon Law.
Biayenda, Emile: b. 1927 at Mpangala, Congo; ord. priest Oct. 26, 1958; national chaplain of Legion of Mary; under house arrest for several months in 1964; studied in France for three years; ord. titular archbishop of Garba and coadjutor of Brazzaville, May 17, 1970; archbishop of Brazzaville, June 14, 1971; cardinal Mar. 5, 1973; titular church, San Mark (in "Agro Laurentino"). Archbishop of Brazzaville, president of Congo Episcopal Conference, member of:
Congregation: Clergy.
Brandao Vilela, Avelar: b. June 13, 1912, Vicosa, Brazil; ord. priest Oct. 27, 1935; professor and spiritual director at diocesan seminary at Aracaju; ord. bishop of Petrolina, Oct. 27, 1946; archbishop of Teresina, Nov. 5, 1955; established 20 social centers and a radio station; introduced agrarian reform of church properties; erected the Institute of Catechetics: Archbishop of Sao Salvador da Bahia, Mar. 25, 1971; president of CELAM, 1967-72; co-president of Medellin Conference, 1968; cardinal Mar. 5, 1973; titular church, Sts. Boniface and Alexius. Archbishop of Sao Salvador da Bahia, member of:
Congregations: Clergy, Causes of Saints, Catholic Education.
Bueno y Monreal, Jose Maria: b. Sept. 11, 1904, Zaragoza, Spain; ord. priest Mar. 19, 1927; ord. bishop of Jaca, Mar. 19, 1946; bishop of Vitoria, May 13, 1950; titular archbishop of Antioch in Pisidia and coadjutor archbishop of Seville, Oct. 27, 1954; archbishop of Seville, Apr. 8, 1957; cardinal Dec. 15, 1958; titular church, Sts. Vitus, Modestus and Crescentia. Archbishop of Seville, member of:
Congregation: Religious and Secular Institutes.
Caggiano, Antonio: b. Jan. 30, 1889, Coronda, Argentina; ord. priest Mar. 23, 1912; general ecclesiastical counselor of Argentine Catholic Action, 1931; military vicar, 1933; ord. bishop of Rosario, Mar. 17, 1935; cardinal Feb. 18, 1946; titular church, St. Lawrence (in Panisperna). Archbishop of Buenos Aires, Aug. 15, 1959, ordinary for Eastern Rite Catholics in Argentina without ordinaries of their own rites, military vicar of Argentina.
Carberry, John J.: b. July 31, 1904, Brooklyn, N. Y.; ord. priest July 28, 1929; ord. titu-

lar bishop of Elis and coadjutor bishop of Lafayette, Ind., July 25, 1956; bishop of Lafayette, Nov. 20, 1957; bishop of Columbus, Jan. 16, 1965; archbishop of St. Louis, Feb. 17, 1968; cardinal Apr. 28, 1969; titular church, St. John the Baptist (de Rossi). Archbishop of St. Louis, member of:
Congregation: Bishops.

Carpino, Francesco: b. May 18, 1905, Palazzolo Acreide, Italy; ord. priest Aug. 14, 1927; ord. titular archbishop of Nicomedia and coadjutor archbishop of Monreale, Apr. 8, 1951; archbishop of Monreale, 1951-61; titular archbishop of Sardica, Jan. 19, 1961; assessor of Sacred Consistorial Congregation, 1961; pro-prefect of Sacred Congregation of the Council, Apr. 7, 1967; cardinal June 26, 1967; titular church, St. Mary Auxiliatrix; archbishop of Palermo, 1967-70. Former archbishop of Palermo, referendary of the Congregation of Bishops, 1970, and member of:
Congregations: Bishops, Clergy.

Casariego, Mario, C.R.S.: b. Feb. 13, 1909, Figueras de Castropol, Spain; ord. priest July 19, 1936; ord. titular bishop of Pudenziana and auxiliary bishop of Guatemala, Dec. 27, 1958; titular archbishop of Perge and coadjutor archbishop of Guatemala, Nov. 12, 1963; archbishop of Guatemala, Dec. 12, 1964; cardinal Apr. 28, 1969; titular church, St. Mary in Aquiro. Archbishop of Guatemala, member of:

Congregation: Causes of Saints.

Cerejeira, Manuel Goncalves: b. Nov. 29, 1888, Lousado,Portugal; ord. priest Apr. 1, 1911; ord. titular archbishop of Mytilene and auxiliary archbishop of Lisbon, June 17, 1928; patriarch of Lisbon, 1929-71; cardinal Dec. 16, 1929; titular church, Sts. Marcellus and Peter. Former patriarch of Lisbon.

Cody, John P.: b. Dec. 24, 1907, St. Louis, Mo.; ord. priest Dec. 8, 1931, Rome, Italy; served in Rome, 1932-38; ord. titular bishop of Apollonia and auxiliary bishop of St. Louis, July 2, 1947; coadjutor bishop of St. Joseph, Mo., Jan. 27, 1954; apostolic administrator of St. Joseph, May 9, 1955; coadjutor bishop of Kansas City-St. Joseph, Aug. 29, 1956; bishop of Kansas City-St. Joseph, 1956-61; titular archbishop of Bostra and coadjutor archbishop of New Orleans, Aug. 10, 1961; apostolic administrator of New Orleans, June 1, 1962; archbishop of New Orleans, Nov. 8, 1964; archbishop of Chicago, June 14, 1965; cardinal June 26, 1967; titular church, St. Cecilia. Archbishop of Chicago, member of:
Congregations: Clergy, Evangelization of Peoples, Divine Worship;
Office: Prefecture of Economic Affairs.

Colombo, Giovanni: b. Dec. 6, 1902, Caronno, Italy; ord. priest May 29, 1926; rector of Milan Seminary, 1953; ord. titular bishop of Filippopoli and auxiliary bishop of Milan, Dec. 7, 1960; archbishop of Milan, Aug. 10,

1963; cardinal Feb. 22, 1965; titular church, Sts. Sylvester and Martin (in Montibus). Archbishop of Milan, member of:
Congregations: Discipline of Sacraments, Catholic Education;
Commission: Revision of Code of Canon Law.

Concha, Luis: b. Nov. 7, 1891, Bogota, Colombia; ord. priest Oct. 28, 1916; ord. bishop of Manizales, Nov. 30, 1935; first archbishop of Manizales, May 10, 1954; archbishop of Bogota, 1959-72; cardinal Jan. 16, 1961; titular church, St. Mary (Nuova). Former archbishop of Bogota, military vicar of Colombia.

Confalonieri, Carlo: b. July 25, 1893, Seveso, Italy; ord. priest Mar. 18, 1916; private secretary to Pius XI for 17 years, to Pius XII for two years; ord. archbishop of L'Aquila, May 4, 1941; transferred to titular archbishopric of Nicopoli al Nesto, Feb. 22, 1950; cardinal Dec. 15, 1958; entered order of cardinal bishops as titular bishop of Palestrina, Mar. 14, 1972; prefect of Sacred Congregation for Bishops, 1967-73. Archpriest of Patriarchal Liberian Basilica, sub-dean of College of Cardinals (1974).

Conway, William: b. Jan. 22, 1913, Belfast, Ireland; ord. priest June 20, 1937; ord. titular bishop of Neve and auxiliary bishop of Armagh, July 27, 1958; archbishop of Armagh and primate of all Ireland, Sept. 9, 1963; cardinal Feb. 22, 1965; titular church, St. Patrick. Archbishop of Armagh, member of:
Congregations: Bishops, Clergy, Evangelization of Peoples, Catholic Education;
Commission: Revision of Code of Canon Law.

Cooke, Terence J.: b. Mar. 1, 1921, New York, N. Y.; ord. priest Dec. 1, 1945; ord. titular bishop of Summa and auxiliary bishop of New York, Dec. 13, 1965; archbishop of New York, Mar. 2, 1968; military vicar for the U.S.; cardinal Apr. 28, 1969; titular church, Sts. John and Paul. Archbishop of New York, member of:
Congregations: Bishops, Oriental Churches;
Commission: Migration and Tourism.

Cooray, Thomas B., O. M. I.: b. Dec. 28, 1901, Periyamulla Negombo, Ceylon; ord. priest June 23, 1929; ord. titular archbishop of Preslavo, Mar. 7, 1946; coadjutor archbishop of Colombo, Ceylon, 1946-47; succeeded as archbishop of Colombo, July 26, 1947; cardinal Feb. 22, 1965; titular church, Sts. Nereus and Achilleus. Archbishop of Colombo, Ceylon (Sri Lanka), member of:
Commission: Revision of Code of Canon Law.

Cordeiro, Joseph: b. Jan. 19, 1918, Bombay, India; ord. priest Aug. 24, 1946; served in educational and other diocesan posts at Karachi, Pakistan; ord. archbishop of Karachi, Aug. 24, 1958, the first native-born prelate in that see; cardinal Mar. 5, 1973; titular church, St. Andrew Apostle ("de Hortis").

Archbishop of Karachi, member of council of general secretariat of Synod of Bishops and member of:
Congregation: Evangelization of Peoples;
Commission: Pontifical Council *Cor Unum.*

Da Costa Nunes, Jose: b. Mar. 15, 1880, Azores; ord. priest July 26, 1903; ord. bishop Nov. 20, 1921; bishop of Macao, 1921-40; archbishop of Goa, primate of the East and patriarch of the East Indies, 1940-53; titular archbishop of Odessus with personal title of patriarch, Dec. 16, 1953; vice-camerlengo of the Holy Roman Church, 1953-62; cardinal Mar. 19, 1962; titular church, St. Prisca.

Darmojuwono, Justin: b. Nov. 2, 1914, Godean, Indonesia; ord. priest May 25, 1947; ord. archbishop of Semarang, Apr. 6, 1964; cardinal June 26, 1967; titular church, Most Holy Names of Jesus and Mary. Archbishop of Semarang, military vicar of Indonesia, member of:
Congregation: Divine Worship;
Secretariat: Non-Christians.

De Araujo Sales, Eugenio: b. Nov. 8, 1920, Acari, Brazil; ord. priest Nov. 21, 1943; ord. titular bishop of Tibica and auxiliary bishop of Natal, Aug. 15, 1954; archbishop of Sao Salvador, 1968-71; cardinal Apr. 28, 1969; titular church, St. Gregory VII. Archbishop of Rio de Janeiro (1971), ordinary for Eastern Rite Catholics in Brazil without ordinaries of their own rites, member of:
Congregations: Bishops, Clergy;
Commission: Social Communications.

Dearden, John F.: b. Oct. 15, 1907, Valley Falls, R. I.; ord. priest Dec. 8, 1932; ord. titular bishop of Sarepta and coadjutor bishop of Pittsburgh, May 18, 1948; bishop of Pittsburgh, Dec. 22, 1950; archbishop of Detroit, Dec. 18, 1958; first president of the National Conference of Catholic Bishops and the United States Catholic Conference, 1966-71; cardinal Apr. 28, 1969; titular church, St. Pius X (alla Balduina). Archbishop of Detroit, member of:
Congregations: Discipline of the Sacraments, Divine Worship;
Secretariat: Non-Christians.

De Furstenberg, Maximilien: b. Oct. 23, 1904, Heerlen, Netherlands; ord. priest Aug. 9, 1931; ord. titular archbishop of Palto and apostolic delegate to Japan, Apr. 25, 1949; internuncio, 1952, when Japan established diplomatic relations with the Vatican; apostolic delegate to Australia, New Zealand and Oceania, Feb. 11, 1960; nuncio to Portugal, 1962-67; cardinal June 26, 1967; titular church, Most Sacred Heart of Jesus (a Castro Pretorio); prefect of the Congregation for the Oriental Churches, 1969-73. Grand Master of Equestrian Order of Holy Sepulchre of Jerusalem, member of:
Council for Public Affairs of Church;
Congregations: Bishops, Religious and Secular Institutes, Evangelization of Peoples;

Commissions: Revision of Code of Canon Law, Revision of Oriental Code of Canon Law, Interpretation of Decrees of Vatican II, State of Vatican City, Institute for Works of Religion.

di Jorio, Alberto: b. July 18, 1884, Rome, Italy; ord. priest Apr. 18, 1908; regent of College of Cardinals, 1948; secretary of the 1958 conclave; cardinal Dec. 15, 1958; titular church, St. Pudentiana; ord. titular archbishop of Castra Nova, Apr. 19, 1962.

Doepfner, Julius: b. Aug. 26, 1913, Hausen, Germany; ord. priest Oct. 29, 1939; ord. bishop of Wuerzburg, Oct. 14, 1948; bishop of Berlin, Jan. 15, 1957; cardinal Dec. 15, 1958; titular church, St. Mary (della Scala). Archbishop of Munich and Freising (1961), member of:
Congregations: Oriental Churches, Clergy, Catholic Education, Evangelization of Peoples;
Commission: Revision of Code of Canon Law.

Duval, Leon-Etienne: b. Nov. 9, 1903, Chenex, France; ord. priest Dec. 18, 1926; ord. bishop of Constantine, Algeria, Feb. 11, 1947; archbishop of Algiers, Feb. 3, 1954; cardinal Feb. 22, 1965; titular church, St. Balbina. Archbishop of Algiers, member of:
Congregations: Discipline of Sacraments, Evangelization of Peoples;
Secretariat: Non-Christians;
Commissions: Revision of Code of Canon Law, Pontifical Council *Cor Unum.*

Enrique y Tarancon, Vicente: b. May 14, 1907, Burriana, Spain; ord. priest Nov. 1, 1929; ord. bishop of Solsona, Mar. 24, 1946; bishop of Oviedo, Apr. 12, 1964; archbishop of Toledo, 1969-71; cardinal Apr. 28, 1969; titular church, St. John Chrysostom. Archbishop of Madrid (1971), member of:
Congregation: Bishops;
Commission: Revision of Code of Canon Law.

Felici, Pericle: b. Aug. 1, 1911, Segni, Italy; ord. priest Oct. 28, 1933; rector of Pontifical Roman Seminary for Legal Studies, 1938-48; judge of Roman Rota, 1947; served on antepreparatory commissions of the Second Vatican Council; ord. titular archbishop of Samosata, Oct. 28, 1960; secretary-general of the Second Vatican Council; accompanied Pope Paul VI on his trip to the UN, Oct. 4, 1965; cardinal June 26, 1967; deacon, St. Apollinare. Member of:
Council for Public Affairs of Church;
Congregations: Doctrine of Faith, Bishops, Discipline of Sacraments, Causes of Saints;
Offices: Administration of Patrimony of Holy See, Vatican II Archives;
Commissions: Revision of Code of Canon Law (President), Revision of Oriental Code of Canon Law, Interpretation of Decrees of Vatican II (President).

Flahiff, George B., C.S.B.: b. Oct. 26, 1905, Paris, Ont., Canada; ord. priest Aug. 17,

1930; professor of medieval history at the University of Toronto and Pontifical Institute of Medieval Studies in Toronto, 1934-54; superior general of Basilian Fathers, 1954; ord. archbishop of Winnipeg, May 31, 1961; president of Canadian Conference of Bishops, 1963-65; cardinal Apr. 28, 1969; titular church, St. Mary della Salute (Primavalle). Archbishop of Winnipeg, member of:
Congregations: Religious and Secular Institutes, Catholic Education.

Florit, Ermenegildo: b. July 5, 1901, Fagagna, Italy; ord. priest Apr. 11, 1925; taught Sacred Scripture at Lateran University from 1929; pro-rector of Lateran University and Institute of Civil and Canon Law, 1951-54; ord. titular archbishop of Hieropolis and coadjutor archbishop of Florence, Sept. 12, 1954; archbishop of Florence, Mar. 19, 1962; cardinal Feb. 22, 1965; titular church, Queen of the Apostles. Archbishop of Florence, member of:
Congregation: Causes of Saints;
Commission: Revision of Code of Canon Law.

Forni, Efrem: b. Jan. 10, 1889, Milan, Italy; ord. priest July 6, 1913; served in Vatican diplomatic service in Portugal and France, 1921-37; ord. titular archbishop of Darnis, Feb. 20, 1938; nuncio to Ecuador, 1937-53; nuncio to Belgium, 1953-62; cardinal Mar. 19, 1962; titular church, Holy Cross in Jerusalem. Member of:
Council for Public Affairs of Church;
Congregations: Bishops, Causes of Saints.

Freeman, James D.: b. Nov. 19, 1907, Sydney, Australia; ord. priest July 13, 1940; ord. titular bishop of Ermopoli minore and auxiliary of Sydney, Jan. 27, 1957; bishop of Armidale, 1968-71; archbishop of Sydney, July 9, 1971; cardinal Mar. 5, 1973; titular church, St. Mary Queen of Peace. Archbishop of Sydney.

Frings, Josef: b. Feb. 6, 1887, Neuss, Germany; ord. priest Aug. 10, 1910; ord. archbishop June 21, 1942; archbishop of Cologne, 1942-69; cardinal Feb. 18, 1946; titular church, St. John (a Porta Latina). Former archbishop of Cologne.

Garrone, Gabriel-Marie: b. Oct. 12, 1901, Aix-les-Bains, France; ord. priest Apr. 11, 1925; captain during World War II, cited for bravery, taken prisoner; rector of major seminary of Chambery, 1947; ord. titular archbishop of Lemno and coadjutor of Toulouse, June 24, 1947; archbishop of Toulouse, 1956-66; pro-prefect of Congregation of Seminaries and Universities, Mar. 24, 1966; cardinal June 26, 1967; titular church, St. Sabina. Prefect of Congregation for Catholic Education, grand chancellor of the Pontifical Gregorian University, member of:
Council for Public Affairs of Church;
Congregations: Doctrine of Faith, Oriental Churches, Bishops, Evangelization of Peoples, Causes of Saints, Religious and Secular Institutes;
Commission: Revision of Code of Canon Law.

Gilroy, Norman Thomas: b. Jan. 22, 1896, Sydney, Australia; ord. priest Dec. 24, 1923; ord. bishop of Port Augusta, Mar. 17, 1935; titular archbishop of Cipsela and coadjutor archbishop of Sydney, July 1, 1937; archbishop of Sydney, 1940-71; cardinal Feb. 18, 1946; titular church, Four Crowned Martyrs. Former archbishop of Sydney, member of:
Commission: Revision of Code of Canon Law.

Gonzalez Martin, Marcelo: b. Jan. 16, 1918, Villanubla, Spain; ord. priest June 29, 1941; taught theology and sociology at Valladolid diocesan seminary; founded organization for construction of houses for poor; ord. bishop of Astorga, Mar. 5, 1961; titular archbishop of Case Mediane and coadjutor of Barcelona, Feb. 21, 1966; archbishop of Barcelona, 1967-71; archbishop of Toledo, Dec. 3, 1971; cardinal Mar. 5, 1973; titular church, Sant'Augustine. Archbishop of Toledo, member of:
Congregation: Evangelization of Peoples.

Gouyon, Paul: b. Oct. 24, 1910, Bordeaux, France; ord. priest Mar. 13, 1937; ord. bishop of Bayonne, Oct. 7, 1957; titular archbishop of Pessinonte and coadjutor archbishop of Rennes, Sept. 6, 1963; archbishop of Rennes, Sept. 4, 1964; cardinal Apr. 28, 1969; titular church, the Nativity (Via Gallia). Archbishop of Rennes, member of:
Secretariats: Christian Unity, Non-Believers;
Commission: Social Communications.

Gracias, Valerian: b. Oct. 23, 1900, Karachi, Pakistan; ord. priest Oct. 3, 1926; ord. titular bishop of Thennesus and auxiliary bishop of Bombay, June 29, 1946; archbishop of Bombay, Dec. 1, 1950; cardinal Jan. 12, 1953; titular church, St. Mary (in Via Lata). Archbishop of Bombay, member of:
Congregation: Discipline of Sacraments;
Secretariat: Non-Christians;
Commission: Revision of Code of Canon Law.

Grano, Carlo: b. Oct. 14, 1887, Rome, Italy; ord. priest July 14, 1912; master of pontifical ceremonies for 26 years; ord. titular archbishop of Thessalonica, Dec. 27, 1958, by Pope John XXIII; nuncio to Italy, 1958-67; cardinal June 26, 1967; titular church, St. Marcellus. Member of:
Council for Public Affairs of Church;
Congregation: Causes of Saints.

Gray, Gordon J.: b. Aug. 10, 1910, Edinburgh, Scotland; ord. priest June 15, 1935; ord. archbishop of Saint Andrews and Edinburgh, Sept. 21, 1951; chairman of International Committee for English in the Liturgy; cardinal Apr. 28, 1969; titular church, St. Clare. Archbishop of Saint Andrews and Edinburgh, member of:

Congregations: Evangelization of Peoples, Divine Worship;
Commission: Social Communications.

Guerri, Sergio: b. Dec. 25, 1905, Tarquinia, Italy; ord. priest Mar. 30, 1929; ord. titular archbishop of Trevi, Apr. 27, 1969; cardinal Apr. 28, 1969; deacon, Holy Name of Mary. Pro-president of Pontifical Commission for State of Vatican City, member of:
Congregations: Oriental Churches, Evangelization of Peoples;
Commission: Social Communications.

Guyot, Louis J.: b. July 7, 1905, Bordeaux, France; ord. priest June 29, 1932; held various offices in Bordeaux diocese; ord. titular bishop of Helenopolis and coadjutor of Constance, May 4, 1949; bishop of Constance, 1950-66; archbishop of Toulouse, Apr. 28, 1966; invested with Legion of Honor by French government; cardinal Mar. 5, 1973; titular church, Saint Agnes Outside the Walls. Archbishop of Toulouse, member of:
Congregations: Clergy; Catholic Education.

Heenan, John: b. Jan. 26, 1905, Ilford, England; ord. priest July 6, 1930; ord. bishop of Leeds, Mar. 12, 1951; archbishop of Liverpool, May 2, 1957; archbishop of Westminster, Sept. 2, 1963; cardinal Feb. 22, 1965; titular church, St. Sylvester (in Capite). Archbishop of Westminster, member of:
Congregation: Bishops;
Commission: Revision of Canon Law.

Hoeffner, Joseph: b. Dec. 24, 1906, Horhausen, Germany; ord. priest Oct. 30, 1932; ord. bishop of Munster, Sept. 14, 1962; titular archbishop of Aquileia and coadjutor archbishop of Cologne, Jan. 6, 1969; archbishop of Cologne, Feb. 24, 1969; cardinal Apr. 28, 1969; titular church, St. Andrew of the Valley. Archbishop of Cologne, member of:
Congregations: Religious and Secular Institutes, Catholic Education;
Secretariat: Non-Believers;
Office: Prefecture of Economic Affairs.

Jubany Arnau, Narciso: b. Aug. 12, 1913, Santa Coloma de Farnes, Spain; ord. priest July 30, 1939; professor of law at Barcelona seminary; served on ecclesiastical tribunal; ord. titular bishop of Ortosia and auxiliary of Barcelona, Jan. 22, 1956; bishop of Gerona, 1964-71; archbishop of Barcelona, 1971; cardinal Mar. 5, 1973; titular church, San Lorenzo (in Damaso). Archbishop of Barcelona, member of:
Congregation: Divine Worship;
Commission: Revision of Code of Canon Law.

Kim, Stephan Sou Hwan: b. May 8, 1922, Tae Gu, Korea; ord. priest Oct. 27, 1947; ord. bishop of Masan, May 31, 1966; archbishop of Seoul, Apr. 9, 1968; cardinal Apr. 28, 1969; titular church, St. Felix of Cantalice (Centocelle). Archbishop of Seoul, member of:
Congregation: Evangelization of Peoples;
Secretariat: Non-Christians.

Knox, James R.: b. Mar. 2, 1914, Bayswater, Australia; ord. priest Dec. 22, 1941 at Rome; forced to remain in Rome because of World War II; chaplain and later vice rector of Pontifical Urban University; secretary of apostolic delegation in Japan; ord. titular archbishop of Melitene, Nov. 8, 1953; apostolic delegate to British Africa, 1953-57; internuncio to India and apostolic delegate to Burma and Ceylon (Sri Lanka), 1957-67; archbishop of Melbourne, Australia, 1967-74; cardinal Mar. 5, 1973; titular church, Santa Maria (in Vallicella). Prefect of Sacred Congregation for Discipline of Sacraments and Divine Worship, member of:
Council for Public Affairs of Church;
Congregations: Bishops, Oriental Churches, Evangelization of Peoples, Catholic Education;
Commissions: Revision of Code of Canon Law, Revision of Oriental Code of Canon Law.

Koenig, Franz: b. Aug. 3, 1905, Rabenstein, Lower Austria; ord. priest Oct. 28, 1933; ord. titular bishop of Livias and coadjutor bishop of Sankt Poelten, Aug. 31, 1952; archbishop of Vienna, May 10, 1956; cardinal Dec. 15, 1958; titular church, St. Eusebius. Archbishop of Vienna, ordinary for faithful of Byzantine Rite living in Austria, president of Secretariat for Non-Believers, member of:
Congregations: Bishops, Evangelization of Peoples;
Commission: Revision of Code of Canon Law.

Krol, John J.: b. Oct. 26, 1910, Cleveland, Ohio; ord. priest Feb. 20, 1937; ord. titular bishop of Cadi and auxiliary bishop of Cleveland, Sept. 2, 1953; archbishop of Philadelphia, Feb. 11, 1961, installed Mar. 22, 1961; cardinal June 26, 1967; titular church, St. Mary (della Merced) and St. Adrian Martyr; vice-president, 1966-72, and president, 1972-74, of NCCB/USCC. Archbishop of Philadelphia, member of:
Congregations: Doctrine of the Faith, Oriental Churches;
Commission: Revision of Code of Canon Law.

Landazuri Ricketts, Juan, O. F. M: b. Dec. 19, 1913, Arequipa, Peru; entered Franciscans, 1933; ord. priest Apr. 16, 1939; ord. titular archbishop of Roina and coadjutor archbishop of Lima, Aug. 24, 1952; archbishop of Lima, May 2, 1955; cardinal Mar. 19, 1962; titular church, St. Mary (in Aracoeli). Archbishop of Lima, member of:
Congregations: Discipline of Sacraments, Clergy, Religious and Secular Institutes;
Commission: Revision of Code of Canon Law.

Leger, Paul Emile, S.S.: b. Apr. 26, 1904, Valleyfield, Quebec, Canada; ord. priest May 25, 1929; rector Canadian College, Rome, 1947; ord. archbishop of Montreal, Apr. 26, 1950; cardinal Jan. 12, 1953; titular church,

St. Mary (of the Angels); resigned as archbishop of Montreal in 1967 to become missionary to lepers. Member of:

Congregations: Discipline of Sacraments, Evangelization of Peoples;

Commissions: Revision of Code of Canon Law, Migration and Tourism.

Lercaro, Giacomo: b. Oct. 28, 1891, Quinto al Mare, Italy; ord. priest July 25, 1914; ord. archbishop of Ravenna, Mar. 19, 1947; archbishop of Bologna, 1952-68; cardinal Jan. 12, 1953; titular church, St. Mary (in Traspontina). Former archbishop of Bologna.

Luciani, Albino: b. Oct. 17, 1912, Forno di Canale, Italy; ord. priest July 7, 1935; taught dogmatic and moral theology at Gregorian Seminary at Belluno; ord. bishop of Vittorio Veneto, Dec. 27, 1958; patriarch of Venice, Dec. 15, 1969; cardinal Mar. 5, 1973; titular church, San Marco (at Piazza Venezia). Patriarch of Venice, member of:

Congregation: Divine Worship.

McCann, Owen: b. June 29, 1907, Woodstock, South Africa; ord. priest Dec. 21, 1935; ord. titular bishop of Stettorio and vicar apostolic of Cape Town, May 18, 1950; first archbishop of Cape Town, Jan. 11, 1951; opponent of apartheid policy; cardinal Feb. 22, 1965; titular church, St. Praxedes. Archbishop of Cape Town, member of:

Congregation: Evangelization of Peoples.

McIntyre, James Francis: b. June 25, 1886, New York, N. Y.; ord. priest May 21, 1921; ord. titular bishop of Cirene and auxiliary bishop of New York, Jan. 8, 1941; titular archbishop of Palto and coadjutor archbishop of New York, July 20, 1946; archbishop of Los Angeles, 1948-70; cardinal Jan. 12, 1953; titular church, St. Anastasia. Former archbishop of Los Angeles.

Malula, Joseph: b. Dec. 12, 1917, Kinshasa, Zaire; ord. priest June 9, 1946; ord. titular bishop of Attanaso and auxiliary bishop of Kinshasa, Sept. 20, 1959; archbishop of Kinshasa. July 7, 1964; cardinal Apr. 28, 1969; titular church, the Protomartyrs (via Aurelia Antica). Archbishop of Kinshasa, member of:

Congregation: Evangelization of Peoples;

Secretariat: Non-Christians.

Manning, Timothy: b. Nov. 15, 1909, Ballingeary, Ireland; completed studies for the priesthood at St. Patrick's Seminary, Menlo Park, Calif.; ord. priest June 16, 1934; became American citizen Jan. 14, 1944; ord. titular bishop of Lesvi and auxiliary of Los Angeles, Oct. 15, 1946; first bishop of Fresno, 1967-69; titular archbishop of Capri and coadjutor of Los Angeles, May 26, 1969; archbishop of Los Angeles, Jan. 21, 1970; cardinal Mar. 5, 1973; titular church, Santa Lucia. Archbishop of Los Angeles, member of:

Congregation: Religious and Secular Institutes.

Marella, Paolo: b. Jan. 25, 1895, Rome, Italy; ord. priest Feb. 23, 1918; aide in Congregation for Propagation of the Faith; on staff of apostolic delegation, Washington, D. C., 1923-33; ord. titular archbishop of Doclea, Oct. 29, 1933; apostolic delegate to Japan, 1933-48, to Australia, New Zealand and Oceania, 1948-53; nuncio to France, 1953-59; cardinal Dec. 14, 1959; entered order of cardinal bishops as titular bishop of Porto and Santa Rufina, Mar. 14, 1972; president of Secretariat for Non-Christians, 1967-73. Archpriest of St. Peter's Basilica, member of:

Council for Public Affairsj1 of Church;

Congregations: Bishops, Evangelization of Peoples;

Tribunal: Apostolic Signatura;

Commissions: Revision of Code of Canon Law, Sacred Art in Italy (Honorary President).

Martin, Joseph: b. Aug. 9. 1891, Orleans, France; ord. priest Dec. 18, 1920; chief military chaplain of French Army's 35th Division, 1939-40; ord. bishop of Le Puy-en-Velay, Apr. 2, 1940; archbishop of Rouen, 1948-68; cardinal Feb. 22, 1965; titular church, St. Teresa, Virgin. Former archbishop of Rouen.

Marty, Francois: b. May 18, 1904, Pachins, France; ord. priest June 28, 1930; ord. bishop of Saint-Flour, May 1, 1952; titular archbishop of Emesa and coadjutor archbishop of Rheims, Dec. 14, 1959; archbishop of Rheims, May 9, 1960; archbishop of Paris, Mar. 26, 1968; cardinal Apr. 28, 1969; titular church, St. Louis of France. Archbishop of Paris, ordinary for Eastern Rite Catholics in France without ordinaries of their own rites, member of:

Congregations: Oriental Churches, Clergy, Divine Worship;

Commission: Revision of Code of Canon Law.

Maurer, Jose Clemente, C.SS.R.: b. Mar. 13, 1900, Puttlingen, Germany; ord. priest Sept. 19, 1925; assigned to Bolivian missions, 1926; became a Bolivian citizen; ord. titular bishop of Cea and auxiliary bishop of La Paz, Apr. 16, 1950; archbishop of Sucre, Oct. 27, 1951; cardinal June 26, 1967; titular church, Most Holy Redeemer and St. Alphonsus. Archbishop of Sucre.

Medeiros, Humberto: b. Oct. 6, 1915, Arrifes, S. Miguel, Azores; came to U.S. at age of 15; became American citizen, 1940; ord. priest June 15, 1946; ord. bishop of Brownsville, Tex., June 9, 1966; archbishop of Boston, Sept. 8, 1970; cardinal Mar. 5, 1973; titular church, Santa Susanna. Archbishop of Boston, member of:

Congregations: Bishops, Catholic Education.

Miranda y Gomez, Miguel Dario: b. Dec. 19, 1895, Leon, Mexico; ord. priest Oct. 28, 1918; ord. bishop of Tulancingo, Dec. 8, 1937; titular archbishop of Selimbra and coadjutor archbishop of Mexico City, Dec. 20, 1955; archbishop of Mexico City, June 28, 1956; president of the Latin American Bish-

ops' Council (CELAM), 1960; cardinal Apr. 28, 1969; titular church, St. Mary of Guadalupe (Montemario). Archbishop of Mexico City, member of:
Congregation: Discipline of Sacraments.

Motta, Carlos Carmelo de Vasconcellos: b. July 16, 1890, Bom Jesus do Amparo, Brazil; ord. priest June 29, 1918; ord. titular bishop of Algiza and auxiliary bishop of Diamantina, Oct. 30, 1932; archbishop of Sao Luis do Maranhao, Dec. 19, 1935; archbishop of Sao Paulo del Brasile, 1944-64; cardinal Feb. 18, 1946; titular church, St. Pancratius. Archbishop of Aparecida (1964).

Mozzoni, Umberto: b. June 29, 1904, Buenos Aires, Argentina; holds Italian citizenship; ord. priest Aug. 14, 1927; professor of theology and canon law at Macerata seminary, Italy; served on Vatican diplomatic staff at Ottawa, London and Lisbon; ord. titular archbishop of Side, Dec. 5, 1954; nuncio to Bolivia, 1954-58, Argentina, 1958-69, Brazil, 1969-73; cardinal Mar. 5, 1973; deacon, St. Eugene. Member of:
Congregations: Oriental Churches, Clergy, Religious and Secular Institutes, Causes of Saints;
Tribunal: Apostolic Signatura;
Commissions: Sanctuaries of Pompei and Loreto (President), Institute for Works of Religion.

Munoz Duque, Anibal: b. Oct. 3, 1908, Santa Rosa de Osos, Colombia; ord. priest Nov. 19, 1933; ord. bishop of Soccoro y San Gil, May 27, 1951; bishop of Bucaramango, 1952-59; bishop of Nueva Pamplona, 1959-68; titular archbishop of Cariana and coadjutor archbishop of Bogota, 1968; archbishop of Bogota, July 29, 1972; cardinal Mar. 5, 1973; titular church, St. Bartholomew. Archbishop of Bogota, military vicar, member of:
Congregation: Discipline of Sacraments.

Munoz Vega, Paolo, S. J.: b. May 23, 1903, Mira, Ecuador; ord. priest July 25, 1933; ord. titular bishop of Ceramo and auxiliary bishop of Quito, Mar. 19, 1964; archbishop of Quito, June 23, 1967; cardinal Apr. 28, 1969; titular church, St. Robert Bellarmine. Archbishop of Quito, member of:
Congregation: Religious and Secular Institutes.

Nasalli Rocca di Corneliano, Mario: b. Aug. 12, 1903, Piacenza, Italy; ord. priest Apr. 9, 1927; ord. titular archbishop of Anzio, Apr. 20, 1969; cardinal Apr. 28, 1969; deacon, St. John the Baptist. Member of:
Congregations: Discipline of Sacraments, Causes of Saints;
Secretariat: Non-Believers.

O'Boyle, Patrick A.: b. July 18, 1896, Scranton, Pa.; ord. priest May 21, 1921; executive director of War Relief Services, NCWC, 1943; ord. archbishop of Washington, Jan. 14, 1948 (retired, 1973); cardinal June 26, 1967; titular church, St. Nicholas (in Carcere). Former archbishop of Washington.

Oddi, Silvio: b. Nov. 14, 1910, Morfasso, Italy; ord. priest May 21, 1933; ord. titular archbishop of Mesembria, Sept. 27, 1953; served in Vatican diplomatic corps, 1953-69; apostolic delegate to Jerusalem, Palestine, Jordan and Cyprus, internuncio to the United Arab Republic, and nuncio to Belgium and Luxembourg; cardinal Apr. 28, 1969; deacon, St. Agatha of the Goths. Member of:
Council for Public Affairs of Church;
Congregations: Bishops, Oriental Churches, Causes of Saints;
Tribunal: Apostolic Signatura;
Commission: State of Vatican City.

Ottaviani, Alfredo: b. Oct. 29, 1890, Rome, Italy; ord. priest Mar. 18, 1916; undersecretary of Congregation for Extraordinary Ecclesiastical Affairs, 1928; substitute secretary of state, 1929; assessor of Sacred Congregation of the Holy Office, 1935-52; prefect of Congregation of Holy Office (now Doctrine of Faith), 1952-68; cardinal Jan. 12, 1953; ord. titular archbishop of Berrea, Apr. 19, 1962; titular church, St. Mary (in Domnica). Prefect emeritus of the Congregation for the Doctrine of the Faith, member of:
Council for Public Affairs of Church;
Congregations: Doctrine of Faith, Bishops;
Commission: Revision of Code of Canon Law.

Otunga, Maurice: b. January, 1923, Chebukwa, Kenya; son of pagan tribal chief; baptized 1935, at age of 12; ord. priest Oct. 3, 1950, at Rome; taught at Kisumu major seminary for three years; attaché in apostolic delegation at Mombasa, 1953-56; ord. titular bishop of Tacape and auxiliary of Kisumu, Feb. 25, 1957; bishop of Kisii, 1960-69; titular archbishop of Bomarzo and coadjutor of Nairobi, Nov. 15, 1969; archbishop of Nairobi, Oct. 24, 1971; cardinal Mar. 5, 1973; titular church, St. Gregory Barbarigo. Archbishop of Nairobi, member of:
Congregations: Discipline of Sacraments, Divine Worship.

Palazzini, Pietro: b. May 19, 1912, Piobbico, Pesaro, Italy; ord. priest Dec. 6, 1934; assistant vice-rector of Pontifical Major Roman Seminary and vice-rector and bursar of Pontifical Roman Seminary for Juridical Studies; professor of moral theology at Lateran University; held various offices in Roman Curia; secretary of Congregation of Council (now Clergy), 1958-73; ord. titular archbishop of Caesarea in Cappadocia, Sept. 21, 1962; author of numerous works on moral theology and law; cardinal Mar. 5, 1973; deacon, St. Jerome. Member of:
Congregations: Discipline of Sacraments, Oriental Churches;
Tribunal: Apostolic Signatura;
Commissions: Revision of Code of Canon Law, Interpretation of Decrees of Vatican II.

Pappalardo, Salvatore: b. Sept. 23, 1918, Villafranca Sicula, Sicily; ord. priest Apr. 12, 1941; entered diplomatic service of secretariat of state, 1947; ord. titular archbishop of Miletus, Jan. 16, 1966; pro-nuncio in Indonesia, 1959-69; president of Pontifical Ecclesiastical Academy, 1969-70; archbishop of Palermo, Oct. 17, 1970; cardinal Mar. 5, 1973; titular church, St. Mary Odigitria of the Sicilians. Archbishop of Palermo, member of:

Congregation: Oriental Churches.

Parecattil, Joseph: b. Apr. 1, 1912, Kidangoor, India; ord. priest Aug. 24, 1939; ord. titular bishop of Aretusa for Syrians and auxiliary bishop of Ernakulam, Nov. 30, 1953; archbishop of Ernakulam (Chaldean-Malabar Rite), July 20, 1956; vice-president of the Indian Bishops' Conference, 1966; appointed one of seven members of Pope Paul VI's advisory council for Eastern Rite churches, 1968; cardinal Apr. 28, 1969; titular church, Our Lady Queen of Peace. Archbishop of Ernakulam of the Chaldean-Malabar Rite, member of:

Congregation: Oriental Churches;

Secretariat: Christian Unity;

Commissions: Revision of Code of Canon Law, Revision of Oriental Code of Canon Law (President).

Parente, Pietro: b. Feb. 16, 1891, Casalnuovo, Italy; ord. priest Mar. 18, 1916; director of Archiepiscopal Seminary at Naples, 1916-26; rector of Pontifical Urban College of Propagation of the Faith, 1934-38; Consultor of the Congregations of the Holy Office, Council, Propagation of the Faith, and Seminaries and Universities; ord. archbishop of Perugia, Oct. 23, 1955; titular archbishop of Tolemaide di Tebaide, Oct. 23, 1959; assessor of Congregation of Holy Office (now Doctrinal Congregation), 1959; cardinal June 26, 1967; titular church, St. Lawrence (in Lucina).

Paupini, Giuseppe: b. Feb. 25, 1907, Mondavio, Italy; ord. priest Mar. 19, 1930; ord. titular archbishop of Sebastopolis in Abasgia, Feb. 26, 1956; served in Vatican diplomatic corps, 1956-69; internuncio to Iran, 1956-57; nuncio to Guatemala and El Salvador, 1957-58, nuncio to Colombia, 1959-69; cardinal Apr. 28, 1969; deacon, All Saints Church. Major penitentiary 1973, member of:

Council for Public Affairs of Church;

Congregation: Causes of Saints;

Commission: State of Vatican City.

Pellegrino, Michele: b. Apr. 25, 1903, Centallo, Italy; ord. priest Sept. 19, 1925; ord. archbishop of Turin, Oct. 17, 1965; cardinal June 26, 1967; titular church, Most Holy Name of Jesus. Archbishop of Turin, member of:

Congregations: Clergy, Divine Worship, Catholic Education.

Philippe, Paul, O.P.: b. Apr. 16, 1905, Paris, France; entered Dominican Order, 1926; ord. priest July 6, 1932; professor at Angelicum, Rome, from 1935; founded Institute of Spirituality for masters of novices at Angelicum, 1950, and school for mistresses of novices, 1953; apostolic visitor of various religious institutes, 1951-56; commissary of the Holy Office, 1955; consultor of various pontifical commissions and congregations from 1958; secretary of Congregation for Religious, 1959; ord. titular archbishop of Heracleopolis Magna, Sept. 21, 1962; secretary of Congregation for Doctrine of Faith, 1967-73; cardinal Mar. 5, 1973; deacon, St. Pius V. Prefect of Congregation for Oriental Churches, 1973, member of:

Congregations: Religious and Secular Institutes, Evangelization of Peoples;

Secretariat: Christian Unity;

Commissions: Revision of Code of Canon Law, Revision of Oriental Code of Canon Law.

Pignedoli, Sergio: b. June 4, 1910, Felina, Italy; ord. priest Apr. 1, 1933; chaplain in Italian navy during World War II; secretary general for organization of 1950 Holy Year; ord. titular archbishop of Iconium, Feb. 11, 1951; nuncio in Bolivia, 1950-54, and Venezuela, 1954-55; auxiliary to Cardinal Montini (now Paul VI) at Milan, 1955-60; apostolic delegate to Central-West Africa, 1960-64, and Canada, 1964-67; secretary of Congregation for Evangelization of Peoples, 1967-73; sent on special mission to Vietnam, 1966; cardinal Mar. 5, 1973; deacon, San Giorgio. President of Secretariat for Non-Christians, 1973, member of:

Congregations: Catholic Education, Evangelization of Peoples, Divine Worship, Causes of Saints;

Secretariat: Christian Unity.

Poletti, Ugo: b. Apr. 19, 1914, Omegna, Italy; ord. priest June 29, 1938; served in various diocesan offices at Novara; ord. titular bishop of Medeli and auxiliary of Novaro, Sept. 14, 1958; president of Pontifical Mission Aid Society for Italy, 1964-67; archbishop of Spoleto, 1967-69; titular archbishop of Cittanova, 1969; served as second viceregent of Rome, 1969-72; pro-vicar general of Rome, 1972, following the sudden death of Cardinal Dell'Acqua; cardinal Mar. 5, 1973; titular church, Sts. Ambrose and Charles. Vicar general of Rome, 1973, archpriest of Patriarchal Lateran Basilica, 1973, grand chancellor of Lateran University, member of:

Congregation: Clergy.

Poma, Antonio: b. June 12, 1910, Villanterio, Italy; ord. priest Apr. 15, 1933; ord. titular bishop of Tagaste and auxiliary bishop of Mantova, Dec. 9, 1951; bishop of Mantova, Sept. 8, 1954; titular archbishop of Gerpiniano and coadjutor archbishop of Bologna, July 16, 1967; archbishop of Bologna, Feb. 12, 1968; cardinal Apr. 28, 1969; titular church, St. Luke (al Prenestino). Archbishop of Bologna, member of:

Congregations: Clergy, Catholic Education.

Primatesta, Raul Francisco: b. Apr. 14, 1919, Capilla del Senor, Argentina; ord.

priest Oct. 25, 1942, at Rome; taught at minor and major seminaries of La Plata; contributed to several theology reviews; ord. titular bishop of Tanais and auxiliary of La Plata, Aug. 15, 1957; bishop of San Rafael, 1961-65; archbishop of Cordoba, Feb. 16, 1965; cardinal Mar. 5, 1973; titular church, St. Mary Sorrowful Virgin. Archbishop of Cordoba, member of:
Congregations: Bishops, Catholic Education, Religious and Secular Institutes.
Quintero, Jose Humberto: b. Sept. 22, 1902, Mucuchies, Venezuela; ord. priest Aug. 22, 1926; ord. titular archbishop of Acrida and coadjutor archbishop of Merida, Dec. 6, 1953; archbishop of Caracas Aug. 31, 1960; cardinal Jan. 16, 1961; titular church, Sts. Andrew and Gregory (al Monte Celio). Archbishop of Caracas.
Raimondi, Luigi: b. Oct. 25, 1912, Acqui-Lussito, Italy; ord. priest June 6, 1936; entered diplomatic service of Holy See, 1938; secretary of nunciature at Guatemala, 1938-42; auditor of apostolic delegation in U.S., 1942-49; consultor and charge d'affaires of internunciature in India, 1949-53; ord. titular archbishop of Tarsus, Jan. 31, 1954; nuncio to Haiti, 1954-67; apostolic delegate to U.S., 1967-73; cardinal Mar. 5, 1973; deacon, Sts. Biagio and Carlo. Prefect of the Sacred Congregation for Causes of Saints, member of:
Council for Public Affairs of Church;
Congregations: Bishops, Evangelization of Peoples.
Rakotomalala, Jerome: b. July 15, 1914, Sainte Marie, Madagascar; ord. priest July 31, 1943; ord. archbishop of Tananarive, May 8, 1960; cardinal Apr. 28, 1969; titular church, St. Mary the Consoler (Casalbertone). Archbishop of Tananarive, member of:
Congregation: Evangelization of Peoples;
Secretariat: Non-Christians.
Renard, Alexandre C.: b. June 7, 1906, Avelin, France; ord. priest July 12, 1931; ord. bishop of Versailles, October 19, 1953; archbishop of Lyons, May 28, 1967; cardinal June 26, 1967; titular church, St. Francis of Paola (ad Montes). Archbishop of Lyons, member of:
Congregations: Religious and Secular Institutes, Evangelization of Peoples.
Ribeiro, Antonio: b. May 21, 1928, Gandarela di Basta, Portugal; ord. priest July 5, 1953; professor of fundamental theology at major seminary at Braga; ord. titular bishop of Tigillava and auxiliary of Braga, Sept. 17, 1967; patriarch of Lisbon, May 10, 1971; cardinal Mar. 5, 1973; titular church, St. Anthony of Padua (in Rome). Patriarch of Lisbon, military vicar member of:
Congregation: Catholic Education;
Commission: Social Communications.
Roberti, Francesco: b. July 7, 1889, Pergola, Italy; ord. priest Aug. 3, 1913; professor of Canon Law at Apollinare, 1918-38; held offices in several Roman Congregations; cardi-

nal Dec. 15, 1958; ord. titular archbishop of Colonnata, Apr. 19, 1962; titular church, the Twelve Apostles; prefect emeritus of Apostolic Signatura.
Rosales, Julio: b. Sept. 18, 1906, Calbayog, Philippines; ord. priest June 2, 1929; ord. bishop of Tagbilaran, Sept. 21, 1946; archbishop of Cebu, Dec. 17, 1949; cardinal Apr. 28, 1969; titular church, Sacred Heart of Jesus (a Vitinia). Archbishop of Cebu, member of:
Congregations: Clergy, Catholic Education;
Secretariat: Non-Christians.
Rossi, Agnelo: b. May 4, 1913, Joaquim Egidio, Brazil; ord. priest Mar. 27, 1937; ord. bishop of Barra do Pirai, Apr. 15, 1956; archbishop of Ribeirao Preto, 1962-64; archbishop of Sao Paulo del Brazil, 1964-70; cardinal Feb. 22, 1965; titular church, Mother of God. Prefect of Congregation for Evangelization of Peoples, grand chancellor of Pontifical Urban University, member of:
Council for Public Affairs of Church;
Congregations: Clergy, Doctrine of Faith, Bishops, Oriental Churches, Causes of Saints, Religious and Secular Institutes, Catholic Education;
Secretariats: Christian Unity, Non-Christians;
Commissions: Revision of Code of Canon Law, Revision of Oriental Code of Canon Law, Institute for Works of Religion.
Roy, Maurice: b. Jan. 25, 1905, Quebec, Canada; ord. priest June 12, 1927; chief of chaplains of Canadian Armed Forces during World War II; ord. bishop of Trois Rivieres, May 1, 1946; military vicar, June 8, 1946; archbishop of Quebec, June 2, 1947; primate of Canada, Jan. 25, 1956; cardinal Feb. 22, 1965; titular church, Our Lady of the Most Holy Sacrament and the Holy Canadian Martyrs. Archbishop of Quebec, primate of Canada, military vicar of Canada, member of:
Congregations: Clergy, Catholic Education;
Council of Laity (President), Commission on Justice and Peace (President);
Commission: Revision of Code of Canon Law.
Rugambwa, Laurean: b. July 12, 1912, Bukongo, Tanzania; ord. priest Dec. 12, 1943; ord. titular bishop of Febiano and vicar apostolic of Lower Kagera, Feb. 10, 1952; bishop of Rutabo, Mar. 25, 1953; cardinal Mar. 28, 1960; titular church, St. Francis (a Ripa); bishop of Bukoba, 1960-68. Archbishop of Dar-es-Salaam, 1968, member of:
Congregation: Causes of Saints;
Commission: Revision of Code of Canon Law.
Salazar Lopez, Jose: b. Jan. 12, 1910, Ameca, Mexico; ord. priest May 26, 1934, in Rome; instrumental in building of new seminary at Guadalajara, the largest in Mexico; vice-rector and later rector of seminary; ord.

titular bishop of Prusiade and coadjutor bishop of Zamora, Aug. 20, 1961; bishop of Zamora, 1967-70; archbishop of Guadalajara, Feb. 21, 1970; cardinal Mar. 5, 1973; titular church, Santa Emerentia. Archbishop of Guadalajara, member of:
Congregation: Divine Worship.
Samore, Antonio: b. Dec. 4, 1905, Bardi, Italy; ord. priest June 10, 1928; served in apostolic nunciatures at Lithuania and Switzerland; worked in Vatican Secretariat of State during World War II; assigned to apostolic delegation in Washington, D.C., 1947; nuncio to Colombia, 1950; ord. titular archbishop of Tirnovo, Apr. 16, 1950; secretary of Congregation of Extraordinary Ecclesiastical Affairs, 1953-67; cardinal June 26, 1967; entered order of cardinal bishops as titular bishop of Sabina and Poggia Mirteto, Dec. 12, 1974; prefect of Congregation for Discipline of Sacraments, 1968-74. Librarian and archivist of Holy Roman Church, 1974, member of:
Council for Public Affairs of Church;
Congregations: Oriental Churches, Bishops, Evangelization of Peoples;
Commission: Revision of Code of Canon Law.
Scherer, Alfred Vicente: b. Feb. 5, 1903, Bom Principio, Brazil; ord. priest Apr. 3, 1926; ord. archbishop of Porto Alegre, Feb. 23, 1947; cardinal Apr. 28, 1969; titular church, Our Lady of La Salette. Archbishop of Porto Alegre, Brazil, member of:
Congregation: Evangelization of Peoples.
Seper, Franjo: b. Oct. 2, 1905, Osijek, Yugoslavia; ord. priest Oct. 26, 1930; secretary of Cardinal Stepinac, 1934-41; rector of Zagreb's major seminary, 1941-51; ord. titular archbishop of Filippopoli and coadjutor archbishop of Zagreb, Sept. 21, 1954; archbishop of Zagreb, 1960-69; cardinal Feb. 22, 1965; titular church, Sts. Peter and Paul (in Via Ostia). Prefect of Congregation for Doctrine of the Faith, chamberlain of College of Cardinals (1974), member of:
Council for Public Affairs of Church;
Congregations: Bishops, Discipline of Sacraments, Clergy, Catholic Education;
Office: Administration of Patrimony of Holy See;
Commissions: Biblical (President), Theological (President), Revision of Code, Interpretation of Decrees of Vatican II.
Shehan, Lawrence J.: b. Dec. 18, 1898, Baltimore, Md.; ord. priest Dec. 23, 1922; ord. titular bishop of Lidda and auxiliary bishop of Baltimore and Washington, Dec. 12, 1945; bishop of Bridgeport, 1953-61; titular archbishop of Nicopolis ad Nestum and coadjutor archbishop of Baltimore, July 10, 1961; archbishop of Baltimore, 1961-74; cardinal Feb. 22, 1965; titular church, St. Clement. Former archbishop of Baltimore, member of:
Commission: Revision of Code of Canon Law.
Sidarouss, Stephanos I, C.M.: b. Feb. 22,

1904, Cairo, Egypt; ord. priest July 2, 1939; ord. titular bishop of Sais, Jan. 25, 1948; auxiliary to the patriarch of Alexandria for the Copts, 1948-58; patriarch of Alexandria, May 10, 1958; cardinal Feb. 22, 1965. Patriarch of Alexandria for the Copts, member of:
Congregation: Oriental Churches;
Commissions: Revision of Code of Canon Law, Revision of Code of Oriental Canon Law.
Silva Henriquez, Raul, S.D.B.: b. Sept. 27, 1907, Talca, Chile; ord. priest July 3, 1938; ord. bishop of Valparaiso, Nov. 29, 1959; archbishop of Santiago de Chile, Mar. 14, 1961; cardinal Mar. 19, 1962; titular church, St. Bernard (alle Terme). Archbishop of Santiago de Chile, member of:
Congregations: Clergy, Divine Worship, Catholic Education;
Commission: Revision of Code of Canon Law.
Siri, Giuseppe: b. May 20, 1906, Genoa, Italy; ord. priest Sept. 22, 1928; ord. titular bishop of Liviade and auxiliary bishop of Genoa, May 7, 1944; archbishop of Genoa, May 14, 1946; cardinal Jan. 12, 1953; titular church, St. Mary (della Vittoria). Archbishop of Genoa, member of:
Congregations: Discipline of Sacraments, Clergy, Catholic Education;
Commission: Revision of Code of Canon Law.
Slipyi or Slipyj, Josyf (Kobernyckyj-Dyckowskyj): b. Feb. 17, 1892, Zazdrist in the Ukraine; ord. priest Sept. 30, 1917; ord. titular archbishop of Serre, Dec. 22, 1939; coadjutor archbishop of Lwow for the Ukrainians, 1939-44; archbishop of Lwow, Nov. 1, 1944; imprisoned 1945-63 for unspecified crimes; released by Soviets and allowed to go to Rome in February, 1963; named major archbishop by Paul VI, 1963; cardinal Feb. 22, 1965; titular church, St. Athanasius. Archbishop of Lwow (not permitted to exercise his office; he resides in Vatican City), major archbishop of the Ukraine.
Staffa, Dino: b. Aug. 14, 1906, Santa Maria in Fabriago, Italy; ord. priest May 25, 1929; judge of Roman Rota, 1944; secretary of Congregation of Seminaries and Universities, 1958-67; ord. titular archbishop of Caesarea in Palestina, Oct. 28, 1960; cardinal June 26, 1967; titular church, Sacred Heart of Christ the King. Prefect of Apostolic Signatura, member of:
Congregations: Oriental Churches, Discipline of Sacraments;
Commission: Revision of Code of Canon Law.
Suenens, Leo Josef: b. July 16, 1904, Brussels, Belgium; ord. priest Sept. 4, 1927; ord. titular bishop of Isinda, Dec. 16, 1945; auxiliary bishop of Mechelen, 1945-61; archbishop of Mechelen-Brussels, 1961; cardinal Mar. 19, 1962; titular church, St. Peter in Chains.

Archbishop of Mechelen-Brussels, military vicar for Belgium; member of:

Congregations: Evangelization of Peoples, Causes of Saints;

Commission: Revision of Canon Law.

Taguchi, Paul Yoshigoro: b. July 20, 1902, Shittsu, Japan; studied at Rome; ord. priest Dec. 22, 1928; returned to Japan, 1931; worked in publications; apostolic administrator of Diocese of Osaka, Nov. 30, 1940; ord. bishop of Osaka, Dec. 14, 1941; first archbishop of Osaka, July 24, 1969, when see was raised to metropolitan rank; cardinal Mar. 5, 1973; titular church, Santa Maria (in Via). Archbishop of Osaka, president of Japanese Episcopal Conference, member of:

Secretariat: Non-Christians.

Taofinu'u, Pio, S.M.: b. Dec. 9, 1923, Falealupo, W. Samoa; ord. priest Dec. 8, 1954; joined Society of Mary, 1955; ord. bishop of Apia, May 29, 1968, the first Polynesian bishop; cardinal Mar. 5, 1973; titular church, Sant' Onofrio (on the Janiculum). Bishop of Apia, member of:

Congregation: Causes of Saints.

Traglia, Luigi: b. Apr. 3, 1895, Albano Laziale, Italy; ord. priest Aug. 10, 1917; clerk of Congregation for Propagation of the Faith, 1927; judge of Roman Rota, 1936; ord. titular archbishop of Cesarea of Palestine and viceregent of Rome, Jan. 6, 1937; cardinal Mar. 28, 1960; chancellor of Holy Roman Church, 1967-73; titular bishop of suburban see of Albano, Mar. 14, 1972, when he entered order of cardinal bishops, and Ostia, Jan. 7, 1974, when he was elected dean of the College of the Cardinals. Dean of College of Cardinals, member of:

Council for Public Affairs of Church;

Congregations: Oriental Churches, Bishops, Discipline of Sacraments, Evangelization of Peoples, Causes of Saints;

Tribunal: Apostolic Signatura;

Commission: State of Vatican City.

Ursi, Corrado: b. July 26, 1908, Andria, Italy; ord. priest July 25, 1931; vice-rector and later rector of the Pontifical Regional Seminary of Molfetta, 1931-51; ord. bishop of Nardo, Sept. 30, 1951; archbishop of Acerenza, Nov. 30, 1961; archbishop of Naples, May 23, 1966; cardinal June 26, 1967; titular church, St. Callistus. Archbishop of Naples, member of:

Congregation: Catholic Education.

Vagnozzi, Egidio: b. Feb. 2, 1906, Rome, Italy; ord. priest Dec. 22, 1928; served in US apostolic delegation; ord. titular archbishop of Mira, May 22, 1949; apostolic delegate to the Philippines, 1949; first nuncio to Philippines, 1951; apostolic delegate to the US, 1958-67; cardinal June 26, 1967; titular church, St. Joseph. President of Prefecture of Economic Affairs of Holy See, member of:

Council for Public Affairs of Church;

Congregation: Oriental Churches;

Tribunal: Apostolic Signatura.

Villot, Jean: b. Oct. 11, 1905, Saint-Amant-Tallende, France; ord. priest Apr. 19, 1930; ord. titular bishop of Vinda and auxiliary bishop of Paris, Oct. 12, 1954; titular archbishop of Bosphorus and coadjutor archbishop of Lyons, Dec. 17, 1959; archbishop of Lyons, 1965-67; cardinal Feb. 22, 1965; entered order of cardinal bishops as titular bishop of Frascati, Dec. 12, 1974. Secretary of State (1969), prefect of Council for Public Affairs of the Church (1969), chamberlain of the Holy Roman Church (1970), member of:

Congregations: Doctrine of Faith, Bishops, Evangelization of Peoples, Causes of Saints;

Office: Administration of Patrimony of Holy See (President);

Commissions: Revision of Code of Canon Law, Revision of Oriental Code of Canon Law, Pontifical Council *Cor Unum* (President), Institute for Works of Religion, State of Vatican City (President).

Violardo, Giacomo: b. May 10, 1898, Govone, Italy; ord. priest June 29, 1923; ord. titular archbishop of Satafi, Mar. 19, 1966; secretary of Congregation for Discipline of the Sacraments, 1966-69; cardinal Apr. 28, 1969; deacon, St. Eustachius. Member of:

Congregations: Discipline of Sacraments, Oriental Churches;

Tribunal: Apostolic Signatura;

Commissions: Revision of Code of Canon Law, Interpretation of Decrees of Vatican II, State of Vatican City.

Volk, Hermann: b. Dec. 27, 1903, Steinheim, Germany; ord. priest Apr. 2, 1927; professor of dogmatic theology at University of Muenster; ord. bishop of Mainz, June 5, 1962; cardinal Mar. 5, 1973; titular church, Saints Fabian and Venazio (at Villa Fiorelli). Bishop of Mainz, member of:

Congregations: Doctrine of Faith, Discipline of Sacraments;

Secretariat: Christian Unity.

Willebrands, Jan: b. Sept. 4, 1909, Bovenkarspel, Netherlands; ord. priest May 26, 1934; ord. titular bishop of Mauriana, June 28, 1964; secretary of Secretariat for Christian Unity, 1960-69; cardinal Apr. 28, 1969; deacon, Sts. Cosmas and Damian. President of Secretariat for Christian Unity (1969), member of:

Congregations: Doctrine of Faith, Discipline of Sacraments, Oriental Churches, Catholic Education, Evangelization of Peoples, Divine Worship;

Commissions: Revision of Code of Canon Law, Revision of Oriental Code of Canon Law..

Wojtyla, Karol: b. May 18, 1920, Wadowice, Poland; ord. priest Nov. 1, 1946; served on faculties of Catholic University of Lublin and University of Cracow; ord. titular bishop of Ombi and auxiliary bishop of Cracow, Sept. 28, 1958; archbishop of Cracow, Jan. 13, 1964; cardinal June 26, 1967; titular church, St. Caesarius (in Palatio). Archbishop of Cracow, member of:

Congregations: Clergy, Divine Worship, Catholic Education.

Wright, John J.: b. July 18, 1909; Dorchester, Mass.; ord. priest Dec. 8, 1935; ord. titular bishop of Egee and auxiliary bishop of Boston, June 30, 1947; bishop of Worcester, Jan. 28, 1950; bishop of Pittsburgh, 1959-69; cardinal Apr. 28, 1969; titular church, Jesus the Divine Teacher. Prefect of Congregation for the Clergy (1969), member of:

Council for Public Affairs of Church;

Congregations: Doctrine of Faith, Bishops, Catholic Education, Evangelization of Peoples;

Commissions: Revision of Code of Canon Law, State of Vatican City, Sanctuaries of Pompei and Loreto, Interpretation of Decrees of Vatican II, Institute for Works of Religion.

Wyszynski, Stefan: b. Aug. 3, 1901, Zuzela, Poland; ord. priest Aug. 3, 1924; ord. bishop of Lublin, May 12, 1946; archbishop of Gniezno and Warsaw, Nov. 12, 1948; cardinal Jan. 12, 1953; titular church, St. Mary (in Trastavere). He was "deposed" by Polish government in fall of 1953, recognized, 1956. Archbishop of Gniezno and Warsaw, primate of Poland, member of:

Congregation: Oriental Churches;

Commission: Revision of Canon Law.

Yu Pin, Paul: b. Apr. 13, 1901, Lan-si Sien, China; ord. priest Dec. 22, 1928; professor of Chinese literature and philosophy at Rome, 1929-36; returned to China, 1936; ord. titular bishop of Sozusa di Palestina and vicar apostolic of Nanking, Sept. 20, 1936; archbishop of Nanking, Apr. 11, 1946; cardinal Apr. 28, 1969; titular church, Jesus the Divine Worker. Archbishop of Nanking (in exile; residing in Taiwan), member of:

Congregation: Evangelization of Peoples;

Secretariat: Non-Christians.

Zoungrana, Paul: b. Sept. 3, 1917, Ougadougou, Upper Volta; ord. priest May 2, 1942; ord. archbishop of Ougadougou at St. Peter's Basilica by John XXIII, May 8, 1960; cardinal Feb. 22, 1965; titular church, St. Camillus de Lellis. Archbishop of Ougadougou, member of:

Congregations: Religious and Secular Institutes, Evangelization of Peoples.

Cardinal Newman Symposium

Pope Paul, in an address Apr. 7, 1975, to 150 participants in a symposium on Cardinal John H. "Newman's Realization of Christian Life," said that his realization was "but another name for a continual effort for the renewal of personal and community life in the spirit of the Gospel and in accordance with the just demands of the present moment of history." Cardinal Newman was born in 1801, entered the Church in 1845, was made a cardinal in 1879, and died in 1890.

CATEGORIES OF CARDINALS
(As of July 30, 1975.)

Information below includes categories of cardinals and dates of consistories at which they were created. Seniority or precedence, except in the case of cardinal bishops, usually depends on order of elevation.

One of these cardinals was named by Pius XI (consistory of Dec. 16, 1929); 12 by Pius XII (consistories of Feb. 18, 1946, and Jan. 12, 1953); 18 by John XXIII (consistories of Dec. 15, 1958, Dec. 14, 1959, Mar. 28, 1960, Jan. 16, 1961, and Mar. 19, 1962); 93 by Paul VI (consistories of Feb. 22, 1965, June 26, 1967, Apr. 28, 1969, and Mar. 5, 1973).

All cardinals are bishops or are ordained bishops after elevation, according to the Motu Proprio, *Cum Gravissima,* of Pope John XXIII (Apr. 15, 1962). For description of categories of Bishop, Priest and Deacon, see index.

Order of Bishops

Bishops of Suburban Sees: Luigi Traglia, Dean (Mar. 28, 1960); Carlo Confalonieri (Dec. 15, 1958); Paolo Marella (Dec. 14, 1959); Jean Villot (Feb. 22, 1965); Antonio Samore (June 26, 1967); Sebastiano Baggio (Apr. 28, 1969).

Eastern Rite Patriarch: Stephanos I Sidarouss, C.M. (Feb. 22, 1965).

Order of Priests

1929 (Dec. 16): Manuel Goncalves Cerejeira.

1946 (Feb. 18): Carlos Carmelo de Vasconcellos Motta, Norman Gilroy, Joseph Frings, Antonio Caggiano.

1953 (Jan. 12): Maurice Feltin, Giuseppe Siri, James McIntyre, Giacomo Lercaro, Stefan Wyszynski, Paul Emile Leger, S.S., Valerian Gracias, Alfredo Ottaviani.

1958 (Dec. 15): Antonio Maria Barbieri, Jose M. Bueno y Monreal, Franz Koenig, Julius Doepfner, Alberto di Jorio, Francesco Roberti.

1960 (Mar. 28): Bernard Jan Alfrink, Laurean Rugambwa.

1961 (Jan. 16): Jose Humberto Quintero, Luis Concha.

1962 (Mar. 19): Jose da Costa Nunes, Efrem Forni, Juan Landazuri Ricketts, O.F.M., Raul Silva Henriquez, S.D.B., Leo Josef Suenens.

1965 (Feb. 22): Josyf Slipyi, Thomas B. Cooray, Maurice Roy, Joseph M. Martin, Owen McCann, Leon-Etienne Duval, Ermenegildo Florit, Franjo Seper, John C. Heenan, Paul Zoungrana, Lawrence J. Shehan, Agnelo Rossi, Giovanni Colombo, William Conway.

1967 (June 26): Gabriel Garrone, Patrick O'Boyle, Egidio Vagnozzi, Maximilien de Furstenberg, Francesco Carpino, Jose Clemente Maurer, C.SS.R., Pietro Parente,

Carlo Grano, Dino Staffa, John J. Krol, John P. Cody, Corrado Ursi, Alfred Bengsch, Justin Darmojuwono, Karol Wojtyla, Michele Pellegrino, Alexandre Renard.

1969 (Apr. 28): Paul Yu Pin, Alfredo Vicente Scherer, Julio Rosales, Gordon J. Gray, Paolo Bertoli, Miguel Dario Miranda y Gomez, Joseph Parecattil, John F. Dearden, Francois Marty;

Jerome Rakotomalala, George Flahiff, Paul Gouyon, Mario Casariego, Vicente Enrique y Tarancon, Joseph Malula, Pablo Muñoz Vega, S.J., Antonio Poma;

John J. Carberry, Terence J. Cooke, Stephan Sou Hwan Kim, Eugenio de Araujo Sales, Joseph Hoeffner, John J. Wright.

1973 (Mar. 5): Albino Luciani, Antonio Ribeiro, James Robert Knox, Avelar Brandao Vilela, Joseph Cordeiro, Anibal Muñoz Duque, Luis Aponte Martinez, Raul Francisco Primatesta, Salvatore Pappalardo, Marcelo Gonzalez Martin, Louis Jean Guyot, Ugo Poletti, Timothy Manning, Paul Yoshigoro Taguchi, Maurice Otunga, Jose Salazar Lopez, Emile Biayenda, Humberto S. Medeiros, Paulo Evaristo Arns, James Darcy Freeman, Narciso Jubany Arnau, Hermann Volk, Pio Taofinu'u.

Order of Deacons

1967 (June 26): Pericle Felici.

1969 (Apr. 28): Silvio Oddi, Giuseppe Paupini, Giacomo Violardo, Jan Willebrands, Mario Nasalli Rocca di Corneliano, Sergio Guerri.

1973 (Mar. 5): Sergio Pignedoli, Umberto Mozzoni, Paul Philippe, Pietro Palazzini, Ferdinando Giuseppe Antonelli.

Ineligible To Vote

As of July 30, 1975, 21 cardinals were ineligible to take part in a papal election in line with the apostolic letter *Ingravescentem Aetatem* effective Jan. 1, 1971, which limited the functions of cardinals after completion of their 80th year.

Cardinals affected were: Barbieri, Caggiano, Cerejeira, Concha, Confalonieri, Da Costa Nunes, Di Jorio, Feltin, Forni, Frings, Grano, Lercaro, McIntyre, Marella, Martin, Motta, Ottaviani, Parente, Roberti, Slipyi, Traglia.

DISTRIBUTION OF CARDINALS

As of July 30, 1975, there were 124 cardinals from approximately 47 countries or areas. Listed below are areas, countries, number and last names.

Europe — 68

Italy (35): Antonelli, Baggio, Bertoli, Carpino, Colombo, Confalonieri, Di Jorio, Felici, Florit, Forni, Grano, Guerri, Lercaro, Luciani, Marella, Mozzoni, Nasalli Rocca di Corneliano, Oddi, Ottaviani, Palazzini, Pappalardo, Parente, Paupini, Pellegrino, Pignedoli, Poletti, Poma, Roberti, Samore, Siri, Staffa, Traglia, Ursi, Vagnozzi, Violardo.

France (9): Feltin, Garrone, Gouyon, Guyot, Martin, Marty, Philippe, Renard, Villot.

Germany (5): Bengsch, Doepfner, Frings, Hoeffner, Volk.

Spain (4): Bueno y Monreal, Enrique y Tarancon, Gonzalez Martin, Jubany Arnau.

Netherlands (3): Alfrink, De Furstenberg, Willebrands.

Portugal (3); Da Costa Nunes (Azores), Goncalves Cerejeira, Ribeiro.

Poland (2): Wyszynski, Wojtyla.

One from each of the following countries: Austria, Koenig; Belgium, Suenens; England, Heenan; Ireland, Conway; Scotland, Gray; Ukraine (now in USSR), Slipyi; Yugoslavia, Seper.

Asia — 9

India (2): Gracias, Parecattil.

One from each of the following countries: China, Yu Pin; Indonesia, Darmojuwono; Japan, Taguchi; Korea, Kim; Pakistan, Cordeiro; Philippines, Rosales; Sri Lanka, Cooray.

Oceania — 4

Australia, (3): Gilroy, Freeman, Knox; Pacific Islands (Western Samoa), Taofinu'u.

Africa — 9

One from each of the following countries: Algeria, Duval; Congo, Biayenda; Egypt (United Arab Republic), Sidarouss; Kenya, Otunga; Malagasy Republic, Rakotomalala; South Africa, McCann; Tanzania, Rugambwa; Upper Volta, Zoungrana; Zaire, Malula.

North America — 17

United States (11): Carberry, Cody, Cooke, Dearden, Krol, McIntyre, Manning, Medeiros, O'Boyle, Shehan, Wright.

Canada (3): Flahiff, Leger, Roy.

Mexico (2): Miranda y Gomez, Salazar Lopez.

Puerto Rico (1): Aponte Martinez.

Central and South America — 17

Brazil (6): Arns, Brandao Vilela, De Araujo Sales, Motta, Rossi, Scherer.

Argentina (2): Caggiano, Primatesta.

Colombia (2): Concha, Munoz Duque.

One from each of the following countries: Bolivia, Maurer; Chile, Silva Henriquez; Ecuador, Munoz Vega, S.J.; Guatemala, Casariego (b. Spain); Peru, Landazuri Ricketts; Uruguay, Barbieri; Venezuela, Quintero.

Cardinals of U.S.

As of July 31, 1975, U.S. cardinals, years of elevation and sees:

James McIntyre, 1953, Los Angeles (retired 1970); Lawrence J. Shehan, 1965, Baltimore (retired 1974); Patrick A. O'Boyle, 1967,

Washington (retired 1973); John J. Krol, 1967, Philadelphia; John P. Cody, 1967, Chicago; John F. Dearden, 1969, Detroit; John J. Carberry, 1969, St. Louis; Terence J. Cooke, 1969, New York; John J. Wright, 1969, prefect of the Congregation for the Clergy; Timothy Manning, 1973, Los Angeles; Humberto S. Medeiros, 1973, Boston.

Deceased cardinals of the United States. Data: years of elevation, sees, years of birth and death.

John McCloskey, 1875, New York, 1810-1885; James Gibbons, 1886, Baltimore, 1834-1921; John Farley, 1911, New York, 1842-1918; William O'Connell, 1911, Boston, 1859-1944; Dennis Dougherty, 1921, Philadelphia, 1865-1951; Patrick Hayes, 1924, New York, 1867-1938; George Mundelein, 1924, Chicago, 1872-1939; John Glennon, 1946, St. Louis, 1862-1946; Edward Mooney, 1946, Detroit, 1882-1958;

Francis Spellman, 1946, New York, 1889-1967; Samuel Stritch, 1946, Chicago, 1887-1958; John O'Hara, C.S.C., 1958, Philadelphia, 1888-1960; Richard Cushing, 1958, Boston, 1895-1970; Albert Meyer, 1959, Chicago, 1903-1965; Aloysius Muench, 1959, Fargo (and papal nuncio), 1889-1962; Joseph Ritter, 1961, St. Louis, 1892-1967; Francis Brennan, 1967, official of Roman Curia, 1894-1968.

REPRESENTATIVES OF THE HOLY SEE

Papal representatives and their functions were the subject of a document entitled *Sollicitudo Omnium Ecclesiarum* which Pope Paul issued on his own initiative under the date of June 24, 1969.

Delegates and Nuncios

Papal representatives "receive from the Roman Pontiff the charge of representing him in a fixed way in the various nations or regions of the world.

"When their legation is only to local churches, they are known as apostolic delegates. When to this legation, of a religious and ecclesial nature, there is added diplomatic legation to states and governments, they receive the title of nuncio, pro-nuncio, and internuncio."

[An apostolic nuncio has the diplomatic rank of ambassador extraordinary and plenipotentiary. Traditionally, because the Vatican diplomatic service has the longest uninterrupted history in the world, a nuncio has precedence among diplomats in the country to which he is accredited and serves as dean of the diplomatic corps on state occasions. Since 1965 pro-nuncios, also of ambassadorial rank, have been assigned to countries in which this prerogative is not recognized.]

(Other representatives, who are covered in the Almanac article, Vatican Representatives to International Organizations, are clerics and lay persons "who form . . . part of a pontifical mission attached to international organizations or take part in conferences and congresses." They are variously called delegates or observers.)

"The primary and specific purpose of the mission of a papal representative is to render ever closer and more operative the ties that bind the Apostolic See and the local churches.

"The ordinary function of a pontifical representative is to keep the Holy See regularly and objectively informed about the conditions of the ecclesial community to which he has been sent, and about what may affect the life of the Church and the good of souls.

"On the one hand, he makes known to the Holy See the thinking of the bishops, clergy, religious and faithful of the territory where he carries out his mandate, and forwards to Rome their proposals and their requests; on the other hand, he makes himself the interpreter, with those concerned, of the acts, documents, information and instructions emanating from the Holy See."

Service and Liaison

Representatives, while carrying out their general and special duties, are bound to respect the autonomy of local churches and bishops. Their service and liaison responsibilities include the following:

• **Nomination of Bishops:** To play a key role in compiling, with the advice of ecclesiastics and lay persons, and submitting lists of names of likely candidates to the Holy See with their own recommendations.

• **Bishops:** To aid and counsel local bishops without interfering in the affairs of their jurisdictions.

• **Episcopal Conferences:** To maintain close relations with them and to assist them in every possible way. (Papal representatives do not belong to these conferences.)

• **Religious Communities of Pontifical Rank:** To advise and assist major superiors for the purpose of promoting and consolidating conferences of men and women religious and to coordinate their apostolic activities.

• **Church-State Relations:** The thrust in this area is toward the development of sound relations with civil governments and collaboration in work for peace and the total good of the whole human family.

The mission of a papal representative begins with appointment and assignment by the pope and continues until termination of his mandate. He acts "under the guidance and according to the instructions of the cardinal secretary of state and prefect of the Council for the Public Affairs of the Church, to whom he is directly responsible for the execution of the mandate entrusted to him by the Supreme Pontiff." Normally, representatives are required to retire at the age of 75.

The Pope said clearly in the document that it was a response to demands made during the Second Vatican Council for clarification of the whole system of papal representation to local churches and governments throughout the world.

At the same time, but without any statement to that effect, the document appeared to be a response to criticism voiced in some quarters about the validity and desirability of this system. It was variously charged that the system interfered with administration in local churches; that it deprived local churches of reasonable independence; that it made the conduct of local church affairs dependent on the opinion of a foreigner in a country; that it violated the principle of subsidiarity; that it reflected an erroneous image of the pope as a would-be political sovereign. Refutation of all these charges was implicit in the broad introduction and specific articles of the document.

NUNCIOS AND DELEGATES

(Sources: *Annuario Pontificio, L'Osservatore Romano,* NC News Service.)

Data, as of July 1, 1975, country, rank of legation (corresponding to rank of legate unless otherwise noted), name of legate (archbishop unless otherwise noted) as available.

Delegate for Papal Representatives: Archbishop Domenico Enrici, former apostolic delegate to Great Britain, was appointed in July, 1973, to the newly created post of Delegate for Papal Representatives, to coordinate papal diplomatic efforts throughout the world. The office entails responsibility for "following more closely through timely visits the activities of papal representatives . . . and encouraging their rapport with the central offices" of the Secretariat of State and the Council for the Public Affairs of the Church.

Africa, North (Libya, Morocco): Algiers, Algeria, Apostolic Delegation; Sante Portalupi.

Africa, South (Botswana, Rhodesia, South Africa, Namibia, Ngwane): Pretoria, Apostolic Delegation; Alfredo Poledrino.

Algeria: Algiers, Nunciature, Sante Portalupi, Pro-Nuncio.

Angola: Luanda, Apostolic Delegation; Giovanni De Andrea.

Antilles: Apostolic Delegation.

Argentina: Buenos Aires, Nunciature; Pio Laghi.

Australia: North Sydney, Nunciature; Gino Paro, Pro-Nuncio (also Apostolic Delegate to Papua-New Guinea).

Austria: Vienna, Nunciature; Opilio Rossi.

Bangladesh: Dacca, Nunciature; Edward Cassidy, Pro-Nuncio (also Pro-Nuncio to China-Taiwan).

Belgium: Brussels, Nunciature; Igino Cardinale.

Bolivia: La Paz, Nunciature; Giuseppe Laigueglia.

Brazil: Brasilia, Nunciature; Carmine Rocco.

Burundi: Bujumbura, Nunciature; Nicolo Rotunno.

Cameroon: Yaounde, Nunciature; Luciano Storero, Pro-Nuncio.

Canada: Ottawa, Nunciature; Guido Del Mestri, Pro-Nuncio.

Central African Republic: Bangui, Nunciature. (The Pro-Nuncio is also Apostolic Delegate to Chad and Congo-Brazzaville.)

Chad: Apostolic Delegation (Delegate resides in Bangui, Central African Republic).

Chile: Santiago, Nunciature; Sotero Sanz Villalba.

China: Taipei (Taiwan), Nunciature; Edward Cassidy, Pro-Nuncio.

Colombia: Bogota, Nunciature; Angelo Palmas.

Congo Republic: Apostolic Delegation (Delegate resides in Bangui, Central African Republic).

Costa Rica: San Jose, Nunciature; Lajos Kada.

Cuba: Havana Nunciature; Mario Tagliaferri.

Cyprus: Nicosia, Nunciature; William A. Carew, Pro-Nuncio (resides in Jerusalem).

Dahomey: Cotonou, Nunciature; Bruno Wustenberg, Pro-Nuncio (resides in Abidjan, Ivory Coast).

Dominican Republic: Santo Domingo, Nunciature; Giovanni Gravelli (also Apostolic Delegate to Puerto Rico).

Ecuador: Quito, Nunciature; Luigi Accogli.

Egypt: Cairo, Nunciature; Achille Glorieux, Pro-Nuncio.

El Salvador: San Salvador, Nunciature; Emanuele Gerada.

Equatorial Guinea: Santa Isabel, Apostolic Delegation; Luciano Storero (resides in Yaounde, Cameroon).

Ethiopia: Addis Ababa, Nunciature; Raymond Etteldorf, Pro-Nuncio.

Finland: Helsinki, Nunciature; Josip Zabkar, Pro-Nuncio (resides in Copenhagen).

France: Paris, Nunciature; Egano Righi Lambertini.

Gabon Republic: Libreville, Nunciature; Luciano Storero, Pro-Nuncio (resides in Yaounde, Cameroon).

Germany: Bonn, Nunciature; Corrado Bafile.

Ghana: Accra, Apostolic Delegation; Girolamo Prigione (resides in Lagos, Nigeria).

Great Britain: London, Apostolic Delegation; Bruno Heim (also Apostolic Delegate to Gibraltar).

Guatemala: Guatemala City, Nunciature; Emanuele Gerada.

Guinea: Conakry, Apostolic Delegation; Bruno Wustenberg (resides in Abidjan, Ivory Coast).

Guinea-Bissau: Apostolic Delegation (Delegate resides at Dakar, Senegal).

Haiti: Port-au-Prince, Nunciature.

Honduras: Tegucigalpa, Nunciature; Gabriel Montalvo.

India: New Delhi, Nunciature; John Gordon, Pro-Nuncio (also Apostolic Delegate to Burma).

Indonesia: Jakarta, Nunciature; Vincenzo Farano, Pro-Nuncio.

Iran: Teheran, Nunciature; Ernesto Gallina, Pro-Nuncio.

Iraq: Baghdad, Nunciature; Jean Rupp, Pro-Nuncio.

Ireland: Dublin, Nunciature; Gaetano Alibrandi.

Italy: Rome, Nunciature; Romolo Carboni.

Ivory Coast: Abidjan, Nunciature; Bruno Wustenberg, Pro-Nuncio (He is also Pro-Nuncio to Dahomey and Apostolic Delegate to Guinea and Togo.).

Japan: Tokyo, Nunciature; Ippolito Rotoli, Pro-Nuncio.

Jerusalem, Palestine, Jordan, Israel: Jerusalem, Apostolic Delegation; William A Carew.

Kenya: Nairobi, Nunciature; Pierluigi Sartorelli, Pro-Nuncio (also Apostolic Delegate to Seychelles Is.).

Korea: Seoul, Nunciature; Luigi Dossena, Pro-Nuncio.

Kuwait: Al Kuwait, Nunciature; Jean Rupp, Pro-Nuncio (resides in Baghdad, Iraq).

Laos, Malaysia and Singapore: Bangkok, Apostolic Delegation; Giovanni Moretti (resides in Bangkok).

Lebanon: Beirut, Nunciature; Alfredo Bruniera.

Lesotho: Maseru, Nunciature; Alfredo Poledrino, Pro-Nuncio (resides in Pretoria, S. Africa).

Liberia: Monrovia, Nunciature; Francis Carroll, S.M.A., Pro-Nuncio (also Apostolic Delegate for Sierra Leone and Gambia).

Luxembourg: Nunciature; Igino Cardinale (resides in Brussels, Belgium).

Malagasy Republic: Tananarive, Nunciature; Michele Cecchini, Pro-Nuncio (also Apostolic Delegate to Reunion).

Malawi: Zomba, Nunciature; Luciano Angeloni, Pro-Nuncio (resides in Zambia).

Mali: Bamako, Apostolic Delegation; Luigi Barbarito (resides in Dakar, Senegal).

Malta: La Valletta, Nunciature; Antonio del Giudice.

Mauritania: Nouakchott, Apostolic Delegation; Luigi Barbarito (resides in Dakar, Senegal).

Mauritius: Port Louis, Nunciature; Michele Cecchini, Pro-Nuncio (resides in Tananarive, Malagasy Republic).

Mexico: Mexico City, Apostolic Delegation; Mario Pio Gaspari.

Mozambique: Laurenco Marques, Apostolic Delegation; Francesco Colasuonna.

Netherlands: The Hague, Nunciature; Angelo Felici, Pro-Nuncio.

New Zealand: Wellington, Nunciature; Angelo Acerbi, Pro-Nuncio (also Apostolic Delegate to Pacific Islands).

Nicaragua: Managua, Nunciature; Gabriel Montalvo.

Niger: Niamey, Nunciature; Luigi Barbarito, Pro-Nuncio (resides in Dakar, Senegal).

Nigeria: Lagos, Apostolic Delegation; Girolamo Prigione.

Pakistan: Islamabad, Nunciature; Joseph Uhac, Pro-Nuncio.

Panama: Panama, Nunciature; Edoardo Rovida.

Paraguay: Asuncion, Nunciature; Joseph Mees.

Peru: Lima, Nunciature; Carlo Furno.

Philippines: Manila, Nunciature; Bruno Torpigliani.

Portugal: Lisbon, Nunciature; Giuseppe Sensi.

Red Sea Region (Somalia, Afars and Issas, part of Arabian Peninsula): Apostolic Delegation; Ubaldo Calabresi (resides in Khartoum, Sudan).

Rwanda: Kigali, Nunciature; Nicolo Rotunno.

Scandinavia (Denmark, Sweden, Norway, Iceland): Copenhagen, Denmark, Apostolic Delegation; Josip Zabkar.

Senegal: Dakar, Nunciature; Luigi Barbarito, Pro-Nuncio. (He is also Pro-Nuncio to Niger and Upper Volta and Apostolic Delegate to Mali and Mauritania.)

Spain: Madrid, Nunciature; Luigi Dadaglio.

Sri Lanka: Colombo, Apostolic Delegation; Carlo Curis.

Sudan: Khartuom, Nunciature; Ubaldo Calabresi, Pro-Nuncio.

Switzerland: Bern, Nunciature; Ambrogio Marchioni.

Syria (Syrian Arab Republic): Damascus, Nunciature; Angelo Pedroni, Pro-Nuncio.

Tanzania: Dar-es-Salaam, Nunciature; Franco Brambilla, Pro-Nuncio.

Thailand: Bangkok, Nunciature; Giovanni Moretti, Pro-Nuncio.

Togo: Lome, Apostolic Delegation, Bruno Wustenberg (resides in Abidjan, Ivory Coast).

Tunisia: Tunis, Nunciature; Sante Portalupi, Pro-Nuncio (resides in Algiers, Algeria).

Turkey: Ankara, Nunciature; Salvatore Asta, Pro-Nuncio.

Uganda: Kampala, Nunciature; Luigi Bellotti, Pro-Nuncio.

United States of America: Washington, D.C., Apostolic Delegation; Jean Jadot.

Upper Volta: Ouagadougou, Nunciature; Luigi Barbarito, Pro-Nuncio (resides in Dakar, Senegal).

Uruguay: Montevideo, Nunciature; Augustine Sepinski, O.F.M.

Venezuela: Caracas, Nunciature; Giovanni Mariani.

Vietnam and Khmer Republic: Saigon, Apostolic Delegation; Henri Lemaitre.

Yugoslavia: Belgrade, Nunciature; Mario Cagna, Pro-Nuncio.

Zaire: Kinshasa, Nunciature; Lorenzo Antonetti.

Zambia: Lusaka, Nunciature; Luciano Angeloni, Pro-Nuncio.

Apostolic Delegate to U.S.

The representative of the Pope to the Catholic Church in the United States is Archbishop Jean Jadot, apostolic delegate. He was born Nov. 23, 1909, in Brussels, Belgium; was ordained to the priesthood Feb. 11, 1934; was appointed titular bishop of Zuri Feb. 23, 1968; received episcopal ordination May 1, 1968; was apostolic delegate for Laos, Malaysia and Singapore (1968-71); held the additional post of pro-nuncio in Thailand (1969-71); was pro-nuncio apostolic in Cameroon and Gabon, and apostolic delegate for Equatorial Guinea (1971-73); was named apostolic delegate to the United States in 1973; is the first non-Italian to hold the post.

The US Apostolic Delegation was established Jan. 21, 1893. It is located at 3339 Massachusetts Ave. N.W., Washington, D.C. 20008.

Archbishop Jadot's predecessors were Archbishops: Francesco Satolli (1893-1896), Sebastiano Martinelli, O.S.O. (1896-1902), Diomede Falconio, O.F.M. (1902-1911), Giovanni Bonzano (1911-1922), Pietro Fumasoni-Biondi (1922-1933), Amleto Cicognani (1933-1958), Egidio Vagnozzi (1958-1967) and Luigi Raimondi (1967-1973).

Amleto Cicognani, for 25 years apostolic delegate to the US, became a cardinal in 1958 and served as papal secretary of state from 1961 to 1969.

DIPLOMATS AT VATICAN

(Sources: *Annuario Pontificio, L'Osservatore Romano,* NC News Service. As of July 1, 1975.)

Algeria: Raouf Boudjakdji, Ambassador.

Argentina: Ricardo Cesar Guardo, Ambassador.

Australia: John Mills McMillan, Ambassador.

Austria: Gordian Gudenus, Ambassador.

Bangladesh: Humayun Rasheed Choudhury, Ambassador.

Belgium: Werner de Merode, Ambassador.

Bolivia: Eduardo Zabalago Canelas, Ambassador.

Brazil: Antonio B. L. Castello Branco, Ambassador.

Burundi: Adolphe Binagana, Ambassador.

Cameroon: Ambassador.

Canada: Paul Tremblay, Ambassador.

Central African Republic: Ambassador.

Chile: Hector Riesle Contreras, Ambassador.

China (Taiwan): Chen Chih-Mai, Ambassador.

Colombia: Antonio Rocha, Ambassador.

Costa Rica: Ambassador.

Cuba: Ambassador.

Cyprus: Polys Modinos, Ambassador.

Dahomey: Virgile-Octave Tevoedjre, Ambassador.

Dominican Republic: Alvaro Logrono Batlle, Ambassador.

Ecuador: Clemente Yerovi Indaburu, Ambassador.

Egypt: Mohamed el Shafei Abdel Hamid, Ambassador.

El Salvador: Gustavo A. Guerrero, Ambassador.

Ethiopia: Ambassador.

Finland: Jussi Makinen, Ambassador.

France: Gerard Almanrich, Ambassador.

Gabon: Ambassador.

Germany: Alexander Böker, Ambassador.

Great Britain: Dugald Malcolm, Minister.

Guatemala: Luis Valladares y Aycinena, Ambassador.

Haiti: Delinois Celestin, Ambassador.

Honduras: Carlos Lopez Contreras, Ambassador.

India: Avtar Singh, Ambassador.

Indonesia: Soebagio Surjaningrat, Ambassador.

Iran: Mehdi Vakil, Ambassador.

Iraq: Hassan Mustafa Al-Nakib, Ambassador.

Ireland: Gerard Wood, Ambassador.

Italy: Gian Franco Pompei, Ambassador.

Ivory Coast: Joseph Amichia, Ambassador.

Japan: Jiri Inagawa, Ambassador.

Kenya: Henry Nzioka, Ambassador.

Korea: Hyun Joon Shin, Ambassador.

Kuwait: Faisal Al Saleh al Mutawa, Ambassador.

Lebanon: Nagib Dahdah, Ambassador.

Lesotho: Ambassador.

Liberia: Reide Wiles, Ambassador.

Lithuania: Stasys Lozoraitis, Jr., first secretary.

Luxembourg: Ambassador.

Malagasy Republic: Jules A. Razafimbahiny, Ambassador.

Malawi: Joe Kachingwe, Ambassador.

Malta: Paolo Farrugia, Ambassador.

Mauritius: Leckraz Teelock, Ambassador.

Monaco: Cesar Charles Solamito, Minister.

Netherlands: Baron Sweder Godfried van Voorst tot Voorst, Ambassador.

New Zealand: Paul Gabites, Ambassador.

Nicaragua: Enrique Fernando Sanchez Salinas, Ambassador.

Niger: Ambassador.

Order of Malta: Count Stanislaus Pecci, Minister.

Pakistan: Mohammad Yousuf, Ambassador.

Panama: Arturo Morgan Morales, Ambassador.
Paraguay: Ambassador.
Peru: Jose Luis de Cossio y Ruiz De Somocurcio, Ambassador.
Philippines: Carlos Valdes, Ambassador.
Portugal: Jose Calvet de Magalhaes, Ambassador.
Rwanda: Ignace Karuhije, Ambassador.
San Marino: Minister.
Senegal: Henry Rene Dodds, Ambassador.
Spain: Gabriel Fernandez de Valderrame y Moreno, Ambassador.
Sudan: Ambassador.
Syria (Arab Republic): Sami al-Droubi, Ambassador.
Tanzania: Daniel Narcis Mtonga Mloka, Ambassador.
Thailand: Sangkadis Diskul, Ambassador.
Tunisia: Abdelmalek Bergaoui, Ambassador.
Turkey: Taha Carim, Ambassador.
Uganda: Miss Bernadette Olowo, Ambassador.
Upper Volta: Pierre Ilboudo, Ambassador.
Uruguay: Abraham Raoul, Ambassador.
Venezuela: Eduardo Tamayo Gascue, Ambassador.
Yugoslavia: Stane Kolman, Ambassador.
Zaire: Lombume Yam Mujwan Kallymazi, Ambassador.
Zambia: Amock Israel Phiri, Ambassador.

U.S. — Vatican Relations

Official relations for trade and diplomatic purposes were maintained by the United States and the Papal States while the latter had the character of and acted like other sovereign powers in the international community.

Consular Relations

Consular relations developed in the wake of an announcement, made by the papal nuncio in Paris to the American mission there Dec. 15, 1784, that the Papal States had agreed to open several Mediterranean ports to US shipping.

US consular representation in the Papal States began with the appointment of John B. Sartori, a native of Rome, in June, 1797. Sartori's successors as consuls were:Felix Cicognani, also a Roman, and Americans George W. Greene, Nicholas Browne, William C. Sanders, Daniel LeRoy, Horatio V. Glentworth, W.J. Stillman, Edwin C. Cushman, David M. Armstrong.

Consular officials of the Papal States who served in the US were: Count Ferdinand Lucchesi, 1826 to 1829, who resided in Washington; John B. Sartori, 1829 to 1841, who resided in Trenton, N.J.; Daniel J. Desmond, 1841 to 1850, who resided in Philadelphia; Louis B. Binsse, 1850 to 1895, who resided in New York.

US recognition of the consul of the Papal States did not cease when the states were absorbed into the Kingdom of Italy in 1871, despite pressure from Baron Blanc, the Italian minister. Binsse held the title until his death Mar. 28, 1895. No one was appointed to succeed him.

Diplomatic Relations

The US Senate approved a recommendation, made by President James K. Polk in December, 1847, for the establishment of a diplomatic post in the Papal States. Jacob L. Martin, the first charge d'affaires, arrived in Rome Aug. 2, 1848, and presented his credentials to Pius IX Aug. 19. Martin, who died within a month, was succeeded by Lewis Cass, Jr. Cass became minister resident in 1854 and served in that capacity until his retirement in 1858.

John P. Stockton, who later became a US Senator from New Jersey, was minister resident from 1858 to 1861. Rufus King was named to succeed him but, instead, accepted a commission as a brigadier general in the Army. Alexander W. Randall of Wisconsin took the appointment. He was succeeded in August, 1862, by Richard M. Blatchford who served until the following year. King was again nominated minister resident and served in that capacity until 1867 when the ministry was ended because of objections from some quarters in the US and failure to appropriate funds for its continuation. J.C. Hooker, a secretary, remained in the Papal States until the end of March, 1868, closing the ministry and performing functions of courtesy.

Myron C. Taylor, appointed in 1939, was Pres. Franklin D. Roosevelt's personal representative to Pope Pius XII. Henry Cabot Lodge, appointed in 1970, was Pres. Richard M. Nixon's personal representative to Pope Paul VI. Neither man had diplomatic status or rank.

VATICAN CITY

The State of Vatican City (Stato della Citta del Vaticano) is the territorial seat of the papacy. The smallest sovereign state in the world, it is situated within the city of Rome, embraces an area of 108.7 acres, and includes within its limits the Vatican Palace, museums, art galleries, gardens, libraries, radio station, post office, bank, astronomical observatory, offices, apartments, service facilities, St. Peter's Basilica, and neighboring buildings between the Basilica and Viale Vaticano.

The extraterritorial rights of Vatican City extend to more than 10 buildings in Rome, including the major basilicas and office buildings of various congregations of the Roman Curia, and to the **Villa of Castel Gandolfo** 15 miles southeast of the City of Rome. Castel Gandolfo is the summer residence of the Holy Father.

The government of Vatican City is in the hands of the reigning pope, who has full executive, legislative and judicial power. The administration of affairs, however, is handled by the Pontifical Commission for the State of Vatican City. The legal system is based on Canon Law; in cases where this code does not obtain, the laws of the City of Rome apply. The City is an absolutely neutral state and enjoys all the rights and privileges of a sovereign power. The Secretariat of State (Papal Secretariat) maintains diplomatic relations with other nations. The citizens of Vatican City, and they alone, owe allegiance to the pope as a temporal head of state.

Cardinals of the Roman Curia residing outside Vatican City enjoy the privileges of extraterritoriality.

The normal population is approximately 1,000. While the greater percentage is made up of priests and religious, there are several hundred lay persons living in Vatican City. They are housed in their own apartments in the City and are engaged in secretarial, domestic, trade and service occupations. About 3,000 persons are employed by the Vatican.

Services of honor and order are performed by the Swiss Guards, who have been charged with responsibility for the personal safety of popes since 1506. Additional police and ceremonial functions are under the supervision of a special office. These functions were formerly handled by the Papal Gendarmes, the Palatine Guard of Honor, and the Guard of Honor of the Pope (Pontifical Noble Guard) which Pope Paul disbanded Sept. 14, 1970.

The **Basilica of St. Peter,** built between 1506 and 1626, is the largest church in Christendom and the site of most papal ceremonies. The pope's own patriarchal basilica, however, is **St. John Lateran,** whose origins date back to 324.

St. Ann's is the parish church of Vatican City.

The **Vatican Library,** one of five in the City, has among its holdings 70,000 manuscripts, 770,000 printed books, and 7,500 incunabula.

The independent temporal power of the pope, which is limited to the confines of Vatican City and small areas outside, was for many centuries more extensive than it is now. As late as the nineteenth century, the pope ruled 16,000 square miles of Papal States across the middle of Italy, with a population of over 3,000,000. In 1870 forces of the Kingdom of Italy occupied these lands which, with the exception of the small areas surrounding the Vatican and Lateran in Rome and the Villa of Castel Gandolfo, became part of the Kingdom by the Italian law of May 13, 1871.

The **Roman Question,** occasioned by this seizure and the voluntary confinement of the pope to the limited papal lands, was finally settled with ratification of the Lateran Agreement on June 7, 1929, by the Italian government and Vatican City and provided a financial indemnity for the former Papal States,

which became recognized as part of Italy. The Lateran Agreement became Article 7 of the Italian Constitution on Mar. 26, 1947.

Papal Flag

The papal flag consists of two equal vertical stripes of yellow and white, charged with the insignia of the papacy on the white stripe — a triple crown or tiara over two crossed keys, one of gold and one of silver, tied with a red cord and two tassels. The divisions of the crown represent the teaching, sanctifying and ruling offices of the pope. The keys symbolize his jurisdictional authority.

The papal flag is a national flag inasmuch as it is the standard of the Supreme Pontiff as the sovereign of the state of Vatican City. It is also universally accepted by the faithful as a symbol of the supreme spiritual authority of the Holy Father.

In a Catholic church, the papal flag is displayed on a staff on the left side of the sanctuary (facing the congregation), and the American flag is displayed on the right.

Vatican Radio

The declared purpose of Vatican Radio Station HVJ is "that the voice of the Supreme Pastor may be heard throughout the world by means of the ether waves, for the glory of Christ and the salvation of souls." Designed by Guglielmo Marconi, the inventor of radio, and supervised by him until his death, the station was inaugurated by Pope Pius XI in 1931.

Vatican Radio operates on international wave lengths, transmits programs in 33 languages, and serves as a channel of communication between the Vatican, church officials and listeners in general in many parts of the world. The station broadcasts about 470 programs a week throughout the world.

The staff of 200 broadcasters and technicians includes 29 Jesuits and is directed by Father Robert Tucci, S.J. Headquarters are located in Vatican City. Studios and offices are at Palazzo Pio, Piazza Pia, 3. The transmitters are situated at Santa Maria di Galeria, a 200-acre site 16 miles from Rome.

1975 Vatican Stamps

The Vatican Philatelic Office scheduled the following issues of stamps for 1975. (Issue date is given where available.)

• Series reproducing some fountains and architectural views of Vatican City, commemorating the European Architectural Heritage Year, issued May 22 in six values (20, 40, 50, 90 and 100 lire) on six different subjects.

• A 300-lira stamp celebrating the solemnity of Pentecost, issued May 22.

• Series commemorating the Ninth International Congress of Christian Archeology, issued Sept. 25 in three values (30, 150 and 200 lire) on three subjects.

• Series commemorating fifth centenary of

founding of Vatican Library, issued Sept. 25 in three values (70, 100, and 250 lire) on three subjects.

• Series commemorating the second centenary of the death of St. Paul of the Cross.

A new type of Aerogram for the Holy Year was also scheduled for release.

Papal Audiences

General audiences are scheduled weekly, on Wednesday at noon.

In Vatican City, they are held in the Audience Hall on the south side of St. Peter's Basilica. The hall, which was opened in 1971, has a seating capacity of 6,800 and a total capacity of 12,000.

From about the middle of July to the middle of September, they are held in a smaller hall at Castel Gandolfo, where the pope spends a working vacation.

General audiences last from about 60 to 90 minutes, during which the pope gives a talk and his blessing. A résumé of the talk, which is usually in Italian, is given in several languages.

Arrangements for papal audiences are handled by an office of the Prefecture of the Apostolic Household.

American visitors can obtain passes for general audiences by applying to the Bishops' Office for United States Visitors to the Vatican, Casa Santa Maria, Via dell'Umilita, 30, 00187 Rome.

Private and group audiences are reserved for dignitaries of various categories and for special occasions.

Publications

Acta Apostolicae Sedis: The only "official commentary" of the Holy See, was established in 1908 for the publication of activities of the Holy See, laws, decrees and acts of congregations and tribunals of the Roman Curia. The first edition was published in January, 1909.

St. Pius X made *AAS* an official organ in 1908. Laws promulgated for the Church ordinarily take effect three months after the date of their publication in this commentary.

The publication, mostly in Latin and Italian, is printed by the Vatican Polyglot Press.

The immediate predecessor of this organ was *Acta Sanctae Sedis*, founded in 1865 and given official status by the Congregation for the Propagation of the Faith in 1904.

Annuario Pontificio: The yearbook of the Holy See. It is edited by the Vatican Secretariat of State and is printed in Italian, with some portions in other languages, by the Vatican Polyglot Press. It covers the worldwide organization of the Church, lists members of the hierarchy, and includes a wide range of statistical information.

The publication of a statistical yearbook of the Holy See dates back to 1716, when a volume called *Notizie* appeared. Publication

under the present title began in 1860, was suspended in 1870, and resumed again in 1872 under the title *Catholic Hierarchy*. This volume was printed privately at first, but has been issued by the Vatican Press since 1885. The title *Annuario Pontificio* was restored in 1912, and the yearbook was called an "official publication" until 1924.

L'Osservatore Romano: The daily newspaper of the Holy See. It began publication July 1, 1861, as an independent enterprise under the ownership and direction of four Catholic laymen headed by Marcantonio Pacelli, vice minister of the interior under Pope Pius IX and a grandfather of the late Pius XII. Leo XIII bought the publication in 1890, making it the "pope's" own newspaper.

The only official material in *L'Osservatore Romano* is that which appears under the heading, "Nostre Informazioni." This includes notices of appointments by the Holy See, the texts of papal encyclicals and addresses by the Holy Father and others, various types of documents, accounts of decisions and rulings of administrative bodies, and similar items. Additional material includes news and comment on developments in the Church and the world. Italian is the language most used.

The bulk of the contents of each edition is determined by a "well defined policy in line with the teaching and the attitudes of the Church . . . which the editorial staff follows with full and direct responsibility," according to Federico Alessandrini, Vatican press officer.

The editorial board is directed by Raimondo Manzini. A staff of about 15 reporters covers Rome news sources. A corps of correspondents provides foreign coverage.

A weekly roundup edition in English was inaugurated in 1968. Other weekly editions are printed in French, Spanish, Portuguese and German.

Vatican Press Office: The establishment of a single Vatican Press Office was announced Feb. 29, 1968, to replace service agencies formerly operated by *L'Osservatore Romano* and an office created for press coverage of the Second Vatican Council. Prof. Federico Alessandrini is the director.

Vatican Polyglot Press: The official printing plant of the Vatican.

The Vatican press was conceived by Marcellus II and Pius IV but was actually founded by Sixtus V on Apr. 27, 1587, to print the Vulgate and the writings of the Fathers of Church and other authors. A Polyglot Press was established in 1626 by the Congregation for the Propagation of the Faith to serve the needs of the Oriental Church. St. Pius X merged both presses under this title.

The plant has facilities for the printing of a wide variety of material in about 30 languages.

Activities of the Holy See: An annual documentary volume covering the activities of the pope — his daily work, general and special audiences, discourses and messages on special occasions, visits outside the Vatican, missionary and charitable endeavors, meetings with diplomats, heads of state and others — and activities of the congregations, commissions, tribunals and offices of the Roman Curia.

Statistical Yearbook of the Church: Issued by the Central Statistics Office of the Church, it contains principal data concerning the presence and work of the Church in the world. The first issue was published in 1972 under the title *Collection of Statistical Tables, 1969.* It is printed in corresponding columns of Italian and Latin. Some of the introductory material is printed in other languages.

VATICAN REPRESENTATIVES

(Sources: *Annuario Pontificio;* NC News Service.)

The Vatican has representatives to a number of quasi-governmental and international organizations.

Governmental Organizations: United Nations (Msgr. Giovanni Cheli, permanent observer); UN Office in Geneva (Msgr. Silvio Luoni, permanent observer); International Atomic Energy Agency (Dr. Hermann Abs, Msgr. Orlano Quilici, delegates); UN Organization for Industrial Development (Msgr. Orlano Quilici, delegate); UN Food and Agriculture Organization (Most Rev. Agostino Ferrari-Toniolo, permanent observer); UN Educational, Scientific and Cultural Organization (Msgr. Luigi Conti, permanent observer);

Council of Europe (Abp. Egano Righi Lambertini, special minister with function of permanent observer); Council for Cultural Cooperation of the Council of Europe (Msgr. Justo Mullor Garcia, delegate); International Institute for the Unification of Private Law (Prof. Pio Ciprotti, delegate); International Committee of Medicine and Pharmacy (Msgr. Victor Heylen); International Union of Official Organizations of Tourism (Rev. Giovanni Arrighi, O.P.); International Geographic Union (Prof. Gastone Imbrighi);

Universal Postal Union; International Telecommunications Union; International Council on Grain; International Union for the Protection of Literary and Artistic Works; International Union for the Protection of Industrial Property; International Organization of Telecommunication via Satellite (Intelsat); European Conference of Postal and Telecommunication Administration (CEPT).

Non-Governmental Organizations: International Committee of Historical Sciences (Msgr. Michele Maccarrone); International Committee of Paleography (Msgr. Jose Ruysschaert); International Committee of the History of Art (Dr. Deocletio Redig de

Campos); International Committee of Anthropological and Ethnological Sciences; International Committee for the Neutrality of Medicine (Rev. Michel Riquet, S.J., permanent observer); International Center of Study for the Preservation and Restoration of Cultural Goods (Dr. Deocletio Redig de Campos); International Council of Monuments and Sites (Dr. Deocletio Redig de Campos, delegate); International Astronomical Union; International Institute of Administrative Sciences; International Technical Committee for Prevention and Extinction of Fires; World Medical Association.

AMERICAN CHURCH

The Church of Santa Susanna was established as the national church for Americans in Rome Feb. 28, 1922, and entrusted to the Paulist Fathers who have served there continuously since then except for several years during World War II.

The golden jubilee of the church was observed May 21, 1972.

VATICAN ASSETS

Cardinal Egidio Vagnozzi, head of the Prefecture for the Economic Affairs of the Holy See, stated in a March, 1975, press interview that the value of the Vatican's "productive assets" throughout the world amounted to less than $125 million.

The cardinal said published reports that the Vatican's revenue-producing assets totaled $10 billion or as much as $20 billion were "completely nonsensical."

Asked by a reporter if the Vatican's productive assets might be worth $500 million, he replied:

"I can tell you that the Holy See's productive assets in Italy and the rest of the world are worth less than a quarter of the amount you mentioned."

The cardinal added that he was not authorized to state the exact amount. He noted that the assets consisted of "mixed property, real estate and movables — stocks and bonds."

Some but not all of the Vatican's investments were transferred in recent years out of Italy to the United States and other countries, in search of a better return.

Commenting on exaggerated speculation about the wealth of the Vatican, Cardinal Vagnozzi said:

"I wish the public, and Catholics in particular, would not believe everything that is written in the papers about the Vatican's finances, because a great deal of what is said is based on hearsay, on indiscretions of ill-informed people, or on estimates for which there is no foundation in fact."

The interview with Cardinal Vagnozzi, a former apostolic delegate to the United States, appeared in *Europa*, a monthly financial supplement published simultaneously by leading European newspapers.

Doctrine of the Catholic Church

Following are excerpts from the first two chapters of the *Dogmatic Constitution on the Church* promulgated by the Second Vatican Council. They describe the relation of the Catholic Church to the Kingdom of God, the nature and foundation of the Church, the People of God, the necessity of membership and participation in the Church for salvation.

Additional subjects in the constitution are treated in other Almanac entries.

I. MYSTERY OF THE CHURCH

". . . By her relationship with Christ, the Church is a kind of sacrament or sign of intimate union with God, and of the unity of all mankind . . ." (No. 1).

". . . He (the eternal Father) planned to assemble in the holy Church all those who would believe in Christ. Already from the beginning of the world the foreshadowing of the Church took place. She was prepared for in a remarkable way throughout the history of the people of Israel and by means of the Old Covenant. Established in the present era of time, the Church was made manifest by the outpouring of the Spirit. At the end of time she will achieve her glorious fulfillment. Then . . . all just men from the time of Adam, 'from Abel, the just one, to the last of the elect,' will be gathered together with the Father in the universal Church" (No. 2).

"When the work which the Father had given the Son to do on earth (cf. Jn. 17:4) was accomplished, the Holy Spirit was sent on the day of Pentecost in order that He might forever sanctify the Church, and thus all believers would have access to the Father through Christ in the one Spirit (cf. Eph. 2:18). . . .

"The Spirit dwells in the Church and in the hearts of the faithful as in a temple (cf. 1 Cor. 3:16; 6:19). . . . The Spirit guides the Church into the fullness of truth (cf. Jn. 16:13) and gives her a unity of fellowship and service. He furnishes and directs her with various gifts, both hierarchical and charismatic, and adorns her with the fruits of His grace (cf. Eph. 4:11-12; 1 Cor. 12:4; Gal. 5:22). By the power of the gospel He makes the Church grow, perpetually renews her, and leads her to perfect union with her Spouse. . . ." (No. 4).

Foundation of the Church

"The mystery of the holy Church is manifest in her very foundation, for the Lord Jesus inaugurated her by preaching the good news, that is, the coming of God's Kingdom, which, for centuries, had been promised in the Scriptures. . . . In Christ's word, in His works, and in His presence this kingdom reveals itself to men. . . .

"The miracles of Jesus also confirm that the kingdom has already arrived on earth. . . .

"Before all things, however, the kingdom is clearly visible in the very person of Christ, Son of God and Son of Man. . . .

"When Jesus rose up again after suffering death on the cross for mankind, He manifested that He had been appointed Lord, Messiah, and Priest forever (cf. Acts 2:36; Hb. 5:6; 7:17-21), and He poured out on His disciples the Spirit promised by the Father (cf. Acts 2:33). The Church, consequently, equipped with the gifts of her Founder and faithfully guarding His precepts . . . receives the mission to proclaim and to establish among all peoples the kingdom of Christ and of God. She becomes on earth the initial budding forth of that kingdom. While she slowly grows, the Church strains toward the consummation of the kingdom and, with all her strength, hopes and desires to be united in glory with her King" (No. 5).

Figures of the Church

"In the Old Testament the revelation of the kingdom had often been conveyed by figures of speech. In the same way the inner nature of the Church was now to be made known to us through various images . . .

". . . The Church is a sheepfold . . . a flock . . . a tract of land to be cultivated, the field of God . . . His choice vineyard . . . the true Vine is Christ . . . the edifice of God . . . the house of God . . . the holy temple (whose members are) . . . living stones . . . this Holy City . . . a bride . . . 'our Mother' . . . the spotless spouse of the spotless Lamb . . . an exile. . ." (No. 6).

"In the human nature which He united to Himself, the Son of God redeemed man and transformed him into a new creation (cf. Gal. 6:15; 2 Cor. 5:17) by overcoming death through His own death and resurrection. By communicating His Spirit to His brothers, called together from all peoples, Christ made them mystically into His own body.

"In that body, the life of Christ is poured into the believers, who, through the sacraments, are united in a hidden and real way to Christ who suffered and was glorified. Through baptism we are formed in the likeness of Christ. . . .

"Truly partaking of the body of the Lord in the breaking of the Eucharistic bread, we are taken up into communion with Him and with one another . . ." (No. 7).

One Body in Christ

"As all the members of the human body, though they are many, form one body, so also are the faithful in Christ (cf. 1 Cor. 12:12). Also, in the building up of Christ's body there is a flourishing variety of members and functions. There is only one Spirit who . . . distributes His different gifts for the welfare of the Church (cf. 1 Cor. 12:1-11). Among these gifts stands out the grace given to the apostles. To their authority, the Spirit Himself subjected even those who were endowed with charisms (cf. 1 Cor. 14). . . .

"The head of this body is Christ . . ." (No. 7).

Mystical Body of Christ

"Christ, the one Mediator, established and ceaselessly sustains here on earth His holy Church, the community of faith, hope, and charity, as a visible structure. Through her He communicates truth and grace to all. But the society furnished with hierarchical agencies and the Mystical Body of Christ are not to be considered as two realities, nor are the visible assembly and the spiritual community, nor the earthly Church and the Church enriched with heavenly things. Rather they form one interlocked reality which is comprised of a divine and a human element. For this reason . . . this reality is compared to the mystery of the incarnate Word. Just as the assumed nature inseparably united to the divine Word serves Him as a living instrument of salvation, so, in a similar way, does the communal structure of the Church serve Christ's Spirit, who vivifies it by way of building up the body (cf. Eph. 4:16).

"This is the unique Church of Christ which in the Creed we avow as one, holy, catholic, and apostolic. After His Resurrection our Savior handed her over to Peter to be shepherded (Jn. 21:17), commissioning him and the other apostles to propagate and govern her (cf. Mt. 28:18, ff.). Her He erected for all ages as 'the pillar and mainstay of the truth' (1 Tm. 3:15). This Church, constituted and organized in the world as a society, subsists in the Catholic Church, which is governed by the successor of Peter and by the bishops in union with that successor, although many elements of sanctification and of truth can be found outside of her visible structure. These elements, however, as gifts properly belonging to the Church of Christ, possess an inner dynamism toward Catholic unity.

". . . the Church, embracing sinners in her bosom, is at the same time holy and always in need of being purified, and incessantly pursues the path of penance and renewal.

"The Church, 'like a pilgrim in a foreign land, presses forward . . .' announcing the cross and death of the Lord until He comes (cf. 1 Cor. 11:26) . . ." (No. 8).

II. THE PEOPLE OF GOD

"At all times and among every people, God has given welcome to whosoever fears Him and does what is right (cf. Acts 10:35). It has pleased God, however, to make men holy and save them not merely as individuals without

any mutual bonds, but by making them into a single people, a people which acknowledges Him in truth and serves Him in holiness. He therefore chose the race of Israel as a people unto Himself. With it He set up a covenant. Step by step He taught this people by manifesting in its history both Himself and the decree of His will, and by making it holy unto Himself. All these things, however, were done by way of preparation and as a figure of that new and perfect covenant which was to be ratified in Christ. . . .

". . . Christ instituted this new covenant, that is to say, the new testament, in His blood (cf. 1 Cor. 11:25), by calling together a people made up of Jew and Gentile, making them one, not according to the flesh but in the Spirit.

"This was to be the new People of God . . . reborn . . . through the Word of the living God (cf. 1 Pt. 1:23) . . . from water and the Holy Spirit (cf. Jn. 3:5-6) . . . 'a chosen race, a royal priesthood, a holy nation, a purchased people. . . . You who in times past were not a people, but are now the people of God' (1 Pt. 2:9-10).

"That messianic people has for its head Christ. . . . Its law is the new commandment to love as Christ loved us (cf. Jn. 13:34). Its goal is the kingdom of God, which has been begun by God Himself on earth, and which is to be further extended until it is brought to perfection by Him at the end of time. . . .

". . . This messianic people, although it does not actually include all men, and may more than once look like a small flock, is nonetheless a lasting and sure seed of unity, hope, and salvation for the whole human race. Established by Christ as a fellowship of life, charity, and truth, it is also used by Him as an instrument for the redemption of all, and is sent forth into the whole world as the light of the world and the salt of the earth (cf. Mt. 5:13-16).

"Israel according to the flesh . . . was already called the Church of God (2 Ezr. 13:1; cf. Nm. 20:4; Dt. 23:1, ff.). Likewise the new Israel . . . is also called the Church of Christ (cf. Mt. 16:18). For He has bought it for Himself with His blood (cf. Acts 20:28), has filled it with His Spirit, and provided it with those means which befit it as a visible and social unity. God has gathered together as one all those who in faith look upon Jesus as the author of salvation and the source of unity and peace, and has established them as the Church, that for each and all she may be the visible sacrament of this saving unity . . ." (No. 9)

Priesthood

". . . The baptized, by regeneration and the anointing of the Holy Spirit, are consecrated into . . . a holy priesthood. . . ."

(All members of the Church participate in

the priesthood of Christ, through the common priesthood of the faithful. See Priesthood of the Laity.)

"Though they differ from one another in essence and not only in degree, the common priesthood of the faithful and the ministerial or hierarchical priesthood are nonetheless interrelated. Each of them in its own special way is a participation in the one priesthood of Christ . . ." (No. 10).

"It is through the sacraments and the exercise of the virtues that the sacred nature and organic structure of the priestly community is brought into operation . . ." (No. 11). (See Role of the Sacraments.)

Prophetic Office

"The holy People of God shares also in Christ's prophetic office. It spreads abroad a living witness to Him, especially by means of a life of faith and charity and by offering to God a sacrifice of praise. . . . The body of the faithful as a whole, anointed as they are by the Holy One (cf. Jn. 2:20, 27), cannot err in matters of belief. Thanks to a supernatural sense of faith which characterizes the People as a whole, it manifests this unerring quality when, 'from the bishops down to the last member of the laity,' it shows universal agreement in matters of faith and morals.

". . . God's People accepts not the word of men but the very Word of God (cf. 1 Thes. 2:13). It clings without fail to the faith once delivered to the saints (cf. Jude 3), penetrates it more deeply by accurate insights, and applies it more thoroughly to life. All this it does under the lead of a sacred teaching authority to which it loyally defers.

"It is not only through the sacraments and Church ministries that the same Holy Spirit sanctifies and leads the People of God. . . . He distributes special graces among the faithful of every rank. By these gifts He makes them fit and ready to undertake the various tasks or offices advantageous for the renewal and upbuilding of the Church. . . . These charismatic gifts . . . are to be received with thanksgiving and consolation, for they are exceedingly suitable and useful for the needs of the Church.

". . . Judgment as to their genuineness and proper use belongs to those who preside over the Church, and to whose special competence it belongs . . . to test all things and hold fast to that which is good (cf. 1 Thes. 5:12; 19-21)" (No. 12).

All Are Called

"All men are called to belong to the new People of God. Wherefore this People, while remaining one and unique, is to be spread throughout the whole world and must exist in all ages, so that the purpose of God's will may be fulfilled. In the beginning God made human nature one. After His children were scattered, He decreed that they should at length be united again (cf. Jn. 11:52). It was for this reason that God sent His Son . . . that He might be Teacher, King, and Priest of all, the Head of the new and universal people of the sons of God. For this God finally sent His Son's Spirit as Lord and Lifegiver. He it is who, on behalf of the whole Church and each and every one of those who believe, is the principle of their coming together and remaining together in the teaching of the apostles and in fellowship, in the breaking of bread and in prayers (cf. Acts 2:42)" (No. 13).

One People of God

"It follows that among all the nations of earth there is but one People of God, which takes its citizens from every race, making them citizens of a kingdom which is of a heavenly and not an earthly nature. For all the faithful scattered throughout the world are in communion with each other in the Holy Spirit. . . . the Church or People of God . . . foster(s) and take(s) to herself, insofar as they are good, the ability, resources and customs of each people. Taking them to herself she purifies, strengthens, and ennobles them . . . This characteristic of universality which adorns the People of God is a gift from the Lord Himself. By reason of it, the Catholic Church strives energetically and constantly to bring all humanity with all its riches back to Christ its Head in the unity of His Spirit.

"In virtue of this catholicity each individual part of the Church contributes through its special gifts to the good of the other parts and of the whole Church. Thus through the common sharing of gifts . . . the whole and each of the parts receive increase. . . .

"All men are called to be part of this catholic unity of the People of God. . . . And there belong to it or are related to it in various ways, the Catholic faithful as well as all who believe in Christ, and indeed the whole of mankind. For all men are called to salvation by the grace of God" (No. 13).

The Catholic Church

"This sacred Synod turns its attention first to the Catholic faithful. Basing itself upon sacred Scripture and tradition, it teaches that the Church . . . is necessary for salvation. For Christ, made present to us in His Body, which is the Church, is the one Mediator and the unique Way of salvation. In explicit terms He Himself affirmed the necessity of faith and baptism (cf. Mk. 16:16; Jn. 3:5) and thereby affirmed also the necessity of the Church, for through baptism as through a door men enter the Church. Whosoever, therefore, knowing that the Catholic Church was made necessary by God through Jesus Christ, would refuse to enter her or to remain in her could not be saved.

"They are fully incorporated into the society of the Church who, possessing the Spirit of Christ, accept her entire system and all the means of salvation given to her, and through union with her visible structure are joined to Christ, who rules her through the Supreme Pontiff and the bishops. This joining is effected by the bonds of professed faith, of the sacraments, of ecclesiastical government, and of communion. He is not saved, however, who, though he is part of the body of the Church, does not persevere in charity. He remains indeed in the bosom of the Church, but . . . only in a 'bodily' manner and not 'in his heart.' . . .

"Catechumens who, moved by the Holy Spirit, seek with explicit intention to be incorporated into the Church are by that very intention joined to her. . . . Mother Church already embraces them as her own" (No. 14).

Other Christians, The Unbaptized

"The Church recognizes that in many ways she is linked with those who, being baptized, are honored with the name of Christian, though they do not profess the faith in its entirety or do not preserve unity of communion with the successor of Peter. . . .

" . . . We can say that in some real way they are joined with us in the Holy Spirit, for to them also He gives His gifts and graces, and is thereby operative among them with His sanctifying power . . ." (No. 15).

"Finally, those who have not yet received the gospel are related in various ways to the People of God. In the first place there is the people to whom the covenants and the promises were given and from whom Christ was born according to the flesh (cf. Rom. 9:4-5). On account of their fathers, this people remains most dear to God, for God does not repent of the gifts He makes nor of the calls He issues (cf. Rom. 11:28-29).

"But the plan of salvation also includes those who acknowledge the Creator. In the first place among these are the Moslems. . . . Nor is God Himself far distant from those who in shadows and images seek the unknown God. . . .

"Those also can attain to everlasting salvation who through no fault of their own do not know the gospel of Christ or His Church, yet sincerely seek God and, moved by grace, strive by their deeds to do His will as it is known to them through the dictates of conscience. Nor does divine Providence deny the help necessary for salvation to those who, without blame on their part, have not yet arrived at an explicit knowledge of God, but who strive to live a good life, thanks to His grace. Whatever goodness or truth is found among them is looked upon by the Church as a preparation for the Gospel. She regards such qualities as given by Him who enlightens all men so that they may finally have life . . ." (No. 16).

THE POPE, TEACHING AUTHORITY, COLLEGIALITY

The Roman Pontiff — the successor of St. Peter as the Vicar of Christ and head of the Church on earth — has full and supreme authority over the universal Church in matters pertaining to faith and morals (teaching authority), discipline and government (jurisdictional authority).

The primacy of the pope is real and supreme power. It is not merely a prerogative of honor — that is, of his being regarded as the first among equals. Neither does primacy imply that the pope is just the presiding officer of the collective body of bishops. The pope is the head of the Church.

Catholic belief in the primacy of the pope was stated in detail in the dogmatic constitution on the Church, *Pastor Aeternus,* approved in 1870 by the fourth session of the First Vatican Council. Some elaboration of the doctrine was made in the *Dogmatic Constitution on the Church* which was approved and promulgated by the Second Vatican Council Nov. 21, 1964. The entire body of teaching on the subject is based on Scripture and tradition and the centuries-long experience of the Church.

Infallibility

The essential points of doctrine concerning infallibility in the Church and the infallibility of the pope were stated by the Second Vatican Council in the *Dogmatic Constitution on the Church,* as follows:

"This infallibility with which the divine Redeemer willed his Church to be endowed in defining a doctrine of faith and morals extends as far as extends the deposit of divine revelation, which must be religiously guarded and faithfully expounded. This is the infallibility which the Roman Pontiff, the head of the college of bishops, enjoys in virtue of his office, when, as the supreme shepherd and teacher of all the faithful, who confirms his brethren in their faith (cf. Lk. 22:32), he proclaims by a definitive act some doctrine of faith or morals. Therefore his definitions, of themselves, and not from the consent of the Church, are justly styled irreformable, for they are pronounced with the assistance of the Holy Spirit, an assistance promised to him in blessed Peter. Therefore they need no approval of others, nor do they allow an appeal to any other judgment. For then the Roman Pontiff is not pronouncing judgment as a private person. Rather, as the supreme teacher of the universal Church, as one in whom the charism of the infallibility of the Church herself is individually present, he is expounding or defending a doctrine of Catholic faith.

"The infallibility promised to the Church resides also in the body of bishops when that body exercises supreme teaching authority with the successor of Peter. To the resultant definitions the assent of the Church can never be wanting, on account of the activity of that same Holy Spirit, whereby the whole flock of Christ is preserved and progresses in unity of faith.

"But when either the Roman Pontiff or the body of bishops together with him defines a judgment, they pronounce it in accord with revelation itself. All are obliged to maintain and be ruled by this revelation, which, as written or preserved by tradition, is transmitted in its entirety through the legitimate succession of bishops and especially through the care of the Roman Pontiff himself.

"Under the guiding light of the Spirit of truth, revelation is thus religiously preserved and faithfully expounded in the Church. The Roman Pontiff and the bishops, in view of their office and of the importance of the matter, strive painstakingly and by appropriate means to inquire properly into that revelation and to give apt expression to its contents. But they do not allow that there could be any new public revelation pertaining to the divine deposit of faith" (No. 25).

Authentic Teaching

The pope rarely speaks *ex cathedra* — that is, "from the chair" of St. Peter, for the purpose of making an infallible pronouncement. More often and in various ways he states authentic teaching in line with Scripture, tradition, the living experience of the Church, and the whole analogy of faith. Of such teaching, the Second Vatican Council said in its *Dogmatic Constitution on the Church* (No. 25):

". . . Religious submission of will and of mind must be shown in a special way to the authentic teaching authority of the Roman Pontiff, even when he is not speaking *ex cathedra*. That is, it must be shown in such a way that his supreme magisterium is acknowledged with reverence, the judgments made by him are sincerely adhered to, according to his manifest mind and will. His mind and will in the matter may be known chiefly either from the character of the documents, from his frequent repetition of the same doctrine, or from his manner of speaking."

With respect to bishops, the constitution said: "They are authentic teachers, that is, teachers endowed with the authority of Christ, who preach to the people committed to them the faith they must believe and put into practice. By the light of the Holy Spirit, they make that faith clear, bringing forth from the treasury of revelation new things and old (cf. Mt. 13:52), making faith bear fruit and vigilantly warding off any errors which threaten their flock (cf. Tm. 4:1-4).

"Bishops, teaching in communion with the Roman Pontiff, are to be respected by all as witnesses to divine and Catholic truth. In matters of faith and morals, the bishops speak in the name of Christ and the faithful are to accept their teaching and adhere to it with a religious assent of soul."

Magisterium—Teaching Authority

Responsibility for teaching doctrine and judging orthodoxy belongs to the official teaching authority of the Church.

This authority is personalized in the pope, the successor of St. Peter as head of the Church, and in the bishops together and in union with the pope, as it was originally committed to Peter and to the whole college of Apostles under his leadership. They are the official teachers of the Church.

Others have auxiliary relationships with the magisterium: theologians, in the study and clarification of doctrine; teachers — priests, religious, lay persons — who cooperate with the pope and bishops in spreading knowledge of religious truth; the faithful, who by their sense of faith and personal witness contribute to the development of doctrine and the establishment of its relevance to life in the Church and the world.

The magisterium, Pope Paul noted in an address at a general audience Jan. 11, 1967, "is a subordinate and faithful echo and secure interpreter of the divine word." It does not reveal new truths, "nor is it superior to Sacred Scripture." Its competence extends to the limits of divine revelation manifested in Scripture and tradition and the living experience of the Church, with respect to matters of faith and morals and related subjects.

Official teaching in these areas is infallible when it is formally defined, for belief and acceptance by all members of the Church, by the pope, acting in the capacity of supreme shepherd of the flock of Christg and when doctrine is proposed and taught with moral unanimity of bishops with the pope in a solemn collegial manner as in an ecumenical council, and/or in the ordinary course of events. Even when not infallibly defined, official teaching in the areas of faith and morals is authoritative and requires religious assent.

The teachings of the magisterium have been documented in creeds, formulas of faith, decrees and enactments of ecumenical and particular councils, various kinds of doctrinal statements, and other teaching instruments. They have also been incorporated into the liturgy, with the result that the law of prayer is said to be a law of belief.

Collegiality

The bishops of the Church, in union with the pope, have supreme teaching and pastoral authority over the whole Church in addition to the authority of office they have for their own dioceses.

This collegial authority is exercised in a solemn manner in an ecumenical council and can be exercised in other ways as well, "provided that the head of the college calls them to collegiate action, or at least so approves or freely accepts the united action of the dispersed bishops, that it is made a true collegiate act."

This doctrine is grounded on the fact that: "Just as, by the Lord's will, St. Peter and the other apostles constituted one apostolic col-

lege, so in a similar way the Roman Pontiff as the successor of Peter, and the bishops as the successors of the apostles are joined together."

Doctrine on collegiality was stated by the Second Vatican Council in the *Dogmatic Constitution on the Church* (Nos. 22 and 23).

REVELATION

Following are excerpts from the *Constitution on Revelation* promulgated by the Second Vatican Council. They describe the nature and process of divine revelation, inspiration and interpretation of Scripture, the Old and New Testaments, and the role of Scripture in the life of the Church.

I. Revelation Itself

". . . God chose to reveal Himself and to make known to us the hidden purpose of His will (cf. Eph. 1:9) by which through Christ, the Word made flesh, man has access to the Father in the Holy Spirit and comes to share in the divine nature (cf. Eph. 2:18; 2 Pt. 1:4). Through this revelation, therefore, the invisible God (cf. Col. 1:15; 1 Tm. 1:17) . . . speaks to men as friends (cf. Ex. 33:11; Jn. 15:14-15) and lives among them (cf. Bar. 3:38) so that He may invite and take them into fellowship with Himself. This plan of revelation is realized by deeds and words having an inner unity: the deeds wrought by God in the history of salvation manifest and confirm the teaching and realities signified by the words, while the words proclaim the deeds and clarify the mystery contained in them. By this revelation then, the deepest truth about God and the salvation of man is made clear to us in Christ, who is the Mediator and at the same time the fullness of all revelation" (No. 2).

"God . . . from the start manifested Himself to our first parents. Then after their fall His promise of redemption aroused in them the hope of being saved (cf. Gn. 3:15), and from that time on He ceaselessly kept the human race in His care, in order to give eternal life to those who perseveringly do good in search of salvation (cf. Rom. 2:6-7). . . . He called Abraham in order to make of him a great nation (cf. Gn. 12:2). Through the patriarchs, and after them through Moses and the prophets, He taught this nation to acknowledge Himself as the one living and true God . . . and to wait for the Savior promised by Him. In this manner He prepared the way for the gospel down through the centuries" (No. 3).

Revelation in Christ

"Then, after speaking in many places and varied ways through the prophets, God 'last of all in these days has spoken to us by His Son' (Hb. 1:1-2). . . . Jesus perfected revelation by fulfilling it through His whole work of making Himself present and manifesting Himself: through His words and deeds, His

signs and wonders, but especially through His death and glorious resurrection from the dead and final sending of the spirit of truth. Moreover, He confirmed with divine testimony what revelation proclaimed: that God is with us to free us from the darkness of sin and death, and to raise us up to life eternal.

"The Christian dispensation, therefore, as the new and definitive covenant, will never pass away, and we now await no further new public revelation before the glorious manifestation of our Lord Jesus Christ (cf. 1 Tm. 6:14; Ti. 2:13)" (No. 4).

II. Transmission of Revelation

". . . God has seen to it that what He had revealed for the salvation of all nations would abide perpetually in its full integrity and be handed on to all generations. Therefore Christ the Lord, in whom the full revelation of the supreme God is brought to completion (cf. 2 Cor. 1:20; 3:16; 4:6), commissioned the apostles to preach to all men that gospel which is the source of all saving truth and moral teaching, and thus to impart to them divine gifts. This gospel had been promised in former times through the prophets, and Christ Himself fulfilled it and promulgated it with His own lips. This commission was faithfully fulfilled by the apostles who, by their oral preaching, by example, and by ordinances, handed on what they had received from . . . Christ . . . or what they had learned through the prompting of the Holy Spirit. The commission was fulfilled, too, by those apostles and apostolic men who under the inspiration of the same Holy Spirit committed the message of salvation to writing" (No. 7).

Tradition

"But in order to keep the gospel forever whole and alive within the Church, the apostles left bishops as their successors, 'handing over their own teaching role' to them. This sacred tradition, therefore, and sacred Scripture of both the Old and the New Testament are like a mirror in which the pilgrim Church on earth looks at God . . ." (No. 7).

". . . The apostolic preaching, which is expressed in a special way in the inspired books, was to be preserved by a continuous succession of preachers until the end of time. Therefore the apostles, handing on what they themselves had received, warn the faithful to hold fast to the traditions which they have learned. . . . Now what was handed on by the apostles includes everything which contributes to the holiness of life, and the increase in faith of the People of God; and so the Church, in her teaching, life, and worship, perpetuates and hands on to all generations all that she herself is, all that she believes" (No. 8).

Development of Doctrine

"This tradition which comes from the apostles develops in the Church with the help of the Holy Spirit. For there is a growth in the understanding of the realities and the words which have been handed down. This happens through the contemplation and study made by believers . . . through the intimate understanding of spiritual things they experience, and through the preaching of those who have received through episcopal succession the sure gift of truth. For, as the centuries succeed one another, the Church constantly moves forward toward the fullness of divine truth until the words of God reach their complete fulfillment in her.

"The words of the holy Fathers witness to the living presence of this tradition, whose wealth is poured into the practice and life of the believing and praying Church. Through the same tradition the Church's full canon of the sacred books is known, and the sacred writings themselves are more profoundly understood and unceasingly made active in her; . . . and the Holy Spirit, through whom the living voice of the gospel resounds in the Church, and through her, in the world, leads unto all truth those who believe and makes the word of Christ dwell abundantly in them (cf. Col. 3:16)" (No. 8).

Tradition and Scripture

"Hence there exist a close connection and communication between sacred tradition and sacred Scripture. For both of them, flowing from the same divine wellspring, in a certain way merge into a unity and tend toward the same end. For sacred Scripture is the word of God inasmuch as it is consigned to writing under the inspiration of the divine Spirit. To the successors of the apostles, sacred tradition hands on in its full purity God's word, which was entrusted to the apostles by Christ the Lord and the Holy Spirit. Thus, led by the light of the Spirit of truth, these successors can in their preaching preserve this word of God faithfully, explain it, and make it more widely known. Consequently, it is not from sacred Scripture alone that the Church draws her certainty about everything which has been revealed. Therefore both sacred tradition and sacred Scripture are to be accepted and venerated with the same sense of devotion and reverence" (No. 9).

"Sacred tradition and sacred Scripture form one sacred deposit of the word of God, which is committed to the Church" (No. 10).

Teaching Authority of Church

"The task of authentically interpreting the word of God, whether written or handed on, has been entrusted exclusively to the living teaching office of the Church, whose authority is exercised in the name of Jesus Christ. This teaching office is not above the word of God, but serves it, teaching only what has been handed on . . . it draws from this one deposit of faith everything which it presents for belief as divinely revealed.

"It is clear, therefore, that sacred tradition, sacred Scripture, and the teaching authority of the Church . . . are so linked and joined together that one cannot stand without the others, and that all together and each in its own way under the action of the one Holy Spirit contribute effectively to the salvation of souls" (No. 10).

III. Inspiration, Interpretation

"Those . . . revealed realities . . . contained and presented in sacred Scripture have been committed to writing under the inspiration of the Holy Spirit. Holy Mother Church, relying on the belief of the apostles, holds that the books of both the Old and New Testament in their entirety, with all their parts, are sacred and canonical because, having been written under the inspiration of the Holy Spirit (cf. Jn. 20:31; 2 Tm. 3:16; 2 Pt. 1:19-21; 3:15-16) they have God as their author and have been handed on as such to the Church herself. In composing the sacred books, God chose men and while employed by Him they made use of their powers and abilities, so that with Him acting in them and through them, they, as true authors, consigned to writing everything and only those things which He wanted" (No. 11).

Inerrancy

"Therefore, since everything asserted by the inspired authors or sacred writers must be held to be asserted by the Holy Spirit, it follows that the books of Scripture must be acknowledged as teaching firmly, faithfully, and without error that truth which God wanted put into the sacred writings for the sake of our salvation. Therefore 'all Scripture is inspired by God and useful for teaching, for reproving, for correcting, for instruction in justice; that the man of God may be perfect, equipped for every good work' (2 Tm. 3:16-17)" (No. 11).

Literary Forms

"However, since God speaks in sacred Scripture through men in human fashion, the interpreter of sacred Scripture, in order to see clearly what God wanted to communicate to us, should carefully investigate what meaning the sacred writers really intended, and what God wanted to mainfest by means of their words.

"... The interpreter must investigate what meaning the sacred writer intended to express and actually expressed in particular circumstances as he used contemporary literary forms in accordance with the situation of his own time and culture. For the correct understanding of what the sacred author wanted to assert, due attention must be paid to the customary and characteristic styles of perceiving, speaking, and narrating which prevailed at the time of the sacred writer, and to the customs men normally followed at that period in their everyday dealings with one another" (No. 12).

Analogy of Faith

"... No less serious attention must be given to the content and unity of the whole of Scripture, if the meaning of the sacred texts is to be correctly brought to light. The living tradition of the whole Church must be taken into account along with the harmony which exists between elements of the faith. ... all of what has been said about the way of interpreting Scripture is subject finally to the judgment of the Church, which carries out the divine commission and ministry of guarding and interpreting the word of God" (No. 12).

IV. The Old Testament

"In carefully planning and preparing the salvation of the whole human race, the God of supreme love, by a special dispensation, chose for Himself a people to whom He might entrust His promises. First He entered into a covenant with Abraham (cf. Gn. 15:18) and, through Moses, with the people of Israel (cf. Ex. 24:8). To this people which He had acquired for Himself, He so manifested Himself through words and deeds as the one true and living God that Israel came to know by experience the ways of God with men. ... The plan of salvation, foretold by the sacred authors, recounted and explained by them, is found as the true word of God in the books of the Old Testament: these books, therefore, written under divine inspiration, remain permanently valuable ..." (No. 14).

Principal Purpose

"The principal purpose to which the plan of the Old Covenant was directed was to prepare for the coming both of Christ, the universal Redeemer, and of the messianic kingdom. ... Now the books of the Old Testament, in accordance with the state of mankind before the time of salvation established by Christ, reveal to all men the knowledge of God and of man and the ways in which God ... deals with men. These books ... show us true divine pedagogy ..." (No. 15).

"... The books of the Old Testament with all their parts, caught up into the proclamation of the gospel, acquire and show forth their full meaning in the New Testament (cf.

Mt. 5:17; Lk. 24:27; Rom. 16:25-26; 2 Cor. 3:14-16) and in turn shed light on it and explain it" (No. 16).

V. The New Testament

"The word of God ... is set forth and shows its power in a most excellent way in the writings of the New Testament. For when the fullness of time arrived (cf. Gal. 4:4), the Word was made flesh and dwelt among us in the fullness of grace and truth (cf. Jn. 1:14). Christ established the Kingdom of God on earth, manifested His Father and Himself by deeds and words, and completed His work by His death, resurrection, and glorious ascension and by the sending of the Holy Spirit. Having been lifted up from the earth, He draws all men to Himself (cf. Jn. 12:32). ... This mystery had not been manifested to other generations as it was now revealed to His holy apostles and prophets in the Holy Spirit (cf. Eph. 3:4-6), so that they might preach the Gospel, stir up faith in Jesus, Christ and Lord, and gather the Church together. To these realities, the writings of the New Testament stand as a perpetual and divine witness" (No. 17).

The Gospels and Other Writings

"... The Gospels have a special preeminence ... for they are the principal witness of the life and teaching of the incarnate Word, our Savior.

"The Church has always and everywhere held and continues to hold that the four Gospels are of apostolic origin. For what the apostles preached ... afterwards they themselves and apostolic men, under the inspiration of the divine Spirit, handed on to us in writing: the foundation of faith, namely, the fourfold Gospel, according to Matthew, Mark, Luke, and John" (No. 18).

"... The four Gospels, ... whose historical character the Church unhesitatingly asserts, faithfully hand on what Jesus Christ, while living among men, really did and taught for their eternal salvation until the day He was taken up into heaven (see Acts 1:1-2). Indeed, after the ascension of the Lord the apostles handed on to their hearers what He had said and done. ... The sacred authors wrote the four Gospels, selecting some things from the many which had been handed on by word of mouth or in writing, reducing some of them to a synthesis, explicating some things in view of the situation of their churches, and preserving the form of proclamation but always in such fashion that they told us the honest truth about Jesus. For their intention in writing was that ... we might know 'the truth' concerning those matters about which we have been instructed (cf. Lk. 1:2-4)" (No. 19).

"Besides the four Gospels, the canon of the New Testament also contains the Epistles of St. Paul and other apostolic writings, composed under the inspiration of the Holy Spirit. In these writings . . . those matters which concern Christ the Lord are confirmed, His true teaching is more and more fully stated, the saving power of the divine work of Christ is preached, the story is told of the beginnings of the Church and her marvelous growth, and her glorious fulfillment is foretold" (No. 20).

VI. Scripture in Church Life

"The Church has always venerated the divine Scriptures just as she venerates the body of the Lord. . . . She has always regarded the Scriptures together with sacred tradition as the supreme rule of faith, and will ever do so. For, inspired by God and committed once and for all to writing, they impart the word of God Himself without change, and make the voice of the Holy Spirit resound in the words of the prophets and apostles. Therefore, like the Christian religion itself, all the preaching of the Church must be nourished and ruled by sacred Scripture . . ." (No. 21).

"Easy access to sacred Scripture should be provided for all the Christian faithful. That is why the Church from the very beginning accepted as her own that very ancient Greek translation of the Old Testament which is named after seventy men (the Septuagint); and she has always given a place of honor to other translations, Eastern and Latin, especially the one known as the Vulgate. But since the word of God should be available at all times, the Church with maternal concern sees to it that suitable and correct translations are made into different languages, especially from the original texts of the sacred books. And if, given the opportunity and the approval of Church authority, these translations are produced in cooperation with the separated brethren as well, all Christians will be able to use them" (No. 22).

Biblical Studies, Theology

The constitution encouraged the development and progress of biblical studies "under the watchful care of the sacred teaching office of the Church." (Such studies have made great progress in recent years.)

It noted also: "Sacred theology rests on the written word of God, together with sacred tradition, as its primary and perpetual foundation," and that "the study of the sacred page is, as it were, the soul of sacred theology" (Nos. 23, 24).

PONTIFICAL BIBLICAL COMMISSION

The Pontifical Biblical Commission, which has been instrumental in directing the course of Catholic biblical scholarship, was established by Leo XIII Oct. 30, 1902, with the apostolic letter *Vigilantiae,* at a time when biblical studies were open to great promise as well as to the threat of Modernism.

The commission was ordered to promote biblical studies; to safeguard the correct interpretation of Scripture, in the pattern of the rule of faith and against the background of sound scholarship; to state positions which had to be held by Catholics on biblical questions; to indicate questions requiring further study and/or those which were open to the judgment of competent scholars. The commission was also authorized to set up standards for biblical studies and to grant degrees in Sacred Scripture.

The commission issued 23 decrees or decisions between 1905 and 1953; letters on the scientific study of the Bible (1941) and the Pentateuch (1948); instructions on teaching Scripture in seminaries (1950), biblical associations (1955), and the historical truth of the Gospels (1964).

Pope St. Pius X stated the authority of decisions of the commission in the letter *Illibatae,* which he issued June 29, 1910, on his own initiative:

"All are bound in conscience to submit to the decisions of the Pontifical Biblical Commission pertaining to doctrine, whether already issued or to be issued in the future, in the same way as to the decrees of the Sacred Congregations (of the Roman Curia) approved by the Pontiff; nor can they avoid the stigma both of disobedience and temerity or be free from grave sin who by any spoken or written words impugn these decisions."

Decisions of the commission regarding points of doctrine are not infallible of themselves. They require religious assent, however, so long as there is no positive evidence that they are wrong. They do not close the door to continuing investigation and study.

The commission was reorganized July 8, 1971, in line with directives issued by Paul VI on his own initiative.

Fifteen new norms changed its structure from a virtually independent office of cardinals aided by lifetime consultors into a group of 20 biblical scholars with five-year terms (renewable) linked with the Congregation for the Doctrine of the Faith. Functionally, however, it remains the same.

The commission:
• receives questions and study topics referred to it by a variety of sources, from the pope to Catholic universities and biblical associations;
• is required to meet in plenary session at least once a year and to submit conclusions reached in such meetings to the pope and the Congregation for the Doctrine of the Faith;
• is under directive to promote relationships with non-Catholic as well as Catholic institutes of biblical studies;
• is to be consulted before any new norms on biblical matters are issued;
• retains its authorization to confer academic degrees in biblical studies.

THE BIBLE

The Catholic canon of the Old Testament consists of:

- The Pentateuch, the first five books: Genesis (Gn.), Exodus (Ex.), Leviticus (Lv.), Numbers (Nm.), Deuteronomy (Dt.).
- Historical Books: Joshua (Jos.), Judges (Jgs.), Ruth (Ru.), 1 and 2 Samuel (Sm.), 1 and 2 Kings (Kgs.), 1 and 2 Chronicles (Chr.), Ezra (Ezr.), Nehemiah (Neh.), Tobit (Tb.), Judith (Jdt.), Esther (Est.), 1 and 2 Maccabees (Mc.).
- Wisdom Books: Job (Jb.), Psalms (Ps.), Proverbs (Prv.), Ecclesiastes (Eccl.), Song of Songs (Song), Wisdom (Wis.), Sirach (Sir.).
- The Prophets: Isaiah (Is.), Jeremiah (Jer.), Lamentations (Lam.), Baruch (Bar.), Ezechiel (Ez.), Daniel (Dn.), Hosea (Hos.), Joel (Jl.), Amos (Am.), Obadiah (Ob.), Jonah (Jon.), Micah (Mi.), Nahum (Na.), Habakkuk (Hb.), Zephaniah (Zep.), Haggai (Hg.), Zechariah (Zec.), Malachi (Mal.).

The Catholic canon of the New Testament consists of:

- The Gospels of Matthew (Mt.), Mark (Mk.), Luke (Lk.), John (Jn.)
- The Acts of the Apostles (Acts).
- The Pauline Letters — Romans (Rom.), 1 and 2 Corinthians (Cor.), Galatians (Gal.), Ephesians (Eph.), Philippians (Phil.), Colossians (Col.), 1 and 2 Thessalonians (Thes.), 1 and 2 Timothy (Tm.), Titus (Ti.), Philemon (Phlm.), Hebrews (Heb.); the Catholic Letters — James (Jas.), 1 and 2 Peter (Pt.), 1, 2 and 3 John (Jn.), Jude (Jude).
- Revelation (Rv.).

Catholic and Other Canons

The Catholic canon of the Old Testament was determined by the tradition of the Church. It was firm by the fifth century, despite some questioning by scholars, and was stated by the African councils of Hippo in 393 and Carthage in 397 and 419, by Innocent I in 405, and by the Council of Florence in 1441. It was defined by the Council of Trent in the dogmatic decree *De Canonicis Scripturis,* Apr. 8, 1546.

The Jews, although they generally accepted 22 or 24 books as sacred in the first century A.D., did not have a definite canon of sacred writings until late in the second or early in the third century. This canon was fixed by the consensus of rabbinical schools.

The canon of the Hebrew Masoretic Text, which is accepted by modern Jews, consists of 24 books, as follows:

- The Law: Genesis, Exodus, Leviticus, Numbers, Deuteronomy.
- The Prophets: earlier prophets — Joshua, Judges, Samuel, Kings; later prophets — Isaiah, Jeremiah, Ezekiel, and 12 others in one book (Hosea, Joel, Amos, Obadiah, Jonah, Micah, Nahum, Habakkuk, Zephaniah, Haggai, Zechariah, Malachi).

- The Writings: Psalms, Job, Proverbs, Ruth, Song of Songs, Ecclesiastes, Lamentations, Esther, Daniel, Ezra-Nehemiah, Chronicles.

This canon does not include a number of books in the Alexandrian collection of sacred writings — viz., 1 and 2 Maccabees, Tobit, Judith, Sirach, Wisdom, Baruch, and portions of Esther and Daniel (chapters 13 and 14). These additional books and passages, contained in the Septuagint version of the Old Testament and called deuterocanonical, are in the Catholic canon.

These books and passages, called deuterocanonical in terminology coined by Sixtus of Siena (1520-1569), were under discussion for some time until questions about their canonicity were settled. Books admitted into the canon with little or no debate were called protocanonical. The canonical status of both categories of books is the same in the Catholic Bible.

The Protestant canon, in an arrangement of 39 books, is the same as the Hebrew canon.

The Old Testament canon has not been definitely settled by the Orthodox. Since the time of the Reformation, however, they have given some preference to the Protestant canon.

The New Testament canon was firm by the end of the fourth century. By the end of the second century all of the New Testament books were generally known and most of them were acknowledged as inspired. The Muratorian Fragment, dating from about 200, listed most of the books recognized in later decrees as canonical. Prior to the end of the fourth century, however, there were controversies over the inspired character of several books — viz., the Letter to the Hebrews, James, Jude, 2 Peter, 2 and 3 John, and Revelation. Controversy over these books ended in the fourth century, and the canon stated by the councils of Hippo and Carthage and reaffirmed by Innocent I in 405 was solemnly defined by the Council of Trent (1545-63).

Although Martin Luther eliminated the aforementioned books from his New Testament canon, they were reinstated by his followers by the year 1700. Anglicans and Calvinists always retained them.

The Greek and Russian Orthodox have the same New Testament canon as the Catholic Church. Some variations exist among other separated Eastern churches.

Languages of the Bible

Hebrew, Aramaic and Greek were the original languages of the Bible. Most of the Old Testament books were written in Hebrew. Portions of Daniel, Ezra, Jeremiah, Esther, and probably the books of Tobit and Judith were written in Aramaic. The Book of Wisdom, 2 Maccabees and all the books of the New Testament were written in Greek.

Manuscripts and Versions

The original writings of the inspired authors have been lost. The Bible has been transmitted through ancient copies called manuscripts and through translations or versions.

Authoritative Greek manuscripts include the Sinaitic and Vatican manuscripts of the fourth century and the Alexandrine and Parisian of the fifth century A. D.

The Septuagint and Vulgate translations are in a class by themselves.

The Septuagint version, a Greek translation of the Old Testament, was begun about 250 and completed about 100 B. C. The work of several Jewish translators at Alexandria, it differed from the Hebrew Bible in the arrangement of books and included several, later called deuterocanonical, which were not acknowledged as sacred by the community at Jerusalem.

The Vulgate was a Latin version of the Old and New Testaments produced from the original languages by St. Jerome from about 383 to 404. It became the most widely used Latin text for centuries and was regarded as basic long before the Council of Trent designated it as authentic and suitable for use in public reading, controversy, preaching and teaching. Because of its authoritative character, it became the basis for many translations into other languages.

Hebrew and Aramaic manuscripts of great antiquity and value have figured more significantly than before in recent scriptural work by Catholic scholars, especially since their use was strongly encouraged, if not mandated, in 1943 by Pius XII in the encyclical *Divino Afflante Spiritu.*

The English translation of the Bible in general use among Catholics until recent years was the *Douay-Rheims,* so called because of the places where it was prepared and published, the New Testament at Rheims in 1582 and the Old Testament at Douay in 1609. The translation was made from the Vulgate text. As revised and issued by Bishop Richard Challoner in 1749 and 1750, it became the standard Catholic English version for about 200 years.

A revision of the Challoner New Testament, made on the basis of the Vulgate text by scholars of the Catholic Biblical Association of America, was published in 1941 in the United States under the sponsorship of the Episcopal Committee of the Confraternity of Christian Doctrine.

New American Bible

A new translation of the entire Bible, the first ever made directly into English from the original languages under Catholic auspices, was projected in 1944 and completed in the fall of 1970 with publication of the *New American Bible.* The Episcopal Committee of the Confraternity of Christian Doctrine spon-

sored the NAB. The translators were members of the Catholic Biblical Association of America and several fellow scholars of other faiths. The typical edition was produced by St. Anthony Guild Press, Paterson, N. J.

Old Testament portions of the NAB were published in separate volumes before undergoing final revision and being bound in one cover. Genesis and Psalms were issued in 1948 and 1950; Genesis to Ruth, in 1952; Job to Sirach, in 1955; the Prophets, in 1961; Samuel to the Maccabees, in 1969. The new translation of the New Testament was issued for the first time in 1970.

Versions of the Bible approved for use in the Catholic liturgy are the *Douay-Rheims,* the *New American Bible, A New Translation from the Latin Vulgate* by Ronald A. Knox, the Catholic edition of the *Revised Standard Version,* and the *Jerusalem Bible.*

The *Jerusalem Bible* is an English translation of a French version based on the original languages. It was published by Doubleday & Co., Inc., which is also working toward completion of the *Anchor Bible.*

The Protestant counterpart of the *Douay-Rheims Bible* was the *King James Bible,* called the *Authorized Version* in England. Originally published in 1611, it was in general use for more than three centuries. Its modern revisions include the *English Revised Version,* published between 1881 and 1885; the *American Revised Version,* 1901, and revisions of the New Testament (1946) and the Old Testament (1952) published in 1957 in the United States as the *Revised Standard Version.*

The latest revision, a translation in the language of the present day made from Greek and Hebrew sources, is the *New English Bible,* published Mar. 16, 1970. Its New Testament portion was originally published in 1961.

Biblical Federation

In November, 1966, Pope Paul commissioned the Secretariat for Promoting Christian Unity to start work for the widest possible distribution of the Bible and to coordinate endeavors toward the production of Catholic-Protestant Bibles in all languages.

The World Catholic Federation for the Biblical Apostolate, established in 1969, sponsors a program designed to create greater awareness among Catholics of the Bible and its use in everyday life. Cardinal Franz Koenig, president of the federation since its inception, agreed to serve in the post for another six years at a four-day plenary meeting of 20 delegates from member organizations early in May, 1972. The meeting was held in Vienna.

The U. S. Center for the Catholic Biblical Apostolate, under the direction of Father Stephen Hartdegen, O.F.M., is related to the Division of Religious Education, U. S. Catholic Conference. Address: 1312 Massachusetts Ave. N. W., Washington, D.C. 20005.

APOCRYPHA

Apocrypha are books which have some resemblance to the canonical books in subject matter and title but which have not been recognized as canonical by the Church. They are characterized by a false claim to divine authority; extravagant accounts of events and miracles alleged to be supplemental revelation; material favoring heresy (especially in "New Testament" apocrypha); minimal, if any, historical value.

Among examples of this type of literature itemized by J. McKenzie, S.J., in *Dictionary of the Bible* are: *the Books of Adam and Eve, Martyrdom of Isaiah, Testament of the Patriarchs, Assumption of Moses, Sibylline Oracles; Gospel of James, Gospel of Thomas, Arabic Gospel of the Infancy, History of Joseph the Carpenter; Acts of John, Acts of Paul, Acts of Peter, Acts of Andrew,* and numerous epistles.

Books of this type are called pseudepigrapha by Protestants. They regard the deuterocanonical books in the Catholic canon of Scripture as apocrypha.

DEAD SEA SCROLLS

The Qumran Scrolls, popularly called the Dead Sea Scrolls, are a collection of manuscripts, all but one of them in Hebrew, found between 1947 and 1956 in caves in the Desert of Juda west of the Dead Sea.

Among the findings were a complete text of Isaiah dating from the second century, B.C., more or less extensive fragments of other Old Testament texts (including the deuterocanonical Tobit), and a commentary on Habakkuk. Until the discovery of these materials, the oldest known Hebrew manuscripts were from the 10th century, A.D.

Also found were messianic and apocalyptic texts, and other writings describing the beliefs and practices of the Essenes, a rigoristic Jewish sect.

The scrolls, dating from about the first century before and after Christ, are important sources of information about Hebrew literature, Jewish history during the period between the Old and New Testaments, and the history of Old Testament texts. They established the fact that the Hebrew text of the Old Testament was fixed before the beginning of the Christian era and have had definite effects in recent critical studies and translations of the Old Testament. Together with other scrolls found at Masada, they are still the subject of intensive study.

A theory was proposed in 1972 by Father Jose O'Callaghan, a Spanish papyrologist, that a scrap of one of the scrolls might be a fragment of St. Mark's Gospel dating from about the year 50. Father Pierre Benoit, O. P., discounted the hypothesis, stating that it was based on an erroneous analysis of a photocopy of the scrap in question.

BOOKS OF THE BIBLE

Old Testament
(Dates are before Christ.)

Pentateuch

The Pentateuch is the collective title of the first five books of the Bible. Substantially, they identify the Israelites as Yahweh's Chosen People, cover their history from Egypt to the threshold of the Promised Land, contain the Mosaic Law and Covenant, and disclose the promise of salvation to come. Principal themes concern the divine promise of salvation, Yahweh's fidelity, and the Covenant. Work on the composition of the Pentateuch was completed in the sixth century.

Genesis: The book of origins, according to its title in the Septuagint. In two parts, covers: religious prehistory, including accounts of the origin of the world and man, the original state of innocence and the fall, the promise of salvation, patriarchs before and after the Deluge, the Tower of Babel narrative, genealogies (first 11 chapters); the covenant with Abraham and patriarchal history from Abraham to Joseph (balance of the 50 chapters). Significant are the themes of Yahweh's universal sovereignty and mercy.

Exodus: Named with the Greek word for departure, is a religious epic which describes the oppression of the 12 tribes in Egypt and their departure, liberation or passover therefrom under the leadership of Moses; Yahweh's establishment of the Covenant with them, making them his Chosen People, through the mediation of Moses at Mt. Sinai; instructions concerning the tabernacle, the sanctuary and Ark of the Covenant; the institution of the priesthood. The book is significant because of its theology of liberation and redemption. In Christian interpretation, the Exodus is a figure of baptism.

Leviticus: Mainly legislative in theme and purpose, contains laws regarding sacrifices, ceremonies of ordination and the priesthood of Aaron, legal purity, the holiness code, atonement, the redemption of offerings, and other subjects. Summarily, Levitical laws provided directives for all aspects of religious observance and for the manner in which the Israelites were to conduct themselves with respect to Yahweh and each other. Leviticus was the liturgical handbook of the priesthood.

Numbers: Taking its name from censuses recounted at the beginning and near the end, is a continuation of Exodus. It combines narrative of the Israelites' desert pilgrimage from Sinai to the border of Canaan with laws related to and expansive of those in Leviticus.

Deuteronomy: The concluding book of the Pentateuch, recapitulates, in the form of a testament of Moses, the Law and much of the desert history of the Israelites; enjoins fidelity to the Law as the key to good or bad fortune for the people; gives an account of the commissioning of Joshua as the successor of Moses. Notable themes concern the election of Israel by Yahweh, observance of the Law, prohibitions against the worship of foreign gods, worship of and confidence in Yahweh, the power of Yahweh in nature. The Deuteronomic Code or motif, embodying all of these elements, was the norm for interpreting Israelite history.

Joshua, Judges, Ruth

Joshua: Records the fulfillment of Yahweh's promise to the Israelites in their conquest, occupation and division of Canaan under the leadership of Joshua. It also contains an account of the return of Transjordanian Israelites and of a renewal of the Covenant. It was redacted in final form probably in the sixth century or later.

Judges: Records the actions of charismatic leaders, called judges, of the tribes of Israel between the death of Joshua and the time of Samuel, and a crisis of idolatry among the people. The basic themes are sin and punishment, repentance and deliverance; its purpose was in line with the Deuteronomic motif, that the fortunes of the Israelites were related to their observance or non-observance of the Law and the Covenant. It was redacted in final form probably in the sixth century.

Ruth: Named for the Gentile (Moabite) woman who, through marriage with Boaz, became an Israelite and an ancestress of David (her son, Obed, became his grandfather). Themes are filial piety, faith and trust in Yahweh, the universality of messianic salvation. Dates ranging from c. 950 to the seventh century have been assigned to the origin of the book, whose author is unknown.

Historical Books

These books, while they contain a great deal of factual material, are unique in their preoccupation with interpreting it, in the Deuteronomic manner, in primary relation to the Covenant on which the nation of Israel was founded and in accordance with which community and personal life were judged.

The books are: Samuel 1 and 2, from the end of Judges (c. 1020) to the end of David's reign (c. 961); Kings 1 and 2, from the last days of David to the start of the Babylonian Exile and the destruction of the Temple (587); Chronicles 1 and 2, from the reign of Saul (c. 1020-1000) to the return of the people from the Exile (538); Ezra and Nehemiah, covering the reorganization of the Jewish community after the Exile (458-397); Maccabees 1 and 2, recounting the struggle against attempted suppression of Judaism (168-142).

Three of the books listed below — Tobit, Judith and Esther — are categorized as religious novels.

Samuel 1 and 2: A single work in concept and contents, containing episodic history of the last two Judges, Eli and Samuel, the establishment and rule of the monarchy under Saul and David, and the political consequences of David's rule. The royal messianic dynasty of David was the subject of Nathan's Oracle in 2 Sm. 7. They were edited in final form probably late in the seventh century or during the Exile.

Kings 1 and 2: Cover the last days of David and the career of Solomon, including the building of the Temple and the history of the kingdom during his reign; stories of the prophets Elija and Elisha; the history of the divided kingdom to the fall of Israel in the North (721) and the fall of Judah in the South (587), the destruction of Jerusalem and the Temple. They reflect the Deuteronomic motif in attributing the downfall of the people to corruption of belief and practice in public and private life. They were completed probably in the sixth century.

Chronicles 1 and 2: A collection of historical traditions interpreted in such a way as to present an ideal picture of one people governed by divine law and united in one Temple worship of the one true God. Contents include genealogical tables from Adam to David, the careers of David and Solomon, coverage of the kingdom of Judah to the Exile, and the decree of Cyrus permitting the return of the people and rebuilding of Jerusalem. Both are related to and were written about 400 by the same author, the Chronicler, who composed Ezra and Nehemiah.

Ezra and Nehemiah: A running account of the return of the people to their homeland after the Exile and of practical efforts, under the leadership of Ezra and Nehemiah, to restore and reorganize the religious and political community on the basis of Israelite traditions, divine worship and observance of the Law. Events of great significance were the building of the second Temple, the building of a wall around Jerusalem, and the proclamation of the Law by Ezra. This restored community was the start of Judaism. Both are related to and were written about 400 by the same author, the Chronicler, who composed Chronicles 1 and 2.

Tobit: Written in the literary form of a novel and having greater resemblance to wisdom than to historical literature, narrates the personal history of Tobit, a devout and charitable Jew in exile, and persons connected with him, viz., his son Tobiah, his kinsman Raguel, and Raguel's daughter Sarah. Its purpose was to teach people how to be good Jews. One of its principal themes is patience under trial, with trust in divine Providence which is symbolized by the presence and action of the angel Raphael. It was written about 200.

Judith: Recounts, in the literary form of a historical novel or romance, the preservation of the Israelites from conquest and ruin through the action of Judith. The essential themes are trust in God for deliverance from danger and emphasis on observance of the Law. It was written probably during the Maccabean period.

Esther: Relates, in the literary form of a historical novel or romance, the manner in which Jews in Persia were saved from annihilation through the central role played by Esther, the Jewish wife of Ahasuerus; a fact commemorated by the Jewish feast of Purim. Like Judith, it has trust in divine Providence as its theme and indicates that God's saving will is sometimes realized by persons acting in unlikely ways. Its origin and date are uncertain; it may have been written about 200 near the beginning of the period of strong Hellenistic influence on the Jews.

Maccabees 1 and 2: While related to some extent because of common subject matter, are quite different from each other.

The first book recounts the background and events of the 40-year (175-135) struggle for religious and political freedom led by Judas Maccabaeus and his brothers against the Hellenist Seleucid kings and some Hellenophiles among the Jews. Victory was symbolized by the rededication of the Temple. Against the background of opposition between Jews and Gentiles, the author equated the survival of belief in the one true God with survival of the Jewish people, thus identifying religion with patriotism. It was written probably by a Palestinian Jew after 104.

The second book supplements the first to some extent, covering and giving a theological interpretation to events from 180 to 162. It explains the feast of the Dedication of the Temple, a key event in the survival of Judaism which is commemorated in the feast of Hanukkah; stresses the primacy of God's action in the struggle for survival; and indicates belief in an afterlife and the resurrection of the body. It was written probably by a Jew of Alexandria after 120.

Wisdom Books

With the exceptions of Psalms and the Song of Songs, the titles listed under this heading are called wisdom books because their purpose was to formulate the fruits of human experience in the context of meditation on sacred Scripture and to present them as an aid toward understanding the problems of life. Hebrew wisdom literature was distinctive from pagan literature of the same type, but it had limitations; these were overcome in the New Testament, which added the dimensions of the New Covenant to those of the Old. Solomon was regarded as the archtype of the wise man.

Job: A dramatic, didactic poem consisting mainly of several dialogues between Job and his friends concerning the mystery involved in the coexistence of the just God, evil, and the suffering of the just. It describes an innocent man's experience of suffering and conveys the truth that faith in and submission to God rather than complete understanding, which is impossible, make the experience bearable; also, that the justice of God cannot be defended by affirming that it is realized in this world. Of uncertain authorship, it was written probably between the fifth and third centuries.

Psalms: A collection of 150 religious songs or lyrics reflecting Israelite belief and piety dating from the time of the monarchy to the post-Exilic period, a span of well over 500 years. The psalms, which are a compendium of Old Testament theology, were used in the temple liturgy and were of several types suitable for the king, hymns, lamentations, expressions of confidence and thanksgiving, prophecy, historical meditation and reflection, and the statement of wisdom. About one-half of them are attributed to David; many, by unknown authors, date from the early post-Exilic period.

Proverbs: The oldest book of the wisdom type in the Bible, consisting of collections of sayings attributed to Solomon and other persons regarding a wide variety of subjects including wisdom and its nature, rules of conduct, duties with respect to one's neighbor, the conduct of daily affairs. It reveals many details of Jewish life. Its nucleus dates from the period before the Exile, but no definite date can be assigned for its final compilation.

Ecclesiastes: A treatise about many subjects whose unifying theme is the vanity of strictly human efforts and accomplishments with respect to the achievement of lasting happiness; the only things which are not vain are fear of the Lord and observance of his commandments. The pessimistic tone of the book is due to the absence of a concept of afterlife. It was written by an unknown author about 250.

Song of Songs: A collection of erotic lyrics reflecting various themes, including the celebration of fidelity and love between man and woman. According to one interpretation, the book is a parable of the love of Yahweh for Israel. It was written by an unknown author after the Exile.

Wisdom: Deals with many subjects including the reward of justice; praise of wisdom, a gift of Yahweh proceeding from belief in him and the practice of his Law; the part played by him in the history of his people, especially in their liberation from Egypt; the folly and shame of idolatry. Its contents are taken from the whole sacred literature of the Jews and represent a distillation of its wisdom based on the law, beliefs and traditions of Israel. Contains the first Old Testament affirmation of an afterlife with God. The last book of the Old Testament to be written, it was probably composed about 50 years before Christ by an unknown author to confirm the faith of the Jewish community in Alexandria.

Sirach: Resembling Proverbs, is a collection of sayings handed on by a grandfather to his grandson. It contains a variety of moral instruction and eulogies of patriarchs and other figures in Israelite history. Its moral maxims apply to individuals, the family and community, relations with God, friendship, education, wealth, the Law, divine worship. Its theme is that true wisdom consists in the Law. (It was formerly called Ecclesiasticus, the Church Book, because of its extensive use by the Church for moral instruction.) It was written in Hebrew between 200 and 175, during a period of strong Hellenistic influence, and was translated into Greek after 132.

The Prophets

These books and the prophecies they contain "express judgments of the people's moral conduct, on the basis of the Mosaic alliance between God and Israel. They teach sublime truths and lofty morals. They contain exhortations, threats, announcements of punishment, promises of deliverance. . . . In the affairs of men, their prime concern is the interests of God, especially in what pertains to the Chosen People through whom the Messiah is to come; hence their denunciations of idolatry and of that externalism in worship which exclude the interior spirit of religion. They are concerned also with the universal nature of the moral law, with personal responsibility, with the person and office of the Messiah, and with the conduct of foreign nations" (*The Holy Bible*, Prophetic Books, CCD Edition, 1961; Preface). There are four major (Isaiah, Jeremiah, Ezekiel, Daniel) and 12 minor prophets (distinguished by the length of books), Lamentations and Baruch. Earlier prophets, mentioned in historical books, include Samuel, Gad, Nathan, Elijah and Elisha.

Before the Exile, prophets were the intermediaries through whom God communicated revelation to the people. Afterwards, prophecy lapsed and the written word of the Law served this purpose.

Isaiah: Named for the greatest of the prophets whose career spanned the reigns of three Hebrew kings from 742 to the beginning of the seventh century, in a period of moral breakdown in Judah and threats of invasion by foreign enemies. It is an anthology of poems and oracles credited to him and a number of followers deeply influenced by him. Of special importance are the prophecies concerning Immanuel (6 to 12), including the prophecy of the virgin birth (7:14). Chapters 40 to 55, called Deutero-Isaiah, are attributed to an anonymous poet toward the end of the Exile; this portion contains the Songs of the Servant. The concluding part of the book (56-66) contains oracles by later disciples. One of many themes in Isaiah concerned the saving mission of the remnant of Israel in the divine plan of salvation. It was edited in its present form by 180.

Jeremiah: Combines history, biography and prophecy in a setting of crisis caused by internal and external factors, viz., idolatry and general infidelity to the Law among the Israelites and external threats from the Assyrians, Egyptians and Babylonians. Jeremiah prophesied the promise of a new covenant as well as the destruction of Jerusalem and the Temple. His career began in 626 and ended some years after the beginning of the Exile. The book, the longest in the Bible, was edited in final form after the Exile.

Lamentations: A collection of five laments or elegies over the fall of Jerusalem and the fate of the people in Exile, written by an unknown eyewitness not long after 587. They convey the message that Yahweh struck the people because of their sins and reflect confidence in his love and power to restore his converted people.

Baruch: Against the background of the already begun Exile, it consists of an introduction and several parts: an exile's prayer of confession and petition for forgiveness and the restoration of Israel; a poem praising wisdom and the Law of Moses; a lament in which Jerusalem, personified, bewails the fate of her people and consoles them with the hope of blessings to come; and a polemic against idolatry. Although ascribed to Baruch, Jeremiah's secretary, it was written by several authors probably in the second century.

Ezekiel: Named for the priest-prophet who prophesied in Babylon from 593 to 571, during the first phase of the Exile. To prepare his fellow early exiles for the impending fall of Jerusalem, he reproached the Israelites for past sins and predicted woes to come upon them. After the destruction of the city, the burden of his message was hope and promise of restoration. Ezekiel had great influence on the religion of Israel after the Exile. The book, which contains the substance of his teaching, had a number of authors and editors.

Daniel: The protagonist is a fictional young Jew, taken early to Babylon where he lived until 537, who figured in a series of edifying stories. The stories, which originated from Israelite tradition, recount the trials and triumphs of Daniel and his three companions, and other episodes including those concerning Susannah, Bel, and the Dragon. The book is more apocalyptic than prophetic: it envisions Israel in glory to come and conveys the message that men of faith can resist temptation and overcome adversity. It states the prophetic themes of right conduct, divine control of men and events, and the final triumph of the kingdom. It was written by an unknown author in the 160's to give moral support to Jews during the persecutions of the Maccabean period.

Hosea: Consists of a prophetic parallel between Hosea's marriage and Yahweh's relations with his people. As the prophet was married to a faithless wife whom he would not give up, Yahweh was bound in Covenant with an idolatrous and unjust Israel whom he would not desert but would chastise for purification. Hosea belonged to the Northern Kingdom of Israel and began his career about the middle of the eighth century. He inaugurated the tradition of describing Yahweh's relation to Israel in terms of marriage.

Joel: Is apocalyptic and eschatological regarding divine judgment, the Day of the Lord, which is symbolized by a ravaging invasion of locusts, the judgment of the nations in the Valley of Josaphat, and the outpouring of the Spirit in the messianic era to come. Its message is that God will vindicate and save Israel, in view of the prayer and repentance of the people, and will punish their enemies. It was composed after the period of Nehemiah.

Amos: Consists of an indictment against foreign enemies of Israel; a strong denunciation of the people of Israel, whose infidelity, idolatry and injustice made them subject to divine judgment and punishment; and a messianic oracle regarding Israel's restoration. Amos prophesied in the Northern Kingdom of Israel, at Bethel, in the first half of the eighth century; chronologically, he was the first of the canonical prophets.

Obadiah: A 21-verse prophecy, the shortest and one of the sternest in the Bible, against the Edomites, invaders of southern Judah and enemies of those returning from the Exile to their homeland. It was redacted in final form no later than the end of the fourth century.

Jonah: A parable of divine mercy with the theme that Yahweh wills the salvation of all, not just a few, men who respond to his call. Its protagonist is a disobedient prophet; forced by circumstances beyond his control to preach penance among Gentiles, he is highly successful in his mission but baffled by the divine concern for those who do not belong to the Chosen People. It was written after the Exile.

Micah: Attacks the injustice and corruption of priests, false prophets, officials and people; announces judgment and punishment to come; foretells the restoration of Israel; refers to the saving remnant of Israel. Micah was a contemporary of Isaiah.

Nahum: Dating from about 613, concerns the destruction of Nineveh in 612 and the overthrow of the Assyrian Empire by the Babylonians.

Habakkuk: Dating from about 605-597, concerns sufferings to be inflicted by oppressors on the people of Judah because of their infidelity to the Lord. It also sounds a note of confidence in the Lord, the Savior, and declares that the just will not perish.

Zephaniah: Exercising his ministry in the second half of the seventh century, during a time of widespread idolatry, superstition and religious degradation, he prophesied impending judgment and punishment for Jerusalem and its people. He prophesied too that a holy remnant of the people (Anawim, mentioned also by Amos) would be spared. Zephaniah was a forerunner of Jeremiah.

Haggai: One of the first prophets after the Exile, Haggai in 520 encouraged the returning exiles to reestablish their community and to complete the second Temple (dedicated in 515), for which he envisioned greater glory, in a messianic sense, than that enjoyed by the original Temple of Solomon.

Zechariah: A contemporary of Haggai, he prophesied in the same vein. A second part of the book, called Deutero-Zechariah and composed by one or more unknown authors, relates a vision of the coming of the Prince of Peace, the Messiah of the Poor.

Malachi: Written by an anonymous author, presents a picture of life in the post-Exilic community between 516 and the initiation of reforms by Ezra and Nehemiah about 432. Blame for the troubles of the community is placed mainly on priests for failure to carry out ritual worship and to instruct the people in the proper manner; other factors were religious indifference and the influence of doubters who were scandalized at the prosperity of the wicked. The vision of a universal sacrifice to be offered to Yahweh (1:11) is interpreted in Christian theology as a prophecy of the sacrifice of the Mass. Malachi was the last of the minor prophets.

OLD TESTAMENT DATES

c. 1800 — c. 1600: Period of the patriarchs (Abraham, Isaac, Jacob).

c. 1600: Israelites in Egypt.

c. 1250: Exodus of Israelites from Egypt.

c. 1210: Entrance of Israelites into Canaan.

c. 1210 — c. 1020: Period of the Judges.

c. 1020 — c. 1000: Reign of Saul, first king.

c. 1000 — c. 961: Reign of David.

c. 961 — 922: Reign of Solomon. Temple built during his reign.

922: Division of the Kingdom into Israel (North) and Judah (South).

721: Conquest of Israel by Assyrians.

587-538: Conquest of Judah by Babylonians. Babylonian Captivity and Exile. Destruction of Jerusalem and the Temple, 587. Captivity ended with the return of exiles, following the decree of Cyrus permitting the rebuilding of Jerusalem.

515: Dedication of the Second Temple.

458-397: Restoration and reform of the Jewish religious and political community; building of the Jerusalem wall, 439. Leaders in the movement were Ezra and Nehemiah.

168-142: Period of the Maccabees; war against Syrians.

142: Independence granted to Jews by Demetrius II of Syria.

135-37: Period of the Hasmonean dynasty.

63: Beginning of Roman rule.

37-4: Period of Herod the Great.

New Testament Books

Gospels

The term Gospel is derived from the Anglo-Saxon *god-spell* and the Greek *euangelion,* meaning good news, good tidings. In Christian use, it means the good news of salvation proclaimed by Christ and the Church, and handed on in written form in the Gospels of Matthew, Mark, Luke and John.

The initial proclamation of the coming of the kingdom of God was made by Jesus in and through his Person, teachings and actions, and especially through his Passion, death and resurrection. This proclamation became the center of Christian faith and the core of the oral Gospel tradition with which the Church spread the good news by apostolic preaching for some 30 years before it was committed to writing by the Evangelists.

According to an Instruction issued by the Pontifical Commission for Biblical Studies Apr. 21, 1964:

• The sacred writers selected from the material at their disposal (the oral Gospel tradition, some written collections of sayings and deeds of Jesus, eyewitness accounts) those things which were particularly suitable to the various conditions (liturgical, catechetical, missionary) of the faithful and the aims they had in mind, and they narrated these things in such a way as to correspond with those circumstances and their aims.

• The life and teaching of Jesus were not simply reported in a biographical manner for the purpose of preserving their memory but were "preached" so as to offer the Church the basis of doctrine concerning faith and morals.

• In their works, the Evangelists presented the true sayings of Jesus and the events of his life in the light of the better understanding they had following their enlightenment by the Holy Spirit. They did not transform Christ into a "mythical" Person, nor did they distort his teaching.

Passion narratives are the core of all the Gospels, covering the suffering, death and resurrection of Jesus as central events in bringing about and establishing the New Covenant. Leading up to them are accounts of the mission of John the Baptizer and the ministry of Jesus, especially in Galilee and finally in Jerusalem before the Passion. The infancy of Jesus is covered by Luke and Matthew with narratives inspired by Old Testament citations appropriate to the birth of the Messiah.

Matthew, Mark and Luke, while different in various respects, have so many similarities that they are called Synoptic; their relationships are the subject of the Synoptic Problem.

Matthew: Written in the 70's or 80's for Jewish Christians, with clear reference to Jewish background and identification of Jesus as the divine Messiah, the fulfillment of the Old Testament. Distinctive are the use of Old Testament citations regarding the Person, activity and teaching of Jesus, and the presentation of doctrine in sermons and discourses. The canonical Matthew was written in Greek, with dependence on Mark.

Mark: The first of the Gospels, dating from about 65. Written for Gentile Christians, it is noted for the realism and wealth of concrete details with which it reveals Jesus as Son of God and Savior more by his actions and miracles than by his discourses. Theologically, it is less refined than the other Gospels.

Luke: Written in the 70's or 80's for Gentile Christians. It is noted for the universality of its address, the insight it provides into the Christian way of life, the place it gives to women, the manner in which it emphasizes Jesus' friendship with sinners and compassion for the suffering.

John: Written sometime in the 90's, is the most sublime and theological of the Gospels, and is different from the Synoptics in plan and treatment. Combining accounts of signs with longer discourses and reflections, it progressively reveals the Person and mission of Jesus — as Word, Way, Truth, Life, Light — in line with the purpose, "to help you believe that Jesus is the Messiah, the Son of God, so that through this faith you may have life in his name" (Jn. 20:31). There are questions about the authorship but no doubt about the Johannine tradition behind the Gospel.

Acts of the Apostles

Acts of the Apostles: Written by Luke in the 70's or 80's as a supplement to his Gospel. It describes the origin and spread of Christian communities through the action of the Holy Spirit from the resurrection of Christ to the time of Paul's first Roman imprisonment in the early 60's.

Letters (Epistles)

These letters, the first documents of the New Testament, were written in response to existential needs of the early Christian communities for doctrinal and moral instruction, disciplinary action, practical advice, and exhortation to true Christian living.

Pauline Letters

These letters, which comprise approximately one-fourth of the New Testament, are primary and monumental sources of the development of Christian theology. Several of them may not have had Paul as their actual author, but evidence of the Pauline tradition behind them is strong. The letters to the Colossians, Philippians, Ephesians and Philemon have been called the "Captivity Letters" because of a tradition that they were written while Paul was under house arrest in Rome from 61 to 63.

Romans: Written in the late 50's from

Corinth on the central significance of Christ and faith in him for salvation, and the relationship of Christianity to Judaism; the condition of mankind without Christ; justification and the Christian life; duties of Christians.

Corinthians 1: Written near the beginning of 57 from Ephesus to counteract factionalism and disorders, it covers community dissensions, moral irregularities, marriage and celibacy, conduct at religious gatherings, the Eucharist, spiritual gifts (charisms) and their function in the Church, charity, the resurrection of the body.

Corinthians 2: Written later in the same year as 1 Cor., concerning Paul's defense of his apostolic life and ministry, and an appeal for a collection to aid poor Christians in Jerusalem.

Galatians: Written probably between 54 and 57 (perhaps earlier, according to some scholars) to counteract Judaizing opinions and efforts to undermine his authority, it asserts the divine origin of Paul's authority and doctrine, states that justification is not through Mosaic Law but through faith in Christ, insists on the practice of evangelical virtues, especially charity.

Ephesians: Written probably between 61 and 63, or perhaps in the 70's, mainly on the Church as the Mystical Body of Christ.

Philippians: Written between 61 and 63 primarily to thank the Philippians for their kindness to him while he was under house arrest in Rome.

Colossians: Written while he was under house arrest in Rome from 61 to 63 to counteract the influence of self-appointed teachers who were watering down doctrine concerning Christ. It includes two highly important Christological passages, a warning against false teachers, and an instruction on the ideal Christian life.

Thessalonians 1 and 2: Written within a short time of each other probably in 51 from Corinth, mainly on doctrine concerning the Parousia, the second coming of Christ.

Timothy 1 and 2, Titus: Written between 65 and 67, or perhaps in the 70's, giving pastoral counsels to Timothy and Titus who were in charge of churches in Ephesus and Crete, respectively. 1 Tm. emphasizes pastoral responsibility for preserving unity of doctrine; 2 Tm. describes Paul's imprisonment in Rome.

Philemon: A private letter written between 61 and 63 to a wealthy Colossian concerning a slave, Onesimus, who had escaped from him; Paul appealed for kind treatment of the man.

Hebrews: Dating from some time between the mid-60's and the 80's, a complex theological treatise on Christology, the priesthood and sacrifice of Christ, the New Covenant, and the pattern for Christian living. Critical opinion is divided as to whether it was addressed to Judaeo or Gentile Christians.

Catholic Letters, Revelation

These seven letters have been called "catholic" because it was thought for some time, not altogether correctly, that they were not addressed to particular communities.

James: Written sometime between the mid-60's and the 80's (although datable before 62 according to some scholars) in the spirit of Hebrew wisdom literature and the moralism of Tobit. An exhortation to practical Christian living, it is also noteworthy for the doctrine it states on good works and its citation regarding anointing of the sick.

Peter 1 and 2: The first letter may have been written in the mid-60's; the second dates from 100 to 125. Addressed to Christians in Asia Minor, both are exhortations to perseverance in the life of faith despite trials and difficulties arising from pagan influences, isolation from other Christians, and false teaching.

John 1: Written sometime in the 90's and addressed to Asian churches, its message is that God is made known to us in the Son and that fellowship with the Father is attained by living in the light, justice and love of the Son.

John 2: Written sometime in the 90's and addressed to a church in Asia, it commends the people for standing firm in the faith and urges them to perseverance.

John 3: Written sometime in the 90's, it appears to represent an effort to settle a jurisdictional dispute in one of the churches.

Jude: Written sometime between the 70's and 90's, it is a brief treatise against erroneous teachings and practices opposed to law, authority and true Christian freedom.

Revelation: Written in the 90's along the lines of Johannine thought, it is a symbolic and apocalyptic treatment of things to come combined with warning but hope and assurance to the Church regarding the coming of the Lord in glory.

BIBLICAL AUTHORSHIP

Some books of the Bible were not written by the authors to whom they have been traditionally attributed; New Testament examples are the Gospels of Matthew and John, Hebrews, 1 and 2 Timothy, Titus, James, Jude.

This fact, which has never been the subject of dogmatic definition by the Church, does not militate against the canonicity of the books, since canonicity concerns the theological matter of inspiration rather than the historical question of human authorship.

Questions concerning authorship are explained in various ways: (1) according to an old custom whereby literary works of importance were sometimes attributed to famous persons so they would get a reading; (2) authorship, by a disciple or school of disciples, of works derived from the doctrine of a master; (3) authorship by persons writing in the spirit and tradition of a master.

GOSPEL PASSAGES

Discourses

The Sermon on the Mount is probably the best known of the many Gospel discourses.

Vindication of his authority (Jn. 2:18-22).

Spiritual rebirth, origin of his teaching, purpose of his coming, judgment on unbelievers; with Nicodemus (Jn. 3:1-21).

Of himself, his mission, everlasting life through him; with a Samaritan woman (Jn. 4:7-30).

Defense of his disciples for not fasting, for plucking corn on the Sabbath (Mt. 9:14-17, 12:1-8; Mk. 2:18-28; Lk. 5:33-39, 6:1-5).

Defense of himself for healing a man with a withered hand on the Sabbath (Mt. 12:9-13; Mk. 3:15; Lk. 6:6-10).

Sermon on the Mount (Mt. 5:1 to 7:29; Lk. 6:20-49).

Testimony concerning John the Baptist (Mt. 11:17-19; Lk. 7:24-35, 16:16).

Instructions for the apostolate (Mt. 10: 5-42; Mk. 6:8-13; Lk. 9:3-6, 10:1-12).

The bread of life (Jn. 6:22-72).

Defense of his claim to divinity (Jn. 5:19-47).

Defense of his disciples against Pharisees (Mt. 15:1-20; Mk. 7:1-23).

Promise of primacy to Peter (Mt. 16:13-20).

Predictions of the Passion and Resurrection (Mt. 16:21-23, 17:21-22, 20:17-19; Mk. 8:31-33, 9:29-31, 10:32-34; Lk. 9:22, 9:44-45, 18:31-34).

Doctrine of the cross (Mt. 16:24-28; Mk. 8:34-39; Lk. 9:23-27).

Scandal (Mt. 18:5-9; Mk. 9:41-49; Lk. 17:1-2).

Fraternal correction (Mt. 18:15-17, 21-22; Lk. 17:3-4).

Conversation with Martha and Mary (Lk. 10:38-42).

The adulteress (Jn. 8:3-11).

Efficacy of prayer (Mt. 7:7-11; Lk. 11:9-13).

Defense of his authority (Mt. 21:23-27; Mk. 11:27-33; Lk. 20:1-8).

Tribute to Caesar (Mt. 22:15-22; Mk. 12:13-17; Lk. 20:20-26).

The great commandment (Mt. 23:34-40; Mk. 12:28-34).

Destruction of Jerusalem and the Temple (Mt. 24:1-3, 15-22, 32-35; Mk. 13:1-20, 28-31; Lk. 21:5-6, 20-24, 29-33).

End of the world and coming of the Son of Man (Mt. 24:4-14, 23-31, 36-51 to 25:1-3; Mk. 13:21-27, 32-37; Lk. 21:7-19, 25-28, 34-36).

Last judgment (Mt. 25:31-46).

Discourses at the Last Supper (Mt. 26:20-29; Mk. 14:17-25; Lk. 22:14-38; Jn. 13:2 to 17:26).

Conferring of primacy on Peter (Jn. 21:15-17).

Commission of the Apostles to teach and baptize (Mt. 28:16-20; Mk. 16:15-18).

Parables

Essential to understanding a parable is identification of its points of reference.

The sower (Mt. 13:1-23; Mk. 4:1-20; Lk. 8:4-15).

The weeds (Mt. 13:24-30, 36-43).

The mustard seed (Mt. 13:31-32; Mk. 4:30-32; Lk. 13:18-19).

The leaven (Mt. 13:33; Lk. 12:20-21).

The treasure (Mt. 13:44).

The pearl (Mt. 13:45-46).

The net (Mt. 13:47-50).

The seed (Mk. 4:26-29).

The house built on rock (Mt. 7:24-27; Lk. 6:47-49).

The two debtors (Lk. 7:41-48).

The unmerciful servant (Mt. 18:21-35).

The good Samaritan (Lk. 10:25-37).

The importunate friend (Lk. 11:5-8).

The rich fool (Lk. 12:16-21).

A barren fig tree (Lk. 13:6-9).

The last seat (Lk. 14:7-11).

The lost sheep (Mt. 18:10-14; Lk. 15:1-7).

The lost coin (Lk. 15:8-10).

The prodigal son (Lk. 15:11-32).

The unjust steward (Lk. 16:1-13).

The rich man (Dives) and Lazarus (Lk. 16:19-31).

The godless judge (Lk. 18:1-8).

The Pharisee and the tax collector. (Lk. 18:9-14).

The laborers in the vineyard (Mt. 20:1-16).

The gold pieces (Lk. 19:11-27).

The two sons (Mt. 21:28-32).

The vine-dressers (Mt. 21:33-46; Mk. 12:1-12; Lk. 20:9-19).

The marriage feast (Mt. 22:1-10; Lk. 14:7-24).

The wedding garment (Mt. 22:11-14).

The great supper (Lk. 14:15-24).

The ten virgins (Mt. 25:1-13).

The talents (Mt. 25:14-30).

Similitudes and Allegories

"Physician, cure yourself" (Lk. 4:23).

The savor of salt (Mt. 5:13; Mk. 9:49; Lk. 14:34-35).

The lamp under a bushel basket (Mt. 5:14-15; Mk. 4:21; Lk. 8:16-18, 11:33-36).

The city on a mountain (Mt. 5:14).

The opponent (Mt. 5:25-26; Lk. 12:58-59).

The lamp of the body (Mt. 6:22-23; Lk. 11:33-36).

The two masters (Mt. 6:24; Lk. 16:13).

A son's request (Mt. 7:9-11; Lk. 11:11-13).

The tree and its fruit (Mt. 7:15-20, 12:33-37; Lk. 6:43-45).

The physician and the sick (Mt. 9:12-13; Mk. 2:17; Lk. 5:31-32).

The bridegroom and the wedding guests (Mt. 9:14-15; Mk. 2:18-20; Lk. 5:33-35).

A patch of raw cloth on an old garment (Mt. 9:16; Mk. 2:21; Lk. 5:36).

New wine in old wineskins (Mt. 9:17; Mk. 2:22; Lk. 5:37-38).

Secrets to be uncovered (Mt. 10:26-27; Mk. 4:22; Lk. 8:17, 12:2-3).
The servant not above the master (Mt. 10:24-25; Lk. 6:40).
The stubborn children (Mt. 11:16-19; Lk. 7:31-35).
The divided kingdom (Mt. 12:25-26; Mk. 3:23-26; Lk. 11:17-18).
The unclean spirit (Mt. 12:43-45; Lk. 11:24-26).
The wise scribe (Mt. 13:52).
The defilement of man (Mt. 15:10-20; Mk. 7:14-23).
Blind guides of blind men (Lk. 6:39; Mt. 15:14).
The children's bread (Mt. 15:26-27; Mk. 7:27-28).
Building a tower (Lk. 14:28-30).
Preparation for war (Lk. 14:31-33).
The watchful servants (Lk. 12:35-38; Mk. 13:34).
Faithful and unfaithful servants (Mt. 24:45-51; Lk. 12:42-48).
The unprofitable servant (Lk. 17:7-10).
The body and the vultures (Mt. 24:28; Lk. 17:37).
The thief (Mt. 24:43-44; Lk. 12:39-40).
The fig tree and the branches (Mt. 24:32-33; Mk. 13:28-29; Lk. 21:29-31).
The good Shepherd (Jn. 10:1-18).
The vine and the branches (Jn. 15:1-17).

Miracles

Changing of water into wine at the marriage feast (Jn. 2:1-11).
Cure of an official's son (Jn. 4:46-54).
Miraculous draft of fishes (Lk. 5:1-11).
The cure of a man possessed by the devil (Mk. 1:23-28; Lk, 4:33-37).
Cure of the fever of Peter's mother-in-law (Mt. 8:14-15; Mk. 1:29-31; Lk. 4:38-39).
Healing of many sick and diseased (Mt. 8:16-17; Mk. 1:32-34; Lk. 4:40-41).
Cure of a leper (Mt. 8:1-4; Mk. 1:40-45; Lk. 5:12-14).
Christ escapes from a mob (Lk. 4:28-30).
Cure of a paralytic (Mt. 9:1-8; Mk. 2:1-12; Lk. 5:18-26).
Cure of a sick man (Jn. 5:1-9).
Cure of a man with a withered hand (Mt. 12:9-13; Mk. 3:1-5; Lk. 6:6-10).
Healing of many sick and diseased (Lk. 6:18-19).
Cure of a centurion's servant (Mt. 8:5-13; Lk. 7:1-10).
Raising to life of a widow's son (Lk. 7:11-17).
Cure of a blind and mute possessed man (Mt. 12:22-37).
Calming of a storm (Mt. 8:23-27; Mk. 4:36-40; Lk. 8:22-25).
Exorcism of unclean spirits (Mt. 8:28-34; Mk. 5:1-15; Lk. 8:26-35).
Cure of a woman with a hemorrhage (Mt. 9:20-22; Mk. 5:25-34; Lk. 8:43-48).
Raising to life of Jairus' daughter (Mt. 9:18-19, 23-26; Mk. 5:20-24, 35-43; Lk. 8:41-42, 49-56).
Cure of two blind men (Mt. 9:27-31).
Exorcism of a mute possessed man (Mt. 9:32-34).
Feeding of over 5,000 with five loaves and two fishes (Mt. 14:13-21; Mk. 6:31-44; Lk. 9:12-17; Jn. 6:1-15).
Walking on the water (Mt. 14:22-33; Mk. 6:45-52; Jn. 6:16-21).
The exorcism of a Canaanite woman's daughter (Mt. 15:21-28; Mk. 7:24-30).
Cure of a deaf mute (Mk. 7:31-37).
Healing of many sick (Mt. 15:29-31).
Feeding of about 4,000 with seven loaves and a few fishes (Mt. 15:32-38; Mk. 8:1-9).
Cure of a blind man (Mk. 8:22-26).
Transfiguration (Mt. 17:1-9; Mk. 9:1-8; Lk. 9:28-36).
Exorcism of a possessed boy (Mt. 17:14-20; Mk. 9:13-28; Lk. 9:37-43).
Temple tax (Mt. 17:23-26).
Escape from his enemies (Jn. 8:59).
Cure of a man born blind (Jn. 9:1-41).
Exorcism of a possessed man (Lk. 11:14-26).
Cure of a crippled woman (Lk. 13:10-17).
Cure of a man afflicted with dropsy (Lk. 14:1-6).
Cure of 10 lepers (Lk. 17:12-19).
Raising of Lazarus to life (Jn. 11:1-44).
Cure of Bartimeus and another blind beggar (Mt. 20:29-34; Mk. 10:46-52; Lk. 18:35-43).
Withering of a barren fig tree (Mt. 21:18-19; Mk. 11:12-14).
Cure of many sick (Mt. 21:14).
Healing of a soldier's ear in the Garden (Mt. 26:51-52; Mk. 14:47; Lk. 22:49-51; Jn. 18:10-11).
Resurrection (Mt. 28:1-10; Mk. 16:1-14; Lk. 24:1-43; Jn. 20:1-20).
Miraculous draft of fishes after the Resurrection (Jn. 21:1-14).
The Ascension (Mk. 16:19; Lk. 24:50-51).

THE FIFTH GOSPEL

Gino Concetti, writing in the Mar. 21, 1974, English edition of *L'Osservatore Romano*, said:

"The geographical and historical setting of Palestine bears a quite special witness (to Christ). It has been said that the Holy Land is itself a gospel, the fifth gospel. The judgment is not an exaggerated one. Everything in Palestine speaks of Christ, his announcement by the prophets, his birth, his life, his miracles, his passion, his death and his resurrection. Those places that Christians have venerated, since the beginning as sacred because sanctified by the Savior, are still able today, 2,000 years later, to re-echo his voice and his message. . . . Direct knowledge of the theatre of the history of salvation will strengthen faith in Christ and facilitate the reunification of peoples."

INTERPRETATION OF THE BIBLE

According to the *Constitution on Revelation* issued by the Second Vatican Council, "the interpreter of Sacred Scripture, in order to see clearly what God wanted to communicate to us, should carefully investigate what meaning the sacred writers really intended, and what God wanted to manifest by means of their words" (No. 12).

Hermeneutics, Exegesis

This careful investigation proceeds in accordance with the rules of hermeneutics, the normative science of biblical interpretation and explanation. Hermeneutics in practice is called exegesis.

The principles of hermeneutics are derived from various disciplines and many factors which have to be considered in explaining the Bible and its parts. These include: the original languages and languages of translation of the sacred texts, through philology and linguistics; the quality of texts, through textual criticism; literary forms and genres, through literary and form criticism; cultural, historical, geographical and other conditions which influenced the writers, through related studies; facts and truths of salvation history; the truths and analogy of faith.

Distinctive to biblical hermeneutics, which differs in important respects from literary interpretation in general, is the premise that the Bible, though written by human authors, is the work of divine inspiration in which God reveals his plan for the salvation of men through historical events and persons, and especially through the Person and mission of Christ.

Textual, Form Criticism

Textual criticism is the study of biblical texts, which have been transmitted in copies several times removed from the original manuscripts, for the purpose of establishing the real state of the original texts. This purpose is served by comparison of existing copies; by application to the texts of the disciplines of philology and linguistics; by examination of related works of antiquity; by study of biblical citations in works of the Fathers of the Church and other authors; and by other means of literary study.

Since about 1920, the sayings of Christ have been a particular object of New Testament study, the purpose being to analyze the forms of expression used by the Evangelists in order to ascertain the words actually spoken by him.

Literary Criticism

Literary criticism aims to determine the origin and kinds of literary composition, called forms or genres, employed by the inspired authors. Such determinations are necessary for decision regarding the nature and purpose and, consequently, the meaning of biblical passages. Underlying these studies is the principle that the manner of writing was conditioned by the intention of the authors, the meaning they wanted to convey, and the then-contemporary literary style, mode or medium best adapted to carry their message — e.g., true history, quasi-historical narrative, poems, prayers, hymns, psalms, aphorisms, allegories, discourses. Understanding these media is necessary for the valid interpretation of their message.

Literal Sense

The key to all valid interpretation is the literal sense of biblical passages. Regarding this matter and the relevance to it of the studies and procedures described above, Pius XII wrote the following in the encyclical *Divino Afflante Spiritu.*

"What the literal sense of a passage is, is not always as obvious in the speeches and writings of ancient authors of the East as it is in the works of our own time. For what they wished to express is not to be determined by the rules of grammar and philology alone nor solely by the context; the interpreter must, as it were, go back wholly in spirit to those remote centuries of the East and with the aid of history, archeology, ethnology, and other sciences accurately determine what modes of writing, so to speak, the authors of that ancient period would be likely to use and in fact did use. . . . In explaining the Sacred Scripture and in demonstrating and proving its immunity from all error (the Catholic interpreter) should make a prudent use of this means, determine to what extent the manner of expression or literary mode adopted by the sacred writer may lead to a correct and genuine interpretation; and let him be convinced that this part of his office cannot be neglected without serious detriment to Catholic exegesis."

The literal sense of the Bible is the meaning in the mind of and intended by the inspired writer of a book or passage of the Bible. This is determined by the application to texts of the rules of hermeneutics. It is not to be confused with word-for-word literalism.

Typical Sense

The typical sense is the meaning which a passage has not only in itself but also in reference to something else of which it is a type or foreshadowing. A clear example is the account of the Exodus of the Israelites: in its literal sense, it narrates the liberation of the Israelites from death and oppression in Egypt; in its typical sense, it foreshadowed the liberation of men from sin through the redemptive death and resurrection of Christ. The typical sense of this and other passages emerged in the working out of God's plan of salvation history. It did not have to be in the mind of the author of the original passage.

Accommodated Senses

Accommodated, allegorical and consequent senses are figurative and adaptive meanings given to books and passages of the Bible for moral and other purposes. Such interpretations involve the danger of stretching the literal sense beyond proper proportions. Hermeneutical principles require that interpretations like these respect the integrity of the literal sense of the passages in question.

In the Catholic view, the final word on questions of biblical interpretation belongs to the teaching authority of the Church. In other views, generally derived from basic principles stated by Martin Luther, John Calvin and other Reformers, the primacy belongs to individual judgment acting in response to the inner testimony of the Holy Spirit, the edifying nature of biblical subject matter, the sublimity and simplicity of the message of salvation, the intensity with which Christ is proclaimed.

Biblical Studies

The first center for biblical studies, in some strict sense of the term, was the School of Alexandria, founded in the latter half of the second century. It was noted for allegorical exegesis. Literal interpretation was a hallmark of the School of Antioch.

St. Jerome, who produced the Vulgate, and St. Augustine, author of numerous commentaries, were the most important figures in biblical studies during the patristic period. By the time of the latter's death, the Old and New Testament canons had been stabilized. For some centuries afterwards, there was little or no progress in scriptural studies, although collections were made of scriptural excerpts from the writings of the Fathers of the Church, and the systematic reading of Scripture became established as a feature of monastic life.

Advances were made in the 12th and 13th centuries with the introduction of new principles and methods of scriptural analysis stemming from renewed interest in Hebraic studies and the application of dialectics.

By the time of the Reformation, the Bible had become the first book set in movable type, and more than 100 vernacular editions were in use throughout Europe.

The Council of Trent

In the wake of the Reformation, the Council of Trent formally defined the Canon of the Bible; it also reasserted the authoritative role of tradition and the teaching authority of the Church as well as Scripture with respect to the rule of faith. In the heated atmosphere of the 16th and 17th centuries, the Bible was turned into a polemical weapon; Protestants used it to defend their doctrines, and Catholics countered with citations in support of the dogmas of the Church. One result of this state of affairs was a lack of substantial progress in biblical studies during the period.

Toward the end of the 17th century, Louis Cappel, a Protestant, introduced a methodology for textual criticism, and Richard Simon, a Catholic, inaugurated modern literary and historical criticism. Their work was poorly regarded, however, and went into eclipse until about the beginning of the 19th century. It was then taken over by men whose work threatened to destroy the credibility of not only the Bible but Christianity itself.

Rationalists, and later Modernists, denied the reality of the supernatural and doctrine concerning inspiration of the Bible, which they generally regarded as a strictly human production expressive of the religious sense and experience of mankind. In their hands, the tools of positive critical research became weapons for biblical subversion. The defensive Catholic reaction to their work had the temporary effect of alienating scholars of the Church from solid advances in archeology, philology, history, textual and literary criticism.

Catholic Developments

Major influences in bringing about a change in Catholic attitude toward use of these disciplines in biblical studies were two papal encyclicals and two institutes of special study, the Ecole Biblique, founded in Jerusalem in 1890, and the Pontifical Biblical Institute established in Rome in 1909. The encyclical *Providentissimus Deus*, issued by Leo XIII in 1893, marked an important breakthrough; in addition to defending the concept of divine inspiration and the formal inspiration of the Scriptures, it encouraged the study of allied and ancillary sciences and techniques for a more fruitful understanding of the sacred writings. The encyclical *Divino Afflante Spiritu*, 50 years later, gave encouragement for the use of various forms of criticism as tools of biblical research. The documents encouraged the work of scholars and stimulated wide communication of the fruits of their study.

Great changes in the climate and direction of biblical studies have occurred in recent years. One of them has been an increase in cooperative effort among Catholic, Protestant, Orthodox and Jewish scholars. Their common investigation of the Dead Sea Scrolls is well known. More recently productive was the collaboration in England of Catholics and Protestants in turning out a Catholic edition of the Revised Standard Version of the Bible.

The development and results of biblical studies in this century have directly and significantly affected all phases of the contemporary renewal movement in the Church. Their influence on theology, liturgy, catechetics, and preaching indicate the importance of their function in the life of the Church.

APOSTLES AND EVANGELISTS

The Apostles were the men selected, trained and commissioned by Christ to preach the Gospel, to baptize, to establish, direct and care for his Church as servants of God and stewards of his mysteries. They were the first bishops of the Church.

St. Matthew's Gospel lists the Apostles in this order: Peter, Andrew, James the Greater, John, Philip, Bartholomew, Thomas, Matthew, James the Less, Jude, Simon and Judas Iscariot. Matthias was elected to fill the place of Judas. Paul became an Apostle by a special call from Christ. Barnabas was called an Apostle.

Two of the Evangelists, John and Matthew, were Apostles. The other two, Luke and Mark, were closely associated with the apostolic college.

Andrew: Born in Bethsaida, brother of Peter, disciple of John the Baptist, a fisherman, the first Apostle called; according to legend, preached the Gospel in Northern Greece, Epirus and Scythia, and was martyred at Patras about 70; in art, is represented with an x-shaped cross, called St. Andrew's Cross; feast, Nov. 30; is honored as the patron of Russia and Scotland.

Barnabas: Originally called Joseph but named Barnabas by the Apostles, among whom he is ranked because of his collaboration with Paul; a Jew of the Diaspora, born on Cyprus; a cousin of Mark and member of the Christian community at Jerusalem, influenced the Apostles to accept Paul, with whom he became a pioneer missionary outside Palestine and Syria, in Antioch, Cyprus and southern Asia Minor; legend says he was martyred on Cyprus during the Neronian persecution; feast, June 11.

Bartholomew (Nathaniel): A friend of Philip; according to various traditions, preached the Gospel in Ethiopia, India, Persia, and Armenia where he was martyred by being flayed and beheaded; in art, is depicted holding a knife, an instrument of his death; feast, Aug. 24 in the Roman Rite, Aug. 25 in the Byzantine Rite.

James the Greater: A Galilean, son of Zebedee, brother of John (with whom he was called a "son of thunder"), a fisherman; with Peter and John, witnessed the raising of Jairus' daughter to life, the transfiguration, the agony of Jesus in the Garden of Gethsemani; first of the Apostles to die, by the sword in 44 during the rule of Herod Agrippa; there is doubt about a journey legend says he made to Spain and also about the authenticity of relics said to be his at Santiago de Compostela; in art, is depicted carrying a pilgrim's bell; feast, July 25 in the Roman Rite, Apr. 30 in the Byzantine Rite.

James the Less: Son of Alphaeus, called "Less" because he was younger in age or shorter in stature than James the Greater; one

of the "catholic" epistles bears his name; was stoned to death in 62 or thrown from the top of the temple in Jerusalem and clubbed to death in 66; in art, is depicted with a club or heavy staff; feast, May 3 in the Roman Rite, Oct. 9 in the Byzantine Rite.

John: A Galilean, son of Zebedee, brother of James the Greater (with whom he was called a "son of thunder"), a fisherman, probably a disciple of John the Baptist, one of the Evangelists, called the "beloved disciple"; with Peter and James the Greater, witnessed the raising of Jairus' daughter to life, the transfiguration, the agony of Jesus in the Garden of Gethsemani; Mary was commended to his special care by Christ; the fourth Gospel, three "catholic" Epistles and Revelation bear his name; according to various accounts, lived at Ephesus in Asia Minor for some time and died a natural death about 100; in art, is represented by an eagle, symbolic of the sublimity of the contents of his Gospel; feast, Dec. 27 in the Roman Rite, May 8 in the Byzantine Rite.

Jude Thaddeus: One of the "catholic" epistles, the shortest, bears his name; various traditions say he preached the Gospel in Mesopotamia, Persia and elsewhere, and was martyred; in art, is depicted with a halberd, the instrument of his death; feast, Oct. 28 in the Roman Rite, June 19 in the Byzantine Rite.

Luke: A Greek convert to the Christian community, called "our most dear physician" by Paul, of whom he was a missionary companion; author of the third Gospel and Acts of the Apostles; the place — Achaia, Bithynia, Egypt — and circumstances of his death are not certain; in art, is depicted as a man, a writer, or an ox (because his Gospel starts at the scene of Temple sacrifice); feast, Oct. 18.

Mark: A cousin of Barnabas and member of the first Christian community at Jerusalem; a missionary companion of Paul and Barnabas, then of Peter; author of the Gospel which bears his name; according to legend, founded the Church at Alexandria, was bishop there and was martyred in the streets of the city; in art, is depicted with his Gospel and a winged lion, symbolic of the voice of John the Baptist crying in the wilderness, at the beginning of his Gospel; feast, Apr. 25.

Matthew: A Galilean, called Levi by Luke and John and the son of Alphaeus by Mark, a tax collector, one of the Evangelists; according to various accounts, preached the Gospel in Judea, Ethiopia, Persia and Parthia, and was martyred; in art, is depicted with a spear, the instrument of his death, and as a winged man in his role as Evangelist; feast, Sept. 21 in the Roman Rite, Nov. 16 in the Byzantine Rite.

Matthias: A disciple of Jesus whom the faithful 11 Apostles chose to replace Judas before the Resurrection; uncertain traditions report that he preached the Gospel in Palestine, Cappadocia or Ethiopia; in art, is represented with a cross and a halberd, the instruments of his death as a martyr; feast, May 14 in the Roman Rite, Aug. 9 in the Byzantine Rite.

Paul: Born at Tarsus, of the tribe of Benjamin, a Roman citizen; participated in the persecution of Christians until the time of his miraculous conversion on the way to Damascus; called by Christ, who revealed himself to him in a special way; became the Apostle of the Gentiles, among whom he did most of his preaching in the course of three major missionary journeys through areas north of Palestine, Cyprus, Asia Minor and Greece; 14 epistles bear his name; two years of imprisonment at Rome, following initial arrest in Jerusalem and confinement at Caesarea, ended with martyrdom, by beheading, outside the walls of the city in 64 or 67 during the Neronian persecution; in art, is depicted in various ways with St. Peter, with a sword, in the scene of his conversion; feasts, June 29, Jan. 25 (Roman Rite).

Peter: Simon, son of Jona, born in Bethsaida, brother of Andrew, a fisherman; called Cephas or Peter by Christ who made him the chief of the Apostles and head of the Church as his vicar; named first in the listings of Apostles in the Synoptic Gospels and the Acts of the Apostles; with James the Greater and John, witnessed the raising of Jairus' daughter to life, the transfiguration, the agony of Jesus in the Garden of Gethsemani; was the first to preach the Gospel in and around Jerusalem and was the leader of the first Christian community there; established a local Church in Antioch; presided over the Council of Jerusalem in 51; wrote two "catholic" epistles to the Christians in Asia Minor; established his see in Rome where he spent his last years and was martyred by crucifixion in 64 or 65 during the Neronian persecution; in art, is depicted carrying two keys, symbolic of his primacy in the Church; feasts, June 29, Feb. 22 (Roman Rite).

Philip: Born in Bethsaida; according to legend, preached the Gospel in Phrygia where he suffered martyrdom by crucifixion; feast, May 3 in the Roman Rite, Nov. 14 in the Byzantine Rite.

Simon: Called the Cananean or the Zealot; according to legend, preached in various places in the Near East and suffered martyrdom by being sawed in two; in art, is depicted with a saw, the instrument of his death, or a book, symbolic of his zeal for the Law; feast, Oct. 28 in the Roman Rite, May 10 in the Byzantine Rite.

Thomas (Didymus): Notable for his initial incredulity regarding the Resurrection and his subsequent forthright confession of the divinity of Christ risen from the dead; according to legend, preached the Gospel in places from the Caspian Sea to the Persian Gulf and eventually reached India where he was martyred near Madras; Thomas Christians trace their origin to him; in art, is depicted kneeling before the risen Christ, or with a carpenter's rule and square; feast, July 3 in the Roman Rite, Oct. 6 in the Byzantine Rite.

JUDAS

The Gospels record only a few facts about Judas, the Apostle who betrayed Christ.

The only non-Galilean among the Apostles, he was from Carioth, a town in southern Juda. He was keeper of the purse in the apostolic band. He was called a petty thief by John. He voiced dismay at the waste of money, which he said might have been spent for the poor, in connection with the anointing incident at Bethany. He took the initiative in arranging the betrayal of Christ. Afterwards, he confessed that he had betrayed an innocent man and cast into the Temple the money he had received for that action. Of his death, Matthew says that he hanged himself; the Acts of the Apostles states that he swelled up and burst open; both reports deal more with the meaning than the manner of his death — the misery of the death of a sinner.

The consensus of speculation over the reason why Judas acted as he did in betraying Christ focuses on disillusionment and unwillingness to accept the concept of a suffering Messiah and personal suffering of his own as an Apostle.

APOSTOLIC FATHERS, FATHERS, DOCTORS OF THE CHURCH

The writers listed below, were outstanding and authoritative witnesses to authentic Christian belief and practice, and played significant roles in giving them expression.

Apostolic Fathers

The Apostolic Fathers were Christian writers of the first and second centuries who are known or believed to have had personal relations with the Apostles, and whose writings echo genuine apostolic teaching.

Chief in importance are: St. Clement (d.c. 97), bishop of Rome and third successor of St. Peter in the papacy; St. Ignatius (50-c.

107), bishop of Antioch and second successor of St. Peter in that see, reputed to be a disciple of St. John; St. Polycarp (69-155), bishop of Smyrna and a disciple of St. John. The authors of the *Didache* and the *Epistle of Barnabas* are also numbered among the Apostolic Fathers.

Other early ecclesiastical writers included: St. Justin, martyr (100-165), of Asia Minor and Rome, a layman and apologist; St. Irenaeus (130-202), bishop of Lyons, who opposed Gnosticism; and St. Cyprian (210-258), bishop of Carthage, who opposed Novatianism.

Fathers and Doctors

The Fathers of the Church were theologians and writers of the first eight centuries who were outstanding for sanctity and learning. They were such authoritative witnesses to the belief and teaching of the Church that their unanimous acceptance of doctrines as divinely revealed has been regarded as evidence that such doctrines were so received by the Church in line with apostolic tradition and Sacred Scripture. Their unanimous rejection of doctrines branded them as heretical. Their writings, however, were not necessarily free of error in all respects.

The greatest of these Fathers were: Sts. Ambrose, Augustine, Jerome and Gregory the Great in the West; Sts. John Chrysostom, Basil the Great, Gregory of Nazianzen and Athanasius in the East.

The Doctors of the Church were ecclesiastical writers of eminent learning and sanctity who have been given this title because of the great advantage the Church has derived from their work. These writings, however, were not necessarily free of error in all respects.

Albert the Great, St. (c. 1200-1280): Born in Swabia, Germany; Dominican; bishop of Regensburg (1260-1262); wrote extensively on logic, natural sciences, ethics, metaphysics, Scripture, systematic theology; contributed to development of Scholasticism; teacher of St. Thomas Aquinas; canonized and proclaimed doctor, 1931; named patron of natural scientists, 1941; called Doctor Universalis, Doctor Expertus; feast, Nov. 15.

Alphonsus Liguori, St. (1696-1787): Born near Naples, Italy; bishop of Agatha of the Goths (1762-1775); founder of the Redemptorists; in addition to his principal work, *Theologiae Moralis,* wrote on prayer, the spiritual life, and doctrinal subjects in response to controversy; canonized, 1839; proclaimed doctor, 1871; named patron of confessors and moralists, 1950; feast, Aug. 1.

Ambrose, St. (c. 340-397): Born in Treves, Germany; bishop of Milan (374-397); one of the strongest opponents of Arianism in the West; his homilies and other writings — on faith, the Holy Spirit, the Incarnation, the sacraments and other subjects — were pastoral and practical; influenced the development of a liturgy at Milan which was named for him; Father and Doctor of the Church; feast, Dec. 7.

Anselm, St. (1033-1109): Born in Aosta, Piedmont, Italy; Benedictine; archbishop of Canterbury (1093-1109); in addition to his principal work, *Cur Deus Homo,* on the atonement and reconciliation of man with God through Christ, wrote about the existence and attributes of God and defended the *Filioque* explanation of the procession of the Holy Spirit from the Father and the Son; canonized, 1494; proclaimed doctor, 1720; called Father of Scholasticism; feast, Apr. 21.

Anthony of Padua, St. (1195-1231): Born in Lisbon, Portugal; first theologian of the Franciscan Order; preacher; canonized, 1232; proclaimed doctor, 1946; called Evangelical Doctor; feast, June 13.

Athanasius, St. (c. 297-373): Born in Alexandria, Egypt; bishop of Alexandria (328-373); participant in the Council of Nicaea I while still a deacon; dominant opponent of Arians whose errors regarding Christ he refuted in *Apology against the Arians, Discourses against the Arians,* and other works; Father and Doctor of the Church; called Father of Orthodoxy; feast, May 2.

Augustine, St. (354-430): Born in Tagaste, North Africa; bishop of Hippo (395-430) after conversion from Manichaeism; works include the autobiographical and mystical *Confessions, City of God,* treatises on the Trinity, grace, passages of the Bible, and doctrines called into question and denied by Manichaeans, Pelagians and Donatists; had strong and lasting influence on Christian theology and philosophy; Father and Doctor of the Church; called Doctor of Grace; feast, Aug. 28.

Basil the Great, St. (c. 329-379): Born in Caesarea, Cappadocia, Asia Minor; bishop of Caesarea (370-379); wrote three books *Contra Eunomium* in refutation of Arian errors, a treatise on the Holy Spirit, many homilies, and several rules for monastic life, on which he had lasting influence; Father and Doctor of the Church; called Father of Monasticism in the East; feast, Jan. 2.

Bede the Venerable, St. (c. 673-735): Born in Northumberland, England; Benedictine; in addition to his principal work, *Ecclesiastical History of the English Nation* (covering the period 597-731), wrote scriptural commentaries; regarded as probably the most learned man in Western Europe of his time; called Father of English History; feast, May 25.

Bernard of Clairvaux, St. (c. 1090-1153): Born near Dijon, France; abbot; monastic reformer, called the second founder of the Cistercian Order; mystical theologian with great influence on devotional life; opponent of the rationalism brought forward by Abelard and others; canonized, 1174; proclaimed doctor, 1830; called Mellifluous Doctor because of his eloquence; feast, Aug. 20.

Bonaventure, St. (c. 1217-1274): Born near Viterbo, Italy; Franciscan; bishop of Albano (1273-1274); cardinal; wrote *Itinerarium Mentis in Deum, De Reductione Artium ad Theologiam, Breviloquium,* scriptural commentaries, additional mystical works affecting devotional life, and a life of St. Francis of Assisi; canonized, 1482; proclaimed doctor, 1588; called Seraphic Doctor; feast, July 15.

Catherine of Siena, St. (c. 1347-1380): Born in Siena, Italy; member of the Third Order of St. Dominic; mystic; authored a long series of letters, mainly concerning spiritual instruction and encouragement, to associates, and

Dialogue, a spiritual testament in four treatises; was active in support of a crusade against the Turks and efforts to end war between papal forces and the Florentine allies; had great influence in inducing Gregory XI to return himself and the Curia to Rome in 1376, to end the Avignon period of the papacy; canonized, 1461; proclaimed the second woman doctor, Oct. 4, 1970; feast, Apr. 29.

Cyril of Alexandria, St. (c. 376-444): Born in Egypt; bishop of Alexandria (412-444); wrote treatises on the Trinity, the Incarnation and other subjects, mostly in refutation of Nestorian errors; made key contributions to the development of Christology; presided at the Council of Ephesus, 431; proclaimed doctor, 1882; feast, June 27.

Cyril of Jerusalem, St. (c. 315-387): Bishop of Jerusalem (350-387); vigorous opponent of Arianism; principal work, *Catecheses,* a prebaptismal explanation of the creed of Jerusalem; proclaimed doctor, 1882; feast, Mar. 18.

Ephraem, St. (c. 306-373): Born in Nisibis, Mesopotamia; counteracted the spread of Gnostic and Arian errors with poems and hymns of his own composition; wrote also on the Eucharist and Mary; proclaimed doctor, 1920; called Deacon of Edessa and Harp of the Holy Spirit; feast, June 9.

Francis de Sales, St. (1567-1622): Born in Savoy; bishop of Geneva (1602-1622); spiritual writer with strong influence on devotional life through treatises such as *Introduction to a Devout Life,* and *The Love of God;* canonized, 1665; proclaimed doctor, 1877; patron of Catholic writers and the Catholic press; feast, Jan. 24.

Gregory Nazianzen, St. (c. 330-c. 390): Born in Arianzus, Cappadocia, Asia Minor; bishop of Constantinople (381-390); vigorous opponent of Arianism; in addition to five theological discourses on the Nicene Creed and the Trinity for which he is best known, wrote letters and poetry; Father and Doctor of the Church; called the Christian Demosthenes because of his eloquence and, in the Eastern Church, The Theologian; feast, Jan. 2.

Gregory I, the Great, St. (c. 540-604): Born in Rome; pope (590-604): wrote many scriptural commentaries, a compendium of theology in the *Book of Morals* based on Job, *Dialogues* concerning the lives of saints, the immortality of the soul, death, purgatory, heaven and hell, and 14 books of letters; enforced papal supremacy and established the position of the pope vis-a-vis the emperor; worked for clerical and monastic reform and the observance of clerical celibacy; Father and Doctor of the Church; feast, Sept. 3.

Hilary of Poitiers, St. (c. 315-368): Born in Poitiers, France; bishop of Poitiers (c. 353-368); wrote *De Synodis,* with the Arian controversy in mind, and *De Trinitate,* the first lengthy study of the doctrine in Latin; introduced Eastern theology to the West; contributed to the development of hymnology; proclaimed doctor, 1851; called the Athanasius of the West because of his vigorous defense of the divinity of Christ against Arians; feast, Jan. 13.

Isidore of Seville, St. (c. 560-636): Born in Cartagena, Spain; bishop of Seville (c. 600-636); in addition to his principal work, *Etymologiae,* an encyclopedia of the knowledge of his day, wrote on theological and historical subjects; regarded as the most learned man of his time; proclaimed doctor, 1722; feast, Apr. 4.

Jerome, St. (c. 343-420): Born in Stridon, Dalmatia; translated the Old Testament from Hebrew into Latin and revised the existing Latin translation of the New Testament to produce the Vulgate version of the Bible; wrote scriptural commentaries and treatises on matters of controversy; regarded as Father and Doctor of the Church from the eighth century; called Father of Biblical Science; feast, Sept. 30.

John Chrysostom, St. (c. 347-407): Born in Antioch, Asia Minor; archbishop of Constantinople (398-407); wrote homilies, scriptural commentaries and letters of wide influence in addition to a classical treatise on the priesthood; proclaimed a doctor by the Council of Chalcedon, 451; called the greatest of the Greek Fathers; named patron of preachers, 1909; called golden-mouthed because of his eloquence; feast, Sept. 13.

John Damascene, St. (c. 675-c. 749): Born in Damascus, Syria; monk; wrote *Fountain of Wisdom,* a three-part work including a history of heresies and an exposition of the Christian faith, three *Discourses against the Iconoclasts,* homilies on Mary, biblical commentaries and treatises on moral subjects; proclaimed doctor, 1890; called Golden Speaker because of his eloquence; feast, Dec. 4.

John of the Cross, St. (1542-1591): Born in Old Castile, Spain; Carmelite; founder of Discalced Carmelites; one of the greatest mystical theologians, wrote *The Ascent of Mt. Carmel — The Dark Night, The Spiritual Canticle, The Living Flame of Love;* canonized, 1726; proclaimed doctor, 1926; called Doctor of Mystical Theology; feast, Dec. 14.

Lawrence of Brindisi, St. (1559-1619): Born in Brindisi, Italy; Franciscan (Capuchin); vigorous preacher of strong influence in the post-Reformation period; 15 tomes of collected works include scriptural commentaries, sermons, homilies and doctrinal writings; canonized, 1881; proclaimed doctor, 1959; feast, July 21.

Leo I, the Great, St. (c. 400-461): Born in Tuscany, Italy; pope (440-461); wrote the *Tome of Leo,* to explain doctrine concerning the two natures and one Person of Christ, against the background of the Nestorian and Monophysite heresies; other works included sermons, letters, and writings against the errors of Manichaeism and Pelagianism; was instrumental in dissuading Attila from sacking Rome in 452; proclaimed doctor, 1574; feast, Nov. 10.

Peter Canisius, St. (1521-1597): Born in Nijmegen, Holland; Jesuit; wrote popular expositions of the Catholic faith in several catechisms which were widely circulated in 20 editions in his lifetime alone; was one of the moving figures in the Counter-Reformation period, especially in southern and western Germany; canonized and proclaimed doctor, 1925; feast, Dec. 21.

Peter Chrysologus, St. (c. 400-450): Born in Imola, Italy; served as archbishop of Ravenna (c. 433-450); his sermons and writings, many of which were designed to counteract Monophysitism, were pastoral and practical; proclaimed doctor, 1729; feast, July 30.

Peter Damian, St. (1007-1072): Born in Ravenna, Italy; Benedictine; cardinal; his writings and sermons, many of which concerned ecclesiastical and clerical reform, were pastoral and practical; proclaimed doctor, 1828; feast, Feb. 21.

Robert Bellarmine, St. (1542-1621): Born in Tuscany, Italy; Jesuit; archbishop of Capua (1602-1605); wrote *Controversies,* a three-volume exposition of doctrine under attack during and after the Reformation, two catechisms and the spiritual work, *The Art of Dying Well,* was an authority on ecclesiology

and Church-state relations; canonized, 1930; proclaimed doctor, 1931; feast, Sept. 17.

Theresa of Avila, St. (1515-1582): Born in Avila, Spain; entered the Carmelite Order, 1535; in the early 1560's, initiated a primitive Carmelite, discalced-Alcantarine reform which greatly influenced men and women religious, especially in Spain; wrote extensively on spiritual and mystical subjects; principal works included her *Autobiography, Way of Perfection, The Interior Castle, Meditations on the Canticle, The Foundations, Visitation of the Discalced Nuns;* canonized, 1614; proclaimed first woman doctor, Sept. 27, 1970; feast, Oct. 15.

Thomas Aquinas, St. (1225-1274): Born near Naples, Italy; Dominican; teacher and writer on virtually the whole range of philosophy and theology; principal works were *Summa contra Gentiles,* a manual and systematic defense of Christian doctrine, and *Summa Theologiae,* a new (at that time) exposition of theology on philosophical principles; canonized, 1323; proclaimed doctor, 1567; called Doctor Communis, Doctor Angelicus, the Great Synthesizer because of the way in which he related faith and reason, theology and philosophy (especially that of Aristotle), and systematized the presentation of Christian doctrine; named patron of Catholic schools and education, 1880; feast, Jan. 28.

CREEDS

Creeds are formal and official statements of Christian doctrine. As summaries of the principal truths of faith, they are standards of orthodoxy and are useful for instructional purposes, for actual profession of the faith, and for expression of the faith in the liturgy.

The classical creeds are the Apostles' Creed and the Creed of Nicaea-Constantinople. Two others are the Athanasian Creed and the Creed of Pius IV.

Apostles' Creed

Text: I believe in God, the Father almighty, Creator of heaven and earth.

And in Jesus Christ, his only Son, our Lord; who was conceived by the Holy Spirit, born of the Virgin Mary, suffered under Pontius Pilate, was crucified, died, and was buried. He descended into hell; the third day he arose again from the dead; he ascended into heaven, sits at the right hand of God, the Father almighty; from thence he shall come to judge the living and the dead.

I believe in the Holy Spirit, the holy Catholic Church, the communion of saints, the forgiveness of sins, the resurrection of the body, and life everlasting. Amen.

Background: The Apostles' Creed reflects the teaching of the Apostles but is not of apostolic origin. It probably originated in the second century as a rudimentary formula of faith professed by catechumens before the reception of baptism. Baptismal creeds in

fourth-century use at Rome and elsewhere in the West closely resembled the present text, which was quoted in a handbook of Christian doctrine written between 710 and 724. This text was in wide use throughout the West by the ninth century. The Apostles' Creed is common to all Christian confessional churches in the West, but is not used in Eastern Churches.

Nicene Creed

The following translation of the Latin text of the creed was prepared by the International Committee on English in the Liturgy.

Text: We believe in one God, the Father, the Almighty, maker of heaven and earth, of all that is seen and unseen.

We believe in one Lord, Jesus Christ, the only Son of God, eternally begotten of the Father, God from God, Light from Light, true God from true God, begotten, not made, one in Being with the Father. Through him all things were made. For us men and for our salvation he came down from heaven: by the power of the Holy Spirit he was born of the Virgin Mary, and became man. For our sake he was crucified under Pontius Pilate; he suffered, died, and was buried. On the third day he rose again in fulfillment of the Scriptures; he ascended into heaven and is seated at the right hand of the Father. He will come again in glory to judge the living and the dead, and his kingdom will have no end.

We believe in the Holy Spirit, the Lord, the giver of life, who proceeds from the Father and the Son. With the Father and the Son he is worshiped and glorified. He has spoken through the prophets.

We believe in one holy catholic and apostolic Church. We acknowledge one baptism for the forgiveness of sins. We look for the resurrection of the dead, and the life of the world to come. Amen.

Background: The Nicene Creed (Creed of Nicaea-Constantinople) consists of elements of doctrine contained in an early baptismal creed of Jerusalem and enactments of the Council of Nicaea (325) and the Council of Constantinople (381). Its strong trinitarian content reflects the doctrinal errors, especially of Arianism, it served to counteract. Theologically, it is much more sophisticated than the Apostles' Creed. Since late in the fifth century, the Nicene Creed has been the only creed in liturgical use in the Eastern Churches. The Western Church adopted it for liturgical use by the end of the eighth century.

The Athanasian Creed

The Athanasian Creed, which has a unique structure, is a two-part summary of doctrine concerning the Trinity and the Incarnation-Redemption bracketed at the beginning and end with the statement that belief in the cited truths is necessary for salvation; it also contains a number of anathemas or condemnatory clauses regarding doctrinal errors. Although attributed to St. Athanasius, it was probably written after his death, between 381 and 428, and may have been authored by St. Ambrose. It is not accepted in the East; in the West, it has place in the liturgy of some other Christian churches as well as in the Roman-Rite Liturgy of the Hours and for the Solemnity of the Holy Trinity.

Creed of Pius IV

The Creed of Pius IV, also called the Profession of Faith of the Council of Trent, was promulgated in the bull *Injunctum Nobis,* Nov. 13, 1564. It is a summary of doctrine defined by the council concerning: Scripture and tradition, original sin and justification, the Mass and sacraments, veneration of the saints, indulgences, the primacy of the See of Rome. It was slightly modified in 1887 to include doctrinal formulations of the First Vatican Council.

REDDITIO OF CREED

The "giving back," by profession, of a baptismal creed by candidates for baptism to a bishop or his representative was one of the immediate preliminaries to reception of the sacrament at the conclusion of the catechumenate in the early Church.

The interrogation concerning truths of faith in the present baptismal rite is reminiscent of this ancient practice.

MORAL OBLIGATIONS

The basic norm of Christian morality is life in Christ. This involves, among other things, the observance of the Ten Commandments, their fulfillment in the twofold law of love of God and neighbor, the implications of the Sermon on the Mount and the whole New Testament, and membership in the Church established by Christ.

The Ten Commandments

The Ten Commandments, the Decalogue, were given by God through Moses to his Chosen People for the guidance of their moral conduct in accord with the demands of the Covenant he established with them as a divine gift. Their observance was essential to participation in the Covenant and the order of salvation based on it.

In the traditional Catholic enumeration and according to Dt. 5:6-21, the Commandments are:

1. "I, the Lord, am your God . . . You shall not have other gods besides me. You shall not carve idols. . . ."
2. "You shall not take the name of the Lord, your God, in vain. . . ."
3. "Take care to keep holy the Sabbath day. . . ."
4. "Honor your father and your mother. . . ."
5. "You shall not kill."
6. "You shall not commit adultery."
7. "You shall not steal."
8. "You shall not bear dishonest witness against your neighbor."
9. "You shall not covet your neighbor's wife."
10. "You shall not desire your neighbor's house or field, nor his male or female slave, nor his ox or ass, nor anything that belongs to him" (summarily, his goods).

Another version of the Commandments, substantially the same, is given in Ex. 20:1-17.

The traditional enumeration of the Commandments in Protestant usage differs from the above. Thus: two commandments are made of the first, as above; the third and fourth are equivalent to the second and third, as above, and so on; and the 10th includes the ninth and 10th, as above.

Love of God and Neighbor

The first three of the commandments deal directly with man's relations with God, viz.: acknowledgment of one true God and the rejection of false gods and idols; honor due to God and his name; observance of the Sabbath as the Lord's day.

The rest cover interpersonal relationships, viz.: the obedience due to parents and, logically, to other persons in authority, and the obligations of parents to children and of persons in authority to those under their care; respect for life and physical integrity; fidelity in marriage, and chastity; justice and rights; truth; internal respect for faithfulness in marriage, chastity, and the goods of others.

Perfection in Christian Life

The moral obligations of the Ten Commandments are complemented by others flowing from the twofold law of love, the whole substance and pattern of Christ's teaching, and everything implied in full and active membership and participation in the community of salvation formed by Christ in his Church. Some of these matters are covered in other sections of the Almanac under appropriate headings.

Precepts of the Church

The precepts of the Church of Roman Rite oblige Catholics to:

1. Assist at Mass on Sundays and holy days of obligation. (Also, to desist from unneces-

sary servile work on these days.)

2. Fast and abstain on the days appointed. (The fasting obligation binds persons from the 21st until the 59th birthday; the days of fast are Ash Wednesday and Good Friday. The abstinence obligation binds from the 14th birthday on these days, and is obligatory for all Fridays in Lent in the U.S.) These regulations, which have been modified in recent years, are penitential in purpose but do not exhaust obligations of penance. Other ways of doing penance are left to personal option.

3. Confess their sins at least once a year.

4. Receive Holy Communion during the Easter time. (In the U.S., the Easter time extends from the First Sunday of Lent to Trinity Sunday.)

5. Contribute to the support of the Church.

6. Observe the laws of the Church concerning marriage.

SOCIAL DOCTRINE

Since the end of the last century, Catholic social doctrine has been formulated in a progressive manner in a number of authoritative documents. Outstanding examples are the encyclicals: *Rerum Novarum,* issued by Leo XIII in 1891; *Quadragesimo Anno,* by Pius XI in 1931; *Mater et Magistra* ("Christianity and Social Progress") and *Pacem in Terris* ("Peace on Earth"), by John XXIII in 1961 and 1963, respectively; and *Populorum Progressio* ("Development of Peoples"), by Paul VI in 1967. Pius XII, among other accomplishments of ideological importance in the social field, made a distinctive contribution with his formulation of a plan for world peace and order in Christmas messages from 1939 to 1941, and in other documentsm

These documents represent the most serious attempts in modern times to systematize the social implications of the Gospel and the rest of divine revelation as well as the socially relevant writings of the Fathers and Doctors of the Church. Their contents are theological penetrations into social life, with particular reference to human rights, the needs of the poor and those in underdeveloped countries, and humane conditions of life, freedom, justice and peace. In some respects, they read like juridical documents; underneath, however, they are Gospel-oriented and pastoral in intention.

Nature of the Doctrine

Pope John, writing in *Christianity and Social Progress,* made the following statement about the nature and scope of the doctrine stated in the encyclicals in particular and related writings in general.

"What the Catholic Church teaches and declares regarding the social life and relationships of men is beyond question for all time valid.

"The cardinal point of this teaching is that

individual men are necessarily the foundation, cause, and end of all social institutions . . . insofar as they are social by nature, and raised to an order of existence that transcends and subdues nature.

"Beginning with this very basic principle whereby the dignity of the human person is affirmed and defended, Holy Church — especially during the last century and with the assistance of learned priests and laymen, specialists in the field — has arrived at clear social teachings whereby the mutual relationships of men are ordered. Taking general norms into account, these principles are in accord with the nature of things and the changed conditions of man's social life, or with the special genius of our day. Moreover, these norms can be approved by all."

The Church in the World

Even more Gospel-oriented and pastoral in a distinctive way is the *Pastoral Constitution on the Church in the Modern World* promulgated by the Second Vatican Council in 1965.

Its purpose was to search out the signs of God's presence and meaning in and through the events of this time in human history. Accordingly, it dealt with the situation of men in present circumstances of profound change, challenge and crisis on all levels of life.

The first part of the constitution developed the theme of the Church and man's calling, and focused attention on the dignity of the human person, the problem of atheism, the community of mankind, man's activity throughout the world, and the serving and saving role of the Church in the world. This portion of the document, it has been said, represents the first presentation by the Church in an official text of an organized Christian view of man and society.

The second part of the document considered several problems of special urgency: fostering the nobility of marriage and the family (see Marriage Doctrine), the proper development of culture, socio-economic life, the life of the political community, the fostering of peace (see Peace and War), and the promotion of a community of nations.

In conclusion, the constitution called for action to implement doctrine regarding the role and work of the Church for the total good of mankind.

Following are a number of key excerpts from the ideological heart of the constitution.

One Human Family and Community: "God, who has fatherly concern for everyone, has willed that all men should constitute one family and treat one another in a spirit of brotherhood....

"For this reason, love for God and neighbor is the first and greatest commandment. Sacred Scripture ... teaches us that the love of God cannot be separated from love of neighbor.... To men growing daily more dependent on one another, and to a world becoming more unified every day, this truth proves to be of paramount importance..." (No. 24).

Human Person Is Central: "Man's social nature makes it evident that the progress of the human person and the advance of society itself hinge on each other. For the beginning, the subject and the goal of all social institutions is and must be the human person, which for its part and by its very nature stands completely in need of social life. This social life is not something added on to man. Hence, through his dealings with others, through reciprocal duties, and through fraternal dialogue he develops all his gifts and is able to rise to his destiny."

Influence of Social Circumstances: "But if by this social life the human person is greatly aided in responding to his destiny, even in its religious dimensions, it cannot be denied that men are often diverted from doing good and spurred toward evil by the social circumstances in which they live and are immersed from their birth. To be sure the disturbances which so frequently occur in the social order result in part from the natural tensions of economic, political, and social forms. But at a deeper level they flow from man's pride and selfishness, which contaminate even the social sphere. When the structure of affairs is flawed by the consequences of sin, man, already born with a bent toward evil, finds there new inducements to sin, which cannot be overcome without strenuous efforts and the assistance of grace" (No. 25).

"Every social group must take account of the needs and legitimate aspirations of other groups, and even of the general welfare of the entire human family."

Human Necessities: "At the same time however, there is a growing awareness of the exalted dignity proper to the human person, since he stands above all things, and his rights and duties are universal and inviolable. Therefore, there must be made available to all men everything necessary for leading a life truly human, such as food, clothing, and shelter; the right to choose a state of life freely and to found a family, the right to education, to employment, to a good reputation, to respect, to appropriate information, to activity in accord with the upright norm of one's own conscience, to protection of privacy and to rightful freedom in matters religious too.

"Hence, the social order and its development must unceasingly work to the benefit of the human person if the disposition of affairs is to be subordinate to the personal realm and not contrariwise, as the Lord indicated when He said that the Sabbath was made for man, and not man for the Sabbath."

Improvement of Social Order: "This social order requires constant improvement. It must be founded on truth, built on justice, and animated by love; in freedom it should grow every day toward a more humane balance. An improvement in attitudes and widespread changes in society will have to take place if these objectives are to be gained.

"God's Spirit, who with a marvelous providence directs the unfolding of time and renews the face of the earth, is not absent from this development. The ferment of the gospel, too, has aroused and continues to arouse in man's heart the irresistible requirements of his dignity" (No. 26).

Regard for Neighbor as Another Self: "Coming down to practical and particularly urgent consequences, this Council lays stress on reverence for man; everyone must consider his every neighbor without exception as another self, taking into account first of all his life and the means necessary to living it with dignity....

"In our times a special obligation binds us to make ourselves the neighbor of absolutely every person, and of actively helping him when he comes across our path...."

Inhuman Evils: "... Whatever is opposed to life itself, such as any type of murder, genocide, abortion, euthanasia, or willful self-destruction, whatever violates the integrity of the human person, such as mutilation, torments inflicted on body or mind, attempts to coerce the will itself; whatever insults human dignity, such as subhuman living conditions, arbitrary imprisonment, deportation, slavery, prostitution, the selling of women and children; as well as disgraceful working conditions, where men are treated as mere tools for profit, rather than as free and responsible persons; all these things and others of their like are infamies indeed. They poison human society, but they do more harm to those who practice them than those who suffer from the injury. Moreover, they are a supreme dishonor to the Creator" (No. 27).

Respect for Those Who Are Different: "Respect and love ought to be extended also to those who think or act differently than we do in social, political, and religious matters. In fact, the more deeply we come to understand their ways of thinking through such courtesy and love, the more easily will we be able to enter into dialogue with them."

Distinction between Error and Person in Error: "This love and good will,, to be sure, must in no way render us indifferent to truth and goodness. Indeed love itself impels the disciples of Christ to speak the saving truth to all men. But it is necessary to distinguish between error, which always merits repudiation, and the person in error, who never loses the dignity of being a person, even when he is flawed by false or inadequate religious notions. God alone is the judge and searcher of hearts; for that reason He forbids us to make judgments about the internal guilt of anyone.

"The teaching of Christ even requires that we forgive injuries, and extends the law of love to include every enemy . . ." (No. 28).

Men Are Equal but Different: "Since all men possess a rational soul and are created in God's likeness, since they have the same nature and origin, have been redeemed by Christ, and enjoy the same divine calling and destiny, the basic equality of all must receive increasingly greater recognition.

"True, all men are not alike from the point of view of varying physical power and the diversity of intellectual and moral resources. Nevertheless, with respect to the fundamental rights of the person, every type of discrimination, whether social or cultural, whether based on sex, race, color, social condition, language, or religion, is to be overcome and eradicated as contrary to God's intent. . . ."

Humane Conditions for All: ". . . Although rightful differences exist between men, the equal dignity of persons demands that a more humane and just condition of life be brought about. For excessive economic and social differences between the members of the one human family and population groups cause scandal, and militate against social justice, equity, and the dignity of the human person, as well as social and international peace.

"Human institutions, both private and public, must labor to minister to the dignity and purpose of man. At the same time let them put up a stubborn fight against any kind of slavery, whether social or political, and safeguard the basic rights of man under every political system. Indeed human institutions themselves must be accommodated by degrees to the highest of all realities, spiritual ones, even though, meanwhile, a long enough time will be required before they arrive at the desired goal" (No. 29).

"Profound and rapid changes make it particularly urgent that no one, ignoring the trend of events or drugged by laziness, content himself with a merely individualistic morality. It grows increasingly true that the obligations of justice and love are fulfilled only if

each person, contributing to the common good, according to his own abilities and the needs of others, also promotes and assists the public and private institutions dedicated to bettering the conditions of human life."

Social Necessities Are Prime Duties: "Let everyone consider it his sacred obligation to count social necessities among the primary duties of modern man, and to pay heed to them. For the more unified the world becomes, the more plainly do the offices of men extend beyond particular groups and spread by degrees to the whole world. But this challenge cannot be met unless individual men and their associations cultivate in themselves the moral and social virtues, and promote them in society. Thus, with the needed help of divine grace, men who are truly new and artisans of a new humanity can be forthcoming" (No. 30).

"In order for individual men to discharge with greater exactness the obligations of their conscience toward themselves and the various groups to which they belong, they must be carefully educated to a higher degree of culture through the use of the immense resources available today to the human race. . . ."

Living Conditions and Freedom: ". . . A man can scarcely arrive at the needed sense of responsibility unless his living conditions allow him to become conscious of his dignity, and to rise to his destiny by spending himself for God and for others. But human freedom is often crippled when a man falls into extreme poverty, just as it withers when he indulges in too many of life's comforts and imprisons himself in a kind of splendid isolation. Freedom acquires new strength, by contrast, when a man consents to the unavoidable requirements of social life, takes on the manifold demands of human partnership, and commits himself to the service of the human community.

"Hence, the will to play one's role in common endeavors should be everywhere encouraged . . ." (No. 31).

Communitarian Character of Life: "God did not create man for life in isolation, but, for the formation of social unity. So also 'it has pleased God to make men holy and save them not merely as individuals, without any mutual bonds, but by making them into a single people, a people which acknowledges Him in truth and serves Him in holiness' *(Dogmatic Constitution on the Church,* No. 9). So from the beginning of salvation history He has chosen men not just as individuals but as members of a certain community. Revealing His mind to them, God called these chosen ones 'His people' (Ex. 3:7-12), and, furthermore, made a covenant with them on Sinai.

"This communitarian character is developed and consummated in the work of Jesus Christ. For the very Word made flesh willed to share in the human fellowship. He was present at the wedding of Cana, visited the house of Zacchaeus, ate with publicans and sinners. He revealed the love of the Father and the sublime vocation of man in terms of the most common of social realities and by making use of the speech and the imagery of plain everyday life. Willingly obeying the laws of His country, He sanctified those human ties, especially family ones, from which social relationships arise. He chose to lead the life proper to an artisan of His time and place.

"In His preaching He clearly taught the sons of God to treat one another as brothers. In His prayers He pleaded that all His disciples might be 'one.' Indeed, as the Redeemer of all, He offered Himself for all even to the point of death. . . . He commanded His apostles to preach to all peoples the gospel message so that the human race might become the Family of God, in which the fullness of the Law would be love."

The Community Founded by Christ: "As the first-born of many brethren and through the gift of His Spirit, He founded after His death and resurrection a new brotherly community composed of all those who receive Him in faith and in love. This he did through His Body, which is the Church. There everyone, as members one of the other, would render mutual service according to the different gifts bestowed on each.

"This solidarity must be constantly increased until that day on which it will be brought to perfection. Then, saved by grace, men will offer flawless glory to God as a family beloved of God and of Christ their Brother" (No. 32).

PEACE AND WAR

The following excerpts, stating principles and objectives of social doctrine concerning peace and war, are from the *Pastoral Constitution on the Church in the Modern World* (Nos. 77 to 82) promulgated by the Second Vatican Council.

Call to Peace: ". . . This Council fervently desires to summon Christians to cooperate with all men in making secure among themselves a peace based on justice and love, and in setting up agencies of peace. This Christians should do with the help of Christ, the Author of peace" (No. 77).

Conditions for Peace: "Peace is not merely the absence of war. Nor can it be reduced solely to the maintenance of a balance of power between enemies. Nor is it brought about by dictatorship. Instead, it is rightly and appropriately called 'an enterprise of justice' (Is. 32:7). Peace results from that harmony built into human society by its divine Founder, and actualized by men as they thirst after ever greater justice.

"The common good of men is in its basic sense determined by the eternal law. Still the concrete demands of this common good are constantly changing as time goes on. Hence peace is never attained once and for all, but

must be built up ceaselessly. Moreover, since the human will is unsteady and wounded by sin, the achievement of peace requires that everyone constantly master his passions and that lawful authority keep vigilant.

"But such is not enough. This peace cannot be obtained on earth unless personal values are safeguarded and men freely and trustingly share with one another the riches of their inner spirits and their talents. A firm determination to respect other men and peoples and their dignity, as well as the studied practice of brotherhood, are absolutely necessary for the establishment of peace. Hence peace is likewise the fruit of love, which goes beyond what justice can provide."

Renunciation of Violence: ". . . We cannot fail to praise those who renounce the use of violence in the vindication of their rights and who resort to methods of defense which are otherwise available to weaker parties too, provided that this can be done without injury to the rights and duties of others or of the community itself . . ." (No. 78).

Mass Extermination: ". . . The Council wishes to recall first of all the permanent binding force of universal natural law and its all-embracing principles. Man's conscience itself gives ever more emphatic voice to these principles. Therefore, actions which deliberately conflict with these same principles, as well as orders commanding such actions, are criminal. Blind obedience cannot excuse those who yield to them. Among such must first be counted those actions designed for the methodical extermination of an entire people, nation, or ethnic minority. These actions must be vehemently condemned as horrendous crimes. The courage of those who openly and fearlessly resist men who issue such commands merits supreme commendation."

International Agreements: "On the subject of war, quite a large number of nations have subscribed to various international agreements aimed at making military activity and its consequences less inhuman. Such are conventions concerning the handling of wounded or captured soldiers, and various similar agreements. Agreements of this sort must be honored. They should be improved upon."

Conscientious Objectors: ". . . It seems right that laws make humane provisions for the case of those who for reasons of conscience refuse to bear arms, provided, however, that they accept some other form of service to the human community."

Legitimate Defense: "Certainly, war has not been rooted out of human affairs. As long as the danger of war remains and there is no competent and sufficiently powerful authority at the international level, governments cannot be denied the right to legitimate defense once every means of peaceful settlement has been exhausted. Therefore, government authorities and others who share public responsibility have the duty to protect the welfare of the people entrusted to their care and to conduct such grave matters soberly.

"But it is one thing to undertake military action for the just defense of the people, and something else again to seek the subjugation of other nations. Nor does the possession of war potential make every military or political use of it lawful. Neither does the mere fact that war has unhappily begun mean that all is fair between the warring parties."

Nature of Military Service: "Those who are pledged to the service of their country as members of its armed forces should regard themselves as agents of security and freedom on behalf of their people. As long as they fulfill this role properly, they are making a genuine contribution to the establishment of peace" (No. 79).

Total War Condemned: ". . . This most holy Synod makes its own the condemnations of total war already pronounced by recent Popes, and issues the following declaration:

"Any act of war aimed indiscriminately at the destruction of entire cities or of extensive areas along with their population is a crime against God and man himself. It merits unequivocal and unhesitating condemnation.

"The unique hazard of modern warfare consists in this: it provides those who possess modern scientific weapons with a kind of occasion for perpetrating just such abominations. Moreover, through a certain inexorable chain of events, it can urge men on to the most atrocious decisions. That such in fact may never happen in the future, the bishops of the whole world, in unity assembled, beg all men, especially government officials and military leaders, to give unremitting thought to the awesome responsibility which is theirs before God and the entire human race" (No. 80).

Retaliation and Deterrence: "Scientific weapons, to be sure, are not amassed solely for use in war. The defensive strength of any nation is considered to be dependent upon its capacity for immediate retaliation against an adversary. Hence this accumulation of arms, which increases each year, also serves, in a way heretofore unknown, as a deterrent to possible enemy attack. Many regard this state of affairs as the most effective way by which peace of a sort can be maintained between nations at the present time."

Arms Race: "Whatever be the case with this method of deterrence, men should be convinced that the arms race in which so many countries are engaged is not a safe way to preserve a steady peace. Nor is the so-called balance resulting from this race a sure and authentic peace. Rather than being eliminated thereby, the causes of war threaten to grow gradually stronger.

"While extravagant sums are being spent for the furnishing of ever new weapons, an adequate remedy cannot be provided for the multiple miseries afflicting the whole modern world. Disagreements between nations are not really and radically healed. On the contrary other parts of the world are infected with them. New approaches initiated by reformed attitudes must be adopted to remove this trap and to restore genuine peace by emancipating the world from its crushing anxiety.

"Therefore, it must be said again: the arms race is an utterly treacherous trap for humanity, and one which injures the poor to an intolerable degree. It is much to be feared that, if this race persists, it will eventually spawn all the lethal ruin whose path it is now making ready . . ." (No. 81).

Outlaw War: "It is our clear duty, then, to strain every muscle as we work for the time when all war can be completely outlawed by international consent. This goal undoubtedly requires the establishment of some universal public authority acknowledged as such by all, and endowed with effective power to safeguard, on the behalf of all, security, regard for justice, and respect for rights."

Multilateral and Controlled Disarmament: "But before this hoped-for authority can be set up, the highest existing international centers must devote themselves vigorously to the pursuit of better means for obtaining common security. Peace must be born of mutual trust between nations rather than imposed on them through fear of one another's weapons. Hence everyone must labor to put an end at last to the arms race, and to make a true beginning of disarmament, not indeed a unilateral disarmament, but one proceeding at an equal pace according to agreement, and backed up by authentic and workable safeguards.

"In the meantime, efforts which have already been made and are still under way to eliminate the danger of war are not to be underrated. On the contrary, support should be given to the good will of the very many leaders who work hard to do away with war, which they abominate. . . ."

Public Opinion: ". . . Men should take heed not to entrust themselves only to the efforts of others, while remaining careless about their own attitudes. For government officials, who must simultaneously guarantee the good of their own people and promote the universal good, depend on public opinion and feeling to the greatest possible extent. It does them no good to work at building peace so long as feelings of hostility, contempt, and distrust, as well as racial hatred and unbending ideologies, continue to divide men and place them in opposing camps.

"Hence arises a surpassing need for renewed education of attitudes and for new inspiration in the area of public opinion. Those who are dedicated to the work of education . . . should regard as their most weighty task the effort to instruct all in fresh sentiments of peace" (No. 82).

Liturgy

The nature and purpose of the liturgy, along with norms for its revision, were the subject matter of the *Constitution on the Sacred Liturgy* promulgated by the Second Vatican Council. The principles and guidelines stated in this document, the first issued by the Council, are summarized here and/or are incorporated in other Almanac entries on liturgical subjects.

Nature and Purpose of Liturgy

"It is through the liturgy, especially the divine Eucharistic Sacrifice, that 'the work of our redemption is exercised.' The liturgy is thus the outstanding means by which the faithful can express in their lives, and manifest to others, the mystery of Christ and the real nature of the true Church . . ." (No. 2).

"The liturgy is considered as an exercise of the priestly office of Jesus Christ. In the liturgy the sanctification of man is manifested by signs perceptible to the senses, and is effected in a way which is proper to each of these signs; in the liturgy full public worship is performed by the Mystical Body of Jesus Christ, that is, by the Head and His members.

"From this it follows that every liturgical celebration, because it is an action of Christ the priest and of His Body the Church, is a sacred action surpassing all others. No other action of the Church can match its claim to efficacy, nor equal the degree of it" (No. 7).

"The liturgy is the summit toward which the activity of the Church is directed; at the same time it is the fountain from which all her power flows. For the goal of apostolic works is that all who are made sons of God by faith and baptism should come together to praise God in the midst of His Church, to take part in her sacrifice, and to eat the Lord's Supper.

". . . From the liturgy, therefore, and especially from the Eucharist, as from a fountain, grace is channeled into us; and the sanctification of men in Christ and the glorification of God, to which all other activities of the Church are directed as toward their goal, are most powerfully achieved" (No. 10).

Full Participation

"Mother Church earnestly desires that all the faithful be led to that full, conscious, and active participation in liturgical celebrations which is demanded by the very nature of the liturgy. Such participation by the Christian people as 'a chosen race, a royal priesthood, a holy nation, a purchased people' (1 Pt. 2:9; cf. 2:4-5), is their right and duty by reason of their baptism.

"In the restoration and promotion of the sacred liturgy, this full and active participation by all the people is the aim to be considered before all else; for it is the primary and indispensable source from which the faithful are to derive the true Christian spirit . . ." (No. 14).

"In order that the Christian people may more securely derive an abundance of graces from the sacred liturgy, holy Mother Church desires to undertake with great care a general restoration of the liturgy itself. For the liturgy is made up of unchangeable elements divinely instituted, and elements subject to change. The latter not only may but ought to be changed with the passing of time if features have by chance crept in which are less harmonious with the intimate nature of the liturgy, or if existing elements have grown less functional.

"In this restoration, both texts and rites should be drawn up so that they express more clearly the holy things which they signify. Christian people, as far as possible, should be able to understand them with ease and to take part in them fully, actively, and as befits a community . . ." (No. 21).

Norms

Norms regarding the reforms concern the greater use of Scripture; emphasis on the importance of the sermon or homily on biblical and liturgical subjects; use of vernacular languages for prayers of the Mass and for administration of the sacraments; provision for adaptation of rites to cultural patterns.

Approval for reforms of various kinds — in liturgical texts, rites, etc. — depends on the Holy See, regional conferences of bishops and individual bishops, according to provisions of law. No priest has authority to initiate reforms on his own. Reforms may not be introduced just for the sake of innovation, and any that are introduced in the light of present-day circumstances should embody sound tradition.

To assure the desired effect of liturgical reforms, training and instruction are necessary for the clergy, religious and the laity. The functions of diocesan and regional commissions for liturgy, music and art are to set standards and provide leadership for instruction and practical programs in their respective fields.

Most of the constitution's provisions regarding liturgical reforms have to do with the Roman Rite. The document clearly respects the equal dignity of all rites, leaving to the Eastern Churches control over their ancient liturgies.

(For coverage of the **Mystery of the Eucharist,** see The Mass; **Other Sacraments,** see separate entries.)

Sacramentals

Sacramentals, instituted by the Church, "are sacred signs which bear a resemblance to the sacraments: they signify effects, particularly of a spiritual kind, which are obtained through the Church's intercession. By them men are disposed to receive the chief effect of the sacraments, and various occasions in life are rendered holy" (No. 60).

"Thus, for well-disposed members of the faithful, the liturgy of the sacraments and sacramentals sanctifies almost every event in their lives; they are given access to the stream of divine grace which flows from the paschal mystery of the passion, death, and resurrection of Christ, the fountain from which all sacraments and sacramentals draw their power. There is hardly any proper use of material things which cannot thus be directed toward the sanctification of men and the praise of God" (No. 61). Some common sacramentals are priestly blessings, blessed palm, candles, holy water, medals, scapulars, prayers and ceremonies of the Roman Ritual.

Liturgy of the Hours

The Liturgy of the Hours (Divine Office) is the public prayer of the Church for praising God and sanctifying the day. Its daily celebration is required as a sacred obligation by men in holy orders and by men and women religious who have professed solemn vows. Its celebration by others is highly commended and is to be encouraged in the community of the faithful.

"By tradition going back to early Christian times, the Divine Office is arranged so that the whole course of the day and night is made holy by the praises of God. Therefore, when this wonderful song of praise is worthily rendered by priests and others who are deputed for this purpose by Church ordinance, or by the faithful praying together with the priest in an approved form, then it is truly the voice of the bride addressing her bridegroom; it is the very prayer which Christ Himself, together with His body, addresses to the Father" (No. 84).

"Hence all who perform this service are not only fulfilling a duty of the Church, but also are sharing in the greatest honor accorded to Christ's spouse, for by offering these praises to God they are standing before God's throne in the name of the Church their Mother" (No. 85).

The Latin text of the Liturgy of the Hours, under revision since 1965, was described by Pope Paul in the apostolic constitution *Canticum Laudis,* dated Nov. 1, 1970. The first of its four complete volumes in the authorized English translation was published in May, 1975.

The revised Liturgy of the Hours consists of:

• Office of Readings, for reflection on the word of God. The principal parts are three psalms, biblical and non-biblical readings.

• Morning and Evening Prayer, called the "hinges" of the Liturgy of the Hours. The principal parts are a hymn, two psalms, an Old or New Testament canticle, a brief biblical reading, Zechariah's canticle (the *Benedictus,* morning) or Mary's canticle (the *Magnificat,* evening), responsories, intercessions and a concluding prayer.

• Prayer during the Day. The principal parts are a hymn, three psalms, a brief biblical reading and one of three concluding prayers corresponding to the time at which the prayer is offered (from 9:00 a.m. to 3:00 p.m.).

• Night Prayer: The principal parts are one or two psalms, a brief biblical reading, Simeon's canticle *(Nunc Dimittis),* a concluding prayer and an antiphon in honor of Mary.

In the new Office, the hours are shorter than they had been, with greater textual variety, meditation aids, and provision for intervals of silence and meditation. The psalms are distributed over a four-week period instead of a week; some psalms, entirely or in part, are not included. Additional canticles from the Old and New Testaments are assigned for Lauds and Vespers, respectively. Additional scriptural texts have been added and variously arranged for greater internal unity, correspondence to readings at Mass, and relevance to events and themes of salvation history. Readings include some of the best material from the Fathers of the Church and other authors and improved selections on the lives of saints.

The book used for recitation of the Office is the **Breviary.**

For coverage of the **Liturgical Year,** see Church Calendar.

Sacred Music

"The musical tradition of the universal Church is a treasure of immeasurable value, greater even than that of any other art. The main reason for this pre-eminence is that, as sacred melody united to words, it forms a necessary or integral part of the solemn liturgy.

". . . Sacred music increases in holiness to the degree that it is intimately linked with liturgical action, winningly expresses prayerfulness, promotes solidarity, and enriches sacred rites with heightened solemnity. The Church indeed approves of all forms of true art, and admits them into divine worship when they show appropriate qualities" (No. 112).

The constitution decreed:

• Vernacular languages for the people's parts of the liturgy, as well as Latin, may be used.

• Participation in sacred song by the whole body of the faithful, and not just by choirs, is to be encouraged and brought about.

• Provisions should be made for proper musical training for clergy, religious and lay persons.

• While Gregorian Chant has a unique dignity and relationship to the Latin liturgy, other kinds of music are acceptable.

• Native musical traditions should be used, especially in mission areas.

• Various instruments compatible with the dignity of worship may be used.

Gregorian Chant: A form and style of chant called Gregorian was the basis and most highly regarded standard of liturgical music for centuries. It originated probably during the formative period of the Roman liturgy and developed in conjunction with Gallican and other forms of chant. Gregory the Great's connection with it is not clear, although it is known that he had great concern for and interest in church music. The earliest extant written versions of Gregorian chant date from the ninth century. A thousand years later, the Benedictines of Solesmes, France, initiated a revival of chant which gave impetus to the modern liturgical movement.

Sacred Art and Furnishings

"Very rightly the fine arts are considered to rank among the noblest expressions of human genius. This judgment applies especially to religious art and to its highest achievement, which is sacred art. By their very nature both of the latter are related to God's boundless beauty, for this is the reality which these human efforts are trying to express in some way. To the extent that these works aim exclusively at turning men's thoughts to God persuasively and devoutly, they are dedicated to God and to the cause of His greater honor and glory" (No. 122).

The objective of sacred art is "that all things set apart for use in divine worship should be truly worthy, becoming, and beautiful, signs and symbols of heavenly realities. . . . The Church has . . . always reserved to herself the right to pass judgment upon the arts, deciding which of the works of artists are in accordance with faith, piety, and cherished traditional laws, and thereby suited to sacred purposes.

". . . Sacred furnishings should worthily and beautifully serve the dignity of worship . . ." (No. 122).

According to the constitution:

• Contemporary art, as well as that of the past, shall "be given free scope in the Church, provided that it adorns the sacred buildings and holy rites with due honor and reverence . . ." (No. 123).

• Noble beauty, not sumptuous display, should be sought in art, sacred vestments and ornaments.

• "Let bishops carefully exclude from the house of god and from other sacred places those works of artists which are repugnant to faith, morals, and Christian piety, and which offend true religious sense either by their distortion of forms or by lack of artistic worth, by mediocrity or by pretense.

• "When churches are to be built, let great care be taken that they be suitable for the celebration of liturgical services and for the active participation of the faithful" (No. 124).

• "The practice of placing sacred images in churches so that they may be venerated by the faithful is to be firmly maintained. Nevertheless, their number should be moderate and their relative location should reflect right order. Otherwise they may create confusion among the Christian people and promote a faulty sense of devotion" (No. 125).

• Artists should be trained and inspired in the spirit and for the purposes of the liturgy.

• The norms of sacred art should be revised. "These laws refer especially to the worthy and well-planned construction of sacred buildings, the shape and construction of altars, the nobility, location, and security of the Eucharistic tabernacle, the suitability and dignity of the baptistery, the proper use of sacred images, embellishments, and vestments . . ." (No. 128).

RITES

A rite is the manner in which liturgical worship is carried out. It includes the forms and ceremonial observances of liturgical worship.

Different rites have evolved in the course of Church history, giving to liturgical worship forms and usages peculiar and proper to the nature of worship itself and to the culture of the faithful in various circumstances of time and place. Thus, there has been development since apostolic times in prayers and ceremonies of the Mass, the administration of the sacraments, requirements for celebration of the Divine Office. Practices within the patriarchates of Antioch, Rome, Alexandria and Constantinople were the principal sources of the rites in present use.

Eastern Rites, described elsewhere in the Almanac, are proper to Eastern Catholic Churches.

The **Roman** or **Latin Rite,** described in this section, prevails in the Western Church. It was derived from Roman practices and the use of Latin as an official language from the third century onward. Other rites in limited use in the Western Church have been the Ambrosian, the Mozarabic, the Lyonnais, the Braga, and rites peculiar to some religious orders like the Dominicans, Carmelites and Carthusians.

The revision of rites in progress since the Second Vatican Council is meant to renew them, not to eliminate the rites of particular churches or to reduce all rites to uniformity.

Reform Tasks: The Congregation for the Sacraments and Divine Worship continued work in 1975 for the completion of a new rite for the dedication of churches and altars, a book of devotional prayers, the martyrology, a fifth volume of the Roman Breviary, a corrected edition of the Roman Missal.

MASS, EUCHARISTIC SACRIFICE AND BANQUET

Declarations of Vatican II

The Second Vatican Council made the following declarations, among others, with respect to the Mass.

"At the Last Supper, on the night when He was betrayed, our Savior instituted the Eucharistic Sacrifice of His Body and Blood. He did this in order to perpetuate the sacrifice of the Cross throughout the centuries until He should come again, and so to entrust to His beloved spouse, the Church, a memorial of His death and resurrection: a sacrament of love, a sign of unity, a bond of charity, a paschal banquet in which Christ is consumed, the mind is filled with grace, and a pledge of future glory is given to us" (*Constitution on the Sacred Liturgy,* No. 47).

". . . As often as the sacrifice of the cross in which 'Christ, our passover, has been sacrificed' (1 Cor. 5:7) is celebrated on an altar, the work of our redemption is carried on. At the same time, in the sacrament of the Eucharistic bread the unity of all believers who form one body in Christ (cf. 1 Cor. 10:17) is both expressed and brought about. All men are called to this union with Christ . . ." (*Dogmatic Constitution on the Church.* No. 3).

". . . The ministerial priest, by the sacred power he enjoys, molds and rules the priestly people. Acting in the person of Christ, he brings about the Eucharistic Sacrifice, and offers it to God in the name of all the people. For their part, the faithful join in the offering of the Eucharist by virtue of their royal priesthood . . ." (*Ibid.,* No. 10).

Declarations of Trent

Among its decrees on the Holy Eucharist, the Council of Trent stated the following points of doctrine on the Mass.

1. There is in the Catholic Church a true Sacrifice, the Mass instituted by Jesus Christ. It is the Sacrifice of His Body and Blood, Soul and Divinity, Himself, under the appearances of bread and wine.

2. This Sacrifice is identical with the Sacrifice of the Cross, inasmuch as Christ is the Priest and Victim in both. A difference lies in the manner of offering, which was bloody upon the Cross and is bloodless on the altar.

3. The Mass is a propitiatory Sacrifice, atoning for sins of the living and dead for whom it is offered.

4. The efficacy of the Mass is derived from the Sacrifice of the Cross, whose super-abundant merits it applies to men.

5. Although the Mass is offered to God alone, it may be celebrated in honor and memory of the saints.

6. Christ instituted the Mass at the Last Supper.

7. Christ ordained the Apostles priests, giving them power and the command to consecrate His Body and Blood to perpetuate and renew the Sacrifice.

ORDER OF MASS

The Mass consists of two principal divisions called the **Liturgy of the Word,** which features the proclamation of the Word of God, and the **Eucharistic Liturgy,** which focuses on the central act of sacrifice in the Consecration and on the Eucharistic Banquet in Holy Communion. (Formerly, these divisions were called, respectively, the **Mass of the Catechumens** and the **Mass of the Faithful.**) In addition to these principal divisions, there are ancillary introductory and concluding rites.

The following description covers the Mass as celebrated with participation by the people. This Order of the Mass was approved by Pope Paul VI in the apostolic constitution *Missale Romanum* dated Apr. 3, 1969, and promulgated in a decree issued Apr. 6, 1969, by the Congregation for Divine Worship. The assigned effective date was Nov. 30, 1969.

Introductory Rites

Entrance: The introductory rites begin with the singing or recitation of an entrance song while the priest approaches the altar, kisses it, and goes to the place where he will be seated. The song consists of one or more scriptural verses stating the theme of the mystery, season or feast commemorated in the Mass.

Greeting: The priest and people make the Sign of the Cross together. The priest then greets them in one of several alternative ways and they reply in a corresponding manner.

Introductory Remarks: At this point, the priest or another of the ministers may introduce the theme of the Mass.

Penitential Rite: The priest and people together acknowledge their sins as a preliminary step toward worthy celebration of the sacred mysteries. This rite includes a brief examination of conscience, a general confession of sin and plea for divine mercy in one of several ways, and a prayer of absolution by the priest. The *Kyrie, eleison* ("Lord, have mercy") is then said if it was not included in one of the foregoing pleas for divine mercy.

Glory to God: A doxology, a hymn of praise to God, sung or said on festive occasions.

Opening Prayer: A prayer of petition offered by the priest on behalf of the worshipping community.

I. Liturgy of the Word

Readings: The featured elements of this liturgy are several readings of passages from the Bible. If three readings are in order, the first is usually from the Old Testament, the second from the New Testament (Epistles, Acts, Revelation), and the third from one of the Gospels; the final reading is always a selection from a Gospel. The first reading(s) is concluded with the formula, "This is the Word of the Lord," to which the people respond, "Thanks be to God." The Gospel reading is concluded with the formula, "This is the Gospel of the Lord," to which the people respond, "Praise to you, Lord Jesus Christ," Between the readings, psalm verses and a Gospel acclamation are sung or said.

Homily: Sermon on a scriptural or liturgical subject; ideally, it should be related to the liturgical service in progress.

Creed: The Nicene profession of faith, by priest and people, on certain occasions.

Prayer of the Faithful: Litany-type prayers of petition, with participation by the people. Called general intercessions, they concern needs of the Church, the salvation of the world, public authorities, persons in need, the local community.

II. Eucharistic Liturgy

Offertory Song: Scriptural verses related to the theme of the Mass, or a suitable hymn, sung or said while things are prepared at the altar for the Eucharistic Liturgy and while the offerings of bread and wine are brought to the altar.

Offertory Procession: Presentation to the priest of the gifts of bread and wine, principally, by participating members of the congregation.

Offering of the Gifts: Consists of the prayers and ceremonies with which the priest offers bread and wine as the elements of the sacrifice to take place during the Eucharistic Prayer and of the Lord's Supper to be shared in Holy Communion. If singing takes place during the offering, the priest can say the prayers and carry out the action silently; if there is no singing, he says the prayers aloud and the people, after each offering, respond with the words, "Blessed be God forever."

Washing of Hands: After offering the bread and wine, the priest cleanses his fingers with water in a brief ceremony of purification.

Pray, Brethren: Prayer that the sacrifice to take place will be acceptable to God. The first part of the prayer is said by the priest; the second, by the people.

Prayer over the Gifts: A prayer of petition offered by the priest on behalf of the worshipping community.

Eucharistic Prayer

Preface: A hymn of praise, introducing the Eucharistic Prayer or Canon, sung or said by the priest following responses by the people. The Order of the Mass contains a variety of prefaces, for use on different occasions.

Holy, Holy, Holy; Blessed Is He: Divine praises sung or said by the priest and people.

Canon: The Eucharistic Prayer of the Mass whose central portion is the Consecration, when the essential act of sacrificial offering

takes place with the changing of bread and wine into the Body and Blood of Christ. The prayers of the Canon, which are said by the celebrant only, commemorate principal mysteries of salvation history and include petitions for the Church, the living and dead, and remembrances of saints. There are four Eucharistic Prayers, for use on various occasions and at the option of the priest. (Additional Canons for Masses with children and for reconciliation were approved in 1975.)

Doxology: A formula of divine praise sung or said by the priest while he holds aloft the chalice containing the consecrated wine in one hand and the paten containing the consecrated host in the other.

Communion Rite

Lord's Prayer: Sung or said by the priest and people.

Prayer for Deliverance from evil: Called an **embolism** because it is a development of the final petition of the Lord's Prayer; said by the priest. It concludes with a memorial of the return of the Lord to which the people respond, "For the kingdom, the power, and the glory are yours, now and forever."

Prayer for Peace: Said by the priest, with corresponding responses by the people. The priest can, in accord with local custom, bid the people to exchange a greeting of peace with each other.

Lamb of God: A prayer for divine mercy sung or said while the priest breaks the consecrated host and places a piece of it into the consecrated wine in the chalice.

Communion: The priest, after saying a preparatory prayer, administers Holy Communion to himself and then to the people, thus completing the sacrifice-banquet of the Mass. (This completion is realized even if the celebrant alone receives the Eucharist.) On giving the Eucharist to the people, the priest says, "The Body of Christ," to each recipient; the customary response is "Amen." If the Eucharist is administered under the forms of bread and wine, the priest says, "The Body and Blood of Christ."

Communion Song: Scriptural verses or a suitable hymn sung or said during the distribution of Holy Communion. After Holy Communion is received, some moments may be spent in silent meditation or in the chanting of a psalm or hymn of praise.

Prayer after Communion: A prayer of petition offered by the priest on behalf of the worshipping community.

Concluding Rite

Announcements: Brief announcements to the people are in order at this time.

Dismissal: Consists of a final greeting by the priest, a blessing, and a formula of dismissal. This rite is omitted if another liturgical action immediately follows the Mass; e.g., a procession, the blessing of the body during a funeral rite.

Some parts of the Mass are changeable with the liturgical season or feast, and are called the **proper** of the Mass. Other parts are said to be **common** because they always remain the same.

Additional Mass Notes

Catholics are seriously obliged to attend Mass in a worthy manner on Sundays and holy days of obligation. Failure to do so without a proportionately serious reason is gravely wrong.

It is the custom for priests to celebrate Mass daily whenever possible. To satisfy the needs of the faithful on Sundays and holy days of obligation, they are authorized to say Mass twice (**bination**) or even three times (**trination**). Bination is also permissible on weekdays. On Christmas and All Souls' Day every priest may say three Masses. Mass may be celebrated in the morning, afternoon or evening.

The **fruits of the Mass,** which in itself is of infinite value, are: **general,** for all the faithful; **special (ministerial),** for the intentions or persons specifically intended by the celebrant; **most special (personal),** for the celebrant himself. On Sundays and certain other days pastors are obliged to offer Mass for their parishioners. If a priest accepts a stipend or offering for a Mass, he is obliged in justice to apply the Mass for the designated intention. Mass may be applied for the living and the dead, or for any good intention.

Mass can be celebrated in several ways: e.g., with people present, without their presence (privately), with two or more priests as co-celebrants (concelebration), with greater or less solemnity.

Some of the various types of Masses are: **for the dead** (Funeral Mass or Mass of Christian Burial, Mass for the Dead — formerly called Requiem Mass); **nuptial,** for married couples, with or after the wedding ceremony; **votive,** to honor a Person of the Trinity, a saint, or for some special intention; **conventual,** the community Mass in houses of solemnly professed religious. A **red Mass** is a Votive Mass of the Holy Spirit, celebrated for members of the legal profession that they might exercise prudence and equity in their official capacities. **Gregorian Masses** are a series of 30 Masses celebrated on 30 consecutive days for a deceased person.

The only day of the year on which Mass is not celebrated is Good Friday. In its place, there is a **Solemn Liturgical Action.**

Places, Altars for Mass

The ordinary place for celebrating the Eucharist is a church or other sacred place, at a permanent or movable altar.

Outside of a sacred place, Mass may be celebrated in an appropriate place at a suitable table covered with a linen cloth and corporal. An **altar stone** containing the relics of saints, which was formerly prescribed, is not required by regulations in effect since the promulgation Apr. 6, 1969, of *Institutio Generalis Missalis Romani.*

A **permanent altar** should have a table of stone, be consecrated, and have enclosed within it relics of some saints.

A **movable altar** may be made of any solid and suitable material. If made of stone and consecrated, it should have enclosed within it relics of some saints; if blessed rather than consecrated, the enclosure of relics is not required.

LITURGICAL VESTMENTS

In the early years of the Church, vestments worn by the ministers at liturgical functions were the same as the garments in ordinary popular use. They became distinctive when their form was not altered to correspond with later variations in popular style. Liturgical vestments are symbolic of the sacred ministry and add appropriate decorum to divine worship.

Mass Vestments

Alb: A body-length tunic of white fabric; a vestment common to all ministers of divine worship.

Amice: A rectangular piece of white cloth worn about the neck, tucked into the collar and falling over the shoulders; worn under the alb.

Chasuble: Originally, a large mantle or cloak covering the body, it is the outer vestment of a priest celebrating Mass or carrying out other sacred actions connected with the Mass.

Cincture: A cord which serves the purpose of a belt, holding the alb close to the body.

Dalmatic: The outer vestment worn by a deacon in place of a chasuble.

Stole: A long, band-like vestment worn about the neck and falling to about the knees. (A stole is used for other functions also.)

The material, form and ornamentation of the aforementioned and other vestments are subject to variation and adaptation, according to norms and decisions of the Holy See and concerned conferences of bishops. The overriding norm is that they should be appropriate for use in divine worship. The customary ornamented vestments are the chasuble, dalmatic and stole.

The minimal vestments required for a priest celebrating Mass are the alb, stole and chasuble.

Liturgical Colors

The colors of outer vestments vary with liturgical seasons, feasts and other circumstances. The colors and their use are:

Green: For the season of the year.

Purple: For Advent and Lent; may also be used in Masses for the dead.

Red: For the Sunday of the Passion, the Wednesday of Holy Week, Good Friday,

Pentecost; feasts of the Passion of Our Lord, the Apostles and Evangelists, martyrs.

Rose: May be used in place of purple on the Third Sunday of Advent (Gaudete Sunday) and the Fourth Sunday of Lent (Laetare Sunday).

White: For Christmastide and Eastertide; feasts and commemorations of Our Lord, except those of the Passion; feasts and commemorations of the Blessed Virgin Mary, angels, saints who are not martyrs, All Saints (Nov. 1), St. John the Baptist (June 24), St. John the Evangelist (Dec. 27), the Chair of St. Peter (Feb. 22), the Conversion of St. Paul (Jan. 25). White may generally be substituted for other colors, and can be used for funeral and other Masses for the dead.

On more solemn occasions, better than ordinary vestments may be used, even though their color (e.g., gold) does not match the requirements of the day.

Considerable freedom is permitted in the choice of colors of vestments worn for votive Masses.

Other Vestments

Cappa Magna: Flowing vestment with a train, worn by bishops and cardinals.

Cassock: A full-length, close-fitting robe worn by priests and other clerics under liturgical vestments and in ordinary use; usually black for priests, purple for bishops and other prelates, red for cardinals, white for the pope. In place of a cassock, priests belonging to religious institutes wear the habit proper to their institute.

Cope: A mantle-like vestment open in front and fastened across the chest; worn by sacred ministers in processions and other ceremonies, as prescribed by appropriate directives.

Gremial: A rectangular veil of silk or linen placed over the knees of a bishop when he is seated during various episcopal ceremonies.

Habit: The ordinary garb of members of religious institutes, analogous to the cassock of diocesan priests; the form of habits varies from institute to institute.

Humeral Veil: A rectangular vestment worn about the shoulders by a deacon. or priest in Eucharistic processions and for other prescribed liturgical ceremonies.

Mitre: A headdress worn at some liturgical functions by bishops, abbots and, in certain cases, other ecclesiastics.

Pallium: A circular band of white wool about two inches wide, with front and back pendants, marked with six crosses, worn about the neck by some major prelates. Symbolic of the fullness of the episcopal office, it is given by the pope on request to patriarchs, primates, archbishops and, rarely, bishops. The pallium is made from the wool of lambs blessed by the pope on the feast of St. Agnes (Jan. 21).

Rochet: A knee-length, white linen-lace

garment of prelates worn under outer vestments.

Surplice: A loose, flowing vestment of white fabric with wide sleeves. For some functions, it is interchangeable with an alb.

Zucchetto: A skullcap worn by bishops and other prelates.

SACRED VESSELS, LINENS

Vessels

Chalice and Paten: The principal sacred vessels required for the celebration of Mass are the **chalice** (cup) and **paten** (plate) in which wine and bread, respectively, are offered, consecrated and consumed. Both should be made of solid and noble material which is not easily breakable or corruptible. Gold coating is required of the interior parts of sacred vessels subject to rust. The cup of a chalice should be made of non-absorbent material.

Vessels for containing consecrated hosts (see below) can be made of material other than solid and noble metal — e. g., ivory, more durable woods — provided the substitute material is locally regarded as noble or rather precious and is suitable for sacred use.

Sacred vessels should be blessed or consecrated, according to prescribed requirements.

Vessels, in addition to the paten, for containing consecrated hosts are:

Ciborium: Used to hold hosts for distribution to the faithful and for reservation in the tabernacle.

Luna, Lunula, Lunette: A small receptacle which holds the sacred host in an upright position in the monstrance.

Monstrance, Ostensorium: A portable receptable so made that the sacred host, when enclosed therein, may be clearly seen, as at Benediction or during extended exposition of the Blessed Sacrament.

Pyx: A watch-shaped vessel used in carrying the Eucharist to the sick.

Linens

Altar Cloth: A white cloth, usually of linen, covering the table of an altar. One cloth is sufficient. Three were used according to former requirements.

Burse: A square, stiff flat case, open at one end, in which the folded corporal is placed; the outside is covered with material of the same kind and color as the outer vestments of the celebrant.

Corporal: A square piece of white linen spread on the altar cloth, on which rest the vessels holding the Sacred Species — the consecrated host(s) and wine — during the Eucharistic Liturgy. The corporal is similarly used whenever the Blessed Sacrament is removed from the tabernacle; e. g., during Benediction the vessel containing the Blessed Sacrament rests on a corporal.

Finger Towel: A white rectangular napkin used by the priest to dry his fingers after cleansing them following the offering of gifts at Mass.

Pall: A square piece of stiff material, usually covered with linen, used to cover the chalice at Mass.

Purificator: A white rectangular napkin used for cleansing sacred vessels after the reception of Communion at Mass.

Veil: The chalice intended for use at Mass is covered with a veil made of the same material as the outer vestments of the celebrant.

THE CHURCH BUILDING

A church is a building set aside and dedicated for purposes of divine worship, the place of assembly for a worshiping community.

A Catholic church is the ordinary place in which the faithful assemble for participation in the Eucharistic Liturgy and other forms of divine worship.

In the early years of Christianity, the first places of assembly for the Eucharistic Liturgy were private homes (Acts 2:46; Rom. 16:5; 1 Cor. 16:5; Col. 4:15) and, sometimes, catacombs. Church building began in the latter half of the second century during lulls in persecution and became widespread after enactment of the Edict of Milan in 313, when it finally became possible for the Church to emerge completely from the underground. The oldest and basic norms regarding church buildings date from about that time.

The essential principle underlying all norms for church building was reformulated by the Second Vatican Council, as follows: "When churches are to be built, let great care be taken that they be suitable for the celebration of liturgical services and for the active participation of the faithful" *(Constitution on the Sacred Liturgy,* No. 124).

This principle was subsequently elaborated in detail by the Congregation for Divine Worship in a document entitled *Institutio Generalis Missalis Romani,* which was approved by Paul VI Apr. 3 and promulgated by a decree of the congregation dated Apr. 6, 1969. Coverage of the following items reflects the norms stated in Chapter V of this document.

Sanctuary: The part of the church where the altar of sacrifice is located, the place where the ministers of the liturgy lead the people in prayer, proclaim the word of God and celebrate the Eucharist. It is set off from the body of the church by a distinctive structural feature — e. g., elevation above the main floor — or by ornamentation. (The traditional **communion rail,** which has been removed in recent years in many churches, served this purpose of demarcation.) The customary location of the sanctuary is at the front of the church; it may, however, be centrally located.

Altar: The main altar of sacrifice and table

of the Lord is the focal feature of the sanctuary and entire church. It stands by itself, so that the ministers can move about it freely, and is so situated that they face the people during the liturgical action. In addition to this main altar, there may also be others; in new churches, these are situated in side chapels or alcoves removed to some degree from the body of the church.

Adornment of the Altar: The altar table is covered with a suitable linen cloth. Required candelabra and a cross are placed upon or near the altar in plain sight of the people and are so arranged that they do not obscure their view of the liturgical action.

Seats of the Ministers: The seat of the celebrant, corresponding with his role as the presiding minister of the assembly, is best located behind the altar and facing the people; it is raised a bit above the level of the altar but must not have the appearance of a throne. The seats of other ministers are also located in the sanctuary.

Ambo, Pulpit: The stand at which scriptural lessons and psalm responses are read, the word of God preached, and the prayer of the faithful offered. It is so placed that the ministers can be easily seen and heard by the people.

Places for the People: Seats and kneeling benches **(pews)** and other accommodations for the people are so arranged that they can participate in the most appropriate way in the liturgical action and have freedom of movement for the reception of Holy Communion. Reserved seats are out of order.

Place for the Choir: Where it is located depends on the most suitable arrangement for maintaining the unity of the choir with the congregation and for providing its members maximum opportunity for carrying out their proper function and participating fully in the Mass.

Tabernacle: The best place for reserving the Blessed Sacrament is in a chapel suitable for the private devotion of the people. If this is not possible, reservation should be at a side altar or other appropriately adorned place. In either case, the Blessed Sacrament should be kept in a tabernacle, i. e., a safe-like, secure receptacle.

Statues: Images of the Lord, the Blessed Virgin Mary and the saints are legitimately proposed for the veneration of the faithful in churches. Their number and arrangement, however, should be ordered in such a way that they do not distract the people from the central celebration of the Eucharistic Liturgy. There should be only one statue of one and the same saint in a church.

General Adornment and Arrangement of Churches: Churches should be so adorned and fitted out that they serve the direct requirements of divine worship and the needs and reasonable convenience of the people.

Other Items

Ambry: A box containing the holy oils, attached to the wall of the sanctuary in some churches.

Baptistery: The place for administering baptism. Some churches have baptisteries adjoining or near the entrance, a position symbolizing the fact that persons are initiated in the Church and incorporated in Christ through this sacrament. Contemporary liturgical practice favors placement of the baptistery near the sanctuary and altar, or the use of a portable font in the same position, to emphasize the relationship of baptism to the Eucharist, the celebration in sacrifice and banquet of the death and resurrection of Christ.

Candles: Used more for symbolical than illuminative purposes, they represent Christ, the light and life of grace, at liturgical functions. They are made of beeswax.

LITURGICAL DEVELOPMENTS

The principal developments covered in this article are enactments of the Holy See and actions related to their implementation in the United States.

Modern Movement

Origins of the modern movement for renewal in the liturgy date back to the 19th century. The key contributing factor was a revival of liturgical and scriptural studies. Of special significance was the work of the Benedictine monks of Solesmes, France, who aroused great interest in the liturgy through the restoration of Gregorian Chant. St. Pius X approved their work in a motu proprio of 1903 and gave additional encouragement to liturgical study and development.

St. Pius X did more than any other single pope to promote early first Communion and the practice of frequent Communion, started the research behind a revised breviary, and appointed a group to investigate possible revisions in the Mass.

The movement attracted some attention in the 1920's and 30's but made little progress.

Significant pioneering developments in the US during the 20's, however, were the establishment of the Liturgical Press, the beginning of publication of *Orate Fratres* (now *Worship*), and the inauguration of the League of the Divine Office by the Benedictines at St. John's Abbey, Collegeville, Minn. Later events of influence were the establishment of the Pius X School of Liturgical Music at Manhattanville College of the Sacred Heart and the organization of a summer school of liturgical music at Mary Manse College by the Gregorian Institute of America. The turning point toward real renewal was reached during and after World War II.

Pius XII gave it impetus and direction, principally through the background teaching in his encyclicals on the *Mystical Body* (1943), *Sacred Liturgy* (1947), and the *Discipline of*

Confessional: A booth-like structure for the hearing of confessions, with separate compartments for the priest and penitents and a grating or screen between them. The use of confessionals became general in the Roman Rite after the Council of Trent.

Crucifix: A cross bearing the figure of the body of Christ, representative of the Sacrifice of the Cross.

Cruets: Vessels containing the wine and water used at Mass. They are placed on a credence table in the sanctuary.

Holy Water Fonts: Receptacles containing holy water, usually at church entrances, for the use of the faithful.

Sanctuary Lamp: A lamp which is kept burning continuously before a tabernacle in which the Blessed Sacrament is reserved, as a sign of the Real Presence of Christ.

Sacred Music (1955), and by means of specific measures affecting the liturgy itself. His work was continued during the pontificates of John XXIII and Paul VI. The Second Vatican Council, in virtue of its *Constitution on the Sacred Liturgy,* inaugurated changes of the greatest significance.

Before and After Vatican II

The most significant liturgical changes made in the years immediately preceding the Second Vatican Council were the following:

(1) Revision of the Rites of Holy Week, for universal observance from 1956.

(2) Modification of the Eucharistic fast and permission for afternoon and evening Mass, in effect from 1953 and extended in 1957.

(3) The Dialogue Mass, introduced in 1958.

(4) Use of popular languages in administration of the sacraments.

(5) Calendar-missal-breviary reform, in effect from Jan. 1, 1961.

(6) Seven-step administration of baptism for adults, approved in 1962.

The *Constitution on the Sacred Liturgy* approved (2,174 to 4) and promulgated by the Second Vatican Council Dec. 4, 1963, marked the beginning of a profound renewal in the Church's corporate worship. Implementation of some of its measures was ordered by Paul VI Jan. 25, 1964, in the motu proprio *Sacram Liturgiam.* On Feb. 29, a special commission, the Consilium for Implementing the Constitution on the Sacred Liturgy, was formed to supervise the execution of the entire program of liturgical reform. Implementation of the program on local and regional levels was left to bishops acting through their own liturgical commissions and in concert with their fellow bishops in national conferences.

Liturgical reform in the United States has been carried out under the direction of the Liturgy Committee, National Conference of Catholic Bishops. Its secretariat, established early in 1965, is located at 1312 Massachusetts Ave. N.W., Washington, D.C. 20005.

Stages of Development

Liturgical development after the Second Vatican Council proceeded in several stages. It started with the formulation of guidelines and directives, and with the translation into vernacular languages of virtually unchanged Latin ritual texts. Then came structural changes in the Mass, the sacraments, the calendar, the Divine Office and other phases of the liturgy. These revisions were just about completed with the publication of a new order for the sacrament of penance in February, 1974. A continuing phase of development, in progress from the beginning, involves efforts to deepen the liturgical sense of the faithful, to increase their participation in worship and to relate it to full Christian life.

Texts and Translations

The master texts of all documents on liturgical reform were in Latin. Effective dates of their implementation depended on the completion and approval of appropriate translations into vernacular languages. English translations were made by the International Committee for English in the Liturgy.

The principal features of liturgical changes and the effective dates of their introduction in the United States are covered below under topical headings. (For expanded coverage of various items, especially the sacraments, see additional entries.)

The Mass

A new Order of the Mass, supplanting the one authorized by the Council of Trent in the 16th century, was introduced in the U.S. Mar. 22, 1970. It had been approved by Paul VI in the apostolic constitution *Missale Romanum,* dated Apr. 3, 1969.

Preliminary and related to it were the following developments.

Mass in English: Introduced Nov. 29, 1964. In the same year, Psalm 42 was eliminated from the prayers at the foot of the altar.

Incidental Changes: The last Gospel (prologue of John) and vernacular prayers following Mass were eliminated Mar. 7, 1965. At the same time, provision was made for the celebrant to say aloud some prayers formerly said silently.

Rubrics: An instruction entitled *Tres Abhinc Annos,* dated May 4 and effective June 29, 1967, simplified directives for the celebration of Mass, approved the practice of saying the canon aloud, altered the Communion and dismissal rites, permitted purple instead of black vestments in Masses for the dead, discontinued wearing of the maniple, and approved in principle the use of vernacular languages for the canon, ordination rites, and lessons of the Divine Office when read in choir.

Canons or Eucharistic Prayers: Three additional Eucharistic prayers authorized May 23, 1968, were approved for use in vernacular translation the following Aug. 15. They have the same basic structure as the traditional Roman Canon, whose use in English was introduced Oct. 22, 1967.

The customary Roman Canon, which dates at least from the beginning of the fifth century and has remained substantially unchanged since the seventh century, is the first in the order of listing of the Eucharistic prayers. It can be used at any time, but is the one of choice for most Sundays, some special feasts like Easter and Pentecost, and for feasts of the Apostles and other saints who are commemorated in the canon. Any preface can be used with it.

The second Eucharistic prayer, the shortest and simplest of all, is best suited for use on weekdays and various special circumstances. It has a preface of its own, but others may be used with it. This canon bears a close resemblance to the one framed by St. Hippolytus about 215.

The third Eucharistic prayer is suitable for use on Sundays and feasts as an alternative to the Roman Canon. It can be used with any preface and has a special formula for remembrance of the dead.

The fourth Eucharistic prayer, the most sophisticated of them all, presents a broad synthesis of salvation history. Based on the Eastern tradition of Antioch, it is best suited for use at Masses attended by persons versed in Sacred Scripture. It has an unchangeable preface.

English translations of three new canons for Masses with children and two for Masses of reconciliation were approved by the Congregation for Divine Worship June 5, 1975, for an experimental period to end with 1977. The choice of one each of the canons was left to the judgment of the National Conference of Catholic Bishops.

Lectionary: A new compilation of scriptural readings and psalm responsories for Mass was introduced Mar. 22, 1970. The *Lectionary* contains a three-year cycle of readings for Sundays and solemn feasts, a two-year weekday cycle, and a one-year cycle for the feasts of saints, in addition to readings for a great variety of Masses, ritual Masses and Masses for various needs. There are also responsorial psalms to follow the first readings, and gospel or alleluia versicles to follow the second readings.

Sacramentary (Missal): The Vatican Polyglot Press began distribution in June, 1970, of the Latin text of a new *Roman Missal,* the first revision published in 400 years. The English translation was authorized for optional use beginning July 1, 1974; the mandatory date for use was Dec. 1, 1974.

The missal is the celebrant's book of prayers and sacramental formulas and does not include the readings of the Mass, such as the Gospel and the Epistle. It contains the texts of entrance songs, prefaces and other prayers of the Mass. The number of prefaces is four times greater than it had been. There are 10 commons (or sets of Mass prayers) of martyrs, two of doctors of the Church, and a dozen for saints or groups of saints of various kinds, such as religious, educators and mothers of families. There are Masses during which certain sacraments are administered and others for religious profession, the Church, the pope, priests, Christian unity, the evangelization of nations, persecuted Christians, and other intentions.

Mass for Special Groups: Reasons and norms for the celebration of Mass at special gatherings of the faithful were the subject of an instruction issued May 15, 1969. Two years earlier, the U.S. Bishops' Liturgy Committee went on record in support of the celebration of Mass in private homes.

Sunday Mass on Saturday: The Congregation for the Clergy, under date of Jan. 10, 1970, granted the request that the faithful, where bishops consider it pastorally necessary or useful, may satisfy the precept of participating in Mass in the late afternoon or evening hours of Saturdays and the days before holy days of obligation.

Trination: The Congregation for the Sacraments, under date of Jan. 20, 1970, granted to all U.S. bishops the authority to permit priests to celebrate Mass three times on Saturdays and days preceding holy days of obligation, on condition that the first and second Masses are celebrated for weddings and/or funerals and the third Mass is celebrated in the evening so that the precept (of participating in Mass) will be satisfied by the faithful.

Mass in Latin: According to notices issued by the Congregation for Divine Worship June 1, 1971, and Oct. 28, 1974: (1) Bishops may permit the celebration of Mass in Latin for mixed-language groups. (2) Priests may celebrate Mass in Latin when people are not present. (3) The approved revised Order of the Mass is to be used in Latin as well as vernacular languages. (4) By way of exception, bishops may permit older and handicapped priests to use the Council of Trent's Order of the Mass in private celebration of the holy Sacrifice.

Inter-Ritual Concelebration: The Apostolic Delegation in Washington, D.C., announced in June, 1971, that it had received authorization to permit priests of Roman and Eastern rites to celebrate Mass together in the rite of the host church. It was understood that the inter-ritual concelebrations would always be "a manifestation of the unity of the Church and of communion among particular churches."

Ordo of the Sung Mass: In a decree dated June 24 and made public Aug. 24, 1972, the Congregation for Divine Worship issued a new *Ordo of the Sung Mass* — containing Gregorian chants in Latin — to replace the *Graduale Romanum.*

Mass for Children: Late in 1973, the Congregation for Divine Worship issued special guidelines for children's Masses, providing accommodations to the mentality and spiritual growth of pre-adolescents while retaining the principal parts and structures of the Mass. The *Directory for Masses with Children* was approved by Paul VI Oct. 22 and was dated Nov. 1, 1973. English versions of three canons for Masses with children were approved by the congregation June 5, 1975, for an experimental period to end with 1977.

Sacraments

The general use of English in administration of the sacraments was approved for the U.S. Sept. 14, 1964. Structural changes of the rites were subsequently made and introduced in the U.S. as follows.

Anointing of the Sick: Revised rites, covering also administration of the Eucharist to sick persons, were approved Nov. 30,. 1972, and published Jan. 18, 1973. The effective date for use of the English prayer formula was Dec. 1, 1974.

Baptism: New rites for the baptism of infants, approved Mar. 19, 1969, were introduced June 1, 1970.

Christian Initiation of Adults: Revised rites were issued Jan. 6, 1972, for the Christian initiation of adults — affecting preparation for and reception of baptism, the Eucharist and confirmation; also, the reception of already baptized adults into the Church. These rites, which were introduced in the U.S. on the completion of English translation, nullified a seven-step baptismal process approved in 1962.

Confirmation: Revised rites, issued Aug. 15, 1971, became mandatory in the U.S. Jan. 1, 1973.

Eucharist: Several enactments concerning the Eucharist have been issued since 1966 when permission was given for the superiors of convents to administer Holy Communion in the absence of priests. Paul VI issued an instruction on *Worship of the Eucharistic Mystery* May 25, 1967, and another on the manner of administering Holy Communion May 20, 1969. Limited permission for lay persons to serve as extraordinary ministers of the Eucharist was given in 1971 and extended in 1972. Also in 1972, instructions were issued regarding administration of the Eucharist to other Christians, and in particular circumstances.

Holy Orders: Revised ordination rites for deacons, priests and bishops, validated by prior experimental use, were approved in 1970. The sacrament of holy orders underwent further revision in 1972 with the elimination of the Church-instituted orders of porter, reader, exorcist, acolyte and sub-deacon, and of the tonsure ceremony symbolic of entrance into the clerical state. The former minor orders of reader and acolyte were changed from orders to ministries.

Matrimony: New rites, issued Mar. 19, 1969, were introduced June 1, 1970. Minor revisions had been made in 1964 in conjunction with a directive for imparting the nuptial blessing at all weddings.

Penance: Ritual revision of the sacraments was completed with the approval by Paul VI Dec. 2, 1973, of new directives for the sacrament of penance or reconciliation. The U.S. Bishops' Committee on the Liturgy set Feb. 27, 1977, as the mandatory date for use of the new rite. The committee also declared that it could be used from Mar. 7, 1976, after adequate preparation of priests and people. Earlier, authorization was given by the Holy See in 1968 for the omission of any reference to excommunication or other censures in the formula of absolution unless there was some indication that a censure had actually been incurred by a penitent.

Additional Developments

Calendar: A revised liturgical calendar, approved by Paul VI Feb. 14 and made public May 9, 1969, went into effect in the U.S. in 1972.

Funeral Rites: Revised rites oriented to the resurrection theme went into effect Nov. 1, 1971.

Holy Week: The English version of revised Holy Week rites went into effect in 1971. They introduced concelebration of Mass, placed new emphasis on commemorating the institution of the priesthood on Holy Thursday, and modified Good Friday prayers for other Christians, Jews and other non-Christians.

Liturgy of the Hours: The background, contents, scope and purposes of the revised Divine Office, called the Liturgy of the Hours, were described by Paul VI in the apostolic constitution *Canticum Laudis,* dated Nov. 1, 1970. A provisional English version, incorporating basic features of the master Latin text, was published in 1971. The first of the four complete volumes of the Hours in English was published in May, 1975; the other three were scheduled for publication before the beginning of Lent, 1976.

Music: An *Instruction on Music in the Liturgy,* dated Mar. 5 and effective May 14, 1967, encouraged congregational singing during liturgical celebrations and attempted to clarify the role of choirs and trained singers. More significantly, the instruction indicated that a major development underway in the liturgy was a gradual erasure of the distinctive lines traditionally drawn between the sung liturgy and the spoken liturgy, between what had been called the high Mass and the low Mass.

In the same year, the U.S. Bishops' Liturgy Committee approved the use of contemporary music, as well as guitars and other suitable instruments, in the liturgy. The Holy See authorized in 1968 the use of musical instruments other than the organ in liturgical services, "provided they are played in a manner suitable to worship."

Oils: The Congregation for Divine Worship issued a directive in 1971 permitting the use of other oils — from plants, seeds or coconuts — instead of the traditional olive oil in administering some of the sacraments. The directive also provided that oils could be blessed at other times than at the usual Mass of Chrism on Holy Thursday, and authorized bishops' conferences to permit priests to bless oils in cases of necessity.

Progress and Problems

Progress toward full implementation of the liturgical renewal envisioned and projected by the Second Vatican Council after 400 years of relatively little liturgical movement has been steady and, on balance, good but not altogether smooth. It has been hindered less by outright opposition than by inadequate pastoral programs of instruction and preparation, foot-dragging and extremes in experimentation. Such factors occasioned a number of official statements intended to counteract their negative effects.

Meaning of Experimentation

Liturgical experimentation, as well as the reluctance of some parties to put into effect the directives of the Second Vatican Council, was one of the subjects covered in a *Pastoral Statement on Liturgical Renewal* issued in May, 1967, by the National Conference of Catholic Bishops. The statement declared:

"Liturgical experimentation has acquired several meanings.... If it means ... privately initiated innovations, it must be disapproved. The Fathers of the council (Vatican II) had no intention whatever of encouraging experiments contrary to liturgical usage and discipline.... Unauthorized liturgical innovations are not genuine experiments at all.... They divert us from the educational work of renewal and from realizing the full potential of the present liturgy. Furthermore, this kind of unauthorized initiative is divisive of the Christian community."

The bishops' statement called for widened liturgical education and greater involvement by congregations in liturgical celebrations.

Norms

A "Third Instruction on the Correct Application of the Constitution on the Sacred Liturgy" was issued by the Congregation for Divine Worship Sept. 3, 1970, to assist bishops in putting liturgical norms — especially those concerning the Mass — into full effect. The document said:

"Liturgical reform is not at all synonymous with so-called desacralization and is not intended as an occasion for what is called secularization. Thus, the liturgy must keep a dignified and sacred character.

"The effectiveness of liturgical actions does not consist in the continual search for newer rites or simpler forms, but in an ever deeper insight into the word of God and the mystery which is celebrated. The priest will assure the presence of God and His mystery in the celebration by following the rites of the Church rather than his own preferences."

The instruction, among other things: stated that no readings of any kind may be substituted for scriptural readings, and that official formulas of the Mass may not be altered; said that the Eucharistic prayer or canon is to be said by the priest alone; noted the Latin-Rite requirement of unleavened wheat bread for the host; provided that women, although they may not serve at the altar, may read scriptural lessons except the Gospel, say prayers of the faithful, make announcements and commentary, be musicians and leaders of song, and act as ushers at Mass; cautioned that experimentation, when necessary and useful, should be carried out in line with prescribed norms.

Eucharistic Prayers

The Congregation for Divine Worship, in an Apr. 27, 1973, letter to the presidents of national conferences of bishops, coupled strong warnings against unauthorized texts with encouragement to employ permissible elements of variety and diversity in the celebration of Mass.

The May *Newsletter* of the U.S. Bishops' Committee on the Liturgy said in comment: "While reserving the decision on additional Eucharistic prayers (only four were approved) strictly to itself, the Holy See . . . 'will not refuse to consider legitimate requests, within the unity of the Roman Rite, and will weigh the petitions presented by episcopal conferences for the preparation and liturgical use of a new Eucharistic prayer in special circumstances; it will propose norms for individual cases.' . . . While the general faculty to permit new Eucharistic prayers is withheld from the episcopal conferences, the possible development for special cases is left open."

Two basic reasons were given against the use of unauthorized texts. "The first is that such a practice weakens Eucharistic and ecclesiastical communion; it is a challenge to both church unity and authority. The second reason, and often the more serious reason, is that many such Eucharistic prayers of private origin are poorly prepared without any sense of the liturgical tradition. Such texts are frequently deficient in the elements of praise and thanksgiving to God . . . just those elements which the liturgical reform has attempted to restore to the Roman liturgy."

Future Directions

Future directions for liturgical renewal were indicated by Archbishop Annibale Bugnini, secretary of the Congregation for Divine Worship, in an article published in the Feb. 7, 1974, edition of *L'Osservatore Romano.* At the conclusion of a review of 10 years of liturgical developments since the Second Vatican Council, he wrote the following.

"So the instructions for the next 10 years could be as follows: careful, methodical catechesis to penetrate Christ's mystery and make it live in souls; special care for the celebrations intended for children and young people, in whom lies the future of the church; progressive involvement of the particular groups in the holy assembly of the People of God; renewal of sacred chant, harmonizing tradition with the new forms, and the real participation of everyone, and not just select groups, in liturgical action; and symbol of the liturgy; respectful and detailed study of the adaptation of the liturgy to the character and traditions of the different peoples, so that it will spring forth spontaneously from their spirit and lose the sense of a superimposition alien to their culture and mentality; loving preparation of liturgical action, so that every congregation will feel it as its own expression, in common charity and in the inspiration of the Spirit; more articulated harmony between Christian piety and liturgical life; generous and joyful involvement of the local churches in the requirements and life of the universal Church, to preserve unity and the necessary cohesion in common prayer.

"The liturgy, like the Church, will not cease to improve itself. Placed by the council on the pastoral plane, having entered the life of the churches as the "summit" and the "fountain" of all her activity, the liturgy cannot but follow the laws of life. Not to progress would be anaemia. Not to renew itself would be death. But progress must be in order, in vital renewal under the breath of the Spirit and in complete adherence to Mother Church."

MASS IN LATIN

In response to requests from the people:

• Father Eugene R. Sinz, pastor of St. Englebert Parish in St. Louis, introduced in September, 1975, a weekly Mass in Latin — with readings and the Prayer of the Faithful in English — with Gregorian Chant. He said: "The Mass is being conducted according to the latest liturgical decrees from Rome. It is consistent with these decrees and with our archdiocesan liturgical commission. There is no objection whatever from Rome or from the chancery to what we are doing."

• In Cleveland, Msgr. Robert C. Blair announced that a Mass in Latin, with singing by the cathedral choir, would be celebrated once a month at St. John's Cathedral, "in conformity" with liturgical decrees.

Sacraments

The sacraments are actions of Christ and his Church which signify grace, cause it in the act of signifying it, and confer it upon persons properly disposed to receive it. They perpetuate the redemptive activity of Christ, making it present and effective. They infallibly communicate the fruit of that activity — namely, grace — to responsive persons with faith. Sacramental actions consist of the union of sensible signs (matter of the sacraments) with the words of the minister (form of the sacraments).

Christ instituted the sacraments: three of them — baptism, Holy Eucharist, penance — directly; the other four — confirmation, holy orders, anointing of the sick, matrimony — through the Church.

Christ is the principal priest or minister of every sacrament; human agents — an ordained priest, baptized persons contracting marriage with each other, any person conferring emergency baptism in a proper manner — are secondary ministers. Sacraments have efficacy from Christ, not from the personal dispositions of their human ministers.

Each sacrament confers sanctifying grace for the special purpose of the sacrament; this is, accordingly, called sacramental grace. It involves a right to actual graces corresponding to the purposes of the respective sacraments.

While sacraments infallibly produce the grace they signify, recipients benefit from them in proportion to their personal dispositions. One of these is the intention to receive sacraments as sacred signs of God's saving and grace-giving action. The state of grace is also necessary for fruitful reception of the Holy Eucharist, confirmation, matrimony, holy orders and anointing of the sick. Baptism is the sacrament in which grace is given in the first instance and original sin is remitted. Penance is the secondary sacrament of reconciliation, in which persons guilty of serious sin after baptism are reconciled with God and the Church, and in which persons already in the state of grace are strengthened in that state.

Role of Sacraments

The Second Vatican Council prefaced a description of the role of the sacraments with the following statement concerning participation by all the faithful in the priesthood of Christ and the exercise of that priesthood by receiving the sacraments (*Dogmatic Constitution on the Church*, Nos. 10 and 11).

". . . The baptized by regeneration and the anointing of the Holy Spirit, are consecrated into a spiritual house and a holy priesthood. Thus through all those works befitting Christian men they can offer spiritual sacrifice and proclaim the power of Him who has called them out of darkness into His marvelous light (cf. 1 Pt. 2:4-10). . . ."

"Though they differ from one another in essence and not only in degree, the common priesthood of the faithful and the ministerial or hierarchical priesthood (of those ordained to holy orders) are nonetheless interrelated. Each of them in its own special way is a participation in the one priesthood of Christ. The ministerial priest, by the sacred power he enjoys, molds and rules the priestly people. Acting in the person of Christ, he brings about the Eucharistic Sacrifice, and offers it to God in the name of all the people. For their part, the faithful join in the offering of the Eucharist by virtue of their royal priesthood. They likewise exercise that priesthood by receiving the sacraments, by prayer and thanksgiving, by the witness of a holy life, and by self-denial and active charity."

"It is through the sacraments and the exercise of the virtues that the sacred nature and organic structure of the priestly community is brought into operation."

Baptism: "Incorporated into the Church through baptism, the faithful are consecrated by the baptismal character to the exercise of the cult of the Christian religion. Reborn as sons of God, they must confess before men the faith which they have received from God through the Church."

Confirmation: "Bound more intimately to the Church by the sacrament of confirmation, they are endowed by the Holy Spirit with special strength. Hence they are more strictly obliged to spread and defend the faith both by word and by deed as true witnesses of Christ."

Eucharist: "Taking part in the Eucharistic Sacrifice, which is the fount and apex of the whole Christian life, they offer the divine Victim to God, and offer themselves along with It. Thus, both by the act of oblation and through holy Communion, all perform their proper part in this liturgical service, not, indeed, all in the same way but each in that way which is appropriate to himself. Strengthened anew at the holy table by the Body of Christ, they manifest in a practical way that unity of God's People which is suitably signified and wondrously brought about by this most awesome sacrament."

Penance: "Those who approach the sacrament of penance obtain pardon from the mercy of God for offenses committed against Him. They are at the same time reconciled with the Church, which they have wounded by their sins, and which by charity, example, and prayer seeks their conversion."

Anointing of the Sick: "By the sacred anointing of the sick and the prayer of her priests, the whole Church commends those who are ill to the suffering and glorified Lord, asking that He may lighten their suffering and save them (cf. Jas. 5:14-16). She exhorts them, moreover, to contribute to the welfare of the whole People of God by associating themselves freely with the passion and death of Christ (cf. Rom. 8:17; Col. 1:24; 2 Tm. 2:11-12; 1 Pt. 4:13)."

Holy Orders: "Those of the faithful who are consecrated by holy orders are appointed to feed the Church in Christ's name with the Word and the grace of God."

Matrimony: "Christian spouses, in virtue of the sacrament of matrimony, signify and partake of the mystery of that unity and fruitful love which exists between Christ and His Church (cf. Eph. 5:32). The spouses thereby help each other to attain to holiness in their married life and by the rearing and education of their children. And so, in their state and way of life, they have their own special gift among the People of God (cf. 1 Cor. 7:7).

"For from the wedlock of Christians there comes the family, in which new citizens of human society are born. By the grace of the Holy Spirit received in baptism these are made children of God, thus perpetuating the People of God through the centuries. The family is, so to speak, the domestic Church. In it parents should, by their word and example, be the first preachers of the faith to their children. They should encourage them in the vocation which is proper to each of them, fostering with special care any religious vocation.

"Fortified by so many and such powerful means of salvation, all the faithful, whatever their condition or state, are called by the Lord, each in his own way, to that perfect holiness whereby the Father Himself is perfect."

Baptism

Baptism is the sacrament of spiritual regeneration by which a person is incorporated in Christ and made a member of His Mystical Body, given grace, and cleansed of original sin. Actual sins and the punishment due for them are remitted also if the person baptized was guilty of such sins (e.g., in the case of a person baptized after reaching the age of reason). The theological virtues of faith, hope and charity are given with grace. The sacrament confers a character on the soul and can be received only once. Baptism has been called a sacrament of the dead because its purpose is to confer sanctifying grace on persons who do not have it.

The matter is the pouring of water. The form is: "I baptize you in the name of the Father and of the Son and of the Holy Spirit."

The minister of solemn baptism is a priest or deacon, but in case of emergency anyone, including a non-Catholic, can validly baptize. The minister pours water on the forehead of the person being baptized and says the words of the form while the water is flowing. The water used in solemn baptism is blessed during the rite.

The Church recognizes as valid baptism by **immersion, aspersion** (sprinkling of the water), or **infusion** (pouring of the water). In the Western Church, i.e., Roman Rite, the method of infusion is prescribed. The Church recognizes as valid baptisms properly performed by non-Catholic ministers. The baptism of infants has always been considered valid and the general practice of infant baptism was well established by the fifth century. Baptism is conferred conditionally when there is doubt about the validity of a previous baptism or the dispositions of the person.

Baptism is necessary for salvation. If a person cannot receive the baptism of water described above, this can be supplied by baptism of blood (martyrdom suffered for the Catholic faith or some Christian virtue) or by baptism of desire (perfect contrition joined with at least the implicit intention of doing whatever God wills that men should do for salvation).

A sponsor is required for the person being baptized. (See Godparents, below).

A person must be validly baptized before he can receive any of the other sacraments.

Christian Initiation of Infants: Infants should be solemnly baptized as soon after birth as conveniently possible. In danger of death, anyone may baptize an infant. If the child survives, the ceremonies of solemn baptism should be supplied.

The sacrament is ordinarily conferred by a priest or deacon of the parents' parish.

Only Catholics, in their 14th year or older, may be **godparents** or sponsors. Only one is required. Two, one of each sex, are permitted. A non-Catholic cannot be a godparent for a Catholic child, but may serve as a witness to the baptism. A Catholic may not be a godparent for a child baptized in a non-Catholic religion, but may be a witness.

The role of godparents in baptismal ceremonies is secondary to the role of the parents. They serve as representatives of the community of faith and with the parents request baptism for the child and perform other ritual functions. Their function after baptism is to serve as proxies for the parents if the parents should be unable or fail to provide for the religious training of the child.

At baptism every child should be given a name with Christian significance, usually the name of a saint, to symbolize newness of life in Christ.

Christian Initiation of Adults: According to the *Ordo Initiationis Christianae Adultorum* ("Rite of the Christian Initiation of Adults") issued by the Congregation for Divine Worship under date of Jan. 6, 1972, adults are prepared for baptism and reception into the Church in several stages:

• An initial period of inquiry, instruction and evangelization.

• The catechumenate, a period of formal instruction and progressive formation in and familiarity with Christian life. It starts with a statement of purpose and includes a rite in which the catechumen is signed with the cross, blessings, exorcisms, and introduction into church for celebration of the word of God.

• Immediate preparation, called a period of purification and enlightenment, from the beginning of Lent to reception of the sacraments of initiation — baptism, confirmation, Holy Eucharist — at Easter. The period is marked by scrutinies, formal giving of the creed and the Lord's Prayer, the choice of a Christian name, and a final statement of intention.

• A final phase whose objective is greater familiarity with Christian life in the Church through observances of the Easter season and association with the community of the faithful.

The priest who baptizes a catechumen can also administer the sacrament of confirmation.

A sponsor is required for the person being baptized.

The *Ordo* also provides a simple rite of initiation for adults in danger of death and for cases in which all stages of the initiation process are not necessary, and guidelines for: (1) the preparation of adults for the sacraments of confirmation and Holy Eucharist in cases where they have been baptized but have not received further formation in the Christian life; (2) for the formation and initiation of children of catechetical age.

The Church recognizes the right of anyone over the age of seven to request baptism and to receive the sacrament after completing a course of instruction and giving evidence of good will. Practically, in the case of minors in a non-Catholic family or environment, the Church accepts them when other circumstances favor their ability to practice the faith — e.g., well-disposed family situation, the presence of another or several Catholics in the family. Those who are not in such favorable circumstances are prudently advised to defer reception of the sacrament until they attain the maturity necessary for independent practice of the faith.

Reception of Baptized Christians: Procedure for the reception of already baptized Christians into full communion with the Catholic Church is distinguished from the catechumenate, since they have received some Christian formation. Instruction and formation are provided as necessary, however; and conditional baptism is administered if there is reasonable doubt about the validity of the person's previous baptism.

In the rite of reception, the person is invited to join the community of the Church in professing the Nicene Creed and is asked to state: "I believe and profess all that the holy Catholic Church believes, teaches, and proclaims as revealed by God." The priest places his hand on the head of the person, states the formula of admission to full communion, confirms (in the absence of a bishop), gives a sign of peace, and administers Holy Communion during a Eucharistic Liturgy.

Confirmation

Confirmation is the sacrament by which a baptized person, through anointing with chrism and the imposition of hands, is endowed with the gifts and special strength of the Holy Spirit for mature Christian living. The sacrament, which completes the Christian initiation begun wth baptism, confers a character on the soul and can be received only once.

According to the apostolic constitution *Divinae Consortium Naturae* dated Aug. 15, 1971, in conjunction with the *Ordo Confirmationis* ("Rite of Confirmation"): "The sacrament of confirmation is conferred through the anointing with chrism on the forehead, which is done by the imposition of the hand (matter of the sacrament), and through the words: 'N . . . . , receive the seal of the Holy Spirit, the Gift of the Father' " (form of the sacrament). On May 5, 1975, bishops' conferences in English-speaking countries were informed by the Congregation for Divine Worship that Pope Paul had approved this English version of the form of the sacrament: "Be sealed with the gift of the Holy Spirit."

The ordinary minister of confirmation in the Roman Rite is a bishop. Priests may be delegated for the purpose. A pastor can confirm a parishioner in danger of death, and a priest can confirm in ceremonies of Christian initiation.

Ideally, the sacrament is conferred during the Eucharistic Liturgy. Elements of the rite include renewal of the promises of baptism, which confirmation ratifies and completes, and the laying on of hands — by symbolic elevation over the heads of those being confirmed — by the confirming bishop and priests participating in the ceremony.

"The entire rite," according to the *Ordo,* "has a twofold meaning. The laying of hands upon the candidates, done by the bishop and the concelebrating priests, expresses the biblical gesture by which the gift of the Holy Spirit is invoked. . . . The anointing with chrism and the accompanying words clearly signify the effect of the Holy Spirit. Signed with the perfumed oil by the bishop's hand, the baptized person receives the indelible character, the seal of the Lord, together with the Spirit who is given and who conforms the person more perfectly to Christ and gives him the grace of spreading the Lord's presence among men."

A sponsor is required for the person being confirmed. This can be one of the baptismal sponsors or another person. Parents can serve as sponsors for their own children.

In the Roman Rite, it has been customary for children to receive confirmation within a reasonable time after first Communion and confession. There is a developing trend, however, to defer confirmation until later when its significance for mature Christian living becomes more evident. In the Eastern Rites, confirmation is administered at the same time as baptism.

The Holy Eucharist

The Holy Eucharist is a sacrifice (see The Mass) and the sacrament in which Christ is present and is received under the appearances of bread and wine.

The matter is bread of wheat, unleavened in the Roman Rite and leavened in the Eastern Rites, and wine of grape. The form consists of the words of consecration said by the priest at Mass: "This is my body. . . . This is the cup of my blood" (according to the traditional usage of the Roman Rite).

Only a priest can consecrate bread and wine so they become the body and blood of Christ. After consecration, however, the Eucharist can be administered by deacons and, for various reasons, by religious and lay persons.

Priests celebrating Mass receive the Eucharist under the appearances of bread and wine. In the Roman Rite, others usually receive under the appearances of bread only, i.e., the consecrated host; in some circumstances, however, they may receive under the appearances of both bread and wine. In Eastern-Rite practice, the faithful generally receive a piece of consecrated leavened bread which has been dipped into consecrated wine (i.e., by intinction).

Conditions for receiving the Eucharist, commonly called **Holy Communion,** are the state of grace, the right intention, and observance of the Eucharistic fast.

The faithful of Roman Rite are required by a precept of the Church to receive the Eucharist at least once a year, during the Easter time (in the US, from the First Sunday of Lent to Trinity Sunday, inclusive).

(See Eucharistic Fast, Mass, Transubstantiation, Viaticum.)

First Communion and Confession: Children are to be prepared for and given opportunity for receiving both sacraments on reaching the age of discretion, at which time they become subject to general norms concerning confession and Communion. This, together with a stated preference for first confession before first Communion, was the central theme of a document published July 9, 1973, by the Congregation for the Discipline of the Sacraments and the Congregation for the Clergy, with the approval of Pope Paul VI.

What the document prescribed was the observance of practices ordered by St. Pius X in the decree *Quam Singulari* of Aug. 8, 1910. Its purpose was to counteract pastoral and catechetical experiments virtually denying children the opportunity of receiving both sacraments at the same time. Termination of such experiments was ordered by the end of the 1972-73 school year.

At the time the document was issued, two- or three-year experiments of this kind — routinely deferring reception of the sacrament of penance until after the first reception of Holy Communion — were in effect in more than half of the dioceses of the U.S.

One reason stated in support of such experiments was the view that children are not capable of serious sin at the age of seven or eight, when Communion is generally received for the first time, and therefore prior reception of the sacrament of penance is not necessary. Another reason was the purpose of making the distinctive nature of the two sacraments clearer to children.

The Vatican view reflected convictions that the principle and practice of devotional reception of penance are as valid for children as they are for adults, and that sound catechetical programs can avoid misconceptions about the two sacraments.

Holy Communion under the Forms of Bread and Wine (by separate taking of the consecrated bread and wine or by intinction, the reception of the host dipped in the wine): Such reception is permitted under conditions stated in instructions issued by the Congregation for Divine Worship (May 25, 1967; June 29, 1970), the *General Instruction on the Roman Missal* (No. 242), and directives of bishops' conferences and individual bishops.

Accordingly, Communion can be administered in this way to: persons being baptized, received into communion with the Church, confirmed, receiving anointing of the sick; couples at their wedding or jubilee; religious at profession or renewal of profession; lay persons receiving an ecclesiastical assignment (e.g., lay missionaries); participants at concelebrated Masses, retreats, pastoral commission meetings; on other special occasions.

Holy Communion Twice a Day: The reception of Holy Communion at Mass a second time on the same day is permitted in accord with provisions of the "Instruction on Facilitating Communion in Particular Circumstances" *(Immensae Caritatis)* approved by Pope Paul VI Jan. 20 and published by the Congregation for Divine Worship Mar. 29, 1973.

The occasions are: Sunday Mass on Saturday evening or a holy day Mass the previous evening; a second Mass on Christmas or Easter, following reception at midnight Mass or the Mass of the Easter Vigil; the evening Mass of Holy Thursday, following reception at the earlier Mass of Chrism; Masses in which baptism, confirmation, holy orders, matrimony, anointing of the sick, first Communion, Viaticum are administered; some Masses for the dead (e.g., of Christian burial, first anniversary); special occasions — consecration of a church or altar, religious profession, conferring an ecclesiastical assignment (e.g., to lay missionaries), feast of Corpus Christi, parochial visitation, canonical visitation or special meetings of religious, Eucharistic and other congresses, pilgrimages, preaching missions; other occasions designated by the local bishop.

Holy Communion and Eucharistic Devotion outside of Mass: These were the subjects of an instruction *(De Sacra Communione et de Cultu Mysterii Eucharistici extra Missam)* dated June 21 and made public Oct. 18, 1973, by the Congregation for Divine Worship.

Holy Communion can be given outside of Mass to persons unable for a reasonable cause to receive it during Mass on a given day. The ceremonial rite is modeled on the structure of the Mass, consisting of a penitential act, a scriptural reading, the Lord's Prayer, a sign or gesture of peace, giving of the Eucharist, prayer and final blessing. Viaticum and Communion to the sick can be given by extraordinary ministers (authorized lay persons) with appropriate rites.

Forms of devotion outside of Mass are exposition of the Blessed Sacrament (by men or women religious, especially, or lay persons in the absence of a priest; but only a priest can give the blessing), processions and congresses with appropriate rites.

Intercommunion: Church policy on intercommunion was stated in an "Instruction on the Admission of Other Christians to the Eucharist," dated June 1 and made public July 8, 1972, against the background of the *Decree on Ecumenism* approved by the Second Vatican Council, and the *Directory on Ecumenism* issued by the Secretariat for Promoting Christian Unity in 1967.

Basic principles related to intercommunion are:

• "There is an indissoluble link between the mystery of the Church and the mystery of the Eucharist, or between ecclesial and Eucharistic communion; the celebration of the Eucharist of itself signifies the fullness of profession of faith and ecclesial communion" (1972 Instruction).

• "Eucharistic communion practiced by those who are not in full ecclesial communion with each other cannot be the expression of that full unity which the Eucharist of its nature signifies and which in this case does not exist; for this reason such communion cannot be regarded as a means to be used to lead to full ecclesial communion" (1972 Instruction).

• The question of reciprocity "arises only with those churches which have preserved the substance of the Eucharist, the sacrament of orders and apostolic succession" (1967 Directory).

• "A Catholic cannot ask for the Eucharist

except from a minister who has been validly ordained" (1967 Directory).

The policy distinguishes between separated Eastern Christians and other Christians.

With Separated Eastern Christians (e.g., Orthodox): These may be given the Eucharist (as well as penance and anointing of the sick) at their request. Catholics may receive these same sacraments from priests of separated Eastern churches if they experience genuine spiritual necessity, seek spiritual benefit, and access to a Catholic priest is morally or physically impossible. This policy (of reciprocity) derives from the facts that the separated Eastern churches have apostolic succession through their bishops, valid priests, and sacramental beliefs and practices in accord with those of the Catholic Church.

With Other Christians (e.g., members of Reformation-related churches, others): Admission to the Eucharist in the Catholic Church, according to the *Directory on Ecumenism,* "is confined to particular cases of those Christians who have a faith in the sacrament in conformity with that of the Church, who experience a serious spiritual need for the Eucharistic sustenance, who for a prolonged period are unable to have recourse to a minister of their own community and who ask for the sacrament of their own accord; all this provided that they have proper dispositions and lead lives worthy of a Christian." The spiritual need is defined as "a need for an increase in spiritual life and a need for a deeper involvement in the mystery of the Church and of its unity."

Circumstances under which Communion may be given to other properly disposed Christians are danger of death, imprisonment, persecution, grave spiritual necessity coupled with no chance of recourse to a minister of their own community. Judgment regarding these and other special circumstances rests with the local bishop.

Catholics cannot ask for the Eucharist from ministers of other Christian churches who have not been validly ordained to the priesthood.

Penance

Penance is the sacrament by which sins committed after baptism are forgiven and a person is reconciled with God and the Church.

A revised ritual for the sacrament — *Ordo Paenitentiae,* published by the Congregation of Divine Worship Feb. 7, 1974 — reiterates standard doctrine concerning the sacrament; emphasizes the social (communal and ecclesial) aspects of sin and conversion, with due regard for personal aspects and individual reception of the sacrament; prescribes three forms for celebration of the sacrament; and presents models for community penitential services.

The Latin version of the ritual, dated Dec.

2, 1973, is already in force. Provision was made for other versions to become effective on appropriate approval of translations by episcopal conferences and the Congregation for Divine Worship.

The U.S. Bishops' Committee on the Liturgy recommended that adequate preparation of priests and people should precede introduction in this country of the revised ritual in English. Recommended dates for its use, after due preparation, were the first Sunday of Lent, 1976 (optional), and the first Sunday of Lent, 1977 (mandatory).

The basic elements of the sacrament are sorrow for sin because of a supernatural motive, confession (of previously unconfessed mortal or grave sins, required; of venial sins also, but not of necessity), and reparation (by means of prayer or other act enjoined by the confessor), all of which comprise the matter of the sacrament; and absolution, which is the form of the sacrament.

The traditional words of absolution remain unchanged at the conclusion of this formula: "God, the Father of mercies, has reconciled the world to himself through the death and resurrection of his Son and has poured forth the Holy Spirit for the forgiveness of sins. May he grant you pardon and peace through the ministry of the Church. And I absolve you from your sins in the name of the Father, and of the Son, and of the Holy Spirit."

The minister of the sacrament is an authorized priest — i.e., one who, besides having the power of orders to forgive sins, also has faculties of jurisdiction granted by an ecclesiastical superior and/or by canon law.

The sacrament can be celebrated in three ways.

• For individuals: The traditional manner remains acceptable but is enriched with additional elements including: reception of the penitent and making of the Sign of the Cross; an exhortation by the confessor to trust in God; a possible reading from Scripture; confession of sins; manifestation of repentance; petition for God's forgiveness through the ministry of the Church and the absolution of the priest; praise of God's mercy, and dismissal in peace. Some of these elements are optional.

• For several penitents, in the course of a community celebration including a liturgy of the Word of God and prayers, individual confession and absolution, and an act of thanksgiving.

• For several penitents, in the course of a community celebration, with general confession and general absolution. This method is reserved for special circumstances in which it is morally or physically impossible for persons to confess and be absolved individually, and in view of their need for reconciliation and reception of the Eucharist. Penitents are required to confess at their next individual confession any grave sins absolved in such a general celebration of the sacrament.

Communal celebrations of the sacrament are not held in connection with Mass.

The place of individual confession, as determined by episcopal conferences in accordance with given norms, can be the traditional confessional or another appropriate setting.

The sacrament is necessary, by the institution of Christ, for the reconciliation of persons guilty of grave sins committed after baptism.

A precept of the Church obliges the faithful guilty of grave sin to confess at least once a year.

The Church favors more frequent reception of the sacrament not only for the reconciliation of persons guilty of serious sins but also for reasons of devotion. Devotional confession — in which venial sins or previously forgiven sins are confessed — serves the purpose of confirming persons in penance and conversion.

Penitential Celebrations: Communal penitential celebrations are designed to emphasize the social dimensions of Christian life — the community aspects and significance of penance and reconciliation.

Elements of such celebrations are community prayer, hymns and songs, scriptural and other readings, examination of conscience, general confession and expression of sorrow for sin, acts of penance and reconciliation, and a form of non-sacramental absolution resembling the one in the penitential rite of the Mass.

If the sacrament is celebrated during the service, there must be individual confession and absolution of sin.

(See Absolution, Confession, Confessional, Confessor, Contrition, Faculties, Forgiveness of Sin, Power of the Keys, Seal of Confession, Sin.)

Anointing of the Sick

This sacrament, promulgated by St. James the Apostle (Jas. 5:13-15), is administered to persons who are dangerously ill. By the anointing with blessed oil and the prayer of a priest, the sacrament confers on the person comforting grace; the remission of venial sins and inculpably unconfessed mortal sins, together with at least some of the temporal punishment due for sins; and, sometimes, results in an improved state of health.

The matter of this sacrament is the anointing with blessed oil (of the sick — olive oil, or vegetable oil if necessary) of the forehead and hands; in cases of necessity, a single anointing of another portion of the body suffices. The form is: "Through this holy anointing and his most loving mercy, may the Lord assist you by the grace of the Holy Spirit so that, when you have been freed from your sins, he may save you and in his goodness raise you up."

Anointing of the sick, formerly called extreme unction, may be received more than once, e.g., in new or continuing stages of serious illness. Ideally, the sacrament should be administered while the recipient is conscious and in conjunction with the sacraments of penance and the Eucharist. It may be administered conditionally even after apparent death.

The sacrament can be administered during a communal celebration in some circumstances, as in a home for the aged.

Pope Paul VI authorized a revision of the rite for administration of the sacrament in the apostolic constitution *Sacram Unctionem Infirmorum* ("Sacred Anointing of the Sick") which was approved Nov. 30, 1972, and made public Jan. 18, 1973. He ordered the new rite into effect as of Jan. 1, 1974. The Latin version of the new rite went into effect Jan. 1, 1974. The provisional English version became effective in the U.S. Dec. 1, 1974.

Matrimony

Coverage of the sacrament of matrimony is given in the articles, Marriage Doctrine of Vatican II, Marriage Laws of the Church, Mixed Marriage Guidelines.

Holy Orders

Holy orders is the sacrament by which spiritual power and grace are given to enable an ordained minister to consecrate the Eucharist, forgive sins, perform other pastoral and ecclesiastical functions, and form the community of the People of God. Holy orders confers a character on the soul and can be received only once. The minister of the sacrament is a bishop.

Holy orders, like matrimony but in a different way, is a social sacrament. As the Second Vatican Council declared in the *Dogmatic Constitution on the Church:*

"For the nurturing and constant growth of the People of God, Christ the Lord instituted in His Church a variety of ministries, which work for the good of the whole body. For those ministers who are endowed with sacred power are servants of their brethren, so that all who are of the People of God, and therefore enjoy a true Christian dignity, can work toward a common goal freely and in an orderly way, and arrive at salvation" (No. 18).

"With their helpers, the priests and deacons, bishops have . . . taken up the service of the community, presiding in place of God over the flock whose shepherds they are, as teachers of doctrine, priests of sacred worship, and officers of good order" (No. 20).

The fullness of the priesthood belongs to those who have received the order of **bishop.** Bishops, in hierarchical union with the pope and their fellow bishops, are the successors of the apostles as pastors of the Church: they have individual responsibility for the care of the local churches they serve and collegial responsibility for the care of the universal Church (see Collegiality). In the ordination or consecration of bishops, the essential form is the imposition of hands by the consecrator(s) and the assigned prayer in the preface of the rite of ordination.

A **priest** is an ordained minister with the power to celebrate Mass, administer the sacraments, preach and teach the word of God, impart blessings, and perform additional pastoral functions, according to the mandate of his ecclesiastical superior.

Concerning priests, the Second Vatican Council stated in the *Dogmatic Constitution on the Church* (No. 28):

". . . The divinely established ecclesiastical ministry is exercised on different levels by those who from antiquity have been called bishops, priests, and deacons. Although priests do not possess the highest degree of the priesthood, and although they are dependent on the bishops in the exercise of their power, they are nevertheless united with the bishops in sacerdotal dignity. By the power of the sacrament of orders, and in the image of Christ the eternal High Priest (Hb. 5:1-10; 7:24; 9:11-28), they are consecrated to preach the gospel, shepherd the faithful, and celebrate divine worship as true priests of the New Testament. . . .

"Priests, prudent cooperators with the episcopal order as well as its aides and instruments, are called to serve the People of God. They constitute one priesthood with their bishop, although that priesthood is comprised of different functions. . . ."

In the ordination of a priest of Roman Rite, the essential matter is the imposition of hands on the heads of those being ordained by the ordaining bishop. The essential form is the accompanying prayer in the preface of the ordination ceremony. Other elements in the rite are the presentation of the implements of sacrifice — the chalice containing wine and the paten containing a host — with accompanying prayers.

Regarding the order of **deacon,** the *Dogmatic Constitution on the Church* (No. 29) stated:

"At a lower level of the hierarchy are deacons, upon whom hands are imposed 'not unto the priesthood, but unto a ministry of service.' For strengthened by sacramental grace, in communion with the bishop and his group of priests, they serve the People of God in the ministry of the liturgy, of the word, and of charity. It is the duty of the deacon, to the extent that he has been authorized by competent authority, to administer baptism solemnly, to be custodian and dispenser of the Eucharist, to assist at and bless marriages in the name of the Church, to bring Viaticum to the dying, to read the sacred Scripture to the faithful, to instruct and exhort the people, to preside at the worship and prayer of the faithful, to administer sacramentals, and to officiate at funeral and burial services. (Deacons are) dedicated to duties of charity and administration. . . ."

". . . The diaconate can in the future be restored as a proper and permanent rank of the hierarchy. It pertains to the competent territorial bodies of bishops, of one kind or another, to decide, with the approval of the Supreme Pontiff, whether and where it is opportune for such deacons to be appointed for the care of souls. With the consent of the Roman Pontiff, this diaconate will be able to be conferred upon men of more mature age, even upon those living in the married state. It may also be conferred upon suitable young men. For them, however, the law of celibacy must remain intact" (No. 29).

The Apostles ordained the first seven deacons (Acts 6:1-6): Stephen, Philip, Prochorus, Nicanor, Timon, Parmenas, Nicholas.

Other Ministries: The Church later assigned ministerial duties to men in several other orders, as:

Subdeacon, with specific duties in liturgical worship, especially at Mass. The order, whose first extant mention dates from about the middle of the third century, was regarded as minor until the 13th century; afterwards, it was called a major order in the West but not in the East.

Acolyte, to serve in minor capacities in liturgical worship; a function now performed by Mass servers.

Exorcist, to perform services of exorcism for expelling evil spirits; a function which came to be reserved to specially delegated priests.

Lector, to read scriptural and other passages during liturgical worship; a function now generally performed by lay persons

Porter, to guard the entrance to an assembly of Christians and to ward off undesirables who tried to gain admittance; an order of early origin and utility but of present insignificance.

Long after it became evident that these positions and functions had fallen into general disuse or did not require clerical ordination, the Holy See started a revision of the orders in 1971. By an indult of Oct. 5, the bishops of the United States were permitted to omit ordaining porters and exorcists. Another indult, dated three days later, permitted the use of revised rites for ordaining acolytes and lectors, and authorized the use of a service celebrating admission to the clerical state in place of the ceremony of tonsure which had previously served this purpose.

To complete the revision, Pope Paul VI abolished Sept. 14, 1972, the orders of porter, exorcist and subdeacon; decreed that laymen, as well as candidates for the diaconate and priesthood, can be installed (rather than ordained) in the ministries (rather than orders) of acolyte and lector; reconfirmed the suppression of tonsure and its replacement with a service of dedication to God and the Church;

and stated that a man enters the clerical state on ordination to the diaconate.

There were no doctrinal obstacles to the Pope's action, because the abolished orders had been instituted by the Church for functional purposes and were not considered to be parts of the sacrament of holy orders.

PERMANENT DIACONATE

Authorization for restoration of the permanent diaconate in the Roman Rite — making it possible for men to become deacons without being required to become priests — was promulgated by Pope Paul VI June 27, 1967, in a document entitled *Sacrum Diaconatus Ordinem* ("Sacred Order of the Diaconate").

The Pope's action implemented the desire expressed by the Second Vatican Council for reestablishment of the diaconate as an independent order in its own right not only to supply ministers for carrying on the work of the Church but also to complete the hierarchical structure of the Church of Roman Rite.

Permanent deacons have been traditional in the Eastern Church. The Western Church, however, which followed the practice of conferring the diaconate only as a sacred order preliminary to the priesthood, did not have them for centuries.

The Pope's document, issued on his own initiative, provided:

• Qualified unmarried men 25 years of age or older may be ordained permanent deacons. They cannot marry after ordination.

• Qualified married men 35 years of age or older may be ordained permanent deacons. The consent of the wife of a prospective deacon is required. A married deacon cannot remarry after the death of his wife.

• Preparation for the diaconate includes a two- or three-year course of study and formation.

• Candidates who are not religious must be affiliated with a diocese.

• Deacons will practice their ministry under the direction of a bishop and the priests with whom they will be associated. (For functions, see the description of deacon, under Holy Orders.)

Restoration of the permanent diaconate in the United States was approved by the Holy See in October, 1968. Shortly afterwards the U.S. bishops established a committee of the same name, which is chaired by Bishop Ernest L. Unterkoefler of Charleston, S.C. The committee operates through a secretariat, of which Msgr. Ernest J. Fiedler is executive director. Its offices are located at 1312 Massachusetts Ave. N. W., Washington, D.C. 20005.

Present Status

The bishops' secretariat reported in June, 1975, that 898 permanent deacons had been ordained in the U.S.; that 74 dioceses had deacons ordained and 60 more were either preparing training programs or were interested in doing so; that a total of 1,841 candidates were in training.

Functions

Deacons have various functions, depending on the nature of their assignments. Liturgically, they can officiate at baptisms, and weddings, can preach and distribute Holy Communion. Some are engaged in religious education work. All are intended to carry out works of charity and pastoral service of one kind or another.

The majority of permanent deacons, 92 percent of whom are married, continue in their secular work. Their ministry of service is developing in three dimensions: of liturgy, of the word, and of charity. Depending on the individual deacon's abilities and preference, he is assigned by his bishop to either a parochial ministry or to one particular field of service. The latter is the most challenging ministry to develop. Deacons are now active in a variety of ministries including those to prison inmates and their families, the sick in hospitals, nursing homes and homes for the aged, alienated youth, the elderly and the poor, and in various areas of legal service to the indigent, of education and campus ministry. A few have been assigned as pastors of multi-county, rural parishes. The unlimited possibilities for diaconal ministry are under realistic assessment, diocese by diocese.

Training Programs

There were 60 training centers for deacons as of June, 1975. The first four were established in 1969. Where feasible, one center may serve two or more dioceses in the formation of diaconal candidates.

Continuing efforts are made to recruit Spanish-speaking, black and other minority candidates in training programs. Of the permanent deacons ordained up to June, 1975, 7 per cent were black, and 12 per cent were Hispanic.

Training programs of spiritual, doctrinal and pastoral formation are generally based on *Permanent Deacons in the United States: Guidelines on Their Formation and Ministry,* published by the Bishops' Committee on the Permanent Diaconate in September, 1971.

Permanent diaconate training programs and their directors, as of June, 1975, were as follows. The listing is alphabetical, by diocese.

Agana: Rev. William D. D'Arcy, P.O. Box 125, Agana, Guam 96910.

Albany: Rev. William Ryan, 40 N. Main Ave., Albany, N.Y. 12203.

Altoona-Johnstown: Rev. Paul L. Panza, The Chancery, Logan Blvd., Hollidaysburg, Pa. 16648.

Amarillo: Rev. James C. Gursynaski, P.O. Box 5644, Amarillo, Tex. 79607.

Arlington: Rev. Msgr. Richard J. Burke, 200 N. Glebe Rd., Arlington, Va. 22203.

Atlanta: Rev. Msgr. Eusebius J. Beltran, 928 Gordon St. S.W., Atlanta, Ga. 30310; also Rev. Joseph A. Sanches, 756 W. Peachtree, N.W., Atlanta, Ga. 30308.

Baltimore: John J. Codd, Sr., P.O. Box 7664, Baltimore, Md. 21207; also Anthony S. Maranto, 5404 Hamlet Ave., Baltimore, Md. 21214.

Baton Rouge: Rev. Leo Guillot, P.O. Box 290, Port Allen, La. 70767.

Birmingham: Rev. Frank J. Muscolino, P.O. Box 2086, Birmingham, Ala., 35201.

Boston: Rev. William C. Burckhart, 345 Waverly St., Belmont, Mass. 02178.

Brooklyn: Rev. James L. Tahaney, 75 Greene Ave., Brooklyn, N.Y. 11238.

Buffalo: Rev. Theodore W. Kraus, 100 S. Elmwood Ave., Buffalo, N.Y. 14202.

Burlington: Rev. Omar L. Dufault, 89 Pearl St., Box 926, Burlington, Vt. 05401.

Camden: Rev. Donald D. Velozo, 1845 Hadden Ave., Camden, N.J. 08101.

Caroline and Marshall Islands (Vicariate Apostolic): Rev. Allen Cameron, S.J., Catholic Mission, Truk, P.O. Box 250, U.S. Trust Territory Pacific 96942.

Charleston: Rev. Thomas Duffy, 119 Broad St., Charleston, S.C. 29401.

Cheyenne: Rev. Carl Beavers, P.O. Box 1117, Florington, Wyo. 82240.

Chicago: Rev. Lawrence J. Gorman, Rev. John Moriarity, 1307 S. Wabash Ave., Chicago, Ill. 60605.

Cincinnati: Rev. John Rea, Mt. St. Mary Seminary, 5440 Moeller Ave., Cincinnati, O. 45212.

Cleveland: Rev. Robert F. Pfeiffer, 1227 Ansel Rd., Cleveland, O. 44108.

Columbus: Rev. Ralph J. Huntzinger, Pontifical College Josephinum, Worthington, O. 43085; also Rev. Thomas Shonbarger, 5277 E. Broad St., Columbus, O. 43213.

Dallas: Rev. Msgr. Robert C. Rehkemper, P.O. Box 19507, Dallas, Tex. 75219.

Denver: Rev. Leo R. Horrigan, 938 Bannock St., Denver, Colo. 80204.

Des Moines: Rev. Duane J. Weiland, P.O. Box 1816, Des Moines, Ia. 50306.

Detroit: Rev. Gary M. Tierney, 1234 Washington Blvd., Detroit, Mich. 48226; also: Rev. Anthony Kosnik, Orchard Lake Seminary, Orchard Lake, Mich. 48034.

El Paso: Rev. John F. Peters, P.O. Box 17548, El Paso, Tex., 79917.

Evansville: Rev. Robert Bultman, 5528 Hogue Rd., Evansville, Ind. 47712.

Fairbanks: Rev. Rene Astruc, S.J., 1500 Birchwood, Anchorage, Alaska 99504.

Fort Wayne-South Bend: Kevin M. Ranaghan, 1035 N. St. Peter, South Bend, Ind. 46617.

Gallup: Rev. Pius Winter, O.F.M., 415 E. Green Ave., Gallup, N.M. 87301.

Galveston-Houston: Don LeFore, 6923 Neff St., Houston, Tex. 77036.

Grand Rapids: Rev. Michael A. Danner, The Christopher House, 2001 Robinson Rd., S.E., Grand Rapids, Mich. 49506.

Green Bay: Rev. Thomas Allen, Sacred Heart Center for Christian Formation, Oneida, Wis. 54155.

Harrisburg: Rev. David T. McAndrew, 610 Church St., Harrisburg, Pa. 17108.

Hartford: Rev. Joseph P. Donahue, 467 Bloomfield Ave., Bloomfield, Conn. 06002.

Helena: Rev. Gary Reller, P.O. Box 1019, Kalispell, Mont. 59901.

Joliet: Rev. Arno Dennerlein, 710 W. Marian St., Joliet, Ill. 60436.

Juneau: Rev. James Cronin, Holy Name Church, P.O. Box 938, Ketchikan, Alaska 99901.

Kalamazoo: Rev. Eugene A. Sears, 215 N. Westnedge Ave., Kalamazoo, Mich. 49006.

Kansas City-St. Joseph: Rev. Patrick Rush, P.O. Box 1037, Kansas City, Mo. 64141.

Los Angeles: Rev. Peter Healy, Catholic Information Center, 809 S. Flower St., Los Angeles, Calif. 90017.

Louisville: Rev. Nick Rice, 2000 Norris Pl., Louisville, Ky. 40205.

Melkite Apostolic Exarchate: Most Rev. Joseph Tawil, 19 Dartmouth St., West Newton, Mass. 02165.

Memphis: Rev. Patrick J. Lynch, 1325 Jefferson Ave., Memphis, Tenn. 38104; also Sr. Jane Edward, 4849 Park Ave., Memphis, Tenn. 38117.

Milwaukee: Rev. Paul Esser, 3257 S. Lake Dr., Milwaukee, Wis. 53207.

Nashville: Rev. James K. Mallett, 2400 - 21st Ave. S., Nashville, Tenn. 37212.

Natchez-Jackson: Rev. Henry Shelton, 2225 Boling St., Jackson, Miss. 39205.

Newark: Rev. Msgr. Richard M. McGuinness, 221 W. Market St., Newark, N.J. 07103.

New Orleans: Rev. Peter J. Calamari, Rev. Crosby Kern, Rev. John C. Favarola, 2901 S. Carrollton Ave., New Orleans, La. 70118.

New York: Rev. Msgr. Austin Vaughan, St. Joseph Seminary, Dunwoodie, Yonkers, N.Y. 10704.

Oakland: Rev. Jerrold F. Kennedy, 2900 Lakeshore Ave., Oakland, Calif. 94610; also: Rev. James Schexnayder, 25580 Campus Dr., Hayward, Calif. 94542.

Oklahoma City: Rev. Philip Bryce, 3214 N. Lake Ave., Oklahoma City, Okla. 73118.

Omaha: Rev. Patrick McCaslin, 5316 N. 14th Ave., Omaha, Nebr. 68110.

Paterson: Rev. Kenneth E. Lasch, 80 13th Ave., Paterson 07504.

Peoria: Rev. J. Thomas Henseler, 904 E. Lake Ave., Peoria Heights, Ill. 61614.

Phoenix: Rev. R. William O'Brien, O. Carm., 400 E. Monroe St., Phoenix, Ariz. 85004.

Pittsburgh: Rev. George E. Saladna, 2900 Noblestown Rd., Pittsburgh, Pa. 15205.

Providence: Rev. John E. Tavares, Seminary College, Warwick, R.I. 02889.

Rapid City: Rev. Laurence Welsh, P.O. Box 752, Rapid City, S.D. 57701.

Richmond: Rev. Edward J. Bobinchock and Rev. N. Robert Quirin, 811 Cathedral Pl., Richmond, Va. 23220.

Rockford: Rev. Lawrence M. Urbaniak, Rural Rt. 2, Box 214-A, Rockford, Ill. 61102.

Saginaw: Rev. Richard Van Mullekom, 2555 Wieneke Rd., Saginaw, Mich. 48603.

St. Cloud: Rev. Kieran Nolan, O.S.B., St. John's University, Collegeville, Minn. 56321.

St. Louis: Rev. Clarence Deddens, 4445 Lindell Blvd., St. Louis, Mo. 63108.

St. Paul-Minneapolis: Rev. Michael J. O'Connell, 226 Summit Ave., St. Paul, Minn. 55102.

Salt Lake City: Revs. John J. Hedderman, Terence F. Moore, Robert J. Bussen and Joseph T. Fitzgerald, 333 E. S. Temple St., Salt Lake City, Utah 84111.

San Antonio: Rev. Alton Rudolph, 2600 W. Woodlawn Ave., San Antonio, Tex. 78284.

San Diego: Rev. Henry F. Fawcett, 5961 Linda Vista Rd., San Diego, Calif. 92110.

San Francisco: Rev. Msgr. Patrick J. O'Shea, 445 Church St., San Francisco, Calif. 94141; also Rev. Anthony E. McGuire, 4609 Alum Rock Ave., San Jose, Calif. 95127.

Santa Fe: Rev. Spencer Stopa, 9101 La Barranca N.E., Albuquerque, N.M. 87111.

Seattle: Rev. Michael G. Ryan, 907 Terry Ave., Seattle, Wash. 97104.

Toledo: Rev. Cleo Schmenk, 1933 Spielbusch Ave., Toledo, O. 43624.

Trenton: Rev. James P. McManimon, 230 Genesee St., Trenton, N.J. 08611.

Tucson: Rev. Charles Gehrman, Regina Cleri Seminary, P.O. Box 17090, Tucson, Ariz. 85731.

Tulsa: Rev. James White, P.O. Box 36, Poteau, Okla. 74953.

Washington: Rev. Msgr. W. George Curlin, 727 5th St. N.W., Washington, D.C. 20001.

Washington/Arlington: Rev. Robert Kearns, S.S.J., Josephite Training Center, 1200 Varnum St., N.E., Washington, D.C. 20017.

Wheeling-Charleston: Rev. Joseph W. Debias, P.O. Box 230, Wheeling, W. Va. 26003.

Worcester: Rev. Paul J. Tougas, 72 Pleasant St., Worcester, Mass. 01608.

Youngstown: Rev. David Rhodes, 144 W. Wood St., Youngstown, O. 44503.

U.S. Has Most Deacons

Of 1,600 permanent deacons in the world, 800 were in the U.S., according to an Aug. 8 1975, Vatican Radio report. Four hundred and 50 were in Europe, 200 in Latin America, about 70 in Africa, and seven in Asia.

MARRIAGE DOCTRINE

The following excerpts, stating key points of doctrine on marriage, are from the *Pastoral Constitution on the Church in the Modern World* (Nos. 48 to 51) promulgated by the Second Vatican Council.

Conjugal Covenant

"The intimate partnership of married life and love has been established by the Creator and qualified by His lawsm It is rooted in the conjugal covenant of irrevocable personal consent. . . .

". . . God Himself is the author of matrimony, endowed as it is with various benefits and purposes. All of these have a very decisive bearing on the continuation of the human race, on the personal development and eternal destiny of the individual members of a family, and on the dignity, stability, peace, and prosperity of the family itself and of human society as a whole. By their very nature, the institution of matrimony itself and conjugal love are ordained for the procreation and education of children, and find in them their ultimate crown.

"Thus a man and a woman . . . render mutual help and service to each other through an intimate union of their persons and of their actions. Through this union they experience the meaning of their oneness and attain to it with growing perfection day by day. As a mutual gift of two persons, this intimate union, as well as the good of the children, imposes total fidelity on the spouses and argues for an unbreakable oneness between them" (No. 48).

Sacrament of Matrimony

"Christ the Lord abundantly blessed this many-faceted love. . . . The Savior of men and the Spouse of the Church comes into the lives of married Christians through the sacrament of matrimony. He abides with them thereafter so that, just as He loved the Church and handed Himself over on her behalf, the spouses may love each other with perpetual fidelity through mutual self-bestowal.

". . . Graced with the dignity and office of fatherhood and motherhood, parents will energetically acquit themselves of a duty which devolves primarily on them, namely education, and especially religious education.

". . . The Christian family, which springs from marriage as a reflection of the loving covenant uniting Christ with the Church, and as a participation in that covenant, will manifest to all men the Savior's living presence in the world, and the genuine nature of the Church . . ." (No. 48).

Conjugal Love

"The biblical Word of God several times urges the betrothed and the married to nourish and develop their wedlock by pure conjugal love and undivided affection. . . .

"This love is an eminently human one since it is directed from one person to another through an affection of the will. It involves the good of the whole person. Therefore it can enrich the expressions of body and mind with a unique dignity, ennobling these expressions as special ingredients and signs of the friendship distinctive of marriage. This love the Lord has judged worthy of special gifts, healing, perfecting, and exalting gifts of grace and of charity.

"Such love, merging the human with the divine, leads the spouses to a free and mutual gift of themselves, a gift proving itself by gentle affection and by deed. Such love pervades the whole of their lives. Indeed, by its generous activity it grows better and grows greater. Therefore it far excels mere erotic inclination, which, selfishly pursued, soon enough fades wretchedly away.

"This love is uniquely expressed and perfected through the marital act. The actions within marriage by which the couple are united intimately and chastely are noble and worthy ones. Expressed in a manner which is truly human, these actions signify and promote that mutual self-giving by which spouses enrich each other with a joyful and a thankful will.

"Sealed by mutual faithfulness and hallowed above all by Christ's sacrament, this love remains steadfastly true in body and in mind, in bright days or dark. It will never be profaned by adultery or divorce. Firmly established by the Lord, the unity of marriage will radiate from the equal personal dignity of wife and husband, a dignity acknowledged by mutual and total love.

"The steady fulfillment of the duties of this Christian vocation demands notable virtue. For this reason, strengthened by grace for holiness of life, the couple will painstakingly cultivate and pray for constancy of love, largeheartedness, and the spirit of sacrifice . . ." (No. 49).

Fruitfulness of Marriage

"Marriage and conjugal love are by their nature ordained toward the begetting and educating of children. Children are really the supreme gift of marriage and contribute very substantially to the welfare of their parents. . . . God Himself . . . wished to share with man a certain special participation in His own creative work. Thus He blessed male and female, saying: 'Increase and multiply' (Gn. 1:28).

"Hence, while not making the other purposes of matrimony of less account, the true practice of conjugal love, and the whole meaning of the family life which results from it, have this aim: that the couple be ready with stout hearts to cooperate with the love of the

Creator and the Savior, who through them will enlarge and enrich His own family day by day.

"Parents should regard as their proper mission the task of transmitting human life and educating those to whom it has been transmitted. They should realize that they are thereby cooperators with the love of God the Creator, and are, so to speak, the interpreters of that love. Thus they will fulfill their task with human and Christian responsibility . . ." (No. 50).

Norms of Judgment

"They will thoughtfully take into account both their own welfare and that of their children, those already born and those which may be foreseen. For this accounting they will reckon with both the material and the spiritual conditions of the times as well as of their state in life. Finally, they will consult the interests of the family group, of temporal society, and of the Church herself.

"The parents themselves should ultimately make this judgment in the sight of God. But in their manner of acting, spouses should be aware that they cannot proceed arbitrarily. They must always be governed according to a conscience dutifully conformed to the divine law itself, and should be submissive toward the Church's teaching office, which authentically interprets that law in the light of the gospel. That divine law reveals and protects the integral meaning of conjugal love, and impels it toward a truly human fulfillment. . . .

"Marriage to be sure is not instituted solely for procreation. Rather, its very nature as an unbreakable compact between persons, and the welfare of the children, both demand that the mutual love of the spouses, too, be embodied in a rightly ordered manner, that it grow and ripen. Therefore, marriage persists as a whole manner and communion of life, and maintains its value and indissolubility, even when offspring are lacking — despite, rather often, the very intense desire of the couple" (No. 50).

Love and Life

"This Council realizes that certain modern conditions often keep couples from arranging their married lives harmoniously, and that they find themselves in circumstances where at least temporarily the size of their families should not be increased. As a result, the faithful exercise of love and the full intimacy of their lives are hard to maintain. But where the intimacy of married life is broken off, it is not rare for its faithfulness to be imperiled and its quality of fruitfulness ruined. For then the upbringing of the children and the courage to accept new ones are both endangered.

"To these problems there are those who presume to offer dishonorable solutions. Indeed, they do not recoil from the taking of life. But the Church issues the reminder that a

true contradiction cannot exist between the divine laws pertaining to the transmission of life and those pertaining to the fostering of authentic conjugal love.

"For God, the Lord of Life, has conferred on men the surpassing ministry of safeguarding life — a ministry which must be fulfilled in a manner which is worthy of men. Therefore from the moment of its conception life must be guarded with the greatest care, while abortion and infanticide are unspeakable crimes. The sexual characteristics of man and the human faculty of reproduction wonderfully exceed the dispositions of lower forms of life. Hence the acts themselves which are proper to conjugal love and which are exercised in accord with genuine human dignity must be honored with great reverence" (No. 51).

Church Teaching

"Therefore when there is question of harmonizing conjugal love with the responsible transmission of life, the moral aspect of any procedure does not depend solely on the sincere intentions or on an evaluation of motives. It must be determined by objective standards. These, based on the nature of the human person and his acts, preserve the full sense of mutual self-giving and human procreation in the context of true love. Such a goal cannot be achieved unless the virtue of conjugal chastity is sincerely practiced. Relying on these principles, sons of the Church may not undertake methods of regulating procreation which are found blameworthy by the teaching authority of the Church in its unfolding of the divine law.

"Everyone should be persuaded that human life and the task of transmitting it are not realities bound up with this world alone. Hence they cannot be measured or perceived only in terms of it, but always have a bearing on the eternal destiny of men" (No. 51).

Humanae Vitae

Marriage doctrine and morality were the subjects of the encyclical *Humanae Vitae* ("Of Human Life") issued by Pope Paul July 29, 1968. Following are a number of key excerpts from the document, which was framed in the pattern of traditional teaching and statements by the Second Vatican Council.

". . . each and every marriage act ('quilibet matrimonii usus') must remain open to the transmission of life" (No. 11).

"Indeed, by its intimate structure, the conjugal act, while most closely uniting husband and wife, capacitates them for the generation of new lives, according to laws inscribed in the very being of man and of woman. By safeguarding both these essential aspects, the unitive and the procreative, the conjugal act preserves in its fullness the sense of true mutual love and its ordination toward man's most high calling to parenthood" (No. 12).

"It is, in fact, justly observed that a conjugal act imposed upon one's partner without regard for his or her condition and lawful desires is not a true act of love, and therefore denies an exigency of right moral order in the relationships between husband and wife. Hence, one who reflects well must also recognize that a reciprocal act of love which jeopardizes the responsibility to transmit life — which God the Creator, according to particular laws, inserted therein — is in contradiction with the design constitutive of marriage and with the will of the Author of life. To use this divine gift, destroying, even if only partially, its meaning and its purpose, is to contradict the nature both of man and of woman and of their most intimate relationship, and therefore it is to contradict also the plan of God and His will" (No. 13).

Forbidden Actions: ". . . the direct interruption of the generative process already begun, and, above all, directly willed and procured abortion, even if for therapeutic reasons, are to be absolutely excluded as licit means of regulating birth.

"Equally to be excluded . . . is direct sterilization, whether perpetual or temporary, whether of the man or of the woman. Similarly excluded is every action which, either in anticipation of the conjugal act, or in its accomplishment, or in the development of its natural consequences, proposes, whether as an end or as a means, to render procreation impossible.

Inadmissible Principles: "To justify conjugal acts made intentionally infecund, one cannot invoke as valid reasons the lesser evil, or the fact that such acts would constitute a whole together with the fecund acts already performed or to follow later and hence would share in one and the same moral goodness. In truth, if it is sometimes licit to tolerate a lesser evil in order to avoid a greater evil or to promote a greater good, it is not licit, even for the gravest reasons, to do evil so that good may follow therefrom; that is, to make into the object of a positive act of the will something which is intrinsically disorder, and hence unworthy of the human person, even when the intention is to safeguard or promote individual, family or social well-being.

"Consequently, it is an error to think that a conjugal act which is deliberately made infecund, and so is intrinsically dishonest, could be made honest and right by the ensemble of a fecund conjugal life" (No. 14).

Rhythm: "If, then, there are serious motives to space out births, which derive from the physical or psychological conditions of husband and wife, or from external conditions, the Church teaches that it is then licit to take into account the natural rhythms immanent in the generative functions, for the use of marriage in the infecund periods only, and in this way to regulate birth without offending" earlier stated principles (No. 16).

Authoritative Teaching: Pope Paul called the foregoing teaching authoritative, although not infallible. He left it open for further study. As a practical norm to be followed, however, he said it involved the binding force of religious assent.

With pastoral concern, the Pope said: "We do not at all intend to hide the sometimes serious difficulties inherent in the life of Christian married persons; for them, as for everyone else, 'the gate is narrow and the way is hard that leads to life.' But the hope of that life must illuminate their way, as with courage they strive to live with wisdom, justice and piety in this present time, knowing that the figure of this world passes away.

"Let married couples, then, face up to the efforts needed, supported by the faith and hope which 'do not disappoint . . . because God's love has been poured into our hearts through the Holy Spirit, who has been given to us.' Let them implore divine assistance by persevering prayer; above all, let them draw from the source of grace and charity in the Eucharist. And, if sin should still keep its hold over them, let them not be discouraged but rather have recourse with humble perseverance to the mercy of God, which is poured forth in the sacrament of penance" (No. 25).

Reactions: Exception was taken to the binding force of the encyclical — notably by the bishops of Belgium, Austria and France, and many theologians — for several reasons: rights of conscience; questions concerning the natural-law concept underlying the encyclical; the thesis of totality; the proposition that contraception may in some cases be the lesser of two evils. All agreed, however, that conscientious objection to the encyclical could not be taken without serious reasons and reflection.

Pope Paul, since publication of the encyclical, has not moved to alter its contents or to mitigate its binding force.

MARRIAGE LAWS

The Catholic Church, in line with the belief that it was established and commissioned by Christ to provide and administer the means of salvation to men, claims jurisdiction over its members in matters pertaining to marriage, which is a sacrament. The purpose of its laws in this area is to safeguard the validity and lawfulness of marriage.

Catholics are bound by all marriage laws of the Church. Non-Catholics, whether baptized or not, are not considered bound by these ecclesiastical laws except in cases of marriage with a Catholic. Certain natural laws, in the Catholic view, bind all men and women, irrespective of their religious beliefs; accordingly, marriage is prohibited before the time of puberty, without knowledge and free mutual consent, in the case of an already existing valid marriage bond, in the case of antecedent and perpetual impotence.

Formalities

These include, in addition to arrangements for the time and place of the marriage ceremony, doctrinal and moral instruction concerning marriage and the recording of data which verifies in documentary form the eligibility and freedom of the persons to marry. Records of this kind, which are confidential, are preserved in the archives of the church where the marriage takes place.

Premarital instructions are the subject matter of Pre-Cana Conferences.

Mixed Marriages

Pastoral experience, which the Catholic Church shares with other religious bodies, confirms the fact that marriages of persons of different beliefs involve special problems related to the continuing religious practice of the concerned persons and to the religious education and formation of their children.

Pastoral measures to minimize these problems include instruction of a non-Catholic party in essentials of the Catholic faith for purposes of understanding. Desirably, some instruction should also be given the Catholic party regarding his or her partner's beliefs.

The Catholic party to a mixed marriage is required to declare his (her) intention of continuing practice of the Catholic faith and to promise to do all in his power to share his faith with children born of the marriage by having them baptized and raised as Catholics. No declarations or promises are required of the non-Catholic party, but he (she) must be informed of the declaration and promise made by the Catholic.

Notice of the Catholic's declaration and promise is an essential part of the application made to a bishop for dispensation from the impediment of mixed religion or disparity of worship (see below).

Mixed marriages may take place with a Nuptial Mass.

A non-Catholic minister may not only attend a marriage but may also address, pray with and give his blessing to the couple following the marriage ceremony.

If a dispensation from the canonical form of marriage is granted by a bishop, a non-Catholic minister can officiate at a mixed marriage.

Banns

The banns are public announcements made in their parish churches, usually on three successive Sundays, of the names of persons who intend to marry. Persons who know of reasons in church law why a proposed marriage should not take place, are obliged to make them known to the pastor.

Marital Consent

The exchange of consent to the marriage contract, which is essential for valid marriage, must be rational, free, true and mutual.

Matrimonial consent can be invalidated by an essential defect, substantial error, the strong influence of force and fear, the presence of a condition or intention against the nature of marriage.

Form of Marriage

A Catholic is required, for validity and lawfulness, to contract marriage — with another Catholic or with a non-Catholic — in the presence of a competent priest or deacon and two witnesses.

There are two exceptions to this law. A Roman Rite Catholic (since Mar. 25, 1967) or an Eastern Rite Catholic (since Nov. 21, 1964) can contract marriage validly in the presence of a priest of a separated Eastern Rite Church, provided other requirements of law are complied with. With permission of the competent Roman-Rite or Eastern-Rite bishop, this form of marriage is lawful, as well as valid. (See Eastern Rite Laws, below.)

With these two exceptions, and aside from cases covered by special permission, the Church does not regard as valid any marriages involving Catholics which take place before non-Catholic ministers of religion or civil officials. (See Mixed Marriage Guidelines.)

An excommunication formerly in force against Catholics who celebrated marriage before a non-Catholic minister was abrogated in a decree issued by the Sacred Congregation for the Doctrine of the Faith on Mar. 18, 1966.

The ordinary place of marriage is the parish of the bride, of the Catholic party in case of a mixed marriage, or of an Eastern Rite groom.

Church law regarding the form of marriage does not affect non-Catholics in marriages among themselves. The Church recognizes as valid the marriages of non-Catholics before ministers of religion and civil officials, unless they are rendered null and void on other grounds.

Impediments

Impediments to marriage are factors which render a marriage unlawful or invalid.

Prohibitory Impediments, which make a marriage unlawful but do not affect validity:

• simple vows of virginity, perpetual chastity, celibacy, to enter a religious order or to receive sacred orders;

• difference of religion, which obtains when one party is a Catholic and the other is a baptized non-Catholic.

The impediment of legal relationship is not in force in the US.

Diriment Impediments, which make a marriage invalid as well as unlawful:

• age, which obtains before completion of the 14th year for a woman and the 16th year for a man;

• impotency, if it is antecedent to the marriage and permanent (this differs from sterility, which is not an impediment);

• the bond of an existing valid marriage;

• disparity of worship, which obtains when one party is a Catholic and the other party is unbaptized;

• sacred orders;

• religious profession of the solemn vow of chastity;

• abduction, which impedes the freedom of the person abducted;

• crime, variously involving elements of adultery, promise or attempt to marry, conspiracy to murder a husband or wife;

• blood relationship in the direct line (father-daughter, mother-son, etc.) and within the third degree of the collateral line (brother-sister, first and second cousins);

• affinity, or relationship resulting from a valid marriage, in any degree of the direct line and within the second degree of the collateral line;

• spiritual relationship arising through baptism — between a godchild and godparent, between the person baptized and the one who performed the baptism;

• public honesty, arising from an invalid marriage or from public or notorious concubinage; it renders either party incapable of marrying relatives of the other in the first and second degrees of the direct line.

Dispensations from Impediments: Persons hindered by impediments either may not or cannot marry unless they are dispensed therefrom in view of reasons recognized in canon law. Local bishops can dispense from the impediments most often encountered (e.g., difference of religion, disparity of worship) as well as others.

Decision regarding some dispensations is reserved to the Holy See.

Separation

A valid and consummated marriage of baptized persons cannot be dissolved by any human authority or any cause other than the death of one of the persons.

In other circumstances:

• 1. A valid but unconsummated marriage of baptized persons, or of a baptized and an unbaptized person, can be dissolved:

a. by the solemn religious profession of one of the persons, made with permission of the pope. In such a case, the bond is dissolved at the time of profession, and the other person is free to marry again;

b. by dispensation from the pope, requested for a grave reason by one or both of the persons. If the dispensation is granted, both persons are free to marry again.

Dispensations in these cases are granted for reasons connected with the spiritual welfare of the concerned persons.

• 2. A legitimate marriage, even consummated, of unbaptized persons can be dissolved in favor of one of them who subsequently receives the sacrament of baptism. This is the Pauline Privilege, so called because it was promulgated by St. Paul (1 Cor. 7:12-15) as a means of protecting the faith of converts. Requisites for granting the privilege are:

a. marriage prior to the baptism of either person;

b. reception of baptism by one person;

c. refusal of the unbaptized person to live in peace with the baptized person and without interfering with his or her freedom to practice the Christian faith. The privilege does not apply if the unbaptized person agrees to these conditions.

• 3. A legitimate and consummated marriage of a baptized and an unbaptized person can be dissolved by the pope in virtue of the Privilege of Faith, also called the Petrine Privilege.

Civil Divorce: Because of the unity and the indissolubility of marriage, the Church denies that civil divorce can break the bond of a valid marriage, whether the marriage involves two Catholics, a Catholic and a non-Catholic, or non-Catholics with each other.

In view of serious circumstances of marital distress, the Church permits an innocent and aggrieved party, whether wife or husband, to seek and obtain a civil divorce for the purpose of acquiring title and right to the civil effects of divorce, such as separate habitation and maintenance, and the custody of children. Permission for this kind of action should be obtained from proper church authority. The divorce, if obtained, does not break the bond of a valid marriage.

Under other circumstances — as would obtain if a marriage was invalid (see Decree of Nullity, below) — civil divorce is permitted for civil effects and as a civil ratification of the fact that the marriage bond really does not exist.

In the United States, according to a decree of the Third Plenary Council of Baltimore, the penalty of excommunication is automatically incurred by persons who attempt to contract marriage after having obtained a divorce from a valid marriage.

Decree of Nullity, sometimes improperly called an annulment. This is a decision by a competent church authority — e.g., a bishop, a diocesan marriage tribunal, the Sacred Roman Rota — that an apparently valid marriage was actually invalid from the beginning because of the unknown or concealed existence, from the beginning, of a diriment impediment, an essential defect in consent, radical incapability for marriage, or a condition placed by one or both of the parties against the very nature of marriage.

Eastern Rite Laws

Marriage laws of the Eastern Church differ in several respects from the legislation of the Roman Rite. The regulations in effect since

May 2, 1949, were contained in the motu proprio *Crebre Allatae* issued by Pius XII the previous February.

According to both the Roman Code of Canon Law and the Oriental Code, marriages between Roman Rite Catholics and Eastern Rite Catholics ordinarily take place in the rite of the groom and have canonical effects in that rite.

Regarding the form for the celebration of marriages between Eastern Catholics and baptized Eastern non-Catholics, the Second Vatican Council declared:

"By way of preventing invalid marriages between Eastern Catholics and baptized Eastern non-Catholics, and in the interests of the permanence and sanctity of marriage and of domestic harmony, this sacred Synod decrees that the canonical 'form' for the celebration of such marriages obliges only for lawfulness. For their validity, the presence of a sacred minister suffices, as long as the other requirements of law are honored" *(Decree on Eastern Catholic Churches,* No. 18).

Marriages taking place in this manner are lawful, as well as valid, with permission of a competent Eastern Rite bishop.

The Rota

The Sacred Roman Rota is the ordinary court of appeal for marriage, and some other cases, which are appealed to the Holy See from lower church courts. Appeals are made to the Rota if decisions by diocesan and archdiocesan courts fail to settle the matter in dispute.

MIXED MARRIAGES

Following are excerpts from a statement, *Implementation of the Apostolic Letter on Mixed Marriages,* approved by the National Conference of Catholic Bishops Nov. 16, 1970, and effective in the US since Jan. 1, 1971. The text of the statement was circulated by NC News Service. The text of the letter on which the statement was based, *Matrimonia Mixta,* was issued by Pope Paul VI Mar. 31, 1970; it appeared in the 1971 edition of the Almanac, pp. 278-81.

Aim of Church

Within marriage the Church seeks always to uphold the strength and stability of marital union and the family which flows from it.

As the Apostolic Letter observes, the "perfect union of mind and full communion of life" to which married couples aspire can be more readily achieved when both partners share the same Catholic belief and life. For this reason, the Church greatly desires that Catholics marry Catholics and generally discourages mixed marriages.

Yet, recognizing that mixed marriages do occur, the Church, upholding the principles of Divine Law, makes special arrangements for them. And, recognizing that these marriages do at times encounter special difficulties, the Church wishes to see that special help and support are extended to the couples concerned.

Pastoral Concern

The Apostolic Letter stresses the importance of individualized support for diverse situations. It recognizes that ". . . the canonical discipline on mixed marriages cannot be uniform and must be adapted . . ." and "the pastoral care to be given to the married people and children of marriage" must also be adapted "according to the distinct circumstances of the married couple and the differing degrees of their ecclesiastical communion." Consequently, pastors, in exercising their ministry in behalf of marriages that unite Catholics and others will do so with zealous concern and respect for the couples involved. They should have an active and positive regard for the holy state in which such couples are united.

In such marriages, the conscientious devotion of the Catholic to the Catholic Church is to be safeguarded, and the conscience of the other partner is to be respected. This is in keeping with the principle of religious liberty. (Cf. *Declaration on Religious Freedom,* No. 30.)

Values in Marriage

The sacred character of all valid marriages, including those which the Church does not consider as sacramental, is recognized.

The broad areas of agreement which unite Christians and Jews in their appreciation of the religious character of marriage should be kept significantly in mind. (Cf. *Joint Statement on Marriage and Family Life in the United States,* issued by the United States Catholic Conference, the National Council of the Churches of Christ, and the Synagogue Council of America, June 8, 1966.)

In this context, it should be clearly noted that, while Catholics are required to observe the Catholic form of marriage for validity, unless dispensed by their bishop, the Catholic Church recognizes the reality of marriages contracted validly among those who are not Christians and among those Christians separated from us.

Sacramental Marriage

In addition to the sacred character of all valid marriages, still more must be said of marriages between a Catholic and another baptized Christian. According to our Catholic tradition, we believe such marriages to be truly sacramental. The Apostolic Letter states that there exists between the persons united in them a special "communion of spiritual benefits." These spiritual bonds in which couples are united are grounded in the "true though imperfect, communion" which exists between the Catholic Church and all who believe in

Christ and are properly baptized (cf. *Decree on Ecumenism,* No. 3). Along with us, such persons are honored by the title of Christian and are rightly regarded as brothers in the Lord. In marriages which unite Catholics and other baptized Christians, the couple should be encouraged to recognize in practical ways what they share together in the life of grace, in faith, hope and charity along with other interior gifts of the Holy Spirit, and that in service to the same Lord they await the salvation which He promised to those who would be His followers.

Difficulties

A number of the particular difficulties faced by Catholics and other Christians in mixed marriages result from the division among Christians. However successful these marriages may be, they do not erase the pain of that wider division. Yet this division need not weaken these marriages; and, given proper understanding, they may lead to a deep spiritual unity between the spouses.

Joint Pastoral Care

In order to aid these couples to come to this deep understanding of their married life together, when possible, their Catholic and other Christian pastors should jointly do all that they can to prepare them for marriage and to support them and their families with all the aids their ministry can provide.

The pastors of the different Christian communities can best bring the couple to a keen awareness of all that they have in common as Christians as well as to a proper appreciation of the gravity of the differences that yet remain between their churches.

In their homes, these couples should be encouraged in practical ways to develop a common life of prayer, calling upon the many elements of spirituality which they share as a common Christian heritage and expressing their own common faith in the Lord, together asking Him to help them grow in their love for each other, to bless their families with the graces they need, and to keep them always mindful of the needs of others. The example of parents united in prayer is especially important for the children whom God may give them. In regard to public worship together in each other's churches, pastors may explain to the couple the provisions made for this by the Holy See in the *Ecumenical Directory.*

Religious Education

Beyond this, parents have the right and the responsibility to provide for the religious education of their children. This right is clearly taught by Vatican II: "Since the family is a society in its own original right, it has the right freely to live its own domestic religious life under the guidance of parents. Parents, moreover, have the right to determine, in accordance with their own religious beliefs, the kind of religious education that their children are to receive" *(Declaration on Religious Freedom,* No. 5).

It is evident that in preparing for a mixed marriage, the couple will have to reach decisions and make specific choices in order to fulfill successfully the responsibility that is theirs toward their children in this respect. It is to be hoped for their own sake that in this matter the couple may reach a common mind.

If this issue is not resolved before marriage, the couple, as sad experience has shown, find a severe strain in their marital life that can subject them to well-meaning but tension-building pressures from relatives on both sides.

If this issue cannot be resolved, there is a serious question whether the couple should marry.

In reaching a concrete decision concerning the baptism and religious education of children, both partners should remember that neither thereby abdicates the fundamental responsibility of parents to see that their children are instilled with deep and abiding religious values.

In this the Catholic partner is seriously bound to act in accord with his faith which recognizes that: "This is the unique Church of Christ which in the Creed we avow as one, holy, catholic and apostolic. After His Resurrection our Savior handed her over to Peter to be shepherded (Jn. 21:17), commissioning him and the other apostles to propagate and govern her (cf. Mt. 28:18, ff.). Her He erected for all ages as 'the pillar and mainstay of the truth,' (1 Tm. 3:15). This Church, constituted and organized in the world as a society, subsists in the Catholic Church, which is governed by the successor of Peter and by the bishops in union with that successor, although many elements of sanctification and of truth can be found outside of her visible structure. These elements, however, as gifts properly belonging to the Church of Christ, possess an inner dynamism toward Catholic unity" *(Dogmatic Constitution on the Church,* No. 8). This faith is the source of a serious obligation in conscience on the part of the Catholic, whose conscience in this regard must be respected.

Norms

Pastoral Responsibility: In every diocese, there shall be appropriate informational programs to explain both the reasons for restrictions upon mixed marriages and the positive spiritual values to be sought in such marriages when permitted. This is particularly important if the non-Catholic is a Christian believer and the unity of married and family life is ultimately based upon the baptism of both wife and husband. If possible, all such programs should be undertaken . . . in conjunction with non-Catholic authorities.

In addition to the customary marriage

preparation programs, it is the serious duty of each one in the pastoral ministry, according to his own responsibility, office or assignment, to undertake:

(a) the spiritual and catechetical preparation, especially in regard to the "ends and essential properties of marriage (which) are not to be excluded by either party" (cf. *Matrimonia Mixta,* No. 6), on a direct and individual basis, of couples who seek to enter a mixed marriage, and

(b) continued concern and assistance to the wife and husband in mixed marriages and to their children, so that married and family life may be supported in unity, respect for conscience, and common spiritual benefit.

In the assistance which he gives in preparation for marriage between a Catholic and a non-Catholic, and his continued efforts to help all married couples and families, the priest should endeavor to be in contact and to cooperate with the minister or religious counselor of the non-Catholic.

Promise: The declaration and promise by the Catholic, necessary for dispensation from the impediment to a mixed marriage (either mixed religion or disparity of worship), shall be made in the following words or their substantial equivalent:

"I reaffirm my faith in Jesus Christ and, with God's help, intend to continue living that faith in the Catholic Church.

"I promise to do all in my power to share the faith I have received with our children by having them baptized and reared as Catholics."

The declaration and promise are made in the presence of a priest or deacon either orally or in writing as the Catholic prefers.

The form of the declaration and promise is not altered in the case of the marriage of a Catholic with another baptized Christian, but the priest should draw the attention of the Catholic to the communion of spiritual benefits in such a Christian marriage. The promise and declaration should be made in the light of the "certain, though imperfect, communion" of the non-Catholic with the Catholic Church because of his belief in Christ and baptism (cf. *Decree on Ecumenism,* No. 3).

Informing the Non-Catholic: At an opportune time before marriage, and preferably as part of the usual premarital instruction, the non-Catholic must be informed of the promises and of the responsibility of the Catholic. No precise manner or occasion of informing the non-Catholic is prescribed. It may be done by the priest, deacon or the Catholic party. No formal statement of the non-Catholic is required. But the mutual understanding of this question beforehand should prevent possible disharmony that might otherwise arise during married life.

The priest who submits the request for dispensation from the impediment to a mixed marriage shall certify that the declaration and

promise have been made by the Catholic and that the non-Catholic has been informed of this requirement. This is done in the following or similar words:

"The required promise and declaration have been made by the Catholic in my presence. The non-Catholic has been informed of this requirement so that it is certain that he (she) is aware of the promise and obligation on the part of the Catholic."

The promise of the Catholic must be sincerely made, and is to be presumed to be sincerely made. If, however, the priest has reason to doubt the sincerity of the promise made by the Catholic, he may not recommend the request for the dispensation and should submit the matter to the local Ordinary.

Form, Ceremony of Marriage: Where there are serious difficulties in observing the Catholic canonical form in a mixed marriage, the local Ordinary of the Catholic party or of the place where the marriage is to occur may dispense the Catholic from the observance of the form for a just pastoral cause. An exhaustive list is impossible, but the following are the types of reasons: to achieve family harmony or to avoid family alienation, to obtain parental agreement to the marriage, to recognize the significant claims of relationship or special friendship with a non-Catholic minister, to permit the marriage in a church that has particular importance to the non-Catholic. If the Ordinary of the Catholic party grants a dispensation for a marriage which is to take place in another diocese, the Ordinary of that diocese should be informed beforehand.

Ordinarily this dispensation from the canonical form is granted in view of the proposed celebration of a religious marriage service. In some exceptional circumstances (e.g., certain Catholic-Jewish marriages) it may be necessary that the dispensation be granted so that a civil ceremony may be performed. In any case, a public form that is civilly recognized for the celebration of marriage is required.

It is not permitted to have two religious marriage services or to have a single service in which both the Catholic marriage ritual and a non-Catholic marriage ritual are celebrated jointly or successively (cf. *Matrimonia Mixta,* No. 13).

With the permission of the local Ordinary and the consent of the appropriate authority of the other church or community, a non-Catholic minister may be invited to participate in the Catholic marriage service by giving additional prayers, blessings, or words of greeting or exhortation. If the marriage is not part of the Eucharistic celebration, the minister may also be invited to read a lesson and/or to preach (cf. *Directory on Ecumenism* Part I, No. 56).

In the case where there has been a dispensation from the Catholic canonical form and the priest has been invited to participate in the non-Catholic marriage service, with the permission of the local Ordinary and the consent of the appropriate authority of the other church or communion, he may do so by giving additional prayers, blessings, or words of greeting and exhortation. If the marriage service is not part of the Lord's Supper or the principal liturgical service of the Word, the priest, if invited, may also read a lesson and/or preach (cf. *Ibid*).

To the extent that Eucharistic sharing is not permitted by the general discipline of the Church, this is to be considered when plans are being made to have the mixed marriage at Mass or not.

Place of Marriage: The ordinary place of marriage is in the parish church or other sacred place. For serious reasons, the local Ordinary may permit the celebration of a mixed marriage, when there has been no dispensation from the canonical form and the Catholic marriage service is to be celebrated, outside a Catholic church or chapel, providing there is no scandal involved and proper delegation is granted (for example, where there is no Catholic church in the area, etc.).

If there has been a dispensation from canonical form, ordinarily the marriage service is celebrated in a non-Catholic church.

PROCEDURAL RULES

Pope Paul VI promulgated, June 11, 1971, a set of 13 rules designed to speed up the handling of cases in which the validity of marriage is questioned. Norms given in the document, which was issued by the Pope on his own initiative and became effective Oct.31, concern "the constitution of ecclesiastical tribunals and . . . the judicial process which will expedite the matrimonial process itself."

The norms do not affect the reasons for the validity or invalidity of marriages, but only the way in which cases of this kind are handled in church courts.

Pope Paul told judges of the Roman Rota Jan. 30, 1975, that national conferences of bishops seemed "unanimously satisfied" with the procedures authorized in 1971. He also said: "We strongly hope that, with the promulgation of the new code of procedures, unnecessary differences among various ecclesiastical regions will be removed."

U. S. Norms

Twenty-three experimental norms — drawn up by the Canon Law Society of America, approved by the National Conference of Catholic Bishops and the Holy See, and in effect since July, 1970 — were broader in some respects than those decreed by Pope Paul. Among other things, they provided for: one-priest tribunals for specific periods of time instead of just for individual cases; dispensation by the NCCB from the need for review of first decisions regarding the validity

or invalidity of a marriage; circumstances affecting the competence of tribunals. Continuing use of the experimental procedural norms was authorized by Paul VI in a letter dated May 22 and announced June 8, 1974 — "until the new order of matrimonial court procedure is promulgated for the Latin Church" in connection with the on-going revision of the Code of Canon Law. Termination of their use had been scheduled for June 30, 1974, following an original authorization for one year and an extension for three more years.

Cases of Non-Consummation

Pope Paul VI promulgated May 31, 1972, norms designed to speed up the handling of cases involving questions about the validity of marriages entered legally but never consummated sexually. The regulations which went into effect July 1, granted local bishops powers previously reserved to the Holy See.

Accordingly local bishops can initiate procedures in cases of this type; testimony and documents are acceptable in any modern language and on tape; physical proof of non-consummation can be omitted if the bishop is satisfied with the statements of the parties and/or witnesses; the number of witnesses is left to the discretion of the bishop.

ERRONEOUS OPINIONS

The Congregation for the Doctrine of the Faith advised bishops throughout the world in August, 1973, that erroneous opinions concerning the indissolubility of marriage were being circulated "in books, Catholic newspapers, and even in seminaries and Catholic schools; and also, in practice, in some ecclesiastical tribunals."

"These opinions," the letter said, "are being used . . . to justify abuses . . . contrary to the present discipline governing the admission to the sacraments of persons who live in irregular (matrimonial) unions."

Among the abuses was a "good conscience procedure" reported from several quarters — i.e., the administration of the sacraments to divorced and remarried Catholics who were unable to obtain a decree of nullity from the Church for their first marriage and were living in a subsequent civil marriage "in good faith."

Accepted norms in force state that the sacraments may be administered to separated or divorced persons who have not remarried; to those who have received a declaration of nullity regarding the previous marriage; and to those who, although remarried, are living in a brother-sister relationship of sexual continence.

DEFENSE OF MARRIAGE

Pope Paul, in an address to judges of the Roman Rota Jan. 30, 1975, said their first concern had to be the defense of values which, "for biblical, theological and rational reasons beyond dispute, bear the character of inviolable authority. These are values which we must recognize as decreed by divine law and which are therefore holy declarations" of the Church's teaching authority. He declared that the "most frequent and serious" task of tribunals was defense of the "indissolubility of a true and perfect marriage, that is, one which is ratified and consummated."

The Holy Father also called the attention of the judges to the need for a "clear and inflexible defense of the institution of marriage and, by consequence, of the institution of the family — the fundamental basis for a moral, healthy and civilized society."

YOUNG MARRIAGE GUIDELINES

In an effort to forestall the break-up of marriages, especially those of young couples, a number of dioceses in the U.S. have formulated and put into effect in recent years special guidelines to be followed with respect to prospective marriages of persons under ages ranging from 18 to 21.

Dioceses which took such action in 1975 included Orlando, Jefferson City, San Antonio, Boston and Davenport. All dioceses in New Jersey instituted a common policy and procedure regarding marriages of persons of all ages; the effective date was Jan. 1, 1976.

The general purpose of the guidelines is to determine and develop the maturity and capabilities of the parties to make the full and permanent commitment of marriage. Specific items cover: advance arrangement for marriage; a period of waiting, to avoid hasty and ill-considered unions; consultation with a priest for discussion and understanding of the doctrine and practice of the Church regarding marriage; participation in Pre-Cana conferences and/or other marriage preparation courses and consultations covering non-sacramental as well as sacramental aspects of marriage.

EUCHARISTIC MINISTERS

The designation of lay men and women to serve as extraordinary ministers of the Eucharist was authorized by Pope Paul in an "Instruction on Facilitating Communion in Particular Circumstances" *(Immensae Caritatis)*, dated Jan. 29, 1973, and published by the Congregation for Divine Worship the following Mar. 29.

Qualified lay persons may serve as extraordinary ministers for specific occasions or extended periods in the absence of a sufficient number of priests and deacons to provide reasonable and appropriate pastoral service in the distribution of Holy Communion, during Mass and outside of Mass (to the sick and shut-ins).

Appointments of extraordinary ministers are made by priests with the approval of the appropriate bishop.

Many parishes and church institutions throughout the United States have extraordinary ministers of the Eucharist.

COMMUNION IN HAND

(Source: *Notitiae*, the official bulletin of the Congregation for Divine Worship.)

The Holy See has approved in recent years the practice of in-hand reception of Holy Communion in regions and countries where it had the approval of the appropriate bishops' conferences. Areas with this practice and the dates of approval are as follows.

Europe

Belgium (May, 1969), France and Germany (June, 1969), The Netherlands and Czechoslovakia (September, 1969), Luxembourg, Scandinavia and Monaco (October, 1969), Austria (February, 1970), Scotland (February, 1975).

Africa

North Africa (October 1969), Central Africa (February, 1970), Gabon (March, 1970), Upper Volta and Niger (February, 1971), Rhodesia (October, 1971), Madagascar (May, 1972), Mozambique (October, 1972), Angola (September, 1973), Zambia (March, 1974), Mali (July, 1974).

Asia and Oceania

Japan (June, 1970), Indonesia (March, 1971), Korea (January, 1974), New Zealand (April, 1974).

Central and South America

Bolivia and Uruguay (October, 1969), Paraguay (September, 1971), Panama (May, 1973), Chile (June, 1973), Costa Rica (September, 1973), Peru and Brazil (March, 1975).

North America

Canada (February, 1970).

Proposals to introduce in-hand reception of Communion in the United States have failed on two occasions to gain the approval of a two-thirds majority vote of the National Conference of Catholic Bishops.

CHANT CENTERS

Msgr. Robert E. Brennan, former archdiocesan director of music, announced in September, 1975, that four Gregorian Chant training centers would be established in the Los Angeles area, in response to "a growing movement" for chant as part of liturgical prayer.

LATIN LITURGY ASSOCIATION

A Latin Liturgy Association, calling for public celebrations of the new order of the Mass in Latin as well as in the vernacular, was established in August 1975, in St. Louis. The group said it was not the intention of the Second Vatican Council to extinguish Latin from the public prayer of the Church.

The Church Calendar

The calendar of the Roman Church consists of an arrangement throughout the year of a series of liturgical seasons and feasts of saints for purposes of divine worship.

The purposes of this calendar were outlined in the *Constitution on the Sacred Liturgy* (Nos. 102-105) promulgated by the Second Vatican Council.

"Within the cycle of a year . . . (the Church) unfolds the whole mystery of Christ, not only from His incarnation and birth until His ascension, but also as reflected in the day of Pentecost, and the expectation of a blessed, hoped-for return of the Lord.

"Recalling thus the mysteries of redemption, the Church opens to the faithful the riches of her Lord's powers and merits, so that these are in some way made present at all times, and the faithful are enabled to lay hold of them and become filled with saving grace" (No. 102).

"In celebrating this annual cycle of Christ's mysteries, holy Church honors with special love the Blessed Mary, Mother of God . . ." (No. 103).

"The Church has also included in the annual cycle days devoted to the memory of the martyrs and the other saints. . . . (who) sing God's perfect praise in heaven and offer prayers for us. By celebrating the passage of these saints from earth to heaven the Church proclaims the paschal mystery as achieved in the saints who have suffered and been glorified with Christ; she proposes them to the faithful as examples who draw all to the Father through Christ, and through their merits she pleads for God's favors" (No. 104).

". . . In the various seasons of the year and according to her traditional discipline, the Church completes the formation of the faithful by means of pious practices for soul and body, by instruction, prayer, and works of penance and mercy. . ." (No. 105).

THE REVISED CALENDAR

Pope Paul announced May 9, 1969, his approval of a reorganization of the liturgical year and calendar for the Roman Rite, in implementation of a directive from the Second Vatican Council in 1964. He made the announcement in a document issued on his own initiative and entitled *Paschalis Mysterii.*

The purpose of the action, the Pope said, was "no other . . . than to permit the faithful to communicate in a more intense way, through faith, hope and love, in 'the whole mystery of Christ which . . . unfolds within the cycle of a year.' "

The motu proprio was dated Feb. 14, 1969. The new calendar was promulgated a month later by a decree of the Congregation for Divine Worship and went into effect Jan. 1, 1970, with provisional modifications. Full im-plementation of all its parts was delayed in 1970 and 1971, pending the completion of work on related liturgical texts. The U.S. bishops ordered the whole new calendar into effect for 1972.

The revised calendar, whose principal architect was Father Pierre Jounel, professor of liturgy at the Catholic University of Paris, involved some restructuring of the liturgical cycles and changes affecting the feasts of saints.

The Seasons

Advent: The liturgical year begins with the First Sunday of Advent, which introduces a season of four weeks or slightly less duration with the theme of expectation of the coming of Christ. During the first two weeks, the final coming of Christ as Lord and Judge at the end of the world is the focus of attention. From Dec. 17 to 24, the emphasis shifts to anticipation of the celebration of his Nativity on the feast of Christmas.

Advent has four Sundays. Since the 10th century, the first Sunday has marked the beginning of the liturgical year in the Western Church. In the Middle Ages, a kind of pre-Christmas fast was in vogue during the season.

Christmastide: Christmastide opens with the feast of the Nativity, Dec. 25, and lasts until the Sunday after Epiphany. The Holy Family is commemorated on the Sunday within the Christmas octave. Jan. 1 — formerly called the Octave Day of the Nativity and, before that, the feast of the Circumcision of Jesus — has the title of Solemnity of Mary the Mother of God. The Epiphany, scheduled for Jan. 6 in the universal calendar, is celebrated in the U.S. on the Sunday between Jan. 2 and 8. The Baptism of the Lord, observed on the Sunday following Epiphany, marks the end of Christmastide.

The period between the end of Christmas-tide and the beginning of Lent belongs to the Ordinary Time of the year. Of variable length, the pre-Lenten phase of this season includes what were formerly called the Sundays after Epiphany and the suppressed Sundays of Septuagesima, Sexagesima and Quinquagesima.

Lent: The penitential season of Lent begins on Ash Wednesday, which occurs between Feb. 4 and Mar. 11, depending on the date of Easter, and lasts until Easter. It has six Sundays and 40 weekdays. The climactic last week is called Holy Week. The last three days (Holy Thursday, Good Friday and Holy Saturday) are called the Paschal Triduum.

The origin of Lenten observances dates back to the fourth century or earlier.

Eastertide: Eastertide, whose theme is resurrection from sin to the life of grace, lasts for

50 days, from Easter to Pentecost. Easter, the first Sunday following the vernal equinox, occurs between Mar. 22 and Apr. 25. The terminal phase of Eastertide, between the feast of the Ascension of the Lord and Pentecost, stresses anticipation of the coming and action of the Holy Spirit.

Ordinary Time: The season of Ordinary Time of the year includes not only the period between the end of Christmastide and the beginning of Lent, as noted above, but also all Sundays after Pentecost to the last Sunday of the liturgical year, which is celebrated as the feast of Christ the King. The number of Sundays before Lent and after Pentecost varies, depending on the date of the key feast of Easter. The overall purpose of the season is to elaborate the themes of salvation history.

The various liturgical seasons are characterized in part by the scriptural readings and Mass prayers assigned to each of them. During Advent, for example, the readings are messianic; during Eastertide, from the Acts of the Apostles, chronicling the Resurrection and the original proclamation of Christ by the Apostles, and from the Gospel of John; during Lent, baptismal and penitential passages. Mass prayers reflect the meaning and purpose of the various seasons.

Feasts of Saints

The feasts of saints are celebrated concurrently with the liturgical seasons and feasts of our Lord. Their purpose always has been to illustrate the paschal mysteries as reflected in the lives of saints, to honor them as heroes of holiness, and to appeal for their intercession. For various reasons, however, the number and variety of feasts distracted attention to some degree from the central mysteries of redemption and the universality of holiness in the Church. To remedy these defects, Pope Paul ordered a number of significant changes affecting the feasts of saints.

In line with revised regulations, some feasts were either abolished or relegated to observance in particular places by local option for one of two reasons: (1) lack of sufficient historical evidence for observance of the feasts; (2) lack of universal significance. More than 40 feasts were eliminated; 92 were made optional for particular places, e.g., the diocese or country in which a saint was martyred; more than 60 were ordered for observance throughout the Roman Rite.

Commenting on the elimination of some feasts, *L'Osservatore Della Domenica,* the Vatican City weekly, said: "Generally, the removal of a name from the calendar does not mean passing judgment on the nonexistence (of a saint) or lack of holiness. Many (saints) have been removed (from the calendar) because all that remains certain about them is their name, and this would say too little to the faithful in comparison with many others.

Other feasts were removed because they lacked universal significance."

Traditional feasts of our Lord have been retained, except for those of the Holy Name and the Precious Blood which were suppressed.

Most feasts of Blessed Mary the Virgin have been retained. Universal observance obtains for the feasts of the Assumption, Immaculate Conception, Birth, Annunciation (of Our Lord), Presentation of the Lord, Visitation, Our Lady of Sorrows, Our Lady of the Rosary, Presentation, Queenship. Local option governs celebration of the memorials of Our Lady of Lourdes, Our Lady of Mt. Carmel, Dedication of (the Basilica of) St. Mary Major, the Immaculate Heart.

St. Joseph, Husband of Mary, is honored universally on Mar. 19 and by local option on another date (feast of St. Joseph the Worker, which may be observed May 1).

The archangels — Michael, Raphael and Gabriel — are honored with a common feast, Sept. 29, instead of with three separate feasts as before. The feast of the Guardian Angels, Oct. 2, stands.

The traditional feasts of the Apostles and Evangelists have been retained, with several date changes. Sts. Peter and Paul, who are honored with a common feast June 29, each has an additional feast on Feb. 22 (Chair of St. Peter) and Jan. 25 (Conversion of St. Paul).

Other saints, as noted above, are honored on universal and optional feasts throughout the year.

The universality of holiness in the Church is reflected in the distribution of feasts among saints of different periods and locations. Sixty-four saints are of the first 10 centuries, 79 of the last 10 centuries. Most represented are the fourth century (25 saints), the 12th (12), the 16th (17), and the 17th (17). Geographically, there are 126 feasts of European saints, 14 of Asians, eight of Africans, four of Americans, and one of a saint of Oceania.

The feast of a saint, as a general rule, is observed on the day of his death *(dies natalis,* day of birth to glory with God in heaven). Exceptions to this rule include the feasts of St. John the Baptist, who is honored on the day of his birth; Sts. Basil the Great and Gregory Nazianzen, and the brother Saints, Cyril and Methodius, who are commemorated in joint feasts.

Application of this general rule in the revised calendar resulted in date changes of some feasts.

Sundays and Feast Days

Sunday is the original Christian feast day because of the unusually significant events of salvation history which took place and are commemorated on the first day of the week — viz., the Resurrection of Christ, the key event of his life and the fundamental fact of

Christianity; and the descent of the Holy Spirit upon the Apostles on Pentecost, the birthday of the Church. The transfer of observance of the Lord's Day from the Sabbath to Sunday was made in apostolic times. The Mass and Liturgy of the Hours (Divine Office) of each Sunday reflect the themes and set the tones of the various liturgical seasons.

Categories of feasts according to dignity and manner of observance are: solemnity (highest, corresponding to former first-class feasts); feast (corresponding to former second-class feasts); memorial (corresponding to former third-class feasts); optional memorial (observable by local choice). Feasts of the first three categories are observed universally in the Roman Rite.

Fixed feasts are those which are regularly celebrated on the same calendar day each year.

Movable feasts are those which are not observed on the same calendar day each year. Examples of these are Easter (the first Sunday after the first full moon following the vernal equinox), Ascension (40 days after Easter), Pentecost (50 days after Easter), Trinity Sunday (first after Pentecost), Christ the King (last Sunday of the liturgical year).

Holy Days of Obligation

Holy days of obligation are special feasts on which Catholics who have reached the age of reason are seriously obliged, as on Sundays, to assist at Mass and to avoid unnecessary servile work. Serious reasons excuse from the observance of either or both of these obligations.

By enactment of the Third Plenary Council of Baltimore, and with the approval of the Holy See, the holy days of obligation observed in the United States are: Christmas, the Nativity of Jesus, Dec. 25; Solemnity of Mary the Mother of God, Jan. 1; Ascension of the Lord; Assumption of Blessed Mary the Virgin, Aug. 15; All Saints' Day, Nov. 1; Immaculate Conception of Blessed Mary the Virgin, Dec. 8.

In addition to these, there are four other holy days of obligation prescribed in the general law of the Church which are not so observed in the U.S.: Epiphany; St. Joseph, Mar. 19; Corpus Christi; Sts. Peter and Paul, June 29.

Ferial, Ember, Rogation Days

Ferial days are weekdays on which no proper feast or vigil is celebrated in the Mass or Liturgy of the Hours (Divine Office). On such days, the Mass may be that of the preceding Sunday, which expresses the liturgical spirit of the season, an optional memorial, a votive Mass, or a Mass for the dead. Ferial days of Advent and Lent are in a special category of their own.

Aside from feast-day considerations, Monday through Friday are called ferial days, and

are consecutively numbered from two to six. The first day of the week is Sunday or the Lord's Day, and the seventh is called the Sabbath.

Ember days originated at Rome about the fifth century, probably as Christian replacements for seasonal festivals of agrarian cults. They were observances of penance, thanksgiving, and petition for divine blessing on the various seasons; they also were occasions of special prayer for clergy to be ordained. These days were observed four times a year: on the Wednesday, Friday and Saturday following the Third Sunday of Advent, the First Sunday of Lent, Pentecost, and the third Sunday of September. In line with the calendar reform of 1969, decision with respect to the observance of ember days rests with the National Conference of Catholic Bishops.

Rogation days originated in France about the fifth century. They were penitential in character and also occasions of prayer for a bountiful harvest and protection against evil. Minor days of rogation were observed on the three days before the feast of the Ascension; Apr. 25 was a day of major rogation. In line with the calendar reform of 1969, decision with respect to the observance of rogation days rests with the National Conference of Catholic Bishops.

Days of Abstinence and Fast

The apostolic constitution *Paenitemini*, in effect since Feb. 23, 1966, authorized the substitution of other works of penance for the customary and common observances of abstinence and fast on various days of the year.

In this country, in line with provisions of the constitution and a 1974 decision of the National Conference of Catholic Bishops, Ash Wednesday and Good Friday are days of fast and abstinence, and all Fridays of Lent are days of abstinence.

The obligation to abstain from meat binds Catholics 14 years of age and older. The obligation to fast, limiting oneself to one full meal and two lighter meals in the course of a day, binds Catholics from the ages of 21 to 59.

BYZANTINE CALENDAR

The Byzantine-Rite calendar has many distinctive features of its own, although it shares common elements with the Roman-Rite calendar—e.g., general purpose, commemoration of the mysteries of faith and of the saints, identical dates for some feasts. Among the distinctive things are the following.

The liturgical year begins on Sept. 1, the **Day of Indiction,** in contrast with the Latin or Roman start on the First Sunday of Advent late in November or early in December. The Advent season begins on Dec. 10.

Cycles of the Year

As in the Roman usage, the dating of feasts follows the Gregorian Calendar. Formerly, until well into this century, the Julian Calendar was used. (The Julian Calendar, which is now about 13 days late, is still used by some Eastern-Rite Churches.)

The year has several cycles, which include proper seasons, the feasts of saints, and series of New Testament readings. All of these elements of worship are contained in liturgical books of the rite.

The ecclesiastical calendar, called the **Menologion,** explains the nature of feasts, other observances and matters pertaining to the liturgy for each day of the year. In some cases, its contents include the lives of saints and the history and meaning of feasts.

The Divine Liturgy (Mass) and Divine Office for the proper of the saints, fixed feasts, and the Christmas season are contained in the **Menaion.** The **Triodion** covers the pre-Lenten season of preparation for Easter; Lent begins two days before the Ash Wednesday observance of the Roman Rite. The **Pentecostarion** contains the liturgical services from Easter to the Sunday of All Saints, the first after Pentecost. The **Evangelion** and **Apostolos** are books in which the Gospels, and Acts of the Apostles and the Epistles, respectively, are arranged according to the order of their reading in the Divine Liturgy and Divine Office throughout the year.

The cyclic progression of liturgical music throughout the year, in successive and repetitive periods of eight weeks, is governed by the **Oktoechos,** the Book of Eight Tones.

Sunday Names

Many Sundays are named after the subject of the Gospel read in the Mass of the day or after the name of a feast falling on the day — e.g., Sunday of the Publican and Pharisee, of the Prodigal Son, of the Samaritan Woman, of St. Thomas the Apostle, and the Fore-Fathers (Old Testament Patriarchs).

Holy Days, Abstinence, Fast

The calendar lists about 28 holy days. Many of the major holy days coincide with those of the Roman calendar, but the feast of the Immaculate Conception is observed on Dec. 9 instead of Dec. 8, and the feast of All Saints falls on the Sunday after Pentecost rather than on Nov. 1. Instead of a single All Souls' Day, there are five All Souls' Saturdays.

According to regulations in effect in the Byzantine-Rite (Ruthenian) Archeparchy of Munhall and its suffragan sees of Passaic and Parma, holy days are obligatory, solemn and simple, and attendance at the Divine Liturgy is required on five obligatory days — the feasts of the Epiphany, the Ascension, Sts. Peter and Paul, the Assumption of the Blessed Virgin Mary, and Christmas. Although attendance at the liturgy is not obligatory on 15 solemn and seven simple holy days, it is recommended.

In the Byzantine-Rite (Ukrainian) Archeparchy of Philadelphia and its suffragan sees of St. Nicholas (Chicago) and Stamford, the obligatory feasts are the Circumcision, Epiphany, Annunciation, Easter, Ascension, Pentecost, Dormition (Assumption of Mary), Immaculate Conception and Christmas.

Lent

The first day of Lent — the Monday before Ash Wednesday of the Roman Rite — and Good Friday are days of strict abstinence for persons between the ages of 21 and 59. No meat, eggs, or dairy products may be eaten on these days.

All persons over the age of 14 must abstain from meat on Fridays during Lent, Holy Saturday, and the vigils of the feasts of Christmas and Epiphany; abstinence is urged, but is not obligatory, on Wednesdays of Lent. The abstinence obligation is not in force on certain "free" or "privileged" Fridays.

Synaxis

An observance without a counterpart in the Roman calendar is the synaxis. This is a commemoration, on the day following a feast, of persons involved with the occasion for the feast — e.g., Sept. 9, the day following the feast of the Nativity of the Blessed Virgin Mary, is the Synaxis of Joachim and Anna, her parents.

Holy Week

In the Byzantine Rite, Lent is liturgically concluded with the Saturday of Lazarus, the day before Palm Sunday, which commemorates the raising of Lazarus from the dead.

On the following Monday, Tuesday and Wednesday, the Liturgy of the Presanctified is prescribed.

On Holy Thursday, the Liturgy of St. Basil the Great is celebrated together with Vespers.

Good Friday, except when the feast of the Annunciation coincides with it, is the only day of the year on which the Divine Liturgy is not celebrated.

On Holy Saturday, the Liturgy of St. Basil the Great is celebrated along with Vespers.

CALENDAR NOTES

The texts of scriptural readings for Mass on Sundays, holy days and some other days are indicated under the respective dates. The second cycle of readings in the Lectionary is prescribed for the 1976 liturgical year; the third cycle is prescribed for the 1977 liturgical year which begins with the first Sunday of Advent, Nov. 28, 1976.

Weekday cycles of readings are the second and first, respectively, for liturgical years 1976 and 1977.

Monthly Prayer Intentions

General and mission intentions recommended by Pope Paul to the prayers of the Apostles of Prayer are given under each month of the 1976 calendar.

JANUARY 1976

1—**Thurs. Solemnity of Mary, Mother of God. Holy day of obligation.** (Nm. 6:22-27; Gal. 4:4-7; Lk. 2:16-21.)

2—Fri. Sts. Basil the Great and Gregory Nazianzen, bishops-doctors; memorial.

3—Sat. Weekday.

4—**Sun. Epiphany of the Lord** (in U.S.); **solemnity.** (Is. 60:1-6; Eph. 3:2-3a, 5-6; Mt. 2:1-12.) [St. Elizabeth Ann Seton; memorial in U.S.]

5—Mon. Bl. John Neumann, bishop; memorial (in U.S.).

6—Tues. Weekday.

7—Wed. Weekday. St. Raymond of Penyafort, priest; optional memorial.

8—Thurs. Weekday.

9—Fri. Weekday.

10—Sat. Weekday.

11—**Sun. Baptism of the Lord; feast.** (Is. 42:1-4, 6-7; Acts 10:34-38; Mk. 1:6b-11.)

12—Mon. Weekday.

13—Tues. Weekday. St. Hilary, bishop-doctor; optional memorial.

14—Wed. Weekday.

15—Thurs. Weekday.

16—Fri. Weekday.

17—Sat. St. Anthony, abbot; memorial.

18—**Second Sunday of the Year.** (1 Sm. 3:3b-10, 19; 1 Cor. 6:13c-15a, 17-20; Jn. 1:35-42.)

19—Mon. Weekday.

20—Tues. Weekday. St. Fabian, pope-martyr, or St. Sebastian, martyr; optional memorials.

21—Wed. St. Agnes, virgin-martyr; memorial.

22—Thurs. Weekday. St. Vincent, deacon-martyr; optional memorial.

23—Fri. Weekday.

24—Sat. St. Francis de Sales, bishop-doctor; memorial.

25—**Third Sunday of the Year.** (Jon. 3:1-5, 10; 1 Cor. 7:29-31; Mk. 1:14-20.) [Conversion of St. Paul, apostle; feast.]

26—Mon. Sts. Timothy and Titus, bishops; memorial.

27—Tues. Weekday. St. Angela Merici, virgin; optional memorial.

28—Wed. St. Thomas Aquinas, priest-doctor; memorial.

29—Thurs. Weekday.

30—Fri. Weekday.

31—Sat. St. John Bosco, priest; memorial.

GENERAL PRAYER INTENTION: That those in the ecumenical field may work with greater hope. (The Week of Prayer for Christian Unity is observed from Jan. 18 to 25; related prayer texts have been issued in recent years by representatives of the Catholic Church and the World Council of Churches.)

MISSION PRAYER INTENTION: That brotherly love among believers may be a missionary call to unity among Christians.

FEBRUARY 1976

1—**Fourth Sunday of the Year.** (Dt. 18:15-20; 1 Cor. 7:32-35; Mk. 1:21-28.)

2—Mon. Presentation of the Lord; feast.

3—Tues. Weekday. St. Blase, bishop-martyr, or St. Ansgar, bishop; optional memorials. (In keeping with long-established custom, throats are blessed on this day, recalling St. Blase's role in saving a boy from choking to death. The blessing in honor and for the intercession of the saint is given with two unlighted candles, fastened like a cross, held to the throat of the person. The priest says the following prayer: "Through the intercession of St. Blase, bishop and martyr, may God deliver you from ailments of the throat and from every other evil. In the name of the Father, and of the Son, and of the Holy Spirit. Amen.")

4—Wed. Weekday.

5—Thurs. St. Agatha, virgin-martyr; memorial.

6—Fri. Sts. Paul Miki and Companions, martyrs; memorial.

7—Sat. Weekday.

8—**Fifth Sunday of the Year.** (Jb. 7:1-4, 6-7; 1 Cor. 9:16-19, 22-23; Mk. 1:29-39.) [St. Jerome Emiliani; optional memorial.]

9—Mon. Weekday.

10—Tues. St. Scholastica, virgin; memorial.

11—Wed. Weekday. Our Lady of Lourdes; optional memorial.

12—Thurs. Weekday.

13—Fri. Weekday.

14—Sat. Sts. Cyril, monk, and Methodius, bishop; memorial.

15—**Sixth Sunday of the Year.** (Lv. 13:1-2, 44-46; 1 Cor. 10:31 to 11:1, Mk. 1:40-45.)

16—Mon. Weekday.

17—Tues. Weekday. Seven Holy Founders of the Servite Order; optional memorial.

18—Wed. Weekday.

19—Thurs. Weekday.

20—Fri. Weekday.

21—Sat. Weekday. St. Peter Damian, bishop-doctor; optional memorial.

22—**Seventh Sunday of the Year.** (Is. 43:18-19, 21-22, 24b-25; 2 Cor. 1:18-22; Mk. 2:1-12.) [Chair of St. Peter; feast.]

23—Mon. St. Polycarp, bishop-martyr; memorial.

24—Tues. Weekday.

25—Wed. Weekday.

26—Thurs. Weekday.

27—Fri. Weekday.

28—Sat. Weekday.

29—**Eighth Sunday of the Year.** (Hos. 2: 16b, 17b, 21-22; 2 Cor. 3:1b-6; Mk. 2:18-22.)

GENERAL PRAYER INTENTION: For our sick brethren and those who have physical handicaps.

MISSION PRAYER INTENTION: That the Western World may gain greater awareness of the superiority of spiritual and moral values over material ones.

MARCH 1976

1—Mon. Weekday.
2—Tues. Weekday.
3—Ash Wednesday. Beginning of Lent. *Fast and abstinence.* (Ashes are blessed this day and imposed on the forehead of the faithful to remind them of their obligation to do penance for sin and to seek spiritual renewal by means of prayer, fasting, good works, and by bearing with patience and for God's purposes the trials and difficulties of everyday life. During the imposition of ashes, the priest says to each recipient: "Turn away from sin and be faithful to the Gospel," or: "Remember, man, you are dust, and to dust you will return." Lent has always been regarded as a special time for penance.)
4—Thurs. Weekday of Lent. [St. Casimir, optional memorial.]
5—Fri. Weekday of Lent. Abstinence.
6—Sat. Weekday of Lent.
7—**First Sunday of Lent.** (Gn. 9:8-15; 1 Pt. 3:18-22; Mk. 1:12-15.) [Sts. Perpetua and Felicity, martyrs; memorial.]
8—Mon. Weekday of Lent. [St. John of God, religious; optional memorial.]
9—Tues. Weekday of Lent. [St. Frances of Rome, religious; optional memorial.]
10—Wed. Weekday of Lent.
11—Thurs. Weekday of Lent.
12—Fri. Weekday of Lent. *Abstinence.*
13—Sat. Weekday of Lent.
14—**Second Sunday of Lent.** (Gn. 22:1-2, 9a, 10-13, 15-18; Rom. 8:31b-34; Mk. 9:2-10.)
15—Mon. Weekday of Lent.
16—Tues. Weekday of Lent.
17—Wed. Weekday of Lent. [St. Patrick, bishop; optional memorial.]
18—Thurs. Weekday of Lent. [St. Cyril of Jerusalem, bishop-doctor; optional memorial.]
19—Fri. St. Joseph; solemnity. Weekday of Lent. *Abstinence.*
20—Sat. Weekday of Lent.
21—**Third Sunday of Lent.** (Ex. 20:1-17; 1 Cor. 1:22-25; Jn. 2:13-25.)
22—Mon. Weekday of Lent.
23—Tues. Weekday of Lent. [St. Turibius, bishop; optional memorial.]
24—Wed. Weekday of Lent.
25—Thurs. Annunciation of the Lord; solemnity. Weekday of Lent.
26—Fri. Weekday of Lent. *Abstinence.*
27—Sat. Weekday of Lent.
28—**Fourth Sunday of Lent.** (2 Chr. 36:14-16, 19-23; Eph. 2:4-10; Jn. 3:14-21.)
29—Mon. Weekday of Lent.
30—Tues. Weekday of Lent.
31—Wed. Weekday of Lent.
PRAYER INTENTIONS: To live more simply; that racial problems in Africa may be solved in the light of justice and love.

APRIL 1976

1—Thurs. Weekday of Lent.
2—Fri. Weekday of Lent. *Abstinence.* [St. Francis of Paola, hermit; optional memorial.]
3—Sat. Weekday of Lent.
4—**Fifth Sunday of Lent.** (Jer. 31:31-34; Heb. 5:7-9; Jn. 12:20-33.) [St. Isidore of Seville, bishop-doctor; optional memorial.]
5—Mon. Weekday of Lent. [St. Vincent Ferrer, priest; optional memorial.]
6—Tues. Weekday of Lent.
7—Wed. Weekday of Lent. [St. John Baptist de la Salle, priest; memorial.]
8—Thurs. Weekday of Lent.
9—Fri. Weekday of Lent. *Abstinence.*
10—Sat. Weekday of Lent.
11—**Sunday of the Passion (Palm Sunday).** (Procession — Mk. 11:1-10 or Jn. 12:12-16; Mass — Is. 50:4-7; Phil. 2:6-11; Mk. 14:1 to 15:47.) [St. Stanislaus, bishop-martyr; optional memorial.] (Holy Week and Easter are the most solemn times in the entire liturgical year.)
12—Monday of Holy Week.
13—Tuesday of Holy Week. [St. Martin I, pope-martyr; optional memorial.]
14—Wednesday of Holy Week.
15—Thursday of Holy Week. Holy Thursday. The Paschal Triduum begins with the evening Mass of the Supper of the Lord.
16—Friday of the Passion of the Lord. Good Friday. *Fast and abstinence.*
17—Holy Saturday. The Easter Vigil.
18—**Easter Sunday; solemnity.** (Acts 10:34a, 37-43; 2 Col. 3:1-4 or 1 Cor. 5:6b-8; Jn. 20:1-9 or Mt. 28:1-10 or (evening) Lk. 24:13-35.)
19—Mon. Weekday.
20—Tues. Weekday.
21—Wed. Weekday. St. Anselm, bishop-doctor; optional memorial.
22—Thurs. Weekday.
23—Fri. Weekday. St. George, martyr; optional memorial.
24—Sat. Weekday. St. Fidelis of Sigmaringen, priest-martyr; optional memorial.
25—**Second Sunday of Easter.** (Acts. 4:32-35; 1 Jn. 5:1-6; Jn. 20:19-31.) [St. Mark, evangelist; feast.]
26—Mon. Weekday.
27—Tues. Weekday.
28—Wed. Weekday. St. Peter Chanel, priest-martyr; optional memorial.
29—Thurs. St. Catherine of Siena, virgin-doctor; memorial.
30—Fri. Weekday. St. Pius V, pope; optional memorial.
GENERAL PRAYER INTENTION: For all those who seek the truth.
MISSION PRAYER INTENTION: That the dialogue between the Church and the great religions of Asia may increase.

MAY 1976

1—Sat. Weekday. St. Joseph, Worker; optional memorial.
2—**Third Sunday of Easter.** (Acts. 3:13-15, 17-19; 1 Jn. 2:1-5a; Lk. 24:35-48.) [St. Athanasius, bishop-doctor; memorial.]
3—Mon. Sts. Philip and James, apostles; feast.
4—Tues. Weekday.
5—Wed. Weekday.
6—Thurs. Weekday.
7—Fri. Weekday.
8—Sat. Weekday.
9—**Fourth Sunday of Easter.** (Acts. 4:8-12; 1 Jn. 3:1-2; Jn. 10:11-18.)
10—Mon. Weekday.
11—Tues. Weekday.
12—Wed. Weekday. Sts. Nereus and Achilleus, martyrs, or St. Pancras, martyr; optional memorials.
13—Thurs. Weekday.
14—Fri. St. Matthias, apostle; feast.
15—Sat. Weekday. St. Isidore the Farmer; optional memorial (in U.S.).
16—**Fifth Sunday of Easter.** (Acts 9:26-31; 1 Jn. 3:18-24; Jn. 15:1-8.)
17—Mon. Weekday.
18—Tues. Weekday. St. John I, pope-martyr; optional memorial.
19—Wed. Weekday.
20—Thurs. Weekday. St. Bernardine of Siena, priest; optional memorial.
21—Fri. Weekday.
22—Sat. Weekday.
23—**Sixth Sunday of Easter.** (Acts 10:25-26, 34-35, 44-48; 1 Jn. 4:7-10; Jn. 15:9-17.)
24—Mon. Weekday.
25—Tues. Weekday. St. Bede the Venerable, priest-doctor, or St. Gregory VII, pope, or St. Mary Magdalene de Pazzi, virgin; optional memorials.
26—Wed. St. Philip Neri, priest; memorial.
27—**Thurs. Ascension of the Lord; solemnity. Holy day of obligation.** (Acts. 1:1-11; Eph. 1:17-23; Mk. 16:15-20.) [St. Augustine of Canterbury, bishop; optional memorial.]
28—Fri. Weekday.
29—Sat. Weekday.
30—**Seventh Sunday of Easter.** (Acts. 1:15-17, 20a, 20c-26; 1 Jn. 4:11-16; Jn. 17:11b-19.)
31—Mon. Visitation of Blessed Mary the Virgin; feast.

GENERAL PRAYER INTENTION: That the right to proper information shall be scrupulously respected in the social communications media. (For the past several years, Pope Paul has designated a World Communications Day in May. For each occasion, he has issued a special statement on the subject.

MISSION PRAYER INTENTION: That human dignity may be fostered in the young churches by the social communications media.

JUNE 1976

1—Tues. St. Justin, martyr; memorial.
2—Wed. Weekday. Sts. Marcellinus and Peter, martyrs; optional memorial.
3—Thurs. Sts. Charles Lwanga and companions; martyrs; memorial.
4—Fri. Weekday.
5—Sat. St. Boniface, bishop-martyr; memorial.
6—**Sun. Pentecost; solemnity.** (Acts. 2:1-11; 1 Cor. 12:3b-7, 12-13; Jn. 20:19-23.) [St. Norbert, bishop; optional memorial.]
7—Mon. (Tenth Week of the Year.) Weekday.
8—Tues. Weekday.
9—Wed. Weekday. St. Ephraem, deacon-doctor; optional memorial.
10—Thurs. Weekday.
11—Fri. St. Barnabas, apostle; memorial.
12—Sat. Weekday.
13—**Sun. Holy Trinity; solemnity.** (Dt. 4:32-34, 39-40; Rom. 8:14-17; Mt. 28:16-20.) [St. Anthony of Padua, priest-doctor; memorial.]
14—Mon. (Eleventh Week of the Year.) Weekday.
15—Tues. Weekday.
16—Wed. Weekday.
17—Thurs. Weekday.
18—Fri. Weekday.
19—Sat. Weekday. St. Romuald, abbot; optional memorial.
20—**Sun. Corpus Christi** (in U.S.); **solemnity.** (Ex. 24:3-8; Heb. 9:11-15; Mk. 14:12-16, 22-26.)
21—Mon. (Twelfth Week of the Year.) St. Aloysius Gonzaga, religious; memorial.
22—Tues. Weekday. St. Paulinus of Nola, bishop, or Sts. John Fisher, bishop-martyr, and Thomas More, martyr; optional memorials.
23—Wed. Weekday.
24—Thurs. Birth of St. John the Baptist; solemnity.
25—Fri. Sacred Heart of Jesus; solemnity.
26—Sat. Weekday. Immaculate Heart of Mary; optional memorial.
27—**Thirteenth Sunday of the Year.** (Wis. 1:13-15, 2:23-24; 2 Cor. 8:7, 9, 13-15; Mk. 5:21-43.) [St. Cyril of Alexandria, bishop-doctor; optional memorial.]
28—Mon. St. Irenaeus, bishop-martyr; memorial.
29—Tues. Sts. Peter and Paul, apostles; solemnity.
30—Wed. Weekday. First Martyrs of the Roman Church; optional memorial.

GENERAL PRAYER INTENTION: That the aged may find their rightful place in society.

MISSION PRAYER INTENTION: That the Church may be able to offer suitable spiritual assistance to immigrants in Northern European countries. (Several special missions are operative among migrant groups.)

JULY 1976

1—Thurs. Weekday.
2—Fri. Weekday.
3—Sat. St. Thomas, apostle; feast.
4—**Fourteenth Sunday of the Year.** (Ez. 2:2-5; 2 Cor. 12:7-10; Mk. 6:1-6.) [St. Elizabeth of Portugal; optional memorial.]
5—Mon. Weekday. St. Anthony Mary Zaccaria, priest; optional memorial.
6—Tues. Weekday. St. Maria Goretti, virgin-martyr; optional memorial.
7—Wed. Weekday.
8—Thurs. Weekday.
9—Fri. Weekday.
10—Sat. Weekday.
11—**Fifteenth Sunday of the Year.** (Am. 7: 12-15; Eph. 1:3-14; Mk. 6:7-13.) [St. Benedict, abbot; memorial.]
12—Mon. Weekday.
13—Tues. Weekday. St. Henry; optional memorial.
14—Wed. Weekday. St. Camillus de Lellis, priest; optional memorial.
15—Thurs. St. Bonaventure, bishop-doctor; memorial.
16—Fri. Weekday. Our Lady of Mt. Carmel; optional memorial.
17—Sat. Weekday.
18—**Sixteenth Sunday of the Year.** (Jer. 23:1-6; Eph. 2:13-18; Mk. 6:30-34.)
19—Mon. Weekday.
20—Tues. Weekday.
21—Wed. Weekday. St. Lawrence of Brindisi, priest-doctor; optional memorial.
22—Thurs. St. Mary Magdalene; memorial.
23—Fri. Weekday. St. Bridget of Sweden, religious; optional memorial.
24—Sat. Weekday.
25—**Seventeenth Sunday of the Year.** (2 Kgs. 4:42-44; Eph. 4:1-6; Jn. 6:1-15.) [St. James the Greater, apostle; feast.]
26—Mon. Sts. Joachim and Ann, parents of Mary; memorial.
27—Tues. Weekday.
28—Wed. Weekday.
29—Thurs. St. Martha; memorial.
30—Fri. Weekday. St. Peter Chrysologus, bishop-doctor; optional memorial.
31—Sat. St. Ignatius of Loyola, priest; memorial.

GENERAL PRAYER INTENTION: For history to be seen in the light of faith. (This intention is in line with the thrust of Catholic observance of this Bicentennial Year, during which new initiatives have been devoted to understanding contemporary conditions in the world and their relation to faith in practice. It is impossible to discern the will of God in the signs of the times — which indicate apostolic opportunities — if history is not viewed in the light of faith.)

MISSION PRAYER INTENTION: That every Christian traveler may be conscious of the responsibility and dynamism in his Christian faith.

AUGUST 1976

1—**Eighteenth Sunday of the Year.** (Ex. 16: 2-4, 12-15; Eph. 4:17, 20-24; Jn. 6:24-35.) [St. Alphonsus Liguori, bishop-doctor; memorial.]
2—Mon. Weekday. St. Eusebius of Vercelli, bishop; optional memorial.
3—Tues. Weekday.
4—Wed. St. John Mary Vianney, Cure of Ars, priest; memorial.
5—Thurs. Weekday. Dedication of St. Mary Major Basilica; optional memorial.
6—Fri. Transfiguration of the Lord; feast.
7—Sat. Weekday. Sts. Sixtus II, pope, and companions, martyrs, or St. Cajetan, priest; optional memorials.
8—**Nineteenth Sunday of the Year.** (1 Kgs. 19:4-8; Eph. 4:30 to 5:2; Jn. 6:41-51.) [St. Dominic, priest; memorial.]
9—Mon. Weekday.
10—Tues. St. Lawrence, deacon-martyr; feast.
11—Wed. St. Clare, virgin; memorial.
12—Thurs. Weekday.
13—Fri. Weekday. Sts. Pontian, pope, and Hippolytus, priest, martyrs; optional memorial.
14—Sat. Weekday.
15—**Sun. Assumption of Blessed Mary the Virgin; solemnity. Holy day of obligation.** (1 Rv. 11: 19a and 12: 1-6a, 10ab; 1 Cor. 15: 20-26; Lk. 1:39-56.)
16—Mon. (Twentieth Week of the Year.) Weekday. St. Stephen of Hungary; optional memorial.
17—Tues. Weekday.
18—Wed. Weekday.
19—Thurs. Weekday. St. John Eudes, priest; optional memorial.
20—Fri. St. Bernard of Clairvaux, abbot-doctor; memorial.
21—Sat. St. Pius X, pope; memorial.
22—**Twenty-First Sunday of the Year.** (Jos. 24:1-2a, 15-17, 18b; Eph. 5:21-32; Jn. 6:60-69.) [Queenship of Blessed Mary the Virgin; memorial.]
23—Mon. Weekday. St. Rose of Lima, virgin; optional memorial.
24—Tues. St. Bartholomew, apostle; feast.
25—Wed. Weekday. St. Louis, or St. Joseph Calasanz, priest; optional memorials.
26—Thurs. Weekday.
27—Fri. St. Monica; memorial.
28—Sat. St. Augustine, bishop-doctor; memorial.
29—**Twenty-Second Sunday of the Year.** (Dt. 4:1-2, 6-8; Jas. 1:17-18, 21b-22, 27; Mk. 7:1-8, 14-15, 21-23. [Beheading of St. John the Baptist; memorial.]
30—Mon. Weekday.
31—Tues. Weekday.

PRAYER INTENTIONS: That young people may find their particular places in service, and consider missionary life as a career.

SEPTEMBER 1976

1—Wed. Weekday.
2—Thurs. Weekday.
3—Fri. St. Gregory the Great, pope-doctor; memorial.
4—Sat. Weekday.
5—**Twenty-Third Sunday of the Year.** (Is. 35:4-7a; Jas. 2:1-5; Mk. 7:31-37.)
6—Mon. Weekday.
7—Tues. Weekday.
8—Wed. Birth of Blessed Mary the Virgin; feast.
9—Thurs. St. Peter Claver, priest; memorial (in U.S.).
10—Fri. Weekday.
11—Sat. Weekday.
12—**Twenty-Fourth Sunday of the Year** (Is. 50:5-9a; Jas. 2:14-18; Mk. 8:27-35.)
13—Mon. St. John Chrysostom, dishop-doctor; memorial.
14—Tues. Triumph of the Cross; feast.
15—Wed. Our Lady of Sorrows; memorial.
16—Thurs. Sts. Cornelius, pope, and Cyprian, bishop, martyrs; memorial.
17—Fri. Weekday. St. Robert Bellarmine, bishop-doctor; optional memorial.
18—Sat. Weekday.
19—**Twenty-Fifth Sunday of the Year.** (Wis. 2:12, 17-20; Jas. 3:16 to 4:3; Mk. 9:30-37.) [St. Januarius, bishop-martyr; optional memorial.]
20—Mon. Weekday.
21—Tues. St. Matthew, apostle; feast.
22—Wed. Weekday.
23—Thurs. Weekday.
24—Fri. Weekday.
25—Sat. Weekday.
26—**Twenty-Sixth Sunday of the Year** (Nm. 11:25-29; Jas. 5:1-6; Mk. 9:38-43, 45, 47-48.) [Sts. Cosmas and Damian, martyrs; optional memorial.]
27—Mon. St. Vincent de Paul, priest; memorial.
28—Tues. Weekday. St. Wenceslaus, martyr; optional memorial.
29—Wed. Sts. Michael, Gabriel and Raphael, archangels; feast.
30—Thurs. St. Jerome, priest-doctor; memorial.

GENERAL PRAYER INTENTION: That all of us might be aware of our responsibility to improve the quality of life for all people. (This responsibility of the "haves" to the "have-nots" is one of the salient points in the social doctrine of the Church which refers, among many other things, to the rights of all people to the God-given gifts of creation. The more a person or society has of this world's goods, the greater is the responsibility, in justice and charity, to share with others who are less fortunate.)

MISSION PRAYER INTENTION: That Latin American countries may find the way to integral social development.

OCTOBER 1976

1—Fri. St. Therese of the Child Jesus, virgin; memorial.
2—Sat. Guardian Angels; memorial.
3—**Twenty-Seventh Sunday of the Year.** (Gn. 2:18-24; Heb. 2:9-11; Mk. 10:2-16.)
4—Mon. St. Francis of Assisi; memorial.
5—Tues. Weekday.
6—Wed. Weekday. St. Bruno, priest; optional memorial.
7—Thurs. Our Lady of the Rosary; memorial.
8—Fri. Weekday.
9—Sat. Weekday. Sts. Denis, bishop, and companions, martyrs, or St. John Leonard, priest; optional memorials]
10—**Twenty-Eighth Sunday of the Year.** (Wis. 7:7-11; Heb. 4:12-13; Mk. 10:17-30.)
11—Mon. Weekday.
12—Tues. Weekday.
13—Wed. Weekday.
14—Thurs. Weekday. St. Callistus I, pope-martyr; optional memorial.
15—Fri. St. Teresa of Avila, virgin-doctor; memorial.
16—Sat. Weekday. St. Hedwig, religious, or St. Margaret Mary Alacoque, virgin; optional memorials.
17—**Twenty-Ninth Sunday of the Year.** (Is. 53:10-11; Heb. 4:14-16; Mk. 10:35-45.) [St. Ignatius of Antioch, bishop-martyr; memorial.]
18—Mon. St. Luke, evangelist; feast.
19—Tues. Sts. Isaac Jogues, John de Brebeuf, priests, and companions, martyrs, memorial (in U.S.); or Weekday. St. Paul of the Cross; optional memorial.
20—Wed. Weekday.
21—Thurs. Weekday.
22—Fri. Weekday.
23—Sat. Weekday. St. John of Capistrano, priest; optional memorial.
24—**Thirtieth Sunday of the Year.** (Jer. 31:7-9; Heb. 5:1-6; Mk. 10:46-52.) [St. Anthony Mary Claret, bishop; optional memorial.]
25—Mon. Weekday.
26—Tues. Weekday.
27—Wed. Weekday.
28—Thurs. Sts. Simon and Jude, apostles; feast.
29—Fri. Weekday.
30—Sat. Weekday.
31—**Thirty-First Sunday of the Year.** (Dt. 6:2-6; Heb. 7:23-28; Mk. 12:28b-34.)

GENERAL PRAYER INTENTION: That the desire to pray may lead to respect for all legitimate forms of prayer, both old and new. (Pope Paul, in numerous talks, has stressed the necessity of prayer in Christian life.)

MISSION PRAYER INTENTION: That October may really be "Mission Month," through increase in missionary concern, prayer and generous aid to the missions.

NOVEMBER 1976

1—**Mon. All Saints; solemnity. Holy day of obligation.** (Rv. 7:2-4, 9-14; 1 Jn. 3:1-3; Mt. 5:1-12a.)

2—Tues. Commemoration of All the Faithful Departed (All Souls Day). Three Masses proper.

3—Wed. Weekday. St. Martin de Porres, religious; optional memorial.

4—Thurs. Weekday. St. Charles Borromeo, bishop; memorial.

5—Fri. Weekday.

6—Sat. Weekday.

7—**Thirty-Second Sunday of the Year.** (1 Kgs. 17:10-16; Heb. 9:24-28; Mk. 12:38-44.)

8—Mon. Weekday.

9—Tues. Dedication of St. John Lateran Basilica; feast.

10—Wed. St. Leo the Great, pope-doctor; memorial.

11—Thurs. St. Martin of Tours, bishop; memorial.

12—Fri. St. Josaphat, bishop-martyr; memorial.

13—Sat. St. Frances X. Cabrini, virgin; memorial (in U.S.).

14—**Thirty-Third Sunday of the Year.** (Dn. 12:1-3; Heb. 10:11-14, 18; Mk. 13:24-32.)

15—Mon. Weekday. St. Albert the Great, bishop-doctor; optional memorial.

16—Tues. Weekday. St. Margaret of Scotland, or St. Gertrude, virgin; optional memorials.

17—Wed. St. Elizabeth of Hungary, religious; memorial.

18—Thurs. Weekday. Dedication of Basilicas of Sts. Peter and Paul; optional memorial.

19—Fri. Weekday.

20—Sat. Weekday.

21—**Sun. Christ the King; solemnity.** (Dn. 7:13-14; Rv. 1:5-8; Jn. 18:33b-37.) [Presentation of Blessed Mary the Virgin; memorial.]

22—Mon. (Thirty-Fourth and Last Week of the Year.) St. Cecilia, virgin-martyr; memorial.

23—Tues. Weekday. St. Clement I, pope-martyr, or St. Columban, abbot; optional memorials.

24—Wed. Weekday.

25—Thurs. Thanksgiving Day Votive Mass (in U.S.). Weekday.

26—Fri. Weekday.

27—Sat. Weekday.

28—**First Sunday of Advent.** (Jer. 33:14-16; 1 Thes. 3:12 to 4:2; Lk. 21:25-28, 34-36.)

29—Mon. Weekday.

30—Tues. St. Andrew, apostle; feast.

PRAYER INTENTIONS: For reverence for all human life (general); that new generations of Christians may preserve missionary tradition and add to it (missions).

DECEMBER 1976

1—Wed. Weekday.

2—Thurs. Weekday.

3—Fri. St. Francis Xavier, priest; memorial.

4—Sat. Weekday. St. John Damascene, priest-doctor; optional memorial.

5—**Second Sunday of Advent.** (Bar. 5:1-9; Phil. 1:4-6, 8-11; Lk. 3:1-6.)

6—Mon. Weekday. St. Nicholas, bishop; optional memorial.

7—Tues. St. Ambrose, bishop-doctor; memorial. ,

8—**Wed. Immaculate Conception of Blessed Mary the Virgin; solemnity. Holy day of obligation.** (Gn. 3:9-15, 20; Eph. 1:3-6, 11-12; Lk. 1:26-38.)

9—Thurs. Weekday.

10—Fri. Weekday.

11—Sat. Weekday. St. Damasus I, pope; optional memorial.

12—**Third Sunday of Advent.** (Zep. 3:14-18a; Phil. 4:4-7; Lk. 3:10-18.) [Our Lady of Guadalupe, memorial in U.S.; St. Jane Frances de Chantal, religious, optional memorial.]

13—Mon. St. Lucy, virgin-martyr; memorial.

14—Tues. St. John of the Cross, priest-doctor; memorial.

15—Wed. Weekday of Advent.

16—Thurs. Weekday of Advent.

17—Fri. Weekday of Advent.

18—Sat. Weekday of Advent.

19—**Fourth Sunday of Advent.** (Mi. 5:1-4a; Heb. 10:5-10; Lk. 1:39-45.)

20—Mon. Weekday of Advent.

21—Tues. Weekday of Advent. [St. Peter Canisius, priest-doctor; optional memorial.]

22—Wed. Weekday of Advent.

23—Thurs. Weekday of Advent. [St. John of Kanty, priest; optional memorial.]

24—Fri. Weekday of Advent.

25—**Sat. Christmas. Birth of the Lord, solemnity. Holy day of obligation.** (Midnight—Is. 9:1-6; Ti. 2:11-14; Lk. 2:1-14. Dawn—Is. 62:11-12; Ti. 3:4-7; Lk. 2:15-20. During the day—Is. 57: 7-10; Heb. 1:1-6; Jn. 1:1-18.)

26—**Sun. Holy Family; feast.** (Sir. 3:2-6, 12-14; Col. 3:12-21; Lk. 2:41-52.) [St. Stephen, first martyr; feast.]

27—Mon. St. John, apostle-evangelist; feast.

28—Tues. Holy Innocents, martyrs; feast.

29—Wed. Fifth Day of Christmas Octave. St. Thomas Becket, bishop-martyr; optional memorial.

30—Thurs. Sixth Day of Christmas Octave.

31—Fri. Seventh Day of Christmas Octave. St. Sylvester I, pope; optional memorial.

PRAYER INTENTIONS: That woman may be able to accomplish her mission in life, for the good of herself and the human community (general); that devotion to Mary may be valued and developed in young churches (missions).

TABLE OF MOVABLE FEASTS

Year	Ash Wednesday	Easter	Ascension	Pentecost	Weeks of Ordinary Time				First Sunday of Advent
					Before Lent		After Pent.		
					Week	Ends	Week	Begins	
1976	Mar. 3	Apr. 18	May 27	June 6	8	Mar. 2	10	June 7	Nov. 28
1977	Feb. 23	Apr. 10	May 19	May 29	7	Feb. 22	9	May 30	Nov. 27
1978	Feb. 8	Mar. 26	May 4	May 14	5	Feb. 7	6	May 15	Dec. 3
1979	Feb. 28	Apr. 15	May 24	June 3	8	Feb. 27	9	June 4	Dec. 2
1980	Feb. 20	Apr. 6	May 15	May 25	6	Feb. 19	8	May 26	Nov. 30
1981	Mar. 4	Apr. 19	May 28	June 7	8	Mar. 3	10	June 8	Nov. 29
1982	Feb. 24	Apr. 11	May 20	May 30	7	Feb. 23	9	May 31	Nov. 28
1983	Feb. 16	Apr. 3	May 12	May 22	6	Feb. 15	8	May 23	Nov. 27
1984	Mar. 7	Apr. 22	May 31	June 10	9	Mar. 6	10	June 11	Dec. 2
1985	Feb. 20	Apr. 7	May 16	May 26	6	Feb. 19	8	May 27	Dec. 1
1986	Feb. 12	Mar. 30	May 8	May 18	5	Feb. 11	7	May 19	Nov. 30
1987	Mar. 4	Apr. 19	May 28	June 7	9	Mar. 3	10	June 8	Nov. 29
1988	Feb. 17	Apr. 3	May 12	May 22	6	Feb. 16	8	May 23	Nov. 27
1989	Feb. 8	Mar. 26	May 4	May 14	5	Feb. 7	6	May 15	Dec. 3
1990	Feb. 28	Apr. 15	May 24	June 3	8	Feb. 27	9	June 4	Dec. 2
1991	Feb. 13	Mar. 31	May 9	May 19	5	Feb. 12	7	May 20	Dec. 1
1992	Mar. 4	Apr. 19	May 28	June 7	9	Mar. 3	10	June 8	Nov. 29
1993	Feb.24	Apr. 11	May 20	May 30	7	Feb. 23	9	May 31	Nov. 28
1994	Feb. 16	Apr. 3	May 12	May 22	6	Feb. 15	8	May 23	Nov. 27
1995	Mar. 1	Apr. 16	May 25	June 4	8	Feb. 28	9	June 5	Dec. 3
1996	Feb. 21	Apr. 7	May 16	May 26	7	Feb. 20	8	May 27	Dec. 1
1997	Feb. 12	Mar. 30	May 8	May 18	5	Feb. 11	7	May 19	Nov. 30
1998	Feb. 25	Apr. 12	May 21	May 31	7	Feb. 24	9	June 1	Nov. 29
1999	Feb. 17	Apr. 4	May 13	May 23	6	Feb. 16	8	May 24	Nov. 28
2000	Mar. 8	Apr. 23	June 1	June 11	9	Mar. 7	10	June 12	Dec. 3
2001	Feb. 28	Apr. 15	May 24	June 3	7	Feb. 27	9	June 4	Dec. 2
2002	Feb. 13	Mar. 31	May 9	May 19	5	Feb. 12	7	May 20	Dec. 1
2003	Mar. 5	Apr. 20	May 29	June 8	8	Mar. 4	10	June 9	Nov. 30
2004	Feb. 25	Apr. 11	May 20	May 30	7	Feb. 24	9	May 31	Nov. 28

Season of Ordinary Time

Weeks between the end of Christmastide and the beginning of Lent, and from the day after Pentecost to the last Sunday of the liturgical year, belong to the season of Ordinary Time. The table indicates the number and terminal date of the week ending the first part, and the number and starting date of the week beginning the second part, of this season. In some years, a week of this season is eliminated because of calendar conditions.

Date of Easter

The Second Vatican Council's *Constitution on the Sacred Liturgy* said there would be no objection "if the feast of Easter were assigned to a particular Sunday of the Gregorian calendar, provided that those whom it may concern, especially the brethren who are not in communion with the Apostolic See, give their assent."

If calendar and related cultural differences between the Roman Catholic and Orthodox Churches were resolved, they could both celebrate Easter on the same day.

The late Orthodox Ecumenical Patriarch Athenagoras of Constantinople proposed that the feast be celebrated each year on the second Sunday of April, but there has been no action on the proposal.

His successor, Demetrios I, and Pope Paul expressed in their 1975 Easter greetings the desire that eventually the Catholic and Orthodox Churches would celebrate the feast at the same time.

With permission of the Holy See in 1975, Catholics in Jordan celebrated Easter on the same day as the Orthodox, May 4, instead of on the Roman calendar date of Mar. 30.

HOLY DAYS AND OTHER FEASTS

The following list includes the six holy days of obligation observed in the United States and additional observances of devotional and historical significance. The dignity or rank of observances is indicated by the terms: **solemnity** (highest in rank, the equivalent of former first class feasts): **feast** (equivalent to former second class feasts); **memorial** (equivalent to former third class feasts, for universal observance); **optional memorial** (for celebration by choice).

All Saints, Nov. 1, holy day of obligation, solemnity. Commemorates all the blessed in heaven, and is intended particularly to honor the blessed who have no special feasts. The background of the feast dates to the fourth century when groups of martyrs, and later other saints, were honored on a common day in various places. In 609 or 610, the Pantheon, a pagan temple at Rome, was consecrated as a Christian church for the honor of Our Lady and the martyrs (later all saints). In 835, Gregory IV fixed Nov. 1 as the date of observance.

All Souls, Commemoration of the Faithful Departed, Nov. 2 (transferable to Nov. 3). The dead were prayed for from the earliest days of Christianity. By the sixth century it was customary in Benedictine monasteries to hold a commemoration of deceased members of the order at Pentecost. A common commemoration of all the faithful departed on the day after All Saints was instituted in 998 by St. Odilo, of the Abbey of Cluny, and an observance of this kind was generally adopted throughout the Church. In 1915, Benedict XV granted priests throughout the world permission to celebrate three Masses for this commemoration. He also granted a special indulgence for the occasion.

Annunciation of the Lord (formerly, Annunciation of the Blessed Virgin Mary), Mar. 25, solemnity. A feast of the Incarnation which commemorates the announcement by the Archangel Gabriel to the Virgin Mary that she was to become the Mother of Christ (Lk. 1:26-38), and the miraculous conception of Christ by her. The feast was instituted about 430 in the East. The Roman observance dates from the seventh century, when celebration was said to be universal.

Ascension of the Lord, movable observance held 40 days after Easter, holy day of obligation, solemnity. Commemorates the Ascension of Christ into heaven 40 days after his Resurrection from the dead (Mk. 16:19; Lk. 24:51; Acts 1:2). The feast recalls the completion of Christ's mission on earth for the salvation of men and his entry into heaven with glorified human nature. The Ascension is a pledge of the final glorification of all who achieve salvation. Documentary evidence of the feast dates from early in the fifth century, but it was observed long before that time in connection with Pentecost and Easter.

Ash Wednesday, movable observance, six and one-half weeks before Easter. It was set as the first day of Lent by St. Gregory the Great (590-604) with the extension of an earlier and shorter penitential season to a total period including 40 weekdays of fasting before Easter. Ashes, symbolic of penance, are blessed and distributed among the faithful during the day. They are used to mark the forehead with the Sign of the Cross, with the reminder: "Remember, man, that you are dust, and unto dust you shall return," or: "Repent, and believe the Good News."

Assumption Aug. 15, holy day of obligation, solemnity. Commemorates the taking into heaven of Mary, soul and body, at the end of her life on earth, a truth of faith that was proclaimed a dogma by Pius XII on Nov. 1, 1950. One of the oldest and most solemn feasts of Mary, it has a history dating back to at least the seventh century when its celebration was already established at Jerusalem and Rome.

Baptism of the Lord, movable, celebrated on the Sunday after Epiphany, feast. Recalls the baptism of Christ by John the Baptist (Mk. 1:9-11), an event associated with the liturgy of the Epiphany. This baptism was the occasion for Christ's manifestation of Himself at the beginning of his public life.

Birth of Mary, Sept. 8, feast. This is a very old feast which originated in the East and found place in the Roman liturgy in the seventh century.

Candlemas Day, Feb. 2. See Presentation of the Lord.

Chair of Peter, Feb. 22, feast. Commemorates establishment of the see of Antioch by Peter. The feast, which has been in the Roman calendar since 336, is a liturgical expression of belief in the episcopacy and hierarchy of the Church.

Christmas, Birth of Our Lord Jesus Christ, Dec. 25, holy day of obligation, solemnity. Commemorates the birth of Christ (Lk. 2:1-20). This event was originally commemorated in the East on the feast of Epiphany or Theophany. The Christmas feast itself originated in the West; by 354 it was certainly kept on Dec. 25. This date may have been set for the observance to offset pagan ceremonies held at about the same time to commemorate the birth of the sun at the winter solstice. Priests may celebrate three Masses on Christmas Day. Christmastide begins with this feast and continues until the Sunday after Epiphany.

Christ the King, movable, celebrated on the last Sunday of the liturgical year, solemnity. Commemorates the royal prerogatives of Christ and is equivalent to a declaration of his rights to the homage, service and fidelity of men in all phases of individual and social life. Pius XI instituted the feast Dec. 11, 1925.

Corpus Christi, movable observance held in the US on the Sunday following Trinity Sunday, solemnity. Commemorates the institution of the Holy Eucharist (Mt. 26:26-28). The feast originated at Liege in 1246 and was extended throughout the Church in the West by Urban IV in 1264. St. Thomas Aquinas composed the Office for the feast.

Dedication of St. John Lateran, Nov. 9, feast. Commemorates the first public consecration of a church, that of the Basilica of the Most Holy Savior by Pope St. Sylvester Nov. 9, 324. The church, as well as the Lateran Palace, was the gift of Emperor Constantine. Since the 12th century it has been known as St. John Lateran, in honor of John the Baptist after whom the adjoining baptistery was named. It was rebuilt by Innocent X (1644-55), reconsecrated by Benedict XIII in 1726, and enlarged by Leo XIII (1878-1903). This basilica is regarded as the church of highest dignity in Rome and throughout the Roman Rite.

Dedication of St. Mary Major, Aug. 5, optional memorial. Commemorates the rebuilding and dedication by Sixtus III (432-40) of a church in honor of Blessed Mary the Virgin. This is the Basilica of St. Mary Major on the Esquiline Hill in Rome. An earlier building was erected during the pontificate of Liberius (352-66); according to legend, it was located on a site covered by a miraculous fall of snow seen by a nobleman favored with a vision of Mary.

Easter, movable celebration held on the first Sunday after the full moon following the vernal equinox (between Mar. 22 and Apr. 25), solemnity with an octave. Commemorates the Resurrection of Christ from the dead (Mk. 16:1-7). The observance of this mystery, kept since the first days of the Church, extends throughout the Easter season which lasts until the feast of Pentecost, a period of 50 days. Every Sunday in the year is regarded as a "little" Easter. The date of Easter determines the dates of movable feasts, such as Ascension and Pentecost, and the number of Sundays after Epiphany and Pentecost.

Easter Vigil (Holy Saturday), day before Easter. Ceremonies are all related to the Resurrection and renewal-in-grace theme of Easter: blessing of the new fire and Paschal Candle, reading of prophecies, blessing of water and the baptismal font, the baptism of converts and renewal of baptismal vows by the faithful, the Litany of the Saints, and the celebration of Mass. The vigil ceremonies are held after sundown, preferably at a time that makes possible the celebration of Mass at midnight.

Epiphany of Our Lord, Jan. 6 or (in the US) a Sunday between Jan. 2 and 8, solemnity. Commemorates the manifestations of the divinity of Christ. It is one of the oldest Christian feasts, with an Eastern origin traceable to the beginning of the third century and antedating the Western feast of Christmas. Originally, it commemorated the manifestations of Christ's divinity — or Theophany — in his birth, the homage of the Magi, and baptism by John the Baptist. Later, the first two of these commemorations were transferred to Christmas when the Eastern Church adopted that feast between 380 and 430. The central feature of the Eastern observance now is the manifestation or declaration of Christ's divinity in his baptism and at the beginning of his public life. The Epiphany was adopted by the Western Church during the same period in which the Eastern Church accepted Christmas. In the Roman Rite, commemoration is made in the Mass of the homage of the wise men from the East (Mt. 2:1-12).

Good Friday, the Friday before Easter, privileged feria of Holy Week. Liturgical elements of the observance are commemoration of the Passion and Death of Christ in the reading of the Passion (according to John), special prayers for the Church and people of all ranks, the veneration of the Cross, and a Communion service. The Solemn Liturgical Action takes place between noon and 9 p.m. This is the only day in the year on which the Eucharistic Liturgy is not celebrated in the Roman Rite.

Guardian Angels, Oct. 2, memorial. Commemorates the angels who protect men from spiritual and physical dangers and assist them in doing good. A feast in their honor celebrated in Spain in the 16th century was extended to the whole Church by Paul V in 1608. In 1670, Clement X set Oct. 2 as the date of observance. Earlier, guardian angels were honored liturgically in conjunction with the feast of St. Michael.

Holy Family, movable observance on the Sunday after Christmas, feast. Commemorates the Holy Family of Jesus, Mary and Joseph as the model of domestic society, holiness and virtue. The devotional background of the feast was very strong in the 17th century. In the 18th century, in prayers composed for a special Mass, a Canadian bishop likened the Christian family to the Holy Family. Leo XIII consecrated families to the Holy Family. In 1921, Benedict XV extended the Divine Office and Mass of the feast to the whole Church.

Holy Innocents, Dec. 28, feast. Commemorates the infants who suffered death at the hands of Herod's soldiers seeking to kill the child Jesus (Mt. 2:13-18). A feast in their honor has been observed since the fifth century.

Holy Thursday, the Thursday before Easter, privileged feria of Holy Week. Commemorates the institution of the Holy Eucharist (which is later celebrated on the special feast of Corpus Christi) and other events of the Last Supper. Ceremonies include the celebration of a principal Mass between 4 and

9 p.m., the washing of feet in imitation of the act of Christ who washed the feet of the Apostles at the Last Supper, the stripping of the altar at the conclusion of Mass. There is also a procession of the Blessed Sacrament to a special place of reposition where It is reserved for veneration by the faithful until the Solemn Liturgical Action on Good Friday. At a special Mass of Chrism, bishops bless oils (of catechumens, chrism, of the sick) for use during the year.

Immaculate Conception, Dec. 8, holy day of obligation, solemnity. Commemorates the fact that Mary, in view of her calling to be the Mother of Christ and in virtue of his merits, was preserved from the first moment of her conception from original sin and was filled with grace from the very beginning of her life. She was the only person so preserved from original sin. The present form of the feast dates from Dec. 8, 1854, when Pius IX defined the dogma of the Immaculate Conception. An earlier feast of the Conception, which testified to long-existing belief in this truth, was observed in the East by the eighth century, in Ireland in the ninth, and subsequently in European countries. In 1846, Mary was proclaimed patroness of the US under this title.

Immaculate Heart of Mary, Saturday following the second Sunday after Pentecost, optional memorial. On May 4, 1944, Pius XII ordered this feast observed throughout the Church in order to obtain Mary's intercession for "peace among nations, freedom for the Church, the conversion of sinners, the love of purity and the practice of virtue." Two years earlier, he consecrated the entire human race to Mary under this title. Devotion to Mary under the title of her Most Pure Heart originated during the Middle Ages. It was given great impetus in the 17th century by the preaching of St. John Eudes, who was the first to celebrate a Mass and Divine Office of Mary under this title. A feast, celebrated in various places and on different dates, was authorized in 1799.

Joachim and Ann, July 26, memorial. Commemorates the parents of Mary. A joint feast, celebrated Sept. 9, originated in the East near the end of the sixth century. Devotion to Ann, introduced in the eighth century at Rome, became widespread in Europe in the 14th century; her feast was extended throughout the Latin Church in 1584. A feast of Joachim was introduced in the West in the 15th century.

John the Baptist, Birth, June 24, solemnity. The precursor of Christ, whose cousin he was, was commemorated universally in the liturgy by the fourth century. He is the only saint, except the Blessed Virgin Mary, whose birthday is observed as a feast. Another feast, on Aug. 29, commemorates his passion and death at the order of Herod (Mk. 6:14-29).

Joseph, Mar. 19, solemnity. Joseph is honored as the husband of the Blessed Virgin Mary, the patron and protector of the universal Church and workman. Devotion to him already existed in the eighth century in the East, and in the 11th in the West. Various feasts were celebrated before the 15th century when Mar. 19 was fixed for his commemoration; this feast was extended to the whole Church in 1621 by Gregory XV. In 1955, Pius XII instituted the feast of St. Joseph the Workman for observance May 1; this feast, which may be celebrated by local option, supplanted the Solemnity or Patronage of St. Joseph formerly observed on the third Wednesday after Easter. St. Joseph was proclaimed protector and patron of the universal Church in 1870 by Pius IX.

Michael, Gabriel and Raphael, Archangels, Sept. 29, feast. A feast bearing the title of Dedication of St. Michael the Archangel formerly commemorated on this date the consecration in 530 of a church near Rome in honor of Michael, the first angel given a liturgical feast. For a while, this feast was combined with a commemoration of the Guardian Angels. The separate feasts of Gabriel (Mar. 24) and Raphael (Oct. 24) were suppressed by the calendar reform of 1969 and this joint feast of the three archangels was instituted.

Octave of Christmas, Jan. 1. See Solemnity of Mary, Mother of God.

Our Lady of Sorrows, Sept. 15, memorial. Recalls the sorrows experienced by Mary in her association with Christ: the prophecy of Simeon (Lk. 2:34-35), the flight into Egypt (Mt. 2:13-21), the three-day separation from Jesus (Lk. 2:41-50), and four incidents connected with the Passion: her meeting with Christ on the way to Calvary, the crucifixion, the removal of Christ's body from the cross, and his burial (Mt. 27:31-61; Mk. 15:20-47; Lk. 23:26-56; Jn. 19:17-42). A Mass and Divine Office of the feast were celebrated by the Servites, especially, in the 17th century, and in 1817 Pius VII extended the observance to the whole Church.

Our Lady of the Rosary, Oct. 7, memorial. Commemorates the Virgin Mary through recall of the mysteries of the Rosary which recapitulate events in her life and the life of Christ. The feast was instituted to commemorate a Christian victory over invading Mohammedan forces at Lepanto on Oct. 7, 1571, and was extended throughout the Church by Clement XI in 1716.

Passion (Palm) Sunday, the Sunday before Easter. Recalls the triumphal entry of Christ into Jerusalem at the beginning of the last week of his life (Mt. 21:1-9). A procession and other ceremonies commemorating this event were held in Jerusalem from very early Christian times and were adopted in Rome by the ninth century, when the blessing of palm for the occasion was introduced. Full liturgical observance includes the blessing of palm and a procession before the principal Mass of the day. The Passion, by Matthew, Mark or Luke, is read during the Mass.

Pentecost, also called **Whitsunday,** movable celebration held 50 days after Easter, solemnity. Commemorates the descent of the Holy Spirit upon the Apostles, the preaching of Peter and the other Apostles to Jews in Jerusalem, the baptism and aggregation of some 3,000 persons to the Christian community (Acts 2:1-41). It is regarded as the birthday of the Catholic Church. The original observance of the feast antedated the earliest extant documentary evidence from the third century.

Peter and Paul, June 29, solemnity. Commemorates the dual martyrdom of Peter by crucifixion and Paul by beheading during the Neronian persecution. This joint commemoration of the two greatest Apostles dates at least from 258 at Rome.

Presentation of the Lord (formerly called Purification of the Blessed Virgin Mary, also Candlemas), Feb. 2, feast. Commemorates the presentation of Jesus in the Temple — according to prescriptions of Mosaic Law (Lv. 12:2-8; Ex. 13:2; Lk. 2:22-32) — and the purification of Mary 40 days after his birth. In the East, where the feast antedated fourth century testimony regarding its existence, it was observed primarily as a feast of Our Lord; in the West, where it was adopted later, it was regarded more as a feast of Mary until the calendar reform of 1969. Its date was set for Feb. 2 after the celebration of Christmas was fixed for Dec. 25, late in the fourth century. The blessing of candles, probably in commemoration of Christ who was the Light to enlighten the Gentiles, became common about the 11th century and gave the feast the secondary name of Candlemas.

Queenship of Mary, Aug. 22, memorial. Commemorates the high dignity of Mary as Queen of heaven, angels and men. Universal observance of the memorial was ordered by Pius XII in the encyclical *Ad Caeli Reginam* Oct. 11, 1954, near the close of a Marian Year observed in connection with the centenary of the proclamation of the dogma of the Immaculate Conception and four years after the proclamation of the dogma of the Assumption. The original date of the memorial was May 31.

Resurrection. See Easter.

Sacred Heart of Jesus, movable observance held on the Friday after Corpus Christi, solemnity. The object of the devotion is the divine Person of Christ, whose heart is the symbol of his love for men — for whom he accomplished the work of Redemption. The Mass and Office now used on the feast were prescribed by Pius XI in 1929. Devotion to the Sacred Heart was introduced into the liturgy in the 17th century through the efforts of St. John Eudes who composed an Office and Mass for the feast. It was furthered as the result of the revelations of St. Margaret Mary

Alacoque after 1675 and by the work of Claude de la Colombiere, S.J. In 1765, Clement XIII approved a Mass and Office for the feast, and in 1856 Pius IX extended the observance throughout the Roman Rite.

Solemnity of Mary, Mother of God, Jan. 1, holy day of obligation, solemnity. The calendar reform of 1969, in accord with Eastern tradition, reinstated the Marian character of this commemoration on the octave day of Christmas. The former feast of the Circumcision, dating at least from the first half of the sixth century, marked the initiation of Jesus (Lk. 2:21) in Judaism and by analogy focused attention on the initiation of persons in the Christian religion and their incorporation in Christ through baptism. The feast of the Solemnity supplants the former feast of the Maternity of Mary observed on Oct. 11.

Transfiguration of the Lord, Aug. 6, feast. Commemorates the revelation of his divinity by Christ to Peter, James and John on Mt. Tabor (Mt. 17:1-9). The feast, which is very old, was extended throughout the universal Church in 1457 by Callistus III.

Trinity, Most Holy, movable observance held on the Sunday after Pentecost, solemnity. Commemorates the most sublime mystery of the Christian faith, i.e., that there are Three Divine Persons — Father, Son and Holy Spirit — in one God (Mt. 28:18-20). A votive Mass of the Most Holy Trinity dates from the seventh century; an Office was composed in the 10th century; in 1334, John XXII extended the feast to the universal Church.

Triumph of the Cross, Sept. 14, feast. Commemorates the finding of the cross on which Christ was crucified, in 326 through the efforts of St. Helena, mother of Constantine; the consecration of the Basilica of the Holy Sepulchre nearly 10 years later: and the recovery in 628 or 629 by Emperor Heraclius of a major portion of the cross which had been removed by the Persians from its place of veneration at Jerusalem. The feast originated in Jerusalem and spread through the East before being adopted in the West. General adoption followed the building at Rome of the Basilica of the Holy Cross "in Jerusalem," so called because it was the place of enshrinement of a major portion of the cross of crucifixion.

Visitation, May 31, feast. Commemorates Mary's visit to her cousin Elizabeth after the Annunciation and before the birth of John the Baptist, the precursor of Christ (Lk. 1:39-47). The feast had a medieval origin and was observed in the Franciscan Order before being extended throughout the Church by Urban VI in 1389. It is one of the feasts of the Incarnation and is notable for its recall of the Magnificat, one of the few New Testament canticles, which acknowledges the unique gifts of God to Mary because of her role in the redemptive work of Christ. The canticle is recited at Vespers in the Liturgy of the Hours.

SAINTS

Biographical sketches of additional saints are under other Almanac titles. See Index.

An asterisk with a feast date indicates that a memorial or feast is observed according to the revised Roman-Rite calendar.

Adjutor, St. (d. 1131): Norman knight; fought in First Crusade; monk-recluse after his return; legendary accounts of incidents on journey to Crusade probably account for his patronage of yachtsmen; Apr. 30.

Agatha, St. (d. c. 250): Sicilian virgin-martyr; her intercession credited in Sicily with stopping eruptions of Mt. Etna; patron of nurses; Feb. 5*.

Agnes, St. (d. c. 304): Roman virgin-martyr; martyred at age of 10 or 12; patron of young girls; Jan. 21*.

Aloysius Gonzaga, St. (1568-1591): Italian Jesuit; died while nursing plague-stricken; canonized 1726; patron of youth; June 21*.

Amand, St. (d. c. 676): Apostle of Belgium; b. France; established monasteries throughout Belgium; Feb. 6.

Andre Grasset de Saint Sauveur, Bl. (1758-1792): Canadian priest; martyred in France, Sept. 2, 1792, during the Revolution; one of a group called the Martyrs of Paris who were beatified in 1926.

Andrew Corsini, St. (1302-1373): Italian Carmelite; bishop of Fiesoli; mediator between quarrelsome Italian states; canonized 1629; Feb. 4.

Andrew Fournet, St. (1752-1834): French priest; co-founder with St. Jeanne Elizabeth des Anges of the Congregation of Daughters of the Cross; canonized 1933; May 13.

Angela Merici, St. (1474-1540): Italian nun; foundress of Institute of St. Ursula, 1535, the first teaching order of nuns in the Church; canonized 1807; Jan. 27*.

Anne Mary Javouhey, Bl. (1779-1851): French virgin; foundress of Institute of St. Joseph of Cluny, 1812; beatified 1950; July 15.

Ansgar, St. (801-865): Bishop, Benedictine monk; b. near Amiens; missionary in Denmark, Sweden, Norway and Northern Germany; apostle of Denmark; Feb. 3*.

Anthony Abbot, St. (c. 251-c. 354): Egyptian hermit; patriarch of all monks; established communities for hermits which became models for monastic life, especially in the East; friend and supporter of St. Athanasius in the latter's struggle with the Arians; Jan. 17*.

Anthony Mary Claret, St. (1807-1870): Spanish priest; founder of Missionary Sons of the Immaculate Heart of Mary (Claretians), 1849; archbishop of Santiago, Cuba, 1851-57; canonized 1950; Oct. 24*.

Anthony Mary Zaccaria, St. (1502-1539): Italian priest; founder of Barnabites (Clerks Regular of St. Paul), 1530; canonized 1897; July 5*.

Apollonia, St. (d. 249): Deaconess of Alexandria; martyred during persecution of Decius; her patronage of dentists probably rests on tradition that her teeth were broken by pincers by her persecutors; Feb. 9.

Augustine of Canterbury, St. (d. 604 or 605): Italian missionary; apostle of the English; sent by Pope Gregory I with 40 monks to evangelize England; arrived there 597; first archbishop of Canterbury; May 27*.

Benedict of Nursia, St. (c. 480-547): Abbot; founder of monasticism in Western Europe; established monastery at Monte Cassino; proclaimed patron of Europe by Paul VI in 1964; July 11*.

Benedict the Black (il Moro), St. (1526-1589): Sicilian Franciscan; born a slave; joined Franciscans as lay brother; appointed guardian and novice master; canonized 1807; Apr. 4.

Bernadette Soubirous, St. (1844-1879): French peasant girl favored with series of visions of Blessed Virgin Mary at Lourdes (see Lourdes Apparitions); joined Institute of Sisters of Notre Dame at Nevers, 1866; canonized 1933; Apr. 16.

Bernard of Menthon, St. (d. 1081): Italian priest; founded Alpine hospices near the two passes named for him; patron of mountaineers; May 28.

Bernardine of Siena, St. (1380-1444): Italian Franciscan; noted preacher and missioner; spread of devotion to Holy Name is attributed to him; represented in art holding to his breast the monogram IHS; canonized 1450; May 20*.

Blase, St. (d. c. 316): Armenian bishop; martyr; the blessing of throats on his feast day derives from tradition that he miraculously saved the life of a boy who had half-swallowed a fish bone; Feb. 3*.

Boniface (Winfrid), St. (d. 754): English Benedictine; bishop, martyr; apostle of Germany; established monastery at Fulda which became center of German missionary work; archbishop of Mainz; martyred near Dukkum in Holland; June 5*.

Brendan, St. (c. 489-583): Irish abbot; founded monasteries; his patronage of sailors probably rests on tradition that he made a seven-year voyage in search of a fabled paradise; called Brendan the Navigator; May 16.

Bridget (Brigid), St. (c. 450-525): Irish nun; founded nunnery at Kildare, the first erected on Irish soil; patron, with Sts. Patrick and Columba, of Ireland; Feb. 1.

Bridget (Birgitta), St. (c. 1303-1373): Swedish mystic; widow; foundress of Order of Our Savior (Brigittines); canonized 1391; wrote *Revelationes,* accounts of her visions; patroness of Sweden; July 23*.

Bruno, St. (1030-1101): German monk; founded Carthusians, 1084, in France; Oct. 6*.

Cabrini, Mother: See Index.

Cajetan of Thiene, St. (1480-1547): Italian lawyer; religious reformer; a founder of Oratory of Divine Love, forerunner of the Theatines; canonized 1671; Aug. 7*.

Callistus I, St. (d. 222): Pope, 217-222; martyr; condemned Sabellianism and other heresies; advocated a policy of mercy toward repentant sinners; Oct. 14*.

Camillus de Lellis, St. (1550-1614): Italian priest; founder of Camillians (Ministers of the Sick); canonized 1746; patron of the sick and of nurses; July 14*.

Casimir, St. (1458-1484): Polish prince; grand duke of Lithuania; noted for his piety; buried at cathedral in Vilna, Lithuania; canonized 1521; patron of Poland and Lithuania; Mar. 4*.

Cassian, St. (d. 298): Roman martyr; an official court stenographer who declared himself a Christian; patron of stenographers; Dec. 3.

Catherine Laboure, St. (1806-1876): French nun; favored with series of visions; first Miraculous Medal (see Index) struck as the result of one of the visions; canonized 1947; Dec. 31.

Catherine of Bologna, St. (1413-1463): Italian Poor Clare; mystic, writer, artist; canonized 1712; patron of artists; Mar. 9.

Cecilia, St. (2nd-3rd century): Roman virgin-martyr; traditional patron of musicians; Nov. 22*.

Charles Borromeo, St. (1538-1584): Italian cardinal; nephew of Pope Pius IV; cardinal bishop of Milan; influential figure in Church reform in Italy; promoted education of clergy; canonized 1610; Nov. 4*.

Charles Lwanga and Companions, Sts. (d. 1886 and 1887): Martyrs of Uganda; pages of King Mwanga of Uganda; Charles Lwanga and 12 companions were martyred near Rubaga, June 3, 1886; the other nine were martyred between May 26, 1886, and Jan. 27, 1887; canonized 1964; first martyrs of black Africa; June 3*.

Christopher, St. (3rd cent.): Early Christian martyr inscribed in Roman calendar about 1550; feast relegated to particular calendars because of legendary nature of accounts of his life; traditional patron of travelers; July 25.

Clare, St. (1194-1253): Foundress of Poor Clares; b. at Assisi; later joined in religious life by her sisters Agnes and Beatrice, and her mother Ortolana; canonized 1255; patroness of television; Aug. 11*.

Clement I, St. (d. c. 100): Pope, 88-97; third successor of St. Peter; wrote important letter to Church in Corinth settling disputes there; venerated as a martyr; Nov. 23*.

Columba, St. (521-597): Irish monk; founded monasteries in Ireland; missionary in Scotland; established monastery at Iona which became the center for conversion of Picts, Scots, and Northern English; Scotland's most famous saint; June 9.

Columban, St. (545-615): Irish monk; scholar; founded monasteries in England and Brittany (famous abbey of Luxeuil), forced into exile because of his criticism of Frankish court; spent last years in northern Italy where he founded abbey at Bobbio; Nov. 23*.

Contardo Ferrini, Bl. (1859-1902): Italian Franciscan tertiary; model of the Catholic professor; beatified 1947; patron of universities; Oct. 17.

Cornelius, St. (d. 253): Pope, 251-253; promoted a policy of mercy with respect to readmission of repentant Christians who had fallen away during the persecution of Decius *(lapsi);* banished from Rome during persecution of Gallus; regarded as a martyr; Sept. 16 (with Cyprian)*.

Cosmas and Damian, Sts. (d. c. 303): Arabian twin brothers; physicians who were martyred during Diocletian persecution; patrons of physicians; Sept. 26*.

Crispin and Crispinian, Sts. (3rd cent.): Early Christian martyrs; said to have met their deaths in Gaul; patrons of shoemakers, a trade they pursued; Oct. 25.

Cyprian, St. (d. 258): Early ecclesiastical writer; b. Africa; bishop of Carthage, 249-258; supported Pope St. Cornelius concerning the readmission of Christians who had apostasized in time of persecution; erred in his teaching that baptism administered by heretics and schismatics was invalid; wrote *De Unitate;* Sept. 16 (with St. Cornelius).*

Cyril and Methodius, Sts.: Greek missionaries; brothers venerated as apostles of the Slavs; Cyril (d. 869) and Methodius (d. 885) began their missionary work in Moravia in 863; developed a Slavonic alphabet; eventually their use of the vernacular in the liturgy was approved; Feb. 14*.

Damasus I, St. (d. 384): Pope, 366-384; opposed Arians and Apollinarians; commissioned St. Jerome to work on Bible translation; developed Roman liturgy; Dec. 11*.

Damian, St.: See Cosmas and Damian, Sts.

David, St. (5th-6th cent.): Welsh monk; founded monastery at Menevia; patron saint of Wales; Mar. 1.

Denis and Companions, Sts. (d. 3rd cent.): Denis, bishop of Paris, and two companions identified by early writers as Rusticus, a priest, and Eleutherius, a deacon; martyred near Paris; Denis is popularly regarded as apostle of France; Oct. 9*.

Dismas, St. (1st cent.): Name given to repentant thief (Good Thief) to whom Jesus promised salvation; regarded as patron of prisoners; Mar. 25.

Dominic, St. (Dominic de Guzman) (1170-1221): Spanish priest; founder of Dominican Order (Friars Preachers), 1215; preached against the Albigensian heresy; a contemporary of St. Francis of Assisi; canonized 1234; Aug. 8*.

Dominic Savio, St. (1842-1857): Italian youth; pupil of St. John Bosco; died before his 15th birthday; canonized 1954; patron of choir boys; Mar. 9.

Dunstan, St. (c. 910-988): English monk; archbishop of Canterbury; initiated reforms in religious life; royal counselor to several kings; considered one of greatest Anglo-Saxon saints; patron of armorers, goldsmiths, locksmiths, jewelers; May 17.

Dymphna, St. (dates uncertain): Nothing certain known of her life; presumably she was an Irish maiden whose relics were discovered at Gheel near Antwerp, Belgium, in the 13th century; since that time many cases of mental illness and epilepsy have been cured at her shrine; patron of those suffering from mental illness; May 15.

Edmund Campion, St. (1540-1581): English Jesuit; convert 1573; martyred at Tyburn; canonized 1970, one of the Forty English and Welsh Martyrs; Dec. 1.

Elizabeth Bayley Seton, St. (1774-1821): American foundress; convert, 1805; founded Sisters of Charity in the U.S.; beatified 1963; canonized Sept. 14, 1975; the first American-born saint; Jan. 4 (U.S.)*.

Elizabeth of Hungary, St. (1207-1231): Queen; became Franciscan tertiary after death of her husband in 1227; devoted life to poor and destitute; a patron of the Third Order of St. Francis; Nov. 17*.

Elizabeth of Portugal, St. (1271-1336): Queen of Portugal; b. Spain; retired to Poor Clare convent as a tertiary after the death of her husband; July 4*.

Erasmus, St. (d. 303): Life surrounded by legend; martyred during Diocletian persecution; patron of sailors; June 2.

Ethelbert, St.(552-676): King of Kent; baptized by St. Augustine 597; issued legal code; furthered spread of Christianity; Feb. 24.

Euphrasia Pelletier, St. (1796-1868): French nun; founded Sisters of the Good Shepherd at Angers, 1829; canonized 1940; Apr. 24.

Eusebius of Vercelli, St. (283-370): Italian bishop; exiled from his see for a time because of his opposition to Arianism; considered a martyr because of sufferings he endured; Aug. 2*.

Fabian, St. (d. 250): Pope, 236-250; martyred under Decius; Jan. 20*.

Felicity, St.: See Perpetua and Felicity, Sts.

Ferdinand III, St. (1198-1252): King of Castile and Leon; waged successful crusade against Mohammedans in Spain; founded university at Salamanca; canonized 1671; May 30.

Fiacre, St. (d. c. 670): Irish hermit; patron of gardeners; Aug. 30.

Fidelis of Sigmaringen, St. (Mark Rey) (1577-1622): German Capuchin; lawyer before he joined the Capuchins; missionary to Swiss Protestants; stabbed to death by peasants who were told he was agent of Austrian emperor; Apr. 24*.

Frances of Rome, St. (1384-1440): Italian model for housewives and widows; happily married for 40 years; after death of her husband in 1436 joined community of Benedictine Oblates she had founded; canonized 1608; patron of motorists; Mar. 9*.

Frances Xavier Cabrini, St. (Mother Cabrini) (1850-1917): American foundress; b. Italy; foundress of Missionary Sisters of the Sacred Heart, 1877; settled in the U.S. 1889; became an American citizen at Seattle 1909; worked among Italian immigrants; canonized 1946, the first American citizen so honored; Nov. 13 (U.S.)*.

Francis Borgia, St. (1510-1572): Spanish Jesuit; joined Jesuits after death of his wife in 1546; became general of the Order, 1565; Oct. 10.

Francis of Assisi, St. (Giovanni di Bernardone) (1182-1226): Founder of the Franciscans, 1209; received stigmata 1224; canonized 1228; one of best known and best loved saints; patron of Catholic Action and of Italy; Oct. 4*.

Francis of Paola, St. (1416-1507): Italian hermit; founder of Minim Friars; Apr. 2*.

Francis Xavier, St. (1506-1552): Spanish Jesuit; missionary to Far East; canonized 1602; patron of foreign missions; considered one of greatest Christian missionaries; Dec. 3*.

Gabriel of the Sorrowful Mother, St. (Francis Possenti) (1838-1862): Italian Passionist; died while a scholastic; canonized 1920; Feb. 27.

Genesius, St. (d. c. 300): Roman actor; according to legend, was converted while performing a burlesque of Christian baptism and was subsequently martyred; patron of actors.

Genevieve, St. (422-500): French nun; a patroness and protectress of Paris; events of her life not authenticated; Jan. 3.

George, St. (d. c. 300): Martyr, probably during Diocletian persecution in Palestine; all other incidents of his life, including story of the dragon, are legendary; patron of England; Apr. 23*.

Gerard Majella, St. (1725-1755): Italian Redemptorist lay brother; noted for supernatural occurrences in his life including bilocation and reading of consciences; canonized 1904; patron of mothers; Oct. 16.

Gertrude, St. (1256-1302): German mystic; writer; helped spread devotion to the Sacred Heart; Nov. 16*.

Gregory VII (Hildebrand), St. (1020?-1085): Pope, 1075-1085; Benedictine monk; adviser to several popes; as pope, strengthened interior life of Church and fought against lay investiture; driven from Rome by Henry IV; died in exile; May 25*.

Gregory the Illuminator, St. (257-332): Martyr; bishop; apostle and patron saint of Armenia; helped free Armenia from the Persians; Sept. 30.

Hedwig, St. (1174-1243): Moravian noblewoman; married duke of Silesia, head of Polish royal family; fostered religious life in country; canonized 1266; Oct. 16*.

Helena, St. (250-330): Empress; mother of Constantine the Great; associated with discovery of the True Cross; Aug. 18.

Henry, St. (972-1024): Bavarian emperor; cooperated with Benedictine abbeys in restoration of ecclesiastical and social discipline; canonized 1146; July 13*.

Hippolytus, St. (d. c. 236): Roman priest; opposed Pope St. Callistus I in his teaching about the readmission of Christians who had apostasized during time of persecution; elected antipope; reconciled before his martyrdom; important ecclesiastical writer; Aug. 13*.

Hubert, St. (d. 727): Bishop; his patronage of hunters is based on legend that he was converted while hunting; Nov. 3.

Hugh of Cluny (the Great), St. (1024-1109): Abbot of Benedictine foundation at Cluny; supported popes in efforts to reform ecclesiastical abuses; canonized 1120; Apr. 29.

Ignatius of Antioch, St. (d. c. 107): Early ecclesiastical writer; martyr; bishop of Antioch in Syria for 40 years; Oct. 17*.

Ignatius of Loyola, St. (1491-1556): Spanish soldier; renounced military career after recovering from wounds received at siege of Pampeluna (Pamplona) in 1521; founded Society of Jesus (Jesuits), 1534, at Paris; canonized 1622; author *The Book of Spiritual Exercises;* July 31*.

Irenaeus of Lyons, St. (130-202): Early ecclesiastical writer; opposed Gnosticism; bishop of Lyons; traditionally regarded as a martyr; June 28*.

Isidore the Farmer, St. (d. 1170): Spanish layman; farmer; canonized 1622; patron of farmers; Oct. 25 (US)*.

Jane Frances de Chantal, St. (1572-1641): French widow; foundress, under guidance of St. Francis de Sales, of Order of the Visitation; canonized 1767; Dec. 12*.

Januarius (Gennaro), St. (d. 304): Bishop of Benevento; martyred during Diocletian persecution; fame rests on liquefaction of some of his blood preserved in a phial at Naples, an unexplained phenomenon which has occurred regularly about 18 times each year for over 400 years; Sept. 19*.

Jerome Emiliani, St. (1481-1537): Venetian priest; founded Somascan Fathers, 1532, for care of orphans; canonized 1767; patron of orphans and abandoned children; Feb. 8*.

Joan of Arc, St. (1412-1431): French heroine, called The Maid of Orleans, La Pucelle; led French army against English invaders; captured by Burgundians, turned over to ecclesiastical court on charge of heresy, found guilty and burned at the stake; her innocence was declared in 1456; canonized 1920; patroness of France; May 30.

John I, St. (d. 526): Pope, 523-526; martyr; May 18*.

John Baptist de la Salle, St. (1651-1719): French priest; founder of Brothers of the Christian Schools, 1680; canonized 1900; Apr. 7*.

John Berchmans, St. (1599-1621): Belgian Jesuit scholastic; patron of Mass servers; canonized 1888; Aug. 13.

John Bosco, St. (1815-1888): Italian priest; founded Salesians, 1864, for education of boys and the Daughters of Mary Auxiliatrix for education of girls; canonized 1934; Jan. 31*.

John Capistran, St. (1386-1456): Italian Franciscan; preacher; papal diplomat; canonized 1690; Oct. 23*.

John Eudes, St. (1601-1680): French priest; founder of Sisters of Our Lady of Charity of Refuge, 1642, and Congregation of Jesus-Mary (Eudists), 1643; canonized 1925; Aug. 19*.

John Fisher, St. (1469-1535): English prelate; theologian; martyr; bishop of Rochester, cardinal; refused to recognize validity of Henry VIII's marriage to Anne Boleyn; upheld supremacy of the pope; beheaded for refusing to acknowledge Henry as head of the Church; canonized 1935; June 22 (with St. Thomas More)*.

John Kanty (Cantius), St. (1395-1473): Polish theologian; canonized 1767; Dec. 23*.

John Leonardi, St. (1550-1609): Italian priest; worked among prisoners and the sick; founded Clerics Regular of the Mother of God; canonized 1938; Oct. 9*.

John Nepomucene, St. (1345-1393): Bohemian priest; regarded as a martyr; canonized 1729; patron of Czechoslovakia; May 16.

John Nepomucene Neumann, Bl. (1811-1860): American prelate; b. Bohemia; ordained in New York 1836; missionary among Germans near Niagara Falls before joining Redemptorists, 1840; bishop of Philadelphia, 1852; first bishop in US to prescribe Forty Hours devotion in his diocese; beatified 1963; Jan. 5 (US)*.

John of God, St. (1495-1550): Portuguese founder; his work among the sick poor led to foundation of Brothers Hospitallers of St. John of God, 1540, in Spain; canonized 1690; patron of sick, hospitals, nurses; Mar. 8*.

John Vianney (Cure of Ars), St. (1786-1859): French parish priest; noted confessor, spent 16 to 18 hours a day in confessional; canonized 1925; patron of parish priests; Aug. 4*.

Josaphat Kuncevyc, St. (1584-1623): Basilian monk; b. Poland; archbishop of Polotsk, Lithuania; worked for reunion of separated Easterners; martyred by mob of schismatics; canonized 1867; Nov. 12*.

Joseph Benedict Cottolengo, St. (1786-1842): Italian priest; established Little Houses of Divine Providence (Piccolo Casa) for care of orphans and the sick; canonized 1934; Apr. 30.

Joseph Cafasso, St. (1811-1860): Italian priest; renowned confessor; promoted devotion to Blessed Sacrament; canonized 1947; June 22.

Joseph Calasanz, St. (1556-1648): Spanish priest; founder of Piarists (Order of Pious Schools); canonized 1767; Aug. 25*.

Joseph of Cupertino, St. (1603-1663): Italian Franciscan; noted for remarkable incidents of levitation; canonized 1767; Sept. 18.

Justin Martyr, St. (100-165): Early ecclesiastical writer; *Apologies for the Christian Religion, Dialog with the Jew Tryphon;* martyred at Rome; June 1*.

Ladislaus, Saint (1040-1095): King of Hungary; supported Pope Gregory VII against Henry IV; canonized 1192; June 27.

Lawrence, St. (d. 258): Widely venerated martyr who suffered death, according to a long-standing but unverifiable legend, by being roasted alive on a gridiron; Aug. 10*.

Leonard of Port Maurice, St. (1676-1751): Italian Franciscan; ascetical writer; preached missions throughout Italy; canonized 1867; patron of parish missions; Nov. 26.

Louis IX, St. (1215-1270): King of France, 1226-1270; participated in Sixth Crusade; patron of Third Order of St. Francis; canonized 1297; Aug. 25*.

Louis de Montfort, St. (1673-1716): French priest; founder of Sisters of Divine Wisdom, 1703, and Missionaries of Company of Mary, 1715; wrote *True Devotion to the Blessed Virgin;* canonized 1947; Apr. 28.

Louise de Marillac, St. (1591-1660): French foundress, with St. Vincent de Paul, of the Sisters of Charity; canonized 1934; Mar. 15.

Lucy, St. (d. 304): Sicilian maiden; martyred during Diocletian persecution; one of most widely venerated early virgin-martyrs; patron of Syracuse, Sicily; invoked by those suffering from eye diseases (based on legend that she offered her eyes to a suitor who admired them); Dec. 13*.

Marcellinus and Peter, Sts. (d.c. 304): Early Roman martyrs; June 2*.

Margaret Clitherow, St. (1556-1586): English martyr; convert shortly after her marriage; one of Forty Martyrs of England and Wales; canonized 1970.

Margaret Mary Alacoque, St. (1647-1690): French nun; spread devotion to Sacred Heart in accordance with revelations made to her in 1675 (see Sacred Heart); canonized 1920; Oct. 16*

Margaret of Scotland, St. (1050-1093): Queen of Scotland; noted for solicitude for the poor and promotion of justice; canonized 1251; Nov. 16*.

Maria Goretti, St. (1890-1902): Italian virgin-martyr; a model of purity; canonized 1950; July 6*.

Mariana Paredes of Jesus, St. (1618-1645): South American recluse; Lily of Quito; canonized, 1950; May 26.

Martha, St. (1st cent.): Sister of Lazarus and Mary of Bethany; Gospel accounts record her concern for homely details; patron of cooks; July 29*.

Martin I, St. (d. 655): Pope, 649; banished from Rome by emperor because of his condemnation of Monothelites; considered a martyr; Apr. 13*.

Martin of Tours, St. (316-397): Bishop of Tours; opposed Arianism and Priscillianism; pioneer of Western monasticism, before St. Benedict; Nov. 11*.

Mary Magdalene, St. (1st cent.): Gospels record her as devoted follower of Christ to whom he appeared after the Resurrection; her identification with Mary of Bethany (sister of Martha and Lazarus) and the woman sinner (Lk 7:36-50) has been questioned; July 22*.

Mary Magdalene de Pazzi, St. (1566-1607): Italian Carmelite nun; recipient of mystical experiences; canonized 1669; May 25*.

Maximilian Kolbe, Bl. (1894-1941): Polish Conventual Franciscan; prisoner at Auschwitz who heroically offered his life in place of a fellow prisoner; beatified 1971.

Methodius, St.: See Index.

Monica, St. (332-387): Mother of St. Augustine; model of a patient mother; her feast is observed in the Roman calendar the day before her son's; Aug. 27*.

Nereus and Achilleus, Sts. (d. c. 100): Early Christian martyrs; soldiers who, according to legend, were baptized by St. Peter; May 12*.

Nicholas of Myra, St. (4th cent.): Bishop of Myra in Asia Minor; one of most popular saints in both East and West; most of the incidents of his life are based on legend; patron of Russia; Dec. 6*.

Nicholas of Tolentino, St. (1245-1365): Italian hermit; famed preacher; canonized 1446; Sept. 10.

Norbert, St. (1080-1134): German bishop; founder of Norbertines or Premonstratensians, 1120; promoted reform of the clergy, devotion to Blessed Sacrament; canonized 1582; June 6*.

Odilia, St. (d. c. 720): Benedictine abbess; according to legend she was born blind, abandoned by her family and adopted by a convent where her sight was miraculously restored; patron of blind; Dec. 13.

Oliver Plunkett, St. (1629-1681): Irish martyr; theologian; archbishop of Armagh and primate of Ireland; beatified 1920; canonized, 1975.

Pancras, St. (d. c. 304): Roman martyr; May 12*.

Paschal Baylon, St. (1540-1592): Spanish Franciscan lay brother; spent life as doorkeeper in various Franciscan friaries; defended doctrine of Real Presence in Blessed Sacrament; canonized 1690; patron of all Eucharistic confraternities and congresses, 1897; May 17.

Patrick, St. (389-461): Famous missionary of Ireland; began missionary work in Ireland about 432; organized the Church there and established it on a lasting foundation; patron of Ireland, with Sts. Bridget and Columba; Mar. 17*.

Paul Miki and Companions, Sts. (d. 1597): Martyrs of Japan; Paul Miki, Jesuit, and twenty-five other priests and laymen were martyred at Nagasaki; canonized 1862, the first canonized martyrs of the Far East; Feb. 6*.

Paul of the Cross, St. (1694-1775): Italian religious; founder of the Passionists; canonized 1867; Oct. 19*.

Paulinus of Nola, St. (d. 451): Bishop of Nola (Spain); writer; June 22*.

Peregrine, St. (1260-1347): Italian Servite; invoked against cancer (he was miraculously cured of cancer of the foot after a vision); canonized 1726; May 1.

Perpetua and Felicity, Sts. (d. 203): Martyrs; Mar. 7*.

Peter Chanel, St. (1803-1841): French Marist; missionary to Oceania, where he was martyred; canonized 1954; Apr. 28*.

Peter Gonzalez, St. (1190-1246): Spanish Dominican; worked among sailors; court chaplain and confessor of King St. Ferdinand of Castile; patron of sailors; Apr. 14.

Peter of Alcantara, St. (1499-1562): Spanish Franciscan; mystic; initiated Franciscan reform; confessor of St. Teresa of Avila; canonized 1669; Oct. 19.

Philip Neri, St. (1515-1595): Italian religious; founded Congregation of the Oratory; considered a second apostle of Rome because of his mission activities there; canonized 1622; May 26*.

Philip of Jesus, St. (1571-1597): Mexican Franciscan; martyred at Nagasaki, Japan; canonized 1862; patron of Mexico City; Feb. 6*.

Pius V, St. (1504-1572): Pope, 1566-1572; enforced decrees of Council of Trent; organized expedition against Turks resulting in victory at Lepanto; canonized 1712; Apr. 30*.

Polycarp, St. (2nd cent.): Bishop of Smyrna; ecclesiastical writer; martyr; Feb. 23*.

Pontian, St. (d. c. 235): Pope, 230-235; exiled to Sardinia by the emperor; regarded as a martyr; Aug. 13 (with Hippolytus)*.

Raymond Nonnatus, St. (d. 1240): Spanish Mercedarian; cardinal; devoted his life to ransoming captives from the Moors; Aug. 31.

Raymond of Penyafort, St. (1175-1275): Spanish Dominican; confessor of Gregory IX; systematized and codified canon law, in effect until 1917; master general of Dominicans, 1238; canonized 1601; Jan. 7*.

Robert Southwell, St. (1561-1595): English Jesuit; poet; martyred at Tyburn; canonized 1970, one of the Forty English and Welsh Martyrs.

Roch, St. (1350-1379): French layman; pilgrim; devoted life to care of plague-stricken; widely venerated; invoked against pestilence; Aug. 17.

Romuald, St. (951-1027): Italian monk; founded Camaldolese Benedictines; June 19*.

Rose of Lima, St. (1586-1617): Peruvian Dominican tertiary; first native-born saint of the New World; canonized 1671; Aug. 23*.

Scholastica, St. (d. c. 559): Sister of St. Benedict; regarded as first nun of the Benedictine Order; Feb. 10*.

Sebastian, St. (3rd cent.): Roman martyr; traditionally pictured as a handsome youth; martyred by being pierced with arrows; patron of athletes; Jan. 20*.

Seven Holy Founders of the Servants of Mary (Buonfiglio Monaldo, Alexis Falconieri, Benedict dell'Antello, Bartholomew Amidei, Ricovero Uguccione, Gerardino Sostegni, John Buonagiunta Monetti): Florentine youths who founded Servites, 1233, in obedience to a vision; canonized 1888; Feb. 17*.

Sixtus II and Companions, Sts. (d. 258): Sixtus, pope 257-258, and four deacons, martyrs; Aug. 7*.

Stanislaus, St. (1030-1079): Polish bishop; martyr; canonized 1253; Apr. 11*.

Stephen, St. (d. c. 33): First Christian martyr; chosen by the Apostles as the first of the seven deacons; stoned to death; Dec. 26*.

Stephen, St. (975-1038): King; apostle of Hungary; welded Magyars into national unity; canonized 1087; Aug. 16*.

Sylvester I, St. (d. 335): Pope 314-335; first ecumenical council held at Nicaea during his pontificate; Dec. 31*.

Tarcisius, St. (d. 3rd cent.): Early martyr; according to tradition, was martyred while carrying the Blessed Sacrament to some Christians in prison; patron of first communicants; Aug. 15.

Therese Couderc, St. (1805-1885): French religious; foundress of the Religious of Our Lady of the Retreat in the Cenacle, 1827; canonized 1970; Sept. 26.

Therese of Lisieux, St. (1873-1897): French Carmelite nun; b. Therese Martin; allowed to enter Carmel at 15, died nine years later of tuberculosis; her "little way" of spiritual perfection became widely known through her spiritual autobiography; despite her obscure life, became one of the most popular saints; canonized 1925; patron of foreign missions; Oct. 1*.

Thomas Becket, St. (1118-1170): English martyr; archbishop of Canterbury; chancellor under Henry II; murdered for upholding rights of the Church; canonized 1173; Dec. 29*.

Thomas More, St. (1478-1535): English martyr; statesman; chancellor under Henry VIII; author of *Utopia;* opposed Henry's divorce, refused to renounce authority of the papacy; beheaded; canonized 1935; June 22 (with St. John Fisher)*.

Timothy, St. (d. c. 97): Bishop of Ephesus; disciple and companion of St. Paul; martyr; Jan. 26*.

Titus, St. (d. c. 96): Bishop; companion of

St. Paul; recipient of one of Paul's epistles; Jan. 26*.

Valentine, St. (d. 269): Priest, physician; martyred at Rome; legendary patron of lovers; Feb. 14.

Vincent, St. (d. 304): Spanish deacon; martyr; Jan. 22*.

Vincent de Paul, St. (1581?-1660): French priest; founder of Congregation of the Mission (Vincentians, Lazarists) and co-founder of Sisters of Charity; declared patron of all charitable organizations and works by Leo XIII; canonized 1737; Sept. 27*.

Vincent Ferrer, St. (1350-1418): Spanish Dominican; famed preacher; Apr. 5*.

Wenceslaus, St. (d. 935): Duke of Bohemia; martyr; patron of Bohemia; Sept. 28*.

Zita, St. (1218-1278): Italian maid; noted for charity to poor; patron of domestics.

SAINTS—PATRONS AND INTERCESSORS

A patron is a saint who is venerated as a special intercessor before God. Most patrons have been so designated as the result of popular devotion and long-standing custom. In many cases, the fact of existing patronal devotion is clear despite historical obscurity regarding its origin. The Church has made official designation of relatively few patrons; in such cases, the dates of designation are given in the list below. The theological background of the patronage of saints includes the dogmas of the Mystical Body of Christ and the Communion of Saints.

Listed below are patron saints of occupations and professions, and saints whose intercession is sought for special needs.

Accountants: St. Matthew.
Actors: St. Genesius.
Advertisers: St. Bernardine of Siena (May 20, 1960).
Alpinists: St. Bernard of Menthon (Aug. 20, 1923).
Altar boys: St. John Berchmans.
Anesthetists: St. Rene Goupil.
Archers: St. Sebastian.
Architects: St. Thomas, Apostle.
Armorers: St. Dunstan.
Art: St. Catherine of Bologna.
Artists: St. Luke, St. Catherine of Bologna.
Astronomers: St. Dominic.
Athletes: St. Sebastian.
Authors: St. Francis de Sales.
Aviators: Our Lady of Loreto (1920), St. Therese of Lisieux, St. Joseph of Cupertino.
Bakers: St. Elizabeth of Hungary, St. Nicholas.
Bankers: St. Matthew.
Barbers: Sts. Cosmas and Damian, St. Louis.
Barren women: St. Anthony of Padua, St. Felicity.
Basket-makers: St. Anthony, Abbot.
Blacksmiths: St. Dunstan.
Blind: St. Odilia, St. Raphael.
Blood banks: St. Januarius.
Bodily ills: Our Lady of Lourdes.
Bookbinders: St. Peter Celestine.
Bookkeepers: St. Matthew.
Booksellers: St. John of God.
Boy Scouts: St. George.
Brewers: St. Augustine of Hippo, St. Luke, St. Nicholas of Myra.
Bricklayers: St. Stephen.
Brides: St. Nicholas of Myra.

Brush makers: St. Anthony, Abbot.
Builders: St. Vincent Ferrer.
Butchers: St. Anthony, Abbot, St. Luke.
Cab drivers: St. Fiacre.
Cabinetmakers: St. Anne.
Cancer patients: St. Peregrine.
Canonists: St. Raymond of Penyafort.
Carpenters: St. Joseph.
Catechists: St. Viator, St. Charles Borromeo, St. Robert Bellarmine.
Catholic Action: St. Francis of Assisi (1916).
Chandlers: St. Ambrose, St. Bernard of Clairvaux.
Charitable societies: St. Vincent de Paul (May 12, 1885).
Children: St. Nicholas of Myra.
Children of Mary: St. Agnes, St. Maria Goretti.
Choir boys: St. Dominic Savio (June 8, 1956), Holy Innocents.
Church: St. Joseph (Dec. 8, 1870).
Clerics: St. Gabriel of the Sorrowful Mother.
Comedians: St. Vitus.
Communications personnel: St. Bernardine.
Confessors: St. Alphonsus Liguori (Apr. 26, 1950), St. John Nepomucene.
Convulsive children: St. Scholastica.
Cooks: St. Lawrence, St. Martha.
Coopers: St. Nicholas of Myra.
Coppersmiths: St. Maurus.
Dairy workers: St. Brigid.
Deaf: St. Francis de Sales.
Dentists: St. Apollonia.
Desperate situations: St. Gregory of Neocaesarea, St. Jude Thaddeus.
Dietitians (in hospitals): St. Martha.
Dyers: Sts. Maurice and Lydia.
Dying: St. Joseph.
Ecologists: St. Francis of Assisi.
Editors: St. John Bosco.
Emigrants: St. Frances Xavier Cabrini, (Sept. 8, 1950).
Epilepsy: St. Vitus.
Engineers: St. Ferdinand III.
Eucharistic congresses and societies: St. Paschal Baylon (Nov. 28, 1897).
Expectant mothers: St. Raymund Nonnatus, St. Gerard Majella.
Eye diseases: St. Lucy.
Falsely accused: St. Raymund Nonnatus.
Farmers: St. George, St. Isidore.

Farriers: St. John Baptist.
Firemen: St. Florian.
Fire prevention: St. Catherine of Siena.
First communicants: St. Tarcisius.
Fishermen: St. Andrew.
Florists: St. Therese of Lisieux.
Forest workers: St. John Gualbert.
Foundlings: Holy Innocents.
Fullers: St. Anastasius the Fuller, St. James the Less.
Funeral directors: St. Joseph of Arimathea, St. Dismas.
Gardeners: St. Adelard, St. Tryphon, St. Fiacre, St. Phocas.
Glassworkers: St. Luke.
Goldsmiths: St. Dunstan, St. Anastasius.
Gravediggers: St. Anthony, Abbot.
Greetings: St. Valentine.
Grocers: St. Michael.
Hairdressers: St. Martin de Porres.
Happy meetings: St. Raphael.
Hatters: St. Severus of Ravenna, St. James the Less.
Haymakers: Sts. Gervase and Protase.
Headache sufferers: St. Teresa of Avila.
Heart patients: St. John of God.
Hospital administrators: St. Basil the Great, St. Frances X. Cabrini.
Hospitals: St. Camillus de Lellis and St. John of God (June 22, 1886), St. Jude Thaddeus.
Housewives: St. Anne.
Hunters: St. Hubert, St. Eustachius.
Infantrymen: St. Maurice.
Innkeepers: St. Amand, St. Martha.
Invalids: St. Roch.
Jewelers: St. Eligius, St. Dunstan.
Journalists: St. Francis de Sales (Apr. 26, 1923).
Jurists: St. John Capistran.
Laborers: St. Isidore, St. James, St. John Bosco.
Lawyers: St. Ivo, St. Genesius, St. Thomas More.
Learning: St. Ambrose.
Librarians: St. Jerome.
Lighthouse keepers: St. Venerius.
Locksmiths: St. Dunstan.
Maids: St. Zita.
Marble workers: St. Clement I.
Mariners: St. Michael, St. Nicholas of Tolentino.
Medical record librarians: St. Raymond of Penyafort.
Medical social workers: St. John Regis.
Medical technicians: St. Albert the Great.
Mentally ill: St. Dymphna.
Merchants: St. Francis of Assisi, St. Nicholas of Myra.
Messengers: St. Gabriel.
Metal workers: St. Eligius.
Millers: St. Arnulph, St. Victor.
Missions, Foreign: St. Francis Xavier (Mar. 25, 1904), St. Therese of Lisieux (Dec. 14, 1927).

Missions, Negro: St. Peter Claver (1896, Leo XIII), St. Benedict the Black.
Missions, Parish: St. Leonard of Port Maurice (Mar. 17, 1923).
Mothers: St. Monica.
Motorcyclists: Our Lady of Grace.
Motorists: St. Christopher, St. Frances of Rome.
Mountaineers: St. Bernard of Menthon.
Musicians: St. Gregory the Great, St. Cecilia, St. Dunstan.
Nail makers: St. Cloud.
Notaries: St. Luke, St. Mark.
Nurses: St. Camillus de Lellis and St. John of God (1930, Pius XI), St. Agatha, St. Raphael.
Nursing and nursing service: St. Elizabeth of Hungary, St. Catherine of Siena.
Orators: St. John Chrysostom (July 8, 1908).
Organ builders: St. Cecilia.
Orphans: St. Jerome Emiliani.
Painters: St. Luke.
Paratroopers: St. Michael.
Pawnbrokers: St. Nicholas.
Pharmacists: Sts. Cosmas and Damian, St. James the Greater.
Pharmacists (in hospitals): St. Gemma Galgani.
Philosophers: St. Justin.
Physicians: St. Pantaleon, Sts. Cosmas and Damian, St. Luke, St. Raphael.
Pilgrims: St. James.
Plasterers: St. Bartholomew.
Poets: St. David, St. Cecilia.
Poison sufferers: St. Benedict.
Policemen: St. Michael.
Poor: St. Lawrence, St. Anthony of Padua.
Poor souls: St. Nicholas of Tolentino.
Porters: St. Christopher.
Possessed: St. Bruno, St. Denis.
Postal employees: St. Gabriel.
Priests: St. Jean-Baptiste Vianney (Apr. 23, 1929).
Printers: St. John of God, St. Augustine of Hippo, St. Genesius.
Prisoners: St. Dismas, St. Joseph Cafasso.
Protector of crops: St. Ansovinus.
Public relations: St. Bernardine of Siena (May 20, 1960).
Public relations (of hospitals): St. Paul, Apostle.
Radiologists: St. Michael (Jan. 15, 1941).
Radio workers: St. Gabriel.
Retreats: St. Ignatius Loyola (July 25, 1922).
Rheumatism: St. James the Greater.
Saddlers: Sts. Crispin and Crispinian.
Sailors: St. Cuthbert, St. Brendan, St. Eulalia, St. Christopher, St. Peter Gonzales, St. Erasmus, St. Nicholas.
Scholars: St. Brigid.
Schools, Catholic: St. Thomas Aquinas (Aug. 4, 1880), St. Joseph Calasanz (Aug. 13, 1948).
Scientists: St. Albert (Aug. 13, 1948).

Sculptors: St. Claude.
Seamen: St. Francis of Paola.
Searchers for lost articles: St. Anthony of Padua.
Secretaries: St. Genesius.
Seminarians: St. Charles Borromeo.
Servants: St. Martha, St. Zita.
Shoemakers: Sts. Crispin and Crispinian.
Sick: St. Michael, St. John of God and St. Camillus de Lellis (June 22, 1886).
Silversmiths: St. Andronicus.
Singers: St. Gregory, St. Cecilia.
Skaters: St. Lidwina.
Skiers: St. Bernard.
Social workers: St. Louise de Marillac (Feb. 12, 1960).
Soldiers: St. Hadrian, St. George, St. Ignatius, St. Sebastian, St. Martin of Tours, St. Joan of Arc.
Speleologists: St. Benedict.
Stenographers: St. Genesius, St. Cassian.
Stonecutters: St. Clement.
Stonemasons: St. Stephen.
Students: St. Thomas Aquinas.
Surgeons: Sts. Cosmas and Damian, St. Luke.
Swordsmiths: St. Maurice.
Tailors: St. Homobonus.
Tanners: Sts. Crispin and Crispinian, St. Simon.
Tax collectors: St. Matthew.
Teachers: St. Gregory the Great, St. John Baptist de la Salle (May 15, 1950).
Telecommunications workers: St. Gabriel (Jan. 12, 1951).
Telegraph/telephone workers: St. Gabriel.
Television: St. Clare of Assisi (Feb. 14, 1958).
Television workers: St. Gabriel.
Tertiaries (Franciscan): St. Louis of France, St. Elizabeth of Hungary.
Theologians: St. Augustine, St. Alphonsus Liguori.
Throat sufferers: St. Blase.
Travelers: St. Anthony of Padua, St. Nicholas of Myra, St. Christopher, St. Raphael.
Travel hostesses: St. Bona (Mar. 2, 1962).
Universities: Blessed Contardo Ferrini.
Vocations: St. Alphonsus.
Watchmen: St. Peter of Alcantara.
Weavers: St. Paul the Hermit, St. Anastasius the Fuller, St. Anastasia.
Wine merchants: St. Amand.
Women in labor: St. Anne.
Women's Army Corps: St. Genevieve.
Workingmen: St. Joseph.
Writers: St. Francis de Sales (Apr. 26, 1923), St. Lucy.
Yachtsmen: St. Adjutor.
Young girls: St. Agnes.
Youth: St. Aloysius Gonzaga (1729, Benedict XIII; 1926, Pius XI), St. John Berchmans, St. Gabriel of the Sorrowful Mother.

Patrons are exemplars of Christian witness as well as intercessors before God.

Patrons of Places

Alsace: St. Odile.
Americas: Our Lady of Guadalupe; St. Rose of Lima.
Argentina: Our Lady of Lujan.
Armenia: St. Gregory Illuminator.
Asia Minor: St. John, Evangelist.
Australia: Our Lady Help of Christians.
Belgium: St. Joseph.
Bohemia: Sts. Wenceslaus, Ludmilla.
Borneo: St. Francis Xavier.
Brazil: Nossa Senhora de Aparecida, Immaculate Conception; St. Peter of Alcantara.
Canada: St. Joseph; St. Anne.
Ceylon (Sri Lanka): St. Lawrence.
Chile: St. James; Our Lady of Mt. Carmel.
China: St. Joseph.
Colombia: St. Peter Claver; St. Louis Bertran.
Corsica: Immaculate Conception.
Czechoslovakia: St. Wenceslaus; St. John Nepomucene; St. Procopius.
Denmark: St. Ansgar; St. Canute.
Dominican Republic: Our Lady of High Grace; St. Dominic.
East Indies: St. Thomas, Apostle.
Ecuador: Sacred Heart.
England: St. George.
Europe: St. Benedict.
Finland: St. Henry.
France: Our Lady of the Assumption; St. Joan of Arc; St. Therese.
Germany: Sts. Boniface, Michael.
Greece: St. Nicholas; St. Andrew.
Holland: St. Willibrord.
Hungary: Blessed Virgin, "Great Lady of Hungary"; St. Stephen, King.
India: Our Lady of Assumption.
Ireland: Sts. Patrick, Brigid and Columba.
Italy: St. Francis of Assisi; St. Catherine of Siena.
Japan: St. Peter Baptist.
Lesotho: Immaculate Heart of Mary.
Lithuania: St. Casimir, Bl. Cunegunda.
Malta: St. Paul; Our Lady of the Assumption.
Mexico: Our Lady of Guadalupe.
Monaco: St. Devota.
Moravia: Sts. Cyril and Methodius.
New Zealand: Our Lady Help of Christians.
Norway: St. Olaf.
Paraguay: Our Lady of Assumption.
Peru: St. Joseph.
Philippines: Sacred Heart of Mary.
Poland: St. Casimir; Bl. Cunegunda; St. Stanislaus of Cracow; Our Lady of Czestochowa.
Portugal: Immaculate Conception; St. Francis Borgia; St. Anthony of Padua; St. Vincent; St. George.
Republic of South Africa: Our Lady of Assumption.
Russia: St. Andrew; St. Nicholas of Myra; St. Therese of Lisieux.

Scandinavia: St. Ansgar.
Scotland: St. Andrew; St. Columba.
Silesia: St. Hedwig.
Slovakia: Our Lady of Sorrows.
South America: St. Rose of Lima.
Spain: St. James; St. Teresa.
Sweden: St. Bridget; St. Eric.
United States: Immaculate Conception.
Uruguay: Our Lady of Lujan.
Wales: St. David.
West Indies: St. Gertrude.

Apostles of Places, Peoples

Alps: St. Bernard of Menthon.
Andalusia (Spain): St. John of Avila.
Antioch: St. Barnabas.
Armenia: St. Gregory the Illuminator; St. Bartholomew.
Austria: St. Severine.
Bavaria: St. Killian.
Brazil: Jose Anchieta.
California: Junipero Serra.
Carinthia (Yugoslavia): St. Virgil.
Colombia: St. Louis Bertran.
Corsica: St. Alexander Sauli.
Crete: St. Titus.
Cyprus: St. Barnabas.
Denmark: St. Ansgar.
England: St. Augustine of Canterbury; St. Gregory the Great.
Ethiopia: St. Frumentius.
Finland: St. Henry.
Florence: St. Andrew Corsini.
France: St. Remigius; St. Martin of Tours; St. Denis.
Friesland (Germany): St. Suitbert; St. Willibrord.
Gaul: St. Irenaeus.
Gentiles: St. Paul.
Georgia (Russia): St. Nino.
Germany: St. Boniface; St. Peter Canisius.
Gothland (Sweden): St. Sigfrid.
Guelderland (Holland): St. Plechelm.
Highlanders (Scotland): St. Columba.
Hungarians (Magyars): St. Stephen, King; St. Gerard; Bl. Astricus.
India: St. Thomas, Apostle.
Indies: St. Francis Xavier.
Ireland: St. Patrick.
Iroquois: Francois Picquit.
Italy: St. Bernardine of Siena.
Japan: St. Francis Xavier.
Malta: St. Paul.
Mexico: The twelve Apostles of Mexico (Franciscans), headed by Fra. Martin de Valencia.
Negro Slaves: St. Peter Claver.
Netherlands: St. Willibrord.
Northumbria (Britain): St. Aidan.
Norway: St. Olaf.
Ottawas (Indians): Fr. Claude Allouez.
Persia: St. Maruthas.
Poland: St. Hyacinth.
Portugal: St. Christian.
Prussia (Slavs): St. Adalbert; St. Bruno of Querfurt.

Rome: St. Philip Neri.
Rumania: St. Nicetas.
Ruthenia: St. Bruno.
Sardinia: St. Ephesus.
Saxony: St. Willihad.
Scandinavia (North): St. Ansgar.
Scotland: St. Palladius.
Slavs: Sts. Cyril and Methodius, St. Adalbert.
Spain: St. James; Sts. Euphrasius and Felix.
Sweden: St. Ansgar.
Switzerland: St. Andeol.
Tournai (Belgium): St. Eligius, St. Piaton.

Emblems of Saints

St. Agatha: Tongs, veil.
St. Agnes: Lamb.
St. Ambrose: Bees, dove, ox, pen.
St. Andrew: Transverse cross.
St. Anne, Mother of the Blessed Virgin: A door.
St. Anthony, Abbot: Bell, hog.
St. Anthony of Padua: Infant Jesus, bread, book, lily.
St. Augustine of Hippo: Dove, child, shell, pen.
St. Barnabas: Stones, ax, lance.
St. Bartholomew: Knife, flayed and holding his skin.
St. Benedict: Broken cup, raven, bell, crosier, bush.
St. Bernard of Clairvaux: Pen, bees, instruments of Passion.
St. Bernardine of Siena: Tablet or sun inscribed with IHS.
St. Blase: Wax, taper, iron comb.
St. Bonaventure: Communion, ciborium, cardinal's hat.
St. Boniface: Oak, ax, book, fox, scourge, fountain, raven, sword.
St. Bridget of Sweden: Book, pilgrim's staff.
St. Bridget of Kildare: Cross, flame over her head, candle.
St. Catherine of Ricci: Ring, crown, crucifix.
St. Catherine of Siena: Stigmata, cross, ring, lily.
St. Cecilia: Organ.
St. Charles Borromeo: Communion, coat of arms with word *Humilitas*.
St. Christopher: Giant, torrent, tree, Child Jesus on his shoulders.
St. Clare of Assisi: Monstrance.
Sts. Cosmas and Damian: A phial, box of ointment.
St. Cyril of Alexandria: Blessed Virgin holding the Child Jesus, pen.
St. Cyril of Jerusalem: Purse, book.
St. Dominic: Rosary, star.
St. Edmund the Martyr: Arrow, sword.
St. Elizabeth of Hungary: Alms, flowers, bread, the poor, a pitcher.
St. Francis of Assisi: Deer, wolf, birds, fish, skull, the Stigmata.

St. Francis Xavier: Crucifix, bell, vessel, Negro.

St. Genevieve: Bread, keys, herd, candle.

St. George: Dragon.

St. Gertrude: Crown, taper, lily.

Sts. Gervase and Protase: Scourge, club, sword.

St. Gregory I (the Great): Tiara, crosier, dove.

St. Helena: Cross.

St. Hilary: Stick, pen, child.

St. Ignatius Loyola: Communion, chasuble, book, apparition of Our Lord.

St. Isidore: Bees, pen.

St. James the Greater: Pilgrim's staff, shell, key, sword.

St. James the Less: Square rule, halberd, club.

St. Jerome: Lion.

St. John Berchmans: Rule of St. Ignatius, cross, rosary.

St. John Chrysostom: Bees, dove, pen.

St. John of God: Alms, a heart, crown of thorns.

St. John the Baptist: Lamb, head cut off on platter, skin of an animal.

St. John the Evangelist: Eagle, chalice, kettle, armor.

St. Josaphat Kuncevyc: Chalice, crown, winged deacon.

St. Joseph, Spouse of the Blessed Virgin: Infant Jesus, lily, rod, plane, carpenter's square.

St. Jude: Sword, square rule, club.

St. Justin Martyr: Ax, sword.

St. Lawrence: Cross, book of the Gospels, gridiron.

St. Leander of Seville: A pen.

St. Liborius: Pebbles, peacock.

St. Longinus: In arms at foot of the cross.

St. Louis IX of France: Crown of thorns, nails.

St. Lucy: Cord, eyes.

St. Luke: Ox, book, brush, palette.

St. Mark: Lion, book.

St. Martha: Holy water sprinkler, dragon.

St. Mary Magdalene: Alabaster box of ointment.

St. Matilda: Purse, alms.

St. Matthew: Winged man, purse, lance.

St. Matthias: Lance.

St. Maurus: Scales, spade, crutch.

St. Meinrad: Two ravens.

St. Michael: Scales, banner, sword, dragon.

St. Monica: Girdle, tears.

St. Nicholas: Three purses or balls, anchor or boat, child.

St. Patrick: Cross, harp, serpent, baptismal font, demons, shamrock.

St. Paul: Sword, book or scroll.

St. Peter: Keys, boat, cock.

St. Philip, Apostle: Column.

St. Philip Neri: Altar, chasuble, vial.

St. Roch: Angel, dog, bread.

St. Rose of Lima: Crown of thorns, anchor, city.

St. Sebastian: Arrows, crown.

Sts. Sergius and Bacchus: Military garb, palm.

St. Simon: Saw, cross.

St. Simon Stock: Scapular.

St. Teresa of Avila: Heart, arrow, book.

St. Therese of Lisieux: Roses entwining a crucifix.

St. Thomas, Apostle: Lance, ax.

St. Thomas Aquinas: Chalice, monstrance, dove, ox, person trampled under foot.

St. Vincent: Gridiron, boat.

St. Vincent de Paul: Children.

St. Vincent Ferrer: Pulpit, cardinal's hat, trumpet, captives.

THE MOTHER OF JESUS IN CATHOLIC UNDERSTANDING

(This article was written for the Catholic Almanac by the Rev. Eamon R. Carroll, O. Carm., professor in the School of Sacred Theology, Catholic University of America.)

Current Catholic understanding about the Virgin Mary, Mother of Jesus, is based on the place the Second Vatican Council gave to the mystery of Mary. The key statements are found in the *Constitution on the Sacred Liturgy* and in the final chapter of the *Dogmatic Constitution on the Church.*

Considering the liturgy and the way in which the Church unfolds the whole mystery of Christ's life in the course of a year — so that the events of redemption are "in some way made present at all times" — the council said: "In celebrating this annual cycle of Christ's mysteries, holy Church honors with special love the Blessed Mary, Mother of God, who is joined by an inseparable bond to the saving work of her Son. In Mary the Church holds up and admires the most excellent fruit of the redemption; in Mary the

Church joyfully contemplates, as in a spotless model, that which the Church herself wholly desires and aspires to be" (*Constitution on the Sacred Liturgy*, No. 103).

In linking respect for Mary to the liturgical celebration of the mystery of Christ in the Church, the council joined doctrine and devotion. The *Dogmatic Constitution on the Church* took a similar approach, with a follow-through from the place of Mary in the communion of saints in the seventh chapter to treatment in the eighth chapter of "The Blessed Virgin Mary, Mother of God, in the Mystery of Christ and the Church." The seventh chapter recalls Mary's place with the risen Christ, as in the eucharistic prayer: "In union with the whole Church we honor Mary, the ever-virgin Mother of Jesus Christ our Lord and God." The eighth chapter opens and closes with the same liturgical theme, on Mary's place among God's friends, and appeals also to the Church, "knowing Mary's role by experience" (*Ibid.*, No. 52) and "contemplating Mary's hidden holiness" *(Ibid.,* No. 64), in support of "the singular cult of Mary that has always existed in the Church" *(Ibid.,* No. 66).

Mary in the Bible

Recent studies by Protestants and Catholics have traced in the Bible a theological portrait of the Mother of Jesus which emphasizes her faith-commitment to God's will and her Son's saving work. Differences in Catholic and Protestant interpretations of the sense in which Mary is joined to the saving work of Jesus underlie different views regarding Mary as a type of the Church.

Not only the stories of the birth and childhood of Jesus in Matthew and Luke but also John's Gospel illustrate the meaning of Mary with respect to Christ and to the Church. In her "pilgrimage of faith," her earthly association with Jesus "even to the cross," Mary was "a type of the Church — in the order of faith, charity and perfect union with Christ" *(Dogmatic Constitution on the Church,* Nos. 58, 63).

The opening chapters of Matthew and Luke are complex reflections on Jesus as Messiah and Redeemer, permeated with the sense of fulfillment of the Old Testament. When the Evangelists composed the Gospels, they worked backwards, beginning with the death and resurrection, then taking up the public life, beginning with Jesus' baptism by John the Baptist, and finally adding the stories of his infancy and childhood — the better to bring out the meaning of the Redeemer's mission. The light of the Easter faith shines with particular strength on these opening chapters, the last to be written down.

In harmony with the Gospel sense of fulfillment, the council referred to Mary as "the exalted daughter of Zion in whom the times are fulfilled, after the long waiting for the promise, and the new economy inaugurated when the Son of God takes on human nature from her in order to free men from sin by the mysteries of His flesh" *(Dogmatic Constitution on the Church,* No. 55). Daughter of Zion in the Old Testament meant the people of Israel. Daughter of her people, Mary of Nazareth fulfills all the longings of Israel for the coming of the Messiah. "She stands out among the Lord's lowly and poor who confidently look for salvation from Him and receive it" *(Ibid.,* No. 55).

Virgin Birth of Christ

Matthew and Luke state the fact of the "virgin birth," that Mary conceived Jesus without a human father — a truth that has formed part of the faith from the earliest creeds to the present teaching and preaching of the Church, in East and West alike.

In her religious and cultural world, it is not likely Mary had previously resolved to remain a virgin; the Old Testament regarded being unmarried as a calamity and childlessness as a disgrace. Mary's question, "How shall this be because I know not man" (Lk. 1:34), is regarded as the inspired reflection of the early Church on the virginal conception of Jesus, comparable to Matthew's account of Joseph's dream-vision (Mt. 1:20). Mary and Joseph accepted as God's will the virginal conception, an unprecedented event that put them both totally at the service of Jesus.

The Gospel offers a comparison between the faith of Abraham — whose son, Isaac, was born of the aged Sara — and Mary's faith in God's power to bring forth the Messiah from her virginal womb. God accomplishes salvation independently of the will of the flesh and of the will of man (Jn. 1:13), though not without a free and loving, if certainly wondering too, acceptance by the humble handmaid of the Lord. God shows his favor when and as he chooses, whether in the barren Sara or in the Virgin Mary, "because nothing shall be impossible with God" (Lk. 1:37 and Gn. 18:14). Jews and Christians honor Abraham as "our father in faith." On Gospel evidence, Mary is "mother in faith, mother of believers."

Mary at Cana and Calvary

John's Gospel pictures Mary at Cana and Calvary, the beginning and end of her Son's public life. In both incidents Jesus addresses her as "woman"; both scenes refer to the "hour" of Jesus' glorification at his death.

Mary's presence at Cana has deeper overtones than her sensitivity to the need for more wine. Jesus' reply to his Mother is an invitation to deepen her faith, to look beyond the failing wine to his messianic career about to begin. The change of water into wine symbolizes the benefits the Savior brings; the marriage feast looks to the "hour" in which the Bridegroom, Christ, will lay down his life in love for his Bride, the Church. Mary is present as the "daughter of Zion" greeting the messianic Bridegroom; she is model of the Church, new People of God, spotless Bride of Christ.

On Calvary Mary stands "by the cross of Jesus," and John records the words of the dying Jesus as he sees her there together with the beloved disciple: "Woman, behold your son. . . . Behold your mother" (Jn. 19:26-27). It is certain that more is meant here than simply our Lord's providing for his Mother's care. The word, "woman," finds an explanation in the Savior's farewell discourse at the Last Supper. To strengthen his followers, Jesus recalled an example from the Bible: "A woman about to give birth has sorrow because her hour has come. But when she has brought forth the child, she no longer remembers the anguish for her joy that a man is born into the world" (Jn. 16:21). Israel's longing for the messianic age was sometimes compared to labor pains. The daughter of Zion had been promised a progeny that would include all races, all nations. The words of Jesus announce the fulfillment of that promise, for Mary on Calvary symbolizes the "woman" who is mother Church, new Israel, new People of God, mother of all, Jew and Gentile.

About Mary's later life, the Scriptures are silent. The last time she appears is in the Acts of the Apostles, at the heart of the band of Apostles praying for the coming of the Holy Spirit at Pentecost. At the overshadowing of the Spirit·at the Annunciation, Mary awaited the birth of Jesus; now she awaits again the coming of the Spirit and the birth of Jesus in His Church. (*Dogmatic Constitution on the Church*, No. 59; *Decree on the Missionary Activity of the Church*, No. 4)

Understanding and Veneration

The process of understanding the mystery of Mary that began in Gospel times has continued in the Church. This is true also of Christian veneration for the Mother of Jesus, shown already in the words of the Magnificat — "All generations shall call me blessed," (Lk. 1:48) — and in the incident from Jesus' public life when the praise of an enthusiastic woman from the crowd is repeated on a deeper level by Jesus himself, "Still happier those who hear the word of God and keep it" (Lk. 11:28). For Luke, no one heard the word of God more perfectly than the Mother of Jesus, as in Elizabeth's praise of Mary's faith: "Of all women you are the most blessed . . . blessed is she who believed that the promise made her by the Lord would be fulfilled" (Lk. 1:42- 45).

The New Eve

The oldest title for Mary after the Gospel is "new Eve." Christian authors as early as the mid-second century compared Mary, the obedient virgin who heard the angel's word, to the first Eve, who heeded the evil angel and disobeyed God. The axiom, "Death through Eve, life through Mary," was coined by the time of St. Jerome.

By the fourth century, Christians were holding that Mary remained a virgin all her life. The Gospels speak of "brethren" of Jesus, but leave their identity undecided — whether they were blood brothers and sisters or cousins. Christian experience of the faith solved the question not by scientific study of the Scriptures but by a contemplative awareness that Mary's commitment to Jesus was lifelong in this virginal sense also.

What is at stake here is an early example of "development of doctrine," and Protestant and Catholic positions still differ strongly on the legitimacy of such a "traditional" interpretation, where the Scriptures are not clear or are even silent.

Two other Roman Catholic beliefs about Mary encounter the same Protestant objection of the seeming silence of the Scriptures: the Immaculate Conception (Mary's freedom from original sin) and the Assumption (Mary's being one with the risen Christ in the fullness of her being, body as well as soul). Both doctrines have been solemnly proclaimed as revealed truth in dogmatic definitions, by Pius IX in 1854 and by Pius XII in 1950.

Mother of God

In early Christian times it was usually the need to defend the mystery of Jesus Christ and of Christian life that called forth from the Church clarifications about the Mother of Jesus. In the fourth century the Christian sense of Mary as model of a life of consecrated virginity led to the understanding that she remained always a virgin. At Ephesus in 431, the third ecumenical council defined the title, "Bearer of God" *(Theotokos)* as revealed truth, precisely to defend the truth that the Son of Mary is actually the Son of God, for Jesus is the God-man. To this day, "Mother of God" remains a title that protects the central truth of the Incarnation, even though some Western Christians find difficulty in the popular use of "Mother of God" for Mary in Catholic and Eastern Orthodox traditions. They fear the conciliar title is not well understood by many who use it, that sometimes it is almost pagan in meaning.

Mother in Order of Grace

As Christianity developed, people turned to Mary as a model of holy response to Christ, as the perfect believer in Jesus. The sense of communion between Mary in heaven and the brethren of her Son on earth grew stronger also. This is what is meant by the "intercession of Mary in the communion of saints" — a mysterious bond between those who are already with the risen Christ and their earthly brothers and sisters still on pilgrimage. Mary's association with Jesus on earth continues now with the risen Lord in a further stage beyond the limitations of the present world. As early as St. Augustine (d. 430), Mary was regarded as the "Mother of the members of Christ" — that is, the members of his Body, which is the Church; for, more than anyone else, she cooperated by her love and faith in the birth of the faithful in the Church, fulfilling the advice of Jesus, "Anyone who does the will of God, that person is my brother and sister and mother" (Mk. 3:35).

In this sense Mary has become "our Mother in the order of grace" *(Dogmatic Constitution on the Church,* No. 61), with a maternity not limited to her life of faith and union with Jesus on earth, but with a "saving role" that continues even "to the eternal fulfillment of the elect" *(Ibid.,* No. 62). "Inseparably joined to the saving work of Christ," is the way the *Constitution on the Sacred Liturgy* states this. What Catholics call Mary's "mediation of grace" is her continuing involvement in God's saving plan.

Views of Theologians

Early Christian authors, like St. Ambrose in the fourth century, expressed the view that Mary was a model to the Church, that her virginal maternity was reflected in the Church's spiritual maternity of the brethren of Christ. In the Middle Ages the likenesses between Mary and the Church were further explored. As the French Cistercian, Blessed Guerric of Igney (d. 1157), put it: "Like the Church of which she is a figure, Mary is Mother of all those who are born to life." Medieval devotion shifted the emphasis from admiration of the holiness of the Mother of God to confidence in her role as all-powerful intercessor, Queen and Mother. Doctrine and devotion to Mary were in accord with the strong sense of community between the Church on earth and the Church triumphant in heaven.

At times devotion to Mary and other saints took bizarre forms, and there were many abuses. When the Reformation took place, calling upon the saints, even St. Mary, for help was rejected by the Reformers as taking away from the unique mediatorship of Christ. Ever since that time, Christians of the West have differed in their understanding of this aspect of the communion of saints.

Ecumenical Considerations

The dogmas of the Immaculate Conception and the Assumption, which remain formidable ecumenical difficulties, are now viewed less as "special privileges," personal and private to Mary, than as saving events that happened to her for the sake of Christ and his Church.

Mary was the child of two human parents, but kept free from original sin. This initial holiness, called the Immaculate Conception, was entirely God's gift to her and is a sign of the love Christ has for his Bride, the Church, which — even though composed of sinners — is "holy Church."

Mary's Assumption means that she is one with the risen Christ in body and soul, that is, in the fullness of her personality. The meaning for the Church is that the Mother of Jesus is "a sign of sure hope and comfort for the pilgrim People of God," showing forth the fullest meaning of being redeemed. Here again Mary is the "spotless image" of the Church responding in joy to the invitation of Christ, himself the "first-fruits from the dead" and the glorious Bridegroom inviting his Church to join him at the Father's right hand. The Church has answered her Lord's invitation in one of her daughters — Mary assumed into heaven — who is "the image and beginning of the Church as she is to be perfected in the world to come" *(Dogmatic Constitution on the Church,* No. 68).

Approach of Vatican II

The Second Vatican Council was highly sensitive to the views and feelings of other Christians when it spoke about the Mother of Jesus. Only once, for example, did it use the difficult term, "Mediatrix," which it explained as strengthening, rather than lessening confidence in Christ, the one Mediator. More significantly, its biblical approach to Mary, with a strong accent on her pilgrimage of faith, is in accord with the pattern of Protestant theology.

Catholics and Protestants, in spite of a common faith in the Trinity and in Christ, are still divided about several main doctrinal issues. In connection with them, the council noted the necessity of remembering "that in Catholic teaching there exists an order or 'hierarchy,' of truths, since they vary in their relationship to the foundation of the Christian faith." *(Decree on Ecumenism,* No. 11). The council also listed these truths in this order: the meaning of redemption, the mystery and ministry of the Church, and the role of Mary in the work of salvation *(Ibid.,* No. 20).

Present indications are that the mystery of Mary in the setting of the larger mystery of Christ and the Church will occupy increasing attention from Catholics, Protestants and Orthodox listening to one another in the Spirit of Jesus — the same Spirit who inspired Mary's prophecy: "All generations shall call me blessed, because he who is mighty has done great things for me" (Lk. 1:48-49).

BISHOPS' PASTORAL LETTER

The article above, by Father Eamon Carroll, O. Carm., was a primary nucleus of the pastoral letter, "Behold your Mother, Woman of Faith," published by the National Conference of Catholic Bishops in 1973. Its contents are also related to the apostolic exhortation *Marialis Cultus* issued by Pope Paul in 1974.

INTERFAITH STATEMENT

L'Osservatore Romano, in its June 13, 1975, edition, highly praised the theological and ecumenical importance of a statement on the role of Mary in the work of redemption. The statement was issued by seven Catholic and six non-Catholic theologians who took part in a round table discussion May 16 during sessions of the International Mariological Congress in Rome.

The statement asserted Mary's "exceptional dignity and efficacy" among human collaborators chosen by God in the work of redemption.

It also defended the practice of offering prayers of intercession to Mary, pointing out that: "Prayers of intercession directed to the Virgin have as their foundation, besides the trust in the Mother of God stirred up by the

Holy Spirit among Christian people, the fact that Mary remains always linked to the work of redemption and therefore to its application across time and space."

The Vatican daily pointed out that, even though the signers of the statement acted in an unofficial capacity, their statement had "its importance both from a theological point of view and from an ecumenical one."

Father Gino Concetti, O.F.M., said in an editorial: "The text places a fundamental importance on theology and specifically on Mariology. . . . In rediscovering the role of Mary, separated Christian communities have a meeting point with the churches that attribute to the Mother of God a veneration equal to her exceptional dignity and efficacy."

Signers of the statement included members of the Greek Orthodox Church, the Evangelical Lutheran Church, the Swedish National Church, the Orthodox Church of Yugoslavia, the Reformed Church in Switzerland and the Evangelical Lutheran Church in West Germany.

APPARITIONS OF THE BLESSED VIRGIN MARY

Only eight of the best known apparitions of the Blessed Virgin Mary are described briefly below.

The sites of the following apparitions have become shrines and centers of pilgrimage. Miracles of the moral and physical orders have been reported as occurring at these places and/or in connection with related practices of prayer and penance.

Banneux, near Liege, Belgium: Mary appeared eight times between Jan. 15 and Mar. 2, 1933, to an 11-year-old peasant girl, Mariette Beco, in a garden behind the family cottage in Banneux, near Liege. She called herself the Virgin of the Poor, and has since been venerated as Our Lady of the Poor, the Sick, and the Indifferent. A small chapel was built by a spring near the site of the apparitions and was blessed Aug. 15, 1933. Approval of devotion to Our Lady of Banneux was given in 1949 by Bishop Louis J. Kerkhofs of Liege, and a statue of that title was solemnly crowned in 1956.

Over 100 sanctuaries throughout the world are dedicated to the honor of Our Lady of Banneux.

The **International Union of Prayer,** for devotion to the Virgin of the Poor, has approximately two million members.

Beauraing, Belgium: Mary appeared 33 times between Nov. 29, 1932, and Jan. 3, 1933, to five children in the garden of a convent school in Beauraing. A chapel, which became a pilgrimage center, was erected on the spot. Reserved approval of devotion to Our Lady of Beauraing was given Feb. 2, 1943, and final approbation July 2, 1949, by Bishop Charue of Namur.

The **Marian Union of Beauraing,** a prayer association for the conversion of sinners, has thousands of members throughout the world (see Pro Maria Committee).

Fatima, Portugal: Mary appeared six times between May 13 and Oct. 13, 1917, to three children in a field called Cova da Iria near Fatima, north of Lisbon. She recommended frequent recitation of the Rosary; urged works of mortification for the conversion of sinners; called for devotion to herself under the title of her Immaculate Heart; asked that the people of Russia be consecrated to her under this title, and that the faithful make a Communion of reparation on the first Saturday of each month.

The apparitions were declared worthy of belief in October, 1930, after a seven-year canonical investigation, and devotion to Our Lady of Fatima was authorized under the title of Our Lady of the Rosary. In October, 1942, Pius XII consecrated the world to Mary under the title of her Immaculate Heart. Ten years later, in the first apostolic letter addressed directly to the peoples of Russia, he consecrated them in a special manner to Mary.

Fatima, with its sanctuary and basilica, ranks with Lourdes as the greatest of modern Marian shrines.

(See First Saturday Devotion.)

Guadalupe, Mexico: Mary appeared four times in 1531 to an Indian, Juan Diego, on Tepeyac hill outside of Mexico City, and instructed him to tell Bishop Zumarraga of her wish that a church be built there. The bishop complied with the request about two years later after being convinced of the genuineness of the apparition by the evidence of a miraculously painted life-size figure of the Virgin on the mantle of the Indian. The mantle bearing the picture has been preserved and is enshrined in the Basilica of Our Lady of Guadalupe, which has a long history as a center of devotion and pilgrimage in Mexico. The shrine church, originally dedicated in 1709 and subsequently enlarged, has the title of basilica.

Benedict XIV, in a decree issued in 1754, authorized a Mass and Office under the title of Our Lady of Guadalupe for celebration on Dec. 12, and named Mary the patroness of New Spain. Our Lady of Guadalupe was designated patroness of Latin America by St. Pius X in 1910 and patroness of the Americas by Pius XII in 1945.

Knock, Ireland: An apparition of Mary, along with the figures of St. Joseph and St. John the Apostle, was witnessed by at least 15 persons in the evening of Aug. 21, 1879, near the parish church of Knock, County Mayo. A commission appointed by the Bishop of Tuam to investigate the matter reported that testimony confirming the apparition was "trustworthy and satisfactory."

La Salette, France: Mary appeared as a sorrowing and weeping figure Sept. 19, 1846, to two peasant children, Melanie Matthieu, 15, and Maximin Giraud, 11, at La Salette in southern France. The message she confided to them, regarding the necessity of penance, was communicated to Pius IX in 1851 and has since been known as the "secret" of La Salette. Bishop de Bruillard of Grenoble declared in 1851 that the apparition was credible, and devotion to Mary under the title of Our Lady of La Salette was authorized. The devotion has been confirmed by popes since the time of Pius IX, and a Mass and Office with this title were authorized in 1942. The shrine church was given the title of minor basilica in 1879.

Lourdes, France: Mary, identifying herself as the Immaculate Conception, appeared 18 times between Feb. 11 and July 16, 1858, to 14-year-old Bernadette Soubirous at the grotto of Massabielle near Lourdes in southern France. Her message concerned the necessity of prayer and penance for the conversion of men. Mary's request that a chapel be built at the grotto and spring was fulfilled in 1862 after four years of rigid examination established the credibility of the apparitions. Devotion under the title of Our Lady of Lourdes was authorized later, and a Feb. 11 feast commemorating the apparitions was instituted by Leo XIII. St. Pius X extended this feast throughout the Church in 1907.

The Church of Notre Dame was made a basilica in 1870, and the Church of the Rosary was built later. The underground Church of St. Pius X, consecrated Mar. 25, 1958, is the second largest church in the world, with a capacity of 20,000 persons.

Our Lady of the Miraculous Medal, France: Mary appeared three times in 1830 to Catherine Laboure in the chapel of the motherhouse of the Daughters of Charity of St. Vincent de Paul, Rue de Bac, Paris. She commissioned Catherine to have made the medal of the Immaculate Conception, now known as the Miraculous Medal, and to spread devotion to her under this title. In 1832, the medal was struck according to the model revealed to Catherine.

Secret of Fatima

Sister Lucy, a Carmelite nun and one of the trio of shepherd children to whom Mary appeared, wrote a three-part account of an apparition which occurred July 13, 1917. The first part concerned a vision of hell. The second dealt with the conversion of the peoples of Russia through devotion to Mary under the title of her Immaculate Heart. The third part was the so-called "secret" which, it was said, was not to be opened until 1960 or the death of Sister Lucy, whichever came first. Presumably, the "secret" was a prophecy of dire events. To date, it has not been disclosed.

Church officials have decried morbid concern about it.

Apparitions Denied

Garabandal: Claims of Vatican support for alleged apparitions of the Blessed Virgin Mary to four young girls at Garabandal, Spain, were denied May 10, 1969, by the Congregation for the Doctrine of the Faith. The congregation, stating that investigation and decision on the matter rested with authorities in the Diocese of Santander, said that it stood by the "official note" authorized by Bishop Vicente Puchol Montiz Aug. 17, 1965. The note said there had been no apparitions of the Blessed Virgin, St. Michael the Archangel or other saints. (It had been reported that the first of several appearances occurred June 18, 1961.) It also said that there was no message of private revelation. (One was reported Oct. 18, 1961.) Summarily, the note stated that all reported incidents were explainable on a natural basis.

Necedah: Reporting in February, 1971, a special commission of the La Crosse diocese agreed with the conclusions of a 1950-1955 investigation that alleged revelations and visions of a woman in Necedah, Wis., were not of supernatural origin. The events were connected with the local Shrine of the Queen of the Holy Rosary, Mediatrix of Peace. The commission recommended that religious worship at the shrine be prohibited. In June, 1972, Bishop Frederick W. Freking warned persistent promoters of the cult of Necedah — organized under the title, For My God and My Country, Inc. — to cease their activities. Because of their failure to do so, he placed seven of them under the penalty of personal interdict in May, 1975. The censure meant that they were barred from the reception of any sacrament except penance.

MARIAN STUDY

The executive committee of the Catholic Biblical Association, at the association's annual convention in Denver in September, 1975, authorized a $1,000 grant to the U.S. Bishops' Committee on Ecumenical and Interreligious Affairs to fund a Catholic-Lutheran study of Mary in the New Testament.

Sponsored by the bishops' committee in collaboration with the national committee of the Lutheran World Federation, the study — like a recent joint study of Peter in the New Testament — will involve biblical scholars of faiths other than Catholic or Lutheran. The Marian study was scheduled for publication by the end of 1976.

The association is committed "to the scientific study of the Bible in conformity with the spirit and instruction of the Catholic Church, which the association acknowledges to be the only divinely appointed custodian and authorized interpreter of the Holy Scripture."

Eastern Catholic Churches

The Eastern Catholic Churches are those which are organized under the major patriarchates of Alexandria, Antioch and Jerusalem (Constantinople, formerly), and the minor patriarchates of Babylon (Iraq) and Cilicia (Turkey).

Origin

The Church had its beginnings in Palestine, whence it spread to other regions of the world. As it spread, certain cities or jurisdictions became key centers of Christian life and missionary endeavor—notably, Jerusalem, Alexandria, Antioch and Constantinople in the East, and Rome in the West — with the result that their practices became diffused throughout their spheres of influence. Various rites originated from these practices which, although rooted in the essentials of Christian faith, were different in significant respects because of their relationships to particular cultural patterns.

Patriarchal Jurisdictions

The main lines of Eastern Church organization and liturgy were drawn before the Roman Empire was separated into Eastern and Western divisions in 292. It was originally co-extensive with the boundaries of the Eastern Empire. Its jurisdictions were those of the patriarchates of Alexandria and Antioch (recognized as such by the Council of Nicaea in 325), and of Jerusalem and Constantinople (given similar recognition by the Council of Chalcedon in 451). These were the major parent bodies of the Eastern Rite Churches which for centuries were identifiable only with limited numbers of nationality and language groups in Eastern Europe, the Middle East and parts of Asia and Africa. Their members are now scattered throughout the world.

Vatican II Decree

The Second Vatican Council, in its *Decree on Eastern Catholic Churches,* stated the following points.

"That Church, Holy and Catholic, which is the Mystical Body of Christ, is made up of the faithful who are organically united in the Holy Spirit through the same faith, the same sacraments, and the same government and who, combining into various groups held together by a hierarchy, form separate Churches or rites. . . . It is the mind of the Catholic Church that each individual Church or rite retain its traditions whole and entire, while adjusting its way of life to the various needs of time and place" (No. 2).

"Such individual Churches, whether of the East or of the West, although they differ somewhat among themselves in what are called rites (that is, in liturgy, ecclesiastical discipline, and spiritual heritage) are, nevertheless, equally entrusted to the pastoral guidance of the Roman Pontiff, the divinely appointed successor of St. Peter in supreme government over the universal Church. They are consequently of equal dignity, so that none of them is superior to the others by reason of rite" (No. 3).

Eastern Heritage: "Each and every Catholic, as also the baptized . . . of every non-Catholic Church or community who enters into the fullness of Catholic communion, should everywhere retain his proper rite, cherish it, and observe it to the best of his ability . . ." (No. 4).

". . . The Churches of the East, as much as those of the West, fully enjoy the right, and are in duty bound, to rule themselves. Each should do so according to its proper and individual procedures . . ." (No. 5).

"All Eastern rite members should know and be convinced that they can and should always preserve their lawful liturgical rites and their established way of life, and that these should not be altered except by way of an appropriate and organic development . . ." (No. 6).

Patriarchs: "The institution of the patriarchate has existed in the Church from the earliest times and was recognized by the first ecumenical Synods.

"By the name Eastern Patriarch is meant the bishop who has jurisdiction over all bishops (including metropolitans), clergy, and people of his own territory or rite, in accordance with the norms of law and without prejudice to the primacy of the Roman Pontiff . . ." (No. 7).

"Though some of the patriarchates of the Eastern Churches are of later origin than others, all are equal in patriarchal dignity. Still the honorary and lawfully established order of precedence among them is to be preserved" (No. 8).

"In keeping with the most ancient tradition of the Church, the Patriarchs of the Eastern Churches are to be accorded exceptional respect, since each presides over his patriarchate as father and head.

"This sacred Synod, therefore, decrees that their rights and privileges should be re-established in accord with the ancient traditions of each Church and the decrees of the ecumenical Synods.

"The rights and privileges in question are those which flourished when East and West were in union, though they should be somewhat adapted to modern conditions.

"The Patriarchs with their synods constitute the superior authority for all affairs of the patriarchate, including the right to establish new eparchies and to nominate bishops of their rite within the territorial bounds of the patriarchate, without prejudice to the inalienable right of the Roman Pontiff to intervene in individual cases" (No. 9).

"What has been said of Patriarchs applies as well, under the norm of law, to major archbishops, who preside over the whole of some individual Church or rite" (No. 10).

Sacraments: "This sacred Ecumenical Synod endorses and lauds the ancient discipline of the sacraments existing in the Eastern Churches, as also the practices connected with their celebration and administration . . ." (No. 12).

"With respect to the minister of holy chrism (confirmation), let that practice be fully restored which existed among Easterners in most ancient times. Priests, therefore, can validly confer this sacrament, provided they use chrism blessed by a Patriarch or bishop" (No. 13).

"In conjunction with baptism or otherwise, all Eastern-Rite priests can confer this sacrament validly on all the faithful of any rite, including the Latin; licitly, however, only if the regulations of both common and particular' law are observed. Priests of the Latin rite, to the extent of the faculties they enjoy for administering this sacrament, can confer it also on the faithful of Eastern Churches, without prejudice to rite. They do so licitly if the regulations of both common and particular law are observed" (No. 14).

"The faithful are bound on Sundays and feast days to attend the divine liturgy or, according to the regulations or custom of their own rite, the celebration of the Divine Praises. That the faithful may be able to satisfy their obligation more easily, it is decreed that this obligation can be fulfilled from the Vespers of the vigil to the end of the Sunday or the feast day . . ." (No. 15).

"Because of the everyday intermingling of the communicants of diverse Eastern Churches in the same Eastern region or territory, the faculty for hearing confession, duly and unrestrictedly granted by his proper bishop to a priest of any rite, is applicable to the entire territory of the grantor, also to the places and the faithful belonging to any other rite in the same territory, unless an Ordinary of the place explicitly decides otherwise with respect to the places pertaining to his rite" (No. 16).

". . . This sacred Synod ardently desires that where it has fallen into disuse the office of the permanent diaconate be restored. The legislative authority of each individual church should decide about the subdiaconate and the minor orders . . ." (No. 17).

"By way of preventing invalid marriages between Eastern Catholics and baptized Eastern non-Catholics, and in the interests of the permanence and sanctity of marriage and of domestic harmony, this sacred Synod decrees that the canonical 'form' for the celebration of such marriages obliges only for lawfulness. For their validity, the presence of a sacred minister suffices, as long as the other requirements of law are honored" (No. 18).

Worship: "Henceforth, it will be the exclusive right of an ecumenical Synod or the Apostolic See to establish, transfer, or suppress feast days common to all the Eastern Churches. To establish, transfer, or suppress feast days for any of the individual Churches is within the competence not only of the Apostolic See but also of a patriarchal or archiepiscopal synod, provided due consideration is given to the entire region and to other individual Churches" (No. 19).

"Until such time as all Christians desirably concur on a fixed day for the celebration of Easter, and with a view meantime to promoting unity among the Christians of a given area or nation, it is left to the Patriarchs or supreme authorities of a place to reach a unanimous agreement, after ascertaining the views of all concerned, on a single Sunday for the observance of Easter" (No. 20).

"With respect to rules concerning sacred seasons, individual faithful dwelling outside the area or territory of their own rite may conform completely to the established custom of the place where they live. When members of a family belong to different rites, they are all permitted to observe sacred seasons according to the rules of any one of these rites" (No. 21).

"From ancient times the Divine Praises have been held in high esteem among all Eastern Churches. Eastern clerics and religious should celebrate these Praises as the laws and customs of their own traditions require. To the extent they can, the faithful too should follow the example of their forbears by assisting devoutly at the Divine Praises" (No. 22).

RITES AND FAITHFUL OF EASTERN CHURCHES

(Principal source of statistics: *Annuario Pontificio.* The statistics are for Eastern-Rite jurisdictions only, and do not include Eastern-Rite Catholics under the jurisdiction of Roman-Rite bishops. Some of the figures reported are only approximate. Some of the jurisdictions listed may be inactive because of government suppression.)

The Byzantine, Alexandrian, Antiochene, Armenian and Chaldean are the five principal rites used in their entirety or in modified form by the various Eastern churches. The number of Eastern Catholics throughout the world is more than 11 million.

Alexandrian Rite

Called the Liturgy of St. Mark, the Alexandrian Rite was modified by the Copts and Melkites, and contains elements of the Byzantine Rite of St. Basil and the liturgies of Sts. Mark, Cyril and Gregory of Nazianzen. The liturgy is substantially that of the Coptic

Church, which is divided into two branches — the Coptic or Egyptian, and the Ethiopian or Abyssinian.

The faithful of this rite are:

COPTS: Returned to Catholic unity about 1741; situated in Egypt, the Near East; liturgical languages are Coptic, Arabic. Jurisdictions (located in Egypt): patriarchate of Alexandria, three dioceses; 107,500.

ETHIOPIANS: Returned to Catholic unity in 1846: situated in Ethiopia, Eritrea, Jerusalem, Somalia; liturgical language is Geez. Jurisdictions (located in Ethiopia): one archdiocese, two dioceses; 95,228.

Antiochene Rite

This is the source of more derived rites than any of the other parent rites. Its origin can be traced to the Eighth Book of the *Apostolic Constitutions* and to the Liturgy of St. James of Jerusalem, which ultimately spread throughout the whole patriarchate and displaced older forms based on the *Apostolic Constitutions.*

The faithful of this rite are:

MALANKARESE: Returned to Catholic unity in 1930; situated in India; liturgical languages are Syriac, Malayalam. Jurisdictions (located in India): one archdiocese, one diocese; 207,672.

MARONITES: United to the Holy See since the time of their founder, St. Maron; have no counterparts among the separated Eastern Christians: situated throughout the world: liturgical languages are Syriac, Arabic. Jurisdictions (located in Lebanon, Cyprus, Egypt, Syria, U.S., Brazil, Australia): patriarchate of Antioch, 14 archdioceses and dioceses, one apostolic administration; 1,425,121. Where no special jurisdictions exist, they are under jurisdiction of local Roman-Rite bishops.

SYRIANS: Returned to Catholic unity in 1781; situated in Asia, Africa, the Americas, Australia; liturgical languages are Syriac, Arabic. Jurisdictions (located in Lebanon, Iraq, Egypt, Syria and Turkey): patriarchate of Antioch, seven archdioceses and dioceses, three patriarchal vicariates; 74,555.

Armenian Rite

Substantially, although using a different language, this is the Greek Liturgy of St. Basil; it is considered an older form of the Byzantine Rite, and incorporates some modifications from the Antiochene Rite.

The faithful of this rite are:

ARMENIANS, exclusively: Returned to Catholic unity during the time of the Crusades; situated in the Near East, Europe, Africa, the Americas, Australasia: liturgical language is Classical Armenian. Jurisdictions (located in Lebanon, Iran, Iraq, Egypt, Syria, Turkey, Poland, France, Greece, Rumania): patriarchate of Cilicia, 8 archdioceses and dioceses, one exarchate, two ordinariates.

Byzantine Rite

Based on the Rite of St. James of Jerusalem and the churches of Antioch, and reformed by Sts. Basil and John Chrysostom, the Byzantine Rite is proper to the Church of Constantinople. (The city was called Byzantium before Constantine changed its name; the modern name is Istanbul.) It is now used by the majority of Eastern Catholics and by the Eastern Orthodox Church (which is not in union with Rome). It is, after the Roman, the most widely used rite.

The faithful of this rite are:

ALBANIANS: Returned to Catholic unity about 1628; situated in Albania; liturgical language is Albanian. Jurisdiction (located in Albania): one apostolic administration.

BULGARIANS: Returned to Catholic unity about 1861; situated in Bulgaria; liturgical language is Old Slavonic. Jurisdiction (located in Bulgaria): one apostolic exarchate.

BYELORUSSIANS, also known as WHITE RUSSIANS: Returned to Catholic unity in the 17th century; situated in Europe, the Americas, Australia; liturgical language is Old Slavonic. They have an apostolic visitor residing at Rome.

GEORGIANS: Returned to Catholic unity in 1861; situated in Georgia (Southern Russia), France; liturgical language is Georgian. They have an apostolic administrator.

GREEKS: Returned to Catholic unity in 1829; situated in Greece, Asia Minor, Europe; liturgical language is Greek. Jurisdictions (located in Greece and Turkey): two exarchates; 3,080.

HUNGARIANS: Descendants of Ruthenians who returned to Catholic unity in 1646; situated in Hungary, the rest of Europe, the Americas; liturgical languages are Greek, Hungarian, English. Jurisdictions (located in Hungary): one diocese and one exarchate: 267,924.

ITALO-ALBANIANS: Have never been separated from Rome; situated in Italy, Sicily, the Americas; liturgical languages are Greek, Italo-Albanian. Jurisdictions (located in Italy): two dioceses, one abbacy; 65,659.

MELKITES: Returned to Catholic unity during the time of the Crusades, but definitive reunion did not take place until early in the 18th century; situated in the Middle East, Asia, Africa, Europe, the Americas, Australia; liturgical languages are Greek, Arabic, English, Portuguese, Spanish. Jurisdictions (located in Syria, Lebanon, Jordan, Israel, U.S., Brazil): patriarchate of Antioch (also has jurisdiction over Melkites in Egypt, Sudan, Jerusalem and Iraq), 15 archdioceses and dioceses, one exarchate; approximately one million.

ROMANIANS: Returned to Catholic unity in 1697; situated in Rumania, the rest of Europe, the Americas; liturgical language is Modern Romanian. Jurisdictions (located in

Rumania): one archdiocese, four dioceses. They have an apostolic visitor in the U.S.

RUSSIANS: Returned to Catholic unity about 1905; situated in Europe, the Americas, Australia, China; liturgical language is Old Slavonic. Jurisdictions (located in Russia and China): two exarchates.

RUTHENIANS, or CARPATHO-RUSSIANS (Rusins): Returned to Catholic unity in the Union of Brest-Litovek, 1596, and the Union of Uzhorod, Apr. 24, 1646; situated in Hungary, Czechoslovakia, elsewhere in Europe, the Americas, Australia; liturgical languages are Old Slavonic, English. Jurisdictions (located in Russia and the U.S.): one archdiocese, three dioceses.

SLOVAKS: Jurisdiction (located in Czechoslovakia): one diocese (also has jurisdiction over Ruthenians, Ukrainians and Hungarians of country).

UKRAINIANS, or GALICIAN RUTHENIANS: Returned to Catholic unity about 1595; situated in Europe, the Americas, Australasia; liturgical languages are Old Slavonic and Ukrainian. Jurisdictions (located in Russian Galicia, Poland, the U.S., Canada, England, Australia, Germany, France, Brazil, Argentina): three archdioceses, nine dioceses, six apostolic exarchates: 4,355,095 (some figures date from 1943).

YUGOSLAVS, SERBS and CROATIANS: Returned to Catholic unity in 1611; situated in Yugoslavia, the Americas; liturgical language is Old Slavonic. Jurisdiction (located in Yugoslavia): one diocese (which also has jurisdiction over all Byzantine-Rite faithful in Yugoslavia); 43,263. They are under the jurisdiction of Ruthenian bishops elsewhere.

Chaldean Rite

This rite, listed as separate and distinct by the Sacred Congregation for the Oriental Churches, was derived from the Antiochene Rite.

The faithful of this rite are:

CHALDEANS: Descendants of the Nestorians, returned to Catholic unity in 1692; situated throughout the Middle East, in Europe, Africa, the Americas; liturgical languages are Syriac, Arabic. Jurisdictions (located in Iraq, Iran, Lebanon, Syria, Turkey): patriarchate of Babylonia, 19 archdioceses and dioceses; 287,470. There are patriarchal vicars for Jordan and Egypt.

SYRO-MALABARESE: Descended from the St. Thomas Christians of India; situated mostly in the Malabar region of India; they use a Westernized and Latinized form of the Chaldean Rite in Syriac and Malayalam. Jurisdictions (located in India): two archdioceses, seven dioceses, six exarchates; 2,116,999.

St. Thomas Christians are so called because they belong to the local church originally formed by the Apostle.

EASTERN JURISDICTIONS

For centuries Eastern-Rite Catholics were identifiable with a limited number of nationality and language groups in certain countries of the Middle East, Eastern Europe, Asia and Africa. The persecution of religion in the Soviet Union since 1917 and in Iron Curtain countries since World War II, however — in addition to decimating and destroying the Church in those places—has resulted in the emigration of many Eastern-Rite Catholics from their homelands. This forced emigration, together with voluntary emigration, has led to the spread of Eastern Rites and their faithful to many other countries.

Europe

(Ukrainian faithful of the Byzantine Rite in Eastern Europe who have no bishop of their own have an apostolic visitor, Archbishop Miroslav Marusyn.)

ALBANIA: Byzantine Rite, apostolic administration.

AUSTRIA: Byzantine Rite, ordinariate.

BULGARIA: Byzantine Rite (Bulgarians), apostolic exarchate.

CZECHOSLOVAKIA: Byzantine Rite (Slovakians and other Byzantine-Rite Catholics), eparchy.

ENGLAND: Byzantine Rite (Ukrainians), apostolic exarchate.

FRANCE: Byzantine Rite (Ukrainians), apostolic exarchate.

Armenian Rite, apostolic exarchate.

Ordinariate for all other Eastern-Rite Catholics.

GERMANY: Byzantine Rite (Ukrainians), apostolic exarchate.

GREECE: Byzantine Rite, apostolic exarchate.

Armenian Rite, ordinariate.

HUNGARY: Byzantine Rite (Hungarians), eparchy, apostolic exarchate.

ITALY: Byzantine Rite (Italo-Albanians), two eparchies, one abbacy.

POLAND: Byzantine Rite, apostolic exarchate.

Armenian Rite, archeparchy.

RUMANIA: Byzantine Rite (Romanians), metropolitan, four eparchies.

Armenian Rite, ordinariate.

RUSSIA: Byzantine Rite (Russians), apostolic exarchate; (Ruthenians), eparchy; (Ukrainians), major archeparchy, two eparchies.

YUGOSLAVIA: Byzantine Rite (Yugoslav and other Byzantine-Rite Catholics), eparchy.

Asia

CHINA: Byzantine Rite (Russians), apostolic exarchate.

CYPRUS: Antiochene Rite (Maronites), archeparchy.

INDIA: Antiochene Rite (Malankarese), metropolitan see, eparchy.

Chaldean Rite (Syro-Malabarese), two metropolitan sees, seven eparchies, six apostolic exarchates.

IRAN: Chaldean Rite (Chaldeans), two metropolitan sees, one archeparchy, one eparchy.

Armenian Rite, eparchy.

IRAQ: Antiochene Rite (Syrians), two archeparchies.

Byzantine Rite (Melkites), patriarchal vicar.

Chaldean Rite (Chaldeans), patriarchate, two metropolitan sees, eight archeparchies and eparchies.

Armenian Rite, archeparchy.

ISRAEL (includes Jerusalem): Antiochene Rite (Syrians), patriarchal vicar; (Maronites), patriarchal vicar.

Byzantine Rite (Melkites), archeparchy, patriarchal vicar.

Chaldean Rite (Chaldeans), patriarchal vicar.

Armenian Rite, patriarchal vicar.

JORDAN: Byzantine Rite (Melkites), archeparchy.

LEBANON: Antiochene Rite (Maronites), patriarchate, seven archeparchies and eparchies; (Syrians), patriarchate.

Byzantine Rite (Melkites), seven metropolitan and archeparchal sees.

Chaldean Rite (Chaldeans), eparchy.

Armenian Rite, patriarchate, eparchy.

SYRIAN ARAB REPUBLIC: Antiochene Rite (Maronites), one archeparchy, one eparchy, one apostolic administration; (Syrians), four archeparchies.

Byzantine Rite (Melkites), patriarchate, four metropolitan sees, one archeparchy.

Chaldean Rite (Chaldeans), eparchy.

Armenian Rite, archeparchy, eparchy, patriarchal vicariate.

TURKEY (Europe and Asia): Antiochene Rite (Syrians), patriarchal vicar.

Byzantine Rite, apostolic exarchate.

Chaldean Rite (Chaldeans), one archeparchy, two eparchies.

Armenian Rite, patriarchate (patriarch resides in Lebanon), archeparchy.

Oceania

AUSTRALIA: Byzantine Rite (Ukrainians), apostolic exarchate.

Antiochene Rite (Maronites), eparchy.

Africa

EGYPTIAN ARAB REPUBLIC: Alexandrian Rite (Copts), patriarchate, three eparchies.

Antiochene Rite (Maronites), eparchy; (Syrians), eparchy.

Byzantine Rite (Melkites), patriarchal vicar.

Chaldean Rite (Chaldeans), patriarchal vicar.

Armenian Rite, eparchy.

ETHIOPIA: Alexandrian Rite (Ethiopians), metropolitan see, two eparchies.

SUDAN: Byzantine Rite (Melkites), patriarchal vicar.

North America

CANADA: Byzantine Rite (Ukrainians), one metropolitan, four eparchies; (Slovaks), apostolic visitor.

UNITED STATES: Antiochene Rite (Maronites), eparchy.

Byzantine Rite (Ukrainians), one metropolitan see, two eparchies; (Ruthenians), one metropolitan see, two eparchies; (Melkites), apostolic exarchate; (Romanians), apostolic visitor.

Other Eastern-Rite Catholics are under the jurisdiction of local Roman-Rite bishops. (See Eastern-Rite Catholics in the United States.)

South America

ARGENTINA: Byzantine Rite (Ukrainians), apostolic exarchate.

Ordinariate for all other Eastern-Rite Catholics.

BRAZIL: Antiochene Rite (Maronites), eparchy.

Byzantine Rite (Melkites), eparchy; (Ukrainians), eparchy.

Ordinariate for all other Eastern-Rite Catholics.

SYNODS, ASSEMBLIES

These assemblies are collegial bodies which have pastoral authority over members of the Eastern Rite Churches.

Patriarchal Synods: Maronites: Antoine Khoraiche, patriarch of Antioch of the Maronites.

Melkites: Maximos V Hakim, patriarch of Antioch of the Melkites.

Chaldeans: Paul II Cheikho, patriarch of Babylonia of the Chaldeans.

Copts: Cardinal Stephanos I Sidarouss, C.M., patriarch of Alexandria of the Copts.

Syrians: Ignace Antoine Hayek, patriarch of Antioch of the Syrians.

Armenians: Ignace Pierre XVI Batanian, patriarch of Cilicia of the Armenians.

Assemblies: Assembly of Ordinaries of the Arab Republic of Egypt: Cardinal Stephanos I Sidarouss, C.M., patriarch of Alexandria of the Copts.

Assembly of Catholic Patriarchs and Bishops of Lebanon.

Assembly of Ordinaries of the Syrian Arab Republic: Maximos V Hakim, patriarch of Antioch of the Melkites.

Conference of the Ukrainian Catholic Hierarchy (Feb. 9, 1962).

Malabarese Episcopal Conference (June 4, 1970): Cardinal Joseph Parecattil, Ernakulam.

Of the collegial bodies listed above, the patriarchal synods have the most authority. In addition to other prerogatives, they have the right to elect bishops and regulate discipline.

EASTERN RITES IN U.S.

(Statistics, from the *Official Catholic Directory, 1975*, are membership figures reported by Eastern-Rite jurisdictions. Additional Eastern-Rite Catholics are included in statistics for Roman-Rite dioceses.)

Byzantine Rite

Ukrainians: There are 283,934 in three jurisdictions in the US: the metropolitan see of Philadelphia (1924, metropolitan 1958) and the suffragan sees of Stamford, Conn. (1956), and St. Nicholas of Chicago (1961).

Ruthenians: There are 287,959 in three jurisdictions in the US: the metropolitan see of Munhall (formerly Pittsburgh, est. 1924; metropolitan and transferred to Munhall, 1969) and the suffragan sees of Passaic, N.J. (1963), and Parma, Ohio (1969). Hungarian and Croatian Byzantine Catholics in the US are also under the jurisdiction of Ruthenian-Rite bishops.

Melkites: In 1975, 21,829 (of approximately 55,000) were reported under the jurisdiction of the exarchate established in 1965, with headquarters at Boston, Mass.

Romanians: There are approximately 5,000 in 18 Romanian Catholic Byzantine Rite parishes in the US, each under the jurisdiction of the Roman-Rite bishop of the territory in which it is located: Cleveland diocese (3 parishes), Detroit (2), Erie (2), Los Angeles (1), Gary (2), Pittsburgh (1), Rockford (2), Trenton (2), and Youngstown (3). No separate statistics are available. The Association of Romanian Catholics of America (see Index) was established in 1948 to preserve the identity of Romanian Catholics within the general framework of the Catholic Church in America. It has petitioned the Holy See for a bishop of the rite in the US. In 1972, the Holy See assigned Msgr. Octavian Barlea as an apostolic visitor to Romanians in the US.

Byelorussians: Have one parish in the US — Christ the Redeemer, Chicago, Ill. — and are under the jurisdiction of the local Roman-Rite bishop.

Russians: Have parishes in California (St. Andrew, El Segundo, and Our Lady of Fatima Center, San Francisco); Illinois (Annunciation Reunion Center, Chicago); Massachusetts (Our Lady of Kazan, Boston); New York (St. Michael's Chapel, Pope John XXIII Reunion Center); and Oregon (Our Lady of Tychvin Chapel, Portland). They are under the jurisdiction of local Roman-Rite bishops.

Antiochene Rite

In 1975, 29,625 (of approximately 153,000) Maronites were reported under the jurisdiction of the eparchy of St. Maron of Detroit (established as an exarchate, 1966; eparchy, 1972).

Armenian Rite

Have parishes in California (Queen of Martyrs, Los Angeles); Massachusetts (Holy Cross, Cambridge); Michigan (St. Vartan, Detroit); New Jersey (Sacred Heart, Paterson); New York (Armenian Catholic Community, 343 W. 25th St., New York, N.Y. 10001); and Pennsylvania (St. Mark, Philadelphia). They are under the jurisdiction of local Roman-Rite bishops.

Chaldean Rite

Have parishes in California (St. Thomas the Apostle, Turlock); Illinois (St. Ephram, Chicago); and Michigan (Mother of God, Detroit). They are under the jurisdiction of local Roman-Rite bishops.

BYZANTINE DIVINE LITURGY

The Divine Liturgy in all rites is based on the consecration of bread and wine by the narration-reactualization of the actions of Christ at the Last Supper. Aside from this fundamental usage, there are differences between the Roman (Latin) Rite and Eastern Rites, and among the Eastern Rites themselves. Following is a general description of the Byzantine Divine Liturgy which is in widest use in the Eastern-Rite Churches.

In the Byzantine, as in all Eastern Rites, the bread and wine are prepared at the start of the Liturgy. The priest does this in a little niche or at a table in the sanctuary. Taking a round loaf of leavened bread stamped with religious symbols, he cuts out a square host and other particles while reciting verses expressing the symbolism of the action. When the bread and wine are ready, he says a prayer of offering and incenses the oblations, the altar, the icons and the people.

At the altar a litany for all classes of people is sung by the priest. The congregation answers, "Lord, have mercy."

The Little Entrance comes next. In procession, the priest leaves the sanctuary carrying the Book of the Gospels, and then returns. He sings prayers especially selected for the day and the feast. These are followed by the solemn singing of the prayer, "Holy God, Holy Mighty One, Holy Immortal One."

The Epistle follows. The Gospel is sung or read by the priest facing the people at the middle door of the sanctuary.

An interruption after the Liturgy of the Catechumens, formerly an instructional period for those learning the faith, is clearly marked. Catechumens, if present, are dismissed with a prayer. Following this are a prayer and litany for the faithful.

The Great Entrance or solemn Offertory Procession then takes place. The priest first says a long silent prayer for himself, in preparation for the great act to come. Again he incenses the oblations, the altar, the icons and people. He goes to the table on the gospel side for the veil-covered paten and chalice. When he arrives back at the sanctuary door, he announces the intention of the Mass in the prayer: "May the Lord God remember all of you in his kingdom, now and forever."

After another litany, the congregation recites the Nicene Creed.

Consecration

The most solemn portion of the sacrifice is introduced by the preface, which is very much like the preface of the Roman Rite. At the beginning of the last phrase, the priest raises his voice to introduce the singing of the Sanctus. During the singing he reads the introduction to the words of consecration.

The words of consecration are sung aloud, and the people sing "Amen" to both consecrations. As the priest raises the Sacred Species in solemn offering, he sings: "Thine of Thine Own we offer unto Thee in behalf of all and for all."

A prayer to the Holy Spirit is followed by the commemorations, in which special mention is made of the all-holy, most blessed and glorious Lady, the Mother of God and ever-Virgin Mary. The dead are remembered and then the living.

A final litany for spiritual gifts precedes the Our Father. The Sacred Body and Blood are elevated with the words, "Holy Things for the Holy." The Host is then broken and commingled with the Precious Blood. The priest recites preparatory prayers for Holy Communion, consumes the Sacred Species, and distributes Holy Communion to the people under the forms of both bread and wine. During this time a communion verse is sung by the choir or congregation.

The Liturgy closes quickly after this. The consecrated Species of bread and wine are removed to the side table to be consumed later by the priest. A prayer of thanksgiving is recited, a prayer for all the people is said in front of the icon of Christ, a blessing is invoked upon all, and the people are dismissed.

VESTMENTS, APPURTENANCES

Sticharion: A long white garment of linen or silk with wide sleeves and decorated with embroidery; formerly the vestment for clerics in minor orders, acolytes, lectors, chanters, and subdeacons; symbolic of purity.

Epitrachelion: A stole with ends sewn together, having a loop through which the head is passed; its several crosses symbolize priestly duties.

Zone: A narrow clasped belt made of the same material as the epitrachelion; symbolic of the wisdom of the priest, his strength against enemies of the Church and his willingness to perform holy duties.

Epimanikia: Ornamental cuffs; the right cuff symbolizing strength, the left, patience and good will.

Phelonion: An ample cape, long in the back and sides and cut away in front; symbolic of the higher gifts of the Holy Spirit.

Antimension: A silk or linen cloth laid on the altar for the Liturgy; it may be decorated with a picture of the burial of Christ and the instruments of his passion; the relics of martyrs are sewn into the front border.

Eileton: A linen cloth which corresponds to the Roman-Rite corporal.

Poterion: A chalice or cup which holds the wine and Precious Blood.

Diskos: A shallow plate, which may be elevated on a small stand, corresponding to the Roman-Rite paten.

Asteriskos: Made of two curved bands of gold or silver which cross each other to form a double arch; a star depends from the junction, which forms a cross; it is placed over the diskos holding the consecrated bread and is covered with a veil.

Veils: Three are used, one to cover the poterion, the second to cover the diskos, and the third to cover both.

Spoon: Used in administering Holy Communion by intinction; consecrated leavened bread is dipped into consecrated wine and spooned onto the tongue of the communicant.

Lance: A metal knife used for cutting up the bread to be consecrated during the Liturgy.

BYZANTINE FEATURES

Art: Named for the empire in which it developed, Byzantine art is a unique blend of imperial Roman and classic Hellenic culture with Christian inspiration. The art of the Greek Middle Ages, it reached a peak of development in the 10th or 11th century. Characteristic of its products, particularly in mosaic and painting, are majesty, dignity, refinement and grace. Its sacred paintings, called icons, are reverenced highly in all Eastern Rites.

Church Building: The classical model of Byzantine church architecture is the Church of the Holy Wisdom (Hagia Sophia), built in Constantinople in the first half of the sixth century and still standing. The square structure, extended in some cases in the form of a cross, is topped by a distinctive onion-shaped dome and surmounted by a triple-bar cross. The altar is at the eastern end of building, where the wall bellies out to form an apse. The altar and sanctuary are separated from the body of the church by a fixed or movable screen, the iconostas, to which icons or sacred pictures are attached (see below).

Clergy: The Byzantine Rite has married as well as celibate priests. In places other than the US, where married candidates have not been accepted for ordination since about 1929, men already married can be ordained to the diaconate and priesthood and can continue in marriage after ordination. Celibate deacons and priests cannot marry after ordination; neither can a married priest remarry after the death of his wife. Bishops must be unmarried.

Iconostas: A large screen decorated with sacred pictures or icons which separates the sanctuary from the nave of a church; its equivalent in the Roman Rite, for thus separating the sanctuary from the nave, is an altar rail.

An iconostas has three doors through which the sacred ministers enter the sanctuary during the Divine Liturgy: smaller (north and south) Deacons' Doors and a large central Royal Door.

The Deacons' Doors usually feature the icons of Sts. Gabriel and Michael; the Royal Door, the icons of the Evangelists — Matthew, Mark, Luke and John. To the right and left of the Royal Door are the icons of Christ the Teacher and of the Blessed Virgin Mary with the Infant Jesus. To the extreme right and left are the icons of the patron of the church and St. John the Baptist (or St. Nicholas of Myra).

Immediately above the Royal Door is a picture of the Last Supper. To the right are six icons depicting the major feasts of Christ, and to the left are six icons portraying the major feasts of the Blessed Virgin Mary. Above the picture of the Last Supper is a large icon of Christ the King.

Some icon screens also have pictures of the 12 Apostles and the major Old Testament prophets surmounted by a crucifixion scene.

Liturgical Language: In line with Eastern tradition, Byzantine practice has favored the use of the language of the people in the liturgy. Two great advocates of the practice were Sts. Cyril and Methodius, apostles of the Slavs, who devised the Cyrillic alphabet and pioneered the adoption of Slavonic in the liturgy.

Sacraments: Baptism is administered by immersion, and confirmation is conferred at the same time. The Eucharist is administered by intinction, i.e., by giving the communicant a piece of consecrated leavened bread which has been dipped into the consecrated wine. When giving absolution in the sacrament of penance, the priest holds his stole over the head of the penitent. Distinctive marriage ceremonies include the crowning of the bride and groom. Ceremonies for anointing the sick closely resemble those of the Roman Rite. Holy orders are conferred by a bishop.

Sign of the Cross: Eastern-Rite Catholics have a distinctive way of making it (see entry in the Glossary). The sign of the cross in conjunction with a deep bow, instead of a genuflection, expresses reverence for the presence of Christ in the Blessed Sacrament.

Theology: The theology of the Eastern Rite Churches is highly mystical and speculative, perhaps more so than that of the Western Church — with which it adheres firmly to the bases of Scripture and apostolic tradition.

EASTERN RITE BRIEFS

NO PATRIARCHATE

Vatican spokesman Federico Alessandrini, at a press conference July 18, 1975, reaffirmed Pope Paul's repeated refusal to make Ukrainian-Rite Cardinal Josyf Slipyi a patriarch. He said in a statement:

"In a recent meeting in Rome . . . groups of Catholic Ukrainians spoke about a Catholic Ukrainian patriarchate, attributing the title to Cardinal Slipyi.

"The issue, raised now for the last 12 years, has already been carefully considered by competent organs of the Holy See which, especially for canonical reasons, have not agreed to the request for a patriarchate with jurisdiction extending to all Ukrainians scattered throughout the world.

"In fact it is known that, according to norms of canon law in force now and confirmed by Vatican Council II, patriarchs have jurisdiction 'within the confines of patriarchal territory.' "

(The cardinal was the archbishop of Lvov since 1949. He was first impeded from administration of the diocese by Soviet detention and then, since 1963, by exile. He could not function in the territory of the Ukraine. It was reported, however, that he signed himself as "Patriarch of the Ukrainians" in his Easter, 1975, pastoral letter.)

"According to the same conciliar decree, the establishment of a patriarchate is reserved to the council or to the Supreme Pontiff. Twice, on July 7, 1971, and May 24, 1975, the Holy Father informed Cardinal Slipyi by letter of his decision in the negative, adding in both cases the expression, *saltem hoc tempore* (at least for now).

"The great majority of Ukrainians — laity, clergy and bishops — have accepted this decision and have understood the reasons of the Holy See. Consequently, whatever may be the aims of some people, a Ukrainian patriarchate does not exist."

Difference of Opinion

Four days before Alessandrini issued this statement, a group supporting the cardinal and calling itself the Ukrainian Patriarchal World Federation for Unity of Church and People held a press conference near the Vatican. One spokesman, Prof. Wasryl Marcus of Loyola University, charged: "The Holy See is represented at the European Security Conference, in Helsinki and Geneva, but we hardly hear a word from the representative of holy Mother Church about the persecution of Ukrainian Catholics in the Soviet Union."

A Ukrainian bishop, in Rome with a pilgrimage of 4,000 of his countrymen, said Marcus did not "represent the majority of the hierarchy, the priests and laity of the Ukrainian Rite."

A non-canonical reason against the establishment of a patriarchate was fear that it might exacerbate, and would be unlikely to improve, the condition of several million Ukrainian Catholics in the Soviet Union where the Rite was forced by the government to merge with the Russian Orthodox Church in 1946.

This reason, along with the canonical reason, against a patriarchate was not acceptable to members of the Society for the Promotion of a Patriarchal System in the Ukrainian Catholic Church. One hundred delegates to a New York convention declared June 8, 1974, that the "Ukrainian Catholic Church in its native territory ... remains undefended by those Vatican authorities who might be expected to provide it with paternal protection." They also objected to the manner in which Ukrainian Catholics in other countries were subject in some respects to Roman-Rite bishops.

PROTEST AGAINST VISIT

Ukrainians protested strongly early in March, 1975, against a tour of several U.S. cities by 19 Soviet clergymen, and also against sponsorship of the tour by the National Council of Churches. The ranking member of the Soviet delegation was Metropolitan Filaret of Kiev-Halych and All Ukraine of the Russian Orthodox Church.

In a Mar. 3 letter to Claire Randall, general secretary of the NCC, Friends of the Ukrainian Catholic University declared: "We assume that, as professional church leaders, you have apprised yourselves of the state of affairs which exists in the Soviet Union in the Church-state arena. Having made this assumption, we are at a loss to understand your motivation in continuing your association with high level church representatives" from the U.S.S.R.

The letter questioned the value of continued dialogue and fellowship with men "who are so obviously the tools of their government and not spokesmen for the believers in the U.S.S.R."

Church Being Used

Archbishop Ambrose Senyshyn of Philadelphia, in a statement to all U.S. Catholic bishops, charged that the Russian Orthodox Church was "totally governed and directed by the atheistic Soviet regime," that the regime was using the church for its own "imperialistic purposes," and that the visiting clergymen were really Soviet agents.

Four Byzantine-Ruthenian bishops said they were "anguished" by the exchange visit of any delegation of Soviet clergymen.

The Ukrainian Orthodox consistory expressed "deep regret" over the NCC's invitation "of overt agents of the Communist regime attired in clerical vestments." Most tragic, the consistory said, was "the fact that the guests of the NCC ... will continue to disseminate lies about the status of the Church in the Soviet Union, especially denying continuous mass persecution of people for their religious convictions."

Protest demonstrations were held in New York City Mar. 8 and in Passaic, N.J., Mar. 9 when the delegation took part in religious services before departing for the Soviet Union.

MARONITE PATRIARCH

Antoine Pierre Khoraiche, 68, bishop of Saida, Lebanon, since 1957, was elected the 71st patriarch of Maronite Catholics Feb. 3, 1975, by the Maronite Episcopal Synod. The successor of Patriarch-Cardinal Paul Pierre Meouchi, who died Jan. 11, he was formally enthroned Feb. 9 at Bkerke, near Beirut. The patriarch's election was officially acknowledged by Pope Paul in a form of recognition known as the extension of ecclesial communion.

SEPARATED EASTERN CHURCHES

Orthodox

Orthodox Churches, the largest and most widespread of the separated Eastern Churches, have much in common with their Eastern Catholic counterparts, including many matters of faith and morals, general discipline, valid orders and sacraments, and liturgy. One important difference is their acceptance of only the first seven ecumenical councils. Another is their rejection of any single supreme head of the Church. They do not acknowledge and hold communion with the pope.

Like their Catholic counterparts, Orthodox Churches are organized in jurisdictions under patriarchs. The patriarchs are the heads of approximately 15 autocephalic and several other autonomous jurisdictions organized along lines of nationality and/or language.

The Ecumenical Patriarch of Constantinople, Dimitrios I, has the primacy of honor among his equal patriarchs but his actual jurisdiction is limited to his own patriarchate. As the spiritual head of worldwide Orthodoxy, he keeps the book of the Holy Canons of the Autocephalous Churches, in which recognized Orthodox Churches are registered, and has the right to call Pan-Orthodox assemblies.

The definitive Orthodox break with Rome dates from 1054.

Top-level relations between the Churches have improved in recent years through the efforts of former Ecumenical Patriarch Athenagoras I, John XXIII, Paul VI and Patriarch Dimitrios I. Pope Paul met with Athenagoras three times before the latter's death in 1972.

The most significant action of both spiritual leaders was their mutual nullification of excommunications imposed by the two Churches on each other in 1054.

The largest Orthodox body in the western hemisphere is the Greek Orthodox Archdiocese of North and South America headed by Archbishop Iakovos, with an estimated membership of some 1.5 million. The second largest is the Orthodox Church of America, with approximately 850,000 members; it was given independent status by the Patriarchate of Moscow May 18, 1970, against the will of Athenagoras I who refused to register it in the book of the Holy Canons of Autocephalous Churches. An additional 650,000 or more Orthodox belong to smaller national and language jurisdictions.

Heads of Orthodox jurisdictions in this hemisphere hold membership in the Standing Conference of Canonical Orthodox Bishops in the Americas.

Jurisdictions

The principal jurisdictions of the Greek, Russian and other Orthodox Churches are as follows.

Greek: Patriarchate of Constantinople, with jurisdiction in Turkey, Crete, the Dodecanese, Western Europe, the Americas, Australia; Dimitrios I is Ecumenical Patriarch.

Patriarchate of Alexandria, with jurisdiction in Egypt and the rest of Africa; there is also a native African Orthodox Church in Kenya and Uganda.

Patriarchate of Antioch (Melkites or Syrian Orthodox), with jurisdiction in Syria, Lebanon, Iraq, Australasia, the Americas; Syrian or Arabic, in place of Greek, is the liturgical language.

Patriarchate of Jerusalem, with jurisdiction in Israel and Jordan.

Churches of Greece, Cyprus and Sinai are autocephalic but maintain relations with their fellow Orthodox.

Russian: Patriarchate of Moscow with jurisdiction centered in the Soviet Union.

Other: Patriarchate of Serbia, with jurisdiction in Yugoslavia, Western Europe, the Americas, Australasia.

Patriarchates of Rumania and Bulgaria.

Katholikate of Georgia, the Soviet Union.

Byelorussians and Ukrainian Byzantines.

Churches of Albania, China, Czechoslovakia, Estonia, Finland, Hungary, Japan, Latvia, Lithuania, Poland.

Other minor communities in various places; e.g., Korea, the US, Carpatho-Russia.

The Armenian Apostolic (Oriental Orthodox) Church in America, with US headquarters in Philadelphia, has 35 parishes in North America.

The Division of Archives and Statistics of the Eastern Orthodox World Foundation reported a 1970 estimate of more than 200 million Orthodox Church members throughout the world. Other sources estimate the total to be approximately 125 million.

Nestorians, Monophysites

Unlike the majority of Eastern Christian Churches, several bodies do not acknowledge all of the first seven ecumenical councils. Nestorians acknowledge only the first two councils; they do not accept the doctrinal definition of the Council of Ephesus concerning Mary as the Mother of God. Monophysite Armenians, Syrians, Copts, Ethiopians and Jacobites acknowledge only the first three councils; they do not accept the doctrinal definition of the Council of Chalcedon concerning the two natures in Christ.

The Armenian Church has communicants in the Soviet Union, the Middle and Far East, the Americas.

The Coptic Church has communicants in Egypt and elsewhere.

The Ethiopian or Abyssinian Church has communicants in Africa, the Middle East, the Americas, India.

The Jacobite Church (West Syrians) has communicants in the Middle East, the Americas, India.

Nestorians (Assyrians) are scattered throughout the world.

It is estimated that there are approximately 10 million or more members of these other Eastern Churches throughout the world. For various reasons, a more accurate determination is not possible.

Conference of Orthodox Bishops

The Standing Conference of Canonical Orthodox Bishops in the Americas was established in 1960 to achieve cooperation among the various ethnic churches. Officers of the conference are Archbishop Iakovos, primate of the Greek Orthodox Archdiocese of North and South America, chairman; Bishop John Martin of the Carpatho-Russian Orthodox Greek Catholic Church, vice-chairman; Bishop Andrei Kuschak of the Ukrainian Orthodox, treasurer; Father Robert G. Stephanopoulos, general secretary.

Member churches of the conference are the: Albanian Orthodox Diocese of America (Ecumenical Patriarchate), American Carpatho-Russian Greek Catholic Diocese, Antiochian Orthodox Christian Archdiocese of New York and All North America, Bulgarian Eastern Orthodox Church, Greek Orthodox Archdiocese of North and South America, Orthodox Church of America, Romanian Orthodox Missionary Episcopate in America, Serbian Orthodox Church in the United States of America and Canada, Ukrainian Orthodox Church of America (Ecumenical Patriarchate), Holy Ukrainian Autocephalic Orthodox Church in Exile.

Patriarchs: High-ranking patriarchs of separated Eastern Churches are Ecumenical Orthodox Patriarch Dimitrios I (Papadopoulos) of Constantinople (Istanbul) and Coptic Orthodox Patriarch Shenouda III (Nazeer Gayed) of Alexandria.

EASTERN ECUMENISM

The Second Vatican Council, in the *Decree on Eastern Catholic Churches,* pointed out the special role they have to play "in promoting the unity of all Christians, particularly Easterners." The document also stated in part:

"The Eastern Churches in communion with the Apostolic See of Rome have a special role to play in promoting the unity of all Christians, particularly Easterners, according to the principles of this sacred Synod's *Decree on Ecumenism* first of all by prayer, then by the example of their lives, by religious fidelity to ancient Eastern traditions, by greater mutual knowledge, by collaboration, and by a brotherly regard for objects and attitudes" (No. 24).

"If any separated Eastern Christian should, under the guidance of grace of the Holy Spirit, join himself to Catholic unity, no more should be required of him than what a simple profession of the Catholic faith demands. A valid priesthood is preserved among Eastern clerics. Hence, upon joining themselves to the unity of the Catholic Church, Eastern clerics are permitted to exercise the orders they possess, in accordance with the regulations established by the competent authority" (No. 25).

"Divine Law forbids any common worship (*communicatio in sacris*) which would damage the unity of the Church, or involve formal acceptance of falsehood or the danger of deviation in the faith, of scandal, or of indifferentism. At the same time, pastoral experience clearly shows that with respect to our Eastern brethren there should and can be taken into consideration various circumstances affecting individuals, wherein the unity of the Church is not jeopardized nor are intolerable risks involved, but in which salvation itself and the spiritual profit of souls are urgently at issue.

"Hence, in view of special circumstances of time, place, and personage, the Catholic Church has often adopted and now adopts a milder policy, offering to all the means of salvation and an example of charity among Christians through participation in the sacraments and in other sacred functions and objects. With these considerations in mind, and 'lest because of the harshness of our judgment we prove an obstacle to those seeking salvation,' and in order to promote closer union with the Eastern Churches separated from us, this sacred Synod lays down the following policy:

"In view of the principles recalled above, Eastern Christians who are separated in good faith from the Catholic Church, if they ask of their own accord and have the right dispositions, may be granted the sacraments of penance, the Eucharist, and the anointing of the sick. Furthermore, Catholics may ask for these same sacraments from those non-Catholic ministers whose Churches possess valid sacraments, as often as necessity or a genuine spiritual benefit recommends such a course of action, and when access to a Catholic priest is physically or morally impossible" (Nos. 26, 27).

"Again, in view of these very same principles, Catholics may for a just cause join with their separated Eastern brethren in sacred functions, things, and places" (No. 28).

"This more lenient policy with regard to common worship involving Catholics and their brethren of the separated Eastern Churches is entrusted to the care and execution of the local Ordinaries so that, by taking counsel among themselves and, if circumstances warrant, after consultation also with the Ordinaries of the separated Churches, they may govern relations between Christians by timely and effective rules and regulations" (No. 29).

ECUMENICAL BRIEFS

Agreed Statement on the Church: Catholic and Orthodox theologians, meeting for their 10th consultation since 1966, issued an "Agreed Statement on the Church" Dec. 10, 1974. One of the central points in the statement was the difference of views regarding the position and status of the Pope and the Patriarch of Constantinople in the hierarchy of their churches.

The statement said:

"The Catholic Church recognizes that the position of Peter in the college of the Apostles finds visible expression in the Bishop of Rome who exercises those prerogatives defined by Vatican Council I within the whole church of Christ in virtue of this primacy.

"The Orthodox Church finds this teaching at variance with its understanding of primacy within the whole church. It appears to destroy the tension between independence and collegiality (in the universal and particular churches). For independence, a basic condition for collegiality, appears to be removed as a consequence of the jurisdictional teaching role attributed to the Patriarch of the West by Vatican Council I. The Orthodox believe that a necessary primacy in the church depends on the consent of the church and is at present exercised by the Patriarch of Constantinople.

"Our two traditions are not easily harmonized. Yet we believe that the Spirit is ever active to show us the way by which we can live together as one and many. We have the hope that we will be open to his promptings wherever they may lead."

The theological consultation was under the joint sponsorship of the U.S. Bishops' Committee for Ecumenical and Interreligious Affairs and the Standing Conference of Canonical Orthodox Bishops in America.

Orthodox Guidelines: A 66-page document

entitled "Guidelines for Orthodox Churches in Ecumenical Relations" was published in February, 1974, by the Standing Conference of Canonical Orthodox Bishops in the Americas. Among the subjects of guidelines were:

• Marriage: Normally marriage in the Orthodox Church "takes place only between members of that Church." There are, however, occasions in which an Orthodox priest may perform a "mixed marriage," under certain conditions. Clergy of other churches may give a blessing or exhort a couple, but do not actually "assist" or "participate" in the marriage service.

• Baptism: Orthodox Churches accept baptism in the name of the Trinity in another church if "proof of the fact of baptism" can be authenticated.

• Eucharist: "Holy Communion will not be sought by Orthodox Christians outside the Church, nor will it be offered to those who do not confess the Orthodox Church as their mother."

• Reciprocity: The "principle of reciprocity" governs preaching in ecumenical situations, meaning that Orthodox priests may preach in non-Orthodox churches and non-Orthodox may speak in Orthodox churches.

Protest of Greek Orthodox Archbishop: United Press International reported July 28, 1975, that Greek Orthodox Archbishop Seraphim of Athens had informed a Vatican official that he was breaking off relationships with the Vatican — ecumenical discussions and cooperation — because of the appointment of Bishop-elect Anargiro Printesis as exarch or head of the approximately 3,000 Byzantine-Rite Catholics of Greece.

The archbishop was quoted as saying: "We cease every relationship with Rome since it believes in the perpetuation of such an ecclesiastical scandal (the Catholic Byzantine Church) in our midst. . . . From now on and until views in accordance with the spirit of respect for the Church of Greece prevail, we will not accept visits by Roman Catholics."

The Byzantine Catholics, grouped together in the 19th century, were regarded with suspicion by the Orthodox.

Archbishop Seraphim apparently felt that the appointment of the new bishop-exarch was for the purpose of increasing Catholic efforts to convert Orthodox to union with Rome.

Dialogues: Between the end of the Second Vatican Council in 1965 and early September, 1975, the Secretariat for Promoting Christian Unity was the Catholic sponsor of at least eight dialogues of Catholic and Orthodox theologians. Participating Orthodox bodies were Russian (four meetings), Coptic (three meetings) and Syrian (one meeting). Improved mutual understanding, but no change in the official teachings of the churches, was the reported result of the dialogues.

WORLD RELIGIOUS POPULATION
(Source: *1974 Britannica Book of the Year.*)

CHRISTIANS, TOTAL: **967,793,450** (North and Central America, 224,933,250; South America, 163,567,000; Europe, 372,425,700; Asia, 87,396,500; Africa, 98,862,000; Oceania, 20,609,000).

Roman Catholic: **551,949,000** (North and Central America, 128,995,500; South America, 157,831,000; Europe, 179,684,000; Asia, 46,456,500; Africa, 34,587,000; Oceania, 4,395,000).

Eastern Orthodox: **91,580,700** (North and Central America, 4,117,000; South America, 54,000; Europe, 67,380,500; Asia, 2,135,000; Africa, 17,410,000; Oceania, 484,000).

Protestant: **324,263,750** (North and Central America, 91,820,750; South America, 5,682,000; Europe, 125,361,000; Asia, 38,805,000; Africa, 46,865,000; Oceania, 15,730,000).

JEWISH: **14,443,925** (North and Central America, 6,344,475; South America, 680,700; Europe, 3,983,750; Asia, 3,064,050; Africa, 297,950; Oceania, 73,000).

MUSLIM: **513,174,500** (North and Central America, 205,000; South America, 185,000; Europe, 4,088,000; Asia, 414,796,000; Africa, 93,328,500; Oceania, 572,000).

ZOROASTRIAN: **181,050** (Asia, 180,600; Africa, 450).

SHINTO: **63,150,000** (North and Central America, 55,000; South America, 90,000; Asia, 63,005,000).

TAOIST: **31,367,700** (North and Central America, 15,000; South America, 12,000; Asia, 31,340,700).

CONFUCIAN: **275,898,865** (North and Central America, 92,165; South America, 90,000; Europe, 40,000; Asia, 275,630,700; Africa, 500; Oceania, 45,500).

BUDDHIST: **223,655,500** (North and Central America, 142,000; South America, 175,000; Europe, 200,000; Asia, 223,136,500; Africa, 2,000).

HINDU: **515,580,500** (North and Central America, 65,000; South America, 470,000; Europe, 300,000; Asia, 513,755,500; Africa, 461,000; Oceania, 529,000).

TOTAL RELIGIOUS POPULATION: **2,605,245,490** (North and Central America, 231,851,890; South America, 165,269,700; Europe, 381,037,450; Asia, 1,612,305,550; Africa, 192,952,400; Oceania, 21,828,500).

TOTAL POPULATION OF WORLD: **3,788,200,000** (North and Central America, 332,000,000; South America, 201,000,000; Europe, 717,000,000; Asia, 2,154,000,000; Africa, 364,000,000; Oceania, 20,200,000).

Protestant Churches

Men, Doctrines, Churches of the Reformation

Some of the leading figures, doctrines and churches of the Reformation are covered below. A companion article covers Major Protestant Churches in the United States.

John Wycliff (c. 1320-1384): English priest and scholar who advanced one of the leading Reformation ideas nearly 200 years before Martin Luther — that the Bible alone is the sufficient rule of faith — but had only an indirect influence on the 16th century Reformers. Supporting belief in an inward and practical religion, he denied the divinely commissioned authority of the pope and bishops of the Church; he also denied the Real Presence of Christ in the Holy Eucharist, and wrote against the sacrament of penance and the doctrine of indulgences. Nearly 20 of his propositions were condemned by Gregory XI in 1377; his writings were proscribed more extensively by the Council of Constance in 1415. His influence was strongest in Bohemia and Central Europe.

John Hus (c. 1369-1415): A Bohemian priest and preacher of reform who authored 30 propositions condemned by the Council of Constance. Excommunicated in 1411 or 1412, he was burned at the stake in 1415. His principal errors concerned the nature of the Church and the origin of papal authority. He spread some of the ideas of Wycliff but did not subscribe to his views regarding faith alone as the condition for justification and salvation, the sole sufficiency of Scripture as the rule of faith, the Real Presence of Christ in the Eucharist, and the sacramental system. In 1457 some of his followers founded the Church of the Brotherhood which later became known as the United Brethren or Moravian Church and is considered the earliest independent Protestant body.

Martin Luther (1483-1546): An Augustinian friar, the key figure in the Reformation. In 1517, as a special indulgence was being preached in Germany, and in view of needed reforms within the Church, he published at Wittenberg 95 theses concerning matters of Catholic belief and practice. Leo X condemned 41 statements from Luther's writings in 1520. Luther, refusing to recant, was excommunicated the following year. His teachings strongly influenced subsequent Lutheran theology, although the norm of Lutheran doctrine is not Luther's teaching alone but the Book of Concord (1580), which consists of the three catholic creeds, plus seven particular symbols or confessions of faith, of which only three are by Luther.

Luther's doctrine included the following:

The sin of Adam, which corrupted human nature radically (but not substantially), has affected every aspect of man's being. Although God holds man responsible for his moral actions, unregenerated man cannot by his innate powers, without the help of divine grace, make himself acceptable to God. Justification, understood as the forgiveness of sins, is by grace for Christ's sake through faith. Faith involves not merely intellectual assent but an act of confidence by the will. Good works are indispensably necessary concomitants of faith, but do not merit salvation. Of the sacraments, Luther retained baptism, penance and the Holy Communion as effective vehicles of the grace of the Holy Spirit; he held that in the Holy Communion the consecrated bread and wine are the Body and Blood of Christ. The rule of faith is the divine revelation in the Sacred Scriptures. He rejected purgatory, indulgences and the invocation of the saints, and held that prayers for the dead have no efficacy.

Lutheran tenets not in agreement with Catholic doctrine were condemned by the Council of Trent.

Anabaptism: Originated in Saxony in the first quarter of the 16th century and spread rapidly through southern Germany. Its doctrine included several key Lutheran tenets but was not regarded with favor by Luther, Calvin or Zwingli. Anabaptists believed that baptism is for adults only and that infant baptism is invalid. Their doctrine of the Inner Light, concerning the direct influence of the Holy Spirit on the believer, implied rejection of Catholic doctrine concerning the sacraments and the nature of the Church. Eighteen articles of faith were formulated in 1632 in Holland. Mennonites are Anabaptists.

Ulrich Zwingli (1484-1531): A priest who triggered the Reformation in Switzerland with a series of New Testament lectures in 1519, later disputations and by other actions. He held the Gospel to be the only basis of truth; rejected the Mass (which he suppressed in 1525 at Zurich), penance and other sacraments; denied papal primacy and doctrine concerning purgatory and the invocation of saints; rejected celibacy, monasticism and many traditional practices of piety. His symbolic view of the Eucharist, which was at odds with Catholic doctrine, caused an irreconcilable controversy with Luther and his followers. Zwingli was killed in a battle between the forces of Protestant and Catholic cantons in Switzerland.

John Calvin (1509-1564): French leader of the Reformation in Switzerland, whose key tenet was absolute predestination of some persons to heaven and others to hell. He rejected Catholic doctrine in 1533 after becoming convinced of a personal mission to reform the Church. In 1536 he published the first edition of *Institutes of the Christian Religion,* a systematic exposition of his doctrine which became the classic textbook of Reformed — as distinguished from Lutheran — theology. To Luther's principal theses — regarding Scripture as the sole rule of faith, the radical corruption of human nature, and justification by faith alone — he added absolute predestination, certitude of salvation for the elect, and the incapability of the elect to lose grace. His Eucharistic theory, which failed to mediate the Zwingli-Luther controversy, was at odds with Catholic doctrine. From 1555 until his death Calvin was the virtual dictator of Geneva, the capital of the non-Lutheran Reformation in Europe.

Arminianism: A modification of the rigid predestinationism of Calvin, set forth by Jacob Arminius (1560-1609) and formally stated in the *Remonstrance* of 1610. Arminianism influenced some Calvinist bodies.

Unitarianism: A 16th century doctrine which rejected the Trinity and the divinity of Christ in favor of a uni-personal God. It claimed scriptural support for a long time but became generally rationalistic with respect to "revealed" doctrine as well as in ethics and its world-view. One of its principal early proponents was Faustus Socinus (1539-1604), a leader of the Polish Brethren.

A variety of communions developed in England in the Reformation and post-Reformation periods.

Anglican Communion: This communion, which regards itself as the same apostolic Church as that which was established by early Christians in England, derived not from Reformation influences but from the renunciation of papal jurisdiction by Henry VIII (1491-1547). His Act of Supremacy in 1534 called Christ's Church an assembly of local churches subject to the prince, who was vested with fullness of authority and jurisdiction. In spite of Henry's denial of papal authority, this Act did not reject substantially other principal articles of faith. Notable changes, proposed and adopted for the reformation of the church, took place in the subsequent reigns of James VI and Elizabeth, with respect to such matters as Scripture as the rule of faith, the sacraments, the nature of the Mass, and the constitution of the hierarchy.

The Anglican Communion is called Episcopal because its prelates have the title and function of bishops. (See Anglican Orders.)

Puritans: Extremists who sought church reform along Calvinist lines in severe simplicity. (Use of the term was generally discontinued after 1660.)

Presbyterians: Basically Calvinistic, called Presbyterian because church polity centers around assemblies of presbyters or elders. John Knox (c. 1513-1572) established the church in Scotland.

Congregationalists: Evangelical in spirit and seeking a return to forms of the primitive church, they uphold individual freedom in religious matters, do not require the acceptance of a creed as a condition for communion, and regard each congregation as autonomous. Robert Browne influenced the beginnings of Congregationalism.

Quakers: Their key belief is in internal divine illumination, the inner light of the living Christ, as the only source of truth and inspiration. George Fox (1624-1691) was one of their leaders in England. Called the Society of Friends, the Quakers are noted for their pacificism.

Baptists: So called because of their doctrine concerning baptism. They reject infant baptism and consider only baptism by immersion as valid. Leaders in the formation of the church were John Smyth (d. 1612) in England and Roger Williams (d. 1683) in America.

Methodists: A group who broke away from the Anglican Communion under the leadership of John Wesley (1703-1791), although some Anglican beliefs were retained. Doctrines include the witness of the Spirit to the individual and personal assurance of salvation. Wesleyan Methodists do not subscribe to some of the more rigid Calvinistic tenets held by other Methodists.

Universalism: A product of 18th-century liberal Protestantism in England. The doctrine is not Trinitarian and includes a tenet that all men will ultimately be saved.

MAJOR PROTESTANT CHURCHES IN THE UNITED STATES

There are more than 250 Protestant church bodies in the United States.

The majority of US Protestants belong to the following denominations: Baptist, Methodist, Lutheran, Presbyterian, Protestant Episcopal, the United Church of Christ, the Christian Church (Disciples of Christ), Holiness Sects.

Baptist Churches

(Courtesy of the Rev. Victor Tupitza, Division of Communication, American Baptist Churches in the U.S.A.)

Baptist churches, comprising the largest of all American Protestant denominations, were first established by John Smyth near the beginning of the 17th century in England. The first Baptist church in America was founded at Providence by Roger Williams in 1639.

Largest of the nearly 30 Baptist bodies in the US are:

The Southern Baptist Convention, 460 James Robertson Parkway, Nashville, Tenn. 37219, with 12.3 million members;

The National Baptist Convention, U.S.A., Inc., 915 Spain St., Baton Rouge, La. 70802, with 6.5 million members;

The National Baptist Convention of America, 1058 Hogan St., Jacksonville, Fla. 32202, with 2.6 million members.

The American Baptist Churches in the U.S.A., Valley Forge, Pa. 19481, with 1.5 million members.

The total number of US Baptists is more than 29 million. The world total is 33 million.

Proper to Baptists is their doctrine on baptism. Called an "ordinance" rather than a sacrament, baptism by immersion is a sign that one has experienced and decided in favor of the salvation offered by Christ. It is administered only to persons who are capable of the experience of faith, which is the sole criterion of salvation and which involves the obligation to a life of virtue. Baptism is not administered to infants.

Baptists do not have a formal creed but generally subscribe to two professions of faith formulated in 1689 and 1832 and are in general agreement with classical Protestant theology regarding Scripture as the sole rule of faith, original sin, justification through faith in Christ, and the nature of the Church. Their local churches are autonomous.

Worship services differ in form from one congregation to another. Usual elements are the reading of Scripture, a sermon, hymns, vocal and silent prayer. The Lord's Supper, called an "ordinance," is celebrated at various intervals.

Methodist Churches

(Courtesy of the Librarian, Commission on Archives and History, and Dr. A. Walz, Statistician.)

Methodism derived from the teaching of John Wesley, an Anglican minister who experienced a new conversion to Christ in 1738. The first self-supporting Methodist congregation was established in London two years later. By the end of the 18th century Methodism was strongly rooted in America.

Methodists, with approximately 14 million members, comprise the second largest Protestant denomination in the US. The United Methodist Church, formed in a merger of the Methodist Church and the Evangelical United Brethren Church in 1968, is the largest of more than 20 bodies, with 10.5 million members; its principal agencies are located in New York, Evanston, Ill., Nashville, Tenn., Washington, D.C., Dayton, O., and Lake Junaluska, N.C. The second largest body, with some 1.5 million communicants, is the African Methodist Episcopal Church; its headquarters are located at 1724 Villa Place, Nashville, Tenn.

Methodism, although it has a base in Calvinistic theology, rejects absolute predestination and maintains that Christ offers grace freely to all men, not just to a select elite. Wesley's distinctive doctrine was the "witness of the Spirit" to the individual soul and personal assurance of salvation. He also emphasized the central themes of conversion and holiness. Methodists are in general agreement with classical Protestant theology regarding

Scripture as the sole rule of faith, original sin, justification through faith in Christ, the nature of the Church, and the sacraments of baptism and the Lord's Supper. Church polity is structured along episcopal, presbyterian and congregational lines. Congregations are free to choose various forms of worship services, which generally follow those in the Book of Common Prayer. Elements of a typical service are readings from Scripture, a sermon, prayers and hymns.

Lutheran Churches

(Courtesy of Erik W. Modean, director of the Lutheran Council News Bureau, 315 Park Ave., New York, N. Y. 10010.)

The actual origin of Lutheranism is generally traced to Oct. 31, 1517, when Martin Luther published a list of 95 theses and tacked them to the door of the church at Wittenberg. This act signaled the beginning of the Reformation in Germany. While the Lutheran Reformers did not intend to establish a new denomination, the subsequent excommunication of Luther and his followers completed the shattering of Western religious unity. The separate institutional existence of the Lutheran Church was necessitated in 1530 when, at the Diet of Augsburg, the Holy Roman Emperor, Charles V, rejected the Augsburg Confession of the Lutherans.

During the 17th century, Lutheranism came to this hemisphere chiefly from its strongholds in Northern and Central Europe. Its membership increased greatly as a result of the immigrations of the 19th century. Lutherans now form the third largest Protestant denomination in the United States, with more than 9 million members.

The three largest Lutheran bodies in the US are:

The Lutheran Church in America, 231 Madison Ave., New York, N.Y. 10016, with 3.2 million members. This body was formed June 28, 1962, by consolidation of the American Evangelical Lutheran Church, the Augustana Evangelical Lutheran Church, the Finnish Evangelical Lutheran Church, and the United Lutheran Church in America.

The Lutheran Church-Missouri Synod, 500 N. Broadway, St. Louis, Mo., with 2.8 million members. This body was formed in 1847.

The American Lutheran Church, 422 S. 5th St., Minneapolis, Minn., with 2.5 million members. This body was formed in April, 1960, by a merger of the American Lutheran Church, the Evangelical Lutheran Church, and the United Evangelical Lutheran Church, joined later by the Lutheran Free Church.

These three bodies participate in the Lutheran Council in the U.S.A., a cooperative agency for theological studies and Christian service in missions, welfare, education and related fields. The LC/USA, formed in 1966, is headquartered in New York City.

The normative statement of Lutheran beliefs is found in the *Book of Concord* (1580). All the major Lutheran bodies in this country subscribe to this collection of symbolical documents, which consists of the three ancient Creeds (Apostles', Nicene and Athanasian), the *Augsburg Confession* (1530), the *Apology of the Augsburg Confession* (1531), the *Smalcald Articles* (1536-1538), the *Treatise on the Authority and Primacy of the Pope* (1537), the *Large and Small Catechisms* (1529), and the *Formula of Concord* (1577), plus the Preface to the *Book of Concord.*

That we "receive forgiveness of sins and become righteous before God by grace, for Christ's sake, through faith," is the central article of faith in the Lutheran confessions. Lutherans believe in two sacraments, baptism and the Holy Eucharist, both of which are visible means of grace. Baptism is necessary for salvation (*Augsburg Confession,* II and IX), and through it a person is born again to newness of life. In the Holy Eucharist, the consecrated bread and wine are the Body and the Blood of Christ (*Smalcald Article* 3, Part Two, VI). The sacraments are "signs and testimonies of God's will toward us for the purpose of awakening and strengthening our faith" (*Augsburg Confession,* XIII). Although private confession is not obligatory, it is regarded as highly beneficial (*Apology,* XIII, 4). The formula reads: "According to the command of our Lord Jesus Christ, I forgive you all your sins in the name of the Father and of the Son and of the Holy Ghost" (*Small Catechism,* V. 28). Through the rite of confirmation, which is not regarded as a sacrament, children and baptized converts are admitted to adult membership in the Lutheran Church.

In the United States, church polity is largely congregation-centered, although national bodies, synods and conferences exercise differing degrees of influence and control over member congregations.

Although forms of worship and ceremonial are not wholly uniform, the commonly followed order of the service consists of Introit, Kyrie, Gloria, collect, (Old Testament lesson), epistle, gospel, creed, sermon, offertory, Great Intercession, preface and Sanctus, consecration, Pax Agnus, distribution of Holy Communion, post communion, Benedicamus and blessing, with interspersed hymns. When Holy Communion is not celebrated, a blessing after the Great Intercession ends the service. Matins and Vespers are used occasionally. The historic vestments are worn to a varying extent. Lutherans follow the church year. Music has always occupied a prominent place in Lutheran liturgical worship and successive generations have built up a rich tradition of church music and hymnody.

Serious differences, regarding biblical interpretation and other subjects, surfaced again at 1975 meetings and discussions of the Lutheran Church-Missouri Synod.

Presbyterian Churches

(Courtesy of Gerald W. Gillette, United Presbyterian Church in the U.S.A.; and Office of the General Assembly, Presbyterian Church in the United States.)

Presbyterians are so called because of their type of church government, by presbyters or elders.

Presbyterianism was founded on Reformed (as distinguished from Lutheran) theological positions laid down by John Calvin. Countries in which it acquired early strength and influence were Switzerland, France, Holland, Scotland and England.

Presbyterianism spread widely in this country in the latter part of the 18th century and afterwards. Presently, it has approximately 4.5 million communicants in nine bodies. The largest of these are:

The United Presbyterian Church in the U.S.A., 475 Riverside Drive, New York, N.Y. 10027, with 3 million members. This body was formed May 28, 1958, by a merger of the Presbyterian Church in the U.S.A and the United Presbyterian Church of North America.

The Presbyterian Church in the United States, 341 Ponce de Leon Boulevard N.E., Atlanta, Ga. 30308, with about 900,000 members.

In Presbyterian doctrine, baptism and the Lord's Supper, viewed as seals of the covenant of grace, are regarded as sacraments. Baptism, which is not necessary for salvation, is conferred on infants and adults. The Lord's Supper is celebrated as a covenant of the Sacrifice of Christ.

The Church is twofold, being invisible and also visible; it consists of all of the elect and all those Christians who are united in Christ as their immediate head.

Presbyterians are in general agreement with classical Protestant theology regarding Scripture as the sole rule of faith, original sin, and justification through faith in Christm

Presbyterian congregations are governed by elders and ministers. On higher levels there are presbyteries, synods and a general assembly with various degrees of authority over local bodies.

Worship services, simple and dignified, include sermons, prayer, reading of the Scriptures and hymns. The Lord's Supper is celebrated at intervals.

Doctrinal developments of the past several years included approval in May, 1967, by the General Assembly of the United Presbyterian Church of a contemporary confession of faith to supplement the historic Westminster Confession. The new confession emphasizes the commitment of the Church and its members to reconciliatory and apostolic works in society.

The Presbyterian-Catholic Consultation is studying "Ethics and the Search for Unity."

Protestant Episcopal Church

(Courtesy of Charles M. Guilbert, Secretary/Treasurer of the General Convention and Custodian of the Standard Book of Common Prayer.)

The Protestant Episcopal Church, also officially known as the Episcopal Church, regards itself as the same apostolic church as that which was established by early Christians in England. It was established in this country during the Revolutionary period. Its constitution and Prayer Book were adopted at a general convention held in 1789. It has approximately 3.4 million members.

Offices of the US executive council are located at 815 Second Ave., New York, N.Y. 10017.

This church, which belongs to the Anglican Communion, subscribes to the branch theory of the Church of Christ, holding that it consists of the Church of Rome, the Eastern Orthodox Church, and the Anglican Communion, and that the heads of these churches are of equal rank in authority.

There is considerable variety in Protestant Episcopal beliefs and practices. Official statements of belief and practice are found in the Apostles' Creed, the Nicene Creed and the Book of Common Prayer, but interpretation is not uniform. Scripture has primary importance with respect to the rule of faith, and some authority is attached to tradition.

All seven sacraments, veneration of the saints, and a great many other Catholic teachings are accepted by some Episcopalians but contested by others.

An episcopal system of church government prevails, where clergymen of lower rank and lay persons also have an active voice in ecclesiastical affairs. The levels of government are the general convention, the executive council, territorial provinces and dioceses, and local parishes. At the parish level, the congregation has the right to select its own rector or pastor.

Liturgical worship is according to the Book of Common Prayer or authorized experimental forms, but ceremonial practices correspond with the doctrinal positions of the various congregations and range from a ceremony similar to the Roman Mass to services of a less elaborate character.

United Church of Christ

(Courtesy of the Rev. David A. Tillyer, Office of Communication, United Church of Christ.)

The 1,867,810-member United Church of Christ was formed in 1957 by a union of the Congregational Christian and the Evangelical and Reformed Churches. The former was originally established by the Pilgrims and the Puritans of the Massachusetts Bay Colony, while the latter was founded in Pennsylvania in the early 1700's by settlers from Central Europe. The denomination has 6,617 congregations throughout the United States.

Its headquarters are located at 297 Park Ave., South, New York, N.Y. 10010.

Its statement of faith recognizes Jesus Christ as "our crucified and risen Lord (who) shared our common lot, conquering sin and death and reconciling the world to himself." It believes in the life after death, and the fact that God "judges men and nations by his righteous will declared through prophets and apostles."

The United Church further believes that Christ calls its members to share in his baptism "and eat at his table, to join him in his passion and victory." Ideally, according to its Lord's Day Service, Communion is to be celebrated weekly. Like other Calvinistic bodies, it believes that Christ is spiritually present in the sacrament.

The United Church is governed along congregational lines, and each local church is autonomous. However, the pronouncements of its biennial General Synod are taken with great seriousness by congregations. Between synods, a 42-member executive council oversees the work of the church.

Christian Church (Disciples of Christ)

(Courtesy of Robert L. Friedly, Executive Director, Office of Communication.)

The Christian Church (Disciples of Christ) originated early in the 1800's from two movements against rigid denominationalism led by Presbyterians Thomas and Alexander Campbell in western Pennsylvania and Barton W. Stone in Kentucky. The two movements developed separately for about 25 years before being merged in 1832.

The church, which identifies itself with the Protestant mainstream, now has approximately 1.3 million members in the US and Canada. The greatest concentration of members in the US is located roughly along the old frontier line, in an arc sweeping from Ohio and Kentucky through the Midwest and down into Oklahoma and Texas.

The general offices of the church are located at 222 South Downey Ave., Box 1986, Indianapolis, Ind. 46206.

The church's persistent concern for Christian unity is based on a conviction expressed in a basic document, *Declaration and Address,* dating from its founding. The document states: "The church of Christ upon earth is essentially, intentionally and constitutionally one."

The Disciples have no official doctrine or dogma. Their worship practices vary widely from more common informal services to what could almost be described as "high church" services. Membership is granted after a simple statement of belief in Jesus Christ and baptism by immersion; many congregations admit un-immersed transfers from other denominations. The Lord's Supper, generally called Communion, is always open to Christians of all persuasions. Lay men and women routinely preside over the Lord's Supper, which is celebrated each Sunday; they often preach and perform other pastoral functions as well. Distinction between ordained and non-ordained members is blurred somewhat because of the Disciples' emphasis on all members of the church as ministers.

The Christian Church is oriented to congregational government, and has a unique structure in which three levels of polity (general, regional and congregational) operate as equals rather than in a pyramid of authority. At the national or international level, it is governed by a general assembly which has voting representation direct from congregations and regions as well as all ordained clergy.

The Holiness Sects

Perfectionist and Pentecostal churches and sects have a total membership of some two million persons in the US.

These groups do not form a denomination in the strict sense of the term, since they are separate and have their own particular characteristics. Classification under a common heading is possible, however, because they all share the same general spirit and spring from a common origin. John Wesley's teaching on justification is the doctrinal thread common to all of these churches — personal holiness, realized in the life of each individual, is the key to a full Christian life. Hence the name, "Holiness Movement." Its origin is traceable to the revival movement of the 19th century.

The Perfectionist branch of this large group includes such foundations as the Church of the Nazarene, the Church of God (Anderson, Ind.), and the Pilgrim Holiness Church. On the Pentecostal side are the Assemblies of God, the numerous Churches of God, and many bodies with the word Pentecostal in their titles. There are also many other very small cults which are similar in spirit to the larger churches.

Among the fundamental Christian doctrines maintained by Holiness believers are those of the Trinity and the divinity of Christ. They accept baptism. Classical Protestantism is reflected in their beliefs regarding the effect of original sin on human nature, the nature of justification, principles of biblical interpretation, and the rejection of tradition.

Some tenets are limited to the Pentecostal and Perfectionist bodies, such as beliefs in the imminent coming of Christ for the second time and a second baptism of the Holy Spirit in which holiness is acquired. There are many different opinions regarding the nature of this holiness.

The Pentecostals hold that justification and holiness are essentially related to the events that accompanied the descent of the Holy Spirit upon the Apostles at Pentecost. Hence, speaking in tongues and other related phenomena are significant.

Women Ordained Priests

A controversial service for the ordination of four women deacons of the Episcopal Church took place Sept. 7, 1975, in Washington, D.C., despite two weeks of public and private efforts by Bishop William F. Creighton to prevent it.

Bishop Creighton, a strong supporter of the ordination of women, counseled waiting until the next Episcopal Convention, set for September, 1976, could act on the matter. He was on record with pledges to ordain women after that, no matter what the convention might decide.

In a pastoral letter read in Washington churches on the morning of the ordination, he asked Episcopalians to boycott the ceremony and urged that the women not be allowed to function as priests in the diocese.

In spite of his plea, a congregation of about 1,000 packed St. Stephen and the Incarnation Church where the service was held.

Earlier in the year, the Rev. William Wendt, pastor of the church, was admonished for allowing the Rev. Alison Cheek, one of 11 women irregularly ordained in Philadelphia in July, 1974, to celebrate Holy Communion there.

At the place in the service where those knowing of "any impediment or crime because of which we should not proceed" were asked to speak, two persons stepped forward with objections to the ordination.

The ordaining Bishop, retired George W. Barrett of Rochester, N.Y., however, said: "In conscience . . . I cannot refuse to act. . . . Equality can certainly not be interpreted as barring one-half of the Christian community from serving as its priests. Without malice . . . with regret for pain caused . . . with determination to do the right as God gives us to see the right, we proceed."

Those ordained were the Revs. Lee McGee, 33, Alison Palmer, 44, and Betty Rosenberg, 30, of Washington, and Diane Tickel, 57, of Anchorage, Alaska.

Heresy Charged

United Press International reported early in October, 1975, that the Rev. Joseph Hirsch, vicar of the Church of the Redeemer in Kansas City, Mo., had announced that he had left the Episcopal Church, taking with him between 25 and 50 parishioners.

The parishioners shared his view that the church had not spoken strongly enough against abortion, that it had been permissive on the issue of ordination of women to the priesthood and toward homosexuals, and that the denomination was afflicted by a "wave of doctrinal heresy" regarding the doctrines of the Virgin Birth of Christ, the Trinity and the Resurrection.

The modern ecumenical movement, which started about 1910 among Protestants and led to formation of the World Council of Churches in 1948, developed outside the mainstream of Catholic interest for many years. It has now become for Catholics as well one of the great religious facts of our time.

The magna charta of ecumenism for Catholics is a complex of several documents which include, in the first place, the *Decree on Ecumenism* promulgated by the Second Vatican Council Nov. 21, 1964. Other enactments underlying and expanding this decree are the *Dogmatic Constitution on the Church,* the *Decree on Eastern Catholic Churches,* and the *Pastoral Constitution on the Church in the Modern World.*

VATICAN II DECREE

The following excerpts from the *Decree on Ecumenism* cover the broad theological background and principles and indicate the thrust of the Church's commitment to ecumenism.

". . . Men who believe in Christ and have been properly baptized are brought into a certain, though imperfect, communion with the Catholic Church. Undoubtedly, the differences that exist in varying degrees between them and the Catholic Church — whether in doctrine and sometimes in discipline, or concerning the structure of the Church — do indeed create many and sometimes serious obstacles to full ecclesiastical communion. These the ecumenical movement is striving to overcome . . ." (No. 3).

Elements Common to Christians

"Moreover some, even very many, of the most significant elements or endowments which together go to build up and give life to the Church herself can exist outside the visible boundaries of the Catholic Church: the written word of God; the life of grace; faith, hope, and charity, along with other interior gifts of the Holy Spirit and visible elements. All of these, which come from Christ and lead back to Him, belong by right to the one Church of Christ" (No. 3).

[In a later passage, the decree singled out a number of elements which the Catholic Church and other churches have in common but not in complete agreement: confession of Christ as Lord and God and as mediator between God and man; belief in the Trinity; reverence for Scripture as the revealed word of God; baptism and the Lord's Supper; Christian life and worship; faith in action; concern with moral questions.]

"The brethren divided from us also carry out many of the sacred actions of the Christian religion. Undoubtedly, in ways that vary according to the condition of each Church or Community, these actions can truly engender a life of grace, and can be rightly described as capable of providing access to the community of salvation.

"It follows that these separated Churches and Communities, though we believe they suffer from defects already mentioned, have by no means been deprived of significance and importance in the mystery of salvation. For the Spirit of Christ has not refrained from using them as means of salvation which derive their efficacy from the very fullness of grace and truth entrusted to the Catholic Church" (No. 3).

Unity Lacking

"Nevertheless, our separated brethren, whether considered as individuals or as Communities and Churches, are not blessed with that unity which Jesus Christ wished to bestow on all those whom He has regenerated and vivified into one body and newness of life — that unity which the holy Scriptures and the revered tradition of the Church proclaim. For it is through Christ's Catholic Church alone, which is the all-embracing means of salvation, that the fullness of the means of salvation can be obtained. It was to the apostolic college alone, of which Peter is the head, that we believe our Lord entrusted all the blessings of the New Covenant, in order to establish on earth the one Body of Christ into which all those should be fully incorporated who already belong in any way to God's People . . ." (No. 3).

What the Movement Involves

"Today, in many parts of the world, under the inspiring grace of the Holy Spirit, multiple efforts are being expended through prayer, word, and action to attain that fullness of unity which Jesus Christ desires. This sacred Synod, therefore, exhorts all the Catholic faithful to recognize the signs of the times and to participate skillfully in the work of ecumenism.

"The 'ecumenical movement' means those activities and enterprises which, according to various needs of the Church and opportune occasions, are started and organized for the fostering of unity among Christians. These are:

• "First, every effort to eliminate words, judgments, and actions which do not respond to the condition of separated brethren with truth and fairness and so make mutual relations between them more difficult.

• "Then, 'dialogue' between competent experts from different Churches and Communities (scholarly ecumenism). . . .

• "In addition, these Communions cooperate more closely in whatever projects a Christian conscience demands for the common good (social ecumenism).

• "They also come together for common prayer, where this is permitted (spiritual ecumenism).

• "Finally, all are led to examine their own faithfulness to Christ's will for the Church and, wherever necessary, undertake with vigor the task of renewal and reform.

". . . It is evident that the work of preparing and reconciling those individuals who wish for full Catholic communion is of its nature distinct from ecumenical action. But there is no opposition between the two, since both proceed from the wondrous providence of God" (No. 4).

Primary Duty of Catholics

"In ecumenical work, Catholics must assuredly be concerned for their separated brethren, praying for them, keeping them informed about the Church, making the first approaches towards them. But their primary duty is to make an honest and careful appraisal of whatever needs to be renewed and achieved in the Catholic household itself, in order that its life may bear witness more loyally and luminously to the teachings and ordinances which have been handed down from Christ through the apostles.

". . . Every Catholic must . . . aim at Christian perfection (cf. Jas. 1:4; Rom. 12:1-2) and, each according to his station, play his part so that the Church . . . may daily be more purified and renewed, against the day when Christ will present her to Himself in all her glory, without spot or wrinkle (cf. Eph. 5:27).

". . . Catholics must joyfully acknowledge and esteem the truly Christian endowments from our common heritage which are to be found among our separated brethren. . . .

"Nor should we forget that whatever is wrought by the grace of the Holy Spirit in the hearts of our separated brethren can contribute to our own edification. Whatever is truly Christian never conflicts with the genuine interests of the faith; indeed, it can always result in a more ample realization of the very mystery of Christ and the Church . . ." (No. 4).

Participation in Worship

Norms concerning participation by Catholics in the worship of other Christian Churches were sketched in this conciliar decree and elaborated in a number of other documents such as: the *Decree on Eastern Catholic Churches,* promulgated by the Second Vatican Council in 1964; *Interim Guidelines for Prayer in Common,* issued June 18, 1965, by the US Bishops' Committee for Ecumenical and Inter-Religious Affairs; a *Directory on Ecumenism,* published in 1967 by the Vatican Secretariat for Promoting Christian Unity; additional communications from the US Bishops' Committee, and numerous sets of guidelines issued locally by and for dioceses throughout the US.

The norms encourage common prayer services for Christian unity and other intentions. Beyond that, they draw a distinction between separated churches of the Reformation tradition and separated Eastern churches, in view of doctrine and practice the Catholic Church has in common with the latter concerning the apostolic succession of bishops, holy orders, liturgy, and other credal matters.

Full participation by Catholics in official Protestant liturgies is prohibited, because it implies profession of the faith expressed in the liturgy. Intercommunion by Catholics at Protestant liturgies is prohibited. Under certain conditions, Protestants may be given Holy Communion in the Catholic Church (see Intercommunion). A Catholic may stand as a witness, but not as a sponsor, in baptism, and as a witness in the marriage of separated Christians. Similarly, a Protestant may stand as a witness, but not as a sponsor, in a Catholic baptism, and as a witness in the marriage of Catholics.

Separated Eastern Churches

The principal norms regarding liturgical participation with separated Eastern Christians are included under Eastern Ecumenism.

ECUMENICAL AGENCIES

Vatican Secretariat

The top-level agency for Catholic ecumenical efforts is the Vatican Secretariat for Promoting Christian Unity, which originated in 1960 as a preparatory commission for the Second Vatican Council. Its purposes are to provide guidance and, where necessary, coordination for ecumenical endeavor by Catholics, and to establish and maintain relations with representatives of other Christian Churches for ecumenical dialogue and action.

The secretariat, first under the direction of Cardinal Augustin Bea, S. J., and now of Cardinal Jan Willebrands, has established firm working relations with a number of representative agencies of other churches, principally the World Council of Churches and the Lutheran World Federation; has joined the Anglican Communion and the Orthodox in dialogue; and is carrying forward with the World Alliance of Reformed Churches (a Presbyterian alliance) studies regarding the possibilities of future dialogue. In the past several years, staff members and representatives of the secretariat have been involved in one way or another in nearly every significant ecumenical enterprise and meeting held throughout the world, including the Fourth General Assembly of the World Council of Churches and the Tenth Lambeth Conference in 1968.

While the secretariat and its counterparts in other churches have focused primary attention on theological and other related problems of Christian unity, they have also begun, and in increasing measure, to emphasize the responsibilities of the churches for greater unity of witness and effort in areas of humanitarian need.

Bishops' Committee

The US Bishops' Committee for Ecumenical and Interreligious Affairs was established by the American hierarchy in 1964. Its purposes are to maintain relationships with other Christian churches and other religious communities at the national level, to advise and assist dioceses in developing and applying ecumenical policies, and to maintain liaison with corresponding Vatican offices — the Secretariats for Christian Unity and Non-Christian Religions.

This standing committee of the National Conference of Catholic Bishops is chaired by Archbishop William W. Baum of Washington. Operationally, the committee is assisted by secretariats headed by the Rev. John F. Hotchkin, secretary for Christian Unity, and the Rev. Edward H. Flannery, secretary for Catholic-Jewish Relations.

The committee co-sponsors several national consultations with other churches and confessional families. These bring together on a regular basis Catholic representatives and their counterparts from the American Baptist Convention, the Christian Church (Disciples of Christ), the Episcopal Church, the Lutheran World Federation (US Committee), the United Methodist Church, the Orthodox Churches, and the Alliance of Reformed Churches (North American area). Reports of consultations conducted under committee auspices are published periodically and are available through the Publications Office of the US Catholic Conference. (See Ecumenical Dialogues.)

The committee has also facilitated regional meetings in conjunction with the Home Mission Board of the Southern Baptist Convention.

The committee relates with the National Council of Churches of Christ, and has sponsored a joint study committee investigating the possibility of Roman Catholic membership in that body.

Advisory and other services are provided by the committee to ecumenical commissions and agencies in dioceses throughout the country.

Through the Secretariat for Catholic-Jewish Relations, the committee is in contact with several national Jewish agencies and bodies. Issues of mutual interest and shared concern are reviewed for the purpose of furthering deeper understanding between the Catholic and Jewish communities.

Through the Secretariat for Non-Christians, moderated by Archbishop Baum, the committee promotes activity in wider areas of dialogue. The Rev. John F. Hotchkin serves as executive secretary for this secretariat.

Offices of the committee are located at 1312 Massachusetts Ave. N. W., Washington, D. C. 20005.

World Council

The World Council of Churches is a fellowship of churches which acknowledge "Jesus Christ as Lord and Savior." It is a permanent organization providing constituent members — in 1975, 271 churches with some 450 million communicants in 90 countries — with opportunities for meeting, consultation and cooperative action with respect to doctrine, worship, practice, social mission, evangelism and missionary work, and other matters of mutual concern.

The WCC was formally established Aug. 23, 1948, in Amsterdam with ratification of a constitution by 147 communions. This action merged two previously existing movements — Life and Work (social mission), Faith and Order (doctrine) — which had initiated practical steps toward founding a fellowship of Christian churches at meetings held in Oxford, Edinburgh and Utrecht in 1937 and 1938. A third movement for cooperative missionary work, which originated about 1910 and, remotely, led to formation of the WCC, was incorporated into the council in 1971 under the title of the International Missionary Council (World Mission and Evangelism).

Four additional general assemblies of the council have been held since the charter meeting of 1948: in Evanston, Ill. (1954), New Delhi, India (1961), Uppsala, Sweden (1968) and Nairobi, Kenya (1975).

Between assemblies, the council operates through a central committee which meets every 12 or 18 months, and an executive committee which meets every six months.

The council continues the work of the International Missionary Council, the Commission on Faith and Order, and the Commission on Church and Society. The structure of the council has three program units: Faith and Witness, Justice and Service, Education and Communication.

Liaison between the council and the Vatican has been maintained since 1966 through a joint working group. Roman Catholic membership in the WCC is a question officially on the agenda of this body. The Joint Commission on Society, Development and Peace (SODEPAX) is an agency of the council and the Pontifical Commission for Justice and Peace. Roman Catholics serve individually as full members of the Commission on Faith and Order and in various capacities on other program committees of the council.

WCC headquarters are located in Geneva, Switzerland. The United States Conference for the World Council of Churches at 475 Riverside Drive, New York, N. Y. 10027, provides liaison between the US churches and Geneva. The WCC also maintains fraternal relations with regional, national and local councils of churches throughout the world.

The Rev. Philip A. Potter, a Methodist from the Island of Dominica, West Indies, was elected secretary general of the WCC in August, 1972.

WCC presidents are: Mrs. Dr. Kiyoko Takeda Cho (Japan), His Holiness German (Yugoslavia), Rev. Dr. Hanns Lilje (Germany), Rev. Dr. Ernest A. Payne (United Kingdom), Rev. Dr. John Coventry Smith (USA), Rt. Rev. A. H. Zulu (South Africa).

National Council

The National Council of The Churches of Christ in the USA, the largest ecumenical organization in the United States, is a cooperative federation of 31 Protestant, Orthodox and Anglican church bodies having about 42 million members.

The NCC, established by the churches in 1950, was structured through the merger of 12 separate cooperative agencies. Presently, through three main program divisions and five commissions, the NCC carries on work in behalf of member churches in home and overseas missions, Christian education and communications, disaster relief and rehabilitation, family life, religious broadcast and film-making, regional and local ecumenism, and other areas.

The NCC is governed by a governing board of approximately 350 members appointed by the constituent churches which meets twice a year.

The NCC's annual budget approximates $16 million, about 60 percent of which is devoted to compassionate ministries of aid and relief to victims of disasters and endemic poverty in lands overseas. The work of the NCC is financially supported for the most part by the member churches and their boards and agencies.

Dr. W. Sterling Cary was elected to a three-year term as president in 1972.

NCC headquarters are located at 475 Riverside Drive, New York, N.Y. 10027.

Consultation

The Consultation on Church Union, officially begun in 1962, is a venture of American churches seeking a united church "truly catholic, truly evangelical, and truly reformed." The nine churches engaged in this process, representing 25 million Christians, are the African Methodist Episcopal Church, the African Methodist Episcopal Zion Church, the Christian Church (Disciples of Christ), the Christian Methodist Episcopal Church, the Episcopal Church, the Presbyterian Church in the United States, the United Church of Christ, the United Methodist Church, and the United Presbyterian Church in the U.S.A.

From 1970 to 1973 the member churches studied the first draft of a plan of union for the proposed Church of Christ Uniting. The responses to this plan, on the one hand, gave evidence of an historic consensus on faith, worship, and ministry; on the other hand, they revealed the need for mature involvement in order to discover the structures of a united church. The 11th plenary at Memphis, April, 1973, called for a future agenda involving the congregations more intimately, explored divisive factors such as racism, and affirmed the doctrinal and liturgical rapprochement already achieved. An affirmation of mutual recognition of membership was accepted and sent to the churches at the 12th plenary held at Cincinnati Nov. 4 to 8, 1974.

Two experimental liturgies, "An Order of Worship for The Proclamation of the Word of God and The Celebration of the Lord's Supper With Commentary" (1968) and "An Order for Holy Baptism" (1973), have been developed. An ecumenical lectionary has also been produced. A joint commission of Roman Catholic and COCU liturgical scholars is preparing an ecumenical marriage rite.

The general secretary of COCU is the Rev. Gerald F. Moede.

Offices are located at 228 Alexander St., Princeton, N.J. 08540.

ECUMENICAL DIALOGUES

(Source: Secretariat for Ecumenical and Interreligious Affairs, National Conference of Catholic Bishops.)

Following is a list of principal consultations, from Mar. 16, 1965, involving representatives of the US Catholic Bishops' Committee for Ecumenical and Interreligious Affairs and representatives of other Christian Churches, with names of the churches, places and dates of meetings, and the subject matter of discussions.

Baptist Convention, American (Division of Cooperative Christianity): (1) De Witt, Mich., Apr. 3, 1967 — American Baptist and Roman Catholic dialogue; a Baptist view of areas of theological agreement. (2) Green Lake, Wis., Apr. 29, 1968 — Baptism and confirmation; Christian freedom and ecclesiastical authority. (3) Schiller Park, Ill., Apr. 28, 1969 — Nature and communication of grace; Christian freedom and ecclesiastical authority; baptism and confirmation.

(4) Atchison, Kan., Apr. 17, 1970 — Role of the Church, resume of years past and the future; Roman Catholic-American Baptist dialogues; observations concerning bilateral ecumenical conversations and the future course of American Baptist-Roman Catholic conversations.

(5) Detroit, Mich., Apr. 23 to 24, 1971 — Theological perspective on clergy and lay issues and relations; theology of the local church; growth in understanding. (6) Liberty,

Mo., Apr. 14 to 15, 1972 — Relationships between Church and State.

Baptists, Southern (Ecumenical Institute, Wake Forest University): (1) Winston-Salem, N. C., May 8, 1969 — Impact of biblical criticism on Roman Catholicism and contemporary Christianity in general; holy use of the word; creeds and the Faith; liturgy and spontaneity in worship; retreat, revival and monasticism; world view of ecumenism. (2) St. Benedict, La., Feb. 4, 1970 — Liturgy and spontaneity in worship; perspectives on Baptist views on Scripture and tradition; the priesthood of all Christians; authority of the Old Testament; Baptist concepts of the Church; retreat, revival and monasticism. (3) Louisville, Ky., May 13, 1970 — The priesthood of all Christians; the ecumenical tide — a pastoral perspective; the enduring meaning of the Old Testament; retreat, revival and monasticism. (4) Daytona Beach, Fla., Feb. 1 to 3, 1971 — Issues and answers, prepared by the Interfaith Witness Department of the Home Mission Board, Southern Baptist Convention. (5) Houston, Tex., Oct. 16 to 18, 1972 — Second regional conference planned in conjunction with the Interfaith Witness Department. (6) Marriottsville, Md., Feb. 4 to 6, 1974 — Third regional conference, planned in conjunction with the Interfaith and Witness Department, concerning different types of reform and their appropriateness at different levels of church life. (7) Menlo Park, Calif. (Oct. 27 to 29, 1975 — Fourth regional conference. The theme: "Conversion to Christ and Life-Long Growth in the Spirit."

Christian Church, Disciples of Christ (Council on Christian Unity): (1) Indianapolis, Ind., Mar. 16, 1967 — A look at Disciples for Catholics. (2) Kansas City, Mo., Sept. 25, 1967 — Roman Catholic view of the nature of unity being sought; opportunities in the contemporary ecumenical movement. (3) St. Louis, Mo., Apr. 29, 1968 — Eucharistic sharing. (4) Washington, D. C., Oct. 16, 1968 — Disciple of Christ inquiry regarding the sacramentality of marriage; pastoral reflections on mixed marriage. (5) New York, N. Y., Apr. 25, 1969 — Recognition and reconciliation of ministries; theological presuppositions concerning ministry among the Disciples; role of the priest in the Catholic community. (6) Columbus, O., Nov. 3 to 5, 1970 — The parish concept in a plan of union (Consultation on Church Union); directions emerging in Catholic parish life. (7) New York, N.Y., June 8 to 10, 1971 — Disciples' theology of baptism; meaning of baptism as liberation, incorporation, empowerment. (8) Indianapolis, Ind., Mar. 8 to 10, 1972 — Ministry of healing and reconciliation as practiced in the two communities. (9) Madison, Wis., June 26 to 28, 1972 — Review and summary of five years of dialogue; planning for future themes. (10) Pleasant Hill, Shaker Town, Ky., May 22 to 24, 1973 — The Church in the New Testament.

Episcopal (The Anglican-Roman Catholic Consultation, Joint Commission on Ecumenical Relations): (1) Washington, D.C., June 22, 1965 — Preliminary discussions. (2) Kansas City, Mo., Feb. 2, 1966 — Eucharist as source or expression of community; Eucharist as sign and cause of unity, and the Church as a Eucharistic fellowship. (3) Providence, R.I., Oct. 10, 1966 — Function of the minister in Eucharistic celebration; minister of the Eucharist. (4) Milwaukee, Wis., May 2, 1967 — Eucharist. (5) Jackson, Miss., Jan. 5, 1968 — Various aspects of the ministerial priesthood and the priesthood of the faithful in Eucharistic celebration; the priest's place and function in the Church's mission of service; the laity in Episcopal Church government. (6) Liberty, Mo., Dec. 2, 1968 — Directions of the ecumenical movement; episcopal symbol of unity in the Christian community; collegiality; Citizens for Educational Freedom; a layman's view of jurisdictional and cultural factors in division; Church and society in contemporary America. (7) Boynton Beach, Fla., Dec. 8, 1969 — All in each place; toward the reconciliation of the Roman Catholic Church and Churches of the Anglican Communion; an approach to designing a Roman Catholic-Episcopal parish; preparation of joint statement on the meeting. (8) Green Bay, Wis., June 17, 1970 — Is the (COCU — Consultation on Church Union) plan of union truly Catholic, with special reference to the priest and the episcopacy?; Anglican-Roman Catholic dialogue — achievement and prognostication. (9) St. Benedict, La., Jan. 26 to 29, 1971 — The primacy of jurisdiction of the Roman Pontiff according to the First Vatican Council; the teaching of the Second Vatican Council concerning the hierarchy of truths; analysis of the ground of "Church Elements: An Ecclesiological Investigation." (10) Liberty, Mo., June 20 to 23, 1971 — Gift of infallibility; sharing in the teaching authority of the Church; official view of episcopacy in the Episcopal Church in the USA; symposium on Hans Kung's *Infallibility? An Inquiry*; dogma as an ecumenical problem; Revelation and statement in Anglicanism; revised working paper on theological truth, propositions and Christian unity; reflections on the teaching ministry of the Church. (11) New York, N.Y., Jan 20 to 24, 1972 — Theological truth, propositions and Christian unity; the Protestant Episcopal Church's view of authority, tradition and the Bible; a comment on the Windsor "Statement of Eucharistic Agreement" issued by the International Anglican-Roman Catholic Consultation. (12) Cincinnati, O., June 12 to 15, 1972 — The notion of *typos* and *typoi* as applied to the forms of the Christian Church; correspondences and differences in the Anglican and Roman Catholic understanding and exercise of teaching authority. (13) Cincinnati, O., Mar. 18 to 22, 1973 — Formulation of a preliminary draft on the purpose of the Church. (14) Vicksburg, Miss., Jan. 6 to 10, 1974 — Formulation of a response to the "Canterbury Statement" of the International Anglican-Roman Catholic Consultation on ministry and ordination; discussion and amendment of a draft on the purpose of the Church; other subjects in a continuing dialogue on the mission of the Church. (15) Cincinnati, O., Nov. 10 to 13, 1974 — Discussion on the nature of authority in Anglicanism and Roman Catholicism. Report prepared on the purpose of the Church. (16) Cincinnati, O., June 22 to 25, 1975 — Special ad hoc consultation on women and orders.

Lutheran, U.S.A. (National Committee of the Lutheran World Federation): (1) Baltimore, Md., Mar. 16, 1965 — Exploratory discussion. (2) Baltimore, Md., July 6, 1965 — Nicene Creed as dogma of the Church. (3) Chicago, Ill., Feb. 10, 1966 — Baptism, in the context of the New Testament; Lutheran understanding; teaching of the Council of Trent. (4) Washington, D.C., Sept. 22, 1966 — Eucharist as sacrifice, in traditional and contemporary Catholic and Lutheran contexts. (5) New York, N.Y., Apr 7, 1967 — Propitiation and five presentations on various aspects of the Eucharist. (6) St. Louis, Mo.. Sept. 29, 1967 — Eucharist. (7) New York, Mar. 8, 1968 — Intercommunion, with respect to Catholic discipline, Lutheran practice, and theological reflections. (8) Williamsburg, Va., Sept. 27, 1968 — Ministry; the competent minister of the Eucharist; scriptural foundations of diakonia (ministry of service). (9) San Francisco, Calif., Feb. 21, 1969 — Apostolic succession in the patristic era and in a contemporary view; Lutheran view of the validity of Lutheran orders; Christian priesthood in the light of documents of the Second Vatican Council. (10) Baltimore, Md., Sept. 26, 1969 — The minister of the Eucharist, according to the Council of Trent; the use of "Church" as applied to Protestant denominations in the documents of Vatican II; Lutheran doctrine of the ministry — Catholic and Reformed; the ordained minister and layman in Lutheranism. (11) St. George, Bermuda, Feb. 19, 1970 — Preparation of joint statement on the ministry. (12) New York, N.Y., May, 1970. (13) Chicago, Ill., Oct. 30 to Nov. 1, 1970. (14) Miami, Fla., Feb. 19 to 22, 1971 — Peter and the New Testament; the papacy in the late pa-

tristic era, Middle Ages, Renaissance; text of the *Dogmatic Constitution on the Church* (Vatican II) with respect to the papacy and infallibility. (15) Seabury, Conn., Sept. 24 to 27, 1971 — An investigation of the concept of divine right *(jus divinum);* teaching of the First Vatican Council on primacy and infallibility; a Lutheran understanding of what papal primacy in the Church might mean. (16) New Orleans, La., Feb. 18 to 21, 1972 — Further discussion of the concept of divine right; ecumenical projections concerning the Petrine office; teaching authority in the Lutheran Church. (17) Minneapolis, Minn., Sept. 22 to 25, 1972 — Further investigation of the Petrine function; councils and conciliarism. (18) San Antonio, Tex., Feb. 16 to 19, 1973 — Discussion of work and papers of the Petrine panel concerning ministry and the Church universal, Catholic and Lutheran interpretive statements; work on papal primacy papers. (19) Allentown, Pa., Sept. 21 to 24, 1973 — Work on a joint statement concerning ministry and the Church universal, the concluding session on this topic; selection of infallibility as the next topic for consideration. (20) Marriottsville, Md., Feb. 15 to 17, 1974 — Start of discussion on infallibility; commissioning of 16 future research papers. (21) Princeton, N.J., Sept. 19 to 22, 1974 — Scriptural studies re infallibility, inquiries into the teachings of early Lutheranism. (22) St. Louis, Mo., Jan. 30 to Feb. 2, 1975 — Historical and systematic studies of the teaching of infallibility. (23) Washington, D.C., Apr. 2 to 3, 1975 — Special meeting of several Lutheran presidents and Catholic bishops to review the work of the scholars' consultation and propose future directions. Press report issued.

(24) Washington, D.C. Sept. 17 to 21, 1975 — Further historical and case studies re infallibility: ecumenical councils and marian definitions. (25) Scottsdale, Ariz., Feb. 19 to 22, 1975 — Infallibility discussion continued.

Methodist (United Methodist Church): (1) Chicago, Ill., June 28, 1966 — Methodists and Roman Catholics: comments for Catholic-Methodist conversation. (2) Chicago, Ill., Dec. 18, 1966 — Salvation, faith and good works; Catholic Church and faith. (3) Lake Junaluska, N. C., June 28, 1967 — Roman Catholic position regarding the Spirit in the Church; mission of the Holy Spirit, in the light of the Second Vatican Council's *Dogmatic Constitution on the Church* and the writings of John Wesley.

(4) New York, N.Y., Dec. 17, 1967 — Three generations of Church-State argumentation. (5) San Antonio, Tex., Sept. 30, 1968 — Shared convictions about education. (6) Delaware, O., Oct. 9, 1969 — Major Methodist ecumenical documents; an appraisal of some documents of Vatican II; racial con-

frontation in Roman Catholicism, Methodism and the National Council of Churches. (7) Chicago, Ill., Jan. 30, 1970 — Review and planning.

(8) Washington, D. C., Dec. 16, 1970 — Completion of a statement of shared convictions about education. Task force meetings during 1971. (9) Cincinnati, O., Feb. 25 to 26, 1972 — Ministry in the United Methodist Church and the spirituality of the ordained ministry; problems of ministry. (10) Dayton, O., Oct. 13 to 14, 1972 — Dialogue on the holiness of the Church and Christian holiness.

(11) Washington, D.C., Mar. 9 to 10, 1973 — Spirituality of the ministry. (12) Washington, D.C., Nov. 1 to 2, 1973 — Start of preparatory work on a consensus statement on spirituality of the ministry.

(13) Washington, D.C., Jan. 30 to Feb. 2, 1975 — Report prepared on Catholic and United Methodist understandings of holiness and spirituality in the ordained ministry. (14) Washington, D.C., Oct. 16 to 18, 1975 — Planning for future consultations.

Orthodox (Standing Conference of Canonical Orthodox Bishops of America): Sept. 9, 1965 — Preliminary discussions. (1) New York, N. Y., Sept. 29, 1966 — Consultation led to appointment of task forces to investigate differences in theological methods, questions of sacramental sharing, possible cooperation in theological education and the formation of seminarians. (2) Worcester, Mass., May 5, 1967 — Theological diversity and unity; intercommunion; common witness in theological education. (3) Maryknoll, N. Y., Dec. 7, 1968 — Eucharist and Church; indissolubility of marriage; Cooperation in theological education.

(4) Worcester, Mass., Dec. 12, 1969 — Orthodox and Catholic views of the Eucharist and membership in the Church; an agreed statement on the Eucharist. (5) New York, N.Y., May 19, 1970 — New Order of the Mass; membership of schismatics and heretics in the ancient Church; current legislation of the Catholic Church and current practices of the Greek Orthodox Church concerning common worship; current legislation of the Catholic Church concerning mixed marriages; Orthodox view of mixed marriages; an agreed statement on mixed marriages.

(6) Brookline, Mass., Dec. 4, 1970 — Ministers, doctrine and practice of matrimony in Eastern and Western traditions. (7) Barlin Acres, Mass., Nov. 3 to 4, 1971 — Ethical issues relating to marriage; revision of an agreed statement on mixed marriages; the primacy of Rome as seen by the Eastern Church.

(8) New York, N.Y., Dec. 6, 1973 — Study of a draft statement on the sanctity of marriage. (9) Washington, D.C., May 23 to 24, 1974 — Dialogical process; witness of the Church on the American scene; approval of an agreed statement on respect for life; Orthodox and Catholic views of contemporary Orthodoxy and Catholicism.

(10) New York, N.Y., Dec. 9 to 10, 1974 — Prepared and issued an agreed statement on the Church. (11) Washington, D.C., May 19 to 20, 1975 — Dialogue on the local church and on the theology of priesthood. (12) New York, N.Y., Jan. 23 to 24, 1976 — Further dialogue on the theology of priesthood, et al.

Presbyterian Reformed (The Roman Catholic-Presbyterian Consultation Group, North American Council of the World Alliance of Reformed Churches): (1) Washington, D.C., July 27, 1965 — Exploratory discussions. (2) Philadelphia, Pa., Nov. 26, 1965 — Role of the Holy Spirit in renewal and reform of the Church. (3) New York, May 12, 1966 — Roman Catholic view of Scripture and tradition; apostolic and ecclesiastical tradition.

(4) Chicago, Ill., Oct. 27, 1966 — Development of doctrine; dialogue, a program of peace, prayer and study for Roman Catholics and Protestants. (5) Collegeville, Minn., Apr. 26, 1967 — Order and ministry in the Reformed tradition; validity of orders; changes in mixed marriage. (6) Lancaster, Pa., Oct. 26, 1967 — Work was begun on a joint statement on ministry. (7) Bristow, Va., May 9, 1968 — Structures and ministries. (8) Allen Park, Mich., Oct. 24, 1968 — Marriage. (9) Charleston, S.C., May 21, 1969 — Validation of ministries and ministry; theological view of marriage.

(10) Macatawa, Mich., Oct. 30, 1969 — Apostles and apostolic succession in the patristic era; report concerning office; divorce and remarriage as understood in the United Presbyterian Church in the USA; the Church and second marriage; recommendations for changes regarding inter-Christian marriages. (11) Morristown, N.J., May 13, 1970 — Joint statements on ministry in the Church and women in Church and society.

(12) Princeton, N.J., Oct. 29 to 30, 1970 — Episcopal/presbyteral polity; episcopacy. (13) Columbus, O., May 13 to 15, 1971 — Ministry in the Church; man-woman relationships; the future of the Church. (14) Richmond, Va., Oct. 28 to 30, 1971 — Reports finalized on women in the Church and ministry in the Church. (15) Oct. 26 to 29, 1972 — The shape of the unity we seek.

(16) Columbus, O., May 30 to June 2, 1973 — Theological and sociological views of the shape of unity we seek. (17) Columbus, O., Oct. 24 to 27, 1973 — Renewed discussion of the previous topic. (18) Columbus, O., May 8 to 11, 1974 — Further discussion of the previous topic in the light of Scripture, tradition, theology and reflection on the total Christian experience; worship and belief; discussion of plans for publication of a book on progress of the dialogue.

(17) Cincinnati, O., Oct. 24 to 26, 1974 — Dialogue on the unity we seek in worship and in structures. (18) Washington, D.C., May 22

to 24, 1975 — Report prepared on the mission and nature of the one Church of Christ, with attention to the unity sought in worship, in structure and in common faith.

ECUMENICAL BRIEFS

Statements: Three ecumenical statements of some importance issued in recent years are the following.

• The "Windsor Statement" on Eucharistic doctrine, published Dec. 31, 1971, by the Anglican-Roman Catholic International Commission of theologians. (For text, see pages 132-33 of the 1973 *Catholic Almanac*.)

• The "Canterbury Statement" on ministry and ordination, published Dec. 13, 1973, by the same commission. (For excerpts, see pages 127-30 of the 1975 *Catholic Almanac*.)

• "Papal Primacy / Converging Viewpoints," published Mar. 4, 1974, by the dialogue group sanctioned by the U.S.A. National Convention of the World Lutheran Federation and the U.S. Bishops' Committee for Ecumenical and Interreligious Affairs. (For excerpts, see pages 130-31 of the 1975 *Catholic Almanac*.)

The statements reflect the views of participants in the dialogues which produced them. They have not been accepted by the respective churches as formulations of doctrine or points of departure for practical changes in discipline.

Covenants: Approximately 100 U.S. Catholic and other Christian parishes, mostly Episcopalian, have established covenant relationships for purposes of mutual contact and cooperation in religious and related affairs.

In Georgia, Bishop Raymond Lessard of Savannah and Episcopal Bishop Paul Reeves signed such a covenant in May, 1975. Its stated purposes are to:

• "Promote serious dialogue between our two dioceses in the spirit of the national and international dialogues between our churches."

• "Encourage all our congregations to enter into covenant relationships with one another. Although we realize that intercommunion has not yet been achieved by our churches, we strongly recommend common prayer together, study together . . . and social witness together."

• "Inaugurate a prayer cycle for the con-

gregations of our two dioceses so that each day we can pray for one another in an ordered way."

World Council of Churches' Assembly: Catholic observers were officially invited to attend the Fifth General Assembly of the World Council of Churches Nov. 23 to Dec. 10, 1975, in Nairobi, Kenya. The meeting, with the theme "Jesus Christ Frees and Unites," was attended by 700 delegates of 271 member bodies in 90 countries.

The four previous assemblies were held in Amsterdam, The Netherlands, in 1948 when the council was founded; Evanston, Ill., in 1954; New Delhi, India, in 1961; and Uppsala, Sweden, in 1968.

Spiritual Ecumenism: Father Herbert Ryan, S.J., keynoting the 11th National Workshop on Christian Unity Mar. 10, 1974, in Charleston, S.C., said that the emphasis in ecumenism had shifted from social action to renewed interest in the spiritual life. He said the ecumenical trend in the 1960's "was for Christian outreach, joint social action . . . because this was seen as a means to carry out the social witness of the Gospel message." Observing that strong enthusiasm for social action had diminished, he said ecumenical efforts needed a new thrust because "Christians in America today have started a search for deepening of their inner lives. This search crosses denominational barriers, and the emerging forms that it has taken — prayer groups, discussion and Bible groups, charismatic fellowships, religious communes — are already thoroughly ecumenical." He called on workshop participants to take up this new "spiritual challenge" while avoiding the pitfalls of "impious withdrawal" from social action. Father Ryan was a member of the Anglican-Roman Catholic International Commission of theologians.

Cardinal Jan Willebrands, addressing a plenary session of the Secretariat for Promoting Christian Unity Feb. 17, 1975, said: "It seems to me that we are witnessing not a slowing-down but a deepening, an interiorization, making for that true interior and spiritual renewal looked upon by the Second Vatican Council as the soul of all ecumenism."

See separate article, Ecumenical Collaboration, under Special Reports.

CATHOLIC-JEWISH RELATIONS

The Second Vatican Council, in addition to the *Decree on Ecumenism* concerning the movement for unity among Christians, stated the mind of the Church on a similar matter in a *Declaration on the Relationship of the Church to Non-Christian Religions.* This document, as the following excerpts indicate, backgrounds the reasons and directions of the Church's regard for the Jews. (Other portions of the document, not cited here, refer to Hindus, Buddhists and Moslems.)

Spiritual Bond

"As this sacred Synod searches into the mystery of the Church, it recalls the spiritual bond linking the people of the New Covenant with Abraham's stock.

"For the Church of Christ acknowledges that, according to the mystery of God's saving design, the beginnings of her faith and her election are already found among the patriarchs, Moses, and the prophets. She professes that all who believe in Christ, Abraham's sons according to faith (cf. Gal. 3:7), are included in the same patriarch's call, and likewise that the salvation of the Church was mystically foreshadowed by the Chosen People's exodus from the land of bondage.

"The Church, therefore, cannot forget that she received the revelation of the Old Testament through the people with whom God in His inexpressible mercy deigned to establish the Ancient Covenant. Nor can she forget that she draws sustenance from the root of that good olive tree onto which have been grafted the wild olive branches of the Gentiles (cf. Rom.11:17-24). Indeed, the Church believes that by His cross Christ, our Peace, reconciled Jew and Gentile, making them both one in Himself (cf. Eph. 2:14-16).

". . . The Jews still remain most dear to God because of their fathers, for He does not repent of the gifts He makes nor of the calls He issues (cf. Rom. 11:28-29). In company with the prophets and the same Apostle (Paul), the Church awaits that day, known to God alone, on which all peoples will address the Lord in a single voice and 'serve him with one accord' (Zeph. 3:9; Cf. Is. 66:23; Ps. 65:4; Rom. 11:11-32).

"Since the spiritual patrimony common to Christians and Jews is thus so great, this sacred Synod wishes to foster and recommend that mutual understanding and respect which is the fruit above all of biblical and theological studies, and of brotherly dialogues.

No Anti-Semitism

"True, authorities of the Jews and those who followed their lead pressed for the death of Christ (cf. Jn. 19:6); still, what happened in His passion cannot be blamed upon all the Jews then living, without distinction, nor upon the Jews of today. Although the Church is the new People of God, the Jews should not be presented as repudiated or cursed by God, as if such views followed from the holy Scriptures. All should take pains, then, lest in catechetical instruction and in the preaching of God's Word they teach anything out of harmony with the truth of the gospel and the spirit of Christ.

"The Church repudiates all persecutions against any man. Moreover, mindful of her common patrimony with the Jews, and motivated by the gospel's spiritual love and by no political considerations, she deplores the hatred, persecutions, and displays of anti-Semitism directed against the Jews at any time and from any source. . . ." (4).

". . . The Church rejects, as foreign to the mind of Christ, any discrimination against men or harassment of them because of their race, color, condition of life, or religion. . . ." (No. 5).

Bishops' Secretariat

The American hierarchy's first move toward implementation of the Vatican II *Declaration on the Relationship of the Church to Non-Christian Religions* was to establish, in 1965, a Subcommission for Catholic-Jewish Relations in the framework of its Commission for Ecumenical and Interreligious Affairs. This subcommission was reconstituted and given the title of secretariat in September, 1967. Its moderator is Bishop Francis J. Mugavero of Brooklyn. The executive director is Father Edward Flannery. The Secretariat for Catholic-Jewish Relations is located at 1312 Massachusetts Ave. N.W., Washington, D.C. 20005.

According to the key norm of a set of guidelines issued by the secretariat Mar. 16, 1967: "The general aim of all Catholic-Jewish meetings (and relations) is to increase our understanding both of Judaism and the Catholic faith, to eliminate sources of tension and misunderstanding, to initiate dialogue or conversations on different levels, to multiply intergroup meetings between Catholics and Jews, and to promote cooperative social action."

WORKSHOP ON RELATIONS

The U.S. Bishops' Secretariat for Catholic-Jewish Relations sponsored the second in a series of national workshops on Christian-Jewish relations Oct. 28 to 30, 1975, in Memphis, Tenn. Participating groups included the Christian-Jewish Relations Office of the National Council of Churches, the National Conference of Christians and Jews, the Diocese of Memphis, the American Jewish Committee and B'nai B'rith. Topics under study were evangelism and Jews, Israel and the Jewish people, local Jewish community contacts, Vatican guidelines on Christian-Jewish relations and anti-Semitism.

See separate article, Catholic-Jewish Relations, under Special Reports.

JUDAISM

Judaism is the religion of the Old Testament and of contemporary Jews. Divinely revealed and with a patriarchal background (Abraham, Isaac, Jacob), it originated with the Mosaic Covenant, was identified with the Israelites, and achieved distinctive form and character as the religion of The Law from this Covenant and reforms initiated by Ezra and Nehemiah after the Babylonian Exile.

Judaism does not have a formal creed but its principal points of belief are clear. Basic is belief in one transcendent God who reveals himself through The Law, the prophets, the life of his people and events of history. The fatherhood of God involves the brotherhood of men. Religious faith and practice are equated with just living according to The

Law. Moral conviction and practice are regarded as more important than precise doctrinal formulation and profession. Formal worship, whose principal act was sacrifice from Canaanite times to 70 A. D., is by prayer, reading and meditating upon the sacred writings, and observance of the Sabbath and festivals.

Judaism has messianic expectations of the complete fulfillment of the Covenant, the coming of God's kingdom, the ingathering of his people, final judgment and retribution for all men. Views differ regarding the manner in which these expectations will be realized—through a person, the community of God's people, an evolution of historical events, an eschatological act of God himself. Individual salvation expectations also differ, depending on views about the nature of immortality, punishment and reward, and related matters.

The sacred books are the 24 books of the Masoretic Hebrew Text of The Law, the Prophets and the Writings (see The Bible). Together, they contain the basic instruction or norms for just living. In some contexts, the term Law or Torah refers only to the Pentateuch (Genesis, Exodus, Leviticus, Numbers, Deuteronomy); in others, it denotes all the sacred books and/or the whole complex of written and oral tradition.

Also of great authority are two Talmuds which were composed in Palestine and Babylon in the fourth and fifth centuries A.D., respectively. They consist of the Mishna, a compilation of oral laws, and the Gemara, a collection of rabbinical commentary on the Mishna. Midrash are collections of scriptural comments and moral counsels.

Priests were the principal official ministers during the period of sacrificial and temple worship. Rabbis were, and continue to be, teachers and leaders of prayer. The synagogue is the place of community worship. The family and home are focal points of many aspects of Jewish worship and practice.

Of the various categories of Jews, Orthodox are the most conservative in adherence to strict religious traditions. Others — Reformed, Conservative, Reconstructionist — are liberal in comparison with the Orthodox. They favor greater or less modification of religious practices in accommodation to contemporary culture and living conditions.

Principal events in Jewish life include the circumcision of males, according to prescriptions of the Covenant; the bar mitzvah which marks the coming-of-age of boys in Judaism at the age of 13; marriage; and observance of the Sabbath and festivals.

Sabbath and Festivals

Observances of the Sabbath and festivals begin at sundown of the previous calendar day and continue until the following sundown.

Sabbath: Saturday, the weekly day of rest prescribed in the Decalogue.

Booths (Tabernacles): A seven-to-nine-day festival in the month of Tishri (Sept.-Oct.), marked by some Jews with Covenant-renewal and reading of The Law. It originated as an agricultural feast at the end of the harvest and got its name from the temporary shelters used by workers in the fields.

Hanukkah (The Festival of Lights, the Feast of Consecration and of the Maccabees): Commemorates the dedication of the new altar in the Temple at Jerusalem by Judas Maccabeus in 165 B.C. The eight-day festival, during which candles in an eight-branch candelabra are lighted in succession, one each day, occurs near the winter solstice, close to Christmas time.

Passover: A seven-day festival commemorating the liberation of the Israelites from Egypt. The narrative of the Exodus, the Haggadah, is read at ceremonial Seder meals on the first and second days of the festival, which begins on the 14th day of Nisan (Mar.-Apr.).

Pentecost (Feast of Weeks): Observed 50 days after Passover. Some Jews regard it as commemorative of the anniversary of the revelation of The Law to Moses.

Purim: A joyous festival observed on the 14th day of Adar (Feb.-Mar.), commemorating the rescue of the Israelites from massacre by the Persians through the intervention of Esther. The festival is preceded by a day of fasting. A gift- and alms-giving custom became associated with it in medieval times.

Rosh Hashana (Feast of the Trumpets, New Year): Observed on the first day of Tishri (Sept.-Oct.), the festival focuses attention on the day of judgment and is marked with meditation on the ways of life and the ways of death. It is second in importance only to the most solemn observance of Yom Kippur, which is celebrated 10 days later.

Yom Kippur (Day of Atonement): The highest holy day, observed with strict fasting. It occurs 10 days after Rosh Hashana.

ISLAM

Islam is the religion of Mohammed and his followers, called Moslems, Muslims, Mohammedans. Islam, meaning submission to God, originated with Mohammed (570-632), an Arabian, who taught that he had received divine revelation and was the last and greatest of the prophets.

Moslems believe in one God. There were six great prophets—Adam, Noah, Abraham, Moses, Jesus and Mohammed—and Mohammed was the greatest. The creed states: "There is no God but Allah and Mohammed is the prophet of Allah."

The principal duties of Moslems are to: profess the faith by daily recitation of the creed; pray five times a day facing in the direction of the holy city of Mecca; give alms; fast daily from dawn to dusk during the month of Ramadan; make a pilgrimage to Mecca once if possible.

Moslems believe in a final judgment, heaven and hell. Polygamy is practiced. Some dietary regulations are in effect. The weekly day of worship is Friday, and the principal service is at noon in a mosque. Moslems do not have an ordained ministry. The general themes of their prayer are adoration and thanksgiving.

The basis of Islamic belief is the Koran, the created word of God revealed to Mohammed by the angel Gabriel over a period of 20 years. The contents of this sacred book are complemented by the Sunna, a collection of sacred traditions, and reinforced by Ijma, the consensus of Moslems which guarantees them against error in matters of belief and practice.

There are several sects of Moslems.

Conciliar Statement

The attitude of the Church toward Islam was stated as follows in the Second Vatican Council's *Declaration on the Relationship of the Church to Non-Christian Religions* (No. 3).

"Upon the Moslems, too, the Church looks with esteem. They adore one God, living and enduring, merciful and all-powerful, Maker of heaven and earth and Speaker to men. They strive to submit wholeheartedly even to His inscrutable decrees, just as did Abraham, with whom the Islamic faith is pleased to associate itself. Though they do not acknowledge Jesus as God, they revere Him as a prophet. They also honor Mary, His virgin mother; at times they call on her, too, with devotion. In addition they await the day of judgment when God will give each man his due after raising him up. Consequently, they prize the moral life, and give worship to God especially through prayer, almsgiving and fasting.

"Although in the course of the centuries many quarrels and hostilities have arisen between Christians and Moslems, this most sacred Synod urges all to forget the past and to strive sincerely for mutual understanding. On behalf of all mankind, let them make common cause of safeguarding and fostering social justice, moral values, peace and freedom."

Dialogue

The purposes of Catholic-Moslem dialogue, which has been rather sketchy, were the subject of joint agreement between the Vatican Secretariat for Non-Christians, and a delegation of the Supreme Council of Islamic Affairs, at a Vatican meeting Dec. 16 to 20, 1970.

Their objectives, as stated in a communique, were to:

• hold regular consultations on Moslem-Christian relations, social, cultural and spiritual questions;

• maintain contact through appointed officers and in other ways;

• do everything possible to develop good relations between Christians and Moslems, in order to strengthen the fraternity existing among believers who share respect for all religious values and faith in God;

• continue efforts for justice and peace in the world.

Representatives of the secretariat and the council denounced every type of discrimination in national and international life. They also expressed hope for the success of efforts to establish peace with justice and honor in the Middle East.

A commission for Vatican-Moslem relations was established in 1974 as part of the Secretariat for Non-Christians.

NON-REVEALED RELIGIONS

Hinduism: The traditional religion of India with origins dating to about 5,000 B.C. Its history is complex, including original Vedic Hinduism, with a sacred literature (Veda) of hymns, incantations and other elements, and with numerous nature gods; Brahmanism, with emphasis on ceremonialism and its power over the gods; philosophical speculation, reflected in the Upanishads, with development of ideas concerning Karma, reincarnation, Brahman, and the manner of achieving salvation; the cults of Vishnu, Shiva and other deities; reforms in Hinduism and in relation to Islam and Christianity.

The principal tenets of Hinduism are open to various interpretations. Karma is the law of the deed, of sowing and reaping, of retribution. It determines the progress of a person toward liberation from the cycle of rebirths necessary for salvation. Liberation is accomplished in stages, through successive rein-

carnations which indicate the previous as well as the existing state of a person. The means of liberation are the practice of ceremonialism and asceticism; faith in, devotion to and worship of the gods Vishnu and Shiva in their several incarnations; and/or knowledge attained through disciplined meditation called Yoga. Salvation, according to philosophical Hinduism, consists in absorption in Brahman, the neuter world-soul. Vishnu, the sungod, and Shiva, the destroyer or generative force of the universe, are the principal popular deities. Ancient belief in nature gods (pantheism) is reflected in sacred respect for some animals. The concept of reincarnation underlies the caste system in Indian society.

There are many sects in Hinduism, which does not have a definite creed. It lends itself easily to syncretism or amalgamation with other beliefs, as evidenced in the 15th century Sikh movement which adopted the monotheism and militancy of Islam. Hindu rituals are various and elaborate, with respect to foods, festivals, pilgrimages, marriage and other life-events.

Buddhism: Originated in the sixth century B.C. in reaction to formalism, pantheism and other trends in Hinduism. The Buddha, the Enlightened One, was Sidartha Gautama, an Indian prince, who sought to explain human suffering and evil and to find a middle way between the extremes of austerity and sensuality.

The four noble truths of Buddhism are: (1) existence involves suffering or pain; (2) suffering comes from craving: (3) craving can be overcome; (4) the way to overcome craving is to follow the "noble eightfold path" of right views, right intention, right speech, right action, right livelihood, right effort, right mindfulness and right concentration.

Karma, the deed-principle of judgment and retribution, and reincarnation are elements of Buddhism. The ultimate objective of life is Nirvana — the absorption of a person in the absolute — which ends the cycles of rebirth.

Buddhism is essentially atheistic and more of a moral philosophy and ethical system than a religion. It has a cultic element in veneration for Buddha. Monasteries, temples and shrines are places of contemplation and ritualistic observance. There are several categories of Buddhist monks and nuns.

Buddhism has many sects. Mahayana Buddhism, with an elaborate ideology, is strong in China, Korea and Japan. Hinayana Buddhism is common in Southeast Asia. Zen Buddhism is highly contemplative. Lamaism in Tibet is a combination of Buddhism and local demonolatry.

Confucianism: An ethical system based on the teachings of Confucius (c. 551-479 B.C.). It is oriented toward the moral perfection of individuals and society, the attainment of the harmony of individual and social life with the harmony of the universe, through conduct governed by the relationships of humanity, justice, ritual and courtesy, wisdom, and fidelity. Originally and basically humanistic, Confucianism was eventually mingled with elements of Chinese religion. It exerted a strong influence on national life in China from 125 to the beginning of the 20th century, despite some periods of decline.

Taoism: Originated in China several centuries before the Christian era and became a fully developed religious system by the fifth century A.D. As a religion of mystery, it developed extreme polytheism, with the Jade Emperor as the highest deity; sought blessings and long life by means of alchemy; fostered superstition and witchcraft; took on organizational and other aspects of Buddhism, with several categories of priests and nuns; exerted strong ethical influence on the lower classes; split into many sects; adopted features from other religions; became the starting point of many secret societies. One of its key tenets — that the way of nature is the guide to human conduct — resulted in a form of quietism opposed to the social concern of Confucianism.

Shinto: The way of the gods, the sum total of the cultic beliefs and practices of the ancestral religion of Japan which originated from nature and ancestor worship. Shinto is pantheistic and has many objects of devotion, the highest being the Ruler of Heaven; is practiced with detailed rituals in public shrines, which are cultic centers; has strong social influence. Sectarian Shinto has about 13 recognized sects and many offshoots. Shinto, with principal concern for this-worldly blessing, has ben affected by Buddhist and Confucian influences.

Eastern cults — with their mysticism and associated disciplines and practices — have recurrent periods of vogue in the West.

Committee for Human Values

In November, 1974, the U.S. National Conference of Catholic Bishops established a distinct standing committee for dialogue and contact with the fields of science and technology as well as with communities of non-religious humanist persuasion.

Prior to 1974, this work had been entrusted to the Bishops' Committee for Ecumenical and Interreligious Affairs and its Secretariat for Human Values.

The new U.S. Bishops' Committee for Human Values is chaired by Bishop Mark Hurley. The offices of the secretariat of this committee are located at 1312 Massachusetts Ave. N.W., Washington, D.C. 20005.

The work of the committee corresponds in part to that of the Vatican Secretariat for Non-Believers.

Guidelines on Human Rights

The Pontifical Commission on Justice and Peace issued a working paper in August, 1975, entitled "The Church and Human Rights" which, while admitting past imperfections in their promotion and defense, defended the Church's basic teaching about them.

The paper said: "There have been periods in the Church's history when . . . the rights of the human person have not been promoted or defended with sufficient clarity or energy." Today, however, "the Church, through her teaching authority and activity, represents an important factor in the field of human rights. . . . Her contribution is keenly appreciated and her comment sought by civil authority."

The paper declared that the mission of the Church "is not to offer concrete solutions in the social, economic and political spheres . . . but to defend and promote the dignity and fundamental rights of the human person."

It also said: "Denunciation of any violation of human rights is the duty of the laity no less than of the hierarchy.

Glossary

A

Abbess: The female superior of a monastic community of nuns; e.g., Benedictines, Poor Clares, some others. Elected by members of the community, an abbess has general authority over her community but no sacramental jurisdiction. Earliest evidence of the use of the title, a feminine derivative of the Aramaic *abba* (father), dates from early in the sixth century.

Abbey: See Monastery.

Abbot: The male superior of a monastic community of men religious; e.g., Benedictines, Cistercians, some others. Elected by members of the community, an abbot has ordinary jurisdiction and general authority over his community. He has some episcopal privileges. The title derives from the Aramaic *abba* (father); first given to the spiritual fathers and guides of hermits in Egypt in the fourth century, it was appropriated in the Rule of St. Benedict to the heads of abbeys and monasteries. Eastern-Rite equivalents of an abbot are a *hegumen* and an *archimandrite*.

A regular abbot is the head of an abbey or monastery. An abbot general or archabbot is the head of a congregation consisting of several monasteries. An abbot primate is the head of the modern Benedictine Confederation. A few regular abbots have jurisdiction over the residents and institutions of a district *(abbacy)* which does not belong to any diocese; jurisdiction of this kind is similar to that of a bishop in his diocese. The only abbot of this kind in the US is the abbot of Belmont Abbey, N.C.

Abjuration: Renunciation of apostasy, heresy or schism by a solemn oath.

Ablution: A term derived from Latin, meaning washing or cleansing, and referring to the cleansing of the hands of a priest celebrating Mass, after the offering of gifts; and to the cleansing of the chalice with water and wine after Communion.

Abortion: The expulsion of a nonviable human fetus from the womb of the mother, with moral implications stemming from the humanity of the fetus from the moment of conception and its consequent right to life.

Accidental expulsion, as in cases of miscarriage, is without moral fault.

Direct abortion, in which a fetus is intentionally removed from the womb, constitutes a direct attack on an innocent human being, a violation of the Fifth Commandment. It is punished in church law by the penalty of excommunication, which is automatically incurred by all baptized persons involved; i.e., the consenting mother and necessary physical and/or moral cooperators. Direct abortion is not justifiable for any reason, e.g.: therapeutic, for the physical and/or psychological welfare of the mother; preventive, to avoid the birth of a defective or unwanted child; social, in the interests of family and/or community.

Indirect abortion, which occurs when a fetus is expelled during medical or other treatment of the mother for a reason other than procuring expulsion, is permissible under the principle of double effect for a proportionately serious reason; e.g., when a medical or surgical procedure is necessary to save the life of the mother.

Absolution: The act by which an authorized priest, acting as the agent of Christ and minister of the Church, grants forgiveness of sins in the sacrament of penance. The essential formula of absolution is: "I absolve you from your sins; in the name of the Father, and of the Son, and of the Holy Spirit. Amen."

Priests receive the power to absolve in virtue of their ordination and the right to exercise this power in virtue of faculties of jurisdiction given them by their bishop, their religious superior, or by canon law. The faculties of jurisdiction can be limited or restricted regarding certain sins and penalties or censures.

In cases of necessity, and also in cases of the absence of their own confessors, Eastern and Roman Rite Catholics may ask for and receive sacramental absolution from a priest of a separated Eastern Church. Separated Eastern Christians may similarly ask for and receive sacramental absolution from an Eastern or Roman Rite priest.

Any priest can absolve a person in danger of death; in the absence of a priest with the usual faculties, this includes a laicized priest or a priest under censure.

(See additional entry under Sacraments.)

Absolution, General: (1) Sacramental absolution given without confession of sin, when confession is impossible. Persons so absolved are required to confess, in their next confession, the mortal sins from which they were so absolved.

(2) A blessing of the Church to which a plenary indulgence is attached, given at the hour of death, and at stated times to members of religious institutes and third orders.

Accessory to Another's Sin: One who culpably assists another in the performance of an evil action. This may be done by counsel, command, provocation, consent, praise, flattery, concealment, participation, silence, defense of the evil done.

Adoration: The highest act and purpose of religious worship, which is directed in love and reverence to God alone in acknowledgment of his infinite perfection and goodness, and of his total dominion over creatures. Adoration, which is also called *latria,* consists of internal and external elements, private and social prayer, liturgical acts and ceremonies, and especially sacrifice.

Adultery: (1) Sexual intercourse between a

married person and another to whom one is not married; a violation of the obligations of chastity and justice. The Sixth Commandment prohibition against adultery is also regarded as a prohibition against all external sins of a sexual nature.

(2) Any sin of impurity (thought, desire, word, action) involving a married person who is not one's husband or wife has the nature of adultery.

Adventists: Members of several Christian sects whose doctrines are dominated by belief in a more or less imminent second advent or coming of Christ upon earth for a glorious 1,000-year reign of righteousness. This reign, following victory by the forces of good over evil in a final Battle of Armageddon, will begin with the resurrection of the chosen and will end with the resurrection of all other men and the annihilation of the wicked. Thereafter, the just will live forever in a renewed heaven and earth. A sleep of the soul takes place between the time of death and the day of judgment. There is no hell. The Bible, in fundamentalist interpretation, is regarded as the only rule of faith and practice.

About six sects have developed in the course of the Adventist movement which originated with William Miller (1782-1849) in the United States. Miller, on the basis of calculations made from the Book of Daniel, predicted that the second advent of Christ would occur between 1843 and 1844. After the prophecy went unfulfilled, divisions occurred in the movement and the Seventh Day Adventists, whose actual formation dates from 1860, emerged as the largest single body. The observance of Saturday instead of Sunday as the Lord's Day dates from 1844.

Advent Wreath: A wreath of laurel, spruce, or similar foliage with four candles which are lighted successively in the weeks of Advent to symbolize the approaching celebration of the birth of Christ, the Light of the World, at Christmas. The wreath originated among German Protestants.

Agape: A Greek word, meaning love, love feast, designating the meal of fellowship eaten at some gatherings of early Christians. Although held in some places in connection with the Mass, the agape was not part of the Mass, nor was it of universal institution and observance. Legislation against it was passed by the Council of Carthage (397) and other councils because of abuses. It was infrequently observed by the fifth century and disappeared altogether between the sixth and eighth centuries. In recent years, a limited revival has taken place in the course of the liturgical and ecumenical movements.

Age of Reason: (1) The time of life when one begins to distinguish between right and wrong, to understand an obligation and take on moral responsibility; seven years of age is the presumption in church law.

(2) Historically, the 18th century period of Enlightenment in England and France, the age of the Encyclopedists and Deists. According to a basic thesis of the Enlightenment, human experience and reason are the only sources of certain knowledge of truth; consequently, faith and revelation are discounted as valid sources of knowledge, and the reality of supernatural truth is called into doubt and/or denied.

Aggiornamento: An Italian word having the general meaning of bringing up to date, renewal, revitalization, descriptive of the processes of spiritual renewal and institutional reform and change in the Church; fostered by the Second Vatican Council.

Agnosticism: A theory which holds that man cannot have certain knowledge of immaterial reality, especially the existence of God and things pertaining to him. Immanuel Kant, one of the philosophical fathers of agnosticism, stood for the position that God, as well as the human soul, is unknowable on speculative grounds; nevertheless, he found practical imperatives for acknowledging God's existence, a view shared by many agnostics. The First Vatican Council declared that the existence of God and some of his attributes can be known with certainty by human reason, even without divine revelation. The word agnosticism was first used, in the sense given here, by T. H. Huxley in 1869.

Agnus Dei: A Latin phrase, meaning Lamb of God.

(1) A title given to Christ, the Lamb (victim) of the Sacrifice of the New Law (on Calvary and in Mass).

(2) A prayer said at Mass before the reception of Holy Communion.

(3) A sacramental. It is a round paschal-candle fragment blessed by the pope. On one side it bears the impression of a lamb, symbolic of Christ. On the reverse side, there may be any one of a number of impressions; e.g., the figure of a saint, the name and coat of arms of the reigning pope. The *agnus dei* may have originated at Rome in the fifth century. The first definite mention of it dates from about 820.

Alleluia: An exclamation of joy derived from Hebrew, All hail to him who is, praise God. It is used in the liturgy and other prayer on joyful occasions during the church year.

Allocution: A formal type of papal address, as distinguished from an ordinary sermon or statement of views.

Alms: An act, gift or service of compassion, motivated by love of God and neighbor, for the help of persons in need; an obligation of charity, which is measurable by the ability of one person to give assistance and by the degree of another's need. Almsgiving, along with prayer and fasting, is regarded as a work of penance as well as an exercise of charity. (See Corporal and Spiritual Works of Mercy.)

Alpha and Omega: The first and last letters

of the Greek alphabet, used to symbolize the eternity of God (Rv. 1:8) and the divinity and eternity of Christ, the beginning and end of all things (Rv. 21:6; 22:13). Use of the letters as a monogram of Christ originated in the fourth century or earlier.

Amen: A Hebrew word meaning truly, it is true. In the Gospels, Christ used the word to add a note of authority to his statements. In other New Testament writings, as in Hebrew usage, it was the concluding word to doxologies. As the concluding word of prayers, it expresses assent to and acceptance of God's will.

Anathema: A Greek word with the root meaning of cursed or separated and the adapted meaning of excommunication, used in church documents, especially the canons of ecumenical councils, for the condemnation of heretical doctrines and of practices opposed to proper discipline.

Anchorite: A kind of hermit living in complete isolation and devoting himself exclusively to exercises of religion and severe penance according to a rule and way of life of his own devising. In early Christian times, anchorites were the forerunners of the monastic life. The closest contemporary approach to the life of an anchorite is that of Carthusian and Camaldolese hermits.

Angels: Purely spiritual beings with intelligence and free will, whose name indicates their mission as ministers of God and ministering spirits to men. They were created before the creation of the visible universe; the devil and bad angels, who were created good, fell from glory through their own fault. In addition to these essentials of defined doctrine, it is held that angels are personal beings; they can intercede for men; fallen angels were banished from God's glory in heaven to hell; bad angels can tempt men to commit sin. The doctrine of guardian angels, although not explicitly defined as a matter of faith, is rooted in long-standing tradition. No authoritative declaration has ever been issued regarding choirs or various categories of angels: according to theorists, there are nine choirs, consisting of seraphim, cherubim, thrones, dominations, principalities, powers, virtues, archangels and angels. In line with scriptural usage, only three angels can be named—Michael, Raphael and Gabriel.

Angelus: A devotion which commemorates the Incarnation of Christ. It consists of three versicles, three Hail Marys and a special prayer, and recalls the announcement to Mary by the Archangel Gabriel that she was chosen to be the Mother of Christ, her acceptance of the divine will, and the Incarnation (Lk. 1:26-38). The Angelus is recited at 6 a.m., noon and 6 p.m. The practice of reciting the Hail Mary in honor of the Incarnation was introduced by the Franciscans in 1263. The *Regina Caeli,* commemorating the joy of

Mary at Christ's Resurrection, replaces the Angelus during the Easter season.

Anger: Passionate displeasure arising from some kind of offense suffered at the hands of another person, frustration or other cause, combined with a tendency to strike back at the cause of the displeasure; a violation of the Fifth Commandment and one of the capital sins if the displeasure is out of proportion to the cause and/or if the retaliation is unjust.

Anglican Orders: Holy orders conferred according to the rite of the Anglican (Episcopal) Church, which Leo XIII declared null and void in the bull *Apostolicae Curae,* Sept. 13, 1896. The orders were declared null because they were conferred according to a rite that was considered substantially defective in form and intent, and because of a break in apostolic succession that occurred when Matthew Parker became head of the Anglican hierarchy in 1559.

In making his declaration, Pope Leo cited earlier arguments against validity made by Julius III in 1553 and 1554 and by Paul IV in 1555. He also noted related directives requiring absolute ordination, according to the Catholic ritual, of convert ministers who had been ordained according to the Anglican Ordinal.

Antichrist: The man of sin, the lawless and wicked antagonist of Christ and the work of God; a mysterious figure of prophecy mentioned in the New Testament. Supported by Satan, submitting to no moral restraints, and armed with tremendous power, Antichrist will set himself up in opposition to God, work false miracles, persecute the People of God, and employ unimaginable means to lead men into error and evil during a period of widespread defection from the Christian faith before the end of time; he will be overcome by Christ. Catholic thinkers have regarded Antichrist as a person, a caricature of Christ, who will lead a final violent struggle against God and His people; they have also applied the title to personal and impersonal forces in history hostile to God and the Church. Official teaching has said little about Antichrist. In 1318, it labeled as partly heretical, senseless, and fanciful the assertions made by the Fraticelli about his coming; in 1415, the Council of Constance condemned the Wycliff thesis that excommunications made by the pope and other prelates were the actions of Antichrist.

Antiphon: (1) A short verse or text, generally from Scripture, recited in the Liturgy of the Hours before and after psalms and canticles.

(2) Any verse sung or recited by one part of a choir or congregation in response to the other part, as in antiphonal or alternate chanting.

Apologetics: The science and art of building and presenting the case for, accounting for, explaining, defending, justifying the reasonableness of the Christian faith, by a wide variety of means including facts of experience, history, science, philosophy. The constant objective of apologetics is preparation for response to God in faith; its ways and means, however, are subject to change in accordance with the various needs of people and different sets of circumstances.

Apostasy: (1) The total and obstinate rejection or abandonment of the Christian faith by a baptized person who continues to call himself a Christian. External manifestation of this rejection constitutes the crime of apostasy, and the person, called an *apostate,* automatically incurs a penalty of excommunication.

(2) Apostasy from orders is the unlawful withdrawal from or rejection of the obligations of the clerical state by a man who has received major orders. The canonical penalty for such apostasy is excommunication.

(3) Apostasy from the religious life occurs when a religious with perpetual vows unlawfully leaves the community with the intention of not returning, or actually remains outside the community for 30 days without permission. The canonical penalty for such apostasy is excommunication.

Apostolate: The ministry or work of an apostle. In Catholic usage, the word is an umbrella-like term covering all kinds and areas of work and endeavor for the service of God and the Church and the good of people. Thus, the apostolate of bishops is to carry on the mission of the Apostles as pastors of the People of God: of priests, to carry out the sacramental and pastoral ministry for which they are ordained; of religious, to follow and do the work of Christ in conformity with the evangelical counsels and their rule of life; of lay persons, as individuals and/or in groups, to give witness to Christ and build up the kingdom of God through practice of their faith, professional competence and the performance of good works in the concrete circumstances of daily life. Apostolic works are not limited to those done within the Church or by specifically Catholic groups, although some apostolates are officially assigned to certain persons or groups and are under the direction of church authorities. Apostolate derives from the commitment and obligation of baptism, confirmation, holy orders, matrimony, the duties of one's state in life, etc.

Archangel: An angel who carries out special missions for God in his dealings with men. Three of them are named in the Bible: Michael, leader of the angelic host and protector of the synagogue; Raphael, guide of Tobiah and healer of his father, who is regarded as the patron of travelers; Gabriel, called the angel of the Incarnation because of his announcement to Mary that she was to be the Mother of Christ.

Archdiocese: An ecclesiastical jurisdiction headed by an archbishop. An archdiocese is usually a metropolitan see, i.e., the principal one of a group of dioceses comprising a province; the other dioceses in the province are suffragan sees.

Archives: Documentary records, and the place where they are kept, of the spiritual and temporal government and affairs of the Church, a diocese, church agencies like the departments of the Roman Curia, bodies like religious institutes, and individual parishes. The collection, cataloguing, preserving, and use of these records are governed by norms stated in canon law and particular regulations. The strictest secrecy is always in effect for confidential records concerning matters of conscience, and documents of this kind are destroyed as soon as circumstances permit.

Archpriest: For some time, before and during the Middle Ages, a priest who took the place of a bishop at liturgical worship. In Europe, the term is sometimes used as an honorary title. It is also an honorary title in Eastern-Rite Churches.

Asceticism: The practice of self-discipline. In the spiritual life, asceticism — by personal prayer, meditation, self-denial, works of mortification, and outgoing interpersonal works — is motivated by love of God and contributes to growth in holiness.

Ashes: Religious significance has been associated with their use as symbolic of penance since Old Testament times. Thus, ashes of palm blessed on the previous Sunday of the Passion are placed on the foreheads of the faithful on Ash Wednesday to remind them to do works of penance, especially during the season of Lent, and that they are dust and unto dust will return. Ashes are a sacramental.

Aspergillum: A vessel or device used for sprinkling holy water. The ordinary type is a metallic rod with a bulbous tip which absorbs the water and discharges it at the motion of the user's hand.

Aspersory: A portable metallic vessel, similar to a pail, for carrying holy water.

Aspiration: Short exclamatory prayer; e.g., My Jesus, mercy.

Atheism: Denial of the existence of God, finding expression in a system of thought (speculative atheism) or a manner of acting (practical atheism) as though there were no God.

The Second Vatican Council, in its *Pastoral Constitution on the Church in the Modern World* (Nos. 19 to 21), noted that a profession of atheism may represent an explicit denial of God. the rejection of a wrong notion of God, an affirmation of man rather than of God, an extreme protest against evil. It said that such a profession might result from acceptance of such propositions as: there is no absolute truth; man can assert nothing, absolutely nothing, about God; everything can be explained by scientific reasoning alone; the whole question of God is devoid of meaning.

The constitution also cited two opinions of

influence in atheistic thought. One of them regards recognition of dependence on God as incompatible with human freedom and independence. The other views belief in God and religion as a kind of opiate which sedates man on earth, reconciling him to the acceptance of suffering, injustice, shortcomings, etc., because of hope for greater things after death, and thereby hindering him from seeking and working for improvement and change for the better here and now.

All of these views, in one way or another, have been involved in the No-God and Death-of-God schools of thought in recent and remote history.

Atonement: The redemptive activity of Christ, who reconciled man with God through his Incarnation and entire life, and especially by his suffering and Resurrection. The word also applies to prayer and good works by which men join themselves with and take part in Christ's work of reconciliation and reparation for sin.

Attributes of God: Perfections of God. God possesses—and is—all the perfections of being, without limitation. Because he is infinite, all of these perfections are one, perfectly united in him. Man, however, because of the limited power of understanding, views these perfections separately, as distinct characteristics—even though they are not actually distinct in God. God is: almighty, eternal, holy, immortal, immense, immutable, incomprehensible, ineffable, infinite, invisible, just, loving, merciful, most high, most wise, omnipotent, omniscient, omnipresent, patient, perfect, provident, supreme, true.

Avarice (Covetousness): A disorderly and unreasonable attachment to and desire for material things; called a capital sin because it involves preoccupation with material things to the neglect of spiritual goods and obligations of justice and charity.

Ave Maria: See Hail Mary.

B

Baldachino: A canopy over an altar.

Beatification: A preliminary step toward canonization of a saint. It begins with an investigation of the candidate's life, writings and heroic practice of virtue, and the certification of at least two miracles worked by God through his intercession. If the findings of the investigation so indicate, the pope decrees that the Servant of God may be called *Blessed* and may be honored locally or in a limited way in the liturgy. Additional procedures lead to canonization (see separate entry).

Beatific Vision: The intuitive, immediate and direct vision and experience of God enjoyed in the light of glory by all the blessed in heaven. The vision is a supernatural mystery.

Beatitude: A literary form of the Old and New Testaments in which blessings are promised to persons for various reasons. Beatitudes are mentioned 26 times in the Psalms, and in other books of the Old Testament. The best known beatitudes — identifying blessedness with participation in the kingdom of God and his righteousness, and descriptive of the qualities of Christian perfection — are those recounted in Mt. 5:3-11 and Lk. 6:20-22.

In Matthew's account, the beatitudes are:

"How blest are the poor in spirit: the reign of God is theirs.

"Blest too are the sorrowing; they shall be consoled.

"(Blest are the lowly; they shall inherit the land.)

"Blest are they who hunger and thirst for holiness; they shall have their fill.

"Blest are they who show mercy; mercy shall be theirs.

"Blest are the single-hearted for they shall see God.

"Blest too are the peacemakers; they shall be called sons of God.

"Blest are those persecuted for holiness' sake; the reign of God is theirs.

"Blest are you when they insult you and persecute you and utter every kind of slander against you because of me."

In Luke's account, the beatitudes are:

"Blest are you poor; the reign of God is yours.

"Blest are you who hunger; you shall be filled.

"Blest are you who are weeping; you shall laugh.

"Blest shall you be when men hate you, when they ostracize you and insult you and proscribe your name as evil because of the Son of Man."

Benediction of the Blessed Sacrament: A short exposition of the Eucharist for adoration by and blessing of the faithful. Devotional practices include the singing of Eucharistic and other hymns, and recitation of the Divine Praises. Benediction, in its present form, dates from about the 15th century and is a form of liturgical worship.

Benedictus: The canticle or hymn uttered by Zechariah at the circumcision of St. John the Baptist (Lk. 1:68-79). It is an expression of praise and thanks to God for sending John as a precursor of the Messiah. The *Benedictus* is recited in the Liturgy of the Hours as part of Lauds.

Bible Service: A devotion consisting essentially of common prayer of a biblical or liturgical character, several readings from Scripture, and a homily on the texts.

Biglietto: A papal document of notification of appointment to the cardinalate.

Biretta: A stiff, square hat with three ridges on top worn by clerics in church and on other occasions.

Blasphemy: Any expression of insult or contempt with respect to God, principally, and to holy persons and things, secondarily; a violation of the honor due to God in the context of the First and Second Commandments.

Blasphemy of the Spirit: Deliberate resistance to the Holy Spirit, called the unforgivable sin (Mt. 12:31) because it makes his saving action impossible. Thus, the only unforgivable sin is the one for which a person will not seek pardon from God.

Blessing: Invocation of God's favor, by official ministers of the Church or by private individuals. Blessings are recounted in the Old and New Testaments, and are common in the Christian tradition. The Church, through its ordained ministers (bishops and priests, especially), invokes divine favor in liturgical blessings; e.g., of the people at Mass, of the gifts to be consecrated at Mass, of persons and things on various occasions. Sacramentals — such as crucifixes, crosses, rosaries, scapulars, medals — are blessed by ministers of the Church for the invocation of God's favor on those who use them in the proper manner. Many types of blessings are listed in the *Roman Ritual.* Private blessings, as well as those of an official kind, are efficacious. Blessings are imparted with the Sign of the Cross and appropriate prayer.

Boat: A small vessel used to hold incense which is to be placed in the censer.

Brief, Apostolic: A papal letter, less formal than a bull, signed for the pope by a secretary and impressed with the seal of the Fisherman's Ring. Simple apostolic letters of this kind are issued for beatifications and with respect to other matters.

Bull, Apostolic: The most solemn form of papal document, beginning with the name and title of the pope (e.g., Paul VI, Servant of the Servants of God), dealing with an important subject, and having attached to it either a leaden seal called a bulla or a red ink imprint of the device on the seal. Bulls are known as apostolic letters with the seal. The seal, on one side, has representations of the heads of Sts. Peter and Paul; on the other side, the name of the reigning pope. Bulls are issued to confer the titles of bishops and cardinals, to promulgate canonizations, and for other purposes. A collection of bulls is called a *bullarium.*

Burial, Ecclesiastical: Interment with church rites and in consecrated ground. Catechumens as well as baptized Catholics have a right to ecclesiastical burial. A non-Catholic partner in a mixed marriage may be buried in a Catholic cemetery with the Catholic partner.

C

Calumny: Harming the name and good reputation of a person by lies; a violation of obligations of justice and truth. Restitution is due for calumny.

Calvary: A knoll about 15 feet high just outside the western wall of Jerusalem where Christ was crucified, so called from the Latin *calvaria* (skull) which described its shape.

Canon: A Greek word meaning rule, norm, standard, measure.

(1) The word designates the Canon of Sacred Scripture, which is the list of books recognized by the Church as inspired by the Holy Spirit.

(2) In the sense of regulating norms, the word designates the body or corpus of Canon Law enacted and promulgated by ecclesiastical authority for the orderly administration and government of the Church. The Code of Canon Law now in force in the Roman Church has been in effect since 1918. It consists of 2,414 canons which are divided into five books covering general rules, ecclesiastical persons, sacred things, trials, crimes and punishments. The code is now under review for the purpose of revision. Eastern-Rite Churches have their own canon law.

(3) The term also designates the four canons, (Eucharistic prayers, anaphoras) of the Mass, the core of the liturgy.

(4) Certain dignitaries of the Church have the title of Canon, and some religious are known as Canons.

Canonization: An infallible declaration by the pope that a person, who died as a martyr and/or practiced Christian virtue to a heroic degree, is now in heaven and is worthy of honor and imitation by all the faithful. Such a declaration is preceded by the process of beatification and another detailed investigation concerning the person's reputation for holiness, his writings, and (except in the case of martyrs) miracles ascribed to his intercession after his death. Miracles are not required for martyrs. The pope can dispense from some of the formalities ordinarily required in canonization procedures (equivalent canonization), as Pope John XXIII did in the canonization of St. Gregory Barbarigo on May 26, 1960. A saint is worthy of honor in liturgical worship throughout the universal Church.

From its earliest years the Church has venerated saints. Public official honor always required the approval of the bishop of the place. Martyrs were the first to be honored. St. Martin of Tours, who died in 397, was the first non-martyr venerated as a saint. The first official canonization by a pope for the universal Church was that of St. Ulrich by John XV in 993. Alexander III reserved the process of canonization to the Holy See in 1171. In 1588 Sixtus V established the Sacred Congregation of Rites for the principal purpose of handling causes for beatification and canonization: this function is now the work of the Congregation for the Causes of Saints. The present procedure is outlined in canons 1999-2141 of the Code of Canon Law and in a 1969 enactment by Paul VI.

The essential portion of a canonization decree states:

"For the honor of the holy and undivided Trinity; for the exaltation of the Catholic faith and the increase of Christian life; with the authority of our Lord Jesus Christ, of the blessed Apostles Peter and Paul, and with our own authority; after mature deliberation and with the divine assistance, often implored; with the counsel of many of our brothers.

"We decree and define that (name) is a saint and we inscribe him (her) in the Catalogue of Saints, stating that he (she) shall be venerated in the universal Church with pious devotion.

"In the name of the Father and of the Son and of the Holy Spirit. Amen."

The official listing of saints and blessed is contained in the *Roman Martyrology* and related decrees issued after its last publication. Butler's unofficial *Lives of the Saints* (1956) contains 2,565 entries.

The Church regards all persons in heaven as saints, not just those who have been officially canonized.

(See Beatification, Saints, Canonizations by Leo XIII and His Successors.)

Canticle: A scriptural chant or prayer differing from the psalms. Three of the canticles prescribed for use in the Liturgy of the Hours are: The *Magnificat* (Lk. 1:46-55), the *Benedictus* (Lk. 1:68-79), and the *Nunc Dimittis* (Lk. 2:29-32.)

Capital Punishment: Punishment for crime by means of the death penalty. The political community, which has authority to provide for the common good, has the right to defend itself and its members against unjust aggression and may in extreme cases punish with the death penalty persons found guilty before the law of serious crimes against individuals and a just social order. Such punishment is essentially vindictive. Its value as a crime-deterrent is a matter of perennial debate. The prudential judgment as to whether or not there should be capital punishment belongs to the civic community. The U.S. Supreme Court ruled June 29, 1972, against the constitutionality of existing statutes on capital punishment. Within 14 months of the decision, which had the effect of staying some 600 executions, 17 states enacted new laws designating as capital offenses mass murder, murder of a policeman, fireman or prison guard, and murder while perpetrating rape, kidnapping, arson or hijacking a commercial vehicle.

Capital Sins: Moral faults which, if habitual, give rise to many more sins. They are: pride, covetousness, lust, anger, gluttony, envy, sloth.

The opposite virtues are: humility, liberality, chastity, meekness, temperance, brotherly love, diligence.

Cardinal Virtues: The four principal moral virtues are prudence, justice, temperance and fortitude.

Catacombs: Underground Christian cemeteries in various cities of the Roman Empire and Italy, especially in the vicinity of Rome; the burial sites of many martyrs and other Christians. Developed from aboveground cemeteries, their passageways, burial niches and assembly rooms were dug out of tuffa, a soft clay which hardened into rock-like consistency on drying. The earliest ones date from the third century; in the fourth, they became the scene of memorial services as the veneration of martyrs increased in popularity; in the seventh and eighth centuries, they were plundered by the Lombards and other invaders. The relics of many martyrs were removed to safer places in the ninth century; afterwards, the catacombs fell into neglect and oblivion until interest in them revived in the 16th century. The catacombs have been excavated extensively, yielding considerable information about early Christian symbolism and art, dating from the third century on, and other aspects of Christian life and practice.

Catafalque: A small structure like a bier, used at services for the dead in the absence of the corpse.

Catechism: A summary of Christian doctrine in question and answer form, used for purposes of instruction.

Catechumen: A person preparing, in a program of instruction and spiritual formation, for baptism and reception into the Church.

Cathedra: A Greek word for chair, designating the chair or seat of a bishop in the principal church of his diocese, which is therefore called a cathedral (see separate entry).

Cathedraticum: The tax paid to a bishop by all churches and benefices subject to him for the support of episcopal administration and for works of charity.

Catholic: A Greek word, meaning universal, first used in the title Catholic Church in a letter written by St. Ignatius of Antioch about 107 to the Christians of Smyrna.

Celebret: A Latin word, meaning Let him celebrate, the name of a document issued by a bishop or other superior stating that a priest is in good standing and therefore should be given opportunity to celebrate Mass or perform other priestly functions.

Celibacy: The unmarried state of life, required in the Roman or Latin Church of candidates for holy orders and of men already ordained to holy orders, for the practice of perfect chastity and total dedication to the service of people in the ministry of the Church. Celibacy is enjoined as a condition for ordination by church discipline and law, not by dogmatic necessity.

In the Roman Church, a consensus in favor of celibacy developed in the early centuries while the clergy included both celibates and men who had been married once. The first local legislation on the subject was enacted by a local council held in Elvira, Spain, about 306; it forbade bishops, priests, deacons and other ministers to have wives. Similar enactments were passed by other local councils from that time on, and by the 12th century particular laws regarded marriage by clerics in major orders to be not only unlawful but also null and void. The latter view was translated by the Second Lateran Council in 1139 into what seems to be the first written universal law making holy orders an invalidating impediment to marriage. In 1563 the Council of Trent ruled definitely on the matter and established the discipline still in force in the Roman Church.

Some exceptions to this discipline have been made in recent years. Several married Protestant ministers who became converts and were subsequently ordained to the priesthood have been permitted to continue in marriage. Married men over the age of 35 can be ordained to the permanent diaconate.

Recent agitation for optional rather than mandatory celibacy for priests has diminished, without change in church law.

Eastern Church discipline on celibacy differs from that of the Roman Church. In line with legislation enacted by the Synod of Trullo in 692 and still in force, candidates for holy orders may marry before becoming deacons and may continue in marriage thereafter, but marriage after ordination is forbidden. Eastern-Rite bishops in the US, however, do not ordain married candidates for the priesthood. Eastern-Rite bishops are unmarried.

Cenacle: The room in Jerusalem where Christ ate the Last Supper with his Apostles.

Censer: A metal vessel with a perforated cover and suspended by chains, in which incense is burned. It is used at some Masses, Benediction of the Blessed Sacrament and other liturgical functions.

Censorship of Books: An exercise of vigilance by the Church for safeguarding authentic religious teaching.

According to a decree issued by the Congregation for the Doctrine of the Faith Apr. 9, 1975, the following regulations are in effect.

(1) Pre-publication clearance is required for: editions of Sacred Scripture, liturgical texts and books of private devotion, catechisms and other writings relating to catechetical instruction. Books dealing with Scripture, theology, canon law, church history and religious or moral disciplines may not be used as basic texts in educational institutions (from elementary to university levels) unless they have been published with the approval of competent church authority.

(2) Pre-publication clearance is recommended for all books on the aforementioned subjects, even though they are not used as basic texts in teaching.

(3) Books or other writings dealing with religion or morals may not be displayed, sold or given out in churches or oratories unless published with the approval of competent ecclesiastical authority.

(4) Except for a just and reasonable cause, Catholics should not write for newspapers, magazines or periodicals which regularly and openly prove to be inimical to the Catholic religion and good morals. The approval of the local bishop is required before clerics or members of religious institutes (who also need the approval of their superior) may write for such publications.

Permission to publish works of a religious character, together with the apparatus of reviewing them beforehand, falls under the authority of the bishop of the place where the writer lives or where the works are published.

Clearance for publication is usually indicated by the terms *Nihil obstat* (Nothing stands in the way) issued by the censor and *Imprimatur* (Let it be printed) authorized by the bishop. The clearing of works for publication does not necessarily imply approval of an author's viewpoint or his manner of handling a subject.

Censures: Spiritual penalties inflicted by the Church on baptized persons for committing certain serious sins, which are classified as crimes in canon law, and for being or remaining obstinate therein. Excommunication, suspension and interdict have been the censures in force since the time of Innocent III (1214). Their intended purposes are to deter persons from committing sins which, more seriously and openly than others, threaten the common good of the Church and its members; to punish and correct offenders; and to provide for the making of reparation for harm done to the community of the Church. Censures may be incurred automatically (*ipso facto*) on the commission of certain offenses for which fixed penalties have been laid down in church law (*latae sententiae*); or they may be inflicted by sentence of a judge (*ferendae sententiae*). Obstinacy in crime—also called contumacy, disregard of a penalty, defiance of church authority — is presumed by law in the commission of crimes for which automatic censures are decreed. The presence and degree of contumacy in other cases, for which judicial sentence is required, is subject to determination by a judge. Absolution can be obtained from any censure, provided the person repents and desists from obstinacy. Absolution may be reserved to the pope, the bishop of a place, or the major superior of an exempt clerical religious institute. In danger of death, any priest can absolve from all censures; in other cases, faculties to absolve from reserved censures can be exercised by competent authorities or given to other priests.

Ceremonies, Master of: One who directs the proceedings of a rite or ceremony during the function.

Chamberlain: (1) The Chamberlain of the Holy Roman Church is a cardinal who administers the property and revenues of the Holy See. On the death of the pope he becomes head of the College of Cardinals and summons and directs the conclave until a new pope is elected.

(2) The Chamberlain of the Sacred College of Cardinals has charge of the property and revenues of the College and keeps the record of business transacted in consistories.

(3) The Chamberlain of the Roman Clergy is the president of the secular clergy of Rome.

Chancellor: Notary of a diocese, who draws up written documents in the government of the diocese; takes care of, arranges and indexes diocesan archives, records of dispensations and ecclesiastical trials.

Chancery (1) A branch of church administration that handles written documents used in the government of a diocese.

(2) The administrative office of a diocese, a bishop's office.

Chapel: A building or part of another building used for divine worship; a portion of a church set aside for the celebration of Mass or for some special devotion.

Chaplain: A priest appointed for the pastoral service of any division of the armed forces, religious communities, institutions, various groups of the faithful.

Chaplet: A term, meaning little crown, applied to a rosary or, more commonly, to a small string of beads used for devotional purposes; e.g., the Infant of Prague chaplet.

Chapter: A general meeting of delegates of religious orders for elections and the handling of other important affairs of their communities.

Charisms: Gifts or graces given by God to men for the good of others and the Church. Examples are special gifts for apostolic work, prophecy, healing, discernment of spirits, the life of evangelical poverty, here-and-now witness to faith in various circumstances of life.

The Second Vatican Council made the following statement about charisms in the *Dogmatic Constitution on the Church* (No. 12):

"It is not only through the sacraments and Church ministries that the same Holy Spirit sanctifies and leads the People of God and enriches it with virtues. Allotting His gifts 'to everyone according as he will' (1 Cor. 12:11), He distributes special graces among the faithful of every rank. By these gifts He makes them fit and ready to undertake the various tasks or offices advantageous for the renewal and upbuilding of the Church, according to the words of the Apostle: 'The manifestation of the Spirit is given to everyone for profit' (1 Cor. 12:7). These charismatic gifts, whether they be the most outstanding or the more simple and widely diffused, are to be received with thanksgiving and consolation, for they are exceedingly suitable and useful for the needs of the Church.

"Still, extraordinary gifts are not to be rashly sought after, nor are the fruits of apostolic labor to be presumptuously expected from them. In any case, judgment as to their genuineness and proper use belongs to those who preside over the Church, and to whose

special competence it belongs, not indeed to extinguish the Spirit, but to test all things and hold fast to that which is good" (cf. 1 Thes. 5:12; 19-21).

Charity: Love of God above all things for his own sake, and love of one's neighbor as oneself because and as an expression of one's love for God; the greatest of the three theological virtues. The term is sometimes also used to designate sanctifying grace.

Chastity: Properly ordered behavior with respect to sex. In marriage, the exercise of the procreative power is integrated with the norms and purposes of marriage. Outside of marriage, the rule is self-denial of the voluntary exercise and enjoyment of the procreative faculty in thought, word or action.

The vow of chastity, which reinforces the virtue of chastity with the virtue of religion, is an evangelical counsel and one of the three vows professed by religious.

Chirograph or Autograph Letter: A letter written by a pope himself, in his own handwriting.

Christ: The title of Jesus, derived from the Greek translation *Christos* of the Hebrew term *Messiah,* meaning the Anointed of God, the Savior and Deliverer of his people. Christian use of the title is a confession of belief that Jesus is the Savior.

Christianity: The sum total of things related to belief in Christ — the Christian religion, Christian churches, Christians themselves, society based on and expressive of Christian beliefs, culture reflecting Christian values.

Christians: The name first applied about the year 43 to followers of Christ at Antioch, the capital of Syria. It was used by the pagans as a contemptuous term. The word applies to persons who profess belief in the divinity and teachings of Christ and who give witness to him in life.

Christian Science: A religious doctrine consisting of Mary Baker Eddy's interpretation and formulation of the actions and teachings of Christ. Its basic tenets reflect Mrs. Eddy's ideas regarding the reality of spirit and its control and domination of what is not spirit. The basic statement of the doctrine is contained in *Science and Health, with Key to the Scriptures,* which she first published in 1875, nine years after being saved from death and healed on reading the New Testament.

Mary Baker Eddy (1821-1910) established the church in 1879, and in 1892 founded at Boston the First Church of Christ, Scientist, of which all other Christian Science churches are branches. The individual churches are self-governing and self-supporting under the general supervision of a board of directors. Services consist of readings of portions of Scripture and *Science and Health.* One of the church's publications, *The Christian Science Monitor,* has a worldwide reputation as a journal of news and opinion.

Church: (1) See several entries under

Church, Catholic. The universal Church is the Church spread throughout the world. The local Church is the Church in a particular locality; e.g., a diocese. Inasmuch as the members of the Church are on earth, in purgatory, or in glory in heaven, the Church is called militant, suffering, or triumphant.

(2) In general, any religious body.

(3) Place of divine worship.

Churching: A rite of thanksgiving in which a blessing is given to women after childbirth. The rite is reminiscent of the Old Testament ceremony of purification (Lv. 12:2-8).

Circumcision: A ceremonial practice symbolic of initiation and participation in the covenant between God and Abraham.

Circumincession: The indwelling of each divine Person of the Holy Trinity in the others.

Clergy: Men ordained to holy orders and assigned to pastoral and other ministries for the service of the people and the Church.

(1) Diocesan or secular clergy are committed to pastoral ministry in parishes and in other capacities in a local church (diocese) under the direction of their bishop, to whom they are bound by a promise of obedience.

(2) Regular clergy belong to religious institutes (orders, congregations, societies) and are so called because they observe the rule (*regula*, in Latin) of their respective institutes. They are committed to the ways of life and apostolates of their institutes. In ordinary pastoral ministry, they are under the direction of local bishops as well as their own superiors.

Clericalism: A term generally used in a derogatory sense to mean action, influence or interference by the Church and the clergy in matters with which they allegedly should not be concerned. Anticlericalism is a reaction of antipathy, hostility, distrust and opposition to the Church and clergy arising from real and/or alleged faults of the clergy, overextension of the role of the laity, or for other reasons.

Cloister: The enclosure of a convent or monastery, which members of the community may not leave or outsiders enter without due permission. Enclosure is of two kinds: papal, in monasteries of religious with solemn vows; episcopal, in the houses of other religious.

Code: A digest of rules or regulations, such as the Code of Canon Law.

Collegiality: The bishops of the Church, in union with and subordinate to the pope — who has full, supreme and universal power over the Church which he can always exercise independently — have supreme teaching and pastoral authority over the whole Church. In addition to their proper authority of office for the good of the faithful in their respective dioceses or other jurisdictions, the bishops have authority to act for the good of the universal Church. This collegial authority is exercised in a solemn manner in an ecumenical council and can also be exercised in other ways sanc-

tioned by the pope. Doctrine on collegiality was set forth by the Second Vatican Council in the *Dogmatic Constitution on the Church.* (See separate entry.)

By extension, the concept of collegiality is applied to other forms of participation and co-responsibility by members of a community.

Commissariat of the Holy Land: A special jurisdiction within the Order of Friars Minor, whose main purposes are the collecting of alms for support of the Holy Places in Palestine and staffing of the Holy Places and missions in the Middle East with priests and brothers. There are 69 such commissariats in 33 countries. One of them has headquarters at Mt. St. Sepulchre, Washington, D.C. Franciscans have had custody of the Holy Places since 1342.

Communion of Faithful, Saints: The communion of all the People of God — on earth, in heavenly glory, in purgatory — with Christ and each other in faith, grace, prayer and good works.

Concelebration: The liturgical act in which several priests, led by one member of the group, offer Mass together, all consecrating the bread and wine. Concelebration has always been common in churches of Eastern Rite. In the Roman Rite, it was long restricted, taking place only at the ordination of bishops and the ordination of priests. The *Constitution on the Sacred Liturgy* issued by the Second Vatican Council set new norms for concelebration.

Concordat: A Church-state treaty with the force of law concerning matters of mutual concern — e.g., rights of the Church, appointment of bishops, arrangement of ecclesiastical jurisdictions, marriage laws, education. Approximately 150 agreements of this kind have been negotiated since the Concordat of Worms in 1122.

Concupiscence: Any tendency of the sensitive appetite. The term is most frequently used in reference to desires and tendencies for sinful sense pleasure.

Confession: Sacramental confession is the act by which a person tells or confesses his sins to a priest who is authorized to give absolution in the sacrament of penance.

Confessor: (1) A male saint who lived a life of eminent sanctity and heroic virtue, but who did not suffer martyrdom for his faith. The first confessor honored as a saint was Martin of Tours.

(2) A priest who administers the sacrament of penance.

Confraternity: An association whose members practice a particular form of religious devotion and/or are engaged in some kind of apostolic work. When a confraternity reaches the stage where affiliations similar to itself are formed and adopt its rules, it takes the name of archconfraternity.

Conscience: Practical judgment concerning

the moral goodness or sinfulness of an action. In the Catholic view, this judgment is made by reference of the action, its attendant circumstances and the intentions of the person to the requirements of divine law as expressed in the Ten Commandments, the summary law of love for God and neighbor, the life and teaching of Christ, and the authoritative teaching and practice of the Church with respect to the total demands of divine Revelation.

A person is obliged: (1) to obey a certain and correct conscience; (2) to obey a certain conscience even if it is inculpably erroneous; (3) not to obey, but to correct, a conscience known to be erroneous or lax; (4) to rectify a scrupulous conscience by following the advice of a confessor and by other measures; (5) to resolve doubts of conscience before acting.

It is legitimate to act for solid and probable reasons when a question of moral responsibility admits of argument (see Probabilism). It is also legitimate to resolve doubts in difficult cases by having recourse to a reflex principle (e.g., by following the manner of acting of a well-informed and well-intentioned group of persons in similar circumstances).

Conscience, Examination of: Self-examination to determine one's spiritual state before God, especially regarding one's sins and faults. It is recommended as a regular practice and is practically necessary in preparing for the sacrament of penance. The *particular examen* is a regular examination to assist in overcoming specific faults and imperfections.

Consecration of a Church: See Dedication of a Church.

Consistory: An assembly of cardinals presided over by the pope. Consistories are secret (pope and cardinals only), semi-public (plus other prelates), and public (plus other attendants).

Constitution: (1) An apostolic or papal constitution is a document in which a pope enacts and promulgates law.

(2) A formal and solemn document issued by an ecumenical council on a doctrinal or pastoral subject, with binding force in the whole Church; e.g., the four constitutions issued by the Second Vatican Council on the Church, liturgy, Revelation, and the Church in the modern world.

(3) The constitutions of religious orders spell out details of and norms drawn from the various rules for the guidance and direction of the life and work of members of each institute.

Consubstantiation: A theory which holds that the Body and Blood of Christ coexist with the substance of bread and wine in the Holy Eucharist. This theory, also called *impanation,* is incompatible with the doctrine of transubstantiation.

Contraception: Anything done by positive interference to prevent sexual intercourse from resulting in conception. Direct contraception is against the order of nature. Indirect contraception — as a secondary effect of medical treatment or other action having a necessary, good, non-contraceptive purpose — is permissible under the principle of the double effect. The practice of rhythm is not contraception because it does not involve positive interference with the order of nature.

Contrition: Sorrow for sin coupled with a purpose of amendment. Contrition arising from a supernatural motive is necessary for the forgiveness of sin.

(1) Perfect contrition is total sorrow for and renunciation of attachment to sin, arising from the motive of pure love of God. Perfect contrition, which implies the intention of doing all God wants done for the forgiveness of sin, is sufficient for the forgiveness of serious sin and the remission of all temporal punishment due for sin. Confession is required before the reception of another sacrament. (The intention to receive the sacrament of penance is implicit — even if unrealized, as in the case of some persons — in perfect contrition.)

(2) Imperfect contrition or attrition is sorrow arising from a quasi-selfish supernatural motive; e.g., the fear of losing heaven, suffering the pains of hell, etc. Imperfect contrition is sufficient for the forgiveness of serious sin when joined with absolution in confession, and sufficient for the forgiveness of venial sin even outside of confession.

Contumely: Personal insult, reviling a person in his presence by accusation of moral faults, by refusal of recognition or due respect; a violation of obligations of justice and charity.

Corporal Works of Mercy: Feeding the hungry, giving drink to the thirsty, clothing the naked, visiting the imprisoned, sheltering the homeless, visiting the sick, burying the dead.

Councils: Bodies representative of various categories of members of the Church which participate with bishops and other church authorities in making decisions and carrying out action programs for the good of the Church and the accomplishment of its mission to its own members and society in general. Examples are priests' senates or councils, councils of religious and lay persons, parish councils, diocesan pastoral councils.

Councils, Plenary: National councils or councils of the bishops of several ecclesiastical provinces, assembled under the presidency of a papal legate to take action related to the life and mission of the Church in the area under their jurisdiction. The membership of such councils is fixed by canon law; their decrees, when approved by the Holy See, are binding in the territory (see Index, Three Plenary Councils of Baltimore).

Councils, Provincial: Meetings of the bishops of a province. The metropolitan, or ranking archbishop, of an ecclesiastical province convenes and presides over such councils in a manner prescribed by canon law to take action related to the life and mission of the Church in the province. Acts and decrees must be approved by the Holy See before being promulgated. Provincial councils should be held at least once every 20 years.

Counsels, Evangelical: Gospel counsels of perfection, especially voluntary poverty, perfect chastity and obedience, which were recommended by Christ to those who would devote themselves exclusively and completely to the immediate service of God. Religious bind themselves by public vows to observe these counsels in a life of total consecration to God and service to people through various kinds of apostolic works.

Counter-Reformation: The period of approximately 100 years following the Council of Trent, which witnessed a reform within the Church to stimulate genuine Catholic life and to counteract effects of the Reformation.

Covenant: A bond of relationship between parties pledged to each other. God-initiated covenants in the Old Testament included those with Abraham, Noah, Moses, Levi, David. The Mosaic (Sinai) covenant made Israel God's Chosen People on terms of fidelity to true faith, true worship, and righteous conduct according to the Decalogue. The New Testament covenant, prefigured in the Old Testament, is the bond men have with God through Christ. All men are called to be parties to this perfect and everlasting covenant, which was mediated and ratified by Christ.

Creation: The production by God of something out of nothing. The biblical account of creation is contained in the first two chapters of Genesis.

Creator: God, the supreme, self-existing Being, the absolute and infinite First Cause of all things.

Creature: Everything in the realm of being is a creature, except God.

Cremation: The reduction of a human corpse to ashes by means of fire. Cremation is not in line with Catholic tradition and practice, even though it is not opposed to any article of faith. It can be permitted for serious reasons. The general practice, however, was forbidden in a decree issued May 19, 1886, by the Sacred Congregation of the Holy Office.

This ruling was incorporated in the Code of Canon Law (Canons 1203, 1240), which generally banned the practice of cremation, forbade following orders for cremation, and deprived of the last rites and ecclesiastical burial those who directed that their bodies be cremated and did not retract the directions.

The principal reason behind the prohibition against cremation was the fact that, historically, the practice had represented an attempt to deny the doctrine of the resurrection of the body. It also appeared to be a form of violence against the body which, as the temple of the Holy Spirit during life, should be treated with reverence.

The Congregation for the Doctrine of the Faith, under date of May 8, 1963, circulated among bishops an instruction which upheld the traditional practices of Christian burial but modified anti-cremation legislation. Cremation may be permitted for serious reasons, of a private as well as public nature, provided it does not involve any contempt of the Church or of religion, or any attempt to deny, question, or belittle the doctrine of the resurrection of the body. The person may receive the last rites and be given ecclesiastical burial. A priest may say prayers for the deceased at the crematorium, but full liturgical ceremonies may not take place there.

Crib: A devotional representation of the birth of Jesus. The custom of erecting cribs is generally attributed to St. Francis of Assisi who in 1223 obtained from Pope Honorius III permission to use a crib and figures of the Christ Child, Mary, St. Joseph, and others, to represent the mystery of the Nativity.

Crosier: The bishop's staff, symbolic of his pastoral office, responsibility and authority.

Crypt: An underground or partly underground chamber; e.g., the lower part of a church used for worship and/or burial.

Cura Animarum: A Latin phrase, meaning care of souls, designating the pastoral ministry and responsibility of bishops and priests.

Curia: The personnel and offices through which (1) the pope administers the affairs of the universal Church, the *Roman Curia* (see separate entry), or (2) a bishop the affairs of a diocese, *diocesan curia.* The principal officials of a diocesan curia are the vicar general of the diocese, the chancellor, officials of the diocesan tribunal or court, examiners, consultors, auditors, notaries.

Custos: A religious superior who presides over a number of convents collectively called a custody. In some religious institutes, a custos may be the deputy of a higher superior.

D

Dean: (1) A priest with supervisory responsibility over a section of a diocese known as a deanery. The post-Vatican II counterpart of a dean is an episcopal vicar.

(2) The senior or ranking member of a group.

Dean of the Sacred College: The president of the College of Cardinals (the ranking cardinal bishop). He is elected by the cardinals holding title to the suburban sees of Rome.

Decision: A judgment or pronouncement on a cause or suit, given by a church tribunal or official with judicial authority. A decision has the force of law for concerned parties.

Declaration: (1) An ecclesiastical document which presents an interpretation of an existing law.

(2) A position paper on a specific subject;

e.g., the three declarations issued by the Second Vatican Council on religious freedom, non-Christian religions, and Christian education.

Decree: An edict or ordinance issued by a pope and/or by an ecumenical council, with binding force in the whole Church; by a department of the Roman Curia, with binding force for concerned parties; by a territorial body of bishops, with binding force for persons in the area; by individual bishops, with binding force for concerned parties until revocation or the death of the bishop.

The nine decrees issued by the Second Vatican Council were combinations of doctrinal and pastoral statements with executive orders for action and movement toward renewal and reform in the Church.

Dedication of a Church: The ceremony whereby a church is solemnly set apart for the worship of God. The custom of dedicating churches had an antecedent in Old Testament ceremonies for the dedication of the Temple, as in the times of Solomon and the Maccabees. The earliest extant record of the dedication of a Christian church dates from early in the fourth century, when it was done simply by the celebration of Mass. Other ceremonies developed later. A church can be dedicated by a simple blessing or a solemn consecration. The rite of consecration is performed by a bishop.

Definitors: Members of the governing council of a religious order, each one having a decisive vote equal to the vote of the general or provincial superior.

Deism: A system of natural religion which acknowledges the existence of God but regards him as so transcendent and remote from man and the universe that divine revelation and the supernatural order of things are irrelevant and unacceptable. It developed from rationalistic principles in England in the 17th and 18th centuries, and had Voltaire, Rousseau and the Encyclopedists among its advocates in France.

Despair: Abandonment of hope for salvation arising from the conviction that God will not provide the necessary means for attaining it, that following God's way of life for salvation is impossible, or that one's sins are unforgivable; a serious sin against the Holy Spirit and the theological virtues of hope and faith, involving distrust in the mercy and goodness of God and a denial of the truths that God wills the salvation of all men and provides sufficient grace for it. Real despair is distinguished from unreasonable fear with respect to the difficulties of attaining salvation, from morbid anxiety over the demands of divine justice, and from feelings of despair.

Detachment: Control of affection for creatures by two principles: (1) supreme love and devotion belong to God; (2) love and service of creatures should be an expression of love for God.

Detraction: Revelation of true but hidden faults of a person without sufficient and justifying reason; a violation of requirements of justice and charity, involving the obligation to make restitution when this is possible without doing more harm to the good name of the offended party. In some cases, e.g., to prevent evil, secret faults may and should be disclosed.

Devil: (1) Lucifer, Satan, chief of the fallen angels who sinned and were banished from heaven. Still possessing angelic powers, he can cause such diabolical phenomena as possession and obsession, and can tempt men to sin.

(2) Any fallen angel.

Devil's Advocate: See Promoter of the Faith.

Devotion: (1) Religious fervor, piety; dedication.

(2) The consolation experienced at times during prayer; a reverent manner of praying.

Devotions: Pious practices of members of the Church include not only participation in various acts of the liturgy but also in other acts of worship generally called popular or private devotions. Concerning these, the Second Vatican Council said in the *Constitution on the Sacred Liturgy* (No. 13): "Popular devotions of the Christian people are warmly commended, provided they accord with the laws and norms of the Church. Such is especially the case with devotions called for by the Apostolic See. Devotions proper to the individual churches also have a special dignity. . . . These devotions should be so drawn up that they harmonize with the liturgical seasons, accord with the sacred liturgy, are in some fashion derived from it, and lead the people to it, since the liturgy by its very nature far surpasses any of them."

Devotions of a liturgical type are Benediction of the Blessed Sacrament, recitation of the Little Office of the Blessed Virgin Mary or of Vespers and Compline. Examples of paraliturgical devotion are a Bible Service or Vigil, and the Angelus, Rosary and Stations of the Cross, which have a strong scriptural basis.

Dies Irae: The opening Latin words, Day of Wrath, of a hymn for requiem Masses, written in the 13th century by the Franciscan Thomas of Celano.

Diocese: A fully organized ecclesiastical jurisdiction under the pastoral direction of a bishop as local ordinary.

Discalced: Of Latin derivation and meaning without shoes, the word is applied to religious orders or congregations whose members go barefoot or wear sandals.

Disciple: A term used sometimes in reference to the Apostles but more often to a larger number of followers (70 or 72) of Christ mentioned in Lk. 10:1.

Disciplina Arcani: A Latin phrase, meaning discipline of the secret and referring to a practice of the early Church, especially during the Roman persecutions, to: (1) conceal Christian truths from those who, it was feared, would misinterpret, ridicule and profane the teachings, and persecute Christians for believing them; (2) instruct catechumens in a gradual manner, withholding the teaching of certain doctrines until the catechumens proved themselves of good faith and sufficient understanding.

Dispensation: The relaxation of a law in a particular case. Laws made for the common good sometimes work undue hardship in particular cases. In such cases, where sufficient reasons are present, dispensations may be granted by proper authorities. Bishops, religious superiors and others may dispense from certain laws; the pope can dispense from all ecclesiastical laws. No one has authority to dispense from obligations of the divine law.

Divination: Attempting to foretell future or hidden things by means of things like dreams, necromancy, spiritism, examination of entrails, astrology, augury, omens, palmistry, drawing straws, dice, cards, etc. Practices like these attribute to creatural things a power which belongs to God alone and are violations of the First Commandment.

Divine Praises: Fourteen praises recited or sung at Benediction of the Blessed Sacrament in reparation for sins of sacrilege, blasphemy and profanity. Some of these praises date from the end of the 18th century.

Blessed be God.

Blessed be his holy Name.

Blessed be Jesus Christ, true God and true Man.

Blessed be the Name of Jesus.

Blessed be his most Sacred Heart.

Blessed be his most Precious Blood.

Blessed be Jesus in the most holy Sacrament of the Altar.

Blessed be the Holy Spirit, the Paraclete.

Blessed be the great Mother of God, Mary most holy.

Blessed be her holy and Immaculate Conception.

Blessed be her glorious Assumption.

Blessed be the name of Mary, Virgin and Mother.

Blessed be St. Joseph, her most chaste Spouse.

Blessed be God in his Angels and in his Saints.

Double Effect Principle: Actions sometimes have two effects closely related to each other, one good and the other bad, and a difficult moral question can arise: Is it permissible to place an action from which two such results follow? It is permissible to place the action, if: the action is good in itself and is directly productive of the good effect; the circumstances are good; the intention of the person is good; the reason for placing the action is proportionately serious to the seriousness of the indirect bad effect. For example: Is it morally permissible for a pregnant woman to undergo medical or surgical treatment for a pathological condition if the indirect and secondary effect of the treatment will be the loss of the child? The reply is affirmative, for these reasons: The action, i.e., the treatment, is good in itself, cannot be deferred until a later time without very serious consequences, and is ordered directly to the cure of critically grave pathology. By means of the treatment, the woman intends to save her life, which she has a right to do. The loss of the child is not directly sought as a means for the cure of the mother but results indirectly and in a secondary manner from the placing of the action, i.e., the treatment, which is good in itself.

The double effect principle does not support the principle that the end justifies the means.

Doxology: (1) The lesser doxology, or ascription of glory to the Trinity, is the Glory be to the Father. The first part dates back to the third or fourth century, and came from the form of baptism. The concluding words, As it was in the beginning, etc., are of later origin.

(2) The greater doxology, Glory to God in the highest, begins with the words of angelic praise at the birth of Christ recounted in the Infancy Narrative (Lk. 2:14). It is often recited at Mass. Of early Eastern origin, it is found in the *Apostolic Constitutions* in a form much like the present.

Dulia: A Greek term meaning the veneration or homage, different in nature and degree from that given to God, paid to the saints. It includes honoring the saints and seeking their intercession with God.

Duty: A moral obligation deriving from the binding force of law, the exigencies of one's state in life, and other sources.

E

Easter Controversy: A three-phase controversy over the time for the celebration of Easter.

Some early Christians in the Near East, called Quartodecimans, favored the observance of Easter on the 14th day of Nisan, the spring month of the Hebrew calendar, whenever it occurred. Against this practice, Pope St. Victor I, about 190, ordered a Sunday observance of the feast.

The Council of Nicaea, in line with usages of the Church at Rome and Alexandria, decreed in 325 that Easter should be observed on the first Sunday following the first full moon of spring.

Uniformity of practice in the West was not achieved until several centuries later, when the British Isles, in delayed compliance with measures enacted by the Synod of Whitby in 664, accepted the Roman date of observance.

Unrelated to the controversy is the fact that some Eastern Christians, in accordance with traditional calendar practices, celebrate

Easter at a different time than the Roman and Eastern-Rite churches.

Easter Duty: The serious obligation binding Catholics of Roman Rite, by a precept of the Church, to receive Holy Communion during the Easter time; in the US, from the first Sunday of Lent to Trinity Sunday.

Easter Water: Holy water blessed with special ceremonies and distributed on the Easter Vigil; used during Easter Week for blessing the faithful and homes.

Ecclesiology: Study of the nature, constitution, members, mission, functions, etc., of the Church.

Ecstasy: An extraordinary state of mystical experience in which a person is so absorbed in God that the activity of the exterior senses is suspended.

Ecumenism: The movement of Christians and their churches toward the unity willed by Christ. The Second Vatican Council called the movement "those activities and enterprises which, according to various needs of the Church and opportune occasions, are started and organized for the fostering of unity among Christians" (*Decree on Ecumenism*, No. 4). Spiritual ecumenism, i.e., mutual prayer for unity, is the heart of the movement. The movement also involves scholarly and pew-level efforts for the development of mutual understanding and better interfaith relations in general, and collaboration by the churches and their members in the social area.

Elevation: The raising of the host after consecration at Mass for adoration by the faithful. The custom was introduced in the Diocese of Paris about the close of the 12th century to offset an erroneous teaching of the time which held that transubstantiation of the bread did not take place until after the consecration of the wine in the chalice. The elevation of the chalice following the consecration of the wine was introduced in the 15th century.

End Justifies the Means: An unacceptable ethical principle which states that evil means may be used to produce good effects.

Envy: Sadness over another's good fortune because it is considered a loss to oneself or a detraction from one's own excellence; one of the seven capital sins, a violation of the obligations of charity.

Epikeia: A Greek word meaning reasonableness and designating a moral theory and practice, a mild interpretation of the mind of a legislator who is prudently considered not to wish positive law to bind in certain circumstances. Use of the principle is justified in practice when the lawgiver himself cannot be appealed to and when it can be prudently assumed that in particular cases, e.g., because of special hardship, he would not wish the law to be applied in a strict manner. Epikeia may not be applied with respect to acts that are intrinsically wrong or those covered by laws which automatically make them invalid.

Episcopate: (1) The office, dignity and sacramental powers bestowed upon a bishop at his ordination.

(2) The body of bishops collectively.

Equivocation: (1) The use of words, phrases, or gestures having more than one meaning in order to conceal information which a questioner has no strict right to know. It is permissible to equivocate (have a broad mental reservation) in some circumstances.

(2) A lie, i.e., a statement of untruth. Lying is intrinsically wrong. A lie told in joking, evident as such, is not wrong.

Eschatology: Doctrine concerning the last things: death, judgment, heaven and hell, and the final state of perfection of the People and Kingdom of God at the end of time.

Eternity: The interminable, perfect possession of life in its totality without beginning or end; an attribute of God, who has no past or future but always is. Man's existence has a beginning but no end and is, accordingly, called immortal.

Ethics: Moral philosophy, the science of the morality of human acts deriving from natural law, the natural end of man, and the powers of human reason. It includes all the spheres of human activity — personal, social, economic, political, etc. Ethics is distinct from but can be related to moral theology, whose primary principles are drawn from divine Revelation.

Eucharistic Congresses: Public demonstrations of faith in the Holy Eucharist. Combining liturgical services, other public ceremonies, subsidiary meetings, different kinds of instructional and inspirational elements, they are unified by central themes and serve to increase understanding of and devotion to Christ in the Eucharist, and to relate this liturgy of worship and witness to life.

International congresses are planned and held under the auspices of a permanent committee for international Eucharistic congresses. Participants include clergy, religious and lay persons from many countries, and representatives of national and international Catholic organizations. Popes have usually been represented by legates, but Paul VI attended two congresses personally, the 38th at Bombay and the 39th at Bogota.

Forty international congresses were held from 1881 to 1973:

Lille (1881), Avignon (1882), Liege (1883), Freiburg (1885), Toulouse (1886), Paris (1888), Antwerp (1890), Jerusalem (1893), Rheims (1894), Paray-le-Monial (1897), Brussels (1898), Lourdes (1899), Angers (1901), Namur (1902), Angouleme (1904), Rome (1905), Tournai (1906), Metz (1907), London (1908), Cologne (1909), Montreal (1910), Madrid (1911), Vienna (1912), Malta (1913), Lourdes (1914), Rome (1922), Amsterdam (1924), Chicago (1926), Sydney (1928), Carthage (1930), Dublin (1932), Buenos Aires (1934), Manila (1937), Budapest (1938), Barcelona (1952), Rio de Janeiro (1955), Munich, Germany (1960), Bombay, India (1964), Bogota, Colombia (1968), Melbourne, Australia (1973).

Eugenics: The science of heredity and environment for the physical and mental improvement of offspring. Extreme eugenics is untenable in practice because it advocates immoral means, such as compulsory breeding of the select, sterilization of persons said to be unfit, abortion, and unacceptable methods of birth regulation.

Euthanasia: Mercy killing, the direct causing of death by painless means for the purpose of ending human suffering. Euthanasia is murder and is totally illicit, for the natural law forbids the direct taking of one's own life or that of an innocent person.

The use of drugs to relieve suffering in serious cases, even when this results in a shortening of life as an indirect and secondary effect, is permissible under conditions of the double effect principle. It is also permissible for a seriously ill person to refuse to follow — or for other responsible persons to refuse to permit — extraordinary medical procedures even though the refusal might entail shortening of life.

Evolution: Scientific theory concerning the development of the physical universe from unorganized matter (inorganic evolution) and, especially, the development of existing forms of vegetable, animal and human life from earlier and more primitive organisms (organic evolution). Various ideas about evolution were advanced for some centuries before scientific evidence in support of the main-line theory of organic evolution, which has several formulations, was discovered and verified in the second half of the 19th century and afterwards. This evidence — from the findings of comparative anatomy and other sciences — confirmed evolution within species and cleared the way to further investigation of questions regarding the processes of its accomplishment. While a number of such questions remain open with respect to human evolution, a point of doctrine not open to question is the immediate creation of the human soul by God.

For some time, theologians regarded the theory with hostility, considering it to be in opposition to the account of creation in the early chapters of Genesis and subversive of belief in such doctrines as creation, the early state of man in grace, and the fall of man from grace. This state of affairs and the tension it generated led to considerable controversy regarding an alleged conflict between religion and science. Gradually, however, the tension was diminished with the development of biblical studies from the latter part of the 19th century onwards, with clarification of the distinctive features of religious truth and scientific truth, and with the refinement of evolutionary concepts.

So far as the Genesis account of creation is concerned, the Catholic view is that the writer(s) did not write as a scientist but as the communicator of religious truth in a manner adapted to the understanding of the people of his time. He used anthropomorphic language, the figure of days and other literary devices to state the salvation truths of creation, the fall of man from grace, and the promise of redemption. It was beyond the competency and purpose of the writer(s) to describe creation and related events in a scientific manner.

Excommunication: A penalty or censure by which a baptized person is excluded from the communion of the faithful, for committing and remaining obstinate in certain sins specified in canon law and technically called crimes. As by baptism a person is made a member of the Church in which there is a communication of spiritual goods, so by excommunication he is deprived of the same spiritual goods until he repents and receives absolution. Even though excommunicated, a person is still responsible for the normal obligations of a Catholic.

Existentialism: A philosophy with radical concern for the problems of individual existence and identity viewed in particular here-and-now patterns of thought which presuppose irrationality and absurdity in human life and the whole universe. It is preoccupied with questions about freedom, moral decision and responsibility against a background of denial of objective truth and universal norms of conduct; is characterized by prevailing anguish, dread, fear, pessimism, despair; is generally atheistic, although its modern originator, Soren Kierkegaard (d. 1855), and Gabriel Marcel attempted to give it a Christian orientation. Pius XII called it "the new erroneous philosophy which, opposing itself to idealism, immanentism and pragmatism, has assumed the name of existentialism, since it concerns itself only with the existence of individual things and neglects all consideration of their immutable essences" (Encyclical *Humani Generis,* Aug. 12, 1950).

Exorcism: (1) Driving out evil spirits; a rite in which evil spirits are charged and commanded on the authority of God and with the prayer of the Church to depart from a person or to cease causing harm to a person suffering from diabolical possession or obsession. The sacramental is officially administered by a priest delegated for the purpose by the bishop of the place. Elements of the rite include the Litany of Saints; recitation of the Our Father, one or more creeds, and other prayers; specific prayers of exorcism; the reading of Gospel passages, and use of the Sign of the Cross. Private exorcism for the liberation of a person from the strong influence of evil spirits, through prayer and the use of sacramentals like holy water, can be done by anyone.

(2) Exorcisms which do not imply the conditions of either diabolical possession or obsession form part of the ceremony of baptism, and are also included in formulas for various blessings; e.g., of water.

F

Faculties: Grants of jurisdiction, or authority, granted by the law of the Church or superiors (pope, bishop, religious superior) for exercise of the powers of holy orders; e.g., priests are given faculties to hear confessions, officiate at weddings; bishops are given faculties to grant dispensations, etc.

Faith: In religion, faith has several aspects. Catholic doctrine calls faith the assent of the mind to truths revealed by God, the assent being made with the help of grace and by command of the will on account of the authority and trustworthiness of God revealing. The term faith also refers to the truths that are believed (content of faith) and to the way in which a person, in response to Christ, gives witness to and expresses his belief in daily life (living faith).

All of these elements, and more, are included in the following statement:

" 'The obedience of faith' (Rom. 16:26; cf. 1:5; 2 Cor. 10:5-6) must be given to God who reveals, an obedience by which man entrusts his whole self freely to God, offering 'the full submission of intellect and will to God who reveals' (First Vatican Council, *Dogmatic Constitution on the Catholic Faith,* Chap. 3), and freely assenting to the truth revealed by Him. If this faith is to be shown, the grace of God and the interior help of the Holy Spirit must precede and assist, moving the heart and turning it to God, opening the eyes of the mind, and giving 'joy and ease to everyone in assenting to the truth and believing it' " (Second Council of Orange, Canon 7) (Second Vatican Council, *Constitution on Revelation,* No. 5). Faith is necessary for salvation.

Faith, Rule of: The norm or standard of religious belief. The Catholic doctrine is that belief must be professed in the divinely revealed truths in the Bible and tradition as interpreted and proposed by the infallible teaching authority of the Church.

Fast, Eucharistic: Eating and the drinking of any liquids except water are prohibited for one hour before the reception of Holy Communion. Water never breaks the Eucharistic fast, which is prescribed for reasons of reverence and preparation. By way of exception, the period of fasting is 15 minutes for the sick and aged, even though not confined to bed or a home, and those caring for them who wish to receive Communion with them but cannot fast for an hour without inconvenience (Instruction, *Immensae Caritatis,* Congregation for the Discipline of the Sacraments, Jan. 29, 1973).

Those who are ill, even though not confined to bed, may take nonalcoholic beverages and liquid or solid medicine before Holy Communion without any time limit.

Father: A title of priests, who are regarded as spiritual fathers because they are the ordinary ministers of baptism, by which persons are born to supernatural life, and because of their pastoral service to people.

Fear: A mental state caused by the apprehension of present or future danger. Grave fear does not necessarily remove moral responsibility for an act, but may lessen it.

First Friday: A devotion consisting of the reception of Holy Communion on the first Friday of nine consecutive months in honor of the Sacred Heart of Jesus and in reparation for sin. (See Sacred Heart, Promises.)

First Saturday: A devotion tracing its origin to the apparitions of the Blessed Virgin Mary at Fatima in 1917. Those practicing the devotion go to confession and, on the first Saturday of five consecutive months, receive Holy Communion, recite five decades of the Rosary, and meditate on the mysteries for 15 minutes.

Fisherman's Ring: A signet ring engraved with the image of St. Peter fishing from a boat, and encircled with the name of the reigning pope. It is not worn by the pope. It is used to seal briefs, and is destroyed after each pope's death.

Forgiveness of Sin: Catholics believe that sins are forgiven by God through the mediation of Christ in view of the repentance of the sinner and by means of the sacrament of penance. (See Penance.)

Fortitude: Courage to face dangers or hardships for the sake of what is good; one of the four cardinal virtues and one of the seven gifts of the Holy Spirit.

Fortune Telling: Attempting to predict the future or the occult by means of cards, palm reading, etc.; a form of divination, prohibited by the First Commandment.

Forum: The sphere in which ecclesiastical authority or jurisdiction is exercised.

(1) External: Authority is exercised in the external forum to deal with matters affecting the public welfare of the Church and its members. Those who have such authority because of their office (e.g., diocesan bishops) are called ordinaries.

(2) Internal: Authority is exercised in the internal forum to deal with matters affecting the private spiritual good of individuals. The sacramental forum is the sphere in which the sacrament of penance is administered; other exercises of jurisdiction in the internal forum take place in the non-sacramental forum.

Franciscan Crown: A seven-decade rosary used to commemorate the seven Joys of the Blessed Virgin: the Annunciation, the Visitation, the Nativity of Our Lord, the Adoration of the Magi, the Finding of the Child Jesus in the Temple, the Apparition of the Risen Christ to his Mother, the Assumption and Coronation of the Blessed Virgin. Introduced in 1422, the Crown originally consisted only of seven Our Fathers and 70 Hail Marys. Two Hail Marys were added to complete the number 72 (thought to be the number of years of Mary's life), and one Our Father, Hail Mary and Glory be to the Father are said for the intention of the pope.

Freedom, Religious: The Second Vatican Council declared that the right to religious freedom in civil society "means that all men are to be immune from coercion on the part of individuals or of social groups and of any human power, in such wise that in matters religious no one is to be forced to act in a manner contrary to his own beliefs. Nor is anyone to be restrained from acting in accordance with his own beliefs, whether privately or publicly, whether alone or in association with others, within due limits" of requirements for the common good. The foundation of this right in civil society is the "very dignity of the human person" (*Declaration on Religious Freedom,* No. 2).

The conciliar statement did not deal with the subject of freedom within the Church. It noted the responsibility of the faithful "carefully to attend to the sacred and certain doctrine of the Church" (No. 14).

Freemasons: A fraternal order which originated in London in 1717 with the formation of the first Grand Lodge of Freemasons. From England, the order spread to Europe and elsewhere. Its original deistic and non-denominational ideology was transformed in Latin countries into a compound of atheism, anticlericalism and irreligion. Since 1877, Grand Orient Freemasonry has been denied recognition by the Scottish and York Rites because of its failure to require belief in God and the immortality of the soul as a condition of membership. In some places, Freemasonry has been regarded as subversive of the state; in Catholic quarters, it has been considered hostile to the Church and its doctrine. In the United States, Freemasonry is generally known as a fraternal and philanthropic order.

Catholics have been forbidden to join the Freemasons, under penalty of excommunication, for serious pastoral reasons. Eight different popes in 17 different pronouncements, and at least six different local councils, condemned Freemasonry. The first condemnation was made by Clement XII in 1738. Eastern Orthodox and many Protestant bodies have also opposed the order.

The existing prohibition against membership in the Freemasons by Catholics was modified by the contents of a letter written in 1974 by Cardinal Franjo Seper, prefect of the Congregation for the Doctrine of the Faith. The letter said that Catholic laymen may join Masonic lodges which do not plot against the Church. The letter also said: "Clerics, religious and members of secular institutes are still forbidden in every case to join any Masonic association."

Free Will: The faculty or capability of making a reasonable choice among several alternatives. Freedom of will underlies the possibility and fact of moral responsibility.

Friar: Term applied to members of mendicant orders to distinguish them from members of monastic orders. (See Mendicants.)

Fruits of the Holy Spirit: Charity, joy, peace, patience, benignity, goodness, longanimity, mildness, faith, modesty, continence, chastity.

G

Gambling: The backing of an issue with a sum of money or other valuables, which is permissible if the object is honest, if the two parties have the free disposal of their stakes without prejudice to the rights of others, if the terms are thoroughly understood by both parties, and if the outcome is not known beforehand. Gambling often falls into disrepute and may be forbidden by civil law, as well as by divine law, because of cheating, fraud and other accompanying evils.

Gehenna: Greek form of a Jewish name, *Gehinnom,* for a valley near Jerusalem, the site of Moloch worship; used as a synonym for hell.

Genuflection: Bending of the knee, a natural sign of adoration or reverence, as when persons genuflect with the right knee in passing before the tabernacle to acknowledge the Eucharistic presence of Christ.

Gethsemani: A Hebrew word meaning oil press, designating the place on the Mount of Olives where Christ prayed and suffered in agony the night before he died.

Gifts of the Holy Spirit: Supernatural habits disposing a person to respond promptly to the inspiration of grace; promised by Christ and communicated through the Holy Spirit, especially in the sacrament of confirmation. They are: wisdom, understanding, counsel, fortitude, knowledge, piety, fear of the Lord.

Gluttony: An unreasonable appetite for food and drink; one of the seven capital sins.

God: The infinitely perfect Supreme Being, uncaused and absolutely self-sufficient, eternal, the Creator and final end of all things. The one God subsists in three equal Persons, the Father and the Son and the Holy Spirit. God, although transcendent and distinct from the universe, is present and active in the world in realization of his plan for the salvation of men, principally through Revelation, the operations of the Holy Spirit, the life and ministry of Christ, and the continuation of Christ's ministry in the Church.

The existence of God is an article of faith, clearly communicated in divine Revelation. Even without this Revelation, however, the Church teaches, in a declaration by the First Vatican Council, that men can acquire certain knowledge of the existence of God and some of his attributes. This can be done on the bases of principles of reason and reflection on human experience.

Non-revealed arguments or demonstrations for the existence of God have been developed from the principle of causality; the contingency of man and the universe; the existence of design, change and movement in the universe; human awareness of moral responsibility; widespread human testimony to the existence of God.

Grace: A free gift of God to men (and angels), grace is a created sharing or participation in the life of God. It is given to men through the merits of Christ and is communicated by the Holy Spirit. It is necessary for salvation. The principal means of grace are the sacraments (especially the Eucharist), prayer and good works.

Sanctifying or habitual grace makes men holy and pleasing to God, adopted children of God, members of Christ, temples of the Holy Spirit, heirs of heaven capable of supernaturally meritorious acts. With grace, God gives men the supernatural virtues and gifts of the Holy Spirit. The sacraments of baptism and penance were instituted to give grace to those who do not have it; the other sacraments, to increase it in those already in the state of grace. The means for growth in holiness, or the increase of grace, are prayer, the sacraments, and good works. Sanctifying grace is lost by the commission of serious sin.

Each sacrament confers sanctifying grace for the special purpose of the sacrament; in this context, grace is called sacramental grace.

Actual grace is a supernatural help of God which enlightens and strengthens a person to do good and to avoid evil. It is not a permanent quality, like sanctifying grace. It is necessary for the performance of supernatural acts. It can be resisted and refused. Persons in the state of serious sin are given actual grace to lead them to repentancem

Grace at Meals: Prayers said before meals, asking a blessing of God, and after meals, giving thanks to God. In addition to traditional prayers for these purposes, many variations suitable for different occasions are possible, at personal option.

H

Habit: (1) A disposition to do things easily, given with grace (and therefore supernatural) and/or acquired by repetition of similar acts.

(2) The garb worn by religious.

Hagiography: Writings or documents about saints and other holy persons.

Hail Mary: A prayer addressed to the Blessed Virgin Mary; also called the *Ave Maria* (Latin equivalent of Hail Mary) and the Angelic Salutation. In three parts, it consists of the words addressed to Mary by the Archangel Gabriel on the occasion of the Annunciation, in the Infancy Narrative (Hail full of grace, the Lord is with you, blessed are you among women.); the words addressed to Mary by her cousin Elizabeth on the occasion of the Visitation (Blessed is the fruit of your womb.); a concluding petition (Holy Mary, Mother of God, pray for us sinners now and at the hour of our death. Amen.). The first two salutations were joined in Eastern Rite formulas by the sixth century, and were similarly used at Rome in the seventh century. Insertion of the name of Jesus at the conclusion of the salutations was probably made by Urban IV about 1262. The present form of the petition was incorporated into the breviary in 1514.

Heaven: The state of those who, having achieved salvation, are in glory with God and enjoy the beatific vision.

The phrase, kingdom of heaven, refers to the order or kingdom of God, grace, salvation.

Hell: The state of punishment of the damned — i.e., those who die in mortal sin, in a condition of self-alienation from God and of opposition to the divine plan of salvation. The punishment of hell begins immediately after death and lasts forever.

Hermit: See Anchorite.

Heroic Act of Charity: The completely unselfish offering to God of one's good works and merits for the benefit of the souls in purgatory rather than for oneself. Thus a person may offer to God for the souls in purgatory all the good works he performs during life, all the indulgences he gains, and all the prayers and indulgences that will be offered for him after his death. The act is revocable at will, and is not a vow. Its actual ratification depends on the will of God.

Heterodoxy: False doctrine, teaching or belief; a departure from truth.

Holy See: (1) The diocese of the pope, Rome.

(2) The pope himself and/or the various officials and bodies of the Church's central administration at Vatican City — the Roman Curia — which act in the name and by authority of the pope.

Holy Spirit: God the Holy Spirit, third Person of the Holy Trinity, who proceeds from the Father and the Son and with whom he is equal in every respect; inspirer of the prophets and writers of sacred Scripture; promised by Christ to the Apostles as their advocate and strengthener; appeared in the form of a dove at the baptism of Christ and as tongues of fire at his descent upon the Apostles; soul of the Church and guarantor, by his abiding presence and action, of truth in doctrine; communicator of grace to men, for which reason he is called the sanctifier.

Holy Water: Water blessed by the Church and used as a sacramental, a practice which originated in apostolic times.

Holy Year: A year during which the pope grants the plenary Jubilee Indulgence to the faithful who fulfill certain conditions. For those who make a pilgrimage to Rome during the year, the conditions are reception of the sacraments of penance and the Eucharist, visits and prayer for the intention of the pope in the basilicas of St. Peter, St. John Lateran, St. Paul and St. Mary Major. For those who do not make a pilgrimage to Rome, the conditions are reception of the sacraments and prayer for the pope during a visit or community celebration in a church designated by the bishop of the locality.

Holy Year observances have biblical counterparts in the Years of Jubilee observed at 50-year intervals by the pre-exilic Israelites — when debts were pardoned and slaves freed (Lv. 25:25-54) — and in sabbatical years observed from the end of the Exile to 70 A.D. — in which debts to fellow Jews were remitted.

The practice of Christians from early times to go on pilgrimage to the Holy Land, the shrines of martyrs and the tombs of the Apostles in Rome influenced the institution of Holy Years. There was also a prevailing belief among the people that every 100th year was a year of "Great Pardon." Accordingly, even before Boniface VIII formally proclaimed the first Holy Year Feb. 22, 1300, scores of thousands of pilgrims were already on the way to or in Rome.

Medieval popes embodied in the observance of Holy Years the practice of good works (reception of the sacraments of penance and the Eucharist, pilgrimages and/or visits to the tombs of the Apostles, and related actions) and spiritual benefits (particularly, special indulgences for the souls in purgatory). These and related practices, with suitable changes for celebrations in local churches, remain staple features of Holy Year observances.

The first three Holy Years were observed in 1300, 1350 and 1390. Subsequent ones were celebrated at 25-year intervals except in 1800 and 1850 when, respectively, the French invasion of Italy and political turmoil made observance impossible. Pope Paul II (1464-1471) set the 25-year timetable. In 1500, Pope Alexander VI prescribed the start and finish ceremonies — the opening and closing of the Holy Doors in the major basilicas on successive Christmas Eves. All but a few of the earlier Holy Years were classified as ordinary. Several, like the one held in 1933 to commemorate the 19th centenary of the death and resurrection of Christ, were in the extraordinary category.

Holy Year 1975 coincided with the 10th anniversary of the closing of the Second Vatican Council. Its themes also coincided with the renewal emphasis which dominated the council, and were related to the main topic — the evangelization of the modern world — on the 1974 agenda of the Synod of Bishops.

Homosexuality: The condition of a person whose sexual orientation is toward persons of the same rather than the opposite sex. Some psychologists regard it as an arrested state of emotional development. The condition, usually discovered during adolescence rather than deliberately caused, is not normal but is not sinful in itself. Homosexual acts against nature are objectively wrong; subjective responsibility for such acts, however, may be conditioned and diminished by compulsion and related factors.

Hope: One of the three theological virtues, by which one firmly trusts that God wills his salvation and will give him the means to attain it.

Hosanna: A Hebrew word, meaning O Lord, save, we pray.

Host, The Sacred: The bread under whose appearances Christ is and remains present in a unique manner after the consecration which takes place during Mass. (See Transubstantiation.)

Humility: A virtue which induces a person to evaluate himself at his true worth, to recognize his dependence on God, and to give glory to God for the good he has and can do.

Hyperdulia: The special veneration accorded the Blessed Virgin Mary because of her unique role in the mystery of Redemption, her exceptional gifts of grace from God, and her pre-eminence among the saints. Hyperdulia is not adoration; only God is adored.

Hypnosis: A mental state resembling sleep, induced by suggestion, in which the subject does the bidding of the hypnotist. Hypnotism is permissible under certain conditions: the existence of a serious reason, e.g., for anesthetic or therapeutic purposes, and the competence and integrity of the hypnotist. Hypnotism may not be practiced for the sake of amusement. Experiments indicate that, contrary to popular opinion, hypnotized subjects may be induced to perform immoral acts which, normally, they would not do.

Hypostatic Union: The union of the human and divine natures in the one divine Person of Christ.

I

Icons: Byzantine-style paintings or representations of Christ, the Blessed Virgin and other saints, venerated in the Eastern Churches where they take the place of statues.

Idolatry: Worship of any but the true God; a violation of the First Commandment.

IHS: In Greek, the first threee letters of the name of Jesus — Iota, Eta, Sigma.

Immortality: The survival and continuing existence of the human soul after death.

Immunity of the Clergy: Exemption of clerics from military duty and civil service.

Impurity: Unlawful indulgence in sexual pleasure. (See Chastity.)

Incardination: The affiliation of a priest to his diocese. Every secular priest must belong to a certain diocese. Similarly, every priest of a religious community must belong to some jurisdiction of his community; this affiliation, however, is not called incardination.

Incarnation: (1) The coming-into-flesh or taking of human nature by the Second Person of the Trinity. He became human as the Son of Mary, being miraculously conceived by the power of the Holy Spirit, without ceasing to be divine. His divine Person hypostatically unites his divine and human natures.

(2) The supernatural mystery coextensive with Christ from the moment of his human conception and continuing through his life on earth; his sufferings and death; his resurrection from the dead and ascension to glory with the Father; his sending, with the Father, of the Holy Spirit upon the Apostles and the Church; and his unending mediation with the Father for the salvation of men.

Incense: A granulated substance which, when burnt, emits an aromatic smoke. It symbolizes the zeal with which the faithful should be consumed, the good odor of Christian virtue, the ascent of prayer to God.

Incest: Sexual intercourse with relatives by blood or marriage; a sin of impurity and also a grave violation of the natural reverence due to relatives. Other sins of impurity (desire, etc.) concerning relatives have the nature of incest.

Index of Prohibited Books: A list of books which Catholics were formerly forbidden to read, possess or sell, under penalty of excommunication. The books were banned by the Holy See after publication because their treatment of matters of faith and morals and related subjects were judged to be erroneous or serious occasions of doctrinal error. Some books were listed in the Index by name; others were covered under general norms. The Congregation for the Doctrine of the Faith declared June 14, 1966, that the Index and its related penalties of excommunication no longer had the force of law in the Church. Persons are still obliged, however, to take normal precautions against occasions of doctrinal error.

The first *Roman Index of Prohibited Books,* which served the same purposes as earlier lists, was published in 1559 by the Holy Office at the order of Paul IV. The Council of Trent, with the approval of the same pope, authorized another Index in 1564. Seven years later, St. Pius V set up a special Congregation for the Reform of the Index and Correction of Books, and gave it universal jurisdiction. In the course of time, many additions and modifications affecting the Index were made. In 1897, Leo XIII issued complete legislation on the subject, and in 1917 Benedict XV turned over to the Congregation of the Holy Office the function of censoring publications in accordance with the provisions of canon law.

Indifferentism: A theory that any one religion is as true and good — or false — as any other religion, and that it makes no difference, objectively, what religion one professes, if any. The theory is completely subjective, finding its justification entirely in personal choice without reference to or respect for objective validity. It is also self-contradictory, since it regards as equally acceptable — or unacceptable — the beliefs of all religions, which in fact are not only not all the same but are in some cases opposed to each other.

Indulgence: According to *The Doctrine and Practice of Indulgences,* an apostolic constitution issued by Paul VI Jan. 1, 1967, an indulgence is the remission before God of the temporal punishment due for sins already forgiven as far as their guilt is concerned, which a follower of Christ — with the proper dispositions and under certain determined conditions — acquires through the intervention of the Church. The Church grants indulgences in accordance with doctrine concerning the superabundant merits of Christ and the saints, the Power of the Keys, and the sharing of spiritual goods in the Communion of Saints.

An indulgence is partial or plenary, depending on whether it does away with either part or all of the temporal punishment due for sin. Both types of indulgences can always be applied to the dead by way of suffrage; the actual disposition of indulgences applied to the dead rests with God.

(1) Partial indulgence: Properly disposed faithful who perform an action to which a partial indulgence is attached obtain, in addition to the remission of temporal punishment acquired by the action itself, an equal remission of punishment through the intervention of the Church. (This grant was formerly designated in terms of days and years.) The proper dispositions for gaining a partial indulgence are sorrow for sin and freedom from serious sin, performance of the required good work, and the intention (which can be general or immediate) to gain the indulgence.

In addition to customary prayers and other good works to which partial indulgences are attached, the *Enchiridion Indulgentiarum* published in 1968 included general grants of partial indulgences to the faithful who: (a) with some kind of prayer, raise their minds to God with humble confidence while carrying out their duties and bearing the difficulties of everyday life; (b) motivated by the spirit of faith and compassion, give of themselves or their goods for the service of persons in need; (c) in a spirit of penance, spontaneously refrain from the enjoyment of things which are lawful and pleasing to them.

(2) Plenary indulgence: To gain a plenary indulgence, it is necessary for a person to be free of all attachment to sin, to perform the work to which the indulgence is attached, and to fulfill the three conditions of sacramental confession, Eucharistic Communion, and prayer for the intention of the pope. The three conditions may be fulfilled several days before or after the performance of the prescribed work, but it is fitting that Communion be received and prayers for the intentions

of the pope be offered on the same day the work is performed. The condition of praying for the pope's intention is fully satisfied by praying one Our Father and one Hail Mary, and sometimes the Creed, but persons are free to choose other prayers.

Four of the several devotional practices for which a plenary indulgence is granted are: (a) adoration of the Blessed Sacrament for at least one-half hour; (b) devout reading of sacred Scripture for at least one-half hour; (c) the Way of the Cross; (d) recitation of the Marian Rosary in a church or public oratory or in a family group, a religious community or pious association. Only one plenary indulgence can be gained in a single day.

Indult: A favor or privilege granted by competent ecclesiastical authority, giving permission to do something not allowed by the common law of the Church.

Infant Jesus of Prague: An 18-inch-high wooden statue of the Child Jesus which has figured in a form of devotion to the Holy Childhood and Kingship of Christ since the 17th century. Of uncertain origin, the statue was presented by Princess Polixena to the Carmelites of Our Lady of Victory Church, Prague, in 1628.

Infused Virtues: The theological virtues of faith, hope, and charity; principles or capabilities of supernatural action, they are given with sanctifying grace by God rather than acquired by repeated acts of a person. They can be increased by practice; they are lost by contrary acts. Natural-acquired moral virtues, like the cardinal virtues of prudence, justice, temperance, and fortitude, can be considered infused in a person whose state of grace gives them supernatural orientation.

Inquisition: A tribunal for dealing with heretics, authorized by Gregory IX in 1231 to search them out, hear and judge them, sentence them to various forms of punishment, and in some cases to hand them over to civil authorities for punishment. The Inquisition was a creature of its time when crimes against faith, which threatened the good of the Christian community, were regarded also as crimes against the state, and when heretical doctrines of such extremists as the Cathari and Albigensians threatened the very fabric of society. The institution, which was responsible for many excesses, was most active in the second half of the 13th century.

Inquisition, Spanish: An institution peculiar to Spain and the colonies in Spanish America. In 1478, at the urging of King Ferdinand, Pope Sixtus IV approved the establishment of the Inquisition for trying charges of heresy brought against Jewish (Marranos) and Moorish (Moriscos) converts. It acquired jurisdiction over other cases as well, however, and fell into disrepute because of irregularities in its functions, cruelty in its sentences, and the manner in which it served the interests of the Spanish crown more than the accused persons and the good of the Church. Protests by the Holy See failed to curb excesses of the Inquisition, which lingered in Spanish history until early in the 19th century.

I N R I: The first letters of words in the Latin inscription atop the cross on which Christ was crucified: (I)esus (N)azaraenus, (R)ex (J)udaeorum — Jesus of Nazareth, King of the Jews.

Insemination, Artificial: The implanting of human semen by some means other than consummation of natural marital intercourse. In view of the principle that procreation should result only from marital intercourse, donor insemination is not permissible. The use of legitimate artificial means to further the fruitfulness of marital intercourse is permissible.

In Sin: The condition of a person called spiritually dead because he does not possess sanctifying grace, the principle of supernatural life, action and meritm Such grace can be regained through repentance.

Instruction: A document containing doctrinal explanations, directive norms, rules, recommendations, admonitions, issued by the pope, a department of the Roman Curia or other competent authority in the Church. To the extent that they so prescribe, instructions have the force of law.

Intercommunion: The common celebration and reception of the Eucharist by members of different Christian churches; a pivotal issue in ecumenical theory and practice. Catholic participation and intercommunion in the Eucharistic liturgy of another church without a valid priesthood and with a variant Eucharistic belief is out of order. Under certain conditions, other Christians may receive the Eucharist in the Catholic Church (see additional Intercommunion entry). Intercommunion is acceptable to some Protestant churches and unacceptable to others.

Interdict: An ecclesiastical penalty imposed on persons and places for certain violations of church law. If the interdict is personal, the interdicted persons may not take part in certain liturgical services, administer or receive certain sacraments. If the interdict is local, persons may not take part in certain liturgical services, administer or receive certain sacraments in the interdicted places.

Interdict is different from excommunication, and does not involve exclusion of a person from the community of the faithful.

Interregnum: The period of time between the death of one pope and the election of his successor. Another term applied to the period is *Sede vacante,* meaning the See (of Rome) being vacant.

Interregnum procedures follow norms contained in two apostolic constitutions: *Vacantis Apostolicae Sedis,* issued by Pius XII Dec. 8, 1945, and *Summi Pontificis Electione,* issued by John XXIII Sept. 5, 1962.

The main concerns during an interregnum

are things connected with the death and burial of the pope, the election of his successor, and the maintenance of ordinary routine for the proper functioning of the Roman Curia.

The chamberlain of the Holy Roman Church takes over the ordinary administration of most Roman affairs. He — or the dean of the College of Cardinals prior to a chamberlain's election by the cardinals — certifies the death of the pope; orders the destruction of the Fisherman's Ring and other personal seals of the pope; and sets in motion the procedures for notifying the world about the pope's death, for funeral preparations, and for summoning the cardinals to a conclave for the election of a new pontiff.

The vicar of Rome exercises ordinary jurisdiction over the diocese.

The congregations, offices and tribunals of the Roman Curia retain ordinary jurisdiction for routine affairs but may not initiate new business during the interregnum.

The secretary of the College of Cardinals replaces the secretary of state and maintains the secretariat in a status quo.

The deceased pope is buried in St. Peter's Basilica within four or five days, following the usual customs for public viewing of the body and the offering of a solemn Mass. Nine consecutive daily Masses are offered for the repose of the pontiff, and the mourning period lasts about 10 days.

The conclave for the election of a new pope begins no later than 18 days after the death of his predecessor. On the election of the new pope, the interregnum comes to an end. (See Papal Election.)

Intinction: A method of administering Holy Communion under the dual appearances of bread and wine, in which the consecrated host is dipped in the consecrated wine before being given to the communicant. The administering of Holy Communion in this manner, which has been traditional in Eastern-Rite liturgies, was authorized in the Roman Rite for various occasions by the *Constitution on the Sacred Liturgy* promulgated by the Second Vatican Council.

Irenicism: Peace-seeking, conciliation, as opposed to polemics; an important element in ecumenism, provided it furthers pursuit of the Christian unity willed by Christ without degenerating into a peace-at-any-price disregard for religious truth.

Irregularity: An impediment to the lawful reception or exercise of holy orders. The Church instituted irregularities — which include apostasy, heresy, homicide, attempted suicide — out of reverence for the dignity of the sacraments.

Itinerarium: Prayers for a spiritually profitable journey.

J

Jansenism: Opinions developed and proposed by Cornelius Jansenius (1585-1638). He held that: human nature was radically and intrinsically corrupted by original sin; some men are predestined to heaven and others to hell; Christ died only for those predestined to heaven; for those who are predestined, the operations of grace are irresistible. Jansenism also advocated an extremely rigorous code of morals and asceticism. The errors were proscribed by Urban VIII in 1642, by Innocent X in 1653, by Clement XI in 1713, and by other popes. Despite these condemnations, the rigoristic spirit of Jansenism lingered for a long time afterwards, particularly in France.

Jehovah's Witnesses: The Witnesses, together with the Watchtower and Bible Tract Society, trace their beginnings to a Bible class organized by Charles Taze Russell in 1872 at Allegheny, Pa. They take their name from a passage in Isaiah (43:12): " 'You are my witnesses,' says Jehovah." They are generally fundamentalist and revivalist with respect to the Bible, and believe that Christ is God's Son but is inferior to God. They place great emphasis on the Battle of Armageddon (as a decisive confrontation of good and evil) that is depicted vividly in Revelation, believing that God will then destroy the existing system of things and that, with the establishment of Jehovah's Kingdom, a small band of 144,000 spiritual sons of God will go to heaven, rule with Christ, and share in some way their happiness with some others.

Each Witness is considered by the society to be an ordained minister charged with the duty of spreading the message of Jehovah, which is accomplished through publications, house-to-house visitations, and other methods. The Witnesses refuse to salute the flag of any nation, regarding this as a form of idolatry, or to sanction blood transfusions even for the saving of life. There are approximately one million Witnesses in more than 22,000 congregations in some 80 countries. The freedom and activities of Witnesses are restricted in some places.

Jesus: The name of Jesus, meaning Savior in Christian usage, derived from the Aramaic and Hebrew *Yeshua* and *Joshua*, meaning *Yahweh* is salvation.

Jesus Prayer: A form of prayer dating back to the fifth century, "Lord Jesus Christ, Son of God, have mercy on me (a sinner)."

Joys of the Blessed Virgin Mary, Seven: (See Franciscan Crown.)

Judgment: (1) Last or final judgment: Final judgment by Christ, at the end of the world and the general resurrection.

(2) Particular judgment: The judgment that takes place immediately after a person's death, followed by entrance into heaven, hell or purgatory.

Jurisdiction: Right, power, authority to rule. Jurisdiction in the Church is of divine institution; has pastoral service for its purpose; includes legislative, judicial and executive authority; can be exercised only by persons with the power of orders.

(1) Ordinary jurisdiction is attached to ecclesiastical offices by law; the officeholders, called ordinaries, have authority over those who are subject to them.

(2) Delegated jurisdiction is that which is granted to persons rather than attached to offices. Its extent depends on the terms of the delegation.

Justice: One of the four cardinal virtues by which a person gives to others what is due to them as a matter of right. (See Cardinal Virtues.)

Justification: The act by which God makes a person just, and the consequent change in the spiritual status of a person, from sin to grace; the remission of sin and the infusion of sanctifying grace through the merits of Christ and the action of the Holy Spirit.

K

Kerygma: Proclaiming the word of God, in the manner of the Apostles, as here and now effective for salvation. This method of preaching or instruction, centered on Christ and geared to the facts and themes of salvation history, is designed to dispose people to faith in Christ and/or to intensify the experience and practice of that faith in those who have it.

Keys, Power of the: Spiritual authority and jurisdiction in the Church, symbolized by the keys of the kingdom of heaven. Christ promised the keys to St. Peter, as head-to-be of the Church (Mt. 16:19), and commissioned him with full pastoral responsibility to feed his lambs and sheep (Jn. 21:15-17), The pope, as the successor of St. Peter, has this power in a primary and supreme manner. The bishops of the Church also have the power, in union with and subordinate to the pope. Priests share in it through holy orders and the delegation of authority.

Examples of the application of the Power of the Keys are the exercise of teaching and pastoral authority by the pope and bishops, the absolving of sins in the sacrament of penance, the granting of indulgences, the imposing of spiritual penalties on persons who commit certain serious sins.

L

Laicization: (1) The process by which a man ordained to holy orders is relieved of the obligations of orders and the ministry and is returned to the status of a lay person. Applications by diocesan clergy are filed with their bishop and forwarded for processing to the congregation of the Roman Curia authorized to grant the indult of laicization.

(2) The process by which a religious is relieved of the obligations of vows and membership in his or her institute. Applications are filed with the proper religious superior and forwarded for processing to the Congre-

gation for Religious which is authorized to grant the appropriate indult.

Languages of the Church: The first language in church use, for divine worship and the conduct of ecclesiastical affairs, was Aramaic, the language of the first Christians in and around Jerusalem. As the Church spread westward, Greek was adopted and prevailed until the third century when it was supplanted by Latin for official use in the West.

According to traditions established very early in churches of the Eastern Rites, many different languages were adopted for use in divine worship and for the conduct of ecclesiastical affairs. The practice was, and still is, to use the vernacular or a language closely related to the common tongue of the people.

In the Western Church, Latin prevailed as the general official language until the promulgation on Dec. 4, 1963, of the *Constitution on the Sacred Liturgy* by the second session of the Second Vatican Council. Since that time, vernacular languages have come into use in the Mass, administration of the sacraments, and the Liturgy of the Hours. The change was introduced in order to make the prayers and ceremonies of divine worship more informative and meaningful to all. Latin, however, remains the official language for administrative and procedural matters.

Law: An ordinance or rule governing the activity of things.

(1) Natural law: Moral norms corresponding to man's nature by which he orders his conduct toward God, neighbor, society and himself. This law, which is rooted in human nature, is of divine origin, can be known by the use of reason, and binds all men having the use of reason. The Ten Commandments are declarations and amplifications of natural law. The primary precepts of natural law, to do good and to avoid evil, are universally recognized, despite differences with respect to understanding and application resulting from different philosophies of good and evil.

(2) Divine positive law: That which has been revealed by God. Among its essentials are the twin precepts of love of God and love of neighbor, and the Ten Commandments.

(3) Ecclesiastical law: That which is established by the Church for the spiritual welfare of the faithful and the orderly conduct of ecclesiastical affairs. (See Canon Law.)

(4) Civil law: That which is established by a socio-political community for the common good.

Lector: A reader of scriptural passages and other selections at Mass and other services of worship.

Legitimation: Removal of the status of illegitimacy; e.g., by marriage of the parents.

Liberalism: A multiphased trend of thought and movement favoring liberty, independence and progress in moral, intellectual, religious, social, economic and political life.

Traceable to the Renaissance, it developed through the Enlightenment, the rationalism of the 19th century, and modernist- and existentialist-related theories of the 20th century. Evaluations of various kinds of liberalism depend on the validity of their underlying principles. Extremist positions — regarding subjectivism, libertinarianism, naturalist denials of the supernatural, and the alienation of individuals and society from God and the Church were condemned by Gregory XVI in the 1830's, Pius IX in 1864, Leo XIII in 1899, and St. Pius X in 1907. There is, however, nothing objectionable about forms of liberalism patterned according to sound principles of Christian doctrine.

Life in Outer Space: Whether rational life exists on other bodies in the universe besides earth, is a question for scientific investigation to settle. The possibility can be granted, without prejudice to the body of revealed truth.

Limbo: The limbo of the fathers was the state of rest and natural happiness after death enjoyed by the just of pre-Christian times until they were admitted to heaven following the Ascension of Christ. Belief in this matter is stated in the Apostles' Creed. The existence of a limbo for unbaptized persons of infant status — a state of rest and natural happiness — has never been formally defined.

Litany: A prayer in the form of responsive petition; e.g., St. Joseph, pray for us, etc. There are seven litanies approved for liturgical use: Litanies of Loreto (Litany of the Blessed Mother), the Holy Name, All Saints, the Sacred Heart, the Precious Blood, St. Joseph, Litany for the Dying. Others may be used privately.

Little Office of the Blessed Virgin Mary: A shortened version of a Liturgy of the Hours honoring the Blessed Virgin. It dates from about the middle of the eighth century.

Liturgical Languages: (See Languages of the Church.)

Loreto, House of: A Marian shrine in Loreto, Italy, consisting of the home of the Holy Family which, according to an old tradition, was transported in a miraculous manner from Nazareth to Dalmatia and finally to Loreto between 1291 and 1294. Investigations conducted shortly after the appearance of the structure in Loreto revealed that its dimensions matched those of the house of the Holy Family missing from its place of enshrinement in a basilica at Nazareth. Among the many popes who regarded it with high honor was John XXIII, who went there on pilgrimage Oct. 4, 1962. The house of the Holy Family is enshrined in the Basilica of Our Lady.

Lust: A disorderly desire for sexual pleasure; one of the seven capital sins.

M

Magi: In the Infancy Narrative of Stm Matthew's Gospel (2:1-12), three wise men from the East whose visit and homage to the Child Jesus at Bethlehem indicated Christ's manifestation of himself to non-Jewish people. The narrative teaches the universality of salvation. The traditional names of the Magi are Caspar, Melchior and Balthasar.

Magnificat: The canticle or hymn uttered by the Virgin Mary after she was greeted by her cousin Elizabeth on the occasion of the Visitation (Lk. 1:46-55). It is an expression of praise, thanksgiving and acknowledgement of the great blessings given by God to Mary, the Mother of the Second Person of the Blessed Trinity made Man.

Martyr: A Greek word, meaning witness, denoting one who voluntarily suffered death for the faith or some Christian virtue.

Martyrology: A catalogue of martyrs and other saints, arranged according to the calendar. The *Roman Martyrology* contains the official list of saints venerated by the Church. Additions to the list are made in beatification and canonization decrees of the Congregation for the Causes of Saints. The Martyrology is being revised to conform with other liturgical books.

Mass for the People: On Sundays and certain feasts throughout the year pastors are required to offer Mass for the faithful committed to their care. If they cannot offer the Mass on these days, they must do so at a later date or provide that another priest offer the Mass.

Master of Novices: The person in charge of the training and formation of candidates for a religious institute during novitiate.

Materialism: Theory which holds that matter is the only reality, and everything in existence is merely a manifestation of matter; there is no such thing as spirit, and the supernatural does not exist. Materialism is incompatible with Christian doctrine.

Meditation: Mental, as distinguished from vocal, prayer, in which thought, affections, and resolutions of the will predominate. There is a meditative element to all forms of prayer, which always involves the raising of the heart and mind to God.

Mendicants: A term derived from Latin and meaning beggars, applied to members of religious orders without property rights; the members, accordingly, worked or begged for their support. The original mendicants were Franciscans and Dominicans in the early 13th century; later, the Carmelites, Augustinians, Servites and others were given the mendicant title and privileges, with respect to exemption from episcopal jurisdiction and wide faculties for preaching and administering the sacrament of penance. The practice of begging is limited at the present time, although it is still allowed with the permission of competent superiors and bishops. Mendicants are supported by free will offerings and income received for spiritual services and other work.

Mercy, Divine: The love and goodness of God, manifested particularly in a time of need.

Merit: In religion, the right to a supernatural reward for good works freely done for a supernatural motive by a person in the state of and with the assistance of grace. The right to such reward is from God, who binds himself to give it. Accordingly, good works, as described above, are meritorious for salvation.

Metempsychosis: Theory of the passage or migration of the human soul after death from one body to another for the purpose of purification from guilt. The theory denies the unity of the soul and human personality, and the doctrine of individual moral responsibility.

Millennium: A thousand-year reign of Christ and the just upon earth before the end of the world. This belief of the Millenarians, Chiliasts, and some sects of modern times is based on an erroneous interpretation of Rv. 20.

Miracles: Observable events or effects in the physical or moral order of things, with reference to salvation, which cannot be explained by the ordinary operation of laws of nature and which, therefore, are attributed to the direct action of God. They make known, in an unusual way, the concern and intervention of God in human affairs for the salvation of men. The most striking examples are the miracles worked by Christ. Numbering about 35, they included his own Resurrection; the raising of three persons to life (Lazarus, the daughter of Jairus, the son of the widow of Naim); the healing of blind, leprous and other persons; nature miracles; and prophecies, or miracles of the intellectual order.

The foregoing notion of miracles, which is based on the concept of a fixed order of nature, was not known by the writers of Sacred Scripture. In the Old Testament, particularly, they called some things miraculous which, according to the definition in contemporary use, may or may not have been miracles. Essentially, however, the occurrences so designated were regarded as exceptional manifestations of God's care and concern for the salvation of his people. The miracles of Christ were miracles in the full sense of the term.

The Church believes it is reasonable to accept miracles as manifestations of divine power for purposes of salvation. God, who created the laws of nature, is their master; hence, without disturbing the ordinary course of things, he can — and has in the course of history before and after Christ — occasionally set aside these laws and has also produced effects beyond their power of operation. The Church does not call miraculous anything which does not admit of easy explanation; on the contrary, miracles are admitted only when the events have a bearing on the order of grace and every possible natural explanation has been tried and found wanting.

(The transubstantiation — i.e., the conversion of the whole substance of bread and wine, their sensible appearances alone remaining, into the Body and Blood of Christ in the act of Consecration at Mass — is not an observable event. Traditionally, however, it has been called a miracle.)

Missal: A liturgical book of Roman Rite also called the *Sacramentary,* containing the celebrant's prayers of the Mass, along with general instructions and ceremonial directives. The Latin text of the new *Roman Missal,* replacing the one authorized by the Council of Trent in the 16th century, was published by the Vatican Polyglot Press in 1970. Its use in English was made mandatory in the U.S. from Dec. 1, 1974. Readings and scriptural responsories formerly in the missal are contained in the *Lectionary.*

Missiology: Study of the missionary nature, constitution and activity of the Church in all aspects: theological reasons for missionary activity, laws and instructions of the Holy See, history of the missions, social and cultural background, methods, norms for carrying on missionary work.

Mission: (1) Strictly, it means being sent to perform a certain work, such as the mission of Christ to redeem mankind, the mission of the Apostles and the Church and its members to perpetuate the prophetic, priestly and royal mission of Christ.

(2) A place where: the Gospel has not been proclaimed; the Church has not been firmly established; the Church, although established, is weak.

(3) An ecclesiastical territory with the simplest kind of canonical organization, under the jurisdiction of the Congregation for the Evangelization of Peoples.

(4) A church or chapel without a resident priest.

(5) A special course of sermons and spiritual exercises conducted in parishes for the purpose of renewing and deepening the spiritual life of the faithful and for the conversion of lapsed Catholics.

Modernism: The "synthesis of all heresies," which appeared near the beginning of the 20th century. It undermines the objective validity of religious beliefs and practices which, it contends, are products of the subconscious developed by mankind under the stimulus of a religious sense. It holds that the existence of a personal God cannot be demonstrated, the Bible is not inspired, Christ is not divine, nor did he establish the Church or institute the sacraments. A special danger lies in modernism, which is still influential, because it uses Catholic terms with perverted meanings. St. Pius X condemned 65 propositions of modernism in 1907 in the decree *Lamentabili* and issued the encyclical *Pascendi* to explain and analyze its errors.

Monastery: The dwelling place, as well as the community thereof, of monks belonging to the Benedictine and Benedictine-related orders like the Cistercians and Carthusians; also, the Augustinians and Canons Regular.

Distinctive of monasteries are: their separation from the world; the papal enclosure or strict cloister; the permanence or stability of attachment characteristic of their members; autonomous government in accordance with a monastic rule, like that of St. Benedict in the West or of St. Basil in the East; the special dedication of its members to the community celebration of the liturgy as well as to work that is suitable to the surrounding area and the needs of its people. Monastic superiors of men have such titles as abbot and prior; of women, abbess and prioress. In most essentials, an abbey is the same as a monastery.

Monk: A member of a monastic order — e.g., the Benedictines, the Benedictine-related Cistercians and Carthusians, and the Basilians, who bind themselves by religious profession to stable attachment to a monastery, the contemplative life and the work of their community. In popular use, the title is wrongly applied to many men religious who really are not monks.

Monotheism: Belief in and worship of one God.

Morality: Conformity or difformity of behavior to standards of right conduct. (See Commandments of God, Precepts of the Church, Conscience, Law.)

Mormons: Members of the Church of Jesus Christ of Latter-Day Saints. The church was established by Joseph Smith (1805-1844) at Fayette, N.Y., three years after he said he had received from an angel golden tablets containing the *Book of the Prophet Mormon.* This book, the Bible, *Doctrine and Covenants,* and *The Pearl of Great Price,* are the basic doctrinal texts of the church. Characteristic of the Mormons are strong belief in the revelations of their leaders, among whom was Brigham Young; a strong community of religious-secular concern; a dual secular and spiritual priesthood, and vigorous missionary activity. The headquarters of the church are located at Salt Lake City, Utah, where the Mormons first settled in 1847.

Mortification: Acts of self-discipline, including prayer, hardship, austerities and penances undertaken for the sake of progress in virtue.

Motu Proprio: A Latin phrase designating a document issued by a pope on his own initiative. Documents of this kind often concern administrative matters.

Mysteries of Faith: Supernatural truths whose existence cannot be known without revelation by God and whose intrinsic truth, while not contrary to reason, can never be wholly understood even after revelation. These mysteries are above reason, not against reason. Among them are the divine mysteries of the Trinity, Incarnation and Eucharist.

Some mysteries — e.g., concerning God's attributes — can be known by reason without revelation, although they cannot be fully understood.

N

Necromancy: Supposed communication with the dead; a form of divination.

Non-Expedit: A Latin expression. It is not expedient (fitting, proper), used to state a prohibition or refusal of permission.

Novena: A term designating public or private devotional practices over a period of nine consecutive days; or, by extension, over a period of nine weeks, in which one day a week is set aside for the devotions.

Novice: A person preparing, in a formal period of trial and formation called the *novitiate,* for membership in a religious institute. The novitiate lasts more than a year and ends with the profession of temporary vows or other temporary commitment to the religious life. Current norms require a total 12-month period of seclusion for novices; to this is added other periods of time spent in apostolic work for the sake of experience. A novice, while acquiring experience of the religious life, is not bound by the obligations of professed members of the institute, is free to leave at any time, and may be discharged at the discretion of competent superiors. The immediate superior of a novice is a master or mistress of novices.

Nun (1) Strictly, a member of a religious order of women with solemn vows (moniales).

(2) In general, all women religious, even those in simple vows who are more properly called sisters.

Nunc Dimittis: The canticle or hymn of Simeon when he saw Christ at the Temple on the occasion of his presentation (Lk. 2:29-32). It is an expression of joy and thanksgiving for the blessing of having lived to see the Messiah. It is one of the canticles prescribed in the Liturgy of the Hours.

O

Oath: Calling upon God to witness the truth of a statement. Violating an oath, e.g., by perjury in court, or taking an oath without sufficient reason, is a violation of the honor due to God.

Obedience: Submission to one in authority. General obligations of obedience fall under the Fourth Commandment. The vow of obedience professed by religious is one of the evangelical counsels.

Obsession, Diabolical: The extraordinary state of one who is seriously molested by evil spirits in an external manner. Obsession is more than just temptation.

Occultism: Practices involving ceremonies, rituals, chants, incantations, other cult-related activities intended to affect the course of nature, the lives of practitioners and others, through esoteric powers of magic, diabolical or other forces; one of many forms of superstition.

Octave: A period of eight days given over

to the celebration of a major feast such as Easter.

Oils, Holy: The oils consecrated by bishops on Holy Thursday or another suitable day, and by priests under certain conditions for use in certain sacraments and consecrations.

(1) The oil of catechumens (olive or vegetable oil), used at baptism and the ordination of priests.

(2) Chrism (olive or vegetable oil mixed with balm), used at baptism, in confirmation, at the ordination of a bishop, in the consecration of churches, altars, altarstones, chalices, patens, and in the blessing of bells.

(3) Oil of the sick (olive or vegetable oil) used in anointing the sick.

Old Catholics: Several sects, including (1) the Church of Utrecht which severed relations with Rome in 1724; (2) the National Polish Church in the US, which had its origin near the end of the 19th century; (3) the Yugoslav Old Catholic Church; (4) especially, a denomination founded by German priests and lay persons who broke away from union with Rome following the First Vatican Council in 1870. The doctrinal reason for the break was strong objection to the dogma of papal infallibility.

The formation of this Old Catholic Church began in 1870 at a public meeting held in Nuremberg under the leadership of A. Dollinger; four years later, episcopal succession was established with the valid consecration of a German bishop by a prelate of the Church of Utrecht. Old Catholics accept the first seven ecumenical councils and doctrine formulated before 1054, but reject communion with the pope and a number of Roman Catholic doctrines and practices. Since 1932, they have had full intercommunion with the Anglican Church. The Roman Church recognizes the validity of Old Catholic orders and other sacraments.

Oratory: A chapel.

Ordinariate: An ecclesiastical jurisdiction for special purposes and people. Examples are the military ordinariate of the US, for service personnel, and Eastern-Rite ordinariates in places where Eastern-Rite dioceses do not exist.

Ordinary: One who has the jurisdiction of an office: the pope, diocesan bishops, vicars general, prelates of missionary territories, vicars apostolic, prefects apostolic, vicars capitular during the vacancy of a see, superiors general, abbots primate and other major superiors of men religious.

Ordination: The consecration of sacred ministers for divine worship and the service of men in things pertaining to God. The power of ordination comes from Christ and the Church, and must be conferred by a minister capable of communicating it.

Organ Transplants: The transplanting of organs from one person to another is permissible for serious reasons provided it is done with the consent of the concerned parties and does not result in the death or essential mutilation of the donor. Advances in methods and technology have increased the range of transplant possibilities in recent years. Despite such progress, unresolved problems have slowed the pace of some transplant practice, especially with respect to the heart. The first successful heart transplant was performed Dec. 3, 1967, on Louis Washkansky, 56, by a team headed by Dr. Christian Barnard in Cape Town, South Africa.

Original Sin: The sin of Adam (Gn. 2:8—3:24), personal to him and passed on to all men as a state of privation of grace. Despite this privation and the related wounding of human nature and weakening of natural powers, original sin leaves unchanged all that man himself is by nature. The scriptural basis of the doctrine was stated especially by St. Paul in 1 Cor. 15:21, ff., and Romans 5:12-21. Original sin is remitted by baptism and incorporation in Christ, through whom grace is given to persons.

O Salutaris Hostia: The first three Latin words, O Saving Victim, of a Benediction hymn.

Oxford Movement: A movement in the Church of England from 1833 to about 1845 which had for its objective a threefold defense of the church as a divine institution, the apostolic succession of its bishops, and the Book of Common Prayer as the rule of faith. The movement took its name from Oxford University and involved a number of intellectuals who authored a series of influential *Tracts for Our Times.* Some of its leading figures — e.g., F. W. Faber, John Henry Newman and Henry Edward Manning — became converts to the Catholic Church. In the Church of England, the movement affected the liturgy, historical and theological scholarship, the status of the ministry, and other areas of ecclesiastical life.

P

Paganism: A term referring to non-revealed religions, i.e., religions other than Christianity, Judaism and Mohammedanism.

Palms: Blessed palms are a sacramental. They are blessed and distributed on the Sunday of the Passion in commemoration of the triumphant entrance of Christ into Jerusalem. Ashes of the burnt palms are used on Ash Wednesday.

Pange Lingua: First Latin words, Sing, my tongue, of a hymn in honor of the Holy Eucharist, used particularly on Holy Thursday and in Eucharistic processions.

Pantheism: Theory that all things are part of God, divine, in the sense that God realizes himself as the ultimate reality of matter or spirit through being and/or becoming all things that have been, are, and will be. The theory leads to hopeless confusion of the Creator and the created realm of being, identifies evil with good, and involves many inherent contradictions.

Papal Election: The Roman Pontiff is elected by the cardinals in secret conclave, being chosen by a two-thirds majority vote (if the number present and voting is exactly divisible by three) or by a two-thirds, plus one, majority (if the number is not exactly divisible by three). This procedure, a modification of former voting methods, was decreed by John XXIII in the apostolic letter *Summi Pontificis Electio*, Sept. 5, 1962.

The conclave, which is held in a sealed-off area of the Vatican Palace, may begin on the 15th day after the death of a pope and must begin no later than the 18th day. Cardinals under the age of 80 are eligible to attend and vote. "The number of cardinals entitled to participate must not exceed 120," Pope Paul VI decreed in an allocution Mar. 5, 1973.

Voting takes place in the Sistine Chapel where four secret ballots are cast each day, two in the morning and two in the afternoon. Voting continues until one of the candidates receives the required majority.

The candidate so elected is asked by the dean of the College of Cardinals whether he accepts the office of the papacy. He becomes pope immediately on giving an affirmative reply. The subsequent coronation is only a ceremonial recognition of the fact that he is the pope. In a ceremony called *adoratio,* the cardinals signify their obedience to the new pontiff in the Sistine Chapel before public announcement of his name is made from the main balcony of the Vatican. The fact of election is first signaled to the outside world by means of white smoke.

The pope is elected for life. If he should resign, which he may do, a new pope is elected. Any male Catholic may be elected, even one who is not a priest. If a layman were elected and accepted the office, he would be ordained as a priest and bishop. If a priest were chosen he would be ordained as a bishop.

Paraclete: A title of the Holy Spirit meaning, in Greek, Advocate, Consoler.

Parental Duties: All duties related to the obligation of parents to provide for the welfare of their children. These obligations fall under the Fourth Commandment.

Parish: A community of the faithful served by a pastor charged with responsibility for providing them with full pastoral service. Most parishes are territorial, embracing all of the faithful in a certain area of a diocese: some are personal or national, for certain classes of people, without strict regard for their places of residence.

Parousia: The coming, or saving presence, of Christ which will mark the completion of salvation history and the coming to perfection of God's kingdom at the end of the world.

Paschal Candle: A large candle, symbolic of the risen Christ, blessed and lighted on the Easter Vigil and placed at the Gospel side of the altar until Ascension Day. It is ornamented with five large grains of incense, representing the wounds of Christ, inserted in the form of a cross; the Greek letters Alpha and Omega, symbolizing Christ the beginning and end of all things, at the top and bottom of the shaft of the cross; and the figures of the current year of salvation in the quadrants formed by the cross.

Paschal Precept: The church law requiring the faithful to receive Holy Communion during the Easter time.

Passion of Christ: Sufferings of Christ, recorded in the four Gospels.

Pastor: An ordained minister charged with responsibility for the doctrinal, sacramental and related service of people committed to his care; e.g., a bishop for the people in his diocese, a priest for the people of his parish.

Pater Noster: The initial Latin words, Our Father, of the Lord's Prayer.

Peace, Sign of: A gesture of greeting — e.g., a handshake — exchanged by the ministers and participants at Mass.

Pectoral Cross: A cross worn on a chain about the neck and over the breast by bishops and abbots as a mark of their office.

Penance or Penitence: (1) The spiritual change or conversion of mind and heart by which a person turns away from sin, and all that it implies, toward God, through a personal renewal under the influence of the Holy Spirit. In the apostolic constitution *Paenitemini,* Pope Paul VI called it "a religious, personal act which has as its aim love and surrender to God." Penance involves sorrow and contrition for sin, together with other internal and external acts of atonement. It serves the purposes of reestablishing in one's life the order of God's love and commandments, and of making satisfaction to God for sin. A divine precept states the necessity of penance for salvation: "Unless you do penance, you shall all likewise perish" (Lk. 13:3) . . . "Be converted and believe in the Gospel" (Mk. 1:15).

In the penitential discipline of the Church, the various works of penance have been classified under the headings of prayer (interior), fasting and almsgiving (exterior). The Church has established minimum requirements for the common and social observance of the divine precept by Catholics — e.g., by requiring them to fast and/or abstain on certain days of the year. These observances, however, do not exhaust all the demands of the divine precept, whose fulfillment is a matter of personal responsibility; nor do they have any real value unless they proceed from the internal spirit and purpose of penance.

Related to works of penance for sins actually committed are works of mortification. The purpose of the latter is to develop — through prayer, fasting, renunciations and similar actions — self-control and detachment from things which could otherwise become occasions of sin.

(2) Penance is a virtue disposing a person to turn to God in sorrow for sin and to carry out works of amendment and atonement.

(3) The sacrament of penance and sacramental penance.

Perjury: Taking a false oath, lying under oath, a violation of the honor due to God.

Persecution, Religious: A campaign waged against a church or other religious body by persons and governments intent on its destruction. The best known campaigns of this type against the Christian Church were the Roman persecutions which occurred intermittently from about 54 to the promulgation of the Edict of Milan in 313. The most extensive persecutions took place during the reigns of Nero, the first major Roman persecutor, Domitian, Trajan, Marcus Aurelius, and Diocletian. Besides the Roman persecutions, the Catholic Church has been subject to many others, including those of the 20th century in Communist-controlled countries.

Peter's Pence: A collection made each year among Catholics for the maintenance of the pope and his works of charity. It was originally a tax of a penny on each house, and was collected on St. Peter's day, whence the name. It originated in England in the eighth century.

Petition: One of the four purposes of prayer. In prayers of petition, persons ask of God the blessings they and others need.

Pharisees: Influential class among the Jews, referred to in the Gospels, noted for their self-righteousness, legalism, strict interpretation of the Law, acceptance of the traditions of the elders as well as the Law of Moses, and beliefs regarding angels and spirits, the resurrection of the dead and judgment. Most of them were laymen, and they were closely allied with the Scribes; their opposite numbers were the Sadducees. The Pharisaic and rabbinical traditions had a lasting influence on Judaism following the destruction of Jerusalem in 70 A.D.

Pious Fund: Property and money originally accumulated by the Jesuits to finance their missionary work in Lower California. When the Jesuits were expelled from the territory in 1767, the fund was appropriated by the Spanish Crown and used to support Dominican and Franciscan missionary work in Upper and Lower California. In 1842 the Mexican government took over administration of the fund, incorporated most of the revenue into the national treasury, and agreed to pay the Church interest of six per cent a year on the capital so incorporated. From 1848 to 1967 the fund was the subject of lengthy negotiations between the US and Mexican governments because of the latter's failure to make payments as agreed. A lump-sum settlement was made in 1967 with payment by Mexico to the US government of more than $700,000, to

be turned over to the Archdiocese of San Francisco.

Polytheism: Belief in and worship of many gods or divinities, especially prevalent in pre-Christian religions.

Poor Box: Alms-box; found in churches from the earliest days of Christianity.

Pope Joan: Alleged name of a woman falsely said to have been pope from 855-858, the years of the reign of Benedict III. The myth was not heard of before the 13th century.

Portiuncula: (1) Meaning little portion (of land), the Portiuncula was the chapel of Our Lady of the Angels near Assisi, Italy, which the Benedictines gave to St. Francis early in the 13th century. He repaired the chapel and made it the first church of the Franciscan Order. It is now enshrined in the Basilica of St. Mary of the Angels in Assisi.

(2) The Portiuncula Indulgence, or Pardon of Assisi, was authorized by Honorius III. Originally, it could be gained for the souls in purgatory only in the chapel of Our Lady of the Angels; by later concessions, it could be gained also in other Franciscan and parish churches. According to legislation now in force, the Portiuncula Indulgence can be gained once on the day of Aug. 2, or on the following Sunday with permission of the bishop of the place. The conditions are, in addition to freedom from attachment to sin: reception of the sacraments of penance and the Eucharist on or near the day; a visit to a parish church on the day, during which the Our Father and Creed are offered for the intentions of the pope.

Possession, Diabolical: The extraordinary state of a person who is tormented from within by evil spirits who exercise strong influence over his powers of mind and body.

Postulant: One of several names used to designate a candidate for membership in a religious institute during the period before novitiate.

Poverty: (1) The quality or state of being poor, in actual destitution and need, or being poor in spirit. In the latter sense, poverty means the state of mind and disposition of persons who regard material things in proper perspective as gifts of God for the support of life and its reasonable enrichment, and for the service of others in need. It means freedom from unreasonable attachment to material things as ends in themselves, even though they may be possessed in small or large measure.

(2) One of the evangelical counsels professed by religious as a vow. It involves the voluntary renunciation of rights of ownership and of independent use and disposal of material goods (solemn vow); or, the right of independent use and disposal, but not of the radical right of ownership (simple vow). Religious institutes provide their members with necessary and useful goods and services from common resources. The manner in which goods

are received and/or handled by religious is determined by poverty of spirit and the rule and constitutions of their institute. Practice of the vow of poverty is undergoing some change in the contemporary renewal in religious life.

Pragmatism: Theory that the truth of ideas, concepts and values depends on their utility or capacity to serve a useful purpose rather than on their conformity with objective standards; also called utilitarianism.

Prayer: The raising of the mind and heart to God in adoration, thanksgiving, reparation and petition. Prayer, which is always mental because it involves thought and love of God, may be vocal, meditative, private and personal, social, and official. The official prayer of the Church as a worshipping community is called the liturgy.

Precepts: Commands or orders given to individuals or communities in particular cases; they establish law for concerned parties. Preceptive documents are issued by the pope, departments of the Roman Curia and other competent authority in the Church.

Presence of God: A devotional practice of increasing one's awareness of the presence and action of God in daily life.

Presumption: A violation of the theological virtue of hope, by which a person striving for salvation either relies too much on his own capabilities or expects God to do things which he cannot do, in keeping with his divine attributes, or does not will to do, according to his divine plan. Presumption is the opposite of despair.

Preternatural Gifts: Exceptional gifts, beyond the exigencies and powers of human nature, enjoyed by Adam in the state of original justice: immunity from suffering and death, superior knowledge, integrity or perfect control of the passions. These gifts were lost as the result of original sin; their loss, however, implied no impairment of the integrity of human nature.

Pride: Unreasonable self-esteem; one of the seven capital sins.

Prie-Dieu: A French phrase, meaning pray God, designating a kneeler or bench suitable for kneeling while at prayer.

Priesthood of the Laity: Lay persons share in the priesthood of Christ in virtue of the sacraments of baptism and confirmation. They are not only joined with Christ for a life of union with him but are also deputed by him for participation in his mission, now carried on by the Church, of worship, teaching, witness and apostolic works. St. Peter called Christians "a royal priesthood" (1 Pt. 2:9) in this connection. St. Thomas Aquinas declared: "The sacramental characters (of baptism and confirmation) are nothing else than certain sharings of the priesthood of Christ, derived from Christ himself."

The priesthood of the laity differs from the official ministerial priesthood of ordained priests and bishops — who have the power of holy orders for celebrating the Eucharist, administering the other sacraments, and providing pastoral care. The ministerial priesthood, by divine commission, serves the universal priesthood. (See Role of Sacraments.)

Primary Option: The life-choice of a person for or against God which shapes the basic orientation of moral conduct.

Prior: A superior or an assistant to an abbot in a monastery.

Privilege: A favor, an exemption from the obligation of a law. Privileges of various kinds, with respect to ecclesiastical laws, are granted by the pope, departments of the Roman Curia and other competent authority in the Church.

Probabilism: A moral system for use in cases of conscience which involve the obligation of doubtful laws. There is a general principle that a doubtful law does not bind. Probabilism, therefore, teaches that it is permissible to follow an opinion favoring liberty, provided the opinion is certainly and solidly probable. Probabilism may not be invoked when there is question of: a certain law or the certain obligation of a law; the certain right of another party; the validity of an action; something which is necessary for salvation.

Pro-Cathedral: A church used as a cathedral.

Promoter of the Faith: An official of the Congregation for the Causes of Saints, whose role in beatification and canonization procedures is to establish beyond reasonable doubt the validity of evidence regarding the holiness of prospective saints and miracles attributed to their intercession.

Prophecies of St. Malachy: These so-called prophecies, listing the designations of 102 popes and 10 antipopes, bear the name they have because they have been falsely attributed to St. Malachy, bishop of Armagh, who died in 1148. Actually, they are forgeries by an unknown author and came to light only in the last decade of the 16th century.

The first 75 prophecies cover the 65 popes and 10 antipopes from Celestine II (1143-1144) to Gregory XIV (1590-91), and are exact with respect to names, coats of arms, birthplaces, and other identifying characteristics. This portion of the work, far from being prophetic, is the result of historical knowledge or hindsight. The 37 designations following that of Gregory are vague, fanciful, and subject to wide interpretation. According to the prophecies, Paul VI, the Flower of Flowers, will have only four successors before the end of the world.

Prophecy: (1) The communication of divine revelation by inspired intermediaries, called prophets, between God and his people. Old Testament prophecy was unique in its origin and because of its ethical and religious content, which included disclosure of the saving will of Yahweh for the people, moral censures and warnings of divine punishment because of sin and violations of the Law and Covenant, in the form of promises, admonitions, reproaches and threats. Although Moses and other earlier figures are called prophets, the period of prophecy is generally dated from the early years of the monarchy to about 100 years after the Babylonian Exile. From that time on the written Law and its interpreters supplanted the prophets as guides of the people. Old Testament prophets are cited in the New Testament, with awareness that God spoke through them and that some of their oracles were fulfilled in Christ. John the Baptist is the outstanding prophetic figure in the New Testament. Christ never claimed the title of prophet for himself, although some people thought he was one. There were prophets in the early Church, and St. Paul mentioned the charism of prophecy in 1 Cor. 14:1-5. Prophecy disappeared after New Testament times. Revelation is classified as the prophetic book of the New Testament.

(2) In contemporary non-scriptural usage, the term is applied to the witness given by persons to the relevance of their beliefs in everyday life and action.

Province: (1) A territory comprising one archdiocese called the metropolitan see and one or more dioceses called suffragan sees. The head of the archdiocese, an archbishop, has metropolitan rights and responsibilities over the province.

(2) A division of a religious order under the jurisdiction of a provincial superior.

Prudence: Practical wisdom and judgment regarding the choice and use of the best ways and means of doing good; one of the four cardinal virtues.

Punishment Due for Sin: The punishment which is a consequence of sin. It is of two kinds:

(1) Eternal punishment is the punishment of hell, to which one becomes subject by the commission of mortal sin. Such punishment is remitted when mortal sin is forgiven.

(2) Temporal punishment is a consequence of venial sin and/or forgiven mortal sin; it is not everlasting and may be remitted in this life by means of penance. Temporal punishment unremitted during this life is remitted by suffering in purgatory.

Purgatory: The state or condition in which those who have died in the state of grace, but with some attachment to sin, suffer for a time before they are admitted to the glory and happiness of heaven. In this state and period of passive suffering, they are purified of unrepented venial sins, satisfy the demands of divine justice for temporal punishment due for sins, and are thus converted to a state of worthiness of the beatific vision.

R

Racism: A theory which holds that any one or several of the different races of the human family are inherently superior or inferior to any one or several of the others. The teaching denies the essential unity of the human race, the equality and dignity of all men because of their common possession of the same human nature, and the participation of all men in the divine plan of redemption. It is radically opposed to the virtue of justice and the precept of love of neighbor. Differences of superiority and inferiority which do exist are the result of accidental factors operating in a wide variety of circumstances, and are in no way due to essential defects in any one or several of the branches of the one human race. The theory of racism, together with practices related to it, is incompatible with Christian doctrine.

Rash Judgment: Attributing faults to another without sufficient reason; a violation of the obligations of justice and charity.

Rationalism: A theory which makes the mind the measure and arbiter of all things, including religious truth. A product of the Enlightenment, it rejects the supernatural, divine revelation, and authoritative teaching by any church.

Recollection: Meditation, attitude of concentration or awareness of spiritual matters and things pertaining to salvation and the accomplishment of God's will.

Relativism: Theory which holds that all truth, including religious truth, is relative, i.e., not absolute, certain or unchanging; a product of agnosticism, indifferentism, and an unwarranted extension of the notion of truth in positive science. Relativism is based on the tenet that certain knowledge of any and all truth is impossible. Therefore, no religion, philosophy or science can be said to possess the real truth; consequently, all religions, philosophies and sciences may be considered to have as much or as little of truth as any of the others.

Relics: The physical remains and effects of saints, which are considered worthy of veneration inasmuch as they are representative of persons in glory with God. First class relics are parts of the bodies of saints, and instruments of their penance and death; second class relics are objects which had some contact with their persons. Catholic doctrine proscribes the view that relics are not worthy of veneration. In line with norms laid down by the Council of Trent and subsequent enactments, discipline concerning relics is subject to control by the Congregation for the Causes of Saints.

Religion: The adoration and service of God as expressed in divine worship and in daily life. Religion is concerned with all of the relations existing between God and man, and between man and man because of the central significance of God. Objectively considered, religion consists of a body of truth which is believed, a code of morality for the guidance of conduct, and a form of divine worship. Subjectively, it is man's total response, theoretically and practically, to the demands of faith; it is living faith, personal engagement, self-commitment to God. Thus, by creed, code and cult, a person orders and directs his life in reference to God and, through what the love and service of God implies, to his fellow men and all things.

Reliquary: A vessel for the preservation and exposition of a relic; sometimes made like a small monstrance.

Reparation: The making of amends to God for sin committed; one of the four ends of prayer and the purpose of penance.

Rescript: A written reply by an ecclesiastical superior regarding a question or request; its provisions bind concerned parties only. Papal dispensations are issued in the form of rescripts.

Reserved Case: A sin or censure, absolution from which is reserved to religious superiors, bishops, the pope, or confessors having special faculties. Reservations are made because of the serious nature and social effects of certain sins and censures.

Restitution: An act of reparation for an injury done to another. The injury may be caused by taking and/or retaining what belongs to another or by damaging either the property or reputation of another. The intention of making restitution, usually in kind, is required as a condition for the forgiveness of sins of injustice, even though actual restitution is not possible.

Ring: In the Church a ring is worn as part of the insignia of bishops, abbots, et al.; by sisters to denote their consecration to God and the Church. The wedding ring symbolizes the love and union of husband and wife.

Ritual: A book of prayers and ceremonies used in the administration of the sacraments and other ceremonial functions. In the Roman Rite, the standard book of this kind is the Roman Ritual. Revisions have been made — e.g., in the rites of baptism — since the Second Vatican Council.

Rogito: The official notarial act or document testifying to the burial of a pope.

Rosary: A form of mental and vocal prayer centered on mysteries or events in the lives of Jesus and Mary. Its essential elements are meditation on the mysteries and the recitation of a number of decades of Hail Marys, each beginning with the Lord's Prayer. Introductory prayers may include the Apostles' Creed, an initial Our Father, three Hail Marys and a Glory be to the Father; each decade is customarily concluded with a Glory be to the Father; at the end, it is customary to say the Hail, Holy Queen and a prayer from the liturgy for the feast of the Blessed Virgin Mary of the Rosary.

The **Mysteries of the Rosary,** which are the subject of meditation, are: (1) Joyful — the Annunciation to Mary that she was to be the Mother of Christ, her visit to Elizabeth, the birth of Jesus, the presentation of Jesus in the Temple, the finding of Jesus in the Temple.

(2) Sorrowful — Christ's agony in the Garden of Gethsemani, scourging at the pillar, crowning with thorns, carrying of the Cross to Calvary, and crucifixion. (3) Glorious — the Resurrection and Ascension of Christ, the descent of the Holy Spirit upon the Apostles, Mary's Assumption into heaven and her crowning as Queen of angels and men.

The complete Rosary, called the Dominican Rosary, consists of 15 decades. In customary practice, only five decades are usually said at one time. Rosary beads are used to aid in counting the prayers without distraction.

The Rosary originated through the coalescence of popular devotions to Jesus and Mary from the 12th century onward. Its present form dates from about the 15th century. Carthusians contributed greatly toward its development; Dominicans have been its greatest promoters.

S

Sabbath: The seventh day of the week, observed by Jews and Sabbatarians as the day for rest and religious observance.

Sacramentary: One of the first liturgical books, containing the celebrant's part of the Mass and rites for administration of the sacraments. The earliest book of this kind, the Leonine Sacramentary, dates from the middle or end of the sixth century.

The sacramentary, incorporating most of the contents of the *Roman Missal,* was reintroduced in the Roman Rite following the promulgation of the *Constitution on the Sacred Liturgy* by the Second Vatican Council.

Sacrarium: A basin with a drain leading directly into the ground; standard equipment of a sacristy.

Sacred Heart, Enthronement: An acknowledgment of the sovereignty of Jesus Christ over the Christian family, expressed by the installation of an image or picture of the Sacred Heart in a place of honor in the home, accompanied by an act of consecration.

Sacred Heart, Promises: Twelve promises to persons having devotion to the Sacred Heart of Jesus, which were communicated by Christ to St. Margaret Mary Alacoque in a private revelation in 1675: (1) I will give them all the graces necessary in their state in life. (2) I will establish peace in their homes. (3) I will comfort them in all their afflictions. (4) I will be their secure refuge during life and, above all, in death. (5) I will bestow abundant blessing upon all their undertakings. (6) Sinners shall find in my Heart the source and the infinite ocean of mercy. (7) By devotion to my Heart tepid souls shall grow fervent. (8) Fervent souls shall quickly mount to high perfection. (9) I will bless every place where a picture of my Heart shall be set up and honored. (10) I will give to priests the gift of touching the most hardened hearts. (11) Those who promote this devotion shall have their names written in my Heart, never to be blotted out. (12) I will grant the grace of final penitence to those who communicate (receive Holy Communion) on the first Friday of nine consecutive months.

Sacrilege: Violation of and irreverence toward a person, place or thing that is sacred because of public dedication to God; a sin against the virtue of religion. Personal sacrilege is violence of some kind against a cleric or religious, or a violation of chastity with a cleric or religious. Local sacrilege is the desecration of sacred places. Real sacrilege is irreverence with respect to sacred things, such as the sacraments and sacred vessels.

Sacristy: A utility room where vestments, church furnishings and sacred vessels are kept and where the clergy vest for sacred functions.

Sadducees: The predominantly priestly party among the Jews in the time of Christ, noted for extreme conservatism, acceptance only of the Law of Moses, and rejection of the traditions of the elders. Their opposite numbers were the Pharisees.

Saints, Cult of: The veneration, called dulia, of holy persons who have died and are in glory with God in heaven; it includes honoring them and petitioning them for their intercession with God. Liturgical veneration is given only to saints officially recognized by the Church; private veneration may be given to anyone thought to be in heaven. The veneration of saints is essentially different from the adoration given to God alone; by its very nature, however, it terminates in the worship of God.

According to the Second Vatican Council's *Dogmatic Constitution on the Church* (No. 50): "It is supremely fitting . . . that we love those friends and fellow heirs of Jesus Christ, who are also our brothers and extraordinary benefactors, that we render due thanks to God for them and 'suppliantly invoke them and have recourse to their prayers, their power and help in obtaining benefits from God through His Son, Jesus Christ, our Lord, who is our sole Redeemer and Savior.' For by its very nature every genuine testimony of love which we show to those in heaven tends toward and terminates in Christ, who is the 'crown of all saints.' Through Him it tends toward and terminates in God, who is wonderful in His saints and is magnified in them."

Salvation: The liberation of men from sin and its effects, reconciliation with God in and through Christ, the attainment of union with God forever in the glory of heaven as the supreme purpose of life and as the God-given reward for fulfillment of his will on earth. Salvation-in-process begins and continues in this life through union with Christ in faith professed and in action; its final term is union with God and the whole community of the saved in the ultimate perfection of God's kingdom. The Church teaches that: God wills

the salvation of all men; men are saved in and through Christ; membership in the Church established by Christ, known and understood as the community of salvation, is necessary for salvation; men with this knowledge and understanding who deliberately reject this Church, cannot be saved. In the context of Catholic belief, the Catholic Church is the Church founded by Christ. (See below, Salvation outside the Church.)

Salvation History: The facts and the record of God's relations with men, in the past, present and future, for the purpose of leading them to live in accordance with his will for the eventual attainment after death of salvation, or everlasting happiness with him in heaven.

The essentials of salvation history are: God's love for all men and will for their salvation; his intervention and action in the world to express this love and bring about their salvation; the revelation he made of himself and the covenant he established with the Israelites in the Old Testament; the perfecting of this revelation and the new covenant of grace through Christ in the New Testament; the continuing action-for-salvation carried on in and through the Mystical Body of Christ, the Church; the communication of saving grace to men through the merits of Christ and the operations of the Holy Spirit in the here-and-now circumstances of daily life and with the cooperation of men themselves.

Salvation outside the Church: The Second Vatican Council covered this subject summarily in the following manner: "Those also can attain to everlasting salvation who through no fault of their own do not know the gospel of Christ or His Church, yet sincerely seek God and, moved by grace, strive by their deeds to do His will as it is known to them through the dictates of conscience. Nor does divine Providence deny the help necessary for salvation to those who, without blame on their part, have not yet arrived at an explicit knowledge of God, but who strive to live a good life, thanks to His grace. Whatever good or truth is found among them is looked upon by the Church as a preparation for the gospel. She regards such qualities as given by Him who enlightens all men so that they may finally have life" *(Dogmatic Constitution on the Church,* No. 16).

Satanism: Worship of the devil, a blasphemous inversion of the order of worship which is due to God alone.

Scandal: Conduct which is the occasion of sin to another person.

Scapular: (1) A part of the habit of some religious orders like the Benedictines and Dominicans; a nearly shoulder-wide strip of cloth worn over the tunic and reaching almost to the feet in front and behind. Originally a kind of apron, it came to symbolize the cross and yoke of Christ.

(2) Scapulars worn by lay persons as a sign of association with religious orders and for

devotional purposes are an adaptation of monastic scapulars. Approved by the Church as sacramentals, they consist of two small squares of woolen cloth joined by strings and are worn about the neck. They are given for wearing in a ceremony of investiture or enrollment. There are nearly 20 scapulars for devotional use: the five principal ones are generally understood to include those of Our Lady of Mt. Carmel (the brown Carmelite Scapular), the Holy Trinity, Our Lady of the Seven Dolors, the Passion, the Immaculate Conception.

Scapular Medal: A medallion with a representation of the Sacred Heart on one side and of the Blessed Virgin Mary on the other. Authorized by St. Pius X in 1910, it may be worn or carried in place of a scapular by persons already invested with a scapular.

Scapular Promise: According to a legend of the Carmelite Order, the Blessed Virgin Mary appeared to St. Simon Stock in 1251 at Cambridge and declared that wearers of the brown Carmelite Scapular would be saved from hell and taken to heaven by her on the first Saturday after death. The validity of the legend has never been the subject of official decision by the Church. Essentially, it expresses belief in the intercession of Mary and the efficacy of sacramentals in the context of truly Christian life.

Schism: Derived from a Greek word meaning separation, the term designates formal and obstinate refusal by a baptized person, called a *schismatic*, to be in communion with the pope and the Church. The canonical penalty is excommunication. One of the most disastrous schisms in history resulted in the definitive separation of the Church in the East from union with Rome about 1054.

Scholasticism: The term usually applied to the Catholic theology and philosophy which developed in the Middle Ages.

Scribes: Hebrew intellectuals noted for their knowledge of the Law of Moses, influential from the time of the Exile to about 70 A.D. Many of them were Pharisees. They were the antecedents of rabbis and their traditions, as well as those of the Pharisees, had a lasting influence on Judaism following the destruction of Jerusalem in 70 A.D.

Scruple: A morbid, unreasonable fear and anxiety that one's actions are sinful when they are not, or more seriously sinful than they actually are. Compulsive scrupulosity is quite different from the transient scrupulosity of persons of tender or highly sensitive conscience, or of persons with faulty moral judgment.

Seal of Confession: The obligation of secrecy which must be observed regarding knowledge of things learned in connection with the confession of sin in the sacrament of penance. The seal covers matters whose revelation would make the sacrament burdensome. Confessors are prohibited, under penalty of excommunication, from making any direct revelation of confessional matter; this prohibition holds, outside of confession, even with respect to the person who made the confession unless the person releases the priest from the obligation. Persons other than confessors are obliged to maintain secrecy, but not under penalty of excommunication. General, non-specific discussion of confessional matter does not violate the seal.

Secularism: A school of thought, a spirit and manner of action which ignores and/or repudiates the validity or influence of supernatural religion with respect to individual and social life. In describing secularism in their annual statement in 1947, the bishops of the United States said in part: " . . . There are many men — and their number is daily increasing — who in practice live their lives without recognizing that this is God's world. For the most part they do not deny God. On formal occasions they may even mention his name. Not all of them would subscribe to the statement that all moral values derive from merely human conventions. But they fail to bring an awareness of their responsibility to God into their thought and action as individuals and members of society. This, in essence, is what we mean by secularism."

See: Another name for diocese or archdiocese.

Seminary: A house of study and formation for men, called seminarians, preparing for the priesthood. Traditional seminaries date from the Council of Trent in the middle of the 16th century; before that time, candidates for the priesthood were variously trained in monastic schools, universities under church auspices, and in less formal ways. At the present time, seminaries are undergoing considerable change for the improvement of academic and formation programs and procedures.

Sermon on the Mount: A compilation of sayings of Our Lord in the form of an extended discourse in Matthew's Gospel (5:1 to 7:27) and, in a shorter discourse, in Luke (6:17-49). The passage in Matthew, called the "Constitution of the New Law," summarizes the living spirit of believers in Christ and members of the kingdom of God. Beginning with the Beatitudes and including the Lord's Prayer, it covers the perfect justice of the New Law, the fulfillment of the Old Law in the New Law of Christ, and the integrity of internal attitude and external conduct with respect to love of God and neighbor, justice, chastity, truth, trust and confidence in God.

Servile Work: Work that is mainly physical and done for the sake of material purposes, in distinction from so-called liberal and artistic work which, although involving physical effort, is of a mental and intellectual nature. Commonly classified as servile are such works as farming, manufacturing, commercial operations, mining, etc. Liberal works are those like studying, teaching, designing, writing, typing, etc. The classification of work as servile or otherwise depends in part on custom and cultural interpretation. The reception of pay for work has nothing to do with its classification. Servile work is prohibited on Sundays and holy days of obligation unless there is sound reason for it.

Seven Last Words of Christ: Words of Christ on the Cross. (1) "Father, forgive them; for they do not know what they are doing." (2) To the penitent thief: "I assure you: today you will be with me in Paradise." (3) To Mary and his Apostle John: "Woman, there is your son . . . There is your mother." (4) "My God, my God, why have you forsaken me?" (5) "I am thirsty." (6) "Now it is finished." (7) "Father, into your hands I commend my spirit."

Shrine, Crowned: A shrine approved by the Holy See as a place of pilgrimage. The approval permits public devotion at the shrine and implies that at least one miracle has resulted from devotion at the shrine. Among the best known crowned shrines are those of the Virgin Mary at Lourdes and Fatima.

Shroud of Turin: A strip of brownish linen cloth, 14 feet, three inches in length and three feet, seven inches in width, bearing the front and back imprint of a human body. A tradition dating from the seventh century, which has not been verified beyond doubt, claims that the shroud is the fine linen in which the body of Christ was wrapped for burial. The early history of the shroud is obscure. It was enshrined at Lirey, France, in 1354 and was transferred in 1578 to Turin, Italy, where it has been kept in the cathedral down to the present time. Scientific investigation, which began in 1898, seems to indicate that the markings on the shroud are those of a human body.

Sick Calls: When a person is confined at home by illness or other cause and is unable to go to church for reception of the sacraments, a parish priest should be informed and arrangements made for him to visit the person at home. Such visitations are common in pastoral practice, both for special needs and for providing persons with regular opportunities for receiving the sacraments.

Prepared for the visit should be: a conveniently placed table covered with a white cloth; on it should be a crucifix, two lighted candles, a glass with water, a spoon and napkin.

The priest, carrying the Blessed Sacrament, should be escorted to and from the sick person by someone carrying a lighted candle. Members of the household should be present when the sick person receives Holy Communion and/or anointing of the sick.

Sign of the Cross: A sign, ceremonial gesture or movement in the form of a cross by which a person confesses faith in the Holy Trinity and Christ, and intercedes for the blessing of himself, other persons, and things. In Roman-Rite practice, a person making the sign touches the fingers of the right hand to his forehead, below the breast, left shoulder and right shoulder while saying: "In the name of the Father, and of the Son, and of the Holy Spirit." The sign is also made with the thumb on the forehead, the lips, and the breast. For the blessing of persons and objects, a large sign of the cross is made by movement of the right hand. In Eastern-Rite practice, the sign is made with the thumb and first two fingers of the right hand joined together and touching the forehead, below the breast, the right shoulder and the left shoulder; the formula generally used is the doxology, "O Holy God, O Holy Strong One, O Immortal One." The Eastern manner of making the sign was general until the first half of the 13th century; by the 17th century, Western practice involved the whole right hand and the reversal of direction from shoulder to shoulder.

Signs of the Times: Contemporary events, trends and features in culture and society, the needs and aspirations of people, all the factors that form the context in and through which the Church has to carry on its saving mission. The Second Vatican Council spoke on numerous occasions about these signs and the relationship between them and a kind of manifestation of God's will, positive or negative, and about subjecting them to judgment and action corresponding to the demands of divine revelation through Scripture, Christ, and the experience, tradition and teaching authority of the Church.

Simony: The deliberate intention and act of selling and/or buying spiritual goods or material things so connected with the spiritual that they cannot be separated therefrom; a violation of the virtue of religion, and a sacrilege, because it wrongfully puts a material price on spiritual things, which cannot be either sold or bought. In church law, actual sale or purchase is subject to censure in some cases. The term is derived from the name of Simon Magus, who attempted to buy from Sts. Peter and John the power to confirm people in the Holy Spirit (Acts 8:4-24).

Sin: (1) Actual sin is rejection of God manifested by free and deliberate violation of his law by thought, word or action. (a) Mortal sin — involving serious matter, sufficient reflection and full consent — results in total alienation from God, making a person dead to sanctifying grace, incapable of performing meritorious supernatural acts and subject to everlasting punishment. (b) Venial sin — involving less serious matter, reflection and consent — does not have such serious consequences.

(2) Original sin is the sin of Adam, with consequences for all men. (See separate entries.)

Sins against the Holy Spirit: Despair of salvation, presumption of God's mercy, impugning the known truths of faith, envy at another's spiritual good, obstinacy in sin, final impenitence. Those guilty of such sins stubbornly resist the influence of grace and, as long as they do so, cannot be forgiven.

Sins, Occasions of: Circumstances (persons, places, things, etc.) which easily lead to sin. There is an obligation to avoid voluntary proximate occasions of sin, and to take precautions against the dangers of unavoidable occasions.

Sins That Cry to Heaven for Vengeance: Willful murder, sins against nature, oppression of the poor, widows and orphans, defrauding laborers of their wages.

Sister: Any woman religious, in popular speech; strictly, the title applies only to women religious belonging to institutes whose members never professed solemn vows. Most of the institutes whose members are properly called sisters were established during and since the 19th century. Women religious with solemn vows, or belonging to institutes whose members formerly professed solemn vows, are properly called nuns.

Sisterhood: A generic term referring to the whole institution of the life of women religious in the Church, or to a particular institute of women religious.

Situation Ethics: A subjective, individualistic ethical theory which denies the binding force of ethical principles as universal laws and preceptive norms of moral conduct, and proposes that morality is determined only by situational conditions and considerations and the intention of the person. In an instruction issued on the subject in May, 1956, the Congregation for the Holy Office said:

"It ignores the principles of objective ethics. This 'New Morality,' it is claimed, is not only the equal of objective morality, but is superior to it.

"The authors who follow this system state that the ultimate determining norm for activity is not the objective order as determined by the natural law and known with certainty from this law. It is instead some internal judgment and illumination of the mind of every individual by which the mind comes to know what is to be done in a concrete situation.

"This ultimate decision of man is, therefore, not the application of the objective law to a particular case after the particular circumstances of a 'situation' have been considered and weighed according to the rules of prudence, as the more important authors of objective ethics teach; but it is, according to them, immediate, internal illumination and judgment.

"With regard to its objective truth and correctness, this judgment, at least in many things, is not ultimately measured, is not to be measured or is not measurable by any objective norm found outside man and independent of his subjective persuasion, but it is fully sufficient in itself. . . .

"Much that is stated in this system of 'Situation Ethics' is contrary to the truth of reality and to the dictate of sound reason. It gives evidence of relativism and modernism, and deviates far from the Catholic teaching handed down through the ages."

Slander: Attributing to a person faults which he does not have; a violation of the obligations of justice and charity, for which restitution is due.

Sloth: One of the seven capital sins; spiritual laziness, involving distaste and disgust for spiritual things; spiritual boredom, which saps the vigor of spiritual life. Physical laziness is a counterpart of spiritual sloth.

Sorcery: A kind of black magic in which evil is invoked by means of diabolical intervention; a violation of the virtue of religion.

Soteriology: The division of theology which treats of the mission and work of Christ as Redeemer.

Species, Sacred: The appearances of bread and wine (color, taste, smell, etc.) which remain after the substance has been changed at the Consecration of the Mass into the Body and Blood of Christ. (See Transubstantiation.)

Spiritism: Attempts to communicate with spirits and departed souls by means of seances, table tapping, ouija boards, and other methods; a violation of the virtue of religion. Spiritualistic practices are noted for fakery.

Spiritual Works of Mercy: Works of spiritual assistance, motivated by love of God and neighbor, to persons in need: counseling the doubtful, instructing the ignorant, admonishing sinners, comforting the afflicted, forgiving offenses, bearing wrongs patiently, praying for the living and the dead.

Stational Churches, Days: Churches, especially in Rome, where the clergy and lay people were accustomed to gather with their bishop on certain days for the celebration of the liturgy. The 25 early titular or parish churches of Rome, plus other churches, each had their turn as the site of divine worship in practices which may have started in the third century. The observances were rather well developed toward the latter part of the fourth century, and by the fifth they included a Mass concelebrated by the pope and attendant priests. On some occasions, the stational liturgy was preceded by a procession from another church called a collecta. There were 42 Roman stational churches in the eighth century, and 89 stational services were scheduled annually in connection with the liturgical seasons. Stational observances fell into disuse toward the end of the Middle Ages. Some revival was begun by John XXIII in 1959 and continued by Paul VI.

Stations of the Cross: A series of meditations on the sufferings of Christ: his condemnation to death and taking up of the Cross; the first fall on the way to Calvary; meeting his Mother; being assisted by Simon of Cyrene, and by Veronica who wiped his face;

the second fall; meeting the women of Jerusalem; the third fall; being stripped and nailed to the Cross; his death; the removal of his body from the Cross and his burial. Depictions of these scenes are mounted in most churches, chapels and in some other places, beneath small crosses.

A person making the Way of the Cross passes before these Stations, or stopping points, pausing at each for meditation. If the Stations are made by a group of people, only the leader has to pass from Station to Station. Prayer for the intentions of the pope is required for gaining the indulgence granted for the Stations.

Those unable to make the Stations in the ordinary manner, because they are impeded from visiting a church or other place where the Stations are, can still practice the devotion by meditating on the sufferings of Christ; praying the Our Father, Hail Mary and Glory for each Station and five times in commemoration of the wounds of Christ; and praying for the intentions of the pope. This practice has involved the use of a Stations Crucifix.

A recent development in this devotion is toward greater awareness of the relation of the Passion to the Resurrection-Ascension; this trend, in some circles, has led to the erection of a 15th—unofficial—station. The concept amounts to an extension of the whole customary thrust of the devotion.

The Stations originated, remotely, from the practice of Holy Land pilgrims who visited the actual scenes of incidents in the Passion of Christ. Representations elsewhere of at least some of these scenes were known as early as the fifth century. Later, the Stations evolved in connection with and as a consequence of strong devotion to the Passion in the 12th and 13th centuries. Franciscans, who were given custody of the Holy Places in 1342, promoted the devotion widely; one of them, St. Leonard of Port Maurice, became known as the greatest preacher of the Way of the Cross in the 18th century. The general features of the devotion were fixed by Clement XII in 1731.

Statutes: Virtually the same as decrees (see separate entry), they almost always designate laws of a particular council or synod rather than pontifical laws.

Stigmata: Marks of the wounds suffered by Christ in his crucifixion, in hands and feet by nails, and side by the piercing of a lance. Some persons, called stigmatists, have been reported as recipients or sufferers of marks like these. The Church, however, has never issued any infallible declaration about their possession by anyone, even in the case of St. Francis of Assisi whose stigmata seem to be the best substantiated and may be commemorated in the Roman-Rite liturgy. Ninety percent of some 300 reputed stigmatists have been women. Judgment regarding the presence, significance, and manner of causation of stigmata would depend, among other things, on irrefutable experimental evidence.

Stipend, Mass: An offering given to a priest for applying the fruits of the Mass according to the intention of the donor. The offering is a contribution to the support of the priest. The disposition of the fruits of the sacrifice, in line with doctrine concerning the Mass in particular and prayer in general, is subject to the will of God. In the early Christian centuries, when Mass was not offered for the intentions of particular persons, the participants made offerings of bread and wine for the sacrifice and their own Holy Communion, and of other things useful for the support of the clergy and the poor. Some offerings may have been made as early as the fourth century for the celebration of Mass for particular intentions, and there are indications of the existence of this practice from the sixth century when private Masses began to be offered. The earliest certain proof of stipend practice, however, dates from the eighth century. By the 11th century, along with private Mass, it was established custom.

Stole Fee: An offering given on certain occasions; e.g., at a baptism, wedding, funeral, for the support of the clergy who administer the sacraments and perform other sacred rites.

Stoup: A vessel used to contain holy water.

Suffragan See: Any diocese, except the archdiocese, within a province.

Suicide: The taking of one's own life; a violation of God's dominion over human life. Ecclesiastical burial is denied to persons who deliberately commit suicide while in full possession of their faculties; it is permitted in cases of doubt.

Supererogation: Good and virtuous actions which go beyond the obligations of duty and the requirements enjoined by God's law as necessary for salvation. Examples of these works are the profession and observance of the evangelical counsels of poverty, chastity, and obedience, and efforts to practice charity to the highest degree.

Supernatural: Above the natural; that which exceeds and is not due or owed to the essence, exigencies, requirements, powers and merits of created nature. While man has no claim on supernatural things and does not need them in order to exist and act on a natural level, he does need them in order to exist and act in the higher order or economy of grace established by God for his salvation.

God has freely given to man certain things which are beyond the powers and rights of his human nature. Examples of the supernatural are: grace, a kind of participation by man in the divine life, by which man becomes capable of performing acts meritorious for salvation; divine revelation by which God manifests himself to man and makes known truth that is inaccessible to human reason alone; faith, by which man believes divine truth because of the authority of God who reveals it through Sacred Scripture and tradition and the teaching of his Church.

Superstition: A violation of the virtue of religion, by which God is worshipped in an unworthy manner or creatures are given honor which belongs to God alone. False, vain, or futile worship involves elements which are incompatible with the honor and respect due to God, such as error, deception, and bizarre practices. Examples are: false and exaggerated devotions, chain prayers and allegedly unfailing prayers, the mixing of unbecoming practices in worship. The second kind of superstition attributes to persons and things powers and honor which belong to God alone. Examples are: idolatry, divination, magic, spiritism, necromancy.

Suspension: A penalty by which a cleric is forbidden to exercise some or all of his powers of orders and jurisdiction, or to accept the financial support of his benefices.

Swearing: Taking an oath; calling upon God to witness the truth of a statement; a legitimate thing to do for serious reasons and under proper circumstances, as in a court of law. To swear without sufficient reason is to dishonor God's name; to swear falsely in a court of law is perjury.

Swedenborgianism: A doctrine developed in and from the writings of Emmanuel Swedenborg (1688-1772), who claimed that during a number of visions he had in 1745 Christ taught him the spiritual sense of Sacred Scripture and commissioned him to communicate it to others. He held that, just as Christianity succeeded Judaism, so his teaching supplemented Christianity. He rejected belief in the Trinity, original sin, the Resurrection, and all the sacraments except baptism and the Eucharist. His followers are members of the Church of the New Jerusalem or of the New Church.

Syllabus, The: (1) When not qualified, the term refers to the list of 80 errors accompanying Pope Pius IX's encyclical *Quanta Cura,* issued in 1864.

(2) The *Syllabus* of St. Pius X in the decree *Lamentabili,* issued by the Holy Office July 4, 1907, condemning 65 heretical propositions of modernism. This schedule of errors was followed shortly by that pope's encyclical *Pascendi,* the principal ecclesiastical document against modernism, issued Sept. 8, 1907.

Synod, Diocesan: Meeting of representative persons of a diocese — priests, religious, lay persons — with the bishop, called by him for the purpose of considering and taking action on matters affecting the life and mission of the Church in the diocese. Persons taking part in a synod have consultative status; the bishop alone is the legislator, with power to authorize synodal decrees. According to canon law, every diocese should have a synod every 10 years.

T

Te Deum: The opening Latin words, Thee, God, of a hymn of praise and thanksgiving prescribed for use in the Office of Readings (Matins of the Liturgy of the Hours) on many Sundays, solemnities and feasts.

Temperance: Moderation, one of the four cardinal virtues.

Temptation: Any enticement to sin, from any source: the strivings of one's own faculties, the action of the devil, other persons, circumstances of life, etc. Temptation itself is not sin. Temptation can be avoided and overcome with the use of prudence and the help of grace.

Thanksgiving: An expression of gratitude to God for his goodness and the blessings he grants; one of the four ends of prayer.

Theism: A philosophy which admits the existence of God and the possibility of divine revelation; it is generally monotheistic and acknowledges God as transcendent and also active in the world. Because it is a philosophy rather than a system of theology derived from revelation, it does not include specifically Christian doctrines, like those concerning the Trinity, the Incarnation and Redemption.

Theological Virtues: The virtues which have God for their direct object: faith, or belief in God's infallible teaching; hope, or confidence in divine assistance; charity, or love of God. They are given to a person with grace in the first instance, through baptism and incorporation in Christ.

Theology: Knowledge of God and religion, deriving from and based on the data of divine Revelation, organized and systematized according to some kind of scientific method. It involves systematic study and presentation of the truths of divine Revelation in Sacred Scripture, tradition, and the teaching of the Church.

The Second Vatican Council made the following declaration about theology and its relation to divine Revelation: "Sacred theology rests on the written word of God, together with sacred tradition, as its primary and perpetual foundation. By scrutinizing in the light of faith all truth stored up in the mystery of Christ, theology is most powerfully strengthened and constantly rejuvenated by that word. For the sacred Scriptures contain the word of God and, since they are inspired, really are the word of God; and thus the study of the sacred page is, as it were, the soul of sacred theology" *(Constitution on Revelation.* No. 24).

Theology has been divided under various subject headings. Some of the major fields have been: dogma, moral, pastoral, ascetics (the practice of virtue and means of attaining holiness and perfection), mysticism (higher states of religious experience). Other subject headings include ecumenism (Christian unity, interfaith relations), ecclesiology (the nature and constitution of the Church), Mariology (doctrine concerning the Blessed Virgin Mary), the sacraments, etc.

Tithing: Contribution of a portion of one's income, originally one-tenth, for purposes of religion and charity. The practice is mentioned 46 times in the Bible. In early Christian times, tithing was adopted in continuance of Old Testament practices of the Jewish people, and the earliest positive church legislation on the subject was enacted in 567. Catholics are bound in conscience to contribute to the support of their church, but the manner in which they do so is not fixed by law. Tithing, which amounts to a pledged contribution of a portion of one's income, has aroused new attention in recent years in the United States.

Titular Sees: Dioceses where the Church once flourished but which later were overrun by pagans or Moslems and now exist only in name or title. Bishops without a territorial or residential diocese of their own; e.g., auxiliary bishops, are given titular sees.

Transfinalization, Transignification: Terms coined to express the sign value of consecrated bread and wine with respect to the presence and action of Christ in the Eucharistic sacrifice and the spiritually vivifying purpose of the Eucharistic banquet in Holy Communion. The theory behind the terms has strong undertones of existential and "sign" philosophy, and has been criticized for its openness to interpretations at variance with the doctrine of transubstantiation and the abiding presence of Christ under the appearances of bread and wine after the sacrifice of the Mass and Communion have been completed. The terms, if used as substitutes for transubstantiation, are unacceptable; if they presuppose transubstantiation, they are acceptable as clarifications of its meaning.

Transubstantiation; "The way Christ is made present in this sacrament (Holy Eucharist) is none other than by the change of the whole substance of the bread into his Body, and of the whole substance of the wine into his Blood (in the Consecration at Mass) . . . this unique and wonderful change the Catholic Church rightly calls transubstantiation" (encyclical *Mysterium Fidei* of Paul VI, Sept. 3, 1965). The first official use of the term was made by the Fourth Council of the Lateran in 1215. Authoritative teaching on the subject was issued by the Council of Trent.

Treasury of the Church: The superabundant merits of Christ and the saints from which the Church draws to confer spiritual benefits, such as indulgences.

Triduum: A three-day series of public or private devotions.

U-Z

Usury: Excessive interest charged for the loan and use of money; a violation of justice.

Veronica: A word resulting from the combination of a Latin word for true, *vera,* and a Greek word for image, *eikon,* designating a likeness of the face of Christ or the name of a woman said to have given him a cloth on which he caused an imprint of his face to appear. The veneration at Rome of a likeness depicted on cloth dates from about the end of the 10th century; it figured in a popular devotion during the Middle Ages, and in the Holy Face devotion practiced since the 19th century. A faint, undiscernible likeness said to be of this kind is preserved in St. Peter's Basilica. The origin of the likeness is uncertain, and the identity of the woman is unknown. Before the 14th century, there were no known artistic representations of an incident concerning a woman who wiped the face of Christ with a piece of cloth while He was carrying the Cross to Calvary.

Viaticum: Holy Communion given to those in danger of death. The word, derived from Latin, means provision for a journey through death to life hereafter.

Vicar General: A prelate appointed by a bishop to help him, as a deputy, in the administration of his diocese. Because of his office, he has the same jurisdictional authority as the bishop except in cases reserved to the bishop by himself or by church law.

Virginity: Observance of perpetual sexual abstinence. The state of virginity, which is embraced for the love of God by religious with a public vow or by others with a private vow, was singled out for high praise by Christ (Mt. 19:10-12) and has always been so regarded by the Church. In the encyclical *Sacra Virginitas,* Pius XII stated: "Holy virginity and that perfect chastity which is consecrated to the service of God is without doubt among the most perfect treasures which the founder of the Church has left in heritage to the society which he established."

Paul VI approved in 1970 a rite in which women can consecrate their virginity "to Christ and their brethren" without becoming members of a religious institute. The *Ordo Consecrationis Virginum,* a revision of a rite promulgated by Clement VII in 1596, is traceable to the Roman liturgy of about 500.

Virtue: A habit or established capability for performing good actions. Virtues are *natural* (acquired and increased by repeating good acts) and/or *supernatural* (given with grace by God).

Vocation: A call to a way of life. Generally, the term applies to the common call of all men, from God, to holiness and salvation. Specifically, it refers to particular states of life, each called a vocation, in which response is made to this universal call; viz., marriage, the religious life and/or priesthood, the single state freely chosen or accepted for the accomplishment of God's will. The term also applies to the various occupations in which persons make a living. The Church supports the freedom of each individual in choosing a particular vocation, and reserves the right to pass on the acceptability of candidates for the priesthood and religious life. Signs or indicators of particular vocations are many, including a person's talents and interests, circumstances and obligations, invitations of grace and willingness to respond thereto.

Vow: A promise made to God with sufficient knowledge and freedom, which has as its object a moral good that is possible and better than its voluntary omission. A person who professes a vow binds himself by the virtue of religion to fulfill his promise. The best known examples of vows are those of poverty, chastity and obedience professed by religious (see Evangelical Counsels, individual entries).

Public vows are made before a competent person, acting as an agent of the Church, who accepts the profession in the name of the Church, thereby giving public recognition to the person's dedication and consecration to God and divine worship. Vows of this kind are either solemn, rendering all contrary acts invalid as well as unlawful; or simple, rendering contrary acts unlawful. Solemn vows are for life; simple vows are for a definite period of time or for life. Vows professed without public recognition by the Church are called private vows. The Church, which has authority to accept and give public recognition to vows, also has authority to dispense persons from their obligations for serious reasons.

Week of Prayer for Christian Unity: Eight days of prayer, from Jan. 18 to 25, for the union of all men in the Church established by Christ. On the initiative of Father Paul James Francis, S.A., of Graymoor, N.Y., it originated in 1908 as the Chair of Unity Octave. In recent years, its observance on an interfaith basis has increased greatly.

Witness, Christian: Practical testimony or evidence given by Christians of their faith in all circumstances of life — by prayer and general conduct, through good example and good works, etc.; being and acting in accordance with Christian belief; actual practice of the Christian faith.

Zucchetto: A skullcap worn by bishops and other prelates.

NFPC

The National Federation of Priests' Councils was organized by 233 delegates from 127 priests' organizations at a charter meeting held in Chicago May 20 and 21, 1968.

Its stated purposes are to:

• give priests' councils, official or unofficial, a representative voice in matters of concern to the Church and with respect to problems facing the nation, including racism and poverty;

• improve communications among priests all over the country;

• coordinate programs of research and make recommendations to priests, bishops and others on specific matters;

• cooperate with lay persons, religious and bishops in meeting the contemporary needs of the Church.

In line with its stated objectives, the organization has developed a variety of programs in such fields as continuing education and the spiritual life of priests, vocations to the priesthood, efforts in behalf of resigned priests, training of presidents of diocesan senates and councils, study of ways to amend the process for the selection of bishop nominees, rural and urban ministry, world peace and justice, corporate responsibility in investment practices.

The NFPC has a membership of about 130 senates, councils and associations, including several provinces of men religious and PADRES, a national priests' group concerned with the needs of the Spanish-speaking. The NFPC publication is *Priests/USA*, a monthly.

The president is Father Reid C. Mayo of Burlington, Vt.

Headquarters are located at 1307 S. Wabash Ave., Chicago, Ill. 60605.

TEAM MINISTRY

This is a form of ministry designed to share responsibility among priests and others in a given pastoral assignment. Experiments and developments connected with it have multiplied since late in the 1960's.

Boston archdiocesan guidelines call team ministry "an arrangement whereby one associate pastor is recommended by the others (and subsequently appointed by the bishop) to be the pastor." Also, that "all priests that staff the parish (should) have a deliberative (decisive) vote in all parish affairs," and that "the parish council should be considered a part of the team ministry."

Another definition, framed by Franciscan Fathers Kenneth F. Kieffer and Isidore Langheim of the Chicago-St. Louis province, said that "team ministry means shared responsibility in all the administrative processes of the ministry — goal-setting, planning, organizing, coordinating, communication, decision-making, directing and evaluating."

Team ministries involving 71 priests in 31 parishes of the Hartford archdiocese, one of the first to experiment with them, were reported to be highly successful in a study published in September, 1975, at the end of a five-year trial period.

Job satisfaction on the part of priests in team ministry was said to be high. So was the quality of pastoral service and relations with parish councils and other organizations of a representative character. No generalizations were contained in the report concerning the comparative merits of team ministry and the traditional pastor-assistant(s) model.

Biographies of Catholics

(In addition to the biographical entries below, others are listed in the Index.)

A

Abelard, Peter (1079-1142); French philosopher, theologian; contributed to scholastic method although he had nominalistic tendencies.

Achillini, Alessandro (1463-1512): Italian physicist, astronomer; inaugurated reaction against Ptolemaic astronomy.

Adam, Karl (1876-1966): German theologian, writer; *Spirit of Catholicism.*

Adenauer, Konrad (1876-1967): German statesman; chancellor of West Germany, 1949-63.

Africanus, Sextus Julius (3rd cent.): Christian historian; wrote history of world from creation to 221 A.D.

Agreda, Mary of (1602-1665): Spanish Poor Clare, mystical writer; *Mystical City of God and the Divine History of the Virgin Mother of God.*

Alan of Walsingham (died 1364): English monk, architect.

Alarcon, Pedro Antonio de (1833-1891): Spanish writer, statesman.

Alberione, Giacomo (1884-1971): Italian priest; founder of Pauline Fathers and Daughters of St. Paul for work in communications field.

Albert or Albrecht (died 1229): Founder and first bishop of Riga, apostle of Livonia.

Albornoz, Gil Alvarez Carillo de (1310-1367): Spanish cardinal, general, statesman; negotiated return of the papal states, 1354; his *Egidian Constitutions* for them prevailed until 1816; archbishop of Toledo.

Alcuin, Albinus (735-804): English scholar; abbot of Tours; educator among Franks.

Alexander of Hales (1180-1245): English theologian, philosopher; first Franciscan teacher at Paris; called Doctor Irrefragabilis.

Alfred the Great (849-899): First Saxon king of England; noted for wise laws, spread of religion and learning.

Allen, Frances (1784-1819): American religious; daughter of Ethan Allen; convert, 1807; professed vows in community of Hospital Sisters at Hotel-Dieu, Montreal, 1810.

Allers, Rudolf (1883-1963): Austrian-born psychologist; d. Maryland; taught at Catholic University of America, 1938-48, and Georgetown University, 1948-63.

Allori, Alessandro (1535-1607) and his son **Cristofano** (1577-1621): Italian painters, Florentine school.

Amiot, Jean Marie (1718-1793): French Jesuit, missionary to China, author.

Ammen, Daniel (1820-1898): American naval officer in Civil War; author.

Ampere, Andre Marie (1775-1836): French physicist; pioneer in electrodynamics; term ampere named for him.

Anderson, William H. (1799-1875): American mathematician and astronomer; on US expedition to Dead Sea, 1848; convert, 1849.

Angelico, Fra (Giovanni da Fiesole) (1387-1455): Italian Dominican painter of religious subjects.

Anglin, Timothy (1822-1896): Canadian journalist and legislator. Father of **Margaret Mary Anglin** (1876-1958): actress, Laetare medalist.

Animuccia, Giovanni (1500?-1571): Italian composer of sacred music.

Apponyi, Albert, Count (1846-1933): Hungarian statesman, parliamentary leader for 40 years; head of Hungary's peace delegation in Paris, 1920.

Argenlieu, Georges Thierry d' (1889-1964): French admiral, Carmelite priest; naval officer in World War I; entered Carmelites, 1920, and ordained priest (Father Louis of the Trinity); recalled to active duty during World War II, fought with Free French; governor general of Indo-China after the war; returned to monastery, 1947.

Arnold, Thomas (1823-1900): English educator; convert, 1856.

Avery, Martha (Moore) (1851-1929): American Socialist, political economist, author; convert, 1903; a founder of the Catholic Truth Guild, 1917.

B

Bacon, Roger (1214-1294): English Franciscan, philosopher, experimental scientist; considered optical and astronomical laws, possibilities of scientific invention, gunpowder.

Baegert, Johann Jacob (1717-1777): Jesuit missionary, ethnographer; author of works on Lower California.

Balboa, Vasco Nunez de (1475-1517): Spanish adventurer; discovered Pacific Ocean, 1513.

Baldwin, Charles Sears (1867-1935): American educator, author; convert, 1934.

Baldwin, Geoffrey P. (1892-1951): American military officer in World Wars I and II; convert, 1937; chief of CARE in Italy.

Banim, John (1798-1842) and **Michael** (1796-1874): First national novelists of Ireland; John called the Scott of Ireland.

Barber, Virgil (1787-1847): American Jesuit; prominent New England Episcopal minister before his conversion, 1816, with his wife and five children; all eventually entered religious life; ordained 1822; established first Catholic church and school in New Hampshire at Claremont. His father **Daniel** (1756-1834) was also an Episcopal minister before he followed the rest of his family into the Church in 1818; wrote *Catholic Worships and Piety Explained.*

Barbour, John (1316?-1395): Scottish poet, author of the epic romance, _The Bruce._

Baring, Maurice (1874-1945): English poet, novelist, critic, author of works on Russia; convert, 1909.

Barry, John (1745-1803): American naval officer, b. Ireland; naval hero in Revolution.

Bartholomeus Anglicus (13th cent.): English Franciscan, author of a medieval encyclopedia of science.

Bartolommeo, Fra (1475-1517): Florentine Dominican, religious painter.

Bayley, James Roosevelt (1814-1877): American prelate; convert, 1842; ordained priest, 1844; bishop of Newark, N. J. 1853-72; archbishop of Baltimore 1872-77.

Bayma, Joseph (1816-1892): Italian Jesuit, mathematician, scientist; author of _Molecular Mechanics._

Bazin, Rene (1853-1932): French novelist, biographer, travel writer; member of French Academy.

Bea, Augustin (1881-1968): German Jesuit, cardinal, Biblical scholar, leader in Christian reunion movement.

Beardsley, Aubrey Vincent (1872-1898): British illustrator; convert, 1895.

Beaton (Bethune), David (1494-1546): Scottish prelate, statesman; cardinal archbishop of St. Andrews; chancellor of Scotland; opposed efforts of Henry VIII to separate Scotland from loyalty to Holy See.

Beauregard, Pierre (1818-1893): American Confederate general; graduate of West Point; superintendent of West Point for five days; resigned to serve with Confederate Army.

Beccaria, Giovanni Battista (1716-1781): Italian physicist; early researcher in electricity.

Becquerel, Antoine Cesar (1788-1878): French physicist, electrochemist; invented the constant cell, a differential galvanometer, an electric thermometer.

Becquerel, Antoine Henri (1852-1908): French physicist; discoverer of radioactivity in uranium; shared 1903 Nobel Prize in physics with the Curies.

Beethoven, Ludwig van (1770-1827): German composer; works include symphonies, concertos and sonatas.

Behaim, Martin (1459-1507): German geographer; constructed a terrestrial globe, 1492.

Bellini, Gentile (1429-1507) and **Giovanni** (1430-1516): Venetian painters.

Belloc, Hilaire (1870-1953): English journalist, essayist, poet, novelist, historian, biographer, critic, apologist.

Benson, Robert Hugh (1871-1914): English author of historical fiction, other works; Anglican clergyman before conversion, 1903; ordained to priesthood, 1904.

Benson, William Shepherd (1855-1932): American naval officer; first chief of naval operations, 1915-19; convert.

Bentley, John Francis (1839-1902): English architect; promoted Gothic revival in England; designed Cathedral of Westminster.

Berengario da Carpi, Jacopo (1470-1530): Italian anatomist; a founder of modern science of anatomy.

Bernanos, Georges (1888-1948): French journalist, novelist; works concerned principally with struggle of the soul against evil.

Bernard, Claude (1813-1878): French physiologist; studied the glycogenic function of the liver, sympathetic nervous system.

Bernini, Giovanni Lorenzo (1598-1680): Italian sculptor of wide influence; architect of St. Peter's.

Bertrand, Louis (1866-1941): French novelist, biographer.

Beschi, Costanzo Giuseppe (1680-1746): Italian Jesuit missionary; famous for linguistic and literary work in the Tamil language.

Besse, Jean Martial Leon (1861-1920): Benedictine monk, historian.

Bianchini, Francesco (1662-1729): Italian astronomer; secretary, under Clement XI, of papal commission for calendar reform.

Bickerstaffe-Drew, Francis (1858-1928): English author (under pseudonym of **John Ayscough**); convert, priest.

Bielski, Marcin (1495-1575): Polish historian, poet.

Bienville, Sieur de (1680-1768); French explorer, governor of Louisiana colony.

Biggs, Richard Keys (1886-1962): American concert organist, composer, choir master; convert.

Billuart, Charles Rene (1685-1757): Belgian Dominican theologian, preacher.

Binet, Jacques Philippe Marie (1786-1856): French mathematician, astronomer; Binet's theorem.

Biondo, Flavio (1388-1463): Italian historian, archaeologist.

Biot, Jean Baptiste (1774-1862): French physicist; studied polarization of light; Biot's law.

Blondel, Maurice (1861-1949): French philosopher; works include _L'Action, La Pensée._

Blowick, John (1889-1972): Irish priest; founder with Bishop Edward Galvin of the Society of St. Columban, 1916.

Bloy, Leon (1846-1917): French writer, social reformer.

Boccaccio, Giovanni (1313-1375): Italian author; known as father of Italian prose; _Decameron._

Boethius, Anicius Manlius (480?-524?): Roman statesman and philosopher; author of _The Consolation of Philosophy._

Boileau-Despreaux, Nicolas (1636-1711): French poet, satirist, critic.

Bolland, John van (1596-1665): Flemish Jesuit; editor of _Acta Sanctorum,_ continued by Bollandists.

Bolzano, Bernard (1781-1848): Bohemian mathematician; formulated theory of functions.

Bona, Giovanni (1609-1674): Italian cardinal, author of liturgical encyclopedia.

Bonaparte, Charles J. (1851-1921): American cabinet official; secretary of navy 1905-06; attorney general, 1906-09.

Bordone, Paris (1500-1571): Venetian painter, pupil of Titian.

Borrus, Christopher (1583-1632): Oceanic geographer.

Boscovich, Ruggiero Giuseppe (1711-1787); Italian Jesuit, astronomer, physicist; offered a molecular theory of matter.

Bosio, Antonio (1575-1629): Italian archaeologist, called Columbus of the Catacombs.

Bossuet, Jacques Benigne (1627-1704): French prelate; pulpit orator, author.

Botticelli, Sandro (1444-1510): Florentine painter.

Bourdaloue, Louis (1632-1704): French Jesuit, pulpit orator.

Bourgeois, Louis (1819-1878): French archaeologist; presented and developed problem of the eoliths, 1863.

Bracton, Henry de (died 1268): English jurist; author of treatise *On the Laws and Customs of England*.

Braille, Louis (1809-1852): Blind French teacher of the blind; inventor of Braille system of raised-point printing.

Bramante, Donato (1444-1514): Italian architect; made plan for reconstruction of St. Peter's.

Branly, Edouard (1846-1940): French physicist; discovered coherer, making wireless telegraphy possible.

Brennan, Francis J. (1894-1968): American cardinal, Roman Curia official; ordained priest, 1920; professor at St. Charles Seminary, Overbrook, Pa., 1920-40; judge, 1940-59, and dean, 1959-67, of the Sacred Roman Rota; ord. bishop June 25, 1967; cardinal, June 26, 1967.

Brentano, Klemens (1778-1842): German poet; rejoined Catholic Church, 1818; recorded revelations of Anne Catherine Emmerich.

Breuil, Henri (1877-1961): French priest, archaeologist; authority on prehistoric art.

Broun, Heywood Campbell (1888-1939): American journalist, author; convert, 1939.

Browne, Charles Farrar (pseud. Artemus Ward) (1834-1867): American humorist, journalist, lecturer.

Brownson, Orestes Augustus (1803-1876): American scholar, essayist, philosopher, controversialist; was successively a Presbyterian, Universalist minister and Unitarian minister before his conversion, 1844.

Bruckner, Anton (1824-1896): Austrian composer and organist.

Brumidi, Constantino (1805-1880): American painter, b. Italy; became naturalized citizen; noted for his frescoes in Capitol at Washington, D.C.

Brunelleschi, Filippo (1377-1466): Italian architect; called founder of Renaissance architecture; established theory of perspective.

Brunetiere, Ferdinand (1849-1906): French critic, editor, professor of literature; convert.

Buck, Edward Eugene (Gene) (1885-1957): American popular song lyricist, producer; president of American Society of Composers, Authors and Publishers (ASCAP), 1924-41.

Budenz, Louis (1891-1972): American journalist; prominent member of American Communist Party, 1935 to 1945, when he was received back into the Church; major witness in the McCarthy hearings in the 1950's.

Bullitt, William C. (1891-1967): American diplomat; first ambassador to Russia; convert shortly before his death.

Burke, John (1859-1937): American jurist, politician; governor of North Dakota, 1907-21; treasurer of US, 1913-21; judge, 1924, and later chief justice of North Dakota supreme court. Represents North Dakota in Statuary Hall.

Burke, Thomas Nicholas (1830-1882): Irish Dominican preacher.

Burnand, Sir Francis Crowley (1836-1917): English playwright; editor of *Punch* (1880-1906), and English *Catholic Who's Who;* convert, 1857.

Burnett, Peter Hardemann (1807-1895): American jurist, politician; judge of Oregon supreme court, first governor of California, member of California supreme court; convert, 1846.

Butler, Alban (1711-1773): English author; *Lives of the Saints.*

Butler, Pierce (1866-1939): American attorney, jurist; associate justice Unted States Supreme Court, 1923-39.

Byrd, William (1540?-1623): English organist, composer; founder of English Madrigal School.

C

Cabeza de Vaca, Alvar Nunez (1490-1557): Spanish explorer; colonial governor in Paraguay.

Cabot, John (1450-1498): Italian navigator; discovered mainland of North America, June 24, 1497.

Cabral, Pedro Alvarez de (1460-1526): Portuguese navigator; discovered Brazil, which he named Vera Cruz.

Caedmon (died 670): First great English Christian poet; lay brother at monastery in Whitby.

Caius (Kees, Keys, Kay, Key), John (1510-1573): English physician; lecturer on anatomy; author.

Cajetan, Tommaso De Vio (1469-1534): Italian cardinal, philosopher, theologian.

Caldani, Leopold Marco Antonio (1725-1813): Italian anatomist, physiologist; furthered anatomical studies on function of spinal cord.

Calderon de La Barca, Pedro (1600-1681): Spanish priest, dramatist; author of over 200 works.

Calvert, Cecil (1605-1675): English proprietor; second Lord Baltimore; responsible for enactment of religious toleration in Maryland colony.

Calvert, George (1580-1632): English proprietor; first Lord Baltimore; held important posts under James I; was granted territory of Baltimore colony but died before grant of charter; convert, 1625.

Camel (Kamel), George Joseph (1661-1706): Moravian Jesuit missionary, botanist; studied plants and natural history of Philippines.

Camoes, Luiz Vaz de (1524-1580): Portuguese poet, dramatist.

Campbell, James (1812-1893): American jurist, cabinet official; US postmaster general, 1853-57.

Cano, Melchior (1509-1560): Spanish Dominican, theologian; called father of fundamental theology.

Canova, Antonio (1757-1822): Italian sculptor of the modern classic school.

Canute (II) the Great (994?-1035): King of Denmark, England, Norway.

Cardano, Girolamo (1501-1576): Italian physician, mathematician.

Cardijn, Joseph (1882-1967): Belgian cardinal, founder of the Young Christian Workers; cardinal, 1965.

Carey, Mathew (1760-1839): American publisher, economist and author, b. Ireland; first extensive US Catholic publisher.

Carnoy, Jean Baptiste (1836-1899): Belgian priest, biologist; pioneer cytologist.

Carpini, Giovanni de Piano (c. 1180-1252): Italian Franciscan, companion of St. Francis; missionary in Germany; papal envoy to Great Khan of the Mongols, 1246; wrote *Liber Tartarorum* recounting in detail the life and customs of the Mongols.

Carrel, Alexis (1873-1944): French surgeon, biologist; developed surgical techniques, experimented on transplantation of organs; author; member Pontifical Academy of Sciences; Nobel Prize for physiology and medicine, 1912.

Carroll, Charles (1737-1832): American statesman; member of Continental Congress, 1776-78; signer of Declaration of Independence; member Maryland Congress and first US Senate, 1789-92. Represents Maryland in Statuary Hall.

Carroll, Daniel (1730-1796): American patriot; brother of Archbishop John Carroll; delegate to Continental Congress, 1780-84; Constitutional Convention, 1787; congressman from Maryland, 1789-91.

Carroll, John (1735-1815): American prelate; ordained priest, 1761; first bishop of the hierarchy of the US (bishop, 1789-1808, and archbishop, 1808-15 of Baltimore); also apostolic administrator of Louisiana and Two Floridas, 1805-15; founder of Georgetown University, 1791.

Carson, Christopher (Kit) (1809-1868): American trapper, scout, Indian agent.

Cartier, Jacques (1491-c. 1557): French explorer of coasts of Labrador and New-

foundland; ascended the St. Lawrence to Montreal.

Caruso, Enrico (1873-1921): Italian operatic tenor.

Cassini, Jean Dominique (1625-1712): French astronomer; first director of Paris observatory; made important discoveries regarding Saturn, parallax of sun.

Cassiodorus, Flavius Aurelius (c. 490-c. 580): Roman statesman, writer, founder of monasteries.

Castelli, Benedetto (c. 1572-1644): Italian Benedictine, mathematician, physicist; authority on hydraulics.

Cauchy, Augustin Louis (1789-1857): French mathematician; did research in calculus, developed wave theory in optics.

Cavalieri, Francesco Bonaventura (1598-1647): Italian religious, mathematician; originated method of indivisibles; forerunner of integral calculus.

Caxton, William (1422-1491): First English printer.

Cellini, Benvenuto (1500-1571): Italian sculptor; worker in gold and bronze.

Cervantes Saavedra, Miguel de (1547-1616): Spanish novelist; *Don Quixote*.

Cesalpino, Andrea (1519-1603): Italian botanist, physician; important contributor to work on plant morphology, physiology; anticipated Linnaean system of classification.

Cezanne, Paul (1839-1906): French painter; a leader of postimpressionism.

Challoner, Richard (1691-1781): English bishop; re-edited Douay Bible.

Champlain, Samuel de (1567-1635): French explorer; Father of New France, founder of Quebec; discovered Lake Champlain.

Champollion, Jean Francois (1790-1832): French Egyptologist; discovered through the Rosetta Stone a system for deciphering hieroglyphics.

Chandler, Joseph Ripley (1792-1880): American journalist, congressman; Grand Master of Free Masons before conversion, 1849; US minister to Naples during administration of Buchanan; US congressman from Pennsylvania, 1849-55.

Charlemagne (742-814): King of the Franks, Emperor of the West, founder of Holy Roman Empire; promoted spread of Christianity, learning; defender of the papacy.

Charles Martel (c. 689-741): Duke of Austrasia, son of Pepin; halted Saracen advance on western Europe at Battle of Tours (732), and thereafter was called Martel *(The Hammer)*; grandfather of Charlemagne.

Chateaubriand, Francois Rene de (1768-1848): French author; influential in history of Romantic Movement.

Chaucer, Geoffrey (1340-1400): Father of English poetry; *Canterbury Tales*.

Chauliac, Guy de (1300-1370): French surgeon; gave authoritative description of bubonic plague, Black Death of 14th century.

Chavez, Dennis (1888-1962): American legislator; member New Mexico State legislature, 1920-30; US congressman, 1931-35; US senator, 1935-62. Represents New Mexico in Statuary Hall.

Cherubini, Maria Luigi (1760-1842): Italian composer of ecclesiastical and operatic works.

Chesterton, Gilbert K. (1874-1936); English essayist, poet, novelist, biographer, journalist; Prince of Paradox; convert, 1922.

Chevreul, Michel Eugene (1786-1889): French chemist; did research in animal fats; discovered margarine, oleine, stearine.

Cimabue, Giovanni (Cenni di Pepo) (1240-1302): Florentine painter; religious subjects.

Claudel, Paul (1868-1955): French author, diplomat; elected to French Academy, 1946.

Clavius, Christopher (1537-1612): Jesuit astronomer, mathematician; introduced decimal point.

Clerke, Agnes Mary (1842-1907): Irish astronomer.

Coady, Moses Michael (1882-1959): Canadian priest, educator; organizer of cooperatives among Canadian fishermen, known as Antigonish movement.

Cobo, Bernabe (1582-1657): Spanish Jesuit, naturalist; author of *History of the New World,* on Latin America.

Cody, Col. William F. (Buffalo Bill) (1846-1917): American Pony Express rider, army guide and scout, hunter, Indian fighter; entered Church just before death.

Collins, Michael (1890-1922): Irish revolutionary leader and soldier.

Colombo, Matteo Realdo (1516-1559): Italian anatomist; discovered pulmonary circulation.

Columbus, Christopher (1451-1506): Genoese explorer; discovered the Americas in 1492.

Connell, Francis J. (1888-1967): American Redemptorist priest, moral theologian, author.

Connelly, Mother Cornelia (1809-1879): American-born foundress; married to Pierce Connelly, an Episcopalian minister; her conversion, 1835, was followed three months later by her husband's; granted permanent separation by Rome and entered convent so her husband could become a priest; sent to England at request of Cardinal Wiseman and founded Society of the Holy Child Jesus, 1846; her husband renounced the priesthood, 1849; his legal attempt to force her to return to married life was unsuccessful.

Constantine the Great (c. 280-337): Roman emperor; granted liberty of worship to Christians by Edict of Milan, 313; established Constantinople as capital of the Eastern Empire.

Copernicus, Nicolaus (1473-1543): Polish astronomer; founder of modern astronomy; taught the revolution of planets around the sun and the rotation of the earth on its axis.

Coppee, Francois (1842-1908): French poet, dramatist, novelist; member of French Academy, 1884.

Cordoba, Francisco Fernandez de (d. 1518?): Spanish explorer; discovered Yucatan, 1517.

Corneille, Pierre (1606-1684): French dramatist; great influence on French tragedy, *Le Cid.*

Corot, Jean Baptiste Camille (1796-1875): French landscape artist.

Correggio, Antonio Allegri (1494-1534): Lombard painter; noted for mastery of light and shade; religious subjects.

Cortez, Hernando (1485-1547): Spanish explorer, soldier; conquered Mexico.

Cory, Herbert Ellsworth (1883-1947): American educator, social scientist, author; convert, 1933.

Coulomb, Charles Augustine (1736-1806): French physicist; investigated electricity and magnetism; stated coulomb's law; the coulomb named for him.

Couperin, Francois (1668-1733): French composer; first great composer for the harpsichord.

Cousin, Jean (1490-1560), and his son **Jean** (1522-1590): French painters, workers in stained glass.

Crashaw, Richard (1613-1649): English poet of metaphysical school; convert, 1646.

Crawford, Francis Marion (1854-1909): American novelist, b. Italy; convert, 1880.

Credi, Lorenz di (1459-1537): Florentine painter; religious subjects.

Creighton, John (1831-1907) and his brother **Edward** (1802-1874): American philanthropists; benefactors of Creighton University; in 1861 took part in laying first telegraph line linking California to rest of the nation.

Cushing, Richard J. (1895-1970): American cardinal; ordained priest, 1921; auxiliary bishop of Boston, 1939-44; archbishop of Boston, 1944-70; cardinal, 1958; founded Missionary Society of St. James the Apostle to recruit diocesan priests for Latin American missions; promoted charitable works especially among exceptional children.

D

Dablon, Claude (1619-1697): French Jesuit missionary in America; superior of Canadian missions.

Daly, Thomas A. (1871-1948): American journalist and poet.

Damien, Father (Joseph de Veuster) (1840-1889): Belgian missionary; joined Picpus Fathers, 1860; from 1873 to his death, devoted his life to caring for lepers on Molokai, in Hawaiian Islands; contracted the disease three years before his death. Represents Hawaii in National Statuary Hall.

Daniel-Rops, Henri (pseud. of Henri Jules Petiot) (1901-1965): French writer on Church history and other subjects; member of French Academy.

Dante Alighieri (1265-1321): Florentine poet; *Divina Commedia, Vita Nuova, De Monarchia.*

Daumer, Georg Friedrich (1800-1875): German writer; anti-Christian works until conversion, 1858; author of *Meine Konversion.*

Davenport, Sir William (1606-1668): English poet and dramatist.

Dawson, Christopher (1889-1970): English author and scholar; convert from Anglicanism, 1914; principal themes of his works are cultural history and the philosophy of religion.

DeGaulle, Charles Andre Joseph Marie (1890-1970): French general, statesman; leader of French forces in World War II; interim president of France, 1945-46; president of Fifth Republic, 1959-69.

Delacroix, Ferdinand Victor Eugene (1799-1863): French painter; romantic school.

Delaroche, Paul (1797-1856): French painter, of the Eclectic school; portrait and historical subjects.

DeRossi, Giovanni Battista (1822-1894): Italian archaeologist; aroused interest in Christian antiquities.

Descartes, Rene (1596-1650): French scientist and philosopher; founder of analytic geometry.

De Soto, Hernando (1500-1542): Spanish explorer; discovered lower course of Mississippi River, 1541.

De Vaux, Roland (1903-1971): French Dominican; biblical archaeologist and exegete; head of Ecole Biblique, Jerusalem; headed international team of scholars who edited Dead Sea Scrolls.

Devlin, Joseph (1872-1934): Irish politician.

Dias, Bartholomew (1450-1500): Portuguese navigator; discovered Cape of Good Hope, 1488.

Dimnet, Ernest (1869-1954): French priest, lecturer, writer.

Dior, Christian (1905-1957): French fashion designer.

Divisch, Wénceslaus (religious name, **Procopius**) (1698-1765): Moravian Premonstratensian monk; erected a lightning rod in 1754, before Franklin's work was known.

Dolci, Carlo (1616-1686): Florentine painter; religious and portrait subjects.

Donatello or **Donato di Niccolo di Betto Bardi** (1386-1466): Italian sculptor; called the founder of modern sculpture.

Dongon, Thomas (1634-1715): Colonial governor of New York, 1682-88; b. Ireland.

Donizetti, Gaetano (1797-1848): Italian operatic composer.

Dooley, Thomas A. (1927-1961): American physician; co-founder of MEDICO, organized to establish medical services in underdeveloped countries; author.

Doria, Andrea (1468-1560): Genoese admiral, statesman; Father of Peace, Liberator of Genoa.

Drexel, Mary Katherine (1858-1955): American missionary; foundress of Sisters of the Blessed Sacrament for Indians and Colored People, 1891.

Drum, Hugh A. (1879-1951): American army officer in World Wars I and II.

Dryden, John (1631-1700): English poet, playwright; poet laureate, 1670; convert, 1686.

Duffy, Sir Charles Gavan (1816-1903): Irish nationalist, political leader in Australia after he emigrated there (1856), author.

Dulong, Pierre Louis (1785-1838): French chemist, physicist; author with Petit of formula determining the specific heat of solids.

Dumas, Jean Baptiste (1800-1884): French chemist; did important research on vapor densities.

Dunne, Peter Finley (1867-1936): American humorist, journalist; creator of Irish philosophical character "Mr. Dooley."

Duns Scotus, John (1256-1308): Scottish scholastic theologian; Franciscan; advanced best theological arguments for doctrine of the Immaculate Conception; known as Doctor Subtilis.

Durer, Albrecht (1471-1528): German painter of Renaissance school, engraver, wood-cut artist; called the inventor of etching.

Durkin, Martin P. (1894-1955): American union leader, cabinet official; secretary of labor, 1953.

Dutton, Ira (Brother Joseph) (1843-1931): American missionary; convert, 1883; assisted Father Damien in work among lepers at Molokai, served there for 42 years, beginning in 1886.

Dwight, Thomas (1843-1911): American surgeon, anatomist; taught anatomy at Harvard and Maine medical schools; convert, 1855.

E

Eck, Johann (1486-1543): German theologian; outstanding opponent of Luther.

Eckhel, Joseph Hilarius (1737-1798): Austrian Jesuit; founder of modern numismatics.

Eichendorff, Joseph von (1788-1857): German lyric poet, novelist, critic.

Elgar, Edward (1857-1934): English composer. *Pomp and Circumstance.*

Emmerich, Anne Catherine (1774-1824): German Augustinian nun, mystic; her visions were recorded by the poet Klemens Brentano.

Endlicher, Stephen (1804-1849): Hungarian botanist, linguist; elaborated a system of classifying plants.

England, John (1786-1842): American prelate, b. Ireland, bishop of Charleston, S. C., 1820-42; founded *United States Catholic Miscellany,* the first US Catholic weekly newspaper; opponent of trusteeism.

Epee, Charles Michel de L' (1712-1789): French priest; developed a sign alphabet for deaf-mutes.

Erasmus, Desiderius (1466-1536): Dutch scholar, Renaissance leader.

Estaing, Jean Baptiste d' (1729-1794): French naval commander; aided Americans during Revolution.

Eustachius, Bartolommeo (1524-1574): Italian anatomist; Eustachian tube, valve, named for him.

Ewing, J. Franklin (1905-1968): American Jesuit priest, anthropologist, missiologist, author.

Ewing, Thomas (1789-1871): American lawyer; US senator from Ohio, 1831-37, 1850-51; secretary of the treasury, 1841; secretary of the interior, 1849-50; convert, 1871.

Eyck, Hubert Van (1366-1426) and his brother **Jan** (1370-1440): Painters, founders of Flemish school; developed process of oil painting; religious and portrait subjects.

F

Faber, Frederick William (1814-1863): British author of spiritual works, hymns; convert, 1845; priest.

Fabre, Jean Henri (1823-1915): French entomologist and author.

Fabricius, Hieronymus (Fabricius ab Aquapendente) (1537-1619): Italian anatomist, surgeon; described valvular system of the veins; teacher of Harvey.

Fallopio, Gabriello (1523-1562): Italian anatomist; discovered Fallopian tubes.

Farley, John (1842-1918): American cardinal, b. Ireland; came to US 1864; ordained priest, 1870; vicar general, 1891, auxiliary, 1895, and archbishop, 1902-18, of New York; cardinal, 1911.

Faye, Herve Auguste Etienne Albans (1814-1902): French astronomer; discovered comet named for him; invented zenithal collimator.

Fenelon, Francois de Salignac de la Mothe (1651-1715): French prelate, writer; archbishop of Cambrai.

Ferrari, Ludovico (1522-1565): Italian mathematician; discovered method of resolving equations of the fourth degree.

Fink, Francis A. (1907-1971): American editor, publisher; associated with *Our Sunday Visitor* from 1930 until his death; president of the Catholic Press Association, 1950-52; recipient of CPA Award in 1971 for his contribution to the Catholic press in the US and Canada.

Fischer, Max (1893-1954): European and American journalist, b. Germany; teacher, author; convert, while a student.

Fitzgibbon, Catherine (Sister Irene) (1823-1896): American religious, b. England; joined Sisters of Charity, 1850; founder and director of Foundling Hospital in New York City, 1869.

FitzSimons, Thomas (1741-1811): American merchant and congressman, b. Ireland; signer of the Constitution; member of first Congress of US.

Fizeau, Armand Hippolyte Louis (1819-1896): French physicist; experimentally determined velocity of light.

Flanagan, Edward Joseph (1886-1948): American priest, b. Ireland; founder of Boys' Town, Nebraska, 1917.

Floyd, John P. (1807-1863): American politician, cabinet official, military leader; governor of Virginia, 1850-53; secretary of war, 1857-61; brigadier general of Confederate Army, 1861; convert, about 1852.

Foch, Ferdinand (1851-1929): French soldier; supreme commander of Allied forces, 1918; led 1918 offensive to victory.

Ford, Francis X. (1892-1952): American Maryknoll missioner; sent to China, 1918; bishop of Kaying, 1935; imprisoned by communists in 1950; he died as a result of his treatment.

Fortunatus of Brescia (1701-1754): Italian Franciscan, pioneer morphologist.

Fortunatus, Venantius Honorius Clementianus (530-610): Latin poet; bishop of Poitiers; wrote the hymn *Vexilla Regis*.

Foster, John G. (1823-1874): American army officer; served with Union army in Civil War; convert, 1861.

Foucauld, Charles Eugene de (1858-1916): French hermit; army officer and explorer in Africa before joining Trappists, 1890; set up hermitage in Sahara among Moslem tribes; killed by desert tribesmen revolting against French; produced studies of Tuareg language and literature.

Foucault, Jean Bernard Leon (1819-1868): French physicist; experimented on light and heat; invented gyroscope, 1852; discovered Foucault electric current.

Fowler, Gene (1891-1960): American journalist, playwright, author.

Francis of Vitoria (1480-1546): Spanish Dominican, theologian; a founder of international law.

Franck, Cesar Auguste (1822-1890): Belgian-French composer; pioneer of modern French instrumental school.

Frassen, Claudius (1620-1711): French Franciscan theologian; author of *Scotus Academicus,* a presentation of the theology of Duns Scotus.

Fraunhofer, Joseph von (1787-1826): Bavarian physicist, optician; discovered Fraunhofer lines; initiated spectrum analysis, the basis of spectrography.

Frechette, Louis Honore (1839-1908): Canadian journalist, poet, prose writer.

Freppel, Charles Emile (1827-1891): French prelate, pulpit orator; bishop of Angers; leader of clerical party; founder of Catholic University of the West (Angers), 1875.

Fresnel, Augustin Jean (1788-1827): French physicist; contributor to science of optics, wave theory of light; introduced compound lenses for lighthouse use.

Froissart, Jean (1337-1410): French historian.

Frontenac, Louis de Buade, Count (1620-

1698): French soldier, colonial governor of New France; encouraged explorations of Joliet, La Salle, others.

G

Gagarin, Ivan Sergeevich (1814-1882): Russian diplomat, writer; convert, 1843; joined Jesuits.

Galilei, Galileo (1564-1642): Italian astronomer, physicist; discovered moon shines with reflected light, observed milky way, four satellites of Jupiter, phases of Venus, sunspots; discovered laws of projectiles, principles of virtual velocities, gave exposition of principles of flotation. Summoned before Inquisition on two occasions for his defense of the Copernican system, an action which at the time was considered irreconcilable with implications of Christian faith.

Galvani, Luigi (1737-1798): Italian physician, physicist; experimented to determine electrical forces involved in muscular movements; founder of galvanism.

Galvin, Edward J. (1882-1956): Irish bishop, missionary in China; co-founder with Father John Blowick of the Columban Fathers, 1916; held under house arrest for three years following Communist takeover of China in 1949; expelled, 1952.

Gama, Vasco da (1469?-1524): Portuguese explorer; discovered new sea route to India.

Garcia, Moreno Gabriel (1821-1875): Ecuadorian journalist, patriot, president of Ecuador; assassinated.

Garrigou-Lagrange, Reginald (1877-1964): French Dominican theologian, philosopher, author of works in all fields of theology; teacher at the University of St. Thomas (Angelicum), Rome, 1909-58; consultor to congregations of the Roman Curia.

Gasquet, Francis Aidan (1846-1929): English Benedictine, cardinal; head of commission for revision of the Vulgate; historian.

Gassendi, Pierre (1592-1655): French philosopher, called Bacon of France; advocate of empirical method.

Gaston, William (1778-1844): American jurist; first student at Georgetown University; North Carolina congressman, judge, member of North Carolina supreme court; responsible for repeal of law which disenfranchised Catholics in his native state, 1835.

Gay-Lussac, Joseph Louis (1778-1850): French chemist, physicist; conducted important research on gases; improved methods of organic analysis.

Geoffrey of Monmouth (1100-1154): English bishop, chronicler; influential in development of national romance in English literature.

Ghiberti, Lorenzo di Cione di Ser Buonaccorso (1378-1455): Florentine painter, sculptor, goldsmith.

Ghirlandajo, Domenico (Domenico de Tommaso Bigordi) (1449-1498): Florentine painter, mosaic and fresco artist; teacher of Michelangelo.

Gibbons, Floyd (1887-1939): American journalist, war correspondent.

Gibbons, James (1834-1921): American cardinal; ordained priest, 1861; vicar apostolic of North Carolina, 1868-72; bishop of Richmond, 1872-77; archbishop of Baltimore 1877-1921; cardinal, 1886; patriot, controversialist, writer; Apostolic Delegate to Third Plenary Council of Baltimore; championed rights of labor.

Gibson, Hugh S. (1883-1954): American diplomat; minister to Poland, ambassador to Belgium, 1927-33, 1937-38, and Brazil; director, Intergovernmental Committee for European Migration; convert, 1938.

Gigli, Beniamino (1890-1957): Italian operatic tenor.

Gill, Eric (1882-1940): English sculptor, engraver, author; convert, 1913.

Gillis, James Martin (1876-1957): American Paulist priest, author, editor, radio orator; editor of the *Catholic World* for 26 years.

Gilmore, Patrick (1829-1892): American bandmaster and composer, b. Ireland.

Giocondo de Verona (1433-1515): Italian Franciscan architect, engineer, antiquarian; architect of St. Peter's.

Gioja, Flavio (14th c.): Italian mariner; contributed to improvement of compass.

Giorgione, Giorgio (1478-1511): Painter of Venetian school.

Giotto di Bondone (1276-1337): Florentine painter, architect, sculptor, fresco artist.

Glennon, John (1862-1946): American cardinal, b. Ireland; ordained priest, 1884; coadjutor bishop of Kansas City, Mo., 1896-1903; archbishop of St. Louis, 1903-46; cardinal, 1946; one of founders of the National Catholic War Council.

Gluck, Christoph Willibald (1714-1787): German operatic composer.

Gobban Saer (560-645): Irish ecclesiastical architect.

Godfrey of Bouillon (1061-1100): French crusader, duke of Lower Lorraine; elected ruler of Jerusalem after its capture in 1099; defender of the Holy Sepulchre.

Goldstein, David (1870-1958): American apologist, b. England; convert, 1905; pioneer of street preaching and Catholic Evidence Guild work; organized the Catholic Truth Guild of Boston, 1917; author.

Goodyear, William Henry (1846-1923): American author, museum curator in New York and Brooklyn, historian; convert, 1880.

Gordon, Andrew (1712-1751): Scottish Benedictine monk; first to use a cylinder of glass to produce frictional electricity; invented electrical chimes.

Gorres, Joseph von (1776-1848): German journalist, literateur.

Gounod, Charles Francois (1818-1893): French composer of operatic and Church music.

Gower, John (1325-1408): English poet.

Goya y Lucientes, Francisco Jose de (1746-

1828): Spanish painter, etcher, lithographer; greatest painter of Spanish national customs.

Greco, El (Kyriakos Theotokopoulos) (1548-1614 or 1625): Greek-born painter of Castillian school.

Gregory of Valencia (1550-1603): Spanish Jesuit, moral theologian; works on usury and lawful rates of interest.

Grijalva, Juan de (1489-1527): Spanish explorer; completed exploration of Yucatan, discovering Mexico.

Grimaldi, Francesco Maria (1618-1663): Italian Jesuit, physicist; discovered diffraction of light.

Guardini, Romano (1885-1968): German priest (b. Italy), theologian, philosopher, author; *The Lord.*

Guido d'Arezzo (995-1050): Benedictine monk, musical theorist; reformer of musical notation.

Guilday, Peter (1884-1947): American priest; leading authority on Church history in US, founder of *Catholic Historical Review.*

Guiney, Louise Imogen (1861-1920): American poet and essayist.

Gurian, Waldemar (1902-1954): American educator and author, b. Russia; convert from Judaism.

Gutenberg, Johann (1400-1468): German printer, inventor of printing from movable type; first to print the Bible, 1452.

H

Haldeman, Samuel Stehman (Felix Aqo, pseud.) (1812-1880): American educator, author; convert, 1843; founder of National Academy of Sciences.

Hannegan, Robert E. (1903-1949): American cabinet official, politician; US postmaster general, 1945-47.

Hardee, William J. (1817-1873): American Confederate general; graduate West Point, 1838; author of *Rifle and Light Infantry Tactics,* used as army textbook at that time.

Harland, Henry (1861-1905): American novelist; used pseudonym **Sidney Luska** in earlier works; convert, 1897.

Harris, Joel Chandler (1848-1908): American journalist, author; creator of Uncle Remus; convert two weeks before his death.

Hassard, John Rose Greene (1836-1888): American journalist, author; convert, 1851; first editor of the *Catholic World.*

Hauy, Rene Just (1743-1822): French priest, mineralogist; a founder of the science of crystallography.

Hawks, Edward F. (1878-1955): American priest, author, b. South Wales; Anglican clergyman before conversion, 1908; ordained priest, 1911.

Haydn, Franz Joseph (1732-1809): Austrian composer; earliest master of symphony and quartet; composer of Austrian national anthem.

Hayes, Carlton J. H. (1882-1964): American historian, educator, diplomat, author; *Political and Social History of Modern Europe;* convert, 1904.

Hayes, Patrick J. (1867-1938): American cardinal; ordained priest, 1892; auxiliary of New York, 1914; ordinary of the armed forces, 1917; archbishop of New York, 1919-38; cardinal, 1924; one of founders of National Catholic Welfare Council.

Healy, George (1813-1894): American portrait painter.

Hebert, Louis Philippe (1850-1917): Canadian sculptor; member of Royal Canadian Academy, 1883.

Hecker, Isaac Thomas (1819-1888): American priest, founder of the Congregation of St. Paul (Paulists); convert, 1844; joined Redemptorists and ordained priest, 1849; founded Paulists 1858 with several companions; first superior, 1858-88; founder of the *Catholic World.*

Heis, Eduard (1806-1877): German astronomer; first ascertained the point of departure of meteors; drew chart of 5,421 stars, with first authentic map of milky way.

Helmont, Jan Baptista van (1577-1644): Flemish physician, chemist; introduced chemical methods in biological studies; introduced word "gas" to designate aeriform fluids.

Hengler, Lawrence (1806-1858): German priest; inventor of horizontal pendulum used in seismographs.

Hennepin, Louis (1640-1701): Belgian Franciscan, explorer; first European to see, describe and depict Niagara Falls; explored Great Lakes region, upper Mississippi.

Henry the Navigator (1394-1460): Portuguese prince; discovered Azores, Madeira, Cape Verde Islands; traced African coast as far as Sierra Leone.

Herdtrich, Christian Wolfgang (1625-1684): Austrian Jesuit missionary; probably wrote first Chinese-Latin dictionary; made Confucius known to Europeans.

Herrera, Francisco de, the Elder (1576-1656): Spanish painter; a founder of the National School of Spain.

Heude, Pierre (1836-1902): French Jesuit missionary, zoologist; authority on land mollusks of China.

Hewit, Augustine Francis (1820-1897); American priest; Congregationalist, Episcopalian minister before conversion, 1846; ordained priest, 1847; assisted Isaac Hecker in founding Paulists.

Heywood, John (1497-1580): English poet, dramatist.

Hill, John Austin (Speakman) (1779-1828): American Dominican, b. England; after conversion joined Dominicans and was ordained priest at Rome; missionary in Ohio.

Holbein, Hans, the Younger (1497-1543): German portrait and historical painter; woodcut artist.

Holland, John Philip (1840-1914): American inventor, b. Ireland; settled at Paterson, N.J.; inventor of first practical submarine.

Hopkins, Gerard Manley (1844-1889): English Jesuit; poet; convert, 1866.

Horner, William Edmonds (1793-1853): American surgeon, anatomist, author; convert, 1839; discovered tensor tarsi, now called Horner's muscle, 1824.

Hubbard, Bernard R. (1889-1962): American Jesuit explorer; called The Glacier Priest; convert, joined Jesuits, 1908; Alaskan explorer; head of Santa Clara Univ. department of geology.

Hugh of St. Victor (1096-1141): Theologian, philosopher, mystic; a founder of scholasticism.

Hughes, John J. (1797-1864): American prelate, b. Ireland; arrived US, 1817; ordained priest, 1826; coadjutor (1837), bishop (1842) and first archbishop (1850-64) of New York; vigorous defender of Catholicism against Know-Nothings and Native Americans; abolished trusteeism; established Catholic school system in his archdiocese; laid cornerstone of St. Patrick's Cathedral (1858).

Hunton, George K. (1888-1967): American lawyer, editor; pioneer in Catholic field for interracial justice.

Hunyady, Janos (1387-1456): Hungarian defender of Christendom against the Turks; assisted at crucial defense of Belgrade, 1456.

Huysmans, Joris Karl (1848-1907): French novelist; convert 1895; Benedictine Oblate.

I

Ingres, Jean (1780-1867): Leading French classical painter; historical subjects.

Innocent III (1161-1216): Pope, 1198-1216; encouraged fourth crusade, promoted efforts against the Albigensians; convoked and presided at the Fourth Lateran Council, 1215; strenuously asserted supremacy of the Church over the state.

Ireland, John (1838-1918): American prelate, b. Ireland; arrived US, 1849; ordained priest, 1861; chaplain in Union army, 1862-63; bishop (1884) and first archbishop (1888-1918) of St. Paul; helped found Catholic University of America (1889); outspoken opponent of national churches.

Ives, Levi Silliman (1797-1867): American Episcopal bishop; convert, 1852; founder of New York Catholic Protectory.

J

Jacopone da Todi (1230-1306): Italian Franciscan poet; *Stabat Mater.*

Jaricot, Pauline (1799-1862): French charitable worker; founded Society for the Propagation of the Faith, 1822, to raise funds for foreign missions.

Jimenez, Juan Ramon (1881-1958): Spanish lyric poet; awarded Nobel Prize for literature, 1956.

John of Austria, Don (1547-1578): Spanish general; commander of fleet that defeated Turks at Lepanto, 1571.

Joliet, Louis (1645-1700): French Canadian explorer of Mississippi with Marquette, 1673.

Jones, Inigo (1573-1652): English architect; designer of stage sets for Ben Jonson and others; introduced Palladian type of architecture in England.

Jorgensen, Johannes (1866-1956): Danish writer; convert, 1896; author of *St. Francis of Assisi.*

Judge, Thomas A. (1868-1933): American priest; founder of Missionary Servants of the Most Blessed Trinity (sisters), 1927, and the Missionary Servants of the Most Holy Trinity (priests and brothers).

Jugan, Jeanne (1792-1879): French foundress; established Little Sisters of the Poor, 1839, to care for aged poor.

Jussieu, Bernard de (1699-1777): French botanist; introduced a natural system for classification of plants.

Justinian I (483-565): Eastern Roman emperor; issued *Corpus Juris Civilis,* code of Roman law.

K

Katona, Stephen (1732-1811): Hungarian Jesuit, historian; author of 40-volume history of Hungary.

Kaye-Smith, Sheila (1887-1956): English author; convert 1929.

Kelly, William (1811-1888): American ironmaster; invented converter for the making of steel; now known as Bessemer's process after Englishman who patented a similar process.

Kenna, John E. (1848-1893): American legislator; private in Confederate Army; US congressman, 1876-80; US senator, 1883-93. Represents West Virginia in Statuary Hall.

Kennedy, John F. (1917-1963): Thirty-fifth president of the United States and first Catholic to hold that office; elected to Congress, 1946, 1948, 1950; to the Senate, 1952, 1958; to the presidency of the US, 1960; assassinated Nov. 22, 1963, at Dallas, Tex.; author; *Why England Slept, Profiles in Courage.*

Kennedy, Joseph P. (1888-1969): American businessman, diplomat; father of John and Robert Kennedy.

Kennedy, Robert F. (1925-1968): American politician, brother of President John F. Kennedy; cabinet official; attorney with justice department, 1951-52; US attorney general, 1961-65; US senator from New York, 1965-68; assassinated while campaigning for Democratic presidential nomination.

Keyes, Edward Lawrence (1843-1924): American physician; convert.

Keyes, Frances Parkinson (1885-1970): American author of popular novels and other works; wrote more than 50 books; convert, 1939.

Kilmer, Alfred Joyce (1886-1918): American poet; convert, 1913, with his wife; killed in action in World War I; works include *Trees and Other Poems.* His wife **Aline Murray Kilmer** (1888-1941): Lecturer, poet; wrote several books of collected verse.

Kir, Felix-Adrien (1876-1968): French priest, politician; mayor of Dijon from 1940.

Kircher, Athanasius (1601-1680): German Jesuit, archaeologist; inventor of magic lantern; stated germ theory of disease.

Knox, Ronald A. (1888-1957): English priest, author; convert, ordained, 1919; translated Vulgate Bible into English.

Kodaly, Zoltan (1882-1967): Hungarian composer; authority on folk music.

Konarski, Stanislaus (1700-1773): Polish priest, educator, author; influential in development of modern Polish literature.

Kosciusko, Tadeusz (1746-1817): Polish patriot; served in Continental Army in American Revolution; headed Polish rebellion, 1794, became dictator; died in Switzerland.

Kreisler, Fritz (1873-1962): American violinist and composer, b. Austria; became US citizen, 1943; convert, 1947.

L

La Bruyere, Jean de (1645-1696): French critic and moralist.

Lacordaire, Jean Baptiste Henri (1802-1861): French Dominican, pulpit orator; member of French Academy.

Laennec, Rene Theophile Hyacinthe (1781-1826): French physician; introduced auscultation, invented stethoscope.

La Farge, John (1835-1910): American artist and author.

La Farge, John (1880-1963): American Jesuit priest, son of artist John La Farge; scholar, author, editor of *America,* 1944-1948; leader in interracial work, a founder and director of the Catholic Interracial Council of New York City, and of the National Catholic Rural Life Conference; author of *The Manner Is Ordinary, The Catholic Viewpoint on Race Relations, An American Amen.*

La Fontaine, Jean de (1621-1695): French poet, known as a fabulist.

Lainez, Diego (1512-1565): Spanish theologian; second general of the Society of Jesus; made important contribution to work of Council of Trent.

Lamarck, Jean Baptiste de Monet, Chevalier de (1744-1829): French botanist, zoologist; originator of evolutionary theory called Lamarckism; divided animals into vertebrates and invertebrates.

Langton, Stephen (d. 1228): English prelate, cardinal archbishop of Canterbury; led English barons against King John; first of the subscribing witnesses to the Magna Charta.

Laplace, Pierre Simon (1749-1827): French astronomer, mathematician; proposed the nebular hypothesis.

LaSalle, Rene Robert Cavelier, Sieur de (1643-1687): French explorer; discovered Ohio River, explored Mississippi River valley.

Lasso, Orlando di (1532-1594): Belgian composer of over 2,000 works.

Lathrop, Rose Hawthorne (Mother Alphon- sa) (1851-1926): American foundress, author; daughter of Nathaniel Hawthorne; convert, 1891, with her husband, **George Parsons Lathrop** (1851-1898); founded Dominican Congregation of St. Rose of Lima (Servants of Relief for Incurable Cancer) after her husband's death; established home at Hawthorne, N.Y.

Latreille, Pierre Andre (1762-1833): French entomologist; classified insects and crustaceans.

Laurier, Sir Wilfrid (1841-1919): Canadian statesman; prime minister, 1896-1911.

Lavigerie, Charles Martial Allemand (1825-1892): French prelate; archbishop of Algiers, 1867; cardinal, 1882; leader in abolition of slavery; founded White Fathers, 1874, for mission work in Africa.

Lavoisier, Antoine Laurent (1743-1794): French chemist; called father of modern chemistry.

Le Fort, Gertrud von (1876-1971): German poet and novelist; convert, 1925; works include *The Veil of Veronica* and *The Song on the Scaffold,* which was the source for the opera *Dialogue of the Carmelites.*

Lehar, Ferenc or **Franz** (1870-1948): Hungarian composer of operettas, orchestral works.

Lemaitre, Jules (1853-1914): French writer, literary and dramatic critic.

Lemcke, Henry (1796-1882): American Benedictine, b. Germany; Lutheran preacher; convert, 1824; ordained priest, 1826; came to US as missionary, 1834; instrumental in bringing first Benedictines to the US; joined Benedictines, 1852.

L'Enfant, Pierre Charles (1754-1825): French engineer; drew up plans for national capital, Washington, D.C.

Leo XIII (1810-1903): Pope, 1878-1903; scholar, statesman, Latinist; author of many encyclicals (see Index).

Leverrier, Urbain Jean Joseph (1811-1877): French astronomer; calculated presence of Neptune; founded the International Meteorological Institute.

Linacre, Thomas (1460-1524): English physician, humanist; assisted in founding of College of Physicians.

Lingard, John (1771-1851): English priest, author of historical works on England.

Linton, Moses L. (1808-1878): American physician; convert, 1844; president of first US Conference of St. Vincent de Paul Society, 1845; organized first medical monthly in US, *The St. Louis Medical and Surgical Journal,* 1848.

Lippi, Fra Filippo (1406-1469): Florentine painter; religious subjects.

Liszt, Franz von (1811-1886): Hungarian piano virtuoso, composer.

Locke, Jesse A. (1859-1952): American educator; Protestant Episcopal minister; convert, 1893.

Lombard, Peter (1100-1160): Italian theologian; bishop of Paris; author of *Sententiarum Libri Quatuor*, a synthesis of theology which exerted wide influence.

Longstreet, James (1821-1904): American army officer; graduate of West Point; resigned commission to serve with Confederate forces; convert, 1877.

Lord, Daniel (1888-1955): American Jesuit; popular writer; associated with editorial staff of *Queen's Work* from 1913 until his death; wrote hundreds of pamphlets; his books include *Played by Ear*, his autobiography.

Lorraine, Claude de (1600-1682): French painter; landscape subjects.

Louis the Great (1326-1382): King of Hungary, 1342-1382, and Poland, 1370-1382.

Loviner, John Forest (1896-1970): American Franciscan priest; founder and director of St. Anthony's Guild; publisher of catechetical materials for the Confraternity of Christian Doctrine; key figure in production of the *New American Bible*.

Lugo, John de (1583-1660): Spanish Jesuit, cardinal, theologian.

M

Mabillon, Jean (1632-1707): French Benedictine, father of science of paleography; author of *Acta Sanctorum Ordinis S. Benedicti.*

McCarran, Patrick A. (1876-1954): American jurist, legislator; chief justice Nevada supreme court, 1917-18; US senator, 1932-54; sponsored Internal Security (McCarran) Act, 1950; co-sponsor of McCarran-Walter Immigration and Nationality Act, 1952. Represents Nevada in Statuary Hall.

McCarthy, Joseph R. (1908-1957): American politician; senator from Wisconsin, 1946 until his death; controversial investigator of Communism in US.

McClellan, William Hildrup (1874-1951): American educator, author; Episcopalian minister; convert, 1908; ordained Jesuit priest, 1918.

McCloskey, John (1810-1885): First American cardinal; ordained priest, 1834; coadjutor bishop of New York x844-47; first bishop of Albany, 1847-64; archbishop of New York, 1864-85, cardinal, 1875.

McCormick, Anne O'Hare (1882-1954): American journalist, b. England of American parents; awarded Pulitzer prize (1937) for European correspondence.

McGivney, Michael Joseph (1852-1890): American priest; founder of Knights of Columbus, 1882.

McGranery, James P. (1895-1963): American congressman, cabinet official; US attorney general, 1952-53.

McGrath, J. Howard (1903-1966): American politician, cabinet official; governor of Rhode Island, 1940-46; US senator, 1946; US attorney general, 1949-52.

McKay, Claude (1890-1948): American Negro poet and novelist, b. Jamaica, B.W.I.; came to US, 1912; author of *A Long Way*

from Home (1937), his autobiography; convert, 1944.

McKenna, Joseph (1843-1926): American jurist, cabinet official; US congressman from California, 1885-92; US circuit judge, 1892-97; US attorney general 1897-98; associate justice US Supreme Court, 1898-1925.

McLoughlin, John (1784-1857): Pioneer settler of Oregon, b. Canada; fur trader, physician; encouraged settlement of Oregon Territory; became American citizen; called Father of Oregon. Represents Oregon in National Statuary Hall.

MacMahon, Marie Edme Patrice Maurice de (1808-1893): Marshal of France, 1859, and president, 1873-1897; military leader in Crimean War, Franco-Prussian War, other campaigns.

McQuaid, Bernard J. (1823-1909): American prelate; ordained priest, 1848; helped found Seton Hall College; chaplain in Civil War; first bishop of Rochester, N.Y., 1868-1909; voted against definition of papal infallibility at Vatican I; promoter of Catholic schools.

Madeleva, Sister M. (**Mary Evaline Wolf**) (1887-1964): American educator, poet; joined Holy Cross Sisters, 1908.

Magellan, Ferdinand (1480-1521): Portuguese navigator; led expedition which first circumnavigated globe; discovered Strait of Magellan, Ladrones, Philippines, where he was slain.

Magsaysay, Ramon (1907-1957): Philippine statesman; crushed the Communist (Huk) Rebellion in 1948-53; third president of the Philippine Republic.

Mahler, Gustav (1880-1911): Bohemian composer and conductor; convert, 1897.

Malherbe, Francois de (1555-1628): French poet; influenced exact usage of language.

Mallinckrodt, Hermann von (1821-1874): German leader of Center Party against Kulturkampf.

Mallory, Stephen Russell (1813-1873): American Confederate political leader, b. Trinidad; US senator from Florida, 1851-1861; resigned when Florida seceded; naval secretary of the Confederacy.

Malory, Sir Thomas (d. 1470): English author of the *Morte d'Arthur.*

Malpighi, Marcello (1628-1694): Italian anatomist; called father of microscopic anatomy.

Malus, Etienne Louis (1775-1812): French engineer, physicist; discovered polarization of light, invented polariscope.

Mangan, James C. (1803-1849): Irish poet.

Manning, Henry Edward (1808-1892): English cardinal, author; convert, 1851.

Mansard, Nicolas Francois (1598-1666): French architect.

Mantegna, Andrea (1431-1506): Italian painter, muralist, engraver; leader of Paduan school.

Manutius, Aldus (1450-1515): Italian scholar, printer, publisher; founded Aldine press.

Manzoni, Alessandro (1785-1873): Italian poet, novelist; *I Promessi Sposi.*

Marconi, Guglielmo (1874-1937): Italian engineer, inventor; outstanding contributor to development of wireless telegraphy, radio; Nobel Prize for physics, 1909.

Mariotte, Edme (1620-1684): French physicist; researcher in hydrodynamics.

Martini, Giambattista (1706-1784): Italian Franciscan, composer of Church music, theorist and teacher.

Masaccio, Tommaso (1401-1428): Italian painter; fresco artist of Florentine school; influenced advance to Renaissance painting; called father of modern art.

Massillon, Jean Baptiste (1663-1742): French preacher; bishop of Clermont.

Matthias Corvinus (Hunyady) (1440-1490): One of Hungary's greatest kings, 1458-1490; repelled Turks, fought against Bohemians, Frederick III; patron of arts, literature; introduced Golden Age in Hungary; founded library.

Mauriac, Francois (1885-1970): French writer; awarded Nobel Prize for literature, 1952; works include the novels *The Desert of Love, The Viper's Triangle.*

Mauro, Fra (d. c. 1459): Italian Camaldolese monk, cosmographer; Fra Mauro Highlands, named for him by 17th century astronomers, was the landing site of Apollo 14.

Maxmilian I, the Great (1573-1651): Duke and elector of Bavaria; opposed Protestant cause; founded Catholic League, 1609.

Mazarin, Jules (1602-1661): French cardinal, statesman; prime minister of France under Louis XIII and Louis XIV; concluded Thirty Years' War by the Treaty of Westphalia; strengthened France as a European power.

Meagher, Thomas F. (1823-1867): American politician and soldier, b. Ireland; came to US, 1852; joined Union forces in Civil War; became brigadier general of Irish Brigade organized by him; territorial secretary of Montana, 1865.

Mendel, Gregor Johann (1822-1884): Austrian Augustinian monk, botanist; formulated Mendelian laws of heredity.

Mercier, Desire Joseph (1851-1926): Belgian prelate, philosopher; cardinal archbishop of Malines; promoter of neo-scholastic philosophy; leader against demands of German invaders in 1914; restored Louvain University after World War I; in 1924 began Malines Conversations, an attempt to unify the Anglican and Roman churches.

Mersenne, Marin (1588-1648): French mathematician.

Merton, Thomas (Father M. Louis) (1915-1968): American Trappist priest and author, b. France; convert, 1939; works include *The Seven Storey Mountain* (his autobiography), *Waters of Siloe, Conjectures of a Guilty By-*

stander, and articles in opposition to nuclear war.

Mestrovic, Ivan (1883-1962): Yugoslav sculptor; religious and mythological subjects, Slav folklore, portrait busts; works include *Pieta* at Notre Dame Univ., where he was a professor from 1955-62.

Metternich, Klemens Wenzel Nepomuk Lothar von (1773-1859): Austrian statesman and diplomat.

Meynell, Alice Thompson (1847-1922): English poet, essayist, leader in Catholic literary revival in England; convert. Her husband, **Wilfrid Meynell** (1852-1948): Journalist, publisher, biographer; he and his wife discovered Francis Thompson; convert.

Mezzofanti, Giuseppe (1774-1849): Italian cardinal, linguist, custodian-in-chief of Vatican Library.

Michelangelo Buonarroti (1475-1564): Italian architect, sculptor, painter, poet; outstanding figure of the Renaissance.

Mikolajczyk, Stanislaus (1901-1967): Polish politician; leader of Polish Peasant party in exile; settled in US, 1947.

Miller, Nathan L. (1868-1953): American politician; governor of New York; convert shortly before death.

Millet, Jean Francois (1814-1875): French painter; landscape and religious subjects.

Minton, Sherman (1890-1965): American jurist; US senator, 1935-40; associate justice US Supreme Court, 1949-56; convert, 1961.

Mistral, Gabriela (pen name of **Lucila Godoy de Alcayaga**) (1889-1957): Chilean poet; Nobel Prize for literature, 1945.

Mitchell, James P. (1902-1964): American cabinet official; labor relations expert; US secretary of labor, 1953-61.

Mitchell, John (1870-1919): American labor leader; president of United Mine Workers; convert, 1907.

Mohler, Johann Adam (1796-1838): German theologian.

Mohr, Josef (1792-1848): Austrian priest, poet; *Silent Night.*

Molina, Luis de (1535-1600): Spanish Jesuit, theologian; author of *Concordia,* expounding a system for the reconciliation of grace and free will, called Molinism.

Mondino (dim. for Raimondo) dei Luicci (1275-c. 1327): Italian anatomist.

Monge, Gaspard (1746-1818): French mathematician; called founder of descriptive geometry.

Montcalm, Marquis Louis Joseph de (1712-1759): French marshal, military commander in Canada; fatally wounded in Battle of Quebec.

Montessori, Maria (1870-1952): Italian physician, educator; originator of Montessori method for education of children.

Monteux, Pierre (1875-1964): American conductor, b. France; US citizen, 1942; led most of the world's greatest orchestras.

Moon, Parker Thomas (1892-1936): American historian, educator, author, editor; convert, 1914.

Moore, Thomas (1779-1852): National lyricist of Ireland.

Moore, Thomas Verner (1877-1969): American priest, psychiatrist, educator, author; joined Carthusians in 1947 — had earlier been a Paulist and Benedictine.

Morgagni, Giovanni Battista (1682-1771): Italian physician; founder of anatomical pathology.

Morley, Sylvanus Griswold (1883-1948): American archeologist; convert.

Moylan, Stephen (1734-1811); American patriot, b. Ireland; immigrated to US 1768; joined Continental Army, 1775; aide-de-camp and secretary to General Washington, 1776; leader of cavalry division.

Mozart, J. C. Wolfgang Amadeus (1756-1791): Austrian composer of more than 600 works in a wide range of forms.

Muench, Aloysius J. (1889-1962): American cardinal; ordained priest, 1913; bishop of Fargo, 1935-59; apostolic visitator and liaison representative between US military government and German hierarchy, 1946; nuncio to Germany, 1951-59; cardinal, 1959.

Muller, Johann (1436-1476): German mathematician, astronomer; assisted in calendar reform.

Muller, Johannes Peter (1801-1858): German physiologist, comparative anatomist.

Murillo, Bartolome Esteban (1617-1682): Spanish artist of the Andalusian school; master of color contrast; religious subjects.

Murphy, Frank (1890-1949): American jurist, cabinet official; mayor of Detroit, 1930-33; US high commissioner to the Philippines, 1935-36; governor of Michigan, 1936-38; US attorney general 1939-40; associate justice of US Supreme Court, 1940-49.

Murphy, John Benjamin (1857-1916): American surgeon; inventor of Murphy button; Laetare Medalist, 1902.

Murray, John C. (1904-1967): American Jesuit priest, educator, theologian, ecumenist, international expert on Church-state relations, author.

Murray, Philip (1886-1952): American labor leader, b. Scotland.

N

Nathan, George Jean (1882-1958): American dramatic critic, editor, author; founder with H. L. Mencken of *The American Mercury*; convert, 1957.

Nelaton, Auguste (1807-1873): French surgeon; inventor of Nelaton probe.

Newman, John Henry (1801-1890): English cardinal, theologian; leader of Oxford Movement; convert, 1845; ordained to priesthood, 1847; founded Oratorians in England; master of prose style; author of historical and apologetical works, poems, novels.

Nicholas of Lyra (1270-1340): Franciscan biblical scholar.

Nieuland, Julius Arthur (1878-1936): American priest of Congregation of Holy Cross, b. Belgium; chemist, botanist; Notre Dame scientist, contributed to invention of Lewisite gas; discovered method for producing synthetic rubber.

Niza, Marcos de (d. 1558): Franciscan missionary, explored parts of Arizona and New Mexico, 1539; accompanied Coronado's expedition.

Nobili, Leopoldo (1784-1835): Italian physicist, inventor of the thermopile.

Noll, John F. (1875-1956): American prelate, author, editor; ordained priest, 1898; bishop of Fort Wayne, Ind., 1925-56; founder and editor of weekly newspaper *Our Sunday Visitor*, 1912; wrote *Father Smith Instructs Jackson*, other books and pamphlets.

Nollet, Jean-Antoine (1700-1770): French priest, physicist; researcher in electricity; invented an electroscope.

Noyes, Alfred (1880-1958): English poet; convert, 1927.

O

O'Callahan, Joseph (1906-1964): American Jesuit priest; Navy chaplain in World War II; awarded the Congressional Medal of Honor, for action aboard the carrier Franklin on Mar. 19, 1945.

Ocampo, Sebastian (1466-1521): Spanish explorer; circumnavigated Cuba, proved its insular character.

O'Connell, Daniel (1775-1847): Irish statesman, nationalist leader; known as the Liberator; responsible for Catholic emancipation, 1829.

O'Connor, (Mary) Flannery (1925-1964): American novelist and short-story writer.

O'Dwyer, Joseph (1841-1898): American physician; developed method of aiding breathing to prevent asphyxia in diphtheria.

Oertel, Abraham (1527-1598): Flemish geographer; publisher of an atlas.

O'Hara, Edwin Vincent (1881-1956): American prelate; ordained priest, 1905; bishop of Great Falls, Mont. 1930-39; bishop of Kansas City, Mo., 1939-56; title of archbishop, 1954; leader in catechetical work in the US; founder of National Catholic Rural Life Conference.

O'Higgins, Bernardo (1778-1842): Chilean soldier, statesman; Liberator of Chile.

Olaf (II) Haraldsson, Saint (995-1030): King of Norway, 1016-1028; attempted conversion of his country; killed in battle; patron of Norway; canonized, 1164.

Orellana, Francisco de (1500-1546): Spanish navigator, explored the Amazon River.

Origen (185-254): Theologian and writer, head of catechetical schools at Alexandria, Caesarea; author of biblical, theological works.

Orosius, Paul (380?-?): Spanish priest; author of book of universal history.

Oursler, Fulton (1893-1952): American author, editor, lecturer; convert 1943; works include *The Greatest Story Ever Told* and *The Greatest Book Ever Written.*

Ozanam, Frederic (1813-1853): French historian; a founder of St. Vincent de Paul Society. (See Index.)

Ozanam, Jacques (1640-1717): French mathematician.

P

Pacioli, Luca (1450?-1520?): Italian Franciscan, mathematician; author of first description of double-entry bookkeeping.

Paderewski, Ignace (1860-1941): Polish pianist, conductor, composer; first premier of Poland after World War I.

Palestrina, Giovanni Pierluigi da (1526-1594): Italian composer of Church music in medieval moods; noted for polyphonic style.

Palladio, Andrea (1518-1580): Italian architect; controlling influence of 17th-century architecture called Palladian.

Palmer, Gretta (1905-1953): American journalist, author; convert, 1946.

Papini, Giovanni (1881-1956): Italian writer; convert, 1918; author of *Life of Christ.*

Pare, Ambroise (1517-1590): French surgeon; called father of modern surgery; introduced artery ligature.

Paris, Bruno Paulin Gaston (1839-1903): French philologist, author.

Parsch, Pius (1884-1954): Austrian Augustinian, theologian, Scripture scholar, liturgist.

Parsons, Wilfrid (1887-1958): American Jesuit priest, editor, author, educator; editor-in-chief of *America*, 1925-36.

Pascal, Blaise (1623-1662): French philosopher, scientist; demonstrated that a column of air has weight; author of *Pensees.*

Pasteur, Louis (1822-1895): French chemist; developed a vaccine against hydrophobia; founded Pasteur Institute; father of bacteriology.

Pastor, Ludwig von (1854-1928): German historian; *The History of the Popes from the Beginning of the Middle Ages.*

Patmore, Coventry (1823-1896): English poet; convert, 1864.

Pazmany, Peter (1570-1637): Hungarian Jesuit, cardinal; leader of Counter Reformation; translated Bible into Hungarian; called founder of modern Hungarian literature.

Peguy, Charles Pierre (1873-1914): French poet and writer; outstanding Catholic defender of Dreyfus; founded the journal *Cahiers de la Quinzaine*; works include *The Mystery of the Charity of Joan of Arc* and religious meditations.

Pelouze, Theophile Jules (1807-1867): French chemist; developed production of guncotton, nitrocellulose.

Pepin the Short (714-768): King of the Franks, son of Charles Martel, father of Charlemagne; first Frank crowned with religious ceremonies; defeated Lombards and restored central Italy to the Holy See.

Perosi, Lorenzo (1872-1956): Italian priest, composer.

Perugino, Il (Pietro Vannucci) (1446-1523): Italian painter; leader of Umbrian school; teacher of Raphael; religious subjects.

Petau (Petavius), Denys (1583-1652): French Jesuit, theologian; called father of the history of dogma.

Petrarch (Francesco Petrarca) (1304-1374): Italian poet.

Piazzi Giuseppe (1746-1826): Italian monk, astronomer; discovered Ceres, first known asteroid.

Picard, Jean (1620-1682): French astronomer; accurately measured degree of a meridian.

Pinturicchio, Bernardino di Betto di Biagio (1454-1513): Italian painter of the Umbrian school; historical and religious subjects.

Pio, Padre (Francesco Forgione) (1887-1968): Italian Capuchin priest; reputed stigmatist.

Pire, Dominique Georges (1910-1969): Belgian priest; awarded Nobel Peace Prize in 1958 for work for displaced persons.

Pisano, Andrea (1270-1348) and his son **Nino** (1315-1368); Italian sculptors.

Pisano, Nicolo (1225-1278): Italian sculptor; works among greatest of Romanesque style. His son, **Giovanni** (1240-1320): Sculptor, architect.

Pitra, Jean Baptiste Francois (1812-1889): French Benedictine, cardinal, scholar.

Pizarro, Francisco (1470-1541): Spanish explorer, conqueror of Peru.

Plumier, Charles (1646-1704): French botanical explorer of Antilles, Central America.

Pole, Reginald (1500-1558): English prelate, cardinal archbishop of Canterbury; opposed divorce of Henry VIII; papal legate, participant in Council of Trent.

Polo, Marco (1245-1324): Early traveler to China, b. Venice; *Book of Marco Polo.*

Ponce de Leon (1460-1521): Spanish explorer; discovered Florida.

Pope, Alexander (1688-1744): English poet; master of the rimed couplet.

Pouget, Jean Francois Albert du, Marquis de Nadaillac (1817-1904): French anthropologist; authority on cave drawings.

Poussin, Nicolas (1594-1665): French painter; historical and landscape subjects.

Price, Thomas Frederick (1860-1919): American missionary; co-founder with Bishop Walsh of the Catholic Foreign Mission Society of America (Maryknoll Fathers); called the Tar Heel Apostle.

Pro, Miguel (1891-1927): Mexican Jesuit; fled Mexico during 1914 Revolution; returned to Mexico, 1926, after his ordination in Belgium; arrested, 1927, and shot to death by police in Mexico City.

Prohaszka, Ottokar (1858-1927): Hungarian bishop; preacher, author.

Provancher, Leon Abel (1820-1892): Canadian priest, naturalist; called father of natural history in Canada.

Puccini, Giacomo (1858-1924): Italian operatic composer.

Pugin, Augustus Welby Northmore (1812-1852): English architect.

Pulaski, Casimir (1748-1779): Polish patriot, fought in American Revolution; called Father of the American Cavalry; fatally wounded at Savannah.

Puvis de Chavannes, Pierre (1824-1898): French muralist.

Q

Quinlan, Thomas (1896-1970): Irish Columban missionary bishop; served in China, 1920-34; prefect apostolic of Chun Cheon, Korea, 1934; interned by Japanese during World War II; imprisoned by North Koreans, 1950-53.

Quinones, Francis (1482-1540): Spanish Franciscan, cardinal, liturgist; worked on revision of breviary.

R

Racine, Jean Baptiste (1639-1699): French dramatic poet.

Rameau, Jean-Philippe (1683-1764): French organist, music theorist, operatic composer.

Randall, James Ryder (1839-1908): American journalist, poet, song writer; _Maryland, My Maryland._

Raphael Santi (1483-1520): Italian painter of religious, portrait, other subjects; architect of St. Peter's; among greatest of Renaissance painters.

Reeve, Arthur Benjamin (1882-1936): American educator, author; convert, 1926.

Regnault, Henri Victor (1810-1878): French chemist, physicist; authority in thermometry.

Reiffenstuel, Anaclete (Johann Georg) (1641-1703): German Franciscan, theologian, canonist.

Reinhold, Hans (1897-1968): American pioneer in liturgical movement, b. Germany; came to US, 1936; naturalized citizen.

Reni, Guido (1575-1642): Italian painter of the Eclectic school; religious and other subjects.

Repplier, Agnes (1858-1950): American author, essayist.

Reymont, Wladislaw (1867-1925): Polish novelist; awarded Nobel Prize for literature in 1924 for _The Peasants._

Ribera, Jose (1588-1652): Spanish painter of Neapolitan school, etcher; religious subjects.

Ricci, Matteo (1552-1610): Italian Jesuit missionary in India and China; introduced Christianity in China; author.

Riccioli, Giovanni Battista (1598-1671): Italian Jesuit, astronomer; introduced some lunar nomenclature in use today.

Richelieu, Armand Jean du Plessis, Duc de (1585-1642): French cardinal, statesman;

founder of the French Academy, 1634.

Ritter, Joseph E. (1892-1967): American cardinal; ordained priest, 1917; auxiliary bishop, 1933, bishop, 1934, and first archbishop, 1944, of Indianapolis; archbishop of St. Louis, 1946-67; cardinal, 1961; ordered desegregation of St. Louis archdiocesan schools, 1957; was outspoken US progressive bishop at Vatican II; first Mass in vernacular in US offered in his diocese.

Robbia, Luca della (1400-1482): Florentine sculptor; developed a glaze for terra cotta ware (Robbia work).

Robinson, William Callyhan (1834-1911): American jurist, author; Episcopalian minister; convert, 1863.

Rochambeau, Jean Baptiste Donatien de Vimeur, Conte de (1725-1807): French general; led French forces sent to aid Americans in Revolution.

Rockne, Knute Kenneth (1888-1931): American football player and coach, b. Norway; immigrated to US, 1893; football coach at Notre Dame University, 1918-31; convert, 1925.

Rodzinski, Artur (1894-1958): American symphony conductor, b. Yugoslavia; became US citizen, 1933.

Rosecrans, William Starke (1819-1898): American army officer; graduate of West Point; army commander during the Civil War; Federal official; convert, 1845.

Rossini, Gioacchino Antonio (1792-1868): Italian operatic composer and innovator in orchestration.

Roualt, Georges (1871-1958): French painter of modern school; convert.

Rubens, Peter Paul (1577-1640): Flemish painter; great colorist, landscape, portrait, historical, religious subjects.

Rubruck, William (1220-1293): French Franciscan missionary and traveler in the East, especially China.

Ruth, George Herman (Babe) (1894-1948): American baseball player and record holder; convert, 1906.

Ruysbroeck, John, Bl. (1293-1381): Flemish mystical theologian; beatified, 1908.

Ryan, Abram J. (1838-1886): American priest, poet; called Poet of the Confederacy.

S

San Gallo, Giuliano Giamberti da (1445-1516); his brother, **Antonio da San Gallo, the Elder** (1455-1534); their nephew, **Antonio da San Gallo, the Younger** (1483-1546): Italian architects.

San Martin, Jose de (1778-1850): South American soldier, statesman; defeated Spanish in Argentina, established independence of Chile, proclaimed independence and called Protector of Peru.

Santorini, Giovanni Domenico (1681-1737): Italian physician, anatomist; discovered emissary veins leading out of sinuses, risory muscles, fissures in external ear.

Sarbiewki, Mathias Casimir (1595-1640): Polish Jesuit, poet; called the Horace of Poland.

Sarto, Andrea del (1486-1531): Florentine painter; great colorist, master of light and shade; religious subjects.

Savage, (Charles) Courtenay (1890-1946): American playwright, author; convert, 1937.

Scanderbeg (George Castriota) (c. 1403-1468): Albanian national hero; leader in Albanian independence movement against Turks.

Scarlatti, Alessandro (1659-1725): Italian operatic composer; called founder of modern opera.

Scheiner, Christoph (1579-1650): German Jesuit, astronomer; made independent discovery of sunspots.

Schlegel, Friedrich von (1772-1829): German Romantic poet, essayist, novelist; convert, 1803.

Schmid, Christoph von (1768-1854): German educator, pioneer writer of children's books.

Schmidt, Wilhelm (1868-1954): German Divine Word priest, ethnologist and historian of religions.

Schubert, Franz Peter (1797-1828): Austrian composer of symphonic and other orchestral works.

Schuman, Robert (1886-1963): French statesman; leader of the Popular Republican Party; Premier of France twice (November, 1947-July, 1948; Aug. 31-Sept. 9, 1948); major figure in post-World War II efforts at European unity; author of Schuman Plan for pooling French and German coal and steel production, a forerunner of the Common Market.

Schuyler, Philippa (1932-1967): American pianist, news correspondent.

Searle, George Mary (1839-1918): American priest and astronomer, b. England of American parents; came to US, 1840; convert, 1866; joined Paulists, 1868; ordained, 1871; director of Vatican Observatory, 1898.

Schwann, Theodor (1810-1882): German anatomist, physiologist; founder of cell theory.

Schwarz, Berthold (13th or 14th c.): German Franciscan; called inventor of gunpowder.

Secchi, Angelo (1818-1878): Italian Jesuit, astronomer; professor at Georgetown University; did spectroscopic work on sun, stars, classification of stars; invented meteorograph.

Segura y Saenz, Pedro (1880-1957): Spanish cardinal, primate of Spain; outspoken critic of Nazism, Fascism and Franco regime.

Seidl, Johann Gabriel (1804-1875): Austrian journalist, poet; author of words for Austrian national anthem.

Semmelweis, Ignaz Philipp (1818-1865): Hungarian physician; pioneer of antiseptic treatment in obstetrics.

Semmes, Raphael (1809-1877): American naval officer, lawyer; commander in US Navy; resigned, 1861, to enter Confederate Navy; commanded the Sumter and the Alabama, commerce destroyers.

Sienkiewicz, Henryk (1846-1916): Polish novelist; awarded Nobel Prize for literature in 1905.

Shea, Sir Ambrose (1815-1905): Canadian political leader; member of House of Assembly of Newfoundland; governor of the Bahamas.

Shea, John Dawson Gilmary (1824-1892): American historian, author; *History of the Catholic Church in the United States.*

Sheridan, Philip H. (1831-1888): American army officer; graduate of West Point; general cavalry commander during the Civil War.

Shevchenko, Taras (1814-1861): Ukrainian poet, nationalist; founder of the Society of Sts. Cyril and Methodius for Ukrainian independence.

Shields, James (1806-1879): American soldier and statesman, b. Ireland; arrived US, 1823, settled in Kaskaskia, Ill.; army officer, politician; general in Mexican War; governor of Oregon Territory, 1849; US senator from Illinois, 1849-55, from Minnesota, 1858-59; moved to California, 1859; brigadier general in Civil War, resigned commission, 1863; moved to Missouri; US senator from Missouri, 1879. Represents Illinois in Statuary Hall.

Shipman, Andrew Jackson (1857-1915): American lawyer, author; convert, 1876; authority on Church law.

Sitwell, Edith (1887-1964): English poet, critic, novelist; convert, 1955.

Skinner, Henrietta Channing Dana (1857-1928): American author; convert, 1878.

Smith, Alfred Emanuel (1873-1944): American politician; governor of New York; Democratic presidential candidate, 1928, the first Catholic ever nominated.

Smith, Ignatius (1886-1957): American Dominican priest, orator, teacher, retreat master.

Smith, Matthew (1891-1960): American priest, editor; founder of Register chain of newspapers.

Sobieski, John III (1624-1696): Polish king, soldier; rescued Vienna from Turks, caused their expulsion from Poland and Hungary.

Spalding, John Lancaster (1840-1916): American prelate; nephew of Martin Spalding, below; author of books on religion, philosophy and social issues; advocate of Catholic parochial school system; served on President Roosevelt's Anthracite Coal Strike Commission, 1902; first bishop of Peoria, 1876-1908, when he resigned because of ill health.

Spalding, Martin J. (1810-1872): American prelate; bishop of Louisville, 1848-64; archbishop of Baltimore, 1864-72; author of numerous books; helped establish American

College of Louvain; advocate of a North American College in Rome and an American Catholic university.

Spallanzani, Lazzaro (1729-1799): Italian naturalist; experimenter on digestion, other functions; disproved theory of spontaneous generation.

Spearman, Frank Hamilton (1859-1937): American author; convert, 1884; Laetare Medalist, 1935.

Spellman, Francis J. (1889-1967): American cardinal; ordained priest, 1916; served in papal secretariat of state, 1925-32; auxiliary of Boston, 1932; archbishop of New York, 1939-67; cardinal, 1946; military vicar of US; author.

Starr, Eliza Allen (1824-1901): American educator, author; convert, 1856; first woman Laetare Medalist, 1885.

Stensen, Niels (Steno, Nicolaus) (1638-1687): Danish bishop, anatomist; discovered excretory duct of parotid glands, convert, 1667.

Stoddard, Charles Warren (1843-1909): American journalist, poet, author; convert, 1867.

Stoddard, John Lawson (1850-1931): American author, lecturer; convert, 1922.

Stone, James Kent (Fr. Fidelis, C.P.) (1840-1921): American missionary priest, author; Episcopalian minister, 1866; convert, 1869; ordained priest, 1872.

Storer, Horatio Robinson (1830-1922): American physician, medical professor, author; convert, 1897.

Stoss, Veit (1440-1533): German sculptor; master wood-carver.

Stradivari, Antonio (1644-1737): Italian violin maker.

Stritch, Samuel (1887-1958): American cardinal; ordained priest, 1910; bishop of Toledo, 1921-30; archbishop of Milwaukee, 1930-39; archbishop of Chicago, 1939-58; cardinal, 1946; first American appointed to the Roman Curia, died before he could take up his post as pro-prefect of the Sacred Congregation for the Propagation of the Faith.

Sturzo, Luigi (1871-1959): Italian priest-statesman.

Suarez, Francisco (1548-1617): Spanish Jesuit, theologian; considered a founder of international law; author of many works; *Doctor Eximius.*

T

Tabb, John Banister (1845-1909): American poet, served in Confederate navy, convert, 1872; ordained priest, 1884.

Taggart, Marion Ames (1866-1945): American author, convert, 1880.

Takamine, Jokichi (1854-1922): Japanese-American chemist; developed Takadiastase, isolated adrenalin; convert.

Talbot, Matthew (1856-1925): Irish layman noted for his sanctity; a reformed alcoholic, is considered a model for those with this condi-

tion; his cause for beatification is under consideration.

Taney, Roger Brooke (1777-1864): American jurist, cabinet official; US attorney general, 1831-33; secretary of the treasury, 1833-34; chief justice United States Supreme Court, 1836-64; associated with the Dred Scott decision, 1857.

Tasso, Torquato (1544-1595): Italian poet.

Teilhard de Chardin, Pierre (1881-1955): French Jesuit; paleontologist and explorer.

Tekakwitha, Kateri (1656-1680): American Indian maiden; Lily of the Mohawks; instructed by Jesuit missionaries and baptized at age of 20; her cause for beatification is under consideration.

Thayer, John (1755-1815): American priest; Protestant chaplain during Revolutionary War; convert, 1783; first native New England priest; missionary in Kentucky; author.

Thomas, Charles Louis Ambrose (1811-1896): Alsatian composer of operatic and other works.

Thomas a Kempis (1380-1471): Dutch Augustinian, considered author of the *Imitation of Christ.*

Thomas of Celano (1200-1255): Italian Franciscan; biographer of St. Francis of Assisi.

Thompson, Francis (1859-1907): English poet; *The Hound of Heaven.*

Tieffentaller, Joseph (1710-1785): Jesuit missionary, geographer.

Tintoretto, Jacopo Robusti (1518-1594): Italian painter of Venetian school; religious and portrait subjects.

Tisserant, Eugene (1884-1972): French cardinal, scholar; librarian and archivist of the Vatican; headed Congregation for the Eastern Churches for more than 20 years; dean of the College of Cardinals, 1951-72; specialist in Oriental languages; member of the French Academy.

Titian or **Tiziano Vecelli** (1477-1576): Italian painter, greatest of the Venetian school; frescoes in wide range of subjects; portraits.

Tobin, Maurice J. (1901-1953): American politician, cabinet official; mayor of Boston, 1937, 1941; governor of Massachusetts, 1944; US secretary of labor, 1949-53.

Tocqueville, Alexis Charles de (1805-1859): French writer, statesman; *La Democratie en Amerique.*

Torricelli, Evangelista (1608-1647): Italian mathematician, physicist; improved telescope, invented barometer.

Toscanelli, Paolo dal Pozzo (1397-1482): Italian physician, geographer; probably aided Columbus.

Toscanini, Arturo (1867-1957): Italian operatic and symphony conductor.

Tulasne, Louis Rene (1815-1885): French botanist; called founder of modern mycology.

U

Undset, Sigrid (1882-1949): Norwegian

novelist; Nobel Prize for literature, 1928; *Kristen Lavransdatter;* convert, 1924.

V

Valentine, Basil (born 1394): Benedictine monk; founder of analytical chemistry.

Vandyke (Van Dyck), Sir Anthony (1599-1641): Flemish associate of Rubens, English court painter; religious and portrait subjects.

Vasari, Giorgio (1511-1574): Italian painter, architect; founder of modern art history and criticism.

Vasquez, Gabriel (1551-1604): Spanish Jesuit, theologian.

Vega, Lope Felix de (Vega) Carpio (1562-1635): Spanish priest, dramatic poet; founder of Spanish national drama.

Velasquez, Diego Rodriguez de Silva y (1599-1660): Spanish painter; master of naturalism; historical, portrait, religious and other subjects.

Verdi, Giuseppe (1813-1901): Italian composer of operatic and other works.

Verne, Jules (1828-1905): French writer; scientific fiction.

Vernier, Pierre (1580-1637): French mathematician; formulated vernier scale for accurate linear and angular magnitude.

Veronese, Paolo (1528-1588): Italian painter of Venetian school; Painter of Pageants; religious frescoes and paintings.

Verrazano, Giovanni da (1485-1528): Italian navigator; explored coast of North America for Francis I of France; claimed by his countrymen to be discoverer of Hudson River.

Verrocchio, Andrea del (1435-1488): Florentine sculptor and painter of Tuscan school.

Vesalius, Andreas (1514-1564): Belgian anatomist; founder of modern anatomy.

Vespucci, Amerigo (1451-1512): Italian navigator; called discoverer of mainland of America, named after him.

Vico, Francesco de (1805-1848): Italian Jesuit, astronomer; discovered six comets.

Viete (Vieta), Francois, Seigneur de La Bigottiere (1540-1603): French mathematician; founder of modern algebra, which he applied to geometry and trigonometry.

Vignola, Giacomo Barozzi da (1507-1573): Italian architect; architectural theorist.

Vincent of Beauvais (1190-1264): French Dominican; author of comprehensive scientific encyclopedia.

Vinci, Leonardo da (1452-1519): Florentine painter, sculptor, architect, engineer, scientist; paintings mainly of religious subjects; founder of science of hydraulics, researcher in meteorology, anatomy, mathematics.

Vladimir, Saint (956-1015): First Christian ruler of Russia.

Volta, Alessandro, Count (1754-1827): Italian physicist; early researcher in electricity; the volt named for him.

Vorosmarty, Michael (1800-1855): Hungarian poet; his lyric poem "Szozat" became a national anthem.

W-Z

Wagner, Robert F. (1877-1953): American public official and judge, b. Nastatten Hessen, Germany; US senator, 1926-49; sponsor of Wagner National Labor Relations Act; convert, 1946.

Waldseemuller, Martin (1470-1518): German cartographer; made first modern atlas; first to use the name America.

Walker, Frank C. (1886-1959): American politician, cabinet official; US postmaster general, 1940-45.

Walsh, James Joseph (1865-1942): American physician, author; *The Thirteenth, the Greatest of Centuries.*

Walsh, William Thomas (1891-1949): American historian.

Walworth, Clarence Augustus (1820-1900): American priest; convert, 1845; ordained, 1848; assisted Isaac Hecker in founding the Paulists, whom he left because of illness; author.

Warren, Leonard (1911-1960): American opera star; convert from Judaism 1942; baritone of Metropolitan Opera.

Wattson, Lewis Thomas (Father James Francis Paul) (1863-1940): American founder; as Episcopalian presbyter, founded Friars of the Atonement, 1899; inaugurated Chair of Unity Octave, 1908; founded St. Christopher's Inn, Garrison, N.Y.; convert with members of his community, 1909; ordained priest, 1910.

Waugh, Evelyn (1903-1966): English writer; convert, 1930.

Weber, Karl Maria von (1786-1826): German composer of operatic and other works; a founder of German opera.

Weigel, Gustave (1900-1964): American Jesuit priest, theologian, author; pioneer in Catholic-Protestant dialogue; consultor of the Vatican Secretariat for Promoting Christian Unity.

White, Edward Douglass (1845-1921): American jurist; US senator, 1891-94; associate justice US Supreme Court, 1894-1910; chief justice, 1910-21; wrote decisions for more than 700 of the 4,000 cases decided during his time on the Court. Represents Louisiana in Statuary Hall.

White, Helen C. (1896-1967): American educator, author.

Wilde, Oscar (1856-1900): Irish poet; dramatist; reconciled to the Church before his death in France.

William of Ockham (Occam) (1300-1349): English Franciscan; philosopher, logician; author of the philosophical axiom, "beings are not to be multiplied without necessity."

William the Conqueror (1027-1087): Duke of Normandy; invaded England, 1066, defeated Harold at Hastings, crowned King of England.

Williams, Michael (1877-1950): American

journalist and author, b. Halifax, Nova Scotia; founded *Commonweal*, 1924.

Winckelmann, Johann Joachim (1717-1768): German art historian, classical archaeologist; convert, 1754.

Windle, Sir Bertram (1858-1929): English scientist; professor at Toronto University, Canada, from 1919; author of works intended to explain relations between scientific progress and Church teaching.

Windthorst, Ludwig (1812-1891): German statesman, leader of Center Party.

Wiseman, Nicholas Patrick (1802-1865): English cardinal, archbishop of Westminster; influenced Catholic revival, encouraged Oxford Movement.

Wynne, Robert J. (1851-1922): American cabinet official; US postmaster general, 1904-05.

Ximenez (Jimenez) de Cisneros, Francisco (1437-1517): Spanish Franciscan, cardinal, statesman.

Yoshida, Shigeru (1878-1967): Japanese statesman; prime minister of Japan, 1946-54; convert shortly before his death.

Zrinyi, Nicholas, Count (1620-1664): Hungarian general, poet; author of first Hungarian epic, *The Fall of Szigets*.

Zurbaran, Francisco de (1598-1664): Spanish painter; religious and monastic portrait subjects.

MISSIONARIES TO THE AMERICAS

Allouez, Claude Jean (1622-1689): French Jesuit; missionary in Canada and midwestern US; preached to 20 different tribes of Indians and baptized over 10,000; vicar general of Northwest.

Altham, John (1589-1640): English Jesuit; missionary among Indians in Maryland.

Anchieta, Jose (1534-1597): Portuguese Jesuit; missionary in Brazil; writer.

Andreis, Felix de (1778-1820): Italian Vincentian; missionary and educator in western US.

Aparicio, Bl. Sebastian (1502-1600): Franciscan brother, born Spain; settled in Mexico, c. 1533; worked as road builder and farmer before becoming Franciscan at about the age of 70; beatified, 1787.

Badin, Stephen T. (1768-1853): French missioner; came to US, 1792, when Sulpician seminary in Paris was closed; ordained, 1793, Baltimore, the first priest ordained in US; missionary in Kentucky, Ohio and Michigan; bought land on which Notre Dame University now stands; buried on its campus.

Baraga, Frederic (1797-1868): Slovenian missionary bishop in US; studied at Ljubljana and Vienna, ordained, 1823; came to US, 1830; missionary to Indians of Upper Michigan; first bishop of Marquette, 1857-1868; wrote Chippewa grammar, dictionary, prayer book and other works.

Bertran, St. Louis (1526-1581): Spanish Dominican; missionary in Colombia and Caribbean, 1562-69; canonized, 1671.

Bourgeoys, Bl. Marguerite (1620-1700): French foundress, missionary; settled in Canada, 1653; founded Congregation of Notre Dame de Montreal, 1658; beatified, 1950.

Brebeuf, St. John de (1593-1649): French Jesuit; missionary among Huron Indians in Canada; martyred by Iroquois, Mar. 16, 1649; canonized, 1930; one of Jesuit North American martyrs.

Cancer de Barbastro, Louis (1500-1549): Spanish Dominican; began missionary work in Middle America, 1533; killed at Tampa Bay, Fla.

Castillo, Bl. John de (1596-1628): Spanish Jesuit; worked in Paraguay Indian mission settlements (reductions); martyred; beatified, 1934.

Catala, Magin (1761-1830): Spanish Franciscan; worked in California mission of Santa Clara for 36 years.

Chabanel, St. Noel (1613-1649): French Jesuit; missionary among Huron Indians in Canada; murdered by renegade Huron, Dec. 8, 1649; canonized, 1930; one of Jesuit North American martyrs.

Chaumonot, Pierre Joseph (1611-1693): French Jesuit; missionary among Indians in Canada.

Claver, St. Peter (1581-1654): Spanish Jesuit; missionary among Negroes of South America and West Indies; canonized, 1888; patron of Catholic missions among Negroes.

Daniel, St. Anthony (1601-1648): French Jesuit; missionary among Huron Indians in Canada; martyred by Iroquois, July 4, 1648; canonized, 1930; one of Jesuit North American martyrs.

De Smet, Pierre Jean (1801-1873): Belgian-born Jesuit; missionary among Indians of northwestern US; served as intermediary between Indians and US government; wrote on Indian culture.

Duchesne, Bl. Rose Philippine (1769-1852): French nun; educator and missionary in the US; established first convent of the Society of the Sacred Heart in the US, at St. Charles, Mo. (later Florissant); founded schools for girls; did missionary work among Indians; beatified, 1940.

Farmer, Ferdinand (family name, Steinmeyer) (1720-1786): German Jesuit; missionary in Philadelphia, where he died; one of the first missionaries in New Jersey.

Flaget, Benedict J. (1763-1850): French Sulpician bishop; came to US, 1792; missionary and educator in US; first bishop of Bardstown, Ky. (now Louisville), 1810-32; 1833-50.

Gallitzin, Demetrius (1770-1840): Russian prince, born The Hague; convert, 1787; ordained priest at Baltimore, 1795; frontier missionary, known as Father Smith; Gallitzin, Pa., named for him.

Garnier, St. Charles (c. 1606-1649): French Jesuit; missionary among Hurons in Canada; martyred by Iroquois, Dec. 7, 1649; canonized, 1930; one of Jesuit North American martyrs.

Gibault, Pierre (1737-1804): Canadian missionary in Illinois and Indiana; aided in securing states of Ohio, Indiana, Illinois, Michigan and Wisconsin for the Americans during Revolution.

Gonzalez, Bl. Roch (1576-1628): Paraguayan Jesuit; worked in Paraguay Indian mission settlements (reductions); martyred; beatified, 1934.

Goupil, St. Rene (1607-1642): French Jesuit brother; missionary companion of St. Isaac Jogues among the Hurons; martyred, Sept. 29, 1642; canonized, 1930; one of Jesuit North American martyrs.

Gravier, Jacques (1651-1708): French Jesuit; missionary among Indians of Canada and midwestern US.

Jogues, St. Isaac (1607-1646): French Jesuit; missionary among Indians in Canada; martyred near present site of Auriesville, N.Y., by Mohawks, Oct. 18, 1646; canonized, 1930; one of Jesuit North American martyrs.

Kino, Eusebio (1645-1711): Italian Jesuit; missionary and explorer in US; arrived Southwest, 1681; established 25 Indian missions, took part in 14 exploring expeditions in northern Mexico, Arizona and southern California; helped develop livestock raising and farming in the area. He was selected in 1965 to represent Arizona in Statuary Hall.

Lalande, St. John (d. 1646): French Jesuit brother; martyred by Mohawks at Auriesville, N. Y., Oct. 19, 1646; canonized, 1930; one of Jesuit North American martyrs.

Lalemant, St. Gabriel (1610-1649): French Jesuit; missionary among the Hurons in Canada; martyred by the Iroquois, Mar. 17, 1649; canonized, 1930; one of Jesuit North American martyrs.

Lamy, Jean Baptiste (1814-1888): French prelate; came to US, 1839; missionary in Ohio and Kentucky; bishop in Southwest from 1850; first bishop (later archbishop) of Santa Fe, 1850-1885. He was nominated in 1951 to represent New Mexico in Statuary Hall.

Las Casas, Bartolome (1474-1566): Spanish Dominican; missionary in Haiti, Jamaica and Venezuela; reformer of abuses against Indians and Negroes; bishop of Chalapas, Mexico, 1544-47; historian.

Manogue, Patrick (1831-1895): Missionary bishop in US, b. Ireland; migrated to US; miner in California; studied for priesthood at St. Mary's of the Lake, Chicago, and St. Sulpice, Paris; ordained, 1861; missionary among Indians of California and Nevada; coadjutor bishop, 1881-84, and bishop, 1884-86, of Grass Valley; first bishop of Sacramento, 1886-1895, when see was transferred there.

Margil, Antonio (1657-1726): Spanish Franciscan; missionary in Middle America; apostle of Guatemala; established missions in Texas.

Marie de l'Incarnation, Ven. (1599-1672): French Ursuline nun; arrived in Canada, 1639; first superior of Ursulines in Quebec; missionary to Indians; writer.

Marquette, Jacques (1637-1675): French Jesuit; missionary and explorer in America; sent to New France, 1666; began missionary work among Ottawa Indians on Lake Superior, 1668; accompanied Joliet down the Mississippi to mouth of the Arkansas, 1673, and returned to Lake Michigan by way of Illinois River; made a second trip over the same route; his diary and map are of historical significance. He was selected in 1895 to represent Wisconsin in Statuary Hall.

Massias, St. John de (1585-1645); Dominican brother, a native of Spain; entered Dominican Friary at Lima, Peru, 1622; served as doorkeeper until his death; beatified, 1837; canonized 1975.

Mazzuchelli, Samuel C. (1806-1864): Italian Dominican; missionary in midwestern US; called Builder of the West; writer.

Membre, Zenobius (1645-1687): French Franciscan; missionary among Indians of Illinois; accompanied LaSalle expedition down the Mississippi (1681-1682) and Louisiana colonizing expedition (1684) which landed in Texas; murdered by Indians.

Nerinckx, Charles (1761-1824): Belgian priest; missionary in Kentucky; founded Sisters of Loretto at the Foot of the Cross.

Nobrega, Manoel (1517-1570): Portuguese Jesuit; leader of first Jesuit missionaries to Brazil, 1549.

Padilla, Juan de (d. 1542): Spanish Franciscan; missionary among Indians of Mexico and southwestern US; killed by Indians in Kansas; protomartyr of the US.

Palou, Francisco (c. 1722-1789): Spanish Franciscan; accompanied Junipero Serra to Mexico, 1749; founded Mission Dolores in San Francisco; wrote history of the Franciscans in California.

Peter of Ghent (d. 1572): Belgian Franciscan brother; missionary in Mexico for 49 years.

Porres, St. Martin de (1569-1639): Peruvian Dominican oblate; his father was a Spanish soldier and his mother a Negro freedwoman from Panama; called wonder worker of Peru; beatified, 1837; canonized, 1962.

Quiroga, Vasco de (1470-1565): Spanish missionary in Mexico; founded hospitals; bishop of Michoacan, 1537.

Ravalli, Antonio (1811-1884): Italian Jesuit; missionary in far-western United States, mostly Montana, for 40 years.

Raymbaut, Charles (1602-1643): French Jesuit; missionary among Indians of Canada and northern US.

Richard, Gabriel (1767-1832): French Sulpician; missionary in Illinois and Michigan; a founder of University of Michigan; elected delegate to Congress from Michigan, 1823; first priest to hold seat in the House of Representatives.

Rodriguez, Bl. Alonso (1598-1628): Spanish Jesuit; missionary in Paraguay; martyred; beatified, 1934.

Rosati, Joseph (1789-1843): Italian Vincentian; missionary bishop in US (vicar apostolic of Mississippi and Alabama, 1822; coadjutor of Louisiana and the Two Floridas, 1823-26; administrator of New Orleans, 1826-29; first bishop of St. Louis, 1826-1843).

Sahagun, Bernardino de (c. 1500-1590): Spanish Franciscan; missionary in Mexico for over 60 years; expert on Aztec archaeology.

Seelos, Francis X. (1819-1867): Redemptorist missionary, born Bavaria; ordained, 1844, at Baltimore; missionary in Pittsburgh and New Orleans.

Serra, Junipero (1713-1784): Spanish Franciscan, b. Majorca; missionary in America; arrived Mexico, 1749, where he did missionary work for 20 years; began work in Upper California in 1769 and established nine of the 21 Franciscan missions along the Pacific coast; baptized some 6,000 Indians and confirmed almost 5,000; a cultural pioneer of California. Represents California in Statuary Hall.

Seghers, Charles J. (1839-1886): Belgian missionary bishop in North America; Apostle of Alaska; archbishop of Oregon City (now Portland), 1880-1884; murdered by berserk companion while on missionary journey.

Solanus, St. Francis (1549-1610): Spanish Franciscan; missionary in Paraguay, Argentina and Peru; Wonder Worker of the New World; canonized, 1726.

Sorin, Edward F. (1814-1893): French priest; member of Congregation of Holy Cross; sent to US in 1841; founder and first president of the University of Notre Dame; missionary in Indiana and Michigan.

Todadilla, Anthony de (1704-1746): Spanish Capuchin; missionary to Indians of Venezuela; killed by Motilones.

Turibius de Mogrovejo, St. (1538-1606): Spanish archbishop of Lima, Peru, c. 1580-1606; canonized 1726.

Twelve Apostles of Mexico (early 16th century): Franciscan priests; arrived in Mexico, 1524: Fathers Martin de Valencia (leader), Francisco de Soto, Martin de la Coruna, Juan Suares, Antonio de Ciudad Rodrigo, Toribio de Benevente, Garcia de Cisneros, Luis de Fuensalida, Juan de Ribas, Francisco Ximenes; Brothers Andres de Coroboda, Juan de Palos.

Valdivia, Luis de (1561-1641): Spanish Jesuit; defender of Indians in Peru and Chile.

Vasques de Espinosa, Antonio (early 17th century): Spanish Carmelite; missionary and explorer in Mexico, Panama and western coast of South America.

Vieira, Antonio (1608-1687): Portuguese Jesuit; preacher; missionary in Peru and Chile; protector of Indians against exploitation by slave owners and traders; considered foremost prose writer of 17th-century Portugal.

White, Andrew (1579-1656): English Jesuit; missionary among Indians in Maryland.

Wimmer, Boniface (1809-1887): German Benedictine; missionary among German immigrants in the US.

Youville, Bl. Marie Marguerite d' (1701-1771): Canadian widow; foundress of Sisters of Charity (Grey Nuns), 1738, at Montreal; beatified, 1959.

Zumarraga, Juan de (1468-1548): Spanish Franciscan; missionary; first bishop of Mexico; introduced first printing press in New World, published first book in America, a catechism for Aztec Indians; extended missions in Mexico and Central America; vigorous opponent of exploitation of Indians; approved of devotions at Guadalupe; leading figure in early church history in Mexico.

FRANCISCAN MISSIONS OF UPPER CALIFORNIA

The 21 Franciscan missions of Upper California were established during the 54-year period from 1769 to 1822. Located along the old El Camino Real, or King's Highway, they extended from San Diego to San Francisco and were the centers of Indian civilization, Christianity and industry in the early history of the state.

Fray Junipero Serra was the great pioneer of the missions of Upper California. He and his successor as superior of the work, Fray Fermin Lasuen, each directed the establishment of nine missions. One hundred and 46 priests of the Order of Friars Minor, most of them Spaniards, labored in the region from 1769 to 1845; 67 of them died at their posts, two as martyrs.

The missions were secularized by the Mexican government in the 1830's but were sub-sequently restored to the Church by the US government. They are now variously used as the sites of parish churches, a university, houses of study and museums.

The names of the missions and the order of their establishment were as follows:

San Diego de Alcala, San Carlos Borromeo (El Carmelo), San Antonio de Padua, San Gabriel Arcangel, San Luis Obispo de Tolosa, San Francisco de Asis (Dolores), San Juan Capistrano;

Santa Clara de Asis, San Buenaventura, Santa Barbara, La Purisima Concepcion de Maria Santisima, Santa Cruz, Nuestra Senora de la Soledad, San Jose de Guadalupe;

San Juan Bautista, San Miguel Arcangel, San Fernando Rey de Espana, San Luis Rey de Francia, Santa Ines, San Rafael Arcangel, San Francisco Solano de Sonoma (Sonoma).

The Church in Countries Throughout the World

(Principal source for statistics: *Annuario Pontificio, 1975.* Other sources are noted in the text. See Index for additional entries on 1975 events in various countries.)

Abbreviation code: archd. — archdiocese; dioc. — diocese; ap. ex. — apostolic exarchate; prel. — prelature; abb. — abbacy; v.a. — vicariate apostolic; p.a. — prefecture apostolic; a.a. — apostolic administration; card. — cardinal; abp. — archbishop; nat. — native; bp. — bishop; priests (dioc. — diocesan or secular priests; rel. — those belonging to religious orders); sem. — seminarians; p.d. — permanent deacons; m. rel. — men religious (include brothers and priests belonging to religious orders); w. rel. — women religious; sch. — schools; inst. — charitable institutes; Caths. — Catholic population; tot. pop. — total population.

Afars and Issas (formerly French Somaliland): French territory in east Africa, on the Gulf of Aden; capital, Djibouti. Christianity in the area, formerly part of Ethiopia, antedated but was overcome by the Arab invasion of 1200. Modern evangelization, begun in the latter part of the 19th century, had meager results. The hierarchy was established in 1955. The territory has an apostolic delegate (to the Red Sea Region).

Dioc., 1; bp., 1; parishes, 12 (5 dioc., 7 rel.); sem., 1; m. rel., 20; w. rel., 39; sch., 7; inst., 4; Caths., 12,000 (8%); tot. pop., (1974 est.), 150,000.

Afghanistan: Republic in south-central Asia; capital, Kabul. Christianity antedated Moslem conquest in the seventh century but was overcome by it. All inhabitants are subject to the law of Islam. Christian missionaries are prohibited. The few Catholics in the country are foreign embassy and technical personnel. Population (UN est., 1973), 18,290,000.

Albania: Communist people's republic in the Balkans, bordering the Adriatic Sea; capital, Tirana. Christianity was introduced before the middle of the fourth century. The Byzantine-Rite Church broke from unity with Rome following the schism of 1054; it has been suppressed. The Latin (Roman) Church, which prevailed in the north, has been wiped out by persecution since 1945, with the expulsion of Italian missionaries; a number of death and prison sentences and other repressive measures against bishops, priests, religious and lay persons; the closing of Catholic schools and a seminary; the cutting of lines of communication with the Holy See. In 1967, the government proclaimed itself the first atheist state in the world.

Archd., 2; dioc., 3; abb., 1; a.a. 1; bp., 3. No statistics are available. The Catholic population was estimated at 143,500 in 1969 by the

CSMC *"World Mission Map"; tot. pop. (1973 est.), 2,350,000.*

Algeria: Republic in northwest Africa: capital, Algiers. Christianity, introduced at an early date, succumbed to Vandal devastation in the fifth century and Moslem conquest in 709, but survived for centuries in small communities into the 12th century. Missionary work was unsuccessful except in service to traders, military personnel and captives along the coast. Church organization was established after the French gained control of the territory in the 1830's. A large number of Catholics were among the estimated million Europeans who left the country after it secured independence from France July 5, 1962. Islam is the state religion. Algeria maintains diplomatic relations with Vatican City.

Archd., 1; dioc., 3; card., 1; bp., 4; parishes, 83; priests, 305 (139 dioc., 166 rel.); p.d., 1; m. rel., 213; w. rel., 1,011; sch., 144; inst., 72; Caths., 65,500 (.4%); tot. pop. (UN est., 1973), 15,770,000.

Andorra: Autonomous principality in the Pyrenees, under the rule of co-princes — the French head of state and the bishop of Urgel, Spain; capital, Andorra la Vella. Christianity was introduced at an early date. Catholicism is the state religion. The principality is under the Spanish diocese of Urgel.

Total pop., 25,000 (almost entirely Catholic).

Angola: Portuguese territory in west Africa; capital, Luanda. Scheduled for independence Nov. 11, 1975. Evangelization by Catholic missionaries, dating from about 1570, reached high points in the 17th and 18th centuries. Apostolic delegation established, 1975.

Archd., 1; dioc., 11; abp., 2 (1 nat.); bp., 11 (3 nat.); parishes, 173; priests, 566 (222 dioc., 344 rel.); sem., 130; m. rel., 484; w. rel., 897; sch., 1,688; inst., 329; Caths., 2,708,906 (45%); tot. pop., 6,019,578.

Antigua: Self-governing state in Caribbean; capital, St. John's.

Dioc., 1; bp., 1; parishes, 11; priests, 12 (1 dioc., 11 rel.); m. rel., 17; w. rel., 10; sch., 7; Caths., 9,456; tot. pop., 130,907. (Figures are for diocese of St. John's, Antigua, and include Antigua, and the British Virgin Islands.)

Arabian Peninsula: Includes Saudi Arabia, Peoples Republic of Yemen, Yemen Arab Republic, Oman, Bahrein, Qatar, United Arab Emirates. Christianity, introduced in various parts of the peninsula in early Christian centuries, succumbed to Islam in the seventh century. The native population is entirely Moslem. The only Christians are foreigners. The peninsula has an apostolic delegate (to the Red Sea Region).

V.a., 1; parishes, 11; priests, 17 (rel.); m. rel., 17; w. rel., 41; sch., 8; Caths., 12,060; tot.

pop., 16,230,000. (Statistics are for the Vicariate Apostolic of Arabia which includes most of the Arabian Peninsula; the vicariate is located in Abu Dhabi, United Arab Emirates.)

Argentina: Republic in southeast South America, bordering on the Atlantic; capital, Buenos Aires. Priests were with the Magellan exploration party and the first Mass in the country was celebrated Apr. 1, 1519. Missionary work began in the 1530's, diocesan organization in the late 1540's, and effective evangelization about 1570. Independence from Spain was proclaimed in 1816. Since its establishment in the country, the Church has been influenced by Spanish cultural and institutional forces, antagonistic liberalism, government interference and opposition; the latter reached a climax during the last five years of the first presidency of Juan Peron (1946-1955). Catholicism is the state religion. Argentina maintains diplomatic relations with Vatican City.

Archd., 12; dioc., 39; prel., 2; ap. ex., 1; ord., 1; card., 2; abp., 11; bp., 52; parishes, 1,999; priests, 5,084 (2,392 dioc., 2,692 rel.); sem., 355; p.d., 11; m. rel., 4,020; w. rel., 12,667; sch., 2,527; inst., 589; Caths., 23,665,502 (90.6%); tot. pop., 26,125,148.

Australia: Commonwealth, member of the British Commonwealth, island continent southeast of Asia; capital, Canberra. The first Catholics in the country were Irish under penal sentence, 1795-1804; the first public Mass was celebrated May 15, 1803. Official organization of the Church dates from 1820. Australia established diplomatic relations with Vatican City in 1973.

Archd., 7; dioc., 20; abb., 1; mission "sui juris," 1; ap. ex., 1; card., 2; abp., 7; bp., 24; parishes, 1,386; priests, 3,587 (2,366 dioc., 1,221 rel.); sem., 413; p.d., 4; m. rel., 3,845; w. rel., 12,185; sch., 1,508; inst., 273; Caths., 3,241,968 (24.4%); tot. pop. (Govt. est., 1974), 13,268,000.

Austria: Republic in central Europe; capital, Vienna. Christianity was introduced by the end of the third century, strengthened considerably by conversion of the Bavarians from about 600, and firmly established in the second half of the eighth century. Catholicism survived and grew stronger as the principal religion in the country in the post-Reformation period, but suffered from Josephinism in the 18th century. Although liberated from much government harassment in the aftermath of the Revolution of 1848, it came under pressure again some 20 years later in the Kulturkampf. During this time the Church became involved with a developing social movement. The Church faced strong opposition from Socialists after World War I and suffered persecution from 1938 to 1945 during the Nazi regime. Some Church-state matters are regulated by a concordat originally concluded in 1934. Austria maintains diplomatic relations with Vatican City.

Archd., 2; dioc., 7; abb., 1; ord., 1; card., 1; abp., 2; bp., 12; parishes, 3,055; priests, 6,219 (3,701 dioc., 2,518 rel.); sem., 429; p.d., 43; m. rel., 3,603; w. rel., 12,772; sch., 327; inst. 1,963; Caths., 6,813,535 (90.2%); tot. pop., 7,551,411.

Azores: North Atlantic island group 750 miles west of Portugal, of which it is part. Christianity was introduced in the second quarter of the 15th century.

Bahamas: Independent (July 10, 1973) island group in the British Commonwealth, consisting of some 700 (30 inhabited) small islands southeast of Florida and north of Cuba; capital, Nassau. On Oct. 12, 1492, Columbus landed on one of these islands, where the first Mass was celebrated in the New World. Organization of the Catholic Church in the Bahamas dates from about the middle of the 19th century.

Dioc., 1; bp., 1; parishes, 60; priests, 56 (19 dioc., 37 rel.); sem., 14; p.d., 2; m. rel., 42; w. rel., 63; sch., 18; inst., 4; Caths., 36,617; tot. pop., 178,000. (Statistics are for the Nassau diocese which includes Turks and Caicos Isd lands.)

Bahrein: Island state in Persian Gulf; capital, Manama. Population, 230,000. Catholic statistics are included in Arabian Peninsula.

Balearic Islands: Spanish province consisting of an island group in the western Mediterranean. Statistics are included in those for Spain.

Bangladesh: Formerly the eastern portion of Pakistan. Officially constituted as a separate nation Dec. 16, 1971; capital, Dacca. Islam is the principal religion; freedom of religion is granted. There were Jesuit, Dominican and Augustinian missionaries in the area in the 16th century. A vicariate apostolic (of Bengali) was established in 1834; the hierarchy was erected in 1950. Bangladesh established diplomatic relations with Vatican City in 1972.

Archd., 1; dioc., 3; abp., 1 (nat.); bp., 3 (nat.); parishes, 64; priests, 138 (36 dioc., 102 rel.); sem., 21; m. rel., 160; w. rel., 379; sch., 324; inst., 65; Caths., 133,763 (.18%); tot. pop. (1974 census), 71,316,517.

Barbados: Parliamentary democracy in the British Commonwealth (independent since 1966), easternmost of the Caribbean islands; capital, Bridgetown. About 70 per cent of the people are Anglicans.

Dioc., 1; bp., 1; parishes, 10; priests, 19 (2 dioc., 17 rel.); sem., 1; m. rel., 32; w. rel., 58; sch., 15; inst., 2; Caths., 24,892; tot. pop., 335,741. (Statistics are for the Bridgetown-Kingston diocese which includes the island of St. Vincent.)

Belgium: Constitutional monarchy in northwestern Europe; capital, Brussels. Christianity was introduced about the first quarter of the fourth century and major evangelization was completed about 730. During the rest of the medieval period the Church had firm diocesan and parochial organization, generally vigorous monastic life, and influential monastic and cathedral schools. Lutherans and Calvinists made some gains during the Reformation period but there was a strong Catholic restoration in the first half of the 17th century, when the country was under Spanish rule. Jansenism disturbed the Church from about 1640 into the 18th century. Josephinism, imposed by an Austrian regime, hampered the Church late in the same century. Repressive and persecutory measures were enforced during the Napoleonic conquest. Freedom came with separation of Church and state in the wake of the Revolution of 1830, which ended the reign of William I. Thereafter, the Church encountered serious problems with philosophical liberalism and political socialism. Catholics have long been engaged in strong educational, social and political movements. Except for one five-year period (1880-1884), Belgium has maintained diplomatic relations with Vatican City since 1835.

Archd., 1; dioc., 7; card., 1; bp., 11; parishes, 3,668; priests, 13,800 (9,171 dioc., 4,629 rel.); sem., 448; p.d., 96; m. rel., 7,098; w. rel., 29,811; Caths., 8,626,958 (89%); tot. pop., 9,683,985.

Belize (formerly British Honduras): Self-governing colony in Central America; capital, Belmopan. Its history has points in common with Guatemala, where evangelization began in the 16th century.

Dioc., 1; bp., 1; parishes, 12; priests, 38; sem., 4; p.d., 1; m. rel., 38; w. rel., 80; sch., 109; inst., 1; Caths., 81,000 (60%); tot. pop., 135,000.

Bermuda: British colony, consisting of 360 islands (20 of them inhabited) nearly 600 miles east of Cape Hatteras; capital, Hamilton. Catholics were not permitted until about 1800. Occasional pastoral care was provided the few Catholics there by visiting priests during the 19th century. Early in the 1900's priests from Halifax began serving the area. A prefecture apostolic was set up in 1953. The first bishop assumed jurisdiction in 1956. The only Catholic school in Bermuda was the first to admit black students, in 1961.

Dioc., 1; bp., 1; parishes, 7; priests, 10 (1 dioc., 9 rel.); m. rel., 9; w. rel., 16; sch., 2; Caths., 8,832 (16.6%); tot. pop., 53,000.

Bhutan: Constitutional monarchy in the Himalayas, northeast of India; capital, Thimphu. Most of the population are Buddhists. Ecclesiastical jurisdiction is under the archdiocese of Shillong-Gauhati, India.

Pop. (1973 est.), 1,150.000.

Bolivia: Republic in central South America; capital, Sucre; seat of government, La Paz. Catholicism, the official religion, was introduced in the 1530's and the first bishopric was established in 1552. Effective evangelization among the Indians, slow to start, reached high points in the middle of the 18th and the

beginning of the 19th centuries and was resumed about 1840. Independence from Spain was proclaimed in 1825, at the end of a campaign that started in 1809. The republic inherited the Spanish right of nominating candidates for bishoprics. Church-state relations are regulated by a 1951 concordat with the Holy See. Bolivia maintains diplomatic relations with Vatican City.

Archd., 2; dioc., 6; prel., 4; v.a., 6; card., 1; abp., 1; bp., 17; parishes, 471; priests, 778 (232 dioc., 546 rel.); sem., 82; p.d., 4; m. rel., 813; w. rel., 1,279; sch., 244; inst., 298; Caths., 5,123,599 (94.2%); tot. pop., 5,441,181.

Botswana: Republic (independent since 1966) in southern Africa, member of the British Commonwealth; capital, Gaborone. Botswana has an apostolic delegate (to South Africa).

Dioc., 1; bp., 1; parishes, 14; priests, 24 (2 dioc., 22 rel.); sem., 1; m. rel., 24; w. rel., 49; sch., 12; inst., 2; Caths., 22,392 (3.4%); tot. pop. (UN est., 1973), 650,000.

Brazil: Republic in northeast South America; capital, Brasilia. One of several priests with the discovery party celebrated the first Mass in the country Apr. 26, 1500. Evangelization began some years later and the first diocese was erected in 1551. During the colonial period, which lasted until 1822, evangelization made some notable progress—especially in the Amazon region between 1680 and 1750—but was seriously hindered by government policy and the attitude of colonists regarding Amazon Indians the missionaries tried to protect from exploitation and slavery. The Jesuits were suppressed in 1782 and other missionaries expelled as well. Liberal anti-Church influence grew in strength. The government gave minimal support but exercised maximum control over the Church. After the proclamation of independence from Portugal in 1822 and throughout the regency, government control was tightened and the Church suffered greatly from dissident actions of ecclesiastical brotherhoods, Masonic anti-clericalism and general decline in religious life. Church and state were separated by the constitution of 1891, proclaimed two years after the end of the empire. The Church carried into the 20th century a load of inherited liabilities and problems amid increasingly difficult political, economic and social conditions affecting the majority of the population. A number of bishops, priests, religious and lay persons have been active in movements for social and religious reform. Brazil maintains diplomatic relations with Vatican City.

Archd., 22; dioc., 140; prel., 41; abb., 2; ord., 1; card., 6; abp., 29; bp., 212; parishes, 6,456; priests, 12,767 (5,110 dioc., 7,657 rel.); sem., 1,052; p.d., 132; m. rel., 11,704; w. rel., 36,000; sch., 4,270; inst., 3,893; Caths., 90,503,669 (88.17%); tot. pop., 102,652,448.

Brunei: State under British protection, on the northern coast of Borneo; capital, Brunei.

Statistics are included in those for Malaysia.

Bulgaria: People's republic in southeastern Europe on the eastern part of the Balkan peninsula; capital, Sofia. Christianity was introduced before 343 but disappeared with the migration of Slavs into the territory. The baptism of Boris I about 865 ushered in a new period of Christianity which soon became involved in switches of loyalty between Constantinople and Rome. Through it all the Byzantine, and later Orthodox, element remained stronger and survived under the rule of Ottoman Turks into the 19th century. The few modern Latin Catholics in the country are traceable to 17th century converts from heresy. The Byzantines are products of a reunion movement of the 19th century. In 1947 the constitution of the new republic decreed the separation of Church and state. Catholic schools and institutions were abolished and foreign religious banished in 1948. A year later the apostolic delegate was expelled. Ivan Romanoff, vicar general of Plovdiv, died in prison in 1952. Bishop Eugene Bossilkoff, imprisoned in 1948, was sentenced to death in 1952; his fate remained unknown until 1975 when the Bulgarian government informed the Vatican that he had died in prison shortly after being sentenced. Roman and Bulgarian Rite vicars apostolic were permitted to attend the Second Vatican Council from 1962 to 1965. All church activity is under surveillance and/or control by the government, which professes to be atheistic. Pastoral and related activities are strictly limited. Most of the population is Orthodox. There was some improvement in Bulgarian-Vatican relations in 1975, following a visit of Bulgarian President Teodor Zivkov to Pope Paul June 19 and talks between Vatican and Bulgarian representatives at the Helsinki Conference in late July. On August 5 Pope Paul appointed two bishops to fill vacant Latin rite sees. This marked the first time since the Communist takeover that all three sees were filled.

Dioc., 1; v.a., 1; ap. ex., 1; bp., 3; Caths. (est.), 65,000 (.75%); tot. pop. (UN est., 1973), 8,620,000.

Burma: Union of Burma, a republic in southeast Asia, on the Bay of Bengal; capital, Rangoon. Christianity was introduced about 1500. Small-scale evangelization had limited results from the middle of the 16th century until the 1850's when effective organization of the Church began. The hierarchy was established in 1955. Buddhism was declared the state religion in 1961, although all other religions are respected. In 1965, church schools were nationalized. In 1966, all foreign missionaries who had entered the country after 1948 for the first time were forced to leave when the government refused to renew their work permits. Despite these setbacks, the Church has shown some progress in recent years. Burma has an apostolic delegate (pronuncio to India).

Archd., 2; dioc., 6; abp., 2 (nat.); bp., 6 (3 nat.); parishes, 145; priests, 189 (140 dioc., 49 rel.); sem., 120; m. rel., 110; w. rel., 582; sch., 248; inst., 760; Caths., 284,769 (.96%); tot. pop., 29,560,000.

Burundi: Republic since 1966, near the equator in east-central Africa; capital, Bujumbura. The first permanent Catholic mission station was established late in the 19th century. Large numbers of persons were received into the Church following the ordination of the first Burundi priests in 1925. The first native bishop was appointed in 1959. Most education takes place in schools under Catholic auspices. During the past several years, the country has been torn by tribal warfare between the Tutsis, the ruling minority, and the Hutus. Burundi maintains diplomatic relations with Vatican City.

Archd., 1; dioc., 5; abp., 1 (nat.); bp., 5 (nat.); parishes, 180; priests, 433 (159 dioc., 274 rel.); sem., 57; m. rel., 425; w. rel., 629; sch., 626; inst., 101; Caths., 1,925,447 (60%); tot. pop., 3,175,365 (Catholic and total population figures are from Fides).

Cambodia: See Khmer Republic.

Cameroon: Republic in west Africa, bordering on the Gulf of Guinea; capital, Yaounde. Effective evangelization began in the 1890's, although Catholics had been in the country long before that time. In the 40-year period from 1920 to 1960, the number of Catholics increased from 60,000 to 700,000. The first native priests were ordained in 1935. Twenty years later the first native bishops were ordained and the hierarchy established. Cameroon maintains diplomatic relations with Vatican City.

Archd., 1; dioc., 13; abp., 1 (nat.); bp., 13 (6 nat.); parishes, 318; priests, 767 (233 dioc., 534 rel.); sem., 146; p.d., 11; m. rel., 783; w. rel., 1,221; sch., 1,185; inst.,203; Caths., 1,498,810 (24.2%); tot. pop.,6,177,391.

Canada: Independent federation in the British Commonwealth, comprising the northern half of North America; capital, Ottawa. (See The Church in Canada.)

Archd., 18; dioc., 51; abb., 1; card., 3; abp., 21; bp., 74; parishes, 4,496; priests, 13,835 (8,015 dioc., 5,820 rel.); sem., 638; p.d., 37; m. rel., 10,867; w. rel., 41,789; sch., 1,777; inst., 413; Caths., 9,435,867 (43.8%); tot. pop., 21,553,162.

Canary Islands: Two Spanish provinces, consisting of seven islands, off the northwest coast of Africa. Evangelization began about 1400. Almost all of the one million inhabitants are Catholics. Statistics are included in those for Spain.

Cape Verde Islands: Independent (July 5, 1975) island group in the Atlantic 300 miles west of Senegal; formerly a Portuguese overseas province; capital, Praia, San Tiago Island. Evangelization began some years before the establishment of the first diocese in 1532.

Dioc., 1; bp., 1; parishes, 30; priests, 53 (18

dioc., 35 rel.); sem., 9; m. rel., 38; w. rel., 34; sch., 53; inst., 3; Caths., 260,000 (97.59%); tot. pop., 266,411.

Caroline and Marshall Islands: US trust territory in the southwest Pacific. Effective evangelization began in the late 1880's.
V.a., 1; bp., 1; parishes, 18; priests, 40 (2 dioc., 38 rel.); sem., 6; p.d., 4; m. rel., 47; w. rel., 43; sch., 2; inst., 14; Caths., 39,831; tot. pop., 114,073.

Central African Republic: Republic (independent since 1960) in central Africa; capital, Bangui. Effective evangelization dates from 1894. The region was organized as a mission territory in 1909. The first native priest was ordained in 1938. The hierarchy was organized in 1955. The Central African Republic maintains diplomatic relations with Vatican City.
Archd., 1; dioc., 4; abp., 1 (nat.); bp., 3; parishes, 78; priests, 190 (31 dioc., 159 rel.); sem., 17; p.d., 1; m. rel., 205; w. rel., 273; sch., 20; inst., 30; Caths., 292,933 (13.9%); tot. pop., 2,099,198.

Ceuta: Spanish possession (city) on the northern tip of Africa, south of Gibraltar. Statistics are included in those for Spain.

Ceylon: See Sri Lanka, Republic of.

Chad: Republic (independent since 1960) in north-central Africa, member of the French Community; capital, N'Djamena (Fort Lamy). Evangelization began in 1929, leading to firm organization in 1947 and establishment of the hierarchy in 1955. Chad has an apostolic delegate (pro-nuncio, Central African Republic).
Archd., 1; dioc., 3; abp., 1; bp., 3; parishes, 67; priests, 167 (25 dioc., 142 rel.); sem., 6; m. rel., 181; w. rel., 199; sch., 60; inst., 32; Caths., 202,196 (5.2%); tot. pop. (UN est., 1973), 3,870,000.

Chile: Republic on the southwestern coast of South America; capital, Santiago. Priests were with the Spanish conquistadores on their entrance into the territory early in the 16th century. The first parish was established in 1547 and the first bishopric in 1561. Overall organization of the Church took place later in the century. By 1650 most of the peaceful Indians in the central and northern areas were evangelized. Missionary work was more difficult in the southern region. Church activity was hampered during the campaign for independence, 1810 to 1818, and through the first years of the new government, to 1830. Later gains were made, into this century, but hindering factors were shortages of native clergy and religious and attempts by the government to control church administration through the patronage system in force while the country was under Spanish control. Separation of Church and state were decreed in the constitution of 1925. Church-state relations were strained during the regime of Marxist president Salvator Allende Gossens (1970-73). He was overthrown in a bloody coup and was reported to have committed suicide Sept. 11, 1973. Conditions remained unsettled under the military government which assumed control after the coup. In April, 1974, the Chilean bishops issued a pastoral letter urging reconciliation in the country and criticizing government policies violating human rights. Chile maintains diplomatic relations with Vatican City.
Archd., 5; dioc., 14; prel., 3; v.a., 2; card., 1; abp., 4; bp., 24; parishes, 914; priests, 2,174 (820 dioc., 1,354 rel.); sem., 139; p.d., 68; m. rel., 2,267; w. rel., 4,745; sch., 811; inst., 276; Caths., 8,807,349 (86.7%); tot. pop., 10,154,050.

China *(This article concerns mainland China which has been under Communist control since 1949):* People's Republic in eastern part of Asia; capital, Peking. Christianity was introduced by Nestorians who had some influence on part of the area from 635 to 845 and again from the 11th century until 1368. John of Monte Corvino started a Franciscan mission in 1294; he was ordained an archbishop about 1307. Missionary activity involving more priests increased for a while thereafter but the Franciscan mission ended in 1368. The Jesuit Matteo Ricci initiated a remarkable period of activity in the 1580's. By 1700 the number of Catholics was reported to be 300,000. The Chinese Rites controversy, concerning the adaptation of rituals and other matters to Chinese traditions and practices, ran throughout the 17th century, ending in a negative decision by mission authorities in Rome. Bl. Francis de Capillas, the protomartyr of China, was killed in 1648. Persecution, a feature of Chinese history as recurrent as changes in dynasties, occurred several times in the 18th century and resulted in the departure of most missionaries from the country. The Chinese door swung open again in the 1840's and progress in evangelization increased with an extension of legal and social tolerance. At the turn of the 20th century, however, the Boxer Rebellion took one or the other kind of toll among an estimated 30,000 victims. Missionary work in the 1900's reached a new high in every respect before the disaster of persecution initiated by Communists before and especially since they established the republic in 1949. The Reds began a savage persecution as soon as they came into power. Among its results were the expulsion of over 5,000 foreign missionaries, 510 of whom were American priests, brothers and nuns; the arrest, imprisonment and harassment of all members of the native religious, clergy and hierarchy; the forced closing of 3,932 schools, 216 hospitals, 781 dispensaries, 254 orphanages, 29 printing presses and 55 periodicals; denial of the free exercise of religion to all the faithful; the detention of hundreds of priests, religious and lay persons in jail and their employment in slave labor; the proscription of the Legion of Mary and other Catholic Action groups for "counterrevolutionary activities" and "crimes against the new China"; complete outlawing of missionary work and pastoral activity. The government formally established a Patriotic Association of Chinese Catholics in July, 1957. Relatively few priests and lay persons joined the organization, which was condemned by Pius XII in 1958. The government formed the nucleus of what it hoped might become the hierarchy of a schismatic Chinese church by "electing" 26 bishops and having them consecrated validly but illicitly between Apr. 13, 1958, and Nov. 15, 1959, without the permission or approval of the Holy See. By Jan. 21, 1962, a total of 42 bishops were consecrated in this manner. In March, 1960, Bishop James E. Walsh, M.M., the last American missionary in China, was sentenced and placed in custody for a period of 20 years. He was released in the summer of 1970.

Archd., 20; dioc., 93; p.a., 29. No Catholic statistics are available. In 1949 there were between 3,500,000-4,000,000 Catholics, about .7 per cent of the total population; the 1969 "CSMC World Mission Map" estimated 3,200,000 Catholics, .5 per cent of the population. The latter figure is only an estimate; there is no way of knowing the actual situation. Tot. pop. (Govt. est., 1974), 800,000,000.

Colombia: Republic in northwest South America, with Atlantic and Pacific borders; capital, Bogota. Evangelization began in 1508. The first two dioceses were established in 1534. Vigorous development of the Church was reported by the middle of the 17th century despite obstacles posed by the multiplicity of Indian languages, government interference through patronage rights and otherwise, rivalry among religious orders and the small number of native priests among the predominantly Spanish clergy. Some persecution, including the confiscation of property, followed in the wake of the proclamation of independence from Spain in 1819. The Church was affected in many ways by the political and civil unrest of the nation through the 19th century and into the 20th. Various aspects of Churchstate relations are regulated by a concordat with the Vatican signed July 12, 1973, and ratified July 2, 1975. The new concordat replaced one which had been in effect with some modifications since 1887. Colombia maintains diplomatic relations with Vatican City.

Archd., 9; dioc., 30; prel., 2; v.a., 9; p.a., 7; card., 2; abp., 8; bp., 51; parishes, 2,079; priests, 5,086 (3,040 dioc., 2,046 rel.); sem., 778; p.d., 4; m. rel., 3,593; w. rel., 16,608; sch., 3,871; inst., 1,342; Caths., 24,067,626 (96%); tot. pop., 25,019,584.(Catholic and total population, figures from the Annuario Pontificio, are higher than those from other sources which report an estimated total population of 23,000,000. The number of Catholics remains between 95 and 96 per cent of the total.)

Comoro Islands: Independent group of islands in Indian Ocean off southeast coast of Africa; capital, Moroni, Grande Comore Island. Former French territory; unilaterally declared its independence July 6, 1975. The majority of the population is Moslem. An apostolic administration for Catholics (formerly under administration of the Ambanja diocese, Malagasy Republic) was established June 20, 1975.

V.a., 1; bp., 1; Caths. (Fides), 2,475; tot. pop. (1974 est.), 286,762.

Congo Republic: Republic in west central Africa, member of the French Community; capital, Brazzaville. Small-scale missionary work with little effect preceded modern evangelization dating from the 1880's. The work of the Church has been affected by political instability, Communist influence, tribalism and hostility to foreigners. The hierarchy was established in 1955. Congo has an apostolic delegate (pro-nuncio, Central African Republic).

Archd., 1; dioc., 2; card., 1 (nat.); bp., 2 (1 nat); parishes, 65; priests, 155 (42 dioc., 113 rel.); sem., 27; m. rel., 146; w. rel., 164; inst., 9; Caths., 447,374 (38%); tot. pop., 1,177,005.

Cook Islands: Self-governing territory of New Zealand, an archipelago of small islands in Oceania. Evangelization by Protestant missionaries started in 1821, resulting in a predominantly Protestant population. The first Catholic missionary work began in 1894. The hierarchy was established in 1966.

Dioc., 1; bp., 1; parishes, 12; priests, 11 (rel.); m. rel., 11; w. rel., 7; sch., 2; Caths., 2,213; tot. pop., 25,217.

Costa Rica: Republic in Central America; capital, San Jose. Evangelization began about 1520 and proceeded by degrees to real development and organization of the Church in the 17th and 18th centuries. The republic became independent in 1838. Twelve years later church jurisdiction also became independent with the establishment of a bishopric in the present capital. Costa Rica maintains diplomatic relations with Vatican City.

Archd., 1; dioc., 3; v.a., 1; abp., 1; bp., 4; parishes, 147; priests, 369 (249 dioc., 120 rel.); sem., 74; m. rel., 185; w. rel., 901; sch., 62; inst., 35; Caths., 1,795,500 (95%); tot. pop. (1973 est.), 1,890,000.

Cuba: Republic under Communist dictatorship, south of Florida; capital, Havana. Effective evangelization began about 1514, leading eventually to the predominance of Catholicism on the island. Native vocations to the priesthood and religious life were unusually numerous in the 18th century but declined in the 19th. The island became independent of Spain in 1902 following the Spanish-American War. Fidel Castro took control of the government Jan. 1, 1959. In 1961, after Cuba was officially declared a socialist state, the University of Villanueva was closed, 350 Catholic schools were nationalized and 136 priests expelled. A greater number of foreign priests and religious had already left the country. Freedom of worship and religious instruction are limited to church premises and no social action is permitted the Church, which survives under surveillance. Cuba maintains diplomatic relations with Vatican City.

Archd., 2; dioc., 4; abp., 2; bp., 6; parishes, 227; priests, 196 (93 dioc., 103 rel.); sem., 47; p.d., 1; m. rel., 144; w. rel., 210; inst., 5; Caths., 4,692,786 (52%); tot. pop. 9,018,121.

Cyprus: Republic in the eastern Mediterranean; capital, Nicosia. Christianity was preached on the island in apostolic times and has a continuous history from the fourth century. Latin and Eastern rites were established but the latter prevailed and became Orthodox after the schism of 1054. Roman and Orthodox Christians have suffered under many governments, particularly during the period of Turkish dominion from late in the 16th to late in the 19th centuries, and from differences between the 80 per cent Greek majority and the Turkish minority. About 80 per cent of the population are Orthodox. Cyprus established diplomatic relations with Vatican City in 1973. Maronite Rite Catholics are under the jurisdiction of the diocese of Cyprus (of the Maronites), whose bishop resides in Lebanon. Roman Rite Catholics are under the jurisdiction of the Roman Rite patriarch of Jerusalem.

There are approximately 6,700 Catholics; total population, 660,000.

Czechoslovakia: Federal socialist republic (since 1969) in Central Europe, consisting of the Czech Socialist Republic, capital Prague; and the Slovak Socialist Republic, capital Bratislava. The republics have local autonomy but are subordinate to the Federal Assembly at Prague made up of representatives from both regions. The Czech and Slovak regions of the country have separate religious and cultural backgrounds. Christianity was introduced in Slovakia in the 8th century by Irish and German missionaries and the area was under the jurisdiction of German bishops. In 863, at the invitation of the Slovak ruler Rastislav who wanted to preserve the cultural and liturgical heritage of the people, Sts. Cyril and Methodius began pastoral and missionary work in the region, ministering to the people in their own language. The saints introduced Old Slovak (Old Church Slavonic) into the liturgy and did so much to evangelize the territory that they are venerated as the apostles of Slovakia. A diocese established at Nitra in 880 had a continuous history except for a century ending in 1024. The Church in Slovakia was severely tested by the Reformation and political upheavals. After World War I, when it became part of the Republic of Czechoslovakia, it was 75 per cent Catholic. In the Czech lands, the martyrdom of Prince Wenceslaus in 929 triggered

the spread of Christianity. Prague has had a continuous history as a diocese since 973. A parish system was organized about the 13th century in Bohemia and Moravia, the land of the Czechs. Mendicant orders strengthened relations with the Latin Rite in the 13th century. In the next century the teachings of John Hus in Bohemia brought trouble to the Church in the forms of schism and heresy, and initiated a series of religious wars which continued for decades following his death at the stake in 1415. Church property was confiscated, monastic communities were scattered and even murdered, ecclesiastical organization was shattered, and so many of the faithful joined the Bohemian Brethren that Catholics became a minority. The Reformation, with the way prepared by the Hussites and cleared by other factors, affected the Church seriously. A Counter Reformation got underway in the 1560's and led to a gradual restoration through the thickets of Josephinism, the Enlightenment, liberalism and troubled politics. In 1920, two years after the establishment of the Republic of Czechoslovakia, the schismatic Czechoslovak Church was proclaimed at Prague, resulting in numerous defections from the Catholic Church in the Czech region. In Ruthenia, 112,000 became Russian Orthodox between 1918 and 1930. Vigorous persecution of the church began in Slovakia before the end of World War II when Communists mounted a 1944 offensive against bishops, priests and religious. In 1945, church schools were nationalized, youth organizations were disbanded, the Catholic press was curtailed, the training of students for the priesthood was seriously impeded. Msgr. Josef Tiso, president of the Slovak Republic, was tried for "treason" in December, 1947, and was executed the following April. Between 1945 and 1949 approximately 10 per cent of the Slovak population spent some time in jail or a concentration camp. Persecution began later in the Czech part of the country, following the accession of the Gottwald regime to power early in 1948. Hospitals, schools and property were nationalized and Catholic organizations were liquidated. A puppet organization was formed in 1949 to infiltrate the Church and implement an unsuccessful plan for establishing a schismatic church. In the same year Archbishop Josef Beran of Prague was placed under house arrest. (He left the country in 1965, was made a cardinal, and died in 1969 in Rome.) A number of theatrical trials of bishops and priests were staged in 1950. All houses of religious were taken over between March, 1950, and the end of 1951. An Eastern Rite diocese, Presov, in Slovakia, was dissolved in 1950 and pressure was applied on the clergy and faithful to join the Orthodox Church. Diplomatic relations with Vatican City were terminated in 1950. About 3,000 priests were deprived of liberty in 1951 and attempts were made to force "peace priests" on the people. In 1958 it was reported that 450 to 500 priests were in jail; an undisclosed number of religious and Byzantine Rite priests had been deported; two bishops released from prison in 1956 were under house arrest; one bishop was imprisoned at Leopoldov and two at the Mirov reformatory. In Bohemia, Moravia and Silesia, five of six dioceses were without ruling bishops; one archbishop and two bishops were active but subject to "supervision"; most of the clergy refused to join the "peace priests." In 1962 only three bishops were permitted to attend the first session of the Second Vatican Council. From January to October, 1968, Church-state relations improved to some extent under the Dubcek regime: a number of bishops were reinstated; some 3,000 priests were engaged in the pastoral ministry, although 1,500 were still barred from priestly work; the "peace priests" organization was disbanded; the Eastern Rite Church, with 147 parishes, was reestablished. In 1969, an end was ordered to rehabilitation trials for priests and religious, but no wholesale restoration of priests and religious to their proper ways of life and work was in prospect. In 1972 the government ordered the removal of nuns from visible but limited apostolates to farms and mental hospitals where they would be out of sight. In 1973, the government allowed the ordination of four bishops — one in the Czech region and three in the Slovak region. Reports from Slovakia late in the same year stated that authorities there had placed severe restrictions on the education of seminarians and the functioning of priests. Government restrictions continued to hamper the work of priests and nuns in 1974 and 1975. Talks between Vatican and Czech officials, begun in 1974, were resumed in 1975 with no noticeable results.

Archd., 2; dioc., 10; a.a., 2; bp., 5; parishes, 4,406; priests, 4,288 (3,704 dioc., 584 rel.); sem., 497; m. rel., 635; w. rel., 4,833; inst., 10; Caths. (est.), 10,935,000 (75%); tot. pop. (UN est., 1973), 14,580,000.

Dahomey: Republic in west Africa, bordering on the Atlantic; member of the French Community; capitals, Cotonou, Porto Novo. Missionary work was very limited from the 16th to the 18th centuries. Effective evangelization dates from 1894. The hierarchy was established in 1955. The majority of Christians are Catholics. Dahomey maintains diplomatic relations with Vatican City.

Archd., 1; dioc., 5; abp., 1 (nat.); bp., 5 (3 nat.); parishes, 88; priests, 186 (89 dioc., 97 rel.); sem., 25; m. rel., 119; w. rel., 331; sch., 48; inst., 43; Caths., 417,887 (14.5%); tot. pop., 2,882,366.

Danzig (Gdansk): Baltic seaport at the mouth of the Vistula River; incorporated into Poland after World War II. The diocese has a Christian history dating from the 10th century. Statistics are included in those for Poland.

Denmark, including the Faroe Islands and Greenland: Constitutional monarchy in northwestern Europe, north of West Germany; capital, Copenhagen. Christianity was introduced in the ninth century and the first diocese for the area was established in 831. Intensive evangelization and full-scale organization of the Church occurred from the second half of the 10th century and ushered in a period of great development and influence in the 12th and 13th centuries. Decline followed, resulting in almost total loss to the Church during the Reformation when Lutheranism became the national religion. Catholics were considered foreigners until religious freedom was legally assured in 1849. Modern development of the Church dates from the second half of the 19th century. About 95 per cent of the population are Evangelical Lutherans. Denmark has an apostolic delegate (to Scandinavia).

Dioc., 1; bp., 1; parishes, 54; priests, 129 (38 dioc., 91 rel.); sem., 4; m. rel., 99; w. rel., 586; sch., 34; inst., 24; Caths., 25,844 (.5%); tot. pop., 5,285,000.

Dominica: Self-governing state in Caribbean; capital, Roseau. Evangelization began in 1642.

Dioc., 1; bp., 1; parishes, 16; priests, 31 (3 dioc., 28 rel.); sem., 3; m. rel., 28; w. rel., 46; sch., 14; inst., 1; Caths., 64,000 (91%); tot. pop., 70,000. (Statistics are for the Roseau diocese which includes the islands of Montserrat, Saint Kitts-Nevis and Anguilla.)

Dominican Republic: Caribbean republic on the eastern two-thirds of the island of Hispaniola, bordering on Haiti; capital, Santo Domingo. Evangelization began shortly after discovery by Columbus in 1492 and church organization, the first in America, was established by 1510. Catholicism is the state religion. The Dominican Republic maintains diplomatic relations with Vatican City.

Archd., 1; dioc., 4; abp., 2; bp., 4; parishes, 174; priests, 479 (98 dioc., 381 rel.); sem., 58; p.d., 4; m. rel., 503; w. rel., 1,260; sch., 265; inst., 72; Caths., 4,186,047 (93.6%); tot. pop., 4,469,300.

Ecuador: Republic on the west coast of South America; capital, Quito. Evangelization began in the 1530's. The first diocese was established in 1545. A synod, one of the first in the Americas, was held in 1570 or 1594. Multiphased missionary work, spreading from the coastal and mountain regions into the Amazon, made the Church highly influential during the colonial period. The Church was practically enslaved by the constitution enacted in 1824, two years after Ecuador, as part of Colombia, gained independence from Spain. Some change for the better took place later in the century, but from 1891 until the 1930's the Church labored under serious liabilities imposed by liberal governments. The concordat of 1866 was violated; foreign missionaries were barred from the country for some time; the property of religious orders was confiscated; education was taken over by the state; traditional state support was refused; legal standing was denied; attempts to control church offices were made through insistence on rights of patronage. A period of harmony and independence for the Church began after agreement was reached on Church-state relations in 1937. Ecuador maintains diplomatic relations with Vatican City.

Archd., 3; dioc., 10; prel., 1; v.a., 5; p.a., 3; card., 1; abp., 2; bp., 20; parishes, 602; priests, 1,338 (591 dioc., 747 rel.); sem., 83; p.d., 5; m. rel., 1,016; w. rel., 4,656; sch., 909; inst., 312; Caths., 6,304,991 (93%); tot. pop., 6,779,561.

Egypt, Arab Republic of: Republic in northeastern Africa, bordering on the Mediterranean; capital, Cairo. Alexandria was the influential hub of a Christian community established by the end of the second century; it became a patriarchate and the center of the Coptic Church, and had great influence on the spread of Christianity in various parts of Africa; Monasticism developed from desert communities of hermits in the third and fourth centuries. Arianism was first preached in Egypt in the 320's. In the fifth century, the Coptic church went Monophysite through failure to accept doctrine formulated by the Council of Chalcedon in 451 with respect to the two natures of Christ. The country was thoroughly Arabized after 640 and was under the rule of Ottoman Turks from 1517 to 1798. English influence was strong during the 19th century. A monarchy established in 1922 lasted about 30 years, ending with the proclamation of a republic in 1953-54. By that time Egypt had become the leader of pan-Arabism against Israel. It waged two unsuccessful wars against Israel in 1948-49 and 1967. Between 1958 and 1961 it was allied with Syria and Yemen, in the United Arab Republic. Islam, the religion of some 90 percent of the population, is the state religion. Egypt maintains diplomatic relations with Vatican City.

Patriarchate, 2 (Alexandria for the Copts and for the Melkites); dioc., 6; v.a., 3; card., 1; bp., 10; parishes, 227; priests, 448 (143 dioc., 305 rel.); sem., 53; m. rel., 435; w. rel., 1,494; sch., 233; inst., 135; Caths. (est.), 140,000 (.4%); tot. pop. (Govt. est., 1973), 35,620,000.

El Salvador: Republic in Central America; capital, San Salvador. Evangelization affecting the whole territory followed Spanish occupation in the 1520's. The country was administered by the captaincy general of Guatemala until 1821 when independence from Spain was declared and it was annexed to Mexico. El Salvador joined the Central American Federation in 1825, decreed its own independence in 1841 and became a republic formally in 1856. El Salvador maintains diplomatic relations with Vatican City.

Archd., 1; dioc., 4; abp., 1; bp., 6; parishes, 213; priests, 403 (203 dioc., 200 rel.); sem., 39;

m. rel., 277; w. rel., 695; sch., 145; inst., 43; Caths., 3,599,010 (92.8%); tot. pop., 3,879,138.

England: Center of the United Kingdom of Great Britain (England, Scotland, Wales) and Northern Ireland, off the northwestern coast of Europe; capital, London. The arrival of St. Augustine of Canterbury and a band of monks in 597 marked the beginning of evangelization. Real organization of the Church took place some years after the Synod of Whitby, held in 663. Heavy losses were sustained in the wake of the Danish invasion in the 780's, but recovery starting from the time of Alfred the Great and dating especially from the middle of the 10th century led to Christianization of the whole country and close Church-state relations. The Norman Conquest of 1066 opened the Church in England to European influence. The 13th century was climactic, but decline had already set in by 1300 when the country had an all-time high of 17,000 religious. In the 14th century, John Wycliff presaged the Protestant Reformation. Henry VIII, failing in 1529 to gain annulment of his marriage to Catherine of Aragon, refused to acknowledge papal authority over the Church in England, had himself proclaimed its head, suppressed all houses of religious, and persecuted persons — Sts. Thomas More and John Fisher, among others — for not subscribing to the Oath of Supremacy and Act of Succession. He held the line on other-than-papal doctrine, however, until his death in 1547. Doctrinal aberrations were introduced during the reign of Edward VI (1547-53), through the Order of Communion, two books of Common Prayer, and the Articles of the Established Church. Mary Tudor's attempted Catholic restoration (1553-58) was a disaster, resulting in the deaths of more than 300 Protestants. Elizabeth (1558-1603) firmed up the Established Church with formation of a hierarchy, legal enactments and multi-phased persecution. One hundred and 11 priests and 62 lay persons were among the casualties of persecution during the underground Catholic revival which followed the return to England of missionary priests from France and The Lowlands. Several periods of comparative toleration ensued after Elizabeth's death. The first of several apostolic vicariates was established in 1685; this form of church government was maintained until the restoration of the hierarchy and diocesan organization in 1850. The revolution of 1688 and subsequent developments to about 1781 subjected Catholics to a wide variety of penal laws and disabilities in religious, civic and social life. The situation began to improve in 1791, and from 1801 Parliament frequently considered proposals for the repeal of penal laws against Catholics. The Act of Emancipation restored citizenship rights to Catholics in 1829. Restrictions remained in force for some time afterwards, however, on public religious worship and activity. The hierarchy was restored in 1850. Since then the Catholic Church, existing side by side with the Established Churches of England and Scotland, has followed a general pattern of growth and development. England has a diplomatic minister to Vatican City; there is an apostolic delegate in England.

Archd., 4; dioc., 13; ap. ex., 1; card., 1; abp., 3; bp., 24; parishes, 2,497; priests, 6,578 (4,258 dioc., 2,320 rel.); sem., 607; p.d., 7; m. rel., 3,102; w. rel., 12,058; sch., 2,684; inst., 334; Caths., 4,060,761 (8.8%); tot. pop., 46,183,104.

Equatorial Guinea: Republic on the west coast of Africa, consisting of Rio Muni on the mainland and the islands of Fernando Po and Annobon in the Gulf of Guinea: capital, Malabo (Santa Isabel). Evangelization began in 1841. Restrictive measures have been enacted against the Church since the country become independent of Spain in 1968.

Dioc., 2; bp., 1 (nat.); parishes, 37; priests, 40 (16 dioc., 24 rel.); sem., 43; m. rel., 36; w. rel., 55; sch., 24; inst., 5; Caths., 235,000 (78%); tot. pop., 300,000.

Ethiopia (Abyssinia): Constitutional monarchy in northeast Africa; capital, Addis Ababa. The country was evangelized by missionaries from Egypt in the fourth century and had a bishop by about 340. Following the lead of its parent body, the Egyptian (Coptic) Church, the Church in the area succumbed to the Monophysite heresy in the sixth century. Catholic influence was negligible for centuries. An ordinariate for the Ethiopian Rite was established in Eritrea in 1930. An apostolic delegation was set up in Addis Ababa in 1937 and several jurisdictions were organized, some under the Congregation for the Oriental Churches and others under the Congregation for the Evangelization of Peoples. Most of the Catholics in the country are in the former Italian colony of Eritrea. Ethiopia maintains diplomatic relations with Vatican City.

Archd., 1; dioc., 2; v.a., 3; p.a., 2; abp., 1; bp., 3; parishes, 165; priests, 470 (156 dioc., 314 rel.); sem. 65; m. rel., 393; w. rel., 647; sch., 246; inst., 128; Caths., 170,846 (.65%); tot. pop. (1973 est.), 26,080,000.

Falkland Islands: British colony off the southern tip of South America.

P.a., 1; parish, 1; priests, 2 (rel.); m. rel., 2; Caths., 203; tot. pop., 1,957.

Fiji: Independent member of the British Commonwealth, 100 inhabited islands in the southwest Pacific; capital, Suva. Marist missionaries began work in 1844 after Methodism had been firmly established. A prefecture apostolic was organized in 1863. The hierarchy was established in 1966.

Archd., 1; abp., 1; bp., 1; parishes, 35; priests, 81 (9 dioc., 72 rel.); sem., 12; m. rel., 133; w. rel., 281; sch., 50; inst., 3; Caths., 46,809 (8.4%); tot. pop., 553,692.

Finland: Republic in northern Europe; capital, Helsinki. Swedes evangelized the country in the 12th century. The Reformation swept the country, resulting in the prohibition of Catholicism in 1595, general reorganization of ecclesiastical life and affairs, and dominance of the Evangelical Lutheran Church. Catholics were given religious liberty in 1781 but missionaries and conversions were forbidden by law. The first Finnish priest since the Reformation was ordained in 1903 in Paris. A vicariate apostolic for Finland was erected in 1920. A law on religious liberty, enacted in 1923, banned the foundation of monasteries. Finland maintains diplomatic relations with Vatican City.

Dioc., 1; bp., 1; parishes, 5; priests, 20 (3 dioc., 17 rel.); sem., 1; m. rel., 22; w. rel., 35; sch., 2; Caths., 3,662 (.08%); tot. pop., 4,634,000.

France: Republic in western Europe; capital, Paris. Christianity was known around Lyons by the middle of the second century. By 250 there were 30 bishoprics. The hierarchy reached a fair degree of organization by the end of the fourth century. Vandals and Franks subsequently invaded the territory and caused barbarian turmoil and doctrinal problems because of their Arianism. The Frankish nation was converted following the baptism of Clovis about 496. Christianization was complete by some time in the seventh century. From then on the Church, its leaders and people, figured in virtually every important development — religious, cultural, political and social — through the periods of the Carolingians, feudalism, the Middle Ages and monarchies to the end of the 18th century. The great University of Paris became one of the intellectual centers of the 13th century. Churchmen and secular rulers were involved with developments surrounding the Avignon residence of the popes and curia from 1309 until near the end of the 14th century and with the disastrous Western Schism that followed. Strong currents of Gallicanism and conciliarism ran through ecclesiastical and secular circles in France; the former was an ideology and movement to restrict papal control of the Church in the country, the latter sought to make the pope subservient to a general council. Calvinism invaded the country about the middle of the 16th century and won a strong body of converts. Jansenism with its rigorous spirit and other aberrations appeared in the next century, to be followed by the highly influential Enlightenment. The Revolution which started in 1789 and was succeeded by the Napoleonic period completely changed the status of the Church, taking a toll of numbers by persecution and defection and disenfranchising the Church in practically every way. Throughout the 19th century the Church was caught up in the whirl of imperial and republican developments and made the victim of official hostility, popular indifference and liberal opposition. In this century, the Church has struggled with problems involving the heritage of the Revolution and its aftermath, the alienation of intellectuals, liberalism, the estrangement of the working classes because of the Church's former identification with the ruling class, and the massive needs of contemporary society. France maintains diplomatic relations with Vatican City.

Archd., 18; dioc., 75; prel., 1; ap. ex., 2; ord., 1; card., 9 abp., 15; bp., 98 parishes, 38,178; priests, 43,680 (36,111 dioc., 7,569 rel.); sem., 1,721; p.d., 18; m. rel., 13,070; w. rel., 92,505; sch., 10,689; inst., 2,230; Caths. (est.), 45,421,230 (86.8%); tot. pop. (Govt. est., 1974), 52,350,000.

Gabon: Republic on the west coast of Equatorial Africa, member of the French Community; capital, Libreville. Sporadic missionary effort took place before 1881 when effective evangelization began. The hierarchy was established in 1955. Gabon maintains diplomatic relations with Vatican City.

Archd., 1; dioc., 3; abp., 1 (nat.); bp., 3 (2 nat.); parishes, 57; priests, 103 (30 dioc., 73 rel.); sem., 1; m. rel., 114; w. rel., 127; sch., 219; inst., 35; Caths., 337,473 (48.7%); tot. pop., 692,530.

Gambia, The: Republic (1970) on the northwestern coast of Africa, smallest state in Africa, member of the British Commonwealth; capital, Banjul. The country was under the jurisdiction of a vicariate apostolic until 1931. The hierarchy was established in 1957. The Gambia has an apostolic delegate (the pro-nuncio to Liberia).

Dioc., 1; bp., 1; parishes, 3; priests, 21(rel.); m. rel., 24; w. rel., 20; sch., 39; inst., 2; Caths., 10,737 (2.1%); tot. pop., 499,000.

Germany: Country in northern Europe partitioned in 1949 into the Communist German Democratic Republic in the East (capital, East Berlin) and the German Federal Republic in the West (capital, Bonn). Christianity was introduced in the third century, if not earlier. Trier, which became a center for missionary activity, had a bishop by 400. Visigoth invaders introduced Arianism in the fifth century but were converted in the seventh century by the East Franks, Celtic and other missionaries. St. Boniface, the apostle of Germany, established real ecclesiastical organization in the eighth century. The Church had great influence during the Carolingian period. Bishops from that time onward began to act in dual roles as pastors and rulers, a state of affairs which led inevitably to confusion and conflict in Church-state relations and perplexing problems of investiture. The Church developed strength and vitality through the Middle Ages but succumbed to abuses which antedated and prepared the ground for the Reformation. Luther's actions from 1517 made Germany a confessional battleground. Religious strife continued until conclusion of the Peace of Westphalia at the end of the Thirty Years' War in 1648. Nearly a century earlier the Peace of Augsburg (1555) had been designed, without success, to assure a degree of tranquillity by recognizing the legitimacy of different religious confessions in different states, depending on the decisions of princes. The implicit principle that princes should control the churches emerged in practice into the absolutism and Josephinism of subsequent years. St. Peter Canisius and his fellow Jesuits spearheaded a Counter Reformation in the second half of the 16th century. Before the end of the century, however, 70 per cent of the population of north and central Germany were Lutheran. Calvinism also had established a strong presence. The Church gained internal strength in a defensive position. Through much of the 19th century, however, its influence was eclipsed by Protestant intellectuals and other influences. It suffered some impoverishment also as a result of shifting boundaries and the secularization of property shortly after 1800. It came under direct attack in the Kulturkampf of the 1870's but helped to generate the opposition which resulted in a dampening of the campaign of Bismarck against it. Despite action by Catholics on the social front and other developments, discrimination against the Church spilled over into the 20th century and lasted beyond World War I. Catholics in politics struggled with others to pull the country through numerous postwar crises. The dissolution of the Center Party, agreed to by the bishops in 1933 without awareness of the ultimate consequences, contributed negatively to the rise of Hitler to supreme power. Church officials protested the Nazi anti-Church and anti-Semitic actions, but to no avail. After World War II Christian leadership had much to do with the recovery of Western Germany. East Germany, gone Communist under Russian auspices, initiated a program of control and repression of the Church in 1948 and 1949. With no prospect of success for measures designed to split bishops, priests, religious and lay persons, the regime has concentrated most of its attention on mind control, especially of the younger generation, by the elimination of religious schools, curtailment of freedom for religious instruction and formation, severe restriction of the religious press, and the substitution since the mid-50's of youth initiation and Communist ceremonies for the rites of baptism, confirmation, marriage, and funerals. Bishops are generally forbidden to travel outside the Republic. The number of priests is decreasing, partly because of reduced seminary enrollments ordered by the government since 1958. In 1973, the Vatican appointed three apostolic administrators and one auxiliary (all titular bishops) for the areas of three West German dioceses located in East Germany. West Germany maintains diplomatic relations with Vatican City.

*Archd., 5; dioc., 18; a.a., 1; ap. ex., 1; card.,
5; abp., 3; bp., 53; parishes, 12,637; priests,
25,278 (18,723 dioc., 6,555 rel.); sem., 1,942;
p.d., 233; m. rel., 10,364; w. rel., 74,040; sch.,
1,582; inst., 18,211.* Catholics number
30,724,360; they constitute approximately 45%
of the West German population of 61,970,000
(UN est., 1973) and 10 per cent of the East
German population of 17,980,000 (UN est.,
1973).

Ghana: Republic on the western coast of
Africa, bordering on the Gulf of Guinea,
member of the British Commonwealth; capital, Accra. Priests visited the country in 1482,
11 years after discovery by the Portuguese,
but missionary effort — hindered by the slave
trade and other factors — was slight until
1880 when systematic evangelization began.
A prefecture apostolic was set up in 1943. The
hierarchy was established in 1950. Ghana has
an apostolic delegate.

*Archd., 1; dioc., 8; abp., 1 (nat.); bp., 8
(nat.); parishes, 144; priests, 367 (111 dioc.,
256 rel.); sem., 156; m. rel., 375; w. rel., 392;
sch., 1,622; inst., 85; Caths., 1,149,867
(12.3%); tot. pop. (UN est., 1973), 9,360,000.*

Gibraltar: British colony on the tip of the
Spanish Peninsula on the Mediterranean.
Evangelization took place after the Moors
were driven out near the end of the 15th century. The Church was hindered by the British
who acquired the colony in 1713. Most of the
Catholics were, and are, Spanish and Italian
immigrants and their descendants. A vicariate
apostolic was organized in 1817. The diocese
was erected in 1910.

*Dioc., 1; bp., 1; parishes, 4; priests, 10 (7
dioc., 3 rel.); m. rel., 12; w. rel., 25; sch., 2;
inst., 4; Caths., 19,812; tot. pop., 29,920.*

Gilbert Islands: British colony in the southwest Pacific in Oceania, consisting of 16 coral
atolls including the Gilbert and Ellice Islands.
French Missionaries of the Sacred Heart
began work in the islands in 1888. A vicariate
for the islands was organized in 1897. The hierarchy was established in 1966.

*Dioc., 1; bp., 1; parishes, 22; priests, 17 (2
dioc., 15 rel.); sem., 2; m. rel., 23; w. rel., 45;
sch., 48; Caths., 28,456; tot. pop., 62,000.*

Greece, including Crete: Kingdom in
southeastern Europe on the Balkan Peninsula; capital, Athens. St. Paul preached the
Gospel at Athens and Corinth on his second
missionary journey and visited the country
again on his third tour. Other Apostles may
have passed through also. Two bishops from
Greece attended the First Council of Nicaea.
After the division of the Roman Empire, the
Church remained Eastern in rite and later
broke ties with Rome as a result of the schism
of 1054. A Latin-Rite jurisdiction was set up
during the period of the Latin Empire of Constantinople, 1204-1261, but crumbled afterwards. Unity efforts of the Council of
Florence had poor results. The country now
has Greek Catholic and Latin jurisdictions.

The Greek Orthodox Church is predominant.
*Archd., 4; dioc., 4; v.a., 1; ap. ex., 1; ord., 1;
abp., 3; bp., 1; parishes, 50; priests, 112 (64
dioc., 48 rel.); sem., 11; m. rel., 93; w. rel.,
180; sch., 38; inst., 24; Caths., 45,605 (.46%);
tot. pop., 9,930,533.*

Greenland: Danish island province northeast of North America; capital, Godthaab.
Catholicism was introduced about 1000. The
first diocese was established in 1124 and a line
of bishops dated from then until 1537. The
first known churches in the western hemisphere, dating from about the 11th century,
were on Greenland; the remains of 19 have
been unearthed. The departure of Scan-
dinavians and spread of the Reformation reduced the Church to nothing. The Moravian
Brethren evangelized the Eskimos from the
1720's to 1901. By 1930 the Danish Church —
Evangelical Lutheran — was in full possession. Since 1930 priests have been in Greenland, which is part of the Copenhagen diocese. There are about 60 Catholics in the area.

Grenada: Independent island state in the
West Indies; capital, St. George's.
*Dioc., 1; bp., 1; parishes, 20; priests, 26 (6
dioc., 20 rel.); sem., 1; m. rel., 29; w. rel., 36;
sch., 34; Caths., 74,000; tot. pop. (UN est.,
1973), 100,000.*

Guadeloupe and Martinique: French overseas departments in the Leeward and Wind-
ward Islands of the West Indies; capitals,
Basse-Terre (Guadeloupe) and Fort-de-
France (Martinique). Catholicism was introduced in the islands in the 16th century.
The hierarchy was established in 1967.
*Archd., 1; dioc., 1; abp., 1; bp., 1; parishes,
96; priests, 207 (97 dioc., 110 rel.); sem., 14;
m. rel., 141; w. rel., 458; sch., 34; inst., 16;
Caths., 624,096 (90%); tot. pop., 687,500.*

Guam: U.S. territory in the southwest Pacific; capital, Agana. The first Mass was offered in the Mariana Islands in 1521. The islands were evangelized by the Jesuits, from
1668, and other missionaries. The first native
Micronesian bishop was ordained in 1970.
*Dioc., 1; bp., 1; parishes, 27; priests, 57 (22
dioc., 35 rel.); sem., 5; p.d., 12; m. rel., 40; w.
rel., 148; sch., 14; inst., 1; Caths., 94,251; tot.
pop., 125,700. (Population figures include U.S.
military personnel.)*

Guatemala: Republic in Central America;
capital, Guatemala City. Evangelization
dates from the beginning of Spanish occupation in 1524. The first diocese, for all Central
American territories administered by the captaincy general of Guatemala, was established
in 1534. The country became independent in
1839, following annexation to Mexico in
1821, secession in 1823 and membership in
the Central American Federation from 1825.
In 1870, a government installed by a liberal
revolution repudiated the concordat of 1853
and took active measures against the Churchm
Separation of Church and state was decreed;
religious orders were suppressed and their

property seized; priests and religious were exiled; schools were secularized. Full freedom was subsequently granted. Guatemala maintains diplomatic relations with Vatican City.

Archd., 1; dioc., 8; prel., 2; a.a., 2; card., 1; bp., 14; parishes, 318; priests, 662 (187 dioc., 475 rel.); sem., 73; p.d., 1; m. rel., 731; w. rel., 1,057; sch., 236; inst., 170; Caths. 4,834,641 (87.2%); tot. pop. (UN est., 1973), 5,540,000.

Guiana, French (Cayenne): French overseas department on the northeast coast of South America; capital, Cayenne. Catholicism was introduced in the 17th century. The Cayenne diocese was established in 1956.

Dioc., 1; bp., 1; parishes, 22; priests, 28 (6 dioc., 22 rel.); sem., 3; m. rel., 23; w. rel., 87; sch., 6; inst., 18; Caths., 42,000; tot. pop. (1973 est.), 60,000.

Guinea: Republic on the west coast of Africa; capital, Conakry. Occasional missionary work followed exploration by the Portuguese about the middle of the 15th century; organized effort dates from 1877. The hierarchy was established in 1955. Following independence from France in 1958, Catholic schools were nationalized, youth organizations banned and missionaries restricted. Foreign missionaries were expelled in 1967. In 1971 Archbishop Tchidimbo of Conakry was sentenced to life imprisonment on a charge of conspiring to overthrow the government. Guinea has an apostolic delegate.

Archd., 1; dioc., 1; p.a., 1; abp., 1 (nat., imprisoned in 1971); bp. 1 (exiled); parishes, 28; priests, 11 (dioc.); sem., 12; m. rel., 4; w. rel., 8; inst., 1; Caths., 40,251 (.95%); tot. pop. (UN est., 1973), 4,210,000.

Guinea-Bissau (formerly Portuguese Guinea): Independent state on the west coast of Africa; capital, Bissau. Catholicism was introduced in the second half of the 15th century but limited missionary work, hampered by the slave trade, had meager results. Missionary work in this century dates from 1933. A prefecture apostolic was established in 1955. Guinea-Bissau has an apostolic delegate.

P.a., 1; parishes, 13; priests, 34 (rel); m. rel., 49; w. rel., 39; sch., 78; inst., 21; Caths., 44,412 (8.7%); tot. pop. (UN est., 1973), 510,000.

Guyana: Republic on the northern coast of South America; capital, Georgetown. In 1899 the Catholic Church and other churches were given equal status with the Church of England and the Church of Scotland, which had sole rights up to that time. Most of the Catholics are Portuguese. The Georgetown diocese was established in 1956, 10 years before Guyana became independent of England. The first native bishop was appointed in 1971.

Dioc., 1; bp., 1; parishes, 23; priests, 75 (10 dioc., 65 rel.); sem., 7; m. rel., 75; w. rel., 73; sch., 62; inst., 13; Caths., 105,000; tot. pop. (UN est., 1973), 780,000.

Haiti: Caribbean republic on the western

third of Hispaniola adjacent to the Dominican Republic; capital, Port-au-Prince. Evangelization followed discovery by Columbus in 1492. Capuchins and Jesuits did most of the missionary work in the 18th century. From 1804, when independence was declared, until 1860, the country was in schism. Relations were regularized by a concordat concluded in 1860, when an archdiocese and four dioceses were established. Factors hindering the development of the Church have been a shortage of native clergy, inadequate religious instruction and the prevalence of voodoo. Political upheavals in the 1960's had serious effects on the Church. Haiti maintains diplomatic relations with Vatican City.

Archd., 1; dioc., 6; abp., 1; bp., 7; parishes, 184; priests, 392 (199 dioc., 193 rel.); sem., 45; p.d., 1; m. rel., 406; w. rel., 775; sch., 814; inst., 248; Caths., 4,420,000 (approximately 85%); tot. pop. (UN est., 1973), 5,200,000.

Honduras: Republic in Central America; capital, Tegucigalpa. Evangelization preceded establishment of the first diocese in the 16th century. Under Spanish rule and after independence from 1823, the Church held a favored position until 1880 when equal legal status was given to all religions. Honduras maintains diplomatic relations with Vatican City.

Archd., 1; dioc., 3; prel., 2; abp., 1; bp., 6; parishes, 106; priests, 204 (66 dioc., 138 rel.); sem., 23; m. rel., 160; w. rel., 348; sch., 53; inst., 79; Caths., 2,942,807 (93%); tot. pop., 3,161,106.

Hong Kong: British crown colony at the mouth of the Canton River, adjacent to the southeast Chinese province of Kwangtung. A prefecture apostolic was established in 1841. Members of the Pontifical Institute for Foreign Missions began work there in 1858. The Hong Kong diocese was erected in 1946.

Dioc., 1; bp., 1; parishes, 40; priests, 335 (63 dioc., 272 rel.); sem., 24; m. rel., 398; w. rel., 793; sch., 289; inst., 39; Caths. 261,890 (6.2%); tot. pop., 4,219,300.

Hungary: People's republic in east central Europe; capital, Budapest. The early origins of Christianity in the country, whose territory was subject to a great deal of change, is not known. Magyars accepted Christianity about the end of the 10th century. St. Stephen I (d. 1038) promoted its spread and helped to organize some of its historical dioceses. Bishops early became influential in politics as well as in the Church. For centuries the country served as a buffer for the Christian West against barbarians from the East, notably the Mongols in the 13th century. Religious orders, whose foundations started from the 1130's, provided the most effective missionaries, pastors and teachers. Outstanding for years were the Franciscans and Dominicans; the Jesuits were noted for their work in the Counter-Reformation from the second half of the 16th century onwards. Hussites and Waldensians prepared the way for the Reformation which struck at almost the same time as the Turks. The Reformation made considerable progress after 1526, resulting in the conversion of large numbers to Lutheranism and Calvinism by the end of the century. Most of them or their descendants returned to the Church later, but many Magyars remained staunch Calvinists. Turks repressed the churches, Protestant as well as Catholic, during a reign of 150 years but they managed to survive. Domination of the Church was one of the objectives of government policy during the reigns of Maria Theresa and Joseph II in the second half of the 18th century; their Josephinism affected Church-state relations until the first World War. More than 100,000 Eastern Rite schismatics were reunited with Rome about the turn of the 18th century. Secularization increased in the second half of the 19th century, which also witnessed the birth of many new Catholic organizations and movements to influence life in the nation and the Church. Catholics were involved in the social chaos and anti-religious atmosphere of the years following World War I, struggling with their compatriots for religious as well as political survival. After World War II Communist strength, which had manifested itself with less intensity earlier in the century, was great long before it forced the legally elected president out of office in 1947 and imposed a Soviet type of constitution on the country in 1949. The campaign against the Church started with the disbanding of Catholic organizations in 1946. In 1948, "Caritas," the Catholic charitable organization, was taken over and all Catholic schools, colleges and institutions were suppressed. Interference in church administration and attempts to split the bishops preceded the arrest of Cardinal Mindszenty on Dec. 26, 1948, and his sentence to life imprisonment in 1949. (He was free for a few days during the unsuccessful uprising of 1956. He then took up residence at the U.S. Embassy in Budapest where he remained until September, 1971, when he was permitted to leave the country. He died in 1975 in Vienna.) In 1950, religious orders and congregations were suppressed and 10,000 religious were interned. At least 30 priests and monks were assassinated, jailed or deported. About 4,000 priests and religious were confined in jail or concentration camps. The government sponsored a national "Progressive Catholic" church and captive organizations for priests and "Catholic Action," which attracted only a small minority. Signs were clear in 1965 and 1966 that a 1964 agreement with the Holy See regarding episcopal appointments had settled nothing. Six bishops were appointed by the Holy See and some other posts were filled, but none of the prelates were free from government surveillance and harassment. Four new bishops were appointed by the Holy See in January and or-

dained in Budapest in February, 1969; three elderly prelates resigned their sees. Shortly thereafter, peace priests complained that the "too Roman" new bishops would not deal with them. Talks between Vatican and Hungarian representatives during the past several years have resulted in the appointment of residential bishops to fill all but two of Hungary's 12 sees.

Archd., 3; dioc., 8; abb., 1; ap. ex., 1; abp., 2; bp., 10; parishes, 2,262; priests, 3,653 (3,374 dioc., 279 rel.); sem., 242; m. rel., 360; w. rel., 96; sch., 7; inst., 102; Caths., 6,182,891 (59%); tot. pop., 10,410,000.

Iceland: Island republic between Norway and Greenland; capital, Reykjavik. Irish hermits were there in the eighth century. Missionaries subsequently evangelized the island and Christianity was officially accepted about 1000. The first bishop was ordained in 1056. The Black Death had dire effects and spiritual decline set in during the 15th century. Lutheranism was introduced from Denmark between 1537 and 1552 and made the official religion. Some Catholic missionary work was done in the 19th century. Religious freedom was granted to the few Catholics in 1874. A vicariate was erected in 1929. Iceland has an apostolic delegate (to Scandinavia).

Dioc., 1; bp., 1; parishes, 2; priests, 8 (2 dioc., 6 rel.); m. rel., 6; w. rel., 53; sch., 3; inst., 3; Caths., 1,050 (.4%); tot. pop., 213,000.

India: Republic on the subcontinent of south central Asia, member of the British Commonwealth; capital, New Delhi. Longstanding tradition credits the Apostle Thomas with the introduction of Christianity in the Kerala area. Evangelization followed the establishment of Portuguese posts and the conquest of Goa in 1510. Jesuits, Franciscans, Dominicans, Augustinians and members of other religious orders figured in the early missionary history. An archdiocese for Goa, with two suffragan sees, was set up in 1558. Five provincial councils were held between 1567 and 1606. The number of Catholics in 1572 was estimated to be 280,000. This figure rose to 800,000 in 1700 and declined to 500,000 in 1800. Missionaries had some difficulties with the British East India Co. which exercised virtual government control from 1757 to 1858. They also had trouble because of a conflict that developed between policies of the Portuguese government, which pressed its rights of patronage in episcopal and clerical appointments, and the Congregation for the Propagation of the Faith, which sought greater freedom of action in the same appointments. This struggle eventuated in the schism of Goa between 1838 and 1857. In 1886, when the number of Catholics was estimated to be one million, the hierarchy for India and Ceylon was restored. Jesuits contributed greatly to the development of Catholic education from the second half of the 19th century. A large percentage of the Catholic population, mostly from the lower castes, is located around Goa and Kerala and farther south. The country is predominantly Hindu. India maintains diplomatic relations with Vatican City.

Patriarchate, 1; archd., 19; dioc., 65; p.a., 2; ap. ex., 6; card., 2; patriarch, 1; abp., 16; bp., 68; parishes, 4,487; priests, 9,686 (5,924 dioc., 3,762 rel.); sem., 2,389; m. rel., 8,063; w. rel., 39,209; sch., 8,245; inst., 3,015; Caths., 8,715,726 (1.5%); tot. pop. (UN est., 1973), 574,220,000.

Indonesia: Republic southeast of Asia, consisting of some 3,000 islands including Kalimantan (most of Borneo), Sulawesi (Celebes), Java, the Lesser Sundas, Moluccas, Sumatra, Timor and West Irian (Irian Jaya, western part of New Guinea); capital, Jakarta. Evangelization by the Portuguese began about 1511. St. Francis Xavier, greatest of the modern missionaries, spent some 14 months in the area. Christianity was strongly rooted in some parts of the islands by 1600. Islam's rise to dominance began at this time. The Dutch East Indies Co., which gained effective control in the 17th century, banned evangelization by Catholic missionaries for some time but Dutch secular and religious priests managed to resume the work. A vicariate of Batavia for all the Dutch East Indies was set up in 1841. About 90 per cent of the population is Moslem. The hierarchy was established in 1961. Indonesia maintains diplomatic relations with Vatican City.

Archd., 7; dioc., 24; p.a., 2; card., 1 (nat.); abp., 6 (3 nat.); bp., 23 (5 nat.); parishes, 455; priests, 1,447 (135 dioc., 1,312 rel.); sem., 247; p.d., 2; m. rel., 2,687; w. rel., 3,788; sch., 4,054; inst., 747; Caths., 2,622,420 (2%); tot. pop., 122,173,997.

Iran: Constitutional monarchy in southwestern Asia, between the Caspian Sea and the Persian Gulf; capital, Teheran. Some of the earliest Christian communities were established in this area outside the (then) Roman Empire. They suffered persecution in the fourth century and were then cut off from the outside world. Nestorianism was generally professed in the late fifth century. Islam became dominant after 640. Some later missionary work was attempted but without success. Religious liberty was granted in 1834, but Catholics were the victims of a massacre in 1918. Islam is the religion of perhaps 98 per cent of the population. In 1964 the country had 100,000 Monophysites, the largest group of Christians, and some 20,000 Nestorians. Catholics belong to the Latin, Armenian and Chaldean rites. Iran (Persia until 1935) maintains diplomatic relations with Vatican City.

Archd., 4; dioc., 2; abp., 4; bp., 1; parishes, 35; priests, 46 (13 dioc., 33 rel.); sem., 2; m. rel., 41; w. rel., 68; sch., 22; inst., 13; Caths., 28,190 (.08%); tot. pop., 32,001,000.

Iraq: Republic in southwestern Asia, between Iran and Saudi Arabia; capital, Bagh-

dad. Some of the earliest Christian communities were established in the area, whose history resembles that of Iran. Catholics belong to the Armenian, Chaldean, Latin and Syrian rites; Chaldeans are most numerous. Islam is the religion of some 90 per cent of the population. Iraq maintains diplomatic relations with Vatican City.

Patriarchate, 1; archd., 8; dioc., 6; patriarch, 1; abp., 8; bp., 6; parishes, 137; priests, 159 (129 dioc., 30 rel.); sem., 91; p.d., 1; m. rel., 53; w. rel., 235; sch., 40; inst., 13; Caths., 287,356 (2.7%); tot. pop. (UN est., 1973), 10,410,000.

Ireland: Republic in the British Isles; capital, Dublin. St. Patrick, who is venerated as the apostle of Ireland, evangelized parts of the island for some years after the middle of the fifth century. Conversion of the island was not accomplished, however, until the seventh century or later. Celtic monks were the principal missionaries. The Church was organized along monastic lines at first, but a movement developed in the 11th century for the establishment of jurisdiction along episcopal lines. By that time many Roman usages had been adopted. The Church gathered strength during the period from the Norman Conquest of England to the reign of Henry VIII despite a wide variety of rivalries, wars, and other disturbances. Henry introduced an age of repression of the faith which continued for many years under several of his successors. The Irish suffered from proscription of the Catholic faith, economic and social disabilities, subjection to absentee landlords and a plantation system designed to keep them from owning property, and actual persecution which took an uncertain toll of lives up until about 1714. Most of those living in the northern part of Ireland became Anglican and Presbyterian in the 1600's but the south remained strong in faith. Some penal laws remained in force until emancipation in 1829. Nearly 100 years later Ireland was divided by two enactments which made Northern Ireland, consisting of six counties, part of the United Kindgom (1920) and gave dominion status to the Irish Free State, made up of the other 26 counties (1922). This state (Eire, in Gaelic) was proclaimed the Republic of Ireland in 1949. The Catholic Church enjoys privileged status but religious freedom is guaranteed for all. Ireland maintains diplomatic relations with Vatican City.

Archd., 4; dioc., 22; card., 1; abp., 3; bp., 26; parishes, 1,213; priests, 5,809 (3,823 dioc., 1,986 rel.); sem., 586; m. rel., 4,880; w. rel., 12,958; sch., 4,625; inst., 340 (preceding figures include Northern Ireland); Caths. (est.), 2,888,940 (94%); tot. pop. (UN est., 1973), 3,030,000.

Ireland, Northern: Part of the United Kingdom, it consists of six of the nine counties of Ulster in the northeast corner of Ireland; capital, Belfast. History is given under Ireland,

above. For recent developments, see Index.
Caths. (approx.), 504,000 (32%); tot. pop., 1,534,000 (other statistics are included in Ireland).

Israel: Parliamentary democracy in the Middle East, at the eastern end of the Mediterranean; capitals, Jerusalem and Tel Aviv (diplomatic). Israel was the birthplace of Christianity, the site of the first Christian communities. Some persecution was suffered in the early Christian era and again during the several hundred years of Roman control. Moslems conquered the territory in the seventh century and, except for the period of the Kingdom of Jerusalem established by Crusaders, remained in control most of the time up until World War I. The Church survived in the area, sometimes just barely, but it did not prosper greatly or show any notable increase in numbers. The British took over the protectorate of the area after World War I. Partition into Israel for the Jews and Palestine for the Arabs was approved by the United Nations in 1947. War broke out a year later with the proclamation of the Republic of Israel. The Israelis won the war and 50 percent more territory than they had originally been ceded. War broke out again for six days in June, 1967, and in October, 1973, resulting in a Middle East crisis that shows few signs of early settlement. Caught in the middle of the conflict are hundreds of thousands of dispossessed Palestinian refugees. Judaism is the faith professed by about 85 percent of the inhabitants; approximately one-third of them are considered observants. Most of the Arab minority are Moslems. The Acre archdiocese for Melkites is situated in Israel. Maronites are subject to the bishop of Tyr, Lebanon. Latins are under the jurisdiction of the Roman patriarchate of Jerusalem. Israel has an apostolic delegate.
Caths., 35,671; tot. pop. (1973 est.), 3,228,000.

Italy: Republic in southern Europe; capital, Rome. A Christian community was formed early at Rome, probably by the middle of the first century. St. Peter established his see there. He and St. Paul suffered death for the faith there in the 60's. The early Christians were persecuted at various times there, as in other parts of the empire, but the Church developed in numbers and influence, gradually spreading out from towns and cities in the center and south to rural areas and the north. Organization, in the process of formation in the second century, developed greatly between the fifth and eighth centuries. By the latter date the Church had already come to grips with serious problems, including doctrinal and disciplinary disputes that threatened the unity of faith, barbarian invasions, and the need for the pope and bishops to take over civil responsibilities because of imperial default. The Church has been at the center of life on the peninsula throughout the cen-

turies. It emerged from underground in 313, with the Edict of Milan, and rose to a position of prestige and lasting influence. It educated and converted the barbarians, preserved culture through the early Middle Ages and passed it on to later times, suffered periods of decline and gained strength through recurring reforms, engaged in military combat for political reasons and intellectual combat for the preservation and development of doctrine, saw and patronized the development of the arts, experienced all human strengths and weaknesses in its members, knew triumph and the humiliation of failure. For long centuries, from the fourth to the 19th, the Church was a temporal as well as spiritual power. This temporal aspect complicated its history in Italy. Since the 1870's, however, when the Papal States were annexed by the Kingdom of Italy, the history became simpler — but remained complicated — as the Church, shorn of temporal power, began to find new freedom for the fulfillment of its spiritual mission. Italy maintains diplomatic relations with Vatican City.
Patriarchate, 1; archd., 56; dioc., over 200; prel., 6; abb., 9; card., 35; abp., 52; bp., 214; parishes, 29,764; priests, 62,839 (41,816 dioc., 21,023 rel.); sem., 7,174; p.d., 16; m. rel., 30,143; w. rel., 152,513; sch., 4,195; inst., 4,308; Caths., 53,730,568 (97%); tot. pop. (Govt. est., 1973), 55,262,000.

Ivory Coast: Republic in western Africa, member of the French Community; capital, Abidjan. The Holy Ghost Fathers began systematic evangelization in 1895. The first native priests from the area were ordained in 1934. The hierarchy was set up in 1955. Ivory Coast maintains diplomatic relations with Vatican City.
Archd., 1; dioc., 7; abp., 1 (nat.); bp., 8 (6 nat.); parishes, 143; priests, 371 (96 dioc., 275 rel.); sem., 53; m. rel., 357; w. rel., 424; sch., 433; inst., 51; Caths., 579,269 (12.7%); tot. pop. (UN est., 1973), 4,640,000.

Jamaica: Parliamentary democracy in the West Indies, member of the British Commonwealth; capital, Kingston. Franciscans and Dominicans evangelized the island from about 1512 until 1655. Missionary work was interrupted after the English took possession but was resumed by Jesuits about the turn of the 19th century. A vicariate apostolic was organized in 1837. The hierarchy was established in 1967.
Archd., 1; dioc., 1; abp., 1; bp., 1; parishes, 35; priests, 128 (24 dioc., 104 rel.); sem., 7; p.d., 2; m. rel., 113; w. rel., 232; sch., 90; inst., 8; Caths., 161,793 (8%); tot. pop. (UN est., 1973), 1,980,000. (Figures include the Cayman Islands.)

Japan: Constitutional monarchy in the northwest Pacific; capital, Tokyo. Jesuits began evangelization in the middle of the 16th century and about 300,000 converts, most of them in Kyushu, were reported at the end of the century. The Nagasaki Martyrs were victims of persecution in 1597. Another persecution took some 4,000 lives between 1614 and 1651. Missionaries, banned for two centuries, returned about the middle of the 19th century and found Christian communities still surviving in Nagasaki and other places in Kyushu. A vicariate was organized in 1846. Religious freedom was guaranteed in 1889. The hierarchy was established in 1891. Japan maintains diplomatic relations with Vatican City.

Archd., 3; dioc., 13; p.a., 1; card., 1; abp., 2; bp., 15; parishes, 707; priests, 1,950 (472 dioc., 1,478 rel.); sem., 103; m. rel., 1,985; w. rel., 6,971; sch., 355; inst., 210; Caths., 358,118 (.3%); tot. pop. (Govt. est., 1973), 108,710,000.

Jerusalem: The entire city, site of the first Christian community, has been under Israeli control since the Israeli-Arab war of June, 1967. There are two patriarchates in the city, Melkite and Latin. Jerusalem has an apostolic delegate.

Jordan: Constitutional monarchy in the Middle East; capital, Amman. Christianity there dates from apostolic times. Survival of the faith was threatened many times under the rule of Moslems from 636 and Ottoman Turks from 1517 to 1918, and in the Islamic Emirate of Trans-Jordan from 1918 to 1949. Since the creation of Israel, some 500,000 Palestinian refugees, some of them Christians, have been in Jordan. Islam is the state religion but religious freedom is guaranteed for all. Jordan has an apostolic delegate.

The statistics which follow are for the Melkite-Rite Catholics of the Archdiocese of Petra and Philadelphia in Jordan. Separate statistics are not available for the Latin (Roman)-Rite Catholics under the jurisdiction of the Latin patriarchate of Jerusalem.

Archd., 1; abp., 1; parishes, 34; priests, 23 (19 dioc., 4 rel.); sem., 1; m. rel., 6; w. rel., 23; sch., 21; inst., 4; Caths., 17,000 (statistics are for the Archdiocese of Petra and Philadelphia for the Melkites); tot. pop., 2,497,000.

Kashmir and Jammu: Statistics included in India.

Kenya: Republic in eastern Africa bordering on the Indian Ocean, member of the British Commonwealth; capital, Nairobi. Systematic evangelization by the Holy Ghost Fathers began in 1892, nearly 40 years after the start of work by Protestant missionaries. The hierarchy was established in 1953. Kenya maintains diplomatic relations with Vatican City.

Archd., 1; dioc., 10; p.a., 2; card., 1 (nat.); bp., 11 (6 nat.); parishes, 224; priests, 757 (148 dioc., 609 rel.); sem., 197; m. rel., 822; w. rel., 1,553; sch., 2,748; inst., 272; Caths., 2,035,379 (16%); tot. pop., 12,623,981.

Khmer Republic (Cambodia): Republic (Oct. 9, 1970) in southeast Asia, bordering on the Gulf of Siam, Thailand, Laos and Vietnam; capital Phnom Penh. Evangelization dating from the second half of the 16th century had limited results, more among Vietnamese than Khmers. Thousands of Catholics of Vietnamese origin were forced to flee in 1970 because of Khmer hostility. The status of the Church remained uncertain following the Khmer Rouge take-over in April, 1975. Buddhism is the state religion. Khmer has an apostolic delegate.

V.a., 1; p.a., 2; bp., 1; parishes, 21; priests, 29 (16 dioc., 13 rel.); sem., 11; m. rel., 16; w. rel., 68; sch., 1; inst., 9; Caths., 16,835 (.2%); tot. pop., 7,000,000.

Korea: Peninsula in eastern Asia, east of China, divided into the (Communist) Democratic People's Republic in the North, formed May 1, 1948, with Pyongyang as its capital; and the Republic of Korea in the South, with Seoul as the capital. Some Catholics may have been in Korea before it became a "hermit kingdom" toward the end of the 16th century and closed its borders to foreigners. The real introduction to Catholicism came through lay converts in the last quarter of the 18th century. A priest arriving in the country in 1794 found 4,000 Catholics there who had never seen a priest. A vicariate was erected in 1831 but was not manned for several years thereafter. There were 15,000 Catholics by 1857. Four persecutions in the 19th century took a terrible toll; several thousands died in the last one, 1866-69. Freedom of religion was granted in 1883 when Korea opened its borders. Progress was made thereafter. The hierarchy was established in 1962. Since the war of 1950-1953, there have been no signs of Catholic life in the North, which has been blanketed by a news blackout. In July, 1972, both Koreas agreed to seek peaceful means of reunification. The South maintains diplomatic relations with Vatican City. Bishop Tji of Won Ju, South Korea, convicted and sentenced to 15 years' imprisonment in 1974 on a charge of inciting to rebellion, was released in February, 1975.

North Korea: Dioc., 2; abb., 1; bp., 1; tot. pop. (UN est., 1973), 15,090,000. No Catholic statistics available; there were an estimated 100,000 Catholics reported in 1969.

South Korea: Archd., 3; dioc., 10; p.a., 1; card., 1; abp., 2; bp., 12; parishes, 499; priests, 838 (510 dioc., 328 rel.); sem., 633; m. rel., 572; w. rel., 2,271; sch., 93; inst., 121; Caths. 953,930 (2.9%); tot. pop. (UN est., 1974), 33,333,333.

Kuwait: Constitutional monarchy (sultanate or sheikdom) in southwest Asia bordering on the Persian Gulf. Remote Christian origins probably date to apostolic times. Islam is the predominant and official religion. Kuwait maintains diplomatic relations with Vatican City.

V.a., 1; parishes, 5; priests, 8 (2 dioc., 6 rel.); m. rel., 6; w. rel., 27; sch., 7; Caths., 17,700;, tot. pop. (UN est., 1973), 880,000.

Laos: Constitutional monarchy in southeast Asia, surrounded by China, Vietnam,

Khmer Republic, Thailand and Burma; capitals, Vientiane (administrative) and Luang Prabang (royal). Systematic evangelization by French missionaries started about 1881; earlier efforts ended in 1688. A vicariate apostolic was organized in 1899 when there were 8,000 Catholics and 2,000 catechumens in the country. Buddhism is the state religion. Laos has an apostolic delegate.

V.a., 4; bp., 5 (2 nat.); parishes, 21; priests, 111 (16 dioc., 95 rel.); sem., 6; m. rel., 107; w. rel., 148; sch., 52; inst., 63; Caths., 37,449 (1%); tot. pop. (UN est., 1973), 3,180,000.

Lebanon: Republic in the Middle East, north of Israel; capital, Beirut. Christianity, introduced in apostolic times, was firmly established by the end of the fourth century and has remained so despite heavy Moslem influence since early in the seventh century. The country is the center of the Maronite Rite. Lebanon maintains diplomatic relations with Vatican City.

There are 17 ecclesiastical jurisdictions in Lebanon serving the following rites: Armenian (1 diocese); Chaldean (1 diocese); Roman (1 vicariate apostolic); Maronite (3 archdioceses and 3 dioceses); Melkite (3 archdioceses, 5 dioceses); the Syrians are served by a patriarchal vicar. The patriarchs of Antioch of the Syrians and Antioch of the Maronites reside in Lebanon.

Caths. 896,775 (30%); tot. pop. (UN est., 1973), 3,213,000.

Lesotho: Constitutional monarchy, an enclave in the southeastern part of the Republic of South Africa; capital, Maseru. Oblates of Mary Immaculate, the first Catholic missionaries in the area, started evangelization in 1862. A prefecture apostolic was organized in 1894. The hierarchy was established in 1951. Lesotho maintains diplomatic relations with Vatican City.

Archd., 1; dioc., 2; abp., 1 (nat.); bp., 2 (1 nat.); parishes, 71; priests, 135 (20 dioc., 115 rel.); sem., 15; m. rel., 200; w. rel., 598; sch., 507; inst., 84; Caths., 433,609; tot. pop., 1,024,828.

Liberia: Republic in western Africa, bordering on the Atlantic; capital, Monrovia. Missionary work and influence, dating interruptedly from the 16th century, were slight before the Society of African Missions undertook evangelization in 1906. Liberia maintains diplomatic relations with Vatican City.

V.a., 2; bp., 2; parishes, 37; priests, 52 (7 dioc., 45 rel.); sem., 8; m. rel., 67; w. rel., 71; sch., 59; inst., 19; Caths., 24,066 (1%); tot. pop. (1973 est.), 1,660,000.

Libya: Arab republic in northern Africa, on the Mediterranean between Egypt and Tunisia; capitals are Tripoli and Benghasi. Christianity was probably preached in the area at an early date but was overcome by the spread of Islam from the 630's. Islamization was complete by 1067 and there has been no Christian influence since then. The Catholics

in the country belong to the foreign colony. Islam is the state religion. Libya has an apostolic delegate (to North Africa).

V.a., 3; p.a., 1; bp., 3; parishes, 1; priests, 7 (rel.); m. rel., 9; w. rel., 80; Caths., 10,500 (.4%); tot. pop., 2,257,000.

Liechtenstein: Constitutional monarchy in central Europe, in the Alps and on the Rhine between Switzerland and Austria; capital, Vaduz. Christianity in the country dates from the fourth century; the area has been under the jurisdiction of Chur, Switzerland, since about that time. The Reformation had hardly any influence in the country. Catholicism is the state religion but religious freedom for all is guaranteed by law. Pop., 22,800.

Luxembourg: Constitutional monarchy in western Europe, between Belgium, Germany and France; capital, Luxembourg. Christianity, introduced in the fifth and sixth centuries, was firmly established by the end of the eighth century. A full-scale parish system was in existence in the ninth century. Monastic influence was strong until the Reformation, which had minimal influence in the country. The Church experienced some adverse influence from the currents of the French Revolution. Luxembourg maintains diplomatic relations with Vatican City.

Dioc., 1; bp., 1; parishes, 274; priests, 521 (416 dioc., 105 rel.); sem., 13; m. rel., 148; w. rel., 1,518; sch., 15; inst., 27; Caths. 326,600 (93%); tot. pop. (UN est., 1973), 350,000.

Macao: Portuguese province in southeast Asia across the Pearl River estuary from Hong Kong. Christianity was introduced by the Jesuits in 1557. Diocese was established in 1576. Macao served as a base for missionary work in Japan and China.

Dioc., 1; parishes, 8; priests, 86 (53 dioc., 33 rel.); sem., 10; m. rel., 52; w. rel., 222; sch., 84; inst., 22; Caths., 30,095; tot. pop. (1973 est.), 280,000.

Madeira Islands: Portuguese province, an archipelago 340 miles west of the northwestern coast of Africa; capital, Funchal. Catholicism has had a continuous history since the first half of the 15th century. Statistics are included in those for Portugal.

Malagasy Republic (Madagascar and adjoining islands): Member of the French Community, off the eastern coast of Africa; capital, Tananarive. Missionary efforts were generally fruitless from early in the 16th century until the Jesuits were permitted to start open evangelization about 1845. A prefecture apostolic was set up in 1850 and a vicariate apostolic in the north was placed in charge of the Holy Ghost Fathers in 1898. There were 100,000 Catholics by 1900. The first native bishop was ordained in 1936. The hierarchy was established in 1955. The Malagasy Republic maintains diplomatic relations with Vatican City.

Archd., 3; dioc., 14; card., 1 (nat.); abp., 2 (nat.); bp., 14 (9 nat.); parishes, 174; priests,

748 (151 dioc., 597 rel.); sem., 97; m. rel., 986; w. rel., 1,610; sch., 1,812; inst., 188; Caths., 1,633,817 (21%); tot. pop. (Govt. est., 1973), 7,655,134.

Malawi: Republic in the interior of eastern Africa, member of the British Commonwealth; capital, Zomba. Missionary work, begun by Jesuits in the late 16th and early 17th centuries, was generally ineffective until the end of the 19th century. The White Fathers arrived in 1889 and later were joined by others. A vicariate was set up in 1897. The hierarchy was established in 1959. Malawi maintains diplomatic relations with Vatican City.

Archd., 1; dioc., 6; abp., 1 (nat.); bp., 6 (4 nat.); parishes, 117; priests, 301 (72 dioc., 229 rel.); sem., 75; m. rel., 330; w. rel., 567; sch., 608; inst., 122; Caths., 944,304 (19.7%); tot. pop. (UN est., 1973), 4,790,000.

Malaysia: Parliamentary democracy in southeastern Asia, member of the British Commonwealth, federation of former states of Malaya, Sabah (former Br. North Borneo), and Sarawak; capital, Kuala Lumpur. Christianity, introduced by Portuguese colonists about 1511, was confined almost exclusively to Malacca until late in the 18th century. The effectiveness of evangelization increased from then on because of the recruitment and training of native clergy. Singapore (see separate entry), founded in 1819, became a center for missionary work. Seventeen thousand Catholics were in the Malacca diocese in 1888. Effective evangelization in Sabah and Sarawak began in the second half of the 19th century. The hierarchy was established in 1973. Malaysia has an apostolic delegate.

Archd., 1; dioc., 2; v.a., 3; abp., 1 (nat.); bp., 5 (3 nat.); parishes, 121; priests, 271 (166 dioc., 105 rel.); sem., 56; p.d., 2; m. rel., 245; w. rel., 488; sch., 327; inst., 45; Caths., 325,644 (2.9%); tot. pop. (UN est., 1972), 10,920,000.

Maldives: Republic, an archipelago 400 miles southwest of India and Ceylon; capital, Male. No serious attempt was ever made to evangelize the area, which is completely Moslem.

Tot. pop. (Govt. est., 1973), 122,673.

Mali: Republic, inland in western Africa; capital, Bamako. Catholicism was introduced late in the second half of the 19th century. Missionary work made little progress in the midst of the predominantly Moslem population. A vicariate was set up in 1921. The hierarchy was established in 1955. Mali has an apostolic delegate.

Archd., 1; dioc., 5; abp., 1 (nat.); bp., 5; parishes, 40; priests, 149 (17 dioc., 132 rel.); sem., 5; m. rel., 155; w. rel., 165; sch., 66; inst., 43; Caths., 44,998 (.86%); tot. pop., 5,193,225.

Malta: Parliamentary democracy, member of the British Commonwealth, 58 miles south of Sicily; capital, Valletta. Early catacombs and inscriptions are evidence of the early introduction of Christianity. St. Paul was shipwrecked on Malta in 60. Saracens controlled the island(s) from 870 to 1090, a period of difficulty for the Church. The line of bishops extends from 1090 to the present. Malta maintains diplomatic relations with Vatican City.

Archd., 1; dioc., 1; abp., 1; bp., 2; parishes, 75; priests, 1,055 (569 dioc., 486 rel.); sem., 96; m. rel., 695; w. rel., 1,557; sch., 83; inst., 31; Caths., 304,193 (95.6%); tot. pop., 318,283.

Mauritania: Islamic republic on the northwest coast of Africa; capital, Nouakchott. With few exceptions, the Catholics in the country are members of the foreign colony.

Dioc., 1; bp., 1; parishes, 5; priests, 9 (2 dioc., 7 rel.); m. rel., 7; w. rel., 13; sch., 2; Caths., 5,900 (.5%); tot. pop., 1,200,000.

Mauritius: Self-governing island state, member of the British Commonwealth, 500 miles east of the Malagasy Republic; capital, Port Louis. Catholicism was introduced by Vincentians in 1722. Port Louis, made a vicariate in 1819, was a jumping-off point for missionaries to Australia, Madagascar and South Africa. Mauritius maintains diplomatic relations with Vatican City.

Dioc., 1; bp., 1; parishes, 24; priests, 90 (52 dioc., 38 rel.); sem., 10; m. rel., 68; w. rel., 311; sch., 67; inst., 15; Caths., 275,000 (33%); tot. pop., 832,000.

Melilla: Spanish possession in northern Africa. Statistics are included in those for Spain.

Mexico (United States of Mexico): Republic in Middle America. Christianity was introduced early in the 16th century. Mexico City, made a diocese in 1530, became the missionary and cultural center of the whole country. Missionary work, started in 1524 and forwarded principally by Franciscans, Dominicans, Augustinians and Jesuits, resulted in the baptism of all persons in the central plateau by the end of the century. Progress there and in the rest of the country continued in the following century but tapered off and went into decline in the 18th century, for a variety of reasons ranging from diminishing government support to relaxations of Church discipline. The wars of independence, 1810-21, in which some Catholics participated, created serious problems of adjustment for the Church. Social problems, political unrest and government opposition climaxed in the constitution of 1917 which practically outlawed the Church. Persecution took serious tolls of life and kept the Church underground, under Calles, 1924-1928, again in 1931, and under Cardenas in 1934. President Camacho, 1940-1946, ended persecution and instituted a more lenient policy. The Church, however, still labors under legal and practical disabilities. Mexico has an apostolic delegate.

Archd., 11; dioc., 50; prel., 6; v.a., 1; p.a., 1; card., 2; abp., 10; bp., 70; parishes, 3,528; priests, 9,254 (6,689 dioc., 2,565 rel.); sem.,

2,360; p.d., 8; m. rel., 4,595; w. rel., 24,627; sch., 2,386; inst., 852; Caths., 51,013,364 (93%); tot. pop. (UN est., 1973), 54,300,000.

Monaco: Constitutional monarchy, an enclave on the Mediterranean coast of France near the Italian border; capital, Monaco-Ville. Christianity was introduced before 1000. Catholicism is the official religion but freedom is guaranteed for all. Monaco has a minister at Vatican City.

Dioc., 1; bp., 1; parishes, 5; priests, 35 (14 dioc., 21 rel.); sem., 1; m. rel., 59; w. rel., 79; sch., 8; inst., 3; Caths. (est.), 27,000 (90%); tot. pop. (1973 est.), 30,000.

Mongolian Peoples' Republic: Republic in north central Asia; capital Ulan Bator. Christianity was introduced by Nestorians. Some Franciscans were in the country in the 13th and 14th centuries, en route to China. Limited evangelization efforts from the 18th century had little success among the Mongols in Outer Mongolia, where Buddhism has predominated for hundreds of years. No Christians were known to be there in 1953. There may be a few Catholics in Inner Mongolia. No foreign missionaries have been in the country since 1953.

Pop. (UN est., 1973), 1,360,000.

Morocco: Constitutional monarchy in northwest Africa with Atlantic and Mediterranean coastlines; capital, Rabat. Christianity was known in the area by the end of the third century. Bishops from Morocco attended a council at Carthage in 484. Catholic life survived under Visigoth and, from 700, Arab rule; later it became subject to influence from the Spanish, Portuguese and French. Islam is the state religion. The hierarchy was established (in 1955). Morocco has an apostolic delegate (to North Africa).

Archd., 2; abp., 2; parishes, 67; priests, 144 (35 dioc., 109 rel.); m. rel., 145; w. rel., 554; sch., 63; inst., 15; Caths., 84,253 (.5%); tot. pop. (UN est., 1973), 16,310,000.

Mozambique: Independent (June 25, 1975) republic in southeast Africa, bordering on the Indian Ocean; former Portuguese territory; capital, Lourenco Marques (Can Phumo). Christianity was introduced by Portuguese Jesuits about the middle of the 16th century. Evangelization continued from then until the 18th century when it went into decline largely because of the Portuguese government's expulsion of the Jesuits. Conditions worsened in the 1830's, improved after 1881, but deteriorated again during the anticlerical period from 1910 to 1925. Conditions improved in 1940, the year Portugal concluded a new concordat with the Holy See and the hierarchy was established. Outspoken criticism by missionaries of Portuguese policies in Mozambique resulted in Church-state tensions in the years immediately preceding independence. The first two native bishops were ordained March 9, 1975. Mozambique has an apostolic delegate.

Archd., 1; dioc., 8; abp., 1 (nat.); bp., 8 (1 nat.); parishes, 231; priests, 552 (90 dioc., 462 rel.); sem., 87; p.d., 2; m. rel., 759; w. rel., 1,219; sch., 4,195; inst., 448; Caths., 1,560,042 (18.2%); tot. pop., 8,550,246.

Namibia (South West Africa): Territory in South Africa in dispute between the Republic of South Africa and the United Nations; capital, Windhoek. The area shares the history of the Republic of South Africa. Namibia (formerly South West Africa) has an apostolic delegate (to South Africa).

V.a., 2; bp., 2; parishes, 43; priests, 74 (3 dioc., 71 rel.); sem., 2; m. rel., 137; w. rel., 378; sch., 110; inst., 84; Caths., 125,464 (15.6%); tot. pop., 800,764.

Nepal: Constitutional monarchy, the only Hindu kingdom in the world, in central Asia south of the Himalayas between India and Tibet; capital, Katmandu. Little is known of the country before the 15th century. Some Jesuits passed through from 1628 and some sections were evangelized in the 18th century, with minimal results, before the country was closed to foreigners. Conversions from Hinduism, the state religion, are not recognized in law. Christian missionary work is not allowed. Any Catholics in the country have been under the jurisdiction of the Patna diocese, India, since 1919.

Tot. pop., (1973 est.), 12,020,000.

Netherlands: Kingdom in northwestern Europe; capital, Amsterdam (seat of the government, The Hague). Evangelization, begun about the turn of the sixth century by Irish, Anglo-Saxon and Frankish missionaries, resulted in Christianization of the country by 800 and subsequent strong influence on The Lowlands. Invasion by French Calvinists in 1572 brought serious losses to the Catholic Church and made the Reformed Church dominant. Catholics suffered a practical persecution of official repression and social handicap in the 17th century. The schism of Utrecht occurred in 1724. Only one-third of the population was Catholic in 1726. The Church had only a skeleton organization from 1702 to 1853, when the hierarchy was re-established. Despite this upturn, cultural isolation was the experience of Catholics until about 1914. From then on new vigor came into the life of the Church, and a whole new climate of interfaith relations began to develop. Before and for some years following the Second Vatican Council, the thrust and variety of thought and practice in the Dutch Church moved it to the vanguard position of "progressive" renewal. The Netherlands maintains diplomatic relations with Vatican City.

Archd., 1; dioc., 6; card., 3; bp., 6; parishes, 1,836; priests, 7,218 (3,239 dioc., 3,979 rel.); sem., 249; p.d., 2; m. rel., 7,148; w. rel., 22,973; sch., 2; Caths., 6,146,311 (44%); tot. pop., 13,968,248.

Netherlands Antilles (Curacao): Autonomous part of the Kingdom of The Netherlands. Consists of two groups of islands in the Caribbean: Curacao, Aruba and Bonaire, off the northern coast of Venezuela; and St. Eustatius, Saba and the southern part of St. Martaan, southeast of Puerto Rico; capital, Willemstad on Curacao. Christianity was introduced in the 16th century. Apostolic delegation was established in 1975.

Dioc., 1; bp., 1; parishes, 35; priests, 53 (5 dioc., 48 rel.); sem., 1; m. rel., 138; w. rel., 222; sch., 191; inst., 16; Caths., 185,000; tot. pop., 230,000.

New Caledonia: French territory consisting of several islands in Oceania east of Queensland, Australia; capital, Noumea. Catholicism was introduced in 1843, nine years after Protestant missionaries began evangelization. A vicariate was organized in 1847. The hierarchy was established in 1966.

Archd., 1; abp., 1; parishes, 36; priests, 59 (10 dioc., 49 rel.); sem., 3; m. rel., 108; w. rel., 224; sch., 70; inst., 14; Caths., 82,000; tot. pop., 126,000.

New Guinea: See Papua — New Guinea.

New Hebrides: Islands in the southwest Pacific, about 500 miles west of Fiji, under joint British-French administration; capital, Vila. Effective, though slow, evangelization by Catholic missionaries began about 1887. A vicariate apostolic was set up in 1904. The hierarchy was established in 1966.

Dioc., 1; bp., 1; priests, 27 (4 dioc., 23 rel.); sem., 2; m. rel., 28; w. rel., 78; sch., 1; inst., 10; Caths., 14,333 (18.3%); tot. pop., 90,000.

New Zealand: Dominion in the British Commonwealth, a group of islands in Oceania 1,200 miles southeast of Australia; capital, Wellington. Protestant missionaries were the first evangelizers. On North Island, Catholic missionaries started work before the establishment of two dioceses in 1848; their work among the Maoris was not organized until about 1881. On South Island, whose first resident priest arrived in 1840, a diocese was established in 1869. These three jurisdictions were joined in a province in 1896. The Marists were the outstanding Catholic missionaries in the area. New Zealand established diplomatic relations with Vatican City in 1973.

Archd., 1; dioc., 3; abp., 1; bp., 4; parishes, 286; priests, 839 (490 dioc., 349 rel.); sem., 89; m. rel., 796; w. rel., 2,347; sch., 313; inst., 40; Caths., 442,069 (14.8%); tot. pop. (1973 est.), 2,961,000.

Nicaragua: Republic in Central America; capital, Managua. Evangelization began shortly after the Spanish conquest about 1524 and eight years later the first bishop took over jurisdiction of the Church in the country. Jesuits were leaders in missionary work during the colonial period, which lasted until the 1820's. Evangelization endeavor increased after establishment of the republic in 1838. In this century it was extended to the Atlantic

coastal area where Protestant missionaries had begun work about the middle of the 1900's. Nicaragua maintains diplomatic relations with Vatican City.

Archd., 1; dioc., 4; prel., 1; v.a., 1; abp., 1; bp., 6; parishes, 173; priests, 320 (103 dioc., 217 rel.); sem., 24; p.d., 6; m. rel., 283; w. rel., 300; sch., 240; inst., 87; Caths., 1,905,493 (92%); tot. pop. (1973 est.), 2,070,000.

Niger: Republic in west central Africa; capital, Niamey. The first mission was set up in 1831. A prefecture apostolic was organized in 1942 and the first diocese was established in 1961. The country is predominantly Moslem. Niger maintains diplomatic relations with Vatican City.

Dioc., 1; bp., 1; parishes, 14; priests, 25 (7 dioc., 18 rel.); m. rel., 35; w. rel., 74; sch., 19; inst., 13; Caths., 12,200 (.2%); tot. pop. (UN est., 1973), 4,300,000.

Nigeria: Republic in western Africa; capital, Lagos. The Portuguese introduced Catholicism in the coastal region in the 15th century. Capuchins did some evangelization in the 17th century but systematic missionary work did not get underway along the coast until about 1840. A vicariate for this area was organized in 1870. A prefecture was set up in 1911 for missions in the northern part of the country where Islam was strongly entrenched. From 1967, when Biafra seceded, until early in 1970 the country was torn by civil war. The hierarchy was established in 1950. Nigeria has an apostolic delegate.

Archd., 3; dioc., 24; p.a., 1; abp., 4 (3 nat.); bp., 25 (19 nat.); parishes, 345; priests, 855 (338 dioc., 517 rel.); sem., 768; m. rel., 712; w. rel., 946; inst., 334; Caths., 3,485,605 (5.8%); tot. pop., 59,291,405.

Norway: Constitutional monarchy in northern Europe, the western part of the Scandinavian peninsula; capital, Oslo. Evangelization begun in the ninth century by missionaries from England and Ireland put the Church on a firm footing about the turn of the 11th century. The first diocese was set up in 1153 and development of the Church progressed until the Black Death in 1349 inflicted losses from which it never recovered. Lutheranism, introduced from outside in 1537 and furthered cautiously, gained general acceptance by about 1600 and was made the state religion. Legal and other measures crippled the Church, forcing priests to flee the country and completely disrupting normal activity. Changes for the better came in the 19th century, with the granting of religious liberty in 1845 and the repeal of many legal disabilities in 1897. Norway was administered as a single apostolic vicariate from 1892 to 1932, when it was divided into three jurisdictions under the supervision of the Congregation for the Propagation of the Faith. Norway has an apostolic delegate (to Scandinavia).

Dioc., 1; v.a., 2; bp., 2; parishes, 29; priests, 65 (19 dioc., 46 rel.); sem., 1; m. rel., 43; w.

rel., 424; sch., 5; inst., 27; Caths., 10,974 (.28%); tot. pop. 3,900,967.

Oman: Independent monarchy in eastern corner of Arabian Peninsula; capital, Muscat. Population (UN est., 1973), 720,000. Catholic statistics are included in Arabian Peninsula.

Pakistan: Islamic republic in southwestern Asia, member of the British Commonwealth; capital, Islamabad. (Formerly included East Pakistan which became the independent nation of Bangladesh in 1971.) Islam, firmly established in the eighth century, is the state religion. Christian evangelization of the native population began about the middle of the 19th century, years after earlier scattered attempts. The hierarchy was established in 1950. Pakistan maintains diplomatic relations with Vatican City.

Archd., 1; dioc., 5; card., 1 (nat.); bp., 7 (2 nat.); parishes, 72; priests, 217 (69 dioc., 148 rel.); sem., 30; m. rel., 223; w. rel., 574; sch., 195; inst., 107; Caths., 359,637 (.5%); tot. pop. (UN est., 1973), 66,750,000.

Panama: Republic in Central America; capital, Panama City. Catholicism was introduced by Franciscan missionaries and evangelization started in 1514. The Panama diocese, oldest in the Americas, was set up at the same time. The Catholic Church has favored status and state aid for missions, charities and parochial schools, but religious freedom is guaranteed to all religions. Panama maintains diplomatic relations with Vatican City.

Archd., 1; dioc., 3; prel., 1; v.a., 1; abp., 1; bp., 6; parishes, 121; priests, 281 (79 dioc., 202 rel.); sem., 22; m. rel., 273; w. rel., 448; sch., 60; inst., 20; Caths., 1,367,974 (87.5%); tot. pop., 1,563,145.

Panama Canal Zone: Under control of the United States, which was given Canal rights following Panamanian independence from Colombia in 1903. Catholic statistics are included in those reported for Panama, above.

Papua-New Guinea: Independent (Sept. 16, 1975) republic (formerly under Australian administration) in southwest Pacific; member of British Commonwealth. Consists of the eastern half of the southwestern Pacific island of New Guinea and the Northern Solomon Islands; capital, Lae. (For statistics on the Indonesian portion of New Guinea, see Indonesia.) Marists began evangelization about 1844 but were handicapped by many factors, including "spheres of influence" laid out for Catholic and Protestant missionaries. A prefecture apostolic was set up in 1896 and placed in charge of the Divine Word Missionaries. The territory suffered greatly during World War II. Hierarchy was established for New Guinea and adjacent islands in 1966. The area has an apostolic delegate (the pronuncio to Australia).

Archd., 3; dioc., 12; abp., 3; bp., 13; parishes, 305; priests, 521 (47 dioc., 474 rel.); sem., 50; p.d., 4; m. rel., 798; w. rel., 943; sch.,

909; inst., 376; Caths., 734,236 (29%); tot. pop., 2,509,318.

Paraguay: Republic in central South America; capital, Asuncion. Catholicism was introduced in 1542, evangelization began almost immediately. A diocese erected in 1547 was occupied for the first time in 1556. On many occasions thereafter dioceses in the country were left unoccupied because of political and other reasons. Jesuits who came into the country after 1609 devised the reductions system for evangelizing the Indians, teaching them agriculture, husbandry, trades and other useful arts, and giving them experience in property use and community life. The reductions were communes of Indians only, under the direction of the missionaries. About 50 of them were established in southern Brazil, Uruguay and northeastern Argentina as well as in Paraguay. They had an average population of three to four thousand. At their peak, some 30 reductions had a population of 100,000. Political officials regarded the reductions with disfavor because they did not control them and feared that the Indians trained in them might foment revolt and upset the established colonial system under Spanish control. The reductions lasted until about 1768 when their Jesuit founders and directors were expelled from Latin America. Church-state relations following independence from Spain in 1811 were tense as often as not because of government efforts to control the Church through continued exercise of Spanish patronage rights and by other means. The Church as well as the whole country suffered a great deal during the War of the Triple Alliance from 1865-70. After that time, the Church had the same kind of experience in Paraguay as in the rest of Latin America with forces of liberalism, anticlericalism, massive educational needs, poverty, a shortage of priests and other personnel. Most recently church leaders have been challenging the government to initiate long-needed economic and social reforms. Paraguay maintains diplomatic relations with Vatican City.

Archd., 1; dioc., 4; prel., 3; v.a., 2; abp., 1; bp., 9; parishes, 238; priests, 458 (187 dioc., 271 rel.); sem., 67; m. rel., 407; w. rel., 740; sch., 288; inst., 106; Caths., 2,248,270 (91%); tot. pop., 2,467,396.

Peru: Republic on the western coast of South America; capital, Lima. An effective diocese became operational in 1537, five years after the Spanish conquest. Evangelization, already underway, developed for some time after 1570 but deteriorated before the end of the colonial period in the 1820's. The first native-born saint of the new world was a Peruvian, Rose of Lima, a Dominican tertiary who died in 1617 and was canonized in 1671. In the new republic founded after the wars of independence the Church experienced problems of adjustment and many of the difficulties that cropped up in other South American countries: government efforts to control it through continuation of the patronage rights of the Spanish crown; suppression of houses of religious and expropriation of church property; religious indifference and outright hostility. The Church was given special status but was not made the established religion. Peru maintains diplomatic relations with Vatican City.

Archd., 7; dioc., 12; prel., 14; card., 1; abp., 6; bp., 37; parishes, 1,081; priests, 2,262 (992 dioc., 1,270 rel.); sem., 250; p.d., 13; m. rel., 1,879; w. rel., 4,755; sch., 822; inst., 472; Caths., 13,893,975 (93%); tot. pop. (UN est., 1973), 14,910,000.

Philippine Islands: Republic, an archipelago of 7,000 islands off the southeast coast of Asia; capital, Quezon City. Systematic evangelization was begun in 1564 and resulted in firm establishment of the Church by the 19th century. During the period of Spanish rule, which lasted from the discovery of the islands by Magellan in 1521 to 1898, the Church experienced difficulties with the patronage system under which the Spanish crown tried to control ecclesiastical affairs through episcopal and other appointments. This system ended in 1898 when the United States gained possession of the islands and instituted a policy of separation of Church and state. Anticlericalism flared late in the 19th century. The Aglipayan schism, an attempt to set up a nationalist church, occurred a few years later, in 1902. The republic maintains diplomatic relations with Vatican City. The country has been under martial law since September 1972.

Archd., 11; dioc., 28; prel., 12; v.a., 4; card., 1; abp., 11; bp., 58; parishes, 1,888; priests, 4,445 (2,175 dioc., 2,270 rel.); sem., 1,964; p.d., 5; m. rel., 3,691; w. rel., 6,952; sch., 1,575; inst., 396; Caths., 32,129,470 (79.9%); tot. pop. (UN est., 1973), 40,220,000.

Poland: People's republic in eastern Europe; capital, Warsaw. The first traces of Christianity date from the second half of the ninth century. Its spread was accelerated by the union of the Slavs in the 10th century. The first bishopric was set up in 968. The Gniezno archdiocese, with suffragan sees and a mandate to evangelize the borderlands as well as Poland, was established in 1000. Steady growth continued thereafter, with religious orders and their schools playing a major role. Some tensions with the Orthodox were experienced. The Reformation, supported mainly by city dwellers and the upper classes, peaked from about the middle of the 16th century, resulting in numerous conversions to Lutheranism, the Reformed Church and the Bohemian Brethren. A successful Counter-Reformation, with the Jesuits in a position of leadership, was completed by about 1632. The movement served a nationalist as well as religious purpose; in restoring religious unity to a large degree, it united the country against potential invaders, the Swedes, Russians and

Turks. The Counter-Reformation had bad side effects, leading to the repression of Protestants long after it was over and to prejudice against Orthodox who returned to allegiance with Rome in 1596 and later. The Church, in the same manner as the entire country, was adversely affected by the partitions of the 18th and 19th centuries. Russification hurt the Orthodox who had reunited with Rome and the Latins who were in the majority. Germans extended their Kulturkampf to the area they controlled. The Austrians exhibited some degree of tolerance. In the republic established after World War I the Church reorganized itself, continued to serve as a vital force in national life, and enjoyed generally harmonious relations with the state. Progressive growth was strong until 1939 when disaster struck in the form of invasion by German and Russian forces and six years of war. In 1945, seven years before the adoption of a Soviet-type of constitution, the Communist-controlled government initiated a policy that included a constant program of atheistic propaganda; a strong campaign against the hierarchy and clergy; the imprisonment in 1948 of 700 priests and even more religious; rigid limitation of the activities of religious; censorship and curtailment of the Catholic press and Catholic Action; interference with church administration and appointments of the clergy; the "deposition" of Cardinal Wyszynski in 1953 and the imprisonment of other members of the hierarchy; the suppression of "Caritas," the Catholic charitable organization; promotion of "Progressive Catholic" activities and a small minority of "patriotic priests." Establishment of the Gomulka regime, the freeing of Cardinal Wyszynski in October, 1956, and the signing of an agreement two months later by bishops and state officials, led to some improvement of conditions. The underlying fact, however, was that the regime conceded to Catholics only so much as was necessary to secure support of the government as a more tolerable evil than the harsh and real threat of a Russian-imposed puppet government like that in Hungary. This has been the controlling principle in Church-state relations. Auxiliary Bishop Ladislaw Rubin of Gniezno sketched the general state of affairs in March, 1968. He said that there was no sign that the government had any intention of releasing its oppressive grip on the Church. As evidence of the "climate of asphyxiation" in the country he cited: persistent questioning of priests by officials concerning their activities; the prohibition against Catholic schools, hospitals and charitable works; the financial burden of a 60 per cent tax on church income. Cardinal Wyszynski denounced "enforced atheism" in a Lenten pastoral in the same year. In May, 1969, the bishops drafted a list of grievances against the government which, they said, were "only some examples of difficulties which demonstrated the situation of the Church in our homeland." The grievances were: refusal of permits to build new churches and establish new parishes; refusal of permission "for the organization of new religion classes"; pressure on Catholics who attend religious ceremonies; censorship and the lack of an independent Catholic daily newspaper; lack of representation in public life; restriction of "freedom to conduct normal pastoral work" in the western portion of the country. There was a move toward improvement in Church-state relations in 1971-72. In 1973, the Polish bishops issued a pastoral letter urging Catholics to resist the official atheism imposed by the government. In 1974 the Polish bishops expressed approval of renewed Vatican efforts at regularizing Church-state relations but insisted that they (the bishops) be consulted on every step of the negotiations. Regular contacts on a working level were established by the Vatican and Poland in 1974.

Archd., 8; dioc., 23; ap. ex., 1; card., 2; abp., 1; bp., 62; parishes, 9,590; priests, 20,666 (16,828 dioc., 3,838 rel.); sem., 2,694; m. rel., 6,232; w. rel., 25,818; sch., 25; inst., 275; Caths., 30,958,807 (92.8%); tot. pop. (UN est., 1973), 33,360,000.

Polynesia, French: French possession in the southern Pacific, including Tahiti and the Marquesas Islands; capital, Papeete. The first phase of evangelization in the Marquesas Islands, begun in 1838, resulted in 216 baptisms in 10 years. A vicariate was organized in 1848 but real progress was not made until after the baptism of native rulers in 1853. Persecution caused missionaries to leave the islands several times. By the 1960's, more than 95 per cent of the population was Catholic. Isolated attempts to evangelize Tahiti were made in the 17th and 18th centuries. Two Picpus Fathers began missionary work in 1831. A vicariate was organized in 1848. By 1908, despite the hindrances of Protestant opposition, disease and other factors, the Church had firm roots.

Archd., 1; dioc., 1; abp., 1; bp., 1; parishes, 82; priests, 45 (8 dioc., 37 rel.); sem., 2; m. rel., 68; w. rel., 61; sch., 21; inst., 5; Caths., 40,015; tot. pop., 130,000.

Portugal: Republic in the western part of the Iberian peninsula; capital, Lisbon. Christianity was introduced before the fourth century. From the fifth century to early in the eighth century the Church experienced difficulties from the physical invasion of barbarians and the intellectual invasion of doctrinal errors in the forms of Arianism, Priscillianism and Pelagianism. The Church survived under the rule of Arabs from about 711 and of the Moors until 1249. Ecclesiastical life was fairly vigorous from 1080 to 1185, and monastic influence became strong. A decline set in about 1450. Several decades later Portugal became the jumping-off place for many missionaries to newly discovered colonies. The Reformation had little effect in the country. Beginning

about 1750, Pombal, minister of foreign affairs and prime minister, mounted a frontal attack on the Jesuits whom he succeeded in expelling from Portugal and the colonies. His anti-Jesuit campaign successful Pombal also attempted, and succeeded to some extent, in controlling the Church in Portugal until his fall from power about 1777. Liberal revolutionaries with anti-Church policies made the 19th century a difficult one for the Church. Similar policies prevailed in Church-state relations in this century until the accession of Salazar to power in 1928. In 1940 he concluded a concordat with the Holy See which regularized Church-state relations but still left the Church in a subservient condition. The prevailing spirit of church authorities in Portugal has been conservative. In 1971 several priests were tried for subversion for speaking out against colonialism and for taking part in guerrilla activities in Angola. A military coup of Apr. 25, 1974, triggered a succession of chaotic political developments which led to an attempt by Communists, after receiving only 18 per cent of the votes cast in a national election, to take over the government in the summer of 1975. Portugal maintains diplomatic relations with Vatican City.

Patriarchate, 1; archd., 2; dioc., 14; card., 3; abp., 3; bp., 17; parishes, 4,314; priests, 4,994 (4,105 dioc., 889 rel.); sem., 489; m. rel., 1,707; w. rel., 7,119; sch., 362; inst., 467; Caths., 8,549,122 (97.7%); tot. pop., 8,748,902.

Puerto Rico: A U.S. commonwealth, the smallest of the Greater Antilles, 885 miles southeast of the southern coast of Florida; capital, San Juan. Following its discovery by Columbus in 1493, the island was evangelized by Spanish missionaries and remained under Spanish ecclesiastical as well as political control until 1898 when it became a possession of the United States. The original diocese, San Juan, was erected in 1511. The present hierarchy was established in 1960.

Archd., 1; dioc., 3; card., 1; bp., 4; parishes, 242; priests, 713 (250 dioc., 463 rel.); sem., 46; m. rel., 605; w. rel., 1,354; sch., 169; inst., 21; Caths., 2,509,748 (86.4%); tot. pop., 2,906,294.

Reunion: French overseas department, 450 miles east of Madagascar; capital, Saint-Denis. Catholicism was introduced in 1667 and some intermittent missionary work was done through the rest of the century. A prefecture apostolic was organized in 1712. Vincentians began work there in 1817 and were joined later by Holy Ghost Fathers. Reunion has an apostolic delegate.

Dioc., 1; bp., 1; parishes, 66; priests, 124 (65 dioc., 59 rel.); sem., 10; m. rel., 110; w. rel., 477; sch., 42; inst., 24; Caths., 443,700; tot. pop., 479,647.

Rhodes: Greek island in the Aegean Sea, 112 miles from the southwestern coast of Asia Minor. A diocese was established about the end of the third century. A bishop from Rhodes attended the Council of Nicaea in 325. Most of the Christians followed the Eastern Churches into schism in the 11th century and became Orthodox. Turks controlled the island from 1522 to 1912. The small Catholic population, for whom a diocese existed from 1328 to 1546, lived in crossfire between Turks and Orthodox. After 1719 Franciscans provided pastoral care for the Catholics, for whom an archdiocese was erected in 1928. Statistics are included in Greece.

Rhodesia: Self-governing state in south central Africa; capital, Salisbury. Earlier unsuccessful missionary ventures preceded the introduction of Catholicism in 1879. Missionaries began to make progress after 1893. The hierarchy was established in 1955. In 1969, four years after the government of Ian Smith made a unilateral declaration of independence from England, a new constitution was enacted for the purpose of assuring continued white supremacy over the black majority. Catholic and Protestant prelates in the country have protested rigorously against the constitution and related enactments as opposed to human rights of the blacks and restrictive of the Church's freedom to carry out its pastoral, educational and social service functions. The first black bishop was ordained in 1973. Rhodesia has an apostolic delegate (to South Africa).

Archd., 1; dioc., 4; p.a. 1; abp., 1; bp., 5 (1 nat.); parishes, 79; priests, 378 (49 dioc., 329 rel.); sem., 79; m. rel., 499 w. rel., 1,043; sch., 180; inst., 162; Caths., 570,468 (10%); tot. pop., 5,547,694.

Rumania: Socialist republic in southeastern Europe; capital, Bucharest. Latin Christianity, introduced in the third century, all but disappeared during the barbarian invasions. The Byzantine Rite was introduced by the Bulgars about the beginning of the eighth century and established firm roots. It eventually became Orthodox, but a large number of its adherents returned later to union with Rome. Attempts to reintroduce the Latin Rite on any large scale have been unsuccessful. Communists took over the government following World War II, forced the abdication of Michael I in 1947, and enacted a Soviet type of constitution in 1952. By that time a campaign against religion was already in progress. In 1948 the government denounced a concordat concluded in 1929, nationalized all schools and passed a law on religions which resulted in the disorganization of Church administration. The 1.5 million-member Rumanian Byzantine Rite Church, by government decree, was incorporated into the Rumanian Orthodox Church, and the Orthodox bishops then seized the cathedrals of Roman Catholic bishops. Five of the six Latin Rite bishops were immediately disposed of by the government, and the last was sentenced to 18 years' imprisonment in

1951, when a great many arrests of priests and laymen were made. Religious orders were suppressed in 1949. Since 1948 more than 50 priests have been executed and 200 have died in prison. One hundred priests were reported in prison at the end of 1958. Some change for the better in Church-state relations was reported after the middle of the summer of 1964, although restrictions were still in effect. About 1,200 priests were engaged in parish work in August, 1965.

Archd., 2; dioc., 8; ord., 1; bp., 2. No recent statistics are available on the number of Catholics. There were an estimated 1,140,000 Catholics (5.9% of the population) in 1969. Tot. pop. (UN est., 1973), 20,830,000.

Rwanda: Republic in east central Africa; capital, Kigali. Catholicism was introduced about the turn of the 20th century. The hierarchy was established in 1959. Intertribal warfare between the ruling Hutus (90 per cent of the population) and the Tutsis (formerly the ruling aristocracy) has plagued the country for several years. Rwanda maintains diplomatic relations with Vatican City.

Archd., 1; dioc., 4; abp., 1; bp., 4 (nat.); parishes, 98; priests, 331 (190 dioc., 141 rel.); sem., 94; p.d., 3; m. rel., 294; w. rel., 657; sch., 1,101; inst., 138; Caths., 1,622,163 (38%); tot. pop., 4,200,000.

Ryukyu Islands: Consists of Okinawa and 72 other islands in western Pacific. Statistics included in Japan.

St. Lucia: British Associated State in West Indies; capital, Castries.

Archd., 1; parishes, 21; priests, 31 (4 dioc., 27 rel.); sem., 4; m. rel., 33; w. rel., 34; sch., 59; inst., 3; Caths., 99,000; tot. pop., 110,000.

St. Pierre and Miquelon: French overseas territory, islands near the southwest coast of Newfoundland. Catholicism was introduced about 1689.

V.a., 1; bp., 1; parishes, 3; priests, 4 (rel.); m. rel., 5; w. rel., 15; sch., 6; inst., 2; Caths., 5,815; tot. pop., 5,840.

Samoa: Includes the independent state of Western Samoa, American Samoa, and the New Zealand dependency of Tokelau in the southwestern Pacific. Catholic missionary work began in 1845. Most of the missions now in operation were established by 1870 when the Catholic population numbered about 5,000. Additional progress was made in missionary work from 1896. The first Samoan priest was ordained in 1892. The hierarchy was established in 1966.

Dioc., 1; card., 1; parishes, 23; priests, 42 (10 dioc., 32 rel.); sem., 9; m. rel., 68; w. rel., 120; sch., 26; inst., 3; Caths., 36,866; tot. pop., 181,587.

San Marino: Republic, a 24-square-mile enclave in northeastern Italy; capital, San Marino. The date of initial evangelization is not known, but a diocese was established by the end of the third century. Ecclesiastically, it forms part of the diocese of Montefeltro in

Italy. San Marino is represented by a minister at Vatican City.

Population (entirely Catholic), 20,000.

Sao Tome and Principe: Portuguese overseas territory, islands off the western coast of Africa in the Gulf of Guinea. Evangelization was begun by the Portuguese who discovered the islands in 1471-72. The Sao Tome diocese was established in 1534.

Dioc., 1; parishes, 44; priests, 13 (rel.); m. rel., 15; w. rel., 19; sch., 8; inst., 2; Caths., 71,470; tot. pop., 77,340.

Saudi Arabia: Monarchy occupying four-fifths of Arabian peninsula; capital, Riyadh. Population (1973 est.), 8,100,000. Catholic statistics are included in Arabian Peninsula.

Scotland: Part of the United Kingdom, in the northern British Isles; capital, Edinburgh. Christianity was introduced by the early years of the fifth century. The arrival of St. Columba and his monks in 563 inaugurated a new era of evangelization which reached into remote areas by the end of the sixth century. He was extremely influential in determining the character of the Celtic Church, which was tribal, monastic, and in union with Rome. Considerable disruption of church activity resulted from Scandinavian invasions in the late eighth and ninth centuries. By 1153 the Scottish Church took a turn away from its insularity and was drawn into closer contact with the European community. Anglo-Saxon religious and political relations, complicated by rivalries between princes and ecclesiastical superiors, were not always the happiest. Religious orders expanded greatly in the 12th century. From shortly after the Norman Conquest of England to 1560 the Church suffered adverse effects from the Hundred Years' War, the Black Death, the Western Schism and other developments. In 1560 parliament abrogated papal supremacy over the Church in Scotland and committed the country to Protestantism in 1567. The Catholic Church was proscribed, to remain that way for more than 200 years, and the hierarchy was disbanded. Defections made the Church a minority religion from that time on. Presbyterian church government was ratified in 1690. Priests launched the Scottish Mission in 1653, incorporating themselves as a mission body under a prefect apostolic and working underground to serve the faithful in much the same way their confreres did in England. About 100 heather priests, trained in clandestine places in the heather country, were ordained by the early 19th century. Catholics got some relief from legal disabilities in 1793 and more later. Many left the country about that time. Some of their numbers were filled subsequently by immigrants from Ireland. The hierarchy was restored in 1878. Scotland, though predominantly Protestant, has a better record for tolerance than Northern Ireland.

Archd., 2; dioc., 6; card., 1; abp., 1; bp., 7;

parishes, 454; priests, 1,150 (906 dioc., 244 rel.); sem., 139; m. rel., 429; w. rel., 1,279; sch., 154; inst., 46; Caths., 816,280 (16%); tot. pop., 5,094,596.*

Senegal: Republic, member of the French Community, in western Africa; capital, Dakar. The country had its first contact with Catholicism through the Portuguese some time after 1460. Some incidental missionary work was done by Jesuits and Capuchins in the 16th and 17th centuries. A vicariate for the area was placed in charge of the Holy Ghost Fathers in 1779. More effective evangelization efforts were accomplished after the Senegambia vicariate was organized in 1863. The hierarchy was established in 1955. Senegal maintains diplomatic relations with Vatican City.

Archd., 1; dioc., 4; abp., 1 (nat.); bp., 3 (nat.); parishes, 57; priests, 207 (60 dioc., 147 rel.); sem., 23; m. rel., 265; w. rel., 502; sch., 128; inst., 112; Caths., 172,509 (4%); tot. pop., 4,230,000.

Seychelles Islands: British colony (scheduled for independence in 1975) of 92 islands in the Indian Ocean 970 miles east of Kenya; capital, Victoria on Mahe. Catholicism was introduced in the 18th century. A vicariate apostolic was organized in 1852. All education in the islands was conducted under Catholic auspices until 1954. The colony has an apostolic delegate (pro-nuncio to Kenya).

Dioc., 1; parishes, 17; priests, 27 (4 dioc., 23 rel.); sem., 1; m. rel., 38; w. rel., 64; sch., 32; inst., 3; Caths., 50,000; tot. pop., 55,000.

Siberia: Republic in the USSR, in northern Asia.

Dioc., 1; v.a. 1.

Sierra Leone: Republic, member of the British Commonwealth, on the western coast of Africa; capital, Freetown. Catholicism was introduced in 1858. Members of the African Missions Society, the first Catholic missionaries in the area, were joined by Holy Ghost Fathers in 1864. Protestant missionaries were active in the area before their Catholic counterparts. Educational work had a major part in Catholic endeavor. The hierarchy was established in 1950. Sierra Leone has an apostolic delegate (the pro-nuncio to Liberia).

Archd., 1; dioc., 2; abp., 1; bp., 2 (1 nat.); parishes, 27; priests, 103 (1 dioc., 102 rel.); sem., 24; m. rel., 120; w. rel., 78; sch., 439; inst., 155; Caths., 54,571 (1.9%); tot. pop. (UN est., 1973), 2,880,000.

Sikkim: Associated state of India in the Himalayas south of Tibet; capital, Gangtok. Some evangelization took place after 1848. Buddhism is the state religion. The territory is under the jurisdiction of the diocese of Darjeeling, India.

Singapore: Independent island republic off the southern tip of the Malay Peninsula; member of the British Commonwealth. Christianity was introduced in the area by

Portuguese colonists about 1511. Singapore was founded in 1819; the first parish church was built in 1846. Singapore has an apostolic delegate.

Archd., 1; abp., 1; parishes, 25; priests, 83 (57 dioc., 26 rel.); sem., 11; m. rel., 79; w. rel., 219; sch., 39; inst., 14; Caths., 77,510 (3.5%); tot. pop., 2,200,000.

Solomon Islands: British protectorate in Oceania; capital, Honiara, on Guadalcanal. Evangelization of the Southern Solomons, begun earlier but interrupted because of violence against them, was resumed by the Marists in 1898. A vicariate apostolic was organized in 1912. A similar jurisdiction was set up for the Western Solomons in 1959. World War II caused a great deal of damage to mission installations. Catholic statistics for the Northern Solomons, where Catholic missionary work started in 1899 and a vicariate was set up in 1930, are included in those reported for Papua-New Guinea.

Dioc., 2; bp., 2; parishes, 30; priests, 40 (5 dioc., 35 rel.); sem., 9; m. rel., 55; w. rel., 137; sch., 75; inst., 28; Caths., 35,060; tot. pop., 205,550.

Somalia: Republic on the eastern coast of Africa; capital, Mogadishu. The country has been Moslem for centuries. Pastoral activity has been confined to immigrants. Schools and hospitals were nationalized in 1972, resulting in the departure of some foreign missionaries. Somalia has an apostolic delegate (to the Red Sea Region).

V.a., 1; parishes, 5; priests, 22 (rel.); m. rel., 25; w. rel., 65; inst., 2; Caths., 3,100; tot. pop. (UN est., 1973), 3,100,000.

Somaliland, French: See Afars and Issas.

South Africa: Republic in the southern part of Africa; capitals, Cape Town (legislative) and Pretoria (administrative). Christianity was introduced by the Portuguese who discovered the Cape of Good Hope in 1498. Boers, who founded Cape Town in 1652, expelled Catholics from the region. There was no Catholic missionary activity from that time until the 19th century. After a period of British opposition, a bishop established residence in 1837 and evangelization got underway thereafter among the Bantus and white immigrants. In recent years church authorities have strongly protested the white supremacy policy of apartheid which seriously infringes the human rights of the native blacks and impedes the Church from carrying out its pastoral, educational and social service functions. The hierarchy was established in 1951. South Africa has an apostolic delegate.

Archd., 4; dioc., 17; abb., 1; p.a., 4; card., 1; abp., 3; bp., 19; parishes, 449; priests, 1,188 (289 dioc., 899 rel.); sem., 58; p.d., 8; m. rel., 1,392; w. rel., 4,544; sch., 761; inst., 328; Caths., 1,639,053 (7.6%); tot. pop., 21,443,416.

South West Africa: See Namibia.

Spain: Nominal monarchy on the Iberian peninsula in southwestern Europe; capital, Madrid. Christians were on the peninsula by 200; some of them suffered martyrdom during persecutions of the third century. A council held in Elvira about 304/6 enacted the first legislation on clerical celibacy in the West. Vandals invaded the peninsula in the fifth century, bringing with them an Arian brand of Christianity which they retained until their conversion following the baptism of their king Reccared, in 589. One of the significant developments of the seventh century was the establishment of Toledo as the primatial see. The Visigoth kingdom lasted to the time of the Arab invasion, 711-14. The Church survived under Moslem rule but experienced some doctrinal and disciplinary irregularities as well as harassment. Reconquest of most of the peninsula was accomplished by 1248; unification was achieved during the reign of Ferdinand and Isabella. The discoveries of Columbus and other explorers ushered in an era of colonial expansion in which Spain became one of the greatest mission-sending countries in history. In 1492, in repetition of anti-Semitic actions of 694, the expulsion of unbaptized Jews was decreed, leading to mass baptisms but a questionable number of real conversions in 1502. (The Jewish minority numbered about 165,000.) Activity by the Inquisition followed. Spain was not seriously affected by the Reformation. Ecclesiastical decline set in about 1650. Anti-Church actions authorized by a constitution enacted in 1812 resulted in the suppression of religious and other encroachments on the leaders, people and goods of the Church. Political, religious and cultural turmoil recurred during the 19th century and into the 20th. A revolutionary republic was proclaimed in 1931, triggering a series of developments which led to civil war from 1936 to 1939. During the conflict, which pitted leftist Loyalists against the forces of Francisco Franco, 6,632 priests and religious and an unknown number of lay persons perished in addition to thousands of victims of combat. One-man, one-party rule, established after the civil war, has come under pressure recently to liberalize its conservative stance and policy with respect to personal liberties and social and economic reforms. Generally conservative church leaders have come under the same pressure from some of their colleagues, priests and lay persons. The Catholic Church is the state religion, but the constitution provides for general religious freedom. Spain maintains diplomatic relations with Vatican City.

Archd., 13; dioc., 50; prel., 1; card., 4; abp., 10; bp., 65; parishes, 22,795; priests, 35,472 (24,285 dioc., 11,187 rel.); sem., 2,348; p.d., 1; m. rel., 20,337; w. rel., 80,052; sch., 6,338; inst., 1,973; Caths. (est.), 34,162,600 (98%); tot. pop. (UN est., 1973), 34,860,000.

Spanish North Africa: Includes the cities of

Ceuta and Melilla on the northern coast of Africa, which are considered part of metropolitan Spain.

Spanish Sahara: Spanish province on the northwestern coast of Africa. Islam is the religion of non-Europeans. A prefecture apostolic was set up in 1954 for the European Catholics there.

P.a., 1; priests, 9 (rel.); m. rel., 10; w. rel., 18; Caths., 16,450. (Figures are for the area covered by the prefecture apostolic of Spanish Sahara.)

Sri Lanka (formerly Ceylon): Independent socialist republic, island southeast of India; capital, Colombo. Effective evangelization began in 1543 and made great progress by the middle of the 17th century. The Church was seriously hampered during the Dutch period from about 1650 to 1795. Anti-Catholic laws were repealed by the British in 1806. The hierarchy was established in 1886. Leftist governments and other factors have worked against the Church since the country became independent in 1948. The high percentage of indigenous clergy and religious has been of great advantage to the Church. Sri Lanka has an apostolic delegate.

Archd., 1; dioc., 6; card., 1 (nat.); bp., 7 (nat.); parishes, 277; priests, 611 (337 dioc., 274 rel.); sem., 121; m. rel., 582; w. rel., 2,333; sch., 92; inst., 106; Caths. (est.), 993,750 (7.5%); tot. pop. (UN est., 1973), 13,250,000.

Sudan: Republic in northeastern Africa, the largest country on the continent; capital, Khartoum. Christianity was introduced from Egypt and gained acceptance in the sixth century. Under Arab rule, it was eliminated in the northern region. No Christians were in the country in 1600. Evangelization attempts begun in the 19th century in the south yielded hard-won results. By 1931 there were nearly 40,000 Catholics there, and considerable progress was made by missionaries after that time. In 1957, a year after the republic was established, Catholic schools were nationalized. An act restrictive of religious freedom went into effect in 1962, resulting in the harassment and expulsion of foreign missionaries. By 1964 all but a few Sudanese missionaries had been forced out of the southern region. The northern area, where Islam predominates, is impervious to Christian influence. Late in 1971 some missionaries were allowed to return to work in the South. Southern Sudan was granted regional autonomy within a unified country in March, 1972, thus ending often bitter fighting between the North and South dating back to 1955. The hierarchy was established in 1974. Sudan maintains diplomatic relations with Vatican City.

Archd., 2; dioc., 4; abp., 2; bp., 3 (nat.); parishes, 81; priests, 127 (57 dioc., 70 rel.); sem., 26; m. rel., 99; w. rel., 189; sch., 27; inst., 17; Caths., 684,998 (4%); tot. pop., 17,000,000.

Surinam (Dutch Guiana): Autonomous part of the Kingdom of The Netherlands, in northern South America; scheduled for independence in November, 1975; capital, Paramaribo, Catholicism was introduced in 1683. Evangelization began in 1817.

Dioc., 1; bp., 1; parishes, 9; priests, 56 (4 dioc., 52 rel.); sem., 2; m. rel., 90; w. rel., 145; sch., 31; inst., 22; Caths., 80,000; tot. pop., 403,000. (Figures are from 1970.)

Swaziland: Constitutional monarchy in southern Africa; almost totally surrounded by the Republic of South Africa; capital, Mbabane. Missionary work was entrusted to the Servites in 1913. A prefecture apostolic was organized in 1923. The hierarchy was established in 1951. Swaziland has an apostolic delegate (to South Africa).

Dioc., 1; bp., 1; parishes, 10; priests, 37 (3 dioc., 34 rel.); sem., 4; m. rel., 46; w. rel., 134; sch., 60; inst., 45; Caths., 41,876 (9%); tot. pop. (1974 est.), 460,000.

Sweden: Kingdom in northwestern Europe; capital, Stockholm. Christianity was introduced by St. Ansgar, a Frankish monk, in 829/30. The Church became well established in the 12th century and was a major influence at the end of the Middle Ages. Political and other factors favored the introduction and spread of the Lutheran Church which became the state religion in 1560. The Augsburg Confession of 1530 was accepted by the government; all relations with Rome, in the country since the 12th century, were severed; monasteries were suppressed; the very presence of Catholics in the country was forbidden in 1617. A decree of tolerance for foreign Catholics was issued about 1781. Two years later a vicariate apostolic was organized for the country. In 1873 Swedes were given the legal right to leave the Lutheran Church and join another Christian church. (Membership in the Lutheran Church is presumed by law unless notice is given of membership in another church.) In 1923 there were only 11 priests and five churches in the country. Since 1952 Catholics have enjoyed almost complete religious freedom. The hierarchy was reestablished in 1953. Hindrances to growth of the Church are the strongly entrenched established church, limited resources, a clergy shortage and the size of the country. Sweden has an apostolic delegate (to Scandinavia). Its Catholic bishop is an American, John E. Taylor, O.M.I.

Dioc., 1; bp., 1; parishes, 26; priests, 96 (27 dioc., 69 rel.); sem., 1; m. rel., 78; w. rel., 224; sch., 2; inst., 18; Caths., 70,265 (.8%); tot. pop., 8,182,230.

Switzerland: Republic in central Europe; capital, Bern. Christianity was introduced in the fourth century or earlier and was established on a firm footing before the barbarian invasions of the sixth century. Constance, established as a diocese in the seventh century, was a stronghold of the faith against the pagan Alamanni, in particular, who were not converted until some time in the ninth century. During this period of struggle with the barbarians, a number of monasteries of great influence were established. The Reformation in Switzerland was triggered by Zwingli in 1519 and furthered by him at Zurich until his death in battle against the Catholic cantons in 1531. Calvin set in motion the forces that made Geneva the international capital of the Reformation and transformed it into a theocracy. Catholics mobilized a Counter-Reformation in 1570, six years after Calvin's death. Struggle between Protestant and Catholic cantons was a fact of Swiss life for several hundred years. The Helvetic Constitution enacted at the turn of the 19th century embodied anti-Catholic measures and consequences, among them the dissolution of 130 monasteries. The Church was reorganized later in the century to meet the threats of liberalism, radicalism and the Kulturkampf. In the process, the Church, even though on the defensive, gained the strength and cohesion that characterizes it to the present time. The six dioceses in the country are immediately subject to the Holy See. In 1973, constitutional articles banning Jesuits from the country and prohibiting the establishment of convents and monasteries were repealed. There is a papal nuncio to Switzerland, but Switzerland does not have a diplomatic officer accredited to Vatican City.

Dioc., 6; abb., 2; bp., 8; parishes, 1,716; priests, 4,444 (2,928 dioc., 1,516 rel.); sem., 285; m. rel., 1,842; w. rel., 10,069; sch., 81; inst., 171; Caths., 3,133,731 (48%); tot. pop., 6,493,080.

Syria: Arab republic in southwest Asia; capital, Damascus. Christian communities were formed in apostolic times. It is believed that St. Peter established a see at Antioch before going to Rome. Damascus became a center of influence. The area was the place of great men and great events in the early history of the Church. Monasticism developed there in the fourth century. So did the Monophysite and Monothelite heresies to which portions of the Church succumbed. Byzantine Syrians who remained in communion with Rome were given the name Melkites. Christians of various persuasions — Jacobites, Orthodox and Melkites — were subject to various degrees of harassment from the Arabs who took over in 638 and from the Ottoman Turks who isolated the country and remained in control from 1516 to the end of World War II. Syria maintains diplomatic relations with Vatican City.

There are 19 ecclesiastical jurisdictions in Syria serving the following rites: Armenian (1 archdiocese, 1 diocese); Chaldean (1 diocese); Roman (1 vicariate apostolic); Maronite (1 patriarchate, whose patriarch resides in Lebanon, 2 archdioceses and 1 apostolic administration); Melkite (1 patriarchate, 5 archdioceses); Syrian (1 patriarchate, whose patriarch resides in Lebanon, 4 archdioceses). Catholics (est.),

206,650; tot. pop. (UN est., 1973), 6,895,000.

Taiwan (Formosa): Location of the Nationalist Government of the Republic of China, an island 100 miles off the southern coast of mainland China; capital, Taipei. Attempts to introduce Christianity in the 17th century were unsuccessful. Evangelization in the 19th century resulted in some 1,300 converts in 1895. Missionary endeavor was hampered by the Japanese who occupied the island following the Sino-Japanese war of 1894-95. Nine thousand Catholics were reported in 1938. Great progress was made in missionary endeavor among the Chinese who emigrated to the island following the Communist take-over of the mainland in 1949. The hierarchy was established in 1952. Nationalist China maintains diplomatic relations with Vatican City.

Archd., 1; dioc., 6; abp., 1; bp., 5; parishes, 435; priests, 780 (224 dioc., 556 rel.); sem., 31; m. rel., 623; w. rel., 1,178; sch., 49; inst., 154; Caths., 299,747 (1.9%); tot. pop., 15,312,622.

Tanzania: Republic (consisting of former Tanganyika on the eastern coast of Africa and former Zanzibar, an island group off the eastern coast); capital, Dar es Salaam. The first Catholic mission in the former Tanganyikan portion of the republic was manned by Holy Ghost Fathers in 1868. The hierarchy was established there in 1953. Zanzibar was the landing place of Augustinians with the Portuguese in 1499. Some evangelization was attempted between then and 1698 when the Arabs expelled all priests from the territory. There was no Catholic missionary activity from then until the 1860's. The Holy Ghost Fathers arrived in 1863 and were entrusted with the mission in 1872. Zanzibar was important as a point of departure for missionaries to Tanganyika, Kenya and other places in East Africa. A vicariate for Zanzibar was set up in 1906. Tanzania maintains diplomatic relations with Vatican City.

Archd., 2; dioc., 21; p.a., 1; a.a., 1; card., 1 (nat.); abp., 1 (nat.); bp., 21 (17 nat.); parishes, 620; priests, 1,248 (500 dioc., 748 rel.); sem., 422; p.d., 1; m. rel., 1,119; w. rel., 2,768; sch., 134; inst., 406; Caths., 2,836,615 (20%); tot. pop., 14,015,613.

Thailand (Siam): Constitutional monarchy in southeastern Asia; capital, Bangkok. The first Christians in the region were Portuguese traders who arrived early in the 16th century. A number of missionaries began arriving in 1554 but pastoral care was confined mostly to the Portuguese until the 1660's. Evangelization of the natives got underway from about that time. A seminary was organized in 1665, a vicariate was set up four years later, and a point of departure was established for missionaries to Tonkin, Cochin China and China. Persecution and death for some of the missionaries ended evangelization efforts in 1688. It was resumed, however, and made progress from 1824 onwards. In 1881 missionaries were sent from Siam to neighboring Laos. The hierarchy was established in 1965. Thailand maintains diplomatic relations with Vatican City.

Archd., 2; dioc., 8; abp., 2 (nat.); bp., 8 (2 nat.); parishes, 220; priests, 319 (106 dioc., 213 rel.); sem., 95; m. rel., 320; w. rel., 1,113; sch., 224; inst., 46; Caths., 161,020 (.4%); tot. pop., 39,565,883.

Tibet: Autonomous region of China in eastern Asia, north of the Himalayas; capital, Lhasa. Christian contact and evangelization attempts have been almost fruitless. Some 1,200 Catholics were reported in Tibet about 1950. Syrians visited the area in the seventh century and evangelization attempts were made by Jesuits, 1624-35 and later, Capuchins, 1707-45, and others afterwards. They all met resistance and some met death. Missionaries do not have access to the country.

Tot. pop., 2,000,000.

Timor, Portuguese: Overseas province in the Malay archipelago; capital, Dili. A Dominican was the first priest in the territory about 1561. Twenty other Dominicans arrived in 1641 and began intensive evangelization. Some of the missionaries exercised civil as well as ecclesiastical authority until early in the 18th century. Anticlerical influences in the Portuguese government forced the missionaries out in 1834. Some improvement in Church-state relations preceded their return in 1874, but in 1910 they were expelled again and the activity of secular priests was restricted. The Catholic population numbered about 19,000 in 1930. Japanese occupation during World War II had an adverse effect on the missions. Dili was made a diocese in 1940.

Dioc., 1; bp., 1; parishes, 3; priests, 50 (42 dioc., 8 rel.); sem., 21; m. rel., 16; w. rel., 48; sch., 51; inst., 4; Caths., 187,540; tot. pop., 633,626.

Togo: Republic on the western coast of Africa; capital, Lome. The first Catholic missionaries in the area, where slave raiders operated for nearly 200 years, were members of the African Missions Society who arrived in 1563. They were followed by Divine Word Missionaries in 1914, when a prefecture apostolic was organized. At that time the Catholic population numbered about 19,000. The African Missionaries returned after their German predecessors were deported following World War I. The first native priest was ordained in 1922. The hierarchy was established in 1955. Togo has an apostolic delegate (to West Africa).

Archd., 1; dioc., 3; abp., 1 (nat.); bp., 3 (2 nat.); parishes, 62; priests, 157 (82 dioc., 75 rel.); sem., 36; m. rel., 116; w. rel., 253; sch., 265; inst., 44; Caths., 429,705 (19.8%); tot. pop., 2,172,148.

Tonga: Polynesian monarchy in the southwestern Pacific, consisting of about 150 islands, member of the British Commonwealth; capital Nuku'alofa. Marists started mis-

sionary work in 1842, some years after Protestants had begun evangelization. By 1880 the Catholic population numbered about 1,700. A vicariate was organized in 1937. The hierarchy was established in 1966.

Dioc., 1; bp., 1; parishes, 13; priests, 20 (6 dioc., 14; rel.); sem., 2; m. rel., 21; w. rel., 68; sch., 15; inst., 2; Caths., 14,372; tot. pop. (UN est., 1973), 90,000.

Trinidad and Tobago: Independent nation, consisting of two islands in the Caribbean, member of the British Commonwealth; capital, Port-of-Spain. The first Catholic church in Trinidad was built in 1591, years after several missionary ventures had been launched and a number of missionaries killed. Capuchins were there from 1618 until about 1802. Missionary work continued after the British gained control early in the 19th century. Cordial relations have existed between the Church and state, both of which have manifested their desire for the development of native clergy.

Archd., 1; abp., 1; parishes, 62; priests, 132 (22 dioc., 110 rel.); sem., 9; m. rel., 141; w. rel., 220; sch., 159; inst., 19; Caths., 366,000; tot. pop. (UN est., 1973), 1,060,000.

Tunisia: Republic on the northern coast of Africa; capital, Tunis. There were few Christians in the territory until the 19th century. A prefecture apostolic was organized in 1843 and the Carthage archdiocese was established in 1884. The Catholic population in 1892 consisted of most of the approximately 50,000 Europeans in the country. When Tunis became a republic in 1956, most of the Europeans left the country. The Holy See and the Tunisian government concluded an agreement in 1964 which changed the Carthage archdiocese into a prelacy and handed over some ecclesiastical property to the republic. A considerable number of Moslem students are in Catholic schools, but the number of Moslem converts to the Church has been small. Tunisia maintains diplomatic relations with Vatican City.

Prel., 1; abp., 1; parishes, 24; priests, 69 (29 dioc., 40 rel.); sem., 1; p.d., 1; m. rel., 59; w. rel., 310; sch., 37; inst., 4; Caths., 20,000 (.36%); tot. pop. (UN est., 1973), 5,510,000.

Turkey: Republic in Asia Minor and southeastern Europe, capital, Ankara. Christian communities were established in apostolic times, as attested in the Acts of the Apostles, some of the Epistles of St. Paul, and Revelation. The territory was the scene of heresies and ecumenical councils, the place of residence of Fathers of the Church, the area in which ecclesiastical organization reached the dimensions of more than 450 sees in the middle of the seventh century. The region remained generally Byzantine except for the period of the Latin occupation of Constantinople from 1204 to 1261, but was conquered by the Ottoman Turks in 1453 and remained under their domination until establishment of the republic in 1923. Christians, always a minority, numbered more Orthodox than Latins; they were all under some restriction during the Ottoman period. They suffered persecution in the 19th and 20th centuries, the Armenians being the most numerous victims. Turkey is overwhelmingly Moslem. Catholics are tolerated to a degree. Turkey maintains diplomatic relations with Vatican City.

Patriarchate, 1 (Cilicia for the Armenians, the patriarch resides in Lebanon); archd., 3; dioc., 1; v.a., 2; missions "sui juris," 1; ap. ex., 1; Caths., 29,000; tot. pop. (UN est., 1973), 37,930,000.

Uganda: Republic in eastern Africa, member of the British Commonwealth; capital, Kampala. The White Fathers were the first Catholic missionaries, starting in 1879. Persecution broke out from 1885 to 1887, taking a toll of 22 Catholic martyrs, who were canonized in 1964, and a number of Anglican victims. (Pope Paul honored all those who died for the faith during a visit to Kampala in 1969.) By 1888, there were more than 8,000 Catholics. Evangelization was resumed in 1894, after being interrupted by war, and proceeded thereafter. The first native African bishop was ordained in 1939. The hierarchy was established in 1953. Church-state relations have been erratic under the regime of Pres. Idi-Amin who has shown both benevolence and hostility toward the Church. Uganda maintains diplomatic relations with Vatican City.

Archd., 1; dioc., 11; abp., 1 (nat.); bp., 11 (9 nat.); parishes, 284; priests, 864 (378 dioc., 486 rel.); sem., 340; m. rel., 829; w. rel., 1,702; sch., 1,705; inst., 131; Caths., 3,544,179 (32.8%); tot. pop. (UN est., 1973), 10,810,000.

Union of Soviet Socialist Republics: Union of 15 Soviet Socialist Republics in northern Eurasia, from the Baltic Sea to the Pacific; Russian capital, Moscow. The Orthodox Church has been predominant in Russian history. It developed from the Byzantine Church before 1064. Some of its members subsequently established communion with Rome as the result of reunion movements but most of them remained Orthodox. The government has always retained some kind of general or particular control of this church. Latins, always a minority, had a little more freedom. From the beginning of the Communist government in 1917, all churches of whatever kind — including Jews and Moslems — became the targets of official campaigns designed to negate their influence on society and/or to eliminate them entirely. An accurate assessment of the situation of the Catholic Church in Russia is difficult to make. Its dimensions, however, can be gauged from the findings of a team of research specialists made public by the Judiciary Committee of the U.S. House of Representatives in 1964. It was reported: "The fate of the Catholic Church in the USSR and countries occupied

by the Russians from 1917 to 1959 shows the following: (a) the number killed: 55 bishops; 12,800 priests and monks; 2.5 million Catholic believers; (b) imprisoned or deported: 199 bishops; 32,000 priests and 10 million believers; (c) 15,700 priests were forced to abandon their priesthood and accept other jobs; and (d) a large number of seminaries and religious communities were dissolved; 1,600 monasteries were nationalized, 31,779 churches were closed. 400 newspapers were prohibited, and all Catholic organizations were dissolved." Several Latin Rite churches are open; e.g., in Moscow, Leningrad, Odessa and Tiflis. An American chaplain is stationed in Moscow to serve Catholics at the U.S. embassy there. Recent reports indicate that, despite repression and attempts at Russification, the strongholds of Catholicism in the USSR are Lithuania (incorporated in the USSR in 1940, together with Estonia and Latvia) and the Ukraine.

Ecclesiastical jurisdictions, 21 (including 7 in Lithuania, 2 in Latvia, 1 in Estonia); card., 1 (Cardinal Slipyi of the Ukraine, living in Rome since his release in 1963 from 18 years' imprisonment); bp., 10 (most of them, including 7 in Lithuania, are apostolic administrators or auxiliaries; some are impeded; 1 bishop was ordained in 1972, Valerians Zondaks, titular bishop of Tabaicara and auxiliary to the apostolic administration of Riga and Liepaja, Latvia); tot. pop. (Govt. est., 1974), 250,900,000. No Catholic statistics are available. Some recent reports estimate the Catholic population of Lithuania to be 3 million, in a total population of 3.1 million.

United Arab Emirates: Independent state along Persian Gulf; capital, Abu Dhabi. Population (UN est., 1973), 210,000. Catholic statistics are included in Arabian Peninsula.

United States: See Catholic History in the United States, Statistics of the Church in the United States.

Upper Volta: Republic inland in western Africa; capital, Ouagadougou. White Fathers started the first missions in 1900 and 1901. White Sisters began work in 1911. A minor and a major seminary were established in 1926 and 1942, respectively. The first native bishop in modern times from West Africa was ordained in 1956 and the first cardinal created in 1965. The hierarchy was established in 1955. Upper Volta established diplomatic relations with Vatican City in 1973.

Archd., 1; dioc., 8; card., 1 (nat.); bp., 9 (7 nat.); parishes, 92; priests, 386 (109 dioc., 277 rel.); sem., 75; m. rel., 430; w. rel., 544; sch., 18; inst., 85; Caths., 357,629 (6%); tot. pop. (UN est., 1973), 5,740,000.

Uruguay: Republic (called the Eastern Republic of Uruguay) on the southeast coast of South America; capital, Montevideo. The Spanish established a settlement in 1624 and evangelization followed. Missionaries followed the reduction pattern to reach the Indians, form them in the faith and train them in agriculture, husbandry, other useful arts, and the experience of managing property and living in community. Montevideo was made a diocese in 1878. The constitution of 1830 made Catholicism the religion of the state and subsidized some of its activities, principally the missions to the Indians. Separation of Church and state was provided for in the constitution of 1917. Uruguay maintains diplomatic relations with Vatican City.

Archd., 1; dioc., 9; card., 1; abp., 1; bp., 11; parishes, 217; priests, 620 (206 dioc., 414 rel.); sem., 33; p.d., 7; m. rel., 643; w. rel., 1,521; sch., 311; inst., 76; Caths., 2,661,191 (89%); tot. pop. (UN est., 1973), 2,990,000.

Vatican City: See separate entry.

Venezuela: Republic in northern South America; capital, Caracas. Evangelization began in 1513-14 and involved members of a number of religious orders who worked in assigned territories, developing missions into pueblos or towns and villages of Indian converts. Nearly 350 towns originated as missions. Fifty-four missionaries met death by violence from the start of missionary work until 1817. Missionary work was seriously hindered during the wars of independence in the second decade of the 19th century and continued in decline through the rest of the century as dictator followed dictator in a period of political turbulence. Restoration of the missions got underway in 1922. The first diocese was established in 1531. Most of the bishops have been native Venezuelans. The first diocesan synod was held in 1574. Church-state relations are regulated by an agreement concluded with the Holy See in 1964. Venezuela maintains diplomatic relations with Vatican City.

Archd., 6; dioc., 17; v.a., 4; card., 1; abp., 6; bp., 28; parishes, 896; priests, 2,134 (872 dioc., 1,262 rel.); sem., 136; m. rel., 1,735; w. rel., 3,839; sch., 956; inst., 144; Caths., 10,786,611 (91.5%); tot. pop., 11,783,840.

Vietnam: Country in southeastern Asia partitioned in 1954 into the Democratic Peoples' Republic of Vietnam in the North (capital, Hanoi) and the Republic of Vietnam in the South (capital, Saigon). Catholicism was introduced in 1533 but missionary work was intermittent until 1615 when Jesuits arrived to stay. One hundred thousand Catholics were reported in 1639. Two vicariates were organized in 1659. A seminary was set up in 1666 and two native priests were ordained two years later. A congregation of native women religious formed in 1670 is still active. Severe persecution broke out in 1698, three times in the 18th century, and again in the 19th. Between 100,000 and 300,000 persons suffered in some way from persecution during the 50 years before 1883 when the French moved in to secure religious liberty for the Catholics. Most of the 117 beatified Martyrs of Vietnam were killed during this 50-year

period. After the French were forced out of Vietnam in 1954, the country was partitioned at the 17th parallel. The North went Communist and the Viet Cong, joined by North Vietnamese regular army troops in 1964, fought to gain control of the South. In 1954 there were approximately 1,114,000 Catholics in the North and 480,000 in the South. More than 650,000 fled to the South to avoid the government repression that silenced the Church in the North. In South Vietnam, the Church continued to develop during the war years. What the Viet Cong victory in South Vietnam will mean to the Church there remains to be seen. Freedom of religious belief and practice was promised by the Revolutionary Government in May, 1975, shortly after its capture of Saigon (Ho Chi Min City). The hierarchy was established in 1960. Vietnam has an apostolic delegate.

North Vietnam: Archd., 1; dioc., 9; abp., 2; bp., 7; Caths. (est.), 800,000; tot. pop. (UN est., 1973), 22,480,000.

South Vietnam: Archd., 2; dioc., 12; abp., 2; bp., 13; parishes, 664; priests, 2,030 (1,605 dioc., 425 rel.); sem., 1,201; m. rel., 2,066; w. rel., 6,571; sch., 1,309; inst., 410; Caths., 1,873,131 (9.7%); tot. pop. (UN est., 1973), 19,370,000.

Virgin Islands: Organized unincorporated U.S. territory, about 34 miles east of Puerto Rico; capital, Charlotte Amalie on St. Thomas (one of the three principal islands). The islands were discovered by Columbus in 1493 and named for St. Ursula and her virgin companions. Missionaries began evangelization in the 16th century. A church on St. Croix dates from about 1660; another, on St. Thomas, from 1774. The Baltimore archdiocese had jurisdiction over the islands from 1804 to 1820 when it was passed on to the first of several places in the Caribbean area. Some trouble arose over a pastoral appointment in the 19th century, resulting in a small schism. The Redemptorists took over pastoral care in 1858; normal conditions have prevailed since.

Prel., 1; bp., 1; parishes, 7; priests, 16 (1 dioc., 15 rel.); sem., 1; m. rel., 17; w. rel., 24; sch., 6; Caths., 26,850; tot. pop., 75,000.

Wales: Part of the United Kingdom, on the western part of the island of Great Britain. Celtic missionaries completed evangelization by the end of the sixth century, the climax of what has been called the age of saints. Welsh Christianity received its distinctive Celtic character at this time. Some conflict developed when attempts were made — and proved successful later — to place the Welsh Church under the jurisdiction of Canterbury; the Welsh opted for direct contact with Rome. The Church made progress despite the depredations of Norsemen in the eighth and ninth centuries. Norman infiltration occurred near the middle of the 12th century, resulting in a century-long effort to establish territorial dioceses and parishes to replace the Celtic organizational plan of monastic centers and satellite churches. The Western Schism produced split views and allegiances. Actions of Henry VIII in breaking away from Rome had serious repercussions. Proscription and penal laws crippled the Church, resulted in heavy defections and touched off a 150-year period of repression in which more than 91 persons died for the faith. Methodism prevailed by 1750. Modern Catholicism came to Wales with Irish immigrants in the 19th century, when the number of Welsh Catholics was negligible. Catholic emancipation was granted in 1829. The hierarchy was restored in 1850.

Archd., 1; dioc., 1; abp., 1; bp., 2; parishes, 171; priests, 370 (212 dioc., 158 rel.); sem., 21; m. rel., 190; w. rel., 734; sch., 106; inst., 23; Caths., 144,642 (5%); tot. pop., 2,824,353.

Wallis and Futuna Islands: French territory in the southwestern Pacific. Marists, who began evangelizing the islands in 1836-7, were the first Catholic missionaries. The entire populations of the two islands were baptized by the end of 1842 (Wallis) and 1843 (Futuna). The first missionary to the latter island was killed in 1841; he was the first martyr of the Pacific. Most of the priests on the islands are native Polynesians. The hierarchy was established in 1966.

Dioc., 1; bp., 1; parishes, 5; priests, 13 (7 dioc., 6 rel.); sem., 1; m. rel., 10; w. rel., 50; sch., 7; Caths., 8,129 (statistics are for the Diocese of Wallis and Futuna).

Yemen: Arab republic in southwestern Arabia; capital, Sana. Christians perished in the first quarter of the sixth century. Moslems have been in control since the seventh century. The state religion is Islam. In 1973, for the first time in 1,400 years, Catholic personnel — priests, religious, lay persons — were invited to work in the country as staff of a government hospital; they were not to engage in proselytizing.

Tot. pop. (UN est., 1973), 7,000,000.

Yemen, Peoples Democratic Republic of: Republic in the southern part of the Arabian peninsula; capitals, Aden and Medinat as-Shaab. No Christian community has existed there since the Moslem conquest of the seventh century. See Arabian Peninsula.

Yugoslavia: Socialist republic in southeastern Europe; capital, Belgrade. Christianity was introduced from the seventh to ninth centuries in the regions which were combined to form the nation after World War I. Since these regions straddled the original line of demarcation for the Western and Eastern Empires (and churches), and since the Reformation had little lasting effect, the Christians are nearly all either Roman Catholics or Byzantines (some in communion with Rome, the majority Orthodox). Yugoslavia was proclaimed a Socialist republic in 1945. Repression of religion became government policy. Between May, 1945, and December, 1950,

persecution took the following toll: almost two-thirds of 22 dioceses lost their bishops; about 348 priests were killed; 200 priests were under arrest and in prison; 12 of 18 seminaries were closed; the Catholic press was confiscated; religious instruction was suppressed in all schools; 300 religious houses and institutions were confiscated, and nuns and other religious driven out; all Church property was expropriated; the ministry of priests was severely restricted and subject to government interference; many thousands of the faithful shared the fate of priests and religious in death, imprisonment and slave labor. Cardinal Stepinac, arrested in 1946 and the symbol of the Church under persecution in Yugoslavia, died Feb. 10, 1960. In an agreement signed June 25, 1966, the government recognized the Holy See's spiritual jurisdiction over the Church in the country and guaranteed to bishops the possibility of maintaining contact with Rome in ecclesiastical and religious matters. The Holy See confirmed the principle that the activity of ecclesiastics, in the exercise of priestly functions, must take place within the religious and ecclesiastical sphere, and that abuse of these functions for political ends would be illegal. Less than two months after the agreement was signed, a group of exiled Croatian priests issued a statement in which they accused the Yugoslav government of failing to abide by it. According to others, an improvement was noticeable. Yugoslavia maintains diplomatic relations with Vatican City.

Archd., 8; dioc., 13; a.a., 1; abp., 9; bp., 21; parishes, 2,443; priests, 3,362 (2,399 dioc., 963 rel.); sem., 774; p.d., 3; m. rel., 1,727; w. rel., 5,177; sch., 4; inst., 10; Caths. (est.) 6,654,690 (31.5%); tot. pop. (Govt. est., 1974), 21,126,000.

Zaire (formerly the Congo): Republic in south central Africa; capital, Kinshasa. Christianity was introduced in 1484 and evangelization began about 1490. The first native bishop in black Africa was ordained in 1518. Subsequent missionary work was hindered by faulty methods of instruction and formation, inroads of the slave trade, wars among the tribes, and Portuguese policy based on the patronage system and having all the trappings of anti-clericalism in the 18th and 19th centuries. Modern evangelization started in the second half of the 19th century. The hierarchy was established in 1959. In the civil disorders which followed independence in 1960, some missions and other church installations were abandoned, thousands of people reverted to tribal religions and many priests and religious were killed. Church-state tensions have developed in recent years because of the Church's criticism of the anti-Christian thrust of Pres. Mobutu's "Africanization" policies. Zaire maintains diplomatic relations with Vatican City.

*Archd., 6; dioc., 42; abp., 5 (4 nat.); bp., 44
(33 nat.); parishes, 778; priests, 2,826 (725
dioc., 2,101 rel.); sem., 491; p.d., 1; m. rel.,
3,176; w. rel., 4,365; sch., 5,538 (nationalized
as of Jan. 1, 1975); inst., 1,353; Caths.,
9,724,200 (40%); tot. pop., 24,056,469.*

Zambia: Republic in central Africa; capital, Lusaka. Portuguese priests did some evangelizing in the 16th and 17th centuries but no results of their work remained in the 19th century. Jesuits began work in the south in the 1880's and White Fathers in the north and east in 1895. Evangelization of the western region began for the first time in 1831. The number of Catholics doubled in the 20 years following World War II. Zambia maintains diplomatic relations with Vatican City.

*Archd., 2; dioc., 6; p.a., 1; abp., 2 (nat.); bp.,
6 (2 nat.); parishes, 215; priests, 455 (71 dioc.,
384 rel.); sem., 33; p.d., 3; m. rel., 537; w. rel.,
562; sch., 574; inst., 126; Caths., 962,162
(20.7%); tot. pop. (UN est., 1973), 4,640,000.*

COMMUNISM

The substantive principles of modern Communism, a theory and system of economics and social organization, were stated about the middle of the 19th century by Karl Marx, author of *The Communist Manifesto* and, with Friedrich Engels, *Das Kapital.*

The elements of Communist ideology include: radical materialism; dialectical determinism; the inevitability of class struggle, which is to be furthered, for the ultimate establishment of a worldwide classless society; common ownership of productive and other goods; the subordination of all persons and institutions to the dictatorship of the collectivity; denial of the rights, dignity and liberty of persons; militant atheism and hostility to religion; utilitarian morality.

Communism in theory and practice has been the subject of many papal documents and statements. Pius IX condemned it in 1846. Leo XIII dealt with it at length in the encyclicals *Quod Apostolici Muneris* in 1878

and *Rerum Novarum* in 1891. Pius XI wrote on the same subject in the encyclicals *Quadragesimo Anno* in 1931 and *Divini Redemptoris* in 1937.

Pius XII, besides writing and speaking about Communism on many occasions, authorized the June 13, 1949, decree of the Congregation of the Holy Office which contained these as well as other provisions: Catholics are forbidden to join the Communist Party; Catholics who knowingly and willingly profess the doctrines of Communism, or defend its principles, or spread its errors are automatically excommunicated. Catholics who join the Communist Party under the force of hard circumstances (as in Iron Curtain countries, for the sake of work needed to support their families) but do not subscribe to its ideology, are not excommunicated.

John XXIII condemned the errors of Communism as intrinsically evil. In the encyclical *Peace on Earth,* however, without going soft on Communism, he sanctioned prudent and cautious efforts to work with Communists for the solution of social and economic problems.

Virtually all of the papal documents on Communism set forth Christian social teachings and urge action for the establishment of a just social order which should be its own best defense against Communism.

During the pontificate of Paul VI, Vatican diplomats have held talks and conducted negotiations with officials of Communist governments in Eastern Europe in efforts to improve the status of the Church, especially in Hungary, Bulgaria and Poland. Results have been partially to the good, particularly with respect to the appointment of several bishops as heads of long-vacant dioceses. Otherwise, negotiations have not substantially eased government suppression of religion.

This policy of seeking a livable accommodation with Communist regimes has been criticized in some quarters which call for a stronger expression of care and concern for people of the "Church of Silence."

THE CHURCH IN PROBLEM AREAS IN 1975

(See related reports in The Church in Countries throughout the World, News Events, other entries, Index.)

Africa

Nigeria: Bishops were continuing efforts to gain control of Catholic schools taken over by the government since 1970.

Rhodesia: Church-state relations remained strained because of the bishops' opposition to the racist policies of the Smith white-supremacy government.

South Africa: Work by the Church remained inhibited by the apartheid policies of the government.

Uganda: The virtually unpredictable President Idi Amin granted permanent residence to five Catholic missionaries in May and ex-

pelled 16 others, Italian Verona Fathers, in July. Meanwhile, a national shrine to the Uganda Martyrs near Kampala was consecrated June 3.

Zaire: President Mobutu Sese Seko, after taking over all Catholic and other schools in January, banned all religious teaching except the cult of Mobutuism. His plan appeared to be to elevate the People's Movement of the Revolution to the status of a national ancestor-worship church of African "authenticity" with himself as the messiah. On Feb. 1, he reacted to two statements issued by the bishops with a warning that he might close down all Catholic churches.

Europe

Communist Nations: Repression prevailed

against the Church and religion in general. Lithuania, a Soviet captive nation since World War II, reported incidents of persecution. The appointment of several bishops resulted from talks between the Vatican and the Bulgarian government, but there was no substantial change in Church-state relations. Similarly, no real softening of hard-line opposition to the Church came from meetings of Vatican officials with representatives of Poland, Czechoslovakia and Hungary.

Portugal: Church leaders appealed for democratic process and an end to violence provoked by Communists seeking to gain total control over the government and military even though they won less than 20 per cent of the popular vote in elections held Apr. 25. One incident in the turmoil was the seizure of the Catholic radio station, *Renascenca,* in the spring.

Spain: Cardinal Vicente Enrique Tarancon of Madrid said in May that leaders and the people were both to blame for the "climate of violence" in the country. Perpetrators of the violence included government police and security officers, Basques seeking independence, social and economic institutions straitjacketed by the Franco regime.

Latin America

Argentina: No Church-state relations were at issue in the turmoil of political, economic and social affairs. The bishops urged efforts to end the violence practiced by extremists, but with little effect.

Bolivia: The military government of Gen. Hugo Banzer ousted a number of missionaries because of their involvement in social activism.

Brazil: The bishops called attention to the prevalence and problem of paganism in the country. They also continued efforts in defense of civil rights and for the preservation of Amazon tribes and their culture against the encroachments of government and economic programs.

Paraguay: The bishops' conference, declaring that charges of subversion by the Church against the government of Gen. Alfredo Stroessner had never been proved, protested against arrests, expulsions and confiscations aimed at Catholic social works.

Middle East

Israel: There was continuing concern over the dwindling presence of Christians as a living community in Jerusalem. Pope Paul noted this in an apostolic exhortation dated Apr. 5, 1974, when he spoke about "the increased needs of the Church in the Holy Land."

Lebanon: The bishops joined other responsible leaders in strong appeals for an end to violence accompanying chaotic political turmoil, as Moslems and Christians contended for control of the government.

Southeast Asia

Vietnam, Cambodia, Laos: The Communist take-over of Southeast Asia ended missionary work in progress there, resulted in the destruction of church facilities, and led to the exodus of thousands of refugees to the United States and other countries. Meager reports from North Vietnam said religion was still alive there. Native clergy were active in the South, but some of them, as well as native seminarians and religious, left the country. No news, except that which concerned the expulsion of missionaries, was forthcoming from the Khmer Republic and Laos.

CATHOLIC WORLD STATISTICS

(Principal source: *Annuario Pontificio, 1975.*)

Patriarchates: 13. Eastern Rites: 8 (Asia, 6; Africa, 2). Roman Rite, 5 (Asia, 2; Europe, 2; West Indies, 1).

Archdioceses: 477 (Asia, 116; Oceania, 14; Africa, 50; Europe, 143; South America, 78; North and Middle America, 76).

Dioceses: 1,729 (Asia, 314; Oceania, 45; Africa, 275; Europe, 526; South America, 284; North and Middle America, 285).

Prelatures: 105 (Asia, 12; Africa, 1; Europe, 8; South America, 70; North and Middle America, 14).

Abbacies: 21 (Asia, 1; Oceania, 1; Africa, 1; Europe, 14; South America, 2; North and Middle America, 2).

Vicariates Apostolic: 76 (Asia, 18; Oceania, 1; Africa, 11; Europe, 5; South America, 36; North and Middle America, 5).

Prefectures Apostolic: 65 (Asia, 36; Africa, 17; South America, 11; North and Middle America, 1).

Apostolic Administrations: 9 (Asia, 1; Africa,

1; Europe, 5; North and Middle America, 2).

Missions "Sui Juris": 4 (Asia, 3; Oceania, 1).

Apostolic Exarchates, Ordinariates: 29 (Asia, 6; Oceania, 1; Europe, 13; South America, 8; North and Middle America, 1).

Cardinals: 122 (Asia, 9; Oceania, 4; Africa, 9; Europe, 67; South America, 15; North and Middle America, 18). As of Sept. 29, 1975.

Archbishops: 434 (Asia, 94; Oceania, 14; Africa, 45; Europe, 110; South America, 69; North and Middle America, 102).

Bishops: 2,189 (Asia, 262; Oceania, 52; Africa, 295; Europe, 673; South America, 464; North and Middle America, 443).

Priests, Total: 421,104 (Asia, 26,273; Oceania, 5,399; Africa, 17,200; Europe, 254,838; South America, 32,863; North and Middle America, 84,531).

Priests, Diocesan: 272,006 (Asia, 13,622; Oceania, 2,988; Africa, 5,082; Europe, 183,419; South America, 14,463; North and Middle America, 52,432).

Priests, Religious: 149,098 (Asia, 12,651;

Oceania, 2,411; Africa, 12,118; Europe, 71,419; South America, 18,400; North and Middle America, 32,099).

Seminarians: 57,051 (Asia, 7,455; Oceania, 605; Africa, 3,783; Europe, 20,914; South America, 2,984; North and Middle America, 21,310).

Permanent Deacons: 1,691 (Asia, 10; Oceania, 24; Africa, 32; Europe, 420; South America, 244; North and Middle America, 961).

Men Religious: 218,120 (Asia, 22,921; Oceania, 6,051; Africa, 18,036; Europe, 114,407; South America, 28,268; North and Middle America, 28,437).

Women Religious: 976,451 (Asia, 77,635; Oceania, 16,737; Africa, 34,445; Europe, 550,010; South America, 87,110; North and Middle America, 210,514).

Catholic Population: 683,000,000 (18.3% of the total world population). Asia, 54,700,000 (2.5%); Oceania, 4,700,000 (23.4%); Africa, 43,000,000 (11.7%); Europe, 261,600,000 (40%); South America, 182,000,000 (92.2%); North and Middle America, 137,000,000 (42%).

Population figures are estimates as of December 31, 1972, and include all persons baptized as Catholics. They are from the Yearbook issued by the Central Statistics Office of the Church.

Totals from the *Annuario Pontificio, 1975,* amounted to more than 696,000,000.

Other sources give a figure that is considerably lower than that reported by the Central Statistics Office. (See Religious Population of the World.)

EPISCOPAL CONFERENCES

(Principal source: *Annuario Pontificio.*)

Listed are countries with conferences, dates when statutes were approved where available, names and sees of presidents (archbishops unless otherwise noted).

AFRICA, North (Feb. 27, 1967): Cardinal Leon-Etienne Duval, Algiers.

AFRICA, South (Apr. 28, 1970): Joseph P. Fitzgerald, Bloemfontein.

ANGOLA and SAO TOME (Nov. 11, 1972): Manuel Nunes Gabriel, Luanda.

ANTILLES (Dec. 10, 1957): Samuel E. Carter, Kingston in Jamaica.

ARAB COUNTRIES: Latin Bishops (Mar. 31, 1967): Patriarch Giacomo Beltritti, Jerusalem.

ARGENTINA (Mar. 9, 1973): Adolfo Servando Tortolo, Parana.

AUSTRALIA (Apr. 3, 1971): Cardinal James Darcy Freeman, Sydney.

AUSTRIA (Oct. 23, 1974): Cardinal Franz Koenig, Vienna.

BANGLADESH (Oct. 18, 1973): Theutonius A. Ganguli, Dacca.

BELGIUM (Aug. 21, 1971): Cardinal Leo Suenens, Mechelen-Brussels.

BOLIVIA (Aug. 19, 1972): Cardinal Jose Clemente Maurer, Sucre.

BRAZIL (Jan. 23, 1971): Alois Lorscheider, Fortaleza.

BULGARIA: Bishop Metodio Dimitrow Stratiew, apostolic exarch, Sofia.

BURMA (Feb. 10, 1967): Gabriel Thohey, Rangoon.

CAMEROON (Apr. 5, 1973): Jean Zoa, Yaounde.

CANADA (Jan. 23, 1955): Jean-Marie Fortier, Sherbrooke.

CENTRAL AFRICAN REPUBLIC: Joachim N'Dayen, Bangui.

CEYLON: See Sri Lanka, Republic of.

CHAD: Paul Dalmais, N'Djamena.

CHILE (June 13, 1970): Cardinal Raul Silva Henriquez, Santiago.

CHINA (Feb. 10, 1967): Cardinal Paul Yu Pin, Nanking.

COLOMBIA (Apr. 2, 1966): Bishop Jose de Jesus Pimiento Rodriguez, Garzon.

CONGO: Cardinal Emile Biayenda, Brazzaville.

COSTA RICA (Oct. 6, 1967): Bishop Roman Arrieta Villalobos, Tileran.

CUBA (Dec. 2, 1972): Bishop Jose Maximino E. Dominguez y Rodriguez, Matanzas.

DAHOMEY: Christophe Adimou, Cotonou.

DOMINICAN REPUBLIC (Oct. 6, 1967): Octavio Beras Rojas, Santo Domingo.

ECUADOR (Mar. 3, 1967): Bernardino Echeverria Ruiz, Guayaquil.

EL SALVADOR (Feb. 22, 1974): Bishop Benjamin Barrera y Reyes, Santa Ana.

ETHIOPIA (Dec. 15, 1966): Asrate M. Yemmeru, Addis Ababa.

FRANCE (Nov. 21, 1966): Cardinal Francois Marty, Paris.

GABON (Oct. 17, 1973): Andre Fernand Anguile, Libreville.

GAMBIA: See Liberia, Sierra Leone and Gambia.

GERMANY (Apr. 22, 1972): Cardinal Julius Doepfner, Munich and Freising. Additional conferences for West Germany and Bavaria, of which Cardinal Doepfner is president; and for Berlin, of which Cardinal Alfred Bengsch, Berlin, is president.

GHANA (Apr. 16, 1973): Bishop Dominic Kodwo Andoh, Accra.

GREAT BRITAIN (June 15, 1968): Cardinal John Heenan, Westminster (England and Wales); Cardinal Gordon J. Gray, St. Andrews and Edinburgh (Scotland).

GREECE (Apr. 17, 1967): Antonio Varthalitis, Corfu, Zante and Cefalonia.

GUATEMALA (Apr. 28, 1973): Bishop Juan Gerardi Conedera, Santa Cruz del Quiche.

GUINEA: Raymond-Marie Tchidimbo, Conakry.

HAITI (Mar. 11, 1972): Bishop Emmanuel Constant, Les Gonaives.

HONDURAS (Mar. 4, 1972): Hector Santos y Hernandez, Tegucigalpa.

HUNGARY (May 3, 1969): Jozsef Ijjas, Kalocsa.

INDIA (Apr. 29, 1967): Cardinal Joseph Parecattil, Ernakulam.

INDONESIA (Aug. 2, 1973): Cardinal Justin Darmojuwono, Semarang.

IRELAND (July 3, 1974): Cardinal William Conway, Armagh.

ITALY (May 8, 1971): Cardinal Antonio Poma, Bologna.

IVORY COAST (Aug. 1, 1973): Bernard Yago, Abidjan.

JAPAN (Aug. 2, 1973): Cardinal Paul Yoshigoro Taguchi, Osaka.

KENYA (Sept. 9, 1974): Cardinal Maurice Otunga, Nairobi (Seychelles Islands included in this conference).

KOREA (Aug. 3, 1973): Cardinal Stephan Sou Hwan Kim, Seoul.

LAOS and KHMER REPUBLIC (CAMBODIA) (Apr. 23, 1971): Bishop Etienne Loosdregt, vicar apostolic, Vientiane.

LATVIA: Bishop Julian Vaivods, apostolic administrator, Riga and Liepaja.

LESOTHO: Alphonsus Morapeli, O.M.I., Maseru.

LIBERIA, SIERRA LEONE and GAMBIA (interterritorial episcopal conference) (Apr. 6, 1973): Thomas J. Brosnahan, Freetown and Bo.

LITHUANIA: Bishop Joseph Matulaitis-Labukas, apostolic administrator, Kaunas and Vilkaviskis.

MALAGASY REPUBLIC (June 18, 1969): Bishop Victor Razafimahatrata, Farafangana.

MALAWI (Oct. 1, 1969): James Chiona, Blantyre.

MALAYSIA and SINGAPORE (Dec. 14, 1967): Bishop Anthony D. Galvin, vicar apostolic, Miri.

MALI (June 15, 1973): Luc Auguste Sangare, Bamako.

MALTA (July 3, 1971): Michele Gonzi, Malta.

MEXICO (Apr. 29, 1972): Cardinal Jose Salazar Lopez, Guadalajara.

MOZAMBIQUE (Apr. 29, 1967): Francesco Nunes Teixeira, Quelimane.

NETHERLANDS (Dec. 2, 1972): Cardinal Bernard Alfrink, Utrecht.

NEW ZEALAND (Sept. 14, 1974): Bishop John P. Kavanaugh, Dunedin.

NICARAGUA (Apr. 8, 1967): Miguel Obando Bravo, Managua.

NIGERIA: Bishop Dominic Ekandem, Ikot Ekpene.

PACIFIC (Jan. 29, 1974): Pierre Martin, former archbishop of Noumea.

PAKISTAN: Cardinal Joseph Cordeiro, Karachi.

PANAMA (Nov. 11, 1972): Bishop Daniel E. Nunez, David.

PAPUA-NEW GUINEA and SOLOMON ISLANDS (Dec. 6, 1966): Bishop Kevin W. Rowell, Aitape.

PARAGUAY (Nov. 7, 1966): Bishop Felipe Santiago Benitez Avalos, Villarrica.

PERU (Feb. 19, 1972): Cardinal Juan Landazuri Ricketts, O.F.M., Lima.

PHILIPPINE ISLANDS (May 21, 1974): Teopista Alberto y Valderramo, Caceres.

POLAND (Mar. 15, 1969): Cardinal Stefan Wyszynski, Gniezno and Warsaw.

PORTUGAL (Jan. 29, 1972): Bishop Manuel D'Almeida Trindade, Aveiro.

PUERTO RICO (June 19, 1971): Cardinal Luis Aponte Martinez, San Juan.

RHODESIA (Aug. 24, 1974): Bishop Ignacio Prieto Vega, Wankie.

RUMANIA: Bishop Aaron Marton, Alba Julia.

RWANDA-BURUNDI (Sept. 5, 1974): Andre Makarakiza, Gitega.

SCANDINAVIA (Apr. 30, 1969): Bishop Paul Verschuren, Helsinki.

SENEGAL-MAURITANIA (Apr. 14, 1973): Hyacinthe Thiandoum, Dakar.

SIERRA LEONE: See Liberia, Sierra Leone and Gambia.

SPAIN (June 15, 1972): Cardinal Vicente Enrique y Tarancon, Madrid.

SRI LANKA, REPUBLIC OF (CEYLON) (Apr. 24, 1970): Cardinal Thomas Cooray, Colombo.

SUDAN (July 15, 1971):

SWITZERLAND (Dec. 12, 1967): Bishop Francois Nestor Adam, Sion.

TANZANIA (Sept. 29, 1969): Bishop James Sangu, Mbeya.

THAILAND (Mar. 28, 1969): Bishop Robert Ratna Bamrungtrakul, Ratchaburi.

TOGO: Robert Dosseh Anyron, Lome.

UGANDA (Sept. 8, 1974): Emmanuel Nsubuga, Kampala.

UNITED STATES OF AMERICA (Dec. 19, 1970): Joseph L. Bernardin, Cincinnati.

UPPER VOLTA and NIGER: Cardinal Paul Zoungrana, Ouagadougou.

URUGUAY (Aug. 19, 1972): Bishop Luis Baccino, San Jose de Mayo.

VENEZUELA (Mar. 29, 1973): Crispulo Benitez Fonturvel, Barquisimeto.

VIETNAM (June 16, 1972): Paul Nguyen van Binh, Saigon.

YUGOSLAVIA (Aug. 26, 1972): Franjo Kuharic, Zagreb.

ZAIRE (Feb. 7, 1969): Bishop Ndamwize Lesambo, Inongo.

ZAMBIA (Feb. 19, 1972): Bishop Medard J. Mazombwe, Chipata.

Territorial Conferences

Territorial as well as national episcopal conferences have been established in some places. Some conferences of this kind are still in the planning stage.

Africa: Association of Member Episcopal Conferences in Eastern Africa (AMECEA): Represents Uganda, Kenya, Tanzania, Zambia and Malawi; Bishop James Odungo, Tororo, Uganda, president.

Symposium of Episcopal Conferences of

Africa and Madagascar (Malagasy Republic) (SECAM): Cardinal Paul Zoungrana, Ougadougou, Upper Volta, president.
Plenary Council of Bishops of West Africa: Abp. Robert Dosseh Anyron, Lome.
Association of Episcopal Conferences of Congo, Central African Republic and Chad: vacant.

Asia: Federation of Asian Bishops' Conferences (FABC): Represents 14 Asian episcopal conferences (excluding the Middle East); headquarters in Hong Kong. Established in 1970; statutes approved experimentally Dec. 6, 1972. Cardinal Stephen Sou Hwan Kim, Seoul, president.

Europe: Council of European Bishops' Conferences: Abp. Roger Etchegaray, Marseilles, France, president.

Central and South America: Latin American Bishops' Conference (Consejo Episcopal LatinoAmericano, CELAM): Established in 1956; statutes approved experimentally Nov. 27, 1969. Represents 22 Latin American national bishops' conferences. Bishop Edoardo Pironio, Mar del Plata, Argentina, president. Address of the secretariat: Apartado Aereo 5278, Bogota, D.E., Colombia.
Episcopal Secretariat of Central America and Panama: Statutes approved experimentally Sept. 26, 1970. Bishop Roman Arrieta Villalobos, Tilaron, Costa Rica, president.

CATHOLIC INTERNATIONAL ORGANIZATIONS

(Source: *The Laity Today,* Bulletin (No. 13-14, 1973) of the Consilium de Laicis, the Vatican Council of the Laity.)

Guidelines

International organizations wanting to call themselves "Catholic" are required to meet standards set by the Vatican's Council of the Laity and to register with and get the approval of the Papal Secretariat of State, according to guidelines published in *Acta Apostolicae Sedis* under date of Dec. 23, 1971. The guidelines were made public in March, 1972.

Among conditions for the right of organizations to "bear the name Catholic" are:
• leaders "will always be Catholics," and candidates for office will be approved by the Secretariat of State;
• adherence by the organization to the Catholic Church, its teaching authority and teachings of the Gospel;
• evidence that the organization is really international with a universal outlook and that it fulfills its mission through its own management, meetings and accomplishments.

The guidelines also stated that leaders of the organizations "will take care to maintain necessary reserve as regards taking a stand or engaging in public activity in the field of politics or trade unionism. Abstention in these fields will normally be the best attitude for them to adopt during their term of office."

The guidelines were in line with a provision stated by the Second Vatican Council in the *Decree on the Apostolate of the Laity:* "No project may claim the name 'Catholic' unless it has obtained the consent of the lawful church authority."

They made it clear that all organizations are not obliged to apply for recognition, but that the Church "reserves the right to recognize as linked with her mission and her aims those organizations or movements which see fit to ask for such recognition."

Conference

Conference of Catholic International Organizations: A permanent body for collaboration among various organizations which seek to promote the development of international life along the lines of Christian principles. Eleven international Catholic organizations participated in its foundation and first meeting in 1927 at Fribourg, Switzerland. In 1951, the conference established its general secretariat and adopted governing statutes which were approved by the Vatican Secretariat of State in 1953.

The general secretariat is located at 1, route du Jura, Fribourg, Switzerland. Other conference addresses are: 1 rue Varembe, 1200 Geneva, Switzerland (Information Center); 9, rue Cler, 750007 Paris, France (International Catholic Center for UNESCO); Avda. Corrientes 524-5, Buenos Aires, Argentina (Liaison Center for Latin America).

International Organizations

Catholic international organizations are listed below. Information includes name, date and place of establishment (when available), address of general secretariat. An asterisk indicates that the organization is a member of the Conference of Catholic International Organizations. Approximately 24 of the organizations have consultative status with other international or regional non-governmental agencies.

Ad Lucem (1932, Lille, France): 12, rue Guy de la Brosse, 75005, Paris, France. Work for the Third World.

Apostleship of Prayer (1849): Borgo Santo Spirito 5, 00193 Rome, Italy. National secretariat in most countries. (See Index.)

Apostolate of Independent Milieus (AIM) (1946, Brussels, Belgium): Piazza San Calisto 16, 00153 Rome, Italy. Evangelization of youth.

Apostolatus Maris* (Apostleship of the Sea) (1922, Glasgow, Scotland): Piazza San Calisto 16, 00153 Rome, Italy. (See Index.)

Associationes Juventutis Salesianae (Associations of Salesian Youth) (1847): Via Maria Ausiliatrice 32, 00152 Turin, Italy.

Blue Army of Our Lady of Fatima*: (See Index.)

Caritas Internationalis* (1951, Rome, Italy): Piazza San Calisto 16, 00153, Rome, Italy. Coordinates relief aid on an international level.

Catholic Fraternity of the Sick and Infirm (1942, Verdun, France): Foyer des Malades, 49 rue Saint-Sauveur, 55100 Verdun, France.

Catholic International Education Office* (1952): 9, rue Guimard, 1040 Brussels, Belgium.

Catholic International Federation for Physical and Sports Education* (1911; present name, 1957): 5, rue Cernuschi, 75017 Paris, France.

Catholic International Union for Social Service* (1925, Milan, Italy): rue de la Poste 111, B-1030 Brussels, Belgium (general secretariat).

"Focolarini" (1943, Trent, Italy): (See Index: Focolare Movement)

General Union of Pastoral Work for Youth (1966): Via Palestro 26, 00185, Rome, Italy.

International Association of Charities of St. Vincent de Paul* (1617, Chatillon les Dombes, France): Chaussee d'Ixelles, 144, B-1050 Brussels, Belgium. (See Index: St. Vincent de Paul Society.)

International Association of Children of Mary (1847): 67 rue de Sevres, 75006 Paris, France.

International Catholic Auxiliaries (1937, Belgium): 91, rue de la Servette, 1202 Geneva, Switzerland.

International Catholic Child Bureau* (1947): 63, Largo Brancaccio, Rome, Italy.

International Catholic Confederation of Hospitals* (1951, Brussels, Belgium): Van Schaek Mathonsingel 4, Nijmegen, Netherlands.

International Catholic Conference of Guiding* (1965): 65, rue de la Glaciere, 75013 Paris, France. Founded by member bodies of interdenominational World Association of Guides and Girl Scouts.

International Catholic Film Organization* (1928, The Hague, The Netherlands): 8, rue de l'Orme, 1040 Brussels, Belgium, (general secretariat). Federation of national Catholic film offices.

International Catholic Girls' Society* (1897): 1, route du Jura, CH 1700 Fribourg, Switzerland. Welfare of Catholic girls living away from home.

International Catholic Migration Commission* (1951): 65, rue de Lausanne, 1202 Geneva, Switzerland. Coordinates Catholic activities to help migrants.

International Catholic Rural Association (1962, Rome): Piazza San Calisto 16, 00153 Rome, Italy. International body for agricultural and rural organizations.

International Catholic Scouters Conference* (1948): 21, rue de Dublin, 1050 Brussels, Belgium.

International Catholic Union of the Press*:

43, rue St. Augustin, 75002 Paris, France. Coordinates and represents at the international level the activities of Catholics and Catholic federations or associations in the field of press and information. Has five specialized branches: International Federation of Catholic Dailies and Periodicals (1928); International Federation of Catholic Journalists (1927); International Federation of Catholic Press Agencies (1950); International Catholic Association of Teachers and Scientific or Technical Research Workers on Information (1968); Federation of Church Press Associations (1974).

International Centre for Studies in Religious Education* (1934-35, Louvain, Belgium), under name Catechetical Documentary Centre; present name, 1956): 186, rue Washington, 1050 Brussels, Belgium. Also referred to as Lumen Vitae Centre; concerned with all aspects of religious formation.

International Christian Union of Business Executives* (1931): 49, avenue d' Auderghem, 1040 Brussels, Belgium.

International Committee of Catholic Nurses* (1933): Square Vercote, 43, 1040 Brussels, Belgium.

International Cooperation for Socio-Economic Development (1965, Rome, Italy): 59-61 Avenue Adolphe Lacomble, 1040 Brussels, Belgium.

International Council of Catholic Men* (Unum Omnes) (1948): Piazza San Calisto 16, 00153 Rome, Italy.

International Crusade for the Blind (1957): 15, rue Mayet, 75006 Paris, France, Coordinates action of Catholic groups and associations for the blind and develops their apostolate.

International Federation of Catholic Parochial Youth Communities (1962, Rome, Italy): Kipdorp 30, Antwerp, Belgium.

International Federation of Catholic Rural Movements (1964, Lisbon, Portugal): 27, rue du Taciturne, 1040 Brussels, Belgium.

International Federation of Catholic Medical Associations (1954): 7 Englewood Road, Upper Darby, Pa. 19082.

International Federation of Catholic Pharmacists* (1954): 60 avenue des Pages, Le Vesinet, France.

International Federation of Catholic Universities* (1949): 77 bis, rue de Grenelle, 75007 Paris, France.

International Federation of Institutes for Social and Socio-Religious Research (1952): rue des Flamandes, 116, Leuven, Belgium.

International Military Apostolate (1967): Kaiserallee, 23, A. 2100 Korneuburg, Austria. Comprised of organizations of military men.

International Movement of Apostolate of Children (1929, France): 8, rue Duguay-Trouin, 75006 Paris, France.

International Movement of Apostolate in "Independent Milieus"* (1963): Piazza San

Calisto 16, 00153 Rome, Italy. Evangelization of adults of the independent milieus (that part of population known as old or recent middle class, aristocracy, bourgeoisie or "white collar").

International Movement of Catholic Agricultural and Rural Youth* (1954, Annevoie, Belgium): Diestsevest 24, Louvain, Belgium (permanent secretariat).

International Young Catholic Students (1946, Fribourg, Switzerland; present name, 1954): 171 rue de Rennes, 75006 Paris, France.

International Young Christian Workers* (1925, Belgium): 26, rue Juste Lipse, 1040 Brussels, Belgium.

Laity and Christian Community (1966, Algiers, Algeria): 98, rue de l'Universite, 75007 Paris, France. Universal brotherhood.

Legion of Mary* (1921, Dublin, Ireland): De Montfort House, North Brunswick St., Dublin, Ireland. (See Index.)

Liga Catholica Internationalis Sobrietas (International Catholic League against Alcoholism) (1897, Brussels, Belgium): Karlstrasse 40, Lorenz-Werthmannhaus, 78 Freiburg/Br., Germany.

Medicus Mundi: Mozartstrasse 9, 51 Aachen, Germany. Place medicine at service of poor.

Movement for a Better World (1952): Centro Internationale Pio XII, Via dei Laghi Km. 10, 00040 Rocca di Papa, Italy. (See Index.)

Our Lady's Teams (Equipes Notre-Dame) (1937, France): 49, rue de la Glaciere, 75013 Paris, France. Movement for spiritual formation of couples.

Pax Christi (1950): Celebesstraat 60, The Hague, The Netherlands. (See Index.)

Pax Romana (1921, Fribourg, Switzerland, divided into two movements, 1947):

International Movement of Catholic Students* (1921): 1 route du Jura, B.P. 453, 1700 Fribourg, Switzerland, For undergraduates.

International Catholic Movement for Intellectual and Cultural Affairs* (1947): 1 route du Jura, Fribourg, Switzerland. For university graduates. Has professional secretariats at: Stradhouderskade 86, Amsterdam, The Netherlands (artists); Biesseltsebaan, 40, Nijmegen, The Netherlands (teachers); 18 rue de Varenne, 75007 Paris, France (engineers); via della Conciliazione 4d, 00193 Rome, Italy (lawyers).

St. Joan's International Alliance* (1911 in England; present title, 1931): 48, chemin des Coudries, 1121 Geneva, Switzerland. (See Index.)

Salesian Cooperators (1876): Via Maria Ausiliatrice 32, 10100 Turin, Italy. Third Salesian family founded by St. John Bosco; Members commit themselves to an apostolate at the service of the Church, giving particular attention to youth in the Salesian spirit and style.

Serra International (1953, in U.S.): (See Index.)

Society of St. Vincent de Paul (1933): 5, rue du Pre-aux-Clercs, 75007 Paris, France.

The Grail (1921), Nijmegen, The Netherlands): 5, Sayad Sokkar St. Matareya, Cairo, Egypt (temporary secretariat). (See Index.).

Third Order of St. Dominic (1285): Convento Santa Sabina, Piazza Pietro d'Illiria, Aventino 00153 Rome, Italy. (See Index.)

Third Order of St. Francis (1221, first Rule approved): Via Maria Mediatrice 25, 00165, Rome, Italy. (See Index.)

UNDA: International Catholic Association for Radio and Television* (1928, Cologne, Germany): rue de Romont 5, C.P. 211, 1701 Fribourg, Switzerland. (See Index.)

Unio Internationalis Laicorum in Servitio Ecclesiae (1965, Aachen, Germany): Breite Strasse 106-110, Postfach 102068, 5 Cologne, Germany. Consists of national and diocesan associations of persons who give professional services to the Church.

Union of Adorers of the Blessed Sacrament (1937): Largo dei Monti Parioli 3, 00197, Rome, Italy.

World Catholic Federation for the Biblical Apostolate (1969, Rome): Silberburgstr, 121 A, D 7000, Stuttgart 1, Germany.

World Federation of Catholic Youth* (1926; present title, 1968, with amalgamation of World Federation of Catholic Young Women and Girls and the International Catholic Youth Federation): 31 avenue de l'Hopital francais, 1080 Brussels, Belgium.

World Federation of Christian Life Communities* (1953): 8, Borgo Santo Spirito, C.P. 9048, Rome, Italy. First Sodality of Our Lady founded in 1563.

World Movement of Christian Workers* (1961): 201, rue Belliard, 1040 Brussels, Belgium.

World Organization of Former Students of Catholic Schools (1967, Rome): 17 rue Michel Charles, 75012 Paris, France.

World Union of Catholic Philosophical Societies* (1948, Amsterdam, The Netherlands): Aignerstrasse 25, 5026 Salzburg, Austria.

World Union of Catholic Teachers* (1951): Piazza San Calisto 16, 00153, Rome, Italy.

World Union of Catholic Women's Organizations* (1910): 20, rue Notre Dame des Champs, 75006 Paris, France.

Regional Organizations

European Association for Catholic Adult Education (1963, Lucerne, Switzerland): Dransdorfer Weg 15/IV, 53 Bonn, Germany.

European Forum of National Committees of the Laity (1968): Mutsaerstraat 32, B 2000 Antwerp, Belgium.

Movimiento Familiar Cristiano (1949-50, Montevideo and Buenos Aires): 7953, C.P. 480, Belo Horizonte, Brazil. Christian Family Movement of Latin America.

The Catholic Church in Canada

The first date in the remote background of the Catholic history of Canada was July 7, 1534, when a priest in the exploration company of Jacques Cartier celebrated Mass on the Gaspe Peninsula.

Successful colonization and the significant beginnings of the Catholic history of the country date from the foundation of Quebec in 1608 by Samuel Champlain and French settlers. Montreal was established in 1642.

The earliest missionaries were Franciscan Recollects and Jesuits who arrived in 1615 and 1625, respectively. They provided some pastoral care for the settlers but worked mainly among the 100,000 Indians — Algonquins and Huron-Iroquois — in the interior and in the Lake Ontario region. Eight Jesuits, the North American Martyrs, were killed in the 1640's. Sulpician Fathers, who arrived in Canada late in the 1640's, played a part in the great missionary period which ended about 1700.

Kateri Tekakwitha, Lily of the Mohawks, the first North American Indian candidate for canonization, died in 1680.

The communities of women religious with the longest histories in Canada are the Canonesses of St. Augustine, since 1637; the Ursulines, since 1639; and the Hospitallers of St. Joseph, since 1642. Communities of Canadian origin are the Congregation of Notre Dame, founded by Marguerite Bourgeoys in 1658, and the Grey Nuns, formed by Mother d'Youville in 1738.

Start of Church Organization

Ecclesiastical organization began with the appointment of Francois Montmorency de Laval as vicar apostolic of New France in 1658 — 26 years after France canceled England's claim to possession of the country. In 1674, Quebec became the first diocese in the territory.

In 1713, the French Canadian population numbered 18,000. In the same year, the Treaty of Utrecht ceded Acadia, Newfoundland and the Hudson Bay Territory to England. The Acadians were scattered among the American Colonies in 1755.

The English acquired possession of Canada and its 70,000 French-speaking inhabitants in virtue of the Treaty of Paris in 1763. Anglo-French and Anglican-Catholic differences and tensions developed. The pro-British government at first refused to recognize the titles of church officials, hindered the clergy in their work and tried to install a non-Catholic educational system. Laws were passed which guaranteed religious liberties to Catholics (Quebec Act of 1774, Constitutional Act of 1791, legislation approved by Queen Victoria in 1851), but it took some time before actual respect for these liberties matched the legal enactments. The initial moderation of government antipathy toward the Church was caused partly by the loyalty of Catholics to the Crown during the American Revolution and the War of 1812.

Growth

The 15 years following the passage in 1840 of the Act of Union, which joined Upper and Lower Canada, were significant. New communities of men and women religious joined those already in the country. The Oblates of Mary Immaculate, missionaries par excellence in Canada, advanced the penetration of the West which had been started in 1818 by Abbe Provencher. New jurisdictions were established, and Quebec became a metropolitan see in 1844. The first Council of Quebec was held in 1851. The established Catholic school system enjoyed a period of growth.

Laval University was inaugurated in 1854 and canonically established in 1876.

Archbishop Taschereau of Quebec was named Canada's first cardinal in 1886.

The apostolic delegation to Canada was set up in 1899. It became a nunciature in 1970, with the establishment of diplomatic relations with the Vatican.

Early in this century, Canada had eight ecclesiastical provinces, 23 dioceses, three vicariates apostolic, 3,500 priests, 2.4 million Catholics, about 30 communities of men religious, and 70 or more communities of women religious. The Church in Canada was phased out of mission status and removed from the jurisdiction of the Congregation for the Propagation of the Faith in 1908.

The greatest concentration of Catholics is in the eastern portion of the country. In the northern and western portions, outside metropolitan centers, there are some of the most difficult parish and mission areas in the world. Bilingual (English-French) differences in the general population are reflected in the Church; for example, in the parallel structures of the Canadian Catholic Conference, which was established in 1943. Quebec is the center of French cultural influence. Many language groups are represented among Catholics, who include about 255,000 members of Eastern Rite in a metropolitan see and four eparchies.

Education, a past source of friction between the Church and the government, is administered by the civil provinces in a variety of arrangements authorized by the Canadian Constitution. Denominational schools have tax support in one way in Quebec and Newfoundland, and in another way in Alberta, Ontario and Saskatchewan. Several provinces provide tax support only for public schools, making private financing necessary for separate church-related schools.

ECCLESIASTICAL JURISDICTIONS OF CANADA

Provinces

Names of ecclesiastical provinces and metropolitan sees in bold face: suffragan sees in parentheses. The Winnipeg archdiocese (Latin) is not a metropolitan see.

Edmonton (Calgary, St. Paul).

Grouard-McLennan (Mackenzie-Ft. Smith, Prince George, Whitehorse).

Halifax (Antigonish, Charlottetown, Yarmouth).

Keewatin-LePas (Churchill-Hudson Bay, Labrador-Schefferville, Moosonee).

Kingston (Alexandria, Peterborough, Sault Ste. Marie).

Moncton (Bathurst, Edmundston, St. John).

Montreal (Joliette, St. Jean-de-Quebec, St. Jerome, Valleyfield).

Ottawa (Hearst, Hull, Mont-Laurier, Pembroke, Rouyn-Noranda, Timmins).

Quebec (Amos, Chicoutimi, Ste.-Anne-de-la-Pocatiere, Trois Rivieres).

Regina (Gravelbourg, Prince Albert, Saskatoon, Abbey of St. Peter).

Rimouski (Gaspe, Hauterive).

St. Boniface (no suffragans).

St. John's (Grand Falls, St. George).

Sherbrooke (Nicolet, St. Hyacinthe).

Toronto (Hamilton, London, St. Catharines, Thunder Bay).

Vancouver (Kamloops, Nelson, Victoria).

Winnipeg — Ukrainian (Edmonton, New Westminster, Saskatoon, Toronto).

Archdioceses, Archbishops

Edmonton, Alta. (St. Albert, 1871; archdiocese, transferred Edmonton, 1912): Joseph N. MacNeil, archbishop, 1973.

Grouard-McLennan, Alta. (v. a. Athabaska-Mackenzie, 1862; Grouard, 1927; archdiocese Grouard-McLennan, 1967); Henri Legare, O.M.I., archbishop, 1972.

Halifax, N. S. (1842; archdiocese, 1852): James M. Hayes, archbishop, 1967.

Keewatin-Le Pas, Man. (v. a., 1910; archdiocese, 1967): Paul Dumouchel, O. M. I., archbishop, 1967.

Kingston, Ont. (1826; archdiocese, 1889): Joseph L. Wilhelm, archbishop, 1966.

Moncton, N.B. (1936): Donat Chiasson, archbishop, 1972.

Montreal, Que. (1836; archdiocese, 1886): Paul Gregoire, archbishop, 1968. Lawrence P. Whelan, Leo Blais, Valerien Belanger, Andre Cimichella, O. S. M., Leonard Crowley, auxiliaries.

Ottawa, Ont. (1847; archdiocese, 1886): Joseph Aurele Plourde, archbishop, 1967.

Quebec, Que. (v. a., 1658; diocese, 1674; archdiocese, 1819; metropolitan, 1844; primatial see, 1956): Cardinal Maurice Roy, archbishop, 1947. Lionel Audet, Laurent Noel, auxiliaries.

Regina, Sask. (1910; archdiocese, 1915): Charles A. Halpin, archbishop, 1973.

Rimouski, Que. (1867; archdiocese, 1946): J. Gilles Ouellet, archbishop, 1973.

St. Boniface, Man. (1847; archdiocese, 1871): Antoine Hacault, archbishop, 1974.

St. John's, Nfld. (p. a., 1784; v. a., 1796; diocese, 1847; archdiocese, 1904): Patrick J. Skinner, C. J. M., archbishop, 1951.

Sherbrooke, Que. (1874; archdiocese, 1951): J.-M. Fortier, archbishop, 1968.

Toronto, Ont. (1841; archdiocese, 1870): Philip F. Pocock, archbishop, 1971. Francis V. Allen, Thomas Fulton, auxiliaries.

Vancouver, B. C. (v. a. British Columbia, 1863; diocese New Westminster, 1890; archdiocese Vancouver, 1908): James F. Carney, archbishop, 1969.

Winnipeg, Man. (1915): Cardinal George B. Flahiff, C. S. B., archbishop, 1961.

Winnipeg, Man. (Ukrainian Byzantine Rite) (Ordinariate of Canada, 1912; ap. ex. Central Canada, 1948; ap. ex. Manitoba, 1951; archdiocese Winnipeg, 1956): Maxim Hermaniuk, C.SS.R., archbishop, 1956.

Dioceses, Bishops

Alexandria, Ont. (1890): Eugene Philippe Larocque, bishop, 1974.

Amos, Que. (1938): Gaston Hains, bishop, 1968.

Antigonish, N. S. (Arichat, 1844; transferred, 1886): William E. Power, bishop, 1960.

Bathurst, N. B. (Chatham, 1860; transferred, 1938): Edgar Godin, bishop, 1969.

Calgary, Alta. (1912): Paul J. O'Byrne, bishop, 1968.

Charlottetown, P. E. I. (1829): Francis J. Spence, bishop, 1970.

Chicoutimi, Que. (1878): Marius Pare, bishop, 1961. Roch Pedneault, auxiliary.

Churchill-Hudson Bay, Man. (p.,a., 1925; v. a. Hudson Bay, 1931; diocese Churchill, 1967; Churchill-Hudson Bay, 1968): Omer Robidoux, O. M. I., bishop, 1970.

Edmonton, Alta. (Ukrainian Byzantine Rite) (ap, ex., 1948; diocese, 1956): Nile Nicholas Savaryn, O.S.B.M., bishop, 1948. Martin Greschuk, auxiliary.

Edmundston, N. B. (1944): Fernand Lacroix, C. J. M., bishop, 1970.

Gaspe, Que. (1922): Bertrand Blanchet, bishop, 1973.

Grand Falls, Nfld. (Harbour Grace, 1856; present title, 1964): Alphonsus Liguori Penney, bishop, 1973.

Gravelbourg, Sask. (1930): Noel Delaquis, bishop, 1974.

Hamilton, Ont. (1856): Paul F. Reding, bishop, 1973.

Hauterive, Que. (p. a., 1882; v. a., 1905; diocese Gulf of St. Lawrence, 1945; name changed, 1960): Jean-Guy Couture, bishop, 1975.

Hearst, Ont. (p. a., 1918; v. a., 1920; diocese, 1938): A. Roger Despatie, bishop, 1973.

Hull, Que. (1963): Adolph Proulx, bishop, 1974.

Joliette, Que. (1904): Rene Audet, bishop, 1968.

Kamloops, B. C. (1945): Adam Exner, O.M.I., bishop, 1974.

Labrador-Schefferville (v. a. Labrador, 1945; diocese, 1967): Peter A. Sutton, O.M.I., bishop, 1974.

London, Ont. (1885; transferred Sandwich, 1859; London, 1869): G. Emmett Carter, bishop, 1964. John Sherlock, auxiliary.

Mackenzie-Fort Smith, N. W. T. (v. a. Mackenzie, 1901; diocese Mackenzie-Fort Smith, 1967): Paul Piché, O. M. I., bishop, 1967.

Mont-Laurier, Que. (1913): Andre Ouellette, bishop, 1965.

Moosonee, Ont. (v. a. James Bay, 1938; diocese Moosonee, 1967): Jules Leguerrier, O. M. I., bishop, 1967.

Nelson, B. C. (1936): Wilfred Emmett Doyle, bishop, 1958.

New Westminster, N.B. (Ukrainian Byzantine Rite) (1974): Jerome Chimy, O.S.B.M., bishop, 1974.

Nicolet, Que. (1885): Joseph A. Martin, bishop, 1950.

Pembroke, Ont. (v.a. 1882; diocese, 1898): Joseph R. Windle, bishop, 1971.

Peterborough, Ont. (1882): Vacant as of Aug. 22, 1975.

Prince Albert, Sask. (v. a., 1890; diocese, 1907): Laurent Morin, bishop, 1959.

Prince George, B. C. (p. a., 1908; v. a. Yukon and Prince Rupert, 1944; diocese Prince George, 1967): J. Fergus O'Grady, O. M. I., bishop, 1967.

Rouyn-Noranda, Que. (1973): Jean-Guy Hamelin, bishop, 1974.

Sainte-Anne-de-la-Pocatiere, Que. (1951): C.-H. Levesque, bishop, 1968.

St. Catharines, Ont. (1958): Thomas J. McCarthy, bishop, 1958.

St. George's, Nfld. (p. a., 1870; v. a., 1890; diocese, 1904): Richard T. McGrath, bishop, 1970.

St. Hyacinthe, Que. (1852): Albert Sanschagrin, O. M. I., bishop, 1967. Louis de Gonzague Langevin, auxiliary.

Saint-Jean-de-Quebec, (1933): Gerard Marie Coderre, bishop, 1955: Robert Lebel, auxiliary.

St. Jerome, Que. (1951): Bernard Hubert, bishop, 1971.

Saint John, N.B. (1842): Arthur J. Gilbert, bishop, 1974.

St. Paul in Alberta (1948): Raymond Roy, bishop, 1972.

Saskatoon, Sask. (1933): James P. Mahoney, bishop, 1967.

Saskatoon, Sask. (Ukrainian Byzantine Rite) (ap. ex., 1951; diocese, 1956): Andrew J. Roborecki, bishop, 1951.

Sault Ste. Marie, Ont. (1904): Alexander Carter, bishop, 1958. Bernard J. Papin, Gerrard Dionne, auxiliaries.

Thunder Bay, Ont. (Ft. William, 1952; transferred, 1970): Norman J. Gallagher, bishop, 1970.

Timmins, Ont. (v. a. Temiskaming, 1908; diocese Haileybury, 1915; present title, 1938): Jacques Landriault, bishop, 1971.

Toronto, Ont. (Ukrainian Byzantine Rite) (ap. ex., 1948; diocese, 1956): Isidore Borecky, bishop, 1948, Michael Rusnak, C.SS.R., auxiliary.

Trois-Rivieres, Que. (1852): Georges-Leon Pelletier, bishop, 1947.

Valleyfield, Que. (1892): Guy Belanger, bishop, 1969.

Victoria, B. C. (diocese Vancouver Is., 1846; archdiocese, 1903; diocese Victoria, 1908): Remi J. De Roo, bishop, 1962.

Whitehorse, Y. T. (v.a., 1944; diocese 1967): Hubert P. O'Connor, O. M. I., bishop, 1971.

Yarmouth, N. S. (1953): Austin Emile Burke, bishop, 1968.

Military Vicariate of Canada (1951): Cardinal Maurice Roy, military vicar.

Abbacy of St. Peter, Muenster, Sask. (1921): Jerome Weber, O. S. B. (blessed, 1960).

BIOGRAPHIES OF CANADIAN BISHOPS

Allen, Francis V.: b. June 25, 1909, Toronto, Ont.; ord. priest June 10, 1933; ord. titular bishop of Avensa and auxiliary bishop of Toronto, Oct. 7, 1954.

Audet, Lionel: b. May 22, 1908, Ste. Marie de Beauce, Que.; ord. priest July 8, 1934; ord. titular bishop of Tibari and auxiliary bishop of Quebec, May 1, 1952.

Audet, Rene: b. Jan. 18, 1920, Montreal, Que.; ord. priest May 30, 1948; ord. titular bishop of Chonochora and auxiliary bishop of Ottawa, July 31, 1963; bishop of Joliette, Jan. 3, 1968.

Baudoux, Maurice: b. July 10, 1902, Louviere, Belgium; ord. priest July 17, 1929; ord.

bishop of St. Paul in Alberta, Oct. 28, 1948; titular archbishop of Preslavus and coadjutor archbishop of St. Boniface, Mar. 4, 1952; archbishop of St. Boniface, Sept. 14, 1955; retired Sept. 7, 1974.

Belanger, Guy: b. Jan. 24, 1928, Valleyfield, Que.; ord. priest May 19, 1951; ord. bishop of Valleyfield, Nov. 23, 1969.

Belanger, Valerien: b. Apr. 6, 1902, Valleyfield, Que.; ord. priest May 29, 1926; ord titular bishop of Cyrene and auxiliary bishop of Montreal, May 11, 1956.

Blais, Leo: b. Apr. 28, 1904, Dollar Bay, Mich.; ord. priest June 14, 1930; ord. bishop of Prince Albert, Aug. 28, 1952; titular bishop of Geron and auxiliary bishop of Montreal, Feb. 28, 1959.

Blanchet, Bertrand: b. Sept. 19, 1932, Saint Thomas de Montmagny, Que.; ord. priest May 20, 1956; ord. bishop of Gaspe, Dec. 8, 1973.

Borecky, Isidore: b. Oct. 1, 1911, Ostrovec, Ukraine; ord. priest July 17, 1938; ord. titular bishop of Amathus in Cypro and exarch of Toronto, May 27, 1948; bishop of Toronto (Ukrainians), Nov. 3, 1956.

Brodeur, Rosario L.: b. Oct. 30, 1889, Acton Vale, Que.; ord. priest June 17, 1916; ord. titular bishop of Mideo and coadjutor bishop of Alexandria, June 30, 1941; bishop of Alexandria, July 27, 1941; retired Oct. 15, 1966.

Burke, Austin Emile: b. Jan. 22, 1922, Sluice Point, N.S.; ord. priest Mar. 25, 1950; ord. bishop of Yarmouth, May 14, 1968.

Cabana, Georges: b. Oct. 22, 1894, Notre Dame de Granby, Que; ord. priest July 28, 1918; ord. titular archbishop of Anchialo and coadjutor archbishop of St. Boniface, June 30, 1941; coadjutor archbishop of Sherbrooke, Jan. 20, 1952; archbishop of Sherbrooke, May 28, 1952; retired Feb. 7, 1968.

Carew, William A.: b. Oct. 23, 1922, St. John's, Nfld., ord. priest June 15, 1947; ord. titular archbishop of Telde, Jan. 4, 1970; nuncio to Rwanda and Burundi, 1970-74; apostolic delegate to Jerusalem and Palestine and pro-nuncio to Cyprus, 1974.

Carney, James F.: b. June 28, 1915, Vancouver, B.C.; ord. priest Mar. 21, 1942; ord. titular bishop of Obori and auxiliary bishop of Vancouver, Feb. 11, 1966; archbishop of Vancouver, Jan. 8, 1969.

Carter, Alexander: b. Apr. 16, 1909, Montreal, Que.; ord. priest June 6, 1936; ord. titular bishop of Sita and coadjutor bishop of Sault Ste. Marie, Feb. 2, 1957; bishop of Sault Ste. Marie, Nov. 22, 1958.

Carter, G. Emmett: b. Mar. 1, 1912, Montreal, Que.; ord. priest May 22, 1937; ord. titular bishop of Altiburo and auxiliary bishop of London, Ont., Feb. 2, 1962; bishop of London, Feb. 17, 1964, installed Mar. 12, 1964.

Caza, Percival: b. Aug. 13, 1896, Saint-Anicet, Que.; ord. priest June 29, 1922; ord. titular bishop of Albule and auxiliary of Valleyfield, Oct. 19, 1948; coadjutor bishop of Valleyfield, 1955; bishop of Valleyfield, Sept. 22, 1966; retired Mar. 18, 1969.

Charbonneau, Paul E.: b. May 4, 1922, Ste. Therese de Blainville, Que.; ord. priest May 31, 1947; ord. titular bishop of Thapsus and auxiliary bishop of Ottawa, Jan. 18, 1961; first bishop of Hull, May 21, 1963; retired Apr. 12, 1973 because of ill health.

Chiasson, Donat: b. Jan. 2, 1930, Paquetville, N.B.; ord. priest May 6, 1956; ord. archbishop of Moncton, June 1, 1972.

Chimy, Jerome I., O.S.B.M.: b. Mar. 12, 1919, Radway, Alta.; ord. priest, June 29, 1944; ord. first bishop of New Westminster,

B.C., for the Ukrainians, Sept. 5, 1974.

Cimichella, Andre, O.S.M.: b. Feb. 21, 1921, Grotte Santo Stefano, Italy; ord. priest May 26, 1945; ord. titular bishop of Quiza and auxiliary of Montreal, July 16, 1964.

Coderre, Gerard Marie: b. Dec. 19, 1904, St. Jacques de Montcalm, Que.; ord. priest May 30, 1931; ord. titular bishop of Aegae and coadjutor bishop of St.-Jean-de-Quebec, Sept. 12, 1951; bishop of St.-Jean-de-Quebec, Feb. 3, 1955.

Couture, Jean-Guy: b. May 6, 1929, Quebec; ord. priest May 30, 1953; ord. bishop of Hauterive, Que., Aug. 15, 1975.

Couturier, Gerard: b. Jan. 12, 1913, St. Louis du Ha Ha, Que; ord. priest Mar. 25, 1938; ord. bishop of Hauterive, Feb. 28, 1957; resigned see Sept. 7, 1974.

Crowley, Leonard: b. Dec. 28, 1921, Montreal, Que.; ord. priest May 31, 1947; ord. titular bishop of Mons and auxiliary bishop of Montreal, Mar. 24, 1971.

Decosse, Aime: b. June 21, 1903, Somerset, Man.; ord. priest July 4, 1926; ord. bishop of Gravelbourg, Jan. 20, 1954; retired May 12, 1973.

Delaquis, Noel: b. Dec. 25, 1934, Notre-Dame-de-Lourdes, Man.; ord. priest 1958; ord. bishop of Gravelbourg, Feb. 19, 1974.

De Roo, Remi J.: b. Feb. 24, 1924, Swan Lake, Man.; ord. priest June 8, 1950; ord. bishop of Victoria, Dec. 14, 1962.

Desmarais, Joseph A.: b. Oct. 31, 1891, Upton, Que.; ord. priest July 25, 1914; ord. titular bishop of Ruspe and auxiliary bishop of St. Hyacinthe, Apr. 22, 1931; bishop of Amos, June 20, 1939; retired Oct. 31, 1968.

Despatie, Alfred Roger : b. Apr. 12, 1927, Sudbury, Ont.; ord. priest Apr. 12, 1952; ord. titular bishop of Usinaza and auxiliary bishop of Sault Ste. Marie, June 28, 1968; bishop of Hearst, Feb. 8, 1973.

Desrochers, Bruno: b. Apr. 17, 1910, St. Louis de Lotbiniere, Que.; ord. priest June 30, 1934; ord. first bishop of Sainte-Anne-de-la-Pocatiere, Sept. 21, 1951; resigned May 24, 1968; vicar general of Sainte-Anne-de-la-Pocatiere.

Dionne, Gerard: b. June 19, 1919, Saint-Basile, N.B.; ord. priest May 1, 1948; ord. titular bishop of Garba and auxiliary bishop of Sault Ste. Marie, Apr. 8, 1975.

Douville, Arthur: b. July 22, 1894, St. Casimir de Portneuf, Que.; ord. priest May 25, 1919; ord. titular bishop of Vita and auxiliary bishop of St. Hyacinthe, Jan. 29, 1940; coadjutor bishop of St. Hyacinthe, Mar. 21, 1942; bishop of St. Hyacinthe, Nov. 27, 1942; retired June 13, 1967.

Doyle, Wilfred E.: b. Feb. 18, 1913, Calgary, Alta.: ord. priest June 5, 1938; ord. bishop of Nelson, Dec. 3, 1958.

Dumouchel, Paul, O.M.I.: b. Sept. 19, 1911, St. Boniface, Man.; ord. priest June 24, 1936; ord. titular bishop of Sufes and vicar apostolic of Keewatin, May 24, 1955; archbishop of Keewatin-Le Pas, July 13, 1967.

Exner, Adam, O.M.I.: b. Dec. 24, 1928, Killaly, Sask.; ord. priest July 7, 1957; ord. bishop of Kamloops, B.C., Mar. 12, 1974.

Flahiff, George F.: (See Cardinals Biographies.)

Fortier, Jean-Marie: b. July 1, 1920, Quebec, Que.; ord. priest June 16, 1944; ord. titular bishop of Pomaria and auxiliary bishop of Ste. Anne-de-la-Pocatiere, Jan. 23, 1961; bishop of Gaspe, Jan. 19, 1965; archbishop of Sherbrooke, Apr. 20, 1968; president of the Canadian Catholic Conference, 1973.

Frenette, Emilien: b. May 6, 1905, Montreal, Que.; ord. priest May 30, 1930; ord. bishop of St. Jerome, Sept. 12, 1951; retired June 11, 1971.

Fulton, Thomas B.: b. Jan. 13, 1918, St. Catharines, Ont.; ord. priest June 7, 1941; ord. titular bishop of Cursola and auxiliary bishop of Toronto, Jan. 6, 1969.

Gagnon, Edouard, P.S.S.: b. Jan. 15, 1918, Port Daniel, Que.; ord. priest Aug. 15, 1940; ord. bishop Mar. 25, 1969; bishop of St. Paul in Alberta 1969-72; rector of Canadian College in Rome, 1972- ; president of Vatican Committee for the Family, 1973.

Gallagher, Norman J.: b. May 24, 1917, Coatbridge, Scotland; ord. priest Mar. 29, 1941; ord titular bishop of Adrasus and auxiliary bishop of Montreal, Sept. 12, 1963; bishop of Thunder Bay, April 22, 1970.

Gilbert, Arthur J.: b. Oct. 26, 1915, Oromocto, N.B.; ord. priest June 3, 1943; ord. bishop of St. John, N.B., June 19, 1974.

Godin, Edgar: b. May 31, 1911, Neguac, N.B.; ord. priest June 15, 1941; ord. bishop of Bathurst, July 25, 1969.

Gregoire, Paul: b. Oct. 24, 1911, Verdun, Que.; ord. priest May 22, 1937; ord. titular bishop of Curubis and auxiliary bishop of Montreal, Dec. 27, 1961; archbishop of Montreal, Apr. 20, 1968.

Greschuk, Martin: b. Nov. 7, 1923, Innisfree, Alta.; ord. priest June 11, 1950; ord. titular bishop of Nazianus and auxiliary bishop of Edmonton of the Ukrainians, Oct. 3, 1974.

Hacault, Antoine: b. Jan. 17, 1926, Bruxelles, Man.; ord. priest May 20, 1951; ord. titular bishop of Media and coadjutor of St. Boniface, Sept. 8, 1964; archbishop of St. Boniface, Sept. 7, 1974.

Hains, Gaston: b. Sept. 10, 1921, Drummondville, Que.; ord. priest June 15, 1946; ord. titular bishop of Belesana and auxiliary bishop of St. Hyacinthe, Oct. 18, 1964; coadjutor bishop of Amos, 1967; bishop of Amos, Oct. 31, 1968.

Halpin, Charles A.: b. Aug. 30, 1930, St. Eustache, Man.; ord. priest May 26, 1956; ord. archbishop of Regina, Nov. 26, 1973.

Hamelin, Jean-Guy: b. Oct. 8, 1925, St. Severin-de-Proulxville, Que.; ord. priest June

11, 1949; ord. first bishop of Rouyn-Noranda, Que., Feb. 9, 1974.

Hayes, James M.: b. May 27, 1924, Halifax, N.S.; ord. priest June 15, 1947; ord. titular bishop of Reperi and apostolic administrator of Halifax, Apr. 20, 1965; archbishop of Halifax, June 22, 1967.

Hermaniuk, Maxim, C.SS.R.: b. Oct. 30, 1911, Nove Selo, Ukraine; ord. priest Sept. 4, 1938; ord. titular bishop of Sinna and exarch of Manitoba (Ukrainians), June 29, 1951; archbishop of Winnipeg (Ukrainians), Nov. 3, 1956.

Hubert, Bernard: b. June 1, 1919, Beloeil, Que.; ord. priest May 30, 1953; ord. bishop of St. Jerome, Sept. 12, 1971.

Jennings, Edward Q.: b. Oct. 4, 1896, Saint John, N.B.; ord. priest Dec. 27, 1925; ord. titular bishop of Sala and auxiliary bishop of Vancouver, June 11, 1941; bishop of Kamloops, Feb. 22, 1946; bishop of Fort William (now Thunder Bay), May 14, 1952; resigned Sept. 18, 1969.

Jordan, Anthony, O.M.I.: b. Nov. 10, 1901, Broxburn, Scotland; ord. priest June w3, 1929; ord. titular bishop of Vada and vicar apostolic of Prince Rupert, B.C., Sept. 8, 1945; titular archbishop of Silyum and coadjutor of Edmonton, Apr. 17, 1955; archbishop of Edmonton, Aug. 11, 1964; retired July 2, 1973.

Lacroix, Fernand, C.J.M.: b. Oct. 16, 1919, Quebec; ord. priest Feb. 10, 1946; ord. bishop of Edmundston, Oct. 20, 1970.

Lacroix, Marc, O.M.I.: b. Apr. 25, 1906, Saint Simon-de-Bagot, Que.; ord. priest May 21, 1933; ord. titular bishop of Roso and vicar apostolic of Hudson Bay, Feb. 22, 1943; bishop of Churchill-Hudson Bay, July 13, 1967; retired Oct. 25, 1968.

Landriault, Jacques: b. Sept. 23, 1921, Alfred, Ont.; ord. priest Feb. 9, 1947; ord. titular bishop of Cadi and auxiliary bishop of Alexandria, July 25, 1962; bishop of Hearst, May 27, 1964; app. bishop of Timmins, Mar. 30, 1971.

Landry, Georges: b. Dec. 3, 1895, Pomquet, N.S.; ord. priest June 24, 1921; ord. bishop of Hearst, May 1, 1946; retired Jan. 14, 1952.

Langevin, Louis-de-Gonzague: b. Oct. 31, 1921, Oka, Que.; ord. priest Feb. 2, 1950; ord. titular bishop of Rosemarkie and auxiliary of St. Hyacinthe Sept. 23, 1974.

Larocque, Eugene Philippe: b. Mar. 27, 1927, Windsor, Ont.; ord. priest June 7, 1952; ord. bishop of Alexandria, Ont., Sept. 3, 1974.

Lebel, Robert: b. Nov. 8, 1924, Trois-Pistoles, Que.; ord. priest June 18, 1950; ord. titular bishop of Alinda and auxiliary of St. Jean de Quebec, May 12, 1974.

Le Blanc, Camille A.: b. Aug. 25, 1898, Neguac, N.B.; ord. priest Apr. 5, 1924; ord. bishop of Bathurst, Sept. 8, 1942; retired Jan. 8, 1969.

Legare, Henri, O.M.I.: b. Feb. 20, 1918,

Willow Bunch, Sask.; ord. priest June 29, 1943; ord. first bishop of Labrador-Schefferville, Sept. 9, 1967; archbishop of Grouard-McLennan, Nov. 21, 1972.

Leguerrier, Jules, O.M.I.: b. Feb. 18, 1915, Clarence Creek, Ont.; ord. priest June 19, 1943; ord. titular bishop of Bavagaliana and vicar apostolic of James Bay, June 29, 1964; first bishop of Moosonee, July 13, 1967.

Levesque, Charles Henri: b. Dec. 29, 1921, St. Andre de Kamouraska, Que.; ord. priest June 13, 1948; ord. titular bishop of Guzabeta and auxiliary bishop of Ste.-Anne-de-la-Pocatiere, Dec. 27, 1965; bishop of Ste.-Anne-de-la-Pocatiere, Aug. 17, 1968.

Levesque, Louis: b. May 27, 1908, Amqui, Que.; ord. priest June 26, 1932; ord. bishop of Hearst, Aug. 15, 1952; titular archbishop of Egnatia and coadjutor of Rimouski, Apr. 13, 1964; archbishop of Rimouski, Feb. 25, 1967; retired Apr. 27, 1973.

Lussier, Philippe, C.SS.R.: b. Oct. 3, 1911, Weedon, Que.; ord. priest Sept. 18, 1937; ord. bishop of St. Paul in Alberta, Aug. 17, 1952; retired Aug. 17, 1968.

McCarthy, Thomas J.: b. Oct. 4, 1905, Goderich, Ont.; ord. priest May 25, 1929; ord. bishop of Nelson, Aug. 1, 1955; bishop of St. Catharines, Nov. 9, 1958.

MacEachern, Malcolm A.: b. Oct. 5, 1901, Broad Cove Chapel, N.S.; ord. priest June 11, 1927; ord. bishop of Charlottetown, Jan. 18, 1955; retired Feb. 24, 1970.

McGrath, Richard T.: b. June 17, 1912, Oderin, Placentia Bay, Nfld.; ord. priest June 24, 1936; ord. bishop of St. George's, Nfld., July 22, 1970.

MacNeil, Joseph N.: b. Apr. 15, 1924, Sydney, N.S.; ord. priest May 23, 1948; ord. bishop of St. John, N.B., June 24, 1969; archbishop of Edmonton, July 6, 1973.

Mahoney, James P.: b. Dec. 7, 1927, Saskatoon, Sack.; ord. priest June 7, 1952; ord. bishop of Saskatoon, Dec. 13, 1967.

Martin, Joseph A.: b. Oct. 4, 1913, Southbridge, Mass.; ord. priest May 18, 1939; ord. titular bishop of Bassiana and coadjutor bishop of Nicolet, Oct. 7, 1950; bishop of Nicolet, Nov. 8, 1950.

Melancon, Georges: b. Apr. 7, 1886, Saint-Guillaume d'Upton, Que.; ord. priest Sept. 12, 1909; ord. bishop of Chicoutimi, July 23, 1940; retired Feb. 18,1961.

Morin, Laurent: b. Feb. 14, 1908, Montreal, Que.; ord. priest May 24, 1934; ord. titular bishop of Arsamosata and auxiliary bishop of Montreal, Oct. 30, 1955; bishop of Prince Albert, Feb. 28, 1959.

Mulvihill, James P., O.M.I.: b. Oct. 15, 1905, Old Chelsea, Ont.; ord. priest, June 24, 1937; ord. titular bishop of Caput Cilla and vicar apostolic of Whitehorse, Jan. 25, 1966; bishop of Whitehorse, July 13, 1967; retired Oct. 15, 1971.

Noel, Laurent: b. Mar. 19, 1920, Saint-Just-de-Bretenieres, Que.; ord. priest June 16, 1944; ord. titular bishop of Agathopolis and auxiliary bishop of Quebec, Aug. 29, 1963.

O'Byrne, Paul J.: b. Dec. 21, 1922, Calgary, Alta.; ord. priest Feb. 21, 1948; ord. bishop of Calgary, Aug. 22, 1968.

O'Connor, Hubert P., O.M.I.: b. Feb. 17, 1928, Huntington, Que.; ord. priest June 5, 1954; ord. bishop of Whitehorse, Dec. 8, 1971.

O'Grady, John Fergus, O.M.I.: b. July 27, 1908, Macton, Ont.; ord. priest June 29, 1934; ord. titular bishop of Aspendus and vicar apostolic of Prince Rupert, Mar. 7, 1956; first bishop of Prince George, July 13, 1967.

O'Neill, Michael C.: b. Feb. 15, 1898, Kemptville, Ont.; ord. priest Dec. 21, 1927; ord. archbishop of Regina, Apr. 14, 1948; retired Sept. 26, 1973.

Ouellet, J. Gilles, P.M.E.: b. Aug. 14, 1922, Bromptonville, Que.; ord. priest June 30, 1946; ord. bishop of Gaspe, Nov. 23, 1968; app. archbishop of Rimouski, Apr. 27, 1973.

Ouellette, Andre: b. Feb. 4, 1913, Salem, Mass.; ord. priest June 11, 1938; ord. titular bishop of Carre and auxiliary bishop of Mont-Laurier, Feb. 25, 1957; bishop of Mont-Laurier, Mar. 27, 1965.

Pappin, Bernard F.: b. July 12, 1928, Westmeath, Ont.; ord. priest May 27, 1954; ord. titular bishop of Aradi and auxiliary bishop of Sault Ste. Marie, Apr. 11, 1975.

Pare, Marius: b. May 22, 1903, Montmagny, Que.; ord. priest July 3, 1927; ord. titular bishop of Aegae and auxiliary bishop of Chicoutimi, May 1, 1956; bishop of Chicoutimi, Feb. 18, 1961.

Parent, Charles Eugene: b. Apr. 22, 1902, Notre Dame-de-Neiges-de-Trois-Pistoles, Que.; ord. priest Mar. 7, 1925; ord. titular bishop of Diana and auxiliary bishop of Rimouski, May 24, 1944; app. archbishop of Rimouski, Mar. 2, 1951; retired Feb. 25, 1967.

Pednault, Roch: b. Apr. 10, 1927, Saint Joseph d'Alma, Que.; ord. priest Feb. 8, 1953; ord. titular bishop of Aggersel and auxiliary of Chicoutimi, Que., June 29, 1974.

Pelletier, Georges Leon: b. Aug. 19, 1904, Saint-Epiphane, Que.; ord. priest July 24, 1931; ord. titular bishop of Hephaestus and auxiliary bishop of Quebec, Feb. 24, 1943; bishop of Trois Rivieres, Sep 26, 1947.

Penney, Alphonsus L.: b. Sept. 27, 1924, St. John's, Nfld.; ord. priest June 29, 1949; ord. bishop of Grand Falls, Jan. 18, 1973.

Piche, Paul, O.M.I.: b. Sept. 14, 1909, Gravelbourg, Sask.; ord. priest Dec. 23, 1934; ord. titular bishop of Orcistus and vicar apostolic of Mackenzie, June 11, 1959; first bishop of Mackenzie-Fort Smith, July 13, 1967.

Plourde, Joseph Aurele: b. Jan. 12, 1915, St. Francois de Madawaska, N.B.; ord. priest May 7, 1944; ord. titular bishop of Lapda and auxiliary bishop of Alexandria, Aug. 26, 1964; archbishop of Ottawa, Jan. 2, 1967.

Pocock, Philip: b. July 2, 1906, St. Thomas,

Ont.; ord. priest June 14, 1930; ord. bishop of Saskatoon, June 29, 1944; titular archbishop of Aprus and coadjutor archbishop of Winnipeg, Aug. 6, 1951; archbishop of Winnipeg, Jan. 14, 1952; titular archbishop of Isauropolis and coadjutor archbishop of Toronto, Feb. 18, 1961; archbishop of Toronto, Mar. 30, 1971.

Power, William E.: b. Sept. 27, 1915; Montreal, Que.; ord. priest June 7, 1941; ord. bishop of Antigonish, July 20, 1960; president Canadian Catholic Conference, 1971-73.

Proulx, Adolph E.: b. Dec. 12, 1927, Hanmer, Ont., Canada; ord. priest Apr. 17, 1954; ord. titular bishop of Missua and auxiliary bishop of Sault Ste. Marie, Feb. 24, 1965; bishop of Alexandria, Apr. 28, 1967; bishop of Hull, Feb. 13, 1974.

Reding, Paul F.: b. Feb. 14, 1925, Hamilton, Ont.; ord. priest June 3, 1950; ord. titular bishop of Liberalia and auxiliary bishop of Hamilton, Sept. 14, 1966; bishop of Hamilton, Sept. 14, 1973.

Robichaud, Norbert: b. Apr. 1, 1905, St. Charles, N.B.; ord. priest May 1, 1931; ord. archbishop of Moncton, Sept. 8, 1942; retired Mar. 23, 1972.

Robidoux, Omer, O.M.L.: b. Dec. 19, 1913 Saint-Pierre-Jolys, Man.; ord. priest June 29, 1939; ord. bishop of Churchill-Hudson Bay, May 21, 1970.

Roborecki, Andrew: b. Dec. 12, 1910, in western Ukraine; arrived Winnipeg, Man., 1912; ord. priest July 18, 1934; ord. titular bishop of Tanais and auxiliary bishop of Ukrainian Catholic Diocese of Central Canada, May 27, 1948; exarch of Saskatchewan, 1951; bishop of Saskatoon (Ukrainians), Nov. 3, 1956.

Routhier, Henri, O.M.I.: b. Feb. 28, 1900, Pincher Creek, Alta.; ord. priest Sept. 7, 1924; ord. titular bishop of Naissus and coadjutor vicar apostolic of Grouard, Sept. 8, 1945; vicar apostolic of Grouard, 1953; archbishop of Grouard-McLennan, July 13, 1967; retired Nov. 21, 1972.

Roy, Maurice: (Cardinals, Biographies.)

Roy, Raymond: b. May 3, 1919, St. Boniface, Man.; ord. priest May 31, 1947; ord. bishop of St. Paul in Alberta, July 18, 1972.

Rusnak, Michael, C.SS.R.: b. Aug. 21, 1921, Beaverdale, Pa.; ord. priest July 3, 1949; ord. titular bishop of Tzernicus and auxiliary bishop of Toronto eparchy and apostolic visitor to Slovak Catholics of Byzantine rite in Canada, Jan. 2, 1965.

Ryan, Joseph F.: b. Mar. 1, 1897, Dundas, Ont.; ord. priest May 21, 1921; ord. bishop of Hamilton, Oct. 19, 1937; retired Mar. 27, 1973.

Sanschagrin, Albert, O.M.I.: b. Aug. 5, 1911, Saint-Tite, Que.; ord. priest May 24, 1936; ord. titular bishop of Bagi and coadjutor bishop of Amos Sept. 14, 1957; bishop of Saint-Hyacinthe, June 13, 1967.

Savaryn, Nile Nicholas, O.S.B.M.: b. May 19, 1905, Stary Sambir, Ukraine; ord. priest Aug. 23, 1931; ord. titular bishop of Jos and auxiliary bishop of the Catholic Ukrainian diocese in Canada, July 1, 1943; bishop of apostolic exarchate for western Canada, 1948; bishop of Edmonton (Ukrainians), Nov. 3, 1956.

Sherlock, John M.: b. Jan. 20, 1926, Brantford, Ont.; ord. priest June 3, 1950; ord. titular bishop of Macriana and auxiliary of London, Ont., Aug. 28, 1974.

Skinner, Patrick J., C.J.M.: b. Mar. 9, 1904, St. John's, Nfld.; ord. priest May 30, 1929; ord. titular bishop of Zenobia and auxiliary bishop of St. John's, Mar. 17, 1950; archbishop of St. John's, Mar. 23, 1951.

Smith, William J.: b. Jan. 2, 1897, Greenfield, Ont.; ord. priest June 16, 1927; ord. bishop of Pembroke, July 25, 1945; retired Feb. 8, 1971.

Spence, Francis J.: b. June 3, 1926, Perth, Ont.; ord. priest, Apr. 16, 1950; ord. titular bishop of Nova and auxiliary bishop of the military vicariate, June 15, 1967; bishop of Charlottetown, Aug. 15, 1970.

Sutton, Peter A., O.M.I.: b. Oct. 18, 1934, Chandler, Que.; ord. priest Oct. 22, 1960; ord. bishop of Labrador-Schefferville, July 18, 1974.

Tessier, Maxime: b. Oct. 9, 1906, St. Sebastien, Que.; ord. priest June 14, 1930; ord. titular bishop of Christopolis and auxiliary bishop of Ottawa, Aug. 2, 1951; coadjutor bishop of Timmins, 1953; bishop of Timmins, May 8, 1955; retired Mar. 24, 1971.

Webster, Benjamin I.: b. Mar. 7, 1898, Spofforth, Eng.; ord. priest May 26, 1923; ord. titular bishop of Paphos and auxiliary bishop of Toronto, Nov. 21, 1946; bishop of Peterborough, Apr. 21, 1954; retired Mar. 12, 1968.

Whelan, Lawrence P.: b. Oct. 16, 1899, Montreal, Que.; ord. priest Dec. 19, 1925; ord. titular bishop of Opus and auxiliary bishop of Montreal, Aug. 15, 1941.

Wilhelm, Joseph L.: b. Nov. 16, 1909, Walkerton, Ont.; ord. priest June 9, 1934; ord. titular bishop of Saccaea and auxiliary bishop of Calgary, Aug. 22, 1963; archbishop of Kingston, Dec. 14, 1966.

Windle, Joseph R.: b. Aug. 28, 1917, Ashdad, Ont.; ord. priest May 16, 1943; ord. titular bishop of Uzita and auxiliary bishop of Ottawa, Jan. 18, 1961; coadjutor bishop of Pembroke, 1969; bishop of Pembroke, Feb. 15, 1971.

Immigration Policy

A commission of the Canadian Catholic Conference recommended in July, 1975, that "redistribution of wealth, and not the control and exclusion of some people" be made the goal of immigration and population policies. They called on Canadians to object to "restrictive and protectionist" immigration and population policies.

CATHOLIC POPULATION STATISTICS OF CANADA

(Source: *Annuario Pontificio.* Archdioceses are indicated by an asterisk. For dioceses marked +, see Canadian Dioceses with Interprovincial Lines.)

Canada's 10 civil provinces and two territories are divided into 17 ecclesiastical provinces consisting of 17 metropolitan sees (archdioceses) and 52 suffragan sees (51 dioceses and one abbacy); there is also one archdiocese immediately subject to the Holy See. (See listing of Ecclesiastical Provinces elsewhere in this section.)

This table presents a regional breakdown of Catholic statistics. In some cases, the totals are approximate because diocesan boundaries fall within several civil provinces.

Civil Province Diocese	Dioc.	Priests Rel.	Tot.	Sems.	Men Rel.	Wom. Rel.	Par- ishes	Cath. Pop.	Total Pop.
Newfoundland	117	42	159	19	145	579	108	179,591	512,145
*St. John's	56	16	72	9	87	366	40	87,300	166,353
Grand Falls	34	—	34	5	13	82	28	34,000	193,500
Saint George's	27	1	28	5	13	90	20	40,791	109,792
Labrador- Schefferville +	—	25	25	—	32	41	20	17,500	42,500
Prince Edward Island									
Charlottetown	79	5	84	4	6	270	58	47,552	111,641
Nova Scotia	318	64	382	14	80	1,133	168	271,564	788,966
*Halifax	96	31	127	5	32	404	50	112,040	414,663
Antigonish	192	13	205	9	28	640	93	124,310	245,795
Yarmouth	30	20	50	—	20	89	25	35,214	128,508
New Brunswick	308	134	442	20	198	1,367	200	296,406	600,598
*Moncton	82	67	149	2	89	440	49	73,998	144,328
Barthurst	88	24	112	5	46	421	70	102,799	116,984
Edmundston	55	25	80	8	41	260	31	49,816	59,286
St. John	83	18	101	5	22	246	50	69,793	280,000
Quebec	4,826	3,245	8,071	346	7,017	28,761	1,887	5,187,771	5,988,731
*Montreal	851	1,380	2,231	63	2,494	9,359	257	1,655,000	2,203,483
*Quebec	961	685	1,646	84	1,420	6,206	276	845,206	857,051
*Rimouski	261	46	307	3	92	1,018	119	161,967	162,979
*Sherbrooke	322	155	477	12	352	1,671	133	212,914	229,174
Amos	71	41	112	—	71	370	78	101,085	106,726
Chicoutimi	315	126	441	77	276	1,125	95	257,221	259,259
Gaspe	101	19	120	6	39	444	69	101,756	111,750
Hauterive	60	32	92	1	61	278	52	90,528	102,824
Hull	205	68	273	4	107	366	56	140,000	180,000
Joliette	155	63	218	8	192	724	85	123,889	126,558
Mont-Laurier	76	40	116	5	106	295	63	69,005	71,205
Nicolet	260	36	296	26	106	1,056	85	154,634	156,150
Rouyn-Noranda	43	28	71	2	58	211	37	53,000	58,920
St. Anne-de-la- Pocatiere	176	12	188	6	37	551	55	89,415	89,629
St. Hyacinthe	272	119	391	18	455	1,847	112	261,460	278,470
St. Jean de Quebec	177	97	274	14	299	848	88	324,000	383,000
St. Jerome	117	119	236	7	304	429	61	181,500	215,843
Trois Rivieres	274	118	392	10	368	1,487	100	229,532	231,981
Valleyfield	129	61	190	—	180	476	66	135,659	163,729
Ontario	1,442	1,360	2,802	150	2,134	5,602	987	2,100,537	7,733,621
*Kingston	77	8	85	9	14	286	51	54,500	265,000
*Ottawa	171	340	511	4	548	1,382	102	261,545	516,045
*Toronto	298	460	758	34	830	580	172	670,000	3,000,000
Alexandria	45	10	55	5	23	142	35	51,430	78,731
Hamilton	155	144	299	22	176	619	107	251,704	1,224,919
Hearst	33	7	40	1	9	85	33	32,952	48,515
London	234	128	362	32	175	915	144	285,961	1,120,825
Moosonee +	2	15	17	—	37	28	11	3,500	15,500
Pembroke +	96	6	102	13	10	315	52	52,043	109,710
Peterborough	49	7	56	6	8	190	33	35,484	283,376

Civil Province Diocese	Dioc.	Priests Rel.	Tot.	Sems.	Men Rel.	Wom. Rel.	Par- ishes	Cath. Pop.	Total Pop.
St. Catharines	52	43	95	4	48	119	42	93,893	380,000
Sault Ste. Marie	128	104	232	12	120	472	98	160,000	348,000
Thunder Bay	24	42	66	3	47	100	37	52,800	200,000
Timmins	78	46	124	5	89	369	70	94,725	143,000
Manitoba	143	235	378	16	306	1,148	169	201,659	996,474
*Keewatin-Le Pas +	—	50	50	—	76	145	4	22,500	63,500
*St. Boniface	82	65	147	8	104	611	70	77,674	303,768
*Winnipeg	61	97	158	8	97	380	79	97,500	612,956
Churchill-Hudson Bay +	—	23	23	—	29	12	16	3,985	16,250
Saskatchewan	196	202	398	19	238	1,009	146	204,461	941,522
*Regina	89	64	153	10	69	314	10	95,000	490,000
Gravelbourg	25	15	40	1	23	125	29	15,906	57,522
Prince Albert	46	44	90	1	49	255	53	40,591	190,000
Saskatoon	36	44	80	7	52	205	42	42,400	185,000
St. Peter Muenster (Abb.)	—	35	35	—	45	110	12	10,564	19,000
Alberta	224	224	448	19	316	1,038	257	318,500	1,710,000
*Edmonton	109	104	213	5	175	668	93	149,500	845,000
*Grouard-McLennan	5	47	52	—	55	101	27	32,500	88,000
Calgary	80	66	146	11	79	194	70	114,000	700,000
St. Paul	30	7	37	3	7	75	67	22,500	77,000
British Columbia	167	172	339	20	233	654	192	346,361	2,101,086
*Vancouver	83	88	171	10	118	373	70	219,890	1,228,525
Kamloops	16	10	26	5	14	45	19	27,000	149,000
Nelson	35	18	53	2	18	35	34	36,451	202,765
Prince George	9	32	41	2	49	53	18	25,020	139,000
Victoria	24	24	48	1	34	148	51	38,000	381,796
Yukon Territory									
Whitehorse +	—	23	23	—	27	20	2	6,328	23,500
Northwest Territories +									
Mackenzie-Ft. Smith	—	44	44	—	71	83	6	20,202	44,878
Eastern Rite (Ukrainian)	195	70	265	11	96	125	316	254,935	—
*Winnipeg	44	5	49	2	5	30	41	60,000	—
Edmonton	40	22	62	3	31	35	147	52,560	—
New Westminster	14	—	14	—	—	—	11	25,000	—
Saskatoon	26	20	46	1	28	42	46	34,175	—
Toronto	71	23	94	5	32	18	71	83,200	—
TOTALS	**8,015**	**5,820**	**13,835**	**638**	**10,867**	**41,789**	**4,496**	**9,435,867**	**21,553,162**

Dioceses with Interprovincial Lines

The following dioceses, indicated by + in the table, have interprovincial lines.

Labrador-Schefferville includes the Labrador region of Newfoundland and the northern part of Quebec province.

Moosonee, Ont., includes part of Quebec province.

Pembroke, Ont., includes one county of Quebec province.

Keewatin-Le Pas includes part of Manitoba and Saskatchewan provinces.

Churchill-Hudson Bay includes part of Northwest Territories.

Whitehorse, Y.T., includes part of British Columbia.

Northwest Territories totals do not include

an area within the boundaries of the Churchill-Hudson Bay diocese.

The Canadian Northland

In a 1975 Labor Day statement, the Administrative Board of the Canadian Catholic Conference urged Canadians to take part in public debate and action for just solutions to the questions of land claims by Indians and Eskimos and responsible stewardship of the country's energy resources. The critical issue, the statement said, is "how these northern energy resources are to be developed — by whom and for whom." They urged that the future of the North "not be determined by colonial patterns of development wherein a powerful few" end up in control.

CANADIAN CATHOLIC CONFERENCE

The Canadian Catholic Conference was established Oct. 12, 1943, as a permanent voluntary association of the bishops of Canada, was given official approval by the Holy See in 1948, and acquired the status of an episcopal conference after the Second Vatican Council.

The CCC acts in two ways: (1) as a strictly ecclesiastical body through which the bishops act together with pastoral authority and responsibility for the Church throughout the country; (2) as an operational secretariat through which the bishops act on a wider scale for the good of the Church and society.

At the top of the CCC organizational table are the president, an executive committee, an administrative board and a plenary assembly. The membership consists of all the bishops of Canada.

Departments and Offices

The CCC's work is planned and co-ordinated by a Pastoral Team of 14 members — six bishops and six staff members (lay and clergy) and the two general secretaries.

The CCC has six departments and four offices all of which work in both French and English: (I) Department for Theology, Liturgy and Canon Law; (II) Department for Education and Communications; (III) Depart-ment for Missions; (IV) Department for Social Life; (V) Department for Internal Relations; (VI) Department for Extraordinary Affairs. Offices for (1) Christian Education (2) Liturgy (3) Missions (4) Social Affairs.

The general secretariat consists of a French and an English general secretary and their assistants and directors of public relations.

Administrative services for purchasing, archives and library, accounting, personnel, publications, printing and distribution are supervised by directors who relate to the general secretaries.

Various advisory councils and committees with mixed memberships of lay persons, religious, priests and bishops also serve the CCC on a variety of topics.

Operations

Meetings for the transaction of business are held twice a year by the plenary assembly, every month except July and August by the executive committee, and four times a year by the administrative board.

Archbishop Jean-Marie Fortier of Sherbrooke is president of the CCC; Bishop G. Emmett Carter of London, Ont., is vice-president.

Headquarters are located at 90 Parent Ave., Ottawa, KIN 7 BI, Canada.

CANADIAN CATHOLIC PUBLICATIONS

(Sources: *Catholic Press Directory,* Canadian Catholic Conference.)

Newspapers

British Columbia Catholic, The, w; 150 Robson St., Vancouver, B.C.; V6B 2A7; 6,784.

Catholic Register, The, w; 67 Bond St., Toronto, Ont.; M5B 1X6; 56,200.

Monitor, The, m; P.O. Box 986, St. John's, Nfld.; 9,946.

New Freeman, The, w; Box 609, St. John, N.B.; 6,058.

Our Sunday Visitor (national), w; Noll Plaza, Huntington, Ind. 46750; 15,424.

Prairie Messenger, w; St. Peter's Press, Muenster, Sask.; SOK 2 YO; 11,952.

Teviskes, Ziburiai, (Lithuanian), w; 941 Dundas St. W., Toronto 3, Ont.; 5,560.

Western Catholic Reporter, w; 9537-76th Ave., Edmonton, Alta., T6C 4H7; 28,188.

Magazines

Annals of Good St. Anne de Beaupre, m; Basilica of St. Anne, Que.; 135,000 (French edition), 75,798 (English edition).

Apostolat, bm; Richelieu, Que., Oblates of Mary Immaculate; 38,000.

Canadian Catholic Institutions, bm; 27 Carlton St., Toronto 2, Ont.; 5,209

Canadian League, The, 5 times a year; 890 St. James St., Winnipeg, Man. R3G 3J7; 102,000.

Centre News, q; 830 Bathurst St., Toronto, Ont.; 2,200.

Christian Communications, 6 times a year; 223 Main St., Ottawa, Ont. K15 1C4; 2,500.

Companion of St. Francis and St. Anthony, m; 15 Chestnut Park Rd., Toronto, Ont.M4W 1W5; Conventual Franciscan Fathers; 10,000.

Field At Home, q; 10 Montcrest Blvd., Toronto Ont. M4K 1J7; 3,117.

Indian Record, 6 times a year; 1301 Wellington Crescent, Winnipeg, Man. R3N-0A9; 2,145.

Kateri, q; P.O. Box 70, Coughnawaga, Que. JO1 1BO; 6,271.

Logos (Ukrainian, English and French), q; 165 Catherine St., Yorkton, Sask.; 380.

Magazine Actualite, m; 2120 Sherbrooke St. E., Montreal 133, Que.; 117,806.

Maintenant, m; 2765 Ch. Cote St., Catherine, Montreal, Que. H3T 1B5.

Martyrs' Shrine Message, q; R. R. No. 1, Midland, Ont.; L4R 4K3; 2,500.

Messager de Saint Antoine, m; Lac-Bouchette, Que. GOW IVO.

Messenger of the Sacred Heart, m; 833 Broadview Ave., Toronto, Ont.; M4K 2P9; 21,200.

Missions Etrangeres, 6 times a year; 59 Rue Desnoyers, Laval, Que.; 57,000.

Oblate Missions, q; 17 Graham Ave., Ottawa KIS 0B6 Ont.; 6,100.

Oratory, 6 times a year; 3800 Ch. Reine-Maries, Montreal Que.; H3V 1H6; 8,600.

Our Family, m; P. O. Box 249, Battleford, Sask.; 50M 0E0; Oblates of Mary Immaculate; 9,151.

Redeemer's Voice, m; 165 Catherine St., Yorkton, Sask.; 1,750.

Regard de Foi, 6 times a year; 5875 Est. rue Sherbrooke, Montreal, Que.; 10,000.

Relations, m; 8100 Blvd., Saint-Laurent, Montreal Que.; H2P 2L9; Jesuit Fathers; 7,427.

Restoration, m; Combermere, P.O. Ont., KOJ ILO; Madonna House; 9,500.

Scarboro Mission Magazine, m; 2685 Kingston Rd., Scarboro, Ont.; M1M 1M4; 45,000.

Spiritan News, 4 times a year; 1537A O'Connor Dr., Toronto, Ont. M4B 2V7; 2,500.

CANADIAN SHRINES

Our Lady of the Cape (Cap de la Madeleine), Queen of the Most Holy Rosary: The Three Rivers, Quebec, parish church, built of fieldstone in 1714 and considered the oldest stone church on the North American continent preserved in its original state, was rededicated June 22, 1888, as a shrine of the Queen of the Most Holy Rosary. Thereafter, the site increased in importance as a pilgrimage and devotional center, and in 1904 St. Pius X decreed the crowning of a statue of the Blessed Virgin which had been donated 50 years earlier to commemorate the dogma of the Immaculate Conception. In 1909, the First Plenary Council of Quebec declared the church a shrine of national pilgrimage. In 1964, the church at the shrine was given the status and title of minor basilica.

St. Anne de Beaupre: The devotional history of this shrine in Quebec, which has been called the "Lourdes of the New World," began with the reported cure of a cripple, Louis Grimont, on Mar. 16, 1658, the starting date of construction work on a small chapel of St. Anne. The original building was successively enlarged and replaced by a stone church which was given the rank of minor basilica in 1888. The present structure, a Romanesque-Gothic basilica, houses the shrine proper in its north transept. The centers of attraction are an eight-foot-high oaken statue and the great relic of St. Anne, a portion of her forearm.

St. Joseph's Oratory: The massive oratory basilica standing on the western side of Mount Royal and overlooking the city of Montreal had its origin in a primitive chapel erected there by Brother Andre, C.S.C., in 1904. Eleven years later, a large crypt was built to accommodate an increasing number of pilgrims, and in 1924 construction work was begun on the large church. A belfry, housing a 60-bell carillon and standing on the site of the original chapel, was dedicated May 15, 1955, as the first major event of the jubilee year observed after the oratory was given the rank of minor basilica.

Martyrs' Shrine: A shrine commemorating several of the Jesuit Martyrs of North America who were killed between 1642 and 1649 in the Ontario and northern New York area is located on the former site of old Forte Sainte Marie. Before its location was fixed near Midland, Ont., in 1925, a small chapel had been erected in 1907 at old Mission St. Ignace to mark the martyrdom of Fathers Jean de Brebeuf and Gabriel Lalemant. This sanctuary has a US counterpart in the Shrine of the North American Martyrs near Auriesville, N.Y., under the care of the Jesuits.

Other shrines and historic churches in Canada include the following.

In Quebec City: the Basilica of Notre Dame, dating from 1650, once the cathedral of a diocese stretching from Canada to Mexico; Notre Dame des Victoires, on the waterfront, dedicated in 1690; the Ursuline Convent, built in 1720, on du Parloir St.

In Montreal: Notre Dame Church, patterned after the famous basilica of the same name in Paris, constructed in 1829; the Shrine of Mary, Queen of All Hearts.

Near Montreal: the Chapel of Mother d'Youville, foundress of the Grey Nuns; Notre Dame de Lourdes, at Rigaud.

CONFERENCE OF RELIGIOUS

The Canadian Religious Conference is a union of major superiors of men and women in Canada. Father Albert Dumont, O.P., is the executive director. Offices are located at 324 Laurier Ave. E., Ottawa, Canada.

AGREEMENT ON BAPTISM

Representatives of the Catholic, Anglican, Lutheran, Presbyterian and United Churches announced in September, 1975, that they had reached an agreement whereby each church would recognize the validity of baptisms conferred according to the established norms of the other churches.

Backgrounding the agreement was a study initiated by the Joint Working Group of the Canadian Council of Churches and the Canadian Catholic Conference. On its completion, it was agreed that baptisms would be recognized when conferred with flowing water — by pouring, sprinkling or immersion — accompanied by the invocation of the Three Persons of the Trinity.

A press release of the Canadian Catholic Conference said: "For the Catholic Church (this step) is an application of decisions taken by the Second Vatican Council."

"These have formed the basis for policies concerning baptism in many countries."

The Catholic Church in the United States

The starting point of the mainstream of Catholic history in the United States was Baltimore at the end of the Revolutionary War, although before that time Catholic explorers had traversed much of the country and missionaries had done considerable work among the Indians in the Southeast, Northeast and Southwest.

Beginning of Organization

Father John Carroll's appointment as superior of the American missions on June 9, 1784, was the first step toward organization of the Church in this country.

At that time, according to a report he made to Rome in 1785, there were approximately 25,000 Catholics in the general population of four million. Many of them had been in the Colonies for several generations. Among them were such outstanding figures as Charles Carroll, a member of the Continental Congress and signer of the Declaration of Independence; Thomas FitzSimons of Philadelphia and Oliver Pollock, the Virginia agent, who raised funds for the militia; Commander John Barry, father of the American Navy, and numerous high-ranking army officers. For the most part, however, Catholics were an unknown minority laboring under legal and social handicaps.

Father Carroll, the brother of Charles Carroll, was named the first American bishop in 1789 and placed in charge of the Diocese of Baltimore, whose boundaries were coextensive with those of the United States. He was consecrated in England Aug. 15, 1790, and installed in his see the following Dec. 12.

Ten years later, Father Leonard Neale became his coadjutor and the first bishop ordained in the United States. Bishop Carroll became an archbishop in 1808 when Baltimore was designated a metropolitan see and the new dioceses of Boston, New York, Philadelphia and Bardstown were established. These jurisdictions were later subdivided, and by 1840 there were, in addition to Baltimore, 15 dioceses, 500 priests and 663,000 Catholics in the general population of 17 million.

Priests and First Seminaries

The number of the 24 original priests was gradually augmented with the arrival of others from France, after the Civil Constitution on the Clergy went into effect there, and other countries. Among the earliest arrivals were several Sulpicians who established the first seminary in the US, St. Mary's, Baltimore, in 1791. By 1815, 30 alumni of the school had been ordained to the priesthood. By that time, two additional seminaries were in operation: Mt. St. Mary's, established in 1809 at Emmitsburg, Md., and St. Thomas, founded two years later, at Bardstown, Ky.

These and similar institutions founded later played key roles in the development and growth of the American clergy.

Early Schools

Early educational enterprises included the establishment in 1791 of a school at Georgetown which later became the first Catholic university in the US; the opening of a secondary school for girls, conducted by Visitation Nuns, in 1792 at Georgetown; and the start of a similar school in the first decade of the 19th century at Emmitsburg, Md., by Saint Elizabeth Ann Seton and the Sisters of Charity of St. Joseph, the first religious community of American foundation.

By the 1840's, which saw the beginnings of the present public school system, more than 200 Catholic elementary schools, half of them west of the Alleghenies, were in operation. From this start, the Church subsequently built the greatest private system of education in the world.

Trusteeism

The initial lack of organization in ecclesiastical affairs, nationalistic feeling among Catholics and the independent action of some priests were factors involved in several early crises.

In Philadelphia, some German Catholics withdrew from one parish in 1789 and founded one of their own, Holy Trinity, which they maintained until 1802. Controversy over the affair reached the point of schism in 1796. Philadelphia was also the scene of the Hogan Schism, which developed in the 1820's when Father William Hogan, with the aid of lay trustees, seized control of St. Mary's Cathedral. His movement, for churches and parishes controlled by other than canonical procedures and run in extra-legal ways, was nullified by a decision of the Pennsylvania Supreme Court in 1822.

Similar troubles seriously disturbed the peace of the Church in other places, principally New York, Baltimore, Buffalo, Charleston and New Orleans.

Dangers arising from the exploitation of lay control were gradually diminished with the extension and enforcement of canonical procedures and with changes in civil law about the middle of the century.

Bigotry

Bigotry against Catholics waxed and waned during the 19th century and into the 20th. The first major campaign of this kind, which developed in the wake of the panic of 1819 and lasted for about 25 years, was mounted in 1830 when the number of Catholic immigrants began to increase to a noticeable degree. Nativist anti-Catholicism generated a great deal of violence, represented by climaxes in loss of life and property in Charlestown, Mass., in 1834, and in Philadelphia 10 years later. Later bigotry was fomented by the Know-Nothings, in the 1850's; the Ku Klux Klan, from 1866; the American Protective Association, from 1887; and the Guardians of Liberty. Perhaps the last eruption of overt anti-Catholicism occurred during the campaign of Alfred E. Smith for the presidency in 1928. Observers feel the issue was laid to rest in the political area with the election of John F. Kennedy to the presidency in 1960.

Growth and Immigration

Between 1830 and 1900, the combined factors of natural increase, immigration and conversion raised the Catholic population to 12 million. A large percentage of the growth figure represented immigrants: some 2.7 million, largely from Ireland, Germany and France, between 1830 and 1880; and another 1.25 million during the 80's when eastern and southern Europeans came in increasing numbers. By the 1860's the Catholic Church, with most of its members concentrated in urban areas, was one of the largest religious bodies in the country.

The efforts of progressive bishops to hasten the acculturation of Catholic immigrants occasioned a number of controversies, which generally centered around questions concerning national or foreign-language parishes. One of them, called Cahenslyism, arose from complaints that German Catholic immigrants were not being given adequate pastoral care.

Immigration continued after the turn of the century, but its impact was more easily cushioned through the application of lessons learned earlier in dealing with problems of nationality and language.

Councils of Baltimore

The bishops of the growing US dioceses met at Baltimore for seven provincial councils between 1829 and 1849.

In 1846, they proclaimed the Blessed Virgin Mary patroness of the United States under the title of the Immaculate Conception, eight years before the dogma was proclaimed.

After the establishment of the Archdiocese of Oregon City in 1846 and the elevation to metropolitan status of St. Louis, New Orleans, Cincinnati and New York, the first of the three plenary councils of Baltimore was held.

The first plenary assembly was convoked on May 9, 1852, with Archbishop Francis P. Kenrick of Baltimore as papal legate. The bishops drew up regulations concerning parochial life, matters of church ritual and ceremonies, the administration of church funds and the teaching of Christian doctrine.

The second plenary council, meeting from Oct. 7 to 21, 1866, under the presidency of Archbishop Martin J. Spalding, formulated a condemnation of several current doctrinal errors and established norms affecting the organization of dioceses, the education and conduct of the clergy, the management of ecclesiastical property, parochial duties and general education.

Archbishop (later Cardinal) James Gibbons called into session the third plenary council which lasted from Nov. 9 to Dec. 7, 1884 Among highly significant results of actions taken by this assembly were the preparation of the line of Baltimore catechisms which became a basic means of religious instruction in this country; legislation which fixed the pattern of Catholic education by requiring the building of elementary schools in all parishes; the establishment of the Catholic University of America in Washington, D.C., in 1889; and the determination of six holy days of obligation for observance in this country.

The enactments of the three plenary councils have had the force of particular law for the Church in the United States.

The Holy See established the Apostolic Delegation at Washington, D.C., on Jan. 24, 1893.

Slavery and Negroes

In the Civil War period, as before, Catholics reflected attitudes of the general population with respect to the issue of slavery. Some supported it, some opposed it, but none were prominent in the Abolition Movement. Gregory XVI had condemned the slave trade in 1839, but no contemporary pope or American bishop published an official document on slavery itself. The issue did not split Catholics in schism as it did Baptists, Methodists and Presbyterians.

Catholics fought on both sides in the Civil War. Five hundred members of 20 or more sisterhoods served the wounded of both sides.

One hundred thousand of the four million slaves emancipated in 1863 were Catholics; the highest concentrations were in Louisiana, about 60,000, and Maryland, 16,000. Three years later, their pastoral care was one of the subjects covered in nine decrees issued by the Second Plenary Council of Baltimore. The measures had little practical effect with respect to integration of the total Catholic community, predicated as they were on the proposition that individual bishops should handle questions regarding segregation in churches and related matters as best they could in the pattern of local customs.

Long entrenched segregation practices continued in force through the rest of the 19th century and well into the 20th. The first effective efforts to alter them were initiated by Cardinal Joseph Ritter of St. Louis in 1947, Cardinal (then Archbishop) Patrick O'Boyle of Washington in 1948, and Bishop Vincent Waters of Raleigh in 1953.

Friend of Labor

The Church became known during the 19th century as a friend and ally of labor in seeking justice for the working man. Cardinal Gibbons journeyed to Rome in 1887, for example, to defend and prevent a condemnation of the Knights of Labor by Leo XIII. The encyclical *Rerum Novarum* was hailed by many American bishops as a confirmation, if not vindication, of their own theories. Catholics have always formed a large percentage of union membership, and some have served unions in positions of leadership.

The American Heresy

Near the end of the century some controversy developed over what was characterized as Americanism or the phantom heresy. It was alleged that Americans were discounting the importance of contemplative virtues, exalting the practical virtues, and watering down the purity of Catholic doctrine for the sake of facilitating convert work.

The French translation of Father Walter Elliott's *Life of Isaac Hecker,* which fired the controversy, was one of many factors that led to the issuance of Leo XIII's *Testem Benevolentiae* in January, 1899, in an attempt to end the matter. It was the first time the orthodoxy of the Church in the US was called into question.

Schism

In the 1890's, serious friction developed between Poles and Irish in Scranton, Buffalo and Chicago, resulting in schism and the establishment of the Polish National Church. A central figure in the affair was Father Francis Hodur, who was excommunicated by Bishop William O'Hara of Scranton in 1898. Nine years later, his ordination by the Old Catholic Archbishop of Utrecht gave the new church its first bishop.

Another schism of the period led to formation of the American Carpatho-Russian Orthodox Greek Catholic Church.

Coming of Age

In 1900, there were 12 million Catholics in the total US population of 76 million, 82 dioceses in 14 provinces, and 12,000 priests and members of about 40 communities of men religious. Many sisterhoods, most of them of European origin and some of American foundation, were engaged in Catholic educational and hospital work, of which they have always been the main support.

The Church in the United States was removed from mission status with promulgation of the apostolic constitution *Sapienti Consilio* by Pope St. Pius X on June 29, 1908.

Before that time, and even into the early 20's, the Church in this country received financial assistance from mission-aid societies in France, Bavaria and Austria. Already,

however, it was making increasing contributions of its own. At the present time, it is the heaviest national contributor to the worldwide Society for the Propagation of the Faith.

American foreign missionary personnel increased from 14 or less in 1906 to 7,148 by 1975 (197 diocesan priests, 3,692 religious priests and brothers, 2,850 sisters, 65 seminarians, 344 lay persons). The first missionary seminary in the US was in operation at Techny, Ill., in 1909, under the auspices of the Society of the Divine Word. Maryknoll, the first American missionary society, was established in 1911 and sent its first priests to China in 1918. Despite these contributions, the Church in the US has not matched the missionary commitment of some other nations.

Bishops' Conference

A highly important apparatus for mobilizing the Church's resources was established in 1917 under the title of the National Catholic War Council. Its name was changed to National Catholic Welfare Conference several years later, but its objectives remained the same: to serve as an advisory and coordinating agency of the American bishops for advancing works of the Church in fields of social significance and impact — education, communications, immigration, social action, legislation, youth and lay organizations.

The forward thrust of the bishops' social thinking was evidenced in a program of social reconstruction they recommended in 1919. By 1945, all but one of their twelve points had been enacted into legislation.

The NCWC was renamed the United States Catholic Conference (USCC) in November, 1966, when the hierarchy also organized itself as a territorial conference with pastoral-juridical authority under the title, National Conference of Catholic Bishops. The USCC is carrying on the functions of the former NCWC.

Pastoral Concerns

The potential for growth of the Church in this country by immigration was sharply reduced but not entirely curtailed after 1921 with the passage of restrictive federal legislation. As a result, the Catholic population became more stabilized and, to a certain extent and for many reasons, began to acquire an identity of its own.

Some increase-from-outside has taken place in the past 50 years, however; from Canada, from central and eastern European countries, and from Puerto Rico and Latin American countries since World War II. This influx, while not as great as that of the 19th century and early 20th, has enriched the Church here with a sizable body of Eastern-Rite Catholics for whom eight ecclesiastical jurisdictions were established between 1924 and 1969. It has also created a challenge for pastoral care of the Spanish-speaking.

The Church continues to grapple with serious pastoral problems in rural areas, where about 600 counties are no-priest land. The National Catholic Rural Life Conference was established in 1922 in an attempt to make the Catholic presence felt on the land, and the Glenmary Society since its foundation in 1939 has devoted itself to this single apostolate. Religious communities and diocesan priests are similarly engaged.

Other challenges lie in the cities and suburbs where 75 percent of the Catholic population lives. Conditions peculiar to each segment of the metropolitan area have developed in recent years as the flight to the suburbs has not only altered some traditional aspects of parish life but has also, in combination with many other factors, left behind a complex of special problems in the inner city.

Phenomena of Change

The Church in the US is presently in a stage of transition from a relatively stable and long established order of life and action to a new order of things. Some of the phenomena of this period are:

• differences in trends and emphasis in theology, and in interpretation and implementation of directives of the Second Vatican Council, resulting in situations of conflict;

• the changing spiritual formation, professional education, style of life and ministry of priests and religious (men and women), which are altering influential patterns of pastoral and specialized service;

• vocations to the priesthood and religious life, which are generally in decline;

• departures from the priesthood and religious life which, while small percentage-wise, are numerous enough to be a matter of serious concern;

• decline of traditional devotional practices;

• exercise of authority along the lines of collegiality and subsidiarity;

• structure and administration, marked by a trend toward greater participation in the life and work of the Church by its members on all levels, from the parish on up;

• alienation from the Church, leading some persons into the catacombs of an underground church, "anonymous Christianity" and religious indifferentism;

• education, undergoing crisis and change in Catholic schools and seeking new ways of reaching out to the young not in Catholic schools and to adults;

• social witness in ministry to the world, which is being shaped by the form of contemporary needs — e.g., race relations, poverty, the peace movement, the Third World;

• ecumenism, involving the Church in interfaith relations on a wider scale than before.

BACKGROUND DATES IN U.S. CATHOLIC CHRONOLOGY

Dates in this section refer mostly to earlier "firsts" and developments in the background of Catholic history in the United States. For other dates, see various sections of the Almanac.

Alabama

1540: Priests crossed the territory with De Soto's expedition.

1560: Five Dominicans in charge of mission at Santa Cruz des Nanipacna.

1682: La Salle claimed territory for France.

1704: Jesuits established first parish church at Fort Louis de la Mobile.

1722: Mobile, formerly under the Quebec diocese, became part of a vicariate apostolic with Florida. Capuchins, Carmelites and Jesuits working there.

1829: Mobile-Birmingham diocese established; made two separate dioceses, 1969.

1830: Spring Hill College, Mobile, established.

1834: Visitation Nuns established an academy at Summerville.

Alaska

1779: Mass celebrated for first time on shore of Port Santa Cruz on lower Bucareli Bay on May 13 by Franciscan John Riobo.

1868: Alaska placed under jurisdiction of Vancouver Island.

1878: Father John Althoff became first resident missionary.

1886: Archbishop Charles J. Seghers, "Apostle of Alaska," murdered by a guide; had surveyed southern and northwest Alaska in 1873 and 1877, respectively.

Sisters of St. Anne first nuns in Alaska.

1894: Alaska made prefecture apostolic.

1901: Jesuits reorganized their missions, established a church at Nome.

1905: Sisters of Providence opened hospital at Nome.

1916: Alaska made vicariate apostolic.

1917: In first ordination in territory, Rev. G. Edgar Gallant raised to priesthood.

1951: Juneau diocese established.

1962: Fairbanks diocese established.

1966: Anchorage archdiocese established.

Arizona

1539: Franciscan Marcos de Niza explored the state.

1540: Franciscans Juan de Padilla, Juan de la Cruz and Marcos de Niza accompanied Coronado expedition through the territory.

1629: Spanish Franciscans began work among Moqui Indians.

1632: Franciscan Martin de Arvide killed by Indians.

1680: Franciscans Jose de Espeleta, Augustin de Santa Maria, Jose de Figueroa and Jose de Trujillo killed in Pueblo Revolt.

1700: Jesuit Eusebio Kino established mission at San Xavier del Bac, near Tucson.

1767: Jesuits expelled; Franciscans took over 10 missions.
1828: Spanish missionaries expelled by Mexican government.
1863: Jesuits returned to San Xavier.
1869: Sisters of Loretto arrived to conduct schools at Bisbee and Douglas.
1897: Tucson diocese established.
1969: Phoenix diocese established.

Arkansas

1541: Priests accompanied De Soto expedition through the territory.
1673: Marquette visited Indians in east.
1686: Henri de Tonti established trading post, first white settlement in territory.
1702: Fr. Nicholas Foucault working among Indians.
1805: Bishop Carroll of Baltimore appointed Administrator Apostolic of Arkansas.
1838: Sisters of Loretto opened first Catholic school.
1843: Little Rock diocese established. There were about 700 Catholics in state, two churches, one priest.
1853: Sisters of Mercy founded St. Mary's Convent at Fort Smith.

California

1542: Cabrillo discovered Upper (Alta) California; name of priest accompanying expedition unknown.
1602: On Nov. 12 Carmelite Andres de la Ascencion offered first recorded Mass in California on shore of San Diego Bay.
1697: Missionary work in Lower and Upper Californias entrusted to Jesuits.
1767: Jesuits expelled from territory. Spanish Crown confiscated their property, including the Pious Fund for Missions. Upper California missions entrusted to Franciscans.
1769: Franciscan Junipero Serra began establishment of Franciscan missions in California, near present San Diego. (See Franciscan Missions of Upper California.)
1775: Franciscan Luis Jayme killed by Indians at San Diego Mission.
1779: Diocese of Sonora, Mexico, which included Upper California, established.
1781: On Sept. 4 an expedition from San Gabriel Mission founded present city of Los Angeles — Pueblo "de Nuestra Senora la Reina de Los Angeles."
Franciscans Francisco Hermenegildo Garces, Juan Antonio Barreneche, Juan Marcello Diaz and Jose Matias Moreno killed by Indians.
1812: Franciscan Andres Quintana killed at Santa Cruz Mission.
1822: Interference and aggression toward missions initiated by Mexican government.
Dedication on Dec. 8 of Old Plaza Church, "Assistant Mission of Our Lady of the Angels," oldest church in Los Angeles.
1833: Missions secularized, finally confiscated.

1840: Pope Gregory XVI established Diocese of Both Californias.
1846: Peter H. Burnett, first governor of California, received into Catholic Church.
1848: Upper California ceded to the United States.
1850: Monterey diocese erected; title changed to Monterey-Los Angeles, 1859; and to Los Angeles, 1922.
1851: University of Santa Clara chartered.
1852: Lower California detached from Monterey diocese.
1853: San Francisco archdiocese established.
1855: US returned confiscated California missions to Church.
1863: Sisters of Notre Dame de Namur opened women's College of Notre Dame at Belmont.
1868: Grass Valley diocese established; transferred to Sacramento in 1886.
1922: Monterey-Fresno diocese established; became separate dioceses, 1967.
1934: Sesquicentennial of Serra's death observed; Serra Year officially declared by Legislature and Aug. 24 observed as Serra Day.
1936: Los Angeles made archdiocese. San Diego diocese established.
1952: Law exempting non-profit, religious-sponsored elementary and secondary schools from taxation upheld in referendum, Nov. 4.
1953: Archbishop James Francis McIntyre of Los Angeles made cardinal by Pius XII.
1962: Oakland, Santa Rosa and Stockton dioceses established.
1973: Archbishop Timothy Manning of Los Angeles made cardinal by Pope Paul VI.

Colorado

1858: First parish in Colorado established.
1864: Sisters of Loretto at the Foot of the Cross, first nuns in the state, established academy at Denver.
1868: Vicariate Apostolic of Colorado and Utah established.
1887: Denver diocese established.
1888: Regis College founded.
1951: Denver made archdiocese.
Pueblo diocese established.

Connecticut

1651: Probably first priest to enter state was Jesuit Gabriel Druillettes; ambassador of Governor of Canada, he participated in a New England Colonial Council at New Haven.
1755: Catholic Acadians, expelled from Nova Scotia, settled in the state.
1791: Rev. John Thayer, first missionary to visit state's Catholics on regular basis, offered Mass at home of Noah Webster.
1808: Connecticut became part of Boston diocese.
1818: Religious freedom established by new constitution, although the Congrega-

tional Church remained, in practice, the state church.

1828: Father Bernard O'Cavanaugh became first resident priest in state.

1829: First Catholic church in state established at Hartford.

Catholic Press of Hartford established.

1843: Hartford diocese established.

1882: Knights of Columbus founded by Father Michael J. McGivney.

1942: Fairfield University founded.

1953: Norwich and Bridgeport dioceses established. Hartford made archdiocese.

1956: Byzantine Rite Exarchate of Stamford established; made eparchy, 1958.

Delaware

1730: Mount Cuba, New Castle County, the scene of Catholic services.

1750: Jesuit mission at Apoquiniminck administered from Maryland.

1772: First permanent parish established at Coffee Run.

1792: French Catholics from Santo Domingo settled near Wilmington.

1816: St. Peter's Church, later the cathedral of the diocese, erected at Wilmington.

1830: Daughters of Charity opened school and orphanage at Wilmington.

1868: Wilmington diocese established.

1869: Visitation Nuns established residence in Wilmington.

District of Columbia

1641: Jesuit Andrew White evangelized Anacosta Indians.

1774: Father John Carroll ministered to Catholics.

1789: Georgetown, first Catholic college in US, established.

1791: Pierre Charles L'Enfant designed the Federal City of Washington. His plans were not fully implemented until the early 1900's.

1792: James Hoban designed the White House.

1794: Father Anthony Caffrey began St. Patrick's Church, first parish church in the new Federal City.

1801: Poor Clares opened school for girls in Georgetown; first school established by nuns in US.

1802: First mayor of Washington, appointed by President Jefferson, was Judge Robert Brent.

1889: Catholic University of America founded.

1893: Apostolic Delegation established with Archbishop Francesco Satolli as the first delegate.

1919: National Catholic Welfare Conference (now the United States Catholic Conference) organized by American hierarchy to succeed National Catholic War Council.

1920: Cornerstone of National Shrine of Immaculate Conception laid.

1939: Washington made archdiocese of equal rank with Baltimore, under direction of same archbishop.

1947: Washington archdiocese received its own archbishop, was separated from Baltimore.

1967: Archbishop Patrick A. O'Boyle of Washington made cardinal by Pope Paul VI.

Florida

1513: Ponce de Leon discovered Florida.

1521: Missionaries accompanying Ponce de Leon and other explorers probably said first Masses within present limits of US.

1528: Franciscans landed on western shore.

1539: Twelve missionaries landed with De Soto at Tampa Bay.

1549: Dominican Luis Cancer de Barbastro and two companions slain by Indians near Tampa Bay.

1565: City of St. Augustine, oldest in US, founded by Pedro Menendez de Aviles, who was accompanied by four secular priests. America's oldest mission, Nombre de Dios, was established.

Father Martin Francisco Lopez de Mendoza Grajales became the first parish priest of St. Augustine, where the first parish in the US was established.

1572: St. Francis Borgia, general of the Society, withdrew Jesuits from Florida.

1606: Bishop Juan de las Cabeyas de Altamirano, O.P., conducted the first episcopal visitation in the US.

1620: The chapel of Nombre de Dios was dedicated to Nuestra Senora de la Leche y Buen Parto (Our Nursing Mother of the Happy Delivery); oldest shrine to the Blessed Mother in the US.

1704: Destruction of Florida's northern missions by English and Indian troops led by Governor James Moore of South Carolina. Franciscans Juan de Parga, Dominic Criodo, Tiburcio de Osorio, Augustine Ponze de Leon, Marcos Delgado and two Indians, Anthony Enixa and Amador Cuipa Feliciano, were slain by the invaders.

1735: Bishop Francis Martinez de Tejadu Diaz de Velasco, auxiliary of Santiago, was the first bishop to take up residence in US, at St. Augustine.

1793: Florida and Louisiana were included in Diocese of New Orleans.

1857: Eastern Florida made a vicariate apostolic.

1870: St. Augustine diocese established.

1917: Convent Inspection Bill passed; repealed 1935.

1958: Miami diocese established.

1968: Miami made metropolitan see; Orlando and St. Petersburg dioceses established.

Georgia

1540: First priests to enter were chaplains with De Soto. They celebrated first Mass within territory of 13 original colonies.

1566: Pedro Martinez, first Jesuit martyr of

the New World, was slain by Indians on Cumberland Island.

1569: Jesuit mission was opened at Guale Island by Father Antonio Sedeno.

1572: Jesuits withdrawn from area.

1595: Five Franciscans assigned to Province of Guale.

1597: Five Franciscan missionaries killed in coastal missions.

1606: Bishop Altamirano, O.P., conducted visitation of the Georgia area.

1612: First Franciscan province in US erected under title of Santa Elena; it included Georgia, South Carolina and Florida.

1655: Franciscans had nine flourishing missions among Indians.

1702: Spanish missions ended as result of English conquest.

1796: Augustinian Father Le Mercier was first post-colonial missionary to Georgia.

1798: Catholics granted right of refuge.

1800: First church erected in Savannah on lot given by city council.

1810: First church erected in Augusta on lot given by State Legislature.

1850: Savannah diocese established; became Savannah-Atlanta, 1937; divided into two separate sees, 1956.

1962: Atlanta made metropolitan see.

Hawaii

1825: Pope Leo XII entrusted missionary efforts in Islands to Sacred Hearts Fathers.

1827: The first Catholic missionaries arrived — Fathers Alexis Bachelot, Abraham Armand and Patrick Short, along with three lay brothers. After three years of persecution, the priests were forcibly exiled.

1836: Father Arsenius Walsh, SS. CC., a British subject, was allowed to remain in Islands but was not permitted to proselytize or conduct missions.

1839: Hawaiian government signed treaty with France granting Catholics freedom of worship and same privileges as Protestants.

1844: Vicariate Apostolic of Sandwich Islands (Hawaii) erected.

1873: Father Damien de Veuster of the Sacred Hearts Fathers arrived in Molokai and spent the remainder of his life working among lepers.

1941: Honolulu diocese established, made a suffragan of San Francisco.

Idaho

1840: Jesuit Pierre de Smet preached to the Flathead and Pend d'Oreille Indians; probably offered first Mass in state.

1842: Jesuit Nicholas Point opened a mission among Coeur d'Alene Indians near Maries.

1863: Secular priests sent from Oregon City to administer to incoming miners.

1867: Sisters of Holy Names of Jesus and Mary opened first Catholic school at Idaho City.

1868: Idaho made a vicariate apostolic.

1870: First church in Boise established. Church lost most of missions among Indians of Northwest Territory when Commission on Indian Affairs appointed Protestant missionaries to take over.

1893: Boise diocese established.

Illinois

1673: Jesuit Jacques Marquette, accompanying Joliet, preached to Indians.

1674: Pere Marquette set up a cabin for saying Mass in what later became City of Chicago.

1675: Pere Marquette established Mission of the Immaculate Conception among Kaskaskia Indians.

1679: La Salle brought with him Franciscans Louis Hennepin, Gabriel de la Ribourde, and Zenobius Membre.

1680: Father Ribourde was killed by Kickapoo Indians.

1689: Jesuit Claude Allouez died after 32 years of missionary activity among Indians of Midwest; he had evangelized 100,000 Indians of 20 different tribes and baptized 10,000. Jesuit Jacques Gravier succeeded Allouez as vicar general of Illinois.

1730: Father Gaston, a diocesan priest, was killed at the Cahokia Mission.

1763: British conquest of the territory resulted in banishment of Jesuits.

1778: Father Pierre Gibault championed Colonial cause in the Revolution and aided greatly in securing states of Ohio, Indiana, Illinois, Michigan and Wisconsin for Americans.

1827: The present St. Patrick's Parish at Ruma, oldest English-speaking Catholic congregation in state, was founded.

1833: Visitation Nuns established residence in Kaskaskia.

1843: Chicago diocese established.

1853: Quincy diocese established; transferred to Alton, 1857; Springfield, 1923.

1860: Quincy College founded.

1877: Peoria diocese established.

1880: Chicago made archdiocese.

1887: Belleville diocese established.

1908: Rockford diocese established. First American Missionary Congress held in Chicago.

1924: Archbishop Mundelein of Chicago made cardinal by Pope Pius XI.

1926: The 28th International Eucharistic Congress, first held in US, convened in Chicago.

1946: Blessed Frances Xavier Cabrini, former resident of Chicago, was canonized; first US citizen raised to dignity of altar. Archbishop Samuel A. Stritch of Chicago made cardinal by Pope Pius XII.

1948: Joliet diocese established.

1958: Cardinal Stritch appointed Pro-Prefect of the Sacred Congregation for the Propagation of the Faith — the first US-born

prelate to be named to the Roman Curia.
1959: Archbishop Albert G. Meyer of Chicago made cardinal by Pope John XXIII.
1961: Eparchy of St. Nicholas of the Ukrainians established at Chicago.
1967: Archbishop John P. Cody of Chicago made cardinal by Pope Paul VI.

Indiana

1679: Recollects Louis Hennepin and Gabriel de la Ribourde entered state.
1686: Land near present Notre Dame University at South Bend given by French government to Jesuits for mission.
1732: Church of St. Francis Xavier founded at Vincennes.
1778: Father Gibault aided George Rogers Clark in campaign against British in conquest of Northwest Territory.
1793: First school in Indiana built at Vincennes by Father John Francis Rivet.
1834: Vincennes diocese, later Indianapolis, established.
1840: Sisters of Providence founded St. Mary-of-the-Woods College for women.
1842: University of Notre Dame founded by Holy Cross Fathers.
1843: Immigration of German farmers to Indiana swelled Catholic population.
1853: First Benedictine community established in state at St. Meinrad.
1857: Fort Wayne diocese established; changed to Fort Wayne-South Bend, 1960.
1944: Indianapolis made archdiocese. Lafayette and Evansville dioceses established.
1957: Gary diocese established.

Iowa

1673: A Peoria village on Mississippi was visited by Pere Marquette.
1679: Fathers Louis Hennepin and Gabriel de la Ribourde visited Indian villages.
1836: First permanent church, St. Raphael's, founded at Dubuque by Dominican Samuel Mazzuchelli.
1837: Dubuque diocese established.
1838: St. Joseph's Mission founded at Council Bluffs by Jesuit Father De Smet.
1843: Sisters of Charity of the Blessed Virgin Mary were first sisterhood in state.
Sisters of Charity opened Clarke College, Dubuque.
1844: Brothers of St. Joseph opened academy for boys at Dubuque.
1850: First Trappist Monastery in state, Our Lady of New Melleray, was begun.
1881: Davenport diocese established.
1882: St. Ambrose College, Davenport, established.
1893: Dubuque made archdiocese.
1902: Sioux City diocese established.
1911: Des Moines diocese established.

Kansas

1542: Franciscan Juan de Padilla, first martyr of the United States, was killed in central Kansas.
1858: St. Benedict's College founded.
1863: Sisters of Charity opened orphanage at Leavenworth, and St. John's Hospital in following year.
1877: Leavenworth diocese established; transferred to Kansas City in 1947.
1887: Dioceses of Concordia (transferred to Salina in 1944) and Wichita established.
1888: Oblate Sisters of Providence opened an orphanage for Negro boys at Leavenworth, first west of Mississippi.
1951: Dodge City diocese established.
1952: Kansas City made archdiocese.

Kentucky

1775: First settlers in Kentucky were Catholics.
1787: Father Charles Francis Whelan, first resident priest, ministered to settlers of Bardstown.
1806: Dominican Fathers built Priory of St. Rose, later founded St. Thomas Aquinas College.
1808: Bardstown diocese established; transferred to Louisville, 1840.
1811: Rev. Guy L. Chabrat became first priest ordained west of the Allegheny Mountains.
1812: Sisters of Loretto founded, first religious community in US without foreign affiliation.
Sisters of Charity of Nazareth founded, the second native community of women founded in the West.
1814: Nazareth College for women established.
1816: Cornerstone of St. Joseph's Cathedral, Bardstown, laid; called "The Cathedral in the Wilderness."
1817: St. Thomas Seminary founded.
1830: Hon. Benjamin J. Webb founded *Catholic Advocate* first Catholic weekly in Kentucky.
1847: Trappist monks took up residence in Gethsemani.
1849: Cornerstone of Cathedral of the Assumption laid at Louisville.
1852: Know-Nothing troubles in state.
1853: Covington diocese established.
1937: Louisville made archdiocese. Owensboro diocese established.
1956: State Court of Appeals upheld right of Catholic Sisters to teach in state's public schools even though they wore religious habits.

Louisiana

1682: La Salle's expedition, accompanied by two priests, completed discoveries of De Soto at mouth of Mississippi. La Salle named territory Louisiana.
1699: French Catholics founded colony of Louisiana.
First recorded Mass offered Mar. 3, by

Franciscan Father Anastase Douay.
1706: Father John Francis Buisson de St. Cosme was killed near Donaldsonville.
1717: Franciscan Anthony Margil established first Indian mission school of San Miguel de Linares.
1718: City of New Orleans founded by Jean Baptiste Le Moyne de Bienville.
1720: First resident priest in New Orleans was the French Recollect Prothais Boyer.
1725: Capuchin Fathers opened school for boys.
1727: Ursuline Nuns founded convent in New Orleans, oldest convent in what is now US; they conducted a school, hospital and orphan asylum.
1793: New Orleans diocese established.
1850: New Orleans made archdiocese.
1853: Natchitoches diocese established; transferred to Alexandria in 1910.
1892: Sisters of Holy Family, a Negro congregation, established at New Orleans.
1912: Loyola University of South established.
1918: Lafayette diocese established.
1925: Xavier University established in New Orleans.
1961: Baton Rouge diocese established.
1962: Catholic schools on all levels desegregated in New Orleans archdiocese.

Maine

1604: First Mass in territory celebrated by Father Nicholas Aubry, accompanying De Monts' expedition which was authorized by King of France to begin colonizing region.
1605: Colony founded on St. Croix Island; two secular priests served as chaplains.
1613: Four Jesuits attempted to establish permanent French settlement near mouth of Kennebec River.
1619: French Franciscans began work among settlers and Indians; driven out by English in 1628.
1630: New England made a prefecture apostolic in charge of French Capuchins.
1633: Capuchin Fathers founded missions on Penobscot River.
1646: Jesuits established Assumption Mission on Kennebec River.
1688: Church of St. Anne, oldest in New England, built at Oldtown.
1704: English soldiers destroyed French missions.
1724: English forces again attacked French settlements, killed Jesuit Sebastian Rale.
1853: Portland diocese established.
1854: Know-Nothing uprising resulted in burning of church in Bath.
1856: Anti-Catholic feeling continued; church at Ellsworth burned.
1864: Sisters of Congregation of Notre Dame from Montreal opened academy at Portland.
1875: James A. Healy, first bishop of

Negro blood consecrated in US, became second Bishop of Portland.

Maryland

1634: Maryland established by Lord Calvert. Two Jesuits among first colonists.
First Mass offered on Island of St. Clement in Lower Potomac by Jesuit Father Andrew White.
St. Mary's founded by English and Irish Catholics.
1641: St. Ignatius Parish founded by English Jesuits at Chapel Point, near Port Tobacco.
1649: Religious Toleration Act passed by Maryland Assembly. It was repealed in 1654 by Puritan-controlled government.
1651: Cecil Calvert, second Lord Baltimore, gave Jesuits 10,000 acres for use as Indian mission.
1658: Lord Baltimore restored Toleration Act.
1672: Franciscans came to Maryland under leadership of Father Massius Massey.
1688: Maryland became royal colony as a result of the Revolution in England; Anglican Church became the official religion (1692); Toleration Act repealed; Catholics disenfranchised and persecuted until 1776.
1784: Father John Carroll appointed prefect apostolic for the territory embraced by new Republic.
1789: Baltimore became first diocese established in US, with John Carroll as first bishop.
1790: Carmelite Nuns founded convent at Port Tobacco, the first in the English-speaking Colonies.
1791: First Synod of Baltimore held.
St. Mary's Seminary, first seminary in US, established.
1793: Rev. Stephen T. Badin first priest ordained by Bishop Carroll.
1800: Jesuit Leonard Neale became first bishop consecrated in present limits of US.
1806: Cornerstone of Assumption Cathedral, Baltimore, was laid.
1808: Baltimore made archdiocese.
1809: St. Joseph's College, first women's college in US, founded.
Sisters of Charity of St. Joseph founded by St. Elizabeth Ann Seton; first native American sisterhood.
1821: Assumption Cathedral, Baltimore, formally opened.
1829: Oblate Sisters of Charity, a Negro congregation, established at Baltimore.
First Provincial Council of Baltimore held; six others followed, in 1833, 1837, 1840, 1843, 1846 and 1849.
1836: Roger B. Taney appointed Chief Justice of Supreme Court by President Jackson.
1852: First of the three Plenary Councils of Baltimore convened. Subsequent councils were held in 1866 and 1884.

1855: German Catholic Central Verein founded.

1886: Archbishop Gibbons of Baltimore made cardinal by Pope Leo XIII.

1965: Archbishop Shehan of Baltimore made cardinal by Pope Paul VI.

Massachusetts

1630: New England made a prefecture apostolic in charge of French Capuchins.

1647: Massachusetts Bay Company enacted an anti-priest law.

1732: Although Catholics were not legally admitted to colony, a few Irish families were in Boston; a priest was reported working among them.

1755-56: Acadians landing in Boston were denied services of a Catholic priest.

1775: General Washington discouraged Guy Fawkes Day procession in which pope was carried in effigy, and expressed surprise that there were men in his army "so void of common sense as to insult the religious feelings of the Canadians with whom friendship and an alliance are being sought."

1780: The Massachusetts State Constitution granted religious liberty, but required a religious test to hold public office and provided for tax to support Protestant teachers of piety, religion and morality.

1788: First public Mass said in Boston on Nov. 2 by Abbe de la Poterie, first resident priest.

1803: Church of Holy Cross erected in Boston with financial aid given by Protestants headed by John Adams.

1808: Boston diocese established.

1831: Irish Catholic immigration increased.

1832: St. Vincent's Orphan Asylum, oldest charitable institution in Boston, opened by Sisters of Mercy.

1834: Ursuline Convent in Charlestown burned by a Nationalist mob.

1843: Holy Cross College founded.

1855: Catholic militia companies disbanded; nunneries' inspection bill passed.

1859: St. Mary's, first parochial school in Boston, opened.

1860: Portuguese Catholics from Azores settled in New Bedford.

1870: Springfield diocese established.

1875: Boston made archdiocese.

1904: Fall River diocese established.

1911: Archbishop O'Connell of Boston made cardinal by Pope Pius X.

1950: Worcester diocese established.

1958: Archbishop Richard J. Cushing of Boston made cardinal by Pope John XXIII.

1966: Apostolic Exarchate for Melkites in the US established, with headquarters in Boston.

1973: Archbishop Humberto S. Medeiros of Boston made cardinal by Pope Paul VI.

Michigan

1641: Jesuits Isaac Jogues and Charles Raymbaut preached to Chippewas; named Sault-Sainte Marie Rapids.

1660: Jesuit Rene Menard opened first regular mission in Lake Superior region.

1668: Pere Marquette founded Sainte Marie Mission at Sault-Sainte Marie.

1671: Pere Marquette founded St. Ignace Mission at Michilimackinac.

1701: Fort Pontchartrain founded on present site of Detroit and placed in command of Antoine de la Mothe Cadillac. The Chapel of Sainte-Anne-de-Detroit founded.

1706: Franciscan Father Delhalle killed by Indians at Detroit.

1823: Father Gabriel Richard elected delegate to Congress from Michigan territory; he was the first priest chosen for the House of Representatives.

1833: Father Frederic Baraga celebrated first Mass in present Grand Rapids.

Detroit diocese established, embracing whole Northwest Territory.

1843: *Western Catholic Register* founded at Detroit.

1845: St. Vincent's Hospital, Detroit, opened by Sisters of Charity.

1848: Cathedral of Sts. Peter and Paul, Detroit, consecrated.

1853: Vicariate Apostolic of Upper Michigan established.

1857: Sault-Ste. Marie diocese established; later transferred to Marquette.

1877: University of Detroit founded.

1882: Grand Rapids diocese established.

1897: Nazareth College for women founded.

1937: Detroit made archdiocese. Lansing diocese established.

1938: Saginaw diocese established.

1946: Archbishop Edward Mooney of Detroit created cardinal by Pope Pius XII.

1949: Opening of St. John's Theological (major) Seminary at Plymouth; this was first seminary in US serving an entire ecclesiastical province (Detroit).

1966: Apostolic Exarchate for Maronites in US established, with headquarters in Detroit; made an eparchy in 1972.

1969: Archbishop John Dearden of Detroit made cardinal by Pope Paul VI.

1971: Gaylord and Kalamazoo dioceses established.

Minnesota

1680: Falls of St. Anthony discovered by Franciscan Louis Hennepin.

1727: First chapel, St. Michael the Archangel, erected near town of Frontenac and placed in charge of French Jesuits.

1732: Fort Charles built; Jesuits ministered to settlers.

1736: Jesuit Jean Pierre Aulneau killed by Indians.

1739: Swiss Catholics from Canada settled near Fort Snelling; Bishop Loras of Dubuque, accompanied by Father Pellamourgues, visited the Fort and administered sacraments.

1841: Father Lucian Galtier built Church of St. Paul, thus forming nucleus of modern city of same name.

1850: St. Paul diocese established.

1851: Sisters of St. Joseph arrived in state.

1857: University of St. John founded.

1888: St. Paul made archdiocese; name changed to St. Paul-Minneapolis in 1966.

1889: Duluth, St. Cloud and Winona dioceses established.

1909: Crookston diocese established.

1958: New Ulm diocese established.

Mississippi

1540: Chaplains with De Soto expedition entered territory.

1682: Franciscans Zenobius Membre and Anastase Douay preached to Taensa and Natchez Indians. Father Membre offered first recorded Mass in the state on Mar. 29, Easter Sunday.

1698: Priests of Quebec Seminary founded missions near Natchez and Fort Adams.

1702: Father Nicholas Foucault murdered by Indians near Fort Adams.

1721: Missions practically abandoned, with only Father Juif working among Yazoos.

1725: Jesuit Mathurin de Petit carried on mission work in northern Mississippi.

1729: Indians tomahawked Jesuit Paul du Poisson near Fort Rosalie; Father Jean Souel shot by Yazoos.

1736: Jesuit Antoine Senat burned at stake by Chickasaws.

1822: Vicariate Apostolic of Mississippi and Alabama established.

1825: Mississippi made a separate vicariate apostolic.

1837: Natchez diocese established (later changed to Natchez-Jackson).

1848: Sisters of Charity opened orphan asylum and school in Natchez.

Missouri

1700: Jesuit Gabriel Marest established a mission among Kaskaskia Indians near St. Louis.

1734: French Catholic miners and traders settled Old Mines and Sainte Genevieve.

1750: Jesuits visited French settlers.

1762: Mission established at St. Charles.

1767: Carondelet mission established.

1770: First church founded at St. Louis.

1811: Jesuits established Indian mission school at Florissant.

1818: Bishop Dubourg arrrived at St. Louis, with Vincentians Joseph Rosati and Felix de Andreis. St. Louis University, the diocesan (Kenrick) seminary and the Vincentian Seminary in Perryville trace their origins to them.

1826: St. Louis diocese established.

1828: Sisters of Charity opened first hospital west of the Mississippi, at St. Louis.

1832: *The Shepherd of the Valley,* first Catholic paper west of the Mississippi.

1845: First conference of Society of St. Vincent de Paul in US founded at St. Louis.

1847: St. Louis made archdiocese.

1865: A Test Oath Law passed by State Legislature (called Drake Convention) to crush Catholicism in Missouri. Law declared unconstitutional by Supreme Court in 1866.

1867: College of St. Teresa for women founded at Kansas City.

1868: St. Joseph diocese established.

1880: Kansas City diocese established.

1946: Archbishop John J. Glennon of St. Louis made cardinal by Pope Pius XII.

1956: Kansas City and St. Joseph dioceses combined into one see. Jefferson City and Springfield-Cape Girardeau dioceses established.

1961: Archbishop Joseph E. Ritter of St. Louis made cardinal by Pope John XXIII.

1969: Archbishop John J. Carberry of St. Louis made cardinal by Pope Paul VI.

Montana

1743: Pierre and Francois Verendrye, accompanied by Jesuit Father Coquart, may have explored territory.

1833: Indian missions handed over to care of Jesuits by Second Provincial Council of Baltimore.

1840: Jesuit Pierre De Smet began missionary work among Flathead and Pend d'Oreille Indians.

1841: St. Mary's Mission established by Father De Smet and two companions on the Bitter Root River in present Stevensville.

1845: Jesuit Antonio Ravalli placed in charge of St. Mary's Mission; Ravalli County named in his honor.

1859: Fathers Point and Hoecken established St. Peter's Mission near the Great Falls.

1869: Sisters of Charity founded a hospital, school and orphanage in Helena.

1877: Vicariate Apostolic of Montana established.

1884: Helena diocese established.

1904: Great Falls diocese established.

1910: Carroll College founded.

1935: Rev. Joseph M. Gilmore became first Montana priest elevated to hierarchy.

Nebraska

1541: Coronado expedition, accompanied by Franciscan Juan de Padilla, reached the Platte River.

1673: Pere Marquette visited Nebraska Indians.

1720: Franciscan Juan Miguel killed by Indians near Columbus.

1855: Father J. F. Tracy administered to Catholic settlement of St. Patrick and to Catholics in Omaha.

1856: Land was donated by Governor Alfred Cumming for a church in Omaha.

1857: Nebraska vicariate apostolic established.
1878: Creighton University established.
1881: Poor Clares, first contemplative group in state, arrived in Omaha.
Duchesne College established.
1885: Omaha diocese established.
1887: Lincoln diocese established.
1912: Kearney diocese established; name changed to Grand Island, 1917.
1917: Father Flanagan founded Boy's Town for homeless boys, an institution which gained national and international recognition in subsequent years.
1945: Omaha made archdiocese.

Nevada

1774: Franciscan missionaries passed through Nevada on way to California missions.
1860: First parish, serving Genoa, Carson City and Virginia City, established.
1862: Rev. Patrick Manogue appointed pastor of Virginia City. He established a school for boys and girls, an orphanage and hospital.
1871: Church erected at Reno.
1931: Reno diocese established.

New Hampshire

1630: Territory made part of a prefecture apostolic embracing all of New England.
1784: State Constitution included a religious test which barred Catholics from public office; local support was provided for public Protestant teachers of religion.
1818: The Barber family of Claremont was visited by their son Virgil (converted to Catholicism in 1816) accompanied by Father Charles Ffrench, O.P. The visit led to the conversion of the entire Barber family.
1823: Father Virgil Barber, minister who became a Jesuit priest, built first Catholic church and school at Claremont.
1830: Church of St. Aloysius erected at Dover.
1853: New Hampshire made part of the Portland diocese.
1858: Sisters of Mercy began to teach school at St. Anne's, Manchester.
1877: Catholics obtained full civil liberty and rights.
1884: Manchester diocese established.
1893: St. Anselm's College founded; St. Anselm's Abbey canonically erected.
1937: Francis P. Murphy became first Catholic governor of New Hampshire.

New Jersey

1668: William Douglass of Bergen was refused a seat in General Assembly because he was a Catholic.
1672: Fathers Harvey and Gage visited Catholics in Woodbridge and Elizabethtown.
1701: Tolerance granted to all but "papists."

1744: Jesuit Theodore Schneider of Pennsylvania visited German Catholics of New Jersey.
1762: Fathers Ferdinand Farmer and Robert Harding working among Catholics in state.
1776: State Constitution tacitly excluded Catholics from office.
1799: Foundation of first Catholic school in state, St. John's at Trenton.
1803: First parish in northern New Jersey founded at Echo Lake.
1814: First church in Trenton erected.
1844: Catholics obtained full civil liberty and rights.
1853: Newark diocese established.
1856: Seton Hall University established.
1881: Trenton diocese established.
1937: Newark made archdiocese. Paterson and Camden dioceses established.
1947: US Supreme Court ruled on N. J. bus case, permitting children attending nonpublic schools to ride on buses and be given other health services provided for those in public schools.
1957: Seton Hall College of Medicine and Dentistry established: the first medical school in state; it was run by Seton Hall until 1965.
1963: Byzantine Eparchy of Passaic established.

New Mexico

1539: Territory explored by Franciscan Marcos de Niza.
1544: Franciscans Juan de la Cruz and Louis de Ubeda, lay brother, killed by Indians.
1581: Franciscans Augustin Rodriguez, Juan de Santa Maria and Francisco Lopez named the region "New Mexico"; they later died at hands of Indians.
1598: Juan de Onate founded a colony at Chamita, where first chapel in state was built.
1609: Santa Fe founded, future headquarters for missions of New Mexico.
1631: Franciscan Pedro de Miranda was killed by Indians.
1632: Franciscan Francisco Letrado was killed by Indians.
1672: Franciscan Pedro de Avila y Ayala was killed by Indians.
1675: Franciscan Alonso Gil de Avila was killed by Indians.
1680: Indians massacred 21 missionaries; missions destroyed.
1684: Franciscan Manuel Beltran was killed by Indians.
1692: Missions restored.
1696: Indians rebelled, massacred five more missionaries.
1850: Jean Baptiste Lamy appointed head of newly established Vicariate Apostolic of New Mexico.
1852: Sisters of Loretto arrived in Santa Fe.
1853: Santa Fe diocese established.

1859: Christian Brothers arrived, established first school for boys in New Mexico (later St. Michael's College).

1*r*5: Sisters of Charity started first orphanage and hospital in Santa Fe. It was closed in 1966.

1875: Santa Fe made archdiocese.

1939: Gallup diocese established.

New York

1524: Giovanni de Verrazano was first white man to enter New York Bay.

1627: Franciscan Joseph d'Aillon discovered oil at Seneca Springs, near Cuba, N. Y.

1642: Jesuits Isaac Jogues and Rene Goupil were mutilated by Mohawks; Rene Goupil was killed by them shortly afterwards. Dutch Calvinists rescued Father Jogues.

1646: Jesuits Isaac Jogues and John Lalande were martyred by Iroquois at Ossernenon, now Auriesville.

1654: The Onondagas were visited by Jesuits from Canada.

1655: First permanent mission established near Syracuse.

1656: Church of St. Mary erected near Lake Onondaga.

Catherine Tekakwitha, "Lily of the Mohawks," was born at Ossernenon, now Auriesville (d. in Canada, 1680).

1658: Indian uprisings destroyed missions among Cayugas, Senecas and Oneidas.

1664: English took New Amsterdam and replaced French priests with their own missionaries.

Duke of York ordered religious freedom in Province of New York.

1667: Missions were restored under protection of Garaconthie, Onondaga chief.

1678: Franciscan Louis Hennepin, first white man to view Niagara Falls, celebrated Mass there.

1682: Thomas Dongan appointed governor by Duke of York.

1683: English Jesuits came to New York, later opened a school.

1700: Although Assembly enacted a bill calling for religious toleration of all Christians in 1683, other penal laws were now enforced against Catholics; all priests were ordered out of the province.

1709: Jesuit missions were abandoned.

1741: Because of an alleged popish plot to burn city of New York, four whites were hanged and 11 Negroes burned at stake.

1777: A rejected amendment of the State Constitution stated that Catholics ought not to hold lands or participate in civil rights unless they swore that no pope or priests may absolve them from allegiance to the state.

1785: Cornerstone was laid for St. Peter's Church, New York City, first permanent structure of Catholic worship in state.

Trusteeism began to cause trouble at New York.

1806: State Test Oath repealed.

1808: New York diocese established.

1828: New York State Legislature enacted a law upholding sanctity of seal of confession.

1834: First native New Yorker to become a secular priest, Rev. John McCloskey, was ordained.

1841: Fordham University and Manhattanville College established.

1847: Albany and Buffalo dioceses established.

1850: New York made archdiocese.

1853: Brooklyn diocese established.

1856: Present St. Bonaventure University and Christ the King Seminary founded at Allegany.

1858: Cornerstone of St. Patrick's Cathedral, New York City, was laid.

1868: Rochester diocese established.

1872: Ogdensburg diocese established.

1875: Archbishop John McCloskey of New York made first American cardinal by Pope Pius IX.

1878: Franciscan Sisters of Allegany were first native American community to send members to foreign missions.

1880: William R. Grace was first Catholic mayor of New York City.

1886: Syracuse diocese established.

1911: Archbishop John M. Farley of New York made cardinal by Pope Pius X.

Catholic Foreign Mission Society of America (Maryknoll) opened a seminary for foreign missions, the first of its kind in US. The Maryknollers were also unique as the first US-established foreign mission society.

1917: Military Ordinariate established with headquarters at New York.

1919: Alfred E. Smith became first elected Catholic governor.

1924: Archbishop Patrick Hayes of New York made cardinal by Pope Pius XI.

1930: Jesuit Martyrs of New York and Canada were canonized on June 29.

1946: Archbishop Francis J. Spellman of New York made cardinal by Pope Pius XII.

1957: Rockville Centre diocese established.

1969: Archbishop Terence Cooke of New York made cardinal by Pope Paul VI.

North Carolina

1526: The Ayllon expedition attempted to establish a settlement on Carolina coast.

1540: De Soto expedition, accompanied by chaplains, entered state.

1776: State Constitution denied office to "those who denied the truths of the Protestant religion."

1805: The few Catholics in state were served by visiting missionaries.

1821: Bishop John England celebrated Mass in the ballroom of the home of William Gaston at New Bern, marking the start of organization of the first parish, St. Paul's, in the state.

1835: William Gaston, State Supreme

Court Justice, succeeded in having repealed the article denying religious freedom.

1852: First Catholic church erected in Charlotte.

1868: North Carolina vicariate apostolic established.

Catholics obtained full civil liberty and rights.

1874: Sisters of Mercy arrived, opened an academy, several schools, hospitals and an orphanage.

1878: Belmont Abbey College founded.

1910: Mary Help of Christians Abbey Nullius established at Belmont.

1924: Raleigh diocese established.

North Dakota

1742: Pierre and Francois Verendrye, accompanied by Jesuit Father Coquart, explored territory.

1818: Canadian priests ministered to Catholics in area.

1839: Jesuit Father De Smet made first of five trips among Mandan and Gros Ventre Indians.

1848: Father George Belcourt, first American resident priest in territory, reestablished Pembena Mission.

1874: Grey Nuns invited to conduct a school at Fort Totten.

1889: Fargo diocese established.

1893: Benedictines founded St. Gall Monastery at Devil's Lake. (It became an abbey in 1903.)

1909: Bismarck diocese established.

1959: Archbishop Aloysius J. Muench, bishop of Fargo, made cardinal by Pope John XXIII.

Ohio

1749: Jesuits in expedition of Celeron de Bienville preached to Indians.

First religious services were held within present limits of Ohio. Jesuits Joseph de Bonnecamp and Peter Potier celebrated Mass at mouth of Little Miami River and in vicinity of Sandusky Bay, respectively.

1751: First Catholic settlement founded among Huron Indians near Sandusky by Father de la Richardie.

1790: Benedictine Pierre Didier ministered to French immigrants.

1812: Bishop Flaget of Bardstown visited and baptized Catholics of Lancaster and Somerset Counties.

1818: Dominican Father Fenwick built St. Joseph's Church and established first Dominican convent in Ohio.

1821: Cincinnati diocese established.

1831: Xavier University founded.

1843: Seven members of Congregation of Most Precious Blood arrived in Cincinnati from France.

1845: Cornerstone laid for St. Peter's Cathedral, Cincinnati; this was first cathedral west of Alleghenies.

1847: Cleveland diocese established.

1850: Cincinnati made archdiocese.

Marianists opened St. Mary's Institute, now University of Dayton.

1865: Sisters of Charity opened hospital in Cleveland, first institution of its kind in city.

1868: Columbus diocese established.

1871: Ursuline College for women opened at Cleveland.

1910: Toledo diocese established.

1935: Archbishop John T. McNicholas, O.P., founded the Institutum Divi Thomae in Cincinnati for fundamental research in natural sciences.

1943: Youngstown diocese established.

1944: Steubenville diocese established.

1969: Byzantine Rite Eparchy of Parma established.

Oklahoma

1540: De Soto expedition, accompanied by chaplains, explored territory.

1541: Coronado expedition, accompanied by Franciscan Juan de Padilla, explored state.

1630: Spanish Franciscan Juan de Salas labored among Indians.

1700: Scattered Catholic families were visited by priests from Kansas and Arkansas.

1874: First Catholic church built by Father Smyth at Atoka.

1876: Prefecture Apostolic of Indian Territory established with Benedictine Isidore Robot as its head.

1886: First Catholic day school for Choctaw and white children opened by Sisters of Mercy at Kribs.

1891: Vicariate Apostolic of Oklahoma and Indian Territory established.

1905: Oklahoma diocese established; title changed to Oklahoma City and Tulsa, 1930.

1917: Benedictine Heights College for women founded.

Carmelite Sisters of St. Theresa of the Infant Jesus were founded at Oklahoma City.

1972: Oklahoma City made archdiocese.

Tulsa diocese established.

Oregon

1603: Vizcaino explored northern Oregon coast.

1774: Franciscan missionaries accompanied Juan Perez on his expedition to coast, and Heceta a year later.

1811: Catholic Canadian trappers and traders with John J. Astor expedition founded first American settlement — Astoria.

1834: Indian missions in Northwest entrusted to Jesuits by Holy See.

1838: Abbe Blanchet appointed vicar general to Bishop of Quebec with jurisdiction over area which included Oregon Territory.

1839: First Mass celebrated at present site of St. Paul.

1843: Oregon vicariate apostolic established.

St. Joseph's College for boys opened.

1844: Jesuit Pierre de Smet established Mission of St. Francis Xavier near St. Paul.

Sisters of Notre Dame de Namur, first to enter Oregon, opened an academy for girls.

1846: Vicariate made an ecclesiastical province with Bishop Blanchet as first Archbishop of Oregon City (now Portland).

Walla Walla diocese established; suppressed in 1853.

1847: First priest was ordained in Oregon.

1848: First Provincial Council of Oregon.

1857: Death of Dr. John McLoughlin, "Father of Oregon."

1865: Rev. H. H. Spalding, a Protestant missionary, published the Whitman Myth to hinder work of Catholic missionaries.

1874: Catholic Indian Mission Bureau established.

1875: St. Vincent's Hospital, first in state, opened at Portland.

1903: Baker diocese established.

1922: Anti-private school bill sponsored by Scottish Rite Masons was passed by popular vote, 115,506 to 103,685.

1925: US Supreme Court declared Oregon anti-private school bill unconstitutional.

1953: First Trappist monastery on West Coast established in Willamette Valley north of Lafayette.

Pennsylvania

1673: Priests from Maryland ministered to Catholics in the Colony.

1682: Religious toleration was extended to members of all faiths.

1720: Jesuit Joseph Greaton became first resident missionary of Philadelphia.

1734: St. Joseph's Church, first Catholic church in Philadelphia, was opened.

1741: Jesuit Fathers Schneider and Wappeler ministered to German immigrants.

1782: St. Mary's Parochial School opened at Philadelphia.

1788: Holy Trinity Church, Philadelphia, was incorporated; first exclusively national church organized in US.

1797: Augustinian Matthew Carr founded St. Augustine parish, Philadelphia.

1799: Prince Demetrius Gallitzin (Father Augustine Smith) built church in western Pennsylvania, at Loretto.

1808: Philadelphia diocese established.

1814: St. Joseph's Orphanage was opened at Philadelphia; first Catholic institution for children in US.

1842: University of Villanova founded by Augustinians.

1843: Pittsburgh diocese established.

1844: Thirteen persons killed, two churches and a school burned in Know-Nothing jiots at Philadelphia.

1846: First Benedictine Abbey in New World founded near Latrobe by Father Boniface Wimmer.

1853: Erie diocese established.

1868: Scranton and Harrisburg dioceses established.

1871: Chestnut Hill College, first for women in state, founded.

1875: Philadelphia made archdiocese.

1901: Altoona-Johnstown diocese established.

1913: Byzantine Rite Apostolic Exarchate of Philadelphia established; became metropolitan see, 1958.

1921: Archbishop Dennis Dougherty made cardinal by Pope Benedict XV.

1924: Byzantine Rite Apostolic Exarchate of Pittsburgh established; made an eparchy in 1963; raised to metropolitan status and transferred to Munhall, 1969.

1951: Greensburg diocese established.

1958: Archbishop John O'Hara, C.S.C., of Philadelphia made cardinal by Pope John.

1961: Allentown diocese established.

1967: Archbishop John J. Krol of Philadelphia made cardinal by Pope Paul VI.

1969: Bishop John J. Wright of Pittsburgh made cardinal by Pope Paul VI and transferred to Curia post.

Rhode Island

1663: Colonial Charter granted freedom of conscience.

1719: Laws denied Catholics the right to hold public office.

1829: St. Mary's Church, Pawtucket, was first Catholic church in state.

1837: Parochial schools inaugurated in state.

First Catholic church in Providence was built.

1851: Sisters of Mercy began work in Rhode Island.

1872: Providence diocese established.

1900: Trappists took up residence in state.

1917: Providence College founded.

South Carolina

1569: Jesuit Juan Rogel was the first resident priest in the territory.

1573: First Franciscans arrived in southeastern section.

1606: Bishop Altamirano conducted visitation of area.

1655: Franciscans had two missions among Indians; later destroyed by English.

1697: Religious liberty granted to all except "papists."

1790: Catholics given right to vote.

1820: Charleston diocese established.

1822: Bishop England founded *U.S. Catholic Miscellany,* first Catholic paper of a strictly religious nature in US.

1830: Sisters of Our Lady of Mercy, first in state, took up residence at Charleston.

1847: Cornerstone of Cathedral of St. John the Baptist, Charleston, was laid.

1861: Cathedral and many institutions destroyed in Charleston fire.

South Dakota

1842: Father Augustine Ravoux began ministrations to French and Indians at Fort Pierre, Vermilion and Prairie du Chien; printed devotional book in Sioux language the following year.

1867: Parish organized among the French at Jefferson.

1878: Benedictines opened school for Sioux children at Fort Yates.

1889: Sioux Falls diocese established.

1902: Lead diocese established; transferred to Rapid City, 1930.

1950: Mount Marty College for women founded.

1952: Blue Cloud Abbey, first Benedictine foundation in state, was dedicated.

Tennessee

1541: Cross planted on shore of Mississippi by De Soto; accompanying the expedition were Fathers John de Gallegos and Louis De Soto.

1682: Franciscan Fathers Membre and Douay accompanied La Salle to present site of Memphis; may have offered the first Masses in the territory.

1800: Catholics were served by priests from Bardstown, Ky.

1822: Non-Catholics assisted in building church in Nashville.

1837: Nashville diocese established.

1843: Sisters of Charity opened a school for girls in Nashville.

1921: Sisters of St. Dominic opened Siena College for women at Memphis.

1940: Christian Brothers College founded at Memphis.

1970: Memphis diocese established.

Texas

1541: Missionaries with De Soto and Coronado entered territory.

1553: Dominicans Diego de la Cruz, Hernando Mendez, Juan Ferrer, Brother Juan de Mina killed by Indians.

1675: Bosque-Larios missionary expedition entered region; Father Juan Larios offered first recorded Mass.

1689: Four Franciscans founded first mission, San Francisco de los Tejas.

1703: Mission San Francisco de Solano founded on Rio Grande.

1717: Franciscan Antonio Margil founded six missions in northeast.

1721: Franciscan Brother Jose Pita killed by Indians at Carnezeria.

1728: Site of San Antonio settled.

1738: Construction of San Fernando Cathedral at San Antonio.

1744: Mission of San Francisco de Solano rebuilt as the Alamo.

1750: Franciscan Francisco Xavier was killed by Indians; so were Jose Ganzabal in

1752, and Alonzo Ferrares and Jose San Esteban in 1758.

1793: Mexico secularized missions.

1825: Government of Texas secularized all Indian missions.

1830: Irish priests ministered to settlements of Refugio and San Patricio.

1841: Vicariate of Texas established.

1847: Ursuline Sisters established their first academy in territory at Galveston. Galveston diocese established.

1852: Oblate Fathers and Franciscans arrived in Galveston to care for new influx of German Catholics. St. Mary's College founded at San Antonio.

1854: Know-Nothing Party began to stir up hatred against Catholics.

1858: Texas Legislature passed law entitling all schools granting free scholarships and meeting state requirements to share in school fund.

1874: San Antonio diocese established.

1881: St. Edward's College founded: became first chartered college in state in 1889. Sisters of Charity founded Incarnate Word College at San Antonio.

1890: Dallas diocese established; changed to Dallas-Ft. Worth, 1953; made two separate dioceses, 1969.

1912: Corpus Christi diocese established.

1914: El Paso diocese established.

1926: San Antonio made archdiocese. Amarillo diocese established.

1947: Austin diocese established.

1961: San Angelo diocese established.

1965: Brownsville diocese established.

1966: Beaumont diocese established.

Utah

1776: Franciscans Silvestre de Escalante and Atanasio Dominguez reached Utah (Salt) Lake; first white men known to enter the territory.

1858: Jesuit Father De Smet accompanied General Harney as chaplain on expedition sent to settle troubles between Mormons and US Government.

1866: On June 29 Father Edward Kelly offered first Mass in Salt Lake City in Mormon Assembly Hall.

1886: Utah vicariate apostolic established.

1891: Salt Lake City diocese established.

1926: College of St. Mary-of-the-Wasatch for women was founded.

Vermont

1609: Champlain expedition passed through territory.

1666: Captain La Motte built fort and shrine of St. Anne on Isle La Motte; Sulpician Father Dollier de Casson celebrated first Mass.

1668: Bishop Laval of Quebec administered confirmation in region; this was the first area in northeastern US to receive an episcopal visit.

1710: Jesuits ministered to Indians near Lake Champlain.

1793: Discriminatory measures against Catholics were repealed.

1830: Father Jeremiah O'Callaghan became first resident priest in state.

1853: Burlington diocese established.

1854: Sisters of Charity arrived to conduct St. Joseph's Orphanage at Burlington.

1904: St. Michael's College founded.

1951: First Carthusian foundation in America established at Whitingham.

Virginia

1526: Dominican Antonio de Montesinos offered first Mass on Virginia soil.

1561: Dominicans visited the coast.

1571: Father John Baptist de Segura and seven Jesuit companions killed by Indians.

1642: Priests outlawed and Catholics denied right to vote.

1689: Capuchin Christopher Plunket was captured and exiled to a coastal island where he died in 1697.

1776: Religious freedom granted.

1791: Father Jean Dubois arrived at Richmond with letters from Lafayette. The House of Delegates was placed at his disposal for celebration of Mass.

1796: A church was built at Alexandria.

1820: Richmond diocese established.

1822: Trusteeism created serious problems in diocese; Bishop Kelly resigned the see.

1848: Sisters of Charity opened an orphan asylum at Norfolk.

1866: School Sisters of Notre Dame and Sisters of Charity opened academies for girls at Richmond.

1974: Arlington diocese established.

Washington

1775: Spaniards explored the region.

1838: Fathers Blanchet and Demers, "Apostles of the Northwest," were sent to territory by archbishop of Quebec.

1840: Log church for Indians was built on Whidby Island, Puget Sound.

1843: Vicariate Apostolic of Oregon, including Washington, was established.

1844: Mission of St. Paul founded at Colville.

Six Sisters of Notre Dame de Namur began work in area.

1850: Nesqually diocese established; transferred to Seattle, 1907.

1856: Sisters of Charity established first permanent school and hospital in Northwest at Fort Vancouver.

1887: Gonzaga University founded.

1913: Spokane diocese established.

1951: Seattle made archdiocese. Yakima diocese established.

West Virginia

1749: Father Joseph de Bonnecamps, accompanying the Bienville expedition, may have offered first Mass in the territory.

1821: First Catholic church in Wheeling.

1838: Sisters of Charity founded school at Martinsburg.

1848: Visitation Nuns established academy for girls at Mt. de Chantal.

1850: Wheeling diocese established; named changed to Wheeling-Charleston, 1974.

Wheeling Hospital incorporated, the oldest Catholic charitable institution in territory.

1955: Wheeling College established.

Wisconsin

1661: Jesuit Rene Menard, first known missionary in the territory, was killed or lost in the Black River district.

1665: Jesuit Claude Allouez founded Mission of the Holy Ghost at La Pointe Chegoimegon, now Bayfield; was the first permanent mission in region.

1673: Father Marquette and Louis Joliet traveled from Green Bay down the Wisconsin and Mississippi rivers.

1762: Suppression of Jesuits in French Colonies closed many missions for 30 years.

1843: Milwaukee diocese established.

1853: St. John's Cathedral, Milwaukee, was built.

1864: Marquette University established.

1868: Green Bay and La Crosse dioceses established.

1875: Milwaukee made archdiocese.

1905: Superior diocese established.

1946: Madison diocese established.

Wyoming

1840: Jesuit Pierre de Smet offered first Mass near Green River.

1851: Father De Smet held peace conference with Indians near Fort Laramie.

1867: Father William Kelly, first resident priest, arrived in Cheyenne and built first church a year later.

1873: Father Eugene Cusson became first resident pastor in Laramie.

1875: Sisters of Charity of Leavenworth opened school and orphanage at Laramie.

1884: Jesuits took over pastoral care of Shoshone and Arapaho Indians.

1887: Cheyenne diocese established.

1949: Weston Memorial Hospital opened near Newcastle.

Catholics in Presidents' Cabinets

(For biographical data on some of these entries, see Index.)

Roger B. Taney, Attorney General 1831-33, Secretary of Treasury 1833-34; app. by Andrew Jackson.

James Campbell, Postmaster General 1853-57; app. by Franklin Pierce.

John B. Floyd, Secretary of War 1857-61; app. by James Buchanan.

Joseph McKenna, Attorney General 1897-98; app. by William McKinley.

Robert J. Wynne, Postmaster General 1904-05; app. by Theodore Roosevelt.

Charles Bonaparte, Secretary of Navy 1905-06, Attorney General 1906-09; app. by Theodore Roosevelt.

James A. Farley, Postmaster General 1933-40; app. by Franklin D. Roosevelt.

Frank Murphy, Attorney General 1939-40; app. by Franklin D. Roosevelt.

Frank C. Walker, Postmaster General 1940-45; app. by Franklin D. Roosevelt.

Robert E. Hannegan, Postmaster General 1945-47; app. by Harry S. Truman.

J. Howard McGrath, Attorney General 1949-52; app. by Harry S. Truman.

Maurice J. Tobin, Secretary of Labor; 1949-53; app. by Harry S. Truman.

James P. McGranery, Attorney General 1952-53; app. by Harry S. Truman.

Martin P. Durkin, Secretary of Labor 1953; app. by Dwight D. Eisenhower.

James P. Mitchell, Secretary of Labor 1953-61; app. by Dwight D. Eisenhower.

Robert F. Kennedy, Attorney General 1961-65; app. by John F. Kennedy, reapp. by Lyndon B. Johnson.

Anthony Celebrezze, Secretary of Health, Education and Welfare 1962-65; app. by John F. Kennedy, reapp. by Lyndon B. Johnson.

John S. Gronouski, Postmaster General 1963-65; app. by John F. Kennedy, reapp. by Lyndon B. Johnson.

John T. Connor, Secretary of Commerce 1965-67; app. by Lyndon B. Johnson.

Lawrence O'Brien, Postmaster General 1965-68; app. by Lyndon B. Johnson.

Walter J. Hickel, Secretary of Interior 1969-71; app. by Richard M. Nixon.

John A. Volpe, Secretary of Transportation 1969-72; app. by Richard M. Nixon.

Maurice H. Stans, Secretary of Commerce, 1969-72; app. by Richard M. Nixon.

Peter J. Brennan, Secretary of Labor, 1973-75; app. by Richard M. Nixon, reapp. by Gerald R. Ford.

Men who became Catholics after leaving Cabinet posts: Thomas Ewing, Secretary of Treasury under William A. Harrison, and Secretary of Interior under Zachary Taylor; Luke E. Wright, Secretary of War under Theodore Roosevelt; Albert B. Fall, Secretary of Interior under Warren G. Harding.

Catholic Justices
of the Supreme Court

(For biographical data on some of these entries, see Index.)

Roger B. Taney, Chief Justice 1836-64; app. by Andrew Jackson.

Edward D. White, Associate Justice 1894-1910, app. by Grover Cleveland; Chief Justice 1910-21, app. by William H. Taft.

Joseph McKenna, Associate Justice 1898-1925; app. by William McKinley.

Pierce Butler, Associate Jusice 1923-39; app. by Warren G. Harding.

Frank Murphy, Associate Justice 1940-49; app. by Franklin D. Roosevelt.

William Brennan, Associate Justice 1956-; app. by Dwight D. Eisenhower.

Sherman Minton, Associate Justice from 1949 to 1956, became a Catholic several years before his death in 1965.

Catholics Represented in
National Statuary Hall

(For biographies, see Index.)

Statues of 12 Catholics deemed worthy of national commemoration by the donating states are among 91 enshrined in National Statuary Hall and other places in the US Capitol. The Hall, formerly the chamber of the House of Representatives, was erected by Act of Congress July 2, 1864.

Donating states, names and years of placement are listed. An asterisk indicates placement of a statue in the Hall itself.

Arizona: Rev. Eusebio Kino, S. J., missionary, 1965.

California: Rev. Junipero Serra, O. F. M.* missionary, 1931.

Hawaii: Father Damien, missionary, 1969.

Illinois: Gen. James Shields, statesman, 1893.

Louisiana: Edward D. White, Justice of the US Supreme Court (1894-1921), 1955.

Maryland: Charles Carroll,* statesman, 1901.

Nevada: Patrick A. McCarran,* statesman, 1960.

New Mexico: Dennis Chavez, statesman, 1966. (Archbishop Jean B. Lamy, pioneer prelate of Santa Fe, was nominated for Hall honor in 1951.)

North Dakota: John Burke,* US treasurer, 1963.

Oregon: Dr. John McLoughlin, pioneer, 1953.

West Virginia: John E. Kenna, statesman, 1901.

Wisconsin: Rev. Jacques Marquette, S. J., missionary, explorer, 1895.

Daniel Carroll Honored

Daniel Carroll, a signer of the U.S. Constitution and brother of John Carroll, the first Catholic bishop in the United States, was honored Oct. 11, 1975, in memorial and dedication ceremonies at the 201-year-old St. John's Parish in Silver Spring, Md. Carroll, who died in 1796, was a delegate to the Continental Congress and the Constitutional Convention, and one of three commissioners appointed to select the site of and to acquire land in the District of Columbia.

CHURCH-STATE DECISIONS OF THE SUPREME COURT

(Among sources of this listing of US Supreme Court decisions was *The Supreme Court on Church and State,* Joseph Tussman, editor; Oxford University Press, New York, 1962.)

Terrett v. Taylor, 9 Cranch 43 (1815): The Court declared unconstitutional an act of the Virginia Legislature which denied property rights to Protestant Episcopal churches in the state. Religious corporations, like other corporations, have rights to their property.

Vidal v. Girard's Executors, 2 Howard 205 (1844): The Court upheld the will of Stephen Girard, which barred ministers of any religion from serving as faculty members or visitors in a school he established for orphans.

Watson v. Jones, 13 Wallace 679 (1872): The Court declared that a member of a religious organization may not appeal to secular courts against a decision made by a church tribunal within the area of its competence.

Reynolds v. United States, 98 US 145 (1879): The Court declared, in reference to the Mormon practice of polygamy, that one may not knowingly violate by external practices the law of the land on religious grounds, since such conduct would make the professed doctrines of belief superior to federal or state law. One must keep the external practice of religion within the framework of laws enacted for the common welfare. This was the first decision rendered on the Free Exercise Clause of the First Amendment.

Davis v. Beason, 133 US 333 (1890): The Court upheld the denial of the right of Mormons to vote in Idaho if they refused to sign a registration oath stating that they were not bigamists or polygamists and would not encourage or preach bigamy or polygamy.

Church of Latter-Day Saints v. United States, 136 US 1 (1890): The Court upheld an Act of Congress which annulled the charter of the Corporation of the Church of Jesus Christ of Latter-Day Saints, and declared "forfeited to the government all its real estate except a small portion used exclusively for public worship" (Tussman, *op. cit.,* p. 33). The Court held that the Corporation continually used its power to violate US laws prohibiting polygamy.

Church of the Holy Trinity v. United States, 143 US 226 (1892): The Court declared it is not "a misdemeanor for a church of this country to contract for the services of a Christian minister residing in another nation" (from the text of the decision).

Bradfield v. Roberts, 175 US 291 (1899): The Court denied that an appropriation of government funds for an institution (Providence Hospital, Washington, D.C.) run by Roman Catholic sisters violated the No Establishment Clause of the First Amendment.

Pierce v. Society of Sisters, 268 US 510 (1925): The Court denied that a state can require children to attend public schools only. The Court held that the liberty of the Constitution forbids standardization by such compulsion, and that the parochial schools involved had claims to protection under the Fourteenth Amendment.

Cochran v. Board of Education, 281 US 370 (1930): The Court upheld a Louisiana statute providing textbooks at public expense for children attending public or parochial schools. The Court held that the children and state were beneficiaries of the appropriations, with incidental secondary benefit going to the schools.

United States v. MacIntosh, 283 US 605 (1931): The Court denied that anyone can place allegiance to the will of God above his allegiance to the government, since such a person could make his own interpretation of God's will the decisive test as to whether he would or would not obey the nation's law. The Court stated that the nation, which has a duty to survive, can require citizens to bear arms in its defense.

Hamilton v. Regents of University of California, 293 US 245 (1934): The Court rejected a "claim to exemption from R.O.T.C. based on conscientious objection to war" (Tussman *op. cit.,* p. 64). If such an exemption were allowed, the liberties of the objector might be extended to the point of refusal to pay taxes in furtherance of a war or any other end condemned by his conscience. This would be an undue exaltation of the right of private judgment.

Cantwell v. Connecticut, 310 US 296 (1940): The Court declared that the right to religious freedom is violated by a statute requiring a person to secure a permit from a government official before soliciting money for alleged religious purposes from someone not of his or her sect. Such a practice would constitute censorship of religion.

Minersville School District v. Gobitis, 310 US 586 (1940): The Court upheld the right of a state to require the salute to the national flag from school children, even from those who refused to do so for sincere religious reasons.

Jones v. City of Opelika, 316 US 584 (1942): The court upheld licensing ordinances in three municipalities against "the claim by Jehovah's Witnesses that they interfere with the free exercise of religion" (Tussman, *op. cit.,* p. 91).

Murdock v. Commonwealth of Pennsylvania, 319 US 105 (1943): In a reversal of the decision handed down in Jones v. City of Opelika, the Court declared the licensing unconstitutional since it violated a freedom guaranteed under the First Amendment. The selling of religious literature by traveling preachers does not make evangelism the equivalent of a commercial enterprise taxable by the State.

Jones v. City of Opelika, 316 US 584 105 (1943): The Court declared that the Constitution denies a city the right to control the expression of men's minds and denies also the right of men to win others to their views through a program of taxes levied against such activity.

Douglas v. City of Jeannette, 319 US 157 (1943): The Court again upheld the proselytizing rights of Jehovah's Witnesses, ruling unconstitutional the action of any public authority in regulating or taxing such activity.

West Virginia State Board of Education v. Barnette, 319 US 624 (1943): In a reversal of the decision handed down in Minersville School District v. Gobitis, the Court declared unconstitutional a state statute requiring of all children a salute to the national flag and a pledge of allegiance which a child may consider contrary to sincere religious beliefs.

Prince v. Commonwealth of Massachusetts, 321 US 158 (1944): The Court upheld a "child-labor regulation against the claim that it prevents a child from performing her religious duty" (Tussman, *op. cit.,* p. 170). The Court asserted a general principle that the state has a wide range of power for limiting parental freedom and authority in things affecting the child's welfare.

United States v. Ballard, 322 US 78 (1944): The Court upheld the general principle that "the truth of religious claims is not for secular authority to determine" (Tussman, *op. cit.,* p. 181).

In Re Summers, 325 US 561 (1945): The Court upheld "the denial, to an otherwise qualified applicant, of admission to the bar on the basis of the applicant's religiously motivated 'conscientious scruples against participation in war' " (Tussman, *op. cit.,* p. 192). The petitioner was barred because he could not in good faith take the prescribed oath to support the Constitution of Illinois which required service in the state militia in times of necessity.

Girouard v. United States, 328 US 61 (1946): In a ruling related to that handed down in United States v. MacIntosh, the Court affirmed the opinion that the refusal of an alien to bear arms does not deny him citizenship.

Everson v. Board of Education, 330 US 1 (1947): The Court upheld the constitutionality of a New Jersey statute authorizing free school bus transportation for parochial as well as public school students. The Court expressed the opinion that the benefits of public welfare legislation, included under such bus transportation, do not run contrary to the concept of separation of Church and State.

McCollum v. Board of Education, 333 US 203 (1948): The Court declared unconstitutional a program for releasing children, with parental consent, from public school classes so they could receive religious instruction on public school premises from representatives of their own faiths.

Zorach v. Clauson, 343 US 306 (1952): The Court upheld the constitutionality of a New York statute permitting, on a voluntary basis, the release during school time of students from public school classes for religious instruction given off public school premises.

Kedroff v. St. Nicholas Cathedral, 344 US 94 (1952): The Court ruled against an action of New York in taking "control of St. Nicholas Cathedral away from the Moscow hierarchy" (Tussman, *op. cit.,* p. 292), on the ground that the controversy involved a matter of church government.

Fowler v. Rhode Island, 345 US 67 (1953): The Court upheld the right of a Jehovah's Witness to preach in a public park against a city ordinance which forbade such preaching. The Court held that the ordinance, as construed and applied, discriminated against the Witness and therefore amounted to preferment by the state of other religious groups.

Torcaso v. Watkins, 367 US 488 (1961): The Court declared unconstitutional a Maryland requirement that one must make a declaration of belief in the existence of God as part of the oath of office for notaries public.

McGowan v. Maryland, 81 Sp Ct 1101; **Two Guys from Harrison v. McGinley,** 81 Sp Ct 1135; **Gallagher v. Crown Kosher Super Market,** 81 Sp Ct 1128; **Braunfield v. Brown,** 81 Sp Ct 1144 (1961): The Court ruled that Sunday closing laws do not violate the No Establishment of Religion Clause of the First Amendment, even though the laws were religious in their inception and still have some religious overtones. The Court held that, "as presently written and administered, most of them, at least, are of a secular rather than of a religious character, and that presently they bear no relationship to establishment of religion as those words are used in the Constitution of the United States."

Engel v. Vitale, 370 US 42 (1962): The Court declared that the voluntary recitation in public schools of a prayer composed by the New York State Board of Regents is unconstitutional on the ground that it violates the No Establishment of Religion Clause of the First Amendment.

Abington Township School District v. Schempp and **Murray v. Curlett,** 83 Sp Ct 1560 (1963): The Court ruled that Bible reading and recitation of the Lord's Prayer in public schools, with voluntary participation by students, are unconstitutional on the ground that they violate the No Establishment of Religion Clause of the First Amendment.

Sherbert v. Verner, 83 A Sp Ct 1790 (1963): The Court ruled that individuals of any religious faith may not, because of their faith or lack of it, be deprived of the benefits of public welfare legislation.

Chamberlin v. Dade County, 1 83 Sp Ct 1864 (1964): The Court reversed a decision of the Florida Supreme Court concerning the constitutionality of prayer and devotional Bible reading in public schools during the school day, as sanctioned by a state statute which specifically related the practices to a sound public purpose.

Board of Education v. Allen, No. 660 (1968): The Court declared constitutional the New York school book loan law which requires local school boards to purchase books with state funds and lend them to parochial and private school students.

Flast v. Cohen, No. 416 (1968): The Court held that individual taxpayers can bring suits to challenge federal expenditures on grounds that they violate the principle of separation of Church and State even though generally taxpayers cannot challenge federal expenditures in court.

Walz v. Tax Commission of New York (1970): The Court upheld the constitutionality of a New York statute exempting church-owned property from taxation.

Earle v. DiCenso, Robinson v. DiCenso, Lemon v. Kurtzman, Tilton v. Richardson (1971): In Earle v. DiCenso and Robinson v. DiCenso, the Court ruled unconstitutional a 1969 Rhode Island statute which provided salary supplements to teachers of secular subjects in parochial schools; in Lemon v. Kurtzman, the Court ruled unconstitutional a 1968 Pennsylvania statute which authorized the state to purchase services for the teaching of secular subjects in nonpublic schools. The principal argument against constitutionality in these cases was that the statutes and programs at issue entailed excessive entanglement of government with religion. In Tilton v. Richardson, the Court held that this argument did not apply to a prohibitive degree with respect to federal grants, under the Higher Education Facilities Act of 1963, for the construction of facilities for nonreligious purposes by four church-related institutions of higher learning, three of which were Catholic, in Connecticut.

Amish Decision (1972): In a case appealed on behalf of Yoder, Miller and Yutzy, the Court ruled that Amish parents were exempt from a Wisconsin statute requiring them to send their children to school until the age of 16. The Court said in its decision that secondary schooling exposed Amish children to attitudes, goals and values contrary to their beliefs, and substantially hindered "the religious development of the Amish child and his integration into the way of life of the Amish faith-community at the crucial adolescent state of development."

Committee for Public Education and Religious Liberty, et al., v. Nyquist, et al., No. 72-694 (1973): The Court ruled that provisions of a 1972 New York statute were unconstitutional on the grounds that they were violative of the No Establishment Clause of the First Amendment and had the "impermissible effect" of advancing the sectarian activities of church-affiliated schools. The programs ruled unconstitutional concerned: (1) maintenance and repair grants, for facilities and equipment, to ensure the health, welfare and safety of students in nonpublic, non-profit elementary and secondary schools serving a high concentration of students from low income families; (2) tuition reimbursement ($50 per grade school child, $100 per high school student) for parents (with income less than $5,000) of children attending nonpublic elementary or secondary schools; tax deduction from adjusted gross income for parents failing to qualify under the above reimbursement plan, for each child attending a nonpublic school.

Sloan, Treasurer of Pennsylvania, et al., v. Lemon, et al., No. 72-459 (1973): The Court ruled unconstituional a Pennsylvania Parent Reimbursement Act for Nonpublic Education which provided funds to reimburse parents (to a maximum of $150) for a portion of tuition expenses incurred in sending their children to nonpublic schools. The Court held that there was no significant difference between this and the New York tuition reimbursement program (above), and declared that the Equal Protection Clause of the Fourteenth Amendment cannot be relied upon to sustain a program held to be violative of the No Establishment Clause.

Levitt, et al., v. Committee for Public Education and Religious Liberty, et al., No. 72-269 (1973): The Court ruled unconstitutional the Mandated Services Act of 1970 under which New York provided $28 million ($27 per pupil from first to seventh grade, $45 per pupil from seventh to 12th grade) to reimburse nonpublic schools for testing, recording and reporting services required by the state. The Court declared that the act provided "impermissible aid" to religion in contravention of the No Establishment Clause.

In related decisions handed down June 25, 1973, the Court: (1) affirmed a lower court decision against the constitutionality of an Ohio tax credit law benefiting parents with children in nonpublic schools; (2) reinstated an injunction against a parent reimbursement program in New Jersey; (3) affirmed South Carolina's right to grant construction loans to church-affiliated colleges, and dismissed an appeal contesting its right to provide loans to students attending church-affiliated colleges (**Hunt v. McNair, Durham v. McLeod**).

Wheeler v. Barrera (1974): The Court ruled that nonpublic school students in Missouri must share in federal funds for educationally deprived students on a comparable basis with public school students under Title I of the Elementary and Secondary Education Act of 1965.

Norwood v. Harrison (93 S. Ct. 2804): The Court ruled that public assistance which avoids the prohibitions of the "effect" and "entanglement" tests (and which therefore does not substantially promote the religious mission of sectarian schools) may be confined to the secular functions of such schools.

Wiest v. Mt. Lebanon School District (1974): The Court upheld a lower court ruling that invocation and benediction prayers at public high school commencement ceremonies do not violate the principle of separation of Church and state.

Meek v. Pittenger (1975): The Court ruled unconstitutional portions of a Pennsylvania law providing auxiliary services for students of nonpublic schools; at the same time, it ruled in favor of provisions of the law permitting textbook loans to students of such schools. In denying the constitutionality of auxiliary services, the Court held that they had the "primary effect of establishing religion" and involved "excessive entanglement" of Church and state officials with respect to supervision; objection was also made against providing such services only on the premises of non-public schools and only at the request of such schools.

THE WALL OF SEPARATION

Thomas Jefferson, in a letter written to the Danbury (Conn.) Baptist Association Jan. 1, 1802, coined the metaphor, "a wall of separation between Church and State," to express a theory concerning interpretation of the religion clauses of the First Amendment: "Congress shall make no law respecting an establishment of religion or prohibiting the free exercise thereof."

The metaphor was cited for the first time in judicial proceedings in 1879, in the opinion by Chief Justice Waite in Reynolds v. United States. It did not, however, figure substantially in the decision.

Accepted as Rule

In 1947 the wall of separation gained acceptance as a constitutional rule, in the decision handed down in Everson v. Board of Education. Associate Justice Black, in describing the principles involved in the No Establishment Clause, wrote:

"Neither a state nor the Federal Government can set up a church. Neither can pass laws which aid one religion, aid all religions, or prefer one religion over another. Neither can force nor influence a person to go to or to remain away from church against his will or force him to profess a belief or disbelief in any religion. No person can be punished for entertaining or professing religious beliefs or disbeliefs, for church attendance or non-attendance. No tax in any amount, large or small, can be levied to support any religious

activities or institutions, whatever they may be called, or whatever form they may adopt to teach or practice religion. Neither a state nor the Federal Government can, openly or secretly, participate in the affairs of any religious organizations or groups and vice versa. In the words of Jefferson, the clause against establishment of religion by law was intended to erect 'a wall of separation between Church and State.' "

Mr. Black's associates agreed with his statement of principles, which were framed without reference to the Freedom of Exercise Clause. They disagreed, however, with respect to application of the principles, as the split decision in the case indicated. Five members of the Court held that the benefits of public welfare legislation — in this case, free bus transportation to school for parochial as well as public school students — did not run contrary to the concept of separation of Church and State embodied in the First Amendment.

Different Opinions

Inside and outside the legal profession, opinion is divided concerning the wall of separation and the balance of the religion clauses of the First Amendment.

The view of absolute separationists, carried to the extreme, would make government the adversary of religion. The bishops of the United States, following the McCollum decision in 1948, said that the wall metaphor had become for some persons the "shibboleth of doctrinaire secularism."

Proponents of governmental neutrality toward religion are of the opinion that such neutrality should not be so interpreted as to prohibit incidental aid to religious institutions providing secular services.

In the realm of practice, federal and state legislatures have enacted measures involving incidental benefits to religious bodies. Examples of such measures are the tax exemption of church property; provision of bus rides, book loans and lunch programs to students in church-related as well as public schools; military chaplaincies; loans to church-related hospitals; the financing of studies by military veterans at church-related colleges under GI bills of rights.

CHURCH TAX EXEMPTION

The exemption of church-owned property was ruled constitutional by the US Supreme Court May 4, 1970, in the case of Walz v. The Tax Commission of New York.

Suit in the case was brought by Frederick Walz, who purchased in June, 1967, a 22-by-29-foot plot of ground in Staten Island valued at $100 and taxable at $5.24 a year. Shortly after making the purchase, Walz instituted a suit in New York State, contending that the exemption of church property from taxation authorized by state law increased his own tax rate and forced him indirectly to support churches in violation of his constitutional right to freedom of religion under the First Amendment. Three New York courts dismissed the suit, which had been instituted by mail. The Supreme Court, judging that it had probable jurisdiction, then took the case.

In a 7-1 decision affecting Church-state relations in every state in the nation, the Court upheld the New York law under challenge.

For and Against

Chief Justice Warren E. Burger, who wrote the majority opinion, said that Congress from its earliest days had viewed the religion clauses of the Constitution as authorizing statutory real estate tax exemption to religious bodies. He declared: "Nothing in this national attitude toward religious tolerance and two centuries of uninterrupted freedom from taxation has given the remotest sign of leading to an established church or religion, and on the contrary it has operated affirmatively to help guarantee the free exercise of all forms of religious beliefs."

Justice William O. Douglas wrote in dissent that the involvement of government in religion as typified in tax exemption may seem inconsequential but: "It is, I fear, a long step down the establishment path. . . . Perhaps I have been misinformed. But, as I read the Constitution and the philosophy, I gathered that independence was the price of liberty."

Burger rejected Douglas' "establishment" fears. If tax exemption is the first step toward establishment, he said, "the second step has been long in coming."

The basic issue centered on the following question: Is there a contradiction between federal constitutional provisions against the establishment of religion, or the use of public funds for religious purposes, and state statutes exempting church property from taxation?

In the Walz' decision, the Supreme Court ruled that there is no contradiction.

Legal Background

The US Constitution makes no reference to tax exemption.

There was no discussion of the issue in the Constitutional Convention nor in debates on the Bill of Rights.

In the Colonial and post-Revolutionary years, some churches had established status and were state-supported. This state of affairs changed with enactment of the First Amendment, which laid down no-establishment as the federal norm. This norm was adopted by the states which, however, exempted churches from tax liabilities.

No establishment, no hindrance, was the early American view of Church-state relationships.

This view, reflected in custom law, was not generally formulated in statute law until the second half of the 19th century, although specific tax exemption was provided for churches in Maryland in 1798, in Virginia in 1800, and in North Carolina in 1806.

The first major challenge to church property exemption was initiated by the Liberal League in the 1870's. It reached the point that President Grant included the recommendation in a State of the Union address in 1875, stating that church property should bear its own proportion of taxes. The plea fell on deaf ears in Congress, but there was some support for the idea at state levels. The exemption, however, continued to survive various challenges.

At the present time, 36 state constitutions contain either mandatory or permissive provisions for exemption. Statutes provide for exemption in all other states.

There has been considerable litigation challenging this special exemption, but most of it focused on whether a particular property satisfied statutory requirements. Few cases before Walz focused on the strictly constitutional question, whether directly under the First Amendment or indirectly under the Fourteenth Amendment.

Objectors to the tax exempt status of churches feel that churches should share, through taxation, in the cost of the ordinary benefits of public services they enjoy, and/or that the amount of "aid" enjoyed through exemption should be proportionate to the amount of social good they do.

Unrelated Income

Taxation of the unrelated business income of churches is a different matter. In a joint statement on this subject issued in May, 1969, the US Catholic Conference and the National Council of Churches said they favored "elimination of the specific exemption of churches from taxation on income from regularly conducted commercial business activities which are unrelated to their exempt functions."

The two groups prefaced the statement with the observation:

"Under existing law many types of organizations are granted exemption from the income tax. Certain exempt organizations, including charitable, educational and some religious organizations, labor unions, business leagues, etc., are nevertheless subjected to tax upon their incomes from any unrelated business; and rents derived from debt-financed property (under leases for periods in excess of five years) are included in unrelated business taxable income.

"The tax upon unrelated business taxable income does not apply to churches, or conventions or associations of churches.

"Such exemption makes available to churches a potential advantage over taxpaying organizations engaged in commercial business activities."

The organizational structure of the Catholic Church in the United States consists of 32 provinces with as many archdioceses (metropolitan sees), 131 suffragan sees (130 dioceses, 1 prelacy), two jurisdictions immediately subject to the Holy See — the Eparchy of St. Maron in Detroit for the Maronites and the Abbacy of Mary Help of Christians (Belmont, N.C.) — 1 apostolic exarchate for the Melkites, and the Military Ordinariate. With the exception of the abbacy, each of these jurisdictions is under the direction of an archbishop or bishop, called an ordinary, who has apostolic responsibility and authority for the pastoral service of the people in his care.

The structure includes the territorial episcopal conference known as the National Conference of Catholic Bishops. In and through this body, which is strictly ecclesiastical and has defined juridical authority, the bishops exercise their collegiate pastorate over the Church in the entire country (see Index).

ECCLESIASTICAL PROVINCES

(Sources: *The Official Catholic Directory, 1975*, NC News Service.)

The 32 ecclesiastical provinces bear the names of archdioceses, i.e., of metropolitan sees.

Anchorage: Archdiocese of Anchorage and suffragan sees of Fairbanks, Juneau. Geographical area: Alaska.

Atlanta: Archdiocese of Atlanta (Ga.) and suffragan sees of Savannah (Ga.), Charlotte and Raleigh (N.C.), Charleston (S.C.). Geographical area: Georgia, North Carolina (except Belmont Abbacy), South Carolina.

Baltimore: Archdiocese of Baltimore (Md.) and suffragan sees of Wilmington (Del.), Arlington and Richmond (Va.), Wheeling-Charleston (W. Va.). Geographical area: Maryland (except five counties), Delaware, Virginia, West Virginia.

Boston: Archdiocese of Boston (Mass.) and suffragan sees of Fall River, Springfield and Worcester (Mass.), Portland (Me.), Manchester (N.H.), Burlington (Vt.). Geographical area: Massachusetts, Maine, New Hampshire, Vermont.

Chicago: Archdiocese of Chicago and suffragan sees of Belleville, Joliet, Peoria, Rockford, Springfield. Geographical area: Illinois.

Cincinnati: Archdiocese of Cincinnati and suffragan sees of Cleveland, Columbus, Steubenville, Toledo, Youngstown. Geographical area: Ohio.

Denver: Archdiocese of Denver (Colo.) and suffragan sees of Pueblo (Colo.), Cheyenne (Wyo.). Geographical area: Colorado, Wyoming.

Detroit: Archdiocese of Detroit and suffragan sees of Gaylord, Grand Rapids, Kalamazoo, Lansing, Marquette, Saginaw. Geographical area: Michigan.

Dubuque: Archdiocese of Dubuque and suffragan sees of Davenport, Des Moines, Sioux City. Geographical area: Iowa.

Hartford: Archdiocese of Hartford (Conn.) and suffragan sees of Bridgeport and Norwich (Conn.), Providence (R.I.). Geographical area: Connecticut, Rhode Island.

Indianapolis: Archdiocese of Indianapolis and suffragan sees of Evansville, Fort Wayne-South Bend, Gary, Lafayette. Geographical area: Indiana.

Kansas City (Kans.): Archdiocese of Kansas City and suffragan sees of Dodge City, Salina, Wichita. Geographical area: Kansas.

Los Angeles: Archdiocese of Los Angeles and suffragan sees of Fresno, Monterey, San Diego. Geographical area: Southern California.

Louisville: Archdiocese of Louisville (Ky.) and suffragan sees of Covington and Owensboro (Ky.), Memphis and Nashville (Tenn.). Geographical area: Kentucky, Tennessee.

Miami: Archdiocese of Miami and suffragan sees of Orlando, St. Augustine, St. Petersburg. Geographical area: Florida.

Milwaukee: Archdiocese of Milwaukee and suffragan sees of Green Bay, La Crosse, Madison, Superior. Geographical area: Wisconsin.

Munhall (Byzantine Rite): Metropolitan See of Munhall, Pa. and Eparchies of Passaic (N.J.), Parma (Ohio).

Newark: Archdiocese of Newark and suffragan sees of Camden, Paterson, Trenton. Geographical area: New Jersey.

New Orleans: Archdiocese of New Orleans (La.) and suffragan sees of Alexandria, Baton Rouge and Lafayette (La.), Birmingham and Mobile (Ala.), Natchez-Jackson (Miss.). Geographical area; Louisiana, Alabama, Mississippi.

New York: Archdiocese of New York and suffragan sees of Albany, Brooklyn, Buffalo, Ogdensburg, Rochester, Rockville Centre, Syracuse. Geographical area: New York.

Oklahoma City: Archdiocese of Oklahoma City (Okla.) and suffragan sees of Tulsa (Okla.) and Little Rock (Ark.). Geographical area: Oklahoma, Arkansas.

Omaha: Archdiocese of Omaha and suffragan sees of Grand Island, Lincoln. Geographical area: Nebraska.

Philadelphia: Archdiocese of Philadelphia and suffragan sees of Allentown, Altoona-Johnstown, Erie, Greensburg, Harrisburg, Pittsburgh, Scranton. Geographical area: Pennsylvania.

Philadelphia (Byzantine Rite): Metropolitan See of Philadelphia (Byzantine Rite) and

Eparchies of St. Nicholas of the Ukrainians in Chicago and Stamford, Conn. The jurisdiction extends to all Ukrainian Catholics in the U.S. from the ecclesiastical province of Galicia in the Ukraine.

Portland: Archdiocese of Portland (Ore.) and suffragan sees of Baker (Ore.), Boise (Ida.), Great Falls and Helena (Mont.). Geographical area: Oregon, Idaho, Montana.

St. Louis: Archdiocese of St. Louis and suffragan sees of Jefferson City, Kansas City-St. Joseph, Springfield-Cape Girardeau. Geographical area: Missouri.

St. Paul and Minneapolis: Archdiocese of St. Paul and Minneapolis (Minn.) and suffragan sees of Crookston, Duluth, New Ulm, St. Cloud and Winona (Minn.), Bismarck and Fargo (N.D.), Rapid City and Sioux Falls (S.D.). Geographical area: Minnesota, North Dakota, South Dakota.

San Antonio: Archdiocese of San Antonio (Tex.) and suffragan sees of Amarillo, Austin, Beaumont, Brownsville, Corpus Christi,

Dallas, Fort Worth, Galveston-Houston and San Angelo (Tex.). Geographical area: Texas (except the Diocese of El Paso).

San Francisco: Archdiocese of San Francisco (Calif.) and suffragan sees of Oakland, Sacramento, Santa Rosa and Stockton (Calif.), Agaña (Guam), Honolulu (Hawaii), Reno (Nev.), Salt Lake City (Utah). Geographical area: Northern California, Nevada, Utah, Hawaii, Guam.

Santa Fe: Archdiocese of Santa Fe (N.M.) and suffragan sees of Gallup (N.M.), Phoenix and Tucson (Ariz.), El Paso (Tex.). Geographical area: New Mexico, Arizona, Diocese of El Paso (Tex.).

Seattle: Archdiocese of Seattle and suffragan sees of Spokane, Yakima. Geographical area: Washington.

Washington: Archdiocese of Washington, D.C., and suffragan see of Prelacy of Virgin Islands. Geographical area: District of Columbia, five counties of Maryland, Virgin Islands.

ARCHDIOCESES, DIOCESES, ARCHBISHOPS, BISHOPS

(Sources: *The Official Catholic Directory, 1975:* NC News Service. As of July 15, 1975.) Archdioceses are indicated by an asterisk.

Albany, N.Y. (1847): Edwin B. Broderick, bishop, 1969.
Former bishops: John McCloskey, 1847-64; John J. Conroy, 1865-77; Francis McNeirny, 1877-94; Thomas M. Burke, 1894-1915; Thomas F. Cusack, 1915-18; Edmund F. Gibbons, 1919-54; William A. Scully, 1954-69.

Alexandria, La. (1853): Lawrence P. Graves, bishop, 1973.
Established at Natchitoches, transferred, 1910.
Former bishops: Augustus M. Martin, 1853-75; Francis X. Leray, 1877-79, administrator, 1879-83; Anthony Durier, 1885-1904; Cornelius Van de Ven, 1904-32; D. F. Desmond, 1933-45; Charles P. Greco, 1946-73.

Allentown, Pa. (1961): Joseph McShea, bishop, 1961.

Altoona-Johnstown, Pa. (1901): James J. Hogan, bishop, 1966.
Established as Altoona, name changed, 1957.
Former bishops: Eugene A. Garvey, 1901-20; John J. McCort, 1920-36; Richard T. Guilfoyle, 1936-57; Howard J. Carroll, 1958-60; J. Carroll McCormick, 1960-66.

Amarillo, Tex. (1926): Lawrence M. DeFalco, bishop, 1963.
Former bishops; Rudolph A. Gerken, 1927-33; Robert E. Lucey, 1934-41; Laurence J. Fitzsimons, 1941-58; John L. Morkovsky, 1958-63.

Anchorage,* Alaska (1966): Joseph T. Ryan, archbishop, 1966.

Arlington, Va. (1974): Thomas J. Welsh, bishop, 1974.

Atlanta,* Ga. (1956; archdiocese, 1962):

Thomas A. Donnellan, archbishop, 1968.
Former ordinaries: Francis E. Hyland, 1956-61; Paul J. Hallinan, first archbishop, 1962-68.

Austin, Tex. (1947): Vincent M. Harris, bishop, 1971.
Former bishop: Louis J. Reicher, 1947-71.

Baker, Ore. (1903): Thomas J. Connolly, bishop, 1971.
Established as Baker City, name changed, 1952.
Former bishops: Charles J. O'Reilly, 1903-18; Joseph F. McGrath, 1919-50; Francis P. Leipzig, 1950-71.

Baltimore,* Md. (1789; archdiocese, 1808): William D. Borders, archbishop, 1974. T. Austin Murphy, auxiliary.
Former ordinaries: John Carroll, 1789-1815, first archbishop; Leonard Neale, 1815-17; Ambrose Marechal, S.S., 1817-28; James Whitfield, 1828-34; Samuel Eccleston, S.S., 1834-51; Francis P. Kenrick, 1851-63; Martin J. Spalding, 1864-72; James R. Bayley, 1872-77; Cardinal James Gibbons, 1877-1921; Michael J. Curley, 1921-47; Francis P. Keough, 1947-61, Cardinal Lawrence J. Shehan, 1961-74.

Baton Rouge, La. (1961): Joseph V. Sullivan, bishop, 1974.
Former bishop: Robert E. Tracy, 1961-74.

Beaumont, Tex. (1966): Warren L. Boudreaux, bishop, 1971.
Former bishop: Vincent M. Harris, 1966-71.

Belleville, Ill. (1887): Albert R. Zuroweste, bishop, 1948.
Former bishops: John Janssen, 1888-1913; Henry Althoff, 1914-47.

Birmingham, Ala. (1969): Joseph G. Vath, bishop, 1969.

Bismarck, N. Dak. (1909): Hilary B. Hacker, bishop, 1957.

Former bishops: Vincent Wehrle, O.S.B., 1910-39; Vincent J. Ryan, 1940-51; Lambert A. Hoch, 1952-56.

Boise, Ida. (1893): Sylvester Treinen, bishop, 1962.

Former bishops: Alphonse J. Glorieux, 1893-1917; Daniel M. Gorman, 1918-27; Edward J. Kelly, 1928-56; James J. Byrne, 1956-62.

Boston,* Mass. (1808; archdiocese, 1875): Cardinal Humberto S. Medeiros, archbishop, 1970. Thomas J. Riley, Joseph F. Maguire, Lawrence J. Riley, Thomas V. Dailey, John M. D'Arcy, Joseph J. Ruocco, John J. Mulcahy, auxiliaries.

Former ordinaries: John L. de Cheverus, 1810-23; Benedict J. Fenwick, S.J., 1825-46; John B. Fitzpatrick, 1846-66; John J. Williams, 1866-1907, first archbishop; Cardinal William O'Connell, 1907-44; Cardinal Richard Cushing, 1944-70.

Bridgeport, Conn. (1953): Walter W. Curtis, bishop, 1961.

Former bishop: Lawrence J. Shehan, 1953-61.

Brooklyn, N.Y. (1853): Francis J. Mugavero, bishop, 1968. John J. Boardman, Charles R. Mulrooney, Joseph P. Denning, John J. Snyder, auxiliaries.

Former bishops: John Loughlin, 1853-91; Charles E. McDonnell, 1892-1921; Thomas E. Molloy, 1921-56; Bryan J. McEntegart, 1957-68.

Brownsville, Tex. (1965): John J. Fitzpatrick, bishop, 1971.

Former bishops: Adolph Marx, 1965; Humberto S. Medeiros, 1966-70.

Buffalo, N.Y. (1847): Edward D. Head, bishop, 1973. Pius A. Benincasa, Bernard J. McLaughlin, auxiliaries.

Former bishops: John Timon, C.M., 1847-67; Stephen V. Ryan, C.M., 1868-96; James E. Quigley, 1897-1903; Charles H. Colton, 1903-15; Dennis J. Dougherty, 1915-18; William Turner, 1919-36; John A. Duffy, 1937-44; John F. O'Hara, C.S.C., 1945-51; Joseph A. Burke, 1952-62; James McNulty, 1963-72.

Burlington, Vt. (1853): John A. Marshall, bishop, 1972.

Former bishops: Louis De Goesbriand, 1853-99; John S. Michaud, 1899-1908; Joseph J. Rice, 1910-38; Matthew F. Brady, 1938-44; Edward F. Ryan, 1945-56; Robert F. Joyce, 1957-71.

Camden, N.J. (1937): George H. Guilfoyle, bishop, 1968. James L. Schad, auxiliary.

Former bishops: Bartholomew J. Eustace, 1938-56; Justin J. McCarthy, 1957-59; Celestine J. Damiano, 1960-67.

Charleston, S.C. (1820): Ernest L. Unterkoefler, bishop, 1964.

Former bishops: John England, 1820-42; Ignatius W. Reynolds, 1844-55; Patrick N. Lynch, 1858-82; Henry P. Northrop, 1883-1916; William T. Russell, 1917-27; Emmet M. Walsh, 1927-49; John J. Russell, 1950-58; Paul J. Hallinan, 1958-62; Francis F. Reh, 1962-64.

Charlotte, N.C. (1971): Michael J. Begley, bishop, 1972.

Cheyenne, Wyo. (1887): Hubert M. Newell, bishop, 1951.

Former bishops: Maurice F. Burke, 1887-93; Thomas M. Lenihan, 1897-1901; James J. Keane, 1902-11; Patrick A. McGovern, 1912-51.

Chicago,* Ill. (1843; archdiocese, 1880): Cardinal John Cody, archbishop, 1965; William E. McManus, Alfred L. Abramowicz, Nevin Hayes, O. Carm., auxiliaries.

Former ordinaries: William Quarter, 1844-48; James O. Van de Velde, S.J., 1849-53; Anthony O'Regan, 1854-58; James Duggan, 1859-70; Thomas P. Foley, administrator, 1870-79; Patrick A. Feehan, 1880-1902, first archbishop; James E. Quigley, 1903-15; Cardinal George Mundelein, 1915-39; Cardinal Samuel Stritch, 1939-58; Cardinal Albert Meyer, 1958-65.

Cincinnati,* Ohio (1821; archdiocese, 1850): Joseph L. Bernardin, archbishop, 1972. Nicholas Elko, Daniel E. Pilarczyk, auxiliaries.

Former ordinaries: Edward D. Fenwick, O.P., 1822-32; John B. Purcell, 1833-83, first archbishop; William H. Elder, 1883-1904; Henry Moeller, 1904-1925; John T. McNicholas, O.P., 1925-50; Karl J. Alter, 1950-69; Paul F. Leibold, 1969-72.

Cleveland, Ohio (1847): James A. Hickey, bishop, 1974. William M. Cosgrove, auxiliary.

Former bishops: L. Amadeus Rappe, 1847-70; Richard Gilmour, 1872-91; Ignatius F. Horstmann, 1892-1908; John P. Farrelly, 1909-21; Joseph Schrembs, 1921-45; Edward F. Hoban, 1945-66; Clarence G. Issenmann, 1966-74.

Columbus, Ohio (1868): Edward J. Herrmann, bishop, 1973. Edward G. Hettinger, auxiliary.

Former bishops: Sylvester H. Rosecrans, 1868-78; John A. Watterson, 1880-99; Henry Moeller, 1900-03; James J. Hartley, 1904-44; Michael J. Ready, 1944-57; Clarence Issenmann, 1957-64; John J. Carberry, 1965-68; Clarence E. Elwell, 1968-73.

Corpus Christi, Tex. (1912): Thomas J. Drury, bishop, 1965.

Former bishops: Paul J. Nussbaum, C.P., 1913-20; Emmanuel B. Ledvina, 1921-49; Mariano S. Garriga, 1949-65.

Covington, Ky. (1853): Richard Ackerman, C.S.Sp., bishop, 1960.

Former bishops: George A. Carrell, S.J., 1853-68; Augustus M. Toebbe, 1870-84; Camillus P. Maes, 1885-1914; Ferdinand Brossart, 1916-23; Francis W. Howard, 1923-44; William T. Mulloy, 1945-59.

Crookston, Minn. (1909): Kenneth J. Po-vish, bishop, 1970.
Former bishops: Timothy Corbett, 1910-38; John H. Peschges, 1938-44; Francis J. Schenk, 1945-60; Laurence A. Glenn, 1960-70.
Dallas, Tex. (1890): Thomas Tschoepe, bishop, 1969.
Former bishops: Thomas F. Brennan, 1891-92; Edward J. Dunne, 1893-1910; Joseph P. Lynch, 1911-54; Thomas K. Gorman, 1954-69.
Davenport, Ia. (1881): Gerald F. O'Keefe, bishop, 1966.
Former bishops: John McMullen, 1881-83; Henry Cosgrove, 1884-1906; James Davis, 1906-26; Henry P. Rohlman, 1927-44; Ralph L. Hayes, 1944-66.
Denver,* Colo. (1887; archdiocese, 1941): James V. Casey, archbishop, 1967. George R. Evans, Richard C. Hanifen, auxiliaries.
Former ordinaries: Joseph P. Machebeuf, 1887-89; Nicholas C. Matz, 1889-1917; J. Henry Tihen, 1917-31; Urban J. Vehr, 1931-67, first archbishop.
Des Moines, Ia. (1911): Maurice J. Dingman, bishop, 1968.
Former bishops: Austin Dowling, 1912-19; Thomas W. Drumm, 1919-33; Gerald T. Bergan, 1934-48; Edward C. Daly, O.P., 1948-64; George J. Biskup, 1965-67.
Detroit,* Mich. (1833; archdiocese, 1937): Cardinal John F. Dearden, archbishop, 1958. Thomas J. Gumbleton, Walter J. Schoenherr, Arthur H. Krawczak, Joseph L. Imesch, auxiliaries.
Former ordinaries: Frederic Rese, 1833-71; Peter P. Lefevere, administrator, 1841-69; Caspar H. Borgess, 1871-88; John S. Foley, 1888-1918; Michael J. Gallagher, 1918-37; Cardinal Edward Mooney, 1937-58, first archbishop.
Dodge City, Kans. (1951): Marion F. Forst, bishop, 1960.
Former bishop: John B. Franz, 1951-59.
Dubuque,* Iowa (1837; archdiocese, 1893): James J. Byrne, archbishop, 1962. Francis J. Dunn, auxiliary.
Former ordinaries: Mathias Loras, 1837-58; Clement Smyth, O.C.S.O., 1858-65; John Hennessy, 1866-1900, first archbishop; John J. Keane, 1900-11; James J. Keane, 1911-29; Francis J. Beckman, 1930-46; Henry P. Rohlman, 1946-54; Leo Binz, 1954-61.
Duluth, Minn. (1889): Paul F. Anderson, bishop, 1969.
Former bishops: James McGolrick, 1889-1918; John T. McNicholas, O.P., 1918-25; Thomas A. Welch, 1926-59; Francis J. Schenk, 1960-69.
El Paso, Tex. (1914): Sidney M. Metzger, bishop, 1942.
Former bishop: Anthony J. Schuler, S.J., 1915-42.
Erie, Pa. (1853): Alfred M. Watson, bishop, 1969.

Former bishops: Michael O'Connor, 1853-54; Josue M. Young, 1854-66; Tobias Mullen, 1868-99; John E. Fitzmaurice, 1899-1920; John M. Gannon, 1920-66; John F. Whealon, 1966-69.
Evansville, Ind. (1944): Francis Raymond Shea, bishop, 1970.
Former bishops: Henry J. Grimmelsman, 1944-65; Paul F. Leibold, 1966-69.
Fairbanks, Alaska (1962): Robert L. Whelan, S.J., bishop, 1968.
Former bishop: Francis D. Gleeson, S.J., 1948-68.
Fall River, Mass. (1904): Daniel A. Cronin, bishop, 1970. James J. Gerrard, auxiliary.
Former bishops: William Stang, 1904-07; Daniel F. Feehan, 1907-34; James E. Cassidy, 1934-51; James L. Connolly, 1951-70.
Fargo, N. Dak. (1889): Justin A. Driscoll, bishop, 1970.
Established at Jamestown, transferred, 1897.
Former bishops: John Shanley, 1889-1909; James O'Reilly, 1910-34; Aloysius J. Muench, 1935-59; Leo F. Dworschak, 1960-70.
Fort Wayne-South Bend, Ind. (1857): Leo A. Pursley, bishop, 1957. Joseph R. Crowley, auxiliary.
Established as Fort Wayne, name changed, 1960.
Former bishops: John H. Luers, 1858-71; Joseph Dwenger, C.Pp. S., 1872-93; Joseph Rademacher, 1893-1900; Herman J. Alerding, 1900-24; John F. Noll, 1925-56.
Fort Worth, Tex. (1969): John J. Cassata, bishop, 1969.
Fresno, Calif. (1967): Hugh A. Donohoe, bishop, 1969. Roger M. Mahoney, auxiliary.
Former bishop: Timothy Manning, 1967-69.
Gallup, N. Mex. (1939): Jerome J. Hastrich, bishop, 1969.
Former bishop: Bernard T. Espelage, O.F.M., 1940-69.
Galveston-Houston, Tex. (1847): John L. Morkovsky, bishop, 1975.
Established as Galveston, name changed, 1959.
Former bishops: John M. Odin, C.M., 1847-61; Claude M. Dubuis, 1862-92; Nicholas A. Gallagher, 1892-1918; Christopher E. Byrne, 1918-50; Wendelin J. Nold, 1950-75.
Gary, Ind. (1957): Andrew G. Grutka, bishop, 1957.
Gaylord, Mich. (1971): Edmund C. Szoka, bishop, 1971.
Grand Island, Neb. (1912): John J. Sullivan, bishop, 1972.
Established at Kearney, transferred, 1917.
Former bishops: James A. Duffy, 1913-31; Stanislaus V. Bona, 1932-44; Edward J. Hunkeler, 1945-51; John L. Paschang, 1951-72.
Grand Rapids, Mich. (1882): Joseph Breitenbeck, bishop, 1969. Joseph C. McKinney, auxiliary.
Former bishops: Henry J. Richter, 1883-

1916; Michael J. Gallagher, 1916-18; Edward D. Kelly, 1919-26; Joseph G. Pinten, 1926-40; Joseph C. Plagens, 1941-43; Francis J. Haas, 1943-53; Allen J. Babcock, 1954-69.

Great Falls, Mont. (1904): Eldon B. Schuster, bishop, 1968.

Former bishops: Mathias C. Lenihan, 1904-30; Edwin V. O'Hara, 1930-39; William J. Condon, 1939-67.

Green Bay, Wis. (1868): Aloysius J. Wycislo, bishop, 1968. John B. Grellinger, Mark Schmitt, auxiliaries.

Former bishops: Joseph Melcher, 1868-73; Francis X. Krautbauer, 1875-85; Frederick X. Katzer, 1886-91; Sebastian G. Messmer, 1892-1903; Joseph J. Fox, 1904-14; Paul P. Rhode, 1915-45; Stanislaus V. Bona, 1945-67.

Greensburg, Pa. (1951): William G. Connare, bishop, 1960. Norbert F. Gaughan, auxiliary.

Former bishop: Hugh L. Lamb, 1951-59.

Harrisburg, Pa. (1868): Joseph T. Daley, bishop, 1971.

Former bishops: Jeremiah F. Shanahan, 1868-86; Thomas McGovern, 1888-98; John W. Shanahan,1899-1916; Philip R. McDevitt, 1916-35; George L. Leech, 1935-71.

Hartford,* Conn. (1843; archdiocese, 1953): John F. Whealon, archbishop, 1969. John F. Hackett, Joseph F. Donnelly, auxiliaries.

Former ordinaries: William Tyler, 1844-49; Bernard O'Reilly, 1850-56; F. P. MacFarland, 1858-74; Thomas Galberry, O.S.A., 1876-78; Lawrence S. McMahon, 1879-93; Michael Tierney, 1894-1908; John J. Nilan, 1910-34; Maurice F. McAuliffe, 1934-44; Henry J. O'Brien, 1945-68, first archbishop.

Helena, Mont. (1884): Vacant as of July 15, 1975.

Former bishops: John B. Brondel, 1884-1903; John P. Carroll, 1904-25; George J. Finnigan, C.S.C., 1927-32; Ralph L. Hayes, 1933-35; Joseph M. Gilmore, 1936-62; Raymond Hunthausen, 1962-75.

Honolulu, Hawaii (1941): John J. Scanlan, bishop, 1968.

Former bishop: James J. Sweeney, 1941-68.

Indianapolis,* Ind. (1834; archdiocese, 1944): George J. Biskup, archbishop, 1970. Established at Vincennes, transferred, 1898.

Former ordinaries: Simon G. Bruté, 1834-39; Celestine de la Hailandiere, 1839-47; John S. Bazin, 1847-48; Maurice de St. Palais, 1849-77; Francis S. Chatard, 1878-1918; Joseph Chartrand, 1918-33; Joseph E. Ritter, 1934-46, first archbishop; Paul C. Schulte, 1946-70.

Jefferson City, Mo. (1956): Michael F. McAuliffe, bishop, 1969.

Former bishop: Joseph Marling, C.Pp.S., 1956-69.

Joliet, Ill. (1948): Romeo Blanchette, bishop, 1966. Raymond J. Vonesh, auxiliary.

Former bishop: Martin D. McNamara, 1949-66.

Juneau, Alaska (1951): Francis T. Hurley, bishop, 1971.

Former bishops: Dermot O'Flanagan, 1951-68; Joseph T. Ryan, administrator, 1968-71.

Kalamazoo, Mich. (1971): Paul V. Donovan, bishop, 1971.

Kansas City,* Kans. (1877; archdiocese, 1952): Ignatius J. Strecker, archbishop, 1969. Established as vicariate apostolic, 1850, became Diocese of Leavenworth, 1877, transferred to Kansas City 1947.

Former ordinaries: J. B. Miege, vicar apostolic, 1851-74; Louis M. Fink, O.S.B., vicar apostolic, 1874-77, first bishop, 1877-1904; Thomas F. Lillis, 1904-10; John Ward, 1910-29; Francis Johannes, 1929-37; Paul C. Schulte, 1937-46; George J. Donnelly, 1946-50; Edward Hunkeler, 1951-69, first archbishop.

Kansas City-St. Joseph, Mo. (Kansas City, 1880; St. Joseph, 1868; united 1956): Charles H. Helmsing, bishop, 1962. George K. Fitzsimons, auxiliary.

Former bishops (Kansas City): John J. Hogan, 1880-1913; Thomas F. Lillis, 1913-38; Edwin V. O'Hara, 1939-56; John P. Cody, 1956-61.

Former bishops (St. Joseph): John J. Hogan, 1868-80, administrator, 1880-93; Maurice F. Burke, 1893-1923; Francis Gilfillan, 1923-33; Charles H. Le Blond, 1933-56.

La Crosse, Wis. (1868): Frederick W. Freking, bishop, 1965.

Former bishops: Michael Heiss, 1868-80; Kilian C. Flasch, 1881-91; James Schwebach, 1892-1921; Alexander J. McGavick, 1921-48; John P. Treacy, 1948-64.

Lafayette, Ind. (1944): Raymond J. Gallagher, bishop, 1965.

Former bishops: John G. Bennett, 1944-57; John J. Carberry, 1957-65.

Lafayette, La. (1918): Gerard L. Frey, bishop, 1973.

Former bishops: Jules B. Jeanmard, 1918-56; Maurice Schexnayder, 1956-72.

Lansing, Mich. (1937): Vacant as of July 15, 1975. James Sullivan, auxiliary.

Former bishops: Joseph H. Albers, 1937-65; Alexander Zaleski, 1965-75.

Lincoln, Neb. (1887): Glennon P. Flavin, bishop, 1967.

Former bishops: Thomas Bonacum, 1887-1911; J. Henry Tihen, 1911-17; Charles J. O'Reilly, 1918-23; Francis J. Beckman, 1924-30; Louis B. Kucera, 1930-57; James V. Casey, 1957-67.

Little Rock, Ark. (1843): Andrew J. McDonald, bishop, 1972.

Former bishops: Andrew Byrne, 1844-62; Edward Fitzgerald, 1867-1907; John Morris, 1907-46; Albert L. Fletcher, 1946-72.

Los Angeles,* Calif. (1840; archdiocese, 1936): Cardinal Timothy Manning, archbishop, 1970. John J. Ward, William R. Johnson, Juan A. Arzube, auxiliaries.

Former ordinaries: Francisco Garcia Diego y Moreno, O.F.M., 1840-46; Joseph S. Alemany, O.P., 1850-53; Thaddeus Amat, C.M., 1854-78; Francis Mora, 1878-96; George T. Montgomery, 1896-1903; Thomas J. Conaty, 1903-15; John J. Cantwell, 1917-47, first archbishop; Cardinal James McIntyre, 1948-70.

Louisville,* Ky. (1808; archdiocese, 1937): Thomas J. McDonough, archbishop, 1967. Charles G. Maloney, auxiliary.
Established at Bardstown, transferred, 1841.
Former ordinaries: Benedict J. Flaget, S.S. 1810-32; John B. David, S.S., 1832-33; Benedict J. Flaget, S.S., 1833-50; Martin J. Spalding, 1850-64; Peter J. Lavialle, 1865-67; William G. McCloskey, 1868-1909; Denis O'Donaghue, 1910-24; John A. Floersh, 1924-67, first archbishop.

Madison, Wis. (1946): Cletus F. O'Donnell, bishop, 1967.
Former bishop: William P. O'Connor, 1946-67.

Manchester, N.H. (1884): Odore J. Gendron, bishop, 1974.
Former bishops: Denis M. Bradley, 1884-1903; John B. Delany, 1904-06; George A. Guertin, 1907-32; John B. Peterson, 1932-44; Matthew F. Brady, 1944-59; Ernest J. Primeau, 1960-74.

Marquette, Mich. (1857): Charles A. Salatka, bishop, 1968.
Former bishops: Frederic Baraga, 1857-68; Ignatius Mrak, 1869-78; John Vertin, 1879-99; Frederick Eis, 1899-1922; Paul J. Nussbaum, C. P., 1922-35; Joseph C. Plagens, 1935-40; Francis Magner, 1941-47; Thomas L. Noa, 1947-68.

Memphis, Tenn. (1970): Carroll T. Dozier, bishop, 1971.

Miami,* Fla. (1958; archdiocese, 1968): Coleman F. Carroll, bishop, 1958, first archbishop, 1968. Rene H. Gracida, auxiliary.

Milwaukee,* Wis. (1843; archdiocese, 1875): William E. Cousins, archbishop, 1959. Leo J. Brust, auxiliary.
Former ordinaries: John M. Henni, 1844-81, first archbishop; Michael Heiss, 1881-90; Frederick X. Katzer, 1891-1903; Sebastian G. Messmer, 1903-30; Samuel A. Stritch, 1930-39; Moses E. Kiley, 1940-53; Albert G. Meyer, 1953-58.

Mobile, Ala. (1829): John L. May, bishop, 1969.
Former bishops: Michael Portier, 1829-59; John Quinlan, 1859-83; Dominic Manucy, 1884; Jeremiah O'Sullivan, 1885-96; Edward P. Allen, 1897-1926; Thomas J. Toolen, 1927-69.

Monterey in California (1967): Harry A. Clinch, bishop, 1967.
Formerly Monterey-Fresno, 1922.
Former bishops (Monterey-Fresno): John J. Cantwell, administrator, 1922-24; John B. MacGinley, first bishop, 1924-32; Philip G.

Sher, 1933-53; Aloysius J. Willinger, 1953-67.

Munhall,* Pa. (Byzantine Rite) (1924; metropolitan, 1969): Stephen J. Kocisko, eparch, 1968, first metropolitan, 1969. John Bilock, auxiliary.
Former ordinaries: Basil Takach 1924-48; Daniel Ivancho, 1948-54; Nicholas T. Elko, 1955-67.

Nashville, Tenn. (1837): James D. Niedergeses, bishop, 1975.
Former bishops: Richard P. Miles, O.P., 1838-60; James Whelan, O.P., 1860-64; Patrick A. Feehan, 1865-80; Joseph Rademacher, 1883-93; Thomas S. Byrne, 1894-1923; Alphonse J. Smith, 1924-35; William L. Adrian, 1936-69; Joseph A. Durick, 1969-75.

Natchez-Jackson, Miss. (1837): Joseph B. Brunini, bishop, 1968. Joseph Howze, auxiliary.
Former bishops: John J. Chanche, S.S., 1841-52; James Van de Velde, S.J., 1853-55; William H. Elder, 1857-80; Francis A. Janssens, 1881-88; Thomas Heslin, 1889-1911; John E. Gunn, S.M., 1911-24; Richard O. Gerow, 1924-67.

Newark,* N.J. (1853; archdiocese, 1937): Peter L. Gerety, archbishop, 1974. John J. Dougherty, Joseph A. Costello, auxiliaries.
Former ordinaries: James R. Bayley, 1853-72; Michael A. Corrigan, 1873-80; Winand M. Wigger, 1881-1901; John J. O'Connor, 1901-27; Thomas J. Walsh, 1928-52, first archbishop; Thomas A. Boland, 1953-74.

New Orleans,* La. (1793; archdiocese, 1850): Philip M. Hannan, archbishop, 1965. L. Abel Caillouet, Harold R. Perry, S. V. D., auxiliaries.
Former ordinaries: Luis Penalver y Cardenas, 1793-1801; John Carroll, administrator, 1809-15; W. Louis Dubourg, S.S., 1815-25; Joseph Rosati, C.M., administrator, 1826-29; Leo De Neckere, C.M., 1829-33; Anthony Blanc, 1835-60, first archbishop; Jean Marie Odin, C.M., 1861-70; Napoleon J. Perche, 1870-83; Francis X. Leray, 1883-87; Francis A. Janssens, 1888-97; Placide L. Chapelle, 1897-1905; James H. Blenk, S.M., 1906-17; John W. Shaw, 1918-34; Joseph F. Rummel, 1935-64; John P. Cody, 1964-65.

New Ulm, Minn. (1957): Alphonse J. Schladweiler, bishop, 1958.

New York,* N.Y. (1808; archdiocese, 1850): Cardinal Terence J. Cooke, archbishop, 1968. John J. Maguire, coadjutor archbishop, 1965. Joseph M. Pernicone, Edward E. Swanstrom, Patrick V. Ahern, James P. Mahoney, Anthony F. Mestice, auxiliaries.
Former ordinaries: Richard L. Concanen, O.P., 1808-10; John Connolly, O.P., 1814-25; John Dubois, S.S., 1826-42; John J. Hughes, 1842-64, first archbishop; Cardinal John McCloskey, 1864-85; Michael A. Corrigan, 1885-1902; Cardinal John Farley, 1902-18; Cardinal Patrick Hayes, 1919-38; Cardinal Francis Spellman, 1939-67.

Norwich, Conn. (1953): Daniel P. Reilly, bishop, 1975.

Former bishops: Bernard J. Flanagan, 1953-59; Vincent J. Hines, 1960-75.

Oakland, Calif. (1962): Floyd L. Begin, bishop, 1962.

Ogdensburg, N. Y. (1872): Stanislaus Brzana, bishop, 1968.

Former bishops: Edgar P. Wadhams, 1872-91; Henry Gabriels, 1892-1921; Joseph H. Conroy, 1921-39; Francis J. Monaghan, 1939-42; Bryan J. McEntegart, 1943-53; Walter P. Kellenberg, 1954-57; James J. Navagh, 1957-63; Leo R. Smith, 1963; Thomas A. Donnellan, 1964-68.

Oklahoma City,* Okla. (1905; archdiocese, 1972): John R. Quinn, 1971, first archbishop 1972.

Former bishops: Theophile Meerschaert, 1905-24; Francis C. Kelley, 1924-48; Eugene J. McGuinness, 1948-57; Victor J. Reed, 1958-71.

Omaha,* Nebr. (1885; archdiocese, 1945): Daniel E. Sheehan, archbishop, 1969.

Former ordinaries: James O'Gorman, O.C.S.O., 1859-74, vicar apostolic; James O'Connor, vicar apostolic, 1876-85, first bishop, 1885-90; Richard Scannell, 1891-1916; Jeremiah J. Harty, 1916-27; Francis Beckman, administrator, 1926-28; Joseph F. Rummel, 1928-35; James H. Ryan, 1935-47, first archbishop; Gerald T. Bergan, 1948-69.

Orlando, Fla. (1968): Thomas J. Grady, bishop, 1974.

Former bishop: William Borders, 1968-74.

Owensboro, Ky. (1937): Henry J. Soenneker, bishop, 1961.

Former bishop: Francis R. Cotton, 1938-60.

Parma, Ohio (Byzantine Rite) (1969): Emil Mihalik, eparch, 1969.

Passaic, N.J. (Byzantine Rite) (1963): Michael J. Dudick, eparch, 1968.

Former bishop: Stephen Kocisko, 1963-68.

Paterson, N. J. (1937): Lawrence B. Casey, bishop, 1966.

Former bishops: Thomas H. McLaughlin, 1937-47; Thomas A. Boland, 1947-52; James A. McNulty, 1953-63; James J. Navagh, 1963-65.

Peoria, Ill. (1877): Edward W. O'Rourke, bishop, 1971.

Former bishops: John L. Spalding, 1877-1908; Edmund M. Dunne, 1909-29; Joseph H. Schlarman, 1930-51; William E. Cousins, 1952-58; John B. Franz, 1959-71.

Philadelphia,* Pa. (1808; archdiocese, 1875): Cardinal John Krol, archbishop, 1961. Gerald V. McDevitt, John J. Graham, Martin Lohmuller, auxiliaries.

Former ordinaries: Michael Egan, O. F. M., 1810-14; Henry Conwell, 1820-42; Francis P. Kenrick, 1842-51; John N. Neumann, C.SS.R., 1852-60; James F. Wood, 1860-83, first archbishop; Patrick J. Ryan, 1884-1911; Edmond F. Prendergast, 1911-18;

Cardinal Dennis Dougherty, 1918-51; Cardinal John O'Hara, C.S.C., 1951-60.

Philadelphia,* Pa. (Byzantine Rite) (1924; metropolitan, 1958): Ambrose Senyshyn, O.S.B.M., metropolitan, 1961. Basil Losten, auxiliary.

Former ordinaries: Stephen Ortynsky, O.S.B.M., 1907-16; Constantine Bohachevsky, 1924-61.

Phoenix, Ariz. (1969): Edward A. McCarthy, bishop, 1969.

Pittsburgh, Pa. (1843): Vincent M. Leonard, bishop, 1969. John B. McDowell, Anthony G. Bosco, auxiliaries.

Former bishops: Michael O'Connor, 1843-53, 1854-60; Michael Domenec, C.M., 1860-76; J. Tuigg, 1876-89; Richard Phelan, 1889-1904; J. F. Regis Canevin, 1904-20; Hugh C. Boyle, 1921-55; John F. Dearden, 1950-58; John J. Wright, 1959-69.

Portland, Me. (1853): Edward C. O'Leary, bishop, 1974.

Former bishops: David W. Bacon, 1855-74; James A. Healy, 1875-1900; William H. O'Connell, 1901-06; Louis S. Walsh, 1906-24; John G. Murray, 1925-31; Joseph E. McCarthy, 1932-55; Daniel J. Feeney, 1955-69; Peter L. Gerety, 1969-74.

Portland,* Ore. (1846): Cornelius M. Power, archbishop, 1974.

Established as Oregon City, name changed, 1928.

Former ordinaries: Francis N. Blanchet, 1846-80 vicar apostolic, first archbishop; Charles J. Seghers, 1880-84; William H. Gross, C.SS.R., 1885-98; Alexander Christie, 1899-1925; Edward D. Howard, 1926-66; Robert J. Dwyer, 1966-74.

Providence, R. I. (1872): Louis E. Gelineau, bishop, 1972. Kenneth A. Angell, auxiliary.

Former bishops: Thomas F. Hendricken, 1872-86; Matthew Harkins, 1887-1921; William A. Hickey, 1921-33; Francis P. Keough, 1934-47; Russell J. McVinney, 1948-71.

Pueblo, Colo. (1941): Charles A. Buswell, bishop, 1959.

Former bishop: Joseph C. Willging, 1942-59.

Raleigh, N. C. (1924): F. Joseph Gossman, bishop, 1975. George E. Lynch, auxiliary.

Former bishops: William J. Hafey, 1925-37; Eugene J. McGuinness, 1937-44; Vincent S. Waters, 1945-75.

Rapid City, S. Dak. (1902): Harold J. Dimmerling, bishop, 1969.

Established at Lead, transferred, 1920.

Former bishops: John Stariha, 1902-09; Joseph F. Busch, 1910-15; John J. Lawler, 1916-48; William T. McCarty, C.SS.R., 1948-69.

Reno, Nev. (1931): Norman McFarland, apostolic administrator, 1974.

Former bishops: Thomas K. Gorman, 1931-52; Robert J. Dwyer, 1952-66; Joseph Green, 1967-74.

Richmond, Va. (1820): Walter F. Sullivan, bishop, 1974. J. Louis Flaherty, auxiliary.

Former bishops: Patrick Kelly, 1820-22; Richard V. Whelan, 1841-50; John McGill, 1850-72; James Gibbons, 1872-77; John J. Keane, 1878-88; Augustine Van de Vyver, 1889-1911; Denis J. O'Connell, 1912-26; Andrew J. Brennan, 1926-45; Peter L. Ireton, 1945-58; John J. Russell, 1958-72.

Rochester, N. Y. (1868): Joseph L. Hogan, bishop, 1969. Dennis W. Hickey, John E. McCafferty, auxiliaries.

Former bishops: Bernard J. McQuaid, 1868-1909; Thomas F. Hickey, 1909-28; John F. O'Hern, 1929-33; Edward F. Mooney, 1933-37; James E. Kearney, 1937-66; Fulton J. Sheen, 1966-69.

Rockford, Ill. (1908): Arthur J. O'Neill, bishop, 1968.

Former bishops: Peter J. Muldoon, 1908-27; Edward F. Hoban, 1928-42; John J. Boylan, 1943-53; Raymond P. Hillinger, 1953-56; Loras T. Lane, 1956-68.

Rockville Centre, N. Y. (1957): Walter P. Kellenberg, bishop, 1957. Vincent J. Baldwin, John R. McGann, auxiliaries.

Sacramento, Calif. (1886): Alden J. Bell, bishop, 1962. John S. Cummins, auxiliary.

Former bishops: Patrick Manogue, 1886-95; Thomas Grace, 1896-1921; Patrick J. Keane, 1922-28; Robert J. Armstrong, 1929-57; Joseph T. McGucken, 1957-62.

Saginaw, Mich. (1938): Francis F. Reh, bishop, 1969.

Former bishops: William F. Murphy, 1938-50; Stephen S. Woznicki, 1950-68.

St. Augustine, Fla. (1870): Paul F. Tanner, bishop, 1968.

Former bishops: Augustin Verot, S.S., 1870-76; John Moore, 1877-1901; William J. Kenny, 1902-13; Michael J. Curley, 1914-21; Patrick J. Barry, 1922-40; Joseph P. Hurley, 1940-67.

St. Cloud, Minn. (1889): George H. Speltz, bishop, 1968. James S. Rausch, auxiliary.

Former bishops: Otto Zardetti, 1889-94; Martin Marty, O.S.B., 1895-96; James Trobec, 1897-1914; Joseph F. Busch, 1915-53; Peter Bartholome, 1953-68.

St. Louis,* Mo. (1826; archdiocese, 1847): Cardinal John J. Carberry, archbishop, 1968. George J. Gottwald, Joseph A. McNicholas, Charles R. Koester, Edward T. O'Meara, auxiliaries.

Former ordinaries: Joseph Rosati, C.M. 1827-43; Peter R. Kenrick, 1843-95, first archbishop; John J. Kain, 1895-1903; Cardinal John Glennon, 1903-46; Cardinal Joseph Ritter, 1946-67.

St. Maron of Detroit (Maronite Rite) (1966; eparchy, 1972): Francis Zayek, exarch, 1966, first eparch, 1972.

St. Nicholas in Chicago (Byzantine Rite Eparchy of St. Nicholas of the Ukrainians) (1961): Jaroslav Gabro, eparch, 1961.

St. Paul and Minneapolis,* Minn. (1850; archdiocese, 1888): John R. Roach, archbishop, 1975. Raymond A. Lucker, auxiliary.

Former ordinaries: Joseph Cretin, 1851-57; Thomas L. Grace, O.P., 1859-84; John Ireland, 1884-1918, first archbishop; Austin Dowling, 1919-30; John G. Murray, 1931-56; William O. Brady, 1956-61; Leo Binz, 1962-75.

St. Petersburg, Fla. (1968): Charles McLaughlin, bishop, 1968.

Salina, Kans. (1887): Cyril J. Vogel, bishop, 1965.

Established at Concordia, transferred, 1944.

Former bishops: Richard Scannell, 1887-91; John J. Hennessy, administrator, 1891-98; John F. Cunningham, 1898-1919; Francis J. Tief, 1921-38; Frank A. Thill, 1938-57; Frederick W. Freking, 1957-64.

Salt Lake City, Utah (1891): J. Lennox Federal, bishop, 1960.

Former bishops: Lawrence Scanlan, 1891-1915; Joseph S. Glass, C.M., 1915-26; John J. Mitty, 1926-32; James E. Kearney, 1932-37; Duane G. Hunt, 1937-60.

San Angelo, Tex. (1961): Stephen A. Leven, bishop, 1969.

Former bishops: Thomas J. Drury, 1962-65; Thomas Tschoepe, 1966-69.

San Antonio,* Tex. (1874; archdiocese, 1926): Francis Furey, archbishop, 1969. Patrick Flores, auxiliary.

Former ordinaries: Anthony D. Pellicer, 1874-80; John C. Neraz, 1881-94; John A. Forest, 1895-1911; John W. Shaw, 1911-18; Arthur Jerome Drossaerts, 1918-40, first archbishop; Robert E. Lucey, 1941-69.

San Diego, Calif. (1936): Leo T. Maher, bishop, 1969. Gilbert Espinoza Chavez, auxiliary.

Former bishops: Charles F. Buddy, 1936-66; Francis J. Furey, 1966-69.

San Francisco,* Calif. (1853): Joseph T. McGucken, archbishop, 1962. William J. McDonald, Norman F. McFarland (apostolic administrator of Reno), auxiliaries.

Former ordinaries: Joseph S. Alemany, O.P., 1853-84; Patrick W. Riordan, 1884-1914; Edward J. Hanna, 1915-35; John Mitty, 1935-61.

Santa Fe,* N. Mex. (1850; archdiocese, 1875): Robert Sanchez, archbishop, 1974.

Former ordinaries: John B. Lamy, 1850-85, first archbishop; John B. Salpointe, 1885-94; Placide L. Chapelle, 1894-97; Peter Bourgade, 1899-1908; John B. Pitaval, 1909-18; Albert T. Daeger, O.F.M., 1919-32; Rudolph A. Gerken, 1933-43; Edwin V. Byrne, 1943-63; James P. Davis, 1964-74.

Santa Rosa, Calif. (1962): Mark J. Hurley, bishop, 1969.

Former bishop: Leo T. Maher, 1962-69.

Savannah, Ga. (1850): Raymond Lessard, bishop, 1973.

Former bishops: Francis X. Gartland, 1850-54; John Barry, 1857-59; Augustin Verot, S.S., 1861-70; Ignatius Persico, O.F.M. Cap., 1870-72; William H. Gross,

C.SS.R., 1873-85; Thomas A. Becker, 1886-99; Benjamin J. Keiley, 1900-22; Michael Keyes, S.M., 1922-35; Gerald P. O'Hara, 1935-59; Thomas J. McDonough, 1960-67; Gerard L. Frey, 1967-72.

Scranton, Pa. (1868): J. Carroll McCormick, bishop, 1966.

Former bishops: William O'Hara, 1868-99; Michael J. Hoban, 1899-1926; Thomas C. O'Reilly, 1928-38; William J. Hafey, 1938-54; Jerome D. Hannan, 1954-65.

Seattle,* Wash. (1850; archdiocese, 1951): Raymond Hunthausen, archbishop, 1975.

Established as Nesqually, name changed, 1907.

Former ordinaries; Augustin M. Blanchet, 1850-79; Aegidius Junger, 1879-95; Edward J. O'Dea, 1896-1932; Gerald Shaughnessy, S.M., 1933-50; Thomas A. Connolly, first archbishop, 1950-75.

Sioux City, Ia. (1902): Frank Greteman, bishop, 1970.

Former bishops: Philip J. Garrigan, 1902-19; Edmond Heelan, 1919-48; Joseph M. Mueller, 1948-70.

Sioux Falls, S. Dak. (1889): Lambert A. Hoch, bishop, 1956.

Former bishops: Martin Marty, O.S.B., 1889-94; Thomas O'Gorman, 1896-1921; Bernard J. Mahoney, 1922-39; William O. Brady, 1939-56.

Spokane, Wash. (1913): Bernard J. Topel, bishop, 1955.

Former bishops: Augustine F. Schinner, 1914-25; Charles D. White, 1927-55.

Springfield-Cape Girardeau, Mo. (1956): Bernard F. Law, bishop, 1973.

Former bishops: Charles Helmsing, 1956-62; Ignatius J. Strecker, 1962-69; William Baum, 1970-73.

Springfield, Ill. (1853): William A. O'Connor, bishop, 1949.

Former bishops: Henry D. Juncker, 1857-68; Peter J. Baltes, 1870-86; James Ryan, 1888-1923; James A. Griffin, 1924-48.

Springfield, Mass. (1870): Christopher J. Weldon, bishop, 1950.

Former bishops: Patrick T. O'Reilly, 1870-92; Thomas D. Beaven, 1892-1920; Thomas M. O'Leary, 1921-49.

Stamford, Conn. (Byzantine Rite) (1956): Joseph M. Schmondiuk, eparch, 1961.

Former eparch: Ambrose Senyshyn, O.S.B.M., 1956-61.

Steubenville, Ohio (1944): John K. Mussio, bishop, 1945.

Stockton, Calif. (1962): Merlin J. Guilfoyle, bishop, 1969.

Former bishop: Hugh A. Donohoe, 1962-69.

Superior, Wis. (1905): George A. Hammes, bishop, 1960.

Former bishops: Augustine F. Schinner, 1905-13; Joseph M. Koudelka, 1913-21; Joseph G. Pinten, 1922-26; Theodore M. Reverman, 1926-41; William P. O'Connor, 1942-46;

Albert G. Meyer, 1946-53; Joseph Annabring, 1954-59.

Syracuse, N. Y. (1886): David F. Cunningham, bishop, 1970. Francis J. Harrison, auxiliary.

Former bishops: Patrick A. Ludden, 1887-1912; John Grimes, 1912-22; Daniel J. Curley, 1923-32; John A. Duffy, 1933-37; Walter A. Foery, 1937-70.

Toledo, Ohio (1910): John A. Donovan, bishop, 1967. Albert H. Ottenweller, auxiliary.

Former bishops: Joseph Schrembs, 1911-21; Samuel A. Stritch, 1921-30; Karl J. Alter, 1931-50; George J. Rehring, 1950-67.

Trenton, N. J. (1881): George W. Ahr, bishop, 1950; John C. Reiss, auxiliary.

Former bishops: Michael J. O'Farrell, 1881-94; James A. McFaul, 1894-1917; Thomas J. Walsh, 1918-28; John J. McMahon, 1928-32; Moses E. Kiley, 1934-40; William A. Griffin, 1940-50.

Tucson, Ariz. (1897): Francis J. Green, bishop, 1960.

Former bishops: Peter Bourgade, 1897-99; Henry Granjon, 1900-22; Daniel J. Gercke, 1923-60.

Tulsa, Okla. (1972): Bernard J. Ganter, bishop, 1973.

Washington,* D.C. (1939): William Baum, archbishop, 1973. Thomas W. Lyons, Eugene A. Marino, S.S.J., auxiliaries.

Former ordinaries: Michael J. Curley, 1939-47; Cardinal Patrick O'Boyle, 1948-73.

Wheeling-Charleston, W. Va. (1850): Joseph H. Hodges, bishop, 1962. James E. Michaels, S.S.C., auxiliary.

Established as Wheeling; name changed, 1974.

Former bishops: Richard V. Whelan, 1850-74; John J. Kain, 1875-93; Patrick J. Donahue, 1894-1922; John J. Swint, 1922-62.

Wichita, Kans. (1887): David M. Maloney, bishop, 1967.

Former bishops: John J. Hennessy, 1888-1920; Augustus J. Schwertner, 1921-39; Christian H. Winkelmann, 1940-46; Mark K. Carroll, 1947-67.

Wilmington, Del. (1868): Thomas Mardaga, bishop, 1968.

Former bishops: Thomas A. Becker, 1868-86; Alfred A. Curtis, 1886-96; John J. Monaghan, 1897-1925; Edmond Fitzmaurice, 1925-60; Michael Hyle, 1960-67.

Winona, Minn. (1889): Loras J. Watters, bishop, 1969.

Former bishops: Joseph B. Cotter, 1889-1909; Patrick R. Heffron, 1910-27; Francis M. Kelly, 1928-49; Edward A. Fitzgerald, 1949-69.

Worcester, Mass. (1950): Bernard J. Flanagan, bishop, 1959. Timothy J. Harrington, auxiliary.

Former bishop: John J. Wright, 1950-59.

Yakima, Wash. (1951): Nicholas E. Walsh, bishop, 1974.

Former bishops: Joseph P. Dougherty, 1951-69; Cornelius M. Power, 1969-74.
Youngstown, Ohio (1943): James W. Malone, bishop, 1968. William A. Hughes, auxiliary.
Former bishops: James A. McFadden, 1943-52; Emmet M. Walsh, 1952-68.
Apostolic Exarchate for Melkites (1966): Archbishop Joseph Tawil, exarch, 1969.
Former exarch: Justin Najmy, 1966-68.
Military Ordinariate (1917): Cardinal Terence J. Cooke, military vicar, 1968. William Moran, military delegate.
Former military vicars: Cardinal Patrick Hayes, 1917-38; Cardinal Francis Spellman, 1939-67.
Abbacy of Belmont, N. C. (1910): Vacant as of July 15, 1975.
Former abbots: Leo M. Haid, O.S.B., 1910-24; Vincent G. Taylor. O.S.B., 1925-59; Walter A. Coggin, O.S.B., 1960-70; Edmund F. McCaffrey, 1970-75.

Military Ordinariate

The Military Ordinariate or Vicariate, is the diocese which serves members of the armed forces of the United States wherever they are. It has jurisdiction over: military and Veterans Administration hospital chaplains; personnel of the armed forces and members of their families and dependents habitually living with them; members of the Coast Guard, National Guard, Air National Guard and Civil Air Patrol when on active dutyg persons living on military installations and/or attached to military offices or VA facilities.

The ordinariate was canonically established on a permanent basis by a decree of the Sacred Consistorial Congregation dated Sept. 8, 1957. Cardinal Terence J. Cooke, Archbishop of New York, is Military Vicar. Offices of the ordinariate are located at 1011 First Ave., New York, N.Y. 10022.

MISSIONARY BISHOPS

Africa

Namibia (South West Africa): Keetmanshoop (vicariate apostolic), Edward F. Schlotterback, O.S.F.S.
Nigeria: Sokoto (diocese), Michael J. Dempsey, O.P.
South Africa: De Aar (diocese), Joseph A. De Palma, S.C.J.
Keimos (diocese), John Minder, O.S.F.S.
Tanzania: Arusha (diocese), Dennis V. Durning, C. S.Sp.
Musoma (diocese), John Rudin, M.M.
Nachingwea (diocese), Bernard R. Cotey, S.D.S.

Asia

Burma: Prome (diocese), Thomas A. Newman, M.S.

China: Chowtsun (diocese), Henry A. Pinger, O.F.M. Expelled.
Wuchow (diocese), Frederick A. Donaghy, M.M. Expelled.
India: Bhagalpur (diocese), Urban McGarry, T.O.R.
Patna (diocese), Augustine F. Wildermuth, S.J.
Indonesia: Agats (diocese), Alphonse A. Sowada, O.S.C.
Korea: Inchon (diocese), William J. McNaughton, M.M.
Cheju-Do (prefecture), Harold W. Henry, S.S.C., ap. admin.
Pakistan: Multan (diocese), Ernest B. Boland, O. P.
Philippine Islands: Marbel (prelacy), Reginald Arliss, C. P.
Tagum (prelacy), Joseph W. Regan, M. M.
Taiwan: Taichung (diocese), William F. Kupfer, M. M.
Thailand: Udon Thani (diocese), Clarence J. Duhart, C. SS. R.
Turkey: Izmir (archdiocese), John H. Boccella, T. O. R.

Central America, West Indies

Bahamas: Nassau (diocese), Paul L. Hagarty, O. S. B.
Belize: Belize (diocese), Robert L. Hodapp, S.J.
Dominican Republic: San Juan de la Maguana (diocese), Thomas F. Reilly, C. SS. R.
Guatemala: Guatemala (archdiocese), Richard J. Ham, M. M., auxiliary.
Huehuetenango (diocese), Hugo Gerbermann, M. M.
Honduras: Comayagua (diocese), Bernardino Mazzarella, O. F. M.
Olancho (prelacy), Nicholas D'Antonio Salza, O.F.M.
Nicaragua: Bluefields (vicariate apostolic), Salvator Schlaefer, O. F. M. Cap.
Virgin Islands: (prelacy), Edward Harper, C. SS. R.

Europe

Sweden: Stockholm (diocese), John E. Taylor, O. M. I.

Oceania

Caroline and Marshall Islands (vicariate apostolic), Martin J. Neylon, S. J.
Fiji Islands: Suva (archdiocese), George H. Pearce, S. M.
New Guinea: Goroko (diocese), John E. Cohill, S. V. D.
Kavieng (diocese), Alfred M. Stemper, M. S. C.
Madang (archdiocese), Adolph A. Noser, S. V. D.
Mendi (diocese), Firmin Schmidt, O. F. M. Cap.
Mount Hagen (diocese), George Bernarding, S. V. D.
Wewak (diocese), Leo Arkfeld, S. V. D.

South America

Bolivia: Coroico (prelacy), Thomas R. Manning, O. F. M.

La Paz (archdiocese), Andrew B. Schierhoff, auxiliary.

Santa Cruz (diocese), Charles A. Brown, M. M., auxiliary.

Brazil: Abaete do Tocantins (prelacy), Angelo Frosi, S. X.

Belem do Para (archdiocese), Jude Prost, O. F. M., auxiliary.

Borba (prelacy), Adrian J. M. Veigle, T. O. R.

Cristalandia (prelacy), James A. Schuck, O. F. M.

Jatai (diocese), Benedict D. Coscia, O. F. M. Mathias Schmidt, O. S. B., auxiliary.

Paranagua (diocese), Bernard Nolker, C. SS. R.

Santarem (prelacy), James C. Ryan, O. F. M.

Sao Salvador da Bahia (archdiocese), Thomas W. Murphy, C.SS.R., auxiliary.

Paraguay: Coronel Oviedo (prelacy), Jerome Pechillo, T. O. R.

Peru: Chimbote (prelacy), James C. Burke, O.P.

Chulucanas (prelacy), John McNabb, O.S.A.

Dioceses with Interstate Lines

Diocesan lines usually fall within a single state and in some cases include a whole state.

The following dioceses, with their statistics as reported in tables throughout the Almanac, are exceptions.

Norwich, Conn., includes Fisher's Island, N.Y.

Wilmington, Del., includes all of Delaware and nine counties of Maryland.

Baltimore, includes all of Maryland except nine counties under the jurisdiction of Wilmington and five under Washington.

Washington, D.C., includes five counties of Maryland.

El Paso, Tex., includes seven counties of New Mexico.

Gallup, N.M., has jurisdiction over several counties of Arizona.

Cheyenne, Wyo., includes all of Yellowstone National Park.

CATHOLIC POPULATION OF THE UNITED STATES

(Source: *The Official Catholic Directory, 1975;* figures as of Jan. 1, 1975. Archdioceses are indicated by an asterisk; for dioceses marked +, see Dioceses with Interstate Lines.)

Section, State Diocese	Catholics	Dioc.	Priests Rel.	Total	Bros.	Sisters	Parishes	Missions
NEW ENGLAND	5,701,190	4,417	2,608	7,025	825	14,193	1,686	223
Maine, Portland	264,538	243	115	358	47	1,037	143	63
New Hampshire, Manchester	261,737	311	102	413	80	1,259	126	39
Vermont, Burlington	150,624	182	127	309	34	367	100	41
Massachusetts	3,037,454	2,335	1,661	3,996	378	8,024	787	52
*Boston	2,004,002	1,460	1,096	2,556	200	5,422	408	19
Fall River	320,000	228	190	418	50	820	113	16
Springfield	370,313	300	172	472	38	1,036	136	15
Worcester	343,139	347	203	550	90	746	130	2
Rhode Island, Providence	605,041	372	260	632	169	1,299	155	7
Connecticut	1,381,796	974	343	1,317	117	2,207	375	21
*Hartford	855,407	611	121	732	73	1,061	221	2
Bridgeport	330,007	223	155	378	21	786	84	4
Norwich+	196,382	140	67	207	23	360	70	15
MIDDLE ATLANTIC	12,909,533	9,933	5,255	15,188	2,454	38,599	3,899	426
New York	6,348,132	4,714	2,672	7,386	1,614	18,641	1,726	208
*New York	1,880,788	1,129	1,070	2,199	832	7,014	407	57
Albany	435,917	459	253	712	120	1,579	210	52
Brooklyn	1,182,514	1,016	448	1,464	338	2,810	227	—
Buffalo	923,392	638	404	1,042	81	2,559	300	—
Ogdensburg	172,679	196	49	245	32	445	122	39
Rochester	358,850	381	170	551	40	1,105	161	29
Rockville Centre	1,004,187	492	130	622	122	2,223	129	10
Syracuse	389,805	403	148	551	49	906	170	21
New Jersey	2,819,026	1,970	906	2,876	351	5,932	683	37
*Newark	1,370,438	845	495	1,340	191	2,742	252	2
Camden	333,867	408	46	454	13	657	123	9
Paterson	312,858	291	255	546	69	1,048	102	6
Trenton	801,863	426	110	536	78	1,495	206	20
Pennsylvania	3,742,375	3,249	1,677	4,926	489	14,026	1,490	181
*Philadelphia	1,376,135	1,041	743	1,784	282	6,141	312	17
Allentown	261,440	301	123	424	30	1,019	152	20

Section, State Diocese	Catholics	Priests Dioc.	Priests Rel.	Total	Bros.	Sisters	Par-ishes	Mis-sions
Pennsylvania								
Altoona-Johnstown..........................	147,509	157	83	240	31	300	120	16
Erie...	212,291	284	67	351	14	859	126	—
Greensburg	227,031	191	113	304	14	420	117	30
Harrisburg	194,100	179	73	252	10	922	103	17
Pittsburgh	962,412	612	357	969	90	3,088	320	24
Scranton..	361,457	484	118	602	18	1,277	240	57
SOUTH ATLANTIC	**2,533,726**	**2,107**	**2,206**	**4,313**	**537**	**7,193**	**1,169**	**277**
Delaware, Wilmington+	**114,563**	**116**	**91**	**207**	**22**	**390**	**52**	**18**
Maryland, *Baltimore..........................	**451,812**	**354**	**443**	**797**	**137**	**2,308**	**150**	**16**
District of Columbia								
*Washington+	**350,733**	**362**	**813**	**1,175**	**197**	**955**	**127**	**3**
Virginia..	**239,964**	**208**	**192**	**400**	**37**	**620**	**138**	**31**
Arlington	144,600	76	89	165	26	220	51	4
Richmond	95,364	132	103	235	11	400	87	27
West Virginia								
Wheeling-Charleston.......................	**95,880**	**131**	**70**	**201**	**7**	**496**	**100**	**53**
North Carolina	**78,282**	**121**	**74**	**195**	**10**	**396**	**117**	**42**
Belmont Abbey	448	2	25	27	3	—	1	—
Charlotte..	39,344	55	35	90	3	259	57	20
Raleigh...	38,490	64	14	78	4	137	59	22
South Carolina, Charleston	**50,838**	**78**	**51**	**129**	**22**	**239**	**66**	**29**
Georgia	**98,666**	**143**	**101**	**244**	**31**	**397**	**86**	**49**
*Atlanta.......................................	61,166	76	65	141	25	200	44	19
Savannah	37,500	67	36	103	6	197	42	30
Florida	**1,052,988**	**594**	**371**	**965**	**74**	**1,392**	**333**	**36**
*Miami	688,700	284	203	487	40	724	125	4
Orlando..	90,617	130	17	147	1	146	58	6
St. Augustine..................................	86,174	92	35	127	—	201	75	16
St. Petersburg	187,497	88	116	204	33	321	75	10
EAST NORTH CENTRAL..................	**10,404,616**	**8,085**	**5,123**	**13,208**	**1,925**	**35,446**	**4,187**	**454**
Ohio...	**2,326,919**	**2,062**	**1,085**	**3,147**	**541**	**8,069**	**956**	**52**
*Cincinnati	511,000	440	443	883	280	2,351	259	—
Cleveland	911,196	641	308	949	133	2,815	237	3
Columbus.......................................	210,163	279	69	348	49	840	121	13
Steubenville...................................	58,000	174	22	196	14	180	73	18
Toledo..	332,977	277	157	434	21	1,281	149	16
Youngstown....................................	303,583	251	86	337	44	602	117	2
Indiana..	**718,183**	**760**	**614**	**1,374**	**214**	**4,133**	**467**	**33**
*Indianapolis	203,386	247	176	423	86	2,079	164	20
Evansville.......................................	89,494	123	22	145	6	561	75	4
Ft. Wayne-South Bend	151,233	130	264	394	72	922	83	5
Gary...	190,265	147	89	236	38	390	85	2
Lafayette..	83,805	113	63	176	12	181	60	2
Illinois..	**3,556,169**	**2,290**	**1,883**	**4,173**	**569**	**10,305**	**1,109**	**122**
*Chicago.....................................	2,466,294	1,261	1,290	2,551	324	6,497	455	5
Belleville..	115,600	176	46	222	33	442	130	19
Joliet..	359,000	215	203	418	138	1,115	110	9
Peoria...	222,832	260	126	386	22	813	172	44
Rockford...	210,939	181	115	296	18	439	99	7
Springfield......................................	181,504	197	103	300	34	999	143	38
Michigan...	**2,289,924**	**1,371**	**691**	**2,062**	**250**	**5,883**	**796**	**121**
*Detroit	1,500,800	649	473	1,122	180	3,550	329	7
Gaylord..	72,000	62	19	81	4	161	59	25
Grand Rapids..................................	145,316	159	46	205	11	685	86	14
Kalamazoo......................................	87,514	59	34	93	17	357	45	18
Lansing	209,404	147	63	210	33	609	81	6
Marquette	99,403	143	21	164	1	215	92	39
Saginaw..	175,487	152	35	187	4	306	104	12
Wisconsin..	**1,513,421**	**1,602**	**850**	**2,452**	**351**	**7,056**	**859**	**126**
*Milwaukee	697,027	654	537	1,191	204	3,872	265	19
Green Bay	324,523	317	178	495	99	1,073	193	30
La Crosse..	206,953	303	56	359	30	1,007	177	22

Section, State Diocese	Catholics	Dioc.	Priests Rel.	Total	Bros.	Sisters	Par- ishes	Mis- sions
Wisconsin								
Madison	202,569	215	52	267	18	604	138	—
Superior	82,349	113	27	140	—	500	86	55
EAST SOUTH CENTRAL	**617,468**	**928**	**466**	**1,394**	**326**	**4,293**	**607**	**150**
Kentucky	**344,189**	**511**	**177**	**688**	**150**	**3,069**	**281**	**51**
*Louisville	191,030	268	125	393	128	1,527	124	22
Covington	104,000	182	32	214	12	981	83	29
Owensboro	49,159	61	20	81	10	561	74	—
Tennessee	**98,509**	**127**	**60**	**187**	**99**	**314**	**87**	**22**
Memphis	42,443	47	28	75	80	166	30	5
Nashville	56,066	80	32	112	19	148	57	17
Alabama	**92,100**	**155**	**160**	**315**	**26**	**526**	**129**	**34**
Birmingham	44,420	65	66	131	12	240	58	19
Mobile	47,680	90	94	184	14	286	71	15
Mississippi, Natchez-Jackson	**82,670**	**135**	**69**	**204**	**51**	**384**	**110**	**43**
WEST NORTH CENTRAL	**3,231,097**	**4,181**	**2,070**	**6,251**	**725**	**15,837**	**2,738**	**523**
Minnesota	**995,012**	**989**	**467**	**1,456**	**151**	**3,625**	**717**	**73**
*St. Paul and Minneapolis	520,416	354	201	555	80	1,461	214	7
Crookston	43,167	52	23	75	—	287	51	29
Duluth	94,208	102	41	143	2	367	82	37
New Ulm	72,937	125	4	129	—	143	95	—
St. Cloud	147,078	168	177	345	56	743	146	—
Winona	117,206	188	21	209	13	624	129	—
Iowa	**527,844**	**955**	**126**	**1,081**	**68**	**2,665**	**541**	**67**
*Dubuque	232,262	408	71	479	60	1,579	194	41
Davenport	105,300	204	24	228	8	528	119	21
Des Moines	78,743	128	15	143	—	218	89	5
Sioux City	111,539	215	16	231	—	340	139	—
Missouri	**763,563**	**943**	**826**	**1,769**	**365**	**4,767**	**493**	**78**
*St. Louis	511,086	557	581	1,138	286	3,648	248	9
Jefferson City	72,714	142	14	156	16	203	92	23
Kansas City-St. Joseph	137,679	166	210	376	55	702	94	14
Springfield- Cape Girardeau	42,084	78	21	99	8	214	59	32
North Dakota	**171,185**	**236**	**91**	**327**	**26**	**803**	**194**	**81**
Bismarck	75,978	90	54	144	23	368	76	48
Fargo	95,207	146	37	183	3	435	118	33
South Dakota	**135,798**	**182**	**125**	**307**	**32**	**627**	**172**	**79**
Rapid City	36,200	49	52	101	8	103	50	48
Sioux Falls	99,598	133	73	206	24	524	122	31
Nebraska	**317,786**	**446**	**185**	**631**	**49**	**1,392**	**280**	**97**
*Omaha	204,372	241	153	394	40	1,034	136	19
Grand Island	52,140	79	7	86	—	150	52	37
Lincoln	61,274	126	25	151	9	208	92	41
Kansas	**319,909**	**430**	**250**	**680**	**34**	**1,958**	**341**	**48**
*Kansas City	138,500	134	165	299	23	833	98	21
Dodge City	32,522	63	10	73	1	214	49	11
Salina	58,618	86	50	136	5	408	98	—
Wichita	90,269	147	25	172	5	503	96	16
WEST SOUTH CENTRAL	**3,579,560**	**1,936**	**1,680**	**3,616**	**584**	**7,187**	**1,483**	**620**
Arkansas, Little Rock	**55,150**	**105**	**64**	**169**	**49**	**535**	**80**	**39**
Louisiana	**1,293,690**	**668**	**582**	**1,250**	**275**	**2,065**	**468**	**173**
*New Orleans	653,378	252	353	605	197	1,280	165	18
Alexandria	73,500	131	42	173	17	255	85	61
Baton Rouge	158,534	91	68	159	22	203	67	25
Lafayette	408,278	194	119	313	39	327	151	69
Oklahoma	**106,266**	**181**	**61**	**242**	**23**	**510**	**124**	**70**
*Oklahoma City	66,395	115	36	151	14	279	74	44
Tulsa	39,871	66	25	91	9	231	50	26
Texas	**2,124,454**	**982**	**973**	**1,955**	**237**	**4,077**	**811**	**338**
*San Antonio	544,883	194	238	432	121	1,611	159	72
Amarillo	72,287	69	22	91	—	138	60	28
Austin	139,080	103	62	165	30	170	81	32

Section, State Diocese	Catholics	Dioc.	Priests Rel.	Total	Bros.	Sisters	Par- ishes	Mis- sions
Texas								
Beaumont....................................	75,000	55	30	85	1	108	37	18
Brownsville	284,148	34	79	113	14	164	59	3
Corpus Christi............................	183,367	69	79	148	14	373	72	46
Dallas...	115,963	97	118	215	9	397	56	14
El Paso+....................................	216,188	88	65	153	19	346	72	49
Fort Worth..................................	72,466	57	39	96	18	208	49	25
Galveston-Houston	352,597	173	211	384	11	520	123	18
San Angelo.................................	68,475	43	30	73	—	42	43	33
MOUNTAIN	**1,559,330**	**1,073**	**789**	**1,862**	**244**	**3,224**	**768**	**641**
Montana	**133,206**	**223**	**66**	**289**	**13**	**292**	**133**	**119**
Great Falls	66,615	86	45	131	3	171	74	72
Helena......................................	66,591	137	21	158	10	121	59	47
Idaho, Boise	**63,596**	**86**	**26**	**112**	**1**	**220**	**66**	**36**
Wyoming, Cheyenne+	**45,000**	**54**	**7**	**61**	**4**	**91**	**39**	**30**
Colorado	**405,701**	**258**	**260**	**518**	**46**	**1,200**	**186**	**104**
*Denver	309,266	163	200	363	36	980	126	42
Pueblo......................................	96,435	95	60	155	10	220	60	62
New Mexico	**356,832**	**168**	**139**	**307**	**123**	**528**	**145**	**278**
*Santa Fe	315,470	138	82	220	93	353	91	233
Gallup+....................................	41,362	30	57	87	30	175	54	45
Arizona	**403,250**	**176**	**214**	**390**	**27**	**630**	**123**	**48**
Phoenix.....................................	229,869	87	132	219	21	304	67	25
Tucson......................................	173,381	89	82	171	6	326	56	23
Utah, Salt Lake City..................	**51,745**	**53**	**40**	**93**	**21**	**132**	**38**	**11**
Nevada, Reno..............................	**100,000**	**55**	**37**	**92**	**9**	**131**	**38**	**15**
PACIFIC	**5,601,968**	**2,831**	**2,621**	**5,452**	**992**	**8,732**	**1,501**	**420**
Washington	**466,654**	**369**	**367**	**736**	**56**	**1,202**	**222**	**69**
*Seattle	344,785	208	254	462	37	620	127	37
Spokane	70,851	93	102	195	19	512	57	25
Yakima	51,018	68	11	79	—	70	38	7
Oregon	**283,893**	**265**	**268**	**533**	**60**	**926**	**156**	**57**
*Portland	260,241	219	255	474	60	825	125	27
Baker	23,652	46	13	59	—	101	31	30
California....................................	**4,604,296**	**2,125**	**1,820**	**3,945**	**762**	**6,122**	**1,008**	**223**
*Los Angeles.............................	2,099,749	690	757	1,447	242	1,959	319	40
*San Francisco..........................	819,250	323	567	890	172	1,719	151	12
Fresno.......................................	284,932	127	41	168	19	189	84	47
Monterey	95,000	89	40	129	25	245	43	12
Oakland....................................	347,420	142	175	317	162	672	84	3
Sacramento	222,426	186	70	256	54	372	90	43
San Diego..................................	563,400	428	102	530	28	701	170	29
Santa Rosa	72,831	85	36	121	56	158	36	25
Stockton....................................	99,288	55	32	87	4	107	31	12
Alaska	**42,125**	**28**	**50**	**78**	**12**	**80**	**49**	**33**
*Anchorage...............................	24,000	13	12	25	4	26	16	10
Fairbanks..................................	13,325	5	35	40	8	34	24	20
Juneau......................................	4,800	10	3	13	—	20	9	3
Hawaii, Honolulu	4205,000	44	116	160	102	402	66	38
EASTERN RITES	**613,347**	**514**	**86**	**600**	**13**	**521**	**477**	**26**
*Philadelphia	166,815	118	9	127	—	191	101	8
*Munhall	150,715	84	9	93	5	150	83	—
Passaic	96,940	82	16	98	3	42	84	2
Stamford...................................	87,250	53	19	72	1	67	57	2
Parma	30,304	51	6	57	—	41	48	4
St. Nicholas..............................	29,869	36	12	48	—	19	36	4
St. Maron of Detroit.................	29,625	59	—	59	—	6	43	4
Melkite Exarchate	21,829	31	15	46	4	5	25	2
MILITARY ORDINARIATE	**1,950,000**	**—**	**—**	**—**	**—**	**—**	**—**	**—**
TOTALS 1975	**48,701,835**	**36,005**	**22,904**	**58,909**	**8,625**	**135,225**	**18,515**	**3,760**
Totals 1974	**48,465,438**	**36,058**	**20,654**	**56,712**	**9,233**	**139,963**	**18,433**	**4,032**
Totals 1965	**45,640,601**	**35,725**	**22,707**	**58,432**	**12,271**	**179,954**	**17,637**	**4,547**

PERCENTAGE OF CATHOLICS IN U.S. POPULATION

(Source: *The Official Catholic Directory, 1975;* figures are as of Jan. 1, 1975. Total general population figures at the end of the table are U.S. Census Bureau estimates for Jan. 1 of the respective years. Archdioceses are indicated by an asterisk; for dioceses marked +, see Dioceses with Interstate Lines.)

Section, State Diocese	Catholic Pop.	Total Pop.	Cath. Pct.	Section, State Diocese	Catholic Pop.	Total Pop.	Cath. Pct.
NEW ENGLAND	**5,701,190**	**13,780,403**	**41.37**	Charlotte	39,344	2,727,500	1.44
				Raleigh	38,490	2,480,393	1.55
Maine, Portland	264,538	993,663	26.62	South Carolina			
New Hampshire				Charleston	50,838	2,726,000	1.86
Manchester	261,737	784,000	33.38	Georgia	98,666	3,580,000	2.76
Vermont, Burlington	150,624	464,200	32.44	*Atlanta	61,166	2,000,000	3.06
Massachusetts	3,037,454	7,499,306	40.50	Savannah	37,500	1,580,000	2.37
*Boston	2,004,002	5,539,700	36.18	Florida	1,052,988	8,790,332	11.98
Fall River	320,000	530,000	60.38	*Miami	688,700	3,600,000	19.13
Springfield	370,313	791,643	46.78	Orlando	90,617	1,590,020	5.70
Worcester	343,139	637,963	53.79	St. Augustine	86,174	1,690,000	5.10
Rhode Island				St. Petersburg	187,497	1,910,312	9.81
Providence	605,041	937,034	64.57				
Connecticut	1,381,796	3,102,200	44.54	**EAST NORTH**			
*Hartford	855,407	1,728,400	49.49	**CENTRAL**	**10,404,616**	**40,660,825**	**25.59**
Bridgeport	330,007	823,600	40.07				
Norwich+	196,382	550,200	35.69	Ohio	2,326,919	10,782,596	21.58
				*Cincinnati	511,000	2,670,727	19.13
MIDDLE ATLANTIC	**12,909,533**	**38,498,121**	**33.53**	Cleveland	911,196	3,004,834	30.32
				Columbus	210,163	1,831,800	11.47
New York	6,348,132	18,687,134	33.97	Steubenville	58,000	550,000	10.55
*New York	1,880,788	5,124,853	36.70	Toledo	332,977	1,443,318	23.07
Albany	435,917	1,472,684	29.60	Youngstown	303,583	1,281,917	23.68
Brooklyn	1,182,514	4,575,560	25.84	Indiana	718,183	5,190,872	13.84
Buffalo	923,392	1,778,355	51.92	*Indianapolis	203,386	2,022,366	10.06
Ogdensburg	172,679	382,353	45.16	Evansville	89,494	435,177	20.56
Rochester	358,850	1,439,600	24.93	Ft. Wayne-South Bend	151,233	973,764	15.53
Rockville Centre	1,004,187	2,705,172	37.12	Gary	190,265	772,685	24.62
Syracuse	389,805	1,208,557	32.25	Lafayette	83,805	986,880	8.49
New Jersey	2,819,026	7,913,966	35.62	Illinois	3,556,169	11,231,439	31.66
*Newark	1,370,438	3,008,805	45.55	*Chicago	2,466,294	5,936,200	41.55
Camden	333,867	1,104,400	30.23	Belleville	115,600	807,682	14.31
Paterson	312,858	1,111,017	28.16	Joliet	359,000	1,027,000	34.96
Trenton	801,863	2,689,744	29.81	Peoria	222,832	1,434,428	15.53
Pennsylvania	3,742,375	11,897,021	31.46	Rockford	210,939	934,938	22.56
*Philadelphia	1,376,135	3,901,000	35.28	Springfield	181,504	1,091,191	16.63
Allentown	261,440	1,000,000	26.14	Michigan	2,289,924	8,936,422	25.62
Altoona-Johnstown	147,509	627,403	23.51	*Detroit	1,500,800	4,502,400	33.33
Erie	212,291	857,035	24.77	Gaylord	72,000	294,968	24.41
Greensburg	227,031	696,803	32.58	Grand Rapids	145,316	899,238	16.16
Harrisburg	194,100	1,585,500	12.24	Kalamazoo	87,514	796,812	10.98
Pittsburgh	962,412	2,295,715	41.92	Lansing	209,404	1,431,786	14.62
Scranton	361,457	933,565	38.72	Marquette	99,403	304,347	32.66
				Saginaw	175,487	706,871	24.83
SOUTH ATLANTIC	**2,533,726**	**31,891,091**	**7.94**	Wisconsin	1,513,421	4,519,496	33.49
				*Milwaukee	697,027	2,006,304	34.74
Delaware, Wilmington+	114,563	807,533	14.19	Green Bay	324,523	728,512	44.55
Maryland, *Baltimore	451,812	2,366,726	19.09	La Crosse	206,953	667,849	30.99
District of Columbia				Madison	202,569	810,276	25.00
*Washington	350,733	2,055,634	17.06	Superior	82,349	306,555	26.86
Virginia	239,964	4,612,226	5.20				
Arlington	144,600	1,200,000	12.05	**EAST SOUTH**			
Richmond	95,364	3,412,226	2.79	**CENTRAL**	**617,468**	**12,794,323**	**4.83**
West Virginia							
Wheeling-Charleston	95,880	1,744,237	5.50	Kentucky	344,189	3,401,469	10.12
North Carolina	78,282	5,208,403	1.50	*Louisville	191,030	1,223,700	15.61
Belmont Abbey	448	510	87.84	Covington	104,000	1,500,000	6.93

Section, State Diocese	Catholic Pop.	Total Pop.	Cath. Pct.	Section, State Diocese	Catholic Pop.	Total Pop.	Cath. Pct.
Kentucky							
Owensboro	49,159	677,769	7.25	Amarillo	72,287	750,000	9.64
Tennessee	98,509	3,858,168	2.55	Austin	139,080	939,600	14.80
Memphis	42,443	1,178,168	3.60	Beaumont	75,000	586,598	12.79
Nashville	56,066	2,680,000	2.09	Brownsville	284,148	355,180	80.00
Alabama	92,100	3,373,006	2.73	Corpus Christi	183,367	527,000	34.79
Birmingham	44,420	2,143,875	2.07	Dallas	115,963	2,505,367	4.63
Mobile	47,680	1,229,131	3.88	El Paso+	216,188	654,000	33.06
Mississippi				Fort Worth	72,466	1,273,800	5.69
Natchez-Jackson	82,670	2,161,680	3.82	Galveston-Houston	352,597	2,598,900	13.57
				San Angelo	68,475	556,961	12.29
WEST NORTH CENTRAL	**3,231,097**	**16,310,730**	**19.81**	**MOUNTAIN**	**1,559,330**	**8,786,326**	**17.75**
Minnesota	995,012	3,764,931	26.43	Montana	133,206	694,330	19.18
*St. Paul and				Great Falls	66,615	351,858	18.93
Minneapolis	520,416	2,017,225	25.80	Helena	66,591	342,472	19.44
Crookston	43,167	215,227	20.06	Idaho, Boise	63,596	770,000	8.26
Duluth	94,208	387,190	24.33	Wyoming, Cheyenne+	45,000	340,000	13.24
New Ulm	72,937	279,054	26.14	Colorado	405,701	2,296,708	17.66
St. Cloud	147,078	349,853	42.04	*Denver	309,266	1,900,000	16.28
Winona	117,206	516,382	22.70	Pueblo	96,435	396,708	24.31
Iowa	527,844	2,781,456	18.98	New Mexico	356,832	950,000	37.56
*Dubuque	232,262	956,078	24.29	*Santa Fe	315,470	710,000	44.43
Davenport	105,300	687,310	15.32	Gallup+	41,362	240,000	17.23
Des Moines	78,743	625,185	12.60	Arizona	403,250	2,062,288	19.55
Sioux City	111,539	512,883	21.75	Phoenix	229,869	1,324,088	17.36
Missouri	763,563	4,709,056	16.21	Tucson	173,381	738,200	23.49
*St. Louis	511,086	1,933,811	26.43	Utah, Salt Lake City	51,745	1,173,000	4.41
Jefferson City	72,714	670,576	10.84	Nevada, Reno	100,000	500,000	20.00
Kansas City-							
St. Joseph	137,679	1,271,000	10.83	**PACIFIC**	**5,601,968**	**27,797,556**	**20.15**
Springfield-Cape							
Girardeau	42,084	833,669	5.05	Washington	466,654	3,421,593	13.64
North Dakota	171,185	617,760	27.71	*Seattle	344,785	2,593,800	13.29
Bismarck	75,978	244,777	31.04	Spokane	70,851	485,983	14.58
Fargo	95,207	372,983	25.53	Yakima	51,018	341,810	14.93
South Dakota	135,798	660,000	20.58	Oregon	283,893	2,312,242	12.28
Rapid City	36,200	178,000	20.34	*Portland	260,241	2,023,742	12.86
Sioux Falls	99,598	482,000	20.66	Baker	23,652	288,500	8.20
Nebraska	317,786	1,513,989	20.99	California	4,604,296	20,933,371	22.00
*Omaha	204,372	711,156	28.74	*Los Angeles	2,099,749	9,407,408	22.32
Grand Island	52,140	297,100	17.55	*San Francisco	819,250	2,542,655	32.22
Lincoln	61,274	505,733	12.12	Fresno	284,932	1,204,652	23.65
Kansas	319,909	2,263,538	14.13	Monterey	95,000	484,363	19.61
*Kansas City	138,500	882,028	15.70	Oakland	347,420	1,737,100	20.00
Dodge City	32,522	206,724	15.73	Sacramento	222,426	1,600,400	13.90
Salina	58,618	353,000	16.61	San Diego	563,400	2,883,937	19.54
Wichita	90,269	821,786	10.98	Santa Rosa	72,831	513,231	14.19
				Stockton	99,288	559,625	17.74
WEST SOUTH CENTRAL	**3,579,560**	**20,308,372**	**17.63**	Alaska	42,125	298,350	14.12
				*Anchorage	24,000	160,000	15.00
Arkansas, Little Rock	55,150	1,923,295	2.87	Fairbanks	13,325	95,350	13.97
Louisiana	1,293,690	3,765,636	34.36	Juneau	4,800	43,000	11.16
*New Orleans	653,378	1,370,980	47.66	Hawaii, Honolulu	205,000	832,000	24.64
Alexandria	73,500	1,083,132	6.79				
Baton Rouge	158,534	612,798	25.87	**EASTERN RITES**	**613,347**	—	—
Lafayette	408,278	698,726	58.43				
Oklahoma	106,266	2,583,414	4.11	**MILITARY**			
*Oklahoma City	66,395	1,451,914	4.57	**ORDINARIATE**	**1,950,000**	—	—
Tulsa	39,871	1,131,500	3.52				
Texas	2,124,454	12,036,027	17.65	**TOTALS 1975**	**48,701,835**	**212,812,000**	**22.88**
*San Antonio	544,883	1,288,621	42.28	**Totals 1974**	**48,465,438**	**211,216,000**	**22.95**
				Totals 1965	**45,640,601**	**193,496,000**	**23.59**

INFANT BAPTISMS AND CONVERTS IN THE UNITED STATES

(Source: *The Official Catholic Directory, 1975;* figures as of Jan. 1, 1975. Archdioceses are indicated by an asterisk; for dioceses marked +, see Dioceses with Interstate Lines.)

Section, State Diocese	Infant Baptisms	Converts
NEW ENGLAND	**82,134**	**2,298**
Maine, Portland	4,872	408
New Hampshire, Manchester	5,107	97
Vermont, Burlington	2,775	152
Massachusetts	43,280	783
*Boston	26,176	394
Fall River	5,632	89
Springfield	5,607	171
Worcester	5,865	129
Rhode Island, Providence	7,443	159
Connecticut	18,657	699
*Hartford	10,903	435
Bridgeport	4,842	132
Norwich+	2,912	132
MIDDLE ATLANTIC	**214,687**	**9,985**
New York	112,172	4,452
*New York	35,010	1,270
Albany	5,046	485
Brooklyn	26,285	524
Buffalo	10,536	675
Ogdensburg	2,982	224
Rochester	6,712	496
Rockville Centre	17,737	299
Syracuse	7,864	479
New Jersey	45,922	1,522
*Newark	19,141	470
Camden	6,502	360
Paterson	6,613	181
Trenton	13,666	511
Pennsylvania	56,593	4,011
*Philadelphia	22,397	1,225
Allentown	4,308	225
Altoona-Johnstown	2,489	311
Erie	4,064	417
Greensburg	3,099	312
Harrisburg	3,379	437
Pittsburgh	11,195	780
Scranton	5,662	304
SOUTH ATLANTIC	**49,605**	**6,762**
Delaware, Wilmington+	2,426	199
Maryland, *Baltimore	7,587	805
District of Columbia		
*Washington+	7,806	1,036
Virginia	5,461	753
Arlington	2,902	328
Richmond	2,559	425
West Virginia		
Wheeling-Charleston	1,732	493
North Carolina	2,014	458
Belmont Abbey	24	6
Charlotte	846	259
Raleigh	1,144	193
South Carolina, Charleston	1,321	349
Georgia	2,499	736
*Atlanta	1,599	360

Section, State Diocese	Infant Baptisms	Converts
Savannah	900	376
Florida	18,759	1,933
*Miami	10,682	645
Orlando	2,638	340
St. Augustine	2,035	481
St. Petersburg	3,404	467
EAST NORTH CENTRAL	**168,462**	**21,785**
Ohio	37,642	5,000
*Cincinnati	8,865	1,050
Cleveland	13,138	1,517
Columbus	3,156	789
Steubenville	1,101	258
Toledo	6,577	855
Youngstown	4,805	531
Indiana	13,824	2,588
*Indianapolis	4,294	1,073
Evansville	1,525	269
Ft. Wayne-South Bend	2,973	456
Gary	3,299	380
Lafayette	1,733	410
Illinois	55,481	7,730
*Chicago	36,068	4,963
Belleville	1,920	380
Joliet	6,306	433
Peoria	4,253	883
Rockford	3,767	375
Springfield	3,167	696
Michigan	34,436	4,136
*Detroit	19,278	1,540
Gaylord	1,409	218
Grand Rapids	3,041	570
Kalamazoo	1,542	371
Lansing	3,767	848
Marquette	1,881	196
Saginaw	3,518	393
Wisconsin	27,079	2,331
*Milwaukee	12,444	882
Green Bay	5,752	391
La Crosse	4,045	447
Madison	3,024	397
Superior	1,814	214
EAST SOUTH CENTRAL	**12,200**	**3,079**
Kentucky	6,595	1,162
*Louisville	3,657	579
Covington	1,904	362
Owensboro	1,034	221
Tennessee	2,094	908
Memphis	941	320
Nashville	1,153	588
Alabama	1,742	633
Birmingham	753	316
Mobile	989	317
Mississippi, Natchez-Jackson	1,769	376
WEST NORTH CENTRAL	**64,101**	**9,346**
Minnesota	20,534	1,828
*St. Paul and Minneapolis	11,333	893

Section, State Diocese	Infant Baptisms	Converts
Minnesota		
Crookston	904	117
Duluth	1,544	134
New Ulm	1,461	162
St. Cloud	2,891	309
Winona	2,401	213
Iowa	10,642	1,550
*Dubuque	4,467	583
Davenport	2,188	335
Des Moines	1,751	309
Sioux City	2,236	323
Missouri	13,108	2,564
*St. Louis	8,213	1,263
Jefferson City	1,494	344
Kansas City-St. Joseph	2,600	634
Springfield-Cape Girardeau	801	323
North Dakota	3,662	451
Bismarck	1,519	146
Fargo	2,143	305
South Dakota	3,203	471
Rapid City	810	112
Sioux Falls	2,393	359
Nebraska	6,520	1,090
*Omaha	4,028	579
Grand Island	1,117	206
Lincoln	1,375	305
Kansas	6,432	1,392
*Kansas City	2,688	568
Dodge City	739	138
Salina	1,210	217
Wichita	1,795	469
WEST SOUTH CENTRAL	**95,771**	**6,478**
Arkansas, Little Rock	1,174	335
Louisiana	24,301	1,619
*New Orleans	11,503	645
Alexandria	1,709	386
Baton Rouge	3,113	257
Lafayette	7,976	331
Oklahoma	2,304	630
*Oklahoma City	1,574	402
Tulsa	730	228
Texas	67,992	3,894
*San Antonio	15,267	456
Amarillo	2,688	162
Austin	2,951	329
Beaumont	1,701	315
Brownsville	8,397	169
Corpus Christi	7,535	187
Dallas	4,165	656
El Paso+	10,958	160
Fort Worth	2,225	260
Galveston-Houston	9,879	1,016
San Angelo	2,226	184
MOUNTAIN	**39,023**	**3,870**
Montana	3,000	441

Section, State Diocese	Infant Baptisms	Converts
Great Falls	1,600	200
Helena	1,400	241
Idaho, Boise	1,888	409
Wyoming, Cheyenne+	1,194	157
Colorado	10,934	884
*Denver	8,432	718
Pueblo	2,502	166
New Mexico	8,132	762
*Santa Fe	6,926	313
Gallup+	1,206	449
Arizona	11,059	756
Phoenix	5,986	459
Tucson	5,073	297
Utah, Salt Lake City	1,308	180
Nevada, Reno	1,508	281
PACIFIC	**127,348**	**8,919**
Washington	7,907	1,322
*Seattle	5,264	965
Spokane	1,374	236
Yakima	1,269	121
Oregon	3,934	728
*Portland	3,359	575
Baker	575	153
California	109,755	6,500
*Los Angeles	60,086	2,604
*San Francisco	10,835	695
Fresno	8,504	348
Monterey	2,409	159
Oakland	5,802	692
Sacramento	4,954	468
San Diego	13,125	1,140
Santa Rosa	1,589	173
Stockton	2,451	221
Alaska	789	80
*Anchorage	357	40
Fairbanks	314	12
Juneau	118	28
Hawaii, Honolulu	4,963	289
EASTERN RITES	**3,863**	**231**
*Philadelphia	695	26
*Munhall	650	72
Passaic	607	19
Stamford	295	9
Parma	467	54
St. Nicholas	292	12
St. Maron of Detroit	554	29
Melkite Exarchate	303	10
MILITARY ORDINARIATE	**19,112**	**2,370**
TOTALS 1975	**876,306**	**75,123**
Totals 1974	**916,564**	**74,741**
Totals 1965	**1,310,413**	**126,209**

New Baptismal Rite: The new baptismal ritual for infants, in line with intentions of the Second Vatican Council, is more suited to the life-situation of the child and parents than the one in previous use. One important feature is the primary emphasis placed on the role of the parents, as distinguished from the complementary role of the sponsors. Another feature is the provision for administering the sacrament during Mass.

U.S. STATISTICAL SUMMARY

(Principal source: *The Official Catholic Directory, 1975.* Comparisons are with figures reported in the previous edition.)

Catholic Population: 48,701,835 (22.88 per cent of the total population); increase, 236,397.

Jurisdictions: 32 archdioceses; 132 dioceses (including Guam); 1 exarchate; 1 prelacy; 1 abbacy; the military ordinariate.

Cardinals: 11 (7 head archiepiscopal sees, 1 is an official in the Roman Curia, 3 are retired).

Archbishops: 58 (32 residential archbishops, including 7 cardinals; 2 titular archbishops — 1 coadjutor and 1 auxiliary; 20 retired, including 3 cardinals; 4 serving outside the U.S.).

Bishops: 324 (219 residential and titular bishops; 52 retired; 53 serving outside the U.S.).

Abbots: 65.

Priests: 58,909; increase, 2,197. Includes: diocesan or secular priests, 36,005 (decrease, 53); religious order priests, 22,904 (increase, 2,250). [The increase in the number of religious order priests reflects the inclusion in the 1975 Directory of priests on missionary duty outside the U.S. according to diocese of origin.]

Brothers: 8,625; decrease, 608.

Sisters: 135,225; decrease, 4,738.

Seminarians: 17,802; decrease, 1,546. Includes: diocesan seminarians, 11,223 (decrease, 542); religious order seminarians, 6,579 (decrease, 1,004).

Infant Baptisms: 876,306; decrease, 40,258.

Converts: 75,123; increase, 382.

Marriages: 385,029; decrease, 21,879.

Deaths: 407,258; decrease, 8,154.

Parishes: 18,515; increase, 82.

Seminaries, Diocesan: 104; decrease, 5.

Religious Seminaries, Novitiates, Scholasticates: 269; decrease, 24.

Colleges and Universities: 251; decrease, 7. Students, 422,243; increase, 15,162.

High Schools: 1,676; decrease, 26. Students, 920,516; increase, 8,786. [Parish and diocesan high schools reported an increase of 13,638 students; private high school enrollment decreased by 4,852.]

Elementary Schools: 8,539; decrease, 108. Students, 2,599,227; decrease, 118,671. [Parochial elementary schools reported an enrollment decrease of 123,646; private elementary school enrollment increased by 4,975.]

Teachers: 171,797; decrease, 2,914. Includes: priests, 6,974 (decrease, 102); scholastics, 434 (decrease, 117); brothers, 3,512 (decrease, 223); sisters, 56,050 (decrease, 3,709); lay teachers, 104,827 (increase, 1,237).

Public School Students in Religious Instruction Programs: 5,082,134; decrease, 171,604. Includes: high school students, 1,093,184 (decrease, 78,138); elementary school students, 3,988,950 (decrease, 93,466).

Catholic Hospitals: 761; decrease, 37. Patients treated, 29,770,269; increase, 2,381,993.

Nurses' Schools: 141; decrease, 12. Student nurses, 19,588; decrease, 540.

Homes for Aged: 463; decrease, 9. Residents, 51,386; increase, 2,173.

Orphanages: 209; children 15,926. Children in Foster Homes: 16,756.

CATHEDRALS IN THE UNITED STATES

A cathedral is the principal church in a diocese, the one in which the bishop has his seat *(cathedra).* He is the actual rector, although many functions of the church, which usually serves a parish, are the responsibility of a priest serving as the administrator. Because of the dignity of a cathedral, the dates of its dedication and its patronal feast are observed throughout a diocese.

The pope's cathedral, the Basilica of St. John Lateran, is the highest-ranking church in the world.

(Archdioceses are indicated by asterisk.)

Albany, N.Y.: Immaculate Conception.

Alexandria, La.: St. Francis Xavier.

Allentown, Pa.: St. Catherine of Siena.

Altoona-Johnstown, Pa.: Blessed Sacrament (Altoona); St. John Gualbert (Johnstown Co-Cathedral).

Amarillo, Tex.: St. Laurence; Sacred Heart (Old Cathedral).

Anchorage,* Alaska: Holy Family.

Arlington, Va: St. Thomas More.

Atlanta,* Ga.: Christ the King.

Austin, Tex.: St. Mary.

Baker, Ore.: St. Francis de Sales.

Baltimore,* Md.: Mary Our Queen; Basilica of the Assumption of the Blessed Virgin Mary (Co-Cathedral).

Baton Rouge, La.: St. Joseph.

Beaumont, Tex.: St. Anthony.

Belleville, Ill.: St. Peter.

Belmont Abbey, N.C.: Mary Help of Christians.

Birmingham, Ala.: St. Paul.

Bismarck, N.D.: Holy Spirit.

Boise, Ida.: St. John the Evangelist.

Boston,* Mass.: Holy Cross.

Bridgeport, Conn.: St. Augustine.

Brooklyn, N.Y.: St. James.

Brownsville, Tex.: Immaculate Conception.

Buffalo, N.Y.: St. Joseph.

Burlington, Vt.: Immaculate Conception (destroyed by fire in 1972).

Camden, N.J.: Immaculate Conception.

Charleston, S.C.: St. John the Baptist.

Charlotte, N.C.: St. Patrick.

Cheyenne, Wyo.: St. Mary.

Chicago,* Ill.: Holy Name.

Cincinnati,* Ohio: St. Peter in Chains.

Cleveland, Ohio: St. John the Evangelist.

Columbus, Ohio: St. Joseph.

Corpus Christi, Tex.: Corpus Christi.
Covington, Ky.: Basilica of the Assumption.
Crookston, Minn.: Immaculate Conception.
Dallas, Tex.: Sacred Heart.
Davenport, Ia.: Sacred Heart.
Denver,* Colo.: Immaculate Conception.
Des Moines, Ia.: St. Ambrose.
Detroit,* Mich.: Blessed Sacrament.
Dodge City, Kans.: Sacred Heart.
Dubuque,* Ia.: St. Raphael.
Duluth, Minn.: Holy Rosary.
El Paso, Tex.: St. Patrick.
Erie, Pa.: St. Peter.
Evansville, Ind.: Most Holy Trinity (Pro-Cathedral).
Fairbanks, Alaska: Sacred Heart.
Fall River, Mass.: St. Mary of the Assumption.
Fargo, N.D.: St. Mary.
Fort Wayne-S. Bend, Ind.: Immaculate Conception (Fort Wayne); St. Matthew (South Bend Co-Cathedral).
Fort Worth, Tex.: St. Patrick.
Fresno, Calif.: St. John.
Gallup, N.M.: Sacred Heart.
Galveston-Houston, Tex.: St. Mary (Galveston); Sacred Heart (Houston Co-Cathedral).
Gary, Ind.: Holy Angels.
Gaylord, Mich.: St. Mary.
Grand Island, Nebr.: Nativity of Blessed Virgin Mary.
Grand Rapids, Mich.: St. Andrew.
Great Falls, Mont.: St. Ann.
Green Bay, Wis.: St. Francis Xavier.
Greensburg, Pa.: Blessed Sacrament.
Harrisburg, Pa.: St. Patrick.
Hartford,* Conn.: St. Joseph.
Helena, Mont.: St. Helena.
Honolulu, Hawaii: Our Lady of Peace.
Indianapolis,* Ind.: Sts. Peter and Paul.
Jefferson City, Mo.: St. Joseph.
Joliet, Ill.: St. Raymond.
Juneau, Alaska: Nativity of the Blessed Virgin Mary.
Kalamazoo, Mich.: St. Augustine.
Kansas City,* Kans.: St. Peter the Apostle.
Kansas City-St. Joseph, Mo.: Immaculate Conception (Kansas City); St. Joseph (St. Joseph Co-Cathedral).
La Crosse, Wis.: St. Joseph.
Lafayette, Ind.: St. Mary.
Lafayette, La.: St. John the Evangelist.
Lansing, Mich.: St. Mary.
Lincoln, Nebr.: Cathedral of the Risen Christ.
Little Rock, Ark.: St. Andrew.
Los Angeles,* Calif.: St. Vibiana.
Louisville,* Ky.: Assumption.
Madison, Wis.: St. Raphael.
Manchester, N.H.: St. Joseph.
Marquette, Mich.: St. Peter.
Memphis, Tenn.: Immaculate Conception.
Miami,* Fla.: St. Mary.
Milwaukee,* Wis.: St. John.

Mobile, Ala.: Immaculate Conception (Minor Basilica).
Monterey, Calif.: San Carlos Borromeo.
Munhall,* Pa. (Byzantine Rite): St. John the Baptist.
Nashville, Tenn.: Incarnation.
Natchez-Jackson, Miss.: Our Lady of Sorrows (Natchez); St. Peter (Jackson Co-Cathedral).
Newark,* N.J.: Sacred Heart.
New Orleans,* La.: Cathedral (Basilica) of St. Louis.
New Ulm, Minn.: Holy Trinity.
New York,* N.Y.: St. Patrick.
Norwich, Conn.: St. Patrick.
Oakland, Calif.: St. Francis de Sales.
Ogdensburg, N.Y.: St. Mary.
Oklahoma City,* Okla.: Our Lady of Perpetual Help.
Omaha,* Nebr.: St. Cecilia.
Orlando, Fla.: St. Charles Borromeo.
Owensboro, Ky.: St. Stephen.
Parma, Ohio (Byzantine Rite): St. John the Baptist.
Passaic, N.J. (Byzantine Rite): St. Michael.
Paterson, N.J.: St. John the Baptist.
Peoria, Ill.: St. Mary.
Philadelphia,* Pa.: Sts. Peter and Paul.
Philadelphia,* Pa. (Byzantine Rite): Immaculate Conception.
Phoenix, Ariz.: Sts. Simon and Jude.
Pittsburgh, Pa.: St. Paul.
Portland, Me.: Immaculate Conception.
Portland,* Ore.: Immaculate Conception.
Providence, R.I.: Sts. Peter and Paul.
Pueblo, Colo.: Sacred Heart.
Raleigh, N.C.: Sacred Heart.
Rapid City, S.D.: Our Lady of Perpetual Help.
Reno, Nev.: St. Thomas Aquinas.
Richmond, Va.: Sacred Heart.
Rochester, N.Y.: Sacred Heart.
Rockford, Ill.: St. Peter.
Rockville Centre, N.Y.: St. Agnes.
Sacramento, Calif.: Blessed Sacrament.
Saginaw, Mich.: St. Mary.
St. Augustine, Fla.: St. Augustine.
St. Cloud, Minn.: St. Mary.
St. Louis,* Mo.: St. Louis.
St. Maron of Detroit (Maronite Rite): St. Maron.
St. Nicholas in Chicago (Byzantine Rite): St. Nicholas.
St. Paul and Minneapolis,* Minn.: St. Paul (St. Paul); Basilica of St. Mary (Minneapolis Co-Cathedral).
St. Petersburg, Fla.: St. Jude the Apostle.
Salina, Kans.: Sacred Heart.
Salt Lake City, Utah: The Madeleine.
San Angelo, Tex.: Sacred Heart.
San Antonio,* Tex.: San Fernando.
San Diego, Calif.: St. Joseph.
San Francisco,* Calif.: St. Mary (Assumption).
Santa Fe,* N.M.: San Francisco de Asis.
Santa Rosa, Calif.: St. Eugene.

Savannah, Ga.: St. John the Baptist.
Scranton, Pa.: St. Peter.
Seattle,* Wash.: St. James.
Sioux City, Ia.: Epiphany.
Sioux Falls, S.D.: St. Joseph.
Spokane, Wash.: Our Lady of Lourdes.
Springfield, Ill.: Immaculate Conception.
Springfield, Mass.: St. Michael.
Springfield-Cape Girardeau, Mo.: St. Agnes (Springfield): St. Mary (Cape Girardeau Co-Cathedral).
Stamford, Conn. (Byzantine Rite): St. Vladimir (Pro-Cathedral).
Steubenville, Ohio: Holy Name.
Stockton, Calif: Annunciation.
Superior, Wis.: Christ the King.
Syracuse, N.Y.: Immaculate Conception.
Toledo, Ohio: Blessed Virgin Mary of the Holy Rosary.
Trenton, N.J.: St. Mary.
Tucson, Ariz.: St. Augustine.
Tulsa, Okla.: Holy Family.
Washington,* D.C.: St. Matthew.
Wheeling-Charleston, W. Va.: St. Joseph (Wheeling); Sacred Heart (Charleston Co-Cathedral).
Wichita, Kans.: Immaculate Conception.
Wilmington, Del.: St. Peter.
Winona, Minn.: Sacred Heart.
Worcester, Mass.: St. Paul.
Yakima, Wash.: St. Paul.
Youngstown, Ohio: St. Columba.
Apostolic Exarchate of the Melkites: Our Lady of the Annunciation (Boston, Mass.).

BASILICAS IN U.S., CANADA

Basilica is a title assigned to certain churches because of their antiquity, dignity, historical importance or significance as centers of worship. Major basilicas have the papal altar and holy door, which is opened at the beginning of a Jubilee Year; minor basilicas enjoy certain ceremonial privileges.

Among the major basilicas are the patriarchal basilicas of St. John Lateran, St. Peter, St. Paul Outside the Walls and St. Mary Major in Rome; St. Francis and St. Mary of the Angels in Assisi, Italy.

The patriarchal basilica of St. Lawrence, Rome, is a minor basilica.

The dates in the listings below indicate when the churches were designated as basilicas.

Minor Basilicas in U.S.

Alabama: Mobile, Cathedral of the Immaculate Conception (Mar. 10, 1962).

California: San Francisco, Mission Dolores (Feb. 8, 1952); Carmel, Old Mission of San Carlos (Feb. 5, 1960).
Illinois: Chicago, Our Lady of Sorrows (May 4, 1956), Queen of All Saints (Mar. 26, 1962).
Indiana: Vincennes, Old Cathedral (Mar. 14, 1970).
Iowa: Dyersville, St. Francis Xavier (May 11, 1956).
Kentucky: Trappist, Our Lady of Gethsemani (May 3, 1949); Covington, Cathedral of Assumption (Dec. 8, 1953).
Louisiana: New Orleans, St. Louis King of France (Dec. 9, 1964).
Maryland: Baltimore, Assumption of the Blessed Virgin Mary (Sept. 1, 1937).
Massachusetts: Roxbury, Perpetual Help ("Mission Church") (Sept. 8, 1954).
Minnesota: Minneapolis. St. Mary (Feb. 1, 1926).
Missouri: Conception, Basilica of Immaculate Conception (Sept. 14, 1940); St. Louis, St. Louis King of France (Jan. 27, 1961).
New York: Brooklyn, Our Lady of Perpetual Help (Sept. 5, 1969); Buffalo, St. Adalbert's (Aug. 11, 1907); Lackawanna, Our Lady of Victory (1926).
Ohio: Carey, Shrine of Our Lady of Consolation (Oct. 21, 1971).
Pennsylvania: Latrobe, St. Vincent Basilica, Benedictine Archabbey (Aug. 22, 1955); Conewago, Basilica of the Sacred Heart (June 30, 1962).
Wisconsin: Milwaukee, St. Josaphat (Mar. 10, 1929).

Minor Basilicas in Canada

Manitoba: St. Boniface, Cathedral Basilica of St. Boniface (June 10, 1949).
Newfoundland: St. John's, Cathedral Basilica of St. John the Baptist.
Nova Scotia: Halifax, St. Mary's Basilica (June 14, 1950).
Ontario: Ottawa, Basilica of Notre Dame; London, St. Peter's Cathedral (Dec. 13, 1961).
Prince Edward Island: Charlottetown, Basilica of St. Dunstan.
Quebec: Sherbrooke, Cathedral Basilica of St. Michael (July 31, 1959). Montreal, Cathedral Basilica of St. James the Greater; St. Joseph of Mount Royal. Cap-de-la-Madeleine, Basilica of Our Lady of the Cape (Aug. 15, 1964). Quebec, Basilica of Notre Dame; St. Anne de Beaupre, Basilica of St. Anne.

CHANCERY OFFICES OF U.S. ARCHDIOCESES AND DIOCESES

A chancery office, under this or another title, is the central administrative office of an archdiocese or diocese.

(Archdioceses are indicated by asterisk.)

Albany, N.Y.: 465 State St., Box 6297, Quail Station. 12206.

Alexandria, La.: 2315 Texas Ave., P. O. Box 5665. 71301.
Allentown, Pa.: 1729 Turner St. 18104.
Altoona-Johnstown, Pa.: Logan Blvd., Hollidaysburg, Pa. 16648.
Amarillo, Tex.: 1800 N. Spring St., P. O. Box 5644. 79107.

Anchorage,* Alaska: 811 Sixth Ave., P. O. Box 2239. 99510.
Arlington, Va.: 200 N. Glebe Rd. 22203.
Atlanta,* Ga.: 756 W. Peachtree St. N.W. 30308.
Austin, Tex.: N. Congress and 16th, P. O. Box 13327. Capitol Sta. 78711.
Baker, Ore.: Baker and First Sts., P. O. Box 826, 97814.
Baltimore,* Md.: 320 Cathedral St. 21201.
Baton Rouge, La.: P. O. Box 2028. 70821.
Beaumont, Tex.: 703 Archie St., P. O. Box 3948. 77704.
Belleville, Ill.: 5312 W. Main St., Box 896. 62203.
Belmont Abbey, N.C.: Belmont, N.C., 28012.
Birmingham, Ala.: P. O. Box 2086. 35201.
Bismarck, N.D.: 420 Raymond St., Box 1575. 58501.
Boise, Ida.: Box 769, 420 Idaho St. 83701.
Boston,* Mass.: 2121 Commonwealth Ave., Brighton, Mass. 02135.
Bridgeport, Conn.: 250 Waldemere Ave. 06604.
Brooklyn, N.Y.: 75 Greene Ave. 11238.
Brownsville, Tex.: P. O. Box 2279. 78520.
Buffalo, N.Y.: 35 Lincoln Parkway. 14222.
Burlington, Vt.: 52 Williams St. 05401.
Camden, N.J.: 1845 Haddon Ave., P. O. Box 709, 01801.
Charleston, S.C.: 119 Broad St. P. O. Box 818. 29402.
Charlotte, N.C.: P. O. Box 3776. 28203.
Cheyenne, Wyo.: Box 426. 82001.
Chicago,* Ill,: 211 E. Chicago Ave. 60611.
Cincinnati,* O.: 29 E. 8th St. 45202.
Cleveland, O.: 350 Chancery Bldg., Cathedral Sq., 1027 Superior Ave. 44114.
Columbus, O.: 198 E. Broad St. 43215.
Corpus Christi, Tex.: 620 Lipan St. 78401.
Covington, Ky.: 1140 Madison Ave., P. O. Box 192. 41012.
Crookston, Minn.: 1200 Memorial Dr., P. O. Box 610. 56716.
Dallas, Tex.: 3915 Lemmon Ave., P. O. Box 19507. 75219.
Davenport, Ia.: St. Vincent Center, 2706 Gaines St. 52801.
Denver,* Colo.: 938 Bannock St. 80204.
Des Moines, Ia.: 2910 Grand Ave., P. O. Box 1816. 50306.
Detroit,* Mich.: 1234 Washington Blvd. 48226.
Dodge City, Kans.: 910 Central Ave., P. O. Box 849. 67801.
Dubuque,* Ia.: 1229 Mt. Loretta Ave. 52001.
Duluth, Minn.: 215 W. 4th St. 55806.
El Paso, Tex.: 1012 N. Mesa St. 79902.
Erie, Pa.: 205 W. 9th St. 16501.
Evansville, Ind.: 219 N. W. Third St. 47708.
Fairbanks, Alaska: 1316 Peger Rd. 99701.
Fall River, Mass.: 47 Underwood St., Box 2577. 02722.

Fargo, N. D.: 1310 Broadway, Box 1750. 58102.
Fort Wayne-South Bend, Ind.: P. O. Box 390, Fort Wayne. 46801.
Fort Worth, Tex.: 1206 Throckmorton St. 76102.
Fresno, Calif.: P. O. Box 1668, 1550 N. Fresno St. 93717.
Gallup, N. Mex.: 406 W. Aztec St., P. O. Box 1338. 87301.
Galveston-Houston, Tex.: 1700 San Jacinto St., Houston. 77002.
Gary, Ind.: 668 Pierce St., P. O. Box 474. 46401.
Gaylord, Mich.: M-32 West, P. O. Box 700. 49735.
Grand Island, Nebr.: 311 W. 17th St., P. O. Box 996. 68801.
Grand Rapids, Mich.: 265 Sheldon Ave. S. E. 49502.
Great Falls, Mont.: 725 Third Ave. N., P. O. Box 1399. 59403.
Green Bay, Wis.: Box 66. 54305.
Greensburg, Pa.: 723 E. Pittsburgh St. 15601.
Harrisburg, Pa.: 111 State St. P. O. Box 2153. 17105.
Hartford,* Conn.: 134 Farmington Ave. 06105.
Helena, Mont.: 612 Harrison Ave., P. O. Box 1729. 59601.
Honolulu, Hawaii: 1184 Bishop St. 96813.
Indianapolis,* Ind.: 1350 N. Pennsylvania St. 46206.
Jefferson City, Mo.: 605 Clark Ave. P. O. Box 417. 65101.
Joliet, Ill.: 425 Summit St. 60435.
Juneau, Alaska: 416 5th St. 99801.
Kalamazoo, Mich.: 215 N. Westnedge. Ave. 49005.
Kansas City,* Kans.: 2220 Central Ave., P. O. Box 2328. 66110.
Kansas City-St. Joseph, Mo.: P. O. Box 1037, Kansas City. 64141.
La Crosse, Wis.: P.O. Box 982. 54601.
Lafayette in Indiana: 610 Lingle Ave. 47902.
Lafayette, La.: P. O. Drawer 3387. 70501.
Lansing, Mich.: 300 W. Ottawa. 48933.
Lincoln, Nebr.: 3400 Sheridan Blvd., P. O. Box 80328. 68501.
Little Rock, Ark.: 2415 N. Tyler St. 72207.
Los Angeles,* Calif.: 1531 W. 9th St. 90015.
Louisville,* Ky.: 212 E. College St., P. O. Box 1073. 40201.
Madison, Wis.: 15 E. Wilson St. 53701.
Manchester, N. H.: 153 Ash St. 03105.
Marquette, Mich.: 444 S. Fourth St., P. O. Box 550. 49855.
Memphis, Tenn.: 1325 Jefferson Ave., 38104.
Miami,* Fla.: 6301 Biscayne Blvd. 33138.
Milwaukee,* Wis.: 345 N. 95th St. 53226.
Mobile, Ala.: 400 Government St., P. O. Box 1966. 36606.

Monterey, Calif.: 580 Fremont Blvd. 93940.

Munhall,* Pa. (Byzantine Rite) 54 Riverview Ave., Pittsburgh. 15214.

Nashville, Tenn.: 2400 21st Ave. S. 37219.

Natchez-Jackson, Miss.: 237 E. Amite St., P. O. Box 2248, Jackson. 39205.

Newark,* N. J.: 31 Mulberry St. 07102.

New Orleans,* La.: 7887 Walmsley Ave. 70125.

New Ulm, Minn.: Chancery Drive. 56073.

New York,* N. Y.: 1011 First Ave. 10022.

Norwich, Conn.: 201 Broadway, P. O. Box 587. 06360.

Oakland, Calif.: 2900 Lakeshore Ave. 94610.

Ogdensburg, N. Y.: 622 Washington St. 13669.

Oklahoma City,* Okla.: 1521 N. Hudson, Oklahoma City. 73103.

Omaha,* Nebr.: 100 N. 62nd St. 68132.

Orlando, Fla.: P. O. Box 7700. 32804.

Owensboro, Ky.: c/o Chancellor's Residence, 4003 Frederica St. 42301.

Parma, Ohio (Byzantine Rite): 1900 Carlton Rd. 44134.

Passaic, N.J. (Byzantine Rite): 101 Market St. 07055.

Paterson, N. J.: 24 De Grasse St. 07505.

Peoria, Ill.: 607 N. E. Madison Ave. 61603.

Philadelphia,* Pa.: 222 N. 17th St. 19103.

Philadelphia,* Pa. (Byzantine Rite): 815 N. Franklin St. 19123.

Phoenix, Ariz.: 400 E. Monroe St. 85004.

Pittsburgh, Pa.: 111 Blvd. of the Allies. 15222.

Portland, Me.: 510 Ocean Ave., Woodfords P. O. Box H. 04103.

Portland in Oregon*: 2838 E. Burnside St. 97207.

Providence, R. I.: Cathedral Sq. 02903.

Pueblo, Colo.: 1426 Grand Ave. 81003.

Raleigh, N. C.: Nazareth Station. 27606.

Rapid City, S. D.: 606 Cathedral Dr., P. O. Box 678. 57701.

Reno, Nev.: 515 Court St. 89501. P. O. Box 1211, 89504.

Richmond, Va.: 807 Cathedral Pl. 23220.

Rochester, N.Y.: 1150 Buffalo Rd. 14624.

Rockford, Ill.: 1245 N. Court St. 61101.

Rockville Centre, N.Y.: 50 N. Park Ave. 11570.

Sacramento, Calif.: 1119 K St., P. O. Box 1706. 95808.

Saginaw, Mich.: 2555 Wieneke Rd. 48603.

St. Augustine, Fla.: Suite 1648, Gulf Life Tower, Jacksonville, Fla. 32207.

St. Cloud, Minn.: P. O. Box 1248. 56301.

St. Louis,* Mo.: 4445 Lindell Blvd. 63108.

St. Maron of Detroit, Mich.: 11470 Kercheval, P. O. Box 3307, Jefferson Sta., Detroit, Mich. 48214.

St. Nicholas in Chicago (Byzantine Rite): 2245 W. Rice St. 60622.

St. Paul and Minneapolis,* Minn.: 226 Summit Ave., St. Paul. 55102.

St. Petersburg, Fla.: 6363 9th Ave. N. 33710. P. O. Box 13109. 33733.

Salina, Kans.: 421 Country Club Rd., P. O. Box 999. 67401.

Salt Lake City, Utah: 333 E. S. Temple. 84111.

San Angelo, Tex.: 116 S. Oakes. Box 1829. 76901.

San Antonio,* Tex.: 9123 Lorene Lane, P. O. Box 32648. 78284.

San Diego, Calif.: Alcala Park. 92110.

San Francisco,* Calif.: 445 Church St. 94114.

Santa Fe,* N. Mex.: 202 Morningside Dr. S. E., Albuquerque. 87108.

Santa Rosa, Calif.: 398 10th St., P. O. Box 1499. 95403.

Savannah, Ga.: 225 Abercorn St., P. O. Box 8789. 31402.

Scranton, Pa.: 300 Wyoming Ave. 18503.

Seattle,* Wash.: 907 Terry Ave. 98104.

Sioux City, Ia.: P. O. Box 1530. 51102.

Sioux Falls, S.D.: 423 N. Duluth Ave. 57104.

Spokane, Wash.: 1023 W. Riverside Ave. 99201.

Springfield, Illinois: 524 E. Lawrence Ave. 62705.

Springfield, Mass.: 76 Elliot St. 01105. P.O. Box 1730, 01101.

Springfield-Cape Girardeau, Mo.: 410 Landers Bldg., Springfield. 65806.

Stamford, Conn. (Byzantine Rite): 161 Glenbrook Rd. 06902.

Steubenville, Ohio: 422 Washington St., P. O. Box 969. 43952.

Stockton, Calif.: 1105 N. Lincoln St. 95203. P. O. Box 4237. 95204.

Superior, Wis.: 1201 Hughitt Ave. 54880.

Syracuse, N.Y.: 240 E. Onondaga St., 13202.

Toledo, Ohio: 2544 Parkwood Ave. 43610.

Trenton, N.J.: 701 Lawrenceville Rd. 08638.

Tucson, Ariz.: 192 S. Stone Ave., Box 31, 85702.

Tulsa, Okla.: P. O. Box 2009. 74101.

Washington,* D.C.: 1721 Rhode Island Ave. N. W. 20036.

Wheeling-Charleston, W. Va.: 1300 Byron St., Wheeling. 26003.

Wichita, Kans.: 424 N. Broadway. 67202.

Wilmington, Del.: P. O. Box 2030. 19899.

Winona, Minn.: 275 Harriet St. 55987.

Worcester, Mass.: 49 Elm St. 01609.

Yakima, Wash.: 228 Liberty Bldg., P.O. Box 901. 98901.

Youngstown, Ohio: 144 W. Wood St. 44503.

Apostolic Exarchate of the Melkites: 19 Dartmouth St., W. Newton, Mass. 02165.

CREDIT UNIONS

The Credit Union National Association, Inc., reported in August, 1975, that there were 834 Catholic credit unions in the United States and 240 in Canada. Many of them were parish organized and operated.

NATIONAL CATHOLIC CONFERENCES

The two conferences described below are related in membership and directive control but distinct in nature, purpose and function.

The National Conference of Catholic Bishops (NCCB) is a strictly ecclesiastical body in and through which the bishops of the United States act together, officially and with authority as pastors of the Church. It is the sponsoring organization of the United States Catholic Conference.

The United States Catholic Conference (USCC) is a civil corporation and operational secretariat in and through which the bishops, together with other members of the Church, act on a wider scale for the good of the Church and society. It is sponsored by the National Conference of Catholic Bishops.

The principal officers of both conferences are: Archbishop Joseph L. Bernardin, president; Cardinal John J. Carberry, vice president; Archbishop Thomas A. Donnellan, treasurer; Bishop James S. Rausch, general secretary.

Headquarters of both conferences are located at 1312 Massachusetts Ave. N. W., Washington, D. C. 20005.

NCCB

The National Conference of Catholic Bishops, established by action of the U.S. hierarchy Nov. 14, 1966, is a strictly ecclesiastical body with defined juridical authority over the Church in this country. It was set up with the approval of the Holy See and in line with directives from the Second Vatican Council. Its constitution was formally ratified during the November, 1967, meeting of the U.S. hierarchy.

The NCCB is the successor to the Annual Meeting of the Bishops of the United States, whose pastoral character was originally approved by Pope Benedict XV Apr. 10, 1919.

The address of the Conference is 1312 Massachusetts Ave. N. W., Washington, D. C. 20005.

Pastoral Council

The conference, one of many similar territorial conferences envisioned in the conciliar *Decree on the Pastoral Office of Bishops in the Church* (No. 38), is "a council in which the bishops of a given nation or territory (in this case, the United States) jointly exercise their pastoral office to promote the greater good which the Church offers mankind, especially through the forms and methods of the apostolate fittingly adapted to the circumstances of the age."

Its decisions, "provided they have been approved legitimately and by the votes of at least two-thirds of the prelates who have a deliberative vote in the conference, and have been recognized by the Apostolic See, are to have juridically binding force only in those cases prescribed by the common law or deter-

mined by a special mandate of the Apostolic See, given either spontaneously or in response to a petition of the conference itself."

All bishops who serve or have served the Church in the U.S., its territories and possessions, have full membership and voting rights in the NCCB.

Officers, Committees

The conference operates through a number of bishops' committees with functions in specific areas of work and concern. Their basic assignments are to prepare materials on the basis of which the bishops, assembled as a conference, make decisions, and to put suitable action plans into effect.

The principal officers are: Archbishop Joseph L. Bernardin, president; Cardinal John J. Carberry, vice president; Archbishop Thomas A. Donnellan, treasurer; Bishop James S. Rausch, general secretary.

These officers, with several other bishops, hold positions on executive-level committees — Executive Committee, the Committee on Budget and Finance, the Committee on Personnel and Administrative Services, and the Committee on Research, Plans and Programs. They also, with other bishops, serve on the NCCB Administrative Committee.

The standing committees and their chairmen (Archbishops and Bishops) are as follows.

American Board of Catholic Missions, William G. Connare.

Arbitration, Edward W. O'Rourke.

Boundaries of Dioceses and Provinces, Joseph L. Bernardin.

Canon Law, Bernard J. Flanagan.

Church in Latin America, John J. Fitzpatrick.

Doctrine, George W. Ahr.

Ecumenical and Interreligious Affairs, William F. Baum.

Human Values, Mark Hurley.

Lay Apostolate, Francis J. Furey.

Liaison with Priests, Religious and Laity, Warren L. Boudreaux.

Liturgy, Walter W. Curtis.

Men Religious, Aloysius J. Wycislo.

Missions, Cardinal Timothy Manning.

Nomination of Bishops, Joseph L. Bernardin.

North American College, Louvain, Edwin Broderick.

North American College, Rome, Daniel A. Cronin.

Pastoral Research and Practices, James Hickey.

Permanent Diaconate, Ernest Unterkoefler.

Priestly Formation, Loras J. Watters.

Priestly Life and Ministry, Thomas J. Grady.

Vocations, John Roach.

Welfare Emergency Relief, Joseph L. Bernardin.

Women Religious, James J. Byrne.

Ad hoc committees and their chairmen are as follows.

Bicentennial, Cardinal John F. Dearden.

Campaign for Human Development, Raymond J. Gallagher.

Farm Labor, Joseph F. Donnelly.

Holy Year, Cardinal Timothy Manning.

Liaison with National Office for Black Catholics, Joseph A. McNicholas.

Migration and Tourism, Robert E. Tracy.

National Catechetical Directory, John F. Whealon.

Nominations to Conference Offices, John L. May.

Pro-Life Activities, Cardinal Terence J. Cooke.

Spanish-Speaking, James S. Rausch.

Women in Society and Church, Michael F. McAuliffe.

USCC

The United States Catholic Conference, Inc. (USCC), is the operational secretariat and service agency of the National Conference of Catholic Bishops for carrying out the civic-religious work of the Church in this country. It is a civil corporation related to the NCCB in membership and directive control but distinct from it in purpose and function.

The address of the Conference is 1312 Massachusettes Ave. N.W., Washington, D.C. 20005.

Service Secretariat

The USCC, as of Jan. 1, 1967, took over the general organization and operations of the former National Catholic Welfare Conference, Inc., whose origins dated back to the National Catholic War Council of 1917. The council underwent some change after World War I and was established on a permanent basis Sept. 24, 1919, as the National Catholic Welfare Council to serve as a central agency for organizing and coordinating the efforts of U.S. Catholics in carrying out the social mission of the Church in this country. In 1923, its name was changed to National Catholic Welfare Conference, Inc., and clarification was made of its nature as a service agency of the bishops and the Church rather than as a conference of bishops with real juridical authority in ecclesiastical affairs.

The Official Catholic Directory states that the USCC assists "the bishops in their service to the Church in this country by uniting the people of God where voluntary collective action on a broad interdiocesan level is needed. The USCC provides an organizational structure and the resources needed to insure coordination, cooperation, and assistance in the public, educational and social concerns of the Church at the national or interdiocesan level."

Officers, Departments

The principal officers of the USCC are Archbishop Joseph L. Bernardin, president; Cardinal John J. Carberry, vice president; Archbishop Thomas A. Donnellan, treasurer; Bishop James S. Rausch, general secretary. These officers, with several other ·bishops, hold positions on executive-level committees — the Executive Committee; the Committee on Research, Plans and Programs; the Committee on Budget and Finance; the Committee on Personnel and Administrative Services. They also serve on the Administrative Board.

The Executive Committee, organized in 1969, is authorized to handle matters of urgency between meetings of the Administrative Board and the general conference, to coordinate items for the agenda of general meetings, and to speak in the name of the USCC.

The major departments and their chairmen (Archbishops and Bishops) are: Communications, Joseph R. Crowley; Education, William D. Borders; Social Development and World Peace, Joseph A. McNicholas. Each department is supervised by a committee composed of an equal number of episcopal and non-episcopal members, including lay persons.

A National Advisory Council of bishops, priests, men and women religious, lay men and women advises the Administrative Board on overall plans and operations of the USCC.

The administrative general secretariat, in addition to other duties, supervises staff-service offices of Finance and Administration, General Counsel, Government Liaison, and Research, Plans and Programs.

USCC committees, bureaus and offices are divisions under the departments, as follows:

• **Communications:** Communications Development, Film and Broadcasting, NC News Service. Creative Services.

• **Education:** Elementary and Secondary Education, Higher Education, Religious Education (Confraternity of Christian Doctrine), Adult Education, Campus and Young Adult Ministry, Family Life, Youth Activities.

• **Social Development and World Peace:** Health Affairs, Chaplains' Services, Justice and Peace, Rural Life, Urban Affairs, Latin America, Migration and Refugee Services.

• **Secretariats:** Spanish-Speaking, Public Affairs (including National Catholic Office for Information).

• **Campaign for Human Development,** for anti-poverty programs.

• **Related Organizations:** National Conference of Catholic Laity, National Catholic Community Service.

Most of the 35 organizations and associations affiliated with the USCC are covered in separate Almanac entries.

The USCC, despite budget cuts and the revamping of some agencies, has not made any substantial reductions in services.

NCCB-USCC REGIONS

For meeting and other operational purposes, the members of the National Conference of Catholic Bishops and the U.S. Catholic Conference are grouped in the following geographical regions.

I. Maine, Vermont, New Hampshire, Massachusetts, Rhode Island, Connecticut.

II. New York.

III. New Jersey, Pennsylvania.

IV. Delaware, District of Columbia, Florida, Georgia, Maryland, North Carolina, South Carolina, Virgin Islands, Virginia, West Virginia.

V. Alabama, Kentucky, Louisiana, Mississippi, Tennessee.

VI. Michigan, Ohio.

VII. Illinois, Indiana, Wisconsin.

VIII. Minnesota, North Dakota, South Dakota, Wyoming, Colorado.

IX. Iowa, Kansas, Missouri, Nebraska.

X. Arizona, Arkansas, New Mexico, Oklahoma, Texas.

XI. California, Hawaii, Nevada, Utah, Caroline-Marshall Islands, Guam.

XII. Idaho, Montana, Alaska, Washington, Oregon.

MEETINGS OF THE CONFERENCE OF BISHOPS

November 18 to 22, 1974

The meeting, held in Washington, D.C., was attended by more than 250 members of the hierarchy. Archbishop Joseph L. Bernardin of Cincinnati was elected to a three-year term as president of the National Conference of Catholic Bishops and the United States Catholic Conference. He succeeded Cardinal John J. Krol of Philadelphia.

The bishops acted on the following items:

Anointing of the Sick: Approved a revision of the "Ethical and Religious Directives for Catholic Health Facilities" with an expansion of the section on the anointing of the sick. The revision, taken from the "Rite of Anointing and Pastoral Care of the Sick," said: "Prudent or probable judgment about the seriousness of an illness is sufficient to justify the anointing of the sick; patients should be anointed before serious surgery, and the sacrament can be repeated if needed; the sacrament should normally be celebrated when the patient is fully conscious; those in danger of death are obliged to receive Communion." The revision was made by the Health Affairs Committee.

Bicentennial Observance: Voted unanimously to accept a report on and to approve plans for the national Catholic observance of the U.S. Bicentennial in 1976. Cardinal John F. Dearden, who presented the report, sketched three key elements of the observance: historical observance by a series of articles on American church history in NC News Service, two network TV productions and a bicentennial calendar; special liturgical observances throughout the year, and especially on July 4, 1976; six liberty and justice hearings to be held in as many cities during 1975 in preparation for a 1976 national conference to be held in Detroit. It was anticipated that recommendations for justice policies and programs would come from the hearings and national conference.

Bilingual Seminaries: Heard an appeal from the Ad Hoc Committee on the Spanish-Speaking for the development of bilingual, bicultural seminaries in every diocese with a seminary and a large Spanish-speaking population. Other recommendations from the committee concerned: special preparatory help for poor and less educated minority students wanting to study for the priesthood; use of Spanish-speaking permanent deacons; use of existing programs — especially the Mexican-American Cultural Center in San Antonio — for the training of priests, religious and lay persons for work among the Spanish-speaking; on-the-job-training work by seminarians among the Spanish-speaking instead of other jobs during vacation periods; continuing education for Anglo priests working among the Spanish-speaking.

Blacks: Received a report concerning a "golden opportunity" for the Church to gain a leadership position in the black community, by Auxiliary Bishop Joseph A. McNicholas of St. Louis, chairman of the Ad Hoc Committee for Liaison with the National Office for Black Catholics.

He urged greater support for the Black Catholics Concerned collection which raised $225,607 in 1973 for the support of the national office. The top priorities of the office, the bishop said, were recruitment of black vocations to the priesthood and religious life, support for black seminarians, and evangelization of the black community.

Campaign for Human Development: Heard a report by Bishop Raymond J. Gallagher of Lafayette, Ind., that the educational phase of the Campaign for Human Development deserved more attention than it was getting. The CHD, in addition to raising and allocating funds for self-help programs, had developed programs to educate people with respect to the nature and causes of poverty.

Capital Punishment: Passed by a vote of 108 to 63 a motion stating: "The U.S. Catholic Conference goes on record in opposition to capital punishment." A statement backgrounding the motion was rejected by a vote of 119 to 103. The statement said it did not mean to challenge the principle that a state could impose capital punishment. However, it said: "We oppose at this time in our nation's history the use of capital punishment on the grounds of the sanctity of life and the human dignity of the person. . . . We urge Catholics and others who share our views to join us in urging" the "prohibition" of capital punishment.

Catholic Relief Services: Received a report from Bishop Edward E. Swanstrom, executive director, that CRS had provided almost $5 million in aid for the famine-stricken Sahelian region of Africa. Also reported was the total value, $154,089,262, of CRS programs for the year which ended June 30, 1974. CRS was able to multiply contributions through matching and additional grants from the U.S. and other governments, foundations and overseas funding sources.

Charismatics: Heard a report urging them to encourage and support the Catholic charismatic movement, but to be alert to possible "dangers" present in it.

Clergy Distribution: Heard a recommendation by Bishop Thomas J. Grady of Orlando, chairman of the Committee on Priestly Life and Ministry, that the bishops set up a committee to study the problems of clergy distribution in the U.S. He said such a study was necessary because of "an existing and increasing shortage of priests," fewer candidates for the priesthood, and lower "perseverance rates" of seminarians. The committee's report also dealt with the needs for spiritual renewal and continuing educaton for priests, more moral support of priests by lay persons, greater flexibility in the life-styles of priests, and positive leadership by bishops in the proper exercise of authority and in setting clear goals and objectives for their dioceses.

Ecumenism: Approved and issued a statement reaffirming support for the ecumenical movement on the 10th anniversary, Nov. 21, of the second Vatican Council's *Decree on Ecumenism.* In the statement the bishops: pledged themselves to work for carrying out the "directives and guidelines" on ecumenism issued by the Holy See; expressed appreciation for the work of bilateral consultations between Catholics and representatives of other Christian religions; praised and promised continuing support for the work of diocesan ecumenical commissions and parishes in ecumenical programs; pledged "constant prayer for Christian unity"; promised to work with other churches in this country and abroad "in responding affirmatively to human need," with particular reference to those suffering from hunger.

Education: Heard Archbishop William D. Borders of Baltimore, chairman of the Education Department, USCC, report that major concerns of the Church in public education were: "the universality of the right to education . . .; positive and prudent sex education; training in special skills; the right of all children to be motivated to appraise moral values with a right conscience and to embrace them with a personal adherence, together with a

deeper knowledge and love of God"; the obligation of Christians "to give their attention with generosity to the entire field of education."

Farm Labor Legislation: Voted unanimously, in a follow-up resolution to another one adopted in 1973, to push for legislation that would "assure the farm workers the right to elections by secret ballot of a union of their choice. We . . . accept as a pastoral necessity our active concern in the solution of an evil that has gone on far too long."

Food Crisis: Voted unanimously to form an ad hoc committee to develop a pastoral response to the world food crisis. The committee, chaired by Cardinal Terence J. Cooke, formulated "The World Food Crisis — Pastoral Plan for Action" which was issued by the NCCB Nov. 21. (See separate heading for text.)

Goals, Priorities: Archbishop Joseph L. Bernardin, just elected president of the NCCB and the USCC, told the bishops Nov. 19 that he saw three priority items for the Church: "seeking new ways of fostering among our people a renewal of faith; restoring a sense of moral values in everyday life; the role of the Church in promoting social justice." Archbishop Bernardin of Cincinnati was elected to a three-year term by a vote of 143 out of a possible 248 on the second ballot cast Nov. 19. Elected at the same time was vice president Cardinal John J. Carberry of St. Louis.

Housing, Interest Rates: Passed a resolution of concern about the housing crisis and high interest rates, and called on the Social Development and World Peace Committee of the USCC to complete a "back-up paper" on these subjects. A prepared statement, which was turned down because it was considered inadequate, had recommended: that the government should do everything possible to make "a decent home for every American" a reality; that private financial institutions should invest more money in cities and place more emphasis on long-term human benefits and less on short-term earnings reports; that the Church should become active in community organization and neighborhood development.

Human Rights: Passed unanimously a resolution to promote the study and circulation of "Human Rights and Reconciliation," a statement issued jointly in October by the 1974 assembly of the Synod of Bishops and Pope Paul. The document dealt with measures necessary for the protection of specific rights to life and to eat, socio-economic rights, politico-cultural rights, and the right to religious liberty.

Human Values: Voted unanimously to establish a new Committee and Secretariat for Human Values but delayed putting the decision into effect until funds become available. The purpose of the committee, it was said, would be to maintain contact and dialogue with persons in science and technology concerning moral and ethical implications in such areas as genetic research, atomic research and computer technology.

Illegal Aliens: Received two reports on illegal aliens, particularly Mexicans. In one, presented by Bishop James S. Rausch, it was said that pressure from the USCC had resulted in a moratorium on deportations of the immediate relatives of legal aliens living in the U.S., pending legislation that would legalize the status of such persons. In the second report Auxiliary Bishop Patrick F. Flores of San Antonio cited opposition to re-establishment of the bracero program which allowed non-residents to work in the U.S. on a temporary basis. And Auxiliary Bishop Gilbert Espinoza Chavez of San Diego said three major and immediate problems concerning illegals were the break-up of families through deportation, the employment of illegals as strike-breakers in California and Arizona, and general harassment of Mexican-Americans because of problems concerning illegal aliens.

International Eucharistic Congress: Heard a request from Cardinal John J. Krol that bishops appoint diocesan coordinators to help prepare for the International Eucharistic Congress to be held in 1976 in Philadelphia. The cardinal said initial plans had already been developed; that his hope was that the congress would be more than just a short period of ceremonial observances; and that it would have a spiritual impact on the nation in its preparation, observance and follow-up.

Meetings: Voted 106 to 52 to return as soon as possible (probably in 1976) to the practice of holding two general meetings a year instead of one such meeting in November and 12 smaller-scale regional meetings in the spring. Reasons for the change were dissatisfaction with the results of spring meetings in 1973 and 1974, and a general feeling that one general meeting a year could not cope with the volume of business to be handled.

Men and Women Religious: Heard reports from liaison committees with the Conference of Major Superiors of Men and the Leadership Conference of Women Religious that men were serving as advisers on 11 bishops' committees, and that two meetings with the sisters' conference had been held for the discussion of mutual concerns such as vocations, financial support for retired sisters, and the apostolic work of sisters.

Missionary and Latin American Aid: Received reports that during the previous year nearly $2 million had been raised for 115 church-approved projects in Latin America, and another $3.6 million for "84 missionary diocesan jurisdictions within the United States and its dependencies" and 16 groups that had the support of diocesan bishops.

Moral Values: Appointed Auxiliary Bishop John B. McDowell of Pittsburgh chairman of an ad hoc committee commissioned to draft a pastoral letter on "Moral Values in Society" for publication in November, 1976. Bishop McDowell said the group "hopes through the proposed pastoral letter to make a significant contribution to the creation of a healthier moral climate."

NCCB and USCC Assessment: Approved by a 109-to-7 vote of diocesan bishops was a resolution to raise diocesan assessments for the NCCB and USCC from six to seven cents per Catholic in 1976. Treasurer Archbishop Thomas A. Donnellan said the additional $450,000 would be necessary to prevent "cutbacks in the programs mandated by the Holy See and by the bishops of this conference."

North American College: Heard Bishop Daniel A. Cronin of Fall River, chairman of the Committee for the North American College, Rome, report that the college might have a deficit of $200,000 by the end of the current academic year. It was also reported that in 1973-74 the college had 182 undergraduate students and 69 graduate student priests; that 80 priests attended three-month sessions of the Institute for Continuing Theological Education; and that 69 bishops participated in a special month-long theological consultation sponsored by the college.

Penance: Accepted recommendations that options be permitted in designating places for confession, according to the needs of penitents and within the norms stated in *Ordo Paenitentiae,* published by the Congregation for Divine Worship Feb. 7, 1974; and that some "appropriate external sign of Penance" be required of penitents when general sacramental absolution is given in unusual circumstances. The bishops rejected by a vote of 140 to 96 a recommendation that each province draw up guidelines for determining when general sacramental absolution would be in order. The bishops, preferring a set of national guidelines, argued that different practices in the various provinces would create serious pastoral confusion.

Permanent Deacons: Received a report from committee chairman Archbishop Daniel E. Sheehan of Omaha that the U.S. has more ordained deacons, 750, than any other country, and that 1,500 candidates were in training programs. Sixty-five dioceses had training programs, and 11 more were preparing programs. It was also reported that the committee — in collaboration with St. John's University School of Divinity, Collegeville, Minn. — had designed a diaconate program for rural dioceses; was translating diaconate guidelines into Spanish; was monitoring the theological studies of deacons and their ministerial experiences; was developing guidelines for brothers wanting to become permanent deacons. The proper form of address, it was said, should be "Permanent Deacon" rather than "Rev. Mr."

Respect Life: Heard a report by Cardinal

John P. Cody of Chicago, chairman of the Ad Hoc Committee for Pro-Life Activities, that the 1974 Respect Life program was "very successful." The report praised the Catholic press for its coverage of the activities and themes of the observance (right to life, the elderly, prisoners, the sick, the handicapped) and diocesan coordinators who arranged local programs.

Rockefeller Nomination: Approved action by the Committee for Population and Pro-Life Affairs in sending a letter to Congressional committees considering the vice-presidential nomination of Nelson A. Rockefeller. The letter asked the committees to question him "on his present position on providing legal protection for unborn human life and ascertaining that he will not use the office of the vice president to promote a personal viewpoint on permissive abortion."

Seminary Programs: Received a report from Bishop Loras J. Watters of Winona, chairman of the Committee on Priestly Formation, which emphasized the importance of a full two-year study of philosophy and a four-year study of theology in seminary programs. Archbishop Joseph Bernardin said at a press conference that some bishops thought academic programs in seminaries had to be upgraded because they had deteriorated in the development of pastoral training programs. In a related statement Archbishop Jean Jadot, apostolic delegate to the U.S., called for greater emphasis on theology and philosophy in seminary training. He said: "We need priests with a deep theological culture, accustomed to serious thinking, trained to grasp not only the 'how' but even more the 'why' of human events in the light of revelation. . . . A solid grounding in philosophy is required for the development of the ability to make a critical evaluation of the discoveries in the natural and social sciences."

Vocation Directors: Heard an appeal from Auxiliary Bishop Raymond J. Vonesh of Joliet, chairman of the Committee on Vocations, for tenures of at least five years for diocesan vocation directors. Short terms and fast turnovers in directors, he said, hinder effective vocational recruitment.

Regional Meetings

The first working draft of a proposed *National Catechetical Directory* was the principal subject of discussions and recommendations at 12 regional meetings of the bishops in April, 1975. Portions of these meetings were open to representative priests, religious and lay persons. (See separate article.)

There was a strong consensus at the Region X meeting, for one, that the first draft of the *National Catechetical Directory* was too technical and should be reworded in more simple and direct language for the benefit of catechist volunteers. It was felt that the draft was too stiff and more suited to professionals than the many more volunteers who eventually would use it.

STATE CATHOLIC CONFERENCES

These conferences are agencies of bishops and dioceses in the various states. Their general purposes are to develop and sponsor cooperative programs designed to cope with pastoral and common-welfare needs, and to represent the dioceses before governmental bodies, the public, and in private sectors. Their membership consists of representatives from the dioceses in the states — bishops, clergy and lay persons in various capacities.

The **National Association of State Catholic Conference Directors** maintains liaison with the general secretariat of the United States Catholic Conference.

Charles M. Phillips of Wisconsin is president.

Alaska Catholic Conference, 416 5th St., Juneau, Alaska 99801; exec. dir., Frank W. Matulich.

Arizona Catholic Conference, 400 E. Monroe St., Phoenix, Ariz. 85004; exec. dir., G. A. (Jack) Bradley.

California Catholic Conference, 926 J St., Suite 1100, Sacramento, Calif. 95814; exec. dir., Bishop John S. Cummins.

Colorado Catholic Conference, 938 Bannock St., Denver, Colo. 80204; Sr. Loretta A. Madden.

Connecticut Catholic Conference, 134 Farmington Ave., Hartford, Conn. 06105; exec. dir., William Wholean.

Florida Catholic Conference, P.O. Box 1571, Tallahassee, Fla. 32302; exec. dir., Thomas A. Horkan.

Georgia Catholic Conference, 335 Ivy St., N.E., Atlanta, Ga. 30303; exec. secy., Cheatham E. Hodges, Jr.

Illinois Catholic Conference, 201 E. Ohio St., Chicago, Ill. 60611; exec. dir., Rev. William J. Lion.

Indiana Catholic Conference, Room 442, Illinois Building, Indianapolis, Ind. 46204; exec. dir., Raymond R. Rufo.

Iowa Catholic Conference, 918 Insurance Exchange Building, Des Moines, Iowa 50309; exec. dir., Timothy McCarthy.

Kansas Catholic Conference, 702 Commercial National Bank Bldg., Kansas City, Kan. 66101; exec. dir., Vincent W. DeCoursey.

Kentucky Catholic Conference, 605 Bank of Commerce Building, Lexington, Ky. 40507; exec. dir. and general counsel, Michael R. Moloney.

Louisiana Catholic Conference, 1100 Chartres St., New Orleans, La. 70116; exec. dir., Emile Comar.

Maryland Catholic Conference, 320 Cathedral St., Baltimore, Md. 21201; exec. dir., James Shaneman.

Massachusetts Catholic Conference, 60 School St., Boston, Mass. 02107; exec. dir., Rev. Michael F. Groden.

Michigan Catholic Conference, P.O. Box 157, Lansing, Mich. 48901; exec. dir., Thomas M. Bergeson.

Minnesota Catholic Conference, 145 University Ave., W., St. Paul, Minn. 55103; exec. dir., John F. Markert.

Missouri Catholic Conference, P.O. Box 1022, Jefferson City, Mo. 65101; acting exec. dir., Louis DeFeo.

Montana Catholic Conference, P.O. Box 404, Helena, Mont. 59601; exec. dir., John Frankino.

Nebraska Catholic Conference, 521 S. 14th St., Lincoln, Nebr. 68508; exec. dir., Paul V. O'Hara.

New Jersey Catholic Conference, 495 W. State St., Trenton, N.J. 08618; exec. dir., Edward J. Leadem.

New York State Catholic Committee, 11 N. Pearl St., Albany, N.Y. 12207; exec. secy., Charles J. Tobin, Jr.

North Dakota Catholic Conference, 304 Ave. A. West, Bismarck, N. Dak. 58501; exec. dir., Edwin C. Becker.

Ohio, Catholic Conference of, 22 South Young St., Columbus, Ohio 43215; exec. dir., Theodore N. Staudt.

Pennsylvania Catholic Conference, 509 N. Second St., Harrisburg, Pa. 17105; exec. dir., Howard J. Fetterhoff.

Tennessee Catholic Conference, 2015 West End Ave., Nashville, Tenn. 37203; acting coordinator, Rev. Philip Breen.

Texas Catholic Conference, 702 Commodore Perry Hotel, Austin, Tex. 78701; exec. dir., Rev. John McCarthy.

Virginia, Office of Lay Activities, 813 Cathedral St., Richmond, Va. 23220; exec. secy., Charles Brower.

Washington Catholic Conference, 301 Security Building, Olympia, Wash. 98501; general counsel, Francis J. Walker.

Wisconsin Catholic Conference, 1245 E. Washington Ave., Madison, Wis. 53703; exec. dir., Charles M. Phillips.

U.S. CATHOLIC CONFERENCE AND PUBLIC AFFAIRS

Based on an article by Jim Castelli, NC News Service.

Following are brief summaries of actions on politics and public affairs by the U.S. Catholic Conference in 1975.

Illegal Aliens: Opposition to a House bill providing penalties for employers of illegal aliens was the main focus of activity. The USCC believed that bill would result in discrimination in hiring against anyone who "looks foreign" and would serve to make illegal aliens "scapegoats" for the country's economic problems.

The USCC effort was massive, including personal lobbying on Capitol Hill and generating support among Catholic groups, other religious bodies and the general public. Past House action indicated that the USCC, which began the fight virtually alone, faced an uphill battle, but USCC-generated pressure helped to delay final action in the House.

Redlining: Msgr. Francis Lally, secretary for Social Development and World Peace, sent a letter to each Senator supporting a mortgage disclosure bill aimed at eliminating "redlining," the practice of refusing mortgage loans in certain neighborhoods. The bill passed the Senate on a vote of 45 to 37. USCC support was significant because it tied into considerable grassroots support from urban Catholics who, along with blacks, were among the major victims of redlining.

Gun Control: The Committee for Social Development and World Peace issued a statement calling for the eventual elimination of handguns and a series of strong interim measures, including registration of handguns, licensing of gun owners and a ban on "Satur-

day Night Specials." The week the statement was issued, *The Nation,* a political opinion weekly, ran an article which analyzed survey data and found that Catholics were less likely than Protestants, particularly affluent Protestants, to own guns and more likely to favor controls. The article called for Catholic Church support on gun control.

Domestic Food Policy: The Administrative Board issued a statement supporting a child nutrition and school lunch bill; the bill was passed over President Ford's veto. The statement also defended the Food Stamp program, clearly rejecting stringent proposals by Sen. James Buckley to prevent most of the newly unemployed from receiving stamps.

International Food Policy: The same statement on food policy supported basic reforms in foreign aid programs, particularly food aid. No action was taken on a House bill embodying many of the proposed reforms, but the USCC said it would be active on a similar bill in the Senate and in the Appropriations Committees of both houses.

Capital Punishment: The USCC was already on record with a one-sentence policy adopted in November, 1974, opposing reinstatement of the death penalty.

Amnesty: The Office for International Justice and Peace in late July prepared a statement supporting in principle a bill in the House which would grant amnesty to war resisters and draft evaders who would sign a statement, under penalty of perjury, that their offenses had been motivated by their opposition to the Vietnam war. Action on the statement was pending.

Biographies of American Bishops

(Sources: Almanac survey, *The Official Catholic Directory*, NC News Service. As of July 15, 1975.)

A

Abramowicz, Alfred L.: b. Jan. 27, 1919, Chicago, Ill.; educ. St. Mary of the Lake Seminary (Mundelein, Ill.), Gregorian Univ. (Rome); ord. priest May 1, 1943; ord. titular bishop of Paestum and auxiliary bishop of Chicago, June 13, 1968.

Ackerman, Richard Henry, C.S.Sp.: b. Aug. 30, 1903, Pittsburgh, Pa.; educ. Duquesne Univ. (Pittsburgh, Pa.), St. Mary's Scholasticate (Norwalk, Conn.), Univ. of Fribourg (Switzerland); ord. priest Aug. 28, 1926; ord. titular bishop of Lares and auxiliary bishop of San Diego, May 22, 1956; app. bishop of Covington, Apr. 4, 1960.

Ahern, Patrick V.: b. Mar. 8, 1919, New York, N.Y.; educ. Manhattan College and Cathedral College (New York City), St. Joseph's Seminary (Yonkers, N. Y.), St. Louis Univ. (St. Louis, Mo.), Notre Dame Univ. (Notre Dame, Ind.); ord. priest Jan. 27, 1945; ord. titular bishop of Naiera and auxiliary bishop of New York, Mar. 19, 1970.

Ahr, George William: b. June 23, 1904, Newark, N.J.; educ. St. Vincent College (Latrobe, Pa.), Seton Hall College (S. Orange, N.J.), North American College (Rome); ord. priest July 29, 1928; ord. bishop of Trenton, Mar. 20, 1950.

Alter, Karl Joseph: b. Aug. 18, 1885, Toledo, O.; educ. St. John's Univ. (Toledo, O.), St. Mary's Seminary (Cleveland, O.); ord. priest June 4, 1910; ord. bishop of Toledo, June 17, 1931; app. archbishop of Cincinnati, June 14, 1950; resigned 1969.

Anderson, Paul F.: b. Apr. 20, 1917, Roslindale, Mass.; educ. Boston College (Chestnut Hill, Mass.), St. John's Seminary (Brighton, Mass.); ord. priest Jan. 6, 1943; ord. titular bishop of Polignando and coadjutor bishop of Duluth, Oct. 17, 1968; bishop of Duluth, Apr. 30, 1969.

Angell, Kenneth A.: b. Aug. 3, 1930, Providence, R.I.; educ. St. Mary's Seminary (Baltimore, Md.); ord. priest May 26, 1956; ord. titular bishop of Septimunicia and auxiliary bishop of Providence, R.I., Oct. 7, 1974.

Arkfeld, Leo, S.V.D.: b. Feb. 4, 1912, Butte, Nebr.; educ. Divine Word Seminary (Techny, Ill.), Sacred Heart College (Girard, Pa.); ord. priest Aug. 15, 1943; ord. titular bishop of Bucellus and vicar apostolic of Central New Guinea, Nov. 30, 1948; name of vicariate changed to Wewak, May 15, 1952; first bishop of Wewak, Nov. 15, 1966.

Arliss, Reginald, C.P.: b. Sept. 8, 1906, East Orange, N.J.; educ. Immaculate Conception Seminary (Jamaica, N.Y.) and other Passionist houses of study; ord. priest Apr.

28, 1934; missionary in China for 16 years, expelled 1951; missionary in Philippines; rector of the Pontifical Philippine College Seminary in Rome, 1961-69; ord. titular bishop of Cerbali and prelate of Marbel, Philippines, Jan. 30, 1970.

Arzube, Juan: b. June 1, 1918, Guayaquil, Ecuador; educ. Rensselaer Polytechnic Institute (Troy, N.Y.), St. John's Seminary (Camarillo, Calif.); ord. priest May 5, 1954; ord. titular bishop of Civitate and auxiliary bishop of Los Angeles, Mar. 25, 1971.

B

Baldwin, Vincent J.: b. July 13, 1907, Brooklyn, N.Y.; educ. Cathedral College (Brooklyn, N.Y.), Institute of Philosophy (Huntington, N.Y.), Capranica College (Rome); ord. priest July 26, 1931, Rome; ord. titular bishop of Bencenna and auxiliary bishop of Rockville Centre, July 26, 1962; app. episcopal vicar, Nov. 3, 1971.

Bartholome, Peter William: b. Apr. 2, 1893, Bellechester, Minn.; educ. Campion College (Prairie du Chien, Wis.), St. Paul Seminary (St. Paul, Minn.), Apollinare (Rome); ord. priest June 12, 1917; ord. titular bishop of Lete and coadjutor bishop of St. Cloud, Mar. 3, 1942; bishop of St. Cloud, May 31, 1953; resigned 1968.

Baum, William W.: b. Nov. 21, 1926, Dallas, Tex.; educ. Kenrick Seminary (St. Louis, Mo.), Angelicum (Rome); ord. priest May 12, 1951; executive director of NCCB commission on ecumenical affairs, 1964-67; appointed member of joint working group of the World Council of Churches and Vatican Secretariat for Promoting Christian Unity, 1965; ord. bishop of Springfield-Cape Girardeau, Apr. 6, 1970; app. archbishop of Washington, Mar. 5, 1973; installed May 9, 1973.

Begin, Floyd L.: b. Feb. 5, 1902, Cleveland, O.; educ. St. John's Cathedral College (Cleveland, O.), North American College and Apolinare (Rome); ord. priest July 31, 1927; ord. titular bishop of Sala and auxiliary bishop of Cleveland, May 1, 1947; app. first bishop of Oakland, Feb. 21, 1962.

Begley, Michael J.: b. Mar. 12, 1909, Mattineague, Mass.; educ. Mt. St. Mary Seminary (Emmitsburg, Md.); ord. priest May 26, 1934; ord. first bishop of Charlotte, N.C., Jan. 12, 1972.

Bell, Alden J.: b. July 11, 1904, Peterborough, Ont., Canada; educ. St. Joseph's College (Mountain View, Calif.), St. Patrick's Seminary (Menlo Park, Calif.), Catholic Univ. (Washington, D.C.); ord. priest May 14, 1932; ord. titular bishop of Rhodopolis and auxiliary bishop of Los Angeles, June 4, 1956; app. bishop of Sacramento, Mar. 30, 1962.

Benincasa, Pius A.: b. July 8, 1913, Niagara

Falls, N.Y.: educ. Propaganda Univ. and Lateran Univ. (Rome); ord. priest Mar. 27, 1937; served in Vatican Secretariat of State, 1954-64; ord. titular bishop of Buruni and auxiliary bishop of Buffalo, June 29, 1964.

Bernardin, Joseph L.: b. Apr. 2, 1928, Columbia, S.C.; educ. St. Mary's Seminary (Baltimore, Md.), Catholic Univ. (Washington, D.C.); ord. priest Apr. 26, 1952; ord. titular bishop of Lugura and auxiliary bishop of Atlanta, Apr. 26, 1966; general secretary of the USCC and NCCB, 1968-72; app. archbishop of Cincinnati, Nov. 21, 1972; installed Dec. 19, 1972; president NCCB/USCC, 1974.

Bernarding, George, S.V.D.: b. Feb. 15, 1912, Carrick, Pa.; educ. Divine Word Seminary (Girard, Pa.); ord. priest Aug. 13, 1939; ord. titular bishop of Belabitene and first vicar apostolic of Mount Hagen, New Guinea, Apr. 21, 1960; first bishop of Mount Hagen, Nov. 15, 1966.

Bilock, John M.: b. June 20, 1916, McAdoo, Pa.; educ. St. Procopius College and Seminary (Lisle, Ill.); ord. priest Feb. 3, 1946; vicar general of Byzantine archeparchy of Munhall, 1969; ord. titular bishop of Pergamum and auxiliary bishop of Munhall, May 15, 1973.

Binz, Leo: b. Oct. 31, 1900, Stockton, Ill.; educ. Loras College (Dubuque, Ia.), St. Mary's Seminary (Baltimore, Md.), Sulpician Seminary (Washington, D.C.), North American College, Propaganda Univ., Gregorian Univ. (Rome); ord. priest Mar. 15, 1924; ord. titular bishop of Pinara and coadjutor bishop and apostolic administrator of Winona, Dec. 21, 1942; app. titular archbishop of Silyum and coadjutor archbishop of Dubuque, Oct. 15, 1949; app. assistant at the papal throne, June 11, 1954; archbishop of Dubuque, Dec. 2, 1954; app. archbishop of St. Paul, Dec. 16, 1961, installed Feb. 28, 1962; title changed to St. Paul and Minneapolis, 1966; retired May 28, 1975.

Biskup, George J.: b. Aug. 23, 1911, Cedar Rapids, Ia.; educ. Loras College (Dubuque, Ia). North American College (Rome), State Univ. of Iowa (Iowa City, Ia); ord. priest Mar. 19, 1937; ord. titular bishop of Hemeria and auxiliary bishop of Dubuque, Apr. 24, 1957; app. bishop of Des Moines, Jan. 30, 1965; app. titular archbishop of Tamalluma and coadjutor of Indianapolis, July 26, 1967; archbishop of Indianapolis, Jan. 14, 1970.

Blanchette, Romeo: b. Jan. 6, 1913, St. George, Ill.; educ. St. Mary of the Lake Seminary (Mundelein, Ill.), Gregorian Univ. (Rome); ord. priest Apr. 3, 1937; vicar general of Joliet, 1950-66; ord. titular bishop of Maxita and auxiliary of Joliet, Apr. 3, 1965; app. bishop of Joliet, July 19, 1966, installed Aug. 31, 1966.

Boardman, John J.: b. Nov. 7, 1894, Brooklyn N.Y.; educ. St. John's College (Brooklyn, N. Y.), St. John's Seminary (Brooklyn, N.Y.); ord. priest May 21, 1921; ord. titular

bishop of Gunela and auxiliary bishop of Brooklyn, June 11, 1952; named assistant at the papal throne; treasurer of the Society for the Propagation of the Faith.

Boccella, John H., T. O. R.: b. June 25, 1912, Castelfranci, Italy; came to US at the age of two; educ. St. Francis College and Seminary (Loretto, Pa.), Angelicum Univ. (Rome), Catholic Univ. (Washington, D.C.); ord. priest Mar. 29, 1941; provincial of Third Order Regular in US, 1945-47; minister general of Third Order Regular, 1947-68; ord. archbishop of Izmir, Turkey, Apr. 17, 1968.

Bokenfohr, John, O.M.I.: b. Jan. 28, 1903, West Point, Nebr.; ord. priest July 11, 1927; ord. bishop of Kimberley, S. Africa, May 3, 1963; resigned July 17, 1974.

Boland, Ernest B., O.P.: b. July 10, 1925, Providence, R. I.; educ. Providence College (Rhode Island), Dominican Houses of Study (Somerset, Ohio; Washington, D. C.); ord. priest June 9, 1955; ord. bishop of Multan, Pakistan, July 25, 1966.

Boland, Thomas A.: b. Feb. 17, 1896, Orange, N.J.; educ. Seton Hall College (South Orange, N.J.), North American College (Rome), Fordham Univ. (New York City); ord. priest Dec. 23, 1922; ord. titular bishop of Irina and auxiliary bishop of Newark, July 25, 1940; app. bishop of Paterson, June 21, 1947; app. archbishop of Newark, Nov. 15, 1952, installed Jan. 14, 1953; resigned Apr. 2, 1974.

Borders, William D.: b. Oct. 9, 1913, Washington, Ind.; educ. St. Meinrad Seminary (St. Meinrad, Ind.), Notre Dame Seminary (New Orleans, La.), Notre Dame Univ. (Notre Dame, Ind.); ord. priest May 18, 1940; ord. first bishop of Orlando, June 14, 1968; app. archbishop of Baltimore, Apr. 2, 1974, installed June 26, 1974.

Bosco, Anthony G.: b. Aug. 1, 1927, New Castle, Pa.; educ. St. Vincent Seminary (Latrobe, Pa.), Lateran Univ. (Rome); ord. priest June 7, 1952; ord. titular bishop of Labicum and auxiliary of Pittsburgh, June 30, 1970.

Boudreaux, Warren L.: b. Jan. 25, 1918, Berwick, La.; educ. St. Joseph's Seminary (St. Benedict, La.), St. Sulpice Seminary (Paris, France), Notre Dame Seminary (New Orleans, La.), Catholic Univ. (Washington, D.C.); ord. priest May 30, 1942; ord. titular bishop of Calynda and auxiliary bishop of Lafayette, La., July 25, 1962; app. bishop of Beaumont, June 5, 1971.

Breitenbeck, Joseph M.: b. Aug. 3, 1914, Detroit, Mich.; educ. University of Detroit, Sacred Heart Seminary (Detroit, Mich.), North American College and Lateran Univ. (Rome), Catholic Univ. (Washington, D.C.); ord. priest May 30, 1942; ord. titular bishop of Tepelta and auxiliary bishop of Detroit, Dec. 20, 1965; app. bishop of Grand Rapids, Oct. 15, 1969, installed Dec. 2, 1969.

Brizgys, Vincas: b. Nov. 10, 1903, Plynial, Lithuania; ord. priest June 5, 1927; ord. titular bishop of Bosano and auxiliary bishop of Kaunas, Lithuania, May 10, 1940; taken into custody and deported to Germany, 1944; liberated by Americans, 1945; US citizen, 1958.

Broderick, Edwin B.: b. Jan. 16, 1917, New York, N. Y.; educ. Cathedral College (New York City), St. Joseph's Seminary (Yonkers, N. Y.), Fordham Univ. (New York City); ord. priest May 30, 1942; ord. titular bishop of Tizica and auxiliary of New York, Apr. 21, 1967; bishop of Albany May 10, 1969.

Brown, Charles, A., M.M.: b. Aug. 20, 1919, New York, N.Y.; educ. Cathedral College (New York City), Maryknoll Seminary (Maryknoll, N. Y.); ord. priest June 9, 1946; ord. titular bishop of Vallis and auxiliary bishop of Santa Cruz, Bolivia, Mar. 27, 1957.

Brunini, Joseph B.: b. July 24, 1909, Vicksburg, Miss.; educ. Georgetown Univ. (Washington, D. C.), North American College (Rome), Catholic Univ. (Washington, D.C.); ord. priest Dec. 5, 1933; ord. titular bishop of Axomis and auxiliary bishop of Natchez-Jackson, Jan. 29, 1957; apostolic administrator of Natchez-Jackson, 1966; app. bishop of Natchez-Jackson, Dec. 2, 1967, installed Jan. 29, 1968.

Brust, Leo J.: b. Jan. 7, 1916, St. Francis, Wis.; educ. St. Francis Seminary (Milwaukee, Wis.), Canisianum (Innsbruck, Austria), Catholic Univ. (Washington, D. C.); ord. priest May 30, 1942; ord. titular bishop of Suelli and auxiliary bishop of Milwaukee. Oct. 16, 1969.

Brzana, Stanislaus J.: b. July 1, 1917, Buffalo, N.Y.; educ. Christ the King Seminary (St. Bonaventure, N.Y.), Gregorian Univ. (Rome); ord. priest June 7, 1941; ord. titular bishop of Cufruta and auxiliary bishop of Buffalo, June 29, 1964; bishop of Ogdensburg, Oct. 22, 1968.

Burke, James C., O.P.: b. Nov. 30, 1926, Wilkes-Barre, Pa.; educ. King's College (Wilkes-Barre, Pa.), Providence College (R.I.); ord. priest June 8, 1956; ord. titular bishop of Lamiggiga and prelate of Chimbote, Peru, May 25, 1967.

Buswell, Charles A.: b. Oct. 15, 1913, Homestead, Okla.; educ. St. Louis Preparatory Seminary (St. Louis, Mo.), Kenrick Seminary (Webster Groves, Mo.), American College, Univ. of Louvain (Belgium); ord. priest July 9, 1939; ord. bishop of Pueblo, Sept. 30, 1959.

Byrne, James J.: b. July 28, 1908, St. Paul, Minn.; educ. Nazareth Hall Preparatory Seminary and St. Paul Seminary (St. Paul, Minn.), Univ. of Minnesota (Minneapolis, Minn.); Louvain Univ. (Belgium); ord. priest June 3, 1933; ord. titular bishop of Etenna and auxiliary bishop of St. Paul, July 2, 1947; app. bishop of Boise, June 16, 1956; app. archbishop of Dubuque, Mar. 19, 1962, installed May 8, 1962.

C

Caillouet, L. Abel.: b. Aug. 2, 1900, Thibodaux, La.; educ. St. Joseph's Preparatory Seminary (St. Benedict, La.), St. Mary's Seminary (Baltimore, Md.), North American College (Rome); ord. priest Mar. 7, 1925; ord. titular bishop of Setea and auxiliary bishop of New Orleans, Oct. 28, 1947.

Carberry, John J.: (See Cardinals, Biographies.)

Carroll, Coleman Francis: b. Feb. 9, 1905, Pittsburgh, Pa.; educ. Duquesne Univ. (Pittsburgh, Pa.), St. Vincent Seminary (Latrobe, Pa.), Catholic Univ. (Washington, D.C.); ord. priest June 15, 1930; ord. titular bishop of Pitanae and auxiliary bishop of Pittsburgh, Nov. 10, 1953; app. first bishop of Miami, installed Oct. 7, 1958; became first archbishop, 1968.

Carroll, Mark K.: b. Nov. 19, 1896, St. Louis, Mo.; educ. St. Louis Preparatory Seminary and St. Louis Theological Seminary (St. Louis, Mo.); ord. priest June 10, 1922; ord. bishop of Wichita, Apr. 23, 1947; retired, 1963, but retained title; resigned, 1967.

Casey, James V.: b. Sept. 22, 1914, Osage, Ia.; educ. Loras College (Dubuque, Ia.), North American College (Rome), Catholic Univ. (Washington, D.C.); ord. priest Dec. 8, 1939; ord. titular bishop of Citium and auxiliary bishop of Lincoln, Apr. 24, 1957; bishop of Lincoln, June 14, 1957; app. archbishop of Denver, Feb. 22, 1967, installed May 17, 1967.

Casey, Lawrence B.: b. Sept. 6, 1905, Rochester, N.Y.; educ. St. Bernard's Seminary (Rochester, N.Y.); ord. priest June 7, 1930; ord. titular bishop of Cea and auxiliary bishop of Rochester, May 5, 1953; app. bishop of Paterson, installed May 12, 1966.

Cassata, John J.: b. Nov. 8, 1908, Galveston, Tex.; educ. St. Mary's Seminary (La Porte, Tex.), North American College, Urbana Univ. and Gregorian Univ. (Rome); ord. priest Dec. 8, 1932; ord. titular bishop of Bida and auxiliary bishop of Dallas-Fort Worth, June 5, 1968; app. bishop of Fort Worth, Aug. 27, 1969, installed Oct. 21, 1969.

Chavez, Gilbert Espinoza: b. May 9, 1932, Ontario, Calif.; educ. St. Francis Seminary (El Cajon, Calif.); Immaculate Heart Seminary (San Diego), Univ. of California; ord. priest Mar. 19, 1960; ord. titular bishop of Magarmel and auxiliary of San Diego, June 21, 1974.

Clinch, Harry A.: b. Oct. 27, 1908, San Anselmo, Calif.; educ. St. Joseph's College (Mountain View, Calif.), St. Patrick's Seminary (Menlo Park, Calif.); ord. priest June 6, 1936; ord. titular bishop of Badiae and auxiliary bishop of Monterey-Fresno, Feb. 27, 1957; app. first bishop of Monterey in California, installed Dec. 14, 1967.

Cody, John P.: (See Cardinals, Biographies.)

Cohill, John Edward, S.V.D.: b. Dec. 13, 1907, Elizabeth, N.J.; educ. Divine Word Seminary (Techny, Ill.); ord. priest Mar. 20, 1936; ord. first bishop of Goroko, New Guinea, Mar. 11, 1967.

Comber, John W., M.M.: b. Mar. 12, 1906, Lawrence, Mass.; educ. St. John's Preparatory College (Danvers, Mass.), Boston College (Boston, Mass.), Maryknoll Seminary (Maryknoll, N.Y.); ord. priest Feb. 1, 1931; superior general of Maryknoll, 1956-66; ord. titular bishop of Foratiana, Apr. 9, 1959.

Connare, William G.: b. Dec. 11, 1911, Pittsburgh, Pa.; educ. Duquesne Univ. (Pittsburgh, Pa.), St. Vincent Seminary (Latrobe, Pa.); ord. priest June 14, 1936; ord. bishop of Greensburg, May 4, 1960.

Connolly, James L.: b. Nov. 15, 1894, Fall River, Mass.; educ. St. Charles College (Catonsville, Md.), St. Mary's Seminary (Baltimore, Md.), Catholic Univ. (Washington, D.C.), Louvain Univ. (Belgium); ord. priest Dec. 21, 1923; rector of St. Paul (Minn.) minor seminary 1940-43, major seminary 1943-45; ord. titular bishop of Mylasa and coadjutor of Fall River, May 24, 1945; bishop of Fall River, May 17, 1951; resigned Oct. 30, 1970.

Connolly, Thomas Arthur: b. Oct. 5, 1899, San Francisco, Calif.; educ. St. Patrick's Seminary (Menlo Park, Calif.), Catholic Univ. (Washington, D.C.); ord. priest June 11, 1926; ord. titular bishop of Sila and auxiliary bishop of San Francisco, Aug. 24, 1939; app. coadjutor bishop of Seattle, Feb. 28, 1948; succeeded as bishop of Seattle, May 18, 1950; first archbishop of Seattle, June 23, 1951; retired Feb. 25, 1975.

Connolly, Thomas J.: b. July 18, 1922, Tonopah, Nev.; educ. St. Patrick's Seminary (Menlo Park, Calif.), Catholic Univ. (Washington, D.C.), Lateran Univ. (Rome); ord. priest Apr. 8, 1947; ord. bishop of Baker, June 30, 1971.

Cooke, Terence J.: (See Cardinals, Biographies.)

Coscia, Benedict Dominic, O.F.M.: b. Aug. 10, 1922, Brooklyn, N.Y.; educ. St. Francis College (Brooklyn, N.Y.), Holy Name College (Washington, D.C.); ord. priest June 11, 1949; ord. bishop of Jatai, Brazil, Sept. 21, 1961.

Cosgrove, William M.: b. Nov. 26, 1916, Canton, Ohio; educ. John Carroll Univ. (Cleveland, O.); ord. priest Dec. 18, 1943; ord. titular bishop of Trisipa and auxiliary bishop of Cleveland, Sept. 3, 1968.

Costello, Joseph A.: b. May 9, 1915, Newark, N.J.; educ. Seton Hall Univ. (S. Orange, N.J.), Immaculate Conception Seminary (Darlington, N.J.); ord. priest June 7, 1941; ord. titular bishop of Choma and auxiliary bishop of Newark, Jan. 24, 1963.

Cotey, Bernard R., S.D.S.: b. June 15, 1921, Milwaukee, Wis.; educ. Divine Savior

Seminary (Lanham, Md.), Marquette Univ. (Milwaukee, Wis.); ord. priest June 7, 1949; ord. first bishop of Nachingwea, Tanzania, Oct. 20, 1963.

Cousins, William E.: b. Aug. 20, 1902, Chicago, Ill.; educ. Quigley Seminary (Chicago, Ill.), St. Mary of the Lake Seminary (Mundelein, Ill.); ord. priest Apr. 23, 1927; ord. titular bishop of Forma and auxiliary bishop of Chicago, Mar. 7, 1949; app. bishop of Peoria, May 21, 1952; archbishop of Milwaukee, Jan. 27, 1959.

Cronin, Daniel A.: b. Nov. 14, 1927, Newton, Mass.; educ. St. John's Seminary (Boston, Mass.), North American College and Gregorian Univ. (Rome); ord. priest Dec. 20, 1952; attaché apostolic nunciature (Addis Ababa), 1957-61; served in papal Secretariat of State, 1961-68; ord. titular bishop of Egnatia and auxiliary bishop of Boston, Sept. 12, 1968; bishop of Fall River, Dec. 16, 1970.

Crowley, Joseph R.: b. Jan. 12, 1915, Fort Wayne, Ind.; educ. St. Mary's College (St. Mary, Ky.), St. Meinrad Seminary (St. Meinrad, Ind.); served in US Air Force, 1942-46; ord. priest May 1, 1953; editor of *Our Sunday Visitor* 1958-67; ord. titular bishop of Maraguis and auxiliary bishop of Fort Wayne-South Bend, Aug. 24, 1971; named vicar general and diocesan director of religious education, Feb. 1, 1972.

Cummins, John S.: b. Mar. 3, 1928, Oakland, Calif.; educ. St. Patrick's Seminary (Menlo Park, Calif.), Catholic Univ. (Washington, D.C.), Univ. of California; ord. priest Jan. 24, 1953; executive director of the California Catholic Conference; ord. titular bishop of Lambaesis and auxiliary bishop of Sacramento, May 16, 1974.

Cunningham, David F.: b. Dec. 3, 1900, Walkerville, Mont.; educ. St. Michael's College (Toronto, Canada), St. Bernard's Seminary (Rochester, N.Y.), Catholic Univ. (Washington, D.C.); ord. priest June 12, 1926; ord. titular bishop of Lampsacus and auxiliary bishop of Syracuse, June 8, 1950; app. coadjutor bishop of Syracuse with right of succession, 1967; bishop of Syracuse, Aug. 4, 1970.

Curtis, Walter W.: b. May 3, 1913, Jersey City, N.J.; educ. Fordham Univ. (New York City), Seton Hall Univ. (South Orange, N.J.), Immaculate Conception Seminary (Darlington, N.J.), North American College and Gregorian Univ. (Rome), Catholic Univ. (Washington, D.C.); ord. priest Dec. 8, 1937; ord. titular bishop of Bisica and auxiliary bishop of Newark, Sept. 24, 1957; app. bishop of Bridgeport, 1961, installed Nov. 21, 1961.

D

Daily, Thomas V.: b. Sept. 23, 1927, Belmont, Mass.; educ. Boston College, St. John's Seminary (Brighton, Mass.); ord. priest Jan. 10, 1952; missionary in Peru for five years as a member of the Society of St. James the Apostle; ord. titular bishop of Bladia and auxiliary bishop of Boston, Feb. 11, 1975.

Daley, Joseph T.: b. Dec. 21, 1915, Connerton, Pa.; educ. St. Charles Borromeo Seminary (Philadelphia, Pa.); ord. priest June 7, 1941; ord. titular bishop of Barca and auxiliary bishop of Harrisburg, Pa., Jan. 7, 1964; coadjutor bishop of Harrisburg, Aug. 2, 1967; bishop of Harrisburg, Oct. 19, 1971.

Danglmayr, Augustine: b. Dec. 11, 1898, Muenster, Tex.; educ. Subiaco College (Arkansas), St. Mary's Seminary (La Porte, Tex.), Kenrick Seminary (St. Louis, Mo.); ord. priest June 10, 1922; ord. titular bishop of Olba, Oct. 7, 1942; auxiliary bishop of Dallas-Ft. Worth, 1942-69.

D'Antonio Salza, Nicholas, O.F.M.: b. July 10, 1916, Rochester, N.Y.; educ. St. Anthony's Friary (Catskill, N.Y.); ord. priest June 7, 1942; ord. titular bishop of Giufi Salaria and prelate of Olancho, Honduras, July 25, 1966.

D'Arcy, John M.: b. Aug. 15, 1932, Brighton, Mass.; educ. Rome; ord. priest Feb. 2, 1957; spiritual director of St. John's Seminary; ord. titular bishop of Mediana and auxiliary bishop of Boston, Feb. 11, 1975.

Dargin, Edward Vincent: b. Apr. 25, 1898, New York, N.Y.; educ. Fordham Univ. (New York City), St. Joseph Seminary (Dunwoodie, N.Y.), Catholic Univ. (Washington, D.C.); ord. priest Sept. 23, 1922; ord. titular bishop of Amphipolis and auxiliary bishop of New York, Oct. 5, 1953; app. episcopal vicar, 1966. Retired.

Davis, James Peter: b. June 9, 1904, Houghton, Mich.; educ. St. Joseph's College (Mountain View, Calif.), St. Patrick's Seminary (Menlo Park, Calif.); ord. priest May 19, 1929; ord. bishop of San Juan, Puerto Rico, Oct. 6, 1943; app. first archbishop of San Juan, July 30, 1960; app. archbishop of Santa Fe, installed Feb. 25, 1964; resigned June 4, 1974.

Dearden, John Francis: (See Cardinals, Biographies.)

De Falco, Lawrence M.: b. Aug. 25, 1915, McKeesport, Pa.; educ. St. Vincent's College (Latrobe, Pa.), St. John's Seminary (Little Rock, Ark.), Gregorian Univ. (Rome); ord. priest June 11, 1942; ord. bishop of Amarillo, May 30, 1963.

Deksnys, Anthony L.: b. May 9, 1906, Buteniskis, Lithuania; educ. Metropolitan Seminary and Theological and Philosophical Faculty at Vytautas the Great Univ. (all at Kaunas, Lithuania), Univ. of Fribourg (Switzerland); ord. priest May 30, 1931; served in US parishes at Mt. Carmel, Pa., and East St. Louis, Ill.; ord. titular bishop of Lavellum, June 15, 1969; assigned to pastoral work among Lithuanians in Western Europe.

Dempsey, Michael J., O.P.: b. Feb. 22, 1912, Providence, R.I.; entered Order of Preachers (Dominicans), Chicago province,

1935; ord. priest June 11, 1942; ord. bishop of Sokoto, Nigeria, Aug. 15, 1967.

Denning, Joseph P.: b. Jan. 4, 1907, Flushing, L. I.; educ. Cathedral College (Brooklyn, N. Y.), Immaculate Conception Seminary (Huntington, L. I.), St. Mary's Seminary (Baltimore, Md.); ord. priest May 21, 1932; ord. titular bishop of Mallus and auxiliary bishop of Brooklyn, Apr. 22, 1959.

De Palma, Joseph A., S.C.J.: b. Sept. 4, 1913, Walton, N. Y.; ord. priest May 20, 1944; superior general of Congregation of Priests of the Sacred Heart, 1959-67; ord. first bishop of De Aar, South Africa, July 19, 1967.

Dimmerling, Harold J.: b. Sept. 23, 1914, Braddock, Pa.; educ. St. Fidelis Preparatory Seminary (Herman, Pa.), St. Charles Seminary (Columbus, O.), St. Francis Seminary (Loretto, Pa.); ord. priest May 2, 1940; ord. bishop of Rapid City, Oct. 30, 1969.

Dingman, Maurice J.: b. Jan. 20, 1914, St. Paul, Ia.; educ. St. Ambrose College (Davenport, Ia.), North American College and Gregorian Univ. (Rome), Catholic Univ. (Washington, D. C.); ord. priest Dec. 8, 1939; ord. bishop of Des Moines, June 19, 1968.

Donaghy, Frederick Anthony, M.M.: b. Jan. 13, 1903, New Bedford, Mass.; educ. Holy Cross College (Worcester, Mass.), St. Mary's Seminary (Baltimore, Md.), Maryknoll Seminary (Maryknoll, N. Y.); ord. priest Jan. 29, 1929; ord. titular bishop of Setea and vicar apostolic of Wuchow, China, Sept. 21, 1939; title changed to bishop of Wuchow, Apr. 11, 1946; expelled by Communists.

Donahue, Stephen Joseph: b. Dec. 10, 1893, New York, N. Y.; educ. Cathedral College (New York, N. Y.), St. Joseph's Seminary (Dunwoodie, N. Y.), North American College (Rome); ord. priest May 22, 1918; ord. titular bishop of Medea and auxiliary bishop of New York, May 1, 1934. Retired.

Donnellan, Thomas A.: b. Jan. 24, 1914, New York, N. Y.; educ. Cathedral College and St. Joseph's Seminary (New York, N. Y.), Catholic Univ. (Washington, D. C.); ord. priest June 3, 1939; ord. bishop of Ogdensburg, Apr. 9, 1964; app. archbishop of Atlanta, installed July 16, 1968.

Donnelly, Joseph F.: b. May 1, 1909, Norwich, Conn.; educ. St. Mary's Seminary and Univ. (Baltimore, Md.), Catholic Univ. (Washington, D.C.), Fairfield Univ. (Fairfield, Conn.); ord. priest June 29, 1934; director of Hartford Archdiocesan Labor Institute 1942-65; chairman of Connecticut State Board of Mediation and Arbitration 1949-65; ord. titular bishop of Nabala and auxiliary bishop of Hartford, Jan. 28, 1965.

Donohoe, Hugh A.: b. June 28, 1905, San Francisco, Calif.; educ. St. Patrick's Preparatory and Major Seminaries (Menlo Park, Calif.), Catholic Univ. (Washington, D. C.); ord. priest June 14, 1930; ord. titular bishop of Taium and auxiliary bishop of San Francisco, Oct. 7, 1947; app. first bishop of Stockton, Jan. 27, 1962; app. bishop of Fresno, Aug. 27, 1969, installed Oct. 7, 1969.

Donovan, John A.: b. Aug. 5, 1911, Chatham, Ont., Canada; educ. Sacred Heart Seminary (Detroit, Mich.), North American College and Gregorian Univ. (Rome); ord. priest Dec. 8, 1935; ord. titular bishop of Rhasus and auxiliary bishop of Detroit, Oct. 26, 1954; app. bishop of Toledo, installed Apr. 18, 1967.

Donovan, Paul V.: b. Sept. 1, 1924, Bernard, Iowa; educ. St. Gregory's Seminary (Cincinnati, Ohio), Mt. St. Mary's Seminary (Norwood, Ohio), Lateran Univ. (Rome); ord. priest May 20, 1950; ord. first bishop of Kalamazoo, Mich., July 21, 1971.

Dougherty, John J.: b. Sept. 16, 1907, Jersey City, N. J.; educ. Seton Hall Univ. (S. Orange, N. J.), Immaculate Conception Seminary (Darlington, N. J.), North American College, Gregorian Univ., Pontifical Biblical Institute (Rome); ord. priest July 23, 1933; ord. titular bishop of Cotenna and auxiliary bishop of Newark, Jan. 24, 1963.

Dozier, Carroll T.: b. Aug. 18, 1911, Richmond, Va.; educ. Holy Cross College (Worcester, Mass.), Gregorian Univ. (Rome); ord. priest, Mar. 19, 1937, Rome; ord. first bishop of Memphis, Jan. 6, 1971.

Driscoll, Justin A.: b. Sept. 30, 1920, Bernard, Ia.; educ. Loras College (Dubuque, Ia.), Catholic Univ. (Washington, D. C.); ord. priest July 28, 1945; president of Loras College, 1967-70; ord. bishop of Fargo, Oct. 28, 1970.

Drury, Thomas J.: b. Jan. 4, 1908, Co. Sligo, Ireland; educ. St. Benedict's College (Atchison, Kans.), Kenrick Seminary (St. Louis, Mo.); ord. priest June 2, 1935; ord. first bishop of San Angelo, Tex., Jan. 24, 1962; app. bishop of Corpus Christi, installed Sept. 1, 1965.

Dudick, Michael J.: b. Feb. 24, 1916, St. Clair, Pa.; educ. St. Procopius College and Seminary (Lisle, Ill.); ord. priest Nov. 13, 1945; ord. bishop of Byzantine Rite Eparchy of Passaic, Oct. 24, 1968.

Duhart, Clarence James, C.SS.R.: b. Mar. 23, 1912, New Orleans, La.; ord, priest June 29, 1937; ord. bishop of Udon Thani, Thailand, Apr. 21, 1966.

Dunn, Francis J.: b. Mar. 22, 1922, Elkader, Ia.; educ. Loras College (Dubuque, Ia.), Kenrick Seminary (St. Louis, Mo.), Angelicum (Rome, Italy); ord. priest Jan. 11, 1948; chancellor of Dubuque, Aug. 27, 1960; ord. titular bishop of Turris Tamallani and auxiliary bishop of Dubuque, Aug. 27, 1969, app. vicar general, Aug. 28, 1969.

Durick, Joseph Aloysius: b. Oct. 13, 1914, Dayton, Tenn.; educ. St. Bernard Minor Seminary (St. Bernard, Ala.), St. Mary's Seminary (Baltimore, Md.), Urban Univ. (Rome); ord. priest May 23, 1940; ord. titular bishop

of Cerbal and auxiliary bishop of Mobile-Birmingham, Mar. 24, 1955; app. coadjutor bishop of Nashville, Tenn., installed Mar. 3, 1964; apostolic administrator, 1966; bishop of Nashville, Sept. 10, 1969; resigned Apr. 4, 1975, to work with prison inmates and their families.

Durning, Dennis V., C.S.Sp.: b. May 18, 1923, Germantown, Pa.; educ. St. Mary's Seminary (Ferndale, Conn.); ord. priest June 3, 1949; ord. first bishop of Arusha, Tanzania, May 28, 1963.

Dworschak, Leo F.: b. Apr. 6, 1900, Independence, Wis.; educ. St. John's Univ. (Collegeville, Minn.), Catholic Univ. (Washington, D.C.); ord. priest May 29, 1926; ord. titular bishop of Tium and coadjutor bishop of Rapid City, Aug. 22, 1946; app. auxiliary bishop of Fargo, Apr. 10, 1947; bishop of Fargo, May 10, 1960; retired, 1970.

Dwyer, Robert Joseph: b. Aug. 1, 1908, Salt Lake City, Utah; educ. St. Patrick's Seminary (Menlo Park, Calif.), Catholic Univ. (Washington, D.C.); ord. priest June 11, 1932; ord. bishop of Reno, Aug. 5, 1952; app. archbishop of Portland, Ore., Dec. 14, 1966, installed Feb. 6, 1967; resigned Jan. 22, 1974.

E

Elko, Nicholas T.: b. Dec. 14, 1909, Donora, Pa.; educ. Duquesne Univ. (Pittsburgh, Pa.), Seminary of Uzhorod (Czechoslovakia); ord. priest Sept. 30, 1934; ord. titular bishop of Apollonias and apostolic administrator of Byzantine-Rite exarchy of Pittsburgh, Mar. 6, 1955; succeeded as exarch of Pittsburgh, Sept. 5, 1955; became eparch when Pittsburgh was raised to eparchy, July, 1963; app. titular archbishop of Dara, 1967, and ordaining prelate for Byzantine Rite in Rome; head of Oriental liturgical commission; app. auxiliary bishop of Cincinnati, Aug. 10, 1971.

Etteldorf, Raymond P.: b. Aug. 12, 1911, Ossian, Ia.; educ. Loras College (Dubuque, Ia.), Gregorian Univ. (Rome); ord. priest Dec. 8, 1937; secretary general of Supreme Council for direction of Pontifical Missionary Works, 1964-68; secretary of Pontifical Commission for Economic Affairs, 1968-69; ord. titular archbishop of Tindari, Jan. 6, 1969; papal representative to New Zealand and the Pacific Islands, 1968-74; pro-nuncio to Ethiopia, 1974.

Evans, George R.: b. Sept. 25, 1922, Denver, Colo.; educ. Notre Dame Univ. (Notre Dame, Ind.), St. Thomas Seminary (Denver, Colo.), Apollinare Univ. (Rome, Italy); ord. priest May 31, 1947; ord. titular bishop of Tubyza and auxiliary bishop of Denver, Apr. 23, 1969.

F

Fearns, John M.: b. June 25, 1897, New York, N.Y.; educ. St. Joseph's Seminary (Yonkers, N.Y.), North American College and Gregorian Univ. (Rome); ord. priest Feb.

19, 1922; ord. titular bishop of Geras and auxiliary bishop of New York, Dec. 10, 1957; app. episcopal vicar, 1966. Retired.

Federal, Joseph Lennox: b. Jan. 13, 1910, Greensboro, N.C.; educ. Belmont Abbey College (Belmont Abbey, N.C.), Niagara Univ. (Niagara Falls, N.Y.), Univ. of Fribourg (Switzerland), North American College and Gregorian Univ. (Rome); ord. priest Dec. 8, 1934; ord. titular bishop of Appiaria and auxiliary bishop of Salt Lake City, Apr. 11, 1951; app. coadjutor with right of succession, May, 1958 bishop of Salt Lake City, Mar. 31, 1960.

Fitzpatrick, John J.: b. Oct. 12, 1918, Trenton, Ont., Canada; educ. Urban Univ. (Rome), Our Lady of the Angels Seminary (Niagara Falls, N.Y.); ord. priest Dec. 13, 1942; ord. titular bishop of Cenae and auxiliary bishop of Miami, Aug. 28, 1968; bishop of Brownsville, Tex., May 28, 1971.

Fitzsimons, George K.: b. 1929, Kansas City, Mo.; educ. Rockhurst College (Kansas City, Mo.), Immaculate Conception Seminary (Conception, Mo.); ord. priest 1961; app. titular bishop of Pertusa and auxiliary bishop of Kansas City-St. Joseph, May 20, 1975.

Flaherty, J. Louis: b. May 13, 1910, Norfolk, Va.; educ. Holy Cross College (Worcester, Mass.), North American College and Gregorian Univ. (Rome), Catholic Univ. (Washington, D.C.); ord. priest Dec. 8, 1936; ord. titular bishop of Tabuda and auxiliary bishop of Richmond, Oct. 5, 1966.

Flanagan, Bernard Joseph: b. Mar. 31, 1908, Proctor, Vt.; educ. Holy Cross College (Worcester, Mass.), North American College (Rome), Catholic Univ. (Washington, D.C.); ord. priest Dec. 8, 1931; ord. first bishop of Norwich, Nov. 30, 1953; app. bishop of Worcester, installed, Sept. 24, 1959.

Flavin, Glennon P.: b. Mar. 2, 1916, St. Louis, Mo.; educ. Kenrick Seminary (St. Louis, Mo.); ord. priest Dec. 20, 1941; ord. titular bishop of Joannina and auxiliary bishop of St. Louis, May 30, 1957; app. bishop of Lincoln, installed Aug. 17, 1967.

Fletcher, Albert Lewis: b. Oct. 28, 1896, Little Rock, Ark.; educ. Little Rock College and St. John's Seminary (Little Rock, Ark.); ord. priest June 4, 1920; ord. titular bishop of Samos and auxiliary bishop of Little Rock, Apr. 25, 1940; bishop of Little Rock, Dec. 7, 1946; resigned July 4, 1972.

Flores, Felixberto C.: b. Jan. 13, 1921, Agana, Guam; educ. St. John's Seminary (Brighton, Mass.), Fordham Univ. (New York); ord. priest Apr. 30, 1949; ord. titular bishop of Stonj, May 17, 1970, and apostolic administrator of the diocese of Agana, Guam; installed second residential bishop of Agana, July 12, 1972.

Flores, Patrick F.: b. July 26, 1929, Ganado, Tex.; educ. St. Mary's Seminary (Houston, Tex.); ord. priest May 26, 1956; ord. titular bishop of Itolica and auxiliary bishop of San Antonio, May 5, 1970; first Mexican-American bishop.

Foery, Walter Andrew: b. July 6, 1890, Rochester, N.Y.; educ. St. Andrew's Preparatory Seminary and St. Bernard's Seminary (Rochester, N.Y.); ord. priest June 10, 1916; ord. bishop of Syracuse, Aug. 18, 1937; resigned 1970.

Forst, Marion F.: b. Sept. 3, 1910, St. Louis, Mo.; educ. St. Louis Preparatory Seminary (St. Louis, Mo.), Kenrick Seminary (Webster Groves, Mo.); ord. priest June 10, 1934; ord. bishop of Dodge City, Mar. 24, 1960.

Franz, John B.: b. Oct. 29, 1896, Springfield, Ill.; educ. Quincy College (Quincy, Ill.), Kenrick Seminary (Webster Groves, Mo.), Catholic Univ. (Washington, D.C.); ord. priest June 13, 1920; ord. first bishop of Dodge City, Aug. 29, 1951; app. bishop of Peoria, installed Nov. 4, 1959; resigned May 24, 1971.

Freking, Frederick W.: b. Aug. 11, 1913, Heron Lake, Minn.; educ. St. Mary's College (Winona, Minn.), North American College and Gregorian Univ. (Rome), Catholic Univ. (Washington, D.C.); ord. priest July 31, 1938; ord. bishop of Salina, Nov. 30, 1957; app. bishop of La Crosse, Dec. 30, 1964, installed Feb. 24, 1965.

Frey, Gerard L.: b. May 10, 1914, New Orleans, La.; educ. Notre Dame Seminary (New Orleans, La.); ord. priest Apr. 2, 1938; ord. bishop of Savannah, Aug. 8, 1967; app. bishop of Lafayette, La., Nov. 7, 1972, installed Jan, 7, 1973.

Frosi, Angelo, S. X.: b. Jan. 31, 1924, Baffano Cremona, Italy; ord. priest May 6, 1948; ord. titular bishop of Magneto, May 1, 1970, and prelate of Abaete do Tocantins, Brazil.

Furey, Francis J.: b. Feb. 22, 1905, Summit Hill, Pa.; educ. St. Charles Borromeo Seminary (Overbrook, Pa.), Pontifical Major Roman Seminary (Rome); ord. priest Mar. 15, 1930; ord. titular bishop of Temnus and auxiliary bishop of Philadelphia, Dec. 22, 1960; app. coadjutor bishop of San Diego with right of succession, July, 1963; bishop of San Diego, 1966-69; archbishop of San Antonio, Aug. 6, 1969.

Furlong, Philip J.: b. Dec. 8, 1892, New York, N.Y.; educ. Cathedral College (New York, N.Y.), St. Joseph's Seminary (Yonkers, N.Y.); ord. priest May 18, 1918; ord. titular bishop of Araxa and auxiliary to military vicar, Jan. 25, 1956. Retired.

G

Gabro, Jaroslav: b. July 31, 1919, Chicago, Ill.; educ. St. Procopius College (Lisle, Ill.), St. Charles College (Catonsville, Md.), St. Basil's College (Stamford, Conn.), St. Josaphat's Seminary and Catholic Univ. (Washington, D.C.); ord. priest Sept. 27, 1945; ord. first eparch of the eparchy of St. Nicholas of the Ukrainians, in Chicago, Oct. 26, 1961, installed Dec. 12, 1961.

Gallagher, Raymond J.: b. Nov. 19, 1912, Cleveland, Ohio; educ. John Carroll Univ. and Our Lady of the Lake Seminary (Cleveland, O.); ord. priest Mar. 25, 1939; secretary of the National Conference of Catholic Charities 1961-65; ord. bishop of Lafayette in Indiana, Aug. 11, 1965.

Ganter, Bernard J.: b. July 17,1928, Galveston, Tex.; educ. Texas A & M Univ. (College Sta., Tex.), St. Mary's Seminary (La Porte, Tex.), Catholic Univ. (Washington, D.C.); ord. priest May 22, 1952; chancellor of Galveston-Houston diocese, 1969-73; ord. first bishop of Tulsa, Feb. 7, 1973.

Gelineau, Louis E.: b. May 3, 1928, Burlington, Vt.; educ. St. Michael's College (Winooski, Vt.), St. Paul's Univ. Seminary (Ottawa, Ont.), Catholic Univ. (Washington, D.C.); ord. priest June 5, 1954; ord. bishop of Providence, R.I., Jan. 26, 1972.

Gendron, Odore: b. 1922, Manchester, N.H.; educ. St. Charles Borromeo Seminary (Sherbrooke, Que., Canada), Univ. of Ottawa, St. Paul Univ. Seminary (Ottawa, Ont., Canada); ord. priest May 31, 1947; ord. bishop of Manchester, Feb. 3, 1975.

Gerbermann, Hugo, M.M.: b. Sept. 11, 1913, Nada, Tex.; educ. St. John's Minor and Major Seminary (San Antonio, Tex.), Maryknoll Seminary (Maryknoll, N.Y.); ord. priest Feb. 7, 1943; missionary work in Ecuador and Guatemala; ord. titular bishop of Amathus and prelate of Huehuetenango, Guatemala, July 22, 1962; first bishop of Huehuetenango, Dec. 23, 1967.

Gerety, Peter L.: b. July 19, 1912, Shelton, Conn.; educ. Sulpician Seminary (Paris, France); ord. priest June 29, 1939; ord. titular bishop of Crepedula and coadjutor bishop of Portland, Me., with right of succession, June 1, 1966; app. apostolic administrator of Portland, 1967; bishop of Portland, Me., Sept. 15, 1969; app. archbishop of Newark, Apr. 2, 1974; installed June 28, 1974.

Gerow, Richard Oliver: b. May 3, 1885, Mobile, Ala.; educ. McGill Institute (Mobile, Ala.), Mt. St. Mary's College (Emmitsburg, Md.), North American College (Rome); ord. priest June 5, 1909; ord. bishop of Natchez-Jackson, Oct. 15, 1924; retired from active administration of diocese, 1966; resigned, 1967.

Gerrard, James J.: b. June 9, 1897, New Bedford, Mass.; educ. St. Laurent College (Montreal, Que.), St. Bernard's Seminary (Rochester, N.Y.); ord. priest May 26, 1923; ord. titular bishop of Forma and auxiliary bishop of Fall River, Mar. 19, 1959.

Gleeson, Francis D., S.J.: b. Jan. 17, 1895, Carrollton, Mo.: educ. Mount St. Michael's Scholasticate (Spokane, Wash.), St. Francis Xavier College (Ona, Spain); entered the Society of Jesus, 1912; ord. priest July 29, 1926; ord. titular bishop of Cotenna and vicar apostolic of Alaska, Apr. 5, 1948; first bishop of Fairbanks, Aug. 8, 1962; retired Nov. 15, 1968.

Glenn, Laurence A,: b. Aug. 25, 1900, Bellingham, Wash.; educ. St. John's Univ. (Collegeville, Minn.), Catholic Univ. (Washington, D.C.); ord. priest June 11, 1927; ord. titular bishop of Tuscamia and auxiliary bishop of Duluth, Sept. 12, 1956; app. bishop of Crookston, Jan. 27, 1960, installed Apr. 20, 1960; resigned 1970.

Glennie, Ignatius T., S.J.: b. Feb. 5, 1907, Mexico City; educ. Mt. St. Michael's Scholasticate (Spokane, Wash.), Pontifical Seminary (Kandy, Ceylon), St. Mary's College (Kurdeong, India); entered Society of Jesus, 1924; ord. priest Nov. 21, 1938; ord. bishop of Trincomalee, Ceylon, Sept. 21, 1947; title of see changed to Trincomalee-Batticaloa (Sri Lanka), 1967; resigned Mar. 25, 1974.

Gorman, Thomas Kiely: b. Aug. 30, 1892, Pasadena, Calif.; educ. St. Mary's Seminary (Baltimore, Md.), Catholic Univ. (Washington, D.C.), Louvain Univ. (Belgium); ord. priest June 23, 1917; ord. bishop of Reno, July 22, 1931; installed as titular bishop of Rhasus and coadjutor bishop of Dallas-Fort Worth, with right of succession, May 8, 1952; bishop of Dallas-Fort Worth, Aug. 20, 1954; resigned 1969.

Gossman, F. Joseph: b. Apr. 1, 1930, Baltimore, Md.: educ. St. Charles College (Catonsville, Md.), St. Mary's Seminary (Baltimore, Md.), North American College (Rome), Catholic Univ. (Washington, D.C.); ord. priest Dec. 17, 1955; ord. titular bishop of Agunto and auxiliary bishop of Baltimore, Sept. 11, 1968; named urban vicar, June 13, 1970; app. bishop of Raleigh April 8, 1975.

Gottwald, George J.: b. May 12, 1914, St. Louis, Mo.; educ. Kenrick Seminary (Webster Groves, Mo.); ord. priest June 9, 1940; ord. titular bishop of Cedamusa and auxiliary bishop of St. Louis, Aug. 8, 1961.

Gracida, Rene H.: b. June 9, 1923, New Orleans, La.; educ. Rice Univ. and Univ. of Houston (Houston, Tex.), Univ. of Fribourg (Switzerland); ord. priest May 23, 1959; ord. titular bishop of Masuccaba and auxiliary bishop of Miami, Jan. 25, 1972.

Grady, Thomas J.: b. Oct. 9, 1914, Chicago, Ill.; educ. St. Mary of the Lake Seminary (Mundelein, Ill.), Gregorian Univ. (Rome), Loyola Univ. (Chicago, Ill.); ord. priest Apr. 23, 1938; ord. titular bishop of Vamalla and auxiliary bishop of Chicago, Aug. 24, 1967; app. bishop of Orlando, Fla., Nov. 11, 1974, installed Dec. 16, 1974.

Graham, John J.: b. Sept. 11, 1913, Philadelphia, Pa.; educ. St. Charles Borromeo Seminary (Philadelphia, Pa.), Pontifical Roman Seminary (Rome, Italy); ord. priest Feb. 26, 1938; ord. titular bishop of Sabrata and auxiliary bishop of Philadelphia, Jan. 7, 1964.

Graner, Lawrence L., C.S.C.: b. Apr. 3, 1901, Franklin, Pa.; educ. Holy Cross Seminary (Notre Dame, Ind.), Holy Cross Mission Seminary (Washington, D.C.); entered Congregation of the Holy Cross, 1924; ord. priest June 24, 1928; ord. bishop of Dacca, India, Apr. 23, 1947; title changed to archbishop of Dacca, July 15, 1950; retired 1967.

Graves, Lawrence P.: b. May 4, 1916, Texarkana, Ark.; educ. St. John's Seminary (Little Rock, Ark.), North American College (Rome), Catholic Univ. (Washington, D.C.); ord. priest June 11, 1942; ord. titular bishop of Vina and auxiliary bishop of Little Rock, Apr. 25, 1969; app. bishop of Alexandria, May 22, 1973, installed July 22, 1973.

Graziano, Lawrence, O.F.M.: b. Apr. 5, 1921, Mt. Vernon, N.Y.; educ. Mt. Alvernia Seminary (Wappingers Falls, N.Y.); ord. priest Jan. 26, 1947; ord. titular bishop of Limata and auxiliary bishop of Santa Ana, El Salvador, Sept. 21, 1961; app. coadjutor bishop of San Miguel, El Salvador, with right of succession, 1965; bishop of San Miguel, Jan. 10, 1968; resigned, 1969; assigned titular see of Valabria.

Greco, Charles Paschal: b. Oct. 29, 1894, Rodney, Miss.; educ. St. Joseph's Seminary (St. Benedict, La.), Louvain Univ. (Belgium), Dominican Univ. (Fribourg, Switzerland); ord. priest July 25, 1918; ord. bishop of Alexandria Feb. 25, 1946; retired May 22, 1973.

Green, Francis J.: b. July 7, 1906, Corning, N.Y.; educ. St. Patrick's Seminary (Menlo Park, Calif.); ord. priest May 15, 1932; ord. titular bishop of Serra and auxiliary bishop of Tucson, Sept. 17, 1953; named coadjutor of Tucson with right of succession, May 11, 1960; bishop of Tucson, Oct. 26, 1960.

Green, Joseph: b. Oct. 13, 1917, St. Joseph, Mich.; educ. St. Joseph Seminary (Grand Rapids, Mich.), St. Gregory Seminary (Cincinnati, O.), St. Mary's Seminary (Norwood, O.), Lateran Univ. (Rome); ord. priest July 14, 1946; ord. titular bishop of Trisipa and auxiliary bishop of Lansing, Aug. 28, 1962; app. bishop of Reno, installed May 25, 1967; resigned Dec. 6, 1974.

Grellinger, John B.: b. Nov. 5, 1899, Milwaukee, Wis.; educ. Marquette Univ. and St. Francis Seminary (Milwaukee, Wis.), Urban Univ. and Gregorian Univ. (Rome); ord. priest July 14, 1929; ord. titular bishop of Syene and auxiliary bishop of Green Bay, July 14, 1949.

Greteman, Frank H.: b. Dec. 25, 1907, Willey, Ia.; educ. Loras Academy and Loras College (Dubuque, Ia.), North American College (Rome), Catholic Univ. (Washington, D.C.); ord. priest Dec. 8, 1932; ord. titular bishop of Vissalsa and auxiliary bishop of Sioux City, May 26, 1965; bishop of Sioux City, Dec. 9, 1970.

Grutka, Andrew G.: b. Nov. 17, 1908, Joliet, Ill.; educ. St. Procopius College and Seminary (Lisle, Ill.), Urban Univ. and Gregorian Univ. (Rome); ord. priest Dec. 5, 1933; app. moderator of lay activities in Gary diocese,

1955; ord. first bishop of Gary, Feb. 25, 1957; app. member of Pontifical Marian Academy, Jan. 5, 1970; elected president of Catholic Communications Foundation, Jan. 6, 1971.

Guilfoyle, George H.: b. Nov. 13, 1913, New York, N.Y.; educ. Georgetown Univ. (Washington, D.C.), Fordham Univ. (New York City), St. Joseph's Seminary (Dunwoodie, N.Y.), Columbia Univ. (New York City); ord. priest Mar. 25, 1944; ord. titular bishop of Marazane and auxiliary bishop of New York, Nov. 30, 1964; app. bishop of Camden, installed Mar. 4, 1968.

Guilfoyle, Merlin J.: b. July 15, 1908, San Francisco, Calif.; educ. St. Joseph's College (Mountain View, Calif.), St. Patrick's Seminary (Menlo Park, Calif.), Catholic Univ. (Washington, D.C.); ord. priest June 10, 1933; ord. titular bishop of Bulla and auxiliary bishop of San Francisco, Sept. 21, 1950; app. bishop of Stockton, Nov. 19, 1969, installed Jan. 13, 1970.

Gumbleton, Thomas J.: b. Jan. 26, 1930, Detroit, Mich.; educ. St. John Provincial Seminary (Detroit, Mich.), Pontifical Lateran Univ. (Rome); ord. priest June 2, 1956; ord. titular bishop of Ululi and auxiliary bishop of Detroit, May 1, 1968.

H

Hacker, Hilary B.: b. Jan. 10, 1913, New Ulm, Minn.; educ. St. Paul Seminary (St. Paul, Minn.), Gregorian Univ. (Rome); ord. priest June 4, 1938; ord. bishop of Bismarck, N. Dak., Feb. 27, 1957.

Hackett, John F.: b. Dec. 7, 1911, New Haven, Conn.; educ. St. Thomas Seminary (Bloomfield, Conn.), Seminaire Ste. Sulpice (Paris); ord. priest June 29, 1936; ord. titular bishop of Helenopolis in Palaestina and auxiliary bishop of Hartford, Mar. 19, 1953.

Hagarty, Paul Leonard, O.S.B.: b. Mar. 20, 1909, Greene, Ia.; educ. Loras College (Dubuque, Ia.), St. John's Seminary and St. John's Univ. (Collegeville, Minn.); entered Order of St. Benedict, 1931; ord. priest June 6, 1936; ord. titular bishop of Arba and vicar apostolic of the Bahamas, Oct. 19, 1950; first bishop of Nassau, July 5, 1960.

Ham, J. Richard, M.M.: b. July 11, 1921, Chicago, Ill.; educ. Maryknoll Seminary (New York); ord. priest June 12, 1948; missionary to Guatemala, 1958; ord. titular bishop of Puzia di Numidia and auxiliary bishop of Guatemala, Jan. 6, 1968.

Hammes, George A.: b. Sept. 11, 1911, St. Joseph Ridge, Wis.; educ. St. Lawrence Seminary (Mt. Calvary, Wis.), St. Louis Preparatory Seminary (St. Louis, Mo.), Kenrick Seminary (Webster Groves, Mo.), Sulpician Seminary, Catholic Univ. (Washington, D.C.); ord. priest May 22, 1937; ord. bishop of Superior, May 24, 1960.

Hanifen, Richard C.: b. June 15, 1931, Denver, Colo,; educ. Regis College and St. Thomas Seminary (Denver, Colo.), Catholic

Univ. (Washington, D.C.), Lateran Univ. (Rome); ord. priest June 6, 1959; ord. titular bishop of Abercorn and auxiliary bishop of Denver, Sept. 20, 1974.

Hannan, Philip M.: b. May 20, 1913, Washington, D.C.; educ. St. Charles College (Catonsville, Md.), Catholic Univ. (Washington, D.C.), North American College (Rome); ord. priest Dec. 8, 1939; ord. titular bishop of Hieropolis and auxiliary bishop of Washington, D.C., Aug. 28, 1956; app. archbishop of New Orleans, installed Oct. 13, 1965.

Harper, Edward, C.SS.R.: b. July 23, 1910, Brooklyn, N.Y.; educ. Redemptorist Houses of Study; ord. priest June 18, 1939; ord. titular bishop of Heraclea Pontica and first prelate of Virgin Islands, Oct. 6, 1960.

Harrington, Timothy J.: b. Dec. 19, 1918, Holyoke, Mass.; educ. Holy Cross College (Worcester, Mass.), Grand Seminary (Montreal, Que.), Boston College School of Social Work; ord. priest Jan. 19, 1946; ord. titular bishop of Rusuca and auxiliary bishop of Worcester, Mass., July 2, 1968.

Harris, Vincent M.: b. Oct. 14, 1913, Conroe, Tex.; educ. St. Mary's Seminary (La Porte, Tex.), North American College and Gregorian Univ. (Rome), Catholic Univ. (Washington, D.C.); ord. priest Mar. 19, 1938; ord. first bishop of Beaumont, Tex., Sept. 28, 1966; app. titular bishop of Rotaria and coadjutor bishop of Austin, Apr. 27, 1971; bishop of Austin, Nov. 15, 1971.

Harrison, Francis J.: b. Aug. 12, 1912; Syracuse, N.Y.; educ. Notre Dame Univ. (Notre Dame, Ind.), St. Bernard's Seminary (Rochester, N.Y.), ord. priest June 4, 1937; ord. titular bishop of Aquae in Numidia and auxiliary bishop of Syracuse, Apr. 22, 1971.

Hastrich, Jerome J.: b. Nov. 13, 1914, Milwaukee, Wis.; educ. Marquette Univ., St. Francis Seminary (Milwaukee, Wis.); ord. priest Feb. 9, 1941; ord. titular bishop of Gurza and auxiliary bishop of Madison, Sept. 3, 1963; app. bishop of Gallup, N.Mex., Sept. 3, 1969.

Hayes, James Thomas Gibbons, S.J.: b. Feb. 11, 1889, New York City; educ. St. Francis Xavier's College (New York City), Jesuit Novitiate (St. Andrew-on-the-Hudson, N.Y.), Jesuit House of Studies (Tronchiennes, Belgium); entered the Society of Jesus, Aug. 14, 1907; ord. priest June 29, 1921; ord. bishop of Cagayan, P.I., June 18, 1933; first archbishop of Cagayan, June 29, 1951; resigned Oct. 13, 1970.

Hayes, Nevin W., O.Carm: b. Feb. 17, 1922, Chicago, Ill.; ord. priest June 8, 1946; prelate nullius of Sicuani, Peru, 1959; ord. titular bishop of Nova Sinna and prelate of Sicuani, Aug. 5, 1965; app. auxiliary bishop of Chicago, Feb. 2, 1971.

Head, Edward D.: b. Aug. 5, 1919, White Plains, N. Y.; educ. Cathedral College, St. Joseph's Seminary, Columbia Univ. (New York City); ord. priest Jan. 27, 1945; director of New York Catholic Charities; ord. titular bishop of Ardsratha and auxiliary bishop of New York, Mar. 19, 1970; app. bishop of Buffalo, Jan. 23, 1973, installed Mar. 19, 1973.

Helmsing, Charles H.: b. Mar. 23, 1908, Shrewsbury, Mo.; educ. St. Louis Preparatory Seminary (St. Louis, Mo.), Kenrick Seminary (Webster Groves, Mo.); ord. priest June 10, 1933; ord. titular bishop of Axomis and auxiliary bishop of St. Louis, Apr. 19, 1949; first bishop of Springfield-Cape Girardeau, Aug. 24, 1956; bishop of Kansas City-St. Joseph, 1962, installed Apr. 3, 1962.

Henry, Harold W., S.S.C.: b. July 11, 1909, Northfield, Minn.; convert, 1922; educ. St. Columban's Seminary (Omaha, Nebr.); ord. priest Dec. 21, 1932; ord. titular bishop of Coridala and vicar apostolic of Kwang Ju, Korea, May 11, 1957; title changed to archbishop of Kwang Ju, 1962, when see was raised to metropolitan rank; transferred to titular see of Thubunae in Numidia, June 28, 1971, and named apostolic administrator of prefecture apostolic of Cheju-Do, Korea.

Herrmann, Edward J.: b. Nov. 6, 1913, Baltimore, Md.; educ. Mt. St. Mary's Seminary (Emmitsburg, Md.), Catholic Univ. (Washington, D.C.); ord. priest June 12, 1947; ord. titular bishop of Lamzella and auxiliary bishop of Washington, D.C., Apr. 26, 1966; app. bishop of Columbus, June 26, 1973.

Hettinger, Edward Gerhard: b. Oct. 14, 1902, Lancaster, O.; educ. St. Vincent's College (Beatty, Pa.); ord. priest June 2, 1928; ord. titular bishop of Teos and auxiliary bishop of Columbus, Feb. 24, 1942.

Hickey, Dennis W.: b. Oct. 28, 1914, Dansville, N.Y.; educ. Colgate Univ. and St. Bernard's Seminary (Rochester, N.Y.); ord. priest June 7, 1941; ord. titular bishop of Rusuccuru and auxiliary bishop of Rochester, N.Y., Mar. 14, 1968.

Hickey, James A.: b. Oct. 11, 1920, Midland, Mich.; educ. Sacred Heart Seminary (Detroit, Mich.), Catholic Univ. (Washington, D.C.), Lateran Univ. and Angelicum (Rome), Michigan State Univ.; ord. priest June 15, 1946; ord. titular bishop of Taraqua and auxiliary bishop of Saginaw, Apr. 14, 1967; rector of North American College, Rome, 1969-74; app. bishop of Cleveland, June 5, 1974; installed July 16, 1974.

Hines, Vincent J.: b. Sept. 14, 1912, New Haven, Conn.; educ. St. Thomas Seminary (Bloomfield, Conn.), St. Sulpice Seminary (Paris), Lateran Univ. (Rome); ord. priest May 2, 1937; ord. bishop of Norwich, Conn., Mar. 17, 1960; resigned June 17, 1975.

Hoch, Lambert A.: b. Feb. 6, 1903, Elkton, S.D.; educ. Creighton Univ. (Omaha, Nebr.), St. Paul Seminary (St. Paul, Minn.); ord. priest May 30, 1928; ord. bishop of Bismarck, Mar. 25, 1952; app. bishop of Sioux Falls Dec. 5, 1956.

Hodapp, Robert L., S.J.: b. Oct. 1, 1910.

Mankato, Minn.; educ. St. Stanislaus Seminary (Florissant, Mo.), St. Louis Univ. (St. Louis, Mo.); ord. priest June 18, 1941; ord. bishop of Belize, June 26, 1958.

Hodges, Joseph H.: b. Oct. 8, 1911, Harper's Ferry, W.Va.; educ. St. Charles College (Catonsville, Md.), North American College (Rome); ord. priest Dec. 8, 1935; ord. titular bishop of Rusadus and auxiliary bishop of Richmond, Oct. 15, 1952; named coadjutor bishop of Wheeling with right of succession, May 24, 1961; bishop of Wheeling, Nov. 23, 1962; title of see changed to Wheeling-Charleston 1974.

Hogan, James J.: b. Oct. 17, 1911, Philadelphia, Pa.; educ. St. Charles College (Catonsville, Md.), St. Mary's Seminary (Baltimore), Gregorian Univ. (Rome), Catholic Univ. (Washington, D.C.); ord. priest Dec. 8, 1937; ord. titular bishop of Philomelium and auxiliary bishop of Trenton, Feb. 25, 1960; app. bishop of Altoona-Johnstown, installed July 6, 1966.

Hogan, Joseph L.: b. Mar. 11, 1916, Lima, N.Y.; educ. St. Bernard's Seminary (Rochester, N.Y.), Canisius College (Buffalo, N.Y.), Angelicum (Rome); ord. priest June 6, 1942; ord. bishop of Rochester, Nov. 28, 1969.

Howard, Edward Daniel: b. Nov. 5, 1877, Cresco, Ia.; educ. St. Joseph's College (Dubuque, Ia.), St. Mary's College (St. Mary's, Kans.), St. Paul Seminary (St. Paul, Minn.); ord. priest June 12, 1906; ord. titular bishop of Isauropolis and auxiliary bishop of Davenport, Apr. 8, 1924; app. archbishop of Oregon City, Apr. 30, 1926; title changed to archbishop of Portland, Sept. 26, 1928; resigned, 1966; assigned titular see of Albule.

Hughes, William A.: b. Sept. 23, 1921, Youngstown, O.; educ. St. Charles College (Catonsville, Md.), St. Mary's Seminary (Cleveland, O.) Notre Dame Univ. (Notre Dame, Ind.); ord. priest Apr. 6, 1946; ord. titular bishop of Inis Cathaig and auxiliary bishop of Youngstown, Sept. 12, 1974.

Howze, Joseph L.: b. Aug. 30, 1924, Daphne, Ala.; convert to Catholicism, 1948; educ. St. Bonaventure Univ. (St. Bonaventure, N.Y.); ord. priest May 7, 1959; ord. titular bishop of Massita and auxiliary bishop of Natchez-Jackson, Jan. 28, 1973.

Hunthausen, Raymond G.: b. Aug. 21, 1921, Anaconda, Mont.; educ. Carroll College (Helena, Mont.), St. Edward's Seminary (Kenmore, Wash.), St. Louis Univ. (St. Louis, Mo.), Catholic Univ. (Washington, D.C.), Fordham Univ. (New York City), Notre Dame Univ. (Notre Dame, Ind.); ord. priest June 1, 1946; ord. bishop of Helena, Aug. 30, 1962; app. archbishop of Seattle, Feb. 25, 1975.

Hurley, Francis T.: b. Jan. 12, 1927, San Francisco, Calif.; educ. St. Patrick's Seminary (Menlo Park, Calif.), Catholic Univ. (Washington, D.C.); ord. priest June 16, 1951; assigned to NCWC in Washington, D.C., 1957; assistant (1958) and later (1968) associate secretary of NCCB and USCC; ord. titular bishop of Daimlaig and auxiliary bishop of Juneau, Alaska, Mar. 19, 1970; app. bishop of Juneau, July 20, 1971.

Hurley, Mark J.: b. Dec. 13, 1919, San Francisco, Calif.; educ. St. Patrick's Seminary (Menlo Park, Calif.), Univ. of California (Berkeley), Catholic Univ. (Washington, D.C.), Lateran Univ. (Rome), Univ. of Portland (Portland, Ore.); ord. priest Sept. 23, 1944; ord. titular bishop of Thunusuda and auxiliary bishop of San Francisco, Jan. 4, 1968; app. bishop of Santa Rosa, Nov. 19, 1969.

I-J

Imesch, Joseph L.: b. June 21, 1931, Detroit, Mich.; educ. Sacred Heart Seminary (Detroit, Mich.), North American College, Gregorian Univ. (Rome); ord. priest Dec. 16, 1956; ord. titular bishop of Pomaria and auxiliary bishop of Detroit, Apr. 3, 1973.

Issenmann, Clarence G.: b. May 30, 1907, Hamilton, O.; educ. St. Joseph's College (Rensselaer, Ind.), St. Gregory's Seminary (Cincinnati, O.), St. Mary of the West Seminary (Norwood, O.); ord. priest June 29, 1932; ord. titular bishop of Phytea and auxiliary bishop of Cincinnati, May 25, 1954; bishop of Columbus, 1957-64; app. titular bishop of Filaca, coadjutor bishop of Cleveland and apostolic administrator "sede plena," 1964; bishop of Cleveland, 1966; resigned June 5, 1974, because of ill health.

Johnson, William R.: b. Nov. 19, 1918, Tonopah, Nev.; educ. Los Angeles College and St. John's Seminary (Camarillo, Calif.), Catholic Univ. (Washington, D.C.); ord. priest May 28, 1944; ord. titular bishop of Blera and auxiliary bishop of Los Angeles, Mar. 25, 1971

Joyce, Robert F.: b. Oct. 7, 1896, Proctor, Vt.; educ. Univ. of Vermont (Burlington, Vt.), Grand Seminary (Montreal, Canada); ord. priest May 26, 1923; ord. titular bishop of Citium and auxiliary bishop of Burlington, Oct. 28, 1954; installed as bishop of Burlington, Feb. 26, 1957; resigned Dec. 14, 1971.

K

Kearney, James Edward: b. Oct. 28, 1884, Red Oak, Ia.; educ. St. Joseph's Seminary (Dunwoodie, N.Y.), Catholic Univ. (Washington, D.C.); ord. priest Sept. 19, 1908; ord. bishop of Salt Lake, Oct. 28, 1932; app. bishop of Rochester, July 31, 1937; retired Oct. 21, 1966.

Kellenberg, Walter P.: b. June 3, 1901, New York, N.Y.; educ. Cathedral College (New York, City), St. Joseph Seminary (Dunwoodie, N.Y.); ord. priest June 2, 1928; ord. titular bishop of Joannina and auxiliary bishop of New York, Oct. 5, 1953; app. bishop of Ogdensburg, Jan. 19, 1954; app. first bishop of Rockville Centre Apr. 16, 1957, installed May 27, 1957.

Kennally, Vincent, S.J.: b. June 11, 1895, Boston, Mass.; educ. Woodstock College (Woodstock, Md.), Weston College (Weston, Mass.); ord. priest June 20, 1928; ord. titular bishop of Sassura and vicar apostolic of the Caroline and Marshall Islands, Mar. 25, 1957; retired Sept. 20, 1971.

Klonowski, Henry T.: b. Mar. 8, 1898, Scranton, Pa.; educ. Univ. of Scranton (Scranton, Pa.), St. Francis Seminary (St. Francis, Wis.), Sts. Cyril and Methodius Seminary (Orchard Lake, Mich.), Capranica College, Angelicum and Gregorian Univ. (Rome); ord. priest Aug. 8, 1920; ord. titular bishop of Daldis and auxiliary bishop of Scranton, July 2, 1947; retired May, 1973.

Kocisko, Stephen: b. June 11, 1915, Minneapolis, Minn.; educ. Nazareth Hall Minor Seminary (St. Paul, Minn.), Pontifical Ruthenian College, Urban Univ. (Rome); ord. priest Mar. 30, 1941; ord. titular bishop of Teveste and auxiliary bishop of apostolic exarchate of Pittsburgh, Oct. 23, 1956; installed as first eparch of the eparchy of Passaic, Sept. 10, 1963; app. eparch of Byzantine-Rite diocese of Pittsburgh, installed Mar. 5, 1968; app. first metropolitan of Munhall, installed June 11, 1969.

Koester, Charles R.: b. Sept. 16, 1915, Jefferson City, Mo.; educ. Conception Academy (Conception, Mo.), St. Louis Preparatory Seminary and Kenrick Seminary (St. Louis, Mo.), North American College (Rome); ord. priest Dec. 20, 1941; ord. titular bishop of Suacia and auxiliary bishop of St. Louis, Feb. 11, 1971.

Krawczak, Arthur H.: b. Feb. 2, 1913, Detroit, Mich.; educ. Sacred Heart Seminary, Sts. Cyril and Methodius Seminary (Orchard Lake, Mich.), Catholic Univ. (Washington, D.C.); ord. priest May 18, 1940; ord. titular bishop of Subbar and auxiliary bishop of Detroit, May 3, 1973.

Krol, John J.: (See Cardinals, Biographies.)

Kupfer, William F., M.M.: b. Jan. 28, 1909, Brooklyn, N.Y.; educ. Cathedral College (Brooklyn, N.Y.) Maryknoll Seminary (Maryknoll, N.Y.); ord. priest June 11, 1933; missionary in China; app. prefect apostolic of Taichung, Formosa, 1951; ord. first bishop of Taichung, July 25, 1962.

L

Lardone, Francesco: b. Jan. 12, 1887, Moretta, Italy; educ. Pontifical Schools of Theology and Canon Law and Royal Univ. (Turin); ord. priest June 29, 1910; became an American citizen, 1937; ord. titular archbishop of Rhizaeum and apostolic nuncio to Haiti and the Dominican Republic, June 30, 1949; app. apostolic nuncio to Peru, Nov. 21, 1953; papal representative to Turkey (first apostolic delegate, then internuncio), 1959-66.

Law, Bernard F.: b. Nov. 4, 1931, Torreon, Mexico; educ. Harvard Univ. (Cambridge, Mass.), St. Joseph Seminary (St. Benedict,

La.), Pontifical College Josephinum (Worthington, O.); ord. priest May 21, 1961; editor of *Mississippi Register* (now *Mississippi Today*), 1963-68; director of NCCB Committee on Ecumenical and Interreligious Affairs, 1968-71; vicar general of Natchez-Jackson diocese, 1971-73; ord. bishop of Springfield-Cape Girardeau, Mo., Dec. 5, 1973.

Leech, George Leo: b. May 21, 1890, Ashley, Pa.; educ. St. Charles Borromeo Seminary (Overbrook, Pa.), Catholic Univ. (Washington, D.C.); ord. priest May 29, 1920; ord. titular bishop of Mela and auxiliary bishop of Harrisburg, Oct. 17, 1935; bishop of Harrisburg Dec. 19, 1935; resigned Oct. 19, 1971; app. titular bishop of Allegheny.

Leipzig, Francis P.: b. June 29, 1895, Chilton, Wis.; educ. St. Francis Seminary (Milwaukee, Wis.), Mt. Angel Seminary (St. Benedict, Ore.), St. Patrick's Seminary (Menlo Park, Calif.); ord. priest Apr. 14, 1920; ord. bishop of Baker, Sept. 12, 1950; retired June 30, 1971.

Lemay, Leo, S.M.: b. Sept. 23, 1909, Lawrence, Mass.; educ. Marist College (Washington, D.C.), Gregorian Univ. (Rome); ord. priest Apr. 15, 1933; ord. titular bishop of Agbia and vicar apostolic of North Solomon Islands, Sept. 21, 1960; first bishop of Bougainville, Nov. 15, 1966; resigned Aug. 6, 1974.

Leonard, Vincent M.: b. Dec. 11, 1908, Pittsburgh, Pa.; educ. Duquesne Univ. (Pittsburgh, Pa.), St. Vincent Seminary (Latrobe, Pa.); ord. priest June 16, 1935; ord. titular bishop of Arsacal and auxiliary bishop of Pittsburgh, Apr. 21, 1964; app. bishop of Pittsburgh, installed July 2, 1969.

Lessard, Raymond W.: b. Dec. 21, 1930, Grafton, N.D.; educ. St. Paul Seminary (St. Paul, Minn.), North American College (Rome); ord. priest Dec. 16, 1956; served on staff of the Congregation for Bishops in the Roman Curia, 1964-73; ord. bishop of Savannah, Apr. 27, 1973.

Leven, Stephen A.: b. Apr. 30, 1905, Blackwell, Okla.; educ. St. Gregory's College (Shawnee, Okla.), St. Benedict's College (Atchison, Kans.), St. Mary's Seminary (La Porte, Tex.), American College (Louvain, Belgium); ord. priest June 10, 1928; ord. titular bishop of Bure and auxiliary bishop of San Antonio, Feb. 8, 1956; app. bishop of San Angelo, Tex., installed Nov. 25, 1969.

Lohmuller, Martin J.: b. Aug. 21, 1919, Philadelphia, Pa.; educ. St. Charles Borromeo Seminary (Philadelphia, Pa.), Catholic Univ. (Washington, D.C.); ord. priest June 3, 1944; ord. titular bishop of Ramsbury and auxiliary bishop of Philadelphia, Apr. 2, 1970.

Losten, Basil: b. May 11, 1930, Chesapeake City, Md.; educ. St. Basil's College (Stamford, Conn.), Catholic University (Washington, D.C.); ord. priest June 10, 1957; ord. titular bishop of Arcadiopolis in Asia and auxiliary bishop of Ukrainian archeparchy of Philadelphia, May 25, 1971.

Lucey, Robert Emmet: b. Mar. 16, 1891, Los Angeles, Calif.; educ. St. Vincent's College (Los Angeles, Calif.), St. Patrick's Seminary (Menlo Park, Calif.), North American College (Rome); ord. priest May 14, 1916; ord. bishop of Amarillo, May 1, 1934; app. archbishop of San Antonio, Jan. 23, 1941; retired June 4, 1969.

Lucker, Raymond A.: b. Feb. 24, 1927, St. Paul, Minn.; educ. St. Paul Seminary (St. Paul, Minn.); University of Minnesota (Minneapolis), Angelicum (Rome); ord. priest June 7, 1952; director of USCC department of education, 1968-71; ord. titular bishop of Meta and auxiliary bishop of St. Paul and Minneapolis, Sept. 8, 1971.

Lynch, George E.: b. Mar. 4, 1917, New York, N.Y.; educ. Fordham Univ. (New York), Mt. St. Mary's Seminary (Emmitsburg, Md.), Catholic Univ. (Washington, D.C.); ord. priest May 29, 1943; ord. titular bishop of Satafi and auxiliary bishop of Raleigh Jan. 6, 1970.

Lyons, Thomas W.: b. Sept. 26, 1923, Washington, D.C.; educ. St. Charles College (Catonsville, Md.), St. Mary's Seminary (Baltimore, Md.); ord. priest May 22, 1948; ord. titular bishop of Mortlach and auxiliary bishop of Washington, D.C., Sept. 12, 1974.

M

McAuliffe, Michael F.: b. Nov. 22, 1920, Kansas City, Mo.; educ. St. Louis Preparatory Seminary (St. Louis, Mo.), Catholic Univ. (Washington, D.C.); ord. priest May 31, 1945; ord. bishop of Jefferson City, Aug. 18, 1969.

McCafferty, John E.: b. Jan. 6, 1920, New York, N.Y.; educ. St. Andrew's and St. Bernard's Seminaries (Rochester, N.Y.), Catholic Univ. (Washington, D.C.); ord. priest Mar. 17, 1945; ord. titular bishop of Tanudaia and auxiliary bishop of Rochester, Mar. 14, 1968.

McCarthy, Edward A.: b. Apr. 10, 1918, Cincinnati, O.; educ. Mt. St. Mary Seminary (Norwood, O.), Catholic Univ. (Washington, D.C.), Lateran and Angelicum (Rome); ord. priest May 29, 1943; ord. titular bishop of Tamascani and auxiliary bishop of Cincinnati, June 15, 1965; first bishop of Phoenix, Ariz., Dec. 2, 1969.

McCauley, Vincent, C.S.C.: b. Mar. 8, 1906, Council Bluffs, Ia.; educ. Notre Dame Univ. (Notre Dame, Ind.), Holy Cross Seminary (Washington, D.C.); ord. priest June 24, 1943; ord. first bishop of Fort Portal, Uganda, May 18, 1961; resigned because of ill health, Dec. 1, 1972; general secretary of Episcopal Conferences of East Africa (AMECEA).

McCormick, J. Carroll: b. Dec. 15, 1907, Philadelphia, Pa.; educ. College Ste. Marie (Montreal), St. Charles Seminary (Overbrook, Pa.), Minor and Major Roman Seminary (Rome); ord. priest July 10, 1932; ord. titular bishop of Ruspae and auxiliary bishop of Philadelphia, Apr. 23, 1947; app. bishop of Altoona-Johnstown, installed Sept. 21, 1960; app. bishop of Scranton, installed May 25, 1966.

McDevitt, Gerald V.: b. Feb. 23, 1917, Philadelphia, Pa.; educ. St. Charles Seminary (Philadelphia, Pa.), Pontifical Roman Seminary (Rome), Catholic Univ. (Washington, D.C.); ord. priest May 30, 1942; ord. titular bishop of Tigias and auxiliary bishop of Philadelphia, Aug. 1, 1962.

McDonald, Andrew J.: b. Oct. 24, 1923, Savannah, Ga.; educ. St. Mary's Seminary (Baltimore, Md.), Catholic Univ. (Washington, D.C.), Lateran Univ. (Rome); ord. priest May 8, 1948; ord. bishop of Little Rock, Sept. 5, 1972.

McDonald, William J.: b. June 17, 1904, Mooncoin, Ireland; educ. St. Kieran's College and Seminary (Kilkenny, Ireland), Catholic Univ. (Washington, D.C.); ord. priest June 10, 1928; rector of Catholic Univ. of America, 1957-67; ord. titular bishop of Aquae Regiae and auxiliary bishop of Washington, May 19, 1964; app. auxiliary bishop of San Francisco, July 26, 1967.

McDonough, Thomas J.: b. Dec. 5, 1911, Philadelphia, Pa.; educ. St. Charles Seminary (Overbrook, Pa.), Catholic Univ. (Washington, D.C.); ord. priest May 26, 1938; ord. titular bishop of Thenae and auxiliary bishop of St. Augustine, Apr. 30, 1947; app. auxiliary bishop of Savannah, Jan. 2, 1957; named bishop of Savannah, installed Apr. 27, 1960; app. archbishop of Louisville, installed May 2, 1967.

McDowell, John B.: b. July 17, 1921, New Castle, Pa.; educ. St. Vincent College, St. Vincent Theological Seminary (Latrobe, Pa.), Catholic Univ. (Washington, D.C.); ord. priest Nov. 4, 1945; ord. titular bishop of Tamazuca, and auxiliary bishop of Pittsburgh, Sept. 8, 1966.

McEleney, John J., S.J.: b. Nov. 13, 1895, Woburn, Mass.; educ. Boston College (Boston, Mass.), Jesuit Scholasticate (New England Province); entered Society of Jesus, 1918; ord. priest June 18, 1930; app. provincial of New England Province, 1944; ord. titular bishop of Zeugma and vicar apostolic of Jamaica, Apr. 15, 1950; title changed to bishop of Kingston, Feb. 29, 1956; archbishop of Kingston, Sept. 14, 1967; retired 1970.

McFarland, Norman F.: b. Feb. 21, 1922, Martinez, Calif.; educ. St. Patrick's Seminary (Menlo Park, Calif.), Catholic Univ. (Washington, D. C.); ord. priest June 15, 1946; ord. titular bishop of Bida and auxiliary bishop of San Francisco, Sept. 8, 1970; apostolic adminstrator of Reno, 1974.

McGann, John R.: b. Dec. 2, 1924, Brooklyn, N.Y.; educ. Cathedral College (Brooklyn, N.Y.), Immaculate Conception Seminary

(Huntington, L.I.); ord. priest June 3, 1950; ord. titular bishop of Morosbisdus and auxiliary bishop of Rockville Centre, Jan. 7, 1971; vicar general and episcopal vicar.

McGarry, Urban, T.O.R.: b. Nov. 11, 1911, Warren, Pa.; ord. priest Oct. 3, 1942, in India; prefect apostolic of Bhagalpur, Aug. 7, 1956; ord. first bishop of Bhagalpur, India, May 10, 1965.

McGucken, Joseph T.: b. Mar. 13, 1902, Los Angeles, Calif.; educ. St. Patrick's Seminary (Menlo Park, Calif.), North American College (Rome); ord. priest Jan. 15, 1928; ord. titular bishop of Sanavus and auxiliary bishop of Los Angeles, Mar. 19, 1941; app. coadjutor bishop of Sacramento with right of succession, Oct. 26, 1955; bishop of Sacramento, Jan. 14, 1957; archbishop of San Francisco, installed Apr. 3, 1962.

McGurkin, Edward A., M.M.: b. June 22, 1905, Hartford, Conn.; educ. Maryknoll Seminary (Maryknoll, N. Y.); ord. priest Sept. 14, 1930; ord. first bishop of Maswa, Tanganyika, Oct. 3, 1956; title of see changed to Shinyanga (Tanzania), 1957; resigned 1975.

McIntyre, J. Francis L.: (See Cardinals, Biographies.)

McKinney, Joseph C.: b. Sept. 10, 1928, Grand Rapids, Mich.: educ. St. Joseph's Seminary (Grand Rapids, Mich.), Seminaire de Philosophie (Montreal, Canada), Urban Univ. (Rome, Italy); ord. priest Dec. 20, 1953; ord. titular bishop of Lentini and auxiliary bishop of Grand Rapids, Sept. 26, 1968.

McLaughlin, Bernard J.: b. Nov. 19, 1912, Buffalo, N.Y.; educ. Urban Univ. (Rome, Italy); ord. priest Dec. 21, 1935, at Rome; ord. titular bishop of Mottola and auxiliary bishop of Buffalo, Jan. 6, 1969.

McLaughlin, Charles B.: b. Sept. 26, 1913, New York, N.Y.; educ. Cathedral College (New York City), St. Joseph's Seminary (Yonkers, N.Y.), St. John's Seminary (Little Rock, Ark.); ord. priest June 6, 1941; ord. titular bishop of Risinium and auxiliary bishop of Raleigh, Apr. 15, 1964; app. first bishop of St. Petersburg, installed June 17, 1968.

McManus, James E., C.SS.R.: b. Oct. 10, 1900, Brooklyn, N.Y.; educ. Redemptorist Preparatory College (North East, Pa.), Mt. St. Alphonsus Seminary (Esopus, N. Y.), Catholic Univ. (Washington, D.C.); entered Congregation of the Most Holy Redeemer, 1921; ord. priest June 19, 1927; ord. bishop of Ponce, Puerto Rico, July 1, 1947; founder of Catholic Univ. of Ponce; transferred to titular see of Benda and app. auxiliary bishop of New York, Nov. 18, 1963; retired 1970.

McManus, William E.: b. Jan. 27, 1914, Chicago, Ill.; educ. St. Mary of the Lake Seminary (Mundelein, Ill.), Catholic Univ. (Washington, D.C.); ord. priest Apr. 15, 1939; ord. titular bishop of Mesarfelta and auxiliary bishop of Chicago, Aug. 24, 1967.

McNabb, John C., O.S.A.: b. Dec. 11,

1925, Beloit, Wis.; educ. Villanova Univ. (Villanova, Pa.), Augustinian College and Catholic Univ. (Washington, D.C.), De Paul Univ. (Chicago, Ill.); ord. priest May 24, 1952; ord. titular bishop of Saia Maggiore and prelate of Chulucanas, Peru, June 17, 1967.

McNaughton, William J., M.M.: b. Dec. 7, 1926, Lawrence, Mass.; educ. Maryknoll Seminary (Maryknoll, N.Y.); ord. priest June 13, 1953; ord. titular bishop of Thuburbo Minus and vicar apostolic of Inchon, Korea, Aug. 24, 1961; title changed to bishop of Inchon, Mar. 10, 1962.

McNicholas, Joseph A.: b. Jan. 13, 1923, St. Louis, Mo.; educ. Cardinal Glennon College, Kenrick Seminary and St. Louis Univ. (all in St. Louis, Mo.); ord. priest June 7, 1949; ord. titular bishop of Scala and auxiliary bishop of St. Louis, Mar. 25, 1969.

McShea, Joseph M.: b. Feb. 22, 1907, Latimer, Pa.; educ. St. Charles Seminary (Philadelphia, Pa.), Major Pontifical Roman Seminary (Rome); ord. priest Dec. 6, 1931; ord. titular bishop of Mina and auxiliary bishop of Philadelphia, Mar. 19, 1952; app. first bishop of Allentown, installed Apr. 11, 1961.

Maginn, Edward J.: b. Jan. 4, 1897, Glasgow, Scotland; educ. Holy Cross College (Worcester, Mass.), St. Joseph's Seminary (Yonkers, N.Y.); ord. priest June 10, 1922; ord. titular bishop of Curium and auxiliary bishop of Albany, Sept. 12, 1957; apostolic administrator of Albany, 1966-69; retired July 8, 1972.

Maguire, John J.: b. Dec. 11, 1904, New York, N.Y.; educ. Cathedral College (New York City), St. Joseph's Seminary (Dunwoodie, N.Y.), North American College (Rome); ord. priest Dec. 22, 1928; ord. titular bishop of Antiphrae and auxiliary bishop of New York, June 29, 1959; app. titular archbishop of Tabalta and coadjutor archbishop of New York, Sept. 15, 1965.

Maguire, Joseph F.: b. Sept. 4, 1919, Boston, Mass.; educ. Boston College, St. John's Seminary (Boston, Mass.); ord. priest June 29, 1945; ord. titular bishop of Macteris and auxiliary bishop of Boston, Feb. 2, 1972.

Maher, Leo T.: b. July 1, 1915, Mount Union, Ia.; educ. St. Joseph's College (Mountain View, Calif.); St. Patrick's Seminary (Menlo Park, Calif.); ord. priest Dec. 18, 1943; ord. first bishop of Santa Rosa, April 5, 1962; bishop of San Diego, Oct. 4, 1969.

Mahoney, James P.: b. Aug. 16, 1925, Kingston, N.Y.; educ. St. Joseph's Seminary (Dunwoodie, N.Y.); ord. priest May 19, 1951; ord. titular bishop of Ipagro and auxiliary bishop of New York, Sept. 15, 1972.

Mahony, Roger M.: b. Feb. 27, 1936, Hollywood, Calif.; educ. St. John's Seminary (Camarillo, Calif.), National Catholic School of Social Service (Catholic Univ., Washington, D.C.); ord. priest May 1, 1962; ord. titular bishop of Tamascani and auxiliary bishop of Fresno, Mar. 19, 1975.

Malone, James W.: b. Mar. 8, 1920, Youngstown, O.; educ. St. Charles Preparatory Seminary (Catonsville, Md.), St. Mary's Seminary (Cleveland, O.), Catholic Univ. (Washington, D.C.); ord. priest May 26, 1945; ord. titular bishop of Alabanda and auxiliary bishop of Youngstown, Mar. 24, 1960; apostolic administrator, 1966; bishop of Youngstown, installed June 20, 1968.

Maloney, Charles G.: b. Sept. 9, 1912, Louisville, Ky.; educ. St. Joseph's College (Rensselaer, Ind.), North American College (Rome); ord. priest Dec. 8, 1937; ord. titular bishop of Capsa and auxiliary bishop of Louisville, Feb. 2, 1955.

Maloney, David M.: b. Mar. 15, 1912, Littleton, Colo.; educ. St. Thomas Seminary (Denver, Colo.), Gregorian Univ. and Apollinare Univ. (Rome); ord. priest Dec. 8, 1936; ord. titular bishop of Ruspe and auxiliary bishop of Denver, Jan. 4, 1961; app. bishop of Wichita, Kans., Dec. 6, 1967.

Manning, Thomas R., O.F.M.: b. Aug. 29, 1922, Baltimore, Md.; educ. Duns Scotus College (Cincinnati, O.), Holy Name College (Washington, D.C.); ord. priest June 5, 1948; ord. titular bishop of Arsamosata and prelate of Coroico, Bolivia, July 14, 1959.

Manning, Timothy: (See Cardinals, Biographies.)

Marcinkus, Paul C.: b. Jan. 15, 1922, Cicero, Ill.; ord. priest May 3, 1947; served in Vatican secretariat from 1952; ord. titular bishop of Orta, Jan. 6, 1969; secretary (1968-71) and president (1971-) of Institute for Works of Religion (Vatican Bank).

Mardaga, Thomas J.: b. May 14, 1913, Baltimore, Md.; educ. St. Charles College (Catonsville, Md.), St. Mary's Seminary (Baltimore, Md.); ord. priest May 14, 1940; ord. titular bishop of Mutugenna and auxiliary bishop of Baltimore, Jan. 25, 1967; app. bishop of Wilmington, installed Apr. 6, 1968.

Marino, Eugene A., S.S.J.: b. May 29, 1934, Biloxi, Miss.; educ. Epiphany Apostolic College and Mary Immaculate Novitiate (Newburgh, N.Y.), St. Joseph's Seminary (Washington, D.C.), Catholic Univ. (Washington, D.C.), Loyola Univ. (New Orleans, La.), Fordham Univ. (New York City); ord. priest June 9, 1962; ord. titular bishop of Walla Walla and auxiliary bishop of Washington, D.C., Sept. 12, 1974.

Marling, Joseph M., C.PP.S.: b. Aug. 31, 1904, Centralia, W. Va.; educ. St. Joseph's College (Collegeville, Ind.), St. Charles Seminary (Carthagena, O.), Catholic Univ. (Washington, D.C.); ord. priest Feb. 21, 1929; ord. titular bishop of Thasus and auxiliary bishop of Kansas City, Mo., Aug. 6, 1947; app. first bishop of Jefferson City, Aug. 24, 1956; resigned 1969; assigned titular see of Lesina.

Marshall, John A.: b. Apr. 26, 1928, Worcester, Mass.; educ. Holy Cross College (Worcester, Mass.), Sulpician Seminary (Montreal), North American College and Gregorian Univ. (Rome), Assumption College (Worcester); ord. priest Dec. 19, 1953; ord. bishop of Burlington, Jan. 25, 1972.

May, John L.: b. Mar. 31, 1922, Evanston, Ill.; educ. St. Mary of the Lake Seminary (Mundelein, Ill.); ord. priest May 3, 1947; general secretary and vice-president of the Catholic Church Extension Society, 1959; ord. titular bishop of Tagarbala and auxiliary bishop of Chicago, Aug. 14, 1967; bishop of Mobile, Ala., Sept. 29, 1969.

Mazzarella, Bernardino N., O.F.M.: b. Apr. 20, 1904, Mirabella Eclano, Italy; educ. St. Anthony Seminary (Catskill, N.Y.), Franciscan Houses of Study (Province of Immaculate Conception); ord. priest June 5, 1931; ord. titular bishop of Hadrianopolis in Pisidia and prelate nullius of Olancho, Honduras, Oct. 18, 1957; installed as first bishop of Comayagua, Honduras, May 17, 1963.

Medeiros, Humberto S.: (See Cardinals, Biographies.)

Mendez, Alfred, C.S.C.: b. June 3, 1907, Chicago, Ill.; educ. Notre Dame Univ. (Notre Dame, Ind.), Institute of Holy Cross (Washington, D.C.); ord. priest June 24, 1935; ord. first bishop of Arecibo, Puerto Rico, Oct. 28, 1960; resigned Jan. 24, 1974.

Mestice, Anthony F.: b. Dec. 6, 1923, New York, N.Y.; educ. St. Joseph Seminary (Yonkers, N.Y.); ord. priest June 4, 1949; ord. titular bishop of Villa Nova and auxiliary bishop of New York Apr. 27, 1973.

Metzger, Sidney Matthew: b. July 11, 1902, Fredericksburg, Tex.; educ. St. John's Seminary (San Antonio, Tex.), North American College (Rome); ord. priest Apr. 3, 1926; ord. titular bishop of Birtha and auxiliary bishop of Santa Fe, Apr. 10, 1940; app. coadjutor bishop of El Paso, Dec. 26, 1941; bishop of El Paso, Dec. 1, 1942.

Michaels, James E., S.S.C.: b. May 30, 1926, Chicago, Ill.; educ. Columban Seminary (St. Columban, Neb.), Gregorian Univ. (Rome); ord. priest Dec. 21, 1951; ord. titular bishop of Verbe and auxiliary bishop of Kwang Ju, Korea, Apr. 14, 1966; app. auxiliary bishop of Wheeling, Apr. 3, 1973; title of see changed to Wheeling-Charleston, 1974.

Mihalik, Emil J.: b. Feb. 6, 1920, Pittsburgh, Pa.; educ. St. Procopius Seminary (Lisle, Ill.), Duquesne Univ. (Pittsburgh, Pa.); ord. priest Sept. 21, 1945; ord. first bishop of Byzantine Rite diocese of Parma, O., June 12, 1969.

Minder, John, O.S.F.S.: b. Nov. 1, 1923, Philadelphia, Pa.; ord. priest June 3, 1950; ord. bishop of Keimos, South Africa, Jan. 10, 1968.

Moran, William J.: b. Jan. 15, 1906, San Francisco, Calif.; educ. St. Patrick's Seminary (Menlo Park, Calif.); ord. priest June 20, 1931; Army chaplain, 1933; ord. titular bishop of Centuria and auxiliary to the military vicar, Dec. 13, 1965.

Morkovsky, John Louis: b. Aug. 16, 1909, Praha, Tex.; educ. St. John's Seminary (San Antonio, Tex.), North American College, Urban Univ. and Gregorian Univ. (Washington, D.C.); ord. priest Dec. 5, 1933; ord titular bishop of Hieron and auxiliary bishop of Amarillo, Feb. 22, 1956; app. bishop of Amarillo, Aug. 27, 1958; titular bishop of Tigava and coadjutor bishop of Galveston-Houston with right of succession, June 11, 1963; apostolic administrator; president Texas Conference of Churches, 1970-72; bishop of Galveston-Houston, Apr. 22, 1975.

Morrow, Louis La Ravoire, S. D. B.: b. Dec. 24, 1892, Weatherford, Tex.; educ. Salesian School and Palafox (Puebla, Mexico); professed in Salesians of St. John Bosco, Sept. 29, 1912; ord. priest May 21, 1921; ord. bishop of Krishnagar, India, Oct. 29, 1939; resigned Oct. 31, 1969.

Mueller, Joseph M.: b. Dec. 1, 1894, St. Louis, Mo.; educ. Pontifical College Josephinum (Worthington, O.); ord. priest June 14, 1919; ord. titular bishop of Sinda and coadjutor bishop of Sioux City, Oct. 16, 1947; bishop of Sioux City, Sept. 20, 1948; resigned Oct. 15, 1970.

Mugavero, Francis John: b. June 8, 1914, Brooklyn, N.Y.; educ. Cathedral College (Brooklyn, N.Y.), Immaculate Conception Seminary (Huntington, N.Y.), Fordham Univ. (New York City); ord. priest May 18, 1940; ord. bishop of Brooklyn, Sept. 12, 1968.

Mulcahy, John J.: b. June 26, 1922, Dorchester, Mass.; educ. St. John's Seminary (Brighton, Mass.); ord. priest May 1, 1947; rector Pope John XXIII Seminary for Delayed Vocations, 1969-73; ord. titular bishop of Penafiel and auxiliary bishop of Boston, Feb. 11, 1975.

Mulrooney, Charles R.: b. Jan. 13, 1906, Brooklyn, N.Y.; educ. Cathedral College (Brooklyn, N.Y.), St. Mary's Seminary (Baltimore, Md.), Sulpician Seminary (Washington, D.C.); ord. priest June 10, 1930; ord. titular bishop of Valentiniana and auxiliary bishop of Brooklyn, April 22, 1959.

Murphy, T. Austin: b. May 11, 1911, Baltimore, Md.; educ. St. Charles College (Catonsville, Md.), St. Mary's Seminary (Baltimore, Md.); ord priest June 10, 1937; ord. titular bishop of Appiaria and auxiliary bishop of Baltimore, July 3, 1962.

Murphy, Thomas W., C.SS.R.: b. Dec. 17, 1917, Omaha, Nebr.; educ. St. Joseph's College (Kirkwood, Mo.); ord. priest June 29, 1943; ord. first bishop of Juazeiro, Brazil, Jan. 2, 1963; resigned Jan. 30, 1974; app. titular bishop of Sululos and auxiliary bishop of Sao Salvador da Bahia, Brazil, Jan. 31, 1974.

Mussio, John K.: b. June 13, 1902, Cincinnati, O.; educ. Xavier Univ. (Cincinnati, O.), Notre Dame Univ. (Notre Dame, Ind.), St. Gregory Preparatory Seminary (Cincinnati,

O.), Mt. St. Mary Seminary (Norwood, O.), Angelicum (Rome); ord. priest Aug. 15, 1935; ord. bishop of Steubenville, May 1, 1945.

N

Nelson, Knute Ansgar, O.S.B.: b. Oct. 1, 1906, Copenhagen, Denmark; educ. Abbey of Maria Laach (Germany), Brown Univ. (Providence, R.I.); professed in the Order of St. Benedict, May 30, 1932; ord. priest May 22, 1937; became an American citizen, Mar. 4, 1941; ord. titular bishop of Bilta and coadjutor bishop of Stockholm, Sweden, Sept. 8, 1947; succeeded as bishop of Stockholm, Oct. 1, 1957; retired; titular bishop of Dura. 1962.

Newell, Hubert M.: b. Feb. 16, 1904, Denver, Colo.; educ. Regis College and St. Thomas Seminary (Denver, Colo.), Catholic Univ. (Washington, D.C.); ord. priest June 15, 1930; ord. titular bishop of Zapara and coadjutor bishop of Cheyenne, Sept. 24, 1947; bishop of Cheyenne, Nov. 10, 1951.

Newman, Thomas A., M.S.: b. Nov. 3, 1903, Waterbury, Conn.; educ. LaSalette Seminary (Ipswich, Mass.), Gregorian Univ. (Rome); ord. priest June 29, 1929; ord. first bishop of Prome, Burma, May 21, 1961.

Neylon, Martin J., S.J.: b. Feb. 13, 1920, Buffalo, N. Y.; ord. priest June 18, 1950; ord. titular bishop of Libertina and coadjutor vicar apostolic of the Caroline and Marshall Islands, Feb. 2, 1970; vicar apostolic of Caroline and Marshall Is., Sept. 20, 1971.

Niedergeses, James D.: b. Feb. 2, 1917, Lawrenceburg, Tenn.; educ. St. Bernard College (St. Bernard, Ala.), St. Ambrose College (Davenport, Ia.), Mt. St. Mary Seminary of the West and Athenaeum (Cincinnati, Ohio); ord. priest 1944; ord. bishop of Nashville May 20, 1975.

Noa, Thomas L.: b. Dec. 18, 1892, Iron Mountain, Mich.; educ. St. Francis Seminary (St. Francis, Wis.), North American College (Rome); ord. priest Dec. 23, 1916; ord. titular bishop of Salona and coadjutor bishop of Sioux City, Mar. 19, 1946; app. bishop of Marquette, Aug. 25, 1947; resigned 1968.

Nold, Wendelin J.: b. Jan. 18, 1900, Bonham, Tex.; educ. St. Mary's Seminary (La Porte, Tex.), North American College (Rome); ord. priest Apr. 11, 1925; ord. titular bishop of Sasima and coadjutor bishop of Galveston, Feb. 25, 1948, succeeded as bishop of Galveston, Apr. 1, 1950; title of see changed to Galveston-Houston, 1959; resigned Apr. 22, 1975.

Nolker, Bernard, C.SS.R.: b. Sept. 25, 1912, Baltimore, Md.; educ. St. Mary's College (North East, Pa.), St. Mary's College (Ilchester, Md.), Mt. St. Alphonsus Seminary (Esopus, N. Y.); ord. priest June 18, 1939; ord. first bishop of Paranagua, Brazil, Apr. 25, 1963.

Noser, Adolph A., S. V. D.: b. July 4, 1900, Belleville, Ill.; educ. Quincy College (Quincy, Ill.), St. Mary's Mission House (Techny, Ill.),

Angelicum (Rome); received into the Society of the Divine Word, 1921; ord. priest Sept. 27, 1925; ord. titular bishop of Capitolias and vicar apostolic of Accra, Gold Coast, British West Africa, Aug. 22, 1947; title changed to bishop of Accra, Apr. 18, 1950; transferred to titular see of Hierpiniana and vicariate apostolic of Alexishaven, New Guinea, Jan. 8, 1953; first archbishop of Madang, Nov. 15, 1966.

O

O'Boyle, Patrick A.: (See Cardinals, Biographies.)

O'Brien, Henry Joseph: b. July 21, 1896, New Haven, Conn.; educ. St. Thomas Seminary (Hartford, Conn.), St. Bernard's Seminary (Rochester, N. Y.), Louvain Univ. (Belgium); ord. priest July 8, 1923; ord. titular bishop of Sita and auxiliary bishop of Hartford, May 14, 1940; bishop of Hartford, Apr., 1945; first archbishop of Hartford, Aug. 6, 1953; retired Nov. 20, 1968.

O'Connor, Martin J.: b. May 18, 1900, Scranton, Pa.; educ. St. Thomas College (Scranton, Pa.), St. Mary's Seminary (Baltimore, Md.), North American College, Urban Univ. and Apollinaris (Rome); ord. priest Mar. 15, 1924; ord. titular bishop of Thespia and auxiliary bishop of Scranton, Jan. 27, 1943; rector of North American College 1946-1964; app. titular archbishop of Laodicea in Syria, Sept. 5, 1959; apostolic nuncio to Malta, 1965-69; president emeritus Pontifical Commission for Social Communication.

O'Connor, William A.: b. Dec. 27, 1903, Chicago, Ill.; educ. Quigley Seminary (Chicago, Ill.), St. Mary of the Lake Seminary (Mundelein, Ill.), Urban Univ. (Rome); ord. priest Sept. 24, 1927; ord. bishop of Springfield, Ill., Mar. 7, 1949.

O'Donnell, Cletus F.: b. Aug. 22, 1917, Waukon, Ia.; educ. St. Mary Seminary (Mundelein, Ill.), Catholic Univ. (Washington, D.C.); ord. priest May 3, 1941; ord. titular bishop of Abritto and auxiliary bishop of Chicago, Dec. 21, 1960; app. bishop of Madison, Feb. 22, 1967, installed Apr. 25, 1967.

O'Keefe, Gerald: b. Mar. 30, 1918, St. Paul, Minn.; educ. College of St. Thomas, St. Paul Seminary (St. Paul, Minn.); ord. priest Jan. 29, 1944; ord. titular bishop of Candyba and auxiliary bishop of St. Paul July 2, 1916; bishop of Davenport, Oct. 20, 1966, installed Jan. 4, 1967.

O'Leary, Edward C.: b. Aug. 21, 1920, Bangor, Me.; educ. Holy Cross College (Worcester, Mass.), St. Paul's Seminary (Ottawa, Canada); ord. priest June 15, 1946; ord. titular bishop of Moglena and auxiliary bishop of Portland, Me., Jan. 25, 1971; app. bishop of Portland, installed Dec. 18, 1974.

O'Meara, Edward T.: b. Aug. 3, 1921, St. Louis, Mo.; educ. Cardinal Glennon College and Kenrick Seminary (St. Louis, Mo.), An-

gelicum (Rome); ord. priest Dec. 21, 1946; app. national director of Society for the Propagation of the Faith, 1967; ord. titular bishop of Thisiduo and auxiliary bishop of St. Louis, Feb. 13, 1972.

O'Neill, Arthur J.: b. Dec. 14, 1917, East Dubuque, Ill.; educ. Loras College (Dubuque, Ia.), St. Mary's Seminary (Baltimore, Md.); ord. priest Mar. 27, 1943; ord. bishop of Rockford, Oct. 11, 1968.

O'Rourke, Edward W.: b. Oct. 31, 1917, Downs, Ill.; educ. St. Mary's Seminary (Mundelein, Ill.), Aquinas Institute of Philosophy and Theology (River Forest, Ill.); ord. priest May 28, 1944; exec. dir. National Catholic Rural Life Conference, 1960-71; ord. bishop of Peoria, July 25, 1971.

Ottenweller, Albert H.: b. Apr. 15, 1916, Stanford, Mont.; educ. St. Joseph's Seminary (Rensselaer, Ind.), Catholic Univ. (Washington, D.C.); ord. priest June 19, 1943; ord. titular bishop of Perdices and auxiliary bishop of Toledo, May 29, 1974.

P

Pardy, James V., M.M.: b. Mar. 9, 1898, Brooklyn, N. Y.; educ. St. Francis College (Brooklyn), Fordham Univ. (New York City), Catholic Univ. (Washington, D.C.); ord. priest. Jan. 26, 1930; ord. titular bishop of Irenopolis and first vicar apostolic of Cheong Ju, Korea, Sept. 16, 1958; title changed to bishop of Cheong Ju, Mar. 10, 1962; retired 1969.

Paschang, John L.: b. Oct. 5, 1895, Hemingford, Nebr.; educ. Conception College (Conception, Mo.), St. John Seminary (Collegeville, Minn.), Catholic Univ. (Washington, D.C.); ord. priest June 12, 1921; ord. bishop of Grand Island, Oct. 9, 1951; resigned July 25, 1972.

Pearce, George H., S.M.: b. Jan. 9, 1921, Brighton, Mass.; educ. Marist College and Seminary (Framington, Mass.); ord. priest Feb. 2, 1947; ord. titular bishop of Attalea in Pamphylia and vicar apostolic of the Samoa and Tokelau Islands, June 29, 1956; title changed to bishop of Apia, 1966; app. archbishop of Suva, Fiji Islands, June 22, 1967.

Pechillo, Jerome, T.O.R.: b. May 16, 1919, Brooklyn, N. Y.; educ. Catholic Univ. (Washington, D. C.); ord. priest June 10, 1947; ord. titular bishop of Novasparsa and prelate of Coronel Oviedo, Paraguay, Jan. 25, 1966.

Pernicone, Joseph M.: b. Nov. 4, 1903, Regalbuto, Sicily; educ. Cathedral College (New York City), St. Joseph's Seminary (Dunwoodie, N.Y.), Catholic Univ. (Washington, D.C.); ord. priest Dec. 18, 1926; ord. titular bishop of Hadrianapolis and auxiliary bishop of New York, May 5, 1954; app. episcopal vicar, 1966.

Perry, Harold R., S. V. D.: b. Oct. 9, 1916, Lake Charles, La.; educ. St. Augustine Seminary (Bay St. Louis, Miss.), St. Mary's Seminary (Techny, Ill.); ord. priest Jan. 6, 1944; app. provincial of southern province of Society of the Divine Word, 1964; ord. titular bishop of Mons in Mauretania and auxiliary bishop of New Orleans, Jan. 6, 1966.

Pilarczyk, Daniel E.: b. Aug. 12, 1934, Dayton, Ohio; educ. St. Gregory's Seminary and Xavier Univ. (Cincinnati, O.); Urban Univ. (Rome); ord. priest Dec. 20, 1959; ord. titular bishop of Hodelm and auxiliary bishop of Cincinnati, Dec. 20, 1974.

Pinger, Henry A., O.F.M.: b. Aug. 16, 1897, Lindsay, Nebr.; educ. Our Lady of Angels Seminary (Cleveland, O.), St. Anthony's Seminary (St. Louis, Mo.); professed in the Order of Friars Minor, June 18, 1918; ord. priest June 27, 1924; ord. titular bishop of Capitolias and vicar apostolic of Chowtsun, China, Sept. 21, 1937; title changed to bishop of Chowtsun, Apr. 11, 1946; imprisoned by Reds in 1951, released in 1956; expelled.

Povish, Kenneth J.: b. Apr. 19, 1924, Alpena, Mich.; educ. St. Joseph's Seminary (Grand Rapids, Mich.), Sacred Heart Seminary (Detroit, Mich.), Catholic Univ. (Washington, D.C.); ord. priest June 3, 1950; ord. bishop of Crookston, Sept. 29, 1970.

Power, Cornelius M.: b. Dec. 18, 1913, Seattle, Wash.; educ. St. Patrick's College (Menlo Park, Calif.), St. Edward's Seminary (Kenmore, Wash.), Catholic Univ. (Washington, D.C.); ord. priest June 3, 1939; ord. bishop of Yakima, May 1, 1969, installed May 29, 1969; app. archbishop of Portland, Ore., Jan. 22, 1974, installed Apr. 17, 1974.

Primeau, Ernest J.: b. Sept. 17, 1909, Chicago, Ill.; educ. Loyola Univ. (Chicago, Ill.), St. Mary of the Lake Seminary (Mundelein, Ill.), Lateran Univ. (Rome); ord. priest Apr. 7, 1934; ord. bishop of Manchester, Feb. 25, 1960; resigned Jan. 30, 1974; app. director of Villa Stritch, Rome, 1974.

Prost, Jude, O.F.M.: b. Dec. 6, 1915, Chicago, Ill.; educ. Our Lady of the Angels Seminary (Cleveland, O.), St. Joseph's Seminary (Teutopolis, Ill.); ord. priest June 24, 1942; ord. titular bishop of Fronta and auxiliary bishop of Belem do Para, Brazil, Nov. 1, 1962.

Pursley, Leo A.: b. Mar. 12, 1902, Hartford City, Ind.; educ. Mt. St. Mary's Seminary (Cincinnati, O.); ord. priest June 11, 1927; ord. titular bishop of Hadrianapolis in Pisidia and auxiliary bishop of Fort Wayne, Sept. 19, 1950; app. apostolic administrator of Fort Wayne, Mar. 9, 1955; installed as bishop of Fort Wayne, Feb. 26, 1957; title of see changed to Fort Wayne-South Bend, 1960.

Q

Quinn, John R.: b. Mar. 28, 1929, Riverside, Calif.; educ. St. Francis Seminary (El Cajon, Calif.), North American College (Rome); ord. priest July 19, 1953; ord. titular bishop of Thisiduo and auxiliary bishop of San Diego, Dec. 12, 1967; bishop of Oklahoma City and Tulsa, Nov. 30, 1971; first archbishop of Oklahoma City, Dec. 19, 1972.

R

Rausch, James S.: b. Sept. 4, 1928, Albany, Minn.; educ. St. Thomas College (St. Paul, Minn.), Univ. of Minnesota (Minneapolis), Gregorian Univ. (Rome); ord. priest June 2, 1956; associate general secretary of USCC, 1970-72; general secretary of NCCB-USCC, 1972-; ord. titular bishop of Summa and auxiliary bishop of St. Cloud, Apr. 26, 1973.

Raya, Joseph M.: b. July 20, 1917, Zahle, Lebanon; educ. St. Louis College (Paris, France), St. Anne's Seminary (Jerusalem); ord. priest July 20, 1941; came to U.S., 1949, became U.S. citizen; ord. archbishop of Acre, Israel, of the Melkites, Oct. 20, 1968; resigned Aug. 20, 1974; assigned titular metropolitan see of Scytopolis.

Regan, Joseph W., M.M.: b. Apr. 5, 1905, Boston, Mass.; educ. Boston College (Boston, Mass.), St. Bernard's Seminary (Rochester, N.Y.), Maryknoll Seminary (Maryknoll, N.Y.); ord. priest Jan. 27, 1929; missionary in China 15 years; in Philippines since 1952; ord. titular bishop of Isinda and prelate of Tagum, Philippine Islands, Apr. 25, 1962.

Reh, Francis F.: b. Jan. 9, 1911, New York, N.Y.; educ. St. Joseph's Seminary (Dunwoodie, N.Y.), North American College and Gregorian Univ. (Rome); ord. priest Dec. 8, 1935; ord. bishop of Charleston, S.C., June 29, 1962; named titular bishop of Macriana in Mauretania, 1964; rector of North American College, 1964-68; bishop of Saginaw, installed Feb. 26, 1969.

Rehring, George John: b. June 10, 1890, Cincinnati, O.; educ. Mt. St. Mary of the West Seminary (Cincinnati, O.), Collegium Angelicum (Rome); ord. priest Mar. 28, 1914; ord. titular bishop of Lunda and auxiliary bishop of Cincinnati, Oct. 7, 1937; app. bishop of Toledo, July 26, 1950; retired 1967.

Reicher, Louis J.: b. June 14, 1890, Piqua, O.; educ. St. Mary's Seminary (Cincinnati, O.), St. Mary's Seminary (La Porte, Tex.); ord. priest Dec. 6, 1918; ord. first bishop of Austin, Apr. 14, 1948; resigned Nov. 15, 1971.

Reilly, Daniel P.: b. May 12, 1928, Providence, R.I.; educ. Our Lady of Providence Seminary (Warwick, R.I.), St. Brieuc Major Seminary (Cotes du Nord, France); ord. priest May 30, 1953; app. bishop of Norwich, June 17, 1975.

Reilly, Thomas F., C.SS.R.: b. Dec. 20, 1908, Boston, Mass.; educ. Mt. St. Alphonsus Seminary (Esopus, N.Y.), Catholic Univ. (Washington, D.C.); ord. priest June 10, 1933; ord. titular bishop of Themisonium and prelate of San Juan de la Maguana, Dominican Republic, Nov. 30, 1956; first bishop of San Juan de la Maguana, Nov. 21, 1969.

Reiss, John C.: b. May 13, 1922, Red Bank,

N.J.; educ. Catholic Univ. (Washington, D.C.), Immaculate Conception Seminary (Darlington, N.J.); ord. priest May 31, 1947; ord. titular bishop of Simidicca and auxiliary bishop of Trenton, Dec. 12, 1967.

Riley, Lawrence J.: b. Sept. 6, 1914; Boston, Mass.; educ. Boston College and St. John's Seminary (Boston, Mass.); ord. priest Sept. 21, 1940; ord. titular bishop of Daimlaig and auxiliary bishop of Boston, Feb. 2, 1972.

Riley, Thomas J.: b. Nov. 30, 1900, Waltham, Mass.; educ. Boston College (Boston, Mass.), St. John's Seminary (Brighton, Mass.), Louvain Univ. (Belgium); ord. priest May 20, 1927; ord. titular bishop of Regiae and auxiliary bishop of Boston, Dec. 21, 1959.

Roach, John R.: b. July 31, 1921, Prior Lake, Minn.; educ. St. Paul Seminary (St. Paul, Minn.); Univ. of Minnesota (Minneapolis); ord. priest June 18, 1946; ord. titular bishop of Cenae and auxiliary bishop of St. Paul and Minneapolis, Sept. 8, 1971; app. archbishop of St. Paul and Minneapolis, May 28, 1975.

Rudin, John J., M.M.: b. Nov. 27, 1916, Pittsfield, Mass.; educ. Maryknoll Seminary (Maryknoll, N.Y.), Gregorian Univ. (Rome); ord. priest June 11, 1944; ord. first bishop of Musoma, Tanzania, Oct. 3, 1957.

Ruocco, Joseph J.: b. Apr. 21, 1922, Boston, Mass.; educ. St. John's Seminary (Brighton, Mass.); ord. priest May 6, 1948; ord. titular bishop of Polignano and auxiliary bishop of Boston, Feb. 11, 1975.

Russell, John J.: b. Dec. 1, 1897, Baltimore, Md.; educ. St. Charles College (Catonsville, Md.), St. Mary's Seminary (Baltimore, Md.), North American College (Rome); ord. priest July 8, 1923; ord. bishop of Charleston, Mar. 14, 1950; bishop of Richmond, July 3, 1958; retired Apr. 30, 1973.

Ryan, James C., O.F.M.: b. Nov. 17, 1912, Chicago, Ill.; educ. St. Joseph's Seraphic Seminary (Westmont, Ill.), Our Lady of the Angels Seminary (Cleveland, O.); ord. priest June 24, 1938; ord. titular bishop of Margo and prelate of Santarem, Brazil, April 9, 1958.

Ryan, Joseph T.: b. Nov. 1, 1913, Albany, N.Y.; educ. Manhattan College (New York City); ord. priest June 3, 1939; national secretary of Catholic Near East Welfare Assn. 1960-65; ord. first archbishop of Anchorage, Alaska, Mar. 25, 1966.

S

Salatka, Charles A.: b. Feb. 26, 1918, Grand Rapids, Mich.; educ. St. Joseph's Seminary (Grand Rapids, Mich.), Catholic Univ. (Washington, D.C.), Lateran Univ. (Rome); ord. priest Feb. 24, 1945; ord. titular bishop of Cariana and auxiliary bishop of Grand Rapids, Mich., Mar. 6, 1962; app. bishop of Marquette, installed Mar. 25, 1968.

Sanchez, Robert: b. Mar. 20, 1934, Socor-ro, N.M.; educ. Immaculate Heart Seminary (Santa Fe, N.M.), Gregorian Univ. (Rome), Catholic Univ. (Washington, D.C.); ord. priest Dec. 20, 1959; ord. archbishop of Santa Fe, N.M., July 25, 1974.

Scanlan, John J.: b. May 24, 1906, County Cork, Ireland; educ. National Univ. of Ireland (Dublin), All Hallows College (Dublin); ord. priest June 22, 1930; U.S. citizen 1938; ord. titular bishop of Cenae and auxiliary bishop of Honolulu, Sept. 21, 1954; bishop of Honolulu, installed May 1, 1968.

Schad, James L.: b. July 20, 1917, Philadelphia, Pa.; educ. St. Mary's Seminary (Baltimore, Md.); ord. priest Apr. 10, 1943; ord. titular bishop of Panatoria and auxiliary bishop of Camden, Dec. 8, 1966.

Schexnayder, Maurice: b. Aug. 13, 1895, Wallace, La.; educ. Chenet Institute (New Orleans, La.), St. Joseph's Seminary (St. Benedict, La.), St. Mary's Seminary (Baltimore, Md.), North American College (Rome); ord. priest Apr. 11, 1925; ord. titular bishop of Tuscamia and auxiliary bishop of Lafayette, La., Feb. 22, 1951; bishop of Lafayette, La., May 24, 1956; retired Nov. 7, 1972.

Schierhoff, Andrew B.: b. Feb. 10, 1922, St. Louis, Mo.; ord. priest Apr. 14, 1948; missionary in Bolivia from 1956; ord. titular bishop of Cerenza and auxiliary of La Paz, Bolivia, Jan. 6, 1969.

Schladweiler, Alphonse: b. July 18, 1902, Milwaukee, Wis.; educ. St. Joseph College (Teutopolis, Ill.), St. Paul's Seminary (St. Paul, Minn.), Univ. of Minnesota (Minneapolis, Minn.); ord. priest June 9, 1929; ord. first bishop of New Ulm, Jan. 29, 1958.

Schlaefer, Salvator, O.F.M. Cap.: b. June 27, 1920, Campbellsport, Wis.; ord. priest June 5, 1946; missionary in Bluefields, Nicaragua from 1947; ord. titular bishop of Fiumepiscense and vicar apostolic of Bluefields, Nicaragua, Aug. 12, 1970.

Schlotterback, Edward F., O.S.F.S.: b. Mar. 2, 1912, Philadelphia, Pa.; educ. Catholic Univ. (Washington, D.C.); ord. priest Dec. 17, 1938; ord. titular bishop of Balanea and vicar apostolic of Keetmanshoop, Namibia, July 11, 1956.

Schmidt, Firmin M., O.F.M.Cap.: b. Oct. 12, 1918, Catherine, Kans.; educ. Catholic Univ. (Washington, D.C.); ord. priest June 2, 1946; app. prefect apostolic of Mendi, Papua-New Guinea, Apr. 3, 1959; ord. titular bishop of Conana and first vicar apostolic of Mendi, Dec. 15, 1965; became first bishop of Mendi when vicariate apostolic was raised to a diocese, Nov. 15, 1966.

Schmidt, Mathias, O.S.B.: b. Apr. 21, 1931, Wortonville, Kans.; ord. priest May 30, 1957; missionary in Brazil; ord. titular bishop of Mutugenna and auxiliary bishop of Jatai, Brazil, Sept. 10, 1972.

Schmitt, Adolph G., C.M.M.: b. Apr. 20, 1905, Bimpar, Bavaria; educ. Aloysianum Preparatory Seminary (Lehr, Bavaria),

Mariannhill Seminary, and University of Wuerzburg (Bavaria); entered Mariannhill Mission Society, 1926; ord. priest Mar. 19, 1931, became citizen, 1945; ord. titular bishop of Nasai and vicar apostolic of Bulawayo, Rhodesia, Apr. 2, 1951; bishop of Bulawayo, Jan. 1, 1955; resigned May 18, 1974.

Schmitt, Mark: b. Feb. 14, 1923, Algoma, Wis., educ. Salvatorian Seminary (St. Nazianz, Wis.), St. John's Seminary (Collegeville, Minn.); ord. priest May 22, 1948; ord. titular bishop of Ceanannus Mor and auxiliary bishop of Green Bay, June 24, 1970.

Schmondiuk, Joseph: b. Aug. 6, 1912, Wall, Pa.; educ. St. Joseph's Preparatory College High School (Philadelphia, Pa.), Pontifical Ruthenian College, Angelicum and Urban Univ. (Rome); ord. priest Mar. 29, 1936; ord. titular bishop of Zeugma in Syria and auxiliary bishop of apostolic exarchate of Philadelphia, Nov. 8, 1956, title of see changed to metropolitan, 1958; app. eparch of Stamford, 1961.

Schoenherr, Walter J.: b. Feb. 28, 1920, Detroit, Mich.; educ. Sacred Heart Seminary (Detroit, Mich.), Mt. St. Mary Seminary (Norwood, O.); ord. priest Oct. 27, 1945; ord. titular bishop of Timidana and auxiliary bishop of Detroit, May 1, 1968.

Schuck, James A., O.F.M.: b. Jan. 17, 1913, Treverton, Pa.; educ. St. Joseph's Seminary (Callicoon, N.Y.), St. Bonaventure's University (St. Bonaventure, N.Y.). Holy Name College (Washington, D.C.); ord. priest June 11, 1940; ord. titular bishop of Avissa and prelate of Cristalandia, Brazil, Feb. 24, 1959.

Schulte, Paul Clarence: b. Mar. 18, 1890, Fredericktown, Mo.; educ. St. Francis Solanus College (Quincy, Ill.), Kenrick Seminary (Webster Groves, Mo.); ord. priest June 11, 1915; ord. bishop of Leavenworth, Sept. 21, 1937; archbishop of Indianapolis, July 27, 1946; resigned Jan. 14, 1970; assigned titular see of Elicrora.

Schuster, Eldon B.: b. Mar. 10, 1911, Calio, N. Dak.; educ. Loras College (Dubuque, Ia.), Catholic Univ. (Washington, D.C.), Oxford Univ. (England), St. Louis Univ. (St. Louis, Mo.); ord. priest May 27, 1937; ord. titular bishop of Amblada and auxiliary bishop of Great Falls, Mont., Dec. 21, 1961; app. bishop of Great Falls, Dec. 2, 1967, installed Jan. 23, 1968.

Senyshyn, Ambrose, O.S.B.M.: b. Feb. 23, 1903, Stary Sambor, Galicia; educ. Monastery Colleges at Krechiev and Iawriev, Dobromil and Crystynopol (Galicia); ord. priest Aug. 23, 1931; ord. titular bishop of Maina and auxiliary bishop of the Ukrainian-Greek Catholic Diocese of the United States, Oct. 22, 1942; app. first bishop of Byzantine Ukrainian Rite exarchate of Stamford, Aug. 8, 1956; eparch of Stamford, 1958; app. metropolitan of Ukrainian archeparchy of Philadelphia, 1961.

Shea, Francis R.: b. Dec. 4, 1913, Knoxville, Tenn.; educ. St. Mary's Seminary (Baltimore, Md.), North American College (Rome), Peabody College (Nashville, Tenn.); ord. priest Mar. 19, 1939; ord. bishop of Evansville, Ind., Feb. 3, 1970.

Sheehan, Daniel E.: b. May 14, 1917, Emerson, Nebr.; educ. Creighton Univ. (Omaha, Nebr.), Kenrick Seminary (Webster Groves, Mo.), Catholic Univ. (Washington, D.C.); ord. priest May 23, 1942; ord. titular bishop of Capsus and auxiliary bishop of Omaha, Mar. 19, 1964; app. archbishop of Omaha, installed Aug. 11, 1969.

Sheen, Fulton J.: b. May 8, 1895, El Paso, Ill.; educ. St. Viator College (Kankakee, Ill.), St. Paul Seminary (St. Paul, Minn.), Catholic Univ. (Washington, D.C.), Louvain Univ. (Belgium), Collegium Angelicum (Rome); ord. priest Sept. 20, 1919; app. national director of the Pontifical Society for the Propagation of the Faith, 1950; ord. titular bishop of Caesariana and auxiliary bishop of New York, June 11, 1951; app. bishop of Rochester, installed Dec. 15, 1966; resigned Oct. 15, 1969; titular archbishop of Newport.

Shehan, Lawrence J.: (See Cardinals.)

Snyder, John J.: b. Oct. 25, 1925, New York, N.Y.; educ. Cathedral College (Brooklyn, N.Y.), Immaculate Conception Seminary (Huntington, N.Y.); ord. priest June 9, 1951; ord. titular bishop of Forlimpopli and auxiliary bishop of Brooklyn, Feb. 2, 1973.

Soenneker, Henry J.: b. May 27, 1907, Melrose, Minn.; educ. Pontifical Josephinum College (Worthington, O.), Catholic Univ. (Washington, D.C.); ord. priest May 26, 1934; ord. bishop of Owensboro, Apr. 26, 1961.

Sowada, Alphonse A., O.S.C.: b. June 23, 1933, Avon, Minn.; educ. Holy Cross Scholasticate (Fort Wayne, Ind.), Catholic Univ. (Washington, D.C.), ord. priest May 31, 1958; missionary in Indonesia from 1958; ord. bishop of Agats, Indonesia, Nov. 23, 1969.

Speltz, George H.: b. May 12, 1912, Altura, Minn.; educ. St. Mary's College, St. Paul's Seminary (St. Paul, Minn.), Catholic Univ. (Washington, D.C.); ord. priest June 2, 1940; ord. titular bishop of Claneus and auxiliary bishop of Winona, Mar. 25, 1963; app. coadjutor bishop of St. Cloud, Apr. 4, 1966; bishop of St. Cloud, Jan. 31, 1968.

Stanton, Martin W.: b. Apr. 17, 1897, Jersey City, N.J.; educ. St. Peter's College (Jersey City, N.J.), Immaculate Conception Seminary (Darlington, N.J.), Fordham Univ. (New York City); ord. priest June 14, 1924; ord. titular bishop of Citium and auxiliary bishop of Newark, Sept. 24, 1957. Retired.

Stemper, Alfred M., M.S.C.: b. Jan. 2, 1913, Black Hammer, Minn.; ord. priest June 26, 1940; ord. titular bishop of Eleutheropolis and vicar apostolic of Kavieng, New Guinea, Oct. 28, 1957; first bishop of Kavieng, Nov. 15, 1966.

Strecker, Ignatius J.: b. Nov. 23, 1917, Spearville, Kans.; educ. St. Benedict's College (Atchison, Kans.), Kenrick Seminary (Webster Groves, Mo.), Catholic Univ. (Washington, D.C.); ord. priest Dec. 19, 1942; ord. bishop of Springfield-Cape Girardeau, Mo., June 20, 1962; archbishop of Kansas City, Kans., Oct. 28, 1969.

Sullivan, James S.: b. July 23, 1929, Kalamazoo, Mich.; ord. priest June 4, 1955; ord. titular bishop of Siccessi and auxiliary bishop of Lansing, Sept. 21, 1972.

Sullivan, John J.: b. July 5, 1920, Horton, Kans.; educ. Kenrick Seminary (St. Louis, Mo.); ord. priest Sept. 23, 1944; vice-president of Catholic Church Extension Society and national director of Extension Lay Volunteers, 1961-68; ord. bishop of Grand Island, Sept. 19, 1972.

Sullivan, Joseph V.: b. Aug. 15, 1919, Kansas City, Mo.; educ. Sulpician Seminary (Washington, D.C.), Catholic Univ. (Washington, D.C.); ord. priest June 1, 1946; ord. titular bishop of Tagamuta and auxiliary bishop of Kansas City-St. Joseph, Apr. 3, 1967; app. Bishop of Baton Rouge, Aug. 13, 1974.

Sullivan, Walter F.: b. June 10, 1928, Washington, D.C.; ord. priest May 9, 1953; ord. titular bishop of Selsea and auxiliary bishop of Richmond, Va., Dec. 1, 1970; app. bishop of Richmond, June 4, 1974.

Swanstrom, Edward E.: b. Mar. 20, 1903, New York, N.Y.; educ. Fordham Univ. (New York City), St. John's Seminary (Brooklyn, N.Y.), New York School of Social Work; ord. priest June 2, 1928; director of Catholic Relief Services; ord. titular bishop of Arba and auxiliary bishop of New York, Oct. 28, 1960.

Szoka, Edmund C.: b. Sept. 14, 1927, Grand Rapids, Mich.; educ. Sacred Heart Seminary (Detroit, Mich.), St. John's Provincial Seminary (Plymouth, Mich.), Lateran Univ. (Rome); ord. priest June 5, 1954; ord. first bishop of Gaylord, Mich., July 20, 1971.

T

Tanner, Paul F.: b. Jan. 15, 1905, Peoria, Ill.; educ. Marquette Univ. (Milwaukee, Wis.), Kenrick Seminary (Webster Groves, Mo.), St. Francis Seminary (Milwaukee, Wis.), Catholic Univ. (Washington, D.C.): ord. priest May 30, 1931; assistant director NCWC Youth Department 1940-45; assistant general secretary of NCWC 1945-58; general secretary of NCWC (now USCC) 1958-68; ord. titular bishop of Lamasba, Dec. 21, 1965; bishop of St. Augustine, Mar. 27, 1968.

Tawil, Joseph: b. Dec. 25, 1913, Damascus, Syria; ord. priest July 20, 1936; ord. titular archbishop of Mira and patriarchal vicar for eparchy of Damascus of the Patriarchate of Antioch for the Melkites, Jan. 1, 1960; apostolic exarch for faithful of the Melkite rite in the US, Oct. 31, 1969.

Taylor, John E., O.M.I.: b. Nov. 15, 1914, East St. Louis, Ill.; educ. Angelicum Univ., Gregorian Univ. (Rome), Univ. of Ottawa (Ottawa, Canada); ord. priest May 25, 1940; ord. bishop of Stockholm, Sweden, Sept. 21, 1962.

Toolen, Thomas Joseph: b. Feb. 28, 1886, Baltimore, Md.; educ. Loyola College and St. Mary's Seminary (Baltimore, Md.), Catholic Univ. (Washington, D.C.); ord. priest Sept. 27, 1910; ord. bishop of Mobile, May 4, 1927; personal title of archbishop conferred, July 14, 1954; retired 1969; assigned titular see of Glastonbury.

Topel, Bernard J.: b. May 31, 1903, Bozeman, Mont.; educ. Carroll College (Helena, Mont.), Grand Seminary (Montreal), Catholic Univ. (Washington, D.C.), Harvard Univ. (Cambridge, Mass.), Notre Dame Univ. (Notre Dame, Ind.); ord. priest June 7, 1927; ord. titular bishop of Binda and coadjutor bishop of Spokane, Sept. 21, 1955; bishop of Spokane, Sept. 25, 1955.

Tracy, Robert E.: b. Sept. 14, 1909, New Orleans, La.; educ. St. Joseph's Preparatory Seminary (St. Benedict, La.), Notre Dame Seminary (New Orleans); ord. priest June 12, 1932; national chaplain of Newman Federation; 1954-56; ord. titular bishop of Sergentiza and auxiliary bishop of Lafayette, La., May 19, 1959; app. first bishop of Baton Rouge, Aug. 10, 1961; resigned Mar. 21, 1974.

Treinen, Sylvester: b. Nov. 19, 1917, Donnelly, Minn.; educ. Crosier Seminary (Onamia, Minn.), St. Paul Seminary (St. Paul, Minn.); ord. priest June 11, 1946; ord. bishop of Boise, July 25, 1962.

Tschoepe, Thomas: b. Dec. 17, 1915, Pilot Point, Tex.; educ. Pontifical College Josephinum (Worthington, O.); ord. priest May 30, 1943; ord. bishop of San Angelo, Tex., Mar. 9, 1966; app. bishop of Dallas, Tex., Aug. 27, 1969.

U-V

Unterkoefler, Ernest L.: b. Aug. 17, 1917, Philadelphia, Pa.; educ. Catholic Univ. (Washington, D.C.); ord. priest May 18, 1944; ord. titular bishop of Latopolis and auxiliary bishop of Richmond, Va., Feb. 22, 1962; app. bishop of Charleston, 1964, installed Feb. 22, 1965.

Vath, Joseph G.: b. Mar. 12, 1918, New Orleans, La.; educ. Notre Dame Seminary (New Orleans, La.), Catholic Univ. (Washington, D.C.); ord. priest June 7, 1941; ord. titular bishop of Novaliciana and auxiliary bishop of Mobile-Birmingham, May 26, 1966; app. first bishop of Birmingham, Oct. 8, 1969.

Veigle, Adrian J.M., T.O.R.: b. Sept. 15, 1912, Lilly, Pa.; educ. St. Francis College (Loretto, Pa.), Pennsylvania State College; ord. priest May 22, 1937; ord. titular bishop of Gigthi and prelate of Borba, Brazil, June 9, 1966.

Vogel, Cyril J.: b. Jan. 15, 1905, Pittsburgh, Pa.; educ. Duquesne Univ. (Pittsburgh, Pa.), St. Vincent's Seminary (Latrobe, Pa.); ord. priest June 7, 1931; ord. bishop of Salina, June 17, 1965.

Vonesh, Raymond J.: b. Jan. 25, 1916, Chicago, Ill.; educ. St. Mary of the Lake Seminary (Mundelein, Ill.). Gregorian Univ. (Rome); ord. priest May 3, 1941; ord. titular bishop of Vanariona and auxiliary bishop of Joliet, Ill., Apr. 3, 1968.

W

Walsh, James Edward, M.M.: b. Apr. 30, 1891, Cumberland, Md.; educ. Mt. St. Mary's College (Emmitsburg, Md.), Maryknoll Foreign Mission Seminary (Maryknoll, N.Y.); entered Catholic Foreign Mission Society (Maryknoll, N.Y.), 1912; ord. priest Dec. 7, 1915; ord. titular bishop of Sata and vicar apostolic of Kongmoon, China, May 22, 1927; superior general of Maryknoll, July 21, 1936, until Aug. 7, 1946; app. general secretary, Catholic Central Bureau, Shanghai, China, Aug. 24, 1948; placed under house arrest in October, 1958, detained in Shanghai hospital; sentenced to 20 years' imprisonment for "espionage," Mar., 1960; released 1970.

Walsh, Nicholas E.: b. Oct. 20, 1916, Burnsville, Minn.; educ. St. Paul Seminary (St. Paul, Minn.), Catholic Univ. (Washington, D.C.), Pontifical Palafoxianum Seminary (Puebla, Mexico), Register College of Journalism (Denver, Colo.); ord. priest June 6, 1942; first editor of *Idaho Register;* diocesan vicar for Mexican Americans; ord. bishop of Yakima, Oct. 28, 1974.

Ward, John J.: b. Sept. 28, 1920, Los Angeles, Calif.; educ. St. John's Seminary (Camarillo, Calif.), Catholic Univ. (Washington, D.C.); ord. priest May 4, 1946; ord. titular bishop of Bria and auxiliary of Los Angeles, Dec. 12, 1963.

Watson, Alfred M.: b. July 11, 1907, Erie, Pa.; educ. St. Mary's Seminary (Baltimore, Md.), Catholic Univ. (Washington, D.C.); ord. priest May 10, 1934; ord. titular bishop of Nationa and auxiliary bishop of Erie, June 29, 1965; app. bishop of Erie, 1969, installed May 13, 1969.

Watters, Loras J.: b. Oct. 14, 1915, Dubuque, Ia.; educ. Loras College (Dubuque, Ia.), Gregorian Univ. (Rome), Catholic Univ. (Washington, D.C.); ord. priest June 7, 1941; ord. titular bishop of Fidoloma and auxiliary bishop of Dubuque, Aug. 26, 1965; bishop of Winona, installed Mar. 13, 1969.

Weldon, Christopher J.: b. Sept. 6, 1905, New York, N.Y.; educ. Montreal College (Canada), St. Joseph's Seminary (Dunwoodie, N.Y.), Catholic Univ. (Washington, D.C.); ord. priest Sept. 21, 1939; ord. bishop of Springfield, Mass., Mar. 24, 1950.

Welsh, Thomas J.: b. Dec. 20, 1921, Weath-

erly, Pa.; educ. St. Charles Borromeo Seminary (Philadelphia, Pa.), Catholic Univ. (Washington, D.C.); ord. priest May 30, 1946; ord. titular bishop of Scattery Island and auxiliary bishop of Philadelphia, Apr. 2, 1970; app. first bishop of Arlington, Va., June 4, 1974, installed Aug. 13, 1974.

Whealon, John F.: b. Jan. 15, 1921, Barberton, O.; educ. St. Charles College (Catonsville, Md.), St. Mary's Seminary (Cleveland, O.); ord. priest May 26, 1945; ord. titular bishop of Andrapa and auxiliary bishop of Cleveland, July 6, 1961; app. bishop of Erie, Dec. 9, 1966, installed Mar. 7, 1967; archbishop of Hartford, installed Mar. 19, 1969.

Whelan, Robert L., S.J.: b. Apr. 16, 1912, Wallace, Ida.; educ. St. Michael's College (Spokane, Wash.), Alma College (Alma, Calif.); ord. priest June 17, 1944; ord. titular bishop of Sicilibba and coadjutor bishop of Fairbanks, Alaska, with right of succession, Feb. 22, 1968; bishop of Fairbanks, Nov. 30, 1968.

Wildermuth, Augustine F., S.J.: b. Feb. 20, 1904, St. Louis, Mo.; educ. St. Stanislaus Seminary (Florissant, Mo.), St. Michael's Scholasticate (Spokane, Wash.), Sacred Heart College (Shembaganur, S. India), St. Mary's College (Kurseong, India), Gregorian Univ. (Rome); entered Society of Jesus, 1922; ord. priest July 25, 1935; ord. bishop of Patna, India, Oct. 28, 1947.

Wright, John J.: (See Cardinals, Biographies.) Prefect of the Sacred Congregation for the Clergy.

Wycislo, Aloysius John: b. June 17, 1908, Chicago, Ill.; educ. St. Mary's Seminary (Mundelein, Ill.), Catholic Univ. (Washington, D.C.); ord. priest Apr. 4, 1934; ord. titular bishop of Stadia and auxiliary bishop of Chicago, Dec. 21, 1960; app. bishop of Green Bay, installed Apr. 16, 1968.

Z

Zayek, Francis: b. Oct. 18, 1920, Manzanillo, Cuba; ord. priest Mar. 17, 1946; ord. titular bishop of Callinicum and auxiliary bishop for Maronites in Brazil, Aug. 5, 1962; named apostolic exarch for Maronites in U.S., with headquarters in Detroit; installed June 11, 1966; first eparch of St. Maron of Detroit, Mar. 25, 1972.

Zuroweste, Albert R.: b. Apr. 26, 1901, East St. Louis, Ill.; educ. St. Francis College (Quincy, Ill.), Kenrick Seminary (Webster Groves, Mo.), Catholic Univ. (Washington, D.C.); ord. priest June 8, 1924; ord. bishop of Belleville, Jan. 29, 1948.

RETIRED U.S. PRELATES

Information, as of July 15, 1975, includes name of the prelate and see held at the time of retirement; archbishops are indicated by an asterisk.

The preferred form of address of retired

prelates is *Former Archbishop* or *Bishop of* (last see held).

Karl J. Alter* (Cincinnati), Peter W. Bartholome (St. Cloud), Leo Binz* (St. Paul and Minneapolis), John Bokenfohr, O.M.I. (Kimberley, S. Africa), Thomas A. Boland* (Newark), Mark K. Carroll (Wichita), James L. Connolly (Fall River), Thomas Connolly* (Seattle), Augustine Danglmayr (Ft. Worth, auxiliary).

Edward V. Dargin (New York, auxiliary), James P. Davis* (Santa Fê), Stephen J. Donahue (New York, auxiliary), Joseph A. Durick (Nashville), Leo P. Dworschak (Fargo), Robert Dwyer* (Portland, Ore.), John M. Fearns (New York, auxiliary), Albert L. Fletcher (Little Rock), Walter A. Foery (Syracuse), John B. Franz (Peoria), Philip J. Furlong (Military Vicariate, delegate).

Richard O. Gerow (Natchez-Jackson), Francis D. Gleeson, S.J. (Fairbanks), Laurence A. Glenn (Crookston), Ignatius T. Glennie, S.J. (Trincomalee-Batticaloa, Sri Lanka), Thomas K. Gorman (Dallas-Ft. Worth), Lawrence L. Graner* (Dacca, Bangladesh), Lawrence Graziano, O.F.M. (San Miguel, El Salvador), Charles P. Greco (Alexandria), Joseph Green (Reno).

James T. Hayes, S.J.* (Cagayan, Philippines), Vincent J. Hines (Norwich), Edward D. Howard* (Portland, Ore.), Clarence G. Issenmann (Cleveland), Robert F. Joyce (Burlington), James E. Kearney (Rochester), Vincent Kennally, S.J. (Caroline and Marshall Islands, vicar apostolic). Henry T. Klonowski (Scranton, auxiliary), George L. Leech (Harrisburg), Francis P. Leipzig (Baker), Leo Lemay, S.M. (Bougainville, Solomon Is.), Robert E. Lucey* (San Antonio).

John J. McEleney, S.J.* (Kingston, Jamaica), Edward A. McGurkin, M.M. (Shinyanga, Tanzania), Cardinal J. Francis McIntyre* (Los Angeles), James E. McManus, C.SS.R. (New York, auxiliary), Edward J. Maginn (Albany, auxiliary), Joseph M. Marling, C.PP.S. (Jefferson City), Alfred Mendez, C.S.C. (Arecibo, P.R.).

Louis La Ravoire Morrow, S.D.B. (Krishnagar, India), Joseph M. Mueller (Sioux City), Knute Ansgar Nelson, O.S.B. (Stockholm, Sweden), Thomas L. Noa (Marquette), Wendelin J. Nold (Galveston-Houston), Cardinal Patrick O'Boyle* (Washington, D.C.), Henry J. O'Brien* (Hartford).

Martin J. O'Connor* (Prefect Emeritus, Pontifical Commission for Social Communications), James V. Pardy, M.M. (Cheong Ju, Korea), John L. Paschang (Grand Island), Ernest J. Primeau (Manchester), Joseph M. Raya* (Acre).

George J. Rehring (Toledo), Louis J. Reicher (Austin), John J. Russell (Richmond), Maurice Schexnayder (Lafayette, La.), Adolph G. Schmitt, C.M.M. (Bulawayo, Rhodesia), Paul C. Schulte* (Indianapolis), Fulton J. Sheen* (Rochester; titular

archbishop, Newport). Cardinal Lawrence J. Shehan* (Baltimore), Martin W. Stanton, (Newark, auxiliary), Thomas J. Toolen* (Mobile-Birmingham; personal title of archbishop), Robert E. Tracy (Baton Rouge), James E. Walsh, M.M. (Kongmoon, China, vicar apostolic).

U.S. BISHOPS OVERSEAS

Cardinal John J. Wright, prefect of the Congregation for the Clergy; Archbishop Raymond P. Etteldorf, pro-nuncio to Ethiopia; Bishop Anthony L. Deksnys, pastoral work among Lithuanians in Western Europe; Bishop Paul C. Marcinkus, president of Institute for Works of Religion (Vatican Bank); Bishop Ernest Primeau, former bishop of Manchester, N.H., director of Villa Stritch, Rome.

BISHOP-BROTHERS

See separate entries for biographical data.

The asterisk indicates brothers who were bishops at the same time.

There have been nine pairs of brother-bishops in the history of the US hierarchy.

Most recently: Francis T. Hurley* of Juneau and Mark J. Hurley* of Santa Rosa, both living; Coleman F. Carroll* present archbishop of Miami, and the late Howard Carroll* of Altoona-Johnstown.

The others, all deceased, were: Francis Blanchet* of Oregon City (Portland) and Augustin Blanchet* of Walla Walla; John S. Foley of Detroit and Thomas P. Foley of Chicago; Francis P. Kenrick,* apostolic administrator of Philadelphia, bishop of Philadelphia and Baltimore, and Peter R. Kenrick* of St. Louis; Matthias C. Lenihan of Great Falls and Thomas M. Lenihan of Cheyenne; James O'Connor, vicar apostolic of Nebraska and bishop of Omaha, and Michael O'Connor of Pittsburgh and Erie; Jeremiah F. and John W. Shanahan, both of Harrisburg; Sylvester J. Espelage, O.F.M.,* of Wuchang, China, who died 10 days after the ordination of his brother, Bernard T. Espelage,* O.F.M., of Gallup.

NORTH AMERICAN COLLEGE

The North American College was founded by the bishops of the United States in 1859 as a residence and house of formation for US seminarians and graduate students in Rome. The first ordination of an alumnus took place June 14, 1862. Pontifical status was granted the college by Leo XIII Oct. 25, 1884.

Students living at the college study theology and related subjects in the various seminaries in Rome, principally at the Pontifical Gregorian University.

The college is directed by an American rector and staff, and operates under the auspices of a US bishops' committee which was set up in 1924.

The present rector, the 14th, is Msgr. Harold P. Darcy.

AMERICAN BISHOPS OF THE PAST

Information includes dates, place of birth if outside the US, date of ordination to the priesthood, sees held, and, in the case of non-residential bishops, the name of the titular see in parentheses.

A

Adrian, William H. (1883-1972): ord. Apr. 15, 1911; bp. Nashville, 1936-69 (ret.).

Albers, Joseph (1891-1965): ord. June 17, 1916; aux. bp. Cincinnati (Lunda), 1929-37; first bp. Lansing, 1937-65.

Alemany, Joseph Sadoc, O.P. (1814-1888): b. Spain; ord. Mar. 11, 1837; bp. Monterey, (now Los Angeles), 1850-53; first abp. San Francisco, 1853-84 (res.).

Alencastre, Stephen P., S.S.CC. (1876-1940): b. Madeira; ord. Ar. 5, 1902; coad. v.a. Sandwich Is. (Arabissus), 1924-36; v.a. Sandwich (now Hawaiian Is.,) 1936-40.

Alerding, Herman J. (1845-1924): b. Germany; ord. Sept. 22, 1869; bp. Fort Wayne, 1900-24.

Allen, Edward P. (1853-1926): ord. Dec. 17, 1881; bp. Mobile, 1897-1926.

Althoff, Henry (1873-1947): ord. July 26, 1902; bp. Belleville, 1914-47.

Amat, Thaddeus, C.M. (1811-1878): b. Spain; ord. Dec. 23, 1837; bp. Monterey (now Los Angeles), 1854-78.

Anderson, Joseph (1865-1927): ord. May 20, 1892; aux. bp. Boston (Oyrina), 1909-27.

Anglim, Robert, C.SS.R. (1922-1973): ord. Jan. 6, 1948; prelate Coari, Brazil (Gaguari), 1966-73.

Annabring, Joseph (1900-1959): b. Hungary; ord. May 3, 1927; bp. Superior, 1954-59.

Appelhans, Stephen A., S.V.D. (1905-1951): ord. May 5, 1932; v.a. East New Guinea (Catula), 1948-51.

Armstrong, Robert J. (1884-1957): ord. Dec. 10, 1910; bp. Sacramento, 1929-57.

Arnold, William R. (1881-1965): ord. June 13, 1908; delegate of US military vicar (Phocaea), 1945-65.

Atkielski, Roman R. (1898-1969): ord. May 30, 1931; aux. bp. Milwaukee (Stobi), 1947-69.

B

Babcock, Allen J. (1898-1969): ord. Mar. 7, 1925; aux. bp. Detroit (Irenopolis), 1947-54; bp. Grand Rapids, 1954-69.

Bacon, David W. (1815-1874): ord. Dec. 13, 1838; first bp. Portland, Me., 1855-74.

Baltes, Peter J. (1827-1886): b. Germany; ord. May 31, 1852; bp. Alton (now Springfield), Ill., 1870-86.

Baraga, Frederic: See Index.

Barron, Edward (1801-1854): b. Ireland; ord. 1829; v.a. The Two Guineas (Constantina), 1842-44 (res.), missionary in US.

Barry, John (1799-1859): b. Ireland; ord.

Sept. 24, 1825; bp. Savannah, 1857-59.

Barry, Patrick J. (1868-1940): b. Ireland; ord. June 9, 1895; bp. St. Augustine, 1922-40.

Baumgartner, Apollinaris, O.F.M. Cap. (1899-1970): ord. May 30, 1926; v.a. Guam (Joppa), 1945-65; first bp. Agana, Guam, 1965-70.

Bayley, James Roosevelt: See Index.

Bazin, John S. (1796-1848): b. France; ord. July 22, 1822; bp. Vincennes (now Indianapolis), 1847-48.

Beaven, Thomas D. (1851-1920): ord. Dec. 18, 1875; bp. Springfield, Mass., 1892-1920.

Becker, Thomas A. (1832-1899): ord. June 18, 1859; first bp. Wilmington, 1868-86; bp. Savannah, 1886-99.

Beckman, Francis J. (1875-1948): ord. June 20, 1902; bp. Lincoln, 1924-30; abp. Dubuque, 1930-46 (res.).

Benjamin, Cletus J. (1909-1961): ord. Dec. 8, 1935; aux. bp. Philadelphia (Binda), 1960-61.

Bennett, John G. (1891-1957): ord. June 27, 1914; first bp. Lafayette, Ind., 1944-57.

Bergan, Gerald T. (1892-1972): ord. Oct. 28, 1915; bp. Des Moines, 1934-38; abp. Omaha, 1948-69 (ret.).

Bidawid, Thomas M. (1910-1971): b. Iraq; ord. May 15, 1935; US citizen; first abp. Ahwaz, Iran (Chaldean Rite), 1968-70: Chaldean patriarchal vicar for United Arab Republic, 1970-71.

Blanc, Anthony (1792-1860): b. France; ord. July 22, 1816; bp. New Orleans, 1835-50; first abp. New Orleans, 1850-60.

Blanchet (brothers): **Augustin M.** (1797-1887): b. Canada; ord. June 3, 1821; bp. Walla Walla, 1846-50; first bp. Nesqually (now Seattle), 1850-79 (res.). **Francis N.** (1795-1883): b. Canada; ord. July 19, 1819; v.a. Oregon Territory (Philadelphia, Adrasus), 1843-46; first abp. Oregon City (now Portland), 1846-80 (res.)

Blenk, James H., S.M. (1856-1917): b. Germany; ord. Aug. 16, 1885; bp. San Juan, 1899-1906; abp. New Orleans, 1906-17.

Boeynaems, Libert H., S.S.CC. (1857-1926): b. Belgium; ord. Sept. 11, 1881; v.a. Sandwich (now Hawaiian) Is. (Zeugma), 1903-26.

Bohachevsky, Constantine (1884-1961): b. Austrian Galicia; ord. Jan. 31, 1909; ap. ex. Ukrainian Byzantine Catholics in US (Amisus), 1924-58; first metropolitan of Byzantine Rite archeparchy of Philadelphia, 1958-61.

Boileau, George, S.J. (1912-1965): ord. June 13, 1948; coad. bp. Fairbanks (Ausuccura), 1964-65.

Bona, Stanislaus (1888-1967): ord. Nov. 1, 1912; bp. Grand Island, 1932-44; coad. bp. Green Bay (Mela), 1944-45; bp. Green Bay, 1945-67.

Bonacum, Thomas (1847-1911): b. Ireland;

ord. June 18, 1870; first bp. Lincoln, 1887-1911.

Borgess, Caspar H. (1826-1890): b. Germany; ord. Dec. 8, 1848; coad. bp. and ap. admin. Detroit (Calydon), 1870-71; bp. Detroit, 1871-87 (res.).

Bourgade, Peter (1845-1908): b. France; ord. Nov. 30, 1869; v.a. Arizona (Thaumacus), 1885-97; first bp. Tucson, 1897-99; abp. Santa Fe, 1899-1908.

Boylan, John J. (1889-1953): ord. July 28, 1915; bp. Rockford, 1943-53.

Boyle, Hugh C. (1873-1950): ord. July 2, 1898; bp. Pittsburgh, 1921-50.

Bradley, Denis (1846-1903): b. Ireland; ord. June 3, 1871; first bp. Manchester, 1884-1903.

Brady, John (1842-1910): b. Ireland; ord. Dec. 4, 1864; aux. bp. Boston (Alabanda), 1891-1910.

Brady, Matthew F. (1893-1959): ord. June 10, 1916; bp. Burlington, 1938-44; bp. Manchester, 1944-59.

Brady, William O. (1899-1961): ord. Dec. 21, 1923; bp. Sioux Falls, 1939-56; coad. abp. St. Paul (Selymbria), June-Oct. 1956; abp. St. Paul, 1956-61.

Brennan, Andrew J. (1877-1956): ord. Dec. 17, 1904; aux. bp. Scranton (Thapsus), 1923-26; bp. Richmond, 1926-45 (res.).

Brennan, Thomas F. (1853-1916): b. Ireland; ord. July 14, 1880; first bp. Dallas, 1891-92; aux. bp. St. John's, Newfoundland (Usula), 1893-1905 (res.).

Broderick, Bonaventure (1868-1943): ord. July 26, 1896; aux. bp. Havana, Cuba (Juliopolis), 1903-05 (res.).

Brondel, John B. (1842-1903): b. Belgium; ord. Dec. 17, 1864; bp. Vancouver Is., 1879-84; first bp. Helena, 1884-1903.

Brossart, Ferdinand (1849-1930): b. Germany; ord. Sept. 1, 1892; bp. Covington, 1916-23 (res.).

Brute, Simon G. (1779-1839): b. France; ord. June 11, 1808; first bp. Vincennes (now Indianapolis), 1834-39.

Buddy, Charles F. (1887-1966): ord. Sept. 19, 1914; first bp. San Diego, 1936-66.

Burke, Joseph A. (1886-1962): ord. Aug. 3, 1912; aux. bp. Buffalo (Vita), 1943-52; bp. Buffalo, 1952-62.

Burke, Maurice F. (1845-1923): b. Ireland; ord. May 22, 1875; first bp. Cheyenne, 1887-93; bp. St. Joseph, 1893-1923.

Burke, Thomas M. (1840-1915): b. Ireland; ord. June 30, 1864; bp. Albany, 1894-1915.

Busch, Joseph F. (1866-1953): ord. July 28, 1889; bp. Lead (now Rapid City), 1910-15; bp. St. Cloud, 1915-53.

Byrne, Andrew (1802-1862): b. Ireland; ord. Nov. 11, 1827; first bp. Little Rock, 1844-62.

Byrne, Christopher E. (1867-1950): ord. Sept. 23, 1891; bp. Galveston, 1918-50.

Byrne, Edwin V. (1891-1963): ord. May 22, 1915; first bp. Ponce, 1925-29; abp. San Juan, 1929-43; abp. Santa Fe, 1943-63.

Byrne, Leo C. (1908-1974): ord. June 10,

1933; aux. bp., St. Louis (Sabadia), 1954-61; coadj. bp. Wichita, 1961-67; coadj. abp. (Plestra) St. Paul and Minneapolis, 1967-74.

Byrne, Patrick J., M.M. (1888-1950): ord. June 23, 1915; apostolic delegate to Korea (Gazera), 1949-50.

Byrne, Thomas S. (1841-1923): ord. May 22, 1869; bp. Nashville, 1894-1923.

C

Canevin, J. F. Regis (1853-1927): ord. June 4, 1879; coad. bp. Pittsburgh (Sabrata), 1903-04; bp. Pittsburgh, 1904-21 (res.).

Cantwell, John J. (1874-1947): b. Ireland; ord. June 18, 1899; bp. Monterey-Los Angeles, 1917-22; bp. Los Angeles, 1917-36; first abp. Los Angeles, 1936-47.

Carrell, George A., S. J. (1803-1868): ord. Dec. 20, 1827; first bp. Covington, 1853-68.

Carroll, Howard J. (1902-1960): ord. Apr. 2, 1927; bp. Altoona-Johnstown, 1958-60.

Carroll, James J. (1862-1913): ord. June 15, 1889; bp. Nueva Segovia, P. I., 1908-12 (res.).

Carroll, John: See Index.

Carroll, John P. (1864-1925): ord. July 7, 1886; bp. Helena, 1904-25.

Cartwright, Hubert J. (1900-1958): ord. June 11, 1927; coad. bp. Wilmington (Neve), 1956-58.

Cassidy, James E. (1869-1951): ord. Sept. 8, 1898; aux. bp. Fall River (Ibora), 1930-34; bp. Fall River, 1934-51.

Chabrat, Guy Ignatius, S.S. (1787-1868): b. France; ord. Dec. 21, 1811; coad. bp. Bardstown (Bolina), 1834-47 (res.).

Chanche, John J., S.S. (1795-1852): ord. June 5, 1819; bp. Natchez (now Natchez-Jackson), 1841-52.

Chapelle, Placide L. (1842-1905): b. France; ord. June 28, 1865; coad. abp. Santa Fe (Arabissus), 1891-94; abp. Santa Fe, 1894-97; abp. New Orleans, 1897-1905.

Chartrand, Joseph (1870-1933): ord. Sept. 24, 1892; coad. bp. Indianapolis (Flavias), 1910-18; bp. Indianapolis, 1918-33.

Chatard, Francis S. (1834-1918): ord. June 14, 1862; bp. Vincennes (now Indianapolis—title changed in 1898), 1878-1918.

Cheverus, John Lefebvre de (1768-1836): b. France; ord. Dec. 18, 1790; bp. Boston, 1810-23 (returned to France, made cardinal 1836).

Christie, Alexander (1848-1925): ord. Dec. 22, 1877; bp. Vancouver Is., 1898-99; abp. Oregon City (now Portland), 1899-1925.

Clancy, William (1802-1847): b. Ireland; ord. May 24, 1823; coad. bp. Charleston (Oreus). 1834-37; v.a. British Guiana, 1837-43.

Collins, John J., S.J. (1856-1934): ord. Aug. 29, 1891; v.a. Jamaica (Antiphellus), 1907-18.

Collins, Thomas P., M.M. (1915-1973): ord. June 21, 1942; v.a. Pando, Bolivia (Sufetula), 1961-68 (res.).

Colton, Charles H. (1848-1915): ord. June 10, 1876; bp. Buffalo, 1903-15.

Conaty, Thomas J. (1847-1915): b. Ireland;

ord. Dec. 21, 1872; rector of Catholic University, 1896-1903; tit. bp. Samos, 1901-03; bp. Monterey-Los Angeles (now Los Angeles), 1903-15.

Concanen, Richard L., O.P. (1747-1810): b. Ireland; ord. Dec. 22, 1770; first bp. New York. 1808-10 (detained in Italy, never reached his see).

Condon, William J. (1895-1967): ord. Oct. 14, 1917; bp. Great Falls, 1939-67.

Connolly, John, O.P. (1750-1825): b. Ireland; ord. Sept. 24, 1774; bp. New York, 1814-25.

Conroy, John J. (1819-1895): b. Ireland; ord. May 21, 1842; bp. Albany, 1865-77 (res.).

Conroy, Joseph H. (1858-1939): ord. June 11, 1881; aux. bp. Ogdensburg (Arindela), 1912-21; bp. Ogdensburg, 1921-39.

Conwell, Henry (1748-1842): b. Ireland; ord. 1776; bp. Philadelphia, 1820-42.

Corbett, Timothy (1858-1939): ord. June 12, 1886; first bp. Crookston, 1910-38 (res.).

Corrigan, Joseph M. (1879-1942): ord. June 6, 1903; rector of Catholic University, 1936-42; tit. bp. Bilta, 1940-42.

Corrigan, Michael A. (1839-1902): ord. Sept. 19, 1863; bp. Newark, 1873-80; coad. abp. New York (Petra), 1880-85; abp. New York, 1885-1902.

Corrigan, Owen (1849-1929): ord. June 7, 1873; aux. bp. Baltimore (Macri), 1908-29.

Cosgrove, Henry (1834-1906): ord. Aug. 27, 1857; bp. Davenport, 1884-1906.

Cote, Philip, S.J. (1896-1970): ord. Aug. 14, 1927; v. a. Suchow, China (Polystylus), 1935-46; first bp. Suchow, 1946-70 (imprisoned by Chinese Communists, 1951; expelled from China, 1953; ap. admin. Islands of Quemoy and Matsu, 1969-70).

Cotter, Joseph B. (1844-1909): b. England; ord. May 3, 1871; first bp. Winona, 1889-1909.

Cotton, Francis R. (1895-1960): ord. June 17, 1920; first bp. Owensboro, 1938-60.

Cowley, Leonard P. (1913-1973): ord. June 4, 1938; aux. bp. St. Paul and Minneapolis, (Pertusa), 1958-73.

Crane, Michael J. (1863-1928): ord. June 15, 1889; aux. bp. Philadelphia (Curium), 1921-28.

Cretin, Joseph (1799-1857): b. France; ord. Dec. 20, 1823; bp. St. Paul, 1851-57.

Crimont, Joseph R., S.J. (1858-1945): b. France; ord. Aug. 26, 1888; v. a. Alaska (Ammaedara), 1917-45.

Crowley, Timothy J., C.S.C. (1880-1945): b. Ireland; ord. Aug. 2, 1906; coad. bp. Dacca (Epiphania), 1927-29; bp. Dacca, 1929-45.

Cunningham, John F. (1842-1919): b. Ireland; ord. Aug. 8, 1865; bp. Concordia, 1898-1919.

Curley, Daniel J. (1869-1932): ord. May 19, 1894; bp. Syracuse, 1923-32.

Curley, Michael J. (1879-1947): b. Ireland; ord. Mar. 19, 1904; bp. St. Augustine, 1914-21; abp. Baltimore, 1921-39; title changed to

abp. Baltimore and Washington, 1939-47.

Curtis, Alfred A. (1831-1908): convert, 1872; ord. Dec. 19, 1874; bp. Wilmington, 1886-96 (res.).

Cusack, Thomas F. (1862-1918): ord. May 30, 1885; aux. bp. New York (Temiscyra), 1904-15; bp. Albany, 1915-18.

Cushing, Richard J.: See Index.

D

Daeger, Albert T., O.F.M. (1872-1932): ord. July 25, 1896; abp. Santa Fe, 1919-32.

Daly, Edward C., O.P. (1894-1964): ord. June 12, 1921; bp. Des Moines, 1948-64.

Damiano, Celestine (1911-1967): ord. Dec. 21, 1935; apostolic delegate to South Africa (Nicopolis in Epiro), 1952-60; bp. Camden, 1960-67.

Danehy, Thomas J., M.M. (1914-1959): ord. Sept. 17, 1939; ap. admin. v. a. Pando, Bolivia (Bita), 1953-59.

David, John B., S.S. (1761-1841): b. France; ord. Sept. 24, 1785; coad. bp. Bardstown (Mauricastrum), 1819-32; bp. Bardstown (now Louisville), 1832-33 (res.).

Davis, James (1852-1926): b. Ireland; ord. June 21, 1878; coad. bp. Davenport (Milopotamus), 1904-06; bp. Davenport, 1906-26.

De Cheverus, John L.: See Cheverus, John.

De Goesbriand, Louis (1816-1899): b. France; ord. July 13, 1840; first bp. Burlington, 1853-99.

De la Hailandiere, Celestine (1798-1882): b. France; ord. May 28, 1825; bp. Vincennes (now Indianapolis), 1839-47 (res.).

Delany, John B. (1864-1906): ord. May 23, 1891; bp. Manchester, 1904-06.

Demers, Modeste, (1809-1871): b. Canada; ord. Feb. 7, 1836; bp. Vancouver Is., 1846-71.

Dempsey, Michael R. (1918-1974): ord. May 1, 1943; aux. bp. Chicago (Truentum), 1968-74,

De Neckere, Leo, C.M. (1799-1833): b. Belgium; ord. Oct. 13, 1822; bp. New Orleans, 1829-33.

De Saint Palais, Maurice (1811-1877): b. France; ord. May 28, 1836; bp. Vincennes (now Indianapolis), 1849-77.

Desmond, Daniel F. (1884-1945): ord. June 9, 1911; bp. Alexandria, 1933-45.

Dinand, Joseph N., S.J. (1869-1943): ord. June 25, 1903; v. a. Jamaica (Selinus), 1927-29 (res.).

Dobson, Robert (1867-1942): ord. May 23, 1891; aux. bp. Liverpool, Eng. (Cynopolis), 1922-42.

Domenec, Michael, C.M. (1816-1878): b. Spain; ord. June 30, 1839; bp. Pittsburgh, 1860-76; bp. Allegheny, 1876-77 (res.).

Donahue, Joseph P. (1870-1959): ord. June 8, 1895; aux. bp. New York (Emmaus), 1945-59.

Donahue, Patrick J. (1849-1922): b. England; ord. Dec. 19, 1885; bp. Wheeling, 1894-1922.

Donnelly, George J. (1889-1950): ord. June

12, 1921; aux. bp. St. Louis (Coela), 1940-46; bp. Leavenworth (now Kansas City — title changed in 1947), 1946-50.

Donnelly, Henry E. (1904-1967): ord. Aug. 17, 1930; aux. bp. Detroit (Tymbrias), 1954-67.

Doran, Thomas F. (1856-1916): ord. July 4, 1880; aux. bp. Providence (Halicarnassus), 1915-16.

Dougherty, Dennis (1865-1951): ord. May 31, 1890; bp. Nueva Segovia, P.I., 1903-08; bp. Jaro, P.I., 1908-15; bp. Buffalo, 1915-18; abp. Philadelphia, 1918-1951; cardinal, 1921.

Dougherty, Joseph P. (1905-1970): ord. June 14, 1930; first bp. Yakima, 1951-69; aux. bp. Los Angeles (Altino), 1969-70.

Dowling, Austin (1868-1930): ord. June 24, 1891; first bp. Des Moines, 1912-19; abp. St. Paul, 1919-30.

Drossaerts, Arthur J. (1862-1940): b. Holland; ord. June 15, 1889; bp. San Antonio 1918-26; first abp. San Antonio, 1926-40.

Drumm, Thomas W. (1871-1933): b. Ireland; ord. Dec. 21, 1901; bp. Des Moines, 1919-33.

Dubois, John, S.S. (1764-1842): b. France; ord. Sept. 28, 1787; bp. New York, 1826-42.

Dubourg, William L., S.S. (1766-1833): b. Santo Domingo; ord. 1788; bp. Louisiana and the Two Floridas (now New Orleans), 1815-25; returned to France; bp. Montauban, 1826-33; abp. Besancon 1833.

Dubuis, Claude M. (1817-1895): b. France; ord. June 1, 1844; bp. Galveston, 1862-92 (res.).

Dufal, Peter, C.S.C. (1822-1898): b. France; ord. Sept. 29, 1852; v.a. Eastern Bengal (Delcon), 1860-78; coad. bp. Galveston, 1878-80 (res.).

Duffy, James A. (1873-1968): ord. May 27, 1899; bp. Kearney (see transferred to Grand Island, 1917), 1913-31 (res.).

Duffy, John A. (1884-1944): ord. June 13, 1908; bp. Syracuse, 1933-37; bp. Buffalo, 1937-44.

Duggan, James (1825-1899): b. Ireland; ord. May 29, 1847; coad. bp. St. Louis (Gabala), 1857-59; bp. Chicago, 1859-80 (res.). Inactive from 1869 because of illness.

Dunn, John J. (1869-1933): ord. May 30, 1896; aux. bp. New York (Camuliana), 1921-33.

Dunne, Edmund M. (1864-1929): ord. June 24, 1887; bp. Peoria, 1909-29.

Dunne, Edward (1848-1910): b. Ireland; ord. June 29, 1871; bp. Dallas, 1893-1910.

Durier, Anthony (1832-1904): b. France; ord. Oct. 28, 1856; bp. Natchitoches (now Alexandria), La., 1885-1904.

Dwenger, Joseph, C.Pp.S. (1837-1893): ord. Sept. 4, 1859; bp. Fort Wayne, 1872-93.

E

Eccleston, Samuel, S.S. (1801-1851): ord. Apr. 24, 1825; coad. bp. Baltimore (Thermae), Sept.-Oct., 1834; abp. Baltimore, 1834-51.

Egan, Michael, O.F.M. (1761-1814): b. Ireland; first bp. Philadelphia, 1810-14.

Eis, Frederick (1843-1926): b. Germany; ord. Oct. 30, 1870; bp. Sault Ste. Marie and Marquette (now Marquette), 1899-1922 (res.).

Elder, William (1819-1904): ord. Mar. 29, 1846; bp. Natchez (now Natchez-Jackson), 1857-80; coad. bp. Cincinnati (Avara), 1880-83; abp. Cincinnati, 1883-1904.

Elwell, Clarence F. (1904-1973): ord. Mar. 17, 1929; aux. bp. Cleveland (Cone) 1962-68; bp. Columbus, 1968-73.

Emmet, Thomas A., S.J. (1873-1950): ord. July 30, 1909; v.a. Jamaica (Tuscamia), 1930-49 (res.).

England, John: See Index.

Escalante, Alonso Manuel, M.M. (1906-1967): b. Mexico; ord. Feb. 1, 1931; v.a. Pando, Bolivia (Sora), 1943-60 (res.).

Espelage (brothers): **Bernard T., O.F.M.** (1892-1971): ord. May 16, 1918; bp. Gallup, 1940-69 (res.). **Sylvester J., O.F.M.** (1877-1940): ord. Jan. 18, 1900; v.a. Wuchang, China (Oreus), 1930-40.

Eustace, Bartholomew J. (1887-1956): ord. Nov. 1, 1914; bp. Camden, 1938-56.

F

Fahey, Leo F. (1898-1950): ord. May 29, 1926; coad. bp. Baker City (Ipsus), 1948-50.

Farley, John: See Index.

Farrelly, John P. (1856-1921): ord. Mar. 22, 1880; bp. Cleveland, 1909-21.

Fedders, Edward L., M.M. (1913-1973): ord. June 11, 1944; prelate Juli, Peru (Antiochia ad Meadrum, 1963-73.

Feehan, Daniel F. (1855-1934): ord. Dec. 29, 1879; bp. Fall River, 1907-34.

Feehan, Patrick A. (1829-1902): b. Ireland; ord. Nov. 1, 1852; bp. Nashville, 1865-80; first abp. Chicago, 1880-1902.

Feeney, Daniel J. (1894-1969): ord. May 21, 1921; aux. bp. Portland, Me. (Sita), 1946-52; coad. bp. Portland, 1952-55; bp. Portland, 1955-69.

Feeney, Thomas J., S.J. (1894-1955): ord. June 23, 1927; v.a. Caroline and Marshall Is. (Agnus), 1951-55.

Fenwick, Benedict J., S.J. (1782-1846): ord. June 11, 1808; bp. Boston, 1825-46.

Fenwick, Edward D., O.P. (1768-1832): ord. Feb. 23, 1793; first bp. Cincinnati, 1822-32.

Fink, Michael, O.S.B. (1834-1904): b. Germany; ord. May 28, 1857; coad. v.a., 1871-74, and v.a., 1874-77, Kansas and Indian Territory (Eucarpia); first bp. Leavenworth (now Kansas City), 1877-1904.

Finnigan, George, C.S.C. (1885-1932): ord. June 13, 1915; bp. Helena, 1927-32.

Fitzgerald, Edward (1833-1907): b. Ireland; ord. Aug. 22, 1857; bp. Little Rock, 1866-1907.

Fitzgerald, Edward A. (1893-1972): ord. July 25, 1916; aux. bp. Dubuque (Cantanus), 1946-49; bp. Winona, 1949-69 (res.).

Fitzgerald, Walter J., S.J. (1883-1947): ord. May 16, 1918; coad. v.a. Alaska (Tymbrias), 1939-45; v.a. Alaska, 1945-47.

Fitzmaurice, Edmond (1881-1962): b. Ireland; ord. May 28, 1904; bp. Wilmington, 1925-60 (res.).

Fitzmaurice, John E. (1837-1920): b. Ireland; ord. Dec. 21, 1862; coad. bp. Erie (Amisus), 1898-99; bp. Erie, 1899-1920.

Fitzpatrick, John B. (1812-1866): ord. June 13, 1840; aux. bp. Boston (Callipolis), 1843-46; bp. Boston, 1846-66.

Fitzsimon, Laurence J. (1895-1958): ord. May 17, 1921; bp. Amarillo, 1941-58.

Flaget, Benedict, S.S.: See Index.

Flannelly, Joseph F. (1894-1973): ord. Sept. 1, 1918; aux. bp. New York (Metelis), 1948-70 (res.).

Flasch, Kilian C. (1831-1891): b. Germany; ord. Dec. 16, 1859; bp. La Crosse, 1881-91.

Floersh, John (1886-1968): ord. June 10, 1911; coad. bp. Louisville (Lycopolis), 1923-24; bp. Louisville, 1924-37; first abp. Louisville, 1937-67 (res.).

Foley (brothers): **John S.** (1833-1918): ord. Dec. 20, 1856; bp. Detroit, 1888-1918. **Thomas** (1822-1879): ord. Aug. 16, 1846; coad. bp. and ap. admin. Chicago (Pergamum), 1870-79.

Foley, Maurice P. (1867-1919): ord. July 25, 1891; bp. Tuguegarao, P.I., 1910-16; bp. Jaro, P.I., 1916-19.

Ford, Francis X., M.M.: See Index.

Forest, John A. (1838-1911): b. France; ord. Apr. 12, 1863; bp. San Antonio, 1895-1911.

Fox, Joseph J. (1855-1915): ord. June 7, 1879, bp. Green Bay, 1904-14 (res.).

G

Gabriels, Henry (1838-1921): b. Belgium; ord. Sept. 21, 1861; bp. Ogdensburg, 1892-1921.

Galberry, Thomas, O.S.A. (1833-1878): b. Ireland; ord. Dec. 20, 1856; bp. Hartford, 1876-78.

Gallagher, Michael J. (1866-1937): ord. Mar. 19, 1893; coad. bp. Grand Rapids (Tiposa in Mauretania), 1915-16; bp. Grand Rapids, 1916-18; bp. Detroit, 1918-37.

Gallagher, Nicholas (1846-1918): ord. Dec. 25, 1868; coad. bp. Galveston (Canopus), 1882-92; bp. Galveston, 1892-1918.

Gannon, John M. (1877-1968): ord. Dec. 21, 1901; aux. bp. Erie (Nilopolis), 1918-20; bp. Erie, 1920-66 (res.).

Garcia Diego y Moreno, Francisco, O.F.M. (1785-1846): b. Mexico; ord. Nov. 14, 1808; bp. Two Californias (now Los Angeles), 1840-46.

Garriga, Mariano S. (1886-1965): ord. July 2, 1911; coad. bp. Corpus Christi (Syene), 1936-49; bp. Corpus Christi, 1949-65.

Garrigan, Philip (1840-1919): b. Ireland;

ord. June 11, 1870; first bp. Sioux City, 1902-19.

Gartland, Francis X. (1808-1854): b. Ireland; ord. Aug. 5, 1832; first bp. Savannah, 1850-54.

Garvey, Eugene A. (1845-1920): ord. Sept. 22, 1869; first bp. Altoona (now Altoona-Johnstown), 1901-20.

Gercke, Daniel J. (1874-1964): ord. June 1, 1901; bp. Tucson, 1923-60 (res.).

Gerken, Rudolph A. (1887-1943): ord. June 10, 1917; first bp. Amarillo, 1927-33; abp. Santa Fe, 1933-43.

Gibbons, Edmund F. (1868-1964): ord. May 27, 1893; bp. Albany, 1919-54 (res.).

Gibbons, James: See Index.

Gilfillan, Francis (1872-1933): b. Ireland; ord. June 24, 1895; coad. bp. St. Joseph (Spiga), 1922-23; bp. St. Joseph 1923-33.

Gill, Thomas E. (1908-1973): ord. June 10, 1933; aux. bp. Seattle (Lambesis) 1956-73.

Gilmore, Joseph M. (1893-1962): ord. July 25, 1915; bp. Helena, 1936-62.

Gilmour, Richard (1824-1891): b. Scotland; ord. Aug. 30, 1852; bp. Cleveland, 1872-91.

Girouard, Paul J., M.S. (1898-1964): ord. July 26, 1927; first bp. Morondava, Madagascar, 1956-64.

Glass, Joseph S., C.M. (1874-1926): ord. Aug. 15, 1897; bp. Salt Lake City, 1915-26.

Glennon, John: See Index.

Glorieux, Alphonse J. (1844-1917): b. Belgium; ord. Aug. 17, 1867; v.a. Idaho (Apollonia), 1885-93; bp. Boise, 1893-1917.

Goesbriand, Louis J. de (1816-1899): b. France; ord. July 13, 1840; first bp. Burlington, 1853-99.

Gorman, Daniel (1861-1927): ord. June 24, 1893; bp. Boise, 1918-27.

Grace Thomas (1841-1921): b. Ireland; ord. June 24, 1876; bp. Sacramento, 1896-1921.

Grace, Thomas L., O.P. (1814-1897): ord. Dec. 21, 1839; bp. St. Paul, 1859-84 (res.).

Granjon, Henry (1863-1922): b. France; ord. Dec. 17, 1887; bp. Tucson, 1900-22.

Griffin, James A. (1883-1948): ord. July 4, 1909; bp. Springfield, Ill., 1924-48.

Griffin, William A. (1885-1950): ord. Aug. 15, aux. bp. Newark (Sanavus), 1938-40; bp. Trenton, 1940-50.

Griffin, William R. (1883-1944): ord. May 25, 1907; aux. bp. La Crosse (Lydda), 1935-44.

Griffiths, James H. (1903-1964): ord. Mar. 12, 1927; aux. bp. New York and delegate of US military vicar (Gaza), 1950-64.

Grimes, John (1852-1922): b. Ireland; ord. Feb. 19, 1882; coad. bp. Syracuse (Hemeria), 1909-12; bp. Syracuse, 1912-22.

Grimmelsman, Henry J. (1890-1972): ord. Aug. 15, 1915; first bp. Evansville, 1945-65 (res.).

Gross, William H., C.SS.R. (1837-1898): ord. Mar. 21, 1863; bp. Savannah, 1873-85; abp. Oregon City (now Portland), 1885-98.

Guertin, George A. (1869-1932): ord. Dec. 17, 1892; bp. Manchester, 1907-32.

Guilfoyle, Richard T. (1892-1957): ord. June 2, 1917; bp. Altoona (now Altoona-Johnstown), 1936-57.

Gunn, John E., S.M. (1863-1924); b. Ireland; ord. Feb. 2, 1890; bp. Natchez (now Natchez-Jackson), 1911-24.

H

Haas, Francis J. (1889-1953): ord. June 11, 1913; bp. Grand Rapids, 1943-53.

Hafey, William (1888-1954): ord. June 16, 1914; first bp. Raleigh, 1925-37; coad. bp. Scranton (Appia), 1937-38; bp. Scranton, 1938-54.

Hagan, John R. (1890-1946): ord. Mar. 7, 1914; aux. bp. Cleveland (Limata), 1946.

Haid, Leo M., O.S.B. (1849-1924): ord. Dec. 21, 1872; v.a. N. Carolina (Messene), 1888-1910; abbot Mary Help of Christians abbacy, 1910-24.

Hallinan, Paul J. (1911-1968): ord. Feb. 20, 1937; bp. Charleston, 1958-62; first abp. Atlanta, 1962-68.

Hanna, Edward J. (1860-1944): ord. May 30, 1885; aux. bp. San Francisco (Titiopolis), 1912-15; abp. San Francisco, 1915-35 (res.).

Hannan, Jerome D. (1896-1965): ord. May 22, 1921; bp. Scranton, 1954-65.

Harkins, Matthew (1845-1921): ord. May 22, 1869; bp. Providence, 1887-1921.

Hartley, James J. (1858-1944): ord. July 10, 1882; bp. Columbus, 1904-44.

Harty, Jeremiah J. (1853-1927): ord. Apr. 28, 1878; abp. Manila, 1903-16; abp. Omaha, 1916-27.

Hayes, Patrick J.: See Index.

Hayes, Ralph L. (1884-1970): ord. Sept. 19, 1909; bp. Helena 1933-35; rector North American College, 1935-44; bp. Davenport, 1944-66 (res.).

Healy, James A. (1830-1900): ord. June 10, 1854; bp. Portland 1875-1900.

Heelan, Edmond (1868-1948): b. Ireland: ord. June 24, 1890; aux. bp. Sioux City (Gerasa), 1919-20; bp. Sioux City, 1920-48.

Heffron, Patrick (1860-1927): ord. Dec. 22, 1884; bp. Winona, 1910-27.

Heiss, Michael (1818-1890): b. Germany; ord. Oct. 18, 1840; bp. La Crosse, 1868-80; coad. abp. Milwaukee, 1880-81; abp. Milwaukee, 1881-90.

Hendrick, Thomas A. (1849-1909): ord. June 7, 1873; bp. Cebu, P.I., 1904-09.

Hendricken, Thomas F. (1827-1886): b. Ireland; ord. Apr. 25, 1853; bp. Providence, 1872-86.

Hennessy, John (1825-1900): b. Ireland; ord. Nov. 1, 1850; bp. Dubuque, 1866-93; first abp. Dubuque, 1893-1900.

Hennessy, John J. (1847-1920): b. Ireland; ord. Nov. 28, 1869; first bp. Wichita, 1888-1920; ap. admin. Concordia (now Salina), 1891-98.

Henni, John M. (1805-1881): b. Switzer-land; ord. Feb. 2, 1829; first bp. Milwaukee, 1844-75; first abp. Milwaukee, 1875-81.

Heslin, Thomas (1845-1911): b. Ireland; ord. Sept. 8, 1869; bp. Natchez (now Natchez-Jackson), 1889-1911.

Heston, Edward L. (1907-73): ord. Dec. 22, 1934; sec. Sacred Congregation for Religious and Secular Institutes, 1969-71; pres. Pontifical Commission for Social Communications, 1971-73; tit. abp. Numidea, 1972.

Hickey, David F., S.J. (1882-1973): ord. June 27, 1917; v.a. Belize, Br. Honduras (Bonitza), 1948-56; first bp. Belize, 1956-57 (res.).

Hickey, Thomas F. (1861-1940): ord. Mar. 25, 1884; coad. bp. Rochester (Berenice), 1905-09; bp. Rochester, 1909-28 (res.).

Hickey, William A. (1869-1933): ord. Dec. 22, 1893; coad. bp. Providence (Claudiopolis), 1919-21; bp. Providence, 1921-33.

Hillinger, Raymond P. (1904-1971): ord. Apr. 2, 1932; bp. Rockford, 1953-56; aux. bp. Chicago (Derbe), 1956-71.

Hoban, Edward F. (1878-1966): ord. July 11, 1903; aux. bp. Chicago (Colonia), 1921-28; bp. Rockford, 1928-42; coad. bp. Cleveland (Lystra), 1942-45; bp. Cleveland, 1945-66.

Hoban, Michael J. (1853-1926): ord. May 22, 1880; coad. bp. Scranton (Halius), 1896-99; bp. Scranton, 1899-1926.

Hogan, John J. (1829-1913): b. Ireland; ord. Apr. 10, 1852; first bp. St. Joseph, 1868-80; first bp. Kansas City, 1880-1913.

Horstmann, Ignatius (1840-1908): ord. June 10, 1865; bp. Cleveland, 1892-1908.

Howard, Francis W. (1867-1944): ord. June 16, 1891; bp. Covington, 1923-44.

Hughes, John J.: See Index.

Hunkeler, Edward J. (1894-1970): ord. June 14, 1919; bp. Grand Island, 1945-51; bp. Kansas City, Kans. 1951-52; first abp. Kansas City, 1952-69 (res.).

Hunt, Duane G. (1884-1960): ord. June 27, 1920; bp. Salt Lake City, 1937-60.

Hurley, Joseph P. (1894-1967): ord. May 29, 1919; bp. St. Augustine, 1940-67.

Hyland, Francis E. (1901-1968): ord. June 11, 1927; aux. bp. Savannah-Atlanta (Gomphi), 1949-56; bp. Atlanta, 1956-61 (res.).

Hyle, Michael W. (1901-1967): ord. Mar. 12, 1927; coad bp. Wilmington, 1958-60; bp. Wilmington, 1960-67.

I

Ireland, John: See Index.

Ireton, Peter L. (1882-1958): ord. June 20, 1906; coad. bp. Richmond (Cyme), 1935-45; bp. Richmond, 1945-58.

J

Janssen, John (1835-1913): b. Germany; ord. Nov. 19, 1858; first bp. Belleville, 1888-1913.

Janssens, Francis A. (1843-1897): b. Holland; ord. Dec. 21, 1867; bp. Natchez, 1881-88; abp. New Orleans, 1888-97.

Jeanmard, Jules B. (1879-1957): ord. June 10, 1903; first bp. Lafayette, La., 1918-56 (res.).

Johannes, Francis (1874-1937): b. Germany; ord. Jan. 3, 1897; coad. bp. Leavenworth (Thasus), 1928-29; bp. Leavenworth (now Kansas City), 1929-37.

Jones, William A., O.S.A. (1865-1921): ord. Mar. 15, 1890; bp. San Juan, 1907-21.

Junger, Aegidius (1833-1895): b. Germany; ord. June 27, 1862; bp. Nesqually (now Seattle), 1879-95.

K

Kain, John J. (1841-1903): ord. July 2, 1866; bp. Wheeling, 1875-93; coad. abp. St. Louis (Oxyrynchus), 1893-95; abp. St. Louis, 1895-1903.

Katzer, Frederick X. (1844-1903): b. Austria; ord. Dec. 21, 1866; bp. Green Bay, 1886-91; abp. Milwaukee, 1891-1903.

Keane, James J. (1856-1929): ord. Dec. 23, 1882; bp. Cheyenne, 1902-11; abp. Dubuque, 1911-29.

Keane, John J. (1839-1918): b. Ireland; ord. July 2, 1866; bp. Richmond, 1878-88; rector of Catholic University, 1888-97; consultor of Congregation for Propagation of the Faith, 1897-1900; abp. Dubuque, 1900-11 (res.).

Keane, Patrick J. (1872-1928): b. Ireland; ord. June 20, 1895; aux. bp. Sacramento (Samaria), 1920-22; bp. Sacramento, 1922-28.

Kearney, Raymond A. (1902-1956): ord. Mar. 12, 1927; aux. bp. Brooklyn (Lysinia), 1935-56.

Keiley, Benjamin J. (1847-1925): ord. Dec. 31, 1873; bp. Savannah, 1900-22 (res.).

Kelleher, Louis J. (1889-1946): ord. Apr. 3, 1915; aux. bp. Boston (Thenae), 1945-46.

Kelley, Francis C. (1870-1948): b. Canada; ord. Aug. 23, 1893; bp. Oklahoma, 1924-48.

Kelly, Edward D. (1860-1926): ord. June 16, 1886; aux. bp. Detroit (Cestrus), 1911-19; bp. Grand Rapids, 1919-26.

Kelly, Edward J. (1890-1956): ord. June 2, 1917; bp. Boise, 1928-56.

Kelly, Francis M. (1886-1950); ord. Nov. 1, 1912; aux. bp. Winona (Mylasa), 1926-28; bp. Winona, 1928-49 (res.).

Kelly, Patrick (1779-1829): b. Ireland; ord. July 18, 1802; first bp. Richmond, 1820-22 (returned to Ireland; bp. Waterford and Lismore, 1822-29).

Kennedy, Thomas F. (1858-1917): ord. July 24, 1887; rector North American College, 1901-17; tit. bp. Hadrianapolis, 1907-15; tit. abp. Seleucia, 1915-17.

Kenny, William J. (1853-1913): ord. Jan 15, 1879; bp. St. Augustine, 1902-13.

Kenrick (brothers): **Francis P.** (1796-1863): b. Ireland; ord. Apr. 7, 1821; coad. bp. Philadelphia (Aratha), 1830-42; bp. Philadelphia, 1842-51; abp. Baltimore, 1851-63. **Peter**

(1806-1896): b. Ireland; ord. Mar. 6, 1932; coad. bp. St. Louis (Adrasus), 1841-43; bp., 1843-47, and first abp. 1847-95, St. Louis (res.).

Keough, Francis P. (1890-1961): ord. June 10, 1916; bp. Providence, 1943-47; abp. Baltimore, 1947-61.

Keyes, Michael, S.M. (1876-1959): b. Ireland; ord. June 21, 1907; bp. Savannah, 1922-35 (res.).

Kiley, Moses E. (1876-1953): b. Nova Scotia; ord. June 10, 1911; bp. Trenton, 1934-40; abp. Milwaukee, 1940-53.

Kogy, Lorenz S., O.M. (1895-1963): b. Georgia, Russia; ord. Nov. 15, 1917; U.S. citizen, 1944; patriarchal vicar for Armenian diocese of Beirut (Comana), 1951-63.

Koudelka, Joseph (1852-1921): b. Austria; ord. Oct. 8, 1875; aux. bp. Cleveland (Germanicoplis), 1908-11; aux. bp. Milwaukee, 1911-13; bp. Superior, 1913-21.

Kowalski, Rembert, O.F.M. (1884-1970): ord. June 22, 1911; v.a. Wuchang, China (Ipsus), 1942-46; first bp. Wuchang, 1946-70 (in exile from 1953).

Kozlowski, Edward (1860-1915): b. Poland; ord. June 29, 1887; aux. bp. Milwaukee (Germia), 1914-15.

Krautbauer, Francis X. (1824-1885): b. Germany; ord. July 16, 1850; bp. Green Bay, 1875-85.

Kucera, Louis B. (1888-1957): ord. June 8, 1915; bp. Lincoln, 1930-57.

L

Lamb, Hugh (1890-1959): ord. May 29, 1915; aux. bp. Philadelphia (Helos), 1936-51; bp. Greensburg, 1951-59.

Lamy, Jean B.: See Index.

Lane, Loras (1910-1968): ord. Mar. 19, 1937; aux. bp. Dubuque (Bencenna), 1951-56; bp. Rockford, 1956-68.

Lane, Raymond A., M.M. (1894-1974): ord. Feb. 8, 1920; v.a. Fushun, Manchukuo (Hypaepa), 1940-46; sup. gen. Maryknoll, 1946-56.

Laval, John M. (1854-1937): b. France; ord. Nov. 10, 1877; aux. bp. New Orleans (Hierocaesarea), 1911-37.

Lavialle, Peter J. (1819-1867): b. France; ord. Feb. 12, 1844; bp. Louisville, 1865-67.

Lawler, John J. (1862-1948): ord. Dec. 19, 1885; aux. bp. St. Paul (Hermopolis), 1910-16; bp. Lead (now Rapid City), 1916-48.

Le Blond, Charles H. (1883-1958): ord. June 29, 1909; bp. St. Joseph, 1933-56 (res.).

Ledvina, Emmanuel (1868-1952): ord. Mar. 18, 1893; bp. Corpus Christi, 1921-49 (res.).

Lefevere, Peter P. (1804-1869): b. Belgium; ord. Nov. 30, 1831; coad. bp. and admin. Detroit (Zela), 1841-69.

Leibold, Paul F. (1914-1972): ord. May 18, 1940; aux. bp. Cincinnati (Trebenna), 1958-66; bp. Evansville, 1966-69; abp. Cincinnati, 1969-72.

Lenihan (brothers): **Mathias C.** (1854-

1943): ord. Dec. 20, 1879; bp. Great Falls, 1904-30 (res.). **Thomas M.** (1844-1901): b. Ireland; ord. Nov. 19, 1868; bp. Cheyenne, 1897-1901.

Leray, Francis X. (1825-1887): b. France; ord. Mar. 19, 1852; bp. Natchitoches (now Alexandria, La.), 1877-79; coad. bp. New Orleans and admin. of Natchitoches (Jonopolis), 1879-83; abp. New Orleans, 1883-87.

Ley, Felix, O.F.M. Cap. (1909-1972): ord. June 14, 1936; ap. admin. Ryukyu Is., (Caporilla), 1968-72.

Lillis, Thomas F. (1861-1938): ord. Aug. 15, 1885; bp. Leavenworth (now Kansas City, Kans.), 1904-10; coad. bp. Kansas City, Mo. (Cibyra), 1910-13; bp. Kansas City, Mo., 1913-38.

Lootens, Louis (1827-1898): b. Belgium; ord. June 14, 1851; v. a. Idaho and Montana (Castabala), 1868-76 (res.).

Loras, Mathias (1792-1858): b. France; ord. Nov. 12, 1815; first bp. Dubuque, 1837-58.

Loughlin, John (1817-1891): b. Ireland; ord. Oct. 18, 1840; first bp. Brooklyn, 1853-91.

Lowney, Denis M. (1863-1918): b. Ireland; ord. Dec. 17, 1887; aux. bp. Providence (Hadrianopolis), 1917-18.

Ludden, Patrick A. (1838-1912): b. Ireland; ord. May 21, 1865; first bp. Syracuse, 1887-1912.

Luers, John (1819-1871): b. Germany; ord. Nov. 11, 1846; first bp. Fort Wayne, 1858-71.

Lynch, Joseph P. (1872-1954): ord. June 9, 1900; bp. Dallas (Dallas-Fort Worth, 1953), 1911-54.

Lynch, Patrick N. (1817-1882): b. Ireland; ord. Apr. 5, 1840; bp. Charleston, 1858-82.

M

McAuliffe, Maurice F. (1875-1944): ord. July 29, 1900; aux. bp. Hartford (Dercos), 1925-34; bp. Hartford, 1934-44.

McCarthy, Joseph E. (1876-1955): ord. July 4, 1903; bp. Portland, Me., 1932-55.

McCarthy, Justin J. (1900-1959): ord. Apr. 16, 1927; aux. bp. Newark (Doberus), 1954-57; bp. Camden, 1957-59.

McCarty, William T., C.SS.R. (1889-1972): ord. June 10, 1915; military delegate (Anea), 1943-47; coad. bp. Rapid City, 1947-48; bp. Rapid City, 1948-69 (res.).

McCloskey, James P. (1870-1945): ord. Dec. 17, 1898, bp. Zamboanga, P.I., 1917-20; bp. Jaro, P.I., 1920-45.

McCloskey, John: See Index.

McCloskey, William G. (1823-1909): ord. Oct. 6, 1852; bp. Louisville, 1868-1909.

McCormick, Patrick J. (1880-1953): ord. July 6, 1904; aux. bp. Washington (Atenia), 1950-53.

McCort, John J. (1860-1936): ord. Oct. 14, 1883; aux. bp. Philadelphia (Azotus), 1912-20; bp. Altoona, 1920-36.

McDevitt, Philip R. (1858-1935): ord. July 14, 1885; bp. Harrisburg, 1916-35.

McDonnell, Charles E. (1854-1921): ord. May 19, 1878; bp. Brooklyn, 1892-1921.

McDonnell, Thomas J. (1894-1961): ord. Sept. 20, 1919; aux. bp. New York (Sela), 1947-51; coad. bp. Wheeling, 1951-61.

McEntegart, Bryan (1893-1968): ord. Sept. 8, 1917; bp. Ogdensburg, 1943-53; rector Catholic University (Aradi), 1953-57; bp. Brooklyn, 1957-68.

McFadden, James A. (1880-1952): ord. June 17, 1905; aux. bp. Cleveland (Bida), 1932-43; first bp. Youngstown, 1943-52.

MacFarland, Francis P. (1819-1874): ord. May 1, 1845; bp. Hartford, 1858-74.

McFaul, James A. (1850-1917): b. Ireland; ord. May 26, 1877; bp. Trenton, 1894-1917.

McGavick, Alexander J. (1863-1948): ord. June 11, 1887; aux. bp. Chicago (Marcopolis), 1899-1921; bp. La Crosse, 1921-48.

McGeough, Joseph F. (1903-1970): ord. Dec. 20, 1930; internuncio Ethiopia, 1957-60; apostolic delegate (Hemesa) S. Africa, 1960-67; nuncio Ireland, 1967-69.

McGill, John (1809-1872): ord. June 13, 1835; bp. Richmond, 1850-72.

MacGinley, John B. (1871-1969): b. Ireland; ord. June 8, 1895; bp. Nueva Caceres, 1910-24; first bp. Monterey-Fresno, 1924-32 (res.).

McGolrick, James (1841-1918): b. Ireland; ord. June 11, 1867; first bp. Duluth, 1889-1918.

McGovern, Patrick A. (1872-1951): ord. Aug. 18, 1895; bp. Cheyenne, 1912-51.

McGovern, Thomas (1832-1898): b. Ireland; ord. Dec. 27, 1861; bp. Harrisburg, 1888-98.

McGrath, Joseph F. (1871-1950): b. Ireland; ord. Dec. 21, 1895; bp. Baker City (now Baker), 1919-50.

McGuinness, Eugene (1889-1957): ord. May 22, 1915; bp. Raleigh, 1937-44; coad. bp. Oklahoma City and Tulsa (Ilium), 1944-48; bp. Oklahoma City and Tulsa, 1948-57.

McLaughlin, Thomas H. (1881-1947): ord. July 26, 1904; aux. bp. Newark (Nisa), 1935-37; first bp. Paterson, 1937-47.

McMahon, John J. (1875-1932): ord. May 20, 1900; bp. Trenton, 1928-32.

McMahon, Lawrence S. (1835-1893): ord. Mar. 24, 1860; bp. Hartford, 1879-93.

McManaman, Edward P. (1900-1964): ord. Mar. 12, 1927; aux. bp. Erie (Floriana), 1948-64.

McMullen, John (1832-1883): b. Ireland; ord. June 20, 1858; first bp. Davenport, 1881-83.

McNamara, John M. (1878-1960): ord. June 21, 1902; aux. bp. Baltimore (Eumenia), 1928-47; aux. bp. Washington, 1947-60.

McNamara, Martin D. (1898-1966): ord. Dec. 23, 1922; first bp. Joliet, 1949-66.

McNeirny, Francis (1828-1894): ord. Aug. 17, 1854; coad. bp. Albany (Rhesaina), 1872-77; bp. Albany, 1877-94.

McNicholas, John T., O.P. (1877-1950): b.

Ireland; ord. Oct. 10, 1901; bp. Duluth, 1918-25; abp. Cincinnati, 1925-50.

McNulty, James A. (1900-1972): ord. July 12, 1925; aux. bp. Newark (Methone), 1947-53; bp. Paterson, 1953-63; bp. Buffalo, 1963-72.

McQuaid, Bernard J.: See Index.

McSorley, Francis J., O.M.I. (1913-1971): ord. May 30, 1939: v.a. Jolo, P.I. (Sozusa), 1958-71.

McVinney, Russell J. (1898-1971): ord. July 13, 1924; bp. Providence, 1948-71.

Machebeuf, Joseph P. (1812-1889): b. France; ord. Dec. 17, 1836; v. a. Colorado and Utah (Epiphania), 1868-1887; first bp. Denver, 1887-89.

Maes, Camillus P. (1846-1915): b. Belgium; ord. Dec. 19, 1868; bp. Covington, 1885-1915.

Magner, Francis (1887-1947): ord. May 17, 1913; bp. Marquette, 1941-47.

Mahoney, Bernard (1875-1939): ord. Feb. 27, 1904; bp. Sioux Falls, 1922-39.

Maloney, Thomas F. (1903-1962): ord. July 13, 1930; aux. bp. Providence (Andropolis), 1960-62.

Manogue, Patrick: See Index.

Manucy, Dominic (1823-1885): ord. Aug. 15, 1850; v. a. Brownsville (Dulma), 1874-84; bp. Mobile, Mar.-Sept., 1884 (res.); reappointed v. a. Brownsville (Maronea) (now diocese of Corpus Christi), 1884-85.

Marechal, Ambrose, S.S. (1766-1828): b. France; ord. June 2, 1792; abp. Baltimore, 1817-28.

Markham, Thomas F. (1891-1952): ord. June 2, 1917; aux. bp. Boston (Acalissus), 1950-52.

Martin, Augustus M. (1803-1875): b. France; ord. May 31, 1828; first bp. Natchitoches (now Alexandria), 1853-75.

Marty, Martin, O.S.B. (1834-1896): b. Switzerland; ord. Sept. 14, 1856; v. a. Dakota (Tiberias), 1880-89; first bp. Sioux Falls, 1889-95; bp. St. Cloud, 1895-96.

Marx, Adolph, (1915-1965): b. Germany; ord. May 2, 1940; aux. bp. Corpus Christi (Citrus), 1956-65; first bp. Brownsville, 1965.

Matz, Nicholas C. (1850-1917): b. France; ord. May 31, 1874; coad. bp. Denver (Telmissus), 1887-89; bp. Denver, 1889-1917.

Meerschaert, Theophile (1847-1924): b. Belgium; ord. Dec. 23, 1871; v. a. Oklahoma and Indian Territory (Sidyma), 1891-1905; first bp. Oklahoma, 1905-24.

Melcher, Joseph (1806-1873): b. Austria; ord. Mar. 27, 1830; first bp. Green Bay, 1868-73.

Messmer, Sebastian (1847-1930): b. Switzerland; ord. July 23, 1871; bp. Green Bay, 1892-1903; abp. Milwaukee, 1903-30.

Meyer, Albert (1903-1965): ord. July 11, 1926; bp. Superior, 1946-53; abp. Milwaukee, 1953-58; abp. Chicago, 1958-65; cardinal, 1959.

Michaud, John S. (1843-1908): ord. June 7,

1873; coad. bp. Burlington (Modra), 1892-99; bp. Burlington, 1899-1908.

Miege, John B., S.J. (1815-1884): b. France; ord. Sept. 12, 1844; v. a. Kansas and Indian Territory (now Kansas City) (Messene), 1851-74 (res.).

Miles, Richard P., O.P. (1791-1860): ord. Sept. 21, 1816; first bp. Nashville, 1838-60.

Minihan, Jeremiah F. (1903-1973); ord. Dec. 21, 1929; aux. bp. Boston (Paphus), 1954-73.

Misner, Paul B., C.M. (1891-1938): ord. Feb. 23, 1919; v.a. Yukiang, China (Myrica), 1935-38.

Mitty, John J. (1884-1961): ord. Dec. 22, 1906; bp. Salt Lake, 1926-32; coad. abp. San Francisco (Aegina), 1932-35; abp. San Francisco, 1935-61.

Moeller, Henry (1849-1925): ord. June 10, 1876; bp. Columbus, 1900-03; coad. abp. Cincinnati (Areopolis), 1903-04; abp. Cincinnati, 1904-25.

Molloy, Thomas E. (1884-1956): ord. Sept. 19, 1908; aux. bp. Brooklyn (Lorea), 1920-21; bp. Brooklyn, 1921-56.

Monaghan, Francis J. (1890-1942): ord. May 29, 1915; coad. bp. Ogdensburg (Mela), 1936-39; bp. Ogdensburg, 1939-42.

Monaghan, John J. (1856-1935): ord. Dec. 18, 1880; bp. Wilmington, 1897-1925 (res.).

Montgomery, George T. (1847-1907): ord. Dec. 20, 1879; coad. bp. Monterey-Los-Angeles (Thmuis), 1894-96; bp. Monterey-Los Angeles (now Los Angeles), 1896-1903; coad. abp. San Francisco (Auxum), 1903-07.

Mooney, Edward (1882-1958): ord. Apr. 10, 1909; ap. del. India (Irenopolis), 1926-31; ap. del. Japan, 1931-33; bp. Rochester, 1933-37; first abp. Detroit, 1937-58; cardinal, 1946.

Moore, John (1835-1901): b. Ireland; ord. Apr. 9, 1860; bp. St. Augustine, 1877-1901.

Mora, Francis (1827-1905): b. Spain; ord. Mar. 19, 1856; coad. bp. Monterey-Los Angeles (Mosynopolis), 1873-78; bp. Monterey-Los Angeles, 1878-96 (res.).

Morris, John (1866-1946): ord. June 11, 1892; coad. bp. Little Rock (Acmonia), 1906-07; bp. Little Rock, 1907-46.

Mrak, Ignatius (1810-1901): b. Austria; ord. July 31; 1837; bp. Sault Ste. Marie and Marquette (now Marquette), 1869-78 (res.).

Muench, Aloysius: See Index.

Muldoon, Peter J. (1862-1927): ord. Dec. 18, 1886; aux. bp. Chicago (Tamasus), 1901-08; first bp. Rockford, 1908-27.

Mullen, Tobias (1818-1900): b. Ireland; ord. Sept. 1, 1844; bp. Erie, 1868-99 (res.).

Mulloy, William T. (1892-1959): ord. June 7, 1916; bp. Covington, 1945-59.

Mundelein, George (1872-1939): ord. June 8, 1895; aux. bp. Brooklyn (Loryma), 1909-15; abp. Chicago, 1915-39; cardinal, 1924.

Murphy, Joseph A., S.J. (1857-1939): b. Ireland; ord. Aug. 26, 1888; v. a. Belize, Br. Honduras (Birtha), 1923-39.

Murphy, William F. (1885-1950): ord. June 13, 1908; first bp. Saginaw, 1938-50.

Murray, John G. (1877-1956): ord. Apr. 14, 1900; aux. bp. Hartford (Flavias), 1920-25; bp. Portland, 1925-31; abp. St. Paul, 1931-56.

N

Navagh, James J. (1901-1965): ord. Dec. 21, 1929; aux. bp. Raleigh (Ombi), 1952-57; bp. Ogdensburg, 1957-63; bp. Paterson, 1963-65.

Neale, Leonard (1746-1817): ord. June 5, 1773; coad. bp. Baltimore (Gortyna), 1800-15; abp. Baltimore, 1815-17.

Neraz, John C. (1828-1894): b. France; ord. Mar. 19, 1853; bp. San Antonio, 1881-1894.

Neumann, John, Bl.: See Index.

Niedhammer, Matthew A., O.F.M. Cap. (1901-1970): ord. June 8, 1927; v. a. Bluefields, Nicaragua (Caloe), 1943-70.

Nilan, John J. (1855-1934): ord. Dec. 2, 1878; bp. Hartford, 1910-34.

Noll, John F.: See Index.

Northrop, Henry P. (1842-1916): ord. June 25, 1865; v.a. North Carolina (Rosalia), 1881-83; bp. Charleston, 1883-1916.

Nussbaum, Paul J., C.P. (1870-1935): ord. May 20, 1894; first bp. Corpus Christi, 1913-20 (res.); bp. Sault Ste. Marie and Marquette (now Marquette), 1922-35.

O

O'Brien, William D. (1878-1962): ord. July 11, 1903; aux. bp. Chicago (Calynda), 1934-62.

O'Connell, Denis J. (1849-1927): b. Ireland; ord. May 26, 1877; aux. bp. San Francisco (Sebaste), 1908-12; bp. Richmond, 1912-26 (res.).

O'Connell, Eugene (1815-1891): b. Ireland; ord. May 21, 1842; v. a. Marysville (Flaviopolis), 1861-68; first bp. Grass Valley, 1868-84 (res.).

O'Connell, William H. (1859-1944): ord. June 7, 1884; bp. Portland, 1901-06; coad. bp. Boston (Constantia), 1906-07; abp. Boston, 1907-44; cardinal, 1911.

O'Connor (brothers), James (1823-1890): b. Ireland; ord. Mar. 25, 1848; v. a. Nebraska (Dibon), 1876-85; first bp. Omaha, 1885-90.

Michael, S.J. (1810-1872): b. Ireland; ord. June 1, 1833; first bp. Pittsburgh, 1843-53; first bp. of Erie, 1853-54; bp. Pittsburgh, 1854-60 (resigned, joined Jesuits).

O'Connor, John J. (1855-1927): ord. Dec. 22, 1877; bp. Newark, 1901-27.

O'Connor, William P. (1886-1973): ord. Mar. 10, 1912; bp. Superior, 1942-46; first bp. Madison, 1946-67 (res.).

O'Dea, Edward J. (1856-1932): ord. Dec. 23, 1882; bp. Nesqually (now Seattle — title changed in 1907), 1896-1932.

Odin, John M., C.M. (1800-1870): b. France; ord. May 4, 1823; v. a. Texas (Claudiopolis), 1842-47; first bp. Galveston, 1847-61; abp. New Orleans, 1861-70.

O'Donaghue, Denis (1848-1925): ord. Sept. 6, 1874; aux. bp. Indianapolis (Pomaria), 1900-10; bp. Louisville, 1910-24 (res.).

O'Dowd, James T. (1907-1950): ord. June 4, 1932; aux. bp. San Francisco (Cea), 1948-50.

O'Farrell, Michael J. (1832-1894): b. Ireland; ord. Aug. 18, 1855; first bp. Trenton, 1881-94.

O'Flanagan, Dermot (1901-1973): b. Ireland; ord. Aug. 27, 1929; first bp. Juneau, 1951-68 (res.).

O'Gara, Cuthbert, C.P. (1886-1968): b. Canada; ord. May 26, 1915; v.a. Yuanling, China (Elis), 1934-46; first bp. Yuanling, 1946-68 (imprisoned, 1951, and then expelled, 1953, by Chinese Communists).

O'Gorman, James, O.C.S.O. (1804-1874): b. Ireland; ord. Dec. 23, 1843; v.a. Nebraska (now Omaha) (Raphanea), 1859-74.

O'Gorman, Thomas (1843-1921): ord. Nov. 5, 1865; bp. Sioux Falls, 1896-1921.

O'Hara, Edwin V.: See Index.

O'Hara, Gerald V. (1888-1963): ord. Apr. 3, 1920; aux. bp. Philadelphia (Heliopolis), 1929-35; bp. Savannah (title changed to Savannah-Atlanta in 1937), 1935-59 (res.); regent of Rumania nunciature, 1946-50 (expelled); nuncio to Ireland, 1951-54; ap. del. to Great Britain, 1954-63.

O'Hara, John F., C.S.C. (1886-1960): ord. Sept. 9, 1916; delegate of US military vicar (Mylasa), 1940-45; bp. Buffalo, 1945-51; abp. Philadelphia, 1951-60; cardinal, 1958.

O'Hara, William (1816-1899): b. Ireland; ord. Dec. 21, 1842; first bp. Scranton, 1868-99.

O'Hare, William F., S.J. (1870-1926): ord. June 25, 1903; v.a. Jamaica (Maximianopolis), 1920-26.

O'Hern, John F. (1874-1933): ord. Feb. 17, 1901; bp. Rochester, 1929-33.

O'Leary, Thomas (1875-1949): ord. Dec. 18, 1897; bp. Springfield, Mass., 1921-49.

Olwell, Quentin, C.P. (1898-1972): ord. Feb. 4, 1923; prelate Marbel, P.I. (Thabraca), 1961-69 (ret.).

O'Regan, Anthony (1809-1866): b. Ireland; ord. Nov. 29, 1834; bp. Chicago, 1854-58 (res.).

O'Reilly, Bernard (1803-1856): b. Ireland; ord. Oct. 16, 1831; bp. Hartford, 1850-56.

O'Reilly, Charles J. (1860-1923): b. Canada; ord. June 29, 1890; first bp. Baker City (now Baker), 1903-18; bp. Lincoln, 1918-23.

O'Reilly, James (1855-1934): b. Ireland; ord. June 24, 1880; bp. Fargo, 1910-34.

O'Reilly, Patrick T. (1833-1892): b. Ireland; ord. Aug. 15, 1857; first bp. Springfield, Mass., 1870-92.

O'Reilly, Peter J. (1850-1924): b. Ireland; ord. June 24, 1877; aux. bp. Peoria (Lebedus), 1900-24.

O'Reilly, Thomas C. (1873-1938): ord. June 4, 1898; bp. Scranton, 1928-38.

Ortynsky, Stephen, O.S.B.M. (1866-1916):

b. Poland; ord. July 18, 1891; first Ukrainian Byzantine Rite bishop in US (Daulia), 1907-16.

O'Shea, John A., C.M. (1887-1969): ord. May 30, 1914; v.a. Kanchow, China (Midila), 1928-46; first bp. Kanchow, 1946-69 (expelled by Chinese Communists, 1953).

O'Shea, William F., M.M. (1884-1945): ord. Dec. 5, 1917; v.a. Heijon, Japan (Naissusz), 1939-45; prisoner of Japanese 1941-42.

O'Sullivan, Jeremiah (1842-1896): b. Ireland; ord. June 30, 1868; bp. Mobile, 1885-96.

P

Paschang, Adolph J., M.M. (1895-1968): ord. May 21, 1921; v.a. Kong Moon, China (Sasima), 1937-46; first bp. Kong Moon, 1946-68 (expelled by Communists, 1951).

Pellicer, Anthony (1824-1880): ord. Aug. 15, 1850; first bp. San Antonio, 1874-80.

Penalver y Cardenas, Luis (1749-1810): b. Cuba; ord. Apr. 4, 1772; first bp. Louisiana and the Two Floridas (now New Orleans), 1793-1801; abp. Guatemala, 1801-06 (res.).

Perche, Napoleon J. (1805-1883): b. France; ord. Sept. 19, 1829; abp. New Orleans, 1870-83.

Persico, Ignatius, O.F.M. Cap. (1823-1895): b. Italy; ord. Jan. 24, 1846; bishop from 1854; bp. Savannah-Atlanta, 1870-72; cardinal, 1893.

Peschges, John H. (1881-1944): ord. Apr. 15, 1905; bp. Crookston, 1938-44.

Peterson, John B. (1871-1944): ord. Sept. 15, 1899; aux. bp. Boston (Hippos), 1927-32; bp. Manchester, 1932-44.

Phelan, Richard (1828-1904): b. Ireland; ord. May 4, 1854; coad. bp. Pittsburgh (Cibyra), 1885-89; bp. Pittsburgh, 1889-1904.

Pitaval, John B. (1858-1928): b. France; ord. Dec. 24, 1881; aux. bp. Santa Fe (Sora), 1902-09; abp. Santa Fe, 1909-18 (res.).

Plagens, Joseph C. (1880-1943): b. Poland; ord. July 5, 1903; aux. bp. Detroit (Rhodiapolis), 1924-35; bp. Sault Ste. Marie and Marquette (title changed to Marquette, 1937), 1935-40; bp. Grand Rapids, 1941-43.

Portier, Michael (1795-1859): b. France; ord. May 16, 1818; v.a. Two Floridas and Alabama (Olena), 1826-29; first bp. Mobile, 1829-59.

Prendergast, Edmond (1843-1918): b. Ireland; ord. Nov. 17, 1865; aux. bp. Philadelphia (Scilium), 1897-1911; abp. Philadelphia, 1911-18.

Purcell, John B. (1800-1883): b. Ireland; ord. May 20, 1826; bp., 1833-50, and first abp., 1850-83, Cincinnati.

Q

Quarter, William (1806-1848): b. Ireland; ord. Sept. 19, 1829; first bp. Chicago, 1844-48.

Quigley, James E. (1855-1915): b. Canada; ord. Apr. 13, 1879; bp. Buffalo, 1897-1903; abp. Chicago, 1903-15.

Quinlan, John (1826-1883): b. Ireland; ord. Aug. 30, 1852; bp. Mobile, 1859-83.

Quinn, William Charles, C.M. (1905-1960): ord. Oct. 11, 1931; v.a. Yukiang, China (Halicarnassus), 1940-46; first bp. Yukiang, 1946-60 (expelled by Chinese Communists, 1951).

R

Rademacher, Joseph (1840-1900): ord. Aug. 2, 1863; bp. Nashville, 1883-93; bp. Fort Wayne, 1893-1900.

Rappe, Louis Amadeus (1801-1877): b. France; ord. Mar. 14, 1829; first bp. Cleveland, 1847-70 (res.).

Ready, Michael J. (1893-1957): ord. Sept. 14, 1918; bp. Columbus, 1944-57.

Reed, Victor J. (1905-1971): ord. Dec. 21, 1929; aux. bp. Oklahoma City and Tulsa (Limasa), 1957-58; bp. Oklahoma City and Tulsa, 1958-71.

Reilly, Edmond J. (1897-1958): ord. Apr. 1, 1922; aux. bp. Brooklyn (Nepte), 1955-58.

Rese, Frederic (1791-1871): b. Germany; ord. Mar. 15, 1823; first bp. Detroit, 1833-71. Inactive from 1841 because of ill health.

Reverman, Theodore (1877-1941): ord. July 26, 1901; bp. Superior, 1926-41.

Reynolds, Ignatius A. (1798-1855): ord. Oct. 24, 1823; bp. Charleston, 1844-55.

Rhode, Paul P. (1871-1945): b. Poland; ord. June 17, 1894; aux. bp. Chicago (Barca), 1908-15; bp. Green Bay, 1915-45.

Rice, Joseph J. (1871-1938): ord. Sept. 29, 1894; bp. Burlington, 1910-38.

Rice, William A., S. J.(1891-1925): ord. Aug. 27, 1925; v.a. Belize, Br. Honduras (Rusicade), 1939-46.

Richter, Henry J. (1838-1916): b. Germany; ord. June 10, 1865; first bp. Grand Rapids, 1883-1916.

Riordan, Patrick W. (1841-1914): b. Canada; ord. June 10, 1865; coad. abp. San Francisco (Cabasa), 1883-84; abp. San Francisco, 1884-1914.

Ritter, Joseph E.: See Index.

Robinson, Pascal C., O. F. M. (1870-1948): b. Ireland; ord. Dec. 21, 1901; ap. visitor to Palestine, Egypt, Syria and Cyprus (Tyana), 1927-29; ap. nuncio to Ireland, 1929-48.

Rohlman, Henry P. (1876-1957): b. Germany; ord. Dec. 21, 1901; bp. Davenport, 1927-44; coad. abp. Dubuque (Macra), 1944-46; abp. Dubuque, 1946-54 (res.).

Rooker, Frederick Z. (1861-1907): ord. July 25, 1888; bp. Jaro, P.I., 1903-07.

Ropert, Gulstan F., SS. CC. (1839-1903): b. France; ord. May 26, 1866; v.a. Sandwich (now Hawaiian) Is. (Panopolis), 1892-1903.

Rosati, Joseph, C. M.: See Index.

Rosecrans, Sylvester (1827-1878): ord. June 5, 1853; aux. bp. Cincinnati (Pompeiopolis), 1862-68; first bp. Columbus, 1868-78.

Rouxel, Gustave A. (1840-1908): b. France; ord. Nov. 4, 1863; aux. bp. New Orleans (Curium), 1899-1908.

Rummel, Joseph (1876-1964): b. Germany;

ord. May 24, 1902; bp. Omaha, 1928-35; abp. New Orleans, 1935-64.

Russell, William T. (1863-1927): ord. June 21, 1889; bp. Charleston, 1917-27.

Ryan, Edward F. (1879-1956): ord. Aug. 10, 1905; bp. Burlington, 1945-56.

Ryan, James (1848-1923): b. Ireland; ord. Dec. 24, 1871; bp. Alton (now Springfield), Ill., 1888-1923.

Ryan, James H. (1886-1947): ord. June 5, 1909; rector Catholic University, 1928-35; tit. bp. Modra, 1933-35; bp., 1935-45, and first abp. Omaha, 1945-47.

Ryan, Patrick J. (1831-1911): b. Ireland; ord. Sept. 8, 1853; coad. bp. St. Louis (Tricomia), 1872-84; abp. Philadelphia, 1884-1911.

Ryan, Stephen, C. M. (1826-1896): b. Canada; ord. June 24, 1849; bp. Buffalo, 1868-96.

Ryan, Vincent J. (1884-1951): ord. June 7, 1912; bp. Bismarck, 1940-51.

S

Salpointe, John B. (1825-1898): b. France; ord. Dec. 20, 1851; v.a. Arizona (Dorylaeum), 1869-84; coad. abp. Santa Fe (Anazarbus), 1884-85; abp. Santa Fe, 1885-94 (res.).

Scanlan, Lawrence (1843-1915): b. Ireland; ord. June 28, 1868; v.a. Utah (Laranda), 1887-91; bp. Salt Lake (now Salt Lake City), 1891-1915.

Scannell, Richard (1845-1916): b. Ireland; ord. Feb. 26, 1871; first bp. Concordia (now Salina), 1887-91; bp. Omaha, 1891-1916.

Schenk, Francis J. (1901-1969): ord. June 13, 1926; bp. Crookston, 1945-60; bp. Duluth, 1960-69.

Scher, Philip G. (1880-1953): ord. June 6, 1904; bp. Monterey-Fresno, 1933-53.

Schinner, Augustine (1863-1937): ord. Mar. 7, 1886; first bp. Superior, 1905-13; first bp. Spokane, 1914-25 (res.).

Schlarman, Joseph H. (1879-1951): ord. June 29, 1904; bp. Peoria, 1930-51.

Schott, Lawrence F. (1907-1963): ord. July 15, 1935; aux. bp. Harrisburg (Eluza), 1956-63.

Schrembs, Joseph (1866-194): b. Germany; ord. June 29, 1889; aux. bp. Grand Rapids (Sophene), 1911; bp. Toledo, 1911-21; bp. Cleveland, 1921-45.

Schuler, Anthony J., S. J. (1869-1944): ord. June 27, 1901; first bp. El Paso, 1915-42 (res.).

Schwebach, James (1847-1921): b. Luxembourg; ord. June 16, 1870; bp. La Crosse, 1892-1921.

Schwertner, August J. (1870-1939): ord. June 12, 1897; bp. Wichita, 1921-39.

Scully, William (1894-1969): ord. Sept. 20, 1919; coad. bp. Albany (Pharsalus), 1945-54; bp. Albany, 1954-69.

Sebastian, Jerome D. (1895-1960): ord. May 25, 1922; aux. bp. Baltimore (Baris in Hellesponto), 1954-60.

Seghers, Charles J.: See Index.

Seidenbusch, Rupert, O. S. B. (1830-1895):

b. Germany; ord. June 22, 1853; v.a. Northern Minnesota (Halia), 1875-88 (res.).

Seton, Robert J. (1839-1927): b. Italy; ord. Apr. 15, 1865; tit. abp. Heliopolis, 1903-27. Grandson of St. Elizabeth Seton.

Shahan, Thomas J. (1857-1932): ord. June 3, 1882; rector, Catholic University of America, 1909-27; tit. bp. Germanicopolis, 1914-32.

Shanahan (brothers): **Jeremiah F.** (1834-1886): ord. July 3, 1859; first bp. Harrisburg, 1868-86. **John W.** (1846-1916): ord. Jan. 2, 1869; bp. Harrisburg, 1899-1916.

Shanley, John (1852-1909): ord. May 30, 1874; first bp. Jamestown (see transferred to Fargo in 1897), 1889-1909.

Shanley, Patrick H., O.C.D. (1896-1970): b. Ireland; ord. Dec. 21, 1930; US citizen; prelate Infanta, P.I. (Sophene), 1953-60 (res.).

Shaughnessy, Gerald, S.M. (1887-1950): ord. June 20, 1920; bp. Seattle, 1933-50.

Shaw, John W. (1863-1934): ord. May 26, 1888; coad. bp. San Antonio (Castabala), 1910-11; bp. San Antonio, 1911-18; abp. New Orleans, 1918-34.

Sheehan, Edward T., C.M. (1888-1933): ord. June 7, 1916; v. a. Yukiang, China (Calydon), 1929-33.

Sheil, Bernard J. (1886-1969): ord. May 21, 1910; aux. bp. Chicago (Pegae), 1928-69; tit. abp. Selge, 1959-69. Founder of Catholic Youth Organization.

Smith, Alphonse (1883-1935): ord. Apr. 18, 1908; bp. Nashville, 1924-35.

Smith, Eustace, O.F.M. (1908-1975): ord. June 12, 1934; v.a. Beirut, Lebanon (Apamea Cibotus), 1958-73.

Smith, Leo R. (1905-1963): ord. Dec. 21, 1929; aux. bp. Buffalo (Marida), 1952-63; bp. Ogdensburg, 1963.

Smyth, Clement, O.C.S.O. (1810-1865):b. Ireland; ord. May 29, 1841; coad. bp. Dubuque (Thennesus), 1857-58; bp. Dubuque, 1858-65.

Spalding, John L.: See Index.

Spalding, Martin J.: See Index.

Spellman, Francis J.: See Index.

Spence, John S. (1909-1973): ord. Dec. 5, 1933; aux. bp. Washington (Aggersel), 1964-73.

Stang, William (1854-1907): b. Germany; ord. June 15, 1878; first bp. Fall River, 1904-07.

Stariha, John (1845-1915): b. Austria; ord. Sept. 19, 1869; first bp. Lead (now Rapid City), 1902-09 (res.).

Steck, Leo J. (1898-1950): ord. June 8, 1924; aux. bp. Salt Lake City (Ilium), 1948-50.

Stock, John (1918-1972): ord. Dec. 4, 1943; aux. bp. Philadelphia (Ukrainian Rite) (Pergamum), 1971-72.

Stritch, Samuel: See Index.

Sullivan, Bernard, S.J. (1889-1970): ord. June 26, 1921; bp. Patna, India, 1929-46 (res.).

Sweeney, James J. (1898-1968): ord. June 20, 1925; first bp. Honolulu, 1941-68.

Swint, John J. (1879-1962): ord. June 23, 1904; aux. bp. Wheeling (Sura), 1922; bp. Wheeling, 1922-62.

T

Takach, Basil (1879-1948): b. Austria-Hungary; ord. Dec. 12, 1902; first ap. ex. Pittsburgh Byzantine Rite exarchy (Zela), 1924-48.

Thill, Francis A. (1893-1957): ord. Feb. 28, 1920; bp. Concordia (title changed to Salina in 1944), 1938-57.

Tief, Francis J. (1881-1965): ord. June 11, 1908; bp. Concordia (now Salina), 1921-38 (res.).

Tierney, Michael (1839-1908): b. Ireland; ord. May 26, 1866; bp. Hartford, 1894-1908.

Tihen, J. Henry (1861-1940): ord. Apr. 26, 1886; bp. Lincoln, 1911-17; bp. Denver, 1917-31 (res.).

Timon, John, C. M. (1797-1867): ord. Sept. 23, 1826; first bp. Buffalo, 1847-67.

Toebbe, Augustus M. (1829-1884): b. Germany; ord. Sept. 14, 1854; bp. Covington, 1870-84.

Treacy, John P. (1890-1964): ord. Dec. 8, 1918; coad. bp. La Crosse (Metelis), 1945-48; bp. La Crosse, 1948-64.

Trobec, James (1838-1921): b. Austria; ord. Sept. 8, 1865; bp. St. Cloud, 1897-1914 (res.).

Tuigg, John (1820-1889): b. Ireland; ord. May 14, 1850; bp. Pittsburgh, 1876-89.

Turner, William (1871-1936): b. Ireland; ord. Aug. 13, 1893; bp. Buffalo, 1919-36.

Tyler, William (1806-1849): ord. June 3, 1829; first bp. Hartford, 1844-49.

V

Van de Velde, James O., S.J. (1795-1855): b. Belgium; ord. Sept. 16, 1827; bp. Chicago, 1849-53; bp. Natchez, 1853-55.

Van de Ven, Cornelius (1865-1932): b. Holland; ord. May 31, 1890; bp. Natchitoches (title changed to Alexandria in 1910), 1904-32.

Van de Vyver, Augustine (1844-1911): b. Belgium; ord. July 24, 1870; bp. Richmond, 1889-1911.

Verdaguer, Peter (1835-1911): b. Spain; ord. Dec. 12, 1862; v. a. Brownsville (Aulon), 1890-1911.

Vehr, Urban J. (1891-1973): ord. May 29, 1915; bp. 1931-41, and first abp. Denver, 1941-67 (res.).

Verot, Augustin, S.S. (1805-1876): b. France; ord. Sept. 20, 1828; v. a. Florida (Danaba), 1858-61; bp. Savannah, 1861-70; bp. St. Augustine, 1870-76.

Vertin, John (1844-1899): b. Austria; ord. Aug. 31, 1866; bp. Sault Ste. Marie and Marquette (now Marquette), 1879-99.

Wade, Thomas, S. M. (1893-1969): ord. June 15, 1922; v. a. Northern Solomons (Barbalissus), 1930-69.

Wadhams, Edgar (1817-1891): convert, 1846; ord. Jan. 15, 1850; first bp. Ogdensburg, 1872-91.

Walsh, Emmet (1892-1968): ord. Jan. 15, 1916; bp. Charleston, 1927-49; coad. bp. Youngstown (Rhaedestus), 1949-52; bp. Youngstown, 1952-68.

Walsh, James A., M.M. (1867-1936): ord. May 20, 1892; co-founder with Thomas F. Price of Maryknoll, first US-established foreign mission society and first sponsor of a US foreign mission seminary; superior of Maryknoll, 1911-36; tit. bp. Syene, 1933-36.

Walsh, Louis S. (1858-1924): ord. Dec. 23, 1882; bp. Portland, Me., 1906-24.

Walsh, Thomas J. (1873-1952): ord. Jan. 27, 1900; bp. Trenton, 1918-28; bp., 1928-37, and first abp., 1937-52, Newark.

Ward, John (1857-1929): ord. July 17, 1884; bp. Leavenworth (now Kansas), 1910-29.

Watterson, John A. (1844-1899): ord. Aug. 9, 1868; bp. Columbus, 1880-99.

Wehrle, Vincent, O.S.B. (1855-1941): b. Switzerland; ord. Apr. 23, 1882; first bp. Bismarck, 1910-39 (res.).

Welch, Thomas A. (1884-1959): ord. June 11, 1909; bp. Duluth, 1925-59.

Whelan, James, O. P. (1822-1878): b. Ireland; ord. Aug. 2, 1846; coad. bp. Nashville (Marcopolis), 1859-60; bp. Nashville, 1860-64 (res.).

Whelan, Richard V. (1809-1874): ord. May 1, 1831; bp. Richmond, 1841-50; bp. Wheeling, 1850-74.

White, Charles (1879-1955): ord. Sept. 24, 1910; bp. Spokane, 1927-55.

Whitfield, James (1770-1834): b. England; ord. July 24, 1809; coad. bp. Baltimore (Apollonia), 1828; abp. Baltimore, 1828-34.

Wigger, Winand (1841-1901): ord. June 10, 1865; bp. Newark, 1881-1901.

Willging, Joseph C. (1884-1959): ord. June 20, 1908; first bp. Pueblo, 1942-59.

Williams, John J. (1822-1907): ord. May 17, 1845; bp., 1866-75, and first abp., 1875-1907, Boston.

Willinger, Aloysius J., C.SS.R. (1886-1973): ord. July 2, 1911; bp. Ponce, P.R., 1929-46; coad. bp. Monterey-Fresno, 1946-53; bp. Monterey-Fresno, 1953-67 (res.).

Winkelmann, Christian H. (1883-1946): ord. June 11, 1907; aux. bp. St. Louis (Sita), 1933-39; bp. Wichita, 1939-46.

Wood, James F. (1813-1883): convert, 1836; ord. Mar. 25, 1844; coad. bp. Philadelphia (Antigonea), 1857-60; bp., 1860-75, and first abp., 1875-83, Philadelphia.

Woznicki, Stephen (1894-1968): ord. Dec. 22, 1917; aux. bp. Detroit (Peltae), 1938-50; bp. Saginaw, 1950-68.

Young, Josue (1808-1866): ord. Apr. 1, 1838; bp. Pittsburgh, 1853-54; bp. Erie, 1854-66.

Zardetti, Otto (1847-1902): b. Switzerland; ord. Aug. 21, 1870; first bp. St. Cloud, 1889-94; abp. Bucharest, Rumania, 1894-95 (res.).

Religious

Religious orders and congregations, collectively called **religious institutes,** are special societies in the Church. Their members, called **religious,** live a community kind of life according to rules and constitutions approved by Church authority and strive for Christian perfection not only by fulfilling the obligations common to all the faithful but also through the profession and observance of public vows of obedience, chastity and poverty. In church law, their way of life is called the state of perfection or the religious life.

Religious Institutes

The particular goal of each institute and the means of realizing it in practice are stated in the rule and constitutions proper to the institute. Local bishops, with permission of the Holy See, can give approval for rules and constitutions of **institutes of diocesan rank.** Pontifical rank belongs to institutes approved by the Holy See. General jurisdiction over all religious is exercised by the Congregation for Religious and Secular Institutes. General legislation concerning religious is contained in Canons 487 to 681 of the Code of Canon Law and in subsequent enactments, especially since the Second Vatican Council.

All religious institutes are commonly called religious orders, despite the fact that there are differences between orders and congregations. The best known **orders** include the Benedictines, Trappists, Franciscans, Dominicans, Carmelites and Augustinians, for men; and the Carmelites, Poor Clares, Dominicans of the Second Order and Visitation Nuns, for women. Members of the orders have solemn vows; their communities have papal enclosure and exemption, and are bound to perform the Liturgy of the Hours (Divine Office) in choir as a common practice. Members of the **congregations** have simple vows. The orders are older than the congregations, which did not appear until the 16th century.

Contemplative institutes devote themselves exclusively to divine worship by prayer, penance and other spiritual exercises in a life of retirement. They do not engage in the active ministry. Examples are the Trappists and Carthusians, the Carmelite and Poor Clare nuns. **Active institutes** are geared primarily for the ministry and many kinds of apostolic work. **Mixed institutes** combine elements of the contemplative and active ways of life. While most institutes of men and women can be classified as active, all of them have some contemplative aspects.

Historical Development

The basis of the life of religious institutes was the invitation Christ extended to men (Mt. 19:16ff.) to follow him with special dedication in a life like his own, which was that of a poor and chaste man under obedience to the Father.

In the earliest years of Christianity, some men and women dedicated themselves to the service of God in a special manner. Among them were holy women, deaconesses and virgins mentioned in the Acts of the Apostles, and confessors and ascetics like St. Clement of Rome, St. Ignatius of Antioch and St. Polycarp.

In the third and fourth centuries, there were traces of a kind of religious profession, and the root idea of the life began to produce significant results in the solitary and community hermitages of Egypt and Syria under the inspiration of men like St. Paul of Thebes, St. Anthony the Abbot and St. Pachomius.

St. Basil, "Father of Monasticism in the East," exerted a deep and still continuing influence on the development of religious life among men and women. His opposite number in the West aas St. Benedict, whose rule or counsels, dating from about 530, set the pattern of monastic life for men and women which prevailed for nearly six centuries and which still endures. Before his time, St. Augustine framed guidelines for community life which are still being followed by some men and women religious.

Mendicant orders, whose members were freer than the monks for works of the active ministry, made their appearance early in the 13th century and began to change some of the established aspects of religious life. Religious women, however, continued to live in the monastic manner.

A significant change in religious life developed in the 16th century when several communities of men with simple rather than solemn vows were approved; among them were **clerics regular** like the Jesuits and Barnabites. Some of these communities are considered to be orders, although they differ in some respects from the older orders.

The Sisters of Charity, in 1633, were the first community of women with simple vows to gain Church approval. Since that time, the number and variety of female communities have greatly increased. Women religious, no longer restricted to the hidden life of prayer, became engaged in many kinds of work including education, health and social service, and missionary endeavor.

Clerical communities of men—i. e., those whose membership is predominantly composed of priests — are similarly active in many types of work. Their distinctive fields are education, home and foreign missions, retreats, special assignments and the communications media, as well as the internal life and conduct of their own communities. They also engage in the ordinary pastoral ministry which is the principal work of diocesan or secular priests.

They are generally called **regular clergy** because of the rule of life (*regula* in Latin) they follow.

Non-clerical or lay institues of men are the various brotherhoods whose non-ordained members (called **lay brothers,** or simply **brothers**) are engaged in educational and hospital work, missionary endeavors, and other special fields.

Some of the institutes of men listed below have a special kind of status because their members, while living a common life like that which is characteristic of religious, do not profess the vows of religious. Examples are the Maryknoll Fathers, the Oratorians of St. Philip Neri, the Paulists and Sulpicians. They are called **societies of the common life without vows.**

RENEWAL OF RELIGIOUS LIFE

Following are key excerpts from the *Decree on the Appropriate Renewal of Religious Life* promulgated by the Second Vatican Council.

Norms

"A life consecrated by a profession of the counsels (of poverty, chastity and obedience) is of surpassing value. Such a life has a necessary role to play in the circumstances of the present age. That this kind of life and its contemporary role may achieve greater good for the Church, this sacred Synod issues the following decrees. They concern only the general principles which must underlie an appropriate renewal of the life and rules of religious communities. These principles apply also to societies living a community life without the exercise of vows, and to secular institutes, though the special character of both groups is to be maintained. After the Council, the competent authority will be obliged to enact particular laws opportunely spelling out and applying what is legislated here" (No. 1).

"The appropriate renewal of religious life involves two simultaneous processes: (1) a continuous return to the sources of all Christian life and to the original inspiration behind a given community and (2) an adjustment of the community to the changed conditions of the times. . . .

"(a) Since the fundamental norm of the religious life is a following of Christ as proposed by the gospel, such is to be regarded by all communities as their supreme law.

"(b) It serves the best interests of the Church for communities to have their own special character and purpose. Therefore loyal recognition and safekeeping should be accorded to the spirit of founders, as also to all the particular goals and wholesome traditions which constitute the heritage of each community.

"(c) All communities should participate in the life of the Church. According to its individual character, each should make its own and foster in every possible way the enterprises and objectives of the Church in such fields as these: the scriptural, liturgical, doctrinal, pastoral, ecumenical, missionary, and social.

"(d) Communities should promote among their members a suitable awareness of contemporary human conditions and of the needs of the Church. . . .

"(e) Since the religious life is intended above all else to lead those who embrace it to an imitation of Christ and to union with God through the profession of the evangelical counsels, the fact must be honestly faced that even the most desirable changes made on behalf of contemporary needs will fail of their purpose unless a renewal of spirit gives life to them. Indeed such an interior renewal must always be accorded the leading role even in the promotion of external works" (No. 2).

"The manner of living, praying, and working should be suitably adapted to the physical and psychological conditions of today's religious and also, to the extent required by the nature of each community, to the needs of the apostolate, the requirements of a given culture, the social and economic circumstances anywhere, but especially in missionary territories."

Allowance should be made for prudent experimentation in the direction of renewal and adaptation (No. 3).

". . . The hope of renewal must be lodged in a more diligent observance of rule and of constitution rather than in a multiplication of individual laws" (No. 4).

Various Communities

"The members of each community should recall above everything else that by their profession of the evangelical counsels they have given answer to a divine call to live for God alone not only by dying to sin (cf. Rom. 6:11) but also by renouncing the world. They have handed over their entire lives to God's service in an act of special consecration which is deeply rooted in their baptismal consecration and which provides an ampler manifestation of it.

"Inasmuch as their self-dedication has been accepted by the Church, they should realize that they are committed to her service as well.

". . . The members of each community should combine contemplation with apostolic love. By the former they adhere to God in mind and heart; by the latter they strive to associate themselves with the work of redemption and to spread the Kingdom of God" (No. 5).

"Members of those communities which are totally dedicated to contemplation give themselves to God alone in solitude and silence and through constant prayer and ready penance. No matter how urgent may be the needs of the active apostolate, such communities will always have a distinguished part to play in Christ's Mystical Body. . . . Their manner of living should be revised according to the aforementioned principles and standards of appropriate renewal, though their withdrawal from the world and the practices of their contemplative life should be maintained at their holiest" (No. 7).

Communities geared for apostolic action "should skillfully harmonize their observances and practices with the needs of the apostolate to which they are dedicated," with due regard for diversity (No. 8). This norm applies to monastic institutes, which should preserve their special character; to communities which "closely join the apostolic life with choral prayer and monastic observances"; and to "the lay religious life, for both men and women" (Nos. 9 and 10).

[See Secular Institutes for a quotation from the decree on the subject.]

The Vows, Authority

"That chastity which is practiced 'on behalf of the heavenly Kingdom' (Mt. 19:12), and which religious profess, deserves to be esteemed as a surpassing gift of grace. For it liberates the human heart in a unique way (cf. 1 Cor. 7:32-35) and causes it to burn with greater love for God and all mankind. It is, therefore an outstanding token of heavenly riches, and also a most suitable way for religious to spend themselves readily in God's service and in works of the apostolate. . . .

"Since the observance of total continence intimately involves the deeper inclinations of human nature, candidates should not undertake the profession of chastity nor be admitted to its profession except after a truly adequate testing period and only if they have the needed degree of psychological and emotional maturity" (No. 12).

"Poverty voluntarily embraced in imitation of Christ provides a witness which is highly esteemed, especially today. Let religious painstakingly cultivate such poverty, and give it new expressions if need be. . . .

". . . Members of a community ought to be poor in both fact and spirit, and have their treasures in heaven (cf. Mt. 6:20).

". . . Communities as such should aim at giving a kind of corporate witness to their own poverty. . . .

"To the degree that their rules and constitutions permit, religious communities can rightly possess whatever is necessary for their temporal life and their mission. Still, let them avoid every appearance of luxury, of excessive wealth, and accumulation of possessions" (No. 13).

"Through the profession of obedience, religious offer to God a total dedication of their own wills as a sacrifice of themselves; they thereby unite themselves with greater steadiness and security to the saving will of God. . . . Under the influence of the Holy Spirit, religious submit themselves to their superiors, whom faith presents as God's representatives, and through whom they are guided into the service of all their brothers in Christ. . . . In this way . . . religious assume a firmer commitment to the ministry of the Church and labor to achieve the mature measure of the fullness of Christ (cf. Eph. 4:13).

"Therefore, in a spirit of faith and of love for God's will, let religious show humble obedience to their superiors in accord with the norms of the rule and constitution. . . . Let them bring to the execution of commands and to the discharge of assignments entrusted to them the resources of their minds and wills, and their gifts of nature and grace. Lived in this manner, religious obedience will not diminish the dignity of the human person but will rather lead it to maturity in consequence of that enlarged freedom which belongs to the sons of God.

". . . Each superior should himself be docile to God's will in the exercise of his office. Let him use his authority in a spirit of service for the brethren. . . . Governing his subjects as God's own sons, and with regard for their human personality, a superior will make it easier for them to obey gladly. Therefore he must make a special point of leaving them appropriately free with respect to the sacrament of penance and direction of conscience. Let him give the kind of leadership which will encourage religious to bring an active and responsible obedience to the offices they shoulder and the activities they undertake. Therefore a superior should listen willingly to his subjects and encourage them to make a personal contribution to the welfare of the community and of the Church. Not to be weakened, however, is the superior's authority to decide what must be done and to require the doing of it.

"Let chapters and councils faithfully acquit themselves of the governing role given to them; each should express in its own way the fact that all members of the community have a share in the welfare of the whole community and a responsibility for it" (No. 14).

MORE SISTERS STAYING

Part of a study conducted under the auspices of the National Sisters Vocation Conference indicated that, although the number of women entering religious life declined between 1965 and 1971, the percentage of those remaining was higher. The study of 1,402 women was published in February, 1975, under the title, "Women Who Have Left Religious Communities: A Study in Role Stress."

Sister Mary Cathleen Toomey, head of the conference, said the retention rate had increased for three principal reasons: the greater maturity of those entering religious life, greater individualization of formation and apostolic programs in the communities, and greater authenticity (less regard for peripheral concerns) in religious life.

RELIGIOUS INSTITUTES OF MEN IN THE UNITED STATES

(Sources: Catholic Almanac survey; *Official Catholic Directory*.)

African Missions, Society of, S.M.A.: Founded 1856, at Lyons, France, by Bishop Melchior de Marion Bressilac. General motherhouse, Rome, Italy; American provincialate, 23 Bliss Ave., Tenafly, N.J. 07670. Missionary work in West Africa, Bahama Islands and inner city parishes.

Assumptionists (Augustinians of the Assumption), AA.: Founded 1845, at Nimes, France, by Rev. Emmanuel d'Alzon; in US, 1946. General motherhouse, Rome, Italy; US province, 329 W. 108th St., New York, N.Y. 10025. Educational, parochial, ecumenical, retreat, foreign mission work.

Atonement, Franciscan Friars of the, S.A.: Founded as an Anglican Franciscan community in 1898 at Garrison, N.Y., by Rev. Paul Wattson. Community corporately received into the Catholic Church in 1909. Motherhouse, Graymoor Christian Unity Center, Garrison N.Y. 10014. Ecumenical, mission, retreat and charitable works.

Augustinians (Order of St. Augustine), O.S.A.: Established canonically in 1256 by Pope Alexander IV; in US, 1796. General motherhouse, Rome, Italy.

St. Thomas of Villanova Province (1796), Villanova, Pa. 19085.

Our Mother of Good Counsel Province (1941), Tolentine Center, 20300 Governors Hwy., Olympia Fields, Ill. 60461.

St. Augustine Province, 3604 Beyer Blvd., San Ysidro, Calif. 92173.

Our Mother of Good Counsel Vice-Province, St. Augustine Priory, Richland, N.J. 08350.

Augustinian Recollects, O.A.R.: Founded 1588; in US, 1944. General motherhouse, Rome, Italy; US provincial residence, 57 Ridgeway Ave., West Orange, N.J. 07052. Missionary, parochial, education work.

Barnabites (Clerics Regular of St. Paul), C.R.S.P.: Founded 1530, in Milan, Italy, by St. Anthony M. Zaccaria. Generalate, Rome, Italy; American headquarters, 40 Agassiz Circle, Buffalo, N.Y. 14214. Parochial, educational, mission work.

Basil the Great, Order of St. (Ukrainian), O.S.B.M.: General motherhouse, Rome, Italy; US province, 31-12 30th St., Long Island City, N.Y. 11106. Parochial work among Byzantine Ukrainian Rite Catholics.

Basilian Fathers (Congregation of the Priests of St. Basil), C.S.B.: Founded 1822, at Annonay, France. General motherhouse, 20 Humewood Dr., Toronto, Ont. M6C 2W2, Canada. Educational, parochial work.

Basilian Salvatorian Fathers: Founded 1684, at Saida, Lebanon, by Eftimios Saifi; in US, 1953. General motherhouse, Saida, Lebanon; American headquarters, East and Pleasant Sts., Methuen, Mass. 01844. Educa-

tional, parochial work among Eastern Rite peoples.

Benedictines (Order of St. Benedict), O.S.B.: Founded 529, in Italy, by St. Benedict of Nursia; in US, 1846.

American Cassinese Federation (1855), Rt. Rev. Martin Burne, O.S.B., pres., St. Mary's Abbey, Morristown, N.J. 07960. 16 abbeys, 2 priories and 2 monasteries in the US.

Benedictine Federation of the Americas (formerly Swiss-American Congregation) (1870), Rt. Rev. David Melancon, O.S.B., pres., St. Joseph Abbey, St. Benedict, La. 70457. 12 abbeys, 1 priory in US.

English Benedictine Congregation: St. Anselm's Abbey, S. Dakota Ave. and 14th St. N.E., Washington, D.C. 20017. Abbey of St. Gregory, Cory's Lane, Portsmouth, R.I. 02871. Priory of St. Mary and St. Louis, 500 S. Mason Rd., St. Louis, Mo. 63141.

Congregation of St. Ottilien for Foreign Missions, St. Paul's Abbey, Newton, N.J. 07860; Benedictine Mission House, Schuyler, Neb. 68661.

Hungarian Congregation, Woodside Priory, 302 Portola Rd., Portola Valley, Calif. 94025.

Congregation of the Annunciation, St. Andrew Priory, Valyermo, Calif. 93563.

Houses not in Congregations: Mount Saviour Monastery, Pine City, N.Y. 14871; Conventual Priory of St. Gabriel the Archangel, Weston, Vt. 05161.

Benedictines, Sylvestrine, O.S.B.: Founded 1231, in Italy by Sylvester Gozzolini. General motherhouse, Rome, Italy; US headquarters, 17320 Rosemont Rd., Detroit, Mich. 48219.

Bethlehem Missionaries, Society of, S.M.B.: Founded 1921, at Immensee, Switzerland, by Rt. Rev. Canon Peter Bondolfi. General motherhouse, Immensee, Switzerland; US headquarters, 5630 E. 17th Pkwy., Denver, Colo. 80220. Foreign mission work.

Blessed Sacrament, Congregation of the, S.S.S.: Founded 1856, at Paris, France, by St. Pierre Julien Eymard; in US, 1900. General motherhouse, Rome, Italy; US headquarters, 184 E. 76th St., New York, N.Y. 10021. Perpetual adoration and Eucharistic apostolate.

Camaldolese Congregation, Cam. O.S.B.: Founded 1012, at Camaldoli, near Arezzo, Italy, by St. Romuald; in US. 1958. General motherhouse, Arezzo, Italy; US foundation, Immaculate Heart Hermitage, Big Sur, Calif. 93920.

Camaldolese Hermits of the Congregation of Monte Corona, Er. Cam.: Founded 1520, from Camaldoli, Italy, by Bl. Paul Giustiniani. General motherhouse, Frascati (Rome), Italy; US foundation, Bloomingdale, O. 43910.

Camillians (Clerics Regular, Ministers of the Sick), O.S.Cam.: Founded 1582, at Rome, by St. Camillus de Lellis; in US, 1923.

General motherhouse, Rome, Italy; North American province, 10100 W. Blue Mound Rd., Wauwatosa, Wis. 53226.

Carmelites (Order of Our Lady of Mt. Carmel), O. Carm.: General motherhouse, Rome, Italy. Educational, charitable work.

Most Pure Heart of Mary Province (1864), 45 E. Dundee Rd., Barrington, Ill. 60010.

St. Elias Province (1931), 69-34 52nd Ave., Maspeth, N.Y. 11378.

Carmelites, Order of Discalced, O.C.D.: Established 1562, a Reform Order of Our Lady of Mt. Carmel; in US, 1935. General motherhouse, Rome, Italy. Parochial, foreign mission work.

St. Therese of Oklahoma Province (1935), 1125 S. Walker St., P.O. Box 26127, Oklahoma City, Okla. 73126.

Washington Province of Discalced Carmelites (1947), 1810 Volney Rd., Youngstown, Ohio 44511.

Anglo-Irish Province, P.O. Box 446, Redlands, Calif. 92373.

Polish Province, 1628 Ridge Rd., Munster, Ind. 46321.

Carthusians, Order of, O. Cart.: Founded 1084, in France, by St. Bruno; in US, 1951. General motherhouse, St. Pierre de Chartreuse, France; US charterhouse, Arlington, Vt. 05250. Cloistered, contemplatives.

Charity, Servants of, S.C.: Founded 1886, in Italy, by Bl. Luigi Guanella. General motherhouse, Rome, Italy; U.S. headquarters, Don Guanella School, Sproul Rd., Springfield, Pa. 19064.

Christ, Society of, S.Ch.: Founded 1932, General Motherhouse, Poznan, Poland; US address, 6100 Dorothy Ave., Detroit, Mich. 48211.

Cistercians, Order of, S.O. Cist.: Founded 1098, by St. Robert. Headquarters, Rome, Italy.

Our Lady of Spring Bank Abbey, 34639 W. Fairview Rd., Oconomowoc, Wis. 53066.

Our Lady of Gerowval Monastery, Rose Hill, Miss. 39356.

Our Lady of Dallas Monastery, Rt. 2, Box 1, Irving, Tex. 75062.

Cistercian Monastery of Our Lady of Fatima, Hainesport, Mt. Laurel Rd. (Mt. Laurel Twp), Moorestown, P.O. 295, N.J. 08057.

Cistercians of the Strict Observance, Order of (Trappists), O.C.S.O.: Founded 1098, in France, by St. Robert; in US, 1848. Generalate, Rome, Italy.

Our Lady of Gethsemani Abbey (1848), Trappist P.O., Ky. 40073.

Our Lady of New Melleray Abbey (1849), Dubuque, Iowa 52001.

St. Joseph's Abbey (1825), Spencer, Mass. 01562.

Holy Spirit Monastery (1944), Conyers, Ga. 30207.

Our Lady of Guadalupe Abbey (1947), Lafayette, Ore. 97127.

Our Lady of the Holy Trinity Abbey

(1947), Huntsville, Utah 84317.

Abbey of the Genesee (1951), Piffard, N.Y. 14533.

Our Lady of Mepkin Abbey (1949), Moncks Corner, S. Car. 29461.

Our Lady of the Holy Cross Abbey (1950), Berryville, Va. 22611.

Our Lady of the Assumption Abbey, Rt. 5, Ava, Mo. 65608.

Our Lady of New Clairvaux Abbey (1955), Vina, Calif. 96092.

St. Benedict's Monastery (1956), Snowmass, Colo. 81654.

Claretians (Missionary Sons of the Immaculate Heart of Mary), C.M.F.: Founded 1849, at Vich, Spain, by St. Anthony Mary Claret. General motherhouse, Rome, Italy. Mission, parochial, educational work.

Western Province, 1119 Westchester Pl., Los Angeles, Calif. 90019.

Eastern Province, 400 N. Euclid Ave. Oak Park, Ill. 60302.

Clerics Regular Minor (Adorno Fathers) C.R.M.: Founded 1589, at Naples, Italy, by Ven. Augustine Adorno and St. Francis Caracciolo. General motherhouse, Rome, Italy; US address, 575 Darlington Ave., Ramsey, N.J. 07446.

Columban Fathers (St. Columban Foreign Mission Society): Founded 1918. US headquarters, St. Columbans, Nebr. 68056. Foreign mission work.

Consolata Society for Foreign Missions, I.M.C.: Founded 1901, at Turin, Italy, by Father Joseph Allamano. General motherhouse, Rome, Italy; US headquarters, P.O. Box C, Lincoln Hwy., Somerset, N.J. 08873.

Crosier Fathers (Canons Regular of the Order of the Holy Cross), O.S.C.: Founded 1210, in Belgium by Bl. Theodore De Celles. Generalate, Amersfoort, Netherlands; US province, 2620 E. Wallen Rd., Fort Wayne, Ind. 46825. Mission, retreat, educational work.

Cross, Congregation of Holy, C.S.C.: Founded 1837, in France; in US, 1841. Generalate, Rome, Italy. Educational and pastoral work; home missions and retreats; foreign missions; social services and apostolate of the press.

Indiana Province (1841), 1304 E. Jefferson Blvd., South Bend, Ind. 46617.

Eastern Province (1952), 835 Clinton Ave., Bridgeport, Conn. 06604.

Southern Province (1968), 812 Audubon St., New Orleans, La. 70118.

Divine Word, Society of the, S.V.D.: Founded 1875, in Holland, by Bl. Arnold Janssen; in US, 1897. General motherhouse, Rome, Italy.

Northern Province of the Blessed Virgin (1964), Techny, Ill. 60082.

Sacred Heart Province (Eastern Province) (1940), 1025 Michigan Ave. N.E., Washington, D.C. 20017.

St. Augustine's Province (Southern Province) (1940), 201 Ruella Ave., Bay St. Louis, Miss. 39520.

St. Therese Province (Western Province) (1964), 2181 W. 25th St., Los Angeles, Calif. 90018.

Dominicans (Order of Friars Preachers), O.P.: Founded early 13th century, in France by St. Dominic. General headquarters, Rome, Italy. Preaching, literary, scientific pursuits.

St. Joseph Province (1806), 869 Lexington Ave., New York, N.Y. 10021.

Holy Name of Jesus Province (1912), 5877 Birch Ct., Oakland, Calif. 94609.

St. Dominic Province (1873), 5375 Notre Dame de Grace Ave., Montreal Que. HAA 1L2, Canada.

St. Albert the Great Province (1939), 1909 S. Ashland Ave., Chicago, Ill. 60608.

Spanish Province, US foundation (1926), P.O. Box 277, San Diego, Tex. 78384.

Edmund, Society of St., S.S.E.: Founded 1843, in France, by Fr. Jean Baptiste Muard. General motherhouse, Edmundite Generalate, Winooski, Vt. 05404. Educational, missionary work.

Eudists (Congregation of Jesus and Mary), C.J.M.: Founded 1643, in France, by St. John Eudes. General motherhouse, Rome, Italy; Canadian province, 6125 1 ère Ave., Charlesbourg, Quebec G1H 2V9, P.Q., Canada. Educational, missionary work.

Francis, Third Order Regular of St., T.O.R.: Founded 1221, in Italy; in US, 1910. General motherhouse, Rome, Italy. Educational, parochial, missionary work.

Most Sacred Heart of Jesus Province (1910), 601 Pitcairn Pl., Pittsburgh, Pa. 15232.

Immaculate Conception Province, 2006 Edgewater Parkway, Silver Springs, Md. 20903.

Commissariat of the Spanish Province of the Immaculate Conception (1924), 205 East Jersey St., Elizabeth, N.J. 07206.

Francis de Sales, Oblates of St., O.S.F.S.: Founded 1871, by Fr. Louis Brisson. General motherhouse, Rome, Italy. Educational work.

Wilmington-Philadelphia Province (1906), 2200 Kentmere Parkway, Box 1452, Wilmington, Del. 19899.

Toledo-Detroit Province (1966), 2109 Richmond Rd., Box 3322, Toledo, Ohio 43607.

Franciscans (Order of Friars Minor), O.F.M.: Founded 1209 in Italy, by St. Francis of Assisi; in US, 1844. General motherhouse, Rome, Italy. Preaching, missionary, educational, parochial, charitable work.

St. John the Baptist Province (1844), 1615 Vine St., Cincinnati, Ohio 45210.

Sacred Heart Province (1858), 3140 Meramec St., St. Louis, Mo. 63118.

Assumption of the Blessed Virgin Mary Province (1887), Pulaski, Wis. 54162.

Most Holy Name of Jesus Province (1901), 135 W. 31st St., New York, N.Y. 10001.

St. Barbara Province (1915), 1500 34th Ave., Oakland, Calif. 94601.

Immaculate Conception Province, 147 Thompson St., New York, N.Y. 10012.

Holy Cross Custody (1912), 1400 Main St., P.O. Box 608, Lemont, Ill. 60439.

Most Holy Savior Custody, 232 S. Home Ave., Pittsburgh, Pa. 15202.

St. John Capistran Commissariat (1928), 1290 Hornberger Ave., Roebling, N.J. 08554.

St. Stephen Transylvanian Commissariat (1948), 517 S. Belle Vista Ave., Youngstown, Ohio 44509.

Holy Family Croatian Custody, (1927), 4848 S. Ellis Ave., Chicago, Ill. 60615.

St. Casimir Lithuanian Vicariate, Kennebunkport, Me. 04046.

Holy Gospel Province (Mexico), US foundation, 2400 Marr St., El Paso, Tex. 79903.

Saints Francis and James Province (Jalisco, Mexico), US foundation, 504 E. Santa Clara St., Hebbronville, Tex. 78361.

Eastern District, Commissariat of the Holy Land, Mt. St. Sepulchre, 14th and Quincy Sts. N.E., Washington, D.C. 20017.

St. Mary of the Angels Custody, Byzantine Slavonic Rite, P.O. Box 70, Sybertsville, Pa. 18251.

Academy of American Franciscan History, P.O. Box 34440, Washington, D.C. 20034.

Franciscans (Order of Friars Minor Capuchin), O.F.M. Cap.: Established in 1528 as a separate jurisdiction of the order founded in 1209 by St. Francis of Assisi; first US province established after 1873. General motherhouse, Rome, Italy. Missionary, parochial work, chaplaincies.

St. Joseph Province (1857), 1740 Mt. Elliott Ave., Detroit, Mich. 48207.

St. Augustine Province (1873), 220 37th St., Pittsburgh, Pa. 15201.

St. Mary Province (1952), 30 Gedney Park Dr., White Plains, N.Y. 10605.

New Jersey Provincial Commissariat (1918), St. Francis Friary, Newton, N.J. 07860.

California Vice-Province (St. Patrick's Province of Ireland), 1721 Hillside Dr., Burlingame, Calif. 94010.

Sts. Adalbert and Stanislaus Province (Warsaw, Poland), Manor Dr., Oak Ridge, N.J. 07438.

Franciscans (Order of Friars Minor Conventual), O.F.M. Conv.: Established in 1517 as a separate jurisdiction of the order founded in 1209 by St. Francis of Assisi; first US foundation, 1852. General curia, Rome, Italy. Missionary, educational, parochial work.

Immaculate Conception Province (1852), 812 N. Salina St., Syracuse, N.Y. 13208.

St. Anthony of Padua Province (1903), 1300 Dundalk Ave., Baltimore, Md. 21222.

St. Bonaventure Province (1939), 955 E. Ringwood Rd., Lake Forest, Ill. 60045.

Our Lady of Consolation Province (1926), Mt. St. Francis, Ind. 47146.

Glenmary Missioners (The Home Missioners of America): Founded 1939, in US. General headquarters, Fairfield, Ohio; mailing address, P.O. Box 40404, Cincinnati, Ohio 45246. Home mission work.

Holy Family, Congregation of the Missionaries of the, M.S.F.: Founded 1895, in Holland, by Rev. John P. Berthier. General motherhouse, Rome, Italy; US headquarters, 10415 Midland Blvd., St. Louis, Mo. 63114. Belated vocations for the missions.

Holy Family, Sons of the, S.F.: Founded 1864, at Barcelona, Spain, by Joseph Manyanet; in US, 1920. General motherhouse, Barcelona, Spain; US address, P.O. Box 1228, Santa Cruz, N. Mex. 87567.

Holy Ghost Fathers, C.S.Sp.: Founded 1703, in Paris, by Claude Francois Poullart des Places; in US, 1872. General motherhouse, Rome, Italy. Missions, education.

Eastern Province (1872), 915 Dorseyville Rd., Pittsburgh, Pa. 15238.

Western Province (1964), 4626 Pennsylvania St., Denver, Colo. 80216.

Holy Ghost, Missionaries of the, M.Sp.S.: Founded 1914, at Mexico City, Mexico, by Felix Rougier. General motherhouse, Mexico City; US headquarters, 4433 Santa Fe Ave., Vernon, Calif. 90058. Missionary work.

Immaculate Heart Missioners (Missionhurst), C.I.C.M.: Founded 1862, by Very Rev. Theophile Verbist. General motherhouse, Rome, Italy; US province, 4651 N. 25th St., Arlington, Va. 22207. Home and foreign mission work.

Jesuits (Society of Jesus), S.J.: Founded 1534, in France, by St. Ignatius Loyola; in US, 1833. Generalate, Rome, Italy. Missionary, educational, literary work.

Maryland Province (1833), 5704 Roland Ave., Baltimore, Md. 21210.

New York Province (1943), 501 E. Fordham Rd., Bronx, N.Y. 10458.

Missouri Province (1863), 4511 W. Pine Blvd., St. Louis, Mo. 63108.

New Orleans Province (1907), 6301 Strafford Pl., P.O. Box 6378, New Orleans, La. 70174.

California Province (1909), College at Prospect Aves., P.O. Box 519, Los Gatos, Calif. 95030.

New England Province (1926), 393 Commonwealth Ave., Boston, Mass. 02115.

Chicago Province, 509 N. Oak Park Ave., Oak Park, Ill. 60302.

Oregon Province (1932), 2222 N.W. Hoyt, Portland, Ore. 97210.

Detroit Province (1955), 602 Boulevard Center Blvd., Cass at W. Grand Blvd., Detroit, Mich. 48202.

Wisconsin Province (1955), 2120 W. Clybourn St., Suite 200, Milwaukee, Wis. 53233.

Joseph, Congregation of St., C.S.J.: General motherhouse, Rome, Italy; US vice prov-

ince, 4706 Case Rd., Avon, Ohio 44011. Parochial, missionary, educational work.

Joseph, Oblates of St., O.S.J.: Founded 1878, in Italy, by Bishop Joseph Marello. General motherhouse, Rome, Italy. Parochial, educational work.

Eastern Province, 28 Memorial Ave., Exeter, Pa. 18643.

Western Province, 1333 58th St., Sacramento, Calif. 95819.

Josephite Fathers, C.J.: General motherhouse, Ghent, Belgium; US foundation, 989 Brookside Ave., Santa Maria, Calif. 93454.

Josephite Fathers (St. Joseph's Society of the Sacred Heart), S.S.J.: Founded 1866, in England, by Cardinal Vaughan; in US, 1871. General motherhouse, 1130 N. Calvert St., Baltimore, Md. 21202. Work in Negro missions.

LaSalette, Missionaries of Our Lady of, M.S.: Founded 1852, by Msgr. de Bruillard; in US, 1892. Motherhouse, Rome, Italy.

Our Lady of Seven Dolors Province (1933), P.O. Box 6127, Hartford, Conn. 06106.

Immaculate Heart of Mary Province (1945), P.O. Box 538, Attleboro, Mass. 02703.

Mary Queen Province (1961), 4650 S. Broadway, St. Louis, Mo. 63111.

Mary Queen of Peace Vice Province (1967), 5270 N. Lake Dr., Milwaukee, Wis. 53217.

Legionaries of Christ (Missionaries of the Sacred Heart of Jesus and the Sorrowful Virgin), L.C.: Founded 1941, in Mexico, by Rev. Maciel. General motherhouse, Rome, Italy; US novitiate, 393 Derby Ave., Orange, Conn. 06477.

Marian Fathers, M.I.C.: Founded 1673; US foundation, 1913. General motherhouse, Rome, Italy. Educational, parochial, mission, publication work.

St. Casimir Province (1930), 6336 S. Kilbourn Ave., Chicago, Ill. 60629.

St. Stanislaus Kostka Province (1948), Eden Hill, Stockbridge, Mass. 01262.

Marianists (Society of Mary; Brothers of Mary), S.M.: Founded 1817, at Bordeaux, France, by Rev William-Joseph Chaminade; in US, 1849. General motherhouse, Rome, Italy. Educational work.

Cincinnati Province (1849), 4435 E. Patterson Rd., Dayton, Ohio 45430.

St. Louis Province (1908), 4538 Maryland Ave., St. Louis, Mo. 63156.

Pacific Province (1948), Cupertino, Calif. 95014.

New York Province (1961), 4301 Roland Ave., Baltimore, Md. 21210.

Mariannhill, Congregation of the Missionaries of, C.M.M.: Trappist monastery, begun in 1882 by Abbot Francis Pfanner in Natal, South Africa, became an independent modern congregation in 1909; in US, 1920. Generalate, Rome, Italy; US-Canadian headquarters, 23715 Ann Arbor Trail, Dearborn Heights, Mich. 48127. Foreign mission work.

Marist Fathers (Society of Mary), S.M.: Founded 1816, at Lyons, France, by Jean Claude Colin; in US, 1863. General motherhouse, Rome, Italy. Educational, foreign mission, pastoral work.

Washington Province (1924), 220 Taylor St. N.E., Washington D.C. 20017.

Northeastern Province (1924), 72 Beacon St., Chestnut Hill, Mass. 02167.

San Francisco Western Province (1961), 625 Pine St., San Francisco, Calif. 94108.

Mary Immaculate, Oblates of, O.M.I.: Founded 1816, in France, by Bl. Charles Joseph Eugene de Mazenod; in US, 1849. General motherhouse, Rome, Italy. Educational, mission work.

Southern US Province (1904), Room 211, 1015 Jackson-Keller Rd., San Antonio, Tex. 98213.

Our Lady of Hope, Eastern Province (1883), 350 Jamaicaway, Boston, Mass. 02130.

St. John the Baptist Province (1921), 216 Nesmith St., Lowell, Mass. 01852.

Central Province (1924), 104 N. Mississippi River Blvd., St. Paul, Minn. 55104.

Western Province (1953), 290 Lenox Ave., Oakland, Calif. 94610.

Italian Province, US foundation, St. Nicholas Church, Palisades Park, N.J. 07650.

Maryknoll Fathers (Catholic Foreign Mission Society of America), M.M.: Founded 1911, in US, by Frs. Thomas F. Price and James A. Walsh. General Center, Maryknoll, N.Y. 10545.

Mekhitarist Order of Vienna, C.M.Vd.: Established 1773. General headquarters, Vienna, Austria; US addresses, Our Lady Queen of Martyrs Church, 1327 Pleasant Ave., Los Angeles, Calif. 90033 and Holy Cross Church, 100 Mt. Auburn St., Cambridge, Mass. 02138. Work among Armenians in US.

Mercedarians (Order of Our Lady of Mercy), O.D.M.: Founded 1218, in Spain, by St. Peter Nolasco. General motherhouse, Rome, Italy; US headquarters, LeRoy, N.Y. 14482.

Mercy, Congregation of Priests of (Fathers of Mercy), C.P.M.: Founded 1808, in France, by Rev. Jean Baptiste Rauzan; in US, 1839. General motherhouse, Cold Spring, N.Y. 10516. Mission work.

Mill Hill Missionaries (St. Joseph's Society for Foreign Missions), M.H.M.: Founded 1866, in England, by Cardinal Vaughan; in US, 1951. General motherhouse, London, England; American headquarters, Albany, N.Y. 12203.

Missionaries of the Holy Apostles, M.Ss.A.: Founded 1962, Washington, D.C., by Eusebe M. Menard. General headquarters, 1335 Quincy St. N.E., Washington, D.C. 20017.

Missionary Fathers of St. Charles, Congregation of the, C.S.: Founded 1887, at Piacenza, Italy, by Bishop John Baptist Scalabrini. General motherhouse, Rome, Italy.

St. Charles Borromeo Province (1888), 27 Carmine St., New York, N.Y. 10014.

St. John Baptist Province (1903), 546 N. East Ave., Oak Park, Ill. 60302.

Monks of the Brotherhood of St. Francis (Monks of New Skete, Byzantine Rite): Founded 1966, in US. New Skete Monastery, Cambridge, N.Y. 12816.

Montfort Fathers (Missionaries of the Company of Mary), S.M.M.: Founded 1715, by St. Louis Marie Grignon de Montfort; in US, 1948. General motherhouse, Rome, Italy; US headquarters, 101-18 104th St., Ozone Park, N.Y. 11416. Mission work.

Oratorian Fathers (Congregation of the Oratory of St. Philip Neri), C.O.: Founded 1575, at Rome, by St. Philip Neri. Central administration, Rome, Italy; a confederation of autonomous houses. US addresses: P.O. Box 11586, Rock Hill, S.C. 29730; P.O. Box 1688, Monterey, Calif. 93940; 4040 Bigelow Blvd., Pittsburgh, Pa. 15213; P.O. Box 211, Yarnell, Ariz. 85362.

Pallottines (Society of the Catholic Apostolate), S.A.C.: Founded 1835, at Rome, by St. Vincent Pallotti. General motherhouse, Rome, Italy. Charitable, educational, parochial, mission work.

Immaculate Conception Province (1952), 309 N. Paca St., Baltimore, Md. 21201.

Mother of God Province (1946), 5424 W. Blue Mound Rd., Milwaukee, Wis. 53208.

Irish Province, US address: 3352 4th St., Wyandotte, Mich. 48192.

Mercy of God Region, 303 Goundry St., North Tonawanda, N.Y. 14120.

Queen of Apostles Province (1909), 448 E. 116th St., New York, N.Y. 10029.

Paraclete, Servants of the, s.P.: Founded 1947, Santa Fe, N.M., archdiocese. General motherhouse, Rome, Italy; US motherhouse, Jemez Springs, N.M. 87025. Devoted to care of priests.

Paris Foreign Missions Society, M.E.P.: Founded 1662, at Paris, France. Headquarters, Paris, France; US establishment, 930 Ashbury St., San Francisco, Calif. 94117. Mission work and training of native clergy.

Passionists (Congregation of the Passion), C.P.: Founded 1720, in Italy, by St. Paul of the Cross. General motherhouse, Rome, Italy.

St. Paul of the Cross Province (1852), 1901 West St., Union City, N.J. 07087.

Holy Cross Province (Western Province), 5700 N. Harlem Ave., Chicago, Ill. 60631.

Patrick's Missionary Society, St., S.P.S.: Founded 1932, at Wicklow, Ireland, by Msgr. Patrick Whitney; in US, 1953. International headquarters, Kiltegan Co., Wicklow, Ireland. US foundations: 70 Edgewater Rd., Cliffside Park, N.J. 07010; 19536 Eric Dr., Saratoga, Calif. 95070; 1347 W. Granville Ave., Chicago, Ill. 60626.

Pauline Fathers (Order of St. Paul the First Hermit), O.S.P.: Founded 1215; established in US, 1955. General motherhouse, Czestochowa, Jasna Gora, Poland; US headquarters, P.O. Box 151, Doylestown, Pa. 18901.

Pauline Fathers (Society of St. Paul for the Apostolate of Communications), S.S.P.: Founded 1914, by Very Rev. James Alberione; in US, 1932. Motherhouse, Rome, Italy; American province, Old Lakeshore Rd., Derby, N.Y. 14047.

Paulists (Missionary Society of St. Paul the Apostle), C.S.P.: Founded 1858, in New York, by Fr. Isaac Thomas Hecker. General offices, 86 Dromore Rd., Scarsdale, N.Y. 10583. Missionary, ecumenical, pastoral work.

Piarists (Order of the Pious Schools), Sch.P.: Founded 1617, at Rome, Italy, by St. Joseph Calasanctius. General motherhouse, Rome, Italy. American headquarters, 1339 Monroe St. N.E., Washington, D.C. 20017. Educational work.

Pontifical Institute for Foreign Missions, P.I.M.E.: Founded 1850, in Italy, at request of Pope Pius XI. General motherhouse, Rome, Italy; US headquarters, 9800 Oakland Ave., Detroit, Mich. 48211. Foreign mission work.

Precious Blood, Society of, C.Pp.S.: Founded 1815, in Italy, by St. Gaspar del Bufalo. General motherhouse, Rome, Italy.

Cincinnati Province, 431 E. Second St., Dayton, O. 45402.

Kansas City Province, Ruth Ewing Rd., Liberty, Mo. 64068.

Pacific Province, 24 Ursuline Rd., Santa Rosa, Calif. 95401.

Atlantic Vicariate, 65 Highland Ave., Rochester, N.Y. 14620.

Premonstratensians (Order of the Canons Regular of Premontre; Norbertines), O. Praem.: Founded 1120, at Premontre, France, by St. Norbert. Generalate, Rome, Italy. Educational, parish work.

St. Norbert Abbey, 1016 N. Broadway, DePere, Wis. 54115.

Daylesford Abbey, 220 S. Valley Rd., Paoli, Pa. 19301.

St. Michael's Seminary and Novitiate, 1042 Star Route, Orange, Calif. 92667.

Providence, Sons of Divine, F.D.P.: Founded 1893, at Tortona, Italy, by Don Aloysius Orione; in US, 1933. General motherhouse, Tortona, Italy; US address, 111 Orient Ave., E. Boston, Mass. 02128.

Redemptorists (Congregation of the Most Holy Redeemer), C.SS.R.: Founded 1732, in Italy, by St. Alphonsus Mary Liguori. General motherhouse, Rome, Italy. Mission work.

Baltimore Province (1850), 7509 Shore Rd., Brooklyn, N.Y. 21209.

St. Louis Province (1875), Box 6, Glenview, Ill. 60025.

Oakland Province (1952), 3696 Clay St., San Francisco, Calif. 94118.

New Orleans Vice-Province, 1527 3rd St., New Orleans, La., 70130.

Resurrectionists (Priests of the Congregation of the Resurrection), C.R.: Founded 1836, in France, under direction of Bogdan Janski. Motherhouse, Rome, Italy; US address, 2250 N. Latrobe Ave., Chicago, Ill. 60639. Parochial, educational, mission work.

Rosminians (Institute of Charity), I.C.: Founded 1828, in Italy, by Antonio Rosmini-Serbati. General motherhouse, Rome, Italy; US address, 2327 W. Heading Ave., Peoria, Ill. 61604. Charitable work.

Sacred Heart, Missionaries of the, M.S.C.: Founded 1854, by Rev. Jules Chevelier. General motherhouse, Rome, Italy; US province, 305 S. Lake St., P.O. Box 270, Aurora, Ill. 60507.

Sacred Heart of Jesus, Priests of the, S.C.J.: Founded 1877, in France. General motherhouse, Rome, Italy; US headquarters, Sacred Heart Monastery, Hales Corners, Wis. 53130. Educational, preaching, mission work.

Sacred Hearts, Fathers of the (Picpus Fathers), SS.CC.: Founded 1805, in France, by Fr. Coudrin. General motherhouse, Rome, Italy. Mission, educational work.

Eastern Province (1946), 3 Adams St. (Box 111), Fairhaven, Mass. 02719.

Western Province (1970), 3 St. James Pk., Los Angeles, Calif. 90018.

Hawaiian Province, Box 797, Kaneohe, Oahu, Hawaii 96744.

Sacred Hearts of Jesus and Mary, Missionaries of the, M.SS.CC.: Founded at Naples, Italy, by Ven. Gaetano Errico. General motherhouse, Rome, Italy; US headquarters, 2249 Shore Rd., Linwood, N.J. 08221.

Salesians of St. John Bosco (Society of St. Francis de Sales), S.D.B.: Founded 1841, by St. John (Don) Bosco. General motherhouse, Rome, Italy.

St. Philip the Apostle Province (1902), 148 Main St., New Rochelle, N.Y. 10802.

San Francisco Province (1926), 1100 Franklin St., San Francisco, Calif. 94109.

Salvatorians (Society of the Divine Savior), S.D.S.: Founded 1881, in Rome, by Fr. Francis Jordan; in US, 1896. General motherhouse, Rome, Italy; US province, 1735 Hi-Mount Blvd., Milwaukee, Wis. 53208. Educational, parochial, mission work; campus ministries, chaplaincies.

Scalabrinians: See Missionary Fathers of St. Charles, Congregation of the.

Servites (Order of Friar Servants of Mary), O.S.M.: Founded 1237, at Florence, Italy, by Seven Holy Founders. Generalate, Rome, Italy. General apostolic ministry.

Eastern Province (1967) 3401 S. Home Ave., Berwyn, Ill. 60402.

Western Province (1967), 5210 Somerset St., Buena Park, Calif. 90621.

Somascan Fathers, C.R.S.: Founded 1534,

at Somasca, Italy, by St. Jerome Emilian. General motherhouse, Rome, Italy; US addresses: 628 Hanover St., Manchester, N.H. 03104; Pine Haven Boys Center, River Rd., Suncook, N.H. 03275.

Sons of Mary Missionary Society: Founded 1952, in the Boston archdiocese, by Rev. Edward F. Garesche, S.J. Headquarters, 567 Salem End Rd., Framingham, Mass. 01701. Dedicated to health of the sick; medical, pastoral and social work in home and foreign missions.

Stigmatine Fathers and Brothers (Congregation of the Sacred Stigmata), C.S.S.: Founded 1816, by Ven. Gaspare Bertoni. General motherhouse, Rome, Italy; US headquarters, 554 Lexington St., Waltham, Mass. 01254. Parish work, Christian living center, information center.

Sulpicians (Society of Priests of St. Sulpice), S.S.: Founded 1641, at Paris, by Rev. Jean Jacques Olier. General motherhouse, Paris, France; US province, 5408 Roland Ave., Baltimore, Md. 21210. Education of seminarians and priests.

Theatines (Congregation of Clerics Regular): C.R.: Founded 1524, at Rome, by St. Cajetan. General motherhouse, Rome, Italy; US headquarters, 1050 S. Birch St., Denver, Colo. 80222.

Trappists: See Cistercians of the Strict Observance.

Trinitarians (Order of the Most Holy Trinity), O.SS.T.: Founded 1198, by St. John of Matha. General motherhouse, Rome, Italy; US headquarters, Park Heights Ave., Box 5710, Baltimore, Md. 21208.

Trinity, Missionary Servants of the Most Holy, S.T.: Founded 1929, by Fr. Thomas Augustine Judge. Generalate, 503 Rock Creek Church Rd. N.W., Washington, D.C. 20010. Home mission work.

Verona Fathers (Sons of the Sacred Heart of Jesus), F.S.C.J.: Founded 1885, in Italy. General motherhouse, Rome, Italy; US headquarters, 8108 Beechmont Ave., Cincinnati, Ohio 45230. Mission work.

Viatorian Fathers (Clerics of St. Viator), C.S.V.: Founded 1831, in France, by Fr. Louis Joseph Querbes. General motherhouse, Rome, Italy; US headquarters, 1212 E. Euclid, Arlington Hts., Ill. 60004. Educational work.

Vincentians (Congregation of the Mission; Lazarists), C.M.: Founded 1625, in Paris, by St. Vincent de Paul; in US, 1867. General motherhouse, Rome, Italy. Educational work.

Eastern Province (1867), 500 E. Chelten Ave., Philadelphia, Pa. 19144.

Western Province (1888), 1849 Cass Ave., St. Louis, Mo. 63106.

Utica Vice-Province (1903), 10475 Cosby Manor Rd., Utica, N.Y. 13502.

American Italian Branch, Our Lady of Pompei Church, 3600 Claremont St., Baltimore, Md. 21224.

American Spanish Branch (Barcelona, Spain), St. Peter's Rectory, 118 Congress St., Brooklyn, N.Y. 11201.

American Spanish Branch (Zaragoza, Spain), Holy Agony Church, 1834 3rd Ave., New York, N.Y. 10029.

Los Angeles Vice-Province (1958), 649 W. Adams Blvd., Los Angeles, Calif. 90007.

New Orleans Vice-Province (1958), P.O. Box 337, Beaumont, Tex. 77709.

Vocationist Fathers (Society of Divine Vocations), S.D.V.: Founded 1920, in Italy; in US, 1962. General motherhouse, Naples, Italy; US address, 170 Broad St., Newark, N.J. 07104.

White Fathers, W.F.: Founded 1868, at Algiers, by Cardinal C.M.A. Lavigerie. General motherhouse, Rome, Italy; US headquarters, 777 Belvidere Ave., Plainfield, N.J. 07062. Foreign missions.

Xaverian Missionary Fathers, S.X.: Founded 1895, by Archbishop Conforti, at Parma, Italy. General motherhouse, Rome, Italy; U.S. province, 12 Helene Ct., Wayne, N.J. 07470. Foreign mission work.

INSTITUTES OF BROTHERS

Alexian Brothers, C.F.A.: Founded 14th century in western Germany and Belgium during the Black Plague. Motherhouse, Aachen, Germany; generalate, Signal Mountain, Tenn. 37377. Hospital and general health work.

Charity, Brothers of, F.C.: Founded 1807, in Belgium, by Canon Peter J. Triest. General motherhouse, Rome, Italy: American District House, 7720 Doe Lane, Philadelphia, Pa. 19118. Charitable, educational work.

Christ the King, Diocesan Brothers of, D.D.C.K.: Founded 1961 by Bishop Albert R. Zuroweste of Belleville, Ill. General motherhouse, P.O. Box 363, Belleville, Ill. 62220.

Christian Brothers, Congregation of, C.F.C. (formerly Christian Brothers of Ireland): Founded 1802 at Waterford, Ireland, by Edmund Ignatius Rice. General motherhouse, Rome, Italy. Educational work.

American Province, Eastern US (1916), 21 Pryor Terr., New Rochelle, N.Y. 10801. 354.

American Province, Western US (1966), Brother Rice Provincialate, 1500 Benicia Rd., Vallejo, Calif. 94590.

Christian Instruction, Brothers of (La Mennais Brothers), F.I.C.: Founded 1817, at Ploermel, France, by Abbe Jean Marie de la Mennais and Abbe Gabriel Deshayes. General motherhouse, Rome, Italy; American province, Notre Dame Institute, Alfred, Me. 04002.

Christian Schools, Brothers of the (Christian Brothers), F.S.C.: Founded 1680, at Reims, France, by St. Jean Baptiste de la Salle. General motherhouse, Rome, Italy; US Conference, 100 De La Salle Dr., P.O. Box 356,

Lockport, Ill. 60441. Educational, charitable work.

Cross, Congregation of Holy, C.S.C.: Founded 1837, in France, by Rev. Basil Moreau; US province, 1841. Generalate, Rome, Italy. Educational work.

Midwest Province (1841), Box 460, Notre Dame, Ind. 46556.

Southwest Province (1956), St. Edward's University, Austin, Tex. 78704.

Eastern Province (1956), 24 Ricardo St., West Haven, Conn. 06516.

Francis, Brothers of Poor of St., C.F.P.: Founded 1857. Motherhouse, Aachen, Germany; US province, Box 120, Mt. Alverno, Fayetteville, Ohio. 45118. Educational work, especially with poor and emotionally disturbed youth.

Francis Xavier, Brothers of St. (Xaverian Brothers), C.F.X.: Founded 1839, in Belgium, by Theodore J. Ryken. Generalate, Rome, Italy. Educational work.

Sacred Heart Province, 10516 Summit Ave., Kensington, Md. 20795.

St. Joseph Province, 704 Brush Hill Rd., Milton, Mass. 02186.

Franciscan Brothers of Brooklyn, O.S.F.: Founded in Ireland; established at Brooklyn, 1858. Generalate, 135 Remsen St., Brooklyn, N.Y. 11201. Educational work.

Franciscan Brothers of the Holy Cross, F.F.S.C.: Founded 1862, in Germany. Generalate, Hausen, Linz Rhein, Germany; US region, St. James Trade School, R.R. 1, Springfield, Ill. 62707. Educational work.

Franciscan Missionary Brothers of the Sacred Heart of Jesus, O.S.F.: Founded 1927, in the St. Louis, Mo., archdiocese. Motherhouse, R.R. 3, Eureka, Mo. 63025. Care of aged, infirm, homeless men and boys.

Good Shepherd, Society of Brothers of the, B.G.S.: Founded 1951, by Bro. Mathias Barrett. Motherhouse, P.O. Box 389, Albuquerque, N.M. 87103. Operate shelters and refuges for aged and homeless men; homes for handicapped men and boys, alcoholic rehabilitation center.

Holy Eucharist, Brothers of the, F.S.E.: Founded in US, 1957. Generalate, P.O. Box 178, Cottonport, La. 71327. Teaching, social, clerical, nursing work.

Immaculate Heart of Mary, Brothers of the, F.I.C.M.: Founded 1948, at Steubenville, Ohio, by Bishop John K. Mussio. Motherhouse, 609 N. 7th St., Steubenville, Ohio 43952. Educational, charitable work.

Immaculate Heart of Mary, Brothers of Charity: Founded 1958, in US. Motherhouse, 201 Highway 60, Riverside, Calif. 92507.

John of God, Hospitaller Order of St., O.H.: Founded 1537, in Spain. General motherhouse, Rome, Italy; US headquarters, 2035 W. Adams Blvd., Los Angeles, Calif. 90018. Nursing work and related fields.

Joseph, Brothers of St., F.S.J.: Founded 1962, in US. Motherhouse, Rt. 13, Box 767, Oklahoma City, Okla. 73132.

Marist Brothers, F.M.S.: Founded 1817, in France, by Bl. Marcellin Champagnat. General motherhouse, Rome, Italy; US address, 1044 Northern Blvd., Roslyn, N.Y. 11576. Educational, social, catechetical work.

Mercy, Brothers of, F.M.M.: Founded 1856, in Germany. General motherhouse, Montabaur, Germany. American headquarters, 4520 Ransom Rd., Clarence, N.Y. 14031. Hospital work.

Mercy, Brothers of Our Lady of, C.F.M.M.: Founded 1844, in The Netherlands by Abp. J. Zwijsen. Generalate, Tilburg, The Netherlands; US region, 2336 South "C" St., Oxnard, Calif. 93030.

Patrician Brothers (Brothers of St. Patrick), F.S.P.: Founded 1808, in Ireland, by Bishop Daniel Delaney; US novitiate, 7820 Bolsa Ave., Midway City, Calif. 92655. Educational work.

Pius X, Brothers of St.: Founded 1952, at La Crosse, Wis., by Bishop John P. Treacy. Motherhouse, Box 438, DeSoto, Wis. 54624. Education, health fields, agriculture, religious education, social work.

Rosary, Brothers of the Holy, F.S.R.: Founded 1956, in US. Address, 101 Boynton Lane, Reno, Nev. 89502.

Sacred Heart, Brothers of the, S.C.: Founded 1821, in France, by Rev. Andre Coindre. General motherhouse, Rome, Italy, Educational work.

New Orleans Province (1847), P.O. Box 89, Bay St. Louis, Miss. 39520.

New England Province (1945), Pascoag, R.I. 02859.

New York Province (1960), R.D. 1, Box 215, Belvidere, N.J. 07823.

MEN SUPERIORS

The Conference of Major Superiors of Men of the USA is a consultative board for discussion of the affairs of men religious in this country, and a liaison body for establishing and maintaining contact among religious institutes and with the Holy See, bishops, diocesan clergy, and Catholic and civic associations. The conference, which was formed in 1956, was officially established Mar. 23, 1960, by decree of the Congregation for Religious and Secular Institutes.

The general objective of the conference is to promote the spiritual and apostolic welfare of religious priests and brothers in the US.

Conference membership consists of 255 major superiors of institutes with a combined total of approximately 40,000 members.

The Rev. Joseph Francis, S.V.D., is president of the conference. The executive secretary is Brother Thomas More Page, C.F.X.

The national secretariat is located at 1330 Massachusetts Ave. N.W., Washington, D.C. 20005.

The annual assembly of the conference was

held June 15 to 19, 1975, in New Orleans. "What Is the Spirit Saying to the Churches?" was the theme of the meeting.

BROTHERS' ASSEMBLY

The National Assembly of Religious Brothers was founded in 1972 as a grassroots organization open to members of all-brother institutes as well as mixed institutes of priests and brothers. It is a service organization for its members and those affected by their apostolates.

The primary objectives of the NARB are: to encourage the development of the spiritual life of all brothers; to promote increased awareness among brothers of their ministerial power for good; to provide a corporate voice for brothers in shaping the future of religious life; to heighten their concern with and involvement in the needs of the Church and society; and to further communication among brothers and provide liaison with various organizations of the Church.

Membership in the assembly is open to brothers in the U.S. and Canada.

The national office is located at 1213 Clover St., Philadelphia, Pa. 19107.

Christian Brother Robert McCann of Albany, N.Y., is president for 1975-77.

"Reconciliation" was the theme of the 1975 convention held June 20 to 23 in New York City.

MEMBERSHIP OF RELIGIOUS INSTITUTES OF MEN

Below are world membership statistics from *Annuario Pontificio, 1975,* of institutes of men of pontifical right with 500 or more members; the number of priests is in parentheses. Also listed are institutes with less than 500 members with houses in U.S.

Most of the institutes reported decreases in membership between 1973 and 1974.

Jesuits (20,604)	29,636
Franciscans (Friars Minor) (15,605)	22,897
Salesians (11,591)	18,959
Franciscans (Capuchins) (9,278)	12,688
Brothers of Christian Schools	12,641
Benedictines (7,058)	10,819
Marist Brothers	7,980
Dominicans (6,084)	7,922
Redemptorists (5,376)	7,233
Oblates of Mary Immaculate (5,086)	6,643
Society of the Divine Word (3,176)	5,301
Vincentians (4,027)	5,176
Holy Spirit, Congregation (3,400)	4,344
Franciscans (Conventuals) (2,745)	4,041
Augustinians (2,827)	3,780
Discalced Carmelites (2,485)	3,529
Passionists (2,557)	3,396
White Fathers (2,867)	3,320
Christian Brothers	3,265
Trappists (1,685)	3,090
Claretians (2,005)	3,042
Priests of the Sacred Heart (1,989)	2,826
Missionaries of the Sacred Heart of Jesus (2,025)	2,771
Brothers of the Sacred Heart (13)	2,470
Marianists (603)	2,458
Holy Cross Fathers (1,044)	2,323
Carmelites (Ancient Observance) (1,698)	2,188
Pallottines (1,433)	2,147
Marists (1,654)	2,081
Hospitallers of St. John of God (115)	1,957
Piarists (1,462)	1,861
Picpus Fathers (1,444)	1,778
Congregation of the Immaculate Heart of Mary (1,412)	1,702
Montfort Fathers (1,288)	1,616
Brothers of Christian Instruction of Ploermel	1,572
Verona Fathers (1,099)	1,569
Brothers of Christian Instruction St. Gabriel (11)	1,568
Society of African Missions (1,352)	1,553
Assumptionists (1,227)	1,500
Cistercians (Common Observance) (953)	1,459
Premonstratensians (1,182)	1,445
Viatorians (483)	1,400
Servants of Mary (989)	1,365
Augustinians (Recollects) (1,066)	1,354
Blessed Sacrament Fathers (885)	1,301
Salvatorians (848)	1,279
Pious Society of St. Paul (500)	1,200
Carmelites of BVM (674)	1,192
Mill Hill Missionaries (970)	1,117
Brothers of Charity	1,116
Missionaries of Holy Family (843)	1,115
Consolata Fathers (853)	1,089
Ministers of Sick (Camillians) (691)	1,081
Columbans (955)	1,075
Oblates of St. Francis de Sales (759)	1,052
Maryknollers (852)	1,042
Little Workers of Divine Providence (732)	1,022
La Salette Missionaries (714)	949
Canons Regular of St. Augustine	920
Franciscans (Third Order Regular) (599)	888
Mercedarians (599)	866
Legionaries of Christ (91)	856
Xaverian Missionary Fathers (609)	832
Brothers of Immaculate Conception	818
Missionaries of Most Precious Blood (629)	788
Congregation of St. Joseph (553)	773
Scalabrinians (599)	766
Brothers of Our Lady of Mercy	747
Pontifical Institute for Foreign Missions (621)	730
Paris Foreign Mission Society (711)	714
Crosier Fathers (453)	632
Sulpicians (624)	624
Brothers of Our Lady of Lourdes	590
Eudists (504)	590
Xaverian Brothers	577
Mariannhill Missionaries (324)	554
Trinitarians (394)	551

Barnabites (414)	531	Glenmary Missioners (75)	116
Servants of Charity (384)	519	Franciscan Bros. of Holy Cross (4)	104
Resurrectionists (338)	498	Basilian Salvatorian Fathers (88)	100
Congr. of St. Basil (Canada) (434)	480	Camaldolese (27)	97
St. Patrick's Mission Society (376)	467	Servants of Holy Paraclete (45)	54
Oratorians (360)	461		

Oratorians (360) 461
Carthusians (267) 450
Stigmatine Fathers (360) 449
Rosminians (313) 434
Somascan Fathers (276) 401
Oblates of St. Joseph (275) 394
Priests of the Sacred Heart
 of Jesus (326) 380
Bethlehem Missionaries (287) 372
Missionaries of Holy Spirit (195) 363
Society of Christ (217) 355
Marian Fathers (249) 346
Paulists (234) 301
Atonement Friars (133) 248
Josephite Fathers (S.S.J.) (196) 237
Vocationist Fathers (172) 235
Missionary Servants of Most
 Holy Trinity (157) 230
Order of St. Paul the First Hermit (120) . 225
Alexian Brothers 221
Sylvestrine Benedictines (143) 207
Bros. of Poor of St. Francis 170
Sons of Holy Family (132) 170
Theatines (120) 163
Brothers of Mercy 162
Josephites (C.J.) (136) 155
Priests of St. Edmund (97) 124

U.S. Membership

As of Jan. 1, 1975, there were 22,904 priests and 8,625 brothers belonging to more than 120 religious institutes of men in the United States.

Institutes reporting more than 500 professed members were: Jesuits (6,243 priests, 613 brothers); Franciscans — Order of Friars Minor (2,238 priests, 560 brothers); Brothers of the Christian Schools (1,784 brothers); Benedictines (1,731 priests, 577 brothers); Redemptorists (1,043 priests, 135 brothers); Dominicans (995 priests, 118 brothers); Oblates of Mary Immaculate (841 priests, 82 brothers); Marianists — Brothers of Mary (840 brothers, 245 priests); Maryknoll (836 priests, 119 brothers); Franciscans — Capuchins (835 priests, 196 brothers); Brothers of the Congregation of Holy Cross (747 brothers); Vincentians (738 priests, 49 brothers); Franciscans — Conventuals (670 priests, 128 brothers); Priests of the Congregation of Holy Cross (637 priests, 73 brothers); Order of St. Augustine (596 priests, 75 brothers); Passionists (560 priests, 81 brothers).

RELIGIOUS INSTITUTES OF WOMEN IN THE UNITED STATES

(Sources: Catholic Almanac survey, *Official Catholic Directory*.)

Africa, Missionary Sisters of Our Lady of (White Sisters), S.A.: Founded 1869, at Algiers, Algeria, by Cardinal Lavigerie; in US, 1929. General motherhouse, Frascati, Italy; US headquarters, 5335 16th St., N.W., Washington, D.C. 20011. Medical, educational, catechetical and social work in Africa.

Agnes, Sisters of St., C.S.A.: Founded 1858, in US, by Caspar Rehrl. General motherhouse, 390 E. Division St., Fond du Lac, Wis. 54935. Educational, hospital, social work.

Ann, Sisters of St., S.S.A.: Founded 1834, in Italy; in US, 1952. General motherhouse, Turin, Italy; US headquarters, Mount St. Ann, Ebensburg, Pa. 15931.

Anne, Sisters of St., S.S.A.: Founded 1850, at Vaudreuil, Que., Canada; in US, 1866. General motherhouse, Lachine, Que., Canada; US address, 720 Boston Post Rd., Marlboro, Mass. 01752. Educational, social work.

Anthony, Missionary Servants of St., M.S.S.A.: Founded 1929, in US, by Rev. Peter Baque. General motherhouse, 100 Peter Baque Rd., San Antonio, Tex. 78209. Social work.

Apostolate, Sisters Auxiliaries of the, A.A.: Founded 1903, in Canada; in US, 1911. General motherhouse, 689 Maple Terr., Monongah, W. Va. 26554. Educational, social work.

Assumption, Little Sisters of the, L.S.A.: Founded 1865, in France; in US, 1891. General motherhouse, Paris, France; US motherhouse, 1195 Lexington Ave., New York, N.Y. 10028. Social work.

Assumption, Oblate Sisters of the, O.A.: Founded in France; in US, 1956. US address, 1015 Pleasant St., Worcester, Mass. 01602.

Assumption, Religious of the, R.A.: Founded 1839, in France; in US, 1919. General motherhouse, Paris, France; US novitiate, 3480 W. Schoolhouse Lane, Germantown, Philadelphia, Pa. 19144. Educational work.

Assumption of the Blessed Virgin, Sisters of the, S.A.S.V.: Founded 1853, in Canada; in US, 1891. General motherhouse, Nicolet, Que., Canada; American province, North Main St., Petersham, Mass. 01366. Educational, mission, social work.

Basil the Great, Sisters of the Order of St. (Munhall Byzantine Rite), O.S.B.M.: Founded fourth century, by St. Basil the Great. Motherhouse, Mount St. Macrina. West National Pike, Uniontown, Pa. 15401. Educational, social work.

Basil the Great, Sisters of the Order of St. (Ukrainian Byzantine Rite), O.S.B.M.: Founded fourth century, in Cappadocia, by St. Basil the Great; in US, 1911. Generalate, Rome, Italy; US motherhouse, 710 Fox

Chase Rd., Philadelphia, Pa. 19111. Educational, social work.

Benedictine Nuns of the Primitive Observance, O.S.B.; Founded c. 529, in Italy; in US, 1948. US motherhouse, Regina Laudis Monastery, Bethlehem, Conn. 06751. Cloistered.

Benedictine Sisters, O.S.B.: Founded c. 529, in Italy; in US, 1852. General motherhouse, Eichstatt, Bavaria, Germany. US addresses: St. Vincent's Archabbey, Latrobe, Pa. 15650; St. Walburga Convent, Boulder, Colo. 80302.

Benedictine Sisters (Bedford, N.H.), O.S.B.: Founded in US, 1957. Regina Pacis, 75 Wallace Rd., Bedford, N.H. 03102.

Benedictine Sisters, Missionary, O.S.B.: Founded 1885. General motherhouse, Tutzing, Bavaria; US motherhouse, 300 N. 18th St., Norfolk, Nebr. 68701.

Benedictine Sisters, Olivetan, O.S.B.: Founded 1887, in US. General motherhouse, Holy Angels Convent, Jonesboro, Ark. 72401. Educational, hospital work.

Benedictine Sisters of Perpetual Adoration of Pontifical Jurisdiction, Congregation of the, O.S.B.: Founded 529, in Italy; in US, 1874. General motherhouse, 8300 Morganford Rd., St. Louis, Mo. 63123.

Benedictine Sisters of Pontifical Jurisdiction, O.S.B.: Founded c. 529, in Italy. No general motherhouse in US. Three congregations:

Congregation of St. Scholastica (1922). Pres., Sister Joan Chittister, O.S.B., Mt. St. Benedict Convent, 6101 E. Lake Rd., Erie, Pa. 16511. Eighteen motherhouses in US.

Congregation of St. Gertrude the Great (1937). St. Scholastica Convent, Fort Smith, Ark. 72901. Thirteen motherhouses in US.

Congregation of St. Benedict (1947). St. Benedict's Priory, St. Joseph, Minn. 56374. Seven motherhouses in US.

Bethany, Congregation of Oblates of, C.O.B.: Founded 1902 in France; in US, 1959. Motherhouse, Canada; US address: 4538 Lindell Blvd., St. Louis, Mo. 63108.

Bethany, Sisters of, C.V.D.: Founded 1928, in El Salvador; in US 1949. US address: 850 N. Hobart Blvd., Los Angeles, Calif. 90029.

Bethlemita Sisters, Daughters of the Sacred Heart of Jesus, S.C.I.F.: Founded 1861, in Guatemala. Motherhouse, Bogota, Colombia; US address, 330 W. Pembroke St., Dallas, Tex. 75208.

Blessed Virgin Mary, Institute of the (Loreto Sisters), I.B.V.M.: Founded 17th century in Bavaria; in US, 1954. General motherhouse, Dublin, Ireland; US address, 6351 N. 27th Ave., Phoenix, Ariz. 85017.

Blessed Virgin Mary, Institute of the (Sisters of Loretto), I.B.V.M.: Founded 1609, in Belgium; in US, 1880. US address, Box 508, Wheaton, Ill. 60187. Educational work.

Bon Secours, Sisters of, C.B.S.: Founded 1824, in France; in US, 1881. General motherhouse, Rome, Italy; US motherhouse, Marriottsville Rd., Marriottsville, Md. 21104. Hospital work.

Bridgettine Sisters (Order of the Most Holy Savior), O.SS.S.: Founded 1344, at Vadstena, Sweden, by St. Bridget; in US, 1957. General motherhouse, Rome, Italy; US address, Vikingsborg, Darien, Conn. 06820.

Brigid, Congregation of St., C.S.B.: Founded 1807, in Ireland; in US, 1953. US regional house, 5118 Loma Linda Dr., San Antonio, Tex. 78201.

Carmel, Congregation of Our Lady of Mount, O. Carm.: Founded 1825, in France; in US, 1833. General motherhouse, P.O. Box 476, Lacombe, La. 70445. Educational work.

Carmel, Institute of Our Lady of Mount, O. Carm.: Founded 1854, in Italy; in US, 1947. General motherhouse, Florence, Italy; US headquarters, 5 Wheatland St., Peabody, Mass. 01960. Domestic work.

Carmelite Missionaries, C.M.: Founded Barcelona, Spain; in US, 1962. General motherhouse, Rome, Italy; US foundation, 106 Abbey St., Winters, Calif. 95694.

Carmelite Missionaries of St. Theresa, C.M.S.T.: Founded 1903, in Mexico. General motherhouse, Mexico City, Mexico; US foundation, 704 Chenevert St., Houston, Tex. 77003.

Carmelite Sisters for the Aged and Infirm, O. Carm.: Founded 1929, at New York, by Cardinal Patrick Hayes, Motherhouse, Avila-on-Hudson, Germantown, N.Y. 12526. Social work.

Carmelite Sisters of Charity, C.a.Ch.: Founded by St. Joaquina de Vedruna. General motherhouse, Rome, Italy; US address, 19950 Anita Ave., Castro Valley, Calif.

Carmelite Sisters of Corpus Christi, O.Carm.: Founded 1908, in England; in US, 1920. US address, 21 Battery St., Newport, R.I. 02840. Home and foreign mission work.

Carmelite Sisters of St. Therese of the Infant Jesus, C.S.T.: Founded 1917, in US. General motherhouse, 1300 Classen Dr., Oklahoma City, Okla. 73103. Educational, social work.

Carmelite Sisters of the Divine Heart of Jesus, C.D.C.J.: Founded 1891, in Germany; in US, 1912. General motherhouse, Sittard, Holland. US provincial houses: 1230 Kavanaugh Pl., Milwaukee, Wis. 52313; 10341 Manchester Rd., St. Louis, Mo. 63122; 4130 Alameda St., Corpus Christi, Tex. 78416. Educational, social, mission work.

Carmelite Sisters of the Sacred Heart, O.C.D.: Founded 1904, in Mexico. General motherhouse, Guadalajara, Mexico; US motherhouse, 920 E. Alhambra Rd., Alhambra, Calif. 91801. Educational, hospital work, day nurseries.

Carmelites, Calced (Carmelite Nuns of the Ancient Observance), O. Carm.: Founded 1452, in The Netherlands; in US, 1930, from

Naples, Italy, convent. Five monasteries in US. Cloistered.

Carmelites, Discalced, O.C.D.: Founded 1562, Spain; in US, 1790. Sixty-five independent monasteries throughout the US. Cloistered.

Casimir, Sisters of St., S.S.C.: Founded 1907, in US. General motherhouse, 2601 W. Marquette Rd., Chicago, Ill. 60629. Educational, hospital, social work.

Cenacle, Congregation of Our Lady of the Retreat in the, R.C.: Founded 1826; in US, 1892. General motherhouse, Rome, Italy. US provinces: The Cenacle, Mt. Kisco, N.Y. 10549; 200 Lake St., Brighton, Mass. 02135; 513 Fullerton Pkwy., Chicago, Ill. 60614.

Charity, Daughters of Divine, F.D.C.: Founded 1868, at Chanty, Austria; in US, 1913. General motherhouse, Rome, Italy. US provinces: 56 Meadowbrook Rd., White Plains, N.Y. 10605; 39 N. Portage Path, Akron, O. 44303; 1315 N. Woodward Ave., Bloomfield Hills, Mich. 48013. Educational, hospital work.

Charity, Irish Sisters of, R.S.C.: Founded 1815, in Ireland; in US, 1953. Motherhouse, Dublin, Ireland; US headquarters, 10664 St. James Dr., Culver City, Calif. 90243.

Charity, Little Missionary Sisters of, P.M.C.: Founded 1915, in Italy; in US, 1949. General motherhouse, Rome, Italy; US headquarters, 120 Orient Ave., E. Boston, Mass. 02128.

Charity, Sisters of (of Seton Hill), S.C.: Founded 1870, at Altoona, Pa., from Cincinnati foundation. Generalate, Mt. Thor Rd., Greensburg, Pa. 15601. Educational, hospital, social work.

Charity, Sisters of (Grey Nuns of Montreal), S.G.M.: Founded 1738, in Canada; in US, 1855. General motherhouse, Pierrefonds, Roxboro 910, Que., Canada; US motherhouse, 10 Pelham Rd., Lexington, Mass. 02173.

Charity, Sisters of (of Leavenworth), S.C.L.: Founded 1858, in US. General motherhouse, Leavenworth, Kans. 66048.

Charity, Sisters of (of Nazareth), S.C.N.: Founded 1812, in US. General motherhouse, Nazareth P. O., Nelson Co., Ky. 40048.

Charity, Sisters of (of St. Augustine), C.S.A.: Founded 1851, at Cleveland, O. General motherhouse, 5232 Broadview Rd., Richfield, O. 44286.

Charity, Sisters of Christian, S.C.C.: Founded 1849, in Germany; in US, 1873. General motherhouse, Rome, Italy. US provinces: Mallinckrodt Convent, Mendham, N.J. 07945; Maria Immaculata Convent, Ridge Rd. at Walnut, Wilmette, Ill. 60011, Educational, other work.

Charity, Vincentian Sisters of, V.S.C.: Founded 1835, in Austria; in US, 1902. General motherhouse, 8200 McKnight Rd., Pittsburgh, Pa. 15237.

Charity, Vincentian Sisters of, V.S.C.: Founded 1928, at Bedford, O. General motherhouse, 1160 Broadway, Bedford, O. 44146.

Charity of Cincinnati, Ohio, Sisters of, S.C.: Founded 1809. General motherhouse, Mt. St. Joseph, Ohio 45051. Educational, hospital, social work.

Charity of Ottawa, Sisters of (Grey Nuns of the Cross), S.C.O.: Founded 1845, at Ottawa, Canada; in US, 1857. General motherhouse, Ottawa, Canada; US provincial house, 975 Varnum Ave., Lowell, Mass. 01854. Educational, hospital work, extended health care.

Charity of Our Lady, Mother of Mercy, Sisters of, S.C.M.M.: Founded 1832, in Holland; in US, 1874. General motherhouse, Rome, Italy; US provincialate, 80 Taylor Ave., East Haven Conn. 06512.

Charity of Our Lady of Mercy, Sisters of, O.L.M.: Founded 1829, in US. General motherhouse, Charleston, S. C. 29412. Educational, hospital work.

Charity of Quebec, Sisters of (Grey Nuns), S.C.Q.: Founded 1849, at Quebec; in US, 1890. General motherhouse, 3400 ave d'Estimauville, Quebec GIC 3X7, Canada. Social work.

Charity of St. Elizabeth, Sisters of (Convent, N.J.), S.C.: Founded 1859, at Newark, N. J. Generalate, Convent, N. J. 07961. Educational, hospital work.

Charity of St. Hyacinthe, Sisters of (Grey Nuns), S.C.S.H.: Founded 1840, at St. Hyacinthe, Canada; in US, 1878. General motherhouse, 665 Ste-Anne St., La Providence (St. Hyacinthe), P. Q., Canada.

Charity of St. Joan Antida, Sisters of, S.C.S.J.A.: Founded 1799, in France; in US, 1932. General motherhouse, Rome, Italy; US motherhouse, 8560 N. 76th Pl., Milwaukee, Wis. 53223.

Charity of St. Louis, Sisters of, S.C.S.L.: Founded 1803, in France; in US, 1910. General motherhouse, Rome, Italy; US provincial house, 422 Robin Ct., Cheshire, Conn. 06410.

Charity of St. Vincent de Paul, Daughters of, D. C.: Founded 1633, in France; in US 1809, at Emmitsburg, Md., by St. Elizabeth Ann Seton. General motherhouse, Paris, France. US provinces: Emmitsburg, Md. 21727; 7800 Natural Bridge Rd., Normandy, St. Louis, Mo. 63121; 9400 New Harmony Rd., Evansville, Ind. 47712; 96 Menands Rd., Albany, N.Y. 12204; 2600 Altamont Rd., Los Altos, Calif. 94022.

Charity of St. Vincent de Paul, Sisters of, Halifax, S.C.H.: Founded 1856, at Halifax, N. S., from Emmitsburg, Md., foundation. Generalate, Mt. St. Vincent, Halifax, N. S., Canada. Educational, hospital, social work.

Charity of St. Vincent de Paul, Sisters of, New York, S.C.: Founded 1817, from Emmitsburg, Md. General motherhouse, Mt. St. Vincent on Hudson, New York, N. Y. 10471. Educational, hospital work.

Charity of the Blessed Virgin Mary, Sisters of, B.V.M.: Founded 1833, in US. General motherhouse, Mt. Carmel, Dubuque, Ia. 52001. Educational work.

Charity of the Incarnate Word, Congregation of the Sisters of, C.C.V.I.: Founded 1869, at San Antonio, Tex., by Bishop C. M. Dubuis. General motherhouse, 4515 Broadway, San Antonio, Tex. 78209.

Charity of the Incarnate Word, Congregation of the Sisters of (Houston, Tex.), C.C.V.I.: Founded 1866, in US, by Bishop C. M. Dubuis. General motherhouse, 6510 Lawndale Ave., Houston, Tex. 77023. Educational, hospital, social work.

Charity of the Sacred Heart, Daughters of, F.C.S.C.J.: Founded 1823, at La Salle de Vihiers, France; in US, 1905. General motherhouse, La Salle de Vihiers, France; US motherhouse, Littleton, N. H. 03561.

Charles Borromeo, Missionary Sisters of St. (Scalabrini Srs.): Founded 1895, in Italy; in US, 1941. American novitiate, 1414 N. 37th Ave., Melrose Park, Ill.

Child Jesus, Sisters of the Poor, P.C.J.: Founded 1844, at Aix-la-Chapelle, Germany; in US, 1924. General motherhouse, Simpelveld, Holland; American provincialate, 4567 Olentangy River Rd., Columbus, O. 43214.

Chretienne, Sisters of Ste., S.S.CH.: Founded 1807, in France; in US, 1903. General motherhouse, Metz, France; American provincial house, 297 Arnold St., Wrentham, Mass. 02093. Educational, hospital, mission work.

Christ, Adorers of the Blood of, A.S.C.: Founded 1834, in Italy; in US, 1870. General motherhouse, Rome, Italy. US provinces: Ruma (P.O. Red Bud R.R.1.), Ill. 62278; 1400 South Sheridan, Wichita, Kans. 67213; Columbia, Pa. 17512. Educational, hospital work.

Christ the King, Sister Servants of, S.S.C.K.: Founded 1936, in US. General motherhouse, Mt. Calvary, Wis. 53057

Christian Doctrine, Sisters of Our Lady of, R.C.D.: Founded 1910, at New York. Motherhouse, Marydell, Suffern, N.Y. 10901.

Christian Education, Religious of, R.C.E.: Founded 1817, in France; in US, 1905. General motherhouse, Paris, France; US provincial residence, 36 Hillcrest Rd., Belmont, Mass. 02178.

Cistercian Nuns: Established in US, 1958. Motherhouse, Frauenthal, Switzerland; in US, Valley of Our Lady Monastery, Rt. 1, Prairie du Sac, Wis. 53378.

Cistercian Nuns of the Strict Observance, Order of, O.C.S.O.: Founded 1125, in France, by St. Stephen Harding; in US, 1949. General motherhouse France. US abbeys: Arnold St. (R.F.D. Box 500), Wrentham, Mass. 02093; Box 97, Sonalta, Ariz. 85637; Whitehorn, Calif. 95489; R.R. 3, Dubuque, Ia. 52001.

Clergy, Congregation of Our Lady, Help of the, C.L.H.C.: Founded 1961, in US. Motherhouse, Maryvale Convent, Maple Ave., Higganum, Conn. 06441.

Clergy, Servants of Our Lady Queen of the, S.R.C.: Founded 1929, in Canada; in US, 1936. General motherhouse, Lac-au-Saumon, Que., GOJ 1MO, Canada.

Colettines: See Franciscan Poor Clare Nuns.

Columban, Missionary Sisters of St., S.S.C.: Founded 1922, in Ireland; in US, 1930. General motherhouse, Wicklow, Ireland; US region, 950 Metropolitan Ave., Hyde Park, Mass. 01236.

Consolata Missionary Sisters, M.C.: Founded 1910, in Italy; in US, 1954. General motherhouse, Turin, Italy; US headquarters, 6801 Belmont Rd., Belmont, Mich. 49306.

Cordi-Marian Missionary Sisters, M.C.M.: Founded 1921, in Mexico; in US, 1926. General motherhouse, 2910 Morales St., Morales, Mexico.

Cross, Daughters of the, D.C.: Founded 1640, in France; in US, 1855. General motherhouse, 1000 Fairview St., Shreveport, La. 71104. Educational work.

Cross, Daughters of, of Liege, F.C.: Founded 1883, in Liege, Belgium; in US, 1958. US address, 165 W. Eaton Ave., Tracy, Calif. 95376.

Cross, Sisters of the Holy, C.S.C.: Founded 1841, at Le Mans, France; in US, 1843. General motherhouse, Notre Dame, Ind. 46556. Educational, hospital work.

Cross and of the Seven Dolors, Sisters of the Holy, C.S.C.: Founded 1847, in Canada; in US, 1881. General motherhouse, Montreal, Que., Canada; US provincial house, Pittsfield, N.H. 03263. Educational work.

Cross and Passion, Sisters of the (Passionist Sisters), C.P.: Founded 1852; in US, 1924. General motherhouse, Bolton, England; US address: Mt. St. Joseph, Wakefield, R.I. 02878

Cross and Passion of Our Lord Jesus Christ, Nuns of the (Passionist Nuns), C.P.: Founded 1771, in Italy, by St. Paul of the Cross; in US, 1910. Five convents in the US. Contemplatives.

Crucified, Augustinian Daughters of the: Founded 1840, in Italy. General motherhouse, Rome, Italy; US novitiate, 420 Lincoln Hwy., Malvern, Pa. 19355.

Cyril and Methodius, Sisters of Sts., SS.C.M.: Founded 1909, in US, by Rev. Matthew Jankola. General motherhouse, Danville, Pa. 17821. Educational, hospital work.

Disciples of the Divine Master, P.D.D.M.: Founded 1924; in US, 1948. General motherhouse, Rome, Italy; US headquarters, 43 West St., Boston, Mass. 02111.

Divine Compassion, Sisters of, R.D.C.: Founded 1886, in US. General motherhouse, 52 N. Broadway, White Plains, N.Y. 10603. Educational work.

Divine Love, Oblates to, Sisters, R.O.D.A.:

Founded 1923, in Italy; in US, 1947. General motherhouse, Rome, Italy; US novitiate, Beekman Rd., Hopewell Junction, N.Y. 12533.

Divine Spirit, Congregation of the, C.D.S.: Founded 1956, in US, by Archbishop John M. Gannon. Motherhouse, 409 W. 6th St., Erie, Pa. 16507. Educational, social work; care of aged.

Dominicans

Dominican Nuns of the Second Order of Perpetual Adoration, O.P.: Founded 1206, in France; in US, 1880. Twelve independent monasteries. Cloistered.

Dominican Oblates of Jesus, D.O.J.: Founded 1946 in Spain, General motherhouse, Madrid, Spain; US foundation, La Salette Convent, 85 New Park Ave., Hartford, Conn. 06106.

Dominican Rural Missionaries, O.P.: Founded 1932, in France; in US, 1951, at Abbeville, La. General motherhouse, Luzarches, France; US motherhouse, 1318 S. Henry St., Abbeville, La. 70510.

Dominican Sisters of Bethany, Congregation, O.P.: Founded 1866, in France. Motherhouse, France; US novitiate, 204 Ridge St., Millis, Mass. 02054.

Dominican Sisters of the Perpetual Rosary, O.P.: Founded 1880, at Calais, France. Eight independent monasteries. Contemplative.

Dominican Sisters of the Presentation, O.P.: Founded 1684, in France; in US, 1906. General motherhouse, Tours, France; US headquarters, 3012 Elm St., Dighton, Mass. 02715. Hospital work.

Dominican Sisters of the Roman Congregation of St. Dominic, O.P.: Founded 1621, in France; in US, 1904. General motherhouse, Rome, Italy; US province, 200 Ivy St., Brookline, Mass. 02146. Educational work.

Eucharistic Missionaries of St. Dominic, O.P.: Founded 1927, in Louisiana. General motherhouse, 1101 Aline St., New Orleans, La. 70115. Parish mission work.

Maryknoll Sisters of St. Dominic, M.M.: Founded 1912, in New York. Center, Maryknoll, N.Y. 10545.

Religious Missionaries of St. Dominic, O.P.: General motherhouse, Rome, Italy. US foundations: 808 S. Wright St., Alice, Texas 78332; 1123 N. Staples St., Corpus Christi, Tex. 78401; 432 N. Oak St., Santa Paula, Calif. 93060.

Sisters of the Third Order of St. Dominic, O.P.: Thirty congregations in the US. Educational, hospital work. Names of congregations are given below, followed by the date of foundation, and location of motherhouse.

St. Catharine of Siena, 1822. St. Catharine, Ky. 40061.

St. Mary of the Springs, 1830. Columbus Ohio 43219.

Most Holy Rosary, 1849. Sinsinawa, Wis. 53824.

Most Holy Name of Jesus, 1850. San Rafael, Calif. 94901.

Holy Cross, 1853. Albany Ave., Amityville, N.Y. 11701.

Most Holy Rosary, 1859. Mt. St. Mary on Hudson, Newburgh, N.Y. 12550.

St. Cecilia, 1860. Eighth Ave. N. and Clay St., Nashville, Tenn. 37208.

St. Mary, 1860. 4601 Cleveland Ave., New Orleans, La. 70119.

St. Catherine of Siena, 1862. 5635 Erie St., Racine, Wis. 53402.

Our Lady of the Sacred Heart, 1873. 1237 W. Monroe St., Springfield, Ill. 62704.

Our Lady of the Rosary, 1876. Sparkill, N.Y. 10976.

Queen of the Holy Rosary, 1876. Mission San Jose, Calif. 94538.

Most Holy Rosary, 1877. Adrian, Mich. 49221.

Our Lady of the Sacred Heart, 1877. 2025 E. Fulton St., Grand Rapids, Mich. 49503.

St. Dominic, 1878. Blauvelt, N.Y. 10913.

Immaculate Conception (Dominican Sisters of the Sick Poor), 1879. P.O. Box 231, Ossining, N.Y. 10562. Social work.

St. Catherine de Ricci, 1880. 2850 N. Providence Rd., Media, Pa. 19063.

Sacred Heart of Jesus, 1881. Mt. St. Dominic, Caldwell, N.J. 07006.

Sacred Heart, 1882. 6501 Almeda Rd., Houston, Tex. 77021.

St. Thomas Aquinas, 1888. 423 E. 152nd St., Tacoma, Wash. 98445.

Most Holy Cross, 1890. P.O. Box 280, Edmonds, Wash. 98020.

St. Catherine of Siena, 1891. 37 Park St., Fall River, Mass. 02721.

St. Rose of Lima (Servants of Relief for Incurable Cancer), 1896. Hawthorne, N.Y. 10532.

Immaculate Conception, 1902. 3600 Broadway, Great Bend, Kans. 67530. Pontifical Institute.

St. Catherine of Siena, 1911. 4600 93rd St., Kenosha, Wis. 53140.

St. Rose of Lima, 1923. 775 Drahner Rd., Oxford, Mich. 48051.

Immaculate Conception, 1929. Biala Nizna, Poland: US provincial house, 9000 W. 81st St., Justice, Ill. 60458.

Immaculate Heart of Mary, 1929. Akron, Ohio 44313.

Immaculate Heart of Mary, W. 3102 Fort George Wright Dr., Spokane, Wash. 99204.

St. Catherine of Siena of Oakford, Republic of South Africa, 1955. General motherhouse, Natal, Republic of South Africa; US motherhouse, 1855 Miramonte Ave., Mountain View, Calif. 94040.

(End, Listing of Dominicans)

Dorothy, Institute of the Sisters of St., S.S.D.: Founded 1834, in Italy; in US, 1911. General motherhouse, Rome, Italy; US motherhouse, Villa Fatima, Taunton, Mass. 02780.

Eucharist, Religious of the, R.E.: Founded 1857, in Belgium; in US, 1900. General motherhouse, Belgium; US foundation, 2907 Ellicott Terr., N.W., Washington, D.C. 20008.

Family, Congregation of the Sisters of the Holy, S.S.F.: Founded 1842, in US. General motherhouse, 6901 Chef Menteur Hway., New Orleans, La. 70126. Educational, hospital work.

Family, Little Sisters of the Holy, P.S.S.F.: Founded 1880, in Canada; in US, 1900. General motherhouse, Sherbrooke, Que., Canada. Domestic work.

Family, Sisters of the Holy, S.H.F.: Founded 1872, in US. General motherhouse, P. O. Box 3248, Mission San Jose, Calif. 94538. Educational, social work.

Family of Nazareth, Sisters of the Holy, C.S.F.N.: Founded 1875, in Italy; in US, 1885. General motherhouse, Rome, Italy. US provinces: 353 N. River Rd., Des Plaines, Ill. 60616; Grant and Frankford Aves., Torresdale, Philadelphia, Pa. 19114; 285 Bellevue Rd., Pittsburgh, Pa. 15229; Marian Heights, 1428-1, Monroe Turnpike, Monroe, Conn. 06868; 1814 Egyptian Way, Box 757, Grand Prairie, Tex. 75050.

Filippini, Religious Teachers, M.P.F.: Founded 1692, in Italy; in US, 1910. General motherhouse, Rome, Italy; US interprovincial motherhouse, Villa Walsh, Morristown, N. J. 07960. Educational work.

Francis de Sales, Oblate Sisters of St., O.S.F.S.: Founded 1866, in France; in US, 1951. General motherhouse, Troyes, France; US headquarters, Childs, Md. 21916. Educational, social work.

Franciscans

Bernardine Sisters of the Third Order of St. Francis, O.S.F.: Founded 1457, at Cracow, Poland; in US, 1894. General motherhouse, 647 Spring Mill Rd., Villanova, Pa. 19085. Educational, hospital, social work.

Congregation of the Servants of the Holy Infancy of Jesus, O.S.F.: Founded 1855, in Germany; in US, 1929. General motherhouse, Wuerzburg, Germany; American motherhouse, P. O. Box 708, Plainfield, N. J. 07061.

Congregation of the Third Order of St. Francis of Mary Immaculate, O.S.F.: Founded 1865, in US, by Fr. Pamphilus da Magliano, O.F.M. General motherhouse, 520 Plainfield Ave., Joliet, Ill. 60435. Educational work.

Conventuals of the Third Order of St. Francis of the Mission of the Immaculate Virgin, O.S.F.: Founded 1893, in New York. General motherhouse, Hastings-on-Hudson, N. Y. 10706. Educational, hospital work.

Daughters of St. Francis of Assisi, D.S.F.: Founded 1890, in Austria-Hungary; in US, 1946. Provincial motherhouse, 507 N. Prairie St., Lacon, Ill. 61540. Nursing, CCD work.

Felician Sisters (Congregation of the Sisters of St. Felix), C.S.S.F.: Founded 1855, in Poland; in US, 1874. General motherhouse, Rome, Italy. US provinces: 36800 Schoolcraft Rd., Livonia, Mich. 48150; 600 Doat St., Buffalo, N.Y. 14211; 3800 Peterson Ave., Chicago, Ill. 60645; South Main St., Lodi, N.J. 07644; 1500 Woodcrest Ave., Coraopolis, Pa. 15108; 1315 Enfield St., Enfield, Conn. 06082; Monument Rd., Ponca City, Okla. 74601.

Franciscan Handmaids of the Most Pure Heart of Mary, F.H.M.: Founded 1917, in US. General motherhouse, 15 W. 124th St., New York, N.Y. 10027. Educational, social work.

Franciscan Hospitaller Sisters of the Immaculate Conception, F.H.I.C.: Founded 1876, in Portugal; in US, 1960. General motherhouse, Oporto, Portugal; US novitiate, 300 S. 17th St., San Jose, Calif. 95112.

Franciscan Missionaries of Mary, F.M.M.: Founded 1877, in India; in US, 1904. General motherhouse, Rome, Italy; US provincialate, 225 E. 45th St., New York, N.Y. 10017. Foreign mission work.

Franciscan Missionaries of Our Lady, O.S.F.: Founded 1854, at Calais, France; in US, 1913. General motherhouse, Desvres, France; US motherhouse, 4200 Essen Lane, Baton Rouge, La. 70809. Hospital work.

Franciscan Missionaries of St. Joseph (Mill Hill Sisters), F.M.S.J.: Founded 1883, at Rochdale, Lancashire, England; in US, 1952. General motherhouse, Eccleshall, Stafford, England; US headquarters, St. Clare Convent, 4 Reber St., Albany, N.Y. 12205.

Franciscan Missionaries of the Divine Motherhood, F.M.D.M.: Founded 1935, in England; US foundation, East Greenbush, N.Y. 12061.

Franciscan Missionary Sisters for Africa, O.S.F.: American foundation, 1953. Generalate, Ireland; US headquarters, 172 Foster St., Brighton, Mass. 02135.

Franciscan Missionary Sisters of Giglio, S.F.M.G.: First foundation in US, 1961. General motherhouse, Assisi, Italy; US address, St. Hyacinth College and Seminary, Granby, Mass. 01033.

Franciscan Missionary Sisters of Our Lady of Sorrows, O.S.F.: Founded 1937, in China, by Bishop R. Palazzi, O.F.M.; in US, 1849. US address, 2385 Laurel Glen Rd., Santa Cruz, Calif. 95060. Educational, social, domestic, retreat and foreign mission work.

Franciscan Missionary Sisters of the Divine Child, F.M.D.C.: Founded 1927, at Buffalo, N.Y., by Bishop William Turner. General motherhouse, 6380 Main St., Williamsville, N.Y. 14221. Educational, social work.

Franciscan Missionary Sisters of the Immaculate Conception, O.S.F.: Founded 1874, in Mexico; in US, 1927. US provincial house, 1519 Woodworth St., San Fernando, Calif. 91340.

Franciscan Missionary Sisters of the Sacred

Heart, F.M.S.C.: Founded 1860, in Italy; in US, 1865. Generalate, Rome, Italy; US provincialate, 120 Franklin St., Peekskill, N.Y. 10566. Educational and social welfare apostolates and specialized services.

Franciscan Poor Clare Nuns (Poor Clares, Order of St. Clare, Poor Clares of St. Colette), P.C., O.S.C., P.C.C.: Founded 1212, at Assisi, Italy, by St. Francis of Assisi; in US, 1875. Proto-monastery, Assisi, Italy; twenty-four autonomous monasteries in the US.

Franciscan Sisters, Daughters of the Sacred Hearts of Jesus and Mary, O.S.F.: Founded 1860, in Germany; in US, 1872. Generalate, Rome, Italy; US motherhouse, P.O. Box 667, Wheaton, Ill. 60187. Educational, hospital, social work.

Franciscan Sisters of Allegany, N.Y., O.S.F.: Founded 1859, at Allegany, N.Y., by Fr. Pamphilus da Magliano, O.F.M. General motherhouse Allegany, N.Y. 14706. Educational, hospital, foreign mission work.

Franciscan Sisters of Baltimore, O.S.F.: Founded 1868, in England; in US, 1881. General motherhouse, 3725 Ellerslie Ave., Baltimore, Md. 21218. Educational work.

Franciscan Sisters of Chicago, O.S.F.: Founded 1894, in US. General motherhouse, 1220 Main St., Lemont, Ill. 60439. Educational, hospital, social work.

Franciscan Sisters of Christian Charity, O.S.F.: Founded 1869, in US. Motherhouse, Rt. 5, Manitowoc, Wis. 54220. Educational, hospital work.

Franciscan Sisters of Little Falls, Minn., O.S.F.: Founded 1891, in US. General motherhouse, Little Falls, Minn. 56345. Health, education, social services.

Franciscan Sisters of Mary Immaculate of the Third Order of St. Francis of Assisi, F.M.I.: Founded 16th century, in Switzerland; in US, 1932. General motherhouse, Rome, Italy; US provincial house, Box 5664, Amarillo, Tex. 79107.

Franciscan Sisters of Our Lady of Perpetual Help, O.S.F.: Founded 1901, in US, from Joliet, Ill., foundation. General motherhouse, 201 Brotherton Lane, St. Louis, Mo. 63135. Educational, hospital work.

Franciscan Sisters of Our Lady of the Holy Angels, B.M.V.A.: Founded 1863, at Neuwied, Germany; in US, 1923. General motherhouse, Rhine, Germany; US motherhouse, 1925 Norfolk Ave., St. Paul, Minn. 55116. Educational, hospital, social work.

Franciscan Sisters of Ringwood, F.S.R.: Founded 1927, at Passaic, N.J. General motherhouse, Mt. St. Francis, Ringwood, N.J. 07456. Educational work.

Franciscan Sisters of St. Elizabeth, F.S.S.E.: Founded 1866, at Naples, Italy; in US, 1919. General motherhouse, Rome; US address, 449 Park Rd., Parsippany, N.J. 07054.

Franciscan Sisters of St. Joseph, F.S.S.J.: Founded 1897, in US. General motherhouse,

5286 S. Park Ave., Hamburg, N.Y. 14075. Educational, hospital work.

Franciscan Sisters of the Atonement, Third Order Regular of St. Francis (Graymoor Sisters), S.A.: Founded 1898, in US, as Anglican community; entered Church, 1909. General motherhouse, Graymoor, Garrison P.O., N.Y. 10524. Mission work.

Franciscan Sisters of the Immaculate Conception, O.S.F.: Founded in Germany; in US, 1928. General motherhouse, Kloster, Bonlanden, Germany; US province, 291 W. North St., Buffalo, N.Y. 14201, E. Aurora, N.Y. 14052.

Franciscan Sisters of the Immaculate Conception, O.S.F.: Founded 1901, in US. General motherhouse, 1000 30th St., Rock Island, Ill. 61201. Hospital work.

Franciscan Sisters of the Immaculate Conception, Missionary, O.S.F.: Founded 1873, in US. General motherhouse, Rome, Italy; US address, 790 Centre St., Newton, Mass. 02158. Educational work.

Franciscan Sisters of the Immaculate Conception and St. Joseph for the Dying, O.S.F.: Founded 1919, in US. General motherhouse, 485 Church St., Monterey, Calif. 93940.

Franciscan Sisters of the Poor, S.F.P.: Founded 1845, at Aix-la-Chapelle, Germany, by Bl. Frances Schervier; in US, 1858. Community service center; 23 Middagh St., Brooklyn, N.Y. 11201. Hospital, social work.

Franciscan Sisters of the Sacred Heart, O.S.F.: Founded 1876, in US. General motherhouse, Mokena, Ill. 60448. Educational, hospital, mission work.

Franciscan Sisters of the Third Order of the Immaculate Conception, F.S.I.C.: Founded 1879, in Spain; in US, 1958. General motherhouse, Murcia, Spain; US foundation, 1525 N. 18th St., Philadelphia, Pa. 19121.

Hospital Sisters of the Third Order of St. Francis, O.S.F.: Founded 1844, in Germany; in US, 1875. General motherhouse, Muenster, Germany; US motherhouse, Box 42, Springfield, Ill. 62705. Hospital work.

Little Franciscan Sisters of Mary, P.F.M.: Founded 1889, in US. General motherhouse, Baie St. Paul, Que., Canada. US province, 55 Moore Ave., Worcester, Mass. Educational, hospital, social work.

Missionaries of the Third Order of St. Francis of Our Lady of the Prairies, O.L.P.: Founded 1960, in US. General motherhouse, Powers Lake, N.D. 58773.

Missionary Sisters of the Immaculate Conception of the Mother of God, S.M.I.C.: Founded 1910, in Brazil; in US, 1922. Generalate, P.O. Box 204, 662 East Dr., Oradell, N.J. 07649. Mission, educational, hospital work.

Mothers of the Helpless, M.D.: Founded 1873, in Spain; in US, 1916. General motherhouse, Valencia, Spain; US address, 432 W. 20th St., New York, N.Y. 10011.

Philip Neri Missionary Teachers, Sisters of

St., R.F.: Founded 1858, in Spain; in US, 1956. Motherhouse, Barcelona, Spain; US novitiate, Route 4, Box 131, Stuart, Fla. 33494.

Poor Clares of Perpetual Adoration, P.C.P.A.: Founded 1854, at Paris, France; in US, 1921, at Cleveland, Ohio. Five monasteries. Contemplative, cloistered, perpetual adoration.

School Sisters of St. Francis, O.S.F.: Founded 1874, in US. General motherhouse, 1501 S. Layton Blvd., Milwaukee, Wis. 53215.

School Sisters of St. Francis (Bethlehem, Pa.), O.S.F.: Founded 1843, in Austria; in US, 1913. General motherhouse, Rome, Italy; US province, Bethlehem, Pa. 18017. Educational work.

School Sisters of St. Francis (Pittsburgh, Pa.), O.S.F.: Founded 1913, in US. Provincial motherhouse, 934 Forest Ave., Pittsburgh, Pa. 15202. Educational, nursing work.

School Sisters of the Third Order of St. Francis (Savannah, Mo.), O.S.F.: Founded 1842, in Austria; in US, 1924. Provincial house, La Verna Hts., Savannah, Mo. 64485. Educational, hospital work.

School Sisters of the Third Order of St. Francis (Panhandle, Tex.), O.S.F.: Founded 1845, in Austria; in US, 1942. General motherhouse, Vienna, Austria; center and novitiate, Sancta Maria Convent, Panhandle, Tex. 79068. Educational, social work.

Sisters of Charity of Our Lady, Mother of the Church, S.C.M.C.: Established 1970, in US. Motherhouse, Baltic, Conn. 06330. Teaching, nursing, care of aged, and dependent children.

Sisters of Our Lady of Mercy (Mercedarians), S.O.L.M.: General motherhouse, Rome, Italy; US addresses: 70 Bay 47th St. Brooklyn, N.Y. 11214; St. Edward School, Pine Hill, N.J. 08021.

Sisters of Mercy of the Holy Cross, S.C.S.C.: Founded 1856, in Switzerland; in US, 1912. General motherhouse, Ingenbohl, Switzerland; US provincial house, Merrill, Wis. 54452.

Sisters of St. Elizabeth, S.S.E.: Founded 1931, at Milwaukee, Wis. General motherhouse, 745 N. Brookfield Rd., Brookfield, Wis. 53005.

Sisters of St. Francis (Clinton, Iowa), O.S.F.: Founded 1868, in US. General motherhouse, Bluff Blvd. and Springdale Dr., Clinton, Ia. 57232. Educational, hospital, social work.

Sisters of St. Francis (Millvale, Pa.), O.S.F.: Founded 1865, Pittsburgh, Pa. General motherhouse, 146 Hawthorne Rd., Millvale P. O., Pittsburgh, Pa. 15209. Educational, hospital work.

Sisters of St. Francis of Christ the King, O.S.F.: Founded 1869, in Austria. General motherhouse, Rome, Italy; US provincial

house, Lemont, Ill. 60439. Educational work, home for aged.

Sisters of St. Francis of Penance and Christian Charity, O.S.F.: Founded 1835, in Holland; in US, 1874. General motherhouse, Rome, Italy. US provinces: 4421 Lower River Rd., Stella Niagara, N.Y. 14144; 2851 W. 52nd Ave., Denver, Colo. 80221; 3910 Bret Harte Dr., P.O. Box 1028, Redwood City, Calif. 94064.

Sisters of St. Francis of Philadelphia, O.S.F.: Founded 1855, at Philadelphia, by Bl. John N. Neumann. General motherhouse, Glen Riddle, Pa. 19037. Educational, hospital work.

Sisters of St. Francis of the Congregation of Our Lady of Lourdes, O.S.F.: Founded 1916, in US. General motherhouse, 6832 Convent Blvd., Sylvania, O. 43560. Educational, hospital work.

Sisters of St. Francis of the Holy Cross, O.S.F.: Founded 1881, in US, by Rev. Edward Daems, O.S.C. General motherhouse, Rt. 1, Green Bay (Bay Settlement), Wis. 54301. Educational, nursing work; home for aged.

Sisters of St. Francis of the Holy Eucharist, O.S.F.: Founded 1424, in Switzerland; in US, 1893. General motherhouse, Ashland and Prewitt Sts., Nevada, Mo. 64772. Educational, social work.

Sisters of St. Francis of the Immaculate Conception, O.S.F.: Founded 1890, in US. General motherhouse, 2408 W. Heading Ave., Peoria, Ill. 61604. Educational, social work.

Sisters of St. Francis of the Immaculate Heart of Mary, O.S.F.: Founded 1241, in Bavaria; in US, 1913. General motherhouse, Rome, Italy; US motherhouse, Hankinson, N.D. 58041. Educational, hospital work.

Sisters of St. Francis of the Martyr St. George, O.S.F.: Founded in 1859, in Germany; in US, 1923. General motherhouse, Thuine, Hanover, Germany; US motherhouse, Alton, Ill. 62002. Social, hospital, foreign mission work.

Sisters of St. Francis of the Perpetual Adoration, O.S.F.: Founded 1863, in Germany; in US, 1875. General motherhouse, Olpe, Germany. US provinces: Box 766, Mishawaka, Ind. 46544; P.O. Box 1060, Colorado Springs, Colo. 80901. Educational, hospital work.

Sisters of St. Francis of the Providence of God, O.S.F.: Founded 1922, in US, by Msgr. M. L. Krusas. General motherhouse, Grove and McRoberts Rds., Pittsburgh, Pa. 15234. Educational, hospital work.

Sisters of St. Joseph of the Third Order of St. Francis, S.S.J.: Founded 1901, in US. General motherhouse, 107 S. Greenlawn Ave., South Bend, Ind. 46617. Educational, hospital work.

Sisters of St. Mary of the Third Order of St. Francis, S.S.M.: Founded 1872, in US. General motherhouse, 1100 Bellevue Ave., St.

Louis, Mo. 63117. Hospital, social work.

Sisters of the Holy Infant Jesus, I.J.: Founded 1662, at Rouen, France; in US, 1950. General motherhouse, Paris, France. US addresses: 20 Reiner St., Colma, Calif. 94014; St. John the Baptist School, Healdsburg, Calif. 95448; St. Veronica's School, South San Francisco, Calif. 94015.

Sisters of the Sorrowful Mother (Third Order of St. Francis), S.S.M.: Founded 1883, in Italy; in US, 1889. General motherhouse, Rome, Italy. US provinces: 6618 N. Teutonia Ave., Milwaukee, Wis. 53209; 9 Pocono Rd., Denville, N.J. 07834; Rt. 3, Box 168, Broken Arrow, Okla. 74012. Educational, hospital work.

Sisters of the Third Franciscan Order Minor Conventuals, O.S.F.: Founded 1860, at Syracuse, N.Y. General motherhouse, 1024 Court St., Syracuse, N.Y. 13208. Educational, hospital work.

Sisters of the Third Order of St. Francis, O.S.F.: Founded 1877, in US, by Bishop John L. Spalding. Motherhouse, Edgewood Hills, E. Peoria, Ill. 61611. Hospital work.

Sisters of the Third Order of St. Francis, O.S.F.: Founded 1894, in US. Motherhouse, Maryville, Mo. 64468. Hospital work.

Sisters of the Third Order of St. Francis, O.S.F.: Founded 1861, at Buffalo, N.Y., from Philadelphia foundation. General motherhouse, 400 Mill St., Williamsville, N.Y. 14221. Educational, hospital work.

Sisters of the Third Order of St. Francis (Oldenburg, Ind.), O.S.F.: Founded 1851, in US. General motherhouse, Oldenburg, Ind. 47036. Educational work.

Sisters of the Third Order of St. Francis of Assisi, O.S.F.: Founded 1849, in US. General motherhouse, 3221 S. Lake Dr., Milwaukee, Wis. 53207. Educational work.

Sisters of the Third Order of St. Francis of Penance and Charity, O.S.F.: Founded 1869, in US, by Rev. Joseph Bihn. Motherhouse, St. Francis Ave., Tiffin, O. 44883. Educational, hospital work.

Sisters of the Third Order of St. Francis of the Holy Family, O.S.F.: Founded 1875, in US. General motherhouse, Dubuque, Ia. 52001. Education, hospital work.

Sisters of the Third Order of St. Francis of the Perpetual Adoration, F.S.P.A.: Founded 1849, in US. General motherhouse, 912 Market St., La Crosse, Wis. 54601. Educational, health care.

Sisters of the Third Order Regular of St. Francis of the Congregation of Our Lady of Lourdes, O.S.F.: Founded 1877, in US. General motherhouse, Assisi Heights, Rochester, Minn. 55901. Education, hospitals.

(End, Listing of Franciscans)

Good Shepherd Sisters (Servants of the Immaculate Heart of Mary), S.C.I.M.: Founded 1850, in Canada; in US, 1882. General motherhouse, Quebec, Canada; Provincial House, Bay View, Saco, Maine 04072. Educational, social work.

Good Shepherd, Sisters of Our Lady of Charity of the, R.G.S.: Founded 1641, in France; in US, 1843. Generalate, Rome, Italy. US provinces: 9517 Leebrook Dr., Cincinnati, O. 45231; Mt. St. Florence, Peekskill, N.Y. 10566; 3601 Reservoir Rd. N. W., Washington, D.C. 10007; 7654 Natural Bridge Rd., St. Louis, Mo. 63121; 5100 Hodgson Rd., St. Paul, Minn. 55112.

Graymoor Sisters: See Franciscan Sisters of the Atonement.

Grey Nuns of the Sacred Heart, G.N.S.H.: Founded 1921, in US. General motherhouse, Quarry Rd., Yardley, Pa. 19067.

Guadalupe, Sisters of, O.L.G.: Founded 1946, in Mexico City. General motherhouse, Mexico City, Mexico; US address, St. Mary's College, Winona, Minn. 55987.

Guardian Angels, Sisters of the Holy, S.A.C.: Founded 1839, in France. General motherhouse, Madrid, Spain; US foundation, 1245 S. Van Ness, Los Angeles, Calif. 90019.

Handmaids of Mary Immaculate, A.M.I.: Founded 1952, in Helena, Montana. Motherhouse, (temporary), Marian Center, Detroit, Mich.

Handmaids of the Precious Blood, Congregation of, H.P.B.: Founded 1947, at Jemez Springs, N. M. General motherhouse, Villa Cor Jesu, Jemez Springs, N. M. 87025.

Helpers, Society of, H.H.S.: Founded 1856, in France; in US, 1892. General motherhouse, Paris, France; US motherhouse, 303 Barry Ave., Chicago, Ill. 60657.

Hermanas Catequistas Guadalupanas, H.C.G.: Founded 1923, in Mexico; in US, 1950. General motherhouse, Mexico; US foundation, 4110 S. Flores, San Antonio, Tex. 78214.

Holy Child Jesus, Society of the, S.H.C.J.: Founded 1846, in England; in US, 1862. General motherhouse, Rome, Italy. US provinces: 1341 Montgomery Ave., Rosemont, Pa. 19010; Westchester Ave., Rye, N. Y. 10580; 5905 N. Commercial St., Portland, Ore. 97217.

Holy Faith, Sisters of the, S.H.F.: Founded 1856, in Ireland; in US, 1953. General motherhouse, Dublin, Ireland; US address, 1050 N. Texas St., Fairfield Calif. 94533.

Holy Ghost, Sisters of the, C.H.G.: Founded 1913, in US, by Most Rev. J. F. Regis Canevin. General motherhouse, 5246 Clarwin Ave., West View, Pittsburgh, Pa. 15229. Educational, nursing work; care of aged.

Holy Ghost and Mary Immaculate, Sister Servants of, S.H.G.: Founded 1893, in US. General motherhouse, 301 Yucca St., San Antonio, Tex. 78203. Education, hospital work.

Holy Heart of Mary, Servants of the, S.S.C.M.: Founded 1860, in France; in US, 1889. General motherhouse, Montreal, Que., Canada; US motherhouse, 145 S. 4th St.,

Kankakee, Ill. 60901. Educational, hospital, social work.

Holy Names of Jesus and Mary, Sisters of the, S.N.J.M.: Founded 1843, in Canada; in US, 1859. General motherhouse, 1420 Mt. Royal Blvd., Outrement, Montreal, Canada; four provinces in US.

Holy Spirit, Daughters of the, D.H.S.: Founded 1706, in France; in US, 1902. General motherhouse, Bretagne, France; US motherhouse, 72 Church St., Putnam, Conn. 06260. Educational work, district nursing.

Holy Spirit, Mission Sisters of the, M.S.Sp.: Founded 1932, at Cleveland, O. Motherhouse, 1030 N. River Rd., Saginaw, Mich. 48603.

Holy Spirit, Missionary Sisters, Servants of the: Founded 1889, in Holland; in US, 1901. Generalate, Rome, Italy; US motherhouse, Techny, Ill. 60082.

Holy Spirit, Sisters of the, C.S.Sp.: Founded 1890, in Rome, Italy; in US, 1929. General motherhouse, 10102 Granger Rd., Garfield Hts., Ohio 44125. Educational, social, nursing work.

Holy Spirit of Perpetual Adoration, Sister Servants of the: Founded 1896, in Holland; in US, 1915. General motherhouse, Steyl, Holland; US motherhouse, 2212 Green St., Philadelphia, Pa. 19130.

Home Mission Sisters of America (Glenmary Sisters): Founded 1952, in US. Motherhouse, 4580 Colerain Ave., Cincinnati, O. 45223.

Home Visitors of Mary, Sisters, H.V.M.: Founded 1949, in Detroit, Mich. Motherhouse, 356 Arden Park, Detroit, Mich. 48002.

Humility of Mary, Congregation of, C.H.M.: Founded 1854, in France; in US, 1864. US address, Ottumwa, Ia. 52501.

Humility of Mary, Sisters of the, H.M.: Founded 1854, in France; in US, 1864. US address, Villa Maria, Pa. 16155.

Immaculate Conception, Little Servant Sisters of the: Founded 1850, in Poland; in US, 1926. General motherhouse, Poland; US motherhouse, 184 Amboy Ave., Woodbridge, N.J. 07095.

Immaculate Conception, Sisters of the, C.I.C.: Founded 1874, in US. General motherhouse, 5205 Avron Blvd., Metairie, La. 70002.

Immaculate Conception of the Blessed Virgin Mary, Sisters of the (Lithuanian), M.I.C.: Founded 1918, at Mariampole, Lithuania; in US, 1936. General motherhouse, Mariampole, Lithuania; US headquarters, Putnam, Conn. 06260.

Immaculate Heart of Mary, Daughters of the, I.H.M.: Founded 1952, in US. General motherhouse, Wintersville, Steubenville P.O., Ohio 43952.

Immaculate Heart of Mary, Missionary Sisters, I.C.M.: Founded 1897, in India; in US, 1919. Generalate, Rome, Italy; US address, 1710 N. Glebe Rd., Arlington, Va.

22207. Educational social, foreign mission work.

Immaculate Heart of Mary, Sisters of the, C.M.F.: Founded 1848, in Spain; in US, 1878. General motherhouse, Barcelona, Spain. US province, 35 E. 15th St., Tucson, Ariz. 85701. Educational work.

Immaculate Heart of Mary, Sisters of the (California Institute of the Most Holy and Immaculate Heart of the B.V.M.), I.H.M.: Founded 1848, in Spain; in US, 1871. Generalate, 3431 Waverly Dr., Los Angeles, Calif. 90027.

Immaculate Heart of Mary, Sisters, Servants of the, I.H.M.: Founded 1845, in US, by Rev. Louis Florent Gillet. US jurisdictions: 610 W. Elm St., Monroe, Mich. 48161; Villa Maria, Immaculata, Pa. 19345; Marywood, Scranton, Pa. 18509; 2857 Palmerston St., Troy, Mich. 48084; 8961 Laurence St., Allen Park, Mich. 48101. Educational work.

Incarnate Word and Blessed Sacrament, Congregation of, I.W.B.S., S.I.W.: Founded 1625, in France; in US, 1853. US motherhouses: 6618 Pearl Rd., Parma Heights, Cleveland, O. 44130; 4600 Bissonnet St., Bellaire, Tex. 77401; 1101 Northeast Water St., Victoria, Tex. 77901; 2930 S. Alameda St., Corpus Christi, Tex. 78404. Educational, hospital work.

Infant Jesus, Sisters of the (Nursing Sisters of the Sick Poor), C.I.J.: Founded 1835, in France; in US, 1905. General motherhouse, 310 Prospect Park W., Brooklyn, N.Y. 11215.

Jeanne d'Arc, Sisters of Ste.: Founded 1914, in America, by Rev. Marie Clement Staub, A.A. General motherhouse, 1681 Chemin St. Louis, Quebec, Canada; US novitiate, 29 Whitman Rd., Worcester, Mass. 01609. Spiritual and temporal service of priests.

Jesus, Congregation of Daughters of, F.J.: Founded 1834, in France; in US, 1904. General motherhouse, Kermaria, Locmine, France; American motherhouse, 9040 84th Ave., Edmonton, Alberta, Canada. Educational, hospital work.

Jesus, Daughters of, F.I.: Founded 1871, in Spain; in US, 1950. General motherhouse, Rome, Italy; US foundation, 115 W. 16th St., Apt. 260, New York, N.Y. 10011.

Jesus, Little Sisters of: Founded 1939, in Sahara; in US, 1952. General motherhouse, Rome, Italy; US headquarters, 700 Irving St. N.W., Washington, D.C. 20017.

Jesus, Society of the Sisters, Faithful Companions of, F.C.J.: Founded 1820, in France; in US, 1896. General motherhouse, Kent, England. US convents: 46 Woodland St., Fitchburg, Mass. 01420; 20 Atkins St., Providence, R.I. 02908; 5 Lincoln St., Centredale, R.I. 02911; Corys Lane, Portsmouth, R.I. 02871.

Jesus Crucified, Congregation of: Founded 1930, in France; in US, 1955. General motherhouse, Brou, France; US foundations: Regina Mundi Priory, Devon, Pa. 19333; St.

Paul's Priory, 61 Narragansett, Newport, R.I.
Jesus Crucified and the Sorrowful Mother, Poor Sisters of, C.J.C.: Founded 1924, in US, by Rev. Alphonsus, C.P. General motherhouse, Thatcher St., Brockton, Mass. 02402. Educational, home nursing work.
Jesus-Mary, Religious of, R.J.M.: Founded 1818, at Lyons, France; in US, 1877. General motherhouse, Rome, Italy; US province, 8908 Riggs Rd., Hyattsville, Md. 20782. Educational work.
Jesus, Mary and Joseph, Missionaries of, M.J.M.J.: Founded 1942, in Spain; in US, 1956. General motherhouse, Madrid, Spain; US regional house, 12940 Up River Rd., Corpus Christi, Tex. 78410.
Jesus the Priest, Oblate Sisters of, O.J.S.: Founded 1937, in Mexico City; in US, 1950. Motherhouse, Mexico City, Mexico; US address, La Salle Institute, Glencoe, Mo. 63038.
John the Baptist, Sisters of St., C.S.J.B.: Founded 1878, in Italy; in US, 1906. General motherhouse, Rome, Italy; US provincialate, Anderson Hill Rd., Purchase, N.Y. 10577. Educational work.
Joseph, Missionary Servants of St., M.S.S.J.: Founded 1874, in Spain; in US, 1957. General motherhouse, Salamanca, Spain; US address, 203 N. Spring St., Falls Church, Va. 22046.
Joseph, Religious Daughters of St., F.S.J.: Founded 1875, in Spain. General motherhouse, Spain; US foundation, 319 Humphreys Ave., Los Angeles, Calif. 90022.
Joseph, Religious Hospitallers of St., R.H.S.J.: Founded 1636, in France; in US, 1894. General motherhouse, 5621 Cantenbury Ave., Montreal, Que., Canada. Hospital work.
Joseph, Sisters of St., C.S.J.: Founded 1650, in France; in US, 1836, at St. Louis. US motherhouses:
637 Cambridge St., Brighton, Mass. 02135; 1515 W. Ogden Ave., La Grange Park, Ill., 60525; 480 S. Batavia St., Orange, Calif. 92666; Mt. St. Joseph Convent, Chestnut Hill, Philadelphia, Pa. 19118.
St. Joseph Convent, Brentwood, N.Y. 11717; 23 Agassiz Circle, Buffalo, N.Y. 14214; Mt. St. Joseph's Convent, Rutland, Vt. 05701; 3430 Rocky River Dr. N.W., Cleveland, O. 44111; Main St. and Division Rd., Tipton, Ind. 46072; Nazareth, Mich. 49074; 362 W. Main St., Watertown, N.Y. 13601; Mt. Gallitzin Motherhouse, Baden, Pa. 15005; 819 W. 8th St., Erie, Pa. 16502.
4095 East Ave., Rochester, N.Y. 14610; 13th and Washington Sts., Concordia, Kans. 66901; Holyoke, Mass. 01040; 1412 E. 2nd St., Superior, Wis. 54880; Pogue Run Rd., Wheeling, W. Va. 26003; 3700 E. Lincoln St., Wichita, Kans. 67218.
Joseph, Sisters of St., C.S.J.: Founded 1823, in France; in US, 1855. General motherhouse, Bourg, France. US provinces: Mary-

wood Rd., Crookston, Minn. 56716; 1200 Mirabeau Ave., New Orleans, La. 70122; 6532 Beechmont Ave., Cincinnati, O. 45230.
Joseph, Sisters of St. (Lyons, France), C.S.J.: Founded 1650, in France; in US, 1906. General motherhouse, Lyons, France; US motherhouse, 93 Halifax St., Winslow, Me. 04901. Educational, hospital work.
Joseph, Sisters of St., of Peace, C.S.J.: Founded 1884, in England. General executive office, 1330 Massachusetts Ave., Suite 101, Washington, D.C. 20005. Educational, hospital, social service work.
Joseph of Carondelet, Sisters of St., C.S.J.: Founded 1650, in France; in US, 1836, at St. Louis, Mo. US headquarters, 2307 S. Lindbergh Blvd., St. Louis, Mo. 63131.
Joseph of Chambery, Sisters of St.: Founded 1650, in France; in US, 1885. Generalate, Rome, Italy; US motherhouse, 27 Park Rd., West Hartford, Conn. 06119. Educational, hospital, social work.
Joseph of Cluny, Sisters of St., S.J.C.: Founded 1807, in France. General motherhouse, Paris, France; US provincial house, Cluny Convent, Brenton Rd., Newport, R.I. 02840.
Joseph of St. Augustine, Fla., Sisters of St., S.S.J.: General motherhouse, 241 St. George St., St. Augustine, Fla. 32084. Educational, hospital, social work.
Joseph of St. Mark, Sisters of St., S.S.J.S.M.: Founded 1845, in France; in US, 1937. General motherhouse, Alsace-Lorraine, France; US motherhouse, 21800 Chardon Rd., Euclid, Cleveland, O. 44117. Social, domestic work.
Lamb of God, Sisters of the, A.D.: Founded 1945, in France; in US, 1958. General motherhouse, France; US foundation, 1516 Parish Ave., Owensboro, Ky. 42301.
Loretto at the Foot of the Cross, Sisters of, S.L.: Founded 1812 in US, by Rev. Charles Nerinckx. General motherhouse, Nerinx, Ky. 40049. Educational work.
Louis, Congregation of Sisters of St., S.S.L.: Founded 1842, in France; in US, 1849. General motherhouse, Monaghan, Ireland; US novitiate, 22300 Mulholland Dr., Woodland Hills, Calif. 91364. Educational work.
Love of God, Sisters of the, R.A.D.: Founded 1864, in Spain; in US, 1958. Motherhouse, Spain; US address, Fairhaven, Mass. 02719.
Marian Sisters of the Diocese of Lincoln: Founded 1954. Motherhouse, 68462 Marycrest, Waverly, Nebr. 68462.
Marian Society of Dominican Catechists, O.P.: Founded 1954. General motherhouse, Boyce, La. 71409. Diocesan community.
Marianites of Holy Cross, Congregation of the Sisters, M.S.C.: Founded 1841, in France; in US, 1843. General motherhouse, Sarthe, France; US provinces: 4123 Woodland Dr., New Orleans, La. 70114; Great Rd., Princeton, N.J. 08540.

Marist Sisters, Congregation of Mary, S.M.: Founded 1824, in France. General motherhouse, Rome, Italy; US convents: Dearborn Hts., Mich. 48125; E. Detroit, Mich.; Wheeling, W. Va. 26002.

Maronite Antonine Sisters: Established in US, 1966. US address, Box 519 N. Lipkey Rd., R.D. 1, North Jackson, Ohio 44451.

Martha of Prince Edward Island, Sisters of St., C.S.M.: Founded 1916, in Canada; in US, 1961. General motherhouse, 141 Mt. Edward Rd., Charlottetown, P.E.I., Canada.

Marthe, Sisters of Sainte (of St. Hyacinthe), S.M.S.H.: Founded 1883, in Canada; in US, 1929. General motherhouse, St. Joseph de Hyacinthe, Que., Canada.

Mary, Company of, O.D.N.: Founded 1607, in France; in US, 1926. General motherhouse, Rome, Italy; US motherhouse, 16791 E. Main St., Tustin, Calif. 92680.

Mary, Daughters of the Heart of, D.H.M.: Founded 1790, in France; in US, 1851. Generalate, Paris, France; US provincialate, 103 E. 20th St., New York, N.Y. 10003. Educational work.

Mary, Little Company of, Nursing Sisters, L.C.M.: Founded 1877, in England; in US, 1893. General motherhouse, Rome, Italy; US provincial house, 9350 S. California Ave., Evergreen Park, Ill. 60642.

Mary, Missionary Sisters of the Society of (Marist Sisters), S.M.S.M.: Founded 1845, at St. Brieuc, France; in US, 1922. General motherhouse, Rome, Italy; US regional house, 357 Grove St., Waltham, Mass. 02154. Foreign missions.

Mary, Servants of, O.S.M.: Founded 13th century, in Italy; in US, 1893. General motherhouse, Rome, Italy; US provincial motherhouse, 7400 Military Ave., Omaha, Nebr.

Mary, Servants of (Servite Sisters), O.S.M.: Founded 1894, in Austria; in US, 1952. General motherhouse, Vienna, Austria; US novitiate, Sublimity, Ore. 97385. Nursing work.

Mary, Servants of (Servite Sisters), O.S.M.: Founded 13th century, in Italy; in US, 1912. General motherhouse, Ladysmith, Wis. 54848.

Mary, Sisters of St., of Oregon, S.S.M.O.: Founded 1886, in Oregon, by Bishop William H. Gross, C.Ss.R. General motherhouse, 4440 S.W. 148th Ave., Beaverton, Ore. 97005. Educational, nursing work.

Mary, Sisters Servants of, O.S.M.: Founded 1861, in Italy; in US, 1916. Generalate, Rome, Italy; US motherhouse, 13811 S. Western Ave., Blue Island, Ill. 60406. Educational, hospital work.

Mary, Sisters Servants of (Trained Nurses), S. de M.: Founded 1851, at Madrid, Spain; in US, 1914. General motherhouse, Rome, Italy; US motherhouse, 800 N. 18th St., Kansas City, Kans. 66102. Home nursing.

Mary and Joseph, Daughters of, D.M.J.: Founded 1817, in Belgium; in US, 1926. Generalate, Rome, Italy; American provincial house, 12935 San Vicente Blvd., Los Angeles, Calif. 90049.

Mary Help of Christians, Daughters of (Salesian Sisters of St. John Bosco), F.M.A.: Founded 1872, in Italy, by St. John Bosco; in US, 1908. General motherhouse, Rome, Italy; US motherhouse, North Haledon, N.J. 07508. Education, youth work.

Mary of Namur, Sisters of St., S.S.M.N.: Founded 1819, at Namur, Belgium; in US, 1863. General motherhouse, Namur, Belgium. US provinces: 1083 Englewood Ave., Renmore, N.Y. 14223; 3300 Hemphill St., Ft. Worth, Tex.

Mary of Providence, Daughters of St., D.S.M.P.: Founded 1872, at Como, Italy; in US, 1913. General motherhouse, Rome, Italy; US provincial house, 4200 N. Austin Ave., Chicago, Ill. 60634. Educational work.

Mary of the Catholic Apostolate, Sisters of the, S.A.C.: Founded 1926 at Schoenstatt, Germany; in US, 1949. General motherhouse, Schoenstatt, Germany. US addresses: Star Route 1, Box 100, Rockport, Tex. 78382; W. 284-N.698 Cherry Lane, Waukesha, Wis. 53186.

Mary of the Immaculate Conception, Daughters of, D.M.: Founded 1904, in US, by Msgr. Lucian Bojnowski. General motherhouse, New Britain, Conn. 06053. Educational, hospital work.

Mary Immaculate, Daughters of (Marianist Sisters), F.M.I.: Founded 1816, in France, by Very Rev. William-Joseph Chaminade. General motherhouse, Rome, Italy; US foundation, 251 W. Ligustrum Dr., San Antonio, Tex. 78228. Educational work.

Mary Immaculate, Religious of, R.M.I.: Founded 1876, in Spain; in US, 1954. General motherhouse, Rome, Italy: US foundation 719 Augusta St., San Antonio, Tex. 78215.

Mary Immaculate, Sisters Servants of, S.S.M.I: Founded 1892, in Austria; in US, 1935. General motherhouse, Rome, Italy; US province, 209 W. Chestnut Hill Ave., Philadelphia, Pa. 19118. Educational, hospital work.

Mary Immaculate of Mariowka, Sister Servants of, S.S.M.I.: Founded 1878 in Poland. General motherhouse, Poland; American provincialate, 1220 Tugwell Dr., Catonsville, Md. 21228.

Mary Reparatrix, Society of, S.M.R.: Founded 1857, in France; in US, 1908. Generalate, Rome, Italy; US province, 14 E. 29th St., New York, N.Y. 10016.

Medical Mission Sisters (Society of Catholic Medical Missionaries, Inc.), S.C.M.M.: Founded 1925, in US. Generalate, Rome, Italy; US headquarters, 8400 Pine Rd., Philadelphia, Pa. 19111. Medical work, especially in mission areas.

Medical Missionaries of Mary, M.M.M.: Founded 1937, in Ireland, by Mother Mary Martin, M.M.M.: in US, 1950. General motherhouse, Drogheda, Ireland; US motherhouse, 1 Arlington St., Winchester, Mass. 01890. Medical aid in missions.

Mercedarian Missionaries of Berriz, M.M.B.: Founded 1930, in Spain; in US, 1946. General motherhouse, Berriz, Spain; US vice provincial house, 918 E. 9th St., Kansas City, Mo. 64106.

Mercy, Daughters of Our Lady of, D.M.: Founded 1837, in Italy, by St. Mary Joseph Rossello; in US, 1919. General motherhouse, Savona, Italy; US motherhouse, Catawba Ave., Newfield, N.J. 08344. Educational, hospital work.

Mercy, Missionary Sisters of Our Lady of, M.O.M.: Founded 1938, in Brazil; in US, 1955. General motherhouse, Brazil; US address, 388 Franklin St., Buffalo, N.Y. 14202.

Mercy, Sisters of, R.S.M.: Founded 1831, in Ireland, by Mother Mary Catherine McAuley. US motherhouses: 634 New Scotland Ave., Albany, N.Y. 12208; 273 Willoughby Ave., Brooklyn, N.Y. 11205; S. 5245 Murphy Rd., Orchard Park, N.Y. 14127; Mansfield Ave., Burlington, Vt. 05401; 1125 Prairie Dr., N.E., Cedar Rapids, Ia. 52402; 444 E. Grandview Blvd., Erie, Pa. 16504; 249 Steele Rd., W. Hartford, Conn. 06117. Windham, N.H. 03087; Merion, Pa. 10968; 3333 Fifth Ave., Pittsburgh, Pa. 15213; 605 Stevens Ave., Portland, Me. 04103; Belmont, N. Car. 28012; 1437 Blossom Rd., Rochester, N.Y. 14610; Rt. 3, Box 3216, Auburn, Calif. 95603. 2300 Adeline Dr., Burlingame, Calif. 94010; US Route 22 at Tirrell Rd., North Plainfield, N.J. 07061; 46 High St., Worcester, Mass. 01608.

Mercy, Sisters of, of the Union in the United States of America, R.S.M.: Founded 1831 in Ireland, by Mother M. Catherine McAuley; union formed in 1929. General motherhouse, 10000 Kentsdale Dr., Box 3446, Bethesda, P.O., Washington, D.C. 20034.

Mercy, Sisters of, Daughters of Christian Charity of St. Vincent de Paul, S.M.D.C.: Founded 1842, in Hungary; US foundation, Rt. 1, Box 353, Hewitt, N.J. 07421.

Mill Hill Sisters: See Franciscan Missionaries of St. Joseph.

Minim Daughters of Mary Immaculate, C.F.M.M.: Founded 1886, in Mexico; in U.S. 1926. General motherhouse, Leon, Guanajuato, Mexico; US address, Box 1865, Nogales, Ariz. 85621.

Misericorde Sisters, S.M.: Founded 1848, in Canada; in US, 1887. General motherhouse. 12435 Ave. Misericorde, Montreal H4J 2G3, Canada. Hospital work.

Mission Helpers of the Sacred Heart, M.H.S.H.: Founded 1890, in US. General motherhouse, 1001 W. Joppa Rd., Towson, Md. 21204. Religious education, social work.

Missionary Catechists of the Sacred Hearts of Jesus and Mary (Violetas), M.C.: Founded

1927, in Mexico; in US, 1943. Motherhouse, Tlalpan, Mexico; US address, 209 W. Murray St., Victoria, Tex. 77901.

Missionary Sisters of the Catholic Apostolate (Pallottine Sisters), S.A.C.: Founded in Rome, 1843; in US, 1912. Generalate, Rome, Italy; US provincialate, Rt. 2, 15270 Old Halls Ferry Rd., Florissant, Mo. 63034.

Most Pure Virgin Mary, Missionary Daughters of the: Founded 1903, at Mexico City; in US, 1916. General motherhouse, Aguascalientes, Mexico. Educational work.

Mother of God, Missionary Sisters of the, M.S.M.G.: Byzantine, Ukrainian Rite, Stamford. Motherhouse, 711-719 N. Franklin St., Philadelphia, Pa. 19123.

Mother of God, Sisters Poor Servants of the, S.M.G.: Founded 1869, at London, England; in US, 1947. General motherhouse, Maryfield, Roehampton, London. US addresses: High Point, N.C. 27260; Norton, Va. 24273; 1800 Geary St., Philadelphia, Pa. 19145. Hospital work.

Nazareth, Poor Sisters of: Founded 1924, in US. General motherhouse, Hammersmith, London, England; US novitiate, 3333 Manning Ave., Los Angeles, Calif. 90064.

Notre Dame, School Sisters de: Founded 1853, in Czechoslovakia; in US, 1910. General motherhouse, Horazdovice, Czechoslovakia; US motherhouse, 3501 State St., Omaha, Nebr. 68112. Educational work.

Notre Dame, School Sisters of, S.S.N.D.: Founded 1833, in Germany; in US, 1847. General motherhouse, Rome, Italy. US provinces: 700 W. Highland Rd., Mequon, Wis. 53092; 6401 N. Charles St., Baltimore, Md. 21212; 320 E. Ripa Ave., St. Louis, Mo. 63125; Good Counsel Hill, Mankato, Minn. 56011; Wilton, Conn. 06897; Rt. 2, Box 4, Irving, Tex. 75060; R.R. 1, DeKalb, Ill. 60115.

Notre Dame, Sisters of, S.N.D.: Founded 1850, at Coesfeld, Germany; in US, 1874. General motherhouse, Rome, Italy. US provinces: 13000 Auburn Rd., Chardon, O. 44024; 1601 Dixie Highway, Covington, Ky. 41011; 3837 Secor Rd., Toledo, O. 43623; 624 W. Potrero Rd., Thousand Oaks, Calif. 91360.

Notre Dame, Sisters of the Congregation of, C.N.D.: Founded 1653, in Canada; in US, 1860. General motherhouse, Montreal, Que., Canada; US motherhouse, 223 West Mountain Rd., Ridgefield, Conn. 06877. Education.

Notre Dame de Namur, Sisters of, S.N.D.: Founded 1803, in France; in US, 1840. General motherhouse, Rome, Italy. US provinces: 328 Dartmouth St., Boston, Mass. 02116; Jeffrey's Neck Rd., Ipswich, Mass. 01938; 1561 N. Benson Rd., Fairfield, Conn. 06430; Ilchester, Md. 21083; 701 E. Columbia Ave., Reading, Cincinnati, O. 45215; 14800 Bohlman Rd., Saratoga, Calif. 95070. Educational work.

Notre Dame de Sion, Congregation of,

N.D.S.: Founded 1843, in France; in US, 1892. Generalate, Rome, Italy; US provincial house, 3823 Locust St., Kansas City, Mo. 64109. Creation of better understanding and relations between Christians and Jews.

Notre Dame des Anges, Missionary Sisters of, M.N.D.A.: Founded 1922, in Canada; in US, 1949. General motherhouse, Lennoxville, Canada; US headquarters, 320 N. Main St., Union City, Conn. 06770.

Our Lady of Sorrows, Sisters of, O.L.S.: Founded 1839, in Italy; in US, 1947. General motherhouse, Rome, Italy; US headquarters, 10450 Ellerbe Rd., Shreveport, La. 71106.

Pallottine Sisters of the Catholic Apostolate, C.S.A.C.: Founded 1843, at Rome, Italy; in US, 1889. General motherhouse, Rome; US motherhouse, Harriman Heights, Harriman, N.Y. 10926. Educational work.

Parish Visitors of Mary Immaculate, P.V.M.I.: Founded 1920, in New York. General motherhouse, Box 658, Monroe, Orange Co., N.Y. 10950. Mission work.

Passionist Sisters: See Cross and Passion, Sisters of the.

Paul, Daughters of St., Missionary Sisters of the Catholic Editions, D.S.P.: Founded 1915, at Alba, Piedmont, Italy; in US, 1932. General motherhouse, Rome, Italy; US provincial house, 50 St. Paul's Ave., Jamaica Plain, Mass. 02130. Apostolate of the communications arts.

Peter Claver, Missionary Sisters of St., S.S.P.C.: Founded 1894; in US, 1914. General motherhouse, Rome, Italy; US address, 667 Woods Mill Rd. S., Chesterfield, Mo. 63017.

Pious Schools, Sisters of, Sch. P.: Founded 1829 in Spain; in US, 1954. General motherhouse, Rome, Italy; US headquarters, 9925 Mason Ave., Chatsworth, Calif. 91311.

Poor, Little Sisters of the, L.S.P.: Founded 1839, in France; in US, 1868. General motherhouse, St. Pern, France. US provinces: 110-30 221st St., Queens Village, N.Y. 11429; 601 Maiden Choice Lane, Baltimore, Md. 21228; 80 W. Baldwin Rd., Palatine, Ill. 60067. Social work.

Poor Clare Missionary Sisters (Misionaras Clarisas), M.C.: Founded Mexico. General motherhouse, Rome, Italy; US novitiate, 11712 Stuart Dr., Garden Grove, Calif. 92640.

Poor Clare Nuns: See Franciscan Poor Clare Nuns.

Poor Clares, P.C.: General motherhouse, Newry, Ireland; US foundation, 37 E. Emerson, Chula Vista, Calif. 92011.

Poor Handmaids of Jesus Christ (Ancilla Domini Sisters), P.H.J.C.: Founded 1851, in Germany; in US, 1868. General motherhouse, Dernbach, Westerwald, Germany; US motherhouse, Donaldson, Ind. 46513. Educational, hospital work.

Precious Blood, Daughters of Charity of the Most: Founded 1872, at Pagani, Italy; in US,

1908. General motherhouse, Rome, Italy; US convent, 1482 North Ave., Bridgeport, Conn. 06604.

Precious Blood, Missionary Sisters of the, C.P.S.: Founded 1885, at Mariannhill, South Africa; in US, 1925. Generalate, Rome, Italy: US motherhouse, New Holland Ave., P.O. Box 43, Shillington, Pa. 19607. Home and foreign mission work.

Precious Blood, Sisters Adorers of the, A.P.B.: Founded 1861, in Canada; in US, 1890. General motherhouses: 2520, rue Girouard, St. Hyacinthe, Que. J2S 7B8, Canada (French); 667 Talbot St., London N6A 2T6, Ont., Canada (English). Contemplatives.

Precious Blood, Sisters of the, C.Pp.S.: Founded 1834, in Switzerland; in US, 1844. Generalate, 4000 Denlinger Rd., Dayton, Ohio 45426. Educational, hospital work.

Precious Blood, Sisters of the Most, C.Pp.S.: Founded 1845, in Steinerberg, Switzerland; in US, 1870. General motherhouse, 204 N. Main St., O'Fallon, Mo. 63366. Educational work.

Presentation, Sisters of St. Mary of the, S.M.P.: Founded 1829, in France; in US, 1903. General motherhouse, Broons, Cotes-du-Nord, France. US motherhouse, Valley City, N. Dak. 58072. Educational, hospital work.

Presentation of Mary, Sisters of the, P.M.: Founded 1796, in France; in US, 1873. General motherhouse, Rome, Italy. US provinces: Manchester, N.H. 03104; Methuen, Mass. 01844.

Presentation of the B.V.M., Sisters of the, P.B.V.M.: Founded 1777, in Ireland; in US, 1854. US motherhouses: 2360 Carter Rd., Dubuque, Ia. 52001; R.D. 2, Box 101, Newburgh, N.Y. 12550; 8931 Callaghan Rd., San Antonio, Tex. 78230; 2340 Turk St., San Francisco, Calif. 94118; Watervliet, N.Y. 12189.

Route 1, Fargo, N. Dak. 58102; 250 S. Davis Dr., P.O. Box 1113, Warner Robbins, Ga. 31093; Aberdeen, S. Dak. 57401; 1300 E. Cedar, Globe, Ariz. 85501; 1555 E. Dana, Mesa, Ariz. 85201; 366 South St., Fitchburg, Mass. 01420.

Providence, Daughters of Divine, F.D.P.: Founded 1832, Italy; in US, 1964. General motherhouse, Rome, Italy; US foundation, 1029 N. Atlanta St., Metairie, La. 70003.

Providence, Missionary Catechists of Divine, M.C.D.P.: Founded 1930, as a filial society; adjunct branch of Sisters of Divine Providence (San Antonio). Formation house, 2318 Castroville Rd., San Antonio, Tex. 78237.

Providence, Oblate Sisters of, O.S.P.: Founded 1829, in US. General motherhouse, 701 Gun Rd., Baltimore, Md. 21227. Educational work.

Providence, Sisters of, S.P.: Founded 1861, in Canada; in US, 1873. General motherhouse, Brightside, Holyoke, Mass. 01040.

Providence, Sisters of, S.P.: Founded 1843, in Canada; in US, 1854. General motherhouse, Montreal, Canada. US provinces: Providence Hts., Pine Lake, Issaquah, Wash. 98027; 9 E. 9th Ave., Spokane, Wash. 99202.

Providence, Sisters of (of St. Mary-of-the-Woods), S.P.: Founded 1806, in France; in US, 1840. General motherhouse, St. Mary-of-the-Woods, Ind. 47876.

Providence, Sisters of Divine, C.D.P.: Founded 1762, in France; in US, 1866. General motherhouse, Box 197, Helotes, Tex. 78023. Educational, hospital work.

Providence, Sisters of Divine, C.D.P.: Founded 1851, in Germany; in US, 1876. General motherhouse, Rome, Italy. US provinces: 9000 Babcock Blvd., Allison Park, Pa. 15101; 8351 Florissant Rd., Normandy, Mo. 63121; Box 2, Rte. 80, Kingston, Mass. 02360. Educational, hospital work.

Providence, Sisters of Divine (of Kentucky), C.D.P.: Founded 1762, in France; in US, 1889. General motherhouse, Moselle, France; US province, Melbourne, Ky. 41059. Educational, hospital work, domestic work.

Redeemer, Oblates of the Most Holy, O.SS.R.: Founded 1864, in Spain. General motherhouse, Spain; US foundation, 60-80 Pond St., Jamaica Plain, Mass. 02130.

Redeemer, Order of the Most Holy, O.SS.R.: Founded 1731, by St. Alphonsus Liguori; in US, 1957. US addresses: Esopus, N.Y. 12429; Liguori, Mo. 63057.

Redeemer, Sisters of the Divine, S.D.R.: Founded 1849, in Niederbronn, France; in US, 1912. General motherhouse, Rome, Italy; US motherhouse, 999 Rock Run Road, Elizabeth, Pa. 15037. Educational, hospital work; care of the aged.

Redeemer, Sisters of the Holy, S.H.R.: Founded 1849, in Alsace; in US, 1924. General motherhouse, Wuerzburg, Germany; US regional house, Huntingdon Valley, Pa. 19006. Personalized medical care in hospitals, homes for aged and private homes.

Refuge, Sisters of Our Lady of Charity of, O.L.C.R.: Founded 1641, at Caen, France; in US, 1855. US federation, P.O. Box 327, Wisconsin Dells, Wis. 53965. Social work.

Religious Conceptionist Missionaries, R.C.M.: Founded 1892, in Spain; in US, 1962. General motherhouse, Madrid, Spain; US foundation, 867 Oxford, Clovis, Calif. 93612.

Reparation of the Congregation of Mary, Sisters of, S.R.C.M.: Founded 1903, in US. Motherhouse, Monsey, N.Y. 10952.

Resurrection, Sisters of the, C.R.: Founded 1891, in Italy; in US, 1900. General motherhouse, Rome, Italy. US provinces: 7432 Talcott Ave., Chicago, Ill. 60631; Castleton-on-Hudson, N.Y. 12033. Educational work.

Rita of the Immaculate Heart, Daughters of St., D.S.R.: Motherhouse, Berry Ave., Versailles, Ky. 40383.

Rosary, Congregation of Our Lady of the Holy, R.S.R.: Founded 1874, in Canada; in US, 1899. General motherhouse, C.P. 2020, Rimouski, Que., Canada. Educational work.

Rosary, Missionary Sisters of Our Lady of the Holy, H.R.S.: Founded 1924, in Ireland; in US, 1954. Motherhouse, Killeshandra, Co. Cavan, Ireland. US novitiate, 214 Ashwood Rd., Villanova, Pa. 19085. African missions.

Sacrament, Missionary Sisters of the Most Blessed, M.SS.S.: General motherhouse, Madrid, Spain; US foundations: 1111 Wordin Ave., Bridgeport, Conn. 06605.

Sacrament, Nuns of the Perpetual Adoration of the Blessed, A.P.: Founded 1807, in Rome, Italy; in US, 1925. US monasteries: 145 N. Cotton Ave., El Paso, Tex. 79901; 771 Ashbury St., San Francisco, Calif. 94117.

Sacrament, Oblate Sisters of the Blessed, O.S.B.S.: Founded 1935, in US; motherhouse, Marty, S.D. 57361. Care of American Indians.

Sacrament, Religious Mercedarians of the Blessed, R.M.S.S.: Founded 1910, in Mexico; in US, 1926. General motherhouse, Mexico City, Mexico; US convent, 222 W. Cevallos St., San Antonio, Tex. 78204.

Sacrament, Servants of the Blessed, S.S.S.: Founded 1858, in France, by St. Pierre Julien Eymard; in US, 1947. General motherhouse, Rome, Italy; US motherhouse, 101 Silver St., Waterville, Me. 04901. Contemplative.

Sacrament, Sisters of the Blessed, for Indians and Colored People, S.B.S.: Founded 1891, in US. General motherhouse, Cornwells Heights, Pa. 19020.

Sacrament, Sisters of the Most Holy, M.H.S.: Founded 1851, in France; in US, 1872. General motherhouse, 409 W. St. Mary Blvd. (P.O. Box 2429), Lafayette, La. 70501.

Sacrament, Sisters Servants of the Blessed, S.S.B.S.: Founded 1904, in Mexico. General motherhouse, Guadalajara, Mexico. US address, 536 Rockwood Ave., Calexico, Calif. 92231.

Sacramentine Nuns (Religious of the Order of the Blessed Sacrament and Our Lady), O.SS.: Founded 1639, in France; in US, 1912. US monasteries: 23 Park Ave., Yonkers, N.Y. 10703; US 31, Conway, Mich. 49722. Perpetual adoration of the Holy Eucharist.

Sacred Heart, Daughters of Our Lady of the: Founded 1882, in France; in US, 1955. General motherhouse, Rome, Italy; US address, 424 E. Browning Rd., Bellmawr, N.J. 08031. Educational work.

Sacred Heart, Missionary Sisters of the (Cabrini Sisters), M.S.C.: Founded 1880, in Italy, by St. Frances Xavier Cabrini; in US, 1889. General motherhouse, Rome, Italy; US provincialate, 223 E. 19th St., New York, N.Y. 10003. Educational, health, social and catechetical work.

Sacred Heart, Religious of the Apostolate of the, R.A.: General motherhouse, Madrid,

Spain; US address, 1120 6th St., Miami Beach, Fla., 33139.

Sacred Heart, Society Devoted to the, S.D.S.H.: Founded 1940, in Hungary; in US, 1956. US motherhouse, 728 S. Hudson Ave., Los Angeles, Calif. 90005. Educational work.

Sacred Heart, Society of the, R.S.C.J.: Founded 1800, in France; in US, 1818. General motherhouse, Rome, Italy. US provinces: 1177 King St., Greenwich, Conn. 06830; 2047 W. Fargo, Chicago, Ill. 60645; 13640 Conway Rd., St. Louis, Mo. 63141; 453 Miller Ave., S. San Francisco, Calif. 94080; 842 Commonwealth Ave., Newton, Mass. 02159. Educational work.

Sacred Heart of Jesus, Apostles of, A.S.C.J.: Founded 1894, in Italy; in US, 1902. General motherhouse, Rome, Italy; US motherhouse, 265 Benham St., Hamden, Conn. 06514. Educational, social work.

Sacred Heart of Jesus, Congregation of Oblates of, O.S.C.: Founded 1843, in France; in US, 1955. US address, 630 N. Dolsea Dr., Clayton, N.J. 08312.

Sacred Heart of Jesus, Handmaids of the, A.C.J.: Founded 1877, in Spain. General motherhouse, Rome, Italy; US province, 2025 Church Rd., Wyncote, Pa. 19095. Educational, retreat work.

Sacred Heart of Jesus, Missionary Sisters of the Most, M.S.C.: Founded 1899, in Germany; in US, 1908. General motherhouse, Rome, Italy; US province, Hyde Park, Reading, Pa. 19605. Educational, hospital, social work.

Sacred Heart of Jesus, Oblate Sisters of the, O.S.H.J.: Founded 1894; in US, 1949. General motherhouse, Rome, Italy; US motherhouse, 50 Warner Rd., Hubbard, Ohio 44425. Educational, social work.

Sacred Heart of Jesus, Servants of the Most: Founded 1894, in Poland; in US, 1959. General motherhouse, Cracow, Poland; US address, 231 Arch St., Cresson, Pa. 16630.

Sacred Heart of Jesus, Sisters of the, S.S.C.J.: Founded 1816, in France; in US, 1903. General motherhouse, St. Jacut, Brittany, France; US provincial house, 5922 Blanco Rd., San Antonio, Tex. 78216. Educational, hospital, domestic work.

Sacred Heart of Jesus and of the Poor, Servants of the (Mexican), S.S.H.J.P.: Founded 1885, in Mexico; in US, 1907. General motherhouse, Apartado 92, Puebla, Pue, Mexico; US regional house, 237 Tobin Pl., El Paso, Tex. 79905.

Sacred Heart of Jesus for Reparation, Congregation of the Handmaids of the: Founded 1918, in Italy; in US, 1958. US address, Sunshine Park, R.D. 3, Steubenville, Ohio 43952.

Sacred Heart of Mary, Religious of the, R.S.H.M.: Founded 1848, in France; in US, 1877. Generalate, Rome, Italy. US provinces: 15 E. 81st St., New York, N.Y. 10028; 945 Tremonto Rd., Santa Barbara, Calif. 93103.

Sacred Hearts, Religious of the Holy Union

of the, S.U.S.C.: Founded 1826, in France; in US, 1886. Generalate, Rome, Italy. US provinces: 492 Rock St., Fall River, Mass. 02720; Main St., Groton, Mass. 01450. Educational work.

Sacred Hearts and of Perpetual Adoration, Sisters of the, SS.CC.: Founded 1797, in France; in US, 1908. General motherhouse, Rome, Italy; US motherhouse, 330 Main St., N. Fairhaven, Mass. 02719. Educational work.

Sacred Hearts of Jesus and Mary, Sisters of the, S.H.J.M.: Established 1953, in US. General motherhouse, Essex, England; US address, 310 San Carlos Ave., El Cerrito, Calif. 94530.

Savior, Company of the, C.S.: Founded 1952, in Spain; in US, 1962. General motherhouse, Madrid, Spain; US foundation, 820 Clinton Ave., Bridgeport, Conn. 06608.

Savior, Sisters of the Divine, S.D.S.: Founded 1888, in Italy; in US, 1895. General motherhouse, Rome, Italy; US motherhouse, 4311 N. 100th St., Milwaukee, Wis. 53222. Educational, hospital work.

Social Service, Sisters of, S.S.S.: Founded 1908, in Hungary; in US, 1926. General motherhouse, 1120 Westchester Pl., Los Angeles, Calif. 90019.

Social Service, Sisters of, S.S.S.: Founded in Hungary, 1923. US motherhouse, 440 Linwood Ave., Buffalo, N.Y. 14209. Social work.

Teresa of Jesus, Society of St., S.T.J.: Founded 1876, in Spain; in US, 1910. General motherhouse, Rome, Italy; US provincial house, 4018 S. Presa St., San Antonio, Tex. 78223.

Thomas of Villanova, Congregation of Sisters of St., S.S.T.V.: Founded 1661, in France; in US, 1948. General motherhouse, Neuilly-sur-Seine, France; US foundation W. Rocks Rd., Norwalk, Conn. 06851.

Trinity, Missionary Servants of the Most Blessed, M.S.B.T.: Founded 1912, in US, by Very Rev. Thomas A. Judge. General motherhouse, 3501 Solly St., Philadelphia, Pa. 19136. Educational, social work.

Trinity, Sisters of the Most Holy, O.Ss.T.: Founded 1198, in Rome; in US, 1920. General motherhouse, Rome, Italy; US motherhouse, 21320 Euclid Ave., Euclid, Ohio 44117. Educational work.

Ursula of the Blessed Virgin, Society of the Sisters of St., S.U.: Founded 1606, in France; in US, 1902. General motherhouse, Tours, France; US novitiate, Rhinebeck, N.Y. 12572. Educational work.

Ursuline Nuns (Roman Union), O.S.U.: Founded 1535, in Italy; in US, 1727. Generalate, Rome, Italy. US provinces: 323 E. 198th St., New York, N.Y. 10458; Crystal Heights Rd., Crystal City, Mo. 63019; 639 Angela Dr., Santa Rosa, Calif. 95401; 71 Lowder St., Dedham, Mass. 02026; 401 Findley St., Toronto, O. 43694.

Ursuline Nuns of the Congregation of Paris, O.S.U.: Founded 1535, in Italy; in US, 1727. US motherhouses: St. Martin, O. 45170; East Miami St., Paola, Kans. 66071; 3115 Lexington Rd., Louisville, Ky. 40206; 2600 Lander Rd., Cleveland, O. 44124; Maple Mount, Ky. 42356; 2413 Collingwood Blvd., Toledo, O. 43620; 4250 Shields Rd., Canfield, O. 44406; 1339 E. McMillan St., Cincinnati, O. 45206.

Ursuline Nuns of the Congregation of Tildonk, Belgium, R.U.: Founded 1535, in Italy; in US, 1924. Generalate, Haecht, Belgium; US address, Blue Point, L.I., N.Y. 11715. Educational, foreign mission work.

Ursuline Sisters, O.S.U.: General motherhouse, Blackrock, Cork, Ireland; US address, Torch Hill Rd., Columbus, Ga. 31903.

Ursuline Sisters of Mount Calvary, O.S.U.: Founded 1535, in Italy; in US, 1910. General motherhouse, Mount Calvary, Germany; US motherhouse, 1026 N. Douglas Ave., Belleville, Ill. 62221. Educational work.

Venerini Sisters, Religious, M.P.V.: Founded 1685, in Italy; in US, 1909. General motherhouse, Rome, Italy; US provincialate; 23 Edward St., Worcester, Mass. 01605.

Verona, Missionary Sisters of, M.S.V.: Founded 1875, in Italy; in US, 1950. US address, 1307 Lakeside Ave., Richmond, Va. 23228. Hospital, social, educational work.

Victory Missionary Sisters, Our Lady of, O.L.V.M.: Founded 1922, in US. Motherhouse, Victory Noll, Box 109, Huntington, Ind. 46750. Educational, social work.

Vincent de Paul, Sisters: See Charity of St. Vincent de Paul, Sisters of.

Visitation Nuns, V.H.M.: Founded 1610, in France; in US, 1799. North American federations: 2002 Bancroft Pkwy., Wilmington, Del. 19806 (Pres., Mother Mary Gabrielle Muth); Visitation Monastery, Springfield, Mo. 65804 (Pres., Mother Anne Madeleine Ernstmann). Contemplative. Educational work.

Visitation of the Congregation of the Immaculate Heart of Mary, Sisters of the, S.V.M.: Founded 1952, in US. Motherhouse, 900 Alta Vista St., Dubuque, Ia. 52201. Educational work.

Vocationist Sisters (Sisters of the Divine Vocations): Founded 1921, in Italy. General motherhouse, Naples, Italy; US foundation, 172 Broad St., Newark, N.J. 07104.

White Sisters: See Africa, Missionary Sisters of Our Lady of.

White Sisters of Charity of St. Vincent de Paul of Zagreb: Founded 1845, in Croatia; in US, 1955. General motherhouse, Zagreb, Yugoslavia; US foundation, 171 Knox Ave., West Seneca, N.Y. 14224.

Wisdom, Daughters of, D.W.: Founded 1703, in France, by St. Louis Marie Grignon de Montfort; in US, 1904. General motherhouse, Vendee, France; US motherhouse, 385 S. Ocean Ave., Islip, N.Y. Educational, hospital work.

Xaverian Missionary Society of Mary, Inc., M.M.: Founded 1945, in Italy; in US, 1954. General motherhouse, Parma, Italy; US address, 242 Salisbury St., Worcester, Mass. 01609.

Xavier Mission Sisters (Catholic Mission Sisters of St. Francis Xavier), X.M.S.: Founded 1946, at Warren, Mich., by Cardinal Edward Mooney. General motherhouse, 35750 Moravian Dr., Fraser, Mich. 48026. Educational, hospital, social work in missions.

ORGANIZATIONS OF WOMEN RELIGIOUS

Leadership of Women

The Leadership Conference of Women Religious in the United States of America is an association of the major superiors of religious communities of women, with the purpose of promoting the spiritual and apostolic welfare of the sisterhoods of the U.S.

Organized in the late 50's and approved by the Congregation for Religious and Secular Institutes June 13, 1962, it has a membership of approximately 600. Its original name, changed in 1971, was the Conference of Major Superiors of Women. With its formerly affiliated Sister Formation Conference, it inaugurated measures for the religious and professional development of sisters and has contributed greatly to the renewal of religious life in this country.

Sister Barbara Thomas, S.C.N., is president of the conference; Sister Mary Daniel Turner, S.N.D. de N., is executive director.

The national secretariat is located at 1330 Massachusetts Ave., N.W., Washington, D.C. 20005.

The 1975 assembly of the conference met Aug. 24 to 28, in St. Paul, Minnesota. Its theme was "Promises to Keep."

Formation Conference

The Sister Formation Conference was organized in 1952 for the purpose of promoting the spiritual and professional formation of American sisters. It is an association of religious engaged in initial and on-going formation work in their communities. The conference seeks to be a forum for exchange and a center for communication and the sharing of resources.

Sister Louise Hageman, O.P., is chairperson of the national leadership board of the conference. Sister Ruth McGoldrick, S.P., is executive director.

The national office is located at 1330 Massachusetts Ave. N.W., Washington, D.C. 20005.

National Assembly

More than 2,000 delegates attending a convention in Cleveland Apr. 17 to 19, 1970, voted overwhelmingly in favor of a proposal to establish the National Assembly of

Women Religious and to make it "a voice" of sisters in the United States.

The assembly's primary goal is "to challenge women religious to communicate a valid concept of the role of the consecrated celibate women in the Church today, and to study, evaluate, establish priorities and make recommendations concerning areas in which women religious are critically needed."

The assembly is intended to be a forum for communication among women religious and "a voice through which they can speak to the Church and to the world."

NAWR's current agenda derives from a comprehensive "Ministry of Justice" resolution adopted at its 1972 convention in Minneapolis and reaffirmed in 1973 in New York. In the statement the sisters committed themselves to "a ministry of justice by the continuous use of our organized power to affect local and international policy for the liberation of all peoples from oppression." The resolution has been put into effect through the sponsorship of regional workshops designed to help sisters bring about significant changes in their respective areas of service.

Membership in the NAWR is open to individual sisters, councils of sisters (official organization of sisters in a diocese), organizations of women religious (de facto groups of sisters which are not official diocesan bodies), clergy and lay associates.

NAWR reported a 1975 membership of 103 diocesan councils and 3,500 individuals. Service publications of the assembly include *NAWR Trends*.

Sister Kathleen Keating is chairperson of NAWR.

Offices are located at 201 E. Ohio St., Chicago, Ill., 60611.

The 1975 NAWR convention was held Aug. 7-10 in San Francisco.

Black Sisters

The National Black Sisters' Conference was organized in August, 1968, for the express purpose of enabling the sisters to determine their priorities in relation to their black people. Its 150 members include black sisters from 123 religious congregations in the United States and Islands.

A major concern of the conference is the development of continuance of black vocations to religious life in the unique contemporary black life style, for fulfillment in bringing about the liberation of black people. The conference conducts an annual institute in sister formation in order to influence the formational and recruitment agendas of white religious congregations. It also publishes vocational material and provides staff members for workshops in these areas.

At the request of Bishop Patrick E. Ekpu of Benin City, Nigeria, the conference provides personnel and technical support for the formation program of the Sisters of the Sacred Heart of Jesus of Nigeria, a newly established indigenous religious congregation.

RARE (Religious Active for Rural Evolvement) — a summer project concerned with problems of southern rural black children — was initiated by the conference in 1974 in southeastern Louisiana.

DESIGN (Development of Educational Services in the Growing Nation), is a subsidiary of the conference and its educational component.

The conference periodically conducts retreats, seminars and workshops on a variety of international and national social and theological issues, including alternative black educational systems, criminal justice, racism, pastoral ministry, etc.

The conference publishes a monthly newsletter for its members entitled *Soulside*.

Sister Helen Marie Christian, R.S.M., is president of the conference. The executive director is Sister Mary Shawn Copeland, O.P.

Headquarters are located at 3508 Fifth Ave. Pittsburgh, Pa. 15213.

National Coalition

Recognition and development of the role of women in the Church and society, along with advocacy for social activism, are the principal characteristics of the National Coalition of American Nuns, organized in July, 1969, under the leadership of Sister Margaret Traxler, S.S.N.D.

Offices are located at 1307 S. Wabash Ave., Chicago, Ill. 60605.

Sisters Uniting

Sisters Uniting, formed in March, 1971, in Chicago, describes itself as a group that works "to facilitate cooperation and coordination" of six national associations: the Association of Contemplative Sisters, the National Sister Formation Conference, the National Sisters Vocation Conference, the National Coalition of American Nuns, the Leadership Conference of Women Religious, and the National Assembly of Women Religious.

Consortium

The Consortium Perfectae Caritatis ("Association of Perfect Love"), named after the Latin title of the Second Vatican Council's *Decree on the Appropriate Renewal of Religious Life*, was organized in March, 1971, at a Washington, D.C., meeting of nearly 150 sisters from 48 communities in the United States and Canada.

The stated purposes of the association are: (1) to bring together those who accept the conciliar documents of Vatican Council II regarding religious life, subsequent papal statements, and interpretations and directives emanating from the Congregation for Religious and Secular Institutes; (2) to communicate and share with each other experiences in implementing the conciliar plan of renewal.

Six hundred sisters attended the 1975 assembly of Consortium held in Chicago Apr. 4 to 6. Theme of the meeting was "The Woman Religious, the Heart of the Institutional Church."

Sister Mary Elise, S.N.D., of Chardon, O., is executive of the group's national council. The mailing address is P.O. Box 1092, Washington, D.C. 20013.

Las Hermanas

Las Hermanas is a national organization of women religious of Hispanic origin formed in 1971 in Houston for the purpose of being "actively present to the ever-changing needs" of the Spanish-speaking.

Accordingly, the organization has three projects in operation: cultural awareness workshops designed to make groups of women religious and civic/governmental agencies more aware of the needs of Spanish-speaking Catholics; Proyecto Mexico, an educational program for Mexican sisters seeking involvement in parish ministry; a nine-month pastoral, educational and renewal institute for priests, religious and lay persons in the Spanish-speaking apostolate.

Las Hermanas, which has sister associates and lay affiliates, is directed by a national coordinating team headed by Sisters Maria de Jesus Ybarra, O.D.N., Mario Barron, C.S.J. and Clarita Trujillo, O.L.V.M.

The national office is located at 14 West Costilla, Colorado Springs, Colo. 80903.

Contemplatives

The Association of Contemplative Sisters was founded by nearly 140 representatives of 57 communities in the US and Canada who took part in a two-week seminar for contemplatives held in August, 1969, at Woodstock College, Md. It has a membership of approximately 700.

The purposes of the association are to encourage and foster healthy development of the contemplative life so that contemplative women may serve the Church more effectively, and to provide a vehicle of communication between the nuns, their communities and the Church at large.

The association publishes the *Contemplative Review,* edited by Sister Mary Roman, Carmelite Monastery, Beckley Hill, Barre, Vt. 05641.

Sister Jean Alice McGoff, O.C.D., is president of the association.

The central office is located at 2500 Cold Spring Rd., Indianapolis, Ind. 46222.

Vocation Conference

The National Sisters Vocation Conference, formed in September, 1970, is a national organization dedicated to deepening the understanding of the role of women, especially women religious, in the Church through work in the vocation apostolate.

The conference seeks to coordinate and provide informational and other services to persons and organizations in the vocation apostolate, and to assist prospective candidates for religious life. A national symposium is held annually in the summer. Its 1975 membership was approximately 1,530.

The national director is Sister M. Cathleen Toomey, R.S.M.

The national office is located at 1307 S. Wabash Ave., Chicago, Ill. 60605.

Other Conferences

International Organizations: The Union of Superiors General (Men), which was established in 1957, had its statutes approved by the Congregation for Religious and Secular Institutes in 1967, and has Pedro Arrupe, S.J., as president; the International Union of Superiors General (Women), which was established in 1965, had its statutes approved in 1967, and has M. Mary Linscott, of the Sisters of Our Lady of Namur, as president.

Regional Organization: The Latin American Confederation of Religious, which was established in 1959, had its statutes approved in 1967, and has Carlos Palmes, S.J., as president.

National Conferences: National conferences of superiors of religious, generally separate for men and women, have been established in 18 countries in Europe, 14 in North and Central America, 10 in South America, 19 in Africa, and 18 in Asia and Oceania.

Vicars' Conference

The National Conference of Vicars for Religious, established in 1972, is a national organization of diocesan officials concerned with religious in their dioceses.

The aims of the conference are: to assist vicars with cooperation, communications services and continuing education; to increase the service of dioceses to religious, and to respond to the needs of religious on regional, national and international levels; to carry on liaison with the Congregation for Religious and Secular Institutes, the National Conference of Catholic Bishops and other organizations concerned with religious.

Approximately 60 priests and sisters attended the 1975 conference held in Milwaukee, Wis., Mar. 9 to 12.

The president of the conference is Father William F. Hughes, 50 N. Park Ave., Rockville Centre, N.Y. 11570.

Father Kevin O'Rourke, O.P., speaking at the national meeting of conference, Mar. 9 to 12, 1975, in Milwaukee, said that on-going revisions of the Code of Canon Law dealing with religious should, when published, be internalized by religious communities in order "to make them effective and Spirit-oriented."

SECULAR INSTITUTES

(Sources: Almanac survey; *Directory of Secular Institutes with Foundations in the U.S.A.*, published by the Publications Office, U.S. Catholic Conference, *Annuario Pontificio*.)

Secular institutes are societies of men and women living in the world who dedicate themselves by vow or promise to observe the evangelical counsels and to carry on apostolic works suitable to their talents and opportunities in the areas of their everyday life.

"Secular institutes are not religious communities but they carry with them in the world a profession of evangelical counsels which is genuine and complete, and recognized as such by the Church. This profession confers a consecration on men and women, laity and clergy, who reside in the world. For this reason they should chiefly strive for total self-dedication to God, one inspired by perfect charity. These institutes should preserve their proper and particular character, a secular one, so that they may everywhere measure up successfully to that apostolate which they were designed to exercise, and which is both in the world and, in a sense, of the world" *(Decree on the Appropriate Renewal of Religious Life,* No. 11; Second Vatican Council).

A secular institute reaches maturity in several stages. It begins as an association of the faithful, technically called a pious union, with the approval of a local bishop. Once it has proved its viability, he can give it the status of an institute of diocesan right, in accordance with norms and permission emanating from the Congregation for Religious and Secular Institutes. On issuance of a separate decree from this congregation, an institute of diocesan right becomes an institute of pontifical right.

Secular institutes, which originated in the latter part of the 18th century, were given full recognition and approval by Pius XII Feb. 2, 1947, in the apostolic constitution *Provida Mater Ecclesia.* On Mar. 25 of the same year a special commission for secular institutes was set up within the Congregation for Religious. Institutes were commended and confirmed by Pius XII in a motu proprio of Mar. 12, 1948, and were the subject of a special instruction issued a week later, Mar. 19, 1948.

The **United States Conference of Secular Institutes (CSI)** was established in October, 1972, following the organization of the World Conference of Secular Institutes in Rome. Its membership is open to all canonically erected secular institutes with members living in the United States. The conference was organized to offer secular institutes an opportunity to exchange experiences, to do research in order to help the Church carry out its mission, and to search for ways and means to make known the existence of secular institutes in the U.S. Address: 7007 Bradley Blvd., Bethesda, Md.

Institutes in the U.S.

Caritas Christi (Cultural Crossroads, Inc.): Originated in Marseilles, 1937; for women. Established as a secular institute of pontifical right Mar. 19, 1955. Address: Rev. Austin Green, O.P., national priest-assistant, 1909 S. Ashland Ave., Chicago, Ill. 60608.

Company of St. Paul: Originated in Milan, Italy, 1920; for lay people and priests. Approved as a secular institute of pontifical right June 30, 1960. Address: P. O. Box 6267, Washington, D.C. 20015.

Company of St. Ursula, Daughters of St. Angela Merici ("The Angelines"): Founded in Brescia, Italy, 1535; for women. Approved as a secular institute of pontifical right 1958. Addresses: Maria Marchetti, Secretary, Via Martinengo da Barco 8, 25100 Brescia, Italy; Angeline Coordinator, Ursuline Academy, 4900 Walnut Hill, Dallas, Tex. 95229.

Cordimarian Filiation (Daughters of the Immaculate Heart of Mary): Originated in Spain, 1850, by. St. Anthony M. Claret; for women. Final approval by the Holy See, Dec. 8, 1959. Address, Rev. Joseph Gallego, C.M.F., 4541 S. Ashland Ave., Chicago, Ill. 60609. International membership of approximately 2,000.

DeSales Secular Institute: Founded in Vienna, Austria, 1940; for women. Pontifical right. Address: Rev. Joseph J. Griffin, O.S.F.S., DeChantal National Center, 2019 Delaware Ave., Wilmington, Del. 19806.

Diocesan Laborer Priests: Approved as a secular institute of pontifical right. The specific aim of the institute is the promotion, sustenance and cultivation of apostolic, religious and priestly vocations. Delegate for U.S., Rev. Ovid Pecherroman, 3706 15th St. N.E., Washington, D.C. 20017.

Institute of Secular Missionaries: Founded in Vitoria, Spain, 1939; for women. Approved as a secular institute, 1955. Address: 601 Greenup St., Covington, Ky. 41011.

Institute of the Heart of Jesus: Originated in France Feb. 2, 1791; restored Oct. 29, 1918; for diocesan priests. Received final approval from the Holy See as a secular institute of pontifical right Feb. 2, 1952. Canon Jean Canivez, superior general. Addresses: Central House, 202 Avenue du Maine, Paris 14me, France; US address, Rev. David Scheider, Notre Dame High School, Batavia, N.Y. 14020. International membership of approximately 1,900. Now experimenting with lay membership.

Mission of Our Lady of Bethany: Founded in Plessis-Chevet, France, 1948; for women. Approved as an institute of diocesan right 1965. Address: Rev. Michael J. Rooney, 370 Common St., Dedham, Mass. 02026.

Missionaries of the Kingship of Christ the King: Under this title are included three distinct and juridically separate institutes founded by Agostino Gemelli, O.F.M. (1878-1959).

(1) Women Missionaries of the Kingship of Christ — Founded in 1919, in Italy; definitively approved as an institute of pontifical rite 1953. Established in 15 countries. U.S. branch established 1950. Age at time of entrance, 21 to 40.

(2) Men Missionaries of the Kingship of Christ — Founded 1928, in Italy, as an institute of diocesan right. U.S. branch established 1962.

(3) Priest Missionaries of the Kingship of Christ — Established in U.S., 1954; approved as institute of diocesan right Feb. 6, 1971. For diocesan priests. Address: Rev. Stephen Hartdegen, O.F.M., Holy Name College, 14th and Shepherd Sts. N.E., Washington, D.C. 20017.

Oblate Missionaries of Mary Immaculate: Founded, 1952, and approved as a secular institute Feb. 2, 1962; for women. Addresses: Oblate Missionaries of Mary Immaculate, 1054 Lisbon St., Lewiston, Me. 04240; 7535 Boulevard Parent, Trois Rivieres, P. Q., Canada. International membership of approximately 1,000.

Rural Parish Workers of Christ the King: Originated in Cottleville, Mo., 1942; for women. An approved secular institute of the Archdiocese of St. Louis. Dedicated to the service of neighbor, especially in rural areas. Address: Box 300, Rt. 1, Cadet, Mo. 63630.

Schoenstatt Sisters of Mary: Originated in Schoenstatt, Germany, 1926; for women. Established as a secular institute of diocesan right May 20, 1948; of pontifical right Oct. 18, 1948. Addresses: Schoenstatt Sisters of Mary, W. 284 N. 698 Cherry Lane, Waukesha, Wis. 53186; House Schoenstatt, Star Rt. 1, Box 100, Rockport, Tex. 78382. International membership of more than 2,600.

Secular Institute of Pius X: Originated in Manchester, N.H., 1940; for priests and laymen. Approved as a secular institute, 1959 (first secular institute of diocesan right founded in the US to be approved by the Holy See). Addresses: P. O. Box 357, Manchester, N.H. 03101. C.P. 1815, Quebec City, P.Q., Canada.

Society of Our Lady of the Way: Originated, 1936; for women. Approved as a secular institute of pontifical right Jan. 3, 1953. Address: Society of Our Lady of the Way, 2339 N. Catalina Ave., Los Angeles, Calif. 90027. International membership of more than 400.

Teresian Institute: Founded in Spain 1911; for women. Address: 235 Cypress St., Newton Centre, Mass. 02159.

Voluntas Dei: Originated in Canada, 1958; for secular priests and laymen. Approved as a secular institute May 6, 1965. Address: Institute Voluntas Dei, 7385, Blvd. Parent, Trois-Rivieres, Que., Canada. International membership of approximately 150.

The *Annuario Pontificio* (1975) lists the following **secular institutes of pontifical right**

which are not established in the US:

For men: Institute of Prado (originated Dec. 25, 1856; decree of praise, Oct. 28, 1959). Christ the King (originated, 1936; decree of praise, Oct. 27, 1963).

For women: Alliance in Jesus through Mary, Apostles of the Sacred Heart, Catechists of the Sacred Heart of Jesus (Ukrainian), Daughters of the Sacred Heart, Daughters of the Queen of the Apostles, Institute of the Blessed Virgin Mary (della Strada), Missionaries of the Sick, Institute of Notre Dame du Travail, Institute of Our Lady of Life, Oblates of Christ the King, Workers of Divine Love, Faithful Servants of Jesus.

Associations

Caritas: Originated in New Orleans, 1950; for women. Address: 3316 Feliciana St., New Orleans, La. 70126.

Daughters of Our Lady of Fatima: Originated in Lansdowne, Pa., 1949; for women. Received diocesan approval, Jan., 1952. Address: Miss Mary C. Long, Fatima House, Rolling Hills Rd., Ottsville, Pa. 18942.

Focolare Movement: Inaugurated in Trent, Italy, in 1943, by Chiara Lubich and a small group of companions; for men and women. Approved as an association of the faithful, 1962. It is not a secular institute by statute, but vows are observed by many single persons among its totally dedicated core membership of 1,500. Centers are located in 30 countries throughout the world. US centers are located in Boston, Chicago (where it was introduced in 1955), and New York. National headquarters : 250 E. 73rd St., Apt. 21D, New York, N.Y. 10021 (women); 206 Skillman Ave., Brooklyn, N.Y. 11211 (men).

Institute of Apostolic Oblates: Founded in Rome, Italy, 1947; for women. Address: 205 S. Pine Dr., Fullerton, Calif. 92633 (provincial house).

Jesus Caritas Fraternity of Fr. Charles de Foucauld: Originated in Ars, France, 1952; for women. Established as an association of perfection May 31, 1962. Address: Miss Patricia M. Collins, 4736 N. Bernard St., Chicago, Ill. 60625. International membership of approximately 550.

Madonna House Apostolate: Originated in Toronto, Canada, 1930; for priests and lay persons. Diocesan pious union. Address: Madonna House, Combermere, Ontario, Canada KOJ ILO — Catherine Doherty (women), Jack Scanlan (men), Rev. J. Callahan (priests). International membership and missions.

Pax Christi: Lay institute of men and women dedicated to witnessing to Christ, with special emphasis on service to the poor in Mississippi. Addresses: St. Francis Center, 708 Ave. I, Greenwood, Miss. 38930; LaVerna House, 2108 Altawoods Blvd., Jackson, Miss. 39204.

THIRD ORDERS SECULAR

Third orders secular are societies of the faithful living in the world who seek to deepen their Christian life and apostolic commitment in association with and according to the spirit of various religious institutes. Members are called Tertiaries, Lay Franciscans, etc. The orders are called "third" because their foundation followed the establishment of the first (for men) and second (for women) religious orders with which they are associated.

Augustine, Third Order Secular of St.: Founded, 13th century; approved Nov. 7, 1400.

Carmel (The Lay Carmelite Order) (Calced): Founded, 13th century; approved by Pope Nicholas V, Oct. 7, 1452. Address: Aylesford, National Scapular Center, I-55 and Cass Ave. N. Westmont, Ill. 60559. Approximately 15,000 members in US.

Carmel, Third Order Secular of Our Blessed Lady of Mt., and St. Teresa of Jesus (Discalced): Rule based on the Carmelite reform established by St. Teresa and St. John of the Cross, 16th century; approved Mar. 23, 1594; rule revised and given for five-year experimental period Oct. 26, 1970. Addresses of provincial directors: 514 Warren St., Brookline, Mass. 02146; Mt. Carmel Center, 4600 W. Davis, Dallas, Tex. 75211; P.O. Box 3079 San Jose, Calif. 95116. Approximately 3,150 members in US.

Dominic, Third Order Secular of St. (The Dominican Laity): Founded in the 13th century. Addresses of provincial directors: 141 E. 65th St., New York, N.Y. 10021; 1909 S. Ashland Ave., Chicago, Ill. 60608; St. Albert's College, 5890 Birch Ct., Oakland, Calif. 94618.

Francis, Third Order Secular of St. (Secular Franciscans): Founded, 1209 by St. Francis of Assisi; approved Aug. 30, 1221. Address: National Secretary, Third Order of St. Francis, 1615 Vine St., Cincinnati, Ohio 45210. Approximately 2.2 million in the world, 55,000 English speaking in North America.

Mary, Third Order of: Founded, Dec. 8, 1850; rule approved by the Holy See, 1857. Addresses of provincial directors: 3875 Harewood Rd., N.E., Washington, D.C. 20017; 7 Harvard St., P. O. Box 66, Charlestown, Mass. 02129; 625 Pine St., San Francisco, Calif. 94108. Approximately 14,000 in the world, 6,600 in US.

Mary, Third Order Secular of Servants of (Servite): Founded, 1233; approved, 1424. Address: Director of Third Order, 323 W. Illinois St., Chicago, Ill. 60610. Approximately 2,500 in US.

Mercy, Secular Third Order of Our Lady of (Mercedarian): Founded, 1219 by St. Peter Nolasco; approved the same year.

Norbert, Third Order of St.: Founded, 1122 by St. Norbert; approved by Pope Honorius II, 1126. Address: St. Norbert Abbey, De Pere, Wis. Approximately 5,300 in US and Canada.

Trinity, Third Order Secular of the Most Holy: Founded, about 1198; approved, 1219. Address: Bro. Gary MacPherson, Holy Trinity Monastery, Pikesville, Md. 21208.

Oblates of St. Benedict are lay persons affiliated with a Benedictine abbey or monastery who strive to direct their lives, as circumstances permit, according to the spirit and Rule of St. Benedict.

MISSION CONTRIBUTIONS

The Congregation for the Evangelization of Peoples announced in April, 1975, that U.S. Catholics increased their annual contribution to the missions in 1974 by three per cent ($610,708) to $21,219,598.33. The American contribution was by far the largest made by the Catholics of any one nation.

FIDES

International Fides Service, the news agency of the Congregation for the Evangelization of Peoples, issues a periodic service of news, comment and background information concerning the missions.

The office address is Via di Propaganda, 1 C, 00187, Rome, Italy.

AGRIMISSIO

Agrimissio is a service agency aiding religious institutes, other organizations (including the Food and Agriculture Organization of the United Nations) and technicians working in rural development in mission territories. It was established in 1970 by the Union of Superiors General, the International Union of Superiors General and the National Catholic Rural Life Conference.

Msgr. Luigi Ligutti, permanent observer of the Holy See to the FAO from 1948 to 1970, is president. Headquarters are located at Piazza S. Calisto, 16, Rome, Italy.

MISSIONARIES EXPELLED

Nine Oblate missionaries, expelled from Laos by the Communist Pathet Lao government, denied in September, 1975, allegations that the people had demonstrated against them.

The information office of the Oblates of Mary Immaculate quoted one of the missionaries as saying: "On the contrary, despite being officially warned to stay away, the people of Luang Prabang showed up en masse at the airport (when the missionaries were leaving) — Christians and Buddhists alike. They stood there in the rain, weeping. None of us will ever forget that scene."

The nine missionaries were part of a group of 29 Italian Oblates expelled by the Communists.

The expulsion of these and other foreign missionaries indicated the need of the Church to recruit and build up native clergy and hierarchy in missionary territories.

Missionary Activity of the Church

The following excerpts concerning the Church's missionary activity are from the decree of the same name promulgated by the Second Vatican Council.

Doctrine

"The pilgrim Church is missionary by her very nature" (No. 2).

Christ "founded His Church as the sacrament of salvation, and sent His apostles into all the world just as He Himself had been sent by His Father (cf. Jn. 20:21). He gave them this command: 'Go, therefore, and make disciples of all nations, baptizing them in the name of the Father, and of the Son, and of the Holy Spirit, teaching them to observe all that I have commanded you' (Mt. 28:19ff). 'Go into the whole world; preach the gospel to every creature. He who believes and is baptized shall be saved, but he who does not believe shall be condemned' (Mk. 16:15ff).

". . . The mission of the Church . . . is fulfilled by that activity which makes her fully present to all men and nations" (No. 5).

" 'Missions' is the term usually given to those particular undertakings by which the heralds of the gospel are sent out by the Church and go forth into the whole world to carry out the task of preaching the gospel and planting the Church among peoples or groups who do not yet believe in Christ. These undertakings are brought to completion by missionary activity and are commonly exercised in certain territories recognized by the Holy See" (and placed under the general direction of the Congregation for the Evangelization of Peoples) (No. 6).

Distinctive Purpose

"The specific purpose of this missionary activity is evangelization and the planting of the Church among those peoples and groups where she has not yet taken root. Thus from the seed which is the Word of God, particular native Churches can be adequately established and flourish the world over, endowed with their own vitality and maturity. Thus too, sufficiently provided with a hierarchy of their own which is joined to a faithful people, and adequately fitted out with requisites for living a full Christian life, they can make their contribution to the good of the Church universal.

". . . Missionary activity among the nations differs from pastoral activity exercised among the faithful, as well as from undertakings aimed at restoring unity among Christians. And yet these two other activities are most closely connected with the missionary zeal of the Church, because the division among Christians damages the most holy cause of preaching the gospel to every creature and blocks the way to the faith for many. Hence, by the same mandate which makes missions necessary, all the baptized are called to be gathered into one flock, and thus to be able to bear unanimous witness before the nations to Christ their Lord. And if they are not yet capable of bearing full witness to the same faith, they should at least be animated by mutual esteem and love" (No. 6).

"Missionary activity is nothing else and nothing less than a manifestation or epiphany of God's will, and the fulfillment of that will in the world and in world history. In the course of this history God plainly works out the history of salvation by means of mission. By the preaching of the word and by the celebration of the sacraments, whose center and summit is the most holy Eucharist, missionary activity brings about the presence of Christ, the Author of salvation" (No. 9).

The three phases of missionary activity are:

• **Christian Witness,** to establish the presence of the Church: "The Church must be present in these groups of men through those of her children who dwell among them or are sent to them. For, wherever they live, all Christians are bound to show forth, by the example of their lives and by the witness of their speech, that new man which they put on at baptism, and that power of the Holy Spirit by whom they were strengthened at confirmation. Thus other men, observing their good works, can glorify the Father (cf. Mt. 5:16) and can better perceive the real meaning of human life and the bond which ties the whole community of mankind together" (No. 11).

• **Preaching the Gospel and Gathering Together the People of God,** through proclamation of the Gospel to conversion and on to transition to full Christian life. In this process: "The Church strictly forbids forcing anyone to embrace the faith, or alluring or enticing people by unworthy techniques. By the same token, she also strongly insists on a person's right not to be deterred from the faith by unjust vexations on the part of others" (No. 13).

• **Forming the Christian Community,** with the objective of developing, sustaining and self-supporting churches in mission lands through the various ministries of lay persons, bishops, priests, deacons and religious (Nos. 15 to 18).

Concerning the role of lay persons, the decree said: "Laymen cooperate in the Church's work of evangelization. As witnesses and at the same time as living instruments, they share in her saving mission. This is especially so if they have been called by God and have been accepted by the bishop for this work" (No. 41).

UNITED STATES FOREIGN MISSIONARIES

(Data on US foreign missionary personnel in the following tables were gathered by, and are reproduced with permission of, the United States Catholic Mission Council, 1325 Massachusetts Ave. N.W., Washington, D.C., 20005.

(For additional information about the Church in mission areas, see News Events and other Almanac entries.)

Field Distribution, 1975

(Under this and following headings, Alaska, Hawaii, etc., are considered abroad because they are outside the 48 contiguous states.)

Africa: Men, 592; women, 473; total, 1,065. Largest numbers in Tanzania, 179; Kenya, 154; Ghana, 112; Zambia, 94; Uganda, 74.

Near East: Men, 41; women, 30; total, 71. Largest numbers in Israel, 25; Lebanon, 16; Yemen, 12.

Far East: Men, 1,254; women, 560; total, 1,814. Largest numbers in Philippines, 526; Japan, 364; Taiwan, 208; India, 177; Korea, 163; Hong Kong, 87.

Oceania: Men, 397; women, 411; total, 808. Largest groups in Hawaii, 255; New Guinea, 243; Caroline Islands, 55; Guam, 54.

Europe: Men, 18; women, 19; total, 37. Largest groups in Finland, 11; Sweden, 10; Denmark, 7.

North America: Men, 110; women, 142; total, 252. Largest group in Alaska, 138.

Caribbean Islands: Men, 354; women, 344; total, 698. Largest groups in Puerto Rico, 350; Jamaica, 155; Haiti, 52.

Central America: Men, 454; women, 280; total, 734. Largest groups in Mexico, 212; Guatemala, 179.

South America: Men, 919; women, 750; total, 1,669. Largest groups in Peru, 492; Brazil, 485; Bolivia, 279; Chile, 196.

Men Religious, 1975

Sixty-nine mission-sending groups had 3,757 priests and brothers in overseas assignments.

Jesuits: 695 in 39 countries; largest group, 118 in Philippines.

Maryknoll Fathers: 647 in 20 countries; largest group, 69 in Tanzania.

Franciscans (O.F.M.): 239 in 17 countries; largest group, 84 in Brazil.

Divine Word Missionaries: 193 in 13 countries; largest group, 68 in New Guinea.

Oblates of Mary Immaculate: 163 in 16 countries; largest group, 30 in Haiti.

Redemptorists: 163 in 6 countries; largest group, 78 in Brazil.

Capuchins (O.F.M. Cap.): 160 in 10 countries; largest group, 39 in Nicaragua.

Marianists: 148 in 12 countries; largest group, 53 in Hawaii.

Benedictines: 111 in 14 countries; largest group, 19 in Guatemala.

Columbans: 93 in 8 countries; largest group, 39 in Philippines.

Dominicans: 70 in 7 countries; largest groups, 21 each in Nigeria and Pakistan.

Holy Cross Fathers: 69 in 8 countries; largest group, 26 in Bangladesh.

Brothers of Christian Schools: 67 in 13 countries; largest group, 24 in Philippines.

Holy Cross Brothers: 64 in 8 countries; largest group, 21 in Brazil.

Holy Ghost Fathers: 62 in 6 countries; largest groups, 26 each in Puerto Rico and Tanzania.

Passionists: 57 in 4 countries; largest group, 30 in Philippines.

La Salette Fathers: 53 in 5 countries; largest group, 16 in Philippines.

Conventual Franciscans (O.F.M. Conv.): 46 in 6 countries; largest group, 15 in Zambia.

Vincentians: 45 in 8 countries; largest group, 27 in Panama.

Marist Fathers: 40 in 8 countries; largest group, 14 in New Guinea.

Marist Brothers: 31 in 7 countries; largest group, 15 in Philippines.

Missionaries of the Sacred Heart: 30 in 2 countries; larger group, 24 in New Guinea.

Sacred Heart Brothers: 30 in 5 countries; largest group, 15 in Zambia.

White Fathers: 28 in 10 countries; largest group, 7 in Tanzania.

African Missionary Fathers: 24 in 2 countries; larger group, 22 in Liberia.

Augustinians: 22 in 2 countries; larger group, 13 in Peru.

Xaverian Brothers: 21 in 2 countries; larger group, 13 in Kenya.

Oblates of St. Francis de Sales: 20 in 3 countries; largest group, 9 in South Africa.

Missionhurst: 20 in 4 countries; largest group, 13 in Dominican Republic.

Forty other mission-sending institutes had 19 or less members in overseas assignments.

Diocesan Priests, 1975

One hundred and 97 diocesan priests from 77 dioceses were in overseas assignments in 1975.

The largest groups were from Boston (26 in 6 countries) and St. Louis (11 in 3 countries).

Many diocesan priests in overseas assignments were members of the **Missionary Society of St. James the Apostle,** founded by Cardinal Richard J. Cushing of Boston in 1958. Its director is Father Dennis A. Dever, 24 Clark St., Boston, Mass. 02109.

Sisters, 1975

One hundred and 67 mission-sending groups had 2,850 sisters in overseas assignments.

Maryknoll Sisters: 513 in 23 countries; largest group, 87 in Hawaii.

Marists: 165 in 15 countries; largest group, 35 in Fiji.

Sisters of the Third Order of St. Dominic: 130 in 18 countries; largest group, 23 in Peru.

School Sisters of Notre Dame: 100 in 16 countries; largest group, 21 in Puerto Rico.

Servants of the Immaculate Heart of Mary: 76 in 8 countries; largest group, 32 in Peru.

Franciscan Missionaries of Mary: 70 in 18 countries; largest group, 10 in Ghana.

Sisters of Notre Dame de Namur: 69 in 7 countries; largest group, 22 in Kenya.

Daughters of Charity: 62 in 11 countries; largest group, 33 in Bolivia.

Medical Mission Sisters: 55 in 13 countries; largest group, 13 in Ghana.

Benedictines: 54 in 10 countries; largest groups, 10 each in Colombia and Guatemala.

Sisters of St. Joseph (Brentwood, N.Y.): 47 in Puerto Rico.

Religious Sisters of Mercy: 44 in 10 countries; largest group, 10 in Panama.

Sisters of the Holy Cross: 41 in 4 countries; largest group, 20 in Brazil.

Ursulines of the Roman Union: 40 in 13 countries; largest group, 8 in Mexico.

Franciscan Sisters of Allegany, N.Y.: 38 in 3 countries; largest group, 23 in Jamaica.

Servants of the Holy Spirit: 36 in 7 countries; largest group, 12 in Ghana.

Sisters of St. Joseph (Carondelet): 36 in 2 countries; larger group, 25 in Peru.

Sisters of the Holy Child Jesus: 35 in 5 countries; largest group, 14 in Nigeria.

Sisters of the Third Franciscan Order, Minor Conventuals (Syracuse, N.Y.): 34 in 3 countries; largest group, 21 in Hawaii.

Religious Sisters of Mercy in the Union in the U.S.A.: 29 in 6 countries; largest groups in Belize and Honduras.

Felician Sisters: 26 in Brazil.

Sisters of Notre Dame: 26 in 2 countries; larger group, 14 in India.

Bernardines: 25 in 3 countries; largest group, 11 in Puerto Rico.

Graymoor Sisters: 23 in 3 countries; largest group, 16 in Canada.

Sisters of the Most Precious Blood (O'Fallon, Mo.): 22 in 3 countries; largest group, 11 in Finland.

Franciscans of the Sorrowful Mother: 20 in 5 countries; largest group, 10 in Barbados.

Sisters of St. Francis of Millvale: 20 in 2 countries; larger group, 18 in Puerto Rico.

Franciscan Sisters of Perpetual Adoration: 19 in 5 countries; largest group, 10 in Guam.

Missionary Sisters of the Immaculate Heart of Mary: 19 in 9 countries; largest group, 5 in Virgin Islands.

Religious Sisters of the Sacred Heart: 19 in 9 countries; largest group, 5 in Japan.

Sisters of St. John the Baptist: 19 in 3 countries; largest group, 9 in Zambia.

One hundred and 36 other mission-sending institutes had 18 or less members in overseas assignments.

Lay Volunteers, 1975

Three hundred and 44 lay volunteers of 28 sponsoring organizations were in overseas assignments in 1975.

Catholic Relief Services: 99 in 45 countries; largest group, 13 in Cambodia.

Jesuit Volunteer Corps: 59 in 4 countries; largest group, 50 in Alaska.

Lay Mission Helpers: 54 in 13 countries; largest group, 12 in New Guinea.

Frontier Apostolate: 33 in Canada.

Catholic Medical Mission Board: 17* in 10 countries; largest group, 4 in Haiti. (*This figure represents only those whose term of service is for at least one year. In addition, 85 short-term volunteers served in 14 countries during the past year.)

Consolata Missioners: 9 in 2 countries; larger group, 8 in Kenya.

Madonna House Apostolate: 7 in 2 countries; larger group, 5 in Grenada.

Milwaukee Latin American Office: 6 in 5 countries; largest group, 2 in Colombia.

Twenty additional sponsoring organizations had 5 or less members in overseas assignments.

U.S. Mission Council

The United States Catholic Mission Council, which took over and expanded functions of the former Mission Secretariat, started operations Sept. 1, 1970, "to provide a forum and organ for the evaluation, coordination and fostering, in the United States, of the worldwide missionary effort of the Church."

Structurally, the council is made up of five seven-member committees representing the National Conference of Catholic Bishops, the Conference of Major Superiors of Men, the Leadership Conference of Women Religious, the National Council of Catholic Laity and mission agencies. Heads of the committees form the executive board which meets at least quarterly to oversee the implementation of policies and programs determined at annual meetings of the whole committee.

Typical activities of the council are educational efforts related to the Church's teaching about its missionary nature, the sponsorship of conferences on theological and pastoral foundations of missionary endeavor, liaison and cooperation with missionary bodies of other Christian churches, the encouragement of mission studies, training programs and refresher courses for departing and returning missionaries, gathering data on missionary activity, and general mission animation.

Rev. Anthony Bellagamba, I.M.C., is executive secretary of the council, with offices at 1325 Massachusetts Ave. N.W., Room 500, Washington, D.C. 20005.

U.S. FOREIGN MISSIONARIES, 1958-1975

Year	Diocesan Priests	Religious Priests	Religious Brothers	Religious Sisters	Seminarians	Lay Persons	Total
1958	19	3477*		2532		96	6124
1960	14	3018	575	2827	170	178	6782
1962	31	3172	720	2764	152	307	7146
1964	80	3438	782	3137	157	532	8126
1966	215	3731	901	3706	201	549	9303
1968	282	3727	869	4150	208	419	9655
1970	373	3117	666	3824	90	303	8373
1972+	246	3182	634	3121	97	376	7656
1973	237	3913*		3012		529	7691
1974	220	3084	639	2916	101	458	7418
1975	197	3023	669	2850	65	344	7148

*Includes religious brothers and seminarians.
+A corrected total for 1972 should read 7937, indicating losses of 436 from 1970 to 1972 and 246 from 1972 to 1973.

FIELD DISTRIBUTION BY AREAS, 1958-1975

	1958	1960	1962	1964	1966	1968	1970	1972	1973	1974	1975
Africa	617	781	901	1025	1184	1157	1141	1107	1229	1121	1065
Far East	1809	1959	2110	2332	2453	2470	2137	1955	1962	1845	1814
Near East	110	111	75	122	142	128	39	59	54	60	71
Oceania	951	986	992	846	953	1027	900	826	811	883	808
Europe	153	203	93	69	38	33	38	39	40	43	37
North America	357	337	224	220	211	251	233	234	253	241	252
Caribbean Islands	928	991	967	1056	1079	1198	1067	819	796	757	698
Central America	392	433	537	660	857	936	738	728	763	752	734
South America	807	981	1247	1796	2386	2455	2080	1889	1783	1716	1669
TOTALS	6124	6782	7146	8126	9303	9655	8373	7656	7691	7418	7148

HOME MISSIONS

The expression "home missions" is applied to places in the U.S. where the local Church is not fully established, i.e., where it does not have resources, human and otherwise, which are needed to begin or, if begun, to survive and grow. These areas share the name "missions" with their counterparts in foreign lands because they too need outside help to provide the personnel and means for making the Church present and active there in carrying out its mission for the salvation of men.

Dioceses in the Southeast, the Southwest, and the Far West are most urgently in need of outside help to carry on the work of the Church. Millions of persons live in counties in which there are no resident priests. Many others live in rural areas beyond the reach and influence of a Catholic center. According to the most recent statistics compiled by the Glenmary Research Center there are 599 priestless counties in the United States. Many states generally thought to be well off from a pastoral standpoint include areas in which the Catholic Church and the ministry of priests are virtually unknown.

About 20 per cent of the total U.S. population and less than three per cent of the Catholic population live within the boundaries of the 17 "most missionary" dioceses of the country. A "Survey of the Catholic Weakness" conducted by the National Catholic Rural Life Conference disclosed that the Catholic Church ranked 33rd among 38 religious bodies in percentage of rural membership.

Mission Workers

A number of forces are at work to meet the pastoral needs of these missionary areas and to establish permanent churches and operating institutions where they are required. In many dioceses, one or more missions and stations are attended from established parishes and are gradually growing to independent status. Priests, brothers and sisters belonging to scores of religious institutes are engaged full-time in the home missions. Lay persons, some of them in affiliation with special groups and movements, are also involved.

Group 7 was organized by the Glenmary Home Missioners for this purpose in 1971. Membership is open to Catholic adults, 21-years-old and older, willing to make a minimum commitment of two years. Twenty-six members of Group 7 are working in Georgia, Mississippi, North Carolina, Tennessee and Virginia.

The Society for the Propagation of the Faith, which conducts an annual collection for mission support in all parishes of the U.S., allocates 40 per cent of this sum for disbursement to home missions through the American Board of Catholic Missions.

The Catholic Church Extension Society provides one million dollars or more a year for the building of mission installations and related needs.

Special mission support is the purpose of the Commission for the Catholic Missions among the Colored People and the Indians.

Diocesan, parochial and high school mission societies frequently undertake projects in behalf of the home missions.

Glenmary Missioners

The Glenmary Home Missioners, founded by Father W. Howard Bishop in 1939, is the only home mission society established for the sole purpose of carrying out the pastoral ministry in small towns and the rural districts of the United States. With 76 priests and 22 professed brothers as of June 1, 1975, the Glenmary Missioners had 41 mission bases and 47 satellite missions in the archdioceses of Atlanta and Cincinnati, and in the dioceses of Altoona-Johnstown, Birmingham, Charlotte, Covington, Dallas, Harrisburg, Little Rock, Nashville, Natchez-Jackson, Tulsa, Owensboro, Savannah and Wheeling-Charleston.

The Rev. Robert C. Berson is president.

National headquarters are located in Fairfield, O. The mailing address is P. O. Box 46404, Cincinnati, O. 45246.

Regional offices for information are at 429 Unquowa Rd., Fairfield, Conn. 06430, and P. O. Box 8, Techny, Ill. 60082.

Sisters

The Glenmary Home Mission Sisters of America, founded July 16, 1952, had 19 professed members engaged in work in six social and catechetical centers, one home nursing center, one house of study and one promotional center, in the archdioceses of Cincinnati and St. Louis, and the dioceses of Charlotte, Columbus, Covington, Dallas, Owensboro and Savannah. Much of this work was concentrated in rural areas where poverty was prevalent. In September, 1971, members of the community began work in religious education research in Nashville and in campus ministry in the Savannah diocese. The community also conducts an associate program for laywomen interested in work in home mission areas for two or more years.

Sister Mary Joseph Wade, elected in 1967, is superior general. The community has headquarters at 4580 Colerain Ave., Cincinnati, Ohio 45223.

Negro Missions

The Commission for Catholic Missions among the Colored People and the Indians reported the following (1974) statistics for 73 dioceses in which it supplied financial assistance: 859,123 Catholics, 667 churches, 970 priests, 24,546 infant baptisms, 5,973 adults received into the Church, 403 schools, 107,313 students. The total number of black Catholics was estimated to be more than 900,000.

The commission, using figures different in some respects from those given above, reported: "A total of 680 churches are maintained for service to entirely or predominantly Negro congregations in eighty-three dioceses. . . . Priests assigned to these *de facto* Negro missions and parishes number slightly more than one thousand. . . . Elementary and high schools are attached to two out of three predominantly Negro missions and parishes. . . . They are staffed by approximately five thousand religious and lay teachers. They and other Catholic schools enroll over 180,000 Negro pupils."

The report, noting that it was impossible to determine "whether, or to what extent indifferent or lapsed Catholics are included in a parish or diocesan report," stated that "at least one out of twenty Negroes is or ought to be Catholic. Fifty years ago the ratio was one out of fifty-five and the reported total was less than two hundred thousand."

The commission report, which was limited in scope, did not cover all aspects of the Church's ministry to the black population, which was estimated to number more than 22 million.

Indian Missions

The Commission for Catholic Missions among the Colored People and the Indians reported the following (1974) statistics for 43 dioceses in which it supplied financial assistance: 155,600 Catholics, 398 churches, 265 priests, 3,680 infant baptisms, 747 adults received into the Church, 39 schools, 6,538 students.

The states with the largest number of missions and Catholic Indians were Arizona, New Mexico, South Dakota and Montana, where almost two-thirds of the reservation Indians now live. Two hundred and seventy-two churches and chapels and 21 schools were maintained with 135 priests engaged in serving more than 70,000 Catholic Indians in these areas. Ninety-two missions and ten schools were located in the states of California, North Dakota, Minnesota, Wisconsin and Wyoming for the estimated 40,000 Catholic Indians there. Alaska had 44 mission churches and chapels and 26 priests to minister to approximately 10,000 Catholic Indians. In other states, the commission reported, "reservations are small; consequently only several schools and from one to five missions are maintained at most of them."

The Catholic mission school played an important part in many of the missions. "Thirty-nine of these," the report stated, "are presently maintained. . . . They are now attended by 6,538 Catholic Indian children from about a hundred Indian congregations."

According to the most recent census reports, it was estimated that 300,000 Indians were living on federal reservations and

307,000 in urban areas. An estimated 25,000 Catholic Indians were not on reservations.

Support Bodies

The Catholic Church Extension Society: This society was established for the purpose of preserving and extending the Church in the US and its dependencies principally through the collection and disbursement of funds for missions. Since the time of its founding in 1905, more than $50 million have been received and expended for this purpose. Disbursements in 1974 amounted to $2.6 million.

Works of the society are supervised by a board of governors consisting of twelve members: Cardinal John Cody, archbishop of Chi-

cago, chancellor; Rev. Joseph A. Cusack, president; five bishops or priests, and five laymen. Society headquarters are located at 1307 S. Wabash Ave., Chicago, Ill. 60605.

Commission for Catholic Missions among the Colored People and the Indians: Organized in 1886, this commission provided financial support ($2,606,000 in 1974) for religious works among Negroes and Indians in the United States. Funds are raised by an annual collection in all parishes of the country.

Cardinal John J. Krol is head of the board of directors. Rev. J. B. Tennelly, S.S., D.D., is secretary. Commission headquarters are located at 2021 H St. N.W., Washington, D.C. 20006.

MINISTRY TO THE SPANISH-SPEAKING

The U.S. Census Bureau, in a report issued in the summer of 1975, indicated that there were approximately 11.2 million persons of Spanish origin in the country. They included about: 60 per cent of Mexican origin; 15 per cent of Puerto Rican origin; 7 per cent of Cuban origin. They comprised about 5 per cent of the nation's population.

According to other estimates, the total figure was considerably higher.

Every state has some Spanish-speaking residents, ranging from 2,000 in North Dakota to more than 2.5 million in California.

Nearly three-fourths of the Spanish-speaking live in California, New Mexico, Texas, Florida and New York.

Most of the Spanish-speaking in the southwestern states are Mexican American. Large numbers of Mexican Americans are also in the Chicago area, Ohio, northern Indiana and southern Michigan.

Puerto Ricans, although concentrated especially in and near New York City, also have large settlements in Chicago and Philadelphia. New York City alone has about three out of every five persons of Puerto Rican birth or parentage in the U.S.

Most persons of Cuban origin live in Florida, particularly in the Miami and Tampa areas. There are smaller concentrations in New York City, northeastern New Jersey, Los Angeles, Long Beach, Calif., Chicago and urban areas of northwestern Indiana.

The vast majority of the Spanish-speaking in the U.S. have been baptized in the Catholic Church.

Variable Conditions

Pastoral ministry to the Spanish-speaking in the United States varies, depending on differences among the people and the availability of personnel to carry it out.

The pattern in cities with large numbers of Spanish-speaking is built around special churches, centers or other agencies where pastoral and additional forms of service are provided in a manner suited to the needs, language and culture of the people. Services in

some places are extensive and include legal advice, job placement, language instruction, recreational and social assistance, specialized counseling, replacement services. In many places, however, even where there are special ministries, the needs are generally greater than the means required to meet them.

Some of the urban dwellers have been absorbed into established parishes and routines of church life and activity. Many Spanish-speaking communities, especially those with transients, remain in need of special ministries.

An itinerant form of ministry best meets the needs of the scores of thousands of migrant workers who follow the crops in various areas of the country. Some of these ministries are carried out from centers and include other services — health, instruction for children, etc. — in addition to opportunities for attending Mass and receiving the sacraments.

Pastoral care for the Spanish-speaking was the central concern of the 1972 Primer Encuentro Nacional Hispano de Pastoral, a national meeting of diocesan bishops and their delegates sponsored by the U.S. Catholic Conference. Needs pinpointed in deliberations were for: greater participation in the Spanish-speaking in leadership and decision-making at all levels in the Church in the U.S.; the development of programs for Christian leadership formation; the establishment of nationally coordinated regional centers of pastoral research and reflection.

Special ministries for the Spanish-speaking have been in operation for a long time in dioceses of the Southwest. The total number of dioceses with such ministries is more than 50. More than 20 others have migrant ministries in operation.

Organizations

NCCB/USCC Secretariat for the Spanish-Speaking: The secretariat influences policy and programs of the American bishops in developing a pastoral response to the Spanish-speaking. It promotes the establishment of diocesan offices and provides communication informational services.

Paul Sedillo, Jr., is director of the national office at 1312 Massachusetts Ave. N.W., Washington, D.C. 20005.

In the Southwest, 55 Mexican-American priests organized **PADRES** in October, 1969, to help the Church identify more closely with the social, economic and educational needs of the Spanish-speaking. PADRES is the abbreviation of the Spanish title, "Padres Asociados para Derechos Religiosos, Educativos y Sociales."

Leadership development among the Spanish-speaking poor is the first of five goals of PADRES, which has a nationwide membership of 1,113 — including 256 Hispanic — priests. Rev. Roberto Peña, O.M.I., is the national chairman. Father Juan Romero is the executive director. Offices are located at 3112 W. Ashby St., San Antonio, Tex. 78228.

An analogous organization of Chicano sisters, **Las Hermanas,** was organized in 1971 (see separate entry).

Mexican American Cultural Center: Founded by the Texas Catholic Conference at a meeting held in Austin Sept. 29, 1971, MACC is a center of research, education, leadership formation and publication. Cooperating with PADRES and Las Hermanas, and with the additional endorsement of the U.S. Catholic Conference, it is dedicated to the liberation and integral development of Mexican-American and other Spanish-speaking peoples. It coordinates programs in social and spiritual development of the Spanish-speaking; bi-cultural/bi-lingual learning environments; community services for cultural and leadership development; intensive courses in pastoral ministry for the Spanish-speaking.

Ruben R. Alfano is program director of the center, which is located at 3019 French Pl., P. O. Box 28185, San Antonio, Tex. 78284.

Miami Apostolate

The Spanish-Speaking Apostolate in metropolitan Miami is one of the most extensive in the country. It serves a population of well over 400,000 people: more than 300,000 Cubans who have established residence there since Fidel Castro rose to power Jan. 1, 1959; a permanent Latin population of more than 50,000; and some 100,000 migrant workers. Directly involved in the apostolate are 96 Spanish-speaking priests and 88 religious brothers and sisters. Spanish-speaking priests are assigned to 39 parishes.

Centro Hispano Catolico (Spanish Catholic Center), founded by Archbishop Coleman F. Carroll in October, 1959, provides many forms of assistance to new arrivals from Latin countries, including: pastoral counseling, orientation to life in the U.S., employment services, medicine-food-clothing distribution, day nursery and kindergarten care, programs for senior citizens, and home visits. Located in the center are Archdiocesan Offices for Immigration Services and the Latin American Affairs Office which fosters cultural relations with Latin American countries.

The staff of the center consists of a chaplain, one Sister of St. Philip Neri, four Sisters of Social Service, and more than a score of lay persons. Sister Suzanne, S.S.S., is supervisor of the center. The executive director and episcopal vicar for Spanish-speaking peoples in the archdiocese is Msgr. Orlando Fernandez. The center is located at 130 N. E. 2nd St., Miami, Fla. 33132.

Officers of the Migration and Refugee Service, U.S. Catholic Conference, in Miami figured largely in the work of receiving and resettling many of the refugees who have come to this country via the Cuban airlift and Spain.

All told, 299,257 persons were resettled between 1961 and the end of 1974. The states with the highest numbers of resettled Cubans were New York (80,961), New Jersey (59,338), California (39,760), and Illinois (22,422).

APPALACHIA COMMITTEE

The Catholic Committee of Appalachia (CCA), chaired by Bishop Michael Begley of Charlotte, consists of bishops, priests, religious and lay persons engaged in ministry in the 13-state region. Appalachia has been defined by Congress as including all of West Virginia and parts of Alabama, Georgia, Kentucky, Maryland, Mississippi, New York, North Carolina, Ohio, Pennsylvania, South Carolina, Tennessee and Virginia.

In 1975, "This Land Is Home to Me: A Pastoral Letter on Powerlessness in Appalachia," was issued by the Catholic bishops of the region.

The CCA belongs to the Commission on Religion in Appalachia, an ecumenical group with members from 17 denominations.

APPALACHIAN INDUSTRIES

Appalachian Industries, specializing in woodworking, was started in 1967 by Father Patrick O'Donnell, a Glenmary Missioner assigned to Lewis and Carter Counties in northeastern Kentucky.

Its purposes are to attract new businesses and to develop local enterprises, thereby giving people of the area reasons to remain in local employment rather than moving to cities for the sake of higher income.

Industries — specializing in custom-designed walnut and cherry tables, benches, chairs in Shaker simplicity and Danish contemporary styles — has a market outlet in Appalachian Studios and runs a retail gift shop in Vanceburg.

Appalachian Studios is located on Route 59 south of Vanceburg. The mailing address is Route 1, Box 6-A, Vanceburg, Ky. 41179.

Education

Following are a résumé and excerpts of the principal themes stated in the Declaration on Christian Education issued by the Second Vatican Council.

All men have an inalienable right to education for personal and social development, and for attainment of their ultimate end (salvation). Christians have a right to a Christian education.

Parents are the primary and principal educators, and the first school is the family in which children learn to live in the society of men and of the Church.

Parents, who entrust others with a share in the work of educating their children, need the help of the community. Civil society, therefore, has the responsibility of aiding parents and secondary educators, as the common good demands, by building schools and providing other educational institutions.

Roles in Education

"The office of educating belongs by a unique title to the Church, not merely because she deserves recognition as a human society capable of educating, but most of all because she has the responsibility of announcing the way of salvation to all men, of communicating the life of Christ to those who believe, and of assisting them with ceaseless concern so that they may grow into the fullness of that same life" (No. 3).

"In discharging her educative function, the Church is preoccupied with all appropriate means to that end. But she is particularly concerned with the means which are proper to herself, of which catechetical training is foremost. . . . The Church seeks to penetrate and ennoble with her own spirit those other means which belong to the common heritage of mankind, and which contribute mightily to the refinement of spirit and the molding of men. Among these are the media of social communication, many groups devoted to spiritual and physical development, youth associations, and especially schools" (No. 4).

"Parents, who have the first and the inalienable duty and right to educate their children, should enjoy true freedom in their choice of schools. Consequently, public authority, which has the obligation to oversee and defend the liberties of citizens, ought to see to it, out of a concern for distributive justice, that public subsidies are allocated in such a way that, when selecting schools for their children, parents are genuinely free to follow their consciences.

"For the rest, it is incumbent upon the state to provide all citizens with the opportunity to acquire an appropriate degree of cultural enrichment, and with the proper preparation for exercising their civic duties and rights. Therefore, the state itself ought to protect the right of children to receive an adequate schooling. . . . must keep in mind the principle of subsidiarity, so that no kind of school monopoly arises. For such a monopoly would militate against the native rights of the human person, the development and spread of culture itself, the peaceful association of citizens, and the pluralism which exists today in very many societies" (No. 6).

"The Church is keenly aware of her very grave obligation to give zealous attention to the moral and religious education of all her children. To those large numbers of them who are being trained in schools which are not Catholic, she needs to be present with her special affection and helpfulness. This she does through the living witness of those who teach and direct such students, through the apostolic activity of their schoolmates, but most of all through the services of the priests and laymen who transmit to them the doctrine of salvation in a way suited to their age and circumstances, and who afford them spiritual assistance through programs which are appropriate under the prevailing conditions of time and setting.

"The Church reminds parents of the serious duty which is theirs of taking every opportunity — or of making the opportunity — for their children to be able to enjoy these helps and to pace their development as Christians with their growth as citizens of the world. For this reason, the Church gives high praise to those civil authorities and civil societies that show regard for the pluralistic character of modern society, and take into account the right of religious liberty, by helping families in such a way that in all schools the education of their children can be carried out according to the moral and religious convictions of each family" (No. 7).

Catholic School Purposes

"The Church's involvement in the field of education is demonstrated especially by the Catholic school. No less than other schools does the Catholic school pursue cultural goals and the natural development of youth. But it has several distinctive purposes.

• "It aims to create for the school community an atmosphere enlivened by the gospel spirit of freedom and charity.

• "It aims to help the adolescent in such a way that the development of his own personality will be matched by the growth of that new creation he became by baptism.

• "It strives to relate all human culture eventually to the news of salvation, so that the light of faith will illumine the knowledge which students gradually gain of the world, of life, and of mankind."

"The Catholic school retains its immense importance in . . . our times." (No. 8).

BASIC TEACHINGS FOR CATHOLIC RELIGIOUS EDUCATION

Following is the text of Basic Teachings for Catholic Religious Education, *a document by the U.S. bishops listing the essential elements of faith which must be stressed in the religious formation of Catholics of all ages. The text, in preparation for two years, was approved by the Congregation for the Clergy and the U.S. bishops, and was released for publication Jan. 11, 1973. It reflects the contents of the* General Catechetical Directory *approved by Pope Paul VI Mar. 18, 1971, and is one of several contributions toward the development of a* National Catechetical Directory *still in preparation.*

(This text, copyrighted by the National Conference of Catholic Bishops, was circulated by the NC Documentary Service, *Origins,* Vol. 2, No. 31.

INTRODUCTION

All religious education is formation in Christ, given to make "faith become living, conscious and active, through the light of instruction." Religious education is proclaiming to others the gospel of the risen Lord, while showing that this "Good News" alone gives meaning to life. So the faith, prayer and lived example of the teacher are of great importance.

No list of documents can bring about real religious education, but certain basic teachings are necessary for doctrinal substance and stability.

This text sets down the principal elements of the Christian message. These basic teachings are here specified by the American bishops, who as bishops hold in the Church special responsibility for determining the content of faith instruction. It is necessary that these basic teachings be central in all Catholic religious instruction, be never overlooked or minimized, and be given adequate and frequent emphasis.

This text makes clear what must be stressed in the religious formation of Catholics of all ages. The bishops have in mind every type of religious education: in the home, in Catholic schools, in programs of the Confraternity of Christian Doctrine, in courses of adult education in religion.

The most effective methodology is expected in teaching basic beliefs. Due consideration should be shown for the listener's level of maturity and understanding. "In this instruction a proper sequence should be observed, as well as a method appropriate to the matter that is being treated, and to the natural disposition, ability, age and circumstances of life of the listener."

It is necessary that the authentic teachings of the Church, and those only, be presented in religious instruction as official Catholic doctrine. Religion texts or classroom teachers should never present merely subjective theorizing as the Church's teaching.

"For this reason, a distinction must be borne in mind between, on the one hand, the area that is devoted to scientific investigation and, on the other, the area that concerns the teaching of the faithful. In the first, experts enjoy the freedom required by their work and are free to communicate to others, in books and commentaries, the fruits of their research. In the second, only those doctrines may be attributed to the Church which are declared to be such by her authentic Magisterium."

This document is not to be confused with either the *General Catechetical Directory* or the planned *National Catechetical Directory* (to which this document will be helpful input). This document should, however, be read in the light of the *General Catechetical Directory,* by which its admittedly limited scope can readily be understood.

This text does not give guidance concerning a hierarchical order of importance of doctrines, or concerning methods of religious instruction. This only specifies the doctrinal basics which the bishops expect in teaching Catholic doctrine. This is intended for parents and catechists, for priests, deacons and religious, for writers and publishers of catechetical texts — to use as adult study and in reviewing the content of religious education programs.

John Henry Cardinal Newman described the knowledge of religion expected in his day: "We want a laity . . . who know their religion, who enter into it, who know just where they stand, who know what they hold and what they do not, who know their creed so well that they can give an account of it, who know so much history that they can defend it."

A century later, the bishops want all this. But they ask and pray for much more — for a laity transformed by the gospel message, who put the gospel to work in every action of their daily lives, whose joy and simplicity and concern for others are so radiant that all men recognize them as Christ's disciples by the love they have for one another.

THREE THEMES

There are three themes, chosen from others, which carry through all religious education. These are:

First Theme: The Importance of Prayer — The People of God have always been a praying people. Religious educators then, who are mature in the faith and faithful to this tradition, will teach prayer. This teaching will take place through experiences of prayer, through the example of prayer, and through the learning of common prayers. Religious education, at home or in the classroom, given by a teacher who values prayer, will provide both the instruction and the experience.

People can pray together as a community when they share some common prayers. So it is important that some of the Church's great prayers be understood, memorized and said frequently. Among these are the Sign of the Cross, the Our Father, the Hail Mary, the Apostles' Creed, an Act of Contrition, and the Rosary.

But there is more to prayer than memorized formulas. Talking with God spontaneously and familiarly, and listening to him, is prayer. Informal prayer, suited to the person's age and capacity, should be explained and encouraged. Praise and thankfulness in prayer bring balance and strength in the difficulties, as well as the joys, of life.

By instruction in prayer, through all levels of religious education. the learner is gradually led on to a more mature prayer — to meditation, contemplation, and union with God.

Second Theme: Participating in the Liturgy — As members of the Christian community, all are called to participate actively in the liturgical prayer of the Church. Religious education therefore must involve the student in his faith community and in that community's liturgy.

Liturgy itself educates. It teaches, it forms community, it forms the individual. It makes possible worship of God and a social apostolate to men.

The Mass, the Church's "great prayer," is the highest, most noble form of the Church's liturgy. Effective instruction will therefore help every Christian participate actively in the eucharistic celebration of his own witnessing faith community.

It is especially important, therefore, that the eucharistic celebration engage younger members of the parish in genuine worship. The parish community takes on new dimension and vitality from their participation in every Mass, especially when the community comes together on Sundays and holy days. The young of the parish are influenced by the example of their elders, and grow by their own full sharing in the Sacrifice of the Mass.

Third Theme: Familiarity with the Holy Bible — A life of prayer is nourished by reading the Bible, which is in itself a form of prayer.

The Word of God is life-giving. It nourishes and inspires, strengthens and sustains. It is the primary source, with Tradition, of Church teaching.

Religious education should encourage love and respect for the Scriptures. This will happen as one is gradually introduced to the Scriptures and given a background knowledge which will prepare him for reading and understanding them. At an appropriate level, each one should have his own copy of the Bible.

In studying and teaching the Bible, the instructor should follow the approach of the Second Vatican Council. The Bible has God as its author and helps us to know and love Jesus Christ.

The Bible is likewise to be taught as a collection of divinely inspired books, each with its human author, its history of composition, and type of literature (or literary form). These help us understand "what meaning the sacred writers really intended, and what God wanted to manifest by means of their words."

The words of St. Paul should describe the Catholic student of religion: "From your infancy you have known the Sacred Scriptures, the source of the wisdom which, through faith in Jesus Christ, leads to salvation. All Scripture is inspired of God and is useful for teaching — for reproof, correction, and training in holiness, so that the man of God may be fully competent and equipped for every good work" (2 Tm. 3:15-16).

Scripture and Tradition stand together as the "one sacred deposit of the word of God, which is committed to the Church." The importance of Tradition is described by the Second Vatican Council: "This Tradition, which comes from the apostles, develops in the Church with the help of the Holy Spirit. For there is a growth in the understanding of the realities and the words which have been handed down . . ." Catholics therefore should be well instructed in Tradition as well as Scripture.

BASIC TEACHINGS

1. The Mystery of the One God — Father, Son, Holy Spirit: The "history of salvation" is the story of God's dealing with men. Through it, the one true God in three Persons — the Father, the Son, the Holy Spirit — reveals himself to man and saves man from sin.

In the Old Testament God revealed himself as the one true personal God, transcendent above this world. By these Old Testament words and actions, God prepared for the later revelation of the Trinity.

This mystery was expressed in the person, words, and works of Jesus Christ. Jesus revealed himself as the eternal and divine Son of God; more fully revealed the Father; and made known a third divine Person, the Holy Spirit, whom the Father and he, as risen Lord, sent to his Church.

Thus, the divine Teacher gives his disciples authoritative knowledge of the true God, and calls them to become sons of God through the gift of the Spirit which he bestows on them.

Catechetical instruction should foster an ever-increasing awareness of the Triune God. It should enable students to grasp, through faith, the great truth that, beginning at baptism, they are called to a lifelong developing intimacy with the three divine Persons.

2. True Worship of God in a World Which Ignores Him: Religious education must stimulate an unshakable belief that God is all-good. "The living God" (Mt. 16:16) is holy, just, and merciful. Infinitely wise and perfect, he has made firm commitments to men and bound them to himself by solemn covenants. He has each of us always in view. He frees us, saves us, and loves us with the love of a father, the love of a spouse. Instruction about God's goodness should awaken joy in the God who is the cause of our eternal hope and should prompt us to worship him.

We worship God especially in the sacred liturgy, offering ourselves to him through our Lord Jesus Christ. We commit ourselves to carrying out his will in our every activity, and to use and increase the talents he has given us. And from his goodness we receive the graces needed to profess the truth in love and to bring forth the fruits of love, justice and peace, all to his glory.

The sad fact is that many people today pay little or no attention to God, while others are persuaded that God is distant, indifferent, or altogether absent. That is because modern life is man-centered, not God-centered. Its climate is unfavorable to faith. Yet, no matter how hidden, some desire for God is lodged in every man.

3. Knowledge of God and the Witness of Christian Love: Sacred Scripture testifies that man can come to know God through the things God has made. The Church holds and teaches that from reflection on created things human reason can come to a knowledge of God as the beginning and end of all that is.

Yet unbelievers need help to find God. They ask, "Show us a sign." We who are committed to Christ can do so, as the first generation Christians did. How? By the compelling witness of a life which shows a steadfast and mature faith in God, which is lived in personal love of Christ, and which carries out works of justice and charity.

True, our final goal is in eternity. But faith in God and union with Christ also entail an obligation to work at solving the problems which beset men here and now. And so Christians must show by their actions that faith in God, far from freeing them of concern for the world's troubles, impels them to be involved and to press for their solution.

4. Jesus Christ, Son of God, the Firstborn of All Creation, and Savior: The greatest of God's works is the taking on of human flesh (incarnation) by his Son, Jesus Christ. The Son came on earth and entered human history so as to renew the world from within and be for it an abiding source of supernatural life and salvation from sin.

He is the firstborn of all creation. He is before all. All things hold together in him, just as all have been created in him, through him, and for him.

Obedient unto death, he was exalted as Lord of all, and through the reality of his resurrection was made known to us as God's Son in power. Being the firstborn of the dead, he gives eternal life to all. In him we are created new men. Through him all creatures will be saved from the slavery of corruption. "There is no salvation in anyone else" (Acts 4:12). Nor has there ever been, from the very beginning.

5. Creation, the Beginning of the History of Man's Salvation: The entire universe was created out of nothing. This includes our world in which salvation and redemption are in fact accomplished through Jesus Christ.

In the Old Testament, God's creative action showed his power and proved that he is always with his people. The creation of angels and of the world is the beginning of the mystery of salvation. And the creation of man is the first gift leading to Christ. In Christ's resurrection from the dead the same all-powerful action of God stands out splendidly.

For this reason, creation is to be presented not in isolation, but as directly relating to the salvation accomplished by Jesus Christ. So, too, when a Christian considers the doctrine of creation, he must not only recall the first action by which God "created the heavens and the earth," but should also remember God's continuing activity as he works out the salvation of men.

God is actively and lovingly present in human history from start to finish, using his limitless power in our behalf. Just as his presence shines forth in the history of Israel, just as he was powerfully at work in the life, death, and resurrection of his Incarnate Son, so is he present among us today and will be for all generations. He will bring his saving work to final completion only at the end of the world, when there will be "new heavens and a new earth."

6. Jesus Christ, the Center of All God's Saving Works: The Christian knows that in Jesus Christ he is joined to all history and all men. The story of man's salvation, set in the midst of the ongoing history of the world, is the carrying out of God's plan for us. Its aim is to form his people into "the whole Christ . . . that perfect man who is Christ come to full stature" (Eph. 4:13).

Realizing this, the Christian addresses himself to his appointed task of making creation give glory to God. He does so to the full extent of his abilities and opportunities, through the power of Jesus the Savior.

7. Jesus Christ, True Man and True God in the Unity of the Divine Person: Head and Lord of the universe, the Son of God was "manifested in the flesh" (1 Tm. 3:16). This is "a wonderful mystery of our faith" *(ibid.).*

The man, Jesus Christ, lived among men. As man, he thought with a human mind, acted with a human will, loved with a human heart. By becoming man, he joined himself in a real way with every human being except in sin. He accorded the human person a degree of respect and concern such as no one before had done.

He lived among men, was close to them, reached out to all — the virtuous and sinners, the poor and the rich, fellow-citizens and foreigners, and was especially solicitous for the suffering and the rejected. In him, God's love for man is seen.

And well it might be. For Jesus is also truly divine. He is not only the perfect man, but God's only-begotten Son: "God from God, light from light, true God from true God, begotten not made, of one substance with the father" (Nicene Creed).

In explaining the incarnation and the divinity of Christ, the teacher must take care to follow Christian Tradition as expressed in Sacred Scripture and by the Fathers and councils of the Church. The instruction should convey the age-old witness of Christian life about this truth: in Christ there is all fullness of divinity.

8. Jesus Christ, Savior and Redeemer of the World: Christ appeared in the history of man and the world, a history subject to sin. Christ steps into the world as God made man, to be its Savior and Redeemer. God so loved sinners that he gave his Son, reconciling the world to himself. It was by the obedience of the Son to the will and command of his Father that all men were saved (cf. Rom. 5:19).

As the Messiah fulfilling Old Testament prophecy and history, Jesus carried out his earthly mission. He preached the gospel of the kingdom of God and summoned men to interior conversion and faith. He persisted in his ministry despite the resistance of religious leaders of his day and their threats on his life.

Out of filial love for his Father and redemptive love of us, he gave himself up to death, and passed through it to the glory of the Father.

By his death and resurrection he redeemed mankind from slavery to sin and to the devil. Risen truly and literally, the Lord became the unfailing source of life and of the outpouring of the Holy Spirit upon the human race. He is the firstborn among many brethren, and created in himself a new humanity.

9. The Holy Spirit in the Church and in the Life of the Christian: The Holy Spirit carries out Christ's work in the world. As Christ is present where a human being is in need (Mt. 25:31, ff.), so the Spirit is at work when persons answer God's invitation to love him and one another. The coming of the consoling Paraclete was promised by Christ. He pledged that the Spirit of Truth would be within us and remain with us. And the Holy Spirit did come at Pentecost, never to depart. The Spirit is present in a special way in the community of those who acknowledge Christ as Lord, the Church. The Church, then, is enlivened by the Spirit. Our lives also

are to be guided by that same Holy Spirit, the Third Person of the Trinity.

Catechetical instruction must underscore the importance and the work of the abiding Spirit of Truth in the Church and in our lives. For this the teachings of the Second Vatican Council will be useful.

10. The Sacraments, Actions of Christ in the Church (the Universal Sacrament): The saving work of Christ is continued in the Church. Through the gift of the Holy Spirit, the Church enjoys the presence of Christ and carries on his ministry and saving mission.

The Church has been entrusted with special means for carrying on Christ's works: namely, the sacraments which he instituted. They are outward signs both of God's grace and man's faith. They effectively show God's intention to sanctify man and man's willingness to receive this sanctification. In this way they bring us God's grace.

The Church itself is in a true sense the universal sacrament. The Church is not only the People of God, but, "by her relationship with Christ, the Church is, as it were, a sacrament (or sign and instruction) of intimate union with God and of the unity of all mankind."

Sacraments are the principal actions through which Christ gives his Spirit to Christians and makes them a holy people. He has entrusted the sacraments to the Church, but they are always to be thought of as actions of Christ himself, from whom they get their power. Thus, it is Christ who baptizes, Christ who offers himself in the Sacrifice of the Mass through the ministry of the priests, and Christ who forgives sins in the sacrament of penance.

"The purpose of the sacraments is to sanctify men, to build up the body of Christ, and finally to give worship to God. Because they are signs, they also instruct . . . the very act of celebrating them disposes the faithful more effectively to receive the grace in a fruitful manner, to worship God duly, and to practice charity. It is therefore of capital importance that the faithful easily understand the sacramental signs, and with great eagerness have frequent recourse to the sacraments, instituted to nourish Christian life."

Catechetical instruction, then, must teach the seven sacraments according to this full meaning. Since they are sacraments of faith, the right attitude of faith must be encouraged, as well as the sincerity and generosity required for celebrating and receiving them worthily.

The sacraments must be seen as sources of grace for individuals and communities, in addition to being remedies for sin and the effects of sin. Therefore, the Christian's union with God in grace is to be presented as in an important measure connected with the sacraments.

11. Religious Instruction on the Sacraments: In religious education each sacrament is to be taught, with careful attention to its individual nature. The instructor should carefully explain the external ritual, or the "sign" for each, and should explain that sacraments, when worthily received, bring God's grace. The teacher should help the student appreciate the lifelong human and ecclesial goal of sacramental living. Such instruction will encourage the students to think about the meaning of the visible signs, as well as the invisible reality of God's saving love which these signs express.

Here, in broad outline, we note:

Baptism is the sacrament of rebirth as a child of God sanctified by the Spirit, of unity with Jesus in his death and resurrection, of cleansing from original sin and personal sins, and of welcome into the community of the Church. It permanently relates him to God with a relationship that can never be erased. It joins him to the priestly, prophetic, and kingly works of Christ.

Confirmation is the sacrament by which those born anew in baptism now receive the seal of the Holy Spirit, the gift of the Father and the Son. Confirmation, as the sealing of the candidate with the Spirit, is linked with the other sacraments of Christian initiation, baptism and the Eucharist. Religious instruction should emphasize the idea of initiation and explain the sealing of the Spirit as preparation for the witness of a mature Christian life, and for the apostolate of living in the world and extending and defending the faith.

Penance brings to the Christian God's merciful forgiveness for sins committed after baptism. Sacramental absolution, which follows upon sincere confession of sin, true sorrow, and resolution not to sin again, is a means of obtaining pardon from God. Usually given to the individual, it also brings about a reconciliation with the faith community, the Church, which is wounded by our sins. Religious instruction should teach this sacrament as bringing individualized direction toward spiritual growth, toward eliminating habits of sin and working for perfection. Confession is for the Catholic the sacramental way of obtaining pardon for sins, of submitting his offenses to the mercy and forgiving grace of God. If one has fallen into serious sin, sacramental confession is the ordinary way established in the Church to reconcile the sinner with Christ and with his Church. It is also true that a sinner can be restored to grace by perfect sorrow or perfect contrition in the sense of the Church's Tradition. Therefore every Catholic, from his early years, should be instructed how to receive and best profit from the regular reception of this sacrament.

Holy Orders in a special way conforms certain members of the People of God to Christ the Mediator. It puts them in positions of special service for building up the Body of Christ and gives a sacred power to fulfill that ministry of service. Through this sacrament Christ bestows a permanent charism of the Holy Spirit enabling the recipients to guide and shepherd the faith community, proclaim and explain the gospel, and guide and sanctify God's people. Representing Christ, they primarily offer the Sacrifice of the Mass. Also as his representatives, they administer the sacrament of penance for the forgiveness of sins, and the sacrament of the anointing of the sick.

The Anointing of the Sick is the sacrament for the seriously ill, infirm and aged. It is best received as soon as the danger of death begins, from either sickness or old age. By this anointing and the accompanying prayers for the restoration of health, the entire Church through the priests asks the Lord to lighten their sufferings, forgive their sins, and bring them to eternal salvation. The Church encourages the sick to contribute to the spiritual good of the entire People of God by associating themselves freely to the sufferings and death of Christ.

12. The Eucharist, Center of All Sacramental Life: The Eucharist has primacy among the sacraments. It is of the greatest importance for uniting and strengthening the Church. The eucharistic celebration is carried out in obedience to the words of Jesus at the Last Supper: "Do this in memory of me."

When a priest pronounces the words of eucharistic consecration, the underlying reality of bread and wine is changed into the body and blood of Christ, given for us in sacrifice. That change has been given the name "transubstantiation." This means that Christ himself, true God and true man, is really and substantially present, in a mysterious way, under the appearances of bread and wine.

This Sacrifice (of the Mass) is not merely a ritual which commemorates a past sacrifice. In it, through the ministry of priests, Christ perpetuates the Sacrifice of the Cross in an unbloody manner. At the same time, the Eucharist is a meal which recalls the Last Supper, celebrates our unity together in Christ, and anticipates the messianic banquet of the kingdom. In the Eucharist Jesus nourishes Christians with his own self, the Bread of Life, so that they may become a people more acceptable to God and filled with greater love of God and neighbor.

To receive the Eucharist worthily the Christian must be in the state of grace (cf. 1 Cor. 11: 27-28).

Having been nourished by the Lord himself, the Christian should with active love eliminate all prejudices and all barriers to brotherly cooperation with others. The Eucharist is a sacrament of unity. It is meant to unite the faithful more closely each day with God and with one another.

The Eucharist, reserved in our churches, is a powerful help to prayer and service of others. Religious instruction should stress the gratitude, adoration and devotion due to the Real Presence of Christ in the Blessed Sacrament reserved.

13. The Sacrament of Matrimony: Particular attention must be given to religious education concerning matrimony. In modern society it is necessary to emphasize that marriage was instituted by the Creator himself and given by him certain purposes, laws and blessings. Students are to be acquainted with the vision and teaching of the Second Vatican Council concerning marriage and the family, concerning the indissolubility of marriage and the evil of divorce.

Christ raised marriage of the baptized to the dignity of a sacrament. The spouses, expressing their personal and irrevocable consent, are the ministers of the sacrament. Therefore they live together in Christ's grace. They imitate — and in a way represent — Christ's own love for his Church. By this sacrament Christian spouses are, as it were, consecrated to uphold the dignity of matrimony and to carry out its duties. It should be made clear that the Church discourages the contracting of mixed marriages in order to encourage a full union of mind and life in matrimony.

Following the Second Vatican Council, the religion teacher should show that marriage is the basis of family life. Special attention should be given to the unity and unbreakable quality of matrimony, as decreed by God. The purposes of marriage should be explained in accord with the teachings of the Second Vatican Council:

"Marriage and conjugal love are by their nature ordained toward the begetting and education of children. . . . Hence, while not making the other purposes of matrimony of less account, the true practice of conjugal love, and the whole meaning of the family life which results from it, have this aim: that the couple be ready with stout hearts to cooperate with the love of the Creator and the Savior, who through them will enlarge and enrich his own family day by day . . . Marriage to be sure is not instituted solely for procreation [but also that] the mutual love of the spouses, too, be embodied in a rightly ordered manner, that it grow and ripen."

Similarly, there must be a clear presentation of the Church's teaching concerning chastity in marriage, moral methods of regulating births, and the protection due to human life once a child has been conceived.

The teacher should explain the vocation of every family to function perfectly as a community — that is, a group of persons sharing life together at a deep, personal level. Each member of the family has this obligation. Such a community will reach out to affect constructively the Church, the civic and the world community.

14. The New Man in the Spirit: When man accepts the Spirit of Christ, God introduces him to a way of life completely new. It empowers a man to share in God's own life. He is joined to the Father and to Christ in a vital union which not even death can break.

The indwelling Holy Spirit gives a man hope and courage, heals his weakness of soul, enables him to master passion and selfishness. The Spirit prompts man to pursue what is good and to advance in such virtues as charity, joy, peace, patience, kindness, longanimity, humility, fidelity, modesty, continence, and chastity. The presence of the Holy Spirit makes prayer possible and effective.

God's dwelling in the soul is a matchless grace and manifold gift. Its effects have been expressed in many ways. Thus, a sinner is said to be "justified by God" or "given new life by the Holy Spirit," or "given a share in Christ's life in himself," or to receive grace. The root meaning is that a person dies to sin, shares in the divinity of the Son through the Spirit of adoption, and enters into close communion with the most Holy Trinity.

In the history of salvation, it is divinely appointed that man is to receive this sanctifying grace of adoption as God's child and to inherit eternal life. Because of the grace of Christ the Savior, man is given supernatural life, meaning and dignity far beyond what his own nature confers.

15. Human and Christian Freedom: God's plan is that man, united with Jesus Christ, should give a free answer to God's call. At the outset, God endowed human nature with freedom. But this has been badly impaired by the sin of humanity, original sin. The resultant weakness is overcome by grace, so that man can live with holiness in the faith of Jesus Christ.

The Church knows that, because of psychological difficulties or external conditions, freedom can be reduced slightly or considerably or altogether. Hence conditions most favorable to the exercise of genuine human freedom must be promoted, not only for man's temporal welfare but also for the higher good of grace and eternal salvation. Accordingly, the Church will seek to communicate a true sense and appreciation of freedom, will defend freedom against unjust force of every kind, and will summon Christians to work together with all men of good will to safeguard freedom.

16. The Sins of Man: In working out his salvation, man finds that the greatest problem is sin.

Original sin is the first obstacle. How does it affect him?

"Although he was made by God in a state of holiness, from the very dawn of history man abused his liberty, at the urging of the evil one. Man set himself against God and sought to find fulfillment apart from God."

"Through one man sin entered the world, and with sin death, death thus coming to all men inasmuch as all sinned" (Rom. 5: 12).

"It is human nature so fallen, stripped of the grace that clothed it, injured in its own natural powers and subjected to the dominion of death, that is transmitted to all men — and it is in this sense that every man is born in sin." This sin of mankind is multitudinous, has caused incalculable sorrow and ruin, and weighs down on every man.

In addition to the effects of original sin, there is personal sin, that committed by the individual. By it a person, acting knowingly and deliberately, violates the moral law. The sinner fails in love of God. He turns away from, or even back from his lifetime goal of doing God's will. He may even, by serious offense (mortal sin), rupture his relationship with the Father.

It is important that the awareness of sin not be lost or lessened. The Christian must have clear knowledge of right and wrong, so as to be able to choose with an informed conscience to love God and avoid offending him.

Religious instruction must not be silent about the reality of sin, the kinds of sin and the degree of gravity and personal wilfulness which indicate mortal sin. Instruction must remind the student of the sufferings and the death on the cross which Christ endured to destroy the effects of sin.

But it must go on to speak eloquently of God's forgiveness. Even though a man sin, he can be pardoned. The power of grace is greater than that of sin. The superabundant love of God restores the penitent and draws him toward salvation.

17. The Moral Life of Christians: Christ directed his apostles to teach the observance of everything that he had commanded. Catechetical instruction must include both the things which are to be believed and those which are to be done or avoided if we are to respond generously to God's love.

Christian morality defines a way of living worthy of a human being and of an adopted son of God. It is a positive response to God, by growing in the new life given through Jesus Christ. It is supported and guided by the grace and gifts of the Holy Spirit.

Christian freedom needs to be guided in questions of day-to-day living. Each person must have a right conscience and follow it. Conscience is not feeling nor self-will, although these may affect the degree of culpability. Conscience is a personal judgment that something is right or wrong because of the will and law of God.

So the conscience of the Catholic Christian must pay respectful and obedient attention to the teaching authority of God's Church. It is the duty of this teaching authority, or magisterium, to give guidance for applying the enduring norms and values of Christian morality to specific situations of everyday life.

The Christian must know that there are moral values which are absolute and never to be disregarded or violated by anyone in any situation. Fidelity to them may require heroism of the sort which we see in the lives of the saints and the deaths of the martyrs.

Obedience to the Holy Spirit includes a faithful observance of the commandments of God, the laws of the Church, and just civil laws. All civil laws are not necessarily just, because at times evil laws permit what God forbids. "Better for us to obey God than men!" (Acts 5:29) Christian witness is especially powerful when it defends the values of God rather than those of the world.

18. The Perfection of Christian Love: The special characteristic of Christian moral teaching is its total relationship to the love of God, or charity. All commandments and norms for this moral teaching are summed up in faith working through charity. Love of God is the soul of morality. God is love, and in God's plan that love reaches out in Jesus Christ, to unite men in mutual love.

It follows, then, that responding freely and perfectly to God and God's will means keeping his commandments and living in his love. It means accepting and practicing the "new commandment" of charity.

Sustained by faith, man is to live a life of love of God and of his fellow men. This is his greatest responsibility, and the source of his greatest dignity. A man's holiness, whatever his vocation or state of life may be, is the perfection of love of God.

Following the Second Vatican Council, religious instruction should speak of the importance for humanity and for the Church of those women and men who, accepting a religious vocation, show in this special and needed way their love of God and true service to mankind. Such instruction should acknowledge the excellence which the Christian message gives to virginity consecrated in Christ.

19. Specifics in the Teaching of Morality: The duties and obligations flowing from love of God and man are to be taught in specific, practical fashion. The follower of Christ is to know the Christian response to the challenges and temptations of contemporary living. The Church has a duty to apply moral principles to current problems, personal and social.

The specifics of morality are to be taught within the overall framework of the Ten Commandments of God and the Sermon on the Mount, especially the Beatitudes (see Appendix A). Also included should be the spiritual and corporal works of mercy, the theological and moral virtues, the seven capital sins, etc. Whatever approach is used, the student should know the Ten Commandments as part of his religious heritage (see Appendix A). Teaching morality also should include instruction on the laws of the Church (see Appendix B). The Bible and the lives of the saints supply concrete examples of moral living.

Toward God the Christian has a lifelong

obligation of love and service. The will of God must be put first in the scale of personal values, and must be kept there throughout life. One must have toward God the attitude of a son to an all-good, all-loving father, and must never think or live as if independent of God. He must gladly give to God genuine worship and true prayer, both liturgical and private.

Man must not put anyone or anything in place of God. This is idolatry, which has its variations in superstition, witchcraft, occultism. Honoring God, man is never to blaspheme nor perjure himself. Honoring God, one is to show respect for persons, places and things related specially to God.

Atheism, heresy, and schism are to be rejected in the light of man's duties to God.

Toward his fellow man the Christian has specific obligations in love. Like Christ, he will show that love by concern for the rights of his fellow man — his freedom, his housing, his food, his health, his right to work, etc. The Christian is to show to all others the justice and charity of Christ — to reach out in the spirit of the Beatitudes to help all others, to build up a better society in the local community and justice and peace throughout the world. His judgment and speech concerning others are to be ruled by the charity due all sons of God. He will respect and obey all lawful authority in the home, in civil society, and in the Church.

Many are the sins against neighbor. It is sinful to be selfishly apathetic toward others in their needs. It is sinful to violate the rights of others — to steal, deliberately damage another's good name or property, cheat, not to pay one's debts. Respecting God's gift of life, the Christian cannot be anti-life and must avoid sins of murder, abortion, euthanasia, genocide, indiscriminate acts of war. He must not use immoral methods of family limitation. Sins of lying, detraction and calumny are forbidden, as are anger, hatred, racism and discrimination. In the area of sexuality, the Christian is to be modest in behavior and dress. In a sex-saturated society, the follower of Christ must be different. For the Christian there can be no premarital sex, fornication, adultery, or other acts of impurity or scandal to others. He must remain chaste, repelling lustful desires and temptations, self-abuse, pornography and indecent entertainment of every description.

Toward self the follower of Christ has certain duties. He must be another Christ in the world of his own day, a living example of Christian goodness. He must be humble and patient in the face of his own imperfections, as well as those of others. He must show a Christlike simplicity toward material things and the affluence of our society. The follower of Christ must be pure in words and actions even in the midst of corruption.

To be guarded against is the capital sin of pride, with its many manifestations. So too with sloth — spiritual, intellectual and physical. The Christian must resist envy of others' success and of their financial and material possessions. He is not to surrender self-control and abuse his bodily health by intemperance in drugs, alcohol, food.

Obviously this listing does not cover all morality or all immorality. But it indicates the practical approach which will help the Christian to form a right conscience, choose always what is right, avoid sin and the occasions of sin, and live in this world according to the Spirit of Christ in love of God.

20. The Church, People of God and Institution for Salvation: The Church, founded by Christ, had its origin in his death and resurrection. It is the new People of God, prepared for in the Old Testament and given life, growth, and direction by Christ in the Holy Spirit. It is the work of God's saving love in Christ.

In the Catholic Church are found the deposit of faith, the sacraments, and the ministries inherited from the apostles. Through these gifts of God, the Church is able to act and grow as a community in Christ, serving mankind and giving men his saving word and activity.

The Church shares in the prophetic office of Christ. Assembled by God's Word, it accepts that Word and witnesses to it in every quarter of the globe. So the Church is missionary by its very nature, and every member of the Church shares the command from Christ to carry the good news to all mankind.

The Church is also a priestly people.

By God's design, it is a society with leaders — i.e., with a hierarchy. As such, it is a people guided by its bishops who are in union with the pope, the bishop of Rome, the vicar of Christ. He has succeeded to the office of Peter in his care and guidance of the whole flock of Christ and is the head of the college of bishops. To them the community of faith owes respect and obedience, for "in exercising his office of father and pastor, a bishop should stand as one who serves."

Religious instruction should treat the role of the pope and of the bishops in their office of teaching, sanctifying and governing the Church. It should explain the gift of infallibility in the Church, and the way and manner in which the teaching authority of the Church guides the faithful in truth.

The Holy Spirit preserves the Church as the body of Christ and his bride, so that — despite the sins of its members — it will never fail in faithfulness to him and will meet him in holiness at the end of the world. The Spirit also helps the Church constantly to purify and renew itself and its members. To help its members, the Spirit-guided Church can modernize in those areas that permit change.

21. The Church as a Community: The

Church is a community sharing together the life of Christ, a people assembled by God. Within this assembly there is a basic equality of all persons. There are different responsibilities in the Church. For example, the ministerial priesthood is essentially different from the "priesthood of the people." But all are united and equal as the one People of God.

In the Church every individual has a call from God, a vocation to holiness. Each deserves respect, since all join in the one cause of Christ. The pope and the bishops coordinate this work, in every rite, diocese, parish and mission. In each, no matter how small or poor or isolated, "Christ is present, and by his power the one, holy, catholic and apostolic Church is gathered together."

22. The Quest for Unity: Christ willed that all who believe in him be one, so that the world might know that he was sent by the Father. Christian unity, then, in faith and love, is God's will. Prayer and work for Christian unity are essential to Catholic life, and religious education must bring this out. Catholics should be deeply, personally concerned over the present, sad divisions of Christians. Catholics should take the first steps in ecumenical dialogue and should try to make the Church more faithful to Christ and to its heritage from the apostles.

We recognize the unique fullness of the Catholic Church which we believe to be the ordinary means of salvation, and which we desire to share with all men. But we also recognize that Catholics can be enriched by the authentic insights into the gospel as witnessed by other religious traditions.

A still wider unity must be a concern of Catholic life and education: the unity of all men under God. Following the Second Vatican Council, religious education must show Christlike respect for all men of good will, beginning with our elder brothers in faith, the Jewish people, and reaching out to those others who with us believe in God.

Religious instruction is, then, to show a sensitive appreciation of the dignity and unique value of every human being. The Church rejects as unchristian any unjust discrimination or injustice because of race, national origin, ethnic origin, color, sex, class, or religion. God has given to every man intrinsic dignity, freedom and eternal importance. "If anyone says, 'My love is fixed on God,' yet hates his brother, he is a liar. One who has no love for the brother he has seen cannot love the God he has not seen" (1 Jn. 4:20).

23. The Church as the Institution for Salvation: The Church is a community of the People of God with Christ as leader and head. It is a structured institution to which Christ has given the mission of bringing the message of salvation to all men. "Established by Christ as a fellowship of life, charity and truth, this messianic people is also used by him as an instrument for the redemption of all, and is sent forth into the whole world as the light of the world and the salt of the earth."

The Church is not of this world, and can never conform itself to this world. But it both speaks and listens to the world, and strives to be seen by the world as faithful to the gospel. So "Christians cannot yearn for anything more ardently than to serve the men of the modern world ever more generously and effectively. Therefore, holding faithfully to the gospel and benefiting from its resources, and united with every man who loves and practices justice, Christians have shouldered a gigantic task demanding fulfillment in this world. Concerning this task they must give a reckoning to him who will judge every man on the last day."

In, but not of this world, the Church is "inspired by no earthly ambition." Only in heaven will it be perfect. Engaged in the world, it always has heaven in view, toward which the People of God are journeying.

24. Mary, Mother of God, Mother and Model of the Church: The Gospel of Luke gives us Mary's words: "My spirit finds joy in God my Savior, for he has looked upon his servant in her lowliness; all ages to come shall call me blessed" (Lk 1: 47-48).

Religious instruction should lead students to see Mary as singularly blessed and relevant to their own lives and needs. Following venerable Christian Tradition as continued in the Second Vatican Council, the teacher should explain the special place of the Virgin Mary in the history of salvation and in the Church.

The "ever-virgin mother of Jesus Christ our Lord and God," she is in the Church in a place highest after Christ, and also is very close to us as our spiritual Mother. In religious instruction there should be explanations of her special gifts from God (being Mother of God, being preserved from all stain of original sin, being assumed body and soul to heaven). The special veneration due to Mary — Mother of Christ, Mother of the Church, our spiritual Mother — should be taught by word and example.

The Church likewise honors the other saints who are already with the Lord in heaven. They inspire us by the heroic example of their lives. To them we pray, asking their intercession with God for us.

The teacher should remind students of reverence toward the bodies of those who have gone before us in death, and our duty of praying for deceased relatives, friends and all the faithful departed.

25. Final Reunion with God: During this earthly life, Christians look forward to their final reunion with God. They long for the coming of "our Lord Jesus Christ, who will give a new form to this lowly body of ours and remake it according to the pattern of his glorified body" (Phil. 3:21).

But the final realities will come about only

when Christ returns with power to bring history to its appointed end. Then as judge of the living and the dead he will hand over his people to the Father. Then only will the Church reach perfection and enter into the fullness of God. Until the Lord's arrival in majesty, "some of his disciples are pilgrims on earth, some have finished this life and are being purified, and others are in glory, beholding clearly God himself Three and One, as he is."

Religious instruction on death, judgment, and eternity should be given in a spirit of consoling hope, as well as salutary fear (cf. Thes. 4:18). The Lord's resurrection means that death has been conquered. So we have reason to live, and to face death, with courage and joy. The renewed funeral liturgy sets the tone for religious instruction on death. In the risen Christ we live, we die, and we shall live again. We look ahead to a homecoming with God our loving Father.

Religious instruction should treat seriously the awesome responsibility which each person has about his eternal destiny. The importance of the individual judgment after death, of the refining and purifying punishments of purgatory, of the dreadful possibility of the eternal death of hell, and of the last judgment should be taught in the light of Christian hope.

On the day of the last judgment each person will fully reach his eternal destiny. Then all of us will be revealed "before the judgment place of Christ, so that each one may receive what he deserves, according to what he has done, good or bad, in his bodily life" (2 Cor. 5:10). Then "the evildoers shall rise to be damned," and "those who have done right shall rise to live" (cf. Jn. 5:29) — to a life eternally with God beyond what the heart of man can imagine, to receive the good things that God has prepared for those who love him.

APPENDIX A

The Ten Commandments of God are of special importance in teaching specifics of morality. The Old Testament, the New Testament and the long use of the Church testify to this. A summary presentation of the Ten Commandments of God taken from the *New American Bible* translation is:

1. I, the Lord, am your God. You shall not have other gods besides me.

2. You shall not take the name of the Lord, your God, in vain.

3. Remember to keep holy the Sabbath day.

4. Honor your father and your mother.

5. You shall not kill.

6. You shall not commit adultery.

7. You shall not steal.

8. You shall not bear false witness against your neighbor.

9. You shall not covet your neighbor's wife.

10. You shall not covet anything that belongs to your neighbor.

The Beatitudes are likewise of particular importance in teaching specifics of morality. The traditional listing of the Beatitudes, as taken from the *New American Bible* translation, is:

1. Blest are the poor in spirit: the reign of God is theirs.

2. Blest are the sorrowing: they shall be consoled.

3. Blest are the lowly: they shall inherit the land.

4. Blest are they who hunger and thirst for holiness: they shall have their fill.

5. Blest are they who show mercy: mercy shall be theirs.

6. Blest are the single-hearted: for they shall see God.

7. Blest are the peacemakers: they shall be called sons of God.

8. Blest are those persecuted for holiness' sake: the reign of God is theirs. (Mt. 5:3-10)

APPENDIX B

From time to time the Church has listed certain specific duties of Catholics. Some duties expected of Catholic Christians today include the following. (Those traditionally mentioned as precepts of the Church are marked with an asterisk.)

1. To keep holy the day of the Lord's resurrection: to worship God by participating in Mass every Sunday and holy day of obligation:* to avoid those activities that would hinder renewal of soul and body, e.g., needless work and business activities, unnecessary shopping, etc.

2. To lead a sacramental life: to receive Holy Communion frequently and the sacrament of penance regularly — minimally, to receive the sacrament of penance at least once a year (annual confession is obligatory only if serious sin is involved)* — minimally, to receive Holy Communion at least once a year between the first Sunday of Lent and Trinity Sunday.*

3. To study Catholic teaching in preparation for the sacrament of confirmation, to be confirmed, and then to continue to study and advance the cause of Christ.

4. To observe the marriage laws of the Church:* to give religious training (by example and word) to one's children; to use parish schools and religious education programs.

5. To strengthen and support the Church:* one's own parish community and parish priests; the worldwide Church and the Holy Father.

6. To do penance, including abstaining from meat and fasting from food on the appointed days.*

7. To join in the missionary spirit and apostolate of the Church.

Progress toward the development of a National Catechetical Directory is described in a separate article; see Index.

CATHOLIC SCHOOLS AND STUDENTS IN THE UNITED STATES

(Source: *The Official Catholic Directory, 1975;* figures as of Jan. 1, 1975. Archdioceses are indicated by an asterisk.)

Section, State Diocese	Univs. Colleges	Students	High Schools	Students	Elem. Schools	Students
NEW ENGLAND	30	47,638	155	74,205	591	167,500
Maine, Portland	2	993	4	1,204	24	6,692
New Hampshire, Manchester	5	3,614	6	2,777	33	10,421
Vermont, Burlington	3	2,431	3	1,479	14	3,407
Massachusetts	9	28,074	94	40,460	282	86,332
*Boston	4	20,373	70	25,923	177	55,597
Fall River	1	2,222	8	3,696	31	8,816
Springfield	1	414	7	5,043	43	13,988
Worcester	3	5,065	9	5,798	31	7,931
Rhode Island, Providence	4	4,734	14	6,661	67	15,635
Connecticut	7	7,792	34	21,624	171	45,013
*Hartford	4	1,565	17	10,644	95	26,486
Bridgeport	2	5,944	11	5,866	55	15,505
Norwich	1	283	6	5,114	21	3,022
MIDDLE ATLANTIC	70	117,672	440	300,760	2,337	833,754
New York	34	46,569	204	145,595	1,036	394,369
*New York	18	17,650	81	61,857	319	117,982
Albany	3	4,532	16	7,424	80	20,506
Brooklyn	2	9,375	29	28,953	190	117,025
Buffalo	7	11,574	32	14,835	169	43,604
Ogdensburg	1	250	5	1,631	30	6,588
Rochester	—	—	9	8,204	89	25,160
Rockville Centre	1	1,055	16	14,997	89	44,351
Syracuse	2	2,133	16	7,694	70	19,153
New Jersey	10	17,073	98	56,335	482	166,846
*Newark	5	15,670	50	24,719	222	79,411
Camden	—	—	12	8,143	71	23,052
Paterson	4	670	15	6,859	71	18,124
Trenton	1	733	21	16,614	118	46,259
Pennsylvania	26	54,030	138	98,830	819	272,539
*Philadelphia	10	24,760	51	60,319	304	145,653
Allentown	2	962	10	6,109	81	17,386
Altoona-Johnstown	2	2,004	3	2,196	41	9,176
Erie	3	5,065	12	4,563	56	15,611
Greensburg	2	1,706	3	1,233	50	9,992
Harrisburg	—	—	11	5,687	60	13,903
Pittsburgh	3	9,496	36	12,663	151	46,112
Scranton	4	10,037	12	6,060	76	14,706
SOUTH ATLANTIC	15	31,180	135	63,309	541	174,714
Delaware, Wilmington	—	—	9	4,655	29	10,706
Maryland, *Baltimore	4	6,476	25	12,785	101	36,664
District of Columbia, *Washington	4	18,882	30	12,632	82	30,346
Virginia	1	620	14	5,084	33	10,793
Arlington	1	620	4	2,475	25	8,502
Richmond	—	—	10	2,609	8	2,291
West Virginia, Wheeling-Charleston	1	567	11	2,801	37	6,485
North Carolina	2	890	3	1,001	40	9,800
Belmont Abbey	1	688	—	—	—	—
Charlotte	1	202	2	779	19	4,902
Raleigh	—	—	1	222	21	4,898
South Carolina, Charleston	—	—	4	1,495	31	6,483
Georgia	—	—	8	3,922	33	9,815
*Atlanta	—	—	3	1,791	15	4,569
Savannah	—	—	5	2,131	18	5,246

Section, State Diocese	Univs. Colleges	Students	High Schools	Students	Elem. Schools	Students
Florida	**3**	**3,745**	**31**	**18,934**	**155**	**53,622**
*Miami	2	2,782	16	9,486	62	25,197
Orlando	—	—	5	2,835	27	7,219
St. Augustine	—	—	3	2,107	27	8,706
St. Petersburg	1	963	7	4,506	39	12,500
EAST NORTH CENTRAL	**51**	**99,525**	**358**	**223,845**	**2,252**	**678,103**
Ohio	**14**	**21,974**	**99**	**65,263**	**546**	**173,792**
*Cincinnati	5	13,048	25	19,835	128	46,776
Cleveland	4	5,379	29	20,695	180	60,166
Columbus	1	959	16	6,780	57	14,767
Steubenville	1	1,033	6	1,606	18	3,790
Toledo	2	766	17	9,988	97	27,986
Youngstown	1	789	6	6,359	66	20,307
Indiana	**9**	**16,322**	**33**	**16,518**	**226**	**54,769**
*Indianapolis	2	1,004	14	6,465	84	19,687
Evansville	—	—	5	2,189	31	6,679
Ft. Wayne-S. Bend	5	12,410	7	4,017	45	11,767
Gary	1	1,844	5	3,311	47	13,080
Lafayette	1	1,064	2	536	19	3,556
Illinois	**12**	**37,252**	**116**	**82,156**	**699**	**235,092**
*Chicago	6	29,352	76	62,717	402	161,407
Belleville	1	728	4	2,132	57	10,888
Joliet	3	5,132	9	3,852	68	19,325
Peoria	—	—	9	4,332	60	14,459
Rockford	—	—	8	4,689	49	13,367
Springfield	2	2,040	10	4,434	63	15,646
Michigan	**8**	**17,020**	**72**	**38,975**	**345**	**106,517**
*Detroit	5	13,704	48	26,887	166	65,649
Gaylord	—	—	5	1,170	20	4,592
Grand Rapids	1	1,630	4	3,386	46	9,839
Kalamazoo	1	520	3	1,448	23	4,316
Lansing	1	1,166	6	3,883	42	11,179
Marquette	—	—	1	124	13	2,734
Saginaw	—	—	5	2,077	35	8,208
Wisconsin	**8**	**6,957**	**38**	**20,933**	**436**	**107,933**
*Milwaukee	4	3,759	16	11,475	177	51,391
Green Bay	2	1,812	10	4,171	104	25,083
La Crosse	1	784	9	4,043	78	16,843
Madison	1	602	3	1,244	54	10,396
Superior	—	—	—	—	23	4,220
EAST SOUTH CENTRAL	**10**	**7,782**	**59**	**25,927**	**296**	**72,033**
Kentucky	**5**	**5,100**	**31**	**13,775**	**162**	**38,310**
*Louisville	3	2,608	11	7,243	80	21,486
Covington	1	1,458	15	4,836	54	11,514
Owensboro	1	1,034	5	1,696	28	5,310
Tennessee	**2**	**1,168**	**10**	**5,465**	**42**	**11,651**
Memphis	1	825	5	3,207	16	5,800
Nashville	1	343	5	2,258	26	5,851
Alabama	**3**	**1,514**	**5**	**3,062**	**52**	**12,964**
Birmingham	2	596	2	1,074	25	5,230
Mobile	1	918	3	1,988	27	7,734
Mississippi, Natchez-Jackson	—	—	13	3,625	40	9,108
WEST NORTH CENTRAL	**36**	**46,548**	**183**	**79,091**	**960**	**229,465**
Minnesota	**9**	**11,144**	**32**	**14,525**	**238**	**59,328**
*St. Paul and Minneapolis	3	4,420	14	9,188	113	36,494
Crookston	—	—	2	384	12	2,004
Duluth	1	1,198	1	477	16	2,209
New Ulm	—	—	3	870	33	5,462
St. Cloud	3	3,389	5	1,172	38	7,874
Winona	2	2,137	7	2,434	26	5,285

Section, State Diocese	Univs. Colleges	Students	High Schools	Students	Elem. Schools	Students
Iowa	**8**	**6,583**	**34**	**14,828**	**173**	**38,902**
*Dubuque	3	2,903	12	6,086	76	19,127
Davenport	4	2,933	8	2,334	34	5,373
Des Moines	—	—	3	2,035	22	5,207
Sioux City	1	747	11	4,373	41	9,195
Missouri	**7**	**18,185**	**50**	**27,061**	**287**	**74,883**
*St. Louis	5	13,594	34	20,009	180	52,201
Jefferson City	—	—	2	859	36	6,927
Kansas City-St. Joseph	2	4,591	11	5,178	47	12,685
Springfield-Cape Girardeau	—	—	3	1,015	24	3,070
North Dakota	**2**	**976**	**9**	**2,780**	**36**	**7,396**
Bismarck	1	660	7	2,078	21	4,427
Fargo	1	316	2	702	15	2,969
South Dakota	**2**	**936**	**6**	**1,717**	**29**	**6,033**
Rapid City	—	—	2	406	4	957
Sioux Falls	2	936	4	1,311	25	5,076
Nebraska	**2**	**5,092**	**34**	**11,419**	**103**	**23,500**
*Omaha	2	5,092	21	8,175	68	18,367
Grand Island	—	—	7	1,504	10	1,392
Lincoln	—	—	6	1,740	25	3,741
Kansas	**6**	**3,632**	**18**	**6,761**	**94**	**19,423**
*Kansas City	3	1,964	7	3,780	42	10,375
Dodge City	1	420	—	—	13	1,798
Salina	1	591	7	933	12	2,071
Wichita	1	657	4	2,048	27	5,179
WEST SOUTH CENTRAL	**12**	**20,326**	**128**	**52,569**	**510**	**154,280**
Arkansas, Little Rock	—	—	**6**	**2,109**	**36**	**6,043**
Louisiana	**4**	**8,010**	**62**	**29,815**	**198**	**79,431**
*New Orleans	4	8,010	30	18,497	105	49,742
Alexandria	—	—	7	2,281	26	6,634
Baton Rouge	—	—	7	2,674	24	10,954
Lafayette	—	—	18	6,363	43	12,101
Oklahoma	**1**	**300**	**5**	**2,220**	**30**	**5,343**
*Oklahoma City	1	300	2	1,054	18	3,162
Tulsa	—	—	3	1,166	12	2,181
Texas	**7**	**12,016**	**55**	**18,425**	**246**	**63,463**
*San Antonio	3	6,972	18	4,798	56	14,783
Amarillo	—	—	2	360	12	1,820
Austin	1	1,410	1	340	15	4,138
Beaumont	—	—	2	624	10	2,123
Brownsville	—	—	2	756	8	2,302
Corpus Christi	—	—	3	732	22	4,381
Dallas	1	1,717	7	3,378	33	10,193
El Paso	—	—	4	1,323	23	4,778
Fort Worth	—	—	3	1,141	15	4,155
Galveston-Houston	2	1,917	11	4,889	46	13,861
San Angelo	—	—	2	84	6	929
MOUNTAIN	**6**	**7,677**	**42**	**14,663**	**208**	**46,734**
Montana	**2**	**2,226**	**7**	**1,751**	**25**	**4,292**
Great Falls	1	982	4	807	19	3,179
Helena	1	1,244	3	944	6	1,113
Idaho, Boise	**1**	**36**	**1**	**426**	**12**	**2,068**
Wyoming, Cheyenne	—	—	**1**	**198**	**8**	**1,933**
Colorado	**1**	**1,089**	**12**	**3,776**	**62**	**15,390**
*Denver	1	1,089	9	3,249	50	13,686
Pueblo	—	—	3	527	12	1,704
New Mexico	**2**	**4,326**	**6**	**2,098**	**33**	**7,789**
*Santa Fe	2	4,326	4	1,836	23	5,773
Gallup	—	—	2	262	10	2,016
Arizona	—	—	**10**	**4,447**	**48**	**10,538**
Phoenix	—	—	7	3,326	27	9,309
Tucson	—	—	3	1,121	21	1,229

Section, State Diocese	Univs. Colleges	Students	High Schools	Students	Elem. Schools	Students
Utah, Salt Lake City	—	—	3	825	9	1,888
Nevada, Reno	—	—	2	1,142	11	2,836
PACIFIC	20	43,577	170	84,734	791	234,384
Washington	4	7,732	14	6,425	91	21,338
*Seattle	2	4,317	9	4,570	64	15,576
Spokane	2	3,415	4	1,420	20	4,233
Yakima	—	—	1	435	7	1,529
Oregon	2	3,402	10	3,893	55	10,695
*Portland	2	3,402	9	3,712	52	10,114
Baker	—	—	1	181	3	581
California	13	28,125	136	70,082	611	190,764
*Los Angeles	4	8,119	67	36,503	269	95,075
*San Francisco	5	15,355	27	14,137	108	33,151
Fresno	—	—	2	1,027	27	5,380
Monterey	—	—	3	1,132	16	3,368
Oakland	3	1,815	11	6,308	55	14,903
Sacramento	—	—	10	3,477	40	13,303
San Diego	1	2,836	9	4,723	71	19,796
Santa Rosa	—	—	5	1,589	13	2,812
Stockton	—	—	2	1,186	12	2,976
Alaska	—	—	2	336	3	501
*Anchorage	—	—	—	—	1	116
Fairbanks	—	—	2	336	1	240
Juneau	—	—	—	—	1	145
Hawaii, Honolulu	1	4,318	8	3,998	31	11,086
EASTERN RITES	1	318	6	1,413	53	8,260
*Philadelphia	1	318	1	402	19	2,615
*Munhall	—	—	—	—	5	1,156
Passaic	—	—	—	—	8	1,273
Stamford	—	—	3	257	10	1,346
Parma	—	—	1	601	6	934
St. Nicholas of Chicago	—	—	1	153	4	899
St. Maron of Detroit	—	—	—	—	1	37
Melkite Exarchate	—	—	—	—	—	—
TOTALS 1975	251	422,243	1,676	920,516	8,539	2,599,227
Totals 1974	258	407,081	1,702	911,730	8,647	2,717,898
Totals 1965	304	384,526	2,455	1,095,519	10,991	4,566,809

REPORT ON CATHOLIC EDUCATION

The status of Catholic educational institutions in the U.S. at the beginning of 1975, 1974 and 1965 were reflected in figures (as of Jan. 1) reported by *The Official Catholic Directory, 1975.*

Colleges and Universities: 251 (7 less than in 1974 and 53 less than in 1965). The decreases were due not only to closings but also to some changes of status from claimed religious affiliation to institutional independence. Students: 422,243 (15,162 more than in 1974 and 37,717 more than in 1965). The all-time high enrollment of 435,716 was registered in 1969.

High Schools: 1,676 (26 less than in 1974 and 779 less than in 1965). Students: 920,516 (8,786 more than in 1974 and 175,003 less than in 1965).

Elementary Schools: 8,539 (108 less than in 1974 and 2,452 less than in 1965). Students:

2,599,227 (118,671 less than in 1974 and 1,967,582 less than in 1965).

Public School Students Receiving Religious Instruction: 5,082,134 (171,604 less than in 1974 and 491,907 more than in 1965). High School Students: 1,093,184 (78,138 less than in 1974 and 211,144 less than in 1965). Elementary School Students: 3,988,950 (93,466 less than in 1974 and 703,051 more than in 1965).

Teachers, Full-Time: 171,797 (2,914 less than in 1974 and 26,959 less than in 1965).

Priests: 6,974 (102 less than in 1974 and 5,372 less than in 1965).

Scholastics: 434 (117 less than in 1974 and 691 less than in 1965).

Brothers: 3,512 (223 less than in 1974 and 2,356 less than in 1965).

Sisters: 56,050 (3,709 less than in 1974 and 48,264 less than in 1965).

Lay persons: 104,827 (1,237 more than in 1974 and 29,724 more than in 1965). Lay teachers comprised 61 per cent of the total faculty in 1975, 59.2 per cent in 1974 and 37.8 per cent in 1965. They outnumbered priests and religious teachers for the first time in 1971 (106,844 to 93,594).

Diminished Declines: Elementary and secondary school data compiled by the National Catholic Educational Association and reported in March, 1975, indicated that declines in schools and students had decreased for three consecutive years, marking an end to more drastic losses from 1965-66 to 1971-72.

Costs: The costs of elementary and secondary education — borne by parents, parochial and diocesan subsidy — have soared in recent years. Some parents have found it economically prohibitive to send their children to available schools. Diocesan administrators, forced to close some schools, have amalgamated and clustered others for regional rather than strictly parochial service. Hardest hit are schools in inner-city areas.

Aside from construction and maintenance expenses, the costliest budget items are salaries for lay teachers whose pay scales are higher than those of priests and religious. Salaries for the latter are rising, however, for a variety of reasons; one of them is the need of religious communities for greater income to provide for the care of their retired teachers.

Sisters Remain Committed

Trends behind the decrease (3,709 in 1975) in the number of sisters teaching in Catholic schools are smaller numbers of young women joining religious communities, the departure of sisters from religious life, and the withdrawal of some sisters from teaching to take up other forms of apostolic work. By and large, however, the decrease does not indicate any wholesale lack of interest on the part of women religious in Catholic education and schools.

Problems and Causes

Causes of enrollment drops include rising costs, population shifts from cities to suburban areas, lower birth rates, and attitudinal changes of parents wondering whether the schools will survive, whether they are worth what they cost, and whether they are really so important for religious as well as general education.

School spokesmen, however, have reaffirmed again and again that Catholic schools will not be phased out of existence.

The National Opinion Research Center in Chicago reported in December, 1974, that 89 per cent of a sampling of 1,000 Catholics rejected "the idea that the Catholic school system is no longer needed in modern-day life."

Questioning continues about the high percentage (60 to 75) of church funds allocated to schools in which less than 50 per cent,

overall, of Catholic children are enrolled while much less is available for religious education programs for public school students and adults.

New Programs Needed

Educators have called attention to past emphasis on the role of Catholic schools in education and the neglect of other aspects of the Church's total teaching function. Programs along the lines envisaged in *To Teach as Jesus Did,* a statement issued by the U.S. bishops in 1972, would extend the Church's educational effort to involve the total community — adults, parents as cooperators in the religious development of their children, college and university students through the campus ministry, lower-level students not in Catholic schools.

Doctrinal Concern

Opinions of parents and educators, as well as bishops who have the prime magisterial responsibility in the Church, remain divided over the merits of some aspects of current religious education programs. At the extremes are those who resist any change at all in traditional catechetical programs and those who appear to be more concerned about ecumenical, psychological and sociological relevance than wholeness of the doctrine which is essential to Catholic belief, practice, experience and witness.

This state of affairs has produced chain reactions of confusion in religious education and, for some parents, lack of confidence in Catholic schools.

U.S. bishops and educators are taking steps to resolve problems of religious education and to provide directives for the teaching of doctrine in line with the *General Catechetical Directory* issued by the Congregation for the Clergy in 1971. In 1972 the bishops published a statement, *To Teach as Jesus Did,* emphasizing the central significance of total Christian education and formation in the pastoral mission of the Church. They followed this up early in 1973 with publication of a document entitled *Basic Teachings for Catholic Religious Education* (see separate entry for text). The best of all of these documents, along with other contents, will form the substance of a future *National Catechetical Directory* (see separate entry).

NCEA

The National Catholic Educational Association, founded in 1904, is a voluntary organization of educational institutions and individuals concerned with Catholic education in the US. Its objectives are to promote and encourage the principles and ideals of Christian education and formation by suitable service and other activities.

The NCEA has 14,000 institutional and individual members. Its official publication is *Momentum.* Numerous service publications are issued to members.

Bishop Cletus F. O'Donnell of Madison,

Wis., is chairman of the association. The Rev. John F. Meyers is president.

Headquarters are located at: Suite 350, One Dupont Circle, Washington, D.C. 20036.

LEGAL STATUS OF CATHOLIC EDUCATION

The right of private schools to exist and operate in the United States is recognized in law. It was confirmed by the U.S. Supreme Court in 1925 when the tribunal ruled (Pierce v. Society of Sisters, see Church-State Decisions of the Supreme Court) that an Oregon state law requiring all children to attend public schools was unconstitutional.

Private schools are obliged to comply with the education laws in force in the various states regarding such matters as required basic curricula, periods of attendance, and standards for proper accreditation.

The special curricula and standards of private schools are determined by the schools themselves. Thus, in Catholic schools, the curricula include not only the subject matter required by state educational laws but also other fields of study, principally, education in the Catholic faith.

The Supreme Court has ruled that the First Amendment to the U.S. Constitution, in accordance with the No Establishment of Religion Clause of the First Amendment, prohibits direct federal and state aid from public funds to church-affiliated schools. (See several cases in Church-State Decisions of the Supreme Court.)

Public Aid

This prohibition does not extend to all child-benefit and public-purpose programs of aid to students of non-public elementary and secondary schools.

Statutes authorizing such programs have been ruled constitutional on the grounds that they:

• have a "secular legislative purpose";
• neither inhibit nor advance religion as a "principal or primary effect";
• do not foster "excessive government entanglement with religion."

Aid programs considered constitutional have provided bus transportaion, textbook loans, school lunches and health services, and "secular, neutral or non-ideological services, facilities and materials provided in common to all school children," public and nonpublic.

Programs of these types were in operation in approximately 28 states, as of December, 1973.

Aid was provided most commonly in the form of auxiliary services such as transportation of students to and from school (23 states), textbook loans (14 states), instructional materials (five states), health services (14 states), guidance and counseling (three states), testing (five states), special education (eight states), vocational education (two

states). A number of states offered free lunch programs and even cooperative central purchasing arrangements.

The effect on these programs of the Supreme Court's decision in Meek v. Pittenger (see separate entry) was not altogether clear in the summer of 1975.

Twenty-two states had no provision for auxiliary services of any kind: Alabama, Alaska, Arizona, Arkansas, Colorado, Florida, Georgia, Hawaii, Idaho, Maryland, Montana, Nevada, North Carolina, Oklahoma, Oregon, South Carolina, Tennessee, Texas, Utah, Virginia, Washington, and Wyoming.

With respect to college and university education in church-affiliated institutions, the Supreme Court has upheld the constitutionality of statutes providing student loans and, under the Federal Higher Education Facilities Act of 1963, construction loans and grants for secular-purpose facilities.

Catholic schools are exempt from real estate taxation in all of the states. Since Jan. 1, 1959, nonprofit parochial and private schools have also been exempt from several federal excise taxes.

Shared Time

In a shared time program of education, students enrolled in Catholic or other church-related schools take some courses (e.g., religion, social studies, fine arts) in their own schools and others (e.g., science, mathematics, industrial arts) in public schools. Such a program, outlined in 1956 by Dr. Erwin L. Shaver of the Massachusetts Council of Churches, has been given serious consideration in recent years by Catholic and other educators. Its constitutionality has not been seriously challenged, but practical problems — relating to teacher and student schedules, transportation, adjustment to new programs, and other factors — are knotty.

Limited shared time programs involving Catholic school students have been in operation since 1927 in Caledonia, Minn., since 1945 in Rutland, Vt., and for a number of years in several communities in Connecticut, Illinois, Michigan, Minnesota, Pennsylvania and Ohio. Since 1964, programs have also been reported operative in Iowa, New Jersey, Oregon, Washington and Wisconsin.

Released Time

Several million children of elementary and high school age of all denominations have the opportunity of receiving religious instruction on released time. Under released time programs they are permitted to leave their public schools during school hours to attend religious instruction classes held off the public school premises. They are released at the request of their parents. Public school authorities merely provide for their dismissal, and take no part in the program.

The first released time program was set up at Gary, Ind., in 1914. In 1905 a proposal had been made by Dr. George U. Wenner, to the Interfaith Conference on Federation, that public school pupils be given a day off a week for religious instruction in their churches. In 1876 a court decision in Vermont left to the discretion of local school boards whether they would release public school students for religious instruction.

In New York, where released time began in 1917, a law was passed in 1940 which authorized school boards to permit the release of public school pupils from class, at the request of their parents, to attend religious instruction off public school premises. The U.S. Supreme Court upheld the constitutionality of the measure in the case of Zorach v. Clauson in 1952.

Released time programs are operative in most states at this time.

ESEA

The first major federal aid to education program in US history containing provisions benefitting parochial school students was enacted by the first session of the 89th Congress and signed into law by President Lyndon B. Johnson on Apr. 11, 1965. The 1965 Elementary and Secondary School Aid Law was passed by the House of Representatives (263 to 153) on Mar. 26 and by the Senate (73 to 18) on Apr. 9.

Provisions

The principal provisions of the $1.3 billion program were stated in three of the eight titles of the law.

• 1. One billion dollars was allocated to public school districts under a formula based chiefly on the number of children in schools who came from families earning less than $2,000 a year. The grant was intended to cover half of the cost of education for each eligible pupil.

Parochial and other private school pupils in the same low-income bracket were to benefit by extensions to them by local public school districts of shared services or facilities. Public school districts were required to take these children into account when making plans to aid needy students.

• 2. About $100 million was provided to buy textbooks for pupils, materials and volumes for school libraries, and some instructional equipment. All were to be owned by a public agency, such as a local school district or library, but they could be loaned to children attending nonpublic schools.

• 3. Another $100 million was to be used to establish educational centers to benefit

both public and private school pupils with cultural enrichment programs and other special services. Public agencies would operate these centers, but the legislation required that private school educators and others from outside the public schools take part in planning for them.

Avoids Impasse

President Johnson presented his program to the Congress on Jan. 12, 1965, in a special message which indicated his intention of avoiding the separation of Church and State impasse which had blocked all earlier aid proposals pertaining to nonpublic, and especially church-affiliated, schools. The aim of the program, under public control, is to serve the public purpose by aiding disadvantaged pupils in public and nonpublic schools.

Program Regulations

Regulations for the administration of programs under the new law were issued Sept. 15, 1965, by the US Office of Education. The leading norms are as follows.

• Participation of Nonpublic School Children: Must be "substantially comparable" to that of public school children.

• Special Projects: Can include "broadened health services, school breakfasts for poor children, and guidance and counseling services" in addition to strictly educational offerings. Public school teachers can go to private schools to offer special services, and mobile or portable equipment can be placed on private school premises temporarily.

• Aid for Textbooks and Library Resources: Materials are to be loaned by public agencies to private school teachers and pupils, not to the schools themselves.

To be distributed to private school pupils on an equal basis with public school student numbers, the materials must be approved for use in public schools and can include books, periodicals, documents, pamphlets, photographic works, musical scores, maps, charts, globes, sound recordings, films and video tapes.

If constitutional restrictions prevent a state from allowing its agencies to act as channels for aid to teachers and pupils in private schools, the regulations provide that the US Commissioner of Education can provide for the distribution of the books and materials himself.

Amendment, Benefits

ESEA, since its passage, has been refunded in several stages and amended in some respects but has remained substantially the same as enacted.

The most recent refunding ($25 billion) was enacted with passage of the Education Amendments of 1974 (H.R. 69) and their signing into law by President Gerald R. Ford

Aug. 21, 1974. The amendments provided, among other things, for the broadening of bilingual education and increased funding for education of the handicapped. They also embodied a forward-funding mechanism to ensure program continuity, and a prohibition against busing past the school nearest a child's home unless a court should find it necessary to protect the constitutional rights of minority children.

The law has benefitted many disadvantaged pupils in public and nonpublic schools. Spokesmen for Catholic education, however, have called attention of the Congress to the fact that provisions of the law have not been applied to a disproportionately large number of eligible students in Catholic schools. (See Wheeler v. Barrera.)

SIGNIFICANT SCHOOL AID DECISIONS

(See several decisions of this type in listing, Church-State Decisions of the Supreme Court.)

The U.S. Supreme Court handed down landmark decisions June 25, 1973, against the constitutionality of programs of aid to nonpublic school education on the elementary and secondary levels in New York and Pennsylvania. Grounds for the decisions were that the programs violated the No Establishment Clause of the First Amendment, that they had the "impermissible effect" of advancing sectarian activities, and that they were generative of religious divisiveness.

New York, Pennsylvania Cases

The decisions struck down provisions in New York statutes for maintenance and repair grants for certain nonpublic school facilities (9 to 0), tuition reimbursement (6 to 3) or tax credits (6 to 3) for parents with children in nonpublic schools, and payment to nonpublic schools for specified services mandated by the state (8 to 1). A Pennsylvania reimbursement program shared the same fate as its New York counterpart (6 to 3).

Voting with the majority in all cases were Justices William O. Douglas, William J. Brennan, Jr., Potter Stewart, Thurgood Marshall, Harry A. Blackmun and Lewis F. Powell, Jr. Chief Justice Warren E. Burger and Justice William H. Rehnquist dissented in the 6 to 3 decisions but joined the majority in the 8 to 1 decision. Justice Byron R. White dissented in all but the 9 to 0 decision.

Rhode Island Ruling

In different decisions with the same thrust, the Court had ruled on June 28, 1971, against the constitutionality of a Rhode Island statute providing salary supplements for teachers of secular subjects in parochial schools in the state, and of a purchase-of-services program for instruction in secular subjects in nonpublic schools in Pennsylvania.

Analysis of Decisions

The New York and Pennsylvania decisions indicated that the Court would strike down any program containing the potential for massive subsidies, either direct or indirect, for education in church-affiliated elementary and secondary schools. So commented Father Charles M. Whelan, S.J., constitutional lawyer and professor of law at Fordham University.

In an analysis of the rulings, Father Whelan said that it seemed "reasonably clear" that all five programs at issue suffered from "three fatal defects":

• "Roman Catholic schools got the lion's share of the benefits."

• The total amount of money involved in the programs, although small, "could easily be expanded to provide massive subsidies for education in parochial schools."

• "There was no way for public schools, parents and students to benefit as well as nonpublic schools, parents and students."

The primary argument against the programs was the "effect" argument. Father Whelan called this a development parallel with the "excessive entanglement" argument in the Lemon decision. He said that the "narrow channel between the Scylla and Charybdis of effect and entanglement" spoken of by Justice Powell (who delivered the majority opinion) will probably "prove too narrow in the immediate future for any new programs specially designed to insure the survival, much less the well-being, of nonpublic elementary and secondary schools."

Meek v. Pittenger

The Supreme Court by a vote of 6 to 3 May 19, 1975, ruled unconstitutional portions of a Pennsylvania law that provided auxiliary services for students of nonpublic schools. The services, budgeted at $12 million, included counseling, testing and psychological services, speech and hearing therapy, teaching and related services for exceptional, handicapped and educationally deprived children.

At the same time, the Court ruled in favor of provisions of the law permitting textbook loans to students of nonpublic schools.

Majority Opinion

The majority opinion written by Justice Potter Stewart said:

• Because 75 per cent of the nonpublic schools receiving services were church-related, the law had the "unconstitutional primary effect of establishing religion."

• "Excessive entanglement would be required for Pennsylvania to be assured that the public school professional staff members who provide the services do not advance the reli-

gious mission of the church-related schools in which they serve."
- Objection was also raised against providing services only on the premises of nonpublic schools and only at the request of such schools.

Burger Dissent

The three dissenting Jusices viewed the majority decision as a threat to the free exercise of religion.

Chief Justice Warren Burger commented: "If the consequences of the Court's holding operated only to penalize institutions with a religious affiliation, the result would be grievous enough; nothing in the religious clauses of the First Amendment permits governmental power to discriminate against or affirmatively stifle religions or religious activity. . . .

"But this holding does more; it penalizes children — children who have the misfortune to have to cope with the learning process under extraordinary physical and psychological burdens, for the most part congenital. This penalty strikes them not because of any act of theirs, but because of their parents' choice of religious exercise."

Noting that affluent parents would be able to afford both the costs of church-related schools and private therapy for handicapped children, while other parents could not, Burger called the decision "a gross violation of Fourteenth Amendment rights" of equal protection under law.

"Extravagant Suggestion"

Burger criticized the majority opinion's "extravagant suggestion of potential entanglement." He wrote: "There is absolutely no support in this record or, for that matter, in ordinary human experience, to support the concern some see with respect to the 'dangers' lurking in extending common, nonsectarian tools of the education process — especially remedial tools — to students in private schools."

The Chief Justice concluded his dissent with the statement: "One can only hope that, at some time in the future, the Court will come to a more enlightened and tolerant view

of the First Amendment's guarantee of free exercise of religion, thus eliminating the denial of equal protection to children in church-sponsored schools, and take a more realistic view that carefully limited aid to children is not a step toward establishing a state religion — at least while this Court sits."

Rehnquist-White Dissent

Justice William Rehnquist, in a dissent joined by Justice Byron White, said the Court had taken an "extreme approach" to the separation of Church and state. He charged: "The Court apparently believes that the Establishment Clause of the First Amendment not only mandates religious neutrality on the part of the government, but also requires that this Court go further and throw its weight on the side of those who believe our society as a whole should be a purely secular one."

Rehnquist was also critical of "the arbitrariness of the percentage approach" in determining whether a law had the primary effect of establishing religion. He noted that the majority of the Court gave no reason for taking such an approach.

Effects of the Decision

Bishop James Rausch, general secretary of the U.S. Catholic Conference, was one of many objectors to the majority decision of the Court. He called it "a great injustice" with the effect of making "handicapped children attending nonpublic schools in Pennsylvania second-class citizens."

The bishop also said that "it is important to bear in mind that the Court's action does not invalidate many forms of government assistance to nonpublic school students which have previously been upheld by the courts."

Unsettled questions remained, however, about the effects of the Meek v. Pittenger decision on these other forms of assistance to students in nonpublic schools.

One indication of possible effects was the action of the Supreme Court May 27, 1975, in remanding to a lower court its prior decision in constitutional support of Ohio's program for auxiliary services in private schools. The lower court was ordered to reconsider the case in the light of the Meek v. Pittenger decision.

UNIVERSITIES AND COLLEGES IN THE UNITED STATES

(Sources: Almanac survey; *The Official Catholic Directory, 1975*.)

Listed below are institutions of higher learning established under Catholic auspices. Some of them are now independent.

Information includes: name of each institution; indication of male (m), female (w), coeducational (c) student body; name of founding group or group with which the institution is affiliated; year of foundation; number of students, in parentheses.

Albertus Magnus College (w): 700 Prospect

St., New Haven, Conn. 06511. Dominican Sisters; 1925 (472).

Albuquerque, University of (c): St. Joseph Pl. N.W., Albuquerque, N.M. 87105. Sisters of St. Francis; 1940 (3,150).

Allentown College of St. Francis de Sales (c); Center Valley, Pa. 18034. Oblates of St. Francis de Sales; 1965 (602).

Alvernia College (c): Reading, Pa. 19607. Bernardine Sisters; 1958 (501).

Alverno College (w): 3401 S. 39th St. Milwaukee, Wis. 53215. School Sisters of St. Francis; 1936; independent (862).

Anna Maria College (c): Sunset Lane, Paxton, Mass. 01612. Sisters of St. Anne; 1946 (835).

Annhurst College (w): R.R. 2 Woodstock, South Woodstock, Conn. 06281. Daughters of the Holy Spirit; 1941 (336).

Aquinas College (c): 1607 Robinson Rd. S. E., Grand Rapids, Mich. 49506. Sisters of St. Dominic; 1922 (1,600).

Assumption College (c): 500 Salisbury St., Worcester, Mass. 01609. Assumptionist Fathers; 1904 (1,721).

Avila College (c): 11901 Wornall Rd., Kansas City, Mo. 64145. Sisters of St. Joseph of Carondelet; 1867 (1,470).

Barat College (w): 700 Westleigh Rd., Lake Forest, Ill. 60045. Society of the Sacred Heart; 1919; independent (770).

Barry College (c): 11300 N. E. 2nd Ave., Miami, Fla. 33161. Dominican Sisters; 1940 (1,450).

Bellarmine College (c): Newburg Rd., Louisville, Ky. 40205; Louisville archdiocese, 1950 (1,350).

Belmont Abbey College (c): Belmont, N. C. 20812. Benedictine Fathers; 1876 (688).

Benedictine College (c): Atchison, Kans. 66002. Benedictines (c. 1,000).

Biscayne College (c): 16400 N. W. 32nd Ave., Miami, Fla. 33054. Augustinian Fathers; 1962 (1,552).

Boston College (University Status) (c): Newton, Mass. 02167. Jesuit Fathers; 1863 (12,749).

Brescia College (c): 120 W. 7th St., Owensboro, Ky. 42301. Ursuline Sisters; 1925 (1,034).

Briar Cliff College (c): W. 33rd and Rebecca Sts., Sioux City, Ia. 51104. Sisters of St. Francis of the Holy Family; 1930 (750).

Cabrini College (c): Radnor, Pa. 19087. Missionary Srs. of Sacred Heart; 1957 (426).

Caldwell College (w): Caldwell, N. J. 07006. Dominican Sisters; 1939 (868).

Canisius College (c): 2001 Main St., Buffalo, N. Y. 14208. Jesuit Fathers; 1870; independent (4,004).

Cardinal Stritch College (c): 6801 N. Yates Rd., Milwaukee, Wis. 52317. Sisters of St. Francis of Assisi; 1932 (1,109).

Carlow College (w): 3333 5th Ave., Pittsburgh, Pa. 15213. Sisters of Mercy; 1929 (800).

Carroll College (c): Helena, Mont. 59601. Diocesan Clergy; 1909 (1,260).

Catholic University of America (c): Fourth St. and Michigan Ave. N.E., Washington, D.C. 20064. Hierarchy of the United States; 1889. Pontifical University (7,030).

Catholic University of Puerto Rico (c): Ponce, P. R. Hierarchy of Puerto Rico; Pontifical University (6,651).

Chaminade College (c): 3140 Waialae Ave.,

Honolulu, Hawaii 96816. Marianists; 1955 (790).

Chestnut Hill College (w): Philadelphia, Pa. 19118. Sisters of St. Joseph; 1871 (534).

Christian Brothers College (c): 650 E. Parkway S., Memphis, Tenn. 38104. Brothers of the Christian Schools; 1871 (750).

Clarke College (w): 1550 Clarke Dr., Dubuque, Iowa 52001. Sisters of Charity; 1843 (600).

Creighton Universtiy (c): 2500 California St., Omaha, Neb. 68178. Jesuit Fathers; 1878 (4,551).

Dallas, University of (c): Irving, Tex. 75060. Private; 1956 (1,717).

Dayton, University of (c): 300 College Park, Dayton, Ohio 45409. Marianists; 1850 (6,733).

De Paul University (c): 2323 N. Seminary Ave., Chicago, Ill. 60614. Vincentians; 1898 (10,010).

Detroit, University of (c): McNicholas Rd. at Livernois, Detroit, Mich. 48221. Jesuit Fathers; 1877 (8,879).

Dominican College of Blauvelt (c): Blauvelt, N. Y. 10913. Dominican Sisters; 1952 (815).

Dominican College of San Rafael (c): San Rafael, Calif. 94901. Dominican Sisters; 1890; independent (769).

Don Bosco College (m): P.O. Box 6, Newton, N.J. 07860. Salesians of St. John Bosco; 1928 (110).

Duquesne University (c): 801 Bluff St., N.W., Pittsburgh, Pa. 15219. Holy Ghost Fathers; 1878 (8,000).

D'Youville College (c): 320 Porter Ave., Buffalo, N. Y. 14201. Grey Nuns of the Sacred Heart; 1908; independent (1,200).

Edgecliff College (c): Edgecliff Victory Pkwy., Cincinnati, Ohio 45206. Sisters of Mercy; 1935 (831).

Edgewood College (c): 855 Woodrow St., Madison, Wis. 53711. Dominican Sisters; 1927 (603).

Emmanuel College (w): 400 The Fenway, Boston, Mass. 02115. Sisters of Notre Dame of Namur; independent (900).

Fairfield University (c): Fairfield, Conn. 06433. Jesuit Fathers; 1942 (4,500).

Felician College (w): S. Main St., Lodi, N.J. 07644. Felician Sisters; 1923 (595).

Fontbonne College (c): Wydown and Big Bend Blvds., St. Louis, Mo. 63105. Sisters of St. Joseph of Carondelet; 1917 (840).

Fordham University (c): Fordham Rd. and Third Ave., New York, N. Y. 10458. Jesuit Fathers; 1841; independent (10,450).

Fort Wright College (c): W. 4000 Randolph Rd., Spokane, Wash. 99204. Sisters of the Holy Names of Jesus and Mary; 1939 (334).

Gannon College (c): 109 W. 6th St., Erie, Pa. 16501. Diocese of Erie; 1944 (3,126).

Georgetown University (c): 37th and O Sts. N.W., Washington, D.C. 20057. Jesuit Fathers; 1789 (10,640).

Georgian Court College (w): Lakewood,

N.J. 08701. Sisters of Mercy; 1908 (733).

Gonzaga University (c): Spokane, Wash. 99202. Jesuit Fathers; 1887 (3,185).

Great Falls, College of (c): 1301 20th St. S., Great Falls, Mont. 59401. Sisters of Charity of Providence; 1932 (1,022).

Gwynedd-Mercy College (c): Gwynedd Valley, Pa. 19437. Sisters of Mercy; 1948 (716).

Holy Cross College (c): Worcester, Mass. 01610. Jesuit Fathers; 1843 (2,475).

Holy Family College (c): Grant and Frankford Aves., Philadelphia, Pa. 19114. Sisters of Holy Family of Nazareth; 1954 (1,000).

Holy Names College (c): 3500 Mountain Blvd., Oakland, Calif. 94619. Sisters of the Holy Names of Jesus and Mary; 1868 (716).

Illinois Benedictine College (c): Lisle, Ill. 60532. Benedictine Fathers; 1890 (1,244).

Immaculata College (w): Immaculata, Pa. 19345. Sisters, Servants of the Immaculate Heart of Mary; 1920 (559).

Incarnate Word College (c): 4301 Broadway, San Antonio, Tex. 78209. Sisters of Charity of the Incarnate Word; 1881 (1,554).

Iona College (c): 715 North Ave., New Rochelle, N.Y. 10801. Congregation of Christian Brothers; 1940; independent (4,600).

John Carroll University (c): North Park and Miramar Blvds., Cleveland, Ohio. 44118. Jesuit Fathers; 1886 (3,671).

Kansas Newman College (formerly Sacred Heart College) (c): 3100 McCormick Ave., Wichita, Kans. 67213. Adorers of the Blood of Christ; 1933 (657).

King's College (c): Wilkes-Barre, Pa. 18702. Holy Cross Fathers; 1946 (2,132).

Ladycliff College (w): Highland Falls, N.Y. 10928. Franciscan Sisters; 1933; independent (467).

La Roche College (c): 9000 Babcock Blvd., Pittsburgh, Pa. 15237. Sisters of Divine Providence; 1963 (620)

La Salle College (c): 20th St. and Olney Ave., Philadelphia, Pa. 19141. Brothers of the Christian Schools; 1863 (6,150)

Le Moyne College (c): Syracuse, N.Y. 13214. Jesuit Fathers; 1946; independent (1,685).

Lewis University (c): Lockport, Ill. 60441. Christian Brothers; 1930 (3,000).

Lone Mountain College (c): 2800 Turk St., San Francisco, Calif. 94118. Religious of the Sacred Heart; 1930 (793).

Loras College (c): 1450 Alta Vista St., Dubuque, Ia. 52001. Archdiocese of Dubuque; 1839 (1,288).

Loretto Heights College (c): 3001 S. Federal Blvd., Denver, Colo. 80236. Sisters of Loretto; 1918; independent (746).

Loyola College (c): 4501 N. Charles St., Baltimore, Md. 21210, Jesuits; 1852 (4,017).

Loyola University (c): 820 N. Michigan Ave., Chicago, Ill. 60611. Jesuit Fathers; 1870 (15,202).

Loyola University (c): 6363 St. Charles Ave., New Orleans, La. 70118. Jesuit Fathers; 1904 (4,215).

Loyola Marymount University (c): 7101 W. 80th St., Los Angeles, Calif. 90045. Jesuit Fathers; Religious of Sacred Heart of Mary, Sisters of St. Joseph of Orange; 1911 (5,305).

Madonna College (c): 3600 Schoolcraft Rd., Livonia, Mich. 48150. Felician Sisters; 1937 (1,399).

Manhattan College (c): 4513 Manhattan College Pkwy., New York, N.Y. 10471. Brothers of the Christian Schools; 1853; independent (4,229). Cooperative program with College of Mt. St. Vincent.

Marian College (c): Fond du Lac, Wis. 54935. Sisters of St. Agnes; 1936 (450).

Marian College (c): 3200 Cold Springs Rd., Indianapolis, Ind. 46222. Sisters of St. Francis (Oldenburg, Ind.); 1937 (653).

Marist College (c): Poughkeepsie, N.Y. 12601. Marist Brothers of the Schools; 1946; independent (1,878).

Marquette University (c): 615 N. 11th St., Milwaukee, Wis. 53233. Jesuit Fathers; 1881; independent (10,987).

Mary College (c): Route 2, Box 119, Bismarck, N.D. 58501. Benedictine Sisters; 1959 (825).

Mary Manse College (c): 2436 Parkwood Ave., Toledo, Ohio 43620. Ursuline Nuns; 1922 (722).

Marycrest College (c): 1607 W. 12th St., Davenport, Iowa 52804. Sisters of the Humility of Mary; 1939 (1,015).

Marygrove College (c): 8425 W. McNicholas Rd., Detroit, Mich. 48221. Sisters, Servants of the Immaculate Heart of Mary; 1910 (991).

Marymount College (w): 2807 N. Glebe Rd., Arlington, Va. 22007. Religious of the Sacred Heart of Mary; 1950 (625).

Marymount College (c): Salina, Kans. 67401. Sisters of St. Joseph of Concordia; 1922 (601).

Marymount College (w): Tarrytown, N.Y. 10591. Religious of the Sacred Heart of Mary; 1907; independent (900).

Marymount Manhattan College (w): 221 E. 71st St., New York, N.Y. 10021. Religious of the Sacred Heart of Mary; 1948; independent (1,316).

Maryville College (c): 13550 Conway Rd., St. Louis, Mo. 63141. Religious of the Sacred Heart; 1872; independent (1,050).

Marywood College (w): Scranton, Pa. 18509. Sisters, Servants of the Immaculate Heart of Mary; 1915 (2,625). Coed in graduate division.

Mater Dei College (c): Riverside Dr., Ogdensburg, N.Y. 13669. Sisters of St. Joseph; 1960 (250).

Medaille College (c): 18 Agassiz Circle, Buffalo, N.Y. 14214; independent (415).

Mercy College (c): 8200 W. Outer Dr., Detroit, Mich. 48219. Sisters of Mercy; 1941 (1,936).

Mercyhurst College (c): 501 E. 38th St., Erie, Pa. 16501. Sisters of Mercy; 1926 (1,477).

Merrimack College (c): North Andover, Mass. 01845. Augustinians; 1947 (2,049).

Misericordia (w): Dallas, Pa. 18612. Sisters of Mercy; 1924 (1,006).

Molloy College (w): 1000 Hempstead Ave., Rockville Centre, N.Y. 11570. Dominican Sisters; 1955 (1,079).

Mount Angel College (c): Mt. Angel, Ore. 97362. Benedictine Sisters; 1954, independent (287).

Mount Marty College (c): Yankton, S.D. 57078. Benedictine Sisters; 1936 (578).

Mt. Mary College (w): 2900 W. Menomonee River Pkwy., Milwaukee, Wis. 53222. School Sisters of Notre Dame; 1913 (1,032).

Mt. Mercy College (c): Elmhurst Dr., Cedar Rapids, Ia. 52402. Sisters of Mercy; 1928 (809).

Mt. St. Agnes College: Merged with Loyola College (Maryland).

Mt. St. Joseph on the Ohio, College of (w): Mt. St. Joseph, Ohio 45051. Sisters of Charity; 1920 (882).

Mt. St. Mary College (w): Hooksett, N.H. 03106. Sisters of Mercy; 1934; independent (201).

Mt. St. Mary College (c): Newburgh, N.Y. 12550. Dominican Sisters; 1954 (825).

Mt. St. Mary College (c): Emmitsburg, Md. 21727. Diocesan Clergy; 1808; independent (1,160).

Mt. St. Mary's College (c): 12001 Chalon Rd., Los Angeles, Calif. 90049. Sisters of St. Joseph of Carondelet; 1925 (1,177).

Mt. St. Vincent, College of (c): Mt. St. Vincent-on-Hudson, New York, N.Y. 10471. Sisters of Charity; 1847; independent (1,050). Coed arrangements with Manhattan College.

Mount Senario College (c): Ladysmith, Wis. 54848. Servants of Mary; independent (243).

Mundelein College (w): 6363 N. Sheridan Rd., Chicago, Ill. 60626. Sisters of Charity of the Blessed Virgin Mary; 1929 (805).

Nazareth College (c): Nazareth, Mich. 49074. Sisters of St. Joseph; 1924 (482).

Nazareth College (w): East Ave., Rochester, N.Y. 14610. Sisters of St. Joseph; 1924; independent (1,917).

New Rochelle, College of (w): 29 Castle Pl., New Rochelle, N.Y. 10801. Ursuline Nuns; 1904; independent (2,949). Coed in some divisions.

Niagara University (c): Niagara Falls, N.Y. 14109. Vincentian Fathers; 1856 (3,759).

Notre Dame, College of (c): Belmont, Calif. 94002. Sisters of Notre Dame de Namur; 1868; independent (1,167).

Notre Dame College (w): 4545 College Rd., Cleveland, Ohio 44121. Sisters of Notre Dame; 1922 (535).

Notre Dame College (w): Manchester, N.H. 03104. Sisters of the Holy Cross; 1950 (400).

Notre Dame College (c): 320 E. Ripa Ave., St. Louis, Mo. 63125. School Sisters of Notre Dame; 1896 (396).

Notre Dame of Maryland, College of (w): 4701 N. Charles St., Baltimore, Md. 21210. School Sisters of Notre Dame; 1873 (667).

Notre Dame, University of (c): Notre Dame, Ind. 46556. Congregation of Holy Cross; 1842 (8,800).

Ohio Dominican College (c): Columbus, Ohio 43219. Dominican Srs.; 1911 (1,000).

Our Lady of Angels College (w): Aston, Pa. 19014. Sisters of St. Francis; 1965 (425).

Our Lady of Holy Cross College (c): 4123 Woodland Dr., New Orleans, La. 70114. Congregation of Sisters Marianites of Holy Cross (777).

Our Lady of the Elms College (w): Chicopee, Mass. 01013. Sisters of St. Joseph; 1928 (420).

Our Lady of the Lake College (c): 411 S.W. 24th St., San Antonio, Tex. 78285. Sisters of Divine Providence; 1912 (2,083).

Portland, University of (c): 5000 N. Willamette Blvd., Portland, Ore. 97203. Holy Cross Fathers; 1901; independent (2,135).

Providence College (c): River Ave. and Eaton St., Providence, R.I. 02918. Dominican Fathers; 1917 (3,104).

Quincy College (c): 1831 College Ave., Quincy, Ill. 62301. Franciscan Fathers; 1860 (1,300).

Regis College (c): W. 50th Ave. and Lowell Blvd. Denver, Colo. 80221. Jesuit Fathers; 1887 (1,100).

Regis College (w): Wellesley St., Weston, Mass. 02193. Sisters of St. Joseph; 1927 (807).

Rivier College (w): Nashua, N.H. 03060. Sisters of the Presentation of Mary; 1933; independent (1,350).

Rockhurst College (c): 5225 Troost Ave., Kansas City, Mo. 64110. Jesuit Fathers; 1910 (2,795).

Rosary College (c): 7900 Division St., River Forest, Ill. 60305. Dominican Sisters; 1901 (1,314).

Rosary Hill College (c): 4380 Main St., Buffalo, N.Y. 14226. Sisters of St. Francis of Penance and Christian Charity; 1947; independent (1,331).

Rosemont College (w): Rosemont, Pa. 19010. Society of the Holy Child Jesus; 1921 (550).

Sacred Heart University (c): Fairfield (P.O. Bridgeport), Conn. 06604. Diocese of Bridgeport; 1963; independent (1,190).

St. Ambrose College (c): Davenport, Ia. 52803. Diocese of Davenport; 1882 (1,342).

St. Anselm's College (c): Manchester N.H. 03102. Benedictine Fathers; 1889 (1,557).

St. Basil's College (m): 195 Glenbrook Rd., Stamford, Conn. 06902. Byzantine Rite Diocese of Stamford; 1939 (23).

St. Benedict College (w): St. Joseph, Minn. 56374. Benedictine Sisters; 1913 (1,362).

St. Bernard College (c): St. Bernard, Ala.

35138. Benedictine Fathers; 1892 (393).

St. Bonaventure University (c): St. Bonaventure, N.Y. 14778. Franciscan Fathers; 1856; independent (2,382).

St. Catherine College (w): 2004 Randolph St., St. Paul, Minn. 55105. Sisters of St. Joseph of Carondelet; 1905 (1,688).

St. Edward's University (c): Austin, Tex. 78704. Holy Cross Brothers; 1885 (1,190).

St. Elizabeth, College of (w): Convent Station, N.J. 07961. Sisters of Charity; 1899; independent (592).

St. Francis, College of (c): 500 Wilcox St., Joliet, Ill. 60435. Sisters of St. Francis of Mary Immaculate; 1925; independent (1,137).

St. Francis College (c): 605 Pool Rd., Biddeford, Me. 04005. Franciscan Fathers; 1953; independent (450).

St. Francis College (c): 180 Remsen St., Brooklyn, N.Y. 11201. Franciscan Brothers; 1884; independent (3,049).

St. Francis College (c): 2701 Spring St., Fort Wayne, Ind. 46808. Sisters of St. Francis; 1890 (1,334).

St. Francis College (c): Loretto, Pa. 15940. Franciscan Fathers; 1847 (1,507).

St. John Fisher College (c): 3690 East Ave., Rochester, N.Y. 14618. Basilian Fathers; 1951; independent (1,500).

St. John's University (c): Grand Central and Utopia Pkwys., Jamaica, N.Y. 11439 (Queens Campus); 300 Howard Ave., Grymes Hill, Staten Island, N.Y. 10301 (Staten Island Campus). Vincentian Fathers; 1870 (14,074).

St. John's University (m): Collegeville, Minn. 56321. Benedictine Fathers; 1857 (1,888). Coed in graduate school.

St. Joseph College (w): 1678 Asylum Ave., West Hartford, Conn. 06117. Sisters of Mercy; 1932 (994). Coed in graduate school.

St. Joseph's College (c): Standish (P.O. N. Windham), Me. 04062. Sisters of Mercy, 1915 (507).

St. Joseph's College (c): Rensselaer, Ind. 47978; Calumet Campus, 4721 Indianapolis Blvd., East Chicago, Ind. 46312. Society of the Precious Blood; 1889 (1,062 at Rensselaer; 1,608 at Calumet Campus, East Chicago).

St. Joseph's College (c): City Ave. at 54th St., Philadelphia, Pa. 19131. Jesuit Fathers; 1851 (5,600).

St. Joseph's College (c): 245 Clinton Ave., Brooklyn, N.Y. 11205. Sisters of St. Joseph; 1916; independent (527).

St. Joseph the Provider, College of (c): Clement Rd., Rutland, Vt. 05701. Sisters of St. Joseph; 1954; independent (195).

St. Leo College (c): St. Leo, Fla. 33574. Benedictine Fathers; 1889; independent (1,070).

St. Louis University (c): 221 N. Grand Blvd., St. Louis, Mo. 63103. Jesuit Fathers; 1818 (10,356).

St. Martin's College (c): Olympia, Wash. 98503. Benedictine Fathers; 1895 (615).

St. Mary, College of (w): 1901 S. 72nd St., Omaha, Neb. 68124. Sisters of Mercy; 1923; independent (498).

St. Mary College (w): Leavenworth, Kans. 66048. Sisters of Charity of Leavenworth; 1923 (535).

St. Mary of the Plains College (c): Dodge City, Kans. 67801. Sisters of St. Joseph of Wichita; 1952 (413).

St. Mary-of-the-Woods College (w): St. Mary-of-the-Woods, Ind. 47876. Sisters of Providence; 1840 (378).

St. Mary's College (w): Notre Dame, Ind. 46556. Sisters of the Holy Cross; 1844 (1,672).

St. Mary's College (c): Orchard Lake, Mich. 48034. Secular Clergy (140).

St. Mary's College (c): Moraga, Calif. 94575. Brothers of the Christian Schools; 1863 (1,066).

St. Mary's College (c): Winona, Minn. 55987. Brothers of the Christian Schools; 1913 (1,125).

St. Mary's Dominican College (w): 7214 St. Charles Ave., New Orleans, La. 70118. Dominican Sisters; 1910 (664).

St. Mary's University (c): 2700 Cincinnati Ave., San Antonio, Tex. 78228. Society of Mary (Marianists); 1852 (3,800).

St. Michael's College (c): Winooski Park, Vt. 05404. Society of St. Edmund; 1904 (1,523).

St. Norbert College (c): De Pere, Wis. 54178. Norbertine Fathers; 1898 (1,400).

St. Peter's College (c): 2641 Kennedy Blvd., Jersey City, N.J. 07306. Jesuit Fathers; 1872 (4,200).

St. Rose, College of (c): 432 Western Ave., Albany, N.Y. 12203. Sisters of St. Joseph of Carondelet; 1920; independent (2,014).

St. Scholastica, College of (c): 1200 Kenwood Ave., Duluth, Minn. 55811. Benedictine Sisters; 1912 (1,117).

St. Teresa, College of (w): Winona, Minn. 55987. Sisters of St. Francis; 1907 (1,077).

St. Thomas, College of (m): St. Paul, Minn. 55101. Archdiocese of St. Paul; 1885 (2,700). Coed in graduate school.

St. Thomas, University of (College Status) (c): 3812 Montrose Blvd., Houston, Tex. 77006. Basilian Fathers; 1947 (1,781).

St. Thomas Aquinas College (c): Sparkill, N.Y. 10976. Dominican Sisters (750).

St. Vincent College (m): Latrobe, Pa. 15650. Benedictine Fathers; 1846 (975).

St. Xavier College (c): 3700 W. 103rd St., Chicago, Ill. 60655. Sisters of Mercy; chartered 1847 (1,400).

Salve Regina College (c): Ochre Point Ave., Newport, R.I. 02840. Sisters of Mercy; 1934 (1,485).

San Diego, University of (c): Alcala Park, San Diego, Calif. 92110. San Diego diocese and Religious of the Sacred Heart; 1949; independent (2,865).

San Francisco, University of (c): 2130 Fulton St., San Francisco, Calif. 94117. Jesuit Fathers; 1855 (5,970).

Santa Clara, University of (c): Santa Clara, Calif. 95053. Jesuit Fathers; 1851 (6,597).

Santa Fe, College of (c): Santa Fe, N. Mex. 87501. Brothers of the Christian Schools; 1947 (1,300).

Scranton, University of (c): Scranton, Pa. 18510. Jesuit Fathers; 1888 (4,031).

Seattle University (c): Broadway and East Madison, Seattle, Wash. 98122. Jesuit Fathers; 1891 (3,344).

Seton Hall University (c): South Orange, N.J. 07079. Diocesan Clergy; 1856 (9,719).

Seton Hill College (w): Greensburg, Pa. 15601. Sisters of Charity of Seton Hill; 1883 (660).

Siena College (c): Loudonville, N.Y. 12211. Franciscan Friars; 1937 (2,104).

Siena Heights College (c): Adrian, Mich. 49221. Dominican Sisters; 1919; independent (1,061).

Silver Lake College of Holy Family (c): R.F.D. 5, Manitowoc, Wis. 54220. Franciscan Sisters of Christian Charity; 1935 (428).

Southern Vermont College (c): Bennington, Vt. 05201. Sisters of St. Joseph; 1926; independent (400). Bachelor and Associate degree programs.

Spalding College (c): 851 S. 4th St., Louisville, Ky. 40203. Sisters of Charity of Nazareth; 1920 (1,130).

Spring Hill College (c): Mobile, Ala. 36608. Jesuit Fathers; 1830 (918).

Steubenville, College of (c): Steubenville, Ohio 43952. Franciscan Fathers; 1946 (999).

Stonehill College (c): North Easton, Mass. 02356. Holy Cross Fathers; 1948; independent (1,650).

Thomas More College (c): Turkey Foot Rd., Box 85, Fort Mitchell, Covington, Ky. 41017. Diocese of Covington; 1921 (1,589).

Trinity College (w): Colchester Ave., Burlington, Vt. 05401. Sisters of Mercy; 1925 (497).

Trinity College (w): Michigan Ave. and Franklin St. N.E., Washington, D.C. 20017. Sisters of Notre Dame de Namur; 1897 (500). Coed in graduate school.

Ursuline College (w): Lander Rd. and Fairmont Blvd., Cleveland, Ohio 44124. Ursuline Nuns; 1871 (425).

Villa Maria College (w): 2551 W. Lake Rd., Erie, Pa. 16505. Sisters of St. Joseph; 1925 (643).

Villanova University (c): Villanova, Pa. 19086. Augustinian Fathers; 1842 (9,910).

Viterbo College (c): La Crosse, Wis. 54601. Franciscan Sisters; 1931 (785).

Walsh College (c): 2020 Easton St. N.W., Canton, Ohio 44720. Brothers of Christian Instruction; 1959 (775).

Wheeling College (c): 316 Washington Ave., Wheeling, W. Va. 26003. Jesuit Fathers; 1954 (531).

White Plains, College of (c): 78 N. Broad-

way, White Plains, N.Y. 10603. Sisters of the Divine Compassion; 1923; independent (675).

Xavier University (c): Victory Pkwy. and Dana Ave., Cincinnati, Ohio 45207. Jesuit Fathers; 1831 (6,022).

Xavier University of Louisiana (c): 7325 Palmetto St., New Orleans, La. 70125. Sisters of Blessed Sacrament; 1925; lay/religious administration board (1,891).

Catholic Junior Colleges

Ancilla Domini College (c): Donaldson, Ind. 46513. Ancilla Domini Sisters; 1937 (250).

Aquinas Junior College (c): Harding Rd., Nashville, Tenn. 37205. Dominican Sisters; 1961 (343).

Cullman College (c): Cullman, Ala. 35055. Benedictine Sisters; 1940 (202).

Donnelly College (c): 1236 Sandusky Ave., Kansas City, Kans. 66102. Archdiocesan College. Benedictine Sisters; 1949 (633).

Elizabeth Seton College (c): 1061 N. Broadway, Yonkers, N.Y. 10701. Sisters of Charity; 1960 (422).

Harriman College (c): Harriman Heights Rd., Harriman, N.Y. 10926. Sisters of the Catholic Apostolate (185).

Hilbert College (c): 5200 S. Park Ave., Hamburg, N.Y. 14075. Franciscan Sisters; 1960; independent (585).

Holy Cross Junior College (c): Notre Dame, Ind. 46556. Brothers of Holy Cross; 1966 (270).

Immaculata College of Washington (w): 4300 Nebraska Ave. N.W., Washington, D.C. Sisters of Providence; 1922 (197).

Lourdes College (w): Sylvania, Ohio 43560. Franciscan Srs.; 1958 (207).

Manor Junior College (w): Fox Chase Manor, Jenkintown, Pa. 19046. Sisters of St. Basil the Great; 1947 (334).

Maria College (w): 700 New Scotland Ave., Albany, N.Y. 12208. Sisters of Mercy; 1963 (487).

Maria Regina College (w): 1024 Court St., Syracuse, N.Y. 13208. Franciscan Sisters; 1963; independent (350).

Marymount College (c): 30800 Palos Verdes Dr. E., Rancho Palos Verdes, Calif. 90274. Religious of the Sacred Heart of Mary (370).

Mt. Aloysius Junior College (c): Cresson, Pa. 16630. Sisters of Mercy; 1939 (500).

Mt. St. Clare College (c): Bluff Blvd., and Springdale Dr., Clinton, Ia. 52732. Sisters of Third Order of St. Francis; 1918 (205).

Ottumwa Heights College (c): Grandview Ave., Ottumwa, Ia. 52501. Sisters of the Humility of Mary; 1925 (375).

Presentation College (c): Aberdeen, S.D. 57401. Sisters of the Presentation; 1951 (370).

St. Catharine College (c): St. Catharine, Ky. 40061. Dominican Sisters; 1931 (132).

St. Gertrude, College of (c): Cottonwood, Ida. 83522. Benedictine Sisters.

St. Gregory's College (c): Shawnee, Okla.

74801. Benedictine Fathers; 1876 (398).

St. Mary's College (c): 200 N. Main St., O'Fallon, Mo. 63366. Sisters of the Most Precious Blood; 1921 (395).

St. Mary's Junior College (c): 2600 S. 6th St., Minneapolis, Minn. 55406 (828).

Springfield College in Illinois (c): 1500 N. Fifth St., Springfield, Ill. 62702. Ursuline Nuns; 1929 (600).

Trocaire College (c): 110 Red Jackett Pkwy., Buffalo, N.Y. 14220. Sisters of Mercy; 1958 (733).

Villa Julie College (c): Green Spring Valley Rd., Stevenson, Md. 21153. Sisters of Notre Dame de Namur; 1952; independent (355).

Villa Maria College of Buffalo (c): 240 Pine Ridge Rd., Buffalo, N.Y. 14225. Felician Srs.; 1960 (405).

CAMPUS MINISTRY

"Campus ministry is a pastoral apostolate of service to the members of the entire college community through concern and care for persons, the proclamation of the Gospel, and the celebration of the liturgy," according to a set of guidelines drawn up by an eight-member commission of the National Catholic Educational Association. The general purpose of the ministry is to make the Church present and active in the academic community.

Ideally, according to the guidelines, elements of the ministry — carried on by teams of priests, men and women religious, and lay persons — include liturgical leadership; pastoral counseling; coordination of expressions and energies for religious life on campus; Christian witness on social and moral issues; objective and independent mediation between various groups on campus; participation in religious aspects of the work of the administration, faculty and students.

Status, Agencies

The dimensions and challenge of the campus ministry are evident from estimates that approximately 75 to 80 per cent of 1.8 million Catholics in colleges and universities are on secular or non-Catholic private campuses. Serving them are about 750 full-time and 1,000 part-time campus ministry personnel.

The Office of Campus and Young Adult Ministries, under the Department of Education of the U.S. Catholic Conference, has responsibility for continuing support of ministry in this field. Rev. Patrick H. O'Neill, O.S.A., is director, with offices at 1312 Massachusetts Ave. N.W., Washington, D.C. 20005.

Information and services are furnished by the National Committee of Diocesan Directors of Campus Ministry. This is a committee of members elected from each of the 12 ecclesiastical regions of the U.S., and is an advisory body to the office.

The autonomous Catholic Campus Ministry Association, whose former equivalent was the National Newman Chaplain's Association, is headed by Rev. Dr. Patrick H. O'Neill, O.S.A., 408 E. Lyman Ave., Winter Park, Fla. 32789.

Training Programs

Frank J. Lewis Chaplains' Schools for Campus Ministry Orientation, held in June, 1975, in New York and California, provided orientation and direction for men and women new to the ministry. Forty campus ministers attended each of the schools, which were funded by the Frank J. Lewis Foundaion.

The National Center for Campus Ministry, for specialized ministerial training and education, serves as a national focus for religious and moral concern in higher education.

Designed by an ecumenical team of chaplains and educators active on public, private and church-related campuses, it is sponsored by the Catholic bishops of the U.S. and is funded by Catholic and non-Catholic individual donors and foundations. It is governed by a board of directors representing major American religious and academic traditions.

The center coordinates local and regional programs of training and continuing education, as well as research projects. Information concerning its operations is available from the National Center for Campus Ministry, 1312 Massachusetts Ave. N.W., Washington, D.C. 20005. Rev. Laurence T. Murphy, M.M., president of the board of trustees, is the interim director.

Newman Background

Special ministry on secular campuses in the U.S. began in 1893 when the first student unit of the Newman movement or apostolate was formed at the University of Pennsylvania. Similar units were formed later at other colleges and universities, and in 1915 various groups throughout the country organized a national student federation. Father John Keough of Philadelphia, who became the first national chaplain of the federation in 1917, was a prime mover in publicizing and developing the movement.

The bishops of the U.S. formally recognized the movement in 1941, and in 1962 approved a National Newman Apostolate structure consisting of: the National Newman Student Federation (dating from 1915), the John Henry Cardinal Newman Honorary Society (1938), the National Newman Chaplains' Association (1950), the National Newman Alumni Association (1957), the National Newman Association of Faculty and Staff (1959), and the National Newman Foundation (1959).

Developments in recent years led to dismantling of the whole Newman structure and its replacement by other organizations and programs considered better related to existing conditions on campuses and in the Church and society in general.

DIOCESAN AND INTERDIOCESAN SEMINARIES

Information, according to states, includes names of archdioceses and dioceses, and names and addresses of seminaries. Types of seminaries, when not clear from titles, are indicated in most cases. Interdiocesan seminaries are generally conducted by religious orders for candidates for the priesthood from several dioceses. The list does not include houses of study only for members of religious communities.

Arizona: Tucson — Regina Cleri Seminary (minor), 8800 E. 22nd St. 85710.

California: Los Angeles — St. John's Seminary (major), 5012 E. Seminary Rd., Camarillo. 93010; St. John's Seminary College, 5118 E. Seminary Rd., Camarillo. 93010; Our Lady Queen of Angels (minor), Box 1071, San Fernando. 91341.

Sacramento — St. Pius X Seminary (minor), Twin Cities Rd. and Midway Ave., Galt. 95632.

San Diego — St. Francis Seminary, 5102 San Pedro Ave. 92111.

San Francisco — St. Patrick's Seminary (major), 320 Middlefield Rd., Menlo Park. 94025; St. Patrick's College Seminary, P.O. Box 151, Mountain View, Calif. 94042. St. Joseph High School (minor), Mountain View, Calif. 94042.

Colorado: Denver — St. Thomas Theological Seminary (major), 1300 S. Steele St. 80210.

Connecticut: Hartford — St. Thomas Seminary (minor), 467 Bloomfield Ave., Bloomfield. 06002.

Stamford Byzantine Rite — Ukrainian Catholic Seminary (major), 161 Glenbrook Rd. 06902; St. Basil's Preparatory School, Clovelly Rd. 06902.

District of Columbia: Washington — Theological School of Catholic University of America, 401 Michigan Ave., N.E. 20064.

Florida: Miami — St. John Vianney Minor Seminary, 2900 S.W. 87th Ave. 33165; St. Vincent de Paul Seminary (major), Military Trail, P.O. Box 460, Boynton Beach. 33435.

Hawaii: Honolulu — St. Stephen's Seminary, P.O. Box 698, Kaneohe. 96744.

Illinois: Belleville — St. Henry's Preparatory Seminary, 5901 W. Main St. 62223.

Chicago — Quigley Preparatory Seminary, 103 East Chestnut St. 60611 (North), 7740 South Western Ave. 60620 (South); St. Mary of the Lake Seminary, Mundelein. 60060; Niles Campus of St. Mary of the Lake Seminary, 7135 N. Harlem Ave. 60631.

Joliet — St. Charles Borromeo Seminary, High School, Rt. 53A and Airport Rd. 60441.

Springfield — Immaculate Conception Seminary, 1903 E. Lakeshore Dr. 62708.

Indiana: Gary — Bishop Noll Institute, 1519 Hoffman St., Hammond. 46320.

Indianapolis — St. Meinrad Major and Minor Seminary (interdiocesan), St. Meinrad. 47577.

Iowa: Davenport — St. Ambrose Seminary, 518 W. Locust St. 52803.

Dubuque — Seminary of St. Pius X, Loras College. 52001.

Kansas: Kansas City — Savior of the World Seminary, 1201 Parallel Ave. 66109.

Kentucky: Covington — Seminary of St. Pius X, Erlanger. 41018.

Louisville — St. Thomas Seminary (preparatory), 1816 Norris Pl. 40205.

Louisiana: Baton Rouge — St. Joseph Cathedral Prep School, 3300 Hundred Oaks Ave. 70821.

Lafayette — Immaculata Seminary (preparatory), Carmel Ave. 70501. Box 3847. 70501.

New Orleans — Notre Dame Seminary, 2901 S. Carrollton Ave. 70118; St. John Vianney Preparatory School, 3810 Monroe St. 70118; St. Joseph Seminary College (interdiocesan), St. Benedict 70457.

Maryland: Baltimore — St. Mary's Seminary and University, 5400 Roland Ave. 21210; Mt. St. Mary's Seminary, Emmitsburg. 21727.

Massachusetts: Boston — St. John's Seminary, Brighton. 02135; St. Clement's Hall, 191 Foster St., Brighton 03135; Pope John XXIII National Seminary, 558 South Ave., Weston. 02193.

Melkite Exarchate — St. Basil's Seminary for Eastern Rites, 30 East St., Methuen. 01844.

Michigan: Detroit — Sacred Heart Seminary College, Inc., 2701 Chicago Blvd. 48206; Sts. Cyril and Methodius Seminary, Orchard Lake. 48034; St. John's Provincial Seminary (major for dioceses in Detroit province), P.O. Box 298, Plymouth. 48170.

Grand Rapids — St. Joseph's Minor Seminary, 600 Burton St., S.E., 49507.

St. Maron of Detroit Eparchy — Our Lady of Lebanon Maronite Seminary, 7164 Alaska Ave. N.W., Washington, D.C. 20012.

Minnesota: St. Cloud — St. John's Seminary, Collegeville. 56321.

St. Paul and Minneapolis — St. Paul Seminary, 2260 Summit Ave., St. Paul. 55105; St. John Vianney Seminary, 2215 Summit Ave., St. Paul. 55105.

Winona — Immaculate Heart of Mary Seminary, Terrace Heights. 55987.

Missouri: Jefferson City — St. Thomas Aquinas Preparatory Seminary, 245 N. Levering Ave. Hannibal. 63401.

Kansas City-St. Joseph — St. John's Diocesan Seminary (high school), 2015 E. 72nd St. Kansas City. 64132.

St. Louis — St. Louis Roman Catholic Theological Seminary (Kenrick Seminary), 7800 Kenrick Rd. 63119; Cardinal Glennon College, (major), 5200 Glennon Dr. 63119; St. Louis Preparatory Seminary, 5200 Shrewsbury Ave. 63119 (South), 3500 St.

Catherine St., Florissant 63033 (North).

Montana: Helena — Diocesan Preparatory Seminary, Carroll College. 59601.

New Jersey: Newark — Immaculate Conception Seminary (major), Darlington. 07446; Seton Hall Divinity School, South Orange. 07079.

New Mexico: Gallup — Cristo Rey Minor Seminary, 406 W. Aztec. 87301; Cristo Rey College Seminary, 205 E. Wilson. 87301.

Santa Fe — Immaculate Heart of Mary Seminary, Mt. Carmel Rd. 87501.

New York: Brooklyn — Cathedral Preparatory Seminary of the Immaculate Conception, 555 Washington Ave. 11238; Cathedral College of the Immaculate Conception, 7200 Douglaston Parkway, Douglaston. 11362; Cathedral Preparatory Seminary of the Immaculate Conception, 56-25 92nd St., Elmhurst. 11373.

Buffalo — Christ the King Seminary (interdiocesan), East Aurora. 14052.

New York — St. Joseph's Seminary (major), Dunwoodie, Yonkers. 10704; Cathedral College (minor), 555 West End Ave. 10024.

Ogdensburg — Wadhams Hall, Riverside Dr. 13669.

Rochester — St. Bernard's Seminary, 2260 Lake Ave. 14612.

Rockville Centre — Immaculate Conception Diocesan Seminary, Lloyd Harbor, Huntington, L.I. 11743; St. Pius X Preparatory Seminary, 1220 Front St., Uniondale, L.I. 11553.

North Dakota: Fargo — Cardinal Muench Seminary, RFD 2. 58102.

Ohio: Cincinnati — Mt. St. Mary's Seminary of the West, 5440 Moeller Ave., Norwood. 45212; St. Gregory's Minor Seminary, 6616 Beechmont Ave., Cincinnati. 45230.

Cleveland — St. Mary's Seminary, 1227 Ansel Rd. 44108; Borromeo Seminary, 28700 Euclid Ave. Wickliffe. 44092.

Columbus — Pontifical College Josephinum (interdiocesan), Worthington. 43085.

Steubenville — St. John Vianney Seminary (major and minor), Bloomingdale. 43910.

Toledo — Seminary of the Holy Spirit, 5201 Airport Highway. 43615.

Pennsylvania: Erie — St. Mark's Seminary, 429 E. Grandview Blvd. 16504.

Munhall Greek Rite — Byzantine Catholic Seminary of Sts. Cyril and Methodius, 3605 Perrysville Ave., Pittsburgh.

Philadelphia — Theological Seminary of St. Charles Borromeo, Overbrook. 19151.

Philadelphia Ukrainian Rite — St. Josaphat's Seminary, 201 Taylor St. N.E., Washington, D.C. 20017.

Pittsburgh — St. Paul Seminary, 2900 Noblestown Rd. 15205; St. Fidelis Seminary (interdiocesan), Herman. 16039.

Scranton — St. Pius X Seminary, Dalton. 18414.

Rhode Island: Providence — Our Lady of Providence Seminary (major), Warwick Neck Ave., Warwick. 02889.

South Dakota: Sioux Falls — Minor Seminary, 3100 W. 41st St. 57105.

Texas: Corpus Christi — Corpus Christi Minor Seminary, Rt. 1, Box 500. 78415.

Dallas — Holy Trinity Seminary (major), P.O. Drawer 5378, Irving. 75062.

El Paso — St. Charles Seminary High School, P.O. Box 17548. 79917.

Galveston-Houston — St. Mary's Seminary, 9845 Memorial Dr. Houston. 77024.

San Antonio — The Assumption Seminary 2600 W. Woodlawn Ave. 78228.

Virginia: Richmond — St. John Vianney Minor Seminary, Rt. 2, Box 389. 23233.

Washington: Seattle — St. Thomas the Apostle (major, for provinces of Seattle, Portland in Oregon and Anchorage, Alaska), Kenmore. 98028; St. Edward's Seminary (minor), Kenmore. 98028.

Spokane — Bishop White Seminary, E. 429 Sharp Ave. 99202.

West Virginia: Wheeling-Charleston — St. Joseph Preparatory Seminary, Rt. 6, Vienna. 26101; Seminary House of Studies, 1252 National Rd., Wheeling. 26003.

Wisconsin: Green Bay — Sacred Heart Center, Oneida. 54155.

Madison — Holy Name Seminary (minor), High Point Rd., R.R. 2. 53711.

Milwaukee — St. Francis School of Pastoral Ministry, 3257 S. Lake Dr. 53207; St. Francis de Sales College, 3501 S. Lake Dr. 53207; De Sales Seminary High School, 3501 S. Lake Dr. 53207.

U.S. SEMINARIES AND STUDENTS, 1962-1975

(Source: *The Official Catholic Directory.*)

Year	Dioc. Seminaries	Total Dioc. Students	Religious Seminaries Scholasticates	Total Rel. Students	Total Seminarians
1962	98	23,662	447	22,657	46,319
1963	107	25,247	454	22,327	47,574
1964	112	26,701	459	22,049	48,750
1965	117	26,762	479	22,230	48,992
1966	126	26,252	481	21,862	48,114
1967	123	24,293	452	21,086	45,379
1968	124	22,232	437	17,604	39,836
1969	122	19,573	407	14,417	33,990
1970	118	17,317	383	11,589	28,906

Year	Dioc. Seminaries	Total Dioc. Students	Religious Seminaries Scholasticates	Total Rel. Students	Total Seminarians
1971	110	14,987	340	10,723	25,710
1972	106	13,554	326	9,409	22,963
1973	107	12,925	304	8,855	21,780
1974	109	11,765	293	7,583	19,348
1975	104	11,223	269	6,579	17,802

Breakdown

The peak enrollment year for diocesan seminaries was 1965, when they had a total of 26,762 students. The comparative figure at the beginning of 1975 was 11,223, a decrease of 58 per cent.

The peak year for seminaries of religious institutes was 1962, when the total enrollment was 22,657. The comparative figure at the beginning of 1975 was 6,579, a decrease of 71 per cent.

The total all-time high enrollment of 48,992 in 1965 was down to 17,802 at the beginning of 1975, a decrease of 63.7 per cent.

Reasons

Many reasons have been advanced for the decline in the number of candidates for the priesthood and religious life.

Obvious ones are defections from both ways of life; the impact of changes rightly or wrongly attributed to the Second Vatican Council; the slow pace of institutional renewal in the priesthood, the religious life and the Church in general, coupled with confused expectations; opportunities for apostolic service in other vocations; the problem of adjusting personalist strivings with the needs for institutional commitment; the difficulty of submitting oneself to the other as well as this-worldly demands of these vocations in the contemporary cultural and social climate.

The basic reason, however, is a crisis of faith, stated Cardinal Gabriel Garrone, prefect of the Congregation for Catholic Education, in a Vatican Radio interview in April, 1972.

He said that the progressive decrease in vocations "is in direct relation to the crisis in the priesthood" and religious life.

This crisis in turn, he added, is "linked to the crisis of faith."

PONTIFICAL UNIVERSITIES

(Principal source: *Annuario Pontificio.*)

These universities, listed according to country of location, have been canonically erected and authorized by the Sacred Congregation for Catholic Education to award degrees in stated fields of study.

Argentina: Catholic University of S. Maria of Buenos Aires (June 16, 1960). Theology, philosophy, psychology, pedagogy, letters, law and political science, economic and social science, physics and mathematics, engineering, fine arts (with music).

Belgium: Catholic University of Louvain (Dec. 9, 1425; 1834), with autonomous institutions for French- (Louvain) and Flemish- (Leuven) speaking. Theology, canon law, philosophy, letters, psychology and educational science, law, economics and social science, medicine, science.

Brazil: Pontifical Catholic University of Rio de Janeiro (Jan. 20, 1947). Theology, philosophy, science and letters, law, social institute, industrial and civil engineering.

Pontifical Catholic University of Rio Grande do Sul, Porto Alegre (Nov. 1, 1950). Philosophy, science and letters, law, political and economic science, engineering, odontology.

Pontifical Catholic University of Sao Paulo (Jan. 25, 1947). Theology, law, philosophy, science and letters, industrial engineering, economic and social science, medicine, journalism.

University of Campinas (Sept. 8, 1956). Philosophy, science, letters, law, economics, odontology, music.

Canada: Laval University, Quebec (Mar. 15, 1876). Theology, philosophy, arts and letters, law, commerce, medicine and pharmacy, science, social science, agriculture and forestry.

St. Paul University, Ottawa (Feb. 5, 1889). Theology, canon law, philosophy, missiology.

University of Sherbrooke (Nov. 21, 1957). Theology, art, law, science, commerce, medicine.

Chile: Catholic University of Chile, Santiago (June 21, 1888). Theology, philosophy, letters, education, juridical, political and social science, physics and mathematics, architecture, agronomy, economics, medicine, technology.

Catholic University of Valparaiso (Nov. 1, 1961). Philosophy and pedagogy, juridical and social science, commerce, physics and mathematics, chemical engineering, polytechnics, architecture, agriculture.

Colombia: Bolivarian Pontifical Catholic University, Medellin (Aug. 16, 1945). Law, social and political science, pedagogy, philosophy, economics and commerce, letters, mechanical, electrical and chemical engineering, architecture and civic planning, fine arts.

Pontifical Xaverian University, Bogota (July 31, 1937). Theology, canon law, philosophy, letters, pedagogy, law, economics, social science, medicine, dentistry, engineering, architecture.

Cuba: Catholic University of St. Thomas of Villanueva, Havana (May 4, 1957). Philosophy and letters, pedagogy and figurative art, law, commercial science, art and economics, science and technology. Taken over by the Castro government in May, 1961.

Ecuador: Catholic University of Ecuador, Quito (July 16, 1954). Law and economics, philosophy, pedagogy and letters, engineering, agriculture.

El Salvador: José Simeón Cañas University, San Salvador (Sept. 15, 1965). Economic science, mechanical, electronic, chemical engineering.

Ethiopia: University of Asmara (Sept. 8, 1960). Letters and pedagogy, juridic, political and economic sciences, mathematics, engineering and architecture.

France: Catholic Faculties of Lille (Nov. 18, 1875). Theology, law, letters, medicine and pharmacy, science, engineering.

Catholic Faculties of Lyons (Nov. 22, 1875). Theology, canon law, philosophy, law and economics, letters, science.

Catholic Institute of Paris (Aug. 11, 1875). Theology, canon law, philosophy, pedagogy, economic and social science, letters, science.

Catholic Institute of Toulouse (Nov. 15,1877). Theology, canon law, philosophy, letters and science.

Catholic University of the West, Angers (Sept. 16, 1875). Theology (philosophy), law, economics, letters, science.

Guatemala: Rafael Landivar University, Guatemala (Oct. 18, 1961). Letters, law, economics, juridic and social science, engineering, political science.

Ireland: St. Patrick's College, Maynooth (Mar. 29, 1896). Theology, canon law, philosophy, arts and science, sociology, education, Celtic studies.

Italy: Catholic University of the Sacred Heart, Milan (Dec. 25, 1920). Jurisprudence, political and social science, economics and commerce, letters and philosophy, medicine and surgery, pedagogy, agriculture.

Japan: *Jochi Daigaku* (University of Sophia), Tokyo (Mar. 29, 1913). Theology, philosophy, letters, languages, law, economics and commerce, science and polytechnics.

Lebanon: St. Joseph University of Beirut (Mar. 25, 1881). Theology, Oriental letters, law, engineering, economics, medicine and pharmacy.

Netherlands: Roman Catholic University, Nijmegen (June 29, 1923). Theology, law, letters, philosophy, medicine, natural science.

Nicaragua: Central American University, Managua (1961). Law, letters and pedagogy, civil and electronic engineering, administrative and economic science, veterinary science.

Panama: University of S. Maria la Antigua, Panama (May 27, 1965). Letters, philosophy and pedagogy, science, administration and commerce.

Paraguay: Catholic University of Our Lady of the Assumption, Asuncion (Feb. 2, 1965). Philosophy and pedagogy, law, political and social science, administrative science.

Peru: Catholic University of Peru, Lima (Sept. 30, 1942). Theology, philosophy, history and letters, jurisprudence and political science, economic and commercial science, civil engineering, education, agriculture.

Philippine Islands: University of Santo Tomas, Manila (Nov. 20, 1645). Theology, canon law, philosophy, pedagogy, law, letters, science, engineering and architecture, fine arts, medicine and surgery, pharmacy, commerce and administration, music.

Poland: Catholic University of Lublin (July 25, 1920). Theology, philosophy, canon law, social-economic sciences, letters.

Portugal: Portuguese Catholic University, Lisbon (Oct. 1, 1971). Theology, philosophy, humane sciences.

Puerto Rico: Catholic University of Puerto Rico, Ponce (Aug. 15, 1972). Arts, science, commerce, pedagogy, law.

Spain: Catholic University of Navarra, Pamplona (Aug. 6, 1960). Theology, canon law, philosophy and letters, jurisprudence, medicine, science, pharmacy, political, economic and commercial science, industrial engineering, agriculture, journalism, Superior Institute of Business Studies.

Pontifical University of Comillas (Mar. 29, 1904). Theology, canon law, philosophy.

Pontifical University of Salamanca (Sept. 25, 1940). Theology, canon law, social sciences, philosophy.

University of Deusto, Bilbao (Aug. 10, 1963). Theology, law, economics and social science, philosophy and letters, science.

Taiwan: Fu Jen Catholic University (Nov. 15, 1923, at Peking; reconstituted at Taipeh, Sept. 8, 1961). Theology, art, law, economics, science.

United States: Catholic University of America, Washington, D. C. (Mar. 7, 1889). Pontifical faculties of theology, canon law, philosophy.

Georgetown University, Washington, D.C. (Mar. 30, 1833). Arts and science, language, law, economics, diplomatic and consular science, medicine and odontology.

Niagara University, Niagara Falls (June 21, 1956). Arts and science, economics, education.

Venezuela: Catholic University "Andres Bello," Caracas (Sept. 29, 1963). Letters and education, law, economics, social science, physical and natural science, pharmacy, civil and industrial engineering, architecture.

National Association of Boards of Education: Founded in 1972, it provides assistance in the formation of parochial and diocesan boards of education, and services. The membership is approximately 2,000. Mary-Angela Harper, Ph.D., is executive director. Address: Suite 350, One Dupont Circle, Washington, D.C. 20036.

Ecclesiastical Faculties

(Source: *Annuario Pontificio*)

These faculties in Catholic seminaries and universities, listed according to country of location, have been canonically erected and authorized by the Sacred Congregation for Catholic Education to award degrees in stated fields of study. In addition to those listed here, there are other faculties of theology or philosophy in state universities and for members of certain religious orders only.

Australia: Faculty of Theology, Sydney (Feb. 2, 1954).

Canada: Institute of Medieval Studies, Toronto (Oct. 18, 1939).

Germany: Theological Faculty, Paderborn (June 11, 1966).

Theological Faculty of the Major Episcopal Seminary, Trier (June 5, 1950).

Philosophical Faculty, Munich (1925; Oct. 25, 1971).

Theological Faculty, Eichstatt (July 25, 1972).

Theological-Philosophical Faculty, Frankfurt (1932; June 7, 1971).

Great Britain: Heythrop College, University of London, London (Nov. 1, 1964). Theology, philosophy.

India: Institute of Philosophy and Theology, Poona (July 27, 1926). Theology, philosophy.

Institute of Theology, Alwaye, Kerala (Feb. 24, 1972).

"Vidyajyoti," Institute of Religious Studies, Delhi (1932; Dec. 9, 1974).

Italy: Interregional Theological Faculty, Milan (Aug. 8, 1935).

Pontifical Theological Faculty of the Most Sacred Heart of Jesus, Cagliari, of the Pontifical Regional Seminary of Sardinia (July 5, 1927).

Pontifical Ambrosian Institute of Sacred Music, Milan (Mar. 12, 1940).

Theological Faculty of Southern Italy, Naples (Mar. 16, 1918, at the Pontifical Campano Seminary; Oct. 31, 1941, at Major Archiepiscopal Seminary). Has Pastoral Ignatian Institute, Messina.

Pontifical Faculty of Educational Science, Turin (Jan. 31, 1966).

Faculty of Philosophy "Aloisianum," Gallarate (1937; Mar. 20, 1974).

Madagascar: Superior Institute of Theology, Ambatoroka (Apr. 21, 1960).

Peru: Pontifical and Civil Faculty of Theology, Lima (July 25, 1571).

Poland: Theological Faculty, Poznan (July 23, 1969).

Spain: Theological Faculty of Barcelona, of the Major Seminary of Barcelona and the College of St. Francis Borgia of San Cugat del Valles (Mar. 7, 1968).

Theological Faculty, Granada (Feb. 11, 1940).

Theological Faculty of the North, of the Metropolitan Seminary of Burgos and the Diocesan Seminary of Vitoria (Feb. 6, 1967).

Theological Faculty "San Vicente Ferrer," Valencia (Jan. 23, 1974).

Switzerland: Theological Faculty, Chur (Jan. 1, 1974).

Theological Faculty, Luzerne (Dec. 25, 1973).

United States: St. Mary's Faculty of Theology, Baltimore (May 1, 1822).

St. Mary of the Lake Faculty of Theology, Chicago (Sept. 30, 1929).

Vietnam, South: Theological Faculty, Dalat (July 31, 1965).

The **Pontifical College Josephinum** (Theological Seminary and Preparatory Department) at Worthington, Ohio, is a regional pontifical seminary. Established Sept. 1, 1888, it is immediately subject to the Holy See.

Institutes of Higher Studies in Rome

(Source: *Annuario Pontificio*.)

Pontifical Gregorian University (1552). Theology, canon law, philosophy, psychology, science of religion, church history, missiology, social sciences. Associated with the university are:

The **Pontifical Biblical Institute** (May 7, 1909), with faculties of Scripture and ancient Oriental studies.

The **Pontifical Institute of Oriental Studies** (Oct. 15, 1917), with faculties of Oriental ecclesiastical studies and Oriental canon law.

Pontifical Lateran University (1773). Theology, canon law, civil law, philosophy, moral theology, literature.

Pontifical Urban University (1627). Theology, philosophy, missiology.

Pontifical University of St. Thomas Aquinas (**Angelicum**) (1580), of the Order of Preachers. Theology, canon law, philosophy, social sciences, spirituality.

Pontifical University Salesianum (May 3, 1940; university designation May 24, 1973), of the Salesians of Don Bosco. Canon law, theology, philosophy, pedagogy, Higher Latin Studies (Feb. 22, 1964).

Pontifical Athenaeum of St. Anselm (1687), of the Benedictines. Theology, philosophy, liturgy, monastic studies.

Pontifical Athenaeum Antonianum (of St. Anthony) (May 17, 1933), of the Order of Friars Minor. Theology, canon law, philosophy, and the affiliated School of Biblical Studies in Jerusalem.

Pontifical Institute of Sacred Music (1911; May 24, 1931).

Pontifical Institute of Christian Archeology (Dec. 11, 1925).

Pontifical Theological Faculty "St. Bonaventure" (Dec. 18, 1587), of the Order of Friars Minor Conventual.

Pontifical Theological Faculty of Sts. Teresa of Jesus and John of the Cross (Teresianum) (July 16, 1935), of the Carmelites. Theology, spirituality.

Pontifical Theological Faculty "Marianum" (1398), of the Servants of Mary.
Pontifical Institute of Arabic Studies (1926), of the White Fathers.

PONTIFICAL ACADEMY OF SCIENCES

(Sources: *Annuario Pontificio*, NC News Service.)

The Pontifical Academy of Sciences was constituted in its present form by Pius XI Oct. 28, 1936, in virtue of *In Multis Solaciis*, a document issued on his own initiative.

Purposes of the academy are to honor pure science and its practitioners, to promote the freedom of pure science and to foster research.

The academy originated as the Accademia Linceorum (lynxes) in Rome Aug. 17, 1603. Pius IX reorganized this body and gave it a new name — Pontificia Accademia dei Nuovi Lincei — in 1847. It was taken over by the Italian state in 1870 and called the Accademia Nazionale dei Lincei, Leo XIII reconstituted it with a new charter in 1887. Pius XI designated the Vatican Gardens as the site of academy headquarters in 1922 and gave it its present title and status in 1936.

In addition to four supernumerary members, membership as of June 10, 1975, numbered 51 in the following countries: U.S., 8; England and France, 7; Italy, 3; Canada, Germany, Japan, Netherlands, and Switzerland, 2 each; Argentina, Australia, Austria, Belgium, Brazil, Greece, Finland, Mexico, Monaco, Pakistan, Peru, Portugal, Spain, Sweden, Vatican City and Venezuela, 1 each.

Scientists from the U.S. who presently hold membership in the Academy are: Edward Adalbert-Doisy, professor of biochemistry at St. Louis University School of Medicine (May 29, 1948); Franco Rasetti, professor emeritus of physics at John Hopkins University, Baltimore, Md. (Oct. 28, 1936); George Speri Sperti, director of the Institutum Divi Thomae in the Athanaeum of Ohio (Oct. 28, 1936); William Wilson Morgan, director of Yerkes Observatory, Williams Bay, Wis. (Sept. 24, 1964); Albert Szent-Gyorgyi, director of muscle research at the Marine Biological Laboratory, Woods Hole, Mass. (Apr. 10, 1970), Rita-Levi Montalcini, professor of biology at St. Louis University (June 24, 1974); Severo Ochoa, professor of biochemistry at New York University (June 24, 1974); Marshall Warren Nierenberg, professor of biochemistry at the National Institutes of Health (Bethesda, Md.) (June 24, 1974).

Deceased U.S. members of the Academy were: George D. Birkhoff, Alexis Carrel, Herbert Sidney Langfeld, Robert A. Millikan, Thomas H. Morgan, Theodore von Karman, Victor F. Hess, Peter Debye, Hugh Stott Taylor.

Other members of the Academy and the dates of their selection are as follows:

Argentina: Luis F. Leloir (Apr. 22, 1968).

Australia: Keith E. Bullen (Apr. 22, 1968).

Austria: Hans Tuppy (Apr. 10, 1970).

Belgium: Christian de Duve (Apr. 16, 1970).

Brazil: Carlos Chagas (Aug. 18, 1961).

Canada: Herbert Charles Best (Apr. 5, 1955); Gerhard Herzberg (Sept. 24, 1964).

England: Hermann Alexander Bruck (Apr. 5, 1955); Paul Adrien Dirac (Aug. 18, 1961); Alan Lloyd Hodgkin (Apr. 22, 1968); Alfred R. Ubbelohde (Apr. 22, 1968); Peter C. C. Garnham (Apr. 10, 1970); Robert Stoneley (Apr. 10, 1970); George Porter (June 24, 1974).

Finland: Arthur Ilmari Virtanen (Apr. 5, 1955).

France: Louis de Broglie (Apr. 5, 1955); Gaston Maurice Julia (Apr. 5, 1955); Jean Lecomte (Sept. 24, 1964); Pierre Raphael Lepine (Sept. 24, 1964); Louis Leprince-Ringuet (Aug. 18, 1961); Georges Chaudron (April 10, 1970); Jerome Lejeune (June 24, 1974).

Germany: Werner Carl Heisenberg (Apr. 5, 1955); Wolfgang Gentner (Apr. 10, 1970).

Greece: George Joakimoglou (Apr. 10, 1970).

Italy: Giovanni Battista Bonino (May 23, 1942); Bettolo Giovanni Battista Marini (Apr. 22, 1968); Mauro Picone (Apr. 10, 1970).

Japan: Paul San-Ichiro Mizushima (Aug. 18, 1961); Hideki Yukawa (Apr. 8, 1961).

Mexico: Manuel Sandoval Vallarta (Aug. 18, 1961).

Monaco: Rudolf L. Mossbauer (Apr. 10, 1970).

Netherlands: F. J. J. Buytendijk (Oct. 28, 1936); Jan Hendrik Oort (Aug. 18, 1961).

Pakistan: Salimuzzanam Siddiqui (Sept. 24, 1964).

Peru: Alberto Hurtado (Aug. 18, 1961).

Portugal: Antonio De Almeida (Apr. 8, 1961).

Spain: Manuel Lora Tomayo (Sept. 24, 1964).

Sweden: Sven Horstadius (Aug. 18, 1961).

Switzerland: Leopold Ruzicka (Dec. 5, 1942); Thomas Lambo (June 24, 1974).

Vatican City: Daniel J. Kelly O'Connell, S.J. (Sept. 24, 1964).

Venezuela: Marcel Roche (Apr. 10, 1970).

Supernumerary members are: Patrick Treanor, S.J., director of the Vatican Observatory; Joseph Junkes, S.J., prefect of the Astrophysics Laboratory of the Vatican Observatory; Alfons Stickler, S.D.B., prefect of the Vatican Library; Msgr. Martino Giusti, prefect of the Secret Vatican Archives.

President of the Academy is Carlos Chagas (Nov. 5, 1972).

Social Services

Catholic Charities is the ordinary title of an umbrella-type of agency which supervises social work under the auspices of archdioceses and dioceses in the United States.

The first central, over-all diocesan agency in the US was established in 1903. There are now more than 500 diocesan and branch agencies of Catholic Charities in this country.

The principal fields of service in which diocesan organizations and their member agencies are engaged are family counseling, child welfare, health services for unmarried mothers, community services, day care centers, neighborhood center programs, and care of the aged. Community organization and social action are also functions of Catholic Charities.

National Conference

The National Conference of Catholic Charities, organized in 1910, serves diocesan organizations by providing a field service, developing a literature, providing an informational service, promoting research, assisting with organization, improving standards, and representing agencies of Catholic Charities among other national organizations and offices, both voluntary and governmental. It has over 500 institutional, 1,500 individual and 650 organizational members.

Closely affiliated with the conference is the National Association of Directors of Catholic Charities and the Conference of Religious, an organization of religious engaged in social and charitable work. Also affiliated are the Society of St. Vincent de Paul of the US, the Association of Ladies of Charity of the US, and the National Christ Child Society.

The conference is the representative of the International Conference of Catholic Charities before the UN Economic and Social Council and before UNICEF. It has consultative status with both agencies.

NCCC initiated steps in 1972 to augment its traditional services to social service agencies with greater emphasis on social action and advocacy.

Msgr. Lawrence J. Corcoran is secretary of the conference.

Offices are located at 1346 Connecticut Ave. N.W., Washington, D.C. 20036.

Vincent de Paul Society

The Society of St. Vincent de Paul, originally called the Conference of Charity, is an association of Catholic laymen devoted to personal service of the poor through the spiritual and corporal works of mercy. The first conference was formed at Paris in 1833 by Frederic Ozanam and his associates.

The first conference in the US was organized in 1845 at St. Louis. There are now approximately 4,200 units of the society in this country, with a membership of about 36,000.

In the past 50 years, members of the society in this country have distributed among poor persons financial and other forms of assistance valued at approximately $180 million.

US Vincentian councils and conferences participating in "twinning" programs assist their poorer counterparts abroad by sending them correspondence, information and financial aid on a continuing basis.

Under the society's revised regulations, women are being admitted to membership. Increasing emphasis is being given to stores and rehabilitation workshops of the society through which persons with marginal income can purchase refurbished goods at minimal cost. Handicapped persons are employed in renovating goods and store operations.

Joseph Rouast of Paris, France, is president of the Council General, the governing body of the society. There are approximately 700,000 members in the world.

The office of the US Superior Council is located at 4140 Lindell Blvd., St. Louis, Mo. 63108.

Service Organizations

Catholic Hospital Association: Founded in 1915, is a service organization for about 830 Catholic-sponsored health care facilities located throughout the United States.

Through research, its monthly *Hospital Progress,* annual meetings and conferences, it keeps institutional and individual members up-to-date on unique Catholic apostolic aspects of medical, moral, educational and professional developments in the health field.

The Catholic Health Services Leadership Program, a major CHA activity, is designed to develop the relationships and maximize the potential strengths and resources of religious congregations, dioceses and their multi-faceted health care facilities and services.

The Catholic Health Assembly (annual meeting) offers CHA constituents the opportunity to dialogue the best methods to strengthen and unify the corporate health commitment of religious congregations and dioceses — the sponsoring groups that operate Catholic hospitals and nursing homes.

Sister Mary Maurita Sengelaub, R.S.M., is president of the association.

Executive offices are located at 1438 S. Grand Boulevard, St. Louis, Mo. 63104.

The Official Catholic Directory, 1975, reported 671 Catholic general hospitals with 161,559 beds treating 29,202,120 patients annually; 90 special hospitals and sanatoria with 7,743 beds treating 468,169; and 141 nurses' schools with 19,588 students.

National Association of Catholic Chaplains: Founded in 1965, it operates under the auspices of the Department of Social Development and World Peace, U.S. Catholic Conference. Membership is approximately 1,600.

The association conducts two pastoral institutes for general hospital chaplains annually, one in Washington, D.C., and another in Menlo Park, Calif. By the summer of 1975, nearly 900 chaplains and pastoral associates had attended these institutes.

Rev. Ralph Karl, O.M.I., of the Columbus State School, Columbus, O., is president of the association. Rev. David Baeten is the executive director.

The office of the association is located at 1312 Massachusetts Ave. N. W., Washington, D.C. 20005.

FACILITIES FOR RETIRED AND AGED PERSONS

This list covers residence, health care and other facilities for the retired and aged under Catholic auspices. Information includes name, type of facility if not evident from the title, address, and total capacity (in parentheses); unless noted otherwise, facilities are for both men and women.

(Sources: Almanac survey, *The Official Catholic Directory, 1975.*)

Alabama: Allen Memorial Home (Nursing Home), 735 S. Washington Ave., Mobile 36603 (50).

Good Samaritan Hospital Nursing Home, 1107 Voeglin St., Selma 36701 (26).

Sacred Heart Home of the Little Sisters of the Poor, 1655 McGill Ave., Mobile 36604 (108).

Villa Mercy (Skilled Nursing Home), Daphne 36526 (45).

Arizona: Sacred Heart Home for the Aged, Little Sisters of the Poor, 1110 N. 16th St., Phoenix 85006 (170).

Villa Maria de Guadalupe Nursing Home, 701 E. Adams St., Tucson 85719 (25).

Arkansas: Benedictine Manor (Retirement Home), 2nd and Grand Sts., Hot Springs 71901 (50).

St. Joseph's Home (Nursing Home), Brinkley 72021 (28).

California: Casa Manana Inn, 3700 N. Sutter St., Stockton 95204 (175).

Catholic Women's Center (Residence for Elderly Single Women), 195 E. San Fernando St., San Jose 95112 (50).

Little Flower Haven (Residential Care Facility for Retired), 8585 La Mesa Blvd., La Mesa 92041 (94).

Little Sisters of the Poor, 2700 E. First St., Los Angeles 90033 (160).

Little Sisters of the Poor, 2647 E. 14th St., Oakland 94601 (100).

Little Sisters of the Poor, 300 Lake St., San Francisco 94118 (186).

Madonna Residence (Hotel for Women over 60), 270 McAllister St., San Francisco 94102 (82).

Marian Residence (Retirement Home), 124 S. College Dr., Santa Maria 93454 (85).

Nazareth House, 2121 N. 1st St., Fresno 93703 (80).

Nazareth House, 3333 Manning Ave., Los Angeles 90064 (107).

Nazareth House, 245 Nova Albion Way, Terra Linda, San Rafael 94903 (109).

Our Lady of Fatima Villa (Nursing Home, Women), 20400 Saratoga-Los Gatos Rd., Saratoga 95070 (85).

Our Lady's Home, 3431 Foothill Blvd., Oakland 94601 (200).

St. Francis Home (Elderly and Retired Women), 1718 W. 6th St., Santa Ana 92703 (71).

Villa Siena, 1855 Miramonte, Mountain View 94040 (23).

Colorado: Little Sisters of the Poor, 3630 W. 30th Ave., Denver 80211 (100).

St. Elizabeth Center (Retirement Home), 2825 W. 32nd Ave., Denver 80211 (95).

Connecticut: Augustana Homes, Simeon Rd., Bethel 06801.

Notre Dame Convalescent Home, West Rocks Rd., Norwalk 06851 (60).

Regina Pacis Villa (Residence), RFD No. 1, Pomfret Center 06259 (16).

St. Joseph Guest Home (Women, Employed and Retired), 311 Greene St., New Haven 06511 (93).

St. Joseph's Home for the Aged, 88 Jackson St., Willimantic 06226 (37).

St. Joseph's Manor (Residence, Rest Home, Chronic Disease Hospital), 6448 Main St., Trumbull 06611 (285).

St. Joseph's Residence, Little Sisters of the Poor, 1365 Enfield St., Enfield, Conn. 06082 (94)

St. Lucian's Home for the Aged, 532 Burritt St., New Britain 06053 (85).

St. Mary's Home (Residence and Health Care Facility), 291 Steele Rd., W. Hartford 06117 (177).

Villa Maria Rest Home for the Aged, West St., Thompson 06277 (30).

Delaware: St. Joseph's Home, Little Sisters of the Poor, 401 N. Bancroft Pkwy., Wilmington 19805 (97).

District of Columbia: St. Joseph's Home, Little Sisters of the Poor, 220 H St., N.E., Washington 20002 (167).

Florida: All Saints Nursing Home for the Aged, 2040 Riverside Ave., Jacksonville 32204 (54).

Cor Jesu Convalescent Center (Skilled

Nursing Facility), 4918 N. Habana Ave., Tampa 33614 (90).

Florida Manor (Residence), P.O. Box 5577, Orlando 32805.

Haven of Our Lady of Peace (Residence and Health Care Facility), 5203 9th Ave., Pensacola 32504 (88).

Lourdes Residence, 305 S. Flagler Dr., W. Palm Beach 33401 (142).

Maria Manor Health Care Center, 10300 4th St. N., St. Petersburg 33702.

Marian Towers, Inc. (Retirement Home), 1705 North Bay Rd., Miami Beach 33160.

Pennsylvania Retirement Residence, 208 Evernia St., W. Palm Beach 33401 (230).

St. Andrew Towers (Retirement Home), 2700 N.W. 99th Ave., Coral Springs 33065.

St. Elizabeth Gardens (Retirement Home), 801 N.E. 33rd St., Pompano Beach 33064.

St. Joseph's Residence, 3485 N.W. 30th St., Ft. Lauderdale 33311.

Villa Maria (Residence), 1050 N.E. 123rd St., N. Miami 33161.

Villa Maria Nursing and Rehabilitation Center, 1050 N.E. 125th St., N. Miami 33161 (180).

Idaho: St. Benedict's Hospital Home for the Aged, Jerome 83338 (40).

Illinois: Addolorato Villa (Residence), Highway 83, McHenry Rd., Wheeling 60090 (103).

Alvernia Manor, 1593 Main St., Lemont 60439 (48).

Holy Family Villa (Residence), Lemont 60439 (108).

Huber Memorial Home (Women), 1000 30th St., Rock Island 61201 (22).

Maryhaven-West (Residence, Nursing Care), 1700 E. Lake St., Glenview 60025 (148).

Mayslake Village (Retirement Facility), 1801 35th St., Oak Brook 60521 (325).

Meredith Memorial Home, Public Square, Belleville 62220 (86).

Mother Theresa Home, 1270 Main St., Lemont 60439 (56).

Our Lady of Angels Retirement Home, 1291 Wyoming, Joliet 60435 (100).

Our Lady of the Snows Apartment Community (Retirement Apartment Community with Lifetime Contract), 9500 Route 460, Belleville 62223 (175).

Rosary Hill Convalescent Home, 9000 W. 81st St., Justice 60458 (60).

St. Andrew Home, 7000 N. Newark Ave., Chicago 60648 (199).

St. Ann's Home and Infirmary, Waukegan and Techny Rds., Techny 60082 (175).

St. Ann's Home for the Aged, 770 State St., Chester 62233 (45).

St. Augustine's Home, Little Sisters of the Poor, 2358 Sheffield Ave., Chicago 60614 (110).

St. Benedict Home (Sheltered and Interme-

diate Care), 6930 W. Touhy Ave., Niles 69648 (52).

St. Joseph's Home for the Elderly, 80 W. Baldwin Rd., Palatine 60067 (208).

St. Joseph's Home for the Aged, 2650 N. Ridgeway Ave., Chicago 60647 (175).

St. Joseph's Home, 2223 W. Heading Ave., Peoria 61604 (200).

St. Joseph's Home for the Aged, 649 E. Jefferson St., Freeport 61032 (118).

St. Joseph's Home, S. 6th St. Rd., Springfield 62703 (93).

St. Patrick's Residence (Sheltered and Intermediate Care; Skilled Nursing Facility), 22 E. Clinton St., Joliet 60431 (207).

Villa Scalabrini (Residence), Northlake 60161 (146).

Villa Saint Cyril (Residence), 1111 St. John's Ave., Highland Park 60035 (80).

Indiana: Providence Home of Our Lady of the Holy Rosary, Jasper 47546 (37).

Providence Retirement Home, 703 E. Spring St., New Albany 47150 (73).

Regina Pacis Home (Residence and Extended and Intermediate Care Facility), 3900 Washington Ave., Evansville 47715 (51).

Sacred Heart Home (Residence and Comprehensive Nursing), R.R. 2, Avilla 46710 (130).

St. Anne Home (Residence and Comprehensive Nursing), 1900 Randalia Dr., Ft. Wayne 46805 (119).

St. Anthony's Rest Home, 201 Franciscan Rd., Crown Point 46307 (122).

St. Augustine Home, Little Sisters of the Poor, 2345 W. 86th St., Indianapolis 46260 (184).

St. John's Home for the Aged, Little Sisters of the Poor, 1236 Lincoln Ave., Evansville 47714 (130).

St. Paul Hermitage (Residence and Comprehensive Nursing), 501 N. 17th St., Beech Grove 46107 (104).

Iowa: The Alverno Residence for Retired Citizens, Clinton 42732 (131).

Bishop Drumm Home for the Aged, 1409 Clark St., Des Moines 50314 (145).

Holy Spirit Retirement Home (Nursing Home), 1701 W. 25th St., Sioux City 51103 (78).

Kahl Home for the Aged and Infirm (Health Facility), 1101 W. 9th St., Davenport 52802 (126).

The Marian Home, 23 N. 7th St., Fort Dodge 50501 (50).

Mary of the Angels Home (Women, Employed and Retired), 605 Bluff St., Dubuque 52001 (92).

Ritter Home for Retired Women, 1837 Sunnyside Ave., Burlington 52601 (10).

St. Anthony Nursing Home, 406 E. Anthony St., Carroll 51401 (78).

St. Francis Home (Custodial, Nursing Home), 901 Davis Ave., Dubuque 52001 (101).

Kansas: Mt. St. Joseph Home for the Aging (Health Care Facility), 2601 Ridge Ave., Kansas City 66102 (47).

St. Ann's Home, 323 E. 5th St., Concordia 66901 (76).

St. John's Rest Home, Victoria 67671 (45).

St. Joseph's Home for the Aging, 924 N. Topeka, El Dorado 67042 (58).

Villa Maria Home for the Aging, 116 S. Central, Mulvane 67110 (57).

Kentucky: Carmel Home (Residence and Nursing Home), Old Hartford Rd., Owensboro 42301 (82).

Carmel Manor (Residence), Carmel Manor St., Ft. Thomas, 41075 (99).

Cardome Residence for Women, Georgetown 40324 (30).

Home for Senior Citizens, P.O. Box R. 1, Philpot 42366 (68).

Madonna Manor Nursing Home, 2344 Amsterdam Rd., Covington 41016 (Cottages for Senior Citizens: 8, with 34 Apartments).

St. Charles Nursing Home, Kyles Lane, Covington 41011 (143).

St. Joseph's Home for the Aged Poor, 622 S. 10th St., Louisville 40203 (185).

St. Margaret of Cortona Home (Women), 1310 Leestown Pike, Lexington 40508 (24).

Taylor Manor Nursing Home, Versailles 40383 (78).

Louisiana: Bethany M.H.S. Nursing Home (Women), P.O. Box 2308, Lafayette 70501 (40).

Christopher Inn Apartments (Residence for Senior Citizens), 2110 Royal St., New Orleans 20116 (250).

Consolata Home (Nursing Home), New Iberia 70560 (74).

Lafon Home of the Holy Family, 1125 N. Tonti St., New Orleans 70119 (75).

Mary-Joseph Residence for the Elderly, 4201 Woodland Dr., New Orleans 70114 (135).

Ollie Steele Burden Manor (Retirement Home and Skilled Nursing Care), 4220 Essen Lane, Baton Rouge 70809 (44).

Our Lady of Prompt Succor Home (Nursing and Extended Care Facility), 751 E. Prudhomme Lane, Opelousas 70570.

St. Charles Nursing Home, P.O. Box 508, Newellton 71357.

St. Joseph's Home (Nursing Home), 2301 Sterlington Rd., Monroe 71201 (110).

St. Margaret's Daughters' Home, 504 Tricou St., New Orleans 70117 (82).

Wynhoven Apartments (Residence for Senior Citizens), 4600 - 10th St., Marrero 70072.

Maine: Deering Pavilion (Apartments for Senior Citizens), 289 Congress St., Portland 04112 (200 units).

Marcotte Nursing Home, 100 Campus Ave., Lewiston 04240 (377).

Mt. St. Joseph Home (Nursing Home),

Highwood St., Waterville 04901 (76).

Northern Maine Security Home (Residence and Intermediate Care Facility), Eagle Lake 04789 (71).

St. John Valley Security Home (Boarding-Nursing Home), 40 Riverview St., Madawaska 04756 (82).

Villa Muir, Home for Women, Bay View, Saco 04072 (15).

Maryland: Carroll Manor (Residence and Nursing Home), 4922 La Salle Rd., Hyattsville 20782 (210).

Little Sisters of the Poor, St. Martin's Home (for the Aged), 601 Maiden Choice Lane, Baltimore 21228 (236).

Sacred Heart Home, 5805 Queens Chapel Rd., Hyattsville 20782 (102).

Stella Maris Hospice (Long-term Geriatrics), 2300 Dulaney Valley Rd., Towson 21204 (355).

Villa Rosa (Nursing Home), Lottsford Vista Rd., Mitchellville 20716 (59).

Massachusetts: Beaven-Kelly Home for Aged Men (Rest Home), 1245 Main St., Brightside, Holyoke 01040 (55).

Catholic Memorial Home, 2446 Highland Ave., Fall River 02720 (293).

Don Orione Home, 111 Orient Ave., East Boston 02128 (180).

D'Youville Manor (Nursing Home), 981 Varnum St., Lowell 01854 (207).

Little Sisters of the Poor, 186 Highland Ave., Somerville 02143 (148).

Madonna Manor (Nursing Home), Washington St., N. Attleboro 02760 (129).

Marian Manor (Nursing Home), 40 Old Harbor St., S. Boston, 02127 (376).

Marian Manor (Nursing Home), 33 Summer St., Taunton 02780 (129).

Maristhill Nursing Home, 66 Newton St., Waltham 02154 (120).

Mary Immaculate Nursing Home, Bennington St., Lawrence 01841 (168).

Mt. St. Vincent Home, Holy Family Rd., Holyoke 01040 (111).

Our Lady's Haven (Nursing Home), 71 Center St., Fairhaven 02719 (131).

Sacred Heart Home, 359 Summer St., New Bedford 02740 (197).

St. Francis Home for Aged, 37 Thorne St., Worcester 01604 (86).

St. Joseph's Manor for Elderly Ladies, 321 Centre St., Dorchester 02122 (95).

St. Joseph's Manor Nursing Home, 261 Thatcher St., Brockton 02154 (56).

St. Luke's Home, 85 Springfield St., Springfield 01105 (192).

St. Patrick's Manor (Nursing Home), 863 Central St., Framingham 01701 (280).

Michigan: Bishop Noa Home for Senior Citizens, Escanaba 49829 (107).

Burtha M. Fisher Home (Residence and Nursing Home), 17550 Southfield Rd., Detroit 48235 (183).

Carmel Hall (Residence and Nursing Home), 2560 Woodward Ave., Detroit 48201 (500).

Kundig Center (Residence), 2936 Ash St., Detroit 48208 (140).

Lourdes Nursing Home, 2380 Watkins Lake Rd., Pontiac 48054 (108).

Marian Hall (Residence), 529 Detroit St., Flint 48502 (114).

Marycrest Manor (Nursing Home), 15475 Middlebelt Rd., Livonia 48154 (92).

Marydale Center for the Aged (Board and Apartments), 3147 Tenth Ave., Port Huron 48060 (44).

St. Ann's Home for Retired People, 2161 Leonard St. N.W., Grand Rapids 49304 (113).

St. Catherine Cooperative House for Elderly Women, 1641 Webb Ave., Detroit 48206 (13).

St. Elizabeth Briarbank (Residence), 1315 N. Woodward Ave., Bloomfield Hills 48013 (56).

St. Francis Home (Nursing Home), 915 N. River Rd., Saginaw 48603 (100).

St. John Vianney Cooperative House for Men, 4806 Mt. Elliot, Detroit 48207 (30).

St. Joseph's Home for the Aged, 4800 Cadieux Rd., Detroit 48224 (100).

Stapleton Center (Residence), 9341 Agnes St., Detroit 48214 (20).

Villa Elizabeth, 2100 Leonard St. N.E., Grand Rapids 49505 (109).

Villa Franciska (Residence, Women), 565 W. Long Lake Rd., Bloomfield Hills 48013 (18).

Minnesota: Assumption Nursing Home, Cold Spring 56320 (68).

Divine Providence Community Home, Sleepy Eye 56085 (40).

Divine Providence Home (Skilled Nursing Home), Ivanhoe 56142 (51).

Holy Trinity Home for Aged, Graceville 56240 (17).

Little Sisters of the Poor (Skilled Nursing and Intermediate Care), 90 Wilkin St., St. Paul 55102 (114).

Madonna Towers (Retirement Apartments), 4001 19th Ave. N.W., Rochester 55901 (145).

Mary Randorf Home of Sacred Heart Parish (Nursing Home), 222 5th St. N., Staples 56479 (84).

Mother of Mercy Nursing Home, Albany 56307 (62).

Regina Nursing Home and Retirement Residence, Hastings 55033 (138).

Sacred Heart Hospice (Nursing Home), 1200 Twelfth St. S.W., Austin 55912 (60).

St. Alexander Nursing Home, 1500 5th St. N., New Ulm 56073 (61).

St. Ann's Home, 330 E. 3rd St., Duluth 55805 (200).

St. Anne Hospice (Residence and Nursing Care), 1347 W. Broadway, Winona 55987 (123).

St. Elizabeth's Hospital and Nursing Home, Campbell Ave., Wabasha 55981 (69).

St. Francis Nursing Home, Breckenridge 56520 (132).

St. Francis Residence, 516 Walsh St., Crookston 56716.

St. Joseph's Home, (Residence and Extended Health Care), 1824 Minnesota Blvd. S.E., St. Cloud 56301 (118).

St. Joseph's Home for the Elderly (Nursing Home), 215 Broadway N.E., Minneapolis 55413 (118).

St. Mary's Extended Care Center, 25512 S. 7th St., Minneapolis 55406 (240).

St. Mary's Home, Winsted 55395 (74).

St. Mary's Home, 1925 Norfolk Ave., St. Paul 55116 (90).

St. Mary's Villa (Nursing Home), Pierz 56364 (66).

St. Otto's Home (Nursing Home), Little Falls 56345 (159).

St. Raphael's Home (Residence and Health Care Facility), 511 9th Ave. N., St. Cloud 56301 (93).

St. Therese Home (Residence and Health Care Facility), 8000 Bass Lake Rd., New Hope 55428 (304).

St. Vincent's Rest Home (Nursing Home), 223 E. 7th St., Crookston 56716 (73).

St. William's Nursing Home, Parkers Prairie 56361 (61).

Villa of St. Francis Nursing Home, Morris 56267 (104).

Missouri: Chariton Apartments (Retirement Apartments), 4249 Michigan Ave., St. Louis 63117 (122 units; 150 residents).

The Alverne (Retirement Home), 1014 Locust St., St. Louis 63101 (251).

LaVerna Heights (Retirement Home and Nursing Care, Women), 104 E. Park Ave., Savannah 64485 (60).

Little Sisters of the Poor, 5331 Highland Ave., Kansas City 64110 (240).

Little Sisters of the Poor, 3225 N. Florissant Ave., St. Louis 63107 (264).

Mercy Villa Professional Nursing Home, 1015 N. Main St., Springfield 65802 (134).

Mother of Good Counsel Home for Chronic Sick, 6825 Natural Bridge Rd., Normandy, 63121 (110).

Our Lady of Mercy Home (Residence and Nursing Home), 918-24 E. 9th St., Kansas City 64106 (126).

Our Lady of Perpetual Help Nursing Home, 3419 Gasconada St., St. Louis 63118 (113).

St. Agnes Home, 10341 Manchester Rd., Kirkwood 63122 (130).

St. Anne Home (Nursing Home), 5351 Page Blvd., St. Louis 63112 (190).

St. Joseph Hill Nursing Care Facility (Men), Highway FF, Eureka 63025 (125).

St. Joseph's Home for the Aged, 1550 W.

Main St., Jefferson City 65101 (70).
St. Joseph's Home for the Aged, 723 First Capitol Dr., St. Charles 63301 (101).

Montana: Holy Family Nursing Home, Holy Family Hospital, St. Ignatius 59865 (4).

Nebraska: Madonna Professional Care Center (Nursing Care), 2200 S. 52nd St., Lincoln 68502 (182).
Mt. Carmel Home, Keens' Memorial (Nursing Home), 18th St., and 5th Ave., Kearney 68847 (74).
New Cassel Retirement Center, 900 N. 90th St., Omaha 68114.
St. Joseph's Home, P.O. Box 1129, Norfolk 68701 (52).
St. Joseph's Home, 320 E. Decatur St., West Point 68788 (60).
St. Joseph's Villa, David City 68632. (44).
St. Vincent's Home, 4500 Ames Ave., Omaha 68104 (259).

New Hampshire: Mount Carmel Nursing Home, 235 Myrtle St., Manchester 03104 (118).
Notre Dame Hospital, Geriatrics Department (Extended Health Care, Women), Manchester 03102 (28).
St. Ann Home, 201 Dover Point Rd., Dover 03820 (52).
St. Francis Home (Nursing Home), Court St., Laconia 03246 (49).
St. Teresa Manor (Nursing Home), 519 Bridge St., Manchester 03104 (50).
St. Vincent de Paul Nursing Home, Providence Ave., Berlin 03570 (72).

New Jersey: Holy Family Residence (Women), New St., P.O. Box 536, W. Paterson 07424 (60).
Little Sisters of the Poor, Shepherd Lane, Totowa 07512.
Mater Dei Nursing Home, Rt. 40, P.O. Newfield, Upper Pittsgrove Township 08344 (64).
Morris Hall, Home for the Aged (Residence and Nursing Home), 2361 Lawrenceville Rd., Lawrenceville 08648 (90).
Mount St. Andrew Villa (Residence), 55 W. Midland Ave., Paramus 07652 (58).
Our Lady's Residence (Nursing Home), Glendale and Clematis Aves., Pleasantville 08232 (104).
St. Ann's Home for the Aged (Residence and Nursing Care, Women), 198 Old Bergen Rd., Jersey City 07305 (105).
St. Joseph's Home (women), Rt. 1, Box 353A, Hewitt 07421.
St. Joseph's Rest Home for Aged Women, 46 Preakness Ave., Paterson 07502 (30).
St. Joseph's Villa, Peapack 07977 (12).
St. Mary's Catholic Home (Skilled Nursing Home), Kresson Rd., Cherry Hill 08034 (94).
Villa Maria (Residence), 641 Somerset St., N. Plainfield 07061 (75).

New Mexico: Good Shepherd Manor (Shelter Care Home for Aged Men), Little Brothers of the Good Shepherd, P.O. Box 10248, Albuquerque 87114 (27).

New York: Bernardine Apartments, 240 E. Onondaga St., Syracuse 13202.
Ferncliff Nursing Home, P.O. Box 386, River Rd., Rhinebeck 12572 (320).
Frances Schervier Home and Hospital, 2975 Independence Ave., New York 10453 (364).
The Heritage (Residence), 1500 Portland Ave., Rochester 14621 (249).
Holy Family Home, 410 Mill St., Williamsville 14221 (96).
Josephine Baird Home (Skilled Nursing Home), 340 W. 55th St., New York 10019 (173).
Little Sisters of the Poor, 391 Central Ave., Albany 12206 (103).
Little Sisters of the Poor, 660 E. 183rd St., Bronx 10458 (200).
Little Sisters of the Poor, 1608 8th Ave., Brooklyn 11215 (152).
Little Sisters of the Poor, 135 W. 106th St., New York 10025 (137).
Little Sisters of the Poor, 110-30 221st St., Queens Village 11429.
Little Sisters of the Poor, 192 9th St., Troy 12180 (110).
Loretto Rest (Residence), E. Brighton and Glen Aves., Syracuse 13205 (206).
Madonna Home of Mercy Hospital (Nursing Home and Extended Care Facility) (120), and Mercy Hospital Health Related Facility (Residence) (58), Watertown 13601.
Madonna Residence for the Elderly, 1 Prospect Park W., Brooklyn, 11215 (290).
Marillac House (Apartments for Active or Retired Senior Citizens), 301 Orchard, Fayetteville 13066 (52 units).
Mary Manning Walsh Home (Nursing Home), 1339 York Ave., New York 10021 (347).
Mercy General Hospital Nursing Home Unit, Tupper Lake 12986 (26).
Mt. Carmel Home (Nursing Home, Women), 539 W. 54th St., New York 10019 (92).
Mt. Loretto Convalescent and Rest Home, R.D., 3, Amsterdam 12010 (87).
Nazareth Nursing Home, 291 W. North St., Buffalo 14201 (100).
Our Lady of Consolation Residence (Nursing Home), Albany and Schlegel Aves., Amityville 11701 (110).
Ozanam Hall Queens Nursing Home, 42-41 201st St., Bayside 11361 (432).
Providence Rest Home (Women), 3304 Waterbury Ave., Bronx 10465 (154).
Resurrection Rest Home (Nursing Home and Health Related Facility), Castleton 12011 (54).
Sacred Heart Home (Health Care Facility) (91), and Brothers of Mercy Apartments for

Elderly (100 units), 4520 Ransom Rd., Clarence 14031.

Sacred Heart Nursing Home, 8 Mickle St., Plattsburgh 12901 (74).

St. Ann's Home (Nursing Home and Extended Care Facility), 1500 Portland Ave., Rochester 14621 (354).

St. Anthony's Home for the Aged, 5285 S. Park Ave., Hamburg 14075 (90).

St. Columban's on the Lake (Retirement Home), Silver Creek 14136 (50).

St. Elizabeth Home, 5539 Broadway, Lancaster 14086 (100).

St. Francis Home (Nursing and Intermediate Care Facility), 147 Reist St., Williamsville 14221 (96).

St. Joseph's Guest House, 350 Cuba Hill Rd., Huntington 11743.

St. Joseph's Home (Nursing Home), 420 Lafayette St., Ogdensburg 13669 (82).

St. Joseph's Villa, 38 Prospect Ave., Catskill 12414.

St. Joseph's Nursing Home, 2535 Genesee St., Utica 13501.

St. Luke Manor for Chronically Ill, 17 Wiard St., Batavia 14020 (20).

St. Patrick's Home for the Aged and Infirm, 66 Van Cortland Park S., Bronx 10463 (214).

St. Teresa's Guest House, 120 Highland Ave., Middletown 10940 (92).

St. Vincent's Home for the Aged, 319 Washington Ave., Dunkirk 14048 (36).

St. Zita's Home (Women), 143 W. 14th St., New York 10011.

Teresian House, Washington Ave. Extension, Albany 12203.

Uihlein Mercy Center (Nursing Home), Lake Placid 12946 (96).

North Carolina: Maryfield Nursing Home, Greensboro Rd., High Point 27260 (60).

North Dakota: Holy Family Guest Home (Nursing Home), Carrington 58421 (40).

Manor St. Joseph (Residence), Edgeley 58533 (50).

St. Anne's Guest Home, 813 Lewis Blvd., Grand Forks 58201 (100).

St. Olaf Guest (Retirement) Home, Powers Lake 58773 (20).

St. Vincent's Nursing Home, 1021 N. 26th St., Bismarck.

Ohio: Alvernia Rest Home, 6765 State Rd., Cleveland 44134 (143).

Assumption Nursing Home, 550 Chalmers Ave., Youngstown 44511 (84).

Francesca Residence (women), 39 N. Portage Path, Akron 44303.

Franciscan Terrace (Residence and Nursing Care), 60 Compton Rd., Cincinnati 45215 (144).

House of Loreto (Nursing Home), 2812 Harvard Ave. N.W., Canton 44709 (98).

Jennings Hall (Skilled Nursing Home),

10204 Granger Rd., Garfield Heights, Cleveland 44125 (122).

Kirby Manor (Retirement Apartments), 11500 Detroit Ave., Cleveland 44102 (202 suites).

Little Sisters of the Poor, 476 Riddle Rd., Cincinnati 45220 (100).

Little Sisters of the Poor, 4291 Richmond Rd., Cleveland 44122 (212).

Maria-Joseph Home for the Aged and Lourdes Hall Nursing Home, 4950 Salem Ave., Dayton 45416 (150).

Mt. St. Joseph (Nursing Home), 21800 Chardon Rd., Cleveland 44117 (100).

Sacred Heart Home, 4900 Navarre Ave., Oregon 43616 (246).

St. Augustine Manor (Nursing Home), 7818 Detroit Ave., Cleveland 44102 (184).

St. Edward Nursing Home, 3131 Smith Rd., Akron 44313 (95).

St. Francis Home for the Aged, 182 St. Francis Ave., Tiffin 44883 (106).

St. Joseph's Hospice for the Aged (Nursing Home), 219 N. Chapel St., Louisville 44641 (58).

St. Margaret's Hall (Residence and Nursing Facility), 1960 Madison Rd., Cincinnati 45206 (145).

St. Raphael Home (Residence and Nursing Facility), 1550 Roxbury Rd., Columbus 43212 (80).

St. Rita's Nursing Home, 880 Greenlawn Ave., Columbus 43223 (100).

St. Theresa Residence for the Aged, 6760 Belkenton Ave., Cincinnati 45236 (125).

Schroder Manor, 1302 Millville Ave., Hamilton 45013 (15).

The Siena Home (Skilled Nursing Home), 235 W. Orchard Spring Dr., Dayton 45415 (98).

Villa Maria Nursing Home, Green Springs 44836 (150).

Villa Sancta Anna Home for Aged, 25000 Chagrin Blvd., Beachwood 44122 (68).

Oklahoma: St. Ann's Nursing Home, 3825 N.W. 19th St., Oklahoma City 74107 (82).

Oregon: Benedictine Nursing Center, S. Main St., Mt. Angel 97362 (105).

Mt. St. Joseph's Residence and Extended Care Center, 3060 S.E. Stark St., Portland 97214 (317).

St. Anthony's Hospital Extended Care Facility, Pendleton 97801 (65).

St. Catherine's Residence and Nursing Center, 3959 Sheridan Ave., North Bend 97459 (99).

St. Elizabeth's Nursing Home, Baker 97814 (49).

Sisters of St. Mary of Oregon Maryville Nursing Home, 14645 S.W. Farmington, Beaverton 97005 (120).

Pennsylvania: Ascension Manor (Apartment House), 911 N. Franklin St., Philadelphia 19123 (140 units).

Blessed John Neumann Nursing Home, 10400 Roosevelt Blvd., Philadelphia 19116 (196).

Christ the King Manor, 1100 W. Long Ave., Du Bois 15801 (100).

Corpus Christi Residence for Women, 7165 Churchland St., Pittsburgh 15206.

Drueding Infirmary, Master and Lawrence Sts., Philadelphia 19122 (50).

Garvey Manor (Nursing Home), Logan Blvd., Hollidaysburg, 16648 (152).

Holy Family Home, Little Sisters of the Poor, 5300 Chester Ave., Philadelphia 19143 (220).

Holy Family Manor (Skilled Nursing Facility), 1200 Spring St., Bethlehem 18018 (200).

Little Flower Manor, Springfield and Providence Rds. Darby 19023 (75).

Little Flower Manor for Diocese of Scranton, 200 S. Meade St., Wilkes-Barre 18702.

Little Sisters of the Poor, 1028 Benton Ave. N.S., Pittsburgh 15212 (163).

Little Sisters of the Poor, 5324 Penn Ave., Pittsburgh 15224 (115).

Little Sisters of the Poor, 2500 Adams Ave., Scranton 18509 (67).

Maria Joseph Manor, Danville 17821 (87).

Marian Manor (Residence and Nursing Care), 2695 Winchester Dr., Pittsburgh 15220 (176).

Mt. Trexler Skilled Nursing Unit of Sacred Heart Hospital, Limeport 18060 (65).

Our Lady Help of Christians Home (Nursing Home, Women), 56th St. and City Line Ave., Philadelphia 19131 (17).

Sacred Heart Manor (Residence and Health Care), 6445 Germantown Ave., Philadelphia 19119 (169).

St. Ann — Villa Laboure (Residence), 449 E. Locust Ave., Philadelphia 19144 (16).

St. Anne Home (Residence and Nursing Care, Women), R.D. 2, Columbia 17512 (120).

St. Anne Home for the Elderly (Skilled Nursing Facility), 685 Angela Dr., Greensburg 15601 (125).

St. Basil's Home for Women, Uniontown 15401 (18).

St. Bernadette Home for the Aged and Convalescent, 1525 N. 18th St., Philadelphia 19121 (174).

St. Ignatius Nursing Home, 4401 Haverford Ave., Philadelphia 19104 (176).

St. Joseph Home for the Aged (Women, Married Couples), Holland, Pa. 18966 (92).

St. Joseph Manor (Skilled Nursing Facility), 1616 Huntingdon Pike, Meadowbrook 19046 (100).

St. Joseph's Residence for Men, 1111 S. Cascade St., New Castle 16101.

St. Leonard's Guest Home, 601 N. Montgomery St., Hollidaysburg 16648 (24).

St. Mary's Home for the Aged, 607 E. 26th St., Erie 16504 (122).

St. Mary's Manor for Sighted and Unsighted, 701 Lansdale Ave., Lansdale 19446 (160).

St. Mary's Villa (Nursing Home), Elmhurst 18416 (121).

Shenango Valley Home for Senior Citizens (Residence and Nursing Care), 2250 Shenango Freeway, Sharon 16146 (100).

Sisters of the Holy Ghost, Home for Aged Women, Hampton Heights, Allison Park 15101 (17).

Villa de Marillac Nursing Home (Women), 5300 Stanton Ave., Pittsburgh 15206 (50).

Villa St. Elizabeth, 1301 Museum Rd., Reading 19602 (49).

Villa Teresa (Nursing Home), 1051 Avila Rd., Harrisburg 17109 (178).

Vincentian Home for the Chronically Ill., Perrymount Rd., Pittsburgh 15237 (153).

Rhode Island: Holy Trinity Home for Aged of the Little Sisters of the Poor, 964 Main St., Pawtucket 02860 (135).

Scalabrini Villa (Rest — Nursing Home), 860 Quidnessett Rd., North Kingstown 02852 (70).

L'Hospice St. Antoine (Residence), Mendon Rd. (P.O. Woonsocket), North Smithfield 02895 (249).

The St. Clare Home for Aged People, 309 Spring St., Newport 02840 (38).

South Carolina: Carter Mary Home, 1660 Ingram Rd., Charleston 29407 (8).

South Dakota: Brady Memorial Home (Intensive Care Nursing Facility), 500 S. Ohlman St., Mitchell 57301 (60).

Maryhouse, Pierre 57501 (47).

Mother Joseph Manor (Skilled Nursing Facility), 1002 North Jay St., Aberdeen 57401 (60).

St. William's Home for the Aged, 101 Viola St., Milbank 57252 (35).

Tekakwitha Nursing Home, Sisseton 57262 (102).

Tennessee: Alexian Brothers Rest Home (Retired Men and Women), Signal Mountain 37377 (97).

Ave Maria Guild Home (Nursing Home), 2805 Charlie Bryan Rd., Memphis 38134 (73).

Texas: Home for Aged Women, 920 S. Oregon St., El Paso 79901 (24).

Mother of Perpetual Help Home (Intermediate Care Facility), 319 E. Madison Ave., Brownsville 78520 (46).

Mt. Carmel Home, 4130 S. Alameda St., Corpus Christi 78411 (92).

The Regis (Retirement Home and Nursing Care), 400 Austin Ave., Waco 76701 (260).

St. Ann's Home for the Aged (Nursing Home), P.O. Box 1338, Panhandle 79068 (52).

St. Anthony's Center (Residence and Extended Health Care), 6301 Almeda Rd., Houston 77021 (279).

St. Benedict's Nursing Home, Alamo and Johnson Sts., San Antonio 78204 (186).

St. Francis Village, Inc. (Retired and Elderly), Crowley. Mailing address — P.O. Box 16310, Ft. Worth 76133 (400).

St. Joseph Residence, 330 W. Pembroke St., Dallas 75208 (49).

San Juan Nursing Home, San Juan 78589 (46).

Utah: St. Joseph Villa (Nursing Home), 474 Westminster Ave., Salt Lake City 84115 (89).

Vermont: Loretto Home for Aged, 59 Meadow St., Rutland 05701 (55).

Michaud Memorial Manor (Residence), Derby Line 05830 (24).

St. Joseph's Home for Aged, 243 N. Prospect St., Burlington 05401 (56).

Virginia: Fulton Catholic Home, Inc. (Aging Poor), 810 Louisiana St., Richmond 23231 (15).

St. Sophia's Home for the Aged, 16 N. Harvie St., Richmond 23220 (114).

Washington: Cathedral Plaza Apartments (Retirement Apartments), W. 1120 Sprague Ave., Spokane 99204 (150).

The Delaney, W. 242 Riverside Ave., Spokane 99201.

The De Paul Retirement Apartments, 4831 35th Ave. S.W., Seattle 98126 (105 units).

Fahy Garden Apartments, Dean and Cedar Sts., Spokane 99201 (30).

Fahy West Apartments, W. 1517 Dean Ave., Spokane 99201 (55).

Highline Nursing Home, 609 Highline Dr., E. Wenatchee 98802 (80).

The Josephinum (Retirement Home), 1902 2nd Ave., Seattle 98101 (228).

Mt. St. Vincent Nursing Center, 4831 35th Ave., N.W., Seattle 98126 (198).

St. Joseph Nursing Home, 1006 North H St., P.O. Box 229, Aberdeen 98520 (33).

St. Joseph Nursing Home, 708 E. Mission Ave., Spokane 99202 (83).

West Virginia: Knights of St. George Home, Wellsburg 26070 (30).

Welty Home for the Aged (Women), 21 Washington Ave., Wheeling 26003 (44).

Wisconsin: Divine Savior Nursing Home, 715 W. Pleasant St., Portage 53901 (106).

The Henry Boyle Catholic Home for the Aged (Nursing Home), 271 N. Park Ave., Fond du Lac 54935 (37).

Hope Nursing Home, 439 Ashford Ave., Lomira 53048 (40).

McCormick Memorial Home for the Aged, 212 Iroquois St., Green Bay 54301 (70).

Marion Heights Nursing Home, 3333 W. Highland Blvd., Milwaukee 53208 (205).

Marycrest (Residence, Women), 600 Third Ave., Durand 54736 (16).

Maryhill Manor Nursing and Retirement Home, 973 Main St., Niagara 54151 (51).

Milwaukee Catholic Home (Retirement Apartments and Skilled Nursing Care), 2301 E. Bradford Ave., Milwaukee 53211 (150).

Nazareth House (Skilled Nursing Facility), Stoughton 53589 (100).

Sacred Heart Hospital Nursing Home, Tomahawk 54487 (31).

St. Ann Rest Home, 2020 S. Muskego Ave., Milwaukee 53204 (54).

St. Anne's Home for the Elderly (Aged Poor), 3800 N. 92nd St., Milwaukee 53222 (220).

St. Camillus Health Center (Skilled Nursing Home), 10100 W. Bluemound Rd., Wauwatosa 53226 (186).

St. Catherine Infirmary (Nursing Home), 5635 Erie St., Racine 53402 (41).

St. Elizabeth Home, 502 St. Lawrence Ave., Janesville 53545.

St. Elizabeth's Nursing Home (Women), 745 N. Brookfield Rd., Brookfield 53005 (18).

St. Francis Home, 709 S. 10th St., La Crosse 54601 (69).

St. Francis Home (Skilled Nursing Facility), 2325 E. 3rd St., Superior 54880 (49).

St. Joan Antida Nursing Home, 6640 W. Beloit Rd., W. Allis 53219 (79).

St. Joseph's Home, 705 Clyman St., Watertown 53094 (88).

St. Joseph's Home, 9244 29th Ave., Kenosha 53140 (82).

St. Joseph's Home, 5301 W. Lincoln Ave., W. Allis 53219 (130).

St. Joseph Home, 5301 W. Lincoln Ave., W. Allis 53219 (130).

St. Joseph Home and Hospital (Skilled Nursing Facility), River Falls 54022 (52).

St. Joseph's Hospital Home for the Aged, Arcadia 54612 (61).

St. Joseph's Nursing Home, 2415 Cass St. La Crosse 54601 (78).

St. Joseph's Nursing Home, 400 Water Ave., Hillsboro 54634 (75).

St. Joseph Residence, Inc. (Nursing Home), 1925 Division St., New London 54961 (107).

St. Mary's Home for the Aged (Residence and Nursing Care), 2005 Division St., Manitowoc 54220 (150).

St. Mary's Nursing Home (Women), 3516 W. Center St., Milwaukee 53210 (130).

St. Mary's Residential Care Home, 203 W. Wisconsin St., Sparta 54656 (30).

St. Mary's Ringling Manor (Nursing Home), 1208 Oak St., Baraboo 53913 (81).

St. Monica's Senior Citizens Home (Retirement Apartments and Rooms), 3920 N. Green Bay Rd., Racine 53404 (102).

St. Paul Home (Residence and Skilled Nursing Home), 509 W. Wisconsin Ave., Kaukauna 54130 (54).

South Milwaukee Nursing Home, 3601 S. Chicago Ave., S. Milwaukee 53172 (96).

Villa Clement (Nursing and Convalescent Center), W. Allis 53214 (190).

Villa Loretto Nursing Home, Mount Calvary 53057.

FACILITIES FOR HANDICAPPED CHILDREN AND ADULTS

Source: *Directory of Catholic Special Facilities and Programs in the United States for Handicapped Children and Adults,* published by the National Catholic Educational Association, One Dupont Circle — Suite 350, Washington, D. C. 20036; edited by the Rev. Msgr. Elmer H. Behrmann, Ph. D., and Sister Ann Dolores Moll, S. L., executive secretary and secretary, respectively, of the Special Education Department, NCEA.

This listing covers facilities and programs with an educational or training concept. Information about other services for the handicapped can generally be obtained from the Catholic Charities Office or its equivalent (c/o Chancery Office) in any diocese. (See Index for listing of addresses of chancery offices in the US.)

Abbreviation code: b, boys; c, coeducational; d, day; g, girls; r, residential. Other information includes chronological age for admission. The number in parentheses at the end of an entry indicates total capacity or enrollment.

Deaf and Hard of Hearing

California: St. Joseph's Center for Deaf and Hard of Hearing, 4025 Grove St., Oakland. 94609.

Illinois: Holy Redeemer Day Classes for Deaf (c; 6-13 yrs.), 9536 S. Millard Ave., Evergreen Park. 60642 (30).

Holy Trinity Day Classes for the Deaf (c; 3-14 yrs.), 1910 W. Taylor, Chicago. 60612 (50).

St. Mary of Perpetual Help High School (day classes, c; 14-20 yrs.), 1023 W. 32nd St., Chicago. 60608 (18).

St. Timothy Day Classes for the Deaf (c; 3-14 yrs.), 6330 N. Washtenaw, Chicago. 60645 (24).

Louisiana: Chinchuba Institute (r&d,c; 2-16 yrs.), P.O. Box 187, Marrero. 70072 (73).

Massachusetts: Boston School for the Deaf (r&d,c; 4 yrs. and older), 800 N. Main St., Randolph. 02368 (304).

Missouri: St. Joseph Institute for the Deaf (r&d,c; 3½-15 yrs.), 1483 82nd Blvd., University City. 63132 (170).

New Jersey: Mt. Carmel Guild Pre-School Deaf Program (d.c), 17 Mulberry St., Newark. 07102 (80).

New York: Cleary School for Deaf Children (d.c; 2½ yrs. and older), 301 Smithtown Blvd., Lake Ronkonkoma, L.I. 11779 (72).

Nassau Day Classes (c; 3-14 yrs.), 75 Post Ave., Westbury. 11590 (54).

St. Francis de Sales School for the Deaf (d.c; 3-16 yrs.), 697 Carroll St., Brooklyn. 11215 (170).

St. Joseph's School for the Deaf (d,c; 3-10 yrs.), 1000 Hutchinson River Pkwy, Bronx. 10465 (270).

St. Mary's School for the Deaf (r&d,c; 3-21 yrs.), 2253 Main St., Buffalo. 14214 (390).

Ohio: St. Rita School for the Deaf (r,c; 4 yrs. and older), 1720 Glendale-Milford Rd., Cincinnati. 45215 (150).

Pennsylvania: Abp. Ryan Memorial Institute for Deaf (r&d,c; pre-school through 8th grade), 3509 Spring Garden St., Philadelphia. 19104 (80).

De Paul Institute (r&d,c; 2-18 yrs.), Castlegate Ave., Pittsburgh. 15226 (173).

Wisconsin: St. John's School for the Deaf (r&d,c; 3-20 yrs.), 3680 S. Kinnickinnic Ave., Milwaukee. 53207 (160).

Emotionally And/Or Socially Maladjusted

Arizona: Good Shepherd School for Girls (r; 12-21 yrs.), 1820 W. Northern Ave., Phoenix. 85021 (189). Also has after care off-campus division.

Arkansas: Monastery of Our Lady of Charity (r,g; 6 yrs. and older), 1125 Malvern Ave., Hot Springs. 71901 (50).

California: Boys Town of the Desert (r; 12-16 yrs.), 14700 Manzanita Park Rd., Beaumont. 92223 (80).

Hanna Boys Center (r; 10-15 yrs.), Box 100, Sonoma. 95476 (120).

Junipero Serra Boys Club (r; 16-18 yrs.), 316 N. Union Ave., Los Angeles. 90026 (32).

Pelletier High School (r,g; 12-18 yrs.), 1500 S. Arlington Ave., Los Angeles. 90019 (105).

Rancho San Antonio (r,b; 12-16 yrs.), 21000 Plummer St., Chatsworth. 91311 (93).

University Mound School for Girls (r; 13-17 yrs.), 501 Cambridge St., San Francisco. 94134 (96).

Colorado: Mt. St. Vincent Home (r,c; 5-14 yrs.), 4159 Lowell Blvd., Denver. 80211 (48).

Neuville Center (r,g; 8th-12th grade), 15151 E. Quincy Ave., Denver. 80232 (60).

Connecticut: Highland Heights—St. Francis Home for Children (r,c; 8-12 yrs.), 651 Prospect St. 06505 (28).

Mt. St. John (r,b; 11-16 yrs.), Kirtland St., Deep River. 06417 (95).

Georgia: Village of St. Joseph (r&d,c; 6-16 yrs.), 2969 Butner Rd. S.W., Atlanta. 30331.

Hawaii: Child Development Center (therapeutic day treatment center; preschool), 2345 Nuuanu Ave., Honolulu. 96817 (10).

Illinois: Group Home—Dominican Sisters of Bethany (r,g; 13-16 yrs.), 1434 W. Estes Ave., Chicago. 60626 (8).

Group Home, The Marcella Residence (g; 14-18 yrs.), 4633 N. Dover, Chicago. 60640 (10).

House of the Good Shepherd, Heart of Mary High School (r,g; 13-18 yrs.), 1126 W. Grace St., Chicago. 60613 (90).

St. Joseph Carondelet Child Center (r,c; 5-14 yrs.), 739 E. 35th St., Chicago. 60616 (48).

Indiana: Father Gibault School for Boys (r;

10-16 yrs.), 5901 Dixie Bee Rd., Terre Haute. 47802 (108).

Hoosier "Boys" Town (r; 10-15 yrs.), Schererville. 46375 (80).

St. Vincent Villa (r.c; 6-13 yrs.), 2000 N. Wells St., Ft. Wayne. 46808 (60).

St. Vincent Villa Pre-School (d,c), 2000 N. Wells St., Ft. Wayne. 46808 (37).

Kentucky: Boys' Haven (r; 14-19 yrs.), 3201 Bardstown Rd., Louisville. 40205 (51).

Maryhurst School (r,g; 13-17 yrs.), 2214 Bank St., Louisville. 40212.

Our Lady of the Highlands (r,g; teen-age high school age),· 938 Highland Ave., Ft. Thomas. 41075 (60).

Louisiana: Our Lady of the River School (r,g), 3225 River Rd., Bridge City. 70094 (60).

Maryland: Christ Child Institute for Children (d,c), Edson Lane, Rockville. 20852 (28).

Good Shepherd Center (r,g; 14-18 yrs.), 4100 Maple Ave., Baltimore. 21227 (120).

Massachusetts: Cushing Hall (r,b; 13-16 yrs.), 279 Tilden Rd., Scituate. 02066 (40). Diagnostic treatment center.

McAuley Nazareth Home for Boys (r; 6-10 yrs.), 77 Mulberry St., Leicester. 01524 (30).

Nazareth Child Study Center (r&d,c; 18 mo.-14 yrs.), 420 Pond St., Jamaica Plain, Mass. 02130 (160).

Our Lady of Lourdes School (r,g; 12-16 yrs.), 280 Tinkham Rd., Springfield. 01129 (80).

Our Lady of Providence Children's Center (r,c; 6-12 yrs.), 2112 Riverdale St., W. Springfield. 01089 (40).

Michigan: Barat House, League of Catholic Women (r,g; 12-16 yrs.), 5250 John R. St., Detroit. 48202 (24).

Boysville of Michigan, Inc. (r; 13-18 yrs.), 8744 Clinton-Macon Rd., Clinton. 49236 (180).

Don Bosco Hall (r,b; 13-17 years.), 10001 Petoskey Ave., Detroit. 48204 (52).

Villa Maria, Sisters of the Good Shepherd (r,g; 13-18 yrs.), 1315 Walker St. N.W., Grand Rapids. 49504 (50).

Vista Maria School (r,g; 12-17 yrs.), 20651 W. Warren Ave., Detroit. 48223 (125).

Minnesota: Carmel Heights (r,g; 13-19 yrs.), 1600 Eighth Ave. East, Duluth. 55805 (20).

Oak Grove High School, Home of the Good Shepherd, (r,g; 14-17 yrs.), 5100 Hodgson Rd., St. Paul. 55112 (60).

St. Cloud Children's Home (r,c; 12-16 yrs.), 1726 7th Ave. S., St. Cloud. 56301 (60).

Missouri: Child Center of Our Lady of Grace (r&d,c; 4-12 yrs.), 7900 Natural Bridge Rd., St. Louis. 63121 (100).

Marillac School (r&d,c; 7-11 yrs.), 310 W. 106th St., Kansas City. 64114 (115 day, 30 boarders).

Marygrove School for Girls (r; 12-17 yrs.), 2705 Mullanphy Lane, Florissant. 63031 (70).

Nebraska: Father Flanagan's Boys' Home (r; 10-16 yrs.), Boys Town, Nebr. 68010 (820).

Mary House (r, g; 14-18 yrs.), 519 S. 40th St., Omaha. 68105. Group home (5).

Walden Center (g, 13-18 yrs.), 602 S. 38th Ave., Omaha. 68105. Short term crisis center.

Nevada: St. Yves High School (r,g; 13-17 yrers.), 7000 North Jones Blvd., Las Vegas, 89106 (60).

New Jersey: Collier School (r,g; 12-17 yrs.), Rest Hill, Wickatunk. 07765 (60).

New York: The Astor Home for Children (r,c; 6-11 yrs., boys; 6-9 yrs., girls), 36 Mill St., Rhinebeck. 12572 (52).

Baker Hall (r,b; 12-17 yrs.), 150 Martin Rd., Lackawanna. 14218 (90).

Holy Angels Home (r,g; 11-17 yrs.), 1326 Winton Rd. N., Rochester. 14609 (39).

LaSalle School for Boys (r&d; 11-18 yrs.), 391 Western Ave., Albany. 12203 (145).

Lincoln Hall (r,b; 12-16 yrs.), Lincolndale. 10540 (270).

Madonna Heights School for Girls (r; 12-16 yrs.), Burrs Lane, Huntington. 11743 (98).

Our Lady of Charity School (r,g; 12-18 yrs.), Hamburg. 14075 (50).

Saint Anne Institute (r,g; 12-18 yrs.), 25 W. Lawrence St., Albany. 12206 (190).

St. Helena's Residence (r,g; 12-17 yrs.), 337 E. 17th St., New York. 10003 (20).

St. John's of Rockaway Beach (r,b; 10-14 yrs.), 144 Beach 111th St., Rockaway Park. 11694 (112). Also conducts group homes in Rockaway and Richmond Hill.

Villa Loretto (r,g; 15½-18 yrs.), Peekskill. 10566 (140).

North Dakota: Home on the Range for Boys (r; 12-18 yrs.), Sentinel Butte. 58654 (49).

Ohio: Carmelita Hall (r,g; 14-19 yrs.), 2903 Ridgewood Dr., Parma. 44134 (16).

Children's Village of St. Vincent de Paul (Parmadale) (r,c; 3-16 yrs.), 6753 State Rd., Parma. 44134 (240).

Marycrest School for Girls (r,g; 14-18 yrs.), 7800 Brookside Rd., Independence. 44131 (70).

Mount Alverno School (r,b; 12-15 yrs.), Mount Alverno Rd., Cincinnati. 45238 (84).

Our Lady of the Woods School, Girls Town of America (r; 13-18 yrs.), 575 N. Bend Rd., Cincinnati. 45224 (80).

Rosemont School (r,g; 12-18 yrs.), 2440 Dawnlight Ave., Columbus. 43211 (92).

St. Anthony Home for Boys (r; 13-17 yrs.), 8301 Detroit Ave. N.W., Cleveland. 44102 (60).

Oklahoma: Tulsa Vianney Girls Residence (r; 12-17 yrs.), 4001 E. 101st St., Tulsa. 74135 (59).

Oregon: Christie School (r,g; 9-16 yrs.), Marylhurst. 97036 (40).

St. Mary's Home for Boys (r; 8-18 yrs.), 16535 S.W. Tualatin Valley Highway, Beaverton. 97005 (40).

Villa St. Rose School for Girls (r; 12-18 yrs.), 597 N. Dekum St., Portland. 97217 (65).

Pennsylvania: Claver School for Girls (r;

13-17 yrs.), 5301 Chew Ave., Philadelphia. 19138 (45).

Gannondale School for Girls (r; 12-17 yrs.), 4635 E. Lake Rd., Erie. 16511 (48).

Gilmary School for Girls (r; 14-18 yrs.), Flaugherty Run Rd., Coraopolis. 15108 (96).

Harborcreek School for Boys (r; 10-15 yrs.), 5712 Iroquois Ave., Harborcreek. 16421 (65).

Lourdesmont School (r,g; 14-17 yrs.), 537 Venard Rd., Clarks Summit. 18411 (60-75).

Pauline Auberle Foundation (r,b; 13-19 yrs.), 1101 Hartman St., McKeesport. 15132 (55).

St. Gabriel Hall (r,b; 10-17 yrs.), P.O. Box 390, Phoenixville. 19460 (177).

St. Michael's School for Boys (r,b; 12-15 yrs.), Hoban Heights. 18620 (100).

Tekakwitha Hills School (r,g; 13-18 yrs.), 8550 Verree Rd., Philadelphia. 19111 (70).

Toner Institute (r,b; 9-13 yrs.), Castlegate Ave., Pittsburgh. 15226 (66).

Tennessee: DeNeuville Heights School for Girls (r; 13-18 yrs.), 3060 Baskin St., Memphis. 38127 (52).

Texas: Mt. St. Michael Jr. and Sr. High School (r,g; 12-18 yrs.), 4500 W. Davis St., Dallas. 75211 (120).

St. Joseph Center (r&d,c; 10-15 yrs.), 901 S. Madison St., Dallas. 75219 (60).

Washington: Good Shepherd Home (r,g; 13-17 yrs.), 4649 Sunnyside Ave. N., Seattle. 98103 (70).

Marian Heights High School (r,g; 13-18 yrs.), 3754 W. Indian Trail Rd., Spokane. 99208 (60). Also conducts a group home.

Morning Star Boys Ranch (r; 11-14 yrs.), Box 781-A Route 3, Spokane. 99203 (30).

Wisconsin: Cedarcrest Girls Residence (r,g; 12-16 yrs.), 8830 W. Bluemound Rd., Milwaukee. 53226 (55).

Our Lady of Charity High School (r,g; 12-21 yrs.), 2640 West Point Rd., Green Bay. 54303 (102).

St. Aemilian Child Care Center, Inc. (r&d,b; 6-12 yrs.), 8901 W. Capitol Dr., Milwaukee. 53222 (47).

St. Charles Boys Home (r; 12-18 yrs.), 151 S. 84th St., Milwaukee. 53214 (56).

St. Joseph's Children's Home (r,c; 6-15 yrs., boys; 6-12 yrs., girls), 1200 15th Ave. E., Superior. 54880 (40).

St. Michael's Home for Children (r,c; 9-18 yrs.), 3222 South Ave., La Crosse. 54601 (83).

St. Vincent Group Home (r,g; 13-21 yrs.), 3310 N. Dousman St., Milwaukee. 53212 (22).

Wyoming: St. Joseph's Children's Home (r,c; 6-13 yrs.), South Main, Torrington. 82240 (45).

Mentally Retarded

California: Helpers of the Mentally Retarded, Inc., 2626 Fulton St., San Francisco. 94118. Conducts two facilities: Helpers Home for Girls (permanent home; 18 years and older), 2626 Fulton St., San Francisco. 94118 (6); Helpers Home for Boys (permanent home; 18 years and older), 383 14th Ave., San Francisco, 94118 (6).

Kennedy Child Study Center (d,c; 5-13 yrs.), 1339 - 20th St., Santa Monica. 90404 (80). Also conducts a developmental nursery (18 mos.-3 yrs.) and a preschool for children from culturally deprived areas (3-5 yrs.).

St. Madeleine Sophie's Preschool Training Center (c; 2-9 yrs.), 2111 E. Madison Ave., El Cajon. 92021 (60).

St. Vincent School (r&d,g; 8-14 yrs.), P.O. Drawer V, 4300 Calle Real, Santa Barbara. 93102 (175).

Tierra del Sol (d,c; 12 yrs. and older), 9919 Sunland Blvd., Sunland. 91040 (100).

Connecticut: Special Education Department, 162 Oak St., Bridgeport. 06604.

Sacred Heart Educational Center (d,c; 5 yrs. to adult), Holy Family Academy, Baltic. 06330 (45).

District of Columbia: Lt. Joseph P. Kennedy Jr. Institute (d,c; 6-18 yrs.), 801 Buchanan St. N.E., Washington. 20017 (120).

St. Gertrude's School of Arts and Crafts (r&d,g; 6-12 yrs.), 4801 Sargent Rd. N.E., Washington. 20017 (48).

Florida: Department of Special Education, 1325 W. Flagler St., Miami. 33135.

Marian Center School for Exceptional Children (r&d,c; 3-14 yrs.), 15701 Northwest 37th Ave., Opa Locka. 33054 (140).

Morning Star School (d,c; 4-15 yrs.), 725 Mickler Rd., Jacksonville. 32211 (70).

Morning Star School (d,c; 4-18 yrs.), 954 Leigh Ave., Orlando. 32804 (45).

Morning Star School (d,c; 4-16 yrs.), 4660 - 80th Ave., N., Pinellas Park. 33565 (50).

Morning Star School (d,c; 4-16 yrs.), 302 E. Linebaugh Ave., Tampa. 33612 (50).

Hawaii: Special Education Center of Oahu (d,c; 4-21 yrs.), 5275 Kalanianole Hwy., P. O. Box 7028, Honolulu. 96821 (80).

Illinois: Bartlett Developmental Learning Center (r&d,c; 6-16 yrs.), 801 W. Bartlett Rd., Bartlett. 60103 (80).

Good Shepherd Manor (permanent home for men; 18 yrs. to death), P.O. Box 260, Momence. 60954 (125).

Kennedy Job Training Center (c; 16 yrs. and older), 123rd and Wolf Rd., Palos Park. 60464 (110).

Lt. Joseph P. Kennedy, Jr., School (r&d,b; 6-12 yrs.), 123rd & Wolf Rd., Palos Park. 60464 (164).

Misericordia Home (r,c; 1 mo.-6 yrs.), 2916 W. 47th St., Chicago. 60632 (136).

Mt. St. Joseph (sheltered care home for older retarded girls and women; 20-45 yrs.), Route 3, Box 261, Lake Zurich. 60047 (158; long waiting list).

St. Agnes Special Education Classes (d,c; 5½-10 yrs.), 3835 S. Washtenaw, Chicago. 60632 (15).

St. Francis School for Exceptional Children (r,c; 6-12 yrs.), 1209 S. Walnut Ave., Freeport. 61032 (27).

St. Jude School (d,c; 6-16 yrs.), 2nd & Spring Ave., Aviston. 62216 (30).

St. Mary of Providence (r&d,g; 4-14 yrs.), 4200 N. Austin Ave., Chicago. 60634 (190).

St. Rose Center (d,g; 6-15 yrs.), 4911 S. Hoyne Ave., Chicago. 60609 (60).

Special Education Program of the East St. Louis Deanery (d,c; 6-16 yrs.), 8213 Church Lane, East St. Louis. 62203 (45).

Indiana: Cara Pre-School (d,c; 4-8 yrs.), 18th and Poplar Sts., Terre Haute. 47803 (13).

Marian Day School (d,c; 6-16 yrs.), 625 Bellemeade Ave., Evansville. 47713 (56).

St. Bavo Special Class (d,c; 6-15 yrs.), 512 W. 8th St., Mishawaka. 46544 (12).

St. Mary Child Center School (d,c; 6-16 yrs.), 311 N. New Jersey St., Indianapolis. 46204 (32).

Trainable and Educable Special Education Classes (d,c; 6-18), P.O. Box 121, Batesville. 47006 (30).

Kansas: Department of Special Education, Diocese of Wichita, 619 S. Maize Rd., Wichita. 67209.

Holy Family Center (d,c; 6-18 yrs.), 619 S. Maize Rd., Wichita. 67209 (65).

Hope, Inc. (d,c; 16 yrs. and older), 1500 Polk, Great Bend. 67530 (35).

Lakemary Center, Inc. (r&d,c; 3-16 yrs.), 100 Lakemary Dr., Paola. 66071 (60r,60d).

Kentucky: Good Counsel School (d,c; 6-16 yrs.), 116 W. 6th St., Covington. 41011 (120).

Laboratory Classes for the Mentally Retarded, Ursuline College (d,c; 4½-15 yrs.), 3105 Lexington Rd., Louisville. 40206 (35-40).

Msgr. Pitt Learning Center (d,c; 5 yrs. and older), 1202 S. Shelby, Louisville. 40203 (70).

Msgr. Pitt Pre-Job Training and Work Study Program (d,c; 16-20 yrs.), 1202 S. Shelby, Louisville. 40203 (20).

Louisiana: Department of Special Education, Archdiocese of New Orleans, 1522 Chippewa St., New Orleans. 70130. Conducts day classes, a special day school, and a vocational rehabilitation center for the mentally retarded.

Department of Special Education, Diocese of Baton Rouge, 555 N. 23rd St., Baton Rouge. 70805. Conducts 12 classes in 6 special centers and a vocational rehabilitation center.

Holy Angels Institute (r,c; teen-age, 14 yrs. and older; nursery, 2 mo. to kindergarten age), 10450 Ellerbe Rd., Shreveport. 71106 (140).

Regina Caeli Center (d,c; 6-16 yrs.), 3903 Kingston, Lake Charles. 70601 (45).

St. Mary's Training School (r,c; 4-16 yrs.), P.O. Box 295, Clarks. 71415 (172).

Maryland: The Benedictine School for Exceptional Children (r,c; 6-16 yrs.), Ridgely. 21660 (100). Also conducts Habilitation Center (r,c; 17-25 yrs.) and a half-way house.

The Education Center (d,c; 6-16 yrs.), 7027 Bellona Ave., Baltimore. 21212 (150).

St. Bernardine Special Education School (d,c; 6-12 yrs.), 3814 Edmondson Ave., Baltimore. 21229 (55).

St. Elizabeth School for Special Education (d,c; 12 yrs. and older), 801 Argonne Dr., Baltimore. 21218 (160).

St. Francis School for Special Education (d,c; 5-13 yrs.), 2226 Maryland Ave., Baltimore. 21218 (92).

St. Maurice Day School (d,c; 5-16 yrs.), 10100 Kendale Dr., Potomac. 20854 (108).

Massachusetts: Cardinal Cushing School and Training Center for Exceptional Children (r&d,c; 6 yrs. and older), Hanover. 02339 (165).

Nazareth Hall on the Cape (d,c; 6-15 yrs.), 261 South St., Hyannis. 02601 (25).

Nazareth Hall for Exceptional Children (d,c; 7-14 yrs.), 887 Highland Ave., Fall River, 02720 (70).

Nazareth Hall School (d,c; 5-16 yrs.), 204 Commonwealth Ave., Attleboro Falls. 02763.

Nazareth Vocational Center (c; 14-21 yrs.), 707 Highland Ave., Fall River. 02720 (24).

Our Lady of Mercy School (d,c; 7-16 yrs.), 25 West Chester St., Worcester. 01605 (90).

St. Coletta Day School (d,c; 7-12 yrs., admission age), 85 Washington St., Braintree. 02184 (58).

Michigan: Department of Special Education, Archdiocese of Detroit, 305 Michigan Ave., Detroit. 48222. Conducts 10 educable classes in 5 centers.

Felician Sisters Home for Mentally Retarded Infants (from birth to 5 yrs.), 1012 S. Jefferson St., Saginaw. 48601. A demonstration project.

Our Lady of Providence School (r&d,g; 6-16 yrs.), 16115 Beck Rd., Northville. 48167 (130).

Robert F. Kennedy High School (c; 14-18 yrs.), 5930 McClellan Ave., Detroit. 48213 (90).

St. Louis School (r,b; 8-14 yrs.), 16195 Old U.S. 12, Chelsea. 48118 (60).

Work Evaluation Program (c; 17 yrs. and older), Holy Trinity School, Lacrosse and 6th St., Detroit. 48226. (10). Vocational program sponsored by Detroit Special Education Dept.

Minnesota: Christ Child School for Exceptional Children (d,c; 4-21 yrs.), 2078 Summit Ave., St. Paul. 55103 (124).

St. Gertrude's School (d,c; 7-16 yrs.), 30 Eighth Ave., S., St. Cloud. 56301 (23).

Missouri: Department of Special Education, Archdiocese of St. Louis, 4472 Lindell Blvd., St. Louis. 63108. Conducts 22 special day classes (c; 6-16 yrs.) and 2 day classes for pre-school children.

Good Shepherd Manor (custodial care facility for boys and men; 16-40 yrs.), 3220 E. 23rd St., Kansas City. 64127 (40).

St. Joseph's Vocational Center (c; 16-21

yrs.), 5341 Emerson Ave., St. Louis. 63120 (124).

St. Mary's Special School (r,c; 6-16 yrs.), 5341 Emerson Ave., St. Louis. 63120 (137).

St. Peter's Special Classes (d,c; 6-15 yrs.), 314 W. High St., Jefferson City. 65101 (30).

Universal Sheltered Workshop, 4208 W. Florissant Ave., St. Louis. 63115. Provides sheltered terminal employment to adult mentally retarded.

Nebraska: Villa Marie School (r&d,c; 7-16 yrs.), Rt. 1, Box 109, Waverly. 68462 (25).

New Jersey: Alhambra Pavilion Day Care and Child Study Center (c; 4-8 yrs.), 21 Centre St., Newark. 07102 (40).

Archbishop Damiano School (d,c; 3½-15 yrs.), 532 Delsea Dr., Westville Grove. 08093 (90).

Child Study Center (d,c; 4-8 yrs.), 272 Main St., Ridgefield Park. 07660 (17).

Department of Special Education, Diocese of Camden, 721 Cooper St., Camden, N.J. 08101. Conducts day classes.

Department of Special Education, Diocese of Paterson (d,c; 3-9 yrs.), 16 Jackson St., Paterson. 07505 (18).

Immaculate Conception Special Class (d,c; 6 yrs. and older), 171 Division St., Trenton. 08611 (11).

McAuley School for Exceptional Children (d,c; 5-9 yrs.), Rt. 22 at Terrill Rd., N. Plainfield. 07061 (30).

Marian Center (d,c; 7-14 yrs.), Delsea Dr. and Chestnut St., Vineland. 08360 (30).

Mount Carmel Guild — Department of Special Education, Archdiocese of Newark, 17 Mulberry St., Newark. 07102. Conducts day classes for the mentally retarded. Also conducts work training programs.

St. Cecilia Special Class (c; 7-13 yrs.), 21 Vernon St., Iselin. 08830 (30).

New Mexico: Notre Dame on the Rio Grande (custodial facility for males, 13 yrs. and older; no maximum age), 305 Lagunita Rd. S.W., Albuquerque. 87105 (15).

St. Joseph's Manor (custodial facility for males, 16 years and older; no maximum age), P.O. Box 487, Bernalillo. 87004. (24).

New York: Cantalician Center for Learning (d,c; 6-18 yrs.), 3233 Main St., Buffalo. 14214 (200).

Catholic Charities Learning Center for Exceptional Children (d,c; 3-6 yrs.), 305 Garfield Pl., Brooklyn. 11215 (18).

Cobb Memorial School (r,c; 6-10 yrs.), Altamont. 12009 (50).

Immaculate Heart of Mary Children's Home (r,c; 6-12 yrs.), William and Kennedy Sts., Buffalo. 14206. Conducts special class for retarded children in the home.

Marianne Hall — Special Education (d,c; 3-15 yrs.), 114 Michaels Ave., Syracuse, 13208 (12).

Maryhaven School for Exceptional Children (r&d,c; 7-16 yrs.), 450 Myrtle Ave., Port Jefferson. 11777 (90). Also conducts a voca-

tional rehabilitation center (d,c; 16 yrs. and older).

St. Catherine Child Care Center (r,c; birth to 5 yrs.), 30 N. Main St., Albany. 12203 (20).

St. Joseph School for Exceptional Children (r&d,c; 7-14 yrs.), Bennett Rd., Dunkirk. 14048 (30).

St. Rita's Home for Children (r,c; birth to 3 yrs.), 2110 Millersport Hwy., Buffalo. 14221 (64).

School for the Disabled (d,c; 5 yrs. and older), Maxwell Rd. — Rt. 9, Newtonville. 12128 (40). For mentally retarded and cerebral palsied.

School of the Holy Childhood (d,c; 7-18 yrs.), 215 Andrews St., Rochester. 14604 (85).

Special Education Department, Diocese of Brooklyn, 345 Adams St., Brooklyn, 11201. Conducts 14 special day classes in 7 parish schools.

Special Education Department, Archdiocese of New York, 451 Madison Ave., New York. 10022. Conducts 13 special day classes in 9 parish schools.

North Carolina: Holy Angels Nursery (r,c; birth to 6 yrs.), Belmont. 28012 (72).

Ohio: Department of Mental Retardation, Diocese of Cleveland, 2346 W. 14th St., Cleveland. 44113.

Good Shepherd Manor (permanent care of men 18 years and older), P.O. Box 387, Wakefield. 45687 (104).

Mary Immaculate School for Exceptional Children (d,c; 6-16 yrs.), 3837 Secor Rd., Toledo. 43623 (100).

Marymount Rehabilitation Services (vocational rehabilitation; 16 yrs. and older), 12215 Granger Rd., Cleveland. 44125.

Mt. Aloysius (r,b; 10-21 yrs.), Tile Plant Rd., New Lexington. 43764 (100).

Our Lady of Angels Special School (d,c; 7-21 yrs.), 3570 Rocky River Dr., Cleveland. 44111. Also conducts Seton High School Work Study Program (c; 16-21 yrs.).

Our Lady of the Elms Special Education (d,c; 6-14 yrs.), 1230 W. Market St., Akron. 44313 (64).

Rose Mary, The Johanna Graselli Rehabilitation and Education Center (r,c; 2-15 yrs.), 19350 Euclid Ave., Cleveland. 44117 (40).

St. John's Villa (d,c; 6-14 yrs.), W. Main St., Carrollton. 44615 (150).

St. Joseph Center (d,c; 7-16 yrs.), 2346 W. 14th St., Cleveland. 44113 (75).

Sheltered Workshop and Training Center (c; 16 yrs. and older), 1904 W. 22nd St., Cleveland. 44143 (25).

Oregon: Emily School for Retarded Children (d,c; 4-18 yrs.), 830 N. E. 47th Ave., Portland. 97213 (30).

Our Lady of Providence Children's Nursing Center (r; nursing care), 830 N. E. 47th Ave., Portland. 97213.

Pennsylvania: Clelian Heights School for Exceptional Children (r&d,c; 6-16 yrs.), R.D. 3, Box 304A, Greensburg. 15601 (100). Also conducts re-socialization program (r&d,g; 16-20 yrs.).

Department of Special Education, Diocese of Pittsburgh, 162 Steuben St., Pittsburgh. 15220. Conducts a program consisting of eight special day classes.

Don Guanella School (r,b; 7-14 yrs.), Sproul Road, Route 27, Springfield. 19064 (200).

McGuire Memorial (r&d,c; infancy to 7 yrs.), 2119 Mercer Rd., New Brighton. 15066 (150).

Mercy Day School: Center for Special Learning (d,c; 6-18 yrs.), 830 S. Woodward St., Allentown. 18103 (80).

Our Lady of Confidence Day School (c; 3-21 yrs.), 1099 W. Luzerne St., Philadelphia. 19140 (240).

St. Anthony School for Exceptional Children (r&d,c; 6-16 yrs.), 13th St. and Hulton Rd., Oakmont. 15139 (150). Also conducts a work adjustment center (c; 16 yrs. and older).

St. Joseph Day School (c; 6-18 yrs.), 619 Mahantongo St., Pottsville. 17901 (40).

St. Joseph's Children and Maternity Hospital Day School (c), 2010 Adams Ave., Scranton. 18509 (24).

St. Katherine School (d,c; 7-17 yrs.), Lancaster and Bowman Ave., Philadelphia. 19151 (270).

St. Mary of Providence Institute (r&d,g; 6-14 yrs.), Elverson. 19520 (120).

Rhode Island: St. Joseph's Pine Harbor (r,c; 3-16 yrs.), Singleton Rd., Pascoag. 02859 (70).

Tennessee: Madonna Day School for Retarded Children (d,c; 7-16), 4189 Leroy, Memphis. 38108 (50).

Texas: Katherine A. Ryan Center for Mentally Retarded Children (d,c), 4301 Broadway, San Antonio. 78209 (40).

Notre Dame of Dallas Special School (d,c; 6-12 yrs.), yrs.), Rt. 2, Box 4, Irving. 75062. (108).

Virginia: St. Coletta School (d,c; 5-18 yrs.), 1305 N. Jackson, Arlington. 22201 (45).

St. Mary's Infant Home (r,c; 3 days-9 yrs.), 317 Chapel St., Norfolk. 23504 (50).

Washington: Antonian School for Special Children (r&d,c; 6-18 yrs.), Cheney Rural Rt. 3, Box 14B, Cheney. 99004 (31).

Marian School (d,c; 6-18 yrs.), Fort Wright College, Spokane. 99204. (45).

Wisconsin: St. Coletta School, Jefferson. 53549. Offers the following programs:

a complete program of special education from kindergarten through elementary and advanced levels (r&d,c);

a work training center in preparation for job placement (r,c; 17-20 yrs.)'

a custodial care center (r,c; 45-85 yrs.);

a half-way house to give guidance and assist with problems (r,c; 18-24 yrs.);

a sheltered workshop to provide employment for the mentally retarded in a sheltered environment (r,c; 25-45 yrs.).

St. Coletta Day School (c; 8-16 yrs.), 1725 N. 54th St., Milwaukee. 53208 (16).

Orthopedically Handicapped

Alabama: Father Purcell Memorial (r,c; birth to 14 yrs.), 1918 Fairview Ave., Montgomery. 36108 (54).

Kentucky: Redwood School and Rehabilitation Center, United Cerebral Palsy of Northern Kentucky, Inc., (d,c; 18 mo. and older), 71 Orphanage Rd., Fort Mitchell, 41017 (77).

Pennsylvania: St. Edmond's Home for Crippled Children (r,c; 2-10 yrs.)., 320 S. Roberts Rd., Rosemont. 19010 (50).

Visually Handicapped

Illinois: Department of Vision and Hearing (itinerant program for the visually handicapped; 6-20 yrs.), 126 N. Desplaines St., Chicago. 60606.

St. Raphael Day School for the Blind (c), 6011 S. Justine St., Chicago. 60636 (6).

Maine: Blind Children's Resource Center, Sacred Heart School (d,c; 6-14 yrs.), 273 Minot Ave., Auburn (15).

Blind Children's Resource Center, Cathedral School (d,c; grades 1-8), 14 Locust St., Portland. 04111 (17).

New Jersey: Mt. Carmel Guild Special Education, Department for the Visually Handicapped (itinerant teaching program for grade and high school children), 17 Mulberry St., Newark. 07102 (56).

St. Joseph's School for the Multiple Handicapped Blind (r&d,c; 4-21 yrs.), 253 Baldwin Ave., Jersey City. 07306 (37).

New York: Catholic Charities Special Services Division (itinerant program, c; 6-20 yrs.), 75 Post Ave., Westbury. 11590 (42).

Catholic Guild for the Blind (itinerant teaching program, c; 5-17 yrs.), 191 Joralemon St., Brooklyn. 11201.

Lavelle School for the Blind (r&d,c; 3-20 yrs.), 221st St. and Paulding Ave., Bronx. 10469 (220).

St. Peter's School Resource Room (c; kindergarten through 8th grade), 2331 Fifth Ave., Troy. 12180 (15).

Pennsylvania: St. Lucy Day School (d,c; 5-14 yrs.), 929 S. Farragut St., Philadelphia. 19143 (49).

JOHN XXIII CENTER

The John XXIII Center for Eastern Christian Studies was established in 1951 by Father Feodor Wilcock and a group of other Eastern-Rite Jesuits. It operates a wide variety of ecumenical activities related to Eastern Christian studies. One of its projects is the John XXIII Institute, believed to be the only academic institution outside of Rome offering a degree in the theology of the Eastern tradition of Christianity.

Father Gino K. Piovesano, S.J., is head of the Center, which is located 2502 Belmont Ave., Fordham Univ., Bronx, N.Y. 10458.

OTHER SOCIAL SERVICES

Cancer Hospitals or Homes: The following homes or hospitals specialize in the care of cancer patients. They are listed according to state.

Penrose Cancer Hospital, Sisters of Charity of Cincinnati, 2215 N. Cascade Ave., Colorado Springs, Colo. 80907.

Our Lady of Perpetual Help Free Cancer Home, Servants of Relief for Incurable Cancer, 760 Washington St., S.W., Atlanta, Ga. 30315 (54).

Rose Hawthorne Lathrop Home, Servants of Relief for Incurable Cancer, 1600 Bay St., Fall River, Mass. 02724 (40).

Our Lady of Good Counsel Free Cancer Home, Servants of Relief for Incurable Cancer, 2076 St. Anthony Ave., St. Paul, Minn. 55104 (49).

Calvary Hospital, Little Company of Mary Sisters, 1600 Macombs Ave., Bronx, N.Y. 10452 (111).

St. Rose's Free Home for Incurable Cancer, Servants of Relief for Incurable Cancer, 71 Jackson St., New York, N.Y. 10002 (94).

Rosary Hill Home, Servants of Relief for Incurable Cancer, Hawthorne, N.Y. 10532 (82).

Holy Family Cancer Home, staffed by Dominican Sisters, Congregation of St. Rose of Lima, 6707 State Rd., Cleveland, O. 44134.

Sacred Heart Free Home for Incurable Cancer, Dominican Sisters, 1315 W. Hunting Park Ave., Philadelphia, Pa. 19140 (60).

Drug Addiction: Rehabilitation centers and outpatient clinics have been established in several dioceses.

Alcoholics: Some priests and religious throughout the U.S. are committed in a special way to the personal rehabilitation and pastoral care of alcoholics through participation in Alcoholics Anonymous and other programs. Facilities for the rehabilitation of alcoholics include:

St. Christopher's Inn, Atonement Friars, Graymoor, Garrison, N.Y. 10524 (capacity, 200).

Matt Talbot Inn, 9305 Superior Ave., Cleveland, Ohio 44106 (capacity, 25 men).

Mt. Carmel Hospital for Alcoholism (40 beds), and Mt. Carmel Rehabilitation Center for Male Alcoholics (100 beds), 396 Straight St., Paterson, N.J. 07501. McNulty House (Halfway House for male alcoholics) 101 Cedar St., Paterson, N.J. 07501. Umbrian Farms (residential treatment for male and female alcoholics), Lafayette, N.J. (capacity 30).

Sacred Heart Rehabilitation Center, 569 Elizabeth St., Detroit, Mich. 48201 (140 beds; 17-week live-in program).

The National Clergy Conference on Alcoholism was established to conduct workshops in various dioceses to instruct priests on ways of dealing with problem drinkers.

Convicts: Priests serve as full- or part-time chaplains in penal and correctional institutions throughout the country. Limited efforts have been made to assist in the rehabilitation of released prisoners in Halfway House establishments.

Facilities for Homeless Men: Representative of places where meals are provided, and in some cases lodging and other services as well, are:

St. Anthony's Dining Room, 121 Golden Gate Ave., San Francisco, Calif. 94102, where more than 11 million free meals have been served since 1950. Founded by Rev. Alfred Boeddeker, O.F.M.

Oznam Inn, Little Brothers of the Good Shepherd, 843 Camp St., New Orleans, La. 70130. Under sponsorship of the St. Vincent de Paul Society.

St. Vincent's Dining Room, 205 E. 2nd St., Reno, Nev. 89501.

St. Vincent's Dining Room, 650 S. Main St., Las Vegas, Nev. 89101.

Good Shepherd Refuge, Little Brothers of the Good Shepherd, 601 2nd St. S.W., Albuquerque, N.M. 87102.

Holy Name Centre for Homeless Men, Inc., 18 Bleeker St., New York, N.Y. 10012. A day shelter for alcoholic, homeless men. Provides social services and aid to transients and those in need. Affiliated with New York Catholic Charities.

St. Christopher Inn, Graymoor, Garrison, N.Y. 10524.

St. John's Hospice for Men, Little Brothers of the Good Shepherd, 1221 Race St., Philadelphia, Pa. 19107.

St. Joseph's House of Hospitality, 1635 Bedford Ave., Pittsburgh, Pa. 15219.

Unwed Mothers: Residential and care services for unwed mothers are the specific work of Sisters of the Good Shepherd in their numerous convents in the U.S.

Organizations for Handicapped

(See separate article for a listing of facilities for the handicapped.)

Blind

The Carroll Center for the Blind (formerly the Catholic Guild for All the Blind): Located at 770 Centre St., Newton, Mass. 02158, the center conducts diagnostic evaluation and rehabilitation programs for blind people over 16 years of age, and maintains programs in community services, volunteer and special services, casework and counseling, and professional training. It offers a large range of services for blind people who are not in residence, and maintains an office of public education and information. The executive director is John A. Reardon.

Xavier Society for the Blind: The Society is located at 154 E. 23rd St., New York, 10010. Founded in 1900 by Rev. Joseph Stadelman,

S.J., it is a center for publications for the blind and maintains a circulating library of approximately 7,000 volumes in Braille, along with a growing list of titles in large type and on tape. Its many publications include *The Catholic Review,* a monthly selection of articles of current interest from the Catholic press presented for the visually handicapped in Braille, on tape, and in large print. Xavier maintains the National Catholic Educational Index, listing all transcribed and recorded textbooks used currently in the overall Catholic educational system. The director of Xavier is Rev. Anthony F..La Bau, S.J.

The Deaf

Approximately 250 priests, 120 sisters and 30 brothers are engaged in special work among some 60,000 deaf persons in the U.S.

International Catholic Deaf Association: Established in 1949, the association has more than 5,000 members in 105 chapters, mostly in the U.S. It is affiliated with the Council of Organizations Serving the Deaf, the recognized official organization of all national associations working with the deaf in this country. In 1971, the ICDA cooperated with the National Association for the Deaf in conducting a census of the deaf funded by the US Department of Health, Education and Wel-fare. New data was sought regarding the number — greatly increased since rubella outbreaks from 1963 to 1965 — location and needs of the deaf, for service planning and programming. The ICDA publishes *The Deaf Catholic,* a bimonthly.

Mentally Retarded

National Apostolate for the Mentally Retarded: Established in 1968, the apostolate has headquarters at Trinity College, P.O. Box 4588, Washington, D.C. 20017. It publishes the quarterly *NAMR Journal* and a monthly newsletter, and has available a bibliography on the religious education of the retarded. Sister M. Therese Harrington is president of the apostolate; the executive director is Rev. Robert Malloy, O.F.M. Cap.

Service Agency

Special Education Department, National Catholic Educational Association: Established in 1954 to coordinate under one agency information and service functions for all areas of special education under Catholic auspices. Prior to 1954, its functions were carried out by a special office of the NCEA. Rev. Msgr. E. H. Behrmann is executive secretary of the department, with offices at 4472 Lindell Blvd., St. Louis, Mo. 63108.

CRIMINAL JUSTICE OFFICE

Bishop Floyd L. Begin of Oakland, voicing strong concern over prison problems in his diocese, established an office dealing with criminal justice in 1975.

A six-page pastoral letter containing more than 50 specific recommendations for Catholic action on corrections and justice accompanied the announcment in September.

The bishop attacked general apathy surrounding the subject as well as penal abuses.

"As followers of Christ," he said, "we should be actively concerned about criminals, prisons and the whole system of criminal justice. The vindictive attitude of 'lock them up and throw away the key' is not consistent with human dignity."

Bishop Begin said that some of the problems were "overcrowded facilities, insufficient alternative programs, indiscriminate pre-trial detention, lack of carefully integrated planning of all these elements, and isolation of the community at large from the concern and efforts of the criminal justice system."

Father Frank M. Buismato, O.F.M., former head of the Center for Peace and Justice in San Francisco, was named director of the new office. His assigned duties included spiritual ministry and support for prisoners and their families, the development of a transportation program for the families of inmates, collaboration with pastors and parish councils on educational and rehabilitation programs, and study of the structure of — and alternatives to — the criminal justice system.

Recommendations made by Bishop Begin were initially developed by the diocesan Social Action Board. The proposals were developed in 1974-75, during which time the board met with representatives of the Alameda and Contra Costa counties' judicial system and criminologists specializing in such matters as juvenile crime, drug addiction and prison reform.

Bishops' Statement

Issues connected with criminal justice and 22 suggested prison reform measures were the subjects of a statement approved by the bishops of the United States at their Nov. 12 to 16, 1973, annual meeting in Washington, D.C.

The statement was one of many on the same subject issued in recent years by individual bishops, the National Federation of Priests' Councils, the Conference of Major Superiors of Men (Religious), numerous organizations of sisters and state Catholic conferences, and other religious and civic associations.

The basic principle underlying the bishops' statement was the premise: "Punishment, in order to fulfill its proper purpose, must fit the nature of the crime; it must be considerate of the offender's human dignity; and it must be tempered by mercy and constantly aimed at reconciliation."

There is great variety in retreat and renewal programs, with orientations ranging from the traditional to teen encounters. Central to all of them are celebration of the liturgy and deepening of a person's commitment to faith and witness in life.

Features of many of the forms are as follows.

Traditional Retreats: Centered around conferences and the direction of a retreat master; oriented to the personal needs of the retreatants; including such standard practices as participation in Mass, reception of the sacraments, private and group prayer, silence and meditation, discussions.

Team Retreat: Conducted by a team of several leaders or directors (priests, religious, lay persons) with division of subject matter and activities according to their special skills and the nature and needs of the group.

Closed Retreat: Involving withdrawal for a period of time — overnight, several days, a weekend — from everyday occupations and activities.

Open Retreat: Made without total disengagement from everyday involvements, on a part-time basis.

Private Retreat: By one person, on a kind of do-it-yourself basis with the one-to-one assistance of a director.

Special Groups: With formats and activities geared to particular groups; e.g., members of Alcoholics Anonymous, vocational groups and apostolic groups.

Marriage Encounters: Usually weekend periods of husband-wife reflection and dialogue; introduced into the US from Spain in 1967.

Charismatic Renewal: Featuring elements of the movement of the same name; "Spirit-oriented"; communitarian and flexible, with spontaneous and shared prayer, personal testimonies of faith and witness.

Christian Community: Characterized by strong community thrust.

Teen Encounters, SEARCH: Formats adapted to the mentality and needs of youth, involving experience of Christian faith and commitment in a community setting.

Christian Maturity Seminars: Similar to teen encounters in basic concept but different to suit persons of greater maturity.

Cursillo: see separate entry.

Movement for a Better World: see separate entry.

Conferences

Retreats International: The first organization for promoting retreats in the US was started in 1904 in California. Its initial efforts and the gradual growth of the movement led to the formation in 1928 of the National Catholic Laymen's Retreat Conference, the forerunner of Retreats International. Henry J. Balling, Jr., president; Lyle M. Becker, executive secretary. Address: 2999 W. Spencer St., Appleton, Wis. 54911.

Retreats International-Women's Division: Successor to the National Laywomen's Retreat Movement, which was founded in 1936 in Chicago as an association of retreat houses, retreat leagues, diocesan organizations, schools and convents conducting or sponsoring retreats for laity and religious. Marjorie Samberg is the president. Bishop Thomas J. Welsh of Arlington, Va., is the episcopal advisor. Mailing address: 229 W. Fulton, Celina, Ohio 45822.

HOUSES OF RETREAT AND RENEWAL

(Sources: Almanac survey: *The Official Catholic Directory, 1975; Directory of Retreat Houses in the United States and Canada*, compiled by Retreats International.)

Abbreviation code: m, men; w, women; mc, married couples; y, youth. Houses and centers without code generally offer facilities to all groups. An asterisk after an abbreviation indicates that the facility is primarily for the group designated but that special groups are also accommodated. Houses furnish information concerning the types of programs they offer.

Alabama: Blessed Trinity Shrine Retreat, P.O. Holy Trinity, Holy Trinity 36859.

Visitation Sacred Heart Retreat House, 2300 Spring Hill Ave., Mobile 36607.

Alaska: Holy Spirit Retreat House, Star Route A, Box 388, Anchorage 99502.

Arizona: Franciscan Renewal Center, Casa de Paz y Bien, 5802 E. Lincoln Dr., Box 220, Scottsdale 85252.

Picture Rocks Retreat — A Christian Renewal Center, 7101 W. Picture Rocks Rd., Cortaro 85230.

Arkansas: The Abbey Retreat (Coury House), Subiaco 72865.

California: Cenacle Retreat House (w*), 5340 Fair Oaks Blvd., Carmichael 95608.

Christ the King Retreat Center, Box 156, Citrus Heights 95610.

Christian Brothers Retreat House (students), 2233 Sulphur Springs Ave., St. Helena 94574.

El Carmelo Retreat House (Christian Renewal Center), 926 E. Highland Ave., P.O. Box 446, Redlands 92373.

El Retiro San Inigo (m), Box 128, Los Altos 94022.

Holy Spirit Retreat House, 4316 Lanai Rd., Encino 91316.

Immaculate Heart Retreat House (w, mc), 3431 Waverly Dr., Los Angeles 90027.

La Casa de Maria, 800 El Bosque Rd., Santa Barbara 93108.

Manresa Retreat House (m*), P.O. Box K, Azusa 91702.

Mary and Joseph Retreat House, 5300 Crest Rd., Rancho Palos Verdes 90274.

Mater Dolorosa Retreat House (m*), 700 N. Sunnyside Ave., Sierra Madre 91024.

New Camaldoli Immaculate Heart Hermitage (m, private), Big Sur 93920.

Old Mission San Luis Rey Retreat, 4050 Mission Ave., San Luis Rey 92860.

Poverello of Assisi Retreat House, 1519 Woodworth St., San Fernando 91340.

Retreat House of the Sacred Heart (w), 920 E. Alhambra Rd., Alhambra 91801.

St. Andrew's Priory Retreat House, Valyermo 93563.

St. Anthony's Retreat House, P.O. Box 248, Three Rivers 93271.

St. Charles Priory, Benet Hill, Oceanside 92054.

St. Clare's Retreat (w*), 2381 Laurel Glen Rd. Santa Cruz 95065.

St. Dominic Savio Retreat House (y), 8301 Arroyo Dr., Rosemead 91770.

St. Francis Retreat (m*), P.O. Box 1070, San Juan Bautista 95045.

St. Raymond's Dominican Retreat (y*), 1666 Hidden Valley Rd., Thousand Oaks 91360.

San Damiano Retreat, P.O. Box 767, Danville 94526.

Serra Retreat (m*), P.O. Box 127, Malibu 90265.

Sisters of Social Service (one-day retreats), 1120 Westchester Pl., Los Angeles 90019.

Vallombrosa Center (w*), 250 Oak Grove Ave., Menlo Park 94025.

Villa Maria del Mar, 2-1918 East Cliff Dr., Santa Cruz 95062.

Colorado: El Pomar Renewal Center, 1661 Mesa Ave., Colorado Springs 80906.

Sacred Heart Retreat House (m), Box 185, Sedalia 80135.

Connecticut: Cenacle Center for Meditation and Spiritual Renewal (w*), Wadsworth St., Box 550,Middletown 06457.

Holy Family Retreat (m*), 303 Tunxis Rd., West Hartford 06107.

Holy Ghost Retreat House (m), Box 607, New Canaan 06840.

Immaculata Retreat House, Route 32, Windham Rd., Willimantic 06226.

Our Lady of Calvary Retreat House (w), Cotton Rd., Farmington 06032.

Villa Maria Retreat House (w*), 159 Sky Meadow Dr., Stamford 06903.

Delaware: St. Francis Renewal Center, 1901 Prior Rd., Wilmington 19809.

District of Columbia: Washington Retreat House (w*), 4000 Harewood Rd. N.E., Washington 20017.

Florida: Cenacle Retreat House, 1400 S. Dixie Highway, Lantana 33462.

Franciscan Center (ecumenical), 3010 Perry Ave., Tampa 33603.

Holy Name Priory (private), San Antonio 33576.

Mary Queen of Apostles Dominican Retreat House, 7275 S.W. 124th St., Kendall 33156.

Our Lady of Florida Retreat House (m*), 1300 US Hwy. No. 1, North Palm Beach 33408.

St. Leo's Abbey (m), St. Leo 33574.

Georgia: Ignatius House, 6700 Riverside Dr. N.W., Atlanta 30328.

Monastery of the Holy Spirit (m), R.R. 1, Conyers 30207.

Illinois: Aylesford Renewal Center, US 66 at Cass Ave., N, Westmont 60559.

Bellarmine Hall (m*), Box 268, Barrington 60010.

Bishop Lane Retreat House, R.R. 2, Box 214 A, Rockford 61102.

Cabrini Contact Center, 9430 Golf Rd., Des Plaines 60016.

Cenacle Retreat House (w), 513 Fullerton Parkway, Chicago 60614.

Cenacle Retreat House (w), 11600 Longwood Dr., Chicago, 60643.

Cenacle Retreat and Conference Center, P.O. Box 340, Warrenville 60555.

Childerley Retreat House (university students), 506 McHenry Rd., Wheeling 60090.

Divine Word Seminary Retreat House, Techny 60082.

King's House, N. 66th St., Belleville 62223.

King's House of Retreats, Box 313, Henry 61537.

La Salle Manor, Christian Brothers Retreat House (y), Plano 60545.

St. Francis Retreat (m*), Mayslake, 1717 31st St., Oak Brook 60521.

St. Mary's Retreat House, P.O. Box 608, 1400 W. Main St., Lemont 60439.

St. Peter's Friary (m), 110 W. Madison St., Chicago 60602.

Tolentine Center, 20300 Governors Highway, Olympia Fields 60461.

Viatorian Villa, 3015 N. Bayview Lane, McHenry 60050.

Villa Redeemer, Box 6, Glenview 60025.

Indiana: Alverna Retreat House, 8140 Spring Mill Rd., Indianapolis 46260.

Lourdes Retreat House (m), Box 156, Cedar Lake 46303.

Our Lady of Fatima Retreat House, 5353

E. 56th St., Indianapolis 46226.
Our Lady of Fatima Retreat House, Notre Dame 46556.
Our Lady of Lourdes Retreat House (m), 12915 Parrish St., P.O. Box 156, Cedar Lake 46303.
St. Jude Guest House, St. Meinrad 47577.
Sarto Retreat Center, 4200 N. Kentucky Ave., Evansville 47711.
Seven Dolors Shrine Retreat House, R.R. 12, Box 31, Valparaiso 46383.

Iowa: American Martyrs Retreat House, P.O. Box 605, Cedar Falls 50613.
Colfax Interfaith Spiritual Center, Box 37, Colfax, 50054.

Kansas: Villa Christi Retreat House, 3033 W. Second St., Wichita 67203.

Kentucky: Marydale Center, Donaldson Rd., Erlanger 41018.
Our Lady of Gethsemani (m, private), The Guestmaster, Abbey of Gethsemani, Trappist 40073.

Louisiana: Abbey Christian Life Center, St. Joseph's Abbey, St. Benedict 70457.
Ave Maria Retreat House, Route 1, Box 0368 AB, Marrero 70072.
Cenacle Retreat House (w), 5500 St. Mary St., Metairie 70004.
Manresa House of Retreats (m), P.O. Box 89, Convent 70723.
Maryhill Retreat House (Christian Life Center), 600 Maryhill Rd., Pineville 71360.
Marywood Retreat House, Route 1, Folsom 70437.
Our Lady of the Oaks Retreat House, P.O. Box D, Grand Coteau 70541.

Maine: St. Paul's Center, Oblate Fathers Retreat House (French-English), 136 State St., Augusta 04330.

Maryland: CYO Retreat House (y*), 15523 York St.,Sparks 21152.
Christian Brothers Retreat House (y), Rt. 15 South, Adamstown 21710.
Loyola Retreat House-on-Potomac (m*), Faulkner 20632. City Office, 1028 Connecticut Ave. N.W., Washington, D.C. 20036.
Manresa-on-Severn, P.O. Box 9, Annapolis 21404.
Marriottsville Spiritual Center (w), Marriottsville 21104.
Pine Lane Spiritual Center (y*), Winchester Rd., Annapolis 21404.
St. Joseph Spiritual Center, 3800 Frederick Ave., Baltimore 21229.

Massachusetts: Calvary Apostolic Center, Passionist Community, 59 South St., Shrewsbury 01545.
Campion Hall Jesuit Retreat House, Great Pond Rd., North Andover 01845.

Cenacle Retreat House, 200 Lake St., Brighton, Boston 02135.
Christian Formation Center, River Rd., Andover 01810
Eastern Point Retreat House, Gonzaga Hall, Gloucester 01930.
Espousal Center, 554 Lexington St., Waltham 02154.
Holy Cross Fathers Retreat House, Washington St., N. Easton 02356.
Jesuit Center, Sullivan Square, Charlestown, Boston 02129.
La Salette Center for Christian Living, 947 Park St., Attleboro 02703.
Loretto Retreat House, Jeffrey's Neck Rd., Ipswich 01938.
Marian Center, 1365 Northampton St., Holyoke 01040.
Miramar Retreat House, Duxbury, 02332.
Mother of God Retreat House (boys), Old Groveland Rd., Bradford 01830.
Mother of Sorrows Retreat House (m, y), 110 Monastery Ave., W. Springfield 01089.
Mt. Carmel Christian Life Center, Oblong Rd., Williamstown 01267.
Sacred Heart Juniorate (boys), Fellows Rd., P.O. Box 271, Ipswich 01938.
St. Gabriel's Retreat House, 159 Washington St., Brighton, Boston 02135.
Salvatorian Center, 30 East St., Methuen 01844.

Michigan: Blessed Sacrament Retreat House, Sacramentine Sisters, Conway 49722.
Capuchin Retreat, Box 188, Washington 48094.
Christian Friendship House (y), 1975 N. River Rd., St. Clare 48079.
Manresa Jesuit Retreat House, 1390 Quarton Rd., Bloomfield Hills 48013.
Mary Reparatrix Retreat Center (w*), 17330 Quincy Ave., Detroit 48221.
Marygrove Renewal Center, Garden 49835.
Monks of Mt. Tabor (private), 4326 Snook Rd., Hadley 48440.
Portiuncula in the Pines, P.O. Box 250, De Witt 48820.
Queen of Angels Retreat, 3400 S. Washington Blvd., Saginaw.
St. Basil's Center, 3990 Giddings Rd., Pontiac 48057.
St. Lazare Retreat House, W. Spring Lake Rd., Spring Lake 49456.
St. Mary's Retreat House (w*), 775 W. Drahner Rd., Oxford 48051.
St. Paul of the Cross Retreat House, 23333 Schoolcraft, Detroit 48223.

Minnesota: Cenacle Retreat House, 1221 Wayzata Blvd., Wayzata 55391.
Christian Brothers Retreat Center (y), Rt. 1, Box 18, Marine-on-St. Croix 55047.
Christian Community Center, Assisi Heights, Rochester 55901.
Epiphany House of Prayer, 266 Summit Ave., St. Paul 55102.

Fiat Retreat House (y), 2120 Park Ave. S., 621 First Ave. S., Minneapolis 55404.

Fitzgerald Center, Immaculate Heart of Mary Seminary, Terrace Heights, Winona 55987.

Franciscan Retreats, Conventual Franciscan Friars, Prior Lake 55372.

Jesuit Retreat House (m), 8243 N. Demontreville Trail, North St. Paul 55109.

King's House of Retreats, 621 S. First Ave., Buffalo 55313.

Maryhill Retreat House, 260 Summit Ave., St. Paul 55102.

St. John Abbey (summer months), Collegeville 56321.

Welch Center (y), 605 N. Central Ave., Duluth 55807.

Mississippi: St. Augustine's (m*), Divine Word Missionaries, Box 311, Bay St. Louis 39520.

Missouri: Cenacle Retreat House (w*), 900 S. Spoede Rd., St. Louis 63131.

Family Life Center, St. Pius X Abbey, Abbey Rd., Pevely 63070.

Holy Family Retreat House, Conception 64432.

Immacolata Retreat House, RFD 4, Box 434, Liberty 64068.

Marianist Apostolic Center, Glencoe 63038.

Our Lady of Assumption Abbey (m), Trappists, Rt. 5, Ava 65608.

Our Lady of the Ozarks, P.O. Box 424, Carthage 64836.

Pallottine Renewal Center, RR 2, 15270, Old Halls Ferry Rd., Florissant 63034.

Passionist Retreat of Our Lady, Retreat House, Passionist Fathers and Brothers, Warrenton 63383.

St. de Chantal Retreat House (w), 1701 South Fort St., Springfield 65807.

The White House Retreat (m), 7400 Christopher Dr., St. Louis 63129.

Montana: Ursuline Retreat Center (w), 2300 Central Ave., Great Falls 59401.

Nebraska: Catholic Women's Retreat League, 1034 S. 38th Ave., Omaha 68105.

Good Counsel, R.R. 1, Box 110, Waverly 68462.

St. Columbans Foreign Mission Society, St. Columbans 68056.

New Hampshire: The Common - St. Joseph Monastery, Peterborough 03458.

New Hampshire Monastery, Hundred Acres, New Boston 03070.

Oblate Fathers Retreat House, Hudson 03051.

St. Francis Friary and Retreat House, 860 Central Rd., Rye Beach 03871.

New Jersey: Blackwood Center, St. Pius X House, Box 216, Blackwood 08012.

Blessed Trinity Missionary Retreat Cenacle (w*), 1190 Long Hill Rd., Stirling 07980.

Carmel Retreat House, 1071 Ramapo Valley Rd., Mahwah; mailing address, P.O. Box 285, Oakland 07436.

Cenacle Retreat House, River Rd., Highland Park 08904.

Christ House, Rt. 15, Lafayette 07848

Good Shepherd Center, 74 Kahdena Rd., Morristown 07960.

Loyola House of Retreats, 161 James St., Morristown 07960.

Queen of Peace Retreat House, Route 206, Newton 07860.

St. Bonaventure Retreat House (m), 174 Ramsey St., Paterson 07501.

St. Joseph's Villa (w), Srs. of St. John the Baptist, Peapack 07977.

San Alfonso Retreat House, 755 Ocean Ave., Long Branch 07740.

Stella Maris Convent, 981 Ocean Ave., Elberon 07741.

Villa Pauline Retreat and Guest House (w*), Hilltop Rd., Mendham 07945.

Xavier Center, Convent Station 07961.

New Mexico: Dominican Retreat House, Our Lady Queen of Peace, 5825 Coors Rd. S.W., Albuquerque 87105.

Holy Cross Retreat House, P.O. Box 158, Mesilla Park 88047.

Our Lady of Guadalupe Monastery (families - pentecostal), Pecos 87552.

New York: Bergamo East Conference Center, Chaminade Rd., Marcy 13403.

Bishop Molloy Retreat House (m), 178th and Wexford Terr., Jamaica, L.I. 11432.

Cardinal Spellman Retreat House, Passionist Fathers, 5801 Palisade Ave., Bronx (Riverdale) 10471.

Cenacle Center for Spiritual Renewal, Cenacle Rd., Lake Ronkonkoma, L.I., 11779.

Cenacle Retreat House, 693 East Ave., Rochester 14607.

Christ the King Retreat House, 500 Brookford Rd., Syracuse 13224.

Cormaria Retreat House (w*), Sag Harbor, L.I. 11963.

Diocesan Cursillo Center (Spanish), 118 Congress St., Brooklyn 11201.

Dominican Retreat House, 1945 Union St., Schenectady 12309.

Gonzaga Retreat House (priests and religious), Monroe 10950.

Jesuit Retreat House, North American Martyrs Shrine, Auriesville 12016.

John XXIII Center for Renewal and Ecumenism, Assumptionists, Cassadaga 14718.

Marian Shrine, Don Bosco Retreat House, Filor's Lane, West Haverstraw 10993.

Monastery of the Precious Blood (w), Ft. Hamilton Parkway and 54th St., Brooklyn 11219.

Mount Alvernia Retreat House, Wappingers Falls 12590.

Mount Augustine Retreat House and Apostolic Center, 144 Campus Rd., Staten Island 10301.

Mount Manresa Retreat House, 239 Fingerboard Rd., Staten Island 10305.

Notre Dame Retreat House, Box 74, Foster Rd., Canandaigua 14424.

Queen of Apostles Retreat House, North Haven, Sag Harbor 11963.

Regina Maria Retreat House (w*), 77 Brinkerhoff St., Plattsburgh 12901.

Retreat House of Mary Reparatrix, 14 E. 29th St., New York 10016.

St. Andrew's House, 89 A St. Andrew's Rd., Walden 12586.

St. Columban's Retreat House, Derby 14047.

St. Francis Retreat House, Capuchin Fathers, Garrison 10524.

St. Gabriel (y*), Burns Rd., Shelter Island Heights 11965.

St. Ignatius Retreat House, 6969 Strickler Rd., Clarence Center 14032.

St. Ignatius Retreat House, Searington Rd., Manhasset, L.I. 11030.

St. Josaphat's Retreat House, East Beach Rd., Glen Cove 11542.

St. Joseph Center (Spanish Center), 523 W. 142nd St., New York 10031.

Stella Maris Retreat House (w), Skaneateles 13152.

Tagaste Monastery Retreat House (m, y), Suffern 10901.

North Carolina: Maryhurst Retreat House (w*), P.O. Box 1390, Pinehurst 28374.

North Dakota: Queen of Peace Retreat, 1310 N. Broadway, Fargo 58102.

Ohio: Catholic Women's Retreat League of Columbus, c/o Miss Josephine Roundtree, president, 92 S. 4th St., Newark 43055.

Franciscan Renewal Center, 320 West St., Carey 43316.

Friarhurst Retreat House, 8136 Wooster Pike, Cincinnati 45227.

Holy Cross Center, Passionist Community, 1055 St. Paul Pl., Cincinnati 45202.

Jesuit Retreat House, 5629 State Rd., Cleveland 44134.

Loyola of the Lakes, 700 Killinger Rd., Clinton 44216.

Loyola Retreat House, P.O. Box 289, Milford 45150.

Maria Stein Retreat-Renewal Center, Box 128, Maria Stein 45860.

Marianist Center, 4435 East Patterson Rd., Dayton 45430.

Mary Reparatrix Retreat House (w*), 3350 Ruther Ave., Cincinnati 45220.

Men of Milford Retreat House (private), Box 348, Milford 45150.

Our Lady of the Pines (w*), 1250 Tiffin St., Fremont 43420.

Sacred Heart, 3128 Logan Ave., Box 3902, Youngstown 44505.

St. Joseph Christian Life Center, 18485 Lake Shore Blvd., Cleveland 44119.

Shrine Center for Renewal, Diocese of Columbus, 5277 E. Broad St., Columbus 43213.

Oregon: Loyola Jesuit Retreat House, 3220 S.E. 43rd St., Portland 97206.

Mt. Angel Abbey, St. Benedict 97373.

Our Lady of Peace Retreat (w*), 3600 S. W. 170th Ave., Beaverton 97005.

Trappist Abbey Retreat (m, y, private), P.O. Box 97, Lafayette 97127.

Pennsylvania: Bl. Raphaela Mary Retreat House, 616 Coopertown Rd., Haverford 19041.

Byzantine Catholic Seminary (m), 3605 Perrysville Ave., Pittsburgh 15214.

Cenacle Retreat House (w*), 4721 Fifth Ave., Pittsburgh 15213.

Convent of the Precious Blood (days of recollection), New Holland Ave., Shillington 19607.

Dominican Retreat House (w*), Ashbourne Rd. and Juniper Ave., Elkins Park 19117.

Mt. St. Ann Retreat, (w*), P.O. Box 328, Ebensburg 15931.

St. Alphonsus Retreat House (m*), Box 218, Tobyhanna 18466 (1,200).

St. Emma Retreat House, 1001 Harvey St., Greensburg 15601.

St. Fidelis Seminary, Herman 16039.

St. Francis Retreat House, 3918 Chipman Rd., Easton 18042.

St. Francis Retreat House (w), Monocacy Manor, Bethlehem 18017.

St. Francis Retreat House, 1201 Beechwood Blvd., Pittsburgh 15206.

St. Gabriel's Retreat House (w), 631 Griffin Pond Rd., Clarks Summit 18411.

St. Joseph's-in-the-Hills (m*), Malvern 19355.

St. Paul of the Cross Retreat House, 148 Monastery Ave., Pittsburgh 15203.

St. Vincent Retreat House (m*, summer), Latrobe 15650.

Villa Maria Retreat House, Box 218, Wernersville 19585.

Villa of Our Lady of the Poconos (w*), Mt. Pocono 18344.

Rhode Island: Corpus Christi Carmel Retreat House, 21 Battery St., Newport 02840.

Ephpheta House — A Center for Renewal, 10 Manville Hill Rd; mailing address, P.O. Box 1, Manville 02838.

Our Lady of Peace Retreat House, Ocean Rd., Narragansett 02882.

South Carolina: Springbank Christian Center, Dominican Retreat House, Kingstree 29556.

Tennessee: Nazareth, House of the Lord, 1306 Dellwood Ave., Memphis 88127.

Texas: Catholic Renewal Center, 4503 Bridge St., Ft. Worth 76103.

Cenacle Retreat House, 420 N. Kirkwood, Houston 77024.

Christian Holiday House, Oblate Fathers, P.O. Box 635, Dickinson 77539.

Holy Name Retreat House (m*), 430 Bunker Hill Rd., P.O. Box 19306, Houston 77024.

Montserrat Jesuit Retreat House, P.O. Box 398, Lake Dallas 75065.

Our Lady of the Pillar Christian Renewal Center, 2507 N.W. 36th St., San Antonio 78228.

Saint Joseph Retreat House, 127 Oblate Dr., San Antonio 78216.

San Juan Retreat House, ("El Rancho Alegre"), Diocese of Brownsville, P.O. Box 998, San Juan 78589.

Utah: Our Lady of the Holy Trinity Retreat House (m), Huntsville 84317.

Virginia: Dominican Retreat, 7103 Old Dominion Dr., McLean 22101.

Franciscan Center for Spiritual Renewal, Rt. 642, Box 825, Winchester 22601..

Holy Family Retreat House, Box 3151, Hampton 23363.

Our Lady of Aquia House, Madonna House Apostolate, Rt. 3, Box 202, Stafford 22554.

St. Ann Retreat House, Bristow 22013.

Spiritual Renewal Center, Rt. 2, Box 388 B, Powhaten 23229.

Washington: Camp Field Retreat Center, P.O. Box 128, Leavenworth 98826.

Immaculate Heart Retreat House, Route 3, Box 653, Spokane 99203.

Palisades Retreat, P.O. Box 2214, Tacoma.

St. Peter the Apostle Diocesan Retreat Center, P.O. Box 86, Cowiche 98923.

Wisconsin: Cenacle Retreat House (w*), 3288 N. Lake Dr., Milwaukee 53211.

Holy Hill Retreat Center, Hubertus 53033.

Holy Name Retreat House (m), Chambers Island; mailing address, 131 S. Madison St., P.O. Box 337, Green Bay 54305.

Jesuit Retreat House (m), 4800 Fahrnwald Rd., Oshkosh 54901.

Marynook — House of the Lord, 500 S. 12th St., Galesville 54630.

Monte Alverno Retreat House, 1000 N. Ballard Rd., Appleton 54911.

Mother of Perpetual Help, 1800 N. Timber Trail Lane, Oconomowoc 53066.

Our Lady of Spring Bank Manor, Cistercian Fathers, Oconomowoc 53066.

St. Anthony Retreat Center, Marathon 54448.

St. Benedict Center (ecumenical retreat and conference center), Fox Bluff, P.O. Box 5070, Madison 53705.

St. Vincent Pallotti Center, Rt. 3, Box 47, Elkhorn 53121.

Siena Center, 5635 Erie St., Racine 53402.

Wyoming: St. Stephen's Indian Mission (private), St. Stephen's 82524.

HOUSE OF PRAYER EXPERIENCE

(Source: Sister Ann E. Chester, I.H.M., HOPE Clearing Center, 70 W. Boston Blvd., Detroit, Mich. 48202: *Exploring Inner Space,* published by the Center.)

The purpose of the House of Prayer Experience (HOPE) movement is to help active religious and priests and lay persons to acquire a contemporary style of contemplative life for renewal, inner growth and a more joyful personal and communal life in the light of the Gospel.

The starting point of participation in the movement is an extended period, from several weeks to several years, of concentration on intensive prayer with a community — a house of prayer experience. The result sought is the development of a style of prayer and contemplation with a carry-over that integrates and permeates religion and life.

Background

HOPE is essentially a movement of the Spirit, a phase of the "New Pentecost" called for by Pope John XXIII. It was born in the hearts of apostolic religious women who were forced by ever-increasing apostolic demands to seek a deeper prayer-life. To meet this need, Father Bernard Haring, C.SS.R., recommended that at least one house of an active congregation have prayer as its essential service, adopting a life-style determined by the needs of prayer rather than by the demands of apostolic work. He took its name from the words of Isaiah, "My house will be called a house of prayer" (Is. 56:7). He first presented this concept at the annual meeting of the Conference of Major Superiors of Women Religious in 1965, offering it as an instrument for renewal in depth.

Early in 1968, the Immaculate Heart of Mary Sisters of Monroe, Mich., organized a clearing center to serve as a focal point for idea exchanges which preceded and led up to a national planning conference in the summer of that year. At the four-day meeting, 156 sisters from 96 congregations in the United States and Canada formulated the rationale of a House of Prayer.

To test the theory, the IHM Sisters sponsored a six-week House of Prayer Experience, called HOPE '69, involving 137 sisters from 19 congregations. Each summer since then an increasing number of these programs, some of them for intercommunity groups, have been sponsored.

Priests of the Detroit archdiocese took part in a Praying-Living-Sharing program in 1970, and similar programs, for Holy Cross Brothers, Carmelites and others, have been conducted since then.

Underlying the movement are the convictions that prayer is necessary to integrate religion and life, and that institutionalized and long-practiced forms of prayer and prayer life are not adequate for religious and priests engaged in apostolic ministries and of lay persons involved in the multiple concerns of life in the world. Hence the emphasis on new forms of prayer, the rejuvenation of traditional forms, and especially the development of a contemplative stance toward life.

Programs

The communities of houses of prayer consist of a relatively stable core of members with an authentic call to a deeper prayer life and of guests who come and go for shorter or longer periods of participation. The stability of the core group, while not a now-and-forever type of commitment, is such as to guarantee continuity in programs and the resources of experienced personnel in conducting them. Experience has shown that the ideal size of a community is relatively small, from seven to nine members; also that, within limits, mixed groups are better than homogeneous ones for realizing the purposes of the movement. The importance of communities bound together by interpersonal relationships of spiritual depth rather than by institutional ties is paramount.

Program elements include the liturgy, meditation, scriptural reading and discussion, shared prayer in the shared life of community, silence and solitude, search for new forms of prayer and for new adaptations of traditional forms — all against the background of existential conditions.

Programs are flexible rather than predetermined, taking shape and finding expression in line with the particular charisms of the participants and their response to the Holy Spirit. In this respect, they differ from conventional retreat exercises and monastic practices.

This flexibility opens the way to particular thrusts with which programs become identified. Thus, some are known for their emphasis on forms of prayer and experience characteristic of charismatic renewal or for the adoption of practices of Eastern spiritual traditions, including yoga and Zen, as an aid to contemplation. Others are identifiable with programs stressing solitude and silence. One of the strongest thrusts is the ministry of prayer, to spread HOPE and to increase participation in its abbreviated (day-long, weekend, etc.) as well as extended programs.

All programs represent efforts to develop prayer and prayer experience in a community of interpersonal relationships which is open to dialogue and involvement with the Church and the world at large.

Representative Houses

Following is a partial list of houses representative of the movement and some of its thrusts. The total number is more than 60.

Visitation House (Immaculate Heart of Mary Sisters), 529 Stewart Rd., Monroe, Mich. 48161; guided retreats, spiritual direction.

Kresge House (intercommunity), 70 W. Boston Blvd., Detroit, Mich. 48202; orientation house, varied ministry of prayer.

Community of HOPE (intercommunity), Xavier Center, Convent Station, N.J. 07961; Pentecostal thrust.

Trinity Center (Missionary Servants of the Most Holy Trinity), 1190 Long Hill Rd., Stirling, N.J. 07980; ecumenical thrust.

Eastern Point House of Prayer, Eastern Point Retreat Center, Gloucester, Mass. 01930; Eastern spirituality thrust.

CANA, PRE-CANA

These special-purpose conferences are not a part of retreat programs, and the movement they represent is not related to the retreat movement. With the latter, however, they share the purpose of deepening religious experience.

Cana Conferences: Cana Conferences for married couples focus on four general areas: the relationships between husband and wife, parents and children, God and the family, society and the family. Treatment of these subjects, techniques of presentation, methods of discussion, and integrated religious activities are determined by the ordinary or special interests of different conference groups. Priests, medical doctors, marriage experts from other disciplines, and married couples may serve as lecturers or discussion leaders. Most conference groups are open to mixed-religion couples.

In some areas, Cana Clubs develop from conference activity. They consist of not more than six couples who meet regularly to discuss the apply principles of Christian Family life to daily living. The movement, called Cana after the marriage feast at Cana (Jn. 2:1-11), traces its origin to Family Renewal Days given in 1943 in New York City by Father John P. Delaney, S.J. The name was changed to Cana Conference by Father Edward Dowling, S.J. The bishops of the United States, in their annual statement in 1949, commended the conferences and urged their promotion throughout the country.

The movement is autonomous and has no central headquarters. It is serviced nationally by the Family Life Division of the US Catholic Conference.

Pre-Cana Conferences: These pre-marriage conferences for engaged couples are analogous to Cana Conferences for married couples, Their purpose is a spiritual, intellectual, emotional, and practical preparation for Christian marriage.

Lay Persons and Their Apostolate

The identity and role of lay persons in the life and mission of the Church were defined in two documents issued by the Second Vatican Council.

According to the *Dogmatic Constitution on the Church* (No. 31):

"The term laity is here understood to mean all the faithful except those in holy orders and those in a religious state sanctioned by the Church. These faithful are by baptism made one body with Christ and are established among the People of God. They are in their own way made sharers in the priestly, prophetic, and kingly functions of Christ. They carry out their own part in the mission of the whole Christian people with respect to the Church and the world.

"A secular quality is proper and special to laymen. . . .

"The laity, by their very vocation, seek the kingdom of God by engaging in temporal affairs and by ordering them according to the plan of God. They live in the world, that is, in each and in all of the secular professions and occupations. They live in the ordinary circumstances of family and social life, from which the very web of their existence is woven.

"They are called there by God so that by exercising their proper function and being led by the spirit of the gospel they can work for the sanctification of the world from within, in the manner of leaven. In this way they can make Christ known to others, especially by the testimony of a life replendent in faith, hope, and charity. The layman is closely involved in temporal affairs of every sort. It is therefore his special task to illumine and organize these affairs in such a way that they may always start out, develop, and persist according to Christ's mind, to the praise of the Creator and the Redeemer."

Call to the Apostolate

In its *Decree on the Lay Apostolate,* the council developed these concepts and outlined the principal features of this apostolate.

"Incorporated into Christ's Mystical Body through baptism and strengthened by the power of the Holy Spirit through confirmation, they are assigned to the apostolate by the Lord Himself. They are consecrated into a royal priesthood and a holy people (cf. 1 Pt. 2:4-10) in order that they may offer spiritual sacrifices through everything they do, and may witness to Christ throughout the world. . . .

"The apostolate is carried on through the faith, hope, and charity which the Holy Spirit diffuses in the hearts of all members of the Church. Indeed, the law of love, which is the Lord's greatest commandment, impels all the faithful to promote God's glory through the

spread of His kingdom and to obtain for all men that eternal life which consists in knowing the only true God and Him whom He sent, Jesus Christ (cf. Jn. 17:3). On all Christians therefore is laid the splendid burden of working to make the divine message of salvation known and accepted by all men throughout the world.

"For the exercise of this apostolate, the Holy Spirit who sanctifies the People of God through the ministry and the sacraments gives to the faithful special gifts as well (cf. 1 Cor. 12:7), 'alloting to everyone according as he will' (1 Cor. 12:11). Thus may the individual, 'according to the gift that each has received, administer it to one another' and become 'good stewards of the manifold grace of God' (1 Pt. 4:10), and build up thereby the whole body in charity (cf. Eph. 4:16). From the reception of these charisms or gifts . . . there arise for each believer the right and duty to use them in the Church and in the world for the good of mankind and for the upbuilding of the Church. In so doing, believers need to enjoy the freedom of the Holy Spirit who 'breathes where he wills' (Jn. 3:8). At the same time, they must act in communion with their brothers in Christ, especially with their pastors" (No. 3).

"The layman's religious program of life should take its special quality from his status as a married man and a family man, or as one who is unmarried or widowed, from his state of health, and from his professional and social activity. He should not cease to develop earnestly the qualities and talents bestowed on him in accord with these conditions of life, and he should make use of the gifts which he has received from the Holy Spirit" (No. 4).

Goals and Methods

"The mission of the Church is not only to bring to men the message and grace of Christ, but also to penetrate and perfect the temporal sphere with the spirit of the gospel" (No. 5).

"The mission of the Church concerns the salvation of men, which is to be achieved by belief in Christ and by His grace. Hence the apostolate of the Church and of all her members is primarily designed to manifest Christ's message by words and deeds and to communicate His grace to the world. . . .

(The lay apostolate) "does not consist only in the witness of one's way of life; a true apostle looks for opportunities to announce Christ by words addressed either to nonbelievers with a view to leading them to faith, or to believers with a view to instructing them and strengthening them, and motivating them toward a more fervent life" (No. 6).

"The temporal order must be renewed in such a way that, without the slightest detriment to its own proper laws (and values), it can be brought into conformity with the higher principles of the Christian life and adapted to the shifting circumstances of time, place, and person. Outstanding among the works of this type of apostolate is that of Christian social action. This sacred Synod desires to see it extended now to the whole temporal sphere, including culture" (No. 7).

"The apostolate of the social milieu, that is, the effort to infuse a Christian spirit into the mentality, customs, laws, and structures of the community in which a person lives, is so much the duty and responsibility of the laity that it can never be properly performed by others" (No. 13).

"The individual apostolate . . . is the origin and condition of the whole lay apostolate, even in its organized expression, and admits

of no substitute" (No. 16).

"The group apostolate is highly important also because the apostolate must often be implemented through joint action, in both the church communities and various other spheres. For the associations established to carry on the apostolate in common sustain their members, form them for the apostolate, and rightly organize and regulate their apostolic work so that much better results can be expected than if each member were to act on his own" (No. 18).

"Deserving of special honor and commendation in the Church are those lay people, single or married, who devote themselves and their professional skill, either permanently or temporarily, to the service of associations and their activities" (No. 22).

USCC-RELATED AGENCIES

The following agencies are engaged in carrying out programs of the United States Catholic Conference. Additional agencies are reported in other Almanac entries.

Religious Education/CCD (Confraternity of Christian Doctrine): Its objective is the religious education of Catholic children who are not in Catholic schools, out-of-school youths and adults. Recent figures indicate that some five and one-half million Catholic children and youths participate in CCD programs from pre-kindergarten through high school.

The modern revival and expansion of the confraternity dates from publication of the encyclical *Acerbo Nimis* by St. Pius X in 1905. His directive that the CCD be established in every parish was incorporated in the Code of Canon Law and reaffirmed by the Second Vatican Council in the *Decree on the Bishops' Pastoral Office in the Church.*

The CCD is a parish-based organization operating under a priest-director and a board or commission of lay persons.

Responsibility for many details of a local CCD unit ideally rests with a lay coordinator or administrator who is a trained professional in theology and/or religious education. This is a recent development in religious education outside the parish school system. Another noteworthy new development in CCD programs is growing emphasis on training parents to prepare their children for reception of First Communion, penance and confirmation.

On the diocesan level, CCD work is coordinated by a director appointed by the bishop, with a staff of assistants — priests, religious, lay persons. In some dioceses, the program operates under an office of religious education or other agency with a similar title. The diocesan office oversees the work of local and regional units, conducts teacher-training courses, issues guidelines for a unified program, conducts diocesan or regional meetings for CCD teachers and other workers.

On the national level, Religious Education/CCD (formerly called the National Center of the Confraternity of Christian Doctrine and since 1969 under the Department of Education, US Catholic Conference) contributes in many ways to the operation of religious education programs throughout the country. On the international level, it participates in programs of the Congregation of the Clergy in the religious education field.

Publications under the direction of Religious Education/CCD include *Living Light,* published by Our Sunday Visitor, Inc., and other publications.

Rev. Thomas Kramer is representative for Religious Education/CCD in the Department of Education, USCC.

Offices are located at 1312 Massachusetts Ave. N.W., Washington, D.C. 20005.

National Council of Catholic Laity: Founded in 1971 by the National Council of Catholic Men and the National Council of Catholic Women. A federation of national lay organizations, diocesan lay councils, pastoral councils on the diocesan and parish basis and individual members. It sponsors national conferences, is a medium through which the laity may speak on issues, and is the counterpart to similar national bodies of priests and sisters. The NCCL publication is *People.*

Principal officers are Jean Eckstein, president; Thomas Simmons and Mrs. Peter Collora, vice-presidents.

Office of the president: 1415 William White Boulevard, Iowa City, Iowa 52240.

National Council of Catholic Men: A federation of more than 9,000 Catholic organizations of men. Through a parish service bureau and a network of diocesan councils, it provides programs of information and action, national conferences and leadership training, and a medium through which Catholic men may be heard nationally on matters of common interest. NCCM is a constituent of the National Council of Catholic Laity.

The president is William H. Sandweg.

Offices are located at 1312 Massachusetts Ave. N.W., Washington, D.C. 20005.

National Council of Catholic Women: A federation of some 10,000 organizations of Catholic women in the U.S.; founded in 1920. NCCW unites Catholic organizations and individual Catholic women of the U.S., develops their leadership potential, assists them to act upon current issues in the Church and society, provides a medium through which Catholic women may speak and act upon matters of common interest, and relates to other national and international organizations in the solution of present-day problems. It is an affiliate of the World Union of Catholic Women's Organizations.

Margaret Mealey is the executive director. The official publication is *Catholic Women*, issued 6 times a year.

National office: 1312 Massachusetts Ave. N.W., Washington, D.C. 20005.

National Catholic Rural Life Conference: Founded in 1923 through the efforts of Bishop Edwin V. O'Hara for the purpose of promoting the general welfare of rural people by a program of extensive services, publications and rural-related activities. Publications include the official monthly *Catholic Rural Life*.

The conference has approximately 5,000 members among rural pastors, farmers, teachers, sociologists, economists, agricultural agents and officials. There are 95 officially appointed diocesan rural life directors.

St. Isidore the Farmer is patron of the conference.

Archbishop Ignatius J. Strecker of Kansas City, Kans., is president. Rev. John J. McRaith is the executive director; Msgr. John G. Weber, executive secretary.

National headquarters are located at 3801 Grand Ave., Des Moines, Ia. 50312.

National Catholic Community Service: Established by the US hierarchy in November, 1940, to serve members of the armed forces, defense production workers and their families. It has continued since then to serve the spiritual, social, welfare and recreational needs of the nation's defense forces, and patients in Veterans' Administration hospitals.

NCCS has responsibility for USO services through staff in locations in the United States and overseas. A VA program is in operation in 150 hospitals throughout the country.

During World War II, in cooperation with the United Service Organizations, NCCS conducted over 500 operations in this country and abroad. It is a member agency of the USO and of the VA Voluntary Service National Advisory Committee.

Alice C. Collins, is the executive director.

Headquarters are located at 237 E. 52nd St., New York, N.Y. 10022.

Catholic Relief Services—USCC: The official overseas aid and development agency of American Catholics; it is a separately incorporated organization of the U.S. Catholic Conference.

CRS was founded in 1943 by the bishops of the United States to help civilians in Europe and North Africa caught in the disruption and devastation of World War II.

Initially, CRS collected, purchased and shipped to war-torn countries huge quantities of food, clothing, medicines and other relief supplies which were distributed to hundreds of thousands of displaced persons, prisoners of war, bombed-out families, widows, orphans and other war victims.

As conditions in Europe improved in the late 1940s and early 1950s, the works conducted by CRS spread to other continents and areas — Asia, Africa and Latin America.

CRS maintains branch offices in 68 countries around the world and, because of its global network of strategically located warehouse facilities, is able to respond instantaneously to meet the needs of those afflicted by disaster or emergencies. Help is given to all those in need regardless of race, creed, color or political affiliation.

In addition to its highly acclaimed disaster relief work, CRS carries on day-to-day development programs in 55 of the poorest countries of the world. These programs, such as "food for work" projects, nutrition-health projects, school-feeding schemes, etc., are designed to help people help themselves and to raise the standards of living not only of the individual but of families and entire communities.

CRS operations are funded, for the most part, from the proceeds of an annual collection — The American Catholic Overseas Aid Appeal — held during the Lenten season in more than 15,000 Catholic churches in the U.S. Support is also received from private philanthropic foundations in the U.S., Europe and Australasia. Assistance from the federal government takes three forms: (a) food availabilities under Title II of Public Law 480; (b) defrayment of ocean freight costs on U.S. government-donated foods and all accredited relief supplies generated by CRS itself; and (c) grants for refugee relief and resettlement.

Each year, CRS also sponsors a nationwide clothing collection during the month of November that yields more than 15 million pounds of used clothing, blankets and material remnants.

In the year ending June 30, 1974, the CRS global program in 70 countries had a total value in excess of $154 million.

Bishop Edward E. Swanstrom, auxiliary of New York, is the executive director.

CRS headquarters are located at 1011 First Ave., New York, N.Y. 10022.

Family Life, USCC Department of Education: Established in 1931 as a central service agency for assisting, developing and coordinating family life programs throughout the United States. It provides information, program models, services and materials for marriage and family life education.

Rev. Donald Conroy is representative for

family life in the Department of Education, USCC.

Headquarters are located at 1312 Massachusetts Ave. N.W., Washington, D.C. 20005.

SPECIAL APOSTOLATES AND GROUPS

Apostleship of the Sea: An international Catholic organization for the moral, social and spiritual welfare of seafarers and those involved in the maritime industry. It was founded in 1920 in Glasgow, Scotland, and formally approved by the Holy See in 1922. It is promoted and directed by the Pontifical Commission for Migrants and Other Travelers, Piazza San Calisto 16, Rome, Italy 00153. The U.S. unit is the National Catholic Apostleship of the Sea Conference established in 1947. It serves 80 port chaplains in 73 U.S. ports on the seacoasts and the Great Lakes. Conference operations include a hospitality and welcoming program as well as counseling and spiritual services carried on by individual port chaplains through Catholic maritime clubs in New York, N.Y.; Mobile, Ala.; Lake Charles and New Orleans, La.; Oakland, San Francisco, San Pedro and Wilmington, Calif.; Seattle, Wash.; and interfaith clubs located in Chicago, Ill.; Milwaukee, and Green Bay, Wis.; Duluth, Minn.; Cleveland, O.; Newark and Port Elizabeth, N.J.; Norfolk, Va.; Jacksonville and Tampa, Fla.; Houston, Galveston, Corpus Christi and Brownsville, Tex. Recent developments have emphasized the interfaith cooperation on the port level in seamen's ministry. The episcopal promoter of the conference is Most Rev. Robert E. Tracy, P.O. Box 39, Lacombe, La. 70445. Rev. James P. Keating, port chaplain of Chicago, is national director and secretary. The national office is located at 9501 S. Ewing Ave., Chicago, Ill. 60617.

Catholic Central Union of America (1855): One of the oldest Catholic lay organizations in the US, the Union is devoted to the development and vigor of Christian principles in personal, social, cultural, economic and civic life. It was the first society ever given an official mandate for Catholic Action by a committee of the American bishops, in 1936. A bureau in St. Louis is the center for the separate but coordinated direction of the Union. The headquarters is also a publishing house (the monthly *Social Justice Review, The Catholic Woman's Journal,* other publications), a library of German-Americana and Catholic Americana, a clearing-house for information, and a center for works of charity. Aid is given to home and foreign missions, and maintenance and direction are provided for St. Elizabeth's Settlement and Day Nursery in St. Louis. Union membership is approximately 18,000. Joseph Gervais of Rochester, N.Y. is president; Harvey J. Johnson is director of the Central Bureau located at 3835 Westminster Place, St. Louis, Mo. 63108. (See also:

National Catholic Women's Union.)

Catholic Medical Mission Board (1928): Founded by Dr. Paluel Flagg and the Rev. Edward Garesche, S.J. Its purposes are to gather and ship medical supplies, and to recruit and assign medical and paramedical personnel to overseas mission hospitals and dispensaries. Since its foundation, it has shipped approximately 35 million pounds of supplies. In 1974, more than $5 million in medicines were shipped to 2,121 mission distribution centers in 36 countries. Also in 1974, 103 medical volunteers were placed in 16 countries; 31 additional volunteers were similarly assigned during the first two months. The Rev. Joseph J. Walter, S.J., is the director. Office: 10 W. 17th Street, New York, N.Y. 10011.

Center for Applied Research in the Apostolate (CARA): A research and development agency in the field of the Church's worldwide religious and social mission. Its purpose is to gather information for the use of decision-makers in evaluating the present status of the Church's mission of service and in planning programs of development toward greater effectiveness of its multiphased ministry in the future. CARA has research and planning programs focused on: church personnel (recruitment, selection training, utilization, effectiveness, retirement, health, due process); overseas areas, with respect to Africa, Oceania, Asia and Latin America; the campus ministry; urban affairs; social theology, diocesan planning, religious life, and other subjects. CARA was incorporated as a non-profit corporation in the District of Columbia Aug. 5, 1964. Offices are located at 1234 Massachusetts Ave., N.W., Washington, D.C. 20005.

Christian Family Movement (CFM) (1947): Originating in Chicago and having a membership of married couples, its purpose is to Christianize family life and create communities conducive to Christian family life. Since 1968, CFM in the US has included couples from all Christian churches. The International Confederation of Christian Family Movements has a membership of 135,000 couples. Ray and Dorothy Maldoon are the US national president couple. National and international headquarters: 1655 Jackson Blvd., Chicago, Ill. 60612. Spanish-speaking CFM, organized in 1969 under the title **Movimiento Familiar Cristiano (MFC),** serves some 2,000 couples in 42 major cities. Headquarters: 1655 Jackson Blvd., Chicago, Ill. 60612.

Christian Life Communities: Formerly

known as Sodalities of Our Lady, they are groups of men and women, adults and youth, joined with other people who are involved or wish to be involved in living their full Christian vocation and commitment in the world. The governing principles and operating norms of Sodalities were revised in the spirit of documents of the Second Vatican Council by the General Council of the World Federation of Sodalities in October, 1967. The new principles were confirmed, on an experimental basis, by Paul VI Mar. 25, 1968. In August, 1970, they were amended by the General Council and submitted to the Holy See for approval. The communities (5,000 in the world, 184 in the US) have greater freedom than previous rules permitted with respect to overall structure, spiritual program (although the Spiritual Exercises of St. Ignatius remain a specific source and characteristic of the spirituality), and apostolic endeavor. The US National Federation functions under lay officers and a board of directors composed of lay persons, priests and religious, with Bishop Louis Gelineau of Providence, R. I., as episcopal moderator. The World Federation office is located in Rome. National office: 3109 S. Grand Blvd., St. Louis, Mo. 63118.

Cursillo Movement: An instrument of Christian renewal designed to form and stimulate persons to engage in apostolic action individually and in the organized apostolate, in accordance with the mission which individuals have to transform the environments in which they live into Christian environments. The movement originated in Spain, where the first cursillo was held near Palma, Mallorca, in 1949. It was introduced in the US in 1957 and is functioning in more than 120 dioceses. The method of the movement involves a three-day weekend called a cursillo and a follow-up program known as the post-cursillo.

The weekend is an intensive experience in Christian community living centered on Christ and built around 15 talks (10 by laymen, five by priests), active participation in discussions and related activities, the celebration of the liturgy. The follow-up program focuses on small weekly reunions of three to five persons and larger group reunions, called ultreyas, in which participants share experiences and insights derived from their prayer life, study and apostolic action. The movement operates within the framework of diocesan and parish pastoral plans, and functions autonomously in each diocese under the direction of the bishop. Responsibility for growth and effectiveness rests with a diocesan leaders' school, a diocesan secretariat, or both. Most Rev. Joseph Green, former bishop of Reno, is episcopal advisor to the movement. Gerry Hughes is coordinator of the National Cursillo Center, P.O. Box 21226, Dallas, Tex. 75211.

Frontier Apostles (1956): Volunteers for a minimum of two years' service in their professional line (priests, sisters and seminarians, lay persons) in the Diocese of Prince George, British Columbia, Canada. More than 1,300 have served since the start of the corps by Bishop Fergus O'Grady; about 80 per cent of 160 now serving are connected with schools of the diocese. Address: Bishop O'Grady, College Rd., Prince George, B.C., Canada.

Grail, The (1921): An international movement of women concerned about the full development of all peoples, working in education, social and cultural areas. Founded by Rev. Jacques van Ginneken, S.J., in The Netherlands, it was introduced in the US in 1940. Grail participants include women from Australia, Belgium, Brazil, Canada, East Africa, Egypt, France, Germany, India, Indonesia, Italy, Japan, Mexico, The Netherlands, Philippines, Portugal, Scotland, South Africa, Switzerland, United States, West Africa. Chairman of the Coordinating Committee, US Grail: Mary A. Kane, US headquarters: Grailville, Loveland, Ohio 45140. International Secretariat: 5, rue Sayed Sokkar, Matareya, Cairo, Egypt.

Group 7 (1971): Started by the Glenmary Home Missioners to recruit Catholic men and women 21 years of age and older for periods of two years or more in the US home mission apostolate, particularly in the 17-state area of Appalachia, the South and Southeast. The purpose of participants is to give individual and group witness to Christian faith in personal and family life, work of their own choice, and community activities. The sponsoring Missioners prepare members for the apostolate, assist them with ongoing educational and instructional programs, and keep them in touch with each other through regular communications. Headquarters: Box 686, Sylva, N.C. 28779.

International Liaison (1965): A placement office for volunteer lay personnel sponsored by the Archdiocese of Newark. It provides liaison services between volunteers and missions and voluntary agencies, with respect to programs in operation in the US and abroad, and has working relations with sister orders in various US dioceses, Canada and campus ministries. In 1973, Maryknoll (Catholic Foreign Mission Society of America) affiliated with International Liaison. Father George Mader is the director. Office: 39 Lackawanna Pl., Bloomfield, N.J. 07003.

Jesuit Volunteer Corps (1956): Established by the Oregon Province of the Jesuits, for service to the underprivileged. There are 250 volunteers working among Eskimos and Indians in Alaska; Indians in the Western states; in inner-city areas, primarily in the Northwest; in Zambia, Africa; in Micronesia and in some Northwest Jesuit high schools. The Rev. L. Gooley, S.J., is the director. Headquarters: P.O. Box 3928, Portland Ore. 97208.

Lay Mission-Helpers Association (1955): It

trains and assigns men and women for work in overseas apostolates for periods of three years. In 1974, 57 members were in overseas assignments and four in home missionsm Overseas assignments included a wide variety of work in Cameroons, Ghana, Kenya, Malawi, Papua-New Guinea, Republic of South Africa, Lesotho, Rhodesia, Sierra Leone, Tanzania, West Irian, Thailand and Micronesia. Affiliated is the Mission Doctors Association, which recruits, prepares and sends Catholic physicians and their families, to mission hospitals and clinics throughout the world for tours of three years. The Rev. Msgr. Lawrence O'Leary is director of both associations. Headquarters: 1531 West Ninth St., Los Angeles, Calif. 90015.

Legion of Mary (1921): Founded at Dublin, its purposes are exclusively spiritual, viz., the sanctification of its members and service to others. It is one of the largest lay organizations in the Church. US address for information: The Legion of Mary, St. Louis Regional Senatus, Box 1313, St. Louis, Mo. 63188. The supreme governing body has offices at De Montfort House, North Brunswick St., Dublin 7, Ireland.

Movement for a Better World (1952): An international movement founded by Rev. Riccardo Lombardi, S.J. Its U.S. contingent of some 20 persons conducts retreats with a distinctive communitarian thrust for the purpose of motivating Christian witness and action for making a better world. U.S. office: 8555-16th St., Suite 402, Silver Spring, Md. 20910. The movement publishes *Atmosphere.*

Opus Dei: An association of Catholic faithful who strive to practice the Christian virtues, in their own states in life and through the exercise of their own professions or occupations in order to carry on an apostolate of witness to Christ. Since the purpose is strictly spiritual, members are free to hold the most diverse views on temporal matters, thus assuring a real pluralism of opinions in all cultural, economic, political and similar areas. Founded by Msgr. Josemaria Escriva de Balaguer in 1928 in Spain, it received full approval from the Holy See June 16, 1950. Members of more than 80 nationalities from all continents form separate branches for men and women. In the US, Opus Dei conducts corporate works in the East, Midwest and on the West coast. The directors' offices are located at 944 Park Ave. (Suite 1400), New York, N.Y. 10028. Elsewhere, the association conducts universities, training schools for farmers and workers, and numerous educational and charitable centers.

Pax Christi (1948): International Catholic peace movement. Originated in Lourdes, France, as a union of French and German Catholics to symbolize a mutual effort to heal wounds inflicted by World War II, spread to Poland and Italy, and acquired its international title when it merged with the English organization Pax. A general secretariat is located at The Hague, The Netherlands. **Pax Christi-USA,** established in 1973, has a membership of 400. Eileen Egan and Gordon C. Zahn are co-chairpersons. *Thirdly Publication* is issued three times a year. Address: 1335 N St. N.W., Washington, D.C. 20005.

Regis College Lay Apostolate (1950): Founded by Sister Mary John Sullivan, C.S.J., it enlists college graduates for a year of teaching service in home and overseas missions. More than 450 lay apostles from Regis College and more than 400 from other colleges have served since the beginning of the program. Headquarters: Regis College, Weston, Mass. 02193

St. Joan's International Alliance (1911): An organization and movement for equal opportunities for women as well as men in all fields — social, economic, political, cultural — and for full participation of women in the service of the Church. It originated in London, England, as The Catholic Women's Suffrage Society, became an international organization with the present title in 1931 and a member of the Conference of International Catholic Organizations in 1973. Membership is open to men and women. The alliance has consultative status with the United Nations. The international secretariat is located in Geneva, Switzerland. The U.S. branch was founded in 1965; its president is Bernice McNeela, P.O. Box 856, Waukegan, Ill. 60085. The press information officer is Frances McGillicuddy, 435 W. 119 St., New York, N.Y. 10027.

Southwest Volunteer Apostolate: Recruits and places volunteers for work among the Indians and Spanish-speaking of the Diocese of Gallup. The executive secretary is Fred Reed. Mailing address: P. O. Box 626, Gallup, N.M.

Young Christian Movement (YCM) (1812): An international apostolic movement, formerly known as the Young Christian Workers, which seeks to train and involve young adults, single and between the ages of 18 and 30, in a variety of people-oriented situations. Groups meet weekly to discuss social and moral issues and to become involved in the solution of problems affecting their individual lives and the community. Membership is international, in 91 countries. The assistant national chaplain is Father Patrick J. O'Connor. The national office is located at 1655 W. Jackson Blvd., Chicago, Ill. 60612. International headquarters: Brussels, Belgium.

Center of Concern (1972): An independent, public-interest group engaging in analysis and advocacy relating to issues of global concern. Discussion is carried on within the framework of social justice. A newsletter, *Focus,* is published bimonthly. William F. Ryan, S.J., is director. Address: 3700 13th St. N.E., Washington, D.C. 20017.

LAOS: An ecumenical agency for training

and recruiting volunteers with professional skills for work in developing nations and in areas of need in the US. LAOS aims to increase public awareness of forces which dehumanize people and to promote action for a world of justice, brotherhood and peace. Address: 4920 Piney Branch Rd. N.W., Washington, D.C. 20011.

CATHOLIC YOUTH ORGANIZATIONS

Angelic Warfare Confraternity (Cord of St. Thomas Confraternity) (1649), 141 E. 65th St., New York, N.Y. 10021. Apostolate for preservation of personal chastity; St. Thomas Aquinas is its patron. Director, Brendan Larnen, O.P.

Black Christian Students (1968): 3517 W. 13th Pl., Chicago, Ill. 60623. For black youth in high schools and parishes in the Chicago area, with emphasis on the Christian dimension of black identity, awareness, culture and future directives. BCS, with plans to spread elsewhere, originated from a group in Young Christian Students, with which it maintains liaison. National Coordinator, Maurice Blackwell; liaison (with YCS), Rev. Vincent J. Giese.

Boy Savior Youth Movement (1874): 30 W. 16th St., New York, N.Y. 10011; 18,000 in 55 schools.

Boy Scouts in the Catholic Church: The National Catholic Committee on Scouting works in cooperation with the Boy Scouts of America, North Brunswick, N.J., in promoting the basic principles of Catholicism among more than one million Catholics among the BSA membership of six million. *Boy's Life.* Committee Chairman, Thomas F. Hawkins, Oak Brook, Ill. National chaplain, Rev. John M. Rice, Messmer High School, 742 W. Capitol Dr., Milwaukee, Wis. 53206.

Camp Fire Girls, Inc. (1910): 1740 Broadway, New York, N.Y. 10019. The Youth Activities representative of the USCC acts as advisor in matters pertaining to Catholic participation in the Camp Fire Girls program. To help young people learn and grow in their individual ways through participation in enjoyable activities. Open to girls from six through high school. Membership: over 600,000 (no exact statistics available on number of Catholic girls participating).

Catholic Central Youth Union of America: 3835 Westminster Pl., St. Louis, Mo. 63108. To develop lay leadership in Catholic social action. Membership: 12-25 age group—approximately 55.

Catholic Youth Organization (CYO): Name of official, parish-centered diocesan Catholic youth programs throughout the country. The National CYO Federation is a constituent member of the Youth Activities section, USCC; 1312 Massachusetts Ave. N.W., Washington, D.C. 20005. CYO promotes a program of spiritual, social and physical activities. The original CYO was organized by Bishop Bernard Sheil of Chicago in 1930.

Columbian Squires (1925): P. O. Drawer 1670, New Haven, Conn. 06507. Junior organization of the Knights of Columbus. To train and develop leadership through active participation in well-organized four-point program of activities. Membership: 13- to 18-year-old Catholic boys. More than 800 circles (local units) active in the U.S., Canada, Puerto Rico, Mexico and the Philippines. *Columbian Squires,* monthly. Director, William L. Piedmont.

Forest Rangers, Catholic Order of Foresters: 305 W. Madison St., Chicago, Ill. 60606. To develop physical, mental and moral lives of members. *Catholic Forester.* Membership: youth up to 16 years of age—approximately 39,000 in 1,170 subordinate courts in U.S. High Chief Ranger, Louis E. Caron.

Girl Scouts of the U.S.A.: 830 Third Ave., New York, N.Y. 10022. Girls from most archdioceses and dioceses in the US and its possessions participate in Girl Scouting. The Youth Activities section, USCC, cooperates with Girl Scouts of the U.S.A. *Girl Scout Leader; The American Girl.* Membership: more than three million (no exact statistics available on number of Catholic girls participating).

Junior Catholic Daughters of America: 10 W. 71st St., New York, N.Y. 10023. A major department of the Catholic Daughters of America. Promote spiritual, cultural and recreational activities under proper leadership; develop articulate Catholic leadership. Membership: Juniors (11 to 18 years old); Juniorettes (6 to 11 years old). National Director, Miss Carole Kelly.

Junior Daughters of Isabella: 375 Whitney Ave., New Haven, Conn. 06511. To promote religious, educational, civic and athletic training of Catholic girls. Membership: Catholic girls 10-22 in junior circles in 11 states and one foreign country.

League of Tarcisians of the Sacred Heart (1917): 3 Adams St., Fairhaven, Mass. 02719. Organize children in their schools as junior apostles of the Sacred Heart. Director, Rev. Francis Larkin, SS. CC.

National Catholic Forensic League (1952): To develop articulate Catholic leaders through an inter-diocesan program of speech and debate activities. *Newsletter,* quarterly. Membership: 900 schools; membership open to Catholic, private and public schools through the local diocesan league. President (1974-76), Robert J. Prior, Msgr. McClancy High School, 71-06 31st Ave., East Elmhurst, N.Y. 11370.

National Christ Child Society Inc. (1886): 5151 Wisconsin Ave. N.W., Washington, D.C. 20016. Founder, Mary V. Merrick. A welfare organization for the care of underprivileged children. Membership: approximately 10,000 adult and junior members in 33 cities in US. President, Mrs. Robert Rasmussen.

Pontifical Association of the Holy Childhood (1843): 800 Allegheny Ave., Pittsburgh, Pa. 15233. Provides mission education programs and materials to children in Catholic elementary schools and religious education programs. *It's Our World*, 4 times a year. National Director, Rev. Francis W. Wright, C.S.Sp.

St. Dominic Savio Classroom Club: Don Bosco, Filor's Lane, West Haverstraw, N.Y. 01993. To promote a program of spiritual, intellectual and recreational activities. *Notes to Savios*, monthly. Membership: students in grades three through ten — 14,000 members, 500 unit clubs, and more than one million in Lay Savio Movement (past Savios) throughout the world.

Young Christian Students: 1655 W. Jackson Blvd., Chicago, Ill. 60612. A student movement for Christian social change. Membership: 500 in high schools and parishes.

Fraternities and Sororities

Alpha Delta Gamma (1924): P. O. Box 54321, Los Angeles, Calif. 90054. Fraternity. *Alphadelity*. Membership: 6,760 in 18 college chapters and 11 alumni associations.

Delta Epsilon Sigma (1939): Loras College, Dubuque, Ia. 52001. National scholastic honor society for students, faculty and alumni of Catholic colleges and universities. Membership: 20,105 in 100 chapters. Secretary, Rev. Dr. Neil W. Tobin.

Kappa Gamma Pi (1926): A national Catholic college women's honor society for graduates who, in addition to academic excellence,

have shown outstanding leadership in extracurricular activities. *Kappa Gamma Pi News*, quarterly. Membership: approximately 16,000 in 123 colleges; 40 alumnae chapters in metropolitan areas. National Moderator, Rev. Cyril F. Meyer, C.M., St. John's Univ., Jamaica, N.Y. 11432. President, Dr. Sally Ann Vonderbrink, 5747 Colerain Ave., Cincinnati, O. 45239.

Phi Kappa Theta (1959): 332 Main St., Worcester, Mass. 01608. National collegiate fraternity with a Catholic heritage. Continuation of Phi Kappa Fraternity, founded at Brown Univ. in 1889, and Theta Kappa Phi Fraternity, founded at Lehigh Univ. in 1919. *The Temple Magazine* quarterly, and newsletter, *The Sun*. Membership: 4,000 undergraduate and 24,000 alumni in 75 collegiate and 25 alumni chapters. President, Rev. J. Raymond Favret. Executive Director, Robert L. Wilcox.

Youth Activities, USCC

The Youth Activities section of the Department of Education of the United States Catholic Conference, established in 1940, is a coordinating and service agency for Catholic youth work throughout the country.

The National CYO Federation is the organization within the section which serves diocesan organizations.

USCC Youth Activities maintains liaison with the U.S. Youth Council, the World Assembly of Youth, the World Federation of Catholic Youth and other groups.

Rev. Rudy Beranek is representative for Youth Activities.

Offices are at 1312 Massachusetts Ave. N.W., Washington, D.C. 20005.

ASSOCIATIONS, MOVEMENTS, SOCIETIES IN THE U.S.

(Principal source: Almanac survey.)

See Index for other associations, movements and societies covered elsewhere.

A

Academy of American Franciscan History (1944), Box 34440, Washington, D.C. 20034. Dir., Rev. Antonine Tibesar, O.F.M.

Academy of California Church History (1946), P.O. Box 1668, Fresno, Calif. 93717. Pres., Msgr. Denis J. Doherty.

Albertus Magnus Guild (1953). Society of Catholic scientists. Pres., Rev. William D. Sullivan, S.J., Boston College, Chestnut Hill, Mass. 02167.

American Benedictine Academy (1947). Scholarly Benedictine society. Pres., Rev. Bede Ernsdorff, O.S.B., St. Martin's College, Olympia, Wash. 98503.

American Catholic Correctional Chaplains Association (1952), 275 in 475 institutions. Pres., Rev. John Foley, Massachusetts Correctional Institution, Box 100, S. Walpole, Mass. 02032.

American Catholic Historical Association

(1919), The Catholic University of America, Washington, D.C. 20064. *The Catholic Historical Review*, quarterly. Pres., Rev. Robert I. Burns, S.J., Sec., Rev. Robert Trisco.

American Catholic Philosophical Association (1926), Catholic University of America, Washington, D.C. 20064; 1,600. *New Scholasticism*, quarterly, *Proceedings*, annually. Pres., Desmond J. FitzGerald, Nat. Sec., George F. McLean, O.M.I.

American Committee on Italian Migration (1952), 9 E. 35th St., New York, N.Y. 10016; 32,000. *ACIM Dispatch*, 4 times a year. Sec., Rev. Joseph A. Cogo, C.S.

American-Lithuanian Roman Catholic Federation (1906), 9050 S. Troy Ave., Evergreen Park, Ill. 60642; 150,000. Pres., Dr. Joseph B. Jerome.

Ancient Order of Hibernians in America, Inc. (1836); 120,000. *National Hibernian Digest*, bimonthly. Pres., John M. Keane; Nat. Sec., John W. Duffy, 235 Wadsworth Ave., New York, N.Y. 10033.

Apostleship of Prayer (1849-France; 1861-US): 114 E. 13th St., New York, N.Y. 10003.

Monthly Leaflet, 1,200,000. Promotes Daily Offering and Sacred Heart devotion.

Apostolate of Christian Action, P.O. Box 24, Fresno, Calif. 93707. *Divine Love,* quarterly. Pres., Stephen Oraze.

Archconfraternity of Christian Mothers (Christian Mothers) (1881), 220 37th St., Pittsburgh, Pa. 15201; over 3,400 branches. Monthly newsletter and quarterly bulletin. Dir. Gen., Very Rev. Bertin Roll, O.F.M. Cap.

Archconfraternity of Our Lady of Perpetual Help and St. Alphonsus (1871), 526 59th St., Brooklyn, N.Y. 11220. 1,250 branches.

Archconfraternity of Perpetual Adoration (1893), St. John's Abbey, Collegeville, Minn. 56321. Dir. Gen., Rt. Rev. John Eidenschink, O.S.B.

Archconfraternity of the Holy Ghost (1912), Holy Ghost Preparatory School, Cornwells Heights, Pa. 19020 (US headquarters). Nat. Dir., Very Rev. Henry J. Brown, C.S.Sp.

Association for Social Economics (formerly the Catholic Economic Association) (1941), De Paul University, 2323 N. Seminary Ave., Chicago, Ill. 60614; 1,000. *Review of Social Economy,* semiannually. Pres. Thomas Hailstones.

Association for the Sociology of Religion (formerly the American Catholic Sociological Society) (1938), Loyola Marymount University, Los Angeles, Calif. 90045. *Sociological Analysis,* quarterly. Exec. Sec., Dr. Loretta Morris.

Association of Catholic Trade Unionists (1937), 58 Washington Square South, New York, N.Y. 10012. Exec. Sec., John C. Donohue.

Association of Marian Helpers (1946), Stockbridge, Mass. 01262; 525,000, mostly in U.S. *The Marian Helpers Bulletin,* quarterly.

Association of Romanian Catholics of America (1948), 4309 Olcott Ave., E. Chicago, Ind. 46312.

B

Blue Army of Our Lady of Fatima (1946), Ave Maria Institute, Washington, N.J. 07882; world-wide membership. *Soul,* bimonthly. Pres., Bishop Joao Pereira Venancio of Leiria (Fatima), Portugal. U.S. Pres., Rev. Msgr. Anthony J. Connell.

C

Canon Law Society of America (1939), 1933 Spielbusch Ave., Toledo, O. 43624. To further research and study in canon law; 1,400. Pres., Rev. John T. Finnegan.

Cardinal Mindszenty Foundation (CMF) (1958), P.O. Box 11321, St. Louis, Mo. 63105. To combat communism with knowledge and facts. Exec. Sec., Eleanor Schlafly.

Catholic Accountants Guild of the Diocese of Brooklyn (1947), 611 Eighth Ave., Brooklyn, N.Y. 11211; 125. Mod., Rev. Msgr. Thomas G. Hagerty. Other similar guilds

have been established in a number of cities.

Catholic Aid Association (1878), 49 W. Ninth St., St. Paul, Minn. 55102; 73,000. *Catholic Aid News,* monthly. Fraternal life insurance society. Pres., F. L. Spanner.

Catholic Alliance for Communications (formerly Catholic Institute of the Press, 1944), 1011 First Ave., New York, N.Y. 10022. To foster Christian principles and action among working members of the communications fields. Pres., Thomas A. Brennan.

Catholic Alumni Clubs International (1957), To advance social, cultural and spiritual wellbeing of members. Membership limited to single Catholics with professional education; 7,000 in 50 clubs in U.S. and Canada. International Pres., R. S. Miller, Jr., 7052 Vernon Ave., St. Louis, Mo. 63130.

Catholic Apostolate of Radio, Television and Advertising (1954), 1011 First Ave., New York, N.Y. 10022; 1,700 in New York City. Pres., Anthony Cervini.

Catholic Art Association (1937), Box 113, Rensselaerville, N.Y. 12147; 800. Pres., Rev. Thomas W. Phelan.

Catholic Audio-Visual Educators Association (CAVE) (1953), Pres., Rev. Joseph Breslin, Cardinal O'Hara High School, Eagle and Spoul Rds., Springfield, Pa. 19064.

Catholic Aviation League of Our Lady of Loreto (1949), O'Hare International Airport, P.O. Box 66123, Chicago, Ill. 60666. Pres., Arthur Fennell.

Catholic Bible Society of America, Inc. (1957), P.O. Box 2296, Dallas, Tex. 75221. Place Bibles in hospitals of Diocese of Dallas and elsewhere. Pres. Mrs. James S. Adams.

Catholic Biblical Association of America (1936), Catholic University of America, Washington, D.C. 20064; 764. *The Catholic Biblical Quarterly.* Pres., Rev. Alexander DiLella, O.F.M.

Catholic Big Brothers, Inc. (of Archdiocese of New York) (1918), 1011 First Ave., New York, N.Y. 10022; Newsletter, quarterly. To provide opportunities for male identification to fatherless boys, 8-15 years of age, through services of qualified adult male volunteers.

Catholic Big Sisters, Inc. (of the Archdiocese of New York), 135 E. 22nd St., New York, N.Y. 10010. Voluntary organization providing adjunctive services to Family Court, for girls up to 16 and boys up to 10 years of age. Dir., Hortense Baffa.

Catholic Business Education Association (1945); 2,001. Vice-Pres., Sister Mary Matthew McCloskey, R.S.M., Box 1169, Vicksburg, Miss. 39180.

Catholic Commission on Intellectual and Cultural Affairs (CCICA) (1946), 620 Michigan Ave. N.E., Washington, D.C. 20064; 325. Exec. Dir., Rev. William J. Rooney.

Catholic Council on Working Life, 1307 S. Wabash Ave., Chicago, Ill. 60605. Pres., Martin Burns.

Catholic Daughters of America (1903), 10

W. 71st St., New York, N.Y. 10023; over 200,000. *Share Magazine.* Nat. Regent, Mrs. Winifred L. Trabeaux.

Catholic Evidence Guild (1918, in England; 1931, in US), c/o 127 W. 31st St., New York, N.Y. 10001. Lay movement for spread of Catholic truth by means of outdoor speaking.

Catholic Family Life Insurance (1868), 1572 E. Capitol Dr., Milwaukee, Wis. 53211; 44,000. *The Family Friend,* quarterly. Pres., David L. Springob.

Catholic Guardian Society (1913), 1011 First Ave., New York, N.Y. 10022. Exec. Dir., James P. O'Neill.

Catholic Home Bureau for Dependent Children (1898), 1011 First Ave., New York, N.Y. 10022. Exec. Dir., Sr. M. Una McCormack.

Catholic Interracial Council of New York, Inc. (1934), 55 Liberty St., New York, N.Y. 10005. *Interracial Review,* quarterly. Pres., Paul R. Screvane, Exec. Dir., John J. Garra.

Catholic Interracial Councils: See National Catholic Conference for Interracial Justice.

Catholic Knights of America (1877), 217 E. 8th St., Cincinnati, O. 45202; 19,560. *Catholic Knights of America Journal,* monthly. Fraternal insurance society.

Catholic Knights of St. George (1881), 709 Brighton Rd., Pittsburgh, Pa. 15233; 67,000. *Knight of St. George,* monthly. Fraternal insurance society. Pres., Joseph J. Miller.

Catholic Kolping Society (1923), 125 N. Stratton La., Mt. Prospect, Ill. 60056; 2,195. *Kolping Banner,* monthly. Fraternal society.

Catholic Lawyers' Guild. Organization usually on a diocesan basis, under different titles.

Catholic League (1943), 1200 N. Ashland Ave., Chicago, Ill. 60622. Exec. Dir., Most Rev. Alfred Abramowicz.

Catholic Library Association (1921), 461 W. Lancaster Avenue, Haverford, Pa., 19041; 4,000. *Catholic Library World,* monthly (Sept.-April), bimonthly (May-June, July-Aug.); *Catholic Periodical and Literature Index.* Pres., James C. Cox, Exec. Dir., Matthew R. Wilt.

Catholic Near East Welfare Association (Near East Missions) (1926), 1011 First Ave., New York, N.Y. 10022. *Near East Missions,* weekly column in 90 diocesan newspapers. Aids missionary activity in 18 countries (under jurisdiction of the Sacred Congregation for the Oriental Church) in Europe, Africa and Asia, including the Holy Land. Nat. Sec., Rev. Msgr. John G. Nolan.

Catholic Negro-American Mission Board (1907), 335 Broadway, Room 1102, New York, N.Y. 10013; 15,000. *Educating in Faith,* monthly. Dir., Rev. Benjamin M. Horton, S.S.J.

Catholic One Parent Organization (COPO) (1961), 39 Lackawanna Pl., Bloomfield, N.J. 07003. To give widows and widowers an opportunity to meet others in the same situation, blending social and spiritual programs. Moderator, Rev. Joseph M. Doyle.

Catholic Order of Foresters (1883), 305 W. Madison St., Chicago, Ill. 60606; 178,634 in 28 states. *The Catholic Forester,* bimonthly. Fraternal and insurance society. High Chief Ranger, Louis E. Caron.

Catholic Pamphlet Society (1938), 2171 Fillmore Ave., Buffalo, N.Y. 14214. Dir., Rev. Paul T. Cronin.

Catholic Peace Fellowship (1964), North Broadway, Upper Nyack, N.Y. 10960; 6,500, *CPF Bulletin.* Peace education and action, development of the pacifist tradition within the Catholic Church. Nat. Sec., Thomas C. Cornell.

Catholic Press Association of the U.S., Inc. (1911), 432 Park Ave. S., New York, N.Y. 10016; 378. *The Catholic Journalist* bimonthly; *Catholic Press Directory,* annually; *Catholic Press Annual.* Pres., Jeremy Harrington, O.F.M., Exec. Dir., James A. Doyle.

Catholic Renascence Society (1940), c/o Exec. Sec., Sister Celestine Cepress, Viterbo College, La Crosse, Wis. 54601. *Renascence,* quarterly.

Catholic School Press Association (1931), 1135 W. Kilbourn Ave., Milwaukee, Wis. 53233. *Catholic School Editor,* quarterly. Dir., Warren G. Bovee.

Catholic Theological Society of America (1946), Office of Secretary, St. Mary of the Lake Seminary, Mundelein, Ill. 60060; 1,092. *Proceedings,* annually. Pres., Rev. Avery Dulles, S.J. (1975-1976).

Catholic Traditionalist Movement (1964), 210 Maple Ave., Westbury, N.Y. 11590.

Catholic Truth Society (1922), 2816 E. Burnside St., Portland, Ore. 97214.

Catholic Union of the Sick in America, Inc. (CUSA) (1947), 184 E. 76th St., New York, N.Y. 10021; 1,200. Admin. Leader, Rev. Joseph La Montagne, S.S.S.

Catholic War Veterans (1935), 2 Massachusetts Ave. N.W., Washington, D.C. 20001; 2,000 posts, *Catholic War Veteran,* bimonthly.

Catholic Worker Movement (1933), 36 E. First St., New York, N.Y. 10003. *The Catholic Worker,* 9 times a year. Lay apostolate founded by Peter Maurin and Dorothy Day; has Houses of Hospitality in 17 U.S. cities and several communal farms in various parts of the country. Promotes pacifism and anarchism in that it is decentralist, and believes in what the popes have termed the principle of subsidiarity, urging decentralization in the school system, community control, and in the economic field credit unions, cooperatives and unions of workers and mutual aid.

Catholic Workman (Katolicky Delnik) (1891), New Prague, Minn. 56071; 18,202. *Catholic Workman,* monthly. Fraternal and insurance society. Pres. Rudy G. Faimon.

Catholic Writers' Guild of America (1919),

65 East 89th St., New York, N. Y. 10028; 200. Exec. Sec., Rev. Bernard J. McMahon.

Catholics United for the Faith (1968), 222 North Ave., New Rochelle, N.Y. 10801; 12,000 in 130 chapters in U.S., 5 in Canada and 1 in Rome. Pres., H. Lyman Stebbins.

Central Association of the Miraculous Medal (1915), 475 E. Chelten Ave., Philadelphia, Pa. 19144. *Miraculous Medal,* quarterly. Dir., Rev. Donald L. Doyle, C.M.

Chaplains' Aid Association, Inc. (1917), 1011 First Ave., New York, N.Y. 10022. Pres., Most Rev. Philip J. Furlong.

Christopher Movement (1945), 12 E. 48th St., New York, N. Y. 10017. Without formal organization or meetings, the movement stimulates personal initiative and responsible action in line with Christian principles, particularly in the fields of education, government, industrial relations and communications. Christopher radio and TV programs are broadcast by 4,000 stations; a million and one-quarter copies of *Christopher News Notes* are distributed seven times a year without subscription fee; 401 weekly newspapers carry the syndicated column *What One Person Can Do;* 24 daily newspapers carry the syndicated column *It's Your Life;* over two million copies of Christopher books are in circulation. Dir., Rev. Richard Armstrong, M.M.

Composers' Forum for Catholic Worship, Inc. (1970), P.O. Box 8554, Sugar Creek, Mo. 64054; 1,000. Research center for the creation of new music for the liturgy. Exec. Dir., Robert I. Blanchard.

Confraternity of the Immaculate Conception of Our Lady of Lourdes (1874), Box 561, Notre Dame, Ind. 46556.

Confraternity of the Most Holy Rosary: See Rosary Altar Society.

Convert Movement Our Apostolate (CMOA) (1945), formerly Convert Makers of America, St. Charles Seminary, 209 Flagg Place, Staten Island, N.Y. 10304. *Bulletin* quarterly. To train and assist lay persons on a parish level to discuss and present the Faith to interested persons on a one-to-one basis.

Crusade for a More Fruitful Preaching and Hearing of the Word of God, Inc. (1937), Allendale, N.J.; *Voices from the Pew,* 2 times a year for seminarians. Pres., Mrs. Barbara Durbin.

Czech Catholic Union of Texas (K.J.T.) (1889), 214 Colorado St., La Grange, Tex. 78945; 15,300. *Nasinec,* weekly, and *K. J. T. News,* monthly. Fraternal and insurance society. Pres., Amos Pavlik.

D

Damien-Dutton Society for Leprosy Aid, Inc. (1944), 214 Commercial Ave., New Brunswick, N.J. 08901; 25,000. *Damien Dutton Call,* quarterly. Provides medicine, rehabilitation and research for conquest of lepro-

sy. Pres., Howard E. Crouch, Dir., Sr. Mary Augustine, S.M.S.M.

Daughters of Isabella (1897), 375 Whitney Ave., New Haven, Conn. 06511; 120,000. Supreme Reg., Mrs. Marie Heyer.

E

Edith Stein Guild, Inc. (1955), Promotes Judaeo-Christian understanding and assists Jewish converts; 860. ESG *Newsletter.* Address, 144-80 Sanford Ave., Flushing, N. Y. 11355.

Enthronement of the Sacred Heart in the Home (1907), 3 Adams St., Fairhaven, Mass. 02719; over 2,000,000. Nat. Dir., Rev. Francis Larkin, SS.CC.

Eucharistic Guard for Nocturnal Adoration (1938), National Center, 800 North Country Club Rd., Tucson, Ariz. 85716. Dir., Rev. James T. Weber.

Eymard League (1948), 194 E. 76 St., New York, N.Y. 10021; approximately 26,000. *Eymard League Bulletin,* quarterly. Nat. Dir., Rev. Ralph A. Lavigne, S.S.S.

F

Family Communion Crusade, Inc. (1950), Barre, Mass. 01005. Exec. Dir., Rev. Hector C. Lemieux, S.S.S.

Family Rosary Crusade (1942), and **Crusade for Family Prayer,** 773 Madison Ave., Albany, N.Y. 12208. Dir., Rev. Patrick Peyton, C.S.C.

Federation of Diocesan Liturgical Commissions (1969), Pevely, Mo. 63070. *Federation Notes.* Exec. Dir., Rev. Maur Burbach, O.S.B.

First Catholic Slovak Ladies' Association, USA (1892), 24950 Chagrin Blvd., Beachwood, Ohio 44122; 100,000. *Fraternally Yours,* monthly. Fraternal insurance society. Exec. Sec., Frances L. Mizenko.

First Catholic Slovak Union (Jednota) (1890), 3289 E. 55th St., Cleveland, Ohio 44127; 115,097. *Jednota,* weekly. Exec. Sec., Stephen F. Ungvarsky.

First Friday Clubs (1936). Organized on local basis; about 90 clubs in US, others elsewhere. Objectives are to spread devotion to the Sacred Heart, encourage members to receive Holy Communion on First Fridays and to meet at breakfast, luncheon or dinner for discussions of Catholic interest.

Franciscan Apostolate of the Way of the Cross (1949), 174 Ramsey St., Paterson, N.J. 07501. Stations Crucifix available on request. Dir., Rev. Cassian J. Kirk, O.F.M.

Friendship House (1938), 21 E. Van Buren St., Chicago, Ill. 60605. *Community,* quarterly. Involved in human relations problems; working for social justice through nonviolence. Co-directors, Jean Bryan and Kevin Reed.

G

Gabriel Richard Institute (1949), 2315 Orleans Ave., Detroit, Mich. 48207. Conducts leadership technique courses in 18 dioceses.

Gregorian Institute of America (1942), 7404 S. Mason Ave., Chicago, Ill. 60638. Pres., Edward J. Harris.

Guard of Honor of the Immaculate Heart of Mary (1932), 135 West 31st St., New York, N.Y. 10001. An archconfraternity approved by the Holy See whose members cultivate devotion to the Blessed Virgin Mary, particularly through a daily Guard Hour of Prayer.

Guild of Catholic Lawyers (1928), Empire State Bldg., 350 Fifth Ave., Room 316, New York, N.Y. 10001; 600. Pres., Marion I. Guilfoyle.

Guild of Our Lady of Ransom (1948), 409 W. Broadway (Room No. 5), S. Boston, Mass. 02127. For aid to inmates and former inmates of Massachusetts prisons. Exec. Dir., and Treas., Rev. John J. Foley.

Guild of St. Paul (1937), 601 Hill'n Dale, Lexington, Ky. 40503; 13,542; Nat. Spir. Dir., Rev. Msgr. Leonard Nienaber; Pres., Robert Parks.

H

Holy Name Society (in US) (1909), 141 E. 65th St., New York, N.Y. 10021; 5,000,000. Promote reverence for and devotion to the Holy Name of Jesus and develop lay apostolate programs in line with renewal aims of the Second Vatican Council, Nat. Dir., Rev. Brendan Larnen, O.P.

Holy Name Society, National Association (NAHNS) (1970), 516 N. Front St., Minersville, Pa. 17954. Association of diocesan and parochial Holy Name Societies. Pres., James T. Flanagan; Exec. Sec., Stephen Andrusisian.

Hungarian Catholic League of America, Inc. (1945), 30 E. 30th St., New York, N.Y. 10016; local branches in 15 states. *Catholic Hungarian Sunday,* weekly.

I

Illinois Club for Catholic Women (1920), 820 North Michigan, Chicago, Ill., 60611. *Triune-News,* monthly. Pres., Mrs. Lydon Wild.

International Catholic Truth Society (1898); 407 Bergen St., Brooklyn, N.Y. 11217. Propagate and preserve the Faith by free distribution of Catholic literature.

Italian Catholic Federation of California, Central Council (1924), 678 Green St., San Francisco, Calif. 94133; 27,000; *Bollettino,* monthly. Sec., Armand De Martini.

J

John Carroll Society, The (1951), 1660 K St. N.W., Washington, D.C. 20006. Sec., Martin J. McNamara, Esq.

Judean Society, Inc., The (1966), 1097 Space Park Way No. 336, Mt. View, Calif. 94043; over 800; "Steps to Effective Living" program booklet, to enrich lives of divorced Catholics. Internatl. Dir. and Foundress, Frances A. Miller.

K

Knights of Peter Claver (1909), Claver Bldg., 1821 Orleans Ave., New Orleans, La. 70116; 17,000. *The Claverite,* bimonthly. Fraternal and aid society. Sup. Knight, Ernest Granger, Sr.

Knights of St. John, Supreme Commandery (1886), 6517 Charles Ave., Parma, O. 44129; Sup. Sec., Brig. Gen. Salvatore La Bianca.

Knights of St. John, Supreme Ladies' Auxiliary (1900), 831 Emmett St., Schenectady, N.Y. 12307; 15,000. Sup. Sec., Miss Adelaide Mahoney.

Knights of the Immaculata (1917), National Center, 8000 39th Ave., Kenosha, Wis. 53141; canonically established with international headquarters in Rome. A pious association for spiritual renewal, personal and social, under the patronage of the Blessed Virgin Mary.

L

Ladies of Charity of the United States, Association of (1960), 1849 Cass Ave., St. Louis, Mo. 63106; 34,000. International Association founded by St. Vincent de Paul in 1617. Pres., Mrs. Dow King, Jr.

League of St. Dymphna, National Shrine of St. Dymphna, Massillon, Ohio 44646. For persons with mental and nervous disorders. Director, Rev. M. M. Herttna.

Lithuanian Catholic Religious Aid, Inc. (1961), 64-09 56th Rd. Maspeth, N.Y. 11378; 194. To assist the persecuted Church in Lithuania. Pres., Most Rev. Vincent Brizgys.

Lithuanian Catholic Alliance (1889), 73 S. Washington St., Wilkes-Barre, Pa. 18701; 154 branches. *Garsas,* monthly. Fraternal insurance organization. Pres., Thomas E. Mack.

Little Flower Mission League (1957), P.O. Box 178, Cottonport, La. 71327. Sponsored by the Brothers of the Holy Eucharist.

Little Flower Society (1923), 11343 S. Michigan Ave., Chicago, Ill. 60628; 40,000, *Little Flower News,* monthly. Nat. Dir., Rev. Quentin Duncan, O. Carm.

Liturgical Conference, The, 1330 Massachusetts Avenue N.W., Washington, D.C. 20005. *Liturgy, Living Worship, Homily Service,* monthlies. Education, research and publication programs for vitalizing and enriching Christian liturgical life, and field service training program. Pres., Elizabeth G. Sullivan.

Loyal Christian Benefit Association (1890), 305 W. 6th St., Erie, Pa. 16512; 56,623. *The Fraternal Leader,* bimonthly. Pres., Miss Bertha M. Leavy.

M

Mariological Society of America (1949), 350. *Marian Studies,* annually. Maria Manor, 10300 - 4th St. N., St. Petersburg, Fla. 33702.

Markham Prayer Card Apostolate (Aposto-

late **To Aid the Dying**) (1931), Franciscan Sisters of the Poor, 60 Compton Rd., Cincinnati, Ohio 45215. Dir., Rev. Herman H. Kenning.

Men of the Sacred Heart (1964), 6026 W. Harwood Ave., Orlando, Fla. 32811; 2,500. *Social Reign,* quarterly; *MSH Newsletter,* monthly. Promote devotion to Sacred Heart. Pres., Albert Barone.

Missionary Association of Catholic Women (1916), 1425 N. Prospect Ave., Milwaukee, Wis. 53202. Pres., Mrs. Joseph Gockel.

Missionary Cenacle Apostolate (M.C.A.) (1909), 3501 Solly Ave., Philadelphia, Pa. 19136; about 1,000.

Missionary Union of the Clergy in the USA (1936), 366 Fifth Ave., New York, N.Y. 10001; *Worldmission,* quarterly. Nat. Dir., Most Rev. Edward T. O'Meara.

Morality in Media, Inc. (1962), 487 Park Ave., New York, N.Y. 10022; 43,000. Newsletter, 8 times a year. To stop traffic in pornography constitutionally and effectively, and promote principles of love, truth and taste in the media. Pres., Rev. Morton A. Hill, S.J.

N

National Alliance of Czech Catholics (1917), 2636 S. Central Park, Chicago, Ill. 60623; 450 parishes. Pres., Mrs. Victoria Voller.

National Association of Church Personnel Administrators (1973), Pres., Rev. Daniel Johnson, 149 Church St., Hamden, Conn. 06514, Sec., Rev. Patrick Sullivan, Box 51, Univ. of Notre Dame, Notre Dame, Ind. 46556.

National Association of Laity (1967), 638 E. 3rd St., Bloomsburg, Pa. 17815. Pres., Dr. Joseph Skehan.

National Association of Priest Pilots (1964), Pres., Rev. Richard Skriba, 5157 S. California Ave., Chicago, Ill. 60632.

National Catholic Bandmasters' Association (1953), Box 523, Notre Dame University, Notre Dame, Ind. 46556. *The School Musician Magazine.*

National Catholic Cemetery Conference (1949), 710 N. River Rd., Des Plaines, Ill. 60016. *The Catholic Cemetery,* monthly. Pres., Rev. Msgr. James P. McKay.

National Catholic Conference for Interracial Justice (1960), 1307 S. Wabash Ave., Chicago, Ill. 60605. *Commitment,* quarterly. Serves 150 Catholic human relations and urban affairs groups; sponsors educational programs on societal problems. Exec. Dir., Rev. James J. Sheehan.

National Catholic Development Conference (1968), 130 E. 40th St., New York, N.Y. 10016. Professional association of organizations and individuals engaged in raising funds for Catholic charitable activities. Pres., Rev. Edwin Dill, S.J. Exec. Dir., George T. Holloway.

National Catholic Guidance Conference

(1962), division of American Personnel and Guidance Association, 1607 New Hampshire Ave. N.W., Washington, D.C. 20009. 868; *Counseling and Values,* and *Newsletter,* quarterlies. Pres., James J. Lee, Univ. of Wisconsin, Madison, Wis. 53706.

National Catholic Music Educators Association (1942), Riggs Bldg., Suite 228, 7411 Riggs Rd., Hyattsville, Md. 20783; affiliate of NCEA; 4,583. *Musart,* quarterly during school year. Pres., Msgr. Donald J. Reagan, Exec. Dir., Sr. Jane Marie Perrot, D.C.

National Catholic Pharmacists Guild of the United States (1962), 325 members; *The Catholic Pharmacist.* Exec. Dir., John P. Winkelmann, 1012 Surrey Hills Dr., St. Louis, Mo. 63117.

National Catholic Society of Foresters (1891), 59 E. Van Buren St., Chicago, Ill. 60605; 76,693; *National Catholic Forester,* bimonthly. A fraternal insurance society. Pres., Mrs. Florence V. Welch.

National Catholic Stewardship Council (1962), 1234 Massachusetts Ave. N.W., Washington, D.C. 20005. To exchange ideas on ways and means of assisting those engaged in promotion of stewardship and support of the Church. Exec. Dir., Rev. Francis A. Novak, C.SS.R.

National Catholic Women's Union (1916), 3835 Westminster Pl., St. Louis, Mo. 63108; 28,000. *The Catholic Woman's Journal,* 10 times a year. Auxiliary of the Catholic Central Union of America.

National Center for Church Vocations (1969), 305 Michigan Ave., Detroit, Mich. 48226. Established by National Conference of Catholic Bishops and the Conferences of Major Superiors of men and women to coordinate Church vocations work in the U.S. Exec. Dir., Rev. Edward J. Baldwin.

National Church Goods Association, 6469 N. Nokomis Ave., Chicago, Ill. 60646. Pres., David R. Malhame.

National Clergy Conference on Alcoholism, 2749 N. Marshfield Ave., Chicago, Ill. 60614. Exec. Dir., Rev. John P. Cunningham.

National Federation of Catholic Physicians' Guilds (1927), 2825 N. Mayfair Rd., Milwaukee, Wis. 53222; 6,700 in 88 autonomous guilds in U.S. and Canada, *Linacre Quarterly.* Pres., John R. Cavanaugh, M.D.

National Federation of Laymen, Inc. (1968), P.O. Box 56058, Chicago, Ill. 60656; representatives in 31 regions of the U.S. Chairman, Edward J. Kraus.

National Guild of Catholic Psychiatrists, Inc. (1949), c/o E. Colbert, M.D., Editor of *Bulletin,* 2021 Santa Monica Blvd., Santa Monica, Calif. 90404; 350. To serve as a bridge between psychiatry and Catholicism. Pres., John Dobson, M.D.

National Organization for Continuing Education of Roman Catholic Clergy, Inc. (1973). Membership, 90 dioceses, 44 religious communities. Pres., Rev. Daniel Danielson, 6401

San Pablo Ave., Oakland, Calif. 94608.
Nocturnal Adoration Society of the United States (1882), 194 E. 76th St., New York, N. Y. 10021; 53,000 in 555 units. Nat. Dir., Rev. Hector C. Lemieux, S.S.S.

O

Order of the Alhambra, International (1904), 4200 Leeds Ave., Baltimore, Md. 21229. 11,000 in U.S. and Canada. Fraternal society dedicated to assisting retarded children. Supreme Commander, Anthony Comorat.

P

Paulist League (1924), 415 W. 59th St., New York, N.Y. 10019; 23,700. Dir., Rev. Edward J. Gorry, C.S.P.

Philangeli (Friends of the Angels) (1949 in England; 1956 in U.S.), 1212 E. Euclid St., Arlington Heights, Ill. 60004; approximately 500,000 in 60 countries. To encourage devotion to the angels. Nat. Dir., Rev. Emmett M. Walsh, C.S.V.

Pious Union of Prayer (1898), St. Joseph's Home, P.O. Box 288, Jersey City, N.J. 07303; 90,000. *Orphans' Messenger and Advocate of the Blind,* quarterly.

Pious Union of the Holy Spirit (1900), 30 Gedney Park Dr., White Plains, N.Y. 10605. Pres., Rev. Jerome McHugh, O.F.M. Cap.

Pontifical Mission for Palestine (1949), c/o Catholic Near East Welfare Association, 1011 First Ave., New York, N.Y. 10022. Field offices in Beirut, Lebanon, Jerusalem and Amman, Jordan. The papal relief agency for 1.5 million Palestinian refugees in Lebanon, Syria, Jordan, and the Gaza Strip. Distributes food, clothing, other essentials; maintains medical clinics, orphanages, libraries, refugee camp schools and chapels, the Pontifical Mission Center for the Blind (Gaza), the Pontifical Mission Libraries (Jerusalem, Bethlehem, Nazareth), the Epheta Institute for Deaf-Mutes (Bethlehem). Pres., Rev. Msgr. John G. Nolan.

Priests' Eucharistic League (1887), 194 E. 76th St., New York, N.Y. 10021; 17,500. *Emmanuel,* monthly. Nat. Dir., Rev. Paul J. Bernier, S.S.S.

Pro Maria Committee (1952), 22 Second Ave., Lowell, Mass. 01854. Promote devotion to Our Lady of Beauraing (See Index). Dir., Rev. J. Debergh, O.M.I.

The Providence Association of the Ukrainian Catholics in America (Ukrainian Catholic Fraternal Benefit Society) (1912), 817 N. Franklin St., Philadelphia, Pa. 19123. *America* (Ukrainian-English).

R

Raskob Foundation for Catholic Activities, Inc. (1945), Kennett Pike and Montchanin Rd., P.O. Box 4019, Wilmington, Del. 19807. Exec. Vice Pres., Gerard S. Garey.
Reparation Society of the Immaculate

Heart of Mary, Inc. (1946), 100 E. 20th St., Baltimore, Md. 21218. *Fatima Findings,* monthly. Dir. Rev. John Ryan, S.J.

Rosary Altar Society (Confraternity of the Most Holy Rosary) (1891, in US), 141 E. 65th St., New York, N. Y. 10021; 3,000,000. *The Rosary Bulletin,* monthly. Prov. Dir., Rev. Brendan Larnen, O.P.

Rosary League (1901), Franciscan Sisters of the Atonement, Graymoor, Garrison, N.Y. 10524. 1,600. *Sparks,* quarterly.

S

Sacred Heart League, Walls, Miss. 38680; 500,000. Promote devotion to the Sacred Heart; through the Auto League it promotes careful, prayerful driving. Dir., Rev. Gregory Bezy, S.C.J.

St. Ansgar's Scandinavian Catholic League (1910), 40 W. 13th St., New York, N.Y. 10011; 2,000. *St. Ansgar's Bulletin,* annually.

St. Anthony's Guild (1924), Paterson, N.J. 07509. *Anthonian,* quarterly. Dir., Rev. Salvator Fink, O.F.M.

St. Apollonia Guild (1958), 2186 Draper Ave., St. Paul, Minn. 55113. For Catholic dentists. Pres., Dr. Terrance L. Tri.

St. Jude League (1928), 221 W. Madison St., Chicago, Ill. 60606. *St. Jude Journal,* bimonthly. Dir., Rev. Mark J. Brummel, C.M.F.

St. Margaret of Scotland Guild, Inc. (1938), Graymoor, Garrison, N.Y. 10524; 2,200. Moderator, Bro. Gerard Hand, S.A.

St. Martin de Porres Guild (1936), 141 E. 65th St., New York, N.Y. 10021. Gen. Dir., Rev. Timothy Shea, O.P.

St. Thomas Aquinas Foundation of the Dominican Fathers of the United States (STAF), 141 E. 65th St., New York, N.Y. 10021. Nat. Mod., Very Rev. Thomas H. McBrien, O.P.

Seraphic Society for Vocations (1944), St. Joseph Franciscan Seminary, P.O. Box 245, Westmont, Ill. 60559. Dir., Bro. Robert Ruzicka, O.F.M.

Serra International (1938), 22 W. Monroe St., Chicago, Ill. 60603; 12,500 members in 380 clubs in more than 27 countries. *Serran,* bimonthly. Fosters vocations to the priesthood, and religious life, trains Catholic lay leadership. Formally aggregated to the Pontifical Society for Priestly Vocations, 1951. Pres., James E. Madigan.

Slovak Catholic Federation of America (1911), One St. Gabriel Circle (off Ingham and Gifford St.), Pittsburgh, Pa. 15212; 300,000. *Good Shepherd (Dobry Pastier),* monthly. The following fraternal organizations hold continuous membership: First Catholic Slovak Union, First Catholic Slovak Ladies Assn.; Slovak Catholic Sokol; Penna. Slovak Catholic Union; Ladies Penna. Slovak Catholic Union; First Slovak Wreath of the Free Eagle.

Slovak Catholic Sokol (1905), 205 Madison

St., Passaic, N.J. 07055; 51,965. *Katolicky Sokol,* weekly; *Priatel Dietok,* monthly.

Society for the Propagation of the Faith (1822), 366 Fifth Ave., New York, N.Y. 10001; 3,000,000 in 160 dioceses in US. *Mission,* bimonthly; *Worldmission,* quarterly. Is subject to direction of Sacred Congregation for the Propagation of the Faith. Nat. Dir., Most Rev. Edward T. O'Meara.

Society of Retired Catholic Persons (1962), 1100 W. Wells St., Milwaukee, Wis. 53233; 6,100. Organization for economic advantage, social activities and apostolic work for retired persons. Pres., Merlin Victora.

Society of St. Peter the Apostle for Native Clergy (1898), 366 Fifth Ave., New York, N.Y. 10001; 160 branches. Organized as the Pope's own mission aid society for the maintenance of diocesan seminaries and diocesan seminarians in mission countries.

Spiritual Life Institute of America (1961), Star Route One, Sedona, Arizona 86336. *Desert Call,* seasonal. An ecumenical movement to foster the contemplative spirit in America. Founder, Rev. William McNamara, O.C.D. Second foundation: Primitive Wilderness Hermitage, Kemptville, Yarmouth Co., Nova Scotia, Canada.

T

Te Deum International (1940), 611 S. 6th St., Springfield, Ill. 62701; 27 chapters. For Catholic adult education on current and international affairs.

Theresians of America (1961), 5326 E. Pershing Ave., Scottsdale, Ariz. 85254; 6,000. Spiritual, intellectual and apostolic organization concerned with the vocation to Christian womanhood in both religious and lay states. Nat. Dir. and founder, Very Rev. Msgr. Elwood C. Voss.

U

Una Voce in the United States (1967), P.O. Box 446, Grand Central Station, New York, N.Y. 10017; 5,000. Pres., John A. McManemin.

United Societies of U.S.A. (1903), 613 Sinclair St., McKeesport, Pa. 15132; 50,005 in 169 lodges in 7 states. *Unity,* quarterly newsletter. Pres., Nicholas M. Kish.

United States Catholic Historical Society (1885), Office of Corresponding Secretary, St. Joseph's Seminary, Yonkers, N.Y. 10704; 250. *Historical Records and Studies* and a monograph series, annually. Pres., Thomas A. Brennan.

V

Vernacular Society (1946), P.O. Box 207, Passaic, N.J. 07055; 500. *Vernacular,* newsletter. Pres., Reinhold Kissner.

W-Y

Western Catholic Union (1877), W.C.U. Bldg., 506-510 Maine St., Quincy, Ill. 62301;

27,110 in 117 branches in 9 states. *Western Catholic Union Record,* monthly.

William J. Kerby Foundation (1941), The Catholic University of America, Washington, D.C. 20017. Pres., Charles Cronin.

Wisconsin Council of Catholic Women (1915), 810 Farwell Dr., Madison, Wis. 53704. Pres., Mrs. Patrick McCormick.

Word of God Institute (1972), 487 Michigan Ave. N.E., Washington, D.C. 20017. For renewed biblical preaching. Dir., Rev. John Burke, O.P.

Young Ladies' Institute (1887), 50 Oak St., San Francisco, Calif. 94102. Grand Sec. Mrs. Sylvia O'Rourke.

Young Men's Institute (1883), 50 Oak St., San Francisco, Calif. 94102; 4,500. *Institute Journal,* bimonthly. Grand Sec., B. G. Merdinger.

Knights of Columbus

The Knights of Columbus, which originated as a fraternal benefit society of Catholic men, was founded by Father Michael J. McGivney and chartered by the General Assembly of Connecticut Mar. 29, 1882.

In line with their general purpose to be of service to the Church, the Knights are active in many apostolic works and community programs.

Since January, 1947, the Knights have sponsored a program of Catholic advertising in secular publications with national circulation. This has brought some 6 million inquiries and led to more than 600,000 enrollments in courses in the Catholic faith. In recent years the Knights have broadened this program to include other media for spreading Christian and religious ideals. As a result substantial contributions have been made to support the work of the John LaFarge Institute in New York, the Catholic Communications Foundation in New York, and the Center for Applied Research in the Apostolate (CARA) in Washington.

K. of C. scholarship funds — two at the Catholic University of America, another for disbursement at other Catholic colleges in the U.S., one at Canadian colleges and another for the Philippines — have provided college educations for more than 1,300 students since 1914.

The order promotes youth activity through sponsorship of the Columbian Squires and through cooperation with other organized youth groups.

K. of C. membership, as of Mar. 1, 1975, was 1,198,460 in 5,912 councils in the U.S., Canada, the Philippines, Cuba, Mexico, Puerto Rico, Panama, Guatemala, Guam and the Virgin Islands. Insurance assets, as of Dec. 31, 1974, amounted to $540,655,788 and total insurance in force, $2,930,225,282.

The Knights' publication, *Columbia,* has the greatest circulation (almost 1.2 million) of any Catholic monthly in the U.S.

John W. McDevitt is Supreme Knight. Virgil C. Dechant is Supreme Secretary.

International headquarters are located at One Columbus Plaza, New Haven, Conn. 06507.

BLACK CATHOLICS

The National Office for Black Catholics, organized in August, 1970, is a central agency with the general purposes of promoting participation by black Catholics in the Church and of making more effective the apostolate of the Church in the black community. Its executive director is Brother Joseph Davis, S.M. Its liaison officer with the National Conference of Catholic Bishops and the U.S. Catholic Conference is Auxiliary Bishop Joseph A. McNicholas of St. Louis. Offices are located at 734 15th St., N.W., Washington, D.C. 20005.

The NOBC has affiliates in various cities throughout the country and a participating membership of approximately 3,000.

Three of its member bodies are:

• The National Black Catholic Clergy Caucus, formed at a charter meeting in April, 1968, in Detroit. Its president, elected in January, 1973, is Auxiliary Bishop Joseph Howze of Natchez-Jackson. Brother Joseph C. Hager, S.M., is the executive director.

• The National Black Catholic Sisters' Conference (see separate entry).

• The National Black Catholic Lay Caucus.

The NOBC, in conjunction with these organizations, sponsored a National Black Catholic Convention in August, 1973, in New Orleans. "Forging Directions" was the theme of the meeting, the first of its kind held since 1894. It was attended by some 400 delegates.

A two-year campaign for the recruitment of black vocations to the priesthood and religious life was inaugurated July 1, 1973, by the NOBC. At that time, there were 171 black priests, two auxiliary bishops, 300 men studying for the priesthood, and 715 sisters. Black Catholics were estimated to number 900,000. Thirty black priests were pastors of all-black or predominantly black parishes. The number of such parishes were about 800.

A Black Catholics Concerned collection, principally in black parishes, was conducted for the second time Oct. 7, 1973, for the support of NOBC activities. Proceeds of the 1972 collection amounted to $209,000.

CATHOLIC RIGHTS LEAGUE

A group of Catholics concerned about anti-Catholic bias and bigotry in the United States announced in May, 1973, the formation of the Catholic League for Religious and Civil Rights.

Patterned after the Jewish Anti-Defamation League and the National Association for the Advancement of Colored People, its stated purpose is to promote and champion the rights of Catholics and of other religious minorities expressed in the Declaration of Independence and the Bill of Rights; and to adopt programs and procedures to correct discriminatory practices against Catholics and others because of their religion.

The major objectives of the league are:

• the right to life for the unborn child, the aged and the handicapped;

• the right of all people to worship according to their consciences without being subjected to ridicule and defamation;

• public assistance for parents who send their children to private schools;

• the right of all religious minorities to be free of religious discrimination;

• the right of doctors, nurses and hospital administrators to follow their consciences — without penalty — in refusing to perform or assist in abortions;

• the right of families to be free of perversion by pornographers and pushers of addictive drugs;

• the right of religious institutions to self-government, and to detemine their religious orientation in matters of policy and employment, where necessary, to preserve their identity and mission.

League founders made it clear that the organization has no official standing with the Church. They said its existence, operations and success would depend entirely on the funding and supportive activity of its membership, which was open to persons of all faiths but was expected to be mostly Catholic.

The league publishes *The Catholic League Newsletter.*

Father Virgil C. Blum, S.J., professor of political science at Marquette University, is president of the league. The executive director is Stuart D. Hubbell, an attorney of Traverse City, Mich. Mario S. Spalatin, an attorney of Milwaukee, Wis., is assistant executive director.

The league's mailing address is 1100 West Wells St., Milwaukee, Wis. 53233.

Jewish Sensitivity Sought

The Catholic League for Religious and Civil Rights appealed in its September, 1975, newsletter to U.S. Jews to show greater sensitivity to the Catholic position on government aid to students in nonpublic schools.

The league expressed agreement with a recent statement by Archbishop Joseph L. Bernardin, that insensitivity by Catholics to Jewish convictions about Israel "would be inexcusable."

"Yet," the letter stated, "five Jewish interest groups . . . committed their resources and statewide organizations in Maryland to the (successful) campaign to repeal . . . fair and constitutional legislation" providing bus rides and secular textbooks to students of Catholic schools.

Communications

Following are excerpts from a 23,000-word Pastoral Instruction on the Mass Media written by the Pontifical Commission for Social Communications and made public June 3, 1971. The most extensive document on the subject ever issued by the Vatican, it supplements and applies the contents of the much shorter Decree on the Instruments of Social Communication promulgated by the Second Vatican Council Dec. 4, 1963. The Latin title of the Instruction is Communio et Progressio ("Unity and Advancement"), from its first two words.

[These excerpts are from the text circulated by NC News Service.]

Purpose of the Media; "The unity and advancement of men living in society: these are the chief aims of social communication and of all the means it uses. These means include the press, the cinema, radio and television."

"In the Christian faith, the unity and brotherhood of man are the chief aims of all communication."

The Common Good: "The total output of the media in any given area should be judged by the contribution it makes to the common good."

Requirements of Communication: "Every communication must comply with certain essential requirements, and these are sincerity, honesty and truthfulness. Good intentions and a clear conscience do not thereby make a communication sound and reliable. A communication must state the truth. It must accurately reflect the situation with all its implications. The moral worth and validity of any communication does not lie solely in its theme or intellectual content. The way in which it is presented, the way in which it is spoken and treated, and even the audience for which it is designed — all these factors must be taken into account."

Every Man a Partner: "The torrent of information and opinion pouring through (the) channels (of communication) makes every man a partner in the business of the human race. This interchange creates the proper conditions for that mutual and sympathetic understanding which leads to universal progress."

Questions: "How can we ensure that (the) swift and haphazard and endless stream of news is properly evaluated and understood? The media are bound to seek a mass audience, and so they often adopt a neutral stance in order to avoid giving offense to any section of their audience. How, in a society that is committed to the rights of dissent, is the distinction between right and wrong, true and false, to be made?"

"How, in the face of competition to capture a large popular audience, are the media to be prevented from appealing to and inflaming the less admirable tendencies in human nature? How can one avoid the concentration of the power to communicate in too few hands, so that any real dialogue is killed? How can one avoid allowing communications made indirectly and through machinery to weaken direct human contact — especially when these communications take the form of pictures and images? When the media invite men to escape into fantasy, what can be done to bring them back to present reality? How can one stop the media from encouraging mental idleness and passivity? And how can one be certain that the incessant appeal to emotion does not sap reason?"

Public Opinion: "The means of social communication are a public forum where every man may exchange ideas. The public expression and the confrontation of different opinions that occur within this dialogue influence and enrich the development of society and further its progress."

"Public opinion is an essential expression of human nature organized in society."

"If public opinion is to emerge in the proper manner, it is absolutely essential that there be freedom to express ideas and attitudes. In accordance with the express teaching of the Second Vatican Council, it is necessary to declare unequivocally that freedom of speech for individuals and groups must be permitted so long as the common good and public morality are not endangered."

Propaganda: "The process of promoting — in what is sometimes referred to as a 'propaganda campaign' — with a view to influencing public opinion is justified only when it serves the truth, promotes causes that are in the public interest, and its objectives and methods accord with the dignity of man."

Weight of Opinions: "Not every opinion that is given publicity should be taken as a true expression of that public opinion which is held by a significant number of people. A number of differing opinions can flourish at the same time in the same area, although one usually has a greater following than the others. The opinion of the majority, however, is not necessarily the best or the closest to the truth."

"Views openly and commonly expressed which reflect the aspirations of the people should always be carefully considered. This is especially binding on those in authority, whether civil or religious."

Right To Be Informed and To Inform: "If public opinion is to be formed in a proper manner, it is necessary that, right from the start, the public be given free access both to the sources and channels of information, and be allowed freedom to express its own views. Freedom of opinion and the right to be informed go hand in hand."

"With the right to be informed goes the

duty to seek information. Information does not simply occur; it has to be sought."

"The right to information is not merely the prerogative of the individual; it is essential to the public interest."

Safety of Correspondents: "The safety of (news) correspondents should be ensured in every possible way because of the service they render to man's right to know about what is happening. This is particularly true in the case of wars, which involve and concern the whole human race. The Church utterly condemns the use of violence against newsmen or against anyone in any way involved in the passing on of news."

Privacy and secrecy: "The right to information is not limitless. It has to be reconciled with other existing rights. There is the right of privacy which protects the private life of families and individuals. There is the right of secrecy which obtains if necessity or professional duty or the common good itself requires it. Indeed, whenever public good is at stake, discretion and discrimination and careful judgment should be used in the preparation of news."

Advertising: Advertising must respect the truth, taking into account accepted advertising conventions."

"If harmful or utterly useless goods are touted to the public, if false assertions are made about goods for sale, if less admirable human tendencies are exploited, those responsible for such advertising harm society and forfeit their good name and credibility. More than this, unremitting pressure to buy articles of luxury can arouse false wants that hurt both individuals and families by making them ignore what they really need. And those forms of advertising which, without shame, exploit the sexual instincts simply to make money, or which seek to penetrate into the subconscious recesses of the mind in a way that threatens the freedom of the individual, these forms of advertising must be shunned. It is desirable that advertisers make definite rules for themselves lest their sales methods affront human dignity or harm the community."

"Serious harm can be done (to developing countries) if advertising and commercial pressure become so irresponsible that communities seeking to rise from poverty to a reasonable standard of living are persuaded to seek this progress by satisfying wants that have been created artificially."

News Reporting: "Not only must news reporting keep to the facts and bear down on the most important ones, but the meaning of what is reported should be brought out by explanation."

Censorship: "Censorship should be used only in the very last extremity."

Communication in the Church: "The Church looks for ways of multiplying and strengthening the bonds of union between her members. For this reason, communication and dialogue among Catholics are indispensable. The Church lives her life in the midst of the whole community of man. She must therefore maintain contacts and lines of communication in order to keep a relationship with the whole human race. This is done both by giving information and by listening carefully to public opinion inside and outside the Church. By holding a continuous discussion with the contemporary world, she tries to help in solving the problems that men face at the present time."

Dialogue and Public Opinion: "Since the Church is a living body, she needs public opinion in order to sustain a giving and taking between her members."

"Catholics should be fully aware of the real freedom to speak their minds which stems from a 'feeling for the faith' and from love."

"Those who exercise authority in the Church will take care to ensure that there is responsible exchange of freely held and expressed opinion among the People of God. More, they will set up norms and conditions for this to take place."

Freedom of Expression: "While the individual Catholic follows the magisterium (teaching authority of the Church), he can and should engage in free research so that he may better understand revealed truths or explain them to a society subject to incessant change."

Constructive Dialogue: "Free dialogue within the Church does no injury to her unity and solidarity. It nurtures concord and the meeting of minds by permitting the free play of the variations of public opinion. But, in order that this dialogue may go on in the right direction, it is essential that charity be in command even when there are differing views. Everyone in this dialogue should be animated by the desire to serve and to consolidate unity and cooperation. There should be a desire to build, not to destroy. There should be a deep love for the Church and a compelling desire for its unity."

Scientific Investigation and Doctrine: "Distinction must be borne in mind between, on the one hand, the area that is devoted to scientific investigation and, on the other, the area that concerns the teaching of the faithful. In the former area, experts enjoy the freedom required by their work and are free to communicate to others in books and commentaries the fruits of their research. In the second area, only those doctrines may be attributed to the Church which are declared to be such by her authentic teaching authority. These doctrines, obviously, can be aired in public without fear."

"It sometimes happens, however, because of the very nature of social communication, that new opinions circulating among theologians at times circulate too soon and in the wrong places. Such opinions, which might be confused with the authentic doctrine of the Church, should be examined critically. It must also be remembered that the real significance of such theories is often badly distorted by popularization and by the style of presentation used in the media."

Flow of Information in the Church: "Since the development of public opinion within the Church is essential, individual Catholics have the right to all the information they need to play their active role in the life of the Church."

The normal flow of life and the smooth functioning of government within the Church requires a steady two-way flow of information between the ecclesiastical authorities at all levels and the faithful as individuals and as organized groups. This applies to the whole world. To make this possible, various institutions are required. These might include news agencies, official spokesmen, meeting facilities, pastoral councils, all properly financed."

Attitude on Secrecy: "On those occasions when the affairs of the Church require secrecy, the rules normal in civil affairs equally apply.

"On the other hand, the spiritual riches which are an essential attribute of the Church demand that the news she gives out . . . be distinguished by integrity, truth and openness. When ecclesiastical authorities are unwilling to give information or are unable to do so, then rumor is unloosed; and rumor is not a bearer of the truth but of dangerous half-truths. Secrecy should therefore be restricted to matters that involve the good name of individuals or that touch upon the rights of people, whether singly or collectively."

Church-World Dialogue: "The Church needs to know contemporary reactions to ideas and events, whether they be Catholic or not. The greater the extent to which the means of social communication reflect these reactions, the more they contribute toward this knowledge required by the Church."

"It is the mission of those with responsible positions in the Church to announce without fail or pause the full truth by the means of social communication, so as to give a true picture of the Church and her life. Since the media are often the only channels of information that exist between the Church and the world, a failure to use them amounts to 'burying the talent given by God.' "

Media and the Gospel: "During his life on earth, Christ showed himself to be the perfect Communicator, while the Apostles used what means of communication were available in their time. It is now necessary that the same message be carried by the means of social communication that are available today. Indeed, it would be difficult to suggest that Christ's command was being obeyed unless all the opportunities offered by the . . . media to extend to vast numbers of people the announcement of his Good News were being used."

The Catholic Press: "The Catholic press . . . can be marvelously effective in bringing a knowledge of the Church to the world and a knowledge of the world to the Church. It does this by imparting information and by stimulating those processes by which public opinion is formed. There is, however, no advantage in founding new publications if quantity is achieved at the cost of quality and if the new injure the old."

"That part of the Catholic press which is of general interest published news and opinions and background articles about all the facets and the problems and worries of modern life. This it does in the light of Christian principles. It is the task of the Catholic press to balance, to complete and, if necessary, to correct the news and comments about religion and the Christian life."

CATHOLIC PRESS STATISTICS

The *1975 Catholic Press Directory,* published by the Catholic Press Association, reported 436 newspapers and magazines in the United States, Canada and the West Indies, with a total circulation of 23,492,737. The figures reflected an increase in the number of newspapers (+2) and an increase of circulation (+56,235); the number of magazines remained unchanged (282) but circulation increased (+669,245).

Newspapers

United States: 145; circulation, 5,109,119.
  National newspapers, 7; circulation, 661,583.
    (National Catholic Register, 87,539; *National Catholic Reporter,* 40,103; *Our Sunday Visitor,* 374,859; *Twin Circle,* 89,897; *The Wanderer,* 47,685; *El Visitante Dominical,* 13,000; *Priests — USA,* 8,500.)
  Diocesan newspapers, 138; circulation, 4,447,536 (includes 7 diocesan editions of *Our Sunday Visitor* with a circulation of 133,707).
Canada and the West Indies: 9, circulation, 154,062.
  National newspaper, Canada, 1 *(Our Sunday Visitor);* circulation, 15,424.
  Weekly newspapers, Canada, 6; circulation, 119,138.
  Weekly newspapers, West Indies, 2; circulation, 19,500.

Magazines

United States and Canada: 282; circulation 18,229,556.
  English-language magazines, 253; circulation, 17,696,763.
  Other-language magazines, 29; circulation, 532,793.
  The magazine with the largest circulation (1,145,558) is *Columbia,* the official organ of the Knights of Columbus.

Among magazines with status in the secular communications field are *America* (weekly; circulation, 42,511) and *Commonweal* (biweekly, circulation, 25,000).

General-interest monthly magazines with large circulation include: *Catholic Digest* (521,879); *Liguorian* (461,728); *St. Anthony Messenger* (266,478); *Family Digest* (156,838);

Sign (133,477); *U.S. Catholic* (50,375).

The oldest Catholic weekly newspaper in the U.S. is *The Pilot* of Boston, established in 1829 (under a different title).

Our Sunday Visitor, Inc., started publication in January, 1975, of *El Visitante de Puerto Rico*, Spanish-language weekly for Puerto Rico.

CATHOLIC NEWSPAPERS AND MAGAZINES IN THE U.S.

(Sources: *Catholic Press Directory, 1975*; Almanac survey; NC News Service.)

Abbreviation code: a, annual; bm, bimonthly; m, monthly; q, quarterly; w, weekly.

Newspapers

Advocate, The, w; 37 Evergreen Pl., E. Orange, N.J. 07018; Newark archdiocese; 43,980.

Alive, m; 400 East Monroe, Phoenix, Ariz. 85004; Phoenix diocese; 10,417.

Anchor, The w; 410 Highland Ave., Fall River, Mass. 02722; Fall River diocese; 24,356.

Arizona Register, biweekly; 64 W. Ochoa St., Tucson, Ariz. 85701; 15,000.

Beacon, The, w; Box A, Pequannock, N.J. 07440; Paterson diocese; 48,008.

Bishop's Bulletin, bm; 423 W. Duluth Ave., Sioux Falls, S. Dak. 57104; 22,000.

Byzantine Catholic World, w; 3643 Perrysville Ave., Pittsburgh, Pa. 15214; Munhall Byzantine archdiocese; 12,900.

Catholic Accent, w; P.O. Box 850, Greensburg, Pa. 15601; Greensburg diocese; 50,599.

Catholic Advance, The, w; 424 N. Broadway, Wichita, Kans. 67202; Wichita diocese; 12,567.

Catholic Banner, w; 119 Broad St., Charleston, S.C. 29401; Charleston diocese; 6,346.

Catholic Bulletin, w; 244 Dayton Ave., St. Paul, Minn. 55102; St. Paul and Minneapolis archdiocese, New Ulm diocese; 53,341.

Catholic Chronicle, w; 1933 Spielbusch Ave., Toledo, O. 43624; Toledo diocese; 50,480.

Catholic Commentator, The, w; P.O. Box 14746, Baton Rouge, La. 70808; Baton Rouge diocese; 37,749.

Catholic Crosswinds, semi-monthly; P.O. Box 194, Pueblo, Colo. 81002; Pueblo diocese; 20,246.

Catholic Exponent, w; 440 Ohio Edison Bldg., Youngstown, O. 44503; Youngstown diocese; 48,074.

Catholic Free Press, w; 247 Mill St., Worcester, Mass. 01602; Worcester diocese; 25,022.

Catholic Herald, The, w; 5890 Newman Ct., Sacramento, Calif. 95819; Sacramento diocese; 12,100.

Catholic Herald Citizen, w; P.O. Box 736, Milwaukee, Wis. 53201; Milwaukee archdiocese; 152,319.

Catholic Herald Citizen — Madison Edition, w; 25 S. Hancock St., Madison, Wis. 53703; 33,706.

Catholic Herald Citizen — Superior Edition, w; 1512 N. 12th St., Superior, Wis. 54880; 21,394.

Catholic Hungarian's Sunday, w; 517 S. Belle Vista Ave., Youngstown, O. 44509; 3,450.

Catholic Key to the News, The, w; P.O. Box 1037, Kansas City, Mo. 64141; Kansas City-St. Joseph diocese; 14,500.

Catholic Light, w; 300 Wyoming Ave., Scranton, Pa. 18503; Scranton diocese; 53,816.

Catholic Messenger, w; 407 Brady St., Davenport, Ia. 52805; Davenport diocese; 27,807.

Catholic Mirror, w; 306 Securities Bldg., Des Moines, Ia. 50309; 17,900.

Catholic Missourian; w; P.O. Box 1107, Jefferson City, Mo. 65101; Jefferson City diocese; 18,205.

Catholic News, The, w; 68 W. Broad St., Mt. Vernon, N.Y. 10552; New York archdiocese; 40,053.

Catholic News-Register, w; 425 Summit St., Joliet, Ill. 60435; Joliet diocese; 9,300.

Catholic Northwest Progress, w; 907 Terry Ave., Seattle, Wash. 98104; Seattle archdiocese, Yakima diocese; 34,285.

Catholic Observer, biweekly; 57 Observer St., Springfield, Mass. 01104; Springfield diocese; 13,698.

Catholic Post, The, w; P.O. Box 1722, Peoria, Ill. 61603; Peoria diocese; 41,315.

Catholic Register, w; Box 126-C, Logan Blvd., Hollidaysburg, Pa. 16648; Altoona-Johnstown diocese.

Catholic Review, w; 320 Cathedral St., Baltimore, Md. 21203; Baltimore archdiocese; 60,614.

Catholic Sentinel, w; 2816 E. Burnside St., Portland, Ore. 97214; Portland archdiocese, 17,301; Baker diocese, 1,750.

Catholic Spirit, The, biweekly; 161 Edgington Lane, Wheeling, W. Va. 26003; Wheeling-Charleston diocese; 21,750.

Catholic Standard, w; 1711 N. St., N.W., Washington, D.C. 20036; Washington archdiocese; 43,513.

Catholic Standard and Times, w; 222 N. 17th St., Philadelphia, Pa. 19103; Philadelphia archdiocese; Allentown diocese; 59,489.

Catholic Star Herald, w; 1845 Haddon Ave., Camden, N.J. 08103; Camden diocese; 36,463.

Catholic Sun, The, w; 204 E. Jefferson St., Syracuse, N.Y. 13202; Syracuse diocese; 42,127.

Catholic Telegraph, w; 326 W. 7th St., Cincinnati, O. 45202; Cincinnati archdiocese; 55,203.

Catholic Times, w; P.O. Box 636, Columbus, O. 43216; Columbus diocese; 34,674.

Catholic Transcript, w; 785 Asylum Ave., Hartford, Conn. 06105; Hartford archdiocese, Bridgeport and Norwich dioceses; 56,314.

Catholic Universe Bulletin, w; 1027 Superior Ave. N.E., Cleveland, O. 44114; Cleveland diocese; 89,790.

Catholic Virginian, w; 14 N. Laurel St., Richmond, Va. 23220; Richmond diocese; 44,534.

Catholic Voice, The, w; 2918 Lakeshore Ave., Oakland, Calif. 94610; Oakland diocese; 84,078.

Catholic Voice, The, w; 6060 N.W. Radial, Omaha, Nebr. 68104; Omaha archdiocese; 51,847.

Catholic Week, w; P.O. Box 349, Mobile, Ala. 36601; Mobile diocese; 9,562.

Catholic Weekly, The, w; P.O. Box 1405, Saginaw, Mich. 48605; Saginaw diocese; 26,772.

Catholic Weekly, The, w; 1628 Lambden Rd., Flint, Mich. 48501; Lansing diocese; 16,112.

Catholic Witness, The, w; 2300 Market St., Harrisburg, Pa. 17103; Harrisburg diocese; 51,000.

Church Today, every 3 weeks; 2315 Texas Ave., Alexandria, La. 71301; Alexandria diocese; 17,600.

Church World, w; Industry Rd., Brunswick, Me. 04011; Portland diocese; 11,080.

Clarion Herald, w; 523 Natchez St., New Orleans, La. 70130; New Orleans archdiocese; 101,249.

Concern, m (exc. Aug.); 153 Ash St., Manchester, N.H. 03105; Manchester diocese; 32,483.

Courier, The, w; P.O. Box 949, Winona, Minn. 55987; Winona diocese; 11,321.

Courier Journal, w; 67 Chestnut St., Rochester, N.Y. 14604; Rochester diocese; 68,190.

Criterion, The, w; P.O. Box 174, Indianapolis, Ind. 46206; Indianapolis archdiocese; 40,046.

Crociato, II (Ital.-Eng.) w; 1 Hanson Pl., Brooklyn, N.Y. 11217; 4,210.

Dakota Catholic Action, 9 times a year; P.O. Box 128, Wilton, N.D. 58579; Bismarck diocese; 15,000.

Denver Catholic Register, w; 938 Bannock St., Denver, Colo. 80201; Denver archdiocese; 23,725.

Dialog, The, w; 1925 Delaware Ave., Wilmington, Del. 19899; Wilmington diocese; 30,000.

Draugas (Lithuanian), daily; 4545 W. 63rd St., Chicago, Ill. 60629; Lithuanian Catholic Press Society.

Eastern Catholic Life, w; 101 Market St., Passaic, N.J. 07055; Passaic Byzantine eparchy; 14,200.

Eastern Kansas Register, The, w; 2220 Central, Kansas City, Kans. 66110; Kansas City archdiocese; 29,747.

Eastern Montana Catholic Register, w; 725 Third Ave. N., Great Falls, Mont. 59403; Great Falls diocese; 6,301.

Eastern Oklahoma Catholic, biweekly; P.O. Box 2009, Tulsa, Okla. 74101; Tulsa diocese.

El Visitante de Puerto Rico, w; 1120 Ashford Ave., Santurce, P.R. 00907; 10,000.

El Visitante Dominical (Spanish), w; Our Sunday Visitor, Inc., Noll Plaza, Huntington, Ind. 46750; 13,000.

Evangelist, The, w; 39 Philip St., Albany, N.Y. 12207; Albany diocese; 92,400.

Florida Catholic, The, w; 620 N. Magnolia Ave., Orlando, Fla. 32802; Orlando and St. Petersburg dioceses; 45,835.

Gary Edition of Our Sunday Visitor, w; 3855 Broadway, Gary, Ind. 46409; 39,079.

Georgia Bulletin, w; 756 W. Peachtree St. N.W., Atlanta, Ga. 30308; Atlanta archdiocese; 14,050.

Globe, The, w; P.O. Box 1678, Sioux City, Ia. 51102; Sioux City diocese; 24,178.

Guardian, The, w; P.O. Box 7417, Little Rock, Ark. 72207; Little Rock diocese; 11,532.

Harmonizer, The, w; Noll Plaza, Huntington, Ind. 46750; Fort Wayne-S. Bend diocese; 24,041.

Hawaii Catholic Herald, w; 1184 Bishop St., Honolulu, H.I. 96813; Honolulu diocese; 11,435.

Idaho Register, w; 420 Idaho St., Boise, Idaho 83702; Boise diocese; 11,592.

Inland Register, w; 1023 W. Riverside, Spokane, Wash. 99201; Spokane diocese; 10,100.

Inside Passage, w; 329 Fifth St., Juneau, Alaska 99801; Juneau and Fairbanks dioceses; 10,006.

Intermountain Catholic Register, The, w; P.O. Box 2489, Salt Lake City, Utah 84110; Salt Lake City diocese; 6,282.

Jednota (Slovak-Eng.), w; 1655 W. Harrisburg Pike, Middletown, Pa. 17057; 38,011.

Lafayette Edition of Our Sunday Visitor, w; 610 Lingle Ave., Lafayette, Ind. 47901; 7,025.

Lake Shore Visitor, w; 2-M Commerce Bldg., Erie, Pa. 16512; Erie diocese; 17,809.

Liberte, La (French-English), biweekly; 275 Holstone St., Fitchburg, Mass. 01421.

Long Island Catholic, The, w; 53 N. Park Ave., Rockville Centre, N.Y. 11570; Rockville Centre diocese; 167,992.

Message, The, w; 208 N.W. Third St., Evansville, Ind. 47708; Evansville diocese; 11,312.

Messenger, The, w; 224 W. Washington St., Belleville, Ill. 62220; Belleville diocese; 22,477.

Messenger, The, w; 1044 Scott St., Covington, Ky. 41012; Covington diocese; 9,902.

Michigan Catholic, The, w; 644 Selden St., Detroit, Mich. 48201; Detroit archdiocese; 103,254.

Mirror, The, w; M.P.O. Box 847, Springfield, Mo. 65801; Springfield-Cape Girardeau diocese; 12,350.

Mississippi Today, w; P.O. Box 2130, Jackson, Miss. 39205; Natchez-Jackson diocese; 23,000.

Monitor, The, w; 441 Church St., San Francisco, Calif. 94114; San Francisco archdiocese, Stockton and Santa Rosa dioceses; 31,232.

Monitor, The, w; 139 N. Warren St., Trenton, N.J. 08607; Trenton diocese; 77,134.

Morning Star, The, w; 515 Cathedral S., Lafayette, La. 70501; Lafayette diocese; 29,319.

Narod Polski (Polish-Eng.) semi-monthly; 984 Milwaukee Ave., Chicago, Ill. 60622; 47,000.

Nasa Nada (Eng.-Croatian), w; 1414 W. 119th St., Crown Point, Ind. 46307; 5,760.

National Catholic Register, w; P.O. Box 25986, Los Angeles, Calif. 90025; 87,539.

National Catholic Reporter, The, w; P.O. Box 281, Kansas City, Mo. 64141; published by laymen; 40,103.

Nevada Register, 3 times a year; P.O. Box 1989, Reno, Nev. 89505; Reno diocese; 3,999.

New Star, The, w; 2208 W. Chicago Ave., Chicago, Ill. 60622; St. Nicholas of Chicago Ukrainian diocese; 11,235.

New World, The, w; 109 N. Dearborn St., Chicago, Ill. 60602; Chicago archdiocese; 136,641.

North Carolina Catholic, w; P.O. Box 10686, Raleigh, N.C. 27605; Raleigh diocese; 5,100.

North Country Catholic, w; P.O. Box 326, Ogdensburg, N.Y. 13699; Ogdensburg diocese; 14,730.

Northwestern Kansas Register, w; P.O. Box 958, Salina, Kans. 67401; Salina diocese; 8,436.

Observer, The, w; P.O. Box 2079, Monterey, Calif. 93940; Monterey diocese; 8,900.

Observer, The, w; 1260 N. Church St., Rockford, Ill. 61101; Rockford diocese; 11,458.

One Voice, w; P.O. Box 10822, Birmingham, Ala. 35202; Birmingham diocese; 11,146.

Our Northland Diocese, m; 1200 Memorial Dr., Crookston, Minn. 56716; Crookston diocese; 12,777.

Our Sunday Visitor, w; Noll Plaza, Huntington, Ind. 46750; national edition and official publication for 7 dioceses; Our Sunday Visitor, Inc.; 374,859.

Outlook, m (Sept.-June); 215 W. 4th St., Duluth, Minn. 55806; Duluth diocese; 25,100.

Pilot, The, w; 49 Franklin St., Boston, Mass. 02110; Boston archdiocese; 91,000.

Pittsburgh Catholic, The, w; 110 Third Ave., Pittsburgh, Pa. 15222; Pittsburgh diocese; 103,485.

Polish American Journal, m; 413 Cedar Ave., Scranton, Pa. 18505; 27,913.

Priests — USA, m; 1307 S. Wabash Ave., Chicago, Ill. 60605; National Federation of Priests' Councils; 8,500.

Providence Visitor, w; 184 Broad St., Providence, R.I. 02903; Providence diocese; 37,500.

Record, The, w; 433 S. 5th St., Louisville, Ky. 40202; Louisville archdiocese; 52,550.

St. Cloud Visitor, w; 810 German St., St. Cloud, Minn. 56301; St. Cloud diocese; 30,407.

St. Joseph's-Blatt (German-Eng.), bm; St. Benedict, Ore. 97373; Manfred F. Ellenberger; 1,422.

St. Louis Review, w; 462 N. Taylor Ave., St. Louis, Mo. 63108; St. Louis archdiocese; 79,635.

Shlakh — The Way, w; 805 N. Franklin St., Philadelphia, Pa. 19123; Philadelphia archeparchy. Stamford and Chicago eparchies; 12,810.

Southern Cross, The, w; P.O. Box 81869, San Diego, Calif. 92138; San Diego diocese; 43,250.

Southern Cross, The, w; P.O. Box 10027; Savannah, Ga. 31402; Savannah diocese; 10,557.

Southern Nebraska Register, w; P.O. Box 80329, Lincoln, Nebr. 68501; Lincoln diocese; 15,915.

Southwest Kansas Register, w; P.O. Box 1317, Dodge City, Kans. 67801; Dodge City diocese; 8,300.

Spirit, The, w; 203 S. Monroe Ave., Green Bay, Wis. 54305; Green Bay diocese; 29,417.

Steubenville Register, w; 419 S. 4th St., Steubenville, O. 43952; Steubenville diocese; 9,250.

Tablet, w; 1 Hanson Pl., Brooklyn, N.Y. 11243; Brooklyn diocese; 108,798.

Tennessee Register, The, w; 421 Charlotte Ave., Nashville, Tenn. 37219; Nashville diocese; 11,368.

Texas Catholic, w; 3915 Lemmon Ave., Dallas, Tex. 75219; Dallas and Fort Worth dioceses; 23,156.

Texas Catholic Herald, The, w; 1700 San Jacinto St., Houston, Tex. 77002; Galveston-Houston diocese; 67,971.

Texas Catholic Herald — Austin Edition,

w; P.O. Box 13327, Capital Sta., Austin, Tex. 78711; Austin diocese; 8,300.

Texas Catholic Herald — Beaumont, w; P.O. Box 3944, Beaumont, Tex. 77704; Beaumont diocese; 14,800.

Texas Concho Register, biweekly; 116 S. Oakes, San Angelo, Tex. 76901; San Angelo diocese; 3,700.

Texas Gulf Coast Catholic, w; P.O. Box 2584, Corpus Christi, Tex. 78403; Corpus Christi diocese; 5,786.

Tidings, The, w; 1530 W. 9th St., Los Angeles, Calif. 90015; Los Angeles archdiocese; 65,001.

Times-Review, The, w; P.O. Box 991, La Crosse, Wis. 54601; La Crosse diocese; 22,700.

Today's Catholic (formerly Alamo Register), w; P.O. Box 12429, San Antonio, Tex. 78212; San Antonio archdiocese; 20,813.

Twin Circle, w; P.O. Box 25986, Los Angeles, Calif. 90025; 89,897.

Upper Peninsula Catholic, w; P.O. Box 548, Marquette, Mich. 49855; Marquette diocese; 11,614.

Vermont Catholic Tribune, w; 209 College St., Burlington, Vt. 05401; Burlington diocese; 28,036.

Voice, The, w; 6201 Biscayne Blvd., Miami, Fla. 33138; Miami archdiocese; 55,105.

Voice of the Southwest, w; P.O. Box 68, Lumberton, N. Mex. 87547; Gallup diocese; 1,599.

Wanderer, The, w; 128 E. 10th St., St. Paul, Minn. 55101; 47,685.

WestMont Word, w; P.O. Box 1729, Helena, Mont. 59601; Helena diocese; 9,830.

West Nebraska Register, w; 411 W. 17th St., Grand Island, Nebr. 68801; Grand Island diocese; 14,142.

West River Catholic, m; 520 Cathedral Dr., Rapid City, S. Dak. 57701; Rapid City diocese; 9,500.

West Texas Register, biweekly; 1800 N. Spring, Amarillo, Tex. 79107; Amarillo diocese; 2,892.

Western Catholic Edition of Our Sunday Visitor, w; 514 E. Lawrence Ave., Springfield, Ill. 62703; Springfield diocese; 39,803.

Western Michigan Catholic, w; 154 Louis St., N.W., Grand Rapids, Mich. 49502; Grand Rapids diocese; 10,500.

Western New York Catholic, w; 531 Virginia St., Buffalo, N.Y. 14202; Buffalo diocese; 39,878.

Witness, The, w; 845 Bluff St., Dubuque, Ia. 52001; Dubuque archdiocese; 22,068.

Wyoming Register, w; P.O. Box 1308, Cheyenne, Wyo. 82001; 5,450.

Magazines, Other Periodicals

Act, 10 times a year; 1655 Jackson Blvd., Chicago, Ill. 60612; 3,300.

A.D. Correspondence, 26 times a year; Notre Dame, Ind. 46556; 4,587.

AIM (Aids in Ministry), q; Box 306, Cranbury, N.J. 08512; 7,173.

America, w; 106 W. 56th St., New York, N.Y. 10019; 42,000.

American Benedictine Review, q; 2nd and Division Sts., Atchison, Kans. 66002; 1,200.

American Ecclesiastical Review, m; 620 Michigan Ave. N.E., Washington, D.C. 20064; 2,100.

American Midland Naturalist, q; Notre Dame, Ind. 46556; 1,650.

Americas, The, q; Box 34440, Washington, D.C. 20034; Academy of American Franciscan History; 1,069.

Amerikanski Slovenec (Slovenian), w; 6117 St. Clair Ave., Cleveland, O. 44103; Slovenian Catholic Union; 15,695.

Annals of Our Lady of the Angels, m; 253 Knickerbocker Rd., Tenafly, N.J. 07670; 17,000.

Anthonian, q; Paterson, N.J. 07509; St. Anthony's Guild; 160,000.

Anthropological Quarterly, q; 620 Michigan Ave. N.E., Washington, D.C. 20064; Catholic Anthropological Conference; 1,000.

Apostolate of Our Lady, m; Carey, O. 43316; Our Lady of Consolation National Shrine; 29,052.

Apostolate of the Little Flower, bm; P.O. Box 5280, 906 Kentucky Ave., bsan Antonio, Tex. 78201; Discalced Carmelite Fathers; 34,840.

Ave Maria (Polish), 6 times a year; 600 Doat St., Buffalo, N.Y. 14211; Felician Srs.; 4,630.

Bells of St. Ann, 3 times a year; Belcourt, N.D. 58316; St. Ann's Indian Mission; 26,466.

Benedictine Orient, bm; 2400 Maple Ave., Lisle, Ill. 60532; 7,372.

Benedictines, q; Mt. St. Scholastica, Atchison, Kans. 66002; 721.

Bernardine Bulletin, The, semiannually; 647 Spring Mill Rd., Villanova, Pa. 19085; Bernardine Srs.; 14,000.

Best Sellers, semimonthly; Univ. of Scranton, Scranton, Pa. 18510; 2,600.

Better World, q; Belford, N.J. 07718; Mary Productions Guild; 3,000.

Bible Today, The, 6 times a year; Liturgical Press, Collegeville, Minn. 56321; 14,260.

Brothers' Newsletter, q; Passionist Monastery, P.O. Box 150, West Springfield, Mass. 01089; National Assembly of Religious Brothers; 3,500.

Call Board, The, 5 times a year; 227 W. 45th St., New York, N.Y. 10036; Catholic Actors' Guild; 1,200.

Catechist, The, m (exc. Dec., June-Aug.); 2285 Arbor Blvd., Dayton, O. 45439; 28,813.

Catholic Action News, m; P.O. Box 1750, Fargo, N. Dak. 58102; Fargo diocese; 17,200.

Catholic Aid News, m; 49 W. 9th St., St. Paul, Minn. 55102; 22,000.

Catholic Apostolate Newsletter, bm; 5424 Blue Mound Rd., Milwaukee, Wis. 53208; Pallottine Fathers; 15,000.

Catholic Biblical Quarterly, q; Catholic University of America, Washington, D.C. 20064; Catholic Biblical Assn.; 3,342.

Catholic Cemetery, The, m; 710 N. River Rd., Des Plaines, Ill. 60016; 2,317.

CCH Echoes, q; 1400 State St., Alton, Ill. 62002; Catholic Children's Home; 250.

Catholic Digest, The, m; P.O. Box 3090, St. Paul, Minn. 55165; 521,879.

Catholic Family Leader, bm; 1312 Massachusetts Ave. N.W., Washington, D.C. 20005; Family Life, USCC; 8,399.

Catholic Forester Magazine, bm; 305 W. Madison St., Chicago, Ill. 60606; Catholic Order of Foresters; 140,000.

Catholic Historical Review, q; Catholic University of America, Washington, D.C. 20064; American Catholic Historical Assn.; 2,250.

Catholic Journalist, The, bm; 432 Park Ave. S., New York, N.Y. 10016; Catholic Press Association; 1,131.

C.K. of A. Journal, m; 217 E. 8th St., Cincinnati, O. 45202; Catholic Knights of America; 18,650.

C.L. of C. Index, m; 2770 E. Main St., Columbus, O. 43209; 7,876.

Catholic Lawyer, q; St. John's University, Jamaica, N.Y. 11432; St. Thomas More Institute for Legal Research; 3,500.

Catholic Library World, m; 461 W. Lancaster Ave., Haverford, Pa. 19041; Catholic Library Association; 3,268.

Catholic Life Magazine, m (exc. July-Aug.); 9800 Oakland Ave., Detroit, Mich. 48211; PIME Missionaries; 15,860.

Catholic Mind, The, m (exc. July-Aug.); 106 W. 56th St., New York, N.Y. 10019; 5,150.

Catholic Near East Magazine, q; 1011 First Ave., New York, N.Y. 10022; 160,000.

Catholic Periodical and Literature Index, bm; 461 W. Lancaster Ave., Haverford, Pa. 19041; Catholic Library Association; 1,769.

Catholic Press Directory, a; 432 Park Ave. S., New York, N.Y. 10016; Catholic Press Assn.; 1,466.

Catholic Quote, m; Valparaiso, Nebr. 68065; 6,500.

Catholic Review (Braille), m; 154 E. 23rd St., New York, N.Y. 10010; Xavier Society for the Blind; 2,800.

Catholic School Editor, The, q; 1135 W. Kilbourn Ave., Milwaukee, Wis. 53233; Catholic School Press Assn.; 300.

Catholic University of America Law Review, q; Washington, D.C. 20064; 1,500.

Catholic War Veteran, bm; 2 Massachusetts Ave. N.W., Washington, D.C. 20001; 100,000.

Catholic Woman's Journal, m; 3835 Westminster Pl., St. Louis, Mo. 63108; 1,344.

Catholic Worker, 9 times a year; 36 E. First St., New York, N.Y. 10003; Dorothy Day; 82,000.

Catholic Workman, m; 107 N. Central Ave., New Prague, Minn. 56071; 7,500.

Charities USA, m; 1346 Connecticut Ave. N.W., Washington, D.C. 20036; National Conference of Catholic Charities.

Chicago Studies, 3 times a year; P.O. Box 665, Mundelein, Ill. 60060; 5,300.

Christopher News Notes, 7 times a year; 12 E. 48th St., New York, N.Y. 10017; The Christophers, Inc.; 1,150,000.

Classical Bulletin, 6 times a year; 221 N. Grand Blvd., St. Louis, Mo. 63103; 1,403.

Classical Folia, biennial; College of Holy Cross, Worcester, Mass. 01610; Institute of Early Christian Iberian Studies; 600.

Claverite, The, bm; 1821 Orleans Ave., New Orleans, La. 70116; Knights of Peter Claver; 13,300.

Columban Mission, m (exc. June, Aug.); St. Columbans, Nebr. 68056; Columban Fathers; 220,000.

Columbia, m; One Columbus Plaza, New Haven, Conn. 06507; Knights of Columbus; 1,145,658.

Columbian, The, w; 188 W. Randolph St., Chicago, Ill. 60601; 24,198.

Comment/Media Today, 9 times a year; 39 Lackawanna Pl., Bloomfield, N.J. 07003; Christian Communications Apostolate; 3,200.

Commitment, q; 1307 S. Wabash Ave., Chicago, Ill. 60605; National Catholic Conference for Interracial Justice; 24,000.

Commonweal, biweekly; 232 Madison Ave., New York, N.Y. 10016; 25,000.

Community, q; 21 E. Van Buren St., Chicago, Ill. 60605; Friendship House; 1,720.

Consolata Missions, q; P.O. Box C, Somerset, N.J. 08873; 32,000.

Continuum, q; St. Xavier College, Chicago, Ill. 60655.

Cord, The, m; St. Bonaventure University, St. Bonaventure, N.Y. 14778; 1,230.

Counseling and Values, q; 802 Finch Bldg., St. Paul, Minn. 55101; National Catholic Guidance Conference, Inc.; 1,926.

Critic, The, bm; 180 N. Wabash Ave., Chicago, Ill. 60601; Thomas More Association; 28,476.

Cross and Crown, q; P.O. Box 627, Oak Park, Ill. 60303; 6,500.

Crossroads Radio, m; 1089 Elm St., W. Springfield, Mass. 01089; 4,570.

Crusader's Almanac, The, q; 1400 Quincy St. N.E., Washington, D.C. 20017; Commissariat of the Holy Land; 85,000.

Damien-Dutton Call, q; 214 Commercial Ave., New Brunswick, N.J. 08901; 13,586.

Daystar, a; 172 Foster St., Brighton, Mass. 02135; Franciscan Missionary Sisters of Africa; 1,800.

Deaf Blind Weekly, The (Braille), w; 154 E. 23rd St., New York, N.Y. 10010; Xavier Society for the Blind; 125.

Desert Call, q; SLIA-Nada, Star Rt. 1, Sedona, Ariz. 86336; Spiritual Life Institute of America; 2,200.

Diakonia, q; Fordham Univ., Bronx, N.Y. 10458; John XXIII Center for Eastern Christian Studies, 1,020.

Divine Love, q; P.O. Box 24, Fresno, Calif. 93707; 200,000.

Divine Word Messenger, q; Bay St. Louis, Miss. 39520; 12,500.

Divine Word Missionaries, q; Techny, Ill. 60082; 197,000.

Educating in Faith, m; 335 Broadway, New York, N.Y. 10013; Catholic Negro-American Mission Board; 16,500.

Emmanuel, m (bm July-Aug.); 194 E. 76th St., New York, N.Y. 10021; Blessed Sacrament Fathers; 17,301.

Encounter, 3 times a year; 200 Lake St., Boston, Mass. 02135; Religious of the Cenacle; 6,500.

Envoy, 6 times a year; Office of Public Relations, Catholic University of America, Washington, D.C. 20064; 52,000.

Eucharist, bm; 194 E. 76th St., New York, N.Y. 10021; 9,614.

Extension, m; 1307 S. Wabash Ave., Chicago, Ill. 60605; Catholic Church Extension Society.

Family, m; 50 St. Paul's Ave., Boston, Mass. 02130; Daughters of St. Paul; 48,000.

Family Digest, m; Noll Plaza, Huntington, Ind. 46750; 156,838.

Family Friend, q; P.O. Box 5663, Milwaukee, Wis. 53211; 22.600.

Fatima Findings, m; 100 E. 20th St., Baltimore, Md. 21218; Reparation Society of the Immaculate Heart of Mary; 4,000.

Folk Mass and Modern Liturgy, 8 times a year; Resource Publications, 6244 Rainbow Dr., San Jose, Calif. 95129; 3,100.

Franciscan Herald, m; 1434 W. 51st St., Chicago, Ill. 60609; Third Order of St. Francis; 4,458.

F.M.A. Focus, q; P.O. Box 598, Mt. Vernon, N.Y. 10550; Franciscan Mission Associates; 488,323.

Franciscan Reporter, q; 3140 Meramec St., St. Louis, Mo. 63138; 34,900.

Franciscan Studies, a; St. Bonaventure, N.Y. 14778; Franciscan Institute; 714.

Fraternal Leader, bm; 305 W. 6th St., Erie, Pa. 16512; Loyal Christian Benefit Association; 45,000.

Friar, m; Butler, N.J. 07405; Franciscan Fathers; 17,640.

Glenmary's Challenge, q; P.O. Box 46404, Cincinnati, O. 45246; Glenmary Home Missioners; 95,000.

Good Shepherd (Slovak and English), m;

205 Madison St., Passaic, N.J. 07055; Slovak Catholic Federation of America; 3,500.

Grain and Fire, q; P.O. Box 178, Cottonport, La. 71327; Brothers of the Holy Eucharist; 600.

Homiletic and Pastoral Review, m; 86 Riverside Dr., New York, N.Y. 10024; 16,732.

Hospital Progress, m; 1438 S. Grand Blvd., St. Louis, Mo. 63104; Catholic Hospital Association; 11,000.

Immaculata, m; 8000 39th Ave., Kenosha, Wis. 53141; Franciscan Fathers; 21,000.

Impact, 6 times a year; 734 15th St., N.W., Washington, D.C. 20005; National Office for Black Catholics; 18,000.

Institute Journal, bm; 50 Oak St., San Francisco, Calif. 94102; Young Men's Institute; 10,000.

It's Our World, 4 times a year; 800 Allegheny Ave., Pittsburgh, Pa. 15233; Pontifical Assn. of the Holy Childhood; 3,000,000.

Jesuit, The, q; 39 E. 83rd St., New York, N.Y. 10028; 304,500.

Jesuit, The (New Orleans Edition), q; 1607 Pere Marquette Bldg., New Orleans, La. 70112; 42,000.

Jesuit Blackrobe, q; 3601 W. Fond du Lac Ave., Milwaukee, Wis. 53216; 46,000.

Jesuit Bulletin, 4 times a year; 4511 W. Pine Blvd., St. Louis, Mo. 63108; Jesuit Seminary Aid Association; 70,149.

Josephite Harvest, The, bm; 1130 N. Calvert St., Baltimore, Md. 21202; Josephite Missionaries; 45,000.

Jurist, The, q; Catholic University of America, Washington, D.C. 20017; School of Canon Law; 2,221.

Katolicky Sokol (Catholic Falcon) (Slovak-English), w; 205 Madison St., Passaic, N.J. 07055; Slovak Catholic Sokol; 19,400.

Katolik (Czech), w; 1637 S. Allport St., Chicago, Ill. 60608; 2,000.

Kinship, q; 4580 Colerain Ave., Cincinnati, O. 45223; Glenmary Home Mission Sisters; 10,500.

Knights of St. John, q; 6517 Charles Ave., Parma, O. 44129; 7,400.

Kolping Banner, m; 125 N. Stratton Lane, Mt. Prospect, Ill. 60056; Catholic Kolping Society; 2,274.

Laivas (Lithuanian), m; 4545 W. 63rd St., Chicago, Ill. 60629.

Land of Cotton, q; 2048 W. Fairview Ave., Montgomery, Ala. 36108; 64,443.

La Paloma, m; 124 Festival, El Paso, Tex. 79912; El Paso diocese newsletter.

Leaves, bm; 23715 Ann Arbor Trail, Dearborn Heights, Mich. '8127; Mariannhill Fathers; 206,400.

Liguorian, m; 1 Liguori Rd., Liguori, Mo. 63057; Redemptorist Fathers; 461,728.

Linacre Quarterly, q; 2825 N. Mayfair Rd., Milwaukee, Wis. 53222; Federation of Catholic Physicians Guilds; 9,720.

Little Bronzed Angel, bm; St. Paul's Indian Mission, Marty, S.D. 53761; Benedictine Fathers; 27,000.

Little Flower Magazine, bm; 1125 S. Walker, Oklahoma City, Okla. 73126; Discalced Carmelite Fathers; 30,000.

Liturgy, 10 times a year, 1330 Massachusetts Ave., N.W. Washington, D.C. 20005; 4,875.

Living Light, The, q; Our Sunday Visitor, Inc., Huntington, Ind. 46750, publisher; edited by Department of Education, USCC; 4,804.

Marian, The, 5 times a year; 4545 W. 63rd St., Chicago, Ill. 60629, Marian Fathers.

Marian Helpers Bulletin, q; Stockbridge, Mass. 01262; Association of Marian Helpers and of the Congregation of Marian Fathers; 737,000.

Marquette Today, q; 1834 W. Wisconsin Ave., Milwaukee, Wis. 53233; 56,000.

Marriage, m; Abbey Press, St. Meinrad, Ind. 47577; 58,000.

Mary Magazine and Aylesford News, bm; Cass Ave. N. at I-55, Westmont, Ill. 60559; Carmelite Fathers; 26,130.

Maryknoll Magazine, m; Maryknoll, N.Y. 10545; Catholic Foreign Mission Society; more than 200,000.

Master's Work, q; Waukegan and Willow Rds. Techny, Ill. 60082; Holy Spirit Missionary Sisters; 6,000.

Mediatrix, q; 6301 12th Ave., Brooklyn, N.Y. 11219; 7,000.

Medical Mission News, bm; 10 W. 17th St., New York, N.Y. 10011; Catholic Medical Mission Board, Inc.; 43,000.

Medical Mission Sisters News, 4 times a year; 8400 Pine Road, Philadelphia, Pa. 19111; 19,250.

Men of Malvern, bm; Malvern, Pa. 19355; 18,000.

Mercy Profile, q; 2303 Grandview Ave., Cincinnati, O. 45206; Sisters of Mercy; 17,000.

Messenger, The, m; 16010 Detroit Ave., Lakewood, O. 44107; 11,300.

Messenger of the Holy Family, bm; 2500 Ashby Rd., St. Louis, Mo. 63114; 4,600.

MHS Review, q; 232 S. Home Ave., Pittsburgh, Pa. 15202; 3,150.

Miesiecznik Franciszkanski (Polish), m; Franciscan Printery, Pulaski, Wis. 54162; Franciscan Fathers; 10,420.

Miraculous Medal, The, q; 475 E. Chelten Ave., Philadelphia, Pa. 19144; Central Association of the Miraculous Medal; 104,000.

Mission, bm; 366 Fifth Ave., New York, N.Y. 10001; Society for Propagation of the Faith; 3,175,000.

Mission, bm; 1663 Bristol Pike, Cornwell Heights, Pa. 19020; Sisters of the Blessed Sacrament; 4,820.

Mission Helper, The, q; 1001 W. Joppa Rd., Baltimore, Md. 21204; Mission Helpers of the Sacred Heart; 7,132.

Missionhurst, 9 times a year; 4651 N. 25th St., Arlington, Va. 22207; Immaculate Heart of Mary Mission Society, Inc.; 350,000.

Mission Intercom, 10 times a year; 1325 Massachusetts Ave. N.W., Washington, D.C. 20005; US Catholic Mission Council; 2,500.

Missionaries of Africa Report, bm; 1622 21st St. N.W., Washington, D.C. 20009; Society of Missionaries of Africa (White Fathers); 19,340.

Modern Schoolman, The, q; 3700 W. Pine Blvd., St. Louis, Mo. 63108; St. Louis University; 900.

Momentum, 4 times a year; Suite 350, One Dupont Circle, Washington, D.C. 20036; National Catholic Educational Asssociation; 15,000.

Mother Cabrini Messenger, bm; 2520 Lakeview Ave., Chicago, Ill. 60614; Mother Cabrini League; 85,000.

Mount Loretto Review, a; 6581 Hylan Blvd., Staten Island, N.Y. 10309; 100,000.

MSC Spotlite, bm; 305 S. Lake St., Aurora, Ill. 60507; Missionaries of the Sacred Heart; 20,000.

Musart, q (during school year); 4637 Eastern Ave. N.W., Washington, D.C. 20018; National Catholic Music Educators Association; 4,000.

Mwangaza, q; 172 Foster St., Brighton, Mass. 02135; Franciscan Missionary Sisters for Africa; 1,800.

My Daily Visitor, m; Noll Plaza, Huntington, Ind. 46750; Our Sunday Visitor, Inc.; 15,112.

Narod (Czech-Eng.), w; 1637 S. Allport St., Chicago, Ill. 60608; Benedictine Abbey Press; 1,450.

National Catholic Forester, bm; 59 E. Van Buren St., Chicago, Ill. 60605; 41,289.

National Jesuit News, m; 5430 S. University, Chicago, Ill. 60615; 6,900.

New Catholic World, bm; 1865 Broadway, New York, N.Y. 10023; 15,000.

New Covenant, m; P.O. Box 102, Main St. Station, Ann Arbor, Mich. 48107; Charismatic Renewal Services; 38,649.

New Scholasticism, q; Notre Dame, Ind. 46556; American Catholic Philosophical Association; 2,550.

News and Views, q; 3900 Westminster Pl.; St. Louis, Mo. 63108; Sacred Heart Program; 210,000.

North American Voice of Fatima, m; 1023 Swann Rd., Youngstown, N.Y. 14174; 13,000.

Notre Dame Magazine, 5 times a year; Notre Dame Univ., Notre Dame, Ind. 46556; 75,000.

Now, q; 35750 Moravian, Fraser, Mich. 48026; Xavier Mission Srs.; 15,592.

Oblate World and Voice of Hope, bm; 350 Jamaica Way, Boston, Mass. 02130; Oblates of Mary Immaculate; 27,000. Southern U.S. Edition, 53,000. Philippine Province Edition, 35,000.

Official Guide to Catholic Educational Institutions, a; 200 Sunrise Highway, Rockville Centre, L.I., N.Y. 11570; 53,625.

Orphan's Messenger and Advocate of the Blind, q; P.O. Box 288, Jersey City, N.J. 07303; St. Joseph's Home, 78,000.

Our Lady of the Snows, bm; 15 S. 59th St., Belleville, Ill. 62223; Shrine of Our Lady of the Snows; 212,000.

Our Lady's Digest, bm; Olivet, Ill. 61860; La Salette Fathers.

Our Lady's Missionary, m; Topsfield Rd., Ipswich, Mass. 01938; La Salette Fathers; 50,000.

Pacemaker, m; 500 17th Ave., Seattle, Wash. 98122; Providence Hospital; 1,000.

Padres' Trail, 6 times a year; St. Michael's Mission, St. Michael, Ariz. 86511; Franciscan Fathers; 6,892.

Paraclete, 5 times a year; P.O. Box 2000, Wheaton, Md. 20902; Holy Ghost Fathers; 155,000.

Parish Visitor, q; 328 W. 71st St., New York, N.Y. 10023; Parish Visitors of Mary Immaculate; 3,000.

Passionist Orbit, q; 5700 N. Harlem Ave., Chicago, Ill. 60631; Passionist Fathers; 52,000.

Pastoral Life, m; Route 224, Canfield, Ohio 44406; Society of St. Paul; 7,640.

Paulist Fathers News, bm; 415 W. 59th St., New York, N.Y. 10019; 23,500.

People, bm; 1312 Massachusetts Ave. N.W., Washington, D.C. 20005; National Council of Catholic Laity; 30,000.

Perpetual Help World, q; 294 E. 150th St., Bronx, N.Y. 10451; Redemptorists.

Perspective, 21, 5 times a year; 400 Sette Dr., Paramus, N.J. 07652; 144,500.

Philosophy Today, q; Carthagena Station, Celina, Ohio 45822; 1,325.

Pilgrim, q; Jesuit Fathers, Auriesville, N.Y. 12016; Shrine of Our Lady of Martyrs; 25,500.

Pope Speaks, The, q; Our Sunday Visitor, Inc., Noll Plaza, Huntington, Ind. 46750 4,270.

Priatel Dietok (Children's Friend) (Slovak), m; 205 Madison St., Passaic, N.J 07055; Junior Catholic Sokol; 7,600.

Priest, The, m; Noll Plaza, Huntington, Ind. 46750; Our Sunday Visitor, Inc.; 9,923.

Probe, m (Oct.-June); 201 E. Ohio St., Chicago, Ill. 60611, NAWR; 3,000.

Professional Placement Newsnotes, bm; 10 W. 17th St., New York, N.Y. 10011; 6,000.

Queen, bm; 40 S. Saxon Ave., Bay Shore, N.Y. 11706; Montfort Fathers; 10,401.

Reign of the Sacred Heart, m; Hales Corners, Wis. 53130; 118,000.

Religion Teacher's Journal, 9 times a year; P.O. Box 180, W. Mystic, Conn. 06388; 35,750.

Religious Book Review, q; Box 296, Williston Park, N.Y. 11596; 9,514.

Renascence, q; Marquette University, Milwaukee, Wis. 53233; Catholic Renascence Society; 748.

Response, The, bm (Sept.-June); 39 Lackawanna Pl., Bloomfield, N.J. 07003; International Liaison of Newark archdiocese; 530.

Review for Religious, bm; 539 N. Grand Blvd., St. Louis, Mo. 63103; 18,932.

Review of Politics, q; Univ. of Notre Dame, Notre Dame, Ind. 46556; 2,100.

Review of Social Economy, semiannual; 2323 N. Seminary Ave., Chicago, Ill. 60614; Association for Social Economics; 990.

Roses and Gold from Our Lady of the Ozarks, m; 1740 Grand Ave., Carthage, Mo. 64836; 36,000.

Roze Maryi (Polish), m; Eden Hill, Stockbridge, Mass. 01262; 7,000.

Sacred Music, q; Route 2, Box 1, Irving, Tex. 75062; 1,300.

St. Anthony Messenger, m; 1615 Republic St., Cincinnati, O. 45210; Franciscan Fathers; 266,000.

St. Joseph's Advocate, q; Mill Hill Missionaries, Albany, N.Y. 12203; 7,500.

St. Maron's Diocese of Detroit- USA/Diocesan Newsletter, bm; 11470 Kercheval, Detroit, Mich. 48214; 4,500.

Salesian Bulletin, bm; 148 Main St., New Rochelle, N.Y. 10802; Salesian Fathers; 120,000.

Salesian Missions, q; 148 Main St., New Rochelle, N.Y. 10802; Salesians of St. John Bosco; 950,000.

Salvatorian Newsletter, The, q; Society of the Divine Savior, Salvatorian Center, Wis. 53061; 221,000.

Sandal Prints, bm; 1820 Mt. Elliott Ave., Detroit, Mich. 48207; Capuchin Fathers; 9,238.

School Guide, a; 68 W. Broad St., Mt. Vernon, N.Y. 10552; 150,000.

School Sister, The, q; Notre Dame of the Lake, Mequon, Wis. 53092; 19,527.

Science Studies, a; St. Bonaventure University, St. Bonaventure, N.Y. 14778; 690.

Scouting Bulletin of the Catholic Committee on Scouting, q; North Brunswick, N.J. 08902; 7,500.

Serenity, q; 601 Maiden Choice Lane, Baltimore, Md. 21228; Little Sisters of the Poor; 35,000.

Share, m (Sept.-June); Maryknoll, N.Y. 10545; Maryknoll Junior Edition; 28,000.

Shepherd's Call, The, q; 601 Second St. S.W., Albuquerque, N.M. 87103; 7,750.

Sign, The, m; Monastery Place, Union City, N.J. 07087; Passionist Fathers; 133,477.

Silent Advocate, bm; St. Rita School for the Deaf, 1720 Glendale-Milford Rd., Cincinnati, O. 45215; 50,000.

Sisters Today, m; St. John's Abbey, Collegeville, Minn. 56321; 21,650.

Social Justice Review, m (exc. July-Aug.); 3835 Westminster Pl., St. Louis, Mo. 63108; Catholic Central Union of America; 1,725.

Sodalis Polonia, 9 times a year; St. Mary's College, Orchard Lake, Mich. 48033; Sts. Cyril and Methodius Seminary; 1,440.

Sons of Mary Missionary Society, q; 567 Salem End Rd., Framingham, Mass. 01701; 2,100.

Sophia, q; 19 Dartmouth St., West Newton, Mass. 02165; Melkite Exarchate in U.S.; 3,000.

Soul, bm; Ave Maria Institute, Washington, N.J. 07882; Blue Army; 100,000.

Spirit, q; Seton Hall University, South Orange, N.J. 08824; poetry magazine; 832.

Spirit and Life, 6 times a year; Clyde, Mo. 64432; Benedictine Srs. of Perpetual Adoration; 7,842.

Spiritual Book News, 8 times a year; Notre Dame, Ind. 46556; 6,137.

Spiritual Life, q; 2131 Lincoln Rd. N.E., Washington, D.C. 20002; Discalced Carmelites; 14,000.

Squires Newsletter, m; Columbus Plaza, New Haven, Conn. 06507; Columbian Squires; 25,103.

Sword, 3 times a year; 31 N. Broadway, Joliet, Ill. 60435; 400.

Theological Studies, q; 3520 Prospect St. N.W., Washington, D.C. 20007; Jesuit Fathers; 7,000.

Theology Digest, q; 3701 Lindell Blvd., St. Louis, Mo. 63108; 8,344.

Theresian, News, The, 6 times a year; 5326 E. Pershing Ave., Scottsdale, Ariz. 85254; 4,400.

Thomist, The, q; 487 Michigan Ave. N.E., Washington, D.C. 20017; Dominican Fathers; 1,100.

Thought, q; 441 E. Fordham Rd., Bronx, N.Y. 10458; Fordham University; 1,500.

Today's Catholic Teacher, m (Sept.-May); 2451 E. River Rd., Suite 200, Dayton, O. 45439; 70,000.

Today's Parish, bm; P.O. Box 180, West Mystic, Conn. 06340; 14,000.

Topic, q; 459 River Rd., Andover, Mass. 01810; Third Order Province of Immaculate Conception; 3,250.

Trinity Missions, q; P.O. Box 30, Silver Springs, Md. 20910; 300,000.

Ultreya Magazine, m; 4500 W. Davis St., Dallas, Tex. 75211. Cursillo Movement; 6,000.

L'Union (French), q; 1 Social St., Woonsocket, R.I. 02895; 35,500.

UNIREA, The Union (Romanian and English), m; 4309 Olcott Ave., East Chicago, Ind. 46312; 2,000.

U.S. Catholic, m; 221 W. Madison St., Chicago, Ill. 60606; Claretian Fathers; 50,375.

Verona Fathers Missions, 4 times a year; 2104 St. Michael's St., Cincinnati, O. 45205; 27,408.

Victorian, q; 780 Ridge Rd., Lackawanna, N.Y. 14218; Our Lady of Victory Homes of Charity; 27,186.

Vox Regis, 3 times a year; St. Bonaventure, N.Y. 14778; Christ the King Seminary; 1,300.

Waif's Messenger, m; 1140 W. Jackson Blvd., Chicago, Ill. 60607; Mission of Our Lady of Mercy; 49,579.

Way — Catholic Viewpoints, 10 times a year; 109 Golden Gate Ave., San Francisco, Calif. 94102; Franciscan Fathers of California, Inc.; 10,051.

Western Catholic Union Record, m; 906 W.C.U. Bldg., Quincy, Ill. 62301; Western Catholic Union; 19,050.

Word of God, w; 2187 Victory Blvd., Staten Island, N.Y. 10314; Society of St. Paul; 30,000.

Working for Boys, q; 601 Winchester St., Newton Highlands, Mass. 02161; Xaverian Brothers; 26,874.

Worldmission, q; 366 5th Ave., New York, N.Y. 10001; Society for the Propagation of the Faith; 2,300.

Worship, 10 times a year; St. John's Abbey, Collegeville, Minn. 56321; 8,160.

Xaverian Missions Newsletter, 9 times a year; 101 Summer St., Holliston, Mass. 01746; Xaverian Missionary Fathers; 24,500.

Your Edmundite Missions Newsletter, bm; 1428 Broad St., Selma, Ala. 36701; Southern Missions of Society of St. Edmund; 72,044.

Youth Program Service, bm; 1312 Massachusetts Ave. N.W., Washington, D.C. 20005; 7,000.

Zeal, q; St. Elizabeth Mission Society of the Sisters of St. Francis, Allegany, N.Y. 14706; 970.

Books

The Official Catholic Directory, annual, P. J. Kenedy and Sons, 866 Third Ave., New York, N.Y. 10022; circulation 13,197. First edition, 1817.

The Catholic Almanac, annual; Our Sunday Visitor, Inc., Huntington, Ind. 46750, publisher; editorial offices, 620 Route 3, Clifton, N.J. 07013. First edition, 1904. (See publication history.)

The American Catholic Who's Who, biennial; NC Publications, 1312 Massachusetts Ave., N.W., Washington, D.C. 20005. First volume, 1934-35; 2,000. Work was under way in 1975 for the publication of a Bicentennial edition as a Catholic event in the national celebration in 1976.

International English Language Periodicals

Australasian Catholic Record, q; St. Patrick's Seminary, Manly, New South Wales, Australia.

Biblical Theology, tri-annual; 44 Old Manse Rd., Newtownabbey, Co. Antrim, N. Ireland BT37 ORX.

Christ to the World, bm; Via G, Nicoterra 31, 00195, Rome, Italy.

Clergy Review, m; 48 Great Peter St., London, S.W. 1, England.

Communio, q; Gonzaga Univ., Spokane, Wash. 99202.

Doctrine and Life, m and **Supplement to Doctrine and Life,** bm; Dominican Publications, St. Saviour's, Dublin 1, Ireland.

Downside Review, q; Newman Bookshop, 87 St. Aldates, Oxford, England.

Dublin Review, q; 14 Howick Place, London, S.W. 1, England.

Eastern Churches Review, semi-annual; 9 Alfred St., Oxford, England.

Furrow, m; St. Patrick's College, Maynooth, Ireland.

Heythrop Journal q; Heythrop College, Cavendish Sq., London W1M, OAN, England.

IDOC International, m; 235 E. 49th St., New York, N.Y. 10017.

International Philosophical Quarterly, q; Fordham University, Bronx, N.Y. 10458.

Irish Theological Quarterly, q; St. Patrick's College, Maynooth, Ireland.

Life and Worship, q; Fowler Wright Books, Ltd., Tenbury Wells, Worcs., England

L'Osservatore Romano, w; Vatican City.

Louvain Studies, semi-annual; Naamsestraat 100, Louvain, Belgium.

Lumen Vitae, q; International Center for Studies in Religious Education, 184, rue Washington, 1050 Brussels, Belgium.

The Middle East Quarterly, 235 E. 49th St., New York, N.Y. 10017.

Month, m; 114 Mount St., London, W. 1, England.

New Blackfriars, m; edited by English Dominicans, Blackfriars, Oxford, England.

One in Christ, q; Benedictine Priory, Priory Close — Southgate, London N. 14 4AT, Eng. (U.S. agency, Grailville, Loveland, O. 45140).

Philosophical Studies, annual; St. Patrick's College, Maynooth, Ireland.

Recusant History, tri-annual; Catholic Record Society, 114 Mount St., London, W. 1, England.

Religion and Society, q; Christian Institute for the Study of Religion and Society, 17 Miller Rd., P.O. Box 604, Bangalore 560 006, S. India.

Scripture in Church, q; Dominican Publications, St. Saviour's, Dublin 1, Ireland.

Studies in Religion/Sciences Religieuses (bilingual), q; Univ. of Toronto Press, Front Campus, Toronto, Ont. M5S 1A6.

Sursum Corda, bm; Box 79, Box Hall, Vic., Australia 3128.

Tablet, The w; 48 Great Peter St., SW1P 2HB, London, England.

Teaching All Nations, q; East Asian Pastoral Institute, Box 1815, Manila, Philippines.

Theology, m; S.P.C.K. Holy Trinity Church, Marylebone Rd., London, N.W. 1, England.

Catholic News Agencies

(Sources: International Catholic Union of the Press, Geneva; Catholic Press Association, U.S.)

Argentina: Agencia Informativa Catolica Argentina (AICA), Rodriguez Pena 846, Casilla de Correo Central 2886, Buenos Aires.

Austria: Katholische Presse-Agentur (Kathpress), Wollzeile 7, Vienna 1.

Belgium: Centre d'Information de Presse (CIP), 38 avenue des Arts, 1040 Bruxelles (Brussels).

Germany: Katholische Nachrichten Agentur (KNA), Kaiser Friedrichstrasse, 9, Bonn.

Great Britain: Catholic Information Office of England and Wales (CIOEW), Avantou House, 9 Bridge St., Pinner, Middlesex.

Hong Kong: Catholic Centre Press Bureau, P.O. Box 2984, Hong Kong.

Hungary: Magyar Kurir, Karolyi w 4-8, Postafiok 41, Budapest V.

Indonesia: Agence "PAX," Dj. Kramat Raya 134, Djakarta IV/5.

Italy: Agenzia Stampa Catholica Associata (ASCA), v. uffici del Vicario 30, I-00186 Rome.

Japan: TO-SEI, 10-1 Rokubancho, Chiyodaku, Tokyo 102.

Mexico: Documentacion e Informacion Catolica, Silos 48, Mexico 13, D.F.

Pakistan: Catholic News Service (CNSP), 111 Depot Lines, Karachi 3.

Spain: Prensa Asociada (PA), Alfonso XI, 4—Apartado 14530, Madrid 14.

LOGOG, Mateo Inurria 15, Apartado 466, Madrid — 16.

Switzerland: Katholische Internationale Presse-Agentur (KIPA), Case Postale 1054 CH 1701, Fribourg.

Centre International de Reportages et d'Information Culturelle (CIRIC), 10, av. de la Gare-des-Eaux Vives, CH-1207 Geneva.

Taiwan: Catholic I-Shi News Agency, 120 Yun-Ho St., Taipeh.

United States of America: NC News Service (NC), 1312 Massachusetts Ave. N.W., Washington, D.C. 20005.

Yugoslavia: Aktusinosti Krscanska Sadasnjost (AKSA), Marulicev TRG 14, Zagreb p.p. 02-748.

Zaire: Documentation et Information Africaine (DIA), B.P. 2598, Kinshasa.

Missions: Agenzia Internationale Fides (AIF), Palazzo di Propagande Fide, Via di Propaganda I-c, Rome, Italy.

Agencies distributing news related to Catholicism as well as other news are:

France: Agence France Presse (AFP), 13 Place de la Bourse, Paris 2e.

Italy: Agenzia Nazionale Stampa Associata (ANSA), Via Propaganda 27, Rome.

U.S. Press Services

NC News Service (NC), established in 1920, provides a worldwide daily news report by wire throughout the continental U.S. and by mail to Canadian and overseas subscribers, serving more than 200 Catholic periodicals, foreign news agencies and Vatican Radio. It also provides feature and photo services; "Origins," a documentary and text service; "Catholic Trends," a fortnightly newsletter to church administrators; "Know Your Faith," a weekly religious education package. NC is represented in all U.S. dioceses and more than 20 foreign countries. It has a three-member bureau in Rome. It is a division of the Communications Department, United States Catholic Conference, with offices at 1312 Massachusetts Ave. N.W., Washington, D.C. 20005. The director and editor-in-chief is A. E. P. Wall.

Religious News Service (RNS) provides Catholic and other religious news in daily foreign and domestic reports, photos and features; "The Religious News Reporter," a

CATHOLIC WRITERS' MARKET
(Source: Almanac survey.)

Editors call the following suggestions to the attention of writers:

Manuscripts should be typewritten, double-spaced, on one side of the page.

Writers should know the editorial policy, purpose and style of the publication to which they submit manuscripts. Sample copies may easily be obtained, often for the mere cost of postage. Some editors suggest that writers send outlines of proposed material, in order to facilitate editorial decision and direction. "Timely" copy should be submitted considerably in advance of the date of proposed publication; some editors advise a period of three months. Authors are urged to avoid sermonizing. Writers should not expect extensive criticism of their work, although they should profit from advice and direction when these are given. Editors are not required to state their reasons for rejecting manuscripts. Replies regarding the acceptance or rejection of copy are usually made within a few weeks.

All writers should send to editors stamped, self-addressed envelopes for the return of material. Those who write to Canadian editors may use international reply coupons, not US stamps.

Payment is made on acceptance or publication. Rates are sometimes variable because of the reputation of the writer, the quality and length of the manuscript, the amount of editorial work required for its final preparation.

America: 106 W. 56th St., New York, N.Y.

weekly 15-minute radio and/or TV package; "The Week in Religion," a feature. RNS was inaugurated in 1933 by the National Conference of Christians and Jews as an independent news agency. Its offices are located at 43 W. 57th St., New York, N.Y. 10019. Lillian R. Block is managing editor.

Eastern Rite Information Service (ER), for Eastern Church news; 2208 W. Chicago Ave., Chicago, Ill. 60622.

Spanish-Language Service: A weekly news summary, *Resumen Semanal de Noticias,* issued by NC News Service, is used by a number of diocesan newspapers. Some papers carry features of their own in Spanish.

BOOK CLUBS

Catholic Book Club (1928), 106 W. 56th St., New York, N.Y. 10019. Sponsors the Campion Award.

Catholic Digest Book Club (1954), Catholic Digest Magazine, P.O. Box 3090, St. Paul, Minn. 55165.

Herald Book Club (1958), Franciscan Herald Press, 1434 W. 51st St., Chicago, Ill. 60609.

Thomas More Book Club (1939), Thomas More Association, 180 N. Wabash Ave., Chicago, Ill. 60601. Sponsors the Thomas More Association Medal.

10019. Ed., Rev. Donald R. Campion, S.J. Weekly, circulation 42,000; $14 per year.

ARTICLES on important public issues evaluated scientifically and morally; serious and authenticated articles on family life, education, religion, and social and political issues with ethical or religious implications; occasionally, "thought" pieces; 1,000-2,000 words—3¢ a word. VERSE, short and modern, befitting a Catholic publication but not necessarily religious—$7.50 and up. No fiction.

American Ecclesiastical Review: 620 Michigan Ave. N.E., Washington, D.C. 20064. Editor-in-chief, Bro. James P. Clifton, C.F.X. Monthly, exc. July-Aug., circulation 2,100; $10 per year.

ARTICLES, mostly theological: 3,000 words.

Annals of St. Anne de Beaupre, The: Basilica of St. Anne, Quebec, Canada. Ed., Rev. J. C. Nadeau, C.SS.R. Monthly, circulation 76,000; $3 per year.

FICTION: Stories of general Catholic interest, preferably with slant on devotion to St. Anne; 1,500-1,600 words — 1½-2¢ a word. ARTICLES of solid general interest to Catholics: on aspects of devotion to St. Anne, relative to history of the devotion in North America or elsewhere: on educational or social problems, or situations that should be of concern to all — especially Christians: 1,200-1,700 words — 2¢ a word, Payment on acceptance; report within a month.

Catechist: 2285 Arbor Blvd., Dayton, O. 45439. Ed., Robert Hawking. Monthly Sept. through May (exc. Dec.), circulation 31,000; $6 per year.

ARTICLES of interest to teachers of religion in parochial schools and CCD programs: 1,500-1,800 words — rate varies. PHOTOGRAPHS, black and white — rate varies.

Catholic Digest: St. Paul, Minn. 55105. Mss. to Rev. Kenneth Ryan, editor. Monthly, circulation 535,000; $4.97 per year.

ARTICLES, factual, of interest to Catholics: 1,500-2,500 words — $200 and up (reprint magazine, uses only two or three original mss per month). PICTURE STORIES, $75 and up. SPECIAL DEPARTMENTS — Open Door, In Our Parish, Hearts Are Trumps, Flights of Fancy, In Our House: short incidents — nominal prices paid to contributors. No fiction or verse.

Catholic Free Press: 247 Mill St. Worcester, Mass. 01602. Ed., Owen J. Murphy, Jr. Weekly, circulation 25,022; $5 per year. Official newspaper of the Diocese of Worcester.

ARTICLES on liturgical subjects, domestic and world affairs, etc.; illustrated features and human interest articles: 500-3,000 words $7-$25. No fiction.

Columban Mission: St. Columbans, Nebr. 68056. Ed., Rev. Peter McPortland. Monthly (exc. June, Aug.); circulation 220,000; $2 per year.

ARTICLES mostly staff written: occasionally accept feature or factual articles on social and religious aspects of Oriental and Latin American life: 2,000 words — $70-$100. PHOTOGRAPHS of Oriental and Latin American subjects and photo stories — $5 each.

Columbia: Columbus Plaza, New Haven, Conn. 06507. Ed., Elmer Von Feldt. Monthly, circulation 1,175,000; $3 per year. Official organ of the Knights of Columbus.

ARTICLES dealing with current events, social problems, Catholic apostolic activities: 1,000-3,000 words (must be accompanied by glossy photos) — $100 to $300. FICTION, Christian viewpoint: up to 3,000 words — up to $300. SATIRE: 1,000 words — $100. CARTOONS, pungent, wordless humor — $25. COVERS — $650.

Commonweal: 232 Madison Ave., New York, N.Y. 10016. Ed., James O'Gara. Bi-weekly, circulation 27,000; $15 per year.

ARTICLES, political, religious and literary subjects: 1,000-3,000 words — 2¢ a word. VERSE, serious poetry of high literary merit — about 40¢ a line.

Cross and Crown: 109 S. Ashland Ave., Chicago, Ill. 60608. Ed., Very Rev. John J. McDonald, O.P. Quarterly, circulation 6,500; $4 per year.

ARTICLES concerning any phase of the spiritual life: minimum 3,000-4,000 words—$4 a page. No fiction or poetry.

Crusader's Almanac: Franciscan Monastery, 1400 Quincy St. N.E., Washington, D.C. 20017. Ed., Rev. Terence W. Kuehn, O.F.M. Quarterly, circulation 105,000; 50¢ per year.

ARTICLES about the Holy Land, Bible and Crusades given preference — 1¢ a word.

Divine Word Messenger: 201 Ruella Ave., Bay Saint Louis, Miss. 39520. Ed., Rev. George G. Wilson, S.V.D. Quarterly, circulation 13,000; $2 per year.

ARTICLES: Catholic Church and American Negro; also general, social, religious, pious, moral themes: 500-1,500 words — 2¢ a word.

Emmanuel; 194 E. 76th Street, New York, N.Y. 10021. Editor-in-Chief, Rev. Raymond A. Tartre, S.S.S. Monthly, bimonthly July-Aug., circulation 17,500; $4 per year.

ARTICLES, clerical spirituality, Eucharistic, pastoral, theological, Scriptural: 2,000-3,000 words — $40.

Eucharist: 194 E. 76th St., New York, N.Y. 10021. Ed., Rev. William J. O'Halloran, S.S.S. Bimonthly, circulation 10,946; $3 per year.

ARTICLES, presenting meaning of Eucharist in Catholic spirituality: average length 1,500 words — 2-3¢ a word.

Family Digest: Noll Plaza, Huntington, Ind. 46750. Ed., Robert A. Willems. Monthly, circulation 156,349; $5 per year.

ARTICLES of timely interest to the young and growing Catholic family — personality profiles, interviews, social concerns, education, humor, inspiration and family interrelationships; 1,000 words or less — 5¢ a word. REPRINTS — $25. PHOTOS, professional quality b/w — $10 each; limited color, $25. PHOTO STORIES — same rates. CARTOONS — $10 each for exclusives. FILLERS — $5 each for exclusives based on personal experience.

Friar: Butler, N.J. 07405. Ed., Rev. Rudolf Harvey, O.F.M. monthly (bimonthly July-Aug.), circulation 20,500; $5 per year.

ARTICLES, Franciscan themes, current events, biography, popular instruction: 2,000 words. Rates vary. CARTOONS.

Hospital Progress: 1438 S. Grand Blvd., St. Louis, Mo. 63104. Ed., R. J. Stephens. Monthly, circulation 17,000; $7 per year. Official journal of the Catholic Hospital Association.

ARTICLES, hospital-oriented; administrative procedures and theories; hospital departmental services: 1,500-5,000 words — $1 per column inch. BOOK REVIEWS, hospital oriented — payment by agreement.

Institute Journal: 50 Oak St., San Francisco, Calif. 94102. Ed., James R. Mullen. Bimonthly, $1 per year.

FICTION — no fixed rate. PHOTOGRAPHS — $15.

It's Our World: 800 Allegheny Ave., Pittsburgh, Pa. 15233. Ed., Thomas F. Haas. Four times a year (two issues: Grades 1-4, 5-8); circulation 3,000,000.

Official publication of Pontifical Association of the Holy Childhood.

ARTICLES, with mission themes suitable for children: 600-800 words — usual rates.

Josephite Harvest, The: 1130 N. Calvert St., Baltimore, Md. 21202. Ed., Rev. John G. Barnett, S.S.J. Bimonthly; circulation 50,000; $2 per year.

ARTICLES concerning the missions: 1¢ a word, and up — by previous arrangement only.

Living Light, The, An Interdisciplinary Review of Christian Education: Published by Our Sunday Visitor, Huntington, Indiana 46750. Editorial offices, Department of Education, 1312 Massachusetts Ave. N.W., Washington D.C. 20005. Quarterly, circulation 4,630; $8 per year.

ARTICLES on religious education, catechetics, Scripture: under 3,000 words — 2¢ per word.

Marian Helpers Bulletin: Eden Hill, Stockbridge, Mass. 01262. Ed., Bro. Robert M. Doyle, M.I.C. Quarterly, circulation over 525,000; $1 per year.

ARTICLES of general interest on devotional, spiritual, moral and social topics: 300-900 words — $25-$35 per article.

Marriage: Abbey Press, St. Meinrad, Ind. 47577. Ed., John J. McHale, Monthly, circulation 58,000; $5.97 per year.

ARTICLES should deal with the relationship between husband and wife; interviews with marriage authorities and interesting couples, profiles, personal essays on marriage: maximum 2,500 words — 5¢ a word minimum.

Maryknoll: Maryknoll, N.Y. 10545. Ed., Rev. Miguel d'Escoto, M.M. Monthly, circulation more than 300,000; $1.00 per year.

ARTICLES must apply in some way to the hopes and aspirations, the culture, the problems and challenges of peoples in Asia, Africa and Latin America: 1,000-1,500 words — average payment, $100. Outline wanted before submission of material. PHOTOS: More interested in photo stories than in individual black and whites and color transparencies. Photo stories — up to $150, black and white; up to $200, color. Individual photos — $15, black and white; $25, color. Transparencies returned after use. Query to be made before sending photos.

Messenger of the Sacred Heart, The: 833 Broadview Ave., Toronto, Ont., Canada, M4K 2P9. Ed., Rev. F.J. Power, S.J. Monthly, circulation 23,000; $3 per year.

FICTION: stories which appeal to men, written with humor—good family reading: maximum, 2,000 words — 2¢ a word. ARTICLES of Catholic interest: 2,500 words — 2¢ a word. Payment upon acceptance.

Miraculous Medal, The: 475 E. Chelten Ave., Philadelphia, Pa. 19144. Ed., Rev. Donald L. Doyle, C.M. Quarterly, circulation 104,000.

FICTION, of general interest. Catholic in principle: 1,500-2,000 words — 2¢ a word and up. VERSE, religious in theme or turn; preferably about Our Lady: maximum 20 lines — 50¢ a line and up. Payment on acceptance. No articles.

My Daily Visitor: Noll Plaza, Huntington, Ind. 46750. Mng. Ed., Paul A. Manoski. Monthly, circulation 15,112; $4 per year.

A pocket-sized booklet of reflections for each day of the month, combined with Mass prayers for the Sundays and holy days of the month.

MATERIAL: Daily reflections based on the feast of the day or the liturgical season: maximum 165 words per page (each day's reflection is printed on a separate page) — $100 for series of reflections.

New Catholic World: 1865 Broadway, New York, N.Y. 10023. Mng. Ed., Robert Heyer. Bimonthly, circulation 16,000; $6 per year. Thematic issues.

FICTION, anything but pietistic: 1,800-2,000 words. ARTICLES, related to themes of issue (query editor): about 1,800-2,000 words. VERSE, not over 22 lines. Rates of payment supplied.

Oblate World and Voice of Hope: 350 Jamaica Way, Boston, Mass. 02130.

Southern U.S. Edition: Co-ed., Rev. John A. Hakey, O.M.I. Five times a year, circulation 53,000; $3 per year.

Philippine Province Edition: Ed., Rev. Martin Walsh, O.M.I.; co-ed., Rev. John A. Hakey, O.M.I. Five times a year, circulation 35,000; $3 per year.

ARTICLES: Photo and mission stories of Oblate Fathers in their missionary work; profiles of Oblate priests and brothers; articles of general Catholic interest — 1½¢-2¢ a word. Finished manuscripts only.

Orphan's Messenger and Advocate of the Blind: St. Joseph's Home, P.O. Box 288, Jersey City, N.J. 07303. Ed., Sr. Eleanor Quin. Quarterly, circulation 94,701; $1 per year.

FICTION, all types, family problems and themes with good morals: 1,000-1,500 words — 1¢ to 2¢ a word. ARTICLES, timely topics or religious: 500-1,000 words — 1¢ to 3¢ a word. PHOTOGRAPHS and DRAWINGS accepted occasionally — rate varies.

Our Family: Box 249, Battleford, Sask., Canada S0M 0E0. Ed., Rev. A. James Materi, O.M.I. Monthly, circulation 10,019; $5 per year.

FICTION, adult only; stories that reflect lives, problems and concerns of audience; love, romance, adventure, intrigue; 1,000-3,000 words — 2¢ a word. ARTICLES related to family living; religion, education, social, biographical, marriage, courtship, domestic, institutional: 1,000-3,000 words — 2¢ a word. POETRY, in the market for many more poems; should deal with man in search for himself, for God, for others, for love, for meaning in life, for commitment: 8-30 lines — $3-$10. PHOTOS — purchased with manuscript as package (extra payment for photos); also in search of individual photos for editorial use. FILLERS — anecdotes of inspirational value, straight exposition, short humor. Write for free Writer's Guide. A sample copy is available for 25¢. Usually buys first North American serial rights; will consider purchasing second or reprint rights.

Our Sunday Visitor: Noll Plaza, Huntington, Ind. 46750. Ed., Richard B. Scheiber. Weekly newspaper-magazine, circulation 350,065; $6.50 per year.

ARTICLES, no limitation on subjects other than those imposed by good taste and orthodoxy. Picture and text stories, profiles of individuals and organizations; articles that reflect moral, cultural, historical, social, economic and certain political concerns about the US and the world; articles on current problems. Practical, factual and anecdotal material is sought: 1,000-1,200 words—$75-$100, usual payment. Queries are preferred to unsolicited completed manuscripts. PHOTOGRAPHS, picture stories preferred rather than individual photos. Picture stories (color) — $100 and up.No fiction or poetry.

Priest, The: Noll Plaza, Huntington, Ind. 46750. Ed., Rev. Jordan Aumann, O.P. (Mss. to the Editor, 1111 N. Richmond St., Chicago, Ill. 60622.) Monthly, circulation 9,923; $8 per year.

ARTICLES of benefit to priests and seminarians in any of the following areas: priestly spirituality, contemporary theology, liturgy, apostolate and ministry, pastoral notes, Scripture. Controversial subject matter acceptable provided it does not go beyond the realm of orthodoxy or respect for authority or demands of fraternal charity: 6-15 double-spaced pages—$25 to $100 (about $5 per manuscript page).

Queen of All Hearts: 40 S. Saxon Ave., Bay Shore, N.Y. 11706. Ed., Rev. James McMillan, S.M.M.; Mng. Ed., Rev. Roger M. Charest S.M.M. Bimonthly; circulation 10,275; $5 per year.

FICTION: short stories, preferably with a Marian theme: 1,000-2,000 words. ARTICLES that bring out the importance of devotion to Mary. PHOTOGRAPHS with human interest, especially relating to the Madonna. VERSE with Marian theme. Payment varies. No artwork or fillers.

Review for Religious: 612 Humboldt Bldg., 539 N. Grand Blvd., St. Louis, Mo. 63103. Ed., D.F.X. Meenan, S.J. Bimonthly, circulation 19,244; $6 per year.

ARTICLES, of interest to religious: 3,000-10,000 words — $6 per printed page.

St. Anthony Messenger: 1615 Republic St., Cincinnati, O. 45210. Ed., Rev. Jeremy Harrington, O.F.M. Monthly, circulation 260,000; $6 per year.

FICTION: Written out of a totally Christian background, illuminating the truth of human nature for adults. No preachiness, sentimentality. FACT ARTICLES: 3,000-3,500 words. Outstanding personalities. Information and comment on major movements in the Church: application of Christian faith to daily life; real-life solutions in the areas of a) family life, education; b) personal living (labor, leisure, art, psychology, spirituality). Human interest narrative. Humor. Photos and picture stories. Query letters welcome.

Salesian Missions: 148 Main St., New Rochelle, New York. Ed., Rev. Edward J. Cappelletti, S.D.B. Quarterly, circulation 950,000; $2 per year.

ARTICLES: mission interest; pertaining to Salesian Society, life, spirit and educational system of St. John Bosco; adolescent interest and education—2¢ a word and up. PHOTOGRAPHS—$5-$6. Suggest queries before submitting material. Payment on acceptance. Early report.

Sign, The: Monastery Pl., Union City, N.J. 07087. Ed., Rev. Augustine P. Hennessy, C.P. Monthly, circulation 155,000; $6 per year.

FICTION of general Catholic interest: 1,000-3,500 words—$200-$300. ARTICLES of Catholic and general interest: 1,000-3,000 words — $200-$300. PHOTOGRAPHS, DRAWINGS

Social Justice Review: 3835 Westminster Pl., St. Louis, Mo. 63108. Ed., Harvey J. Johnson, Monthly, exc. July-Aug., circulation 1,741; $6 per year.

ARTICLES: research, editorial and review: 2,000-4,000 words—$3 per column. No fiction.

Spiritual Life: 2131 Lincoln Rd., N.E., Washington, D.C. 20002. Ed., Rev. Christopher Latimer, O.C.D. Quarterly, circulation 14,000; $5 per year.

ARTICLES, must follow scope of magazine: 3,000-5,000 words — rate varies. Sample copy and instructions for writers sent upon request.

Today's Catholic Teacher: 2451 E. River Rd., Suite 200, Dayton, O. 45439. Ed., Ruth A. Matheny. Monthly Sept. through May (exc. Dec.), circulation 70,000; $6 per year.

ARTICLES of professional and personal interest to teachers, administrators, pastors, parish councils and school board members concerning Catholic schools and CCD programs: 600-800 words, 1,500-3,000 words—$20-$75. Premium payment for superior content and writing presentation. Black and white photos helpful. Payment on publication.

WAY—Catholic Viewpoints: 109 Golden Gate Ave. San Francisco, Calif. 94102. Ed., Simon Scanlon, O.F.M. Ten times a year, circulation 8,404; $4 per year.

ARTICLES, in keeping with the purpose of the magazine, to bear effective witness to the ideals and aims of the Order of St. Francis: to view the world through Christian eyes; to point up the relationship between abstract belief and concrete action in the modern world: 1,500-2,200 words—$30 to $50. PHOTOGRAPHS: bought with articles.

Working for Boys: 601 Winchester St., Newton Highlands, Mass. 02161. Ed., Brother Jerome, C.F.X. (Mss. to Bro. Jason, C.F.X., Assoc. Ed., Xaverian Brothers High School, Westwood, Mass, 02090.) Quarterly, circulation 26,874; 25¢ per year.

FICTION, preferably seasonal: 800-1,000 words—3¢ a word. ARTICLES, preferably seasonal: All Souls, Christmas, Easter, Summer: 800-1,000 words—3¢ a word. VERSE, seasonal, 4-16 lines—25¢-50¢ a line.

Worship: St. John's Abbey, Collegeville, Minn. 56321. Ed., Rev. Aelred Tegels, O.S.B. Monthly (exc. July-Aug.), circulation 9,000; $8 per year.

ARTICLES related to the engagement of the magazine in ongoing study of both the theoretical and pastoral dimensions of liturgy; examines historical traditions of worship in their doctrinal context, the experience of worship in Christian churches, the findings of contemporary theology, psychology, communications, cultural anthropology, and sociology insofar as they have a bearing on public worship: 3,000-5,000 words—2¢ a word for commissioned articles. No fiction or poetry.

STATUS OF CATHOLIC BOOK PUBLISHING

Religious publishing is "booming," but "the sales pattern of Catholic books is a pallid imitation of the rip-roaring success of their Protestant counterparts," according to John J. Delaney, retiring editorial director of the Catholic department of Doubleday & Co., Inc. He was the recipient in September, 1975, of the 22nd annual Thomas More Medal "for the most distinguished contribution to Catholic literature."

Thomas More Medalist

Delaney was honored with the award by the Thomas More Association for his work in producing Doubleday's Image Book reprint series since 1954. He was also cited for his encouragement of writers, co-authorship of *A Dictionary of Catholic Biography,* general editorship of the *Catholic Viewpoint* and *Catholic Perspective* series, and responsibility in the U.S. publication of the *Jerusalem Bible.*

Paucity of Authors

The principal reason why Catholic books "continue plodding along," said Delaney, is that "there is an appalling paucity of publishable Catholic authors."

In an article published in the *National Catholic Reporter,* he stated: "Just as happened with the Protestant publishing scene of the past two or three years, the market for Catholic books has revived. But, unfortunately, unlike our Protestant colleagues, we do not have enough competent Catholic authors to provide books for this market."

Reasons

Among the reasons Delaney gave for the lack of Catholic authors were:

• The period since the Second Vatican Council "has seen change, uncertainty, questioning, groping, renewal, renovation, revolution, if you like, unlike anything the Church has experienced in centuries," and many men and women who might have been writing "have been too involved in the processes of renewal and reform to have time to write."

• This period "has witnessed an exodus of men and women from the Church and from their accustomed state who normally might be expected to produce books." Many earlier best-selling Catholic titles were written by priests and nuns, Delaney said. "But in a period when many religious had renounced their roles as priests and nuns and many of those who remained were redefining their roles in religion, little time or energy was left for the most demanding of man's endeavors — writing."

Disappearance of Publishers

• The "disappearance of many of the old-line Catholic publishers," such as Bruce, P. J. Kenedy, Benziger Brothers, Herder and Herder, and Helicon. "No longer were the editors of these publishers out in the field coaxing, cajoling, giving out with ideas — doing the myriad things a good editor does to get books into existence." The drop in the number of publishing firms also meant that "potential authors were seriously limited in finding publishers for their work."

• Many magazines that "had published original Catholic writing went out of business" and others cut down the amount of material they would accept for publication. "With this curtailment of sources offering publication, one more disheartening obstacle was added to an already formidable list facing one aspiring to a career of writing in the Catholic field."

The Financial Side

• "Increasingly, the allurement of general publishing, especially to lay authors, was brighter than religious publishing. For many years, the financial return in the religious field, and particularly in the Catholic field, generally speaking, was meager compared to the financial return from general publishing."

• When priests and nuns, a main source of readership of Catholic books, "became involved as they did in renewal and reform efforts, they spent less time reading" and more money on material things.

• Authors have sought to write for a

broader Christian market than for the strictly Catholic market, and the consequence has been "a loss of authors who are capable and competent in the Catholic field."

• To secure federal and state funds, many Catholic colleges have declared themselves secular colleges. "When the educational milieu changes from religious to secular, one of

the consequences may be a loss of authors for Catholic publishing."

Good Market, Few Authors

"So now," Delaney said, "those of us who are left involved in Catholic publishing are faced with the curious situation of a real revival of interest in Catholic books when very few publishable authors exist to meet that demand."

RADIO, TELEVISION, THEATRE

Radio

Christian in Action: Originated in 1941, produced in cooperation with the Office for Film and Broadcasting, NCCB/USCC. A 15-minute weekly program currently employing a youth-oriented music and commentary format; heard on more than 50 stations (ABC).

Christopher Radio Program: Produced by Rev. Richard Armstrong, M.M. Features 15-minute interview-discussion series, weekly, on 700 stations; a one-minute Christopher "Thought for Today," daily, on more than 2,100 stations. Address: 12 E. 48th St., New York, N.Y. 10017.

Crossroads: Originated in 1954 as the Hour of the Crucified, produced by the Passionist Fathers and Brothers. Weekly, on nearly 325 stations and Armed Forces Radio. Director: Rev. Cyril Schweinberg, C.P.; Associate Director: Bro. Damian Carroll, C.P. Address: 1089 Elm St., West Springfield, Mass. 01089.

Encuentro (Spanish-language version of Crossroads): Originated in October, 1972. Weekly, on over 30 Spanish-language stations in U.S. and Latin America. Producer: Bro. John Regis McHale, C.P. Address: 1089 Elm St., W. Springfield, Mass. 01089.

Guideline: Produced in cooperation with the Office for Film and Broadcasting, NCCB/USCC. Weekly program designed to set forth the teachings of the Catholic Church and to discuss issues the Church faces in the contemporary world; heard on approximately 90 stations (NBC).

Sacred Heart Program: Originated in 1939, produced by the Jesuit Fathers. Features five 15-minute programs and one half-hour program weekly on radio, and one 15-minute TV program weekly. Director, Rev. Denis E. Daly, S.J. Address: 3900 Westminster Place, St. Louis, Mo. 63108.

Television

Directions: Originated in 1960, this weekly half-hour program sustains a news-oriented approach to reporting social, moral and religious issues within a Catholic context. The Office for Film and Broadcasting, NCCB/USCC, cooperates in the production of some 11 segments a year, in addition to interfaith and seasonal specials; carried at variable dates on more than 100 stations (ABC).

Look Up and Live: Originated in 1954, this

half-hour series sustains a variety of formats from dramatizations to studio discussions. The Office for Film and Broadcasting, NCCB/USCC, cooperates in producing 14 half-hours a year, in addition to interfaith and seasonal specials; carried on approximately 120 stations (CBS).

Religious Specials: The Office for Film and Broadcasting, NCCB/USCC, cooperates in the production of four one-hour Catholic specials a year and occasional seasonal or trifaith presentations. These programs offer a varied format: film, dramatizations, panel discussions, music and commentary, etc. Catholic portions are telecast on approximately 175 stations (NBC).

Theatre

The Blackfriars Theatre: The oldest experimental theatre under Catholic auspices in the United States, suspended operations in March, 1972, 32 years after it became the first off-Broadway theatre in New York City. Founded in 1931 in Washington, D.C., under the sponsorship of the Blackfriars Guild, it produced 75 original plays in 41 years; the last one, which opened Feb. 23, 1972, was *The Red Hat.* The Guild founders and long-time promoters of the theatre were Dominican Fathers Urban Nagle (1905-65) and Thomas F. Carey (1904-72). President, Rev. Terence Quinn, O.P. Address: 141 E. 65th St., New York, N.Y. 10021.

Catholic University Speech and Drama Department: Established in 1937. Offers degree courses in theatre arts, produces five plays a year in The Hartke Theatre, has touring company of graduates (see National Players). Acting chairman of the department, Donald J. Waters. Address: Catholic University of America, Washington, D.C. 20064.

National Players: Originated in 1949, is the professional touring company of graduates of the Catholic University Speech and Drama Department; oldest classical touring company in the US. Operates a theatre at Olney, Md.

Catholic Actors' Guild of America, Inc.: Established in 1914 to provide varied services to people in the theatre. Has more than 1,000 members, publishes *The Call Board* bimonthly. President, Cyril Ritchard. Address: Piccadilly Hotel, 227 W. 45th St., New York,

N.Y. 10036. The Actors' Chapel is located in St. Malachy's Church, 239 W. 49th St., New York, N.Y.

Communications Services

Christopher TV Series, "Christopher Closeup": Originated in 1951. Half-hour and quarter-hour interviews in color, weekly, on 150 stations. Address: 12 E. 48th St., New York, N.Y. 10017.

Father Peyton's Family Theater Productions: Films for TV, for sale and rental. Address: 7201 Sunset Blvd., Hollywood, Calif. 90046.

Franciscan Communications Center: An audio-visual media center of the Franciscan movement, dedicated to the production of public service broadcasting material and audio-visual media for religious education. Creators and producers of TeleSPOTS and AudioSPOTS, 10- to 60-second public service messages for radio and TV; TeleKETICS films and media kits (Images of Faith, Lifelines, etc.), for religious, moral and value education, Address: 1229 South Santee St., Los Angeles, Calif. 90015.

Mary Productions "Airtime": Originated in 1950. Offers royalty-free scripts for stage, film, radio and tape production. Address: Mary Productions Guild, 58 Lenison Ave., Belford, N.J. 07718.

Paulist Communications: Contracts with dioceses and parishes to provide public service programs free to radio stations and scripts to priest-broadcasters; contacts stations for dioceses. Address: P.O. Box 1057, Pacific Palisades, Calif. 90272.

Paulist Productions: Producers and distributors of the INSIGHT Film Series (available for TV at no charge), and the educational series VIGNETTES. Purchase and rental information available. Address: P.O. Box 1057, Pacific Palisades, Calif. 90272.

Sacred Heart Program — TV: Originated in 1954, produced by the Jesuit Fathers. Director, Rev. Denis E. Daly, S.J. Address: 3900 Westminster Pl., St. Louis, Mo. 63108.

St. Bernardine Communicators Guild: Offers vocation tapes to individuals and organizations for broadcast on local stations. Address: 6801 N. Yates Rd., Milwaukee, Wis. 53217.

Tele-Vue I Productions: Films for TV, mostly educational, for sale and rental. Address: Rev. Paul W. Stauder, Box 24, East St. Louis, Ill. 62202.

Catholic Television Network (CTN): Instructional TV operations have been established in the following archdioceses and dioceses. Archdioceses are indicated by an asterisk.

Boston,* Mass.: Rev. James Hawker, Director, 468 Beacon St. 02115.

Brooklyn, N.Y.: Mr. Michael J. Hurley, Director, 500 19th St. 11215.

Chicago,* Ill.: Mr. Charles E. Hinds, Executive Director, One N. Wacker Dr. 60606.

Detroit,* Mich.: Rev. John B. Zwers,

Director, 305 Michigan Ave. 48226.

Los Angeles,* Calif.: Mr. David Moore, 1520 W. Ninth St. 90015.

Miami,* Fla.: Msgr. Joseph H. O'Shea, Director, 6200 Northeast 4th Ct. 33138.

Milwaukee,* Wis.: Rev. Guy Gurath, Director, 12666 W. Beloit Rd., New Berlin, Wis. 53151.

New York,* N.Y.: Sr. M. Irene Fugazy, Director, Seminary Ave., Yonkers, N.Y. 10704.

Rockville Centre, N.Y.: Dr. Francis J. Ryan, Director, 1345 Admiral Lane, Uniondale, N.Y. 11553.

San Francisco,* Calif.: Msgr. Pierre Du Maine, Director, 443 Church St. 94114.

UNDA-USA: A national professional and autonomous Catholic association for broadcasters and allied communicators organized in 1972. It succeeded the Catholic Broadcasters Association of America which in 1948 had replaced the Catholic Forum of the Air organized in 1938. It is a member of the international Catholic association for radio and television known as UNDA (the Latin word for "wave," symbolic of air waves of communication). UNDA-USA publishes a newsletter five times a year for members and presents the Gabriel Awards (see Index) annually for excellence in broadcasting. President, Sister Maureen Rodgers, O.P., 305 Michigan Ave., Detroit, Mich. 48226.

Office for Film and Broadcasting (OFB): A unit of the Department of Communication of the United States Catholic Conference.

OFB serves as the principal instrument of the USCC for the exercise of a national pastoral ministry which aims (a) generally, at developing the unique potential that these media possess for contributing to mutual understanding and progress among men, and (b) specifically, at the utilization of these media for communicating the Gospel to the men of our day.

OFB provides a national service of information, training and cooperation for diocesan communications offices throughout the country. SHARE, a packet of film and broadcasting information, is published twice monthly.

For the motion picture medium, OFB publishes the twice-monthly *Catholic Film Newsletter* which reviews all current nationally released 35 mm films and provides information about resources for film utilization and education (16 mm films, books, magazines, festivals). The critical reviews are addressed to the moral as well as artistic dimensions of motion pictures and are the result of a consensus based on the reactions of OFB's professional staff and board of consultors. All films reviewed are also classified according to the OFB rating system. Film classification supplements appear every two months as part of the *Newsletter*. In addition, the publication carries information and evaluative studies on trends and issues pertinent to television, with an emphasis on educational material.

The office maintains a 16mm film library of Catholic program material and a consultation service for educational and religious film program directors.

For the broadcast media, OFB is responsible for cooperating with the three major networks (NBC, ABC, and CBS) in the production of all regularly scheduled network radio and television programs involving Catholic participation (see Radio and Television).

For the Catholic press, OFB publishes a weekly film/broadcast service consisting of reviews, information, articles and photos. Special projects are undertaken with individual publications, religious and general.

OFB also plays a liaison role for the NCCB/USCC with the film and broadcasting industries, national media, and religious agencies and organizations. It is a member of OCIC and UNDA, the international Catholic organizations for film and broadcasting, respectively. Consultations and information services are also provided for the Pontifical Commission for Social Communications and the communications offices of national episcopal conferences throughout the world.

Rev. Patrick J. Sullivan, S.J., is the director.

Address: 1011 First Ave., New York, N.Y. 10022.

Foundation

The Catholic Communications Foundation (CCF) was established by the Catholic Fraternal Benefit Societies in 1968 in New York to lend support and assistance to development of the broadcasting apostolate of the Church.

The CCF, in addition to making financial grants (more than $450,000 from 1966 to 1974) for religious programs and programming services, has promoted the development of diocesan communications capabilities and has funded scholarship programs at the Institute for Religious Communications at Loyola University, New Orleans.

CCF officers are Bishop John A. Donovan, chairman of the board; Bishop Andrew A. Grutka, president and treasurer; Richard T. Tobin and Charles E. Reilly, Jr., executive vice president and secretary, respectively. James R. Bastis is staff coordinator. Serving on the board are several US bishops, communications executives, and representatives of the fraternal societies.

Address: Suite 1224, 500 Fifth Ave., New York, N.Y. 10036.

DIOCESAN COMMUNICATIONS OFFICES, DIRECTORS

(Principal source: *1975/76 Directory of Catholic Communications Personnel,* published by the National Catholic Office for Information. Archdioceses are designated by an asterisk.)

Alabama: Birmingham — Rev. Martin Muller (Communications), Box 6147, Birmingham 35209.

Mobile — Rev. Michael J. Dyer (Ed., *The Catholic Week*), Rev. Robert L. Anderson, S.J. (Radio-TV), 557 Dauphin St., Mobile 36602.

Alaska: Anchorage* — Rev. Richard Saudis, 811 6th Ave., Box 2239, Anchorage 99510.

Fairbanks — Rev. James E. Poole, S.J., Box 101, Nome 99762.

Juneau — Miss Carol Crater (Ed., *Inside Passage*), 416 5th St., Juneau 99801.

Arizona: Phoenix — Jerry Burns (Media Director), 400 E. Monroe, Phoenix 85004.

Tucson — Ms. Marguerite Bantlin (Information), 64 W. Ochoa St., Tucson 85701.

Arkansas: Little Rock — Msgr. B. Francis McDevitt (Communications, Radio-TV), 617 Louisiana St., Little Rock 72201.

California: Fresno — Mr. Joseph Jasmin (Information), Box 4273, Fresno 93744.

Los Angeles* — Rev. John C. Urban (Communications), 1531 W. 9th St., Los Angeles 90015.

Monterey — Rev. Dennis M. Gilbert (Communications), 14 Stone St., Salinas 93901; Rev. Felix Migliazzo (Ed., *The Observer*), Box 88, Monterey 93940.

Oakland — Mr. William Bettencourt (Public Relations), Rev. Richard Mangini, 2900 Lakeshore Ave., Oakland 94610.

Sacramento — Rev. James T. Murphy (Information), Box 1407, Sacramento 95807; Rev. James F. Church (Radio-TV), 1121 K St., Sacramento 95814.

San Diego — Deacon Michael Newman (Communications), Box 81869, San Diego 92138; Rev. Eugene Fischer (Radio-TV), P.O. Box 11277, San Diego 92111.

San Francisco* — Rev. Miles Riley (Communications Center); Rev. Harry G. Schlitt (Radio-TV), Sister Janet Marie (Film and Audio Distributor), 50 Oak St., San Francisco 94102; Gerard E. Sherry (Information), 441 Church St., San Francisco 94114.

Santa Rosa — Msgr. Walter J. Tappe, 398 10th St., Box 1297, Santa Rosa 95403.

Stockton — Rev. Lawrence J. McGovern (Information), Box 4237, 1105 N. Lincoln St., Stockton 95204.

Colorado: Denver* — Rev. C. B. Woodrich (Information), 938 Bannock St., Denver 80204; Rev. Maurice J. McInerney (Radio-TV), 29 W. Kiowa St., Colorado Springs 80902.

Pueblo — Ms. Geraldine Carrigan (Communications; Ed., *Catholic Crosswinds*), 1725 Spruce, Pueblo 81004.

Connecticut: Bridgeport — Rev. Alfred J.

Sienkiewicz (Radio-TV), 385 Scofieldtown Rd., Stamford 06903.

Hartford* — Rev. Edmund S. Nadolny (Communications), 785 Asylum Ave., Hartford 06105.

Norwich — Sr. Roberta McGrath (Communications), 201 Hickory St., Norwich 06360.

Stamford (Ukrainian Diocese) — Msgr. Emil Manastersky, 161 Glenbrook Rd., Stamford 06902.

Delaware: Wilmington — Mr. F. Eugene Donnelly (Communications), Box 2030, Wilmington 19899

District of Columbia: Washington* — Rev. Maurice T. Fox (Communications), 1721 Rhode Island Ave. N.W., Washington 20036; Msgr. Leonard F. Hurley (Radio-TV), Box 18, Germantown, Md. 20767.

Florida: Miami* — Mr. John E. Shields (Public Relations), 6301 Biscayne Blvd., Miami 33138; Msgr. Joseph H. O'Shea (Radio-TV), Rev. Jose Hernando (Spanish Speaking Radio-TV), Rev. Frank E. Cahill (Programming and Production), 6200 Northeast 4th Ct., Miami 33138.

Orlando — Rev. Patrick Murray (Communications), Box 1527, Ormond Beach 32074.

St. Augustine — Rev. R. Joseph James (Diocesan News Service, Radio-TV), Box 8625, Jacksonville 32211.

St. Petersburg — Msgr. J. Keith Symons, Box 13109, St. Petersburg 33733.

Georgia: Atlanta* — Rev. Peter A. Dora (Ed., *The Georgia Bulletin*), 756 W. Peachtree St. N.W., Atlanta 30308.

Savannah — Rev. Francis J. Donohue (Communications), Box 9207, Savannah 31402.

Hawaii: Honolulu — Msgr. Francis A. Marzen, 1184 Bishop St., Honolulu 96813.

Idaho: Boise — Rev. David L. Riffle (Communications Center), 6003 Overland, Boise 83705; Rev. David J. Kundtz (Information), Box 2835, Boise 83701.

Illinois: Belleville — Rev. James Blazine (Communications), 5312 W. Main St. P.O. Box 986, Belleville 62223.

Chicago* — Rev. James P. Roache (Communications), Rev. John S. Banahan (Radio-TV), Box 1979, Chicago 60690.

Joliet — Rev. Edwin J. Joyce, 425 Summit St., Joliet 60435; Rev. William F. Irwin, St. Patrick Church, Wilton Center, R.R. No. 1, Manhattan 60442.

Peoria — Rev. Tom Royer, 612 E. Park Ave., Champagne 61820.

Rockford — Rev. Thomas Monahan (Communications), 1245 N. Court St., Rockford 61101.

St. Nicholas in Chicago for Ukrainians — Msgr. Jaroslav Swyschuk (Eastern Rite Information Bureau), 2208 W. Chicago Ave., Chicago 60622.

Springfield — Rev. Richard L. Paynic (Information), Box 15, Springfield 62705.

Indiana: Evansville — Rev. Joseph L. Ziliak (Information), 208 N.W. 3rd St., Evansville 47708; Rev. Jean F. Vogler (Radio-TV), 3109 Bayard Park Dr., Evansville 47714.

Fort Wayne-South Bend — Msgr. James P. Conroy (Communications), Noll Plaza, Huntington 46750.

Gary — Rev. John J. Savio, 6060 Miller Ave., Gary 46403.

Indianapolis* — Mr. Charles J. Schisla (Communications), 136 W. Georgia St., Indianapolis 46225.

Lafayette — Rev. Paul Dehner (Information), 3810 W. Jefferson Rd., Kokomo 46901.

Iowa: Davenport — Rev. Francis C. Henricksen (Communications), 407 Brady St., Box 939, Davenport 52805.

Des Moines — Sister Janet M. Hudspeth, O.P. (Communications), 2910 Grand Ave., Box 1816, Des Moines 50306.

Dubuque* — Rev. John W. Dalton, 1229 Mt. Loretta Ave. Dubuque 52001.

Sioux City — Mr. Lewis E. Heifner, 710 19th St., Box 1678, Sioux City 51102; Msgr. Frank Brady (Radio-TV), 1212 Morningside Ave., Sioux City 51106.

Kansas: Dodge City — Msgr. A. J. Felling (Communications), Box 849, Dodge City 67801.

Kansas City* — Rev. H. J. Wickey (Information), Box 2329, Kansas City 66110.

Salina — Rev. L. E. Pierce (Information), Box 958, Salina 67401.

Wichita — Rev. Eugene J. Gerber, 424 N. Broadway, Wichita 67202.

Kentucky: Covington — Rev. Patrick A. Doyle, 1044 Scott St., Covington 41012; Rev. David Macpherson (Radio-TV), Thomas More College, P.O. Box 85, Covington 41017.

Louisville* — Rev. John H. Morgan, 1305 W. Market St., Louisville 40203.

Owensboro — Msgr. George Hancock (Information), 4003 Frederica St., Owensboro 42301; Rev. Leonard Reisz (Radio-TV), St. Edward Church, 510 Eddings St., Fulton 42041.

Louisiana: Alexandria — Mr. Al Nassif (Information), Box 5047, Alexandria 71301.

Baton Rouge — Rev. Gerald Lefebure (Information), Box 14746, Baton Rouge 70808.

Lafayette — Rev. Richard Greene (Communications), Box 3223, Lafayette 70501.

New Orleans* — Mr. Thomas M. Finney (Communications, Public Relations), 7887 Walmsley Ave., New Orleans 70125; Rev. Brian Highfill (Radio-TV), Box 4014, Houma 70360.

Maine: Portland — Mr. Clarence F. McKay (Communications), 510 Ocean Ave., Portland 04103.

Maryland: Baltimore* — Mr. James E. Shaneman (Information), Rev. John Geaney, C.S.P. (Telecommunications), 320 Cathedral St., Baltimore 21201.

Massachusetts: Boston* — Mr. George E. Ryan (News Bureau), 49 Franklin St., Boston

02110; Msgr. Walter L. Flaherty (Radio-TV), 55 Chapel St., Newton 02160.

Fall River — Msgr. Daniel F. Shalloo (Information), P.O. Box 7, Fall River 02722; Rev. John F. Hogan, (TV), 494 Slocum Rd., N. Dartmouth 02747.

Springfield — Msgr. David P. Welch, 57 Observer St., Box 1570, Springfield 01101; Rev. Cyril Schweinberg, C.P. (Radio-TV), 1089 Elm St., W. Springfield 01089.

Worcester — Rev. John W. Barrett (Communications), 49 Elm St., Worcester 01609.

Melkite Apostolic Exarchate — Rev. James E. King, 19 Dartmouth St., W. Newton 02165.

Michigan: Detroit* — Mr. John F. Lynch (Communications), Sr. Maureen Rogers, O.P. (Radio-TV), 305 Michigan Ave., Detroit 48226.

Gaylord — Rev. David Gemuend, Box 700, Gaylord 49735.

Grand Rapids — Msgr. Hugh M. Beahan, 423 First St. N.W., Grand Rapids 49504.

Kalamazoo — Rev. Robert E. Consani (Communications), 200 E. Front St., Mattawan 49071.

Lansing — Rev. Donald L. Eder (Communications), Chancery Office, 505 N. Capitol Ave., Lansing 48933.

Marquette — Sr. Clare Mess (Communications), Box 280, Marquette 49855.

Saginaw — Sr. Jan Stobbart, O.P. (Communications), Mr. Robert Young (Press Officer), 2555 Wieneke Rd., Saginaw 48603.

St. Maron's Diocese of Detroit (Maronite Rite) — Msgr. Joseph Abi-Nader, Box 14082 — Jefferson Sta., Detroit 48214.

Minnesota: Crookston — Rev. John O'Toole, Box 605, Crookston 56716.

Duluth — Rev. George M. Schroeder (Information), 215 W. 4th St., Duluth 55806.

New Ulm — Rev. Donald J. Eichinger (Communications), Church of the Japanese Martyrs, Sleepy Eye 56085.

St. Cloud — Ms. Rosemary Borgert (Information), 810 St. Germain St., Box 1068, St. Cloud 56301.

St. Paul and Minneapolis* — Rev. Robert C. Nygaard (Communications), 226 Summit Ave., St. Paul 55102.

Winona — Msgr. W. T. Magee (Communications), Box 949, Winona 55987.

Mississippi: Natchez-Jackson — Mrs. Janna Avalon, Box 2130, Jackson 39205.

Missouri: Jefferson City — Rev. Hugh Behan (Information), Box 1107, Jefferson City 65101; Rev. John Long (Communications), Box 417, Jefferson City 65101.

Kansas City-St. Joseph — Rev. John Weiss, Box 1037, Kansas City 64141.

St. Louis* — Rev. Edward O'Donnell (Information), 462 N. Taylor Ave., St. Louis 63108; Rev. Joseph M. O'Brien (Radio-TV), 4140 Lindell Blvd., St. Louis 63108.

Springfield-Cape Girardeau — Mr. Robert

G. Lee (Communications), M.P.O. Box 847, Springfield 65801.

Montana: Great Falls — Rev. Richard Hopkins, 725 3rd Ave. N., Box 2107, Great Falls 59403.

Helena — Mrs. Frances H. Voss (Communications), Box 1175, Helena 59601.

Nebraska: Grand Island — Rev. Bernard M. Berger (Communications), P.O. Box 477, Grand Island 68801.

Lincoln — Rev. James D. Dawson (Information), Box 80328, Lincoln 68501.

Omaha* — Sister Patricia Kowalski (Communications), 100 N. 62nd St., Omaha 68132.

Nevada: Reno — Rev. Lawrence M. Quilici (Communications), 1111 Michael Way, Las Vegas 89108.

New Hampshire: Manchester — Rev. Philip P. Bruni (Communications), 153 Ash St., Manchester 03105.

New Jersey: Camden — Mr. Charles Germain (Information), 1845 Haddon Ave., Box 709, Camden 08101.

Newark* — Rev. James A. Pindar (Communications), 31 Mulberry St., Newark 07102.

Passaic (Byzantine Rite Eparchy) — Msgr. Thomas Dolinay 101 Market St., Passaic 07055.

Paterson — Rev. Ronald Amandolare (Acting Dir., Communications Center), Rev. Bruce Welch (Radio Programming), 74 Kahdena Rd., Morristown 07960; Mr. Gerald M. Costello (Information), 163-165 Newark-Pompton Turnpike (Box A), Pequannock 07440.

Trenton — Msgr. William E. Maguire, 139 N. Warren St., Trenton 08608.

New Mexico: Gallup — Rev. Cormac Antram, O.F.M., Box 48, Houck 86506.

Santa Fe* — Ms. Eileen Stanton (Communications), 202 Morningside Dr. S.E., Albuquerque 87110.

New York: Albany — Rev. William H. Kennedy (Communications), 40 N. Main Ave., Albany 12203.

Brooklyn — Rev. Thomas J. Flanagan (Public Information), Mr. Frank DeRosa (Media Relations), 75 Greene Ave., Brooklyn 11238.

Buffalo — Rev. Robert E. Nesslin (Communications), 531 Virginia St., Buffalo 14202; Msgr. John J. McMahon (Radio-TV), 100 S. Elmwood Ave., Buffalo 14202.

New York* — Msgr. Eugene V. Clark (Communications), Rev. Jose Alvarez (Spanish Media), 1011 First Ave., New York, N.Y. 10022.

Ogdensburg — Rev. David W. Stinebrickner (Information), 622 Washington St., Ogdensburg 13669; Rev. John L. Downs (Radio-TV), St. Cecilia's Rectory, 23 Grove St., Adams 13605.

Rochester — Rev. Michael F. Conboy (Information), 1150 Buffalo Rd., Rochester 14624; Rev. Louis J. Hohman (Episcopal Advisor), 67 Chestnut St., Rochester 14604.

Rockville Centre — Rev. Daniel S. Hamilton (Information), 53 N. Park Ave., Box 395, Rockville Centre 11571; Rev. William J. Ayres (Radio-TV), 40 Grove Pl., Babylon 11702.

Syracuse — Msgr. Robert F. Lavin, 240 E. Onondaga St., Syracuse 13202.

North Carolina: Charlotte — Rev. William G. Wellein, 335 Springdale Ave., Winston-Salem 27104.

Raleigh — Rev. James F. Keenan, Box 1149, Washington 27889.

Belmont Abbey — Rev. Peter Stragand, O.S.B., Belmont 28012.

North Dakota: Bismarck — Rev. John J. Owens, Box 128, Wilton 58579.

Fargo — Sister Mary Ethel Paulus (Ed., *Catholic Action News*), Box 1750, Fargo 58102

Ohio: Cincinnati* — Mr. Daniel J. Kane (Communications), Rev. Theodore Kosse (Radio-TV), 426 E. 5th St., Cincinnati 45202.

Cleveland — Rev. Joseph Kraker (Communications), Mr. J. Jerome Lackamp (Radio-TV), 1027 Superior Ave., Cleveland 44114.

Columbus — Rev. James P. Hanley (Communications), Ms. Leni Koloski (Public Relations, Information), Rev. Michael Reis (Radio-TV), 197 E. Gay St., Columbus 43215.

Parma (Byzantine Rite Eparchy) — Rev. Joseph Pohorlak, 5390 W. 220th St., Fairview Park 44126.

Steubenville — Rev. James C. Marshall, 422 Washington St., Box 969, Steubenville 43952.

Toledo — Mr. Jim Richards (Information), 2544 Parkwood Ave., Toledo 43610.

Youngstown — Mr. Patrick DiSalvatore (Communications), Sister Nancy Dawson, O.S.U. (Radio-TV), 144 W. Wood St., Youngstown 44114.

Oklahoma: Oklahoma City* — Rev. David F. Monahan (Communications), Box 887, Oklahoma City 73101.

Tulsa — Rev. William K. Skeehan (Communications), Box 45672, Tulsa 74145.

Oregon: Baker — Rev. Joseph B. Hayes, St. Patrick Church, Box 730, Vale 97918.

Portland* — Rev. Donald Happe, Rev. Leo Remington (Radio-TV), 2838 E. Burnside, Portland 97214.

Pennsylvania: Allentown — Msgr. Vincent E. Lewellis (Information), 1729 Turner St., Allentown 18104.

Altoona-Johnstown — Msgr. Edward W. O'Malley (Information), 126C Logan Blvd., Hollidaysburg 16648.

Erie — Msgr. E. James Caldwell (Publicity and Information), Box 4047, Erie 16512.

Greensburg — Mr. John Quigley (Communications), Ms. Colleen Wood (Radio-TV), Box 850, Greensburg 15601.

Harrisburg — Rev. David T. McAndrew (Communications), 4800 Union Deposit Rd., Harrisburg 17105.

Munhall* (Byzantine Rite) — Msgr. Edward V. Rosack (Information), 624 Park Rd., Cambridge 15003; Most Rev. John M. Bilock (Radio-TV), 54 Riverview Ave., Pittsburgh 15214.

Philadelphia* — Mr. Edward F. Devenney (Communications), Rev. Leo J. McKenzie (Radio-TV), 222 North 17th St., Philadelphia 19103.

Philadelphia* (Ukrainian) — Rev. Ronald Popivchak, 519 Union Ave., Bridgeport 19405.

Pittsburgh — Msgr. Daniel H. Brennan (Communications), Mr. Joseph Williams (Public Information), 111 Boulevard of the Allies, Pittsburgh 15222.

Scranton — Rev. Joseph P. Gilgallon, 300 Wyoming Ave., Box 708, Scranton 18503.

Rhode Island: Providence — Mr. Brian L. Wallin (Communications), Cathedral Square, Providence 02903.

South Carolina: Charleston — Rev. Robert J. Millard (Communications), 1529 Assembly St., Columbia 29201.

South Dakota: Rapid City — Rev. William J. O'Connell, Box 678, Rapid City 57701.

Sioux Falls — Msgr. Louis J. Delahoyde, 423 N. Duluth Ave., Sioux Falls 57104.

Tennessee: Memphis — Msgr. Paul W. Clunan (Communications), 203 S. White Station Rd., Memphis 38117.

Nashville — Mr. Joseph A. Sweat (Public Affairs), 2400 21st Ave. S., Nashville 37212.

Texas: Amarillo — Msgr. Leroy T. Matthiesen (Information), Msgr. Richard F. Vaughan (Radio-TV), Box 5644, 1800 N. Spring, Amarillo 79107.

Austin — Rev. Victor Goertz (Ed., *Texas Catholic Herald*), 1401 Washington Ave., Waco 76702.

Beaumont — Rev. Earl D. Mudd, P.O. Box 3948, Beaumont 77704.

Brownsville — Mr. Allan Porter (Communications), Box 2279, Brownsville 78520.

Corpus Christi — Mr. John J. Foley (Public Relations), 818 Antelope, Corpus Christi 78401.

Dallas — Mr. Norman D. Phillips (Information), Box 19507, Dallas 75219; Mr. Ed Hallack, KDFW, 400 N. Griffin St., Dallas 75202.

El Paso — Mr. Andrew Sparke (Information), 1013 E. San Antonio, El Paso 79901.

Fort Worth — Rev. Eugene Witkowski, 1206 Throckmorton St., Ft. Worth 76102; Mr. Jerry Thomas, KTVT Channel 11, 4801 W. Freeway, Ft. Worth 76107.

Galveston-Houston — Msgr. John L. Fos, Mr. Paul Kelly (Radio-TV), 1700 San Jacinto St., Houston 77002.

San Angelo — Mr. Frank Trudo (Communications), 1705 Kenwood Dr., San Angelo 76901.

San Antonio* — Rev. Brian Wallace

(Communications), P.O. Box 12429, San Antonio 78212.

Utah: Salt Lake City — Msgr. W. H. McDougall (Information), 331 E. S. Temple St., Salt Lake City 84111; Rev. Thomas J. Meersman (Radio-TV), Box 477, Kearns 84118.

Vermont: Burlington — Rev. Joseph T. Sullivan (Communications), 52 Williams St., Burlington 05401.

Virginia: Arlington — Msgr. Richard J. Burke, 200 N. Glebe Rd., Arlington 22203.

Richmond — Mr. Bob Edwards (Communications), 907 Terry Ave., Seattle 98104.

Washington: Seattle* — Rev. James Eblen (Communications), 907 Terry Ave., Seattle 98104.

Spokane — Mr. Dan Morris, W. 1023 Riverside Ave., P.O. Box 48, Spokane 99210.

Yakima — Rev. Robert J. Shields, Box 50067, Zillah 98953.

West Virginia: Wheeling — Mr. Frank L. Sweeney, Box 230, Wheeling 26003.

Wisconsin: Green Bay — Mr. Reinhart J. Wessing (Communications), Box 909, Green Bay 54305.

La Crosse — Rev. Dennis J. Lynch (Communications), 1732 State St., La Crosse 54601.

Madison — Rev. Joseph P. Higgins, Box 111, Madison 53701; Rev. Stephen Umhoefer (Radio-TV), High Point Rd. Rt. 2, Madison 53711.

Milwaukee* — Msgr. Ralph R. Schmit (Radio-TV), 4063 N. 64th St., Milwaukee 53216.

Superior — Rev. Robert Urban (Information), 1512 N. 12th St., Superior 54880.

Wyoming: Cheyenne — Rev. Philip Colibraro (Information), Box 97, Pine Bluffs 82082.

Delaware Valley Catholic Office for Television and Radio: Interdiocesan agency of the Archdiocese of Philadelphia and the dioceses of Allentown, Pa.; Camden and Trenton, N.J.; and Wilmington, Del. Director, Rev. Leo J. McKenzie, 222 North 17th St., Philadelphia, Pa. 19103.

National Office

The National Catholic Office for Information, successor to the NCWC Bureau of Information, serves as the official spokesman for both the United States Catholic Conference and the National Conference of Catholic Bishops in relating to the news media.

The office prepares and distributes news releases; handles inquiries from the press; arranges news media coverage of bishops' meetings; offers public information and public relations counsel on a day-to-day basis to the office of the general secretary of the USCC and the NCCB, and to other agencies and staff members; performs a number of special research and writing functions on behalf of the conferences and their staffs.

The office also provides services and coordination for diocesan information offices.

William Ryan is director of the office, which is located at 1312 Massachusetts Ave. N.W., Washington, D.C. 20005.

JESUITS' GENERAL CONGREGATION

The Rome headquarters of the Society of Jesus released June 24, 1975, a letter from Cardinal Jean Villot, papal secretary of state, expressing Pope Paul's views about the results of the 32nd general congregation in the history of the society.

Also released were the Latin texts of 15 decrees approved by the law-making body, which concluded three months of sessions on Mar. 7. The major decrees concerned the character and mission of the Jesuits in the contemporary world, and the vow of poverty.

Cardinal Villot said in his letter that one of the "well known events" connected with the congregation's deliberations was a controversy with the Pope over the fourth vow, professed by some but not all Jesuits, of obedience to special missions of the Pope. The congregation had wished that the vow, peculiar to the society, be extended to all Jesuit priests. The Holy Father, however, judged that such a change would run counter to the basic tradition of the society.

Written exchanges on the subject preceded the congregation's acceptance of the Pope's decision.

Superior General Father Pedro Arrupe agreed with the Pope. "I am sure the Pope is

right on this," he said at a press conference on Mar. 13.

Cardinal Villot's letter:

• Included some "special recommendations relative to certain decrees."

• Expressed approval on an experimental basis of a poverty decree which drew a distinction between income for Jesuit institutions and Jesuit communities.

• In a recommendation concerning decrees on Jesuit "identity" and mission in work for social justice, said the Pope declared that, "without doubt, advancement of justice is connected with evangelization. ... There is (however) no need, certainly, to exalt more than is proper the advancement of men and their social progress on a temporal plane, with damage to the essential significance which the Church gives to evangelization, that is, to the integral announcement of the Gospel. ... This in a special way regards Society of Jesus, instituted principally for a spiritual and supernatural end, to which all other activity is subordinated. ...

"Nor should it be forgotten that it is the task of priests to inspire lay Catholics, to whom belongs the major responsibility for the advancement of justice. The tasks proper to each must not be confused."

Honors and Awards

Pontifical Orders

The Pontifical Orders of Knighthood are secular orders of merit whose membership depends directly on the pope. Details regarding the various orders are handled by a special agency in the Secretariat of Briefs, an office in the Papal Secretariat of State.

Supreme Order of Christ (Militia of Our Lord Jesus Christ): The highest of the five pontifical orders of knighthood, the Supreme Order of Christ was approved Mar. 14, 1319, by John XXII as a continuation in Portugal of the suppressed Order of Templars. Members were religious with vows and a rule of life until the order lost its religious character toward the end of the 15th century. Since that time it has existed as an order of merit. Paul VI, in 1966, restricted awards of the order to Christian heads of state.

Order of the Golden Spur (Golden Militia): Although the original founder is not certainly known, this order is one of the oldest knighthoods. Indiscriminate bestowal and inheritance diminished its prestige, however, and in 1841 Gregory XVI replaced it with the Order of St. Sylvester and gave it the title of Golden Militia. In 1905 St. Pius X restored the Order of the Golden Spur in its own right, separating it from the Order of St. Sylvester. Paul VI, in 1966, restricted awards of the order to Christian heads of state.

Order of Pius IX: Founded by Pius IX June 17, 1847, the order is awarded for outstanding services for the Church and society, and may be given to non-Catholics as well as Catholics. The title to nobility formerly attached to membership was abolished by Pius XII in 1939. In 1957 Pius XII instituted the Class of the Grand Collar as the highest category of the order; in 1966, Paul VI restricted this award to heads of state "in solemn circumstances." The other three classes are of Knights of the Grand Cross, Knight Commanders with and without emblem, and Knights. The new class was created to avoid difficulties in presenting papal honors to Christian or non-Christian leaders of high merit.

Order of St. Gregory the Great: First established by Gregory XVI in 1831 to honor citizens of the Papal States, the order is conferred on persons who are distinguished for personal character and reputation, and for notable accomplishment. The order has civil and military divisions, and three classes of knights.

Order of St. Sylvester: Instituted Oct. 31, 1841, by Gregory XVI to absorb the Order of the Golden Spur, this order was divided into two by St. Pius X in 1905, one retaining the name of St. Sylvester and the other assuming the title of Golden Militia. Membership consists of three degrees: Knights of the Grand Cross, Knight Commanders with and without emblem, and Knights.

Ecclesiastical Order

Order of the Holy Sepulchre: Critical opinion is divided regarding various details of the history of the order. It is certain, however, that these knights first appeared in the Holy Land and were in existence at the end of the 11th century. Some assign earlier dates or origin, claiming as founders St. James the Apostle, first bishop of Jerusalem, and St. Helena, builder of the Basilica of the Holy Sepulchre. Others hold that Godfrey of Bouillon instituted the order in 1099 and that it took its name from the Holy Sepulchre where its members were knighted.

The order lost a great deal of prestige after the fall of the Latin Kingdom of Jerusalem and the consequent departure of the knights from the Holy Land. It was united with the Knights of St. John in 1489, came under the grand mastership of Alexander VI in 1496 and shortly thereafter was split into three national divisions, German, French and Spanish. Pius IX re-established the Latin patriarchate of Jerusalem in 1847 and gave the patriarch the faculty of conferring the order of knighthood. This right had been held by the Franciscan custos following the appointment of the Friars as guardians of the Holy Land in 1342. Three classes of membership were designated in 1868. Leo XIII later instituted the Cross of Honor (which does not confer knighthood) in three classes — gold, silver and bronze — and also the Dames of the Holy Sepulchre. From 1907 to 1928 the pope was grand master, an office now held by a cardinal. Revised statutes for the order went into effect in 1949, 1962 and 1967. The 1949 constitution enjoined the knights "to revive in modern form the spirit and ideal of the Crusades with the weapons of faith, the apostolate, and Christian charity."

The Order of the Holy Sepulchre now has five classes: 12 Knights of the Collar and four degrees, with separate divisions of each for men and women — Grand Cross, Commanders with Plaque, Commanders and Knights. Three honorary decorations are awarded, vis., Palm of the Order, Cross of Merit (which may be bestowed on non-Catholics), and the Pilgrim's Shell.

Investiture ceremonies combine a profession of faith with the ancient ritual of knighthood dubbing. Candidates do not take monastic vows but pledge an upright Christian life and loyalty to the pope.

The grand master of the order is Cardinal Maximilien de Furstenberg.

There are four lieutenancies of the order in the United States.

Knights of Malta

The Sovereign Military Hospitaller Order of St. John of Jerusalem of Rhodes and of Malta traces its origin to a group of men who maintained a Christian hospital in the Holy Land in the 11th century. The group was approved as a religious order — the Hospitallers of St. John — by Paschal II in 1113.

The order, while continuing its service to the poor, principally in hospital work, assumed military duties in the following century and included knights, chaplains and sergeants-at-arms among its members. All the knights were professed monks with the vows of poverty, chastity and obedience. Headquarters were located in the Holy Land until the last decade of the 13th century and on Rhodes after 1308 (whence the title, Knights of Rhodes).

After establishing itself on Rhodes, the order became a sovereign power like the sea republics of Italy and the Hanseatic cities of Germany, flying its own flag, coining its own money, floating its own navy, and maintaining diplomatic relations with many nations.

The order was forced to abandon Rhodes in 1522 after the third siege of the island by the Turks under Sultan Suliman I. Eight years later, the Knights were given the island of Malta, where they remained as a bastion of Christianity until near the end of the 18th century. Headquarters have been located in Rome since 1834.

The title of Grand Master of the Order, in abeyance for some time, was restored by Leo XIII in 1879. A more precise definition of both the religious and the sovereign status of the order was embodied in a new constitution of 1961 and a code issued in 1966.

Religious aspects of the order are subject to regulation by the Holy See. At the same time the sovereignty by the order, which is based on international law, is recognized by the Holy See and by 40 countries with which full diplomatic relations are maintained.

The four main classifications of members are: Knights of Justice, who are religious with the vows of poverty, chastity and obedience;

Knights of Obedience, who make a solemn promise of obedience to the Grand Master; Knights of Honor and Devotion and of Grace and Devotion, of noble lineage; and Knights of Magistral Grace. There are also chaplains, Dames and Donats of the order.

The order, with five grand priories, three sub-priories and 36 national associations, is devoted to hospital and charitable work of all kinds in some 60 countries.

The Grand Master, who is the sovereign head of the order, has the title of Most Eminent Highness with the rank of Cardinal. He must be of noble lineage and under solemn vows for a minimum period of 10 years.

The present Grand Master is Fra' Angelo de Mojana di Cologna, a lawyer of Milan, who was elected for life May 8, 1962, by the Council of State.

The address of headquarters of the order is Via Condotti, Palazzo Malta, 00187 Roma, Italia.

Papal Medals

Pro Ecclesia et Pontifice: This decoration ("For the Church and the Pontiff") had its origin in 1888 as a token of the golden sacerdotal jubilee of Leo XIII; he bestowed it on those who had assisted in the observance of his jubilee and on persons responsible for the success of the Vatican Exposition. The medal bears the likeness of Leo XIII on one side; on the other, the tiara, the papal keys, and the words *Pro Ecclesia et Pontifice.* Originally, the medal was issued in gold, silver or bronze. St. Pius X ordered that it be of gold only. It is awarded in recognition of service to the Church and the papacy.

Benemerenti: Several medals ("To a well-deserving person") have been conferred by popes for exceptional accomplishment and service. The medals, which are made of gold, silver or bronze, bear the likeness and name of the reigning pope on one side; on the other, a laurel crown and the letter "B."

These two medals may be given by the pope to both men and women. Their bestowal does not convey any title or honor of knighthood.

AMERICAN CATHOLIC AWARDS

Aquinas Medal, by the American Catholic Philosophical Association for outstanding contributions to the field of Catholic philosophy.

Jacques Maritain (1951), Etienne Gilson (1952), Gerald Smith, S.J. (1955), Gerald B. Phelan (1959), Rudolf Allers (1960), James A. McWilliams, S.J. (1961) Charles De Koninck (1964), James Collins (1965).

Martin C. D'Arcy (1967), Dr. Josef Pieper (1968), Leo R. Ward (1969), Bernard Lonergan, S.J. (1970), Henry B. Veatch (1971), Joseph Owens, C.SS.R. (1972), A. Hilary Armstrong (1973), Cornelio Fabro (1974), Anton Pegis (1975).

Bellarmine Medal (1955), by Bellarmine College (Louisville, Ky.), to persons in national or international affairs who, in controversial matters, exemplify the characteristics of St. Robert Bellarmine in charity, justice and temperance.

Jefferson Caffrey (1955), Gen. Carlos Romulo (1956), US Rep. John W. McCormack (1957), Frank M. Folsom (1958), Robert D. Murphy (1959), James P. Mitchell (1960), Frederick H. Boland (1961);

Gen. Alfred M. Gruenther (1962), Henry Cabot Lodge (1963), R. Sargent Shriver (1964), Irene Dunne (1965), Sen. Everett M. Dirksen (1966), Nicholas Katzenbach (1967),

Danny Thomas (1968), J..Irwin Miller(1969), Theodore M. Hesburgh, C.S.C. (1970), Sen. John Sherman Cooper (1971), (no award, 1972), Dr. William B. Walsh (1973).

Borromeo Award (1960), by Carroll College (Helena, Mont.), for zeal, courage and devotion in the spirit of St. Charles Borromeo.

William D. Murray (1960), Robert E. Sullivan (1961), Vincent H. Walsh (1962), Leo V. Kelly (1963), Joseph A. Kimmet (1964), Dr. W. E. Long (1965), Frank E. Blair (1968), Gough, Booth, Shanahan and Johnson (1971), Egon E. Mallman, S.J. (1973), Christian Brothers of Ireland (1974), Most Rev. Raymond Hunthausen (1975).

Campion Award (1955), by the Catholic Book Club for distinguished service in Catholic letters.

Jacques Maritain (1955), Helen C. White (1956), Paul Horgan (1957), James Brodrick, S.J. (1958), Sister M. Madeleva (1959), Frank J. Sheed and Maisie Ward (1960), John La Farge, S.J. (1961), Harold C. Gardiner, S.J. (1962);

T. S. Eliot (1963), Barbara Ward (1964), Msgr. John T. Ellis (1965), John Courtney Murray, S.J. (1966), Phyllis McGinley (1967), Dr. George N. Shuster (1968), G. B. Harrison (1970), Walter and Jean Kerr (1971), Karl Rahner, S.J. (1974).

Cardinal Gibbons Medal (1949) by the Alumni Association of the Catholic University of America for distinguished and meritorious service to the Church, the United States or the Catholic University.

Carlton J. H. Hayes (1949), Gen. Carlos P. Romulo (1950), Fulton Oursler (1951), Most Rev. Fulton J. Sheen (1953), J. Edgar Hoover (1954), Gen. J. Lawton Collins (1955), US Sen. John F. Kennedy and Ignatius Smith, O.P. (1956), Most Rev. Bryan J. McEntegart (1957), Thomas E. Murray (1958);

Gen. Alfred M. Gruenther (1959), Karl F. Herzfeld (1960), Charles G. Fenwick (1961), Luke E. Hart (1962), John W. McCormack (1963), John A. McCone (1964), R. Sargent Shriver (1965), James J. Norris (1967), Danny Thomas (1968), Theodore Hesburgh, C.S.C. (1969), Dr. Carroll Hochwalt (1970), Danny Thomas (1971), Cardinal Patrick O'Boyle (1972), Helen Hayes (1973), Sen. Mike Mansfield (1974).

Cardinal Spellman Award (1947), by the Catholic Theological Society for outstanding achievement in the field of theology.

Revs. Francis J. Connell, C.SS.R., Emmanuel Doronzo, O.M.I., Gerald Yelle, S.S., William R. O'Connor, John C. Murray, S.J. (1947); Eugene Burke, C.S.P. (1948), Bernard J. J. Lonergan, S.J. (1949), John C. Murray, S.J. (1950), Msgr. William R. O'Connor (1951), Emmanuel Doronzo, O.M.I. (1952), Gerald Kelly, S.J. (1953), Francis J. Connell, C.SS.R. (1954), Edmond D. Benard (1955), John C. Ford, S.J. (1956);

Gerard Yelle, S.S. (1957), Msgr. Joseph C.

Fenton (1958), Juniper Carol, O.F.M. (1959), Rev. John Quasten (1960), Cyril C. Vollert, S.J. (1961), Walter J. Burghardt, S.J. (1962), Rev. Francis Dvornik (1963), Barnabas Ahern, C.P. (1964), Godfrey Diekmann, O.S.B. (1965), Paul K. Meagher, O.P. (1966), John L. McKenzie, S.J. (1967), Dr. Martin R. P. McGuire (1968), Richard A. McCormick, S.J. (1969), Avery Dulles, S.J. (1970), Raymond E. Brown, S.S. (1971).

For recipients after 1971, see John Courtney Murray Award.

Catholic Action Medal (1934), by St. Bonaventure University (St. Bonaventure, N.Y.).

Alfred E. Smith (1934), Michael Williams (1935), Joseph Scott (1936), Patrick Scanlan (1937), George J. Gillespie (1938), William F. Montavon (1939), John J. Craig (1940), John S. Burke (1941), Dr. George Speri Sperti (1942), Francis P. Matthews (1943);

Jefferson Caffrey (1944), John A. Coleman (1945), David Goldstein (1946), Clement Lane (1947), Paul W. Weber (1948), Bruce M. Mohler (1949), Edward M. O'Connor (1950), Richard F. Pattee (1951), James M. O'Neill (1952), John E. Swift (1953);

Frank M. Folsom (1954), Walter L. McGuiness (1955), Carlton J. H. Hayes (1956), Thomas E. Murray (1957), Paul V. Murray (1958), Dr. John L. Madden (1959), Christopher H. Dawson (1960), Stephen Kuttner (1961), Charles De Koninck (1962), Lt. Gen. G. Trudeau (1963), Frank J. Sheed (1964), Danny Thomas (1965), Walter and Jean Kerr (1966), Sir Hugh Stott Taylor (1967), Maurice Lavanoux (1968).

CIP Award (1948), by the Catholic Institute of the Press (now the Catholic Alliance for Communications) for service in the communications media.

Bob Considine (1948), Neil MacNeil (1949), Fulton Oursler (1950), Leo McCarey (1951), Dr. James M. O'Neill (1952), H. I. Phillips (1953), Martin Quigley (1954), Gene Lockhart (1955), Jim Bishop (1956), Arthur Daley and Red Smith (1957);

Clare Boothe Luce (1958), John La Farge, S.J. (1959), Phyllis McGinley (1960), Edwin O'Connor (1961), Barrett McGurn (1962), Paul Horgan (1963), Daniel Callahan (1964), NBC-TV and CBS-TV (1965), Gary MacEoin (1966).

Cecilia Medal (1952), by the Music Department of Boys Town (Nebr.) for outstanding work in liturgical music.

Winifred T. Flanagan (1952), Dom Francis Missia (1953), Omer Westendorf (1954), Dom Ermin Vitry (1955), William A. Reilly (1956), Flor Peeters (1957), Roger Wagner (1958), Most Rev. Gerald T. Bergan (1959), Francis T. Brunner, C.SS.R. (1960), Jean Langlois (1961);

James B. Welch (1962), W. Ripley Dorr (1963), C. Alexander Peloquin (1964), Dr. Louise Cuyler (1965), Dr. Eugene Selhorst (1966), Dr. Paul Manz (1967), Myron J. Roberts (1968), Norman T. Letter (1969), Rev. Elmer Pfeil (1969), Rev. Richard Schuler (1970).

Christian Culture Award (1941), by Assumption University (Canada) to outstanding exponents of Christian ideals.

Sigrid Undset (1941), Jacques Maritain (1942), Philip Murray (1943), Frank J. Sheed (1944), Arnold M. Walter (1945), Henry Ford II (1946), George S. Sperti (1947), Richard Pattee (1948), Etienne Gilson (1949), Paul Doyon (1950), Christopher Dawson (1951), John C.H. Wu (1952);

Charles Malik (1953), Ivan Mestrovic (1954), F. W. Foerster (1955), Paul Martin (1956), Robert Speaight (1957), Allen Tate (1958), Barbara Ward (1959), John Cogley (1960), Peter Drucker (1961), Benjamin E. Mays (1962), John Quincy Adams (1963);

William Foxwell Albright (1964), Dr. Karl Stern (1965), John Howard Griffin (1966), Edith K. Peterkin (1967), Dr. Mircea Eliade (1968), Dr. James D. Collins (1969), Dorothy Day (1970), Dr. Marshall McLuhan (1971), James M. Cameron (1972), Jean Vanier (1973), Robert J. Kreyche (1974).

Christian Wisdom Award (1958), by Loyola University (Chicago) to outstanding American or European theologians.

John C. Murray, S.J. (1958), Martin C. D'Arcy, S.J. (1959), Gustave A. Weigel, S.J. (1960), Etienne Gilson (1962).

Collegian Award (1949), by "The Collegian," weekly student newspaper of La Salle College (Phila.), for public service in the field of communications.

Ed Sullivan (1949), Morley Cassidy (1950), Bob Considine (1951), Red Smith (1952), George Sokolsky (1953), Edward R. Murrow (1954), David Lawrence (1955), Jim Bishop (1956), Richard W. Slocum (1957), Chet Huntley (1958);

John C. O'Brien (1959), Walter Cronkite (1960), David Brinkley (1961), James Reston (1962), Charles Collingwood (1963), Art Buchwald (1964), Nancy Dickerson (1965), Charles Schulz (1966), Sandy Grady (1967), Harrison E. Salisbury (1968), Ralph W. Howard (1969).

Damien-Dutton Award (1953), by the Damien-Dutton Society for service toward conquest of leprosy or for the promotion of better understanding of social problems connected with the disease.

Stanley Stein (1953), Joseph Sweeney, M.M. (1954), Sister Marie Suzanne (1955), Dr. Perry Burgess (1956), John Farrow (1957), Dr. H. Windsor Wade (1958), Sister Hilary Ross (1959), Msgr. Louis J. Mendelis (1960), Dr. Kensuke Mitsuda (1961), Pierre d'Orgeval, SS.CC. (1962);

Eunice Weaver (1963), Dr. Robert Cochrane (1964), John F. Kennedy, posthumously (1965), The Peace Corps (1966), Dr. Howard A. Rusk (1967), Dr. Frans Hemerijckx (1968), Dr. Victor G. Heiser (1969),

Dr. Dharmendra (1970), Dr. Chapman H. Binford (1971), Dr. Patricia Smith (1972), Dr. Jacinto Convit (1973), Dr. Jose N. Rodriguez (1974), Dr. Oliver Hasselblad (1975).

Edith Stein Award (1955), by the Edith Stein Guild for service toward better understanding between Christians and Jews.

Sister Noemi de Sion (1956), Authur B. Klyber, C.SS.R. (1957), Rev. John M. Oesterreicher (1958), John J. O'Connor (1959), Victor J. Donovan, C.P. (1960), Jacques and Raissa Maritain (1961), Gerard E. Sherry (1962), Mother Kathryn Sullivan, R.S.C.J. (1963), Paulist Press (1964), Rev. Edward N. Flannery (1965), Mother Katherine Hargrove, R.S.C.J. (1966), Gregory Baum, O.S.A. (1967), Sr. Rose Albert Thering (1968), Msgr. Vincent O. Genova (1969), Dr. Joseph Lichten (1970), Philip Scharper (1971), Rabbi Marc Tanenbaum (1972), Leon Paul (1973).

Emmanuel D'Alzon Medal (1954), by Assumptionists to persons exemplifying the ideals of their founder.

Jacques Maritain (1954), Michael F. Doyle (1955), Cardinal Richard J. Cushing (1956), Mother Mary St. Elizabeth (1956), Most Rev. John J. Wright (1959), Paolino Gerli (1960), Most Rev. Honoré van Waeyenbergh (1961), J. Peter Grace (1963), Danny Thomas (1967), Miss Mary Dowd, posthumously (1970), Most Rev. Bernard J. Flanagan (1974).

Father McKenna Award (1950), by the national headquarters of the Holy Name Society, for outstanding service to the society's ideals.

Msgr. John J. Murphy, Msgr. Henry J. Watterson, Msgr. Frederic J. Allchin (1950), Eustace Struckhoff, O.F.M., Msgr. Joseph A. McCaffrey, Msgr. Francis P. Connelly, Rev. Raymond E. Jones, Msgr. Joseph E. Maguire, Msgr. Edward J. Kelly, Msgr. J. Frederick Kriebs, Rev. Thomas E. O'Connell, Very Rev. Charles L. Elslander, Rev. Joseph J. Heim, Msgr. F. Borgias Lehr (1951);

Rev. Francis J. Hannegan (1954), Rev. Charles A. Hoot, Rev. Louis A. Hinnebusch, O.P., Rev. John O. Purcell, Rev. Paul M. Lackner (1955), Msgr. F. J. Timoney (1958), Rev. Thomas F. McNicholas (1960), James A. Quinn, O.P., and Rev. John C. Griffith (1961), Msgr. Joseph A. Aughney (1962), Msgr. Cornelius P. Higgins (1963), Msgr. Charles P. Mynaugh (1964), Msgr. Charles P. Muth, Rev. Patrick J. Foley (1971), Rev. Msgr. Robert T. Kickham (1973).

Franciscan International Award (1958), by the Conventual Franciscans (Prior Lake, Minn.) for outstanding contributions to the American way of life.

Mr. and Mrs. Ignatius A. O'Shaughnessy (1959), Archbishop William O. Brady (1960), Lawrence Welk (1961), Charles Kellstad (1962), Dr. Finn J. Larsen (1963), Dr. Charles W. Mayo (1964), Ara Parseghian (1965), F. K. Weyerhaueser (1966);

Alcoholics Anonymous (1967), James T. Griffin (1968), George S. Harris (1969), Baroness Catherine DeHueck Doherty (1970), Harry Reasoner (1971), Dr. Billy Graham (1972), Dr. and Mrs. John C. Willke (1973), Gov. Patrick J. Lucey (1974).

Good Samaritan Award (1968), by the National Catholic Development Conference to recognize the concern for one's fellowman exemplified by the Good Samaritan.

Bishop Edward E. Swanstrom (1968), Berard Scarborough, O.F.M. (1969), Bishop Joseph B. Whelan, C.S.Sp. (1970), Mother Teresa (1971), Bishop Michael R. Dempsey (1972), Msgr. Ralph W. Beiting (1973), Rev. Daniel Egan, S.A. (1974).

Hoey Awards (1942), by the Catholic Interracial Council of New York (55 Liberty St., New York, N.Y. 10004) for the promotion of interracial justice.

Frank A. Hall and Edward La Salle (1942), Philip Murray and Ralph H. Metcalfe (1943), Mrs. Edward V. Morrell and John L. Yancey (1944), Paul D. Williams and Richard Barthe (1945), Richard Reid and Charles L. Rawlings (1946), Julian J. Reiss and Clarence T. Hunter (1947), Mrs. Anna McGarry and Ferdinand L. Rousseve (1948), John J. O'Connor and M. C. Clarke (1949), J. Howard McGrath and Lou Montgomery (1950), Mrs. Roger L. Putnam and Francis M. Hammond (1951);

Charles F. Vatterot, Jr., and Joseph J. Yancey (1952), Joseph J. Morrow and John B. King (1953), Mrs. Gladys D. Woods and Collins J. Seitz (1954), Millard F. Everett and Dr. James W. Hose (1955), Frank M. Folsom and Paul G. King (1956), George Meany and James W. Dorsey (1957), James T. Harris and Robert S. Shriver, Jr. (1958), Percy H. Steele, Jr., and John P. Nelson (1959);

William Duffy, Jr., and George A. Moore (1960), Ralph Fenton and Mrs. Osma Spurlock (1961), Benjamin Muse and Dr. Eugene T. Reed (1962), James T. Carey and Percy H. Williams (1963), Arthur J. Holland and Frederick O'Neal (1964), Gerard E. Sherry and James R. Dumpson (1965), Jane M. Hoey and Mrs. Roy Wilkins (1966), Dr. Frank Horne and Lt. Gov. Malcolm Wilson (1967), E. H. Molisani and John Strachan (1968);

Harold E. McGannon and Hulan E. Jack (1969), George P. McManus, Alfred B. Del Bello, Maceo A. Thomas and Cleo Joseph L. Froix, M.D. (1970), Most Rev. Francis J. Mugavero and Most Rev. Harold R. Perry (1971), Joseph F. Crangle and Alen E. Pinado (1972), Meade H. Esposito and Robert B. Boyd (1973), Hon. Harold A. Stevens and Thomas Van Arsdale (1974).

Honor et Veritas Award (1959), by the Catholic War Veterans to outstanding Americans.

Cardinal Francis J. Spellman (1960), Gen. Douglas MacArthur (1961), U. S. Sen. Thomas J. Dodd (1962), Gen. William West-

moreland (1966), Dean Rusk (1967), Col. Martin T. Riley (1968), Theodore M. Hesburgh (1969), Kenneth D. Wells (1970), Danny Thomas (1971), Thomas V. Cuite (1972), Lawrence Welk (1973).

Insignis Medal (1951), by Fordham University for extraordinary distinction in the service of God through excellence in professional performance.

Dr. Carlos Espinosa Davila, Arthur H. Hayes (1955), Pierre Harmel, Victor Andres Belaunde (1956), M. E. Michelet (1957), Daniel Linehan, S.J., Dr. Victor F. Hess (1958), Dr. George N. Shuster, John H. Tully, Albert Conway (1959), Charles F. Vatterot, Cardinal Agagianian, Charles Norman and Lucy W. Shaffer, David C. Cronin, S.J. (1960);

Cardinal Spellman (1961), Edward P. Gilleran (1962), Joseph A. Martino, William J. Tracy (1963), Brother James M. Kenny, S.J., and Austin Ripley (1966), Vincent T. Lombardi (1967), Melkite Patriarch Maximos V Hakim of Antioch (1968), Joseph and Marian Kaiser (1970), Joseph P. Routh (1973).

John Courtney Murray Award (1972), by the Catholic Theological Society for distinguished achievement in theology. Originated in 1947 as the Cardinal Spellman Award.

Rev. Charles E. Curran (1972), Bernard Lonergan, S.J. (1973), George A. Tavard, A.A. (1974), Rev. Carl Peter (1975).

John Gilmary Shea Prize (1944), by the American Catholic Historical Association for scholarly works on the history of the Catholic Church broadly considered.

Carlton J. H. Hayes (1946), John H. Kennedy (1950), George W. Pare (1951), Rev. Philip Hughes (1954), Annabelle M. Melville (1955), Rev. John Tracy Ellis (1956), Rev. Thomas J. McAvoy, C.S.C. (1957), Rev. John M. Daley, S.J. (1958), Rev. Robert A. Graham, S.J. (1959);

Rev. Maynard Geiger, O.F.M. (1960), Rev. John C. Murray, S.J. (1961), Francis Dvornik (1962), Oscar Halecki (1963), Helen C. White (1964), John T. Noonan (1965), Rev. Robert I. Burns, S.J. (1966 and 1967), Rev. Edward S. Surtz, S.J. (1968), Robert Brentano (1969), David M. Kennedy (1970), Jaroslav Pelikan (1971), John T. Noonan (1972), Robert E. Quirk (1973), Bro. Thomas W. Spalding, C.F.X. (1974).

John La Farge Memorial Award for Interracial Justice (1965), by the Catholic Interracial Council of New York.

Cardinal Francis J. Spellman (1965), U.S. Sen. Jacob K. Javits (1966), Gov. Nelson Rockefeller (1967), George F. Meany (1968), Whitney M. Young, Jr. (1969), Harry Van Arsdale, Jr. (1970), John V. Lindsay (1971), Earl W. Brydges (1972), Louis K. Lefkowitz (1973), Arthur Levitt (1974), Robert F. Wagner (1975).

Laetare Medal (1883), by the University of Notre Dame for distinguished accomplishment for Church or nation by an American Catholic.

John Gilmary Shea (1883), Patrick J. Keeley (1884), Eliza Allen Starr (1885), Gen. John Newton (1886), Edward Preuss (1887), Patrick V. Hickey (1888), Mrs. A. H. Dorsey (1889), William J. Onahan (1890), Daniel Dougherty (1891), Henry F. Brownson (1892);

Patrick Donahoe (1893), Augustin Daly (1894), Mrs. James Sadlier (1895), Gen. William S. Rosecrans (1896), Dr. Thomas A. Emmet (1897), Timothy E. Howard (1898), Mary G. Caldwell (1899), John Creighton (1900), Wm. B. Cochran (1901), Dr. J. B. Murphy (1902);

Charles J. Bonaparte (1903), Richard C. Kerens (1904), Thomas B. Fitzpatrick (1905), Dr. Francis Quinlan (1906), Katherine E. Conway (1907), James C. Monaghan (1908), Frances Tiernan (Christian Reid) (1909), Maurice F. Egan (1910), Agnes Repplier (1911), Thomas M. Mulry (1912);

Charles G. Hebermann (1913), Edward Douglass White (1914), Mary V. Merrick (1915), Dr. James J. Walsh (1916), Admiral William S. Benson (1917), Joseph Scott (1918), George Duval (1919), Dr. Lawrence F. Flick (1920), Elizabeth Nourse (1921), Charles F. Neil (1922);

Walter G. Smith (1923), Charles D. Maginnis (1924), Dr. Edward F. Zahm (1925), Edward N. Hurley (1926), Margaret Anglin (1927), 129Jack J. Spalding (1928), Alfred E. Smith 130(1929), Frderick P. Kenkel (1930), James 131J. Phelan (1931), Dr. Stephen J. Maher (1932);

John McCormack (1933), Mrs. Nicholas F. Brady (1934), Frank Spearman (1935), Richard Reid (1936), Jeremiah Ford (1937), Dr. Irvin Abell (1938), Josephine Brownson (1939), Gen. Hugh A. Drum (1940), William T. Walsh (1941), Helen C. White (1942);

Thomas F. Woodlock (1943), Anne O'Hare McCormick (1944), G. Howland Shaw (1945), Carlton J. H. Hayes (1946), William G. Bruce (1947), Frank C. Walker (1948), Irene Dunne (Mrs. Francis Griffin) (1949), Gen. Joseph L. Collins (1950), John H. Phelan, (1951), Thomas E. Murray (1952);

I. A. O'Shaughnessy (1953), Jefferson Caffrey (1954), George Meany (1955), Gen. Alfred M. Gruenther (1956), Clare Boothe Luce (1957), Frank M. Folsom (1958), Robert D. Murphy (1959), George N. Shuster (1960), Pres. John F. Kennedy (1961), Dr. Francis J. Braceland (1962):

Adm. George W. Anderson, Jr. (1963), Phyllis McGinley (1964), Frederick D. Rossini (1965), Mr. and Mrs. Patrick F. Crowley (1966), J. Peter Grace (1967), R. Sargent Shriver (1968), Justice William J. Brennan, Jr. (1969), Dr. William D. Walsh (1970), Walter and Jean Kerr (1971), Dorothy Day (1972), Rev. John A. O'Brien (1973), James A. Farley (1974), Sister Ann Ida Gannon, B.V.M. (1975).

Magnificat Medal (1947), by Mundelein College (Chicago) to Catholic college alumnae for leadership in social action.

Mrs. Henry Mannix (1948), Mrs. Felix H. Lapeyre (1949), Mrs. Mary B. Finan (1950), Mrs. John J. Daly (Mary Tinley) (1951), Mrs. K. Cary Clem (1952), Mrs. Robert E. Garritty (1953), Dr. Jeannette E. Vidal (1954), Mrs. Ben Regan (1955), Marion McCandless (1956), Mrs. Donald Gunn (1957);

Ellen Collins (1958), Ruth M. Fox (1959), Margaret J. Mealey (1960), Mrs. George Vergara (1961), Josephine Sobrino (1962), Mrs. Patrick F. Crowley (1963), Ann M. Lally (1964).

Marianist Award (1949), by the University of Dayton for outstanding contributions to Mariology (until 1966); for outstanding contributions to mankind (from 1967).

Juniper Carol, O.F.M. (1950), Daniel A. Lord, S.J. (1951), Patrick J. Peyton, C.S.C. (1952), Roger Brien, S.G.G. (1953), Emil Neubert, S.M. (1954), Joseph A. Skelly, C.M. (1955), Frank Duff (1956), Eugene F. Kennedy and John McShain (1957), Winifred A. Feely (1958), Abp. John F. Noll (1959), Eamon R. Carroll, O. Carm. (1960), Coley Taylor (1961), Abbe Rene Laurentin (1963), Philip C. Hoelle, S.M. (1964), Cyril O. Vollert, S.J. (1965), Eduardo Frei Montalvo (1967).

Marian Library Medal (1953), by the Marian Library of the University of Dayton for books in English on the Blessed Virgin Mary. Starting in 1971, the medal will be awarded every four years, at the time of an International Mariological Congress, to a scholar for Mariological studies.

Most Rev. Fulton J. Sheen (1953), Msgr. John S. Kennedy (1954), Rev. William G. Most (1955), Ruth Cranston (1956), Juniper Carol, O.F.M. (1957), Donald C. Sharkey and Joseph Debergh, O.M.I. (1958);

Edward O'Connor, C.S.C. (1959), John J. Delaney (1960), Sister Mary Pierre, S.M. (1961), Marion A. Habig, O.F.M. (1962), Titus F. Cranny, S.A. (1963), Hilda C. Graef (1964), Edward Schillebeeckx, O.P. (1965), Cyril Vollert, S.J. (1966), Thomas O'Meara, O.P. (1967), Charles Balic, O. F. M. (1971).

Mater et Magistra Award (1963), by the College of Mt. St. Joseph on the Ohio to women for social action in the pattern and spirit of the encyclical *Mater et Magistra.*

Jane Hoey (1963), Mary Dolan (1964), Mrs. Anne Fremantle (1966), Margaret Mealey (1967), Mrs. Arthur L. Zepf, Sr. (1968), Alice R. May (1969), Mother Teresa (1974).

Mendel Medal (1928), by Villanova University for scientists.

Dr. John A. Kolmer (1929), Dr. Albert F. Zahm (1930), Dr. Karl F. Herzfeld (1931), Dr. Francis P. Garvan (1932), Dr. Hugh Stott Taylor (1933), Abbe Georges Lemaitre

(1934), Dr. Francis Owen Rice (1935), Rev. Julius A. Nieuwland, C.S.C. (1936), Pierre Teilhard de Chardin, S.J. (1937), Dr. Thomas Parran (1938);

Rev. John M. Cooper (1939), Dr. Peter J. W. Debye (1940), Dr. Eugene M. K. Geiling (1941), Dr. Joseph A. Becker (1942), Dr. George Speri Sperti (1943), Dr. John C. Hubbard (1946), Frank N. Piasecki (1954), James B. Macelwane, S.J. (1955), Dr. William J. Thaler (1960), Dr. James A. Shannon (1961), Maj. Robert M. White (1963), Dr. Charles A. Hufnagel (1965), Dr. Alfred M. Bongiovanni (1968).

Msgr. John P. Monaghan Social Action Award by the Assn. of Catholic Trade Unionists; originally (1948), the Quadragesimo Anno Medal.

John Quincy Adams (1948), Brother Justin, F.S.C. (1949), Joseph Bierne (1950), Rev. Raymond A. McGowan (1951), Philip Murray (1952), Charles M. Halloran (1953), US Sen. Robert F. Wagner, Sr. (1954), Rev. John P. Monaghan (1955), John C. Cort (1956), Msgr. Joseph F. Connolly (1957);

George Meany (1958), Robert F. Kennedy (1959), Thomas Carey (1960), James B. Carey (1961), Rev. Joseph Hammond (1966), Paul Jennings (1967), Matthew Guinan (1968), David Sullivan (1969), Vincent McDonnell (1970).

Peace Award (1950), by the Third Order Secular of St. Francis.

Myron C. Taylor (1950), John Foster Dulles (1951), John W. McCormack (1952), John C. Wu (1953), Ralph Bunche (1954), John R. Gariepy (1956), Most Rev. Richard J. Cushing (1957), Patrick McGeehan, Sr. (1958), Victor Andres Belaunde (1959), J. Edgar Hoover (1960), George K. Hunton (1961);

Mrs. Lester Auberlin (1962), Rev. Martin Luther King (1963), Most Rev. John J. Wright (1964), Pope Paul VI (1965), Cardinal Wyszynski (1966), Bishop Fred Pierce Corson (1967), Robert F. Kennedy, posthumously (1968), Msgr. Robert Fox (1969), Bishop James Walsh, M.M. (1970), Jean Vanier (1972), Mother Teresa of Calcutta (1974).

Peter Guilday Prize (1972), by the American Catholic Historical Association for articles accepted by the editors of the *Catholic Historical Review* which are the first scholarly publications of their authors.

James P. Gaffey (1972), B. Robert Kreiser (1974).

Pius XII Marian Award (1955), by the Montfort Fathers for promotion of the devotion of consecration to the Immaculate Heart of Mary.

Denis M. McAuliffe, O. P. (1955), James M. Keane, O. S. M. (1956), Rev. John Cantwell (1957), Marie Delicia Unson (1958), Rev. Herman J. Vincent of St. Henry's Parish, Bridge City, Tex., and parishioners of St. Helen's Mission, Orangefield, Tex. (1959),

Leo Dillon (1960), De Montfort Groups of Detroit, Mich., and Rev. Thomas Kerwin, their spiritual director (1961), Frank Duff (1965), Mr. and Mrs. Thomas F. Larkin, Jr. (1973).

Poverello Medal (1949), by The College of Steubenville (Ohio), "in recognition of great benefactions to humanity, exemplifying in our age the Christ-like spirit of charity which filled the life of St. Francis of Assisi."

Alcoholics Anonymous Fellowship (1949), Edward F. Hutton (1950), the Court of Last Resort, New York, N. Y. (1951), The Lions International (1952), Variety Clubs International (1953), Llewellyn J. Scott (1954), Dr. Jonas E. Salk and Associates (1955), Mother Anna Dengel (1956), Catherine de Hueck Doherty (1957), D. M. Hamill (1958);

Daniel W. Egan, T. O. R. (1959, posthumously), Mrs. Emma C. Zeis (1960), Donald H. McGannon (1961), Jane Wyatt (1962), Birgit Nilsson (1963), Arthur Joseph Rooney (1964), Joe E. Brown (1965), Project Hope (1966), Lena F. Edwards (1967), VISTA (1968), Jack Twyman (1969), The Salvation Army (1970), Most Rev. John K. Mussio (1971), Bro. George J. Hungerman, F.M.S.I., M.D. (1972), The Dismas Committee of the St. Vincent de Paul Society (1973).

Regina Medal (1959), by the Catholic Library Association for outstanding contributions to children's literature.

Eleanor Farjeon (1959), Anne Carroll Moore (1960), Padraic Colum (1961), Frederick G. Melcher (1962), Ann Nolan Clark (1963), May Hill Arbuthnot (1964), Ruth Sawyer Durand (1965), Leo Politi (1966), Bertha Mahoney Miller (1967), Marguerite de Angeli (1968), Lois Lenski (1969), Ingri and Edgar Parin d'Aulaire (1970), Tasha Tudor (1971) Miendert DeJong (1972); Frances Clarke Sayers (1973), Robert McCloskey (1974), Lynd Ward and May McNeer (1975).

Rerum Novarum Award (1949), by St. Peter's College (Jersey City, N. J.) for outstanding work in the interests of industrial peace.

Raymond Reiss (1949), Justin McAghon (1950), Frederick W. Mansfield (1951), Most Rev. Karl J. Alter (1952), Martin P. Durkin (1953), Christopher M. Hoey (1954), James P. Mitchell (1955), George Meany (1956), Henry Ford II (1957), Hugh E. Sheridan (1958);

Joseph F. Finnegan (1959), Cardinal Richard Cushing (1960), Joseph D. Keenan (1961), (no award 1962), Louis C. Seaton (1963).

Richard Reid Memorial Award (1963), by the Catholic Institute of the Press (now the Catholic Alliance for Communications) in memory of its cofounder.

Thomas A. Brennan (1963), James A. Connolly (1964), John J. Sheehan (1965), Arthur Hull Hays (1966), Victor L. Ridder (1968), Bob Considine, (1969).

The Saint De La Salle Medal, by Manhattan College, for significant contribution to the moral, cultural or educational life of the nation.

John F. Brosnan (1951), Cardinal Francis Spellman (1952), Most Rev. Joseph P. Donahue (1953), Most Rev. Edwin V. O'Hara, posthumously (1950), Sr. Mary Emil, I.H.M. (1957), Msgr. Joseph E. Schieder (1958), Very Rev. Bro. Bertrand, O. S. F. (1959), Dr. Roy J. Deferrari (1960).

John Courtney Murray, S.J. (1961), Bro. Clair Stanislaus, F.S.C. (1962), Most Rev. Bryan J. McEntegart (1963), Sr. M. Rose Eileen, C.S.C. (1964), Mother Kathryn Sullivan, R.S.C.J. (1965), Bro. Bernard Peter, F.S.C. (1966), Dr. William Hughes Mulligan (1967), C. Alfred Koob, O. Praem. (1968), Theodore M. Hesburgh, C.S.C. (1970), Most Rev. Edwin B. Broderick (1971), Very Rev. Bro. Charles Henry, F.S.C. (1972), Mary Shea Giordano (1973), Dorothy Day (1974), Henry Viscardi, Jr. (1975).

St. Francis de Sales Award (1959), by the Catholic Press Association for distinguished contribution to Catholic journalism.

Dale Francis (1959), Frank A. Hall (1960), John C. Murray, S.J. (1961), Albert J. Nevins, M.M. (1962), Floyd Anderson (1963), Rev. Patrick O'Connor (1964), John Cogley (1965), Joseph Breig (1966), John Reedy, C.S.C. (1967), Bishop James P. Shannon (1968), no award (1969), Msgr. Robert G. Peters (1970), Francis A. Fink (1971), Jeremy Harrington, O.F.M. (1972), Robert E. Burns (1973), Gerard E. Sherry (1974), John B. Sheerin, C.S.P. (1975).

St. Francis Xavier Medal (1954), by Xavier University (Cincinnati) to persons exemplifying the spirit of St. Francis Xavier.

Most Rev. Fulton J. Sheen, Rev. Leo Kampsen, Msgr. Frederick G. Hochwalt (1954), James Keller, M.M. (1955), Gen. Carlos P. Romulo (1956), Stan Musial, Aloysius A. Breen, S.J., Edwin G. Becker (1957), Msgr. (Maj. Gen.) Patrick J. Ryan, Msgr. (Maj. Gen.) Terrence P. Finnegan, Msgr. (Rear Adm.) George A. Rosso (1958);

Neal Ahern and T. L. Bouscaren, S.J. (1959), Celestine J. Steiner, S.J. (1960), Philip J. Scharper (1961), Charles Dismas Clark, S.J. (1962), Pres. John F. Kennedy (posthumously) and J. Paul Spaeth (1963), James B. Donovan (1964), Charles H. Keating, Jr. (1965), Frank Blair (1967), Martin H. Work (1968), Lt. Col. William A. Anders (1969), Bishop James E. Walsh, M.M. (1970), Lawrence Welk, Rev. Msgr. Ralph N. Beiting (1971), Paul L. O'Connor, S.J. (1972), James F. Maguire, S.J., Edward P. VonderHaar (posthumously) (1973), Daniel J. O'Conor, Jr., G. Milton Wurzelbacher (1974).

St. Vincent de Paul Medal (1948), by St. John's University (Jamaica, N.Y.), for outstanding service to Catholic charities.

Francis D. McGarey (1948), John A. Coleman (1949), Aloysius L. Fitzpatrick (1950), Frank J. Lewis (1951), Howard W. Fitzpatrick (1952), Richard F. Mulroy (1953), Harry J. Kirk (1954), Bernard J. Keating (1955), John M. Nolan (1956), John R. Gariepy (1957);

Charles E. McCarthy (1958), Frederick V. Goess (1959), Maurice J. Costello (1960), Thomas F. Hanley (1961), John J. Lynch (1962), William A. Walters (1963), George E. Heneghen (1964), James A. Quigney (1965), Henry J. Shields (1966);

Eugene McGovern (1967), George J. Krygier (1968), James A. Cousins (1969), Edward T. Reilly (1970), T. Raber Taylor (1971), Luke J. Smith (1972), William C. Rohrkemper (1973), Edward V. Murtagh (1974).

Serra Award of the Americas (1947), by the Academy of American Franciscan History for service to Inter-American good will.

Sumner Welles (1947), Pablo Martinez del Rio (1948), Dr. Herbert E. Bolton (1949), Gabriela Mistral (1950), Carlos E. Castaneda (1951), Victor A. Belaunde (1952), Clarence Haring (1953), Alceu Amoroso Lima (1954), France V. Scholes (1956);

Silvio Zavala (1957), John Tate Lanning (1958), John Basadre (1959), Arthur Preston Whitaker (1960), Marcel Bataillon (1961), Javier Malagon y Barcelo (1962), Dr. George P. Hammond (1964), Augustin Millares Carlo (1970).

Signum Fidei Medal (1942), by the Alumni Association of La Salle College (Phila.) for noteworthy contributions to the advancement of humanitarian principles in keeping with Christian tradition.

Brother E. Anselm, F.S.C. (1942), Karl H. Rogers (1943), Very Rev. Edward V. Stanford, O.S.A. (1944), Mrs. Edward V. Morrell (1945), Cardinal Dennis Dougherty (1946), Max Jordan (1947), John J. Sullivan (1948), Dr. Louis H. Clerf (1949), Most Rev. Gerald P. O'Hara (1950), Most Rev. Fulton J. Sheen (1951);

John H. Harris (1952), James Keller, M.M. (1953), John M. Haffert (1954), Dr. Francis J. Braceland (1955), Matthew H. McCloskey (1956), Henry Viscardi, Jr. (1957), no award (1958), Dr. Joseph J. Toland, Jr. (1959), Luke E. Hart (1960), Joseph E. McCafferty (1961);

Martin H. Work (1962), R. Sargent Shriver (1963), Mother M. Benedict, M.D. (1964), Sen. Eugene McCarthy (1965), William B. Ball (1966), Frank Folsom (1967), Rev. Leon H. Sullivan (1968), Rev. William J. Finley (1969);

Dr. James W. Turpin (1970), Lisa A. Richette, Esq. (1971), Rev. Melvin Floyd (1972), Elwood E. Kieser, C.S.P. (1973), Msgr. Philip J. Dowling (1974), James C. Giuffre, M.D. (1975).

Soteriological Award (1967), by the Confraternity of the Passion (Third Order of the Passionists, St. Michael's Monastery, Union City, N. J.) for outstanding exemplification of sharing in the Passion of Christ in contemporary society.

Most Rev. Cuthbert M. O'Gara, C.P. (1967), Mrs. Martin Luther King, Jr. (1968), Veronica's Veil Players (1969), Mother Mary Teresa Benedetti, C.P. (1970), Dr. Billy Graham (1971), Mrs. Flo Kuhn (1972), Rev. Martin J. Tooker, C.P. (1973), Mrs. Mary Sloan (1974).

Stella Maris Medal (1960), by Mary Manse College (Toledo, O.) for service.

Alice R. May (1960), Emma Endres Kountz (1961), Elizabeth M. Zepf (1962), Judge Geraldine F. Macelwane (1963), Ven. Mother Mary Adelaide, O.S.F. (1964), Marian Rejent, M.D. (1966), Mrs. Irene Hubbard McCarthy (1967), Sr. Ruth Hickey, S.G.M. (1969), Mrs. Ella Phillips Stewart (1970), Sr. M. Lawrence Wilson (1971), Mrs. Carol Pietrykowski (1972), Miss Rita O'Grady (1973), Mildred L. Bayer, R.N. (1975).

Sword of Loyola (1964), by Loyola University of Chicago to person or persons exemplifying Ignatius of Loyola's courage, dedication and service.

J. Edgar Hoover (1964), Col. James McDivitt and Maxim A. Paget (1965), Lt. Dieter Dengler (1966), Brig. Gen. David Sarnoff (1967), Capt. Edward V. Rickenbacker (1968), Dr. Thomas C. Paine and William Anders (1969), Most Rev. Fulton J. Sheen (1970), Helen Hayes (1971), James F. Maguire, S.J. (1972), Mr. and Mrs. Foster McGaw (1973).

Thomas More Association Medal (1954), by the Thomas More Association for distinguished contribution to Catholic literature during the year.

Doubleday and Co., Inc. (1954), Alfred A. Knopf, Inc. (1955), P. J. Kenedy and Sons, Inc. (1956), Farrar, Straus and Cudahy, Inc. (1957), Hawthorn Books (1958), Sheed and Ward, Inc. (1959), J. B. Lippincott Co. (1960), Doubleday and Co., Inc. (1961), Random House, Inc. (1962);

William Morrow and Co., Inc. (1963), Harper and Row (1964), Farrar, Straus and Giroux (1965), Doubleday and Co., Inc. (1966), Herder and Herder (1967), Hans Kueng (1968), John L. McKenzie, S.J. (1969), Daniel Callahan (1970). Daniel Berrigan, S.J. (1971), Andrew Greeley and Eugene Kennedy, M.M. (1972), Graham Greene (1973), Piers Paul Read (1974).

Vercelli Medal (1947), by the Holy Name Society for distinguished service to ideals of the society.

William Bruce, Paul M. Brennan, Joseph Scott, Stephen Barry, Patrick Kennedy (1947), R. W. Hoogstraet (1948), William H. Collins (1949), Ward D. Hopkins (1950), Charles A. Burkholder, James C. Connell, James T. Vocelle, Edwin J. Allen, Fred A. Muth, Austin J. Roche, Michael Lawlor (1951), Michael L. Roche (1953), Maurice J.

O'Sullivan, Lucien T. Vivien, Jr. (1954); John A. Lee, Sr., Daniel M. Hamill, Clarence F. Boggan, Louis J. Euler, Henry J. McGreevy, Ralph F. Nunlist (1955), James J. McDonnell (1957), Joseph J. Wilson (1958), William J. Meehan (1959), Paul Meade (1960), William T. Tavares (1961), David M. Martin (1962), Bert M. Walz (1963), Herbert Michelbrook (1964), Alfred A. McGarraghy (1965), Frank J. Beuerlein (1968), Humbert J. Campana (1970), Richard Asmus (1971), Charles J. Little (1973), William J. Burke, Jr. (1974).

CPA AWARDS

Catholic Press Association Awards for material published in 1974 were presented during the 65th CPA convention held May 13 to 16, 1975, in New York City.

Newspapers

Awards were presented in three categories of circulation: 1-13,000; 13,001-38,000; over 38,000.

General excellence: *Prairie Messenger,* Muenster, Saskatchewan, Canada (1-13,000); *North Country Catholic,* Ogdensburg, N.Y. (13,001-38,000); *National Catholic Reporter,* Kansas City, Mo.; *The Beacon,* Paterson, N.J. (over 38,000).

Best front page: *B.C. Catholic,* Vancouver, B.C., Canada (1-13,000); *Catholic Sentinel,* Portland, Ore. (13,001-38,000); *National Catholic Reporter,* Kansas City, Mo. (over 38,000).

Best campaign in the public interest: *Church World,* Portland, Me. (1-13,000), for series on world hunger; *The Witness,* Dubuque, Ia. (13,001-38,000), for series on drug abuse in Dubuque; *Catholic Bulletin,* St. Paul, Minn. (over 38,000), for campaign on abortion issue.

Awards without reference to circulation categories:

Best news report originating with a newspaper: *The Monitor,* San Francisco, Calif., for "Successful Exorcism Reported Locally," by Gerard E. Sherry.

Best in-depth background or interpretative reporting: *Long Island Catholic,* Rockville Centre, N.Y., for "Spanish Speaking and Church: Still a Gap," by Carol Speranza.

Best editorial: *The Advocate,* Newark, N.J., for "The Rights of Homosexuals"; *The Catholic Transcript,* Hartford, Conn., for "Pardoning of a President."

Best editorial page or section: *Tennessee Register,* Nashville, Tenn.

Best human interest feature story: *The Morning Star,* Lafayette, La., for "A Christmas Story: Nursing Home Patients Give Hope and Joy to Others," by Barbara Lenox.

Culture, arts and leisure column originating with a newspaper: *Church World,* Portland, Me., for columns by Thomas P. McDonnell.

Spiritual Life column originating with a newspaper: *Concern*, Manchester, N.H., for "The Question Corner," by Rev. Richard J. Chagnon.

General commentary column originating with a newspaper: *Catholic Chronicle*, Toledo, O., for "Rome Should Discuss Celibacy," by Fr. Robert Kirtland; *Concern*, Manchester, N.H., for "Loneliness Revisited," by Paul A. Dowd.

Syndicated column originating with a newspaper: "Essays in Theology," by Richard P. McBrien; syndicated by *The Catholic Transcript*, Hartford, Conn.

Best news story, background piece, column, editorial or treatment dealing with world justice and peace: *The Evangelist*, Albany, N.Y., for feature on world hunger.

Best coverage of themes of the Holy Year: *The Observer*, Monterey, Calif.

Best youth coverage: *The Catholic Register*, Toronto, Canada, for *Catholic Youth Register*, edited by Dan Mothersill.

Best photo story originating with a newspaper: *Clarion Herald*, New Orleans, La., for "Photos of Marching Band," by Frank Methe (photos); George Gurtner (text), Louis Aguirre (design).

Best photograph originating with a newspaper: *The Catholic News*, New York, N.Y., for "A Religious Vocation Can Get You Life," by Chris Sheridan.

Best example of circulation promotion: *The New World*, Chicago, Ill.

Best special issue, section or supplement: *The Tablet*, Brooklyn, N.Y.

Best example of effective advertising promotion: *Catholic Standard*, Washington, D.C.

Magazines

General excellence: *Marriage and Family Living* (general interest); *Maryknoll* (missions); *National Jesuit News* and *Paulist Fathers News* (religious orders); *Momentum* (professional and special interest); *Homiletic and Pastoral Review* (religious and clergy); *Theological Studies* (scholarly); *Queen* (devotional).

Best color cover: *St. Anthony Messenger* (four-color); *Sign* (two- or three-color); *Glenmary's Challenge* (single color).

Best short story: *U.S. Catholic*, for "Whalen's Complaint," by Desmond O'Grady.

Best article originating with a magazine: *Sign*, for "Justice Is a Personal Decision," by Robert C. Aldridge.

Best editorial: *U.S. Catholic*, for editorial by Robert E. Burns on Cardinal Wright's remarks about the ordination of Episcopal women.

Best regular column originating with a magazine: *Commonweal*, for Washington Report: "Post-Watergate Reconstruction-Media," by Sisyphus.

Best single photo originating with a magazine: *U.S. Catholic*, for "Boy on Stairs," by Paul Conklin (photos) and Glenn Heinlein (design).

Best photo story originating with a magazine: *U.S. Catholic*, for "The Tribe that Nobody Knows," by Paul Conklin.

Best illustration of an article, story or poem either with art work or photography: *Folk Mass and Modern Liturgy*, for "The Charismatic Movement," illustrated by George F. Colopy.

Best Poetry: *Maryknoll*, for "The Inca of Machu Pichu," by Donald J. Casey.

Best treatment of evangelism: *St. Anthony Messenger*, for "A New Look at Evangelism: An Interview with Samuel Rayan, S.J.," by Jack Wintz.

Best treatment of family life: *St. Anthony Messenger*, for "Hope for the Troubled American Family," by Lawrence H. Fuchs, Ph.D.

Best special issue, section or supplement: *St. Anthony Messenger*, for "The American Family," March issue.

Best single piece of promotion: *The Catechist*.

Books

Biography: *Thomas Merton, Monk*, Brother Patrick Hart, Sheed and Ward.

History: *Islam under the Crusaders*, Robert I. Burns, Princeton University Press.

Christian family: *The Courage To Be Married*, Jonathan Hanaghan, Abbey Press.

Theology: *The Spirit of Eastern Christendom*, Jaroslav Pelikan, University of Chicago Press.

Liturgy: *The Sacraments Today*, Juan Luis Segundo, S.J., Orbis Books.

Fiction: *The Good Shepherd*, Thomas Fleming, Doubleday & Co., Inc.

Christian living: *To Barbara with Love: Prayers and Reflections by a Believer for a Skeptic*, Joan Bel Geddes, Doubleday & Co., Inc.

Scripture: *A Theology of the Old Testament*, John L. McKenzie, Doubleday & Co., Inc.

Christian ethics: *Process and Permanence in Ethics*, Alfons Deeken, S.J., Paulist Press.

Prayer life: *Silent Music: The Science of Meditation*, by William Johnston, S.J. Harper and Row.

Youth and children's books: *Stepka and the Fire*, Dorothy Van Woerkom, Concordia.

El Visitante Dominical

The Spanish-language edition of *Our Sunday Visitor* was awarded the Tom Wallace Plaque of the Inter-American Press Association Oct. 22, 1975, during the 31st general assembly of the association in Sao Paulo, Brazil. The paper, which began publication Apr. 14, 1974, was honored for its "extraordinary effort to bring about greater understanding, closer Christian brotherhood and respect for human rights in the Americas."

CHRISTOPHER AWARDS

Christopher Awards were presented Feb. 27, 1975, in New York City to 81 producers, directors and writers for their work in television, films and books. The award is a bronze medallion inscribed with the Christopher motto, "It is better to light one candle than to curse the darkness."

Award winners were selected on the basis of their affirmation of the highest values of the human spirit, artistic and technical accomplishment, and a significant degree of public acceptance of their work.

Special Christopher Awards were presented to John J. Delaney, editorial director, Catholic and Image Books, Doubleday and Co., Inc., on the occasion of Image Books' 20th anniversary, for achievement in bringing quality religious writings to readers at reasonable cost; and Earl Hamner, Jr., for consistent advocacy of sound human values in his writing.

Books for Adults

Lester R. Brown, with Erik P. Eckholm, *By Bread Alone;* Praeger.

Lynn Caine, *Widow,* Morrow.

John R. Coleman, *Blue-Collar Journal: A College President's Sabbatical;* Lippincott.

Adele Faber and Elaine Mazlish, *Liberated Parents/Liberated Children;* Grosset and Dunlap.

James T. Flexner, *Washington, the Indispensable Man;* Little, Brown.

Lawrence LeShan, *How to Meditate: A Guide to Self-Discovery;* Little, Brown.

Senator Charles H. Percy, *Growing Old in the Country of the Young;* McGraw-Hill.

Theodore Rosengarten, *All God's Dangers: The Life of Nate Shaw;* Knopf.

Jonathan D. Spence, *Emperor of China;* Knopf.

Hiltgunt Zassenhaus, *Walls: Resisting the Third Reich — One Woman's Story;* Beacon.

Books for Young People

Uni Shulevitz, *Dawn,* Farrar, Straus and Giroux; picture book.

Charlotte Zolotow, *My Grandson Lew,* illustrated by William P. Du Bois; Harper and Row; ages 6 to 8.

Helen Coutant, *First Snow,* illustrated by Vo-Dinh; Knopf; ages 8 to 12.

Ann E. Weiss, *Save the Mustangs;* Julian Messner; ages 8 to 12.

Mary Rodgers, *A Billion for Boris;* Harper and Row; ages 12 and up.

Motion Pictures

"That's Entertainment," United Artists; Jack Haley, Jr.; family.

"Where the Lilies Bloom," United Artists; Robert B. Radnitz, William Graham, Earl Hamner, Jr.; family.

"Antonia: A Portrait of the Woman," Phoenix Films; Judy Collins, Jill Godmilow; adults and adolescents.

"Conrack," Twentieth Century Fox; Martin Ritt, Harniet Frank, Jr., Irving Ravetch; adults and adolescents.

"Harry and Tonto," Twentieth Century Fox; Paul Mazursky, Josh Greenfeld; adults and adolescents.

"The Wild and the Brave," Tomorrow Entertainment; Natalie and Eugene Jones; adults and adolescents.

"Scenes from a Marriage," Cinema V; Ingmar Bergman; adults.

Television

"ABC News Close-up on Children: A Case of Neglect"; Av Weston, Pamela Hill, Brit Hume.

"The Autobiography of Miss Jane Pittman," CBS; Bob Christiansen, Rick Rosenberg, John Korty, Tracy Keenan Wynn.

"The Bridge of Adam Rush," ABC; Daniel Wilson, Larry Elikann, Lee Kalcheim.

"Bushman of the Kalahari," ABC; Nicholas Clapp, Dennis B. Kane, Robert M. Young, John Marshall.

"CBS Reports: Caution: Drinking Water May Be Dangerous to Your Health"; Perry Wolff, Judy Crichton.

"Drink, Drank, Drunk," Public Broadcasting Service; Tom Skinner, Charles Hauck, Jack Kuney, John Boni.

"The Fragile Mind," ABC; Laurence D. Savadove, Alan Landsburg, Kay Hoffman, Fritz Roland.

"IBM Presents Clarence Darrow," NBC; Mike Merrick, Don Gregory, John Rich, David W. Rintels.

"The Little House on the Prairie," NBC; Ed Friendly, Michael Landon, Blanche Hanalis.

"Marlo Thomas and Friends in Free To Be ... You and Me," ABC; Marlo Thomas, Carole Hart, Bill Davis.

"The Migrants," CBS; Tom Gries, Lanford Wilson.

"On Death and Dying," NBC; Rev. Patrick J. Sullivan, S.J., Doris Ann, Martin Hoade, Philip Scharper.

"Robinson Crusoe," NBC; Cedric Messina, James McTaggart.

"Tell Me Where It Hurts," CBS; Herbert Hirschman, Paul Bogart, Fay Kanin.

"Tornado! 4:40 p.m., Xenia, Ohio," NBC; George Murray, Patrick Trese.

GABRIEL AWARDS

Gabriel Awards are presented annually for excellence in radio and television broadcasting by UNDA-USA, the Catholic fraternal association for broadcasters and allied communicators.

Awards presented May 22, 1975, for outstanding achievement in the 1974 broadcasting year are listed below.

Television

"CBS Playhouse 90: The Migrants," CBS.

"Competition," Diocese of Youngstown and WFMJ-TV, Youngstown, Ohio.

"Drink, Drank, Drunk," WQED-TV, Pittsburgh, and PBS.

"CBS Reports: Caution: Drinking Water May Be Dangerous to Your Health," CBS News.

"Montage: The Lingering Heart," WKYC-TV, Cleveland, Ohio.

"Arizona Biography: Sierra," KOOL-TV, Phoenix, Ariz.

"To Be Truly Human," Canadian Broadcasting Corp.

"The Lady They Call the 'B,' " Ontario Educational Communications Authority.

"Celebrating Tomorrow's Hope," Religious Broadcasting Commission, Seattle, Wash.

"New Fire," Archdiocese of Omaha for KETV.

"The Cay," NBC.

"Cozmics: Waves," WCVB-TV, Boston, Mass.

"Homefront III," Bonneville International Corporation for the Church of Jesus Christ of Latter-Day Saints.

Station Award: WCVB-TV, Boston, Mass.

Special Award for Continuing Outstanding Achievement in Syndicated Religious Series: "Insight," Paulist Productions, Pacific Palisades, Calif.

Radio

"The Beginning," Metro Detroit Council of Churches and WCAR Radio.

"Update: Vietnam Retrospective," ABC.

"Journey to Ararat," KFWB Radio, Hollywood, Calif.

"Back to Bloody Harlan," WWVA, Wheeling, W. Va.

"The Liberated Woman," NBC and United States Catholic Conference.

"Lovenotes for Listeners," KCBS-FM for Archdiocesan Communications Center, San Francisco, Calif.

"Homefront III," Bonneville International Corporation for The Church of Jesus Christ of Latter-Day Saints.

"To Whom It May Concern," KSFO Radio for the Archdiocesan Communications Center, San Francisco, Calif.

In addition, 14 other TV and 3 radio programs were awarded certificates of merit by UNDA.

A **Personal Achievement Award** was presented to Frederick Wiseman, Documentary Film Maker, Zipporah Films, Boston, Mass.

OBSCENITY LAWS AND THE SUPREME COURT

Between 1967 and the beginning of the 1972-73 term, five Supreme Court Justices handed down 22 or more decisions in which they overturned obscenity convictions in 14 states and overruled 98 jurists of lower courts.

These rulings, along with the following decisions of the entire Supreme Court, served as precedents for decisions handed down June 21, 1973, in Miller v. California, Paris Adult Theater v. Slaton, and related cases.

Roth Test

Roth v. United States, Alberts v. California (1957): The Court ruled that obscene literature is not within the area of speech or press protected by the Constitution. The ruling was based on the observation: "Implicit in the history of the First Amendment is the rejection of obscenity as utterly without redeeming social importance. This rejection for that reason is mirrored in the universal judgment that obscenity should be restrained."

The Court gave this test of obscenity: "Whether to the average person, applying community standards, the dominant theme of the material taken as a whole appeals to prurient interest."

In connection with this definition, the Court indicated that material relating to sex is not necessarily obscene. Determiing standards of obscenity were said to be:

• The quality of the material must be of such a nature that it has the inherent "capacity to attract individuals eager for a forbidden look: that is, it must consist of material which goes substantially beyond customary limits of candor in the description or representation of nudity, sex or shameful acts."

• It must be offensive to the community conscience and not merely to a group in the community. This standard, however, does not outlaw the enactment of statutes designed to prevent the deliberate distribution of obscene literature to children.

• The offensive material must constitute the dominant theme. Unrelated excerpts or incidental passages are not sufficient to render a book obscene.

Smith v. California: The Court ruled unconstitutional a Los Angeles ordinance making it a criminal offense to have an obscene book in one's possession for the purpose of sale, on the ground that the ordinance did not make "knowledge" of the obscene contents an essential element of the crime.

Roth Test Modified

Manual Enterprises v. Day (1962): The Court reversed a Circuit Court of Appeals decision which had substantiated findings of the Post Office Department that homosexual material could not be mailed because it was obscene and because the magazine in question indicated where obscene material could be obtained. One opinion supporting the decision held that the allegedly objectionable material was not of such a nature as to be considered "patently offensive" by community standards of the nation. This line of thought represented a modification of the community standards test stated in Roth.

Jacobellis v. Ohio (1964): The Court reversed the conviction of a motion picture operator for exhibiting "The Lovers." The opinion noted that "a work cannot be proscribed unless it is utterly without social importance," and that the term "community standards" used in Roth does not refer to a local standard but rather to a national standard.

Tralins v. Gerstein, Grove Press, Inc., v. Gerstein: The Court ruled that Florida courts had erred in finding two publications obscene, *Pleasure Is My Business* and *Tropic of Cancer.*

Three major decisions were handed down Mar. 21, 1966, when the Court sustained the convictions of **Ralph Ginzburg,** publisher of *Eros* magazine, and **Edward Mishkin,** publisher of books on sadism and masochism, while reversing a Massachusetts ban on John Clelan's 18th century novel, *Fanny Hill.*

In the Ginzburg ruling it said that, when material is neither obviously obscene nor obviously not obscene, courts may take the advertising and promotional activities of distributors into account as an indication of their intentions.

In the Mishkin case, the Court said legal obscenity is present when the material appeals to the prurient interest of the special audience to which it is addressed.

In the *Fanny Hill* decision, the Court declared that the presence of "redeeming social value" can render a work immune to a ban on grounds of obscenity

1973 Decisions

The trend of Court decisions from 1957 was progressively permissive, with modification of the initial Roth test with the concept of national community standards and standards of "redeeming social values."

The Court reversed this trend with five 5 to 4 decisions on representative obscenity cases June 21, 1973.

In **Miller v. California** (No. 70-73), the Court ruled:

• Obscenity laws can be enforced against the publication and sale of works which "appeal to the prurient interest in sex, which portray (specifically defined) sexual conduct in a patently offensive way, and which, taken as a whole, do not have serious literary, artistic, political or scientific value."

• A jury of "average persons, applying contemporary community (rather than national) standards," can determine prurient appeal or patent offensiveness.

• "Some redeeming social value" is not available as a defense against prosecution for obscenity, as it had been since 1966.

In **Paris Adult Theater v. Slaton** (No. 71-1051), the Court ruled:

• States can assume, in the absence of clear proof to the contrary, that there is a causal connection between obscene material and crime and anti-social behavior.

• No constitutional doctrine of privacy protects the display of obscene material in public places.

At the time of the Court's decisions in 1973, at least 15 states had laws in line with the stated guidelines, 19 had statutes containing the "utterly without redeeming social value" clause, and 12 or more had no legal definition of obscenity.

Subsequent decisions by the Supreme Court and other courts, along with related legislative actions, have failed, practically, to frame a definition of obscenity precise enough to be applied by law enforcement officials and lower courts with a minimum number of appeals. However, there have been convictions, with relatively negligible penalties — and many appeals.

X-Rated Movies

The Supreme Court, in a 6 to 3 vote, struck down a Jacksonville, Fla., ordinance in June, 1975, banning the showing of X-rated films in drive-in theaters where they could be seen by non-customers.

In writing the majority decision, Justice Louis Powell said the law violated First Amendment guarantees of freedom of speech.

The law prohibited the showing of certain types of films if they could be seen from highways or other public places.

Powell said the law was too broad in scope and that it was unconstitutional for the state "to shield the public from some kinds of speech on the grounds that they are more offensive than others."

"We conclude," he declared, "that the limited privacy interests of persons on the public streets cannot justify this censorship of otherwise protected speech on the basis of its content."

In a dissent, Chief Justice Warren Burger said it was "absurd" to say that the ordinance acted to suppress ideas.

"The First Amendment interests in this case are trivial at best," he said.

Burger called the majority ruling "rigidly simplistic" — a mechanistic application of principles generated by concern for freedom of speech to "the unique visual medium to which the Jacksonville ordinance is directed."

In a separate dissent, Justice Byron White said that, if the majority decision were taken literally, "the state may not forbid 'expressive' nudity on the public streets . . . or any other public place, since other persons in those places at that time have a 'limited privacy interest' and may merely look the other way."

The Court, on the same day it delivered the Jacksonville decision, dismissed an appeal to a lower court ruling which defended a ban on nudity on public beaches, parks or streets in Santa Barbara, Calif.

PRESS BRIEFS

• The first regular transmission of a complete daily religious news service from the United States to Europe was inaugurated May 9, 1975, by NC News Service.

Teletype reception of the NC report, averaging more than 7,000 news and feature stories annually, was scheduled at Vatican Radio and the NC Rome Bureau. A.E.P. Wall, news director and editor-in-chief, indicated that future extension of the wire to serve clients in London might be possible.

The new European service began on the eve of World Communications Day, May 11, and of the convention of the Catholic Press Association, with Associated Church Press.

• One report issued at the 1975 Catholic Press Association convention, with Associated Church Press Service, disclosed that the average diocesan newspaper in the U.S. lost more than $13,000 in 1974 because of increased costs. The finding came from a survey of 50 newspapers.

ABBREVIATIONS

A.A.: Augustinianus Assumptionis; Augustinians of the Assumption (Assumptionists).

A.A.S.: "Acta Apostolicae Sedis"; Acts of the Apostolic See.

A.B.: Artium Baccalaureus; Bachelor of Arts.

Abb.: abbacy.

Abp.: Archbishop.

A.D.: Anno Domini; in the year of the Lord.

ad lib.: ad libitum; at your own choice.

A.M.: Artium Magister; Master of Arts.

A.M.D.G.: Ad majorem Dei gloriam; to the greater glory of God.

Ap.: Apostle.

A.U.C.: Ab Urbe Condita; from the founding of the city.

A.V.: Authorized Version (of the Bible).

b: born.

B.A.: Bachelor of Arts.

B.C.: Before Christ.

B.C.L.: Bachelor of Canon (Civil) Law.

Bl.: Blessed.

Bp.: Bishop.

Bro.: Brother.

B.S.: Bachelor of Science.

B.V.M: Blessed Virgin Mary.

c.: circa; about.

CARA: Center for Applied Research in the Apostolate.

C.E.: Common or Christian Era.

CCC: Canadian Catholic Conference.

CCD: Confraternity of Christian Doctrine.

CEF: Citizens for Educational Freedom.

C.F.A.: Congregatio Fratrum Cellitarum seu Alexianorum; Alexian Brothers.

CFM: Christian Family Movement.

C.F.X.: Congregatio Fratrum S. Francisci Xaverii; Xaverian Brothers.

C.I.C.: Codex Iuris Canonici; Code of Canon Law.

C.I.C.M: Congregatio Immaculati Cordis Mariae; Congregation of the Immaculate Heart of Mary (Scheut Fathers).

C.J.: Congregatio Josephitarum Gerardimontensium; Josephite Fathers (of Belgium).

C.J.M.: Congregation of Jesus and Mary (Eudists).

C.M.: Congregation of the Mission (Vincentians or Lazarists).

C.M.F.: Cordis Mariae Filius; Missionary Sons of the Immaculate Heart of Mary.

C.M.M.: Congregatio Missionariorum de Mariannhill; Missionaries of Mariannhill.

CMSM: Conference of Major Superiors of Men.

C.O.: Congregatio Oratorii; Oratorian Fathers.

COCU: Consultation on Church Union.

C.P.: Congregation of the Passion.

CPA: Catholic Press Association.

CPF: Catholic Press Features.

C.P.M.: Congregatio Presbyterorum a Misericordia; Congregation of the Fathers of Mercy.

C.PP.S.: Congregatio Missionariorum Pretiosissimi Sanguinis; Society of the Precious Blood.

C.R.: Congregation of the Resurrection.

C.R.M.: Clerics Regular Minor.

CRS: Catholic Relief Services.

C.R.S.P.: Clerics Regular of St. Paul (Barnabite Fathers).

C.S.: Missionaries of St. Charles.

C.S.B.: Congregation of St. Basil (Basilians).

C.S.C.: Congregatio Sanctae Crucis; Congregation of Holy Cross.

C.S.P.: Paulist Fathers.

C.S.S.: Congregation of the Sacred Stigmata: (Stigmatine Fathers and Brothers).

C.SS.R.: Congregatio Sanctissimi Redemptoris; Congregation of the Most Holy Redeemer (Redemptorists).

C.S.Sp.: Congregatio Sancti Spiritus; Congregation of the Holy Ghost.

C.S.V.: Clerks of St. Viator (Viatorians).

C.Y.O.: Catholic Youth Organization.

D.C.L.: Doctor Canonicae (Civilis) Legis; Doctor of Canon (Civil) Law.

Doctor Divinitatis; Doctor of Divinity.

D.N.J.C.: Dominus noster Jesus Christus; Our Lord Jesus Christ.

Doct.: Doctor.

D.O.M.: Deo Optimo Maximo; To God, the Best and Greatest.

D.V.: Deo volente; God willing.

e.g.: exempli gratia; for example.

ER: Eastern Rite News Service.

Er. Cam.: Congregatio Monachorum Eremitarum Camaldulensium; Monk Hermits of Camaldoli.

et al.: et alii or et aliae; and others.
exc.: except.

f., ff.: following.
F.D.P.: Filii Divini Providentiae; Sons of Divine Providence.
F.M.S.: Fratris Maristarum a Scholis; Marist Brothers.
F.M.S.I.: Filii Mariae Salutis Infirmorum; Sons of Mary, Health of the Sick.
Fr.: Father, or Friar.
F.S.C.: Fratres Scholarum Christianorum; Brothers of the Christian Schools (Christian Brothers).
F.S.C.J.: Congregatio Filiorum S. Cordis Jesu; Sons of the Sacred Heart (Verona Fathers).

I.C.: Institute of Charity (Rosminians).
ICEL: International Committee on English in the Liturgy.
i.e.: id est; that is.
IHS: Iesus Hominem Salvator; Jesus, the Savior of Men.
I.M.C.: Institutum Missionum a Consolata; Consolata Society for Foreign Missions.
I.N.R.I.: Iesus Nazarenus, Rex Iudaeorum; Jesus of Nazareth, King of the Jews.

J.C.D.: Juris Canonici Doctor; Doctor of Canon Law.
J.C.L.: Juris Canonici Licentiatus; Licentiate in Canon Law.
J.M.J.: Jesus, Mary, Joseph.
J.U.D.: Juris Utriusque Doctor; Doctor of Both Civil and Canon Laws.

K. of C.: Knights of Columbus.
K.H.S.: Knight of the Holy Sepulchre.
K.P.: Knight of Pius IX.
K.S.G.: Knight of St. Gregory.
K.S.S.: Knight of St. Sylvester.

LCWR: Leadership Conference of Women Religious.
LL.B.: Legum Baccalaureus; Bachelor of Laws.
LL.D.: Legum Doctor; Doctor of Laws.
LWF: Lutheran World Federation.

M.E.P.: Societe des Missions Etrangeres de Paris; Paris Foreign Missions Society.
M.H.M.: Mill Hill Missionaries.
M.I.C.: Congregatio Clericorum Regularium Marianorum sub titulo Immaculatae Conceptionis Beatae Mariae Virginis; Marian Fathers.
MM: Martyrs.
M.M.: Catholic Foreign Mission Society (Maryknoll Missioners).
M.S.: Missionaries of Our Lady of La Salette.
M.S.C.: Missionaries of the Sacred Heart.
M.S.F.: Congregatio Missionarorum a Sancta Familia; Missionaries of the Holy Family.
Msgr.: Monsignor.

NAB: New American Bible.
NAWR: National Association of Women Religious.
NC: National Catholic News Service.
NCC: National Council of Churches.
NCCB: National Conference of Catholic Bishops.
NCCL: National Catholic Council of the Laity.
NCCM: National Council of Catholic Men.
NCCS: National Catholic Community Service.
NCCW: National Council of Catholic Women.
NCEA: National Catholic Educational Association.
NCRLC: National Catholic Rural Life Conference.
NEB: New English Bible.
NFPC: National Federation of Priests' Councils.
NOBC: National Office for Black Catholics.
N.T.: New Testament.

O.A.R.: Order of Augustinian Recollects.
O.Carm.: Ordo Carmelitarum; Order of Calced Carmelites (Carmelites).
O.Cart.: Ordo Cartusiensis; Carthusian Order.
O.C.D.: Ordo Carmelitarum Discalceatorum; Order of Discalced Carmelites.
O.C.S.O.: Order of Cistercians of the Strict Observance (Trappists). Other Cistercisions are of the Common Observance.
O. de M.: Ordo B. Mariae de Merced; Order of Mercy (Mercedarians).
O.F.M.: Order of Friars Minor (Franciscans).
O.F.M.Cap.: Order of Friars Minor Capuchin (Capuchins).
O.F.M. Conv.: Order of Friars Minor Conventual (Conventuals).
O.H.: Ordo Hospitalarius S. Joannis de Deo; Hospitaller Order of St. John of God.
O.M.I.: Oblates of Mary Immaculate.
O.P.: Order of Preachers (Dominicans).
O. Praem: Order of Premonstratensians (Norbertines).
O.S.A.: Order of Hermits of St. Augustine (Augustinians).
O.S.B.: Order of St. Benedict (Benedictines).
O.S.B.M.: Ordo Sancti Basilii Magni; Order of St. Basil the Great.
O.S.C: Ordo S. Crucis; Order of the Holy Cross (Crosier Fathers).
O.S.Cam: Order of St. Camillus (Camillians).
O.S.F.: Order of St. Francis; Franciscan Brothers; also various congregations of Franciscan Sisters.
O.S.F.S.: Oblates of St. Francis de Sales.
O.S.J.: Oblates of St. Joseph.
O.S.M.: Order of Servants of Mary (Servites).
O.S.P. Order of St. Paul the First Hermit (Pauline Fathers).
O.SS.T.: Ordo Sanctissimae Trinitatis Re-

demptionis Captivorum; Order of the Most Holy Trinity (Trinitarians).

O.T.: Old Testament.

P.A.: Protonotary Apostolic.

Ph.D.: Philosophiae Doctor; Doctor of Philosophy.

P.I.M.E.: Pontificium Institutum pro Missionibus Exteris; Pontifical Institute for Foreign Missions; Missionaries of Sts. Peter and Paul.

Pont. Max.: Pontifex Maximus; Supreme Pontiff.

PP., Pp.: Papa (Pope).

R.C.: Roman Catholic.

R.I.P.: Requiescat in pace; may he [she] rest in peace.

RNS: Religious News Service.

R.P.: Reverendus Pater (Reverend Father).

R.V.: Revised Version (of the Bible).

S.A.: Societas Adunationis (Franciscan Friars of the Atonement).

S.A.C.: Societatis Apostolatus Catholici; Society of the Catholic Apostolate (Pallottines).

Sch.P. or S.P.: Ordo Clericorum Regularum Pauperum Matris Dei Scholarum Piarum; Piarist Fathers.

S.C.J.: Congregatio Sacerdotum a Corde Jesu; Congregation of Priests of the Sacred Heart.

S.D.B.: Salesians of Don Bosco.

S.D.S.: Society of the Divine Savior (Salvatorians).

S.D.V.: Society of Divine Vocations.

S.F.: Congregatio Filiorum Sacrae Familiae; Sons of the Holy Family.

S.J.: Society of Jesus (Jesuits).

S.M.: Society of Mary (Marists); Society of Mary (Marianists).

S.M.A.: Societas Missionum ad Afros; Society of African Missions.

S.M.B.: Societas Missionaria de Bethlehem; Society of Bethlehem Missionaries.

S.M.M.: Societas Mariae Montfortana; Company of Mary (Montfort Fathers).

S.O.Cist: Sacer Ordo Cisterciensis; Cistercians of the Common Observance.

SODEPAX: Joint Commission for Society, Development and Peace.

S.P.: Piarist Fathers; Servants of the Holy Paraclete.

Sr.: Sister.

S.S.: Society of St. Sulpice (Sulpicians).

SS.CC.: Congregatio Sacrorum Cordium; Fathers of the Sacred Hearts.

S.S.E.: Society of St. Edmund.

S.S.J.: Societas Sancti Joseph SSmi Cordis; St. Joseph's Society of the Sacred Heart (Josephites).

S.S.L.: Sacrae Scripturae Licentiatus; Licentiate in Sacred Scripture.

S.S.P: Society of St. Paul.

S.S.S.: Sacerdoti del Sanctissimo Sacramento; Congregation of the Blessed Sacrament.

S., St.; SS., Sts.: Saint; Saints.

S.T.: Missionarii Servi Sanctissimae Trinitatis; Missionary Servants of the Most Holy Trinity.

S.T.B.: Sacrae Theologiae Baccalaureus; Bachelor of Sacred Theology.

S.T.D.: Sacrae Theologiae Doctor; Doctor of Sacred Theology.

S.T.L.: Sacrae Theologiae Licentiatus; Licentiate in Sacred Theology.

S.T.M.: Sacrae Theologiae Magister; Master of Sacred Theology.

S.V.D.: Societas Verbi Divini; Society of the Divine Word.

S.X.: Xaverian Missionary Fathers.

T.O.R.: Third Order Regular of St. Francis.

T.O.S.F.: Tertiary of Third Order of St. Francis.

UN: United Nations.

UNCTAD: United Nations Conference on Trade and Development.

UNESCO: United Nations Educational, Scientific and Cultural Organization.

UNICEF: United Nations Children's Fund.

USCC: United States Catholic Conference.

V.A.: Vicar Apostolic.

Ven.: Venerable.

V.F.: Vicar Forane.

V.G.: Vicar General.

V.T.: Vetus Testamentum; Old Testament.

WCC: World Council of Churches.

W.F.: White Fathers.

Y.C.M.: Young Christian Movement.

Zip Codes

These abbreviations have been approved for use with ZIP Code numbers.

Alabama, AL; Alaska, AK; Arizona, AZ; Arkansas, AR; California, CA; Colorado, CO; Connecticut, CT; Delaware, DE; District of Columbia, DC; Florida, FL;

Georgia, GA; Guam, GU; Hawaii, HI; Idaho, ID; Illinois, IL; Indiana, IN; Iowa, IA; Kansas, KS; Kentucky, KY; Louisiana, LA;

Maine, ME; Maryland, MD; Massachusetts, MA; Michigan, MI; Minnesota, MN; Mississippi, MS; Missouri, MO; Montana, MT; Nebraska, NB; Nevada, NV;

New Hampshire, NH; New Jersey, NJ; New Mexico, NM; New York, NY; North Carolina, NC; North Dakota, ND; Ohio, OH; Oklahoma, OK; Oregon, OR; Pennsylvania, PA;

Puerto Rico, PR; Rhode Island, RI; South Carolina, SC; South Dakota, SD; Tennessee, TN; Texas, TX; Utah, UT; Vermont, VT; Virginia, VA; Virgin Islands, VI;

Washington, WA; West Virginia, WV; Wisconsin, WI; Wyoming, WY.

TITLES AND FORMS OF ADDRESS IN LETTERS

For Churchmen

In general, it has been customary for Catholics to add the words "in Christ" to the appropriate conclusions of formal letters to ecclesiastical dignitaries, priests and religious. "Asking Your Excellency's blessing" and similar forms have also been customary.

Given below are forms of proper address, salutation and conclusion.

Patriarchs: His Beatitude (Christian Name and Surname), Patriarch of (See City); Your Beatitude; Asking the Apostolic Blessing of Your Beatitude, I am, Yours respectfully, (Name).

Cardinals: His Eminence (Christian Name) Cardinal (Surname); (if he is an archbishop or bishop, include Title of the See); Your Eminence; Asking the Blessing of Your Eminence, I am, Yours respectfully, (Name).

Archbishops and Bishops: The Most Rev. (Name), Archbishop or Bishop of (Name of See); Your Excellency; Asking Your Excellency's Blessing, I am, Yours respectfully, (Name).

Abbots: The Right Rev. (Name), Abbot of (Name of Abbey); Right Reverend and dear Abbot; I am, Yours respectfully, (Name).

Monsignors: The Rev. Monsignor or Monsignor (Name); Reverend and dear Monsignor; I am, Yours respectfully, (Name).

Rectors of Seminaries, Heads of Colleges: The Very Rev. (Name); Very Reverend and dear Father; I am, Yours respectfully, (Name).

Provincials of Religious Orders: The Very Rev. Father Provincial, (Name, Title of Order); Very Reverend and dear Father Provincial; I am, Yours respectfully, (Name).

Diocesan Clergy: The Rev. (Name); Reverend and dear Father; Respectfully yours, (Name).

Regular Clergy: The Rev. (Name); Reverend and dear Father (Religious Name); Respectfully yours, (Name). Benedictine and Cistercian Monks and Canons Regular are addressed as The Rev. Dom (Name).

Clerics in Major Orders below the Priesthood: The Reverend (Religious Name) or The Reverend Mr. (Name). Reverend Sir or Dear Mr. (Name); Respectfully yours, (Name).

Brothers and Sisters: Brother or Sister (Name); Dear Brother or Sister (Religious Name); Respectfully yours, (Name).

Protestant Minister: The Reverend (Name), Reverend Sir; Very truly yours, (Name).

Rabbi: Rabbi (Name): Reverend Sir; Very truly yours, (Name).

For Others

President: The President; Dear Mr. President; Yours very truly, (Name).

Vice-President: The Vice-President; Dear Mr. Vice-President; Yours very truly, (Name).

Member of Cabinet: The Honorable (Name), Secretary of (Name of Department); Dear Mr. (or Madam) Secretary; Yours very truly, (Name).

Ambassador: The Honorable, or His Excellency, for Ambassador of foreign country (Name), Ambassador to (Name of Country); Dear Mr. Ambassador (Your Excellency, for ambassador of foreign country); Yours very truly, (Name).

Senator: The Honorable (Name), United States Senate; My dear Senator, Dear Mr. (or Madam) Senator; Yours very truly, (Name).

Congressman: The Honorable (Name), United States House of Representatives, Dear Sir (Madam); Yours very truly, (Name).

Member of Supreme Court: The Honorable (Name), United States Supreme Court; Dear Mr. Justice; Yours very truly (Name).

Judge: The Honorable (Name), Name of Court; Dear Sir, Dear Judge (Name); Yours very truly, (Name).

Governor: The Honorable (Name), Governor of (Name of State); Dear Sir; Yours very truly, (Name).

Mayor: The Honorable (Name), Mayor of (Name of City); Dear Sir; Yours very truly, (Name).

Military and Naval Officers: Rank, for general and commissioned officers, (Name); Dear Sir; Yours very truly, (Name). Warrant officers and flight officers are addressed as Mister; non-commissioned officers, by their titles.

King: His Majesty (Name); Sir, or May it please Your Majesty; Yours very truly, (Name).

Ecclesiastical Titles

According to instructions issued by Pope Paul Mar. 28, 1969, titles used by him with reference to cardinals, bishops and other church dignitaries are limited to: "Our Venerable Brother," "Venerable Brother," "Beloved Son."

Customary titles still stand for cardinals and bishops; e.g., "Eminence," "Excellency," "Most Reverend," "Lord Cardinal." "Monsignor," is used for prelates of honor and chaplains of the pope.

Recent changes in the life styles of religious have been accompanied by changes in titles of superiors. In some institutes, general superiors are known as presidents and the heads of convents as coordinators. Many superiors have relinquished the title of mother. Many institutes no longer require their members to adopt a religious name for use in place of a given name, and it has become customary for religious, sisters and brothers, to use family names.

BICENTENNIAL BOOKS FROM OUR SUNDAY VISITOR

OUR AMERICAN CATHOLIC HERITAGE
by Albert J. Nevins, M.M.

What can you as a Catholic tell your children or friends about their American Catholic heritage? Quite frankly, it's an enormous task without the help of OUR AMERICAN CATHOLIC HERITAGE. In this one epic volume you can find all the time-honored Catholic heroes, spotlighted from over 500 years of American Catholic history. In essence, OUR AMERICAN CATHOLIC HERITAGE is the spirit of America viewed from a Catholic perspective. And like gifted story-telling, each revealing page captures your interest and imagination. More than 475 photos, illustrations, maps and charts lend added depth and visual explanation to the multitude of fascinating stories. Order OUR AMERICAN CATHOLIC HERITAGE now, for yourself and for your loved ones. Clothbound, no. 838 . . . $20.00 / paperbound, no. 878..$5.95

A NATION BUILT ON GOD
by Edward J. Melvin, C.M.

Since the Declaration of Independence, belief in God has been the guiding force behind our laws. Yet today, asserts Father Melvin, the liberties upon which this nation was built are being eroded. Writing from an ecumenical stance, and using basic American documents, he points to the Founding Fathers' philosophy, a philosophy they were certain must be followed and preserved if the nation was to endure. A NATION BUILT ON GOD is a timely report to the American people; highlighting the key historical message of the Bicentennial commemoration. Clothbound, no. 870 ....$4.95

SAINTS OF THE AMERICAS
by Marion A. Habig, O.F.M.

Here in one complete volume are the lives of *all* the American saints and blessed, recaptured by one of the Church's noted historians. Every effort has been made to assure that the accounts of martyrdom or the lives of the saints are in accord with the facts of history. Perhaps "stranger than fiction," these stories are nevertheless *"true"* histories of the men and women of the New World whose exemplary lives are an inspiration to all. Modern readers, turned off by pious accounts of legendary marvels, will appreciate the thrust this thoroughly researched and highly interesting volume takes. A joy to read and an informative experience, its value is enhanced by excellent illustrations, bibliography and five topical appendices. Clothbound, no. 880 ....$9.95

If your bookseller does not have these titles, you may order them by sending listed price (we pay postage and handling) to: Sales Service Department / Noll Plaza / Huntington, Indiana 46750. Enclose check or money order — do not send cash. Be sure to ask for our free book list!